ELEMENTS OF
Literature

FOURTH COURSE
WITH READINGS IN
WORLD LITERATURE

We have not even to
risk the adventure alone,
for the heroes of all time
have gone before us.

— from "The Monomyth"
by Joseph Campbell

HOLT, RINEHART AND WINSTON
Harcourt Brace & Company

Austin • New York • Orlando • Atlanta • San Francisco • Boston • Dallas • Toronto • London

Special Contributors

Janet Burroway wrote an Elements of Literature essay on nonfiction and instructional materials on individual nonfiction selections. Ms. Burroway is a novelist and teacher who has also written children's books and a popular textbook called *Writing Fiction.* Ms. Burroway has taught at the University of Sussex, England; the University of Illinois; and the Writer's Workshop at the University of Iowa. She is currently Robert O. Lawton Distinguished Professor at Florida State University in Tallahassee. Her novels include *The Buzzards* (nominated for the Pulitzer Prize), *Raw Silk* (nominated for the National Book Award), *Opening Nights,* and *Cutting Stone.*

Richard Cohen wrote Elements of Literature essays on nonfiction and instructional material on individual selections. Mr. Cohen is an educational writer and editor as well as a novelist. Mr. Cohen has written a college creative-writing textbook, *Writer's Mind: Crafting Fiction,* and the novels *Domestic Tranquility, Don't Mention the Moon,* and *Say You Want Me.* A graduate of the University of Michigan, he has taught creative writing at the University of Wisconsin, Madison.

David Adams Leeming wrote the introductions "Greek Drama: Out of Ritual" and "The Myth of Oedipus," as well as instructional material on *Antigone.* He also wrote the introduction to the Bible and instructional material on the selections in "Traditions! Readings in World Literature." Dr. Leeming was for many years a Professor of English and Comparative Literature at the University of Connecticut. He is the author of several books on mythology, including *Mythology: The Voyage of the Hero; The World of Myth;* and *Encyclopedia of Creation Myths.* For several years Dr. Leeming taught English at Robert College in Istanbul, Turkey. He also served as secretary and assistant to the writer James Baldwin in New York and Istanbul. He has published two biographies, *James Baldwin* and *Amazing Grace: A Biography of Beauford Delaney.*

Writers

The writers prepared instructional materials for the text under the supervision of Dr. Probst and the editorial staff.

Ellen Ashdown
Educational Writer and Editor
Tallahassee, Florida

Elaine Goldenberg
Educational Writer and Editor
Cambridge, Massachusetts

Phyllis Goldenberg
Educational Writer and Editor
Miami, Florida

Lynn Hovland
Former Teacher
Educational Writer and Editor
Berkeley, California

Carole Lambert
Journalist and Educational
 Writer and Editor
Waterville, Maine

Carroll Moulton
Former Teacher
Educational Writer and Editor
Southampton, New York

Pam Ozaroff
Educational Writer and Editor
Newton Center, Massachusetts

Mairead Stack
Educational Writer and Editor
New York, New York

Diane Tasca
Educational Writer and Editor
Palo Alto, California

Acknowledgments

For permission to reprint copyrighted material, grateful acknowledgment is made to the following sources:

American Heritage: Quote by Roger Rosenblatt from "How Have We Changed?" from *American Heritage,* vol. 45, no. 8, December 1994. Copyright © 1994 by American Heritage.

Harry Belafonte: Quote by Harry Belafonte from "What Did We Lose?" from *Life,* vol. 16, no. 4, April 1993. Copyright 1993 by Harry Belafonte.

Julian Bond: Quote by Julian Bond from "What Did We Lose?" from *Life,* vol. 16, no. 4, April 1993. Copyright © 1993 by Julian Bond.

The Christian Science Publishing Society: From Devon McNamara's review of *Angela's Ashes* by Frank McCourt from *The* *Christian Science Monitor,* 1996. Copyright © 1996 by The Christian Science Publishing Society. All rights reserved.

Don Congdon Associates, Inc.: Quote "You can't have 'plot'. . ." by Ray Bradbury.

Barbara Sande Dimmitt: From telephone interview with Barbara Sande Dimmitt conducted on October 21, 1998 by Holt, Rinehart and Winston.

The Gale Group: From "Anne Tyler" from *Contemporary Authors,* vols. 33–36, edited by Ann Evory. Copyright © 1973, 1978 by Gale Research Company. All rights reserved. From "Louis L'Amour" from *Contemporary Authors,* vols. 37–40, edited by Ann Evory. Copyright © 1973, 1979 by Gale Research Company. All rights reserved. Quote by

Acknowledgments (continued)

Tim O'Brien from *Contemporary Authors, New Revision Series*, vol. 58, edited by Daniel Jones and John D. Jorgenson. Copyright © 1997 by Gale Research Inc.

Davis Grossberg, Attorney-in-fact for the Heirs of Alan Jay Lerner: From lyrics from *Camelot* by Alan Jay Lerner and Frederick Loewe. Copyright © 1961 by Alan Jay Lerner and Frederick Loewe. CAUTION: Professionals and amateurs are hereby warned that *Camelot*, being fully protected under the Copyright Laws of the United States of America, the British Empire, including the Dominion of Canada, and all other countries of the Berne and Universal Copyright Conventions, is subject to royalty. All rights, including professional, amateur, motion picture, recitation, lecturing, public reading, radio and television broadcasting, and the rights of translation into foreign languages, are strictly reserved. Particular emphasis is laid on the question of readings, permission for which must be secured in writing.

Harcourt Brace & Company: From "Study of the Text" from *Shakespeare: Major Plays and the Sonnets,* edited by G. B. Harrison. Copyright © 1948 by Harcourt Brace & Company; copyright renewed © 1976 by G. B. Harrison.

Hill and Wang, a division of Farrar, Straus & Giroux, Inc.: From "I've Known Rivers" from *The Big Sea* by Langston Hughes. Copyright © 1940 by Langston Hughes; copyright renewed © 1968 by Arna Bontemps and George Houston Bass.

Limelight Editions: From "Cast, Crew and Personnel" from *From Option to Opening,* Fourth Edition, Revised, by Donald C. Farber. Copyright © 1977 by Donald C. Farber.

Sterling Lord Literistic, Inc.: Comment on "A Presentation of Whales" by Barry Lopez. Copyright © 1994 by Barry Lopez.

Michael T. Marsden: From "The Popular Western as a Cultural Artifact" by Michael T. Marsden from *Arizona and the West: A Quarterly Journal of History,* vol. 20, no. 3, Autumn 1978. Copyright © 1978 by Michael T. Marsden.

Merrill Publishing Company: From *The Humanist Tradition in World Literature,* edited by Stephen L. Harris. Copyright © 1970 by Charles E. Merrill Publishing Company, Columbus, OH.

NEA Today: Quote by Amy Tan from "Meet:" from *NEA Today,* vol. 10, no. 3, October 1991. Copyright © 1991 by the National Education Association of the United States.

Thomas Nelson and Sons Ltd.: From the Introduction and Footnotes to *Julius Caesar, the Arden Edition of the Works of William Shakespeare,* edited by T. S. Dorsch. First published in 1955 by Methuen & Co. Ltd.

The New York Times Company: From "A Man of His Words," book review of *Borges: A Reader,* edited by Emir Rodriguez Monegal and Alastair Reid, by James Atlas from *The New York Times,* October 25, 1981. Copyright © 1981 by The New York Times Company. From "Characters Dangerously Like Us," book review of *The Progress of Love* by Alice Munro, by Joyce Carol Oates from *The New York Times,* September 14, 1986. Copyright © 1986 by The New York Times Company. From "Hometown Horrors," book review of *Friend of My Youth* by Alice Munro, by Bharati Mukherjee from *The New York Times,* March 18, 1990. Copyright © 1990 by The New York Times Company. From "TV Notes: Father-Son Story" by Eleanor Blau from *The New York Times,* June 9, 1998. Copyright © 1998 by The New York Times Company.

Newsweek, Inc.: From "It May Be a Bell Tolling for Me" from *Newsweek,* April 22, 1968. Copyright © 1968 by Newsweek, Inc. All rights reserved. From page 2 from *Newsweek: The Sixties* by the Editors of Newsweek. Copyright © by Newsweek, Inc. All rights reserved.

W. W. Norton & Company, Inc.: From *Shakespeare: A Life in Drama* by Stanley Wells. Copyright © 1995 by Stanley Wells.

Pocket Books, a division of Simon & Schuster, Inc.: From "Julius Caesar: A Modern Perspective" by Coppelia Kahn from *The Tragedy of Julius Caesar* by William Shakespeare. Copyright © 1992 by The Folger Shakespeare Library. From *All the Other Things I Really Need to Know I Learned from Watching Star Trek: The Next Generation* by Dave Marinaccio. Copyright © 1998 by Dave Marinaccio. From Introduction from *Star Trek The Next Generation: The Continuing Mission* by Judith and Garfield Reeves-Stevens. Copyright © 1997 by Paramount Pictures.

Random House, Inc.: From Epilogue by Alex Haley and quote by Malcolm X from *The Autobiography of Malcolm X* by Malcolm X, with the assistance of Alex Haley. Copyright © 1964 by Alex Haley and Malcolm X; copyright © 1965 by Alex Haley and Betty Shabazz.

Red Crane Books, Santa Fe, NM: From *Working in the Dark: Reflections of a Poet of the Barrio* by Jimmy Santiago Baca. Copyright © 1992 by Jimmy Santiago Baca.

Simon & Schuster, Inc.: From "Notes, Chapter 1" from *Admiral Death* by Hanson Baldwin. Copyright 1938 by Hanson Baldwin.

Gloria Steinem: Quote by Alice Walker from "Do You Know This Woman? She Knows You: A Profile of Alice Walker" by Gloria Steinem from *Ms.,* June 1982. Copyright © 1982 by Ms. Foundation for Education and Communication, Inc.

Viking Penguin, a division of Penguin Putnam Inc.: From "Edgar Allan Poe" from *Studies in Classic American Literature* by D. H. Lawrence. Copyright 1923 by Thomas Seltzer, Inc., copyright renewed 1950 by Frieda Lawrence. Copyright © 1961 by The Estate of the late Mrs. Frieda Lawrence.

Warner Bros. Publications Inc., Miami, FL 33014: From lyrics from *Camelot* by Alan Lerner and Frederick Loewe. Copyright © 1960, 1961 and renewed © 1988 by Alan Jay Lerner (ASCAP) & Frederick Loewe (ASCAP). All rights administered by Chappell & Co. (ASCAP). All rights reserved.

A. P. Watt, Ltd., on behalf of The Royal Literary Fund: From Introduction from *Tellers of Tales: 100 Short Stories for the United States, England, France, Russia and Germany,* edited by W. Somerset Maugham. Copyright 1939 by W. Somerset Maugham.

SOURCES CITED:

From *Reaching Judgment at Nuremberg* by Bradley F. Smith. Published by Basic Books, Inc., Publishers, New York, 1977.

From appendix to *Cancer Ward* by Aleksandr Solzhenitsyn. Published by Farrar, Straus and Giroux, Inc., New York, 1969.

Quote by Julia Alvarez from *Contemporary Literary Criticism*, vol. 93, edited by Brigham Narins, et al. Published by Gale Research, Inc., Detroit, MI, 1996.

From "Robert Anderson" by Michael Witkoski from *Twentieth-Century American Dramatists,* Part 1: A–J, edited by John MacNicholas. Published by Gale Research, Inc., Detroit, MI, 1981.

Quote by Edward Hoagland about Anne Tyler from *Contemporary Literary Criticism, Yearbook 1989,* edited by Roger Matuz. Published by Gale Research, Inc., Detroit, MI, 1990.

From *Pilgrim at Tinker Creek* by Annie Dillard. Published by HarperCollins, New York, NY, 1974.

From a review of *The Unexpected Salami* by Laurie Gwen Shapiro from *Kirkus Reviews,* vol. LXVI, no. 6, March 15, 1998. Published by Kirkus Associates, LP, New York, 1998.

Quote by Pat Mora from "Conserving Natural and Cultural Diversity: The Prose and Poetry of Pat Mora" by Patrick D. Murphy from *MELUS,* Spring 1996. Published by MELUS, Amherst, MA, 1996.

From "Viewing the Visual Arts," book review of *You Can't Keep a Good Woman Down* by Alice Walker, by Katha Pollitt from *The New York Times,* May 24, 1981.

From "Amy Tan Walks in Two Worlds" by Sarah Lyall from *The New York Times.*

From *Shakespeare's Living Art* by Rosalie L. Colie. Published by Princeton University Press, Princeton, NJ, 1974.

From interview with Doris Lessing from *Counterpoint* by Roy Newquist. Published by Rand McNally, Chicago, 1964.

From "Call of the Sea" by Roger Rosenblatt from *Time,* October 5, 1998. Published by Time, Inc., New York, 1998.

From "From the Dark Carnival to the Machineries of Joy" by Orson Scott Card from *The Washington Post,* Book World, November 2, 1980.

CONTENTS

The Short-Story Collections

Collection 1

Hard Choices

COLLECTION PLANNING GUIDE T6A–T6D

COMMUNICATIONS WORKSHOPS

Collection 2

Hearts That Love

COLLECTION PLANNING GUIDE T92A–T92D

COMMUNICATIONS WORKSHOPS

Collection 3

Exiles, Castaways, and Strangers

COLLECTION PLANNING GUIDE T170A–T170D

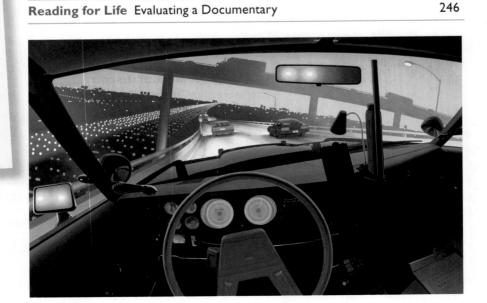

Collection 4

Breakthroughs

COLLECTION PLANNING GUIDE T246A–T246D

COMMUNICATIONS WORKSHOPS

Language/Grammar Links

The Nonfiction Collections

Collection 5

Becoming Myself

COLLECTION PLANNING GUIDE T342A–T342D

COMMUNICATIONS WORKSHOPS

Language/Grammar Links

- Watch Your Tone **352**
- Specific and Proper Nouns **364**
- Voice—a Bit o' Poetry **375**

Collection 6

Being There!
COLLECTION PLANNING GUIDE T386A–T386D

Language/Grammar Links

• Combining Narration and Exposition **408**

• Technical Vocabulary— Widgets, Whatsits, Thingamajigs **432**

• Topic Sentences **444**

COMMUNICATIONS WORKSHOPS

Collection 7

Making a Point
COLLECTION PLANNING GUIDE T454A–T454D

Language/Grammar Links
- Connotations Give Loaded Words Their Punch **467**
- Streamlining Your Prose **478**
- Setting Off Parenthetical Information **488**

The Poetry Collections

Collection 8

How to Live

COLLECTION PLANNING GUIDE T504A–T504D

Collection 9

Can This Be Love?

COLLECTION PLANNING GUIDE T546A–T546D

Language/Grammar Link
• Inverted Sentences—
  Variety and
  Challenge **563**

Collection 10

Dreams—Lost and Found
COLLECTION PLANNING GUIDE T586A–T586D

COMMUNICATIONS WORKSHOPS

The Drama Collection

Collection 11

Doing the Right Thing

COLLECTION PLANNING GUIDE T634A–T634D

COMMUNICATIONS WORKSHOP

COMMUNICATIONS WORKSHOPS

William Shakespeare

William Shakespeare's Life: A Biographical Sketch *by* Robert Anderson 762

The Elizabethan Stage *by* Robert Anderson 765

The Play: The Results of Violence 769

■ **Reading Skills and Strategies**
How to Read Shakespeare 771

Collection 12

Ambition or Honor?
COLLECTION PLANNING GUIDE T772A–T772D

COMMUNICATIONS WORKSHOPS

Language/Grammar Link
• Watch for Parallel Structure **915**

Traditions!
Readings in World Literature

Collection 13
Sources of Wisdom
COLLECTION PLANNING GUIDE T901A–T901D

Collection 14

Finding Our Heroes

COLLECTION PLANNING GUIDE T946A–T946D

COMMUNICATIONS WORKSHOPS

**Language/Grammar
Links**

- A Changing
Language: English
Word Origins **971**

- Commas and
Appositives **980**

Resource Center

Readings in World Literature

Below is a listing of the readings in world literature contained in this book. For ease of reference, these selections are listed separately and organized by geographic region.

The Leader in Literature Presents

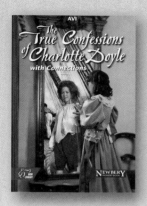

HRW LIBRARY

WITH CONNECTIONS THAT MATTER

Attractive hardcover editions with contemporary art that captures students' imaginations

Readings from a variety of authors and genres—poems, short stories, essays, memoirs, biographical sketches, interviews, and many more—that complement the theme

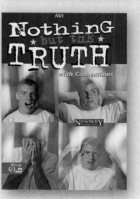

Study guides with support for both the novel and the Connections:

- Pacing suggestions, vocabulary activities, inclusion strategies, and cross-curricular and multimedia projects

- Reproducible masters for reading skills, vocabulary, literary elements, and assessments

- One-page news sheets, Novel Notes, that provide high-interest background information relating to historical, cultural, or literary elements of the novel

ELEMENTS OF
Literature

OVER THE YEARS, *Elements of Literature* has earned the trust of teachers across the country and generated tremendous enthusiasm in the literature and language arts classroom. *The success of this unique program is due in large part to the authentic authorship team that shaped it. In no other literature textbook can you find the expertise of professional writers* who have made the instruction focused and connected. These authors have given *Elements of Literature* its unique voice—a voice that speaks to students and gets them excited about reading and writing.

CREATED BY LEADING EDUCATORS AND AUTHORS

Robert Anderson, John Malcolm Brinnin, and John Leggett, program authors since the inception of *Elements of Literature,* have been determined to involve students in the experience of literature, reflected in the program's respectful tone to students. The authors' motivational approach to instruction, through the use of anecdotes, story, and media, has helped establish the literary framework of this outstanding literature series. Dr. Robert Probst, respected nationally for his response approach, has been instrumental in shaping the student-centered pedagogy of the program. His commitment to making literature meaningful to students and relevant to their lives and experiences is the central focus of *Elements of Literature.*

AN INCREASED EMPHASIS ON READING SKILLS

With this edition of *Elements of Literature,* Dr. Richard Vacca, national reading and literacy expert, joins the authorship team. As special advisor, Dr. Vacca assisted in developing the conceptual framework for the reading strand in the *Pupil's Editions* for grades nine through twelve. Dr. Kylene Beers, well known for her expertise in the area of reading, brings to the program the classroom experiences necessary to answer an increasingly urgent need in today's classrooms—reaching struggling and reluctant readers. Dr. Beers helped to integrate the strong reading development strand in the *Pupil's* and *Annotated Teacher's Editions* with a major new program component, *Reading Skills and Strategies: Reaching Struggling Readers.* This invaluable resource binder includes model lessons, instructional transparencies, and easy readings that help teach students the strategies needed to develop good reading skills.

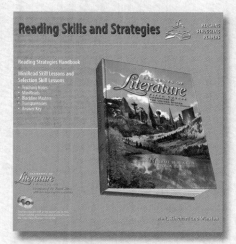

The lessons in *Reading Skills and Strategies: Reaching Struggling Readers* correlate directly to the *Pupil's Edition* and provide a more thorough and detailed approach for students who are having difficulty. The binder includes the following resources:

- **MiniRead Skill Lessons** are based on short, easy selections enabling students to practice the reading strategies in a less-challenging situation. A complete lesson plan models instruction for the teacher.

- **Selection Skill Lessons** provide opportunities for students to apply the reading strategies they've learned to the literature selections in their textbook.

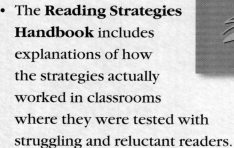

- The **Reading Strategies Handbook** includes explanations of how the strategies actually worked in classrooms where they were tested with struggling and reluctant readers.

- The **QuickGuide** provides a concise, convenient reference guide for using the instructional materials effectively.

Expanding the Role

THIS EDITION OF *Elements of Literature* expands the role of technology, bringing students face-to-face with the media that will shape their understanding of the role of language in their world.

INTERNET RESOURCES ENCOURAGE INVOLVEMENT

The *Elements of Literature* Web resources extend, enhance, and support the series by linking students to carefully researched resources.

When students use the **go.hrw.com** logo and keyword from their textbook, they will be instantly linked to specific resources ranging from biographical information about authors, to extensions of in-text activities and writing assignments, to cross-curricular support for selections. These Internet connections provide a fun and easy way to reach relevant sites without spending valuable time surfing the Web.

INTERACTIVE CD-ROMS MAKE GRAMMAR AND WRITING PRACTICE FUN

The **Language Workshop Interactive Multimedia CD-ROMs** offer a complete course of study in grammar, usage, and mechanics. Sound effects, animation, fine art, and other visuals complement interactive exercises so that students actually enjoy honing their grammar skills.

The **Writer's Workshop Interactive Multimedia CD-ROMs** guide students step-by-step through eight different writing assignments, such as writing a personal narrative, an informative report, or a persuasive essay.

MULTIMEDIA RESOURCES MAKE LITERATURE COME ALIVE

The **Audio CD Library** includes professional readings of nearly every selection in the textbook and reflects a wide range of genres, periods, and cultures.

The **Visual Connections Videocassette Program** features video segments directly related to course content. Author biographies, interviews, historical summaries, and cross-curricular connections enrich and extend instruction.

# of Technology

THE ALL-IN-ONE RESOURCE TOOL

The new **One-Stop Planner CD-ROM with Test Generator** is an all-in-one, comprehensive management tool that makes planning your lessons easier and more efficient. Two CD-ROMs for each grade level include all your teaching resources—organized in easy-to-understand, point-and-click menus.

Here are just a few of the teaching resources you can access on the **One-Stop Planner:**

- Editable lesson plans, importable into several word-processing formats
- Video previews of the *Visual Connections Videocassette Program*
- *Viewing and Representing* Transparencies and Worksheets
- Selection Tests and Answer Keys

LESSON PLANS FOR EVERY CLASSROOM NEED

Lesson Plans Including Strategies for English-Language Learners are designed to help make literature more accessible to students whose first language is not English.

Block Scheduling Lesson Plans help you manage instruction and activities for each day of the 90-day block.

ASSESSMENT TOOLS MATCHED TO THE WAY YOU TEACH

Elements of Literature provides a rich variety of assessment tools—including traditional, alternative, and standardized—that allows you to eval-uate students' performance according to your teaching methods.

- *Formal Assessment*
- *Portfolio Management System with Rubrics for Assignments*
- *Standardized Test Preparation* and *Preparation for College Admission Exams*
- *Test Generator* (included on the One-Stop Planner CD-ROM)

ADDITIONAL TEACHING RESOURCES

Elements of Literature includes an array of flexible resources correlated to the *Pupil's Edition*.

- *Workshop Resources Transparencies and Worksheets*
- *Literary Elements Transparencies and Worksheets*
- *Daily Oral Grammar Transparencies and Worksheets*
- *Viewing and Representing* (Fine Art Transparencies and Worksheets, and the HRW Multimedia Presentation Maker)
- *Language Handbook Worksheets*
- *Grammar and Language Links Worksheets*
- *Cross-Curricular Activities*
- *Words to Own Worksheets*
- *Graphic Organizers for Active Readers*
- *Spelling and Decoding Worksheets (for grades 6–8)*

Literature

AN INVITATION TO A DIALOGUE

Dr. Robert Probst, *Georgia State University*

The classroom is the place for students to learn to read and reflect on visions of human possibilities offered them by the great literature and to begin to tell their own visions and stories.

Literature and Life

Surely, of all the arts, literature is most immediately implicated with life itself. The very medium through which the author shapes the text—language—is grounded in the shared lives of human beings. Language is the bloodstream of a common culture, a common history.

— LOUISE ROSENBLATT

Mathematicians, scientists, and engineers build bridges and send people to the moon, statisticians calculate our insurance premiums and life expectancies, and accountants figure our taxes and amortize our house payments, but the poets, dramatists, novelists, and story-writers have nonetheless remained at the center of life. They bind us together as a society, and they define us as individuals within that society.

When we're very young we need stories almost as much as we need food and protection. Stories entertain us and help us sleep, but they also teach us how to get through the world. They tell us there are pots of gold waiting for us at the end of the rainbow, and they warn us about the trolls hiding under the bridges. They teach us about hope, fear, courage, and all the other elements of our lives. As we grow out of childhood, the great stories, poems, and plays of the world's literature encourage us to reflect on the issues that have intrigued men and women for centuries, inviting us into a continuing dialogue about human experience. When we're older, our own stories represent what we've done, capturing for us what we've made of our lives. Some we'll tell happily, some we'll tell with great pain, and some we may not tell at all, but they're all important because they are a way of making sense of our lives.

If literature is the ongoing dialogue about what it means to be human, then the language arts classroom is society's invitation to students to join that conversation. The texts we use represent the reflections of the world's cultures on the nature of human experience, and the writings we elicit from our students are their first efforts to join in that reflection. The classroom is the place for students to learn to read and reflect on visions of human possibilities offered them by the great literature and to begin to tell their own stories.

Literature offers an invitation to reflect, but it doesn't offer formulas to memorize or answers to write dutifully in notes so that later on, when life presents us with problems, we can pull out our tattered old notebooks and find our path sketched out for us. Literature is an invitation to a dialogue.

That, perhaps more than any other reason, is why it's so important that we teach literature and writing well. It's too easy to avoid the responsible thought demanded by the significant issues, too tempting to accept someone else's formulation of the truth. "Life imitates art," Richard Peck said in a speech in New Orleans in 1974, "especially bad art." By that he meant, I think, that we may too often give in to tempting laziness and allow our lives to be governed by visions of human possibilities that we take from film, television, or graffiti. The problem for teachers, of course, is to lead students not simply to absorb unthinkingly what art offers, but to reflect on it.

This textbook series tries to support teachers' efforts to lead students to think, to feel, and to take responsibility for themselves. It will have much in common with other textbooks. After all, we'd miss "The Raven" if he didn't land croaking on our window sill one morning just before homeroom, and twelfth grade wouldn't be the same without an evening or two around the hearth with Beowulf. But if this series has much in common with other textbooks, it will also have much that differs—including new authors, perhaps authors we haven't met before, exploring lives and circumstances that previously may not have been well represented in the pages of school texts. And similarly, there will be familiar approaches to teaching—perhaps specific activities—that we've all come to rely upon, but there will be other suggestions that emphasize aspects of literary experience, writing, and discussion that may not have been prominent in other books.

Principles of the Program

❶ First among the principles of the program is that *the subject matter of the language arts classroom is human experience comprehended and expressed in language.* The classroom invites the student into the dialogue about the big issues of human experience. The content of literature is the content of our days, and we think and feel about these issues before we enter the classroom and open the text.

When we do finally come to the text, it offers students an opportunity to begin to make sense of experience and to see it captured in the literature.

❷ Implicit in this vision of the language arts is a second principle, *that learning in the English classroom is a creative act,* requiring students to make things with language. Reading literature is a process of engaging the text, weighing it against the experiences readers bring to it.

Similarly, writing isn't simply a matter of learning and applying the rules of grammar and usage or of memorizing the structure and strategies of narratives, descriptions, and arguments.

Literature offers us access to hidden experiences and perceptions.

❸ *The third principle focuses on the encounter between student and content.* It doesn't focus exclusively on the information and skills that have at times provided the framework for our instruction.

Nor, on the other hand, is teaching planned with thought only for the student's interests, needs and desires, and thus organized around whatever concerns happen to predominate at the moment. It is, to borrow Rosenblatt's term, transactional.

❹ For this series, *the integration of the several aspects of the English language arts program* is the fourth governing principle. Literature can't be taught effectively without work in composition. Writing, without the inspiration offered by good literature, remains shallow and undeveloped. Oral language has to be acquired in the context of groups working collaboratively. And so, these texts will suggest ways of interrelating instruction in literature, writing, and language.

Working With the Series

You will find, as you work with selections in this textbook, that students have immediate responses to what they've read. That may be the place to start. The students' responses are very likely to lead you back to the issues you would have wanted to discuss anyway, and so the questions we've suggested might be addressed naturally during the flow of the discussion. Look for the potential in students' reactions and their questions even before turning to the questions in the "First Thoughts" section. Then, the questions in the text can extend or expand the discussion.

The same might be said about the writing. The series has been designed so that experiences with literature, with writing, and with group processes will often be interconnected. We hope that the literature will inspire and shape the students' writing, that their writing will lead back to further reading, and that the discussions and group activities suggested will build a supportive community in which all this work can take place.

The objective in all of this is for students to be able to draw upon their literary heritage and their developing skill with written and spoken language so that, as humane and reasoning people, they may be responsibly engaged with the world around them. If the language arts class helps to achieve that goal, we should be well satisfied with our labors. ❈

Reaching Struggling Readers

AN INTERVIEW WITH

DR. KYLENE BEERS

Dr. Kylene Beers

from the Editor's Desk

As we have listened to teachers over the past few years, one dominant issue has emerged: How do we teach literature to struggling readers? In our search for an answer, we read the research, attended workshops, and interviewed teachers and students. It was obvious that fill-in-the-blank drill worksheets weren't the answer. It was time for a change, but nothing we encountered seemed to offer a real solution to the problem of teaching literature to struggling readers.

Finally, one day Dr. Robert Probst suggested we contact Dr. Kylene Beers. He told us she knew a great deal about reading and might be the person with the answers. During our first meeting with Dr. Beers, she explained the link between reading skills and strategies and discussed the difference she had seen strategies make in the lives of struggling readers. She made a lot of sense to those of us who can recite whole sections of the *Iliad* but had never heard the words *reading* and *strategy* in the same sentence. A year and a half later we see the results of that first meeting: the *Reading Skills and Strategies: Reaching Struggling Readers* binder. This wasn't the easiest project in the history of publishing. Drill worksheets would have been easier to produce, but it was time for a change—time to turn struggling readers into successful ones.

Here are some of the questions we asked Dr. Beers during the course of this project.

The curriculum demands on English teachers are enormous. Teachers often ask us why they should add reading skills and strategies to an already loaded course.

❝I used to ask myself the same thing. Twenty years ago, when I began teaching, I expected that I'd carefully guide excited students through the prose and poetry of literary giants like Whitman, Emerson, Dickinson, Thoreau, Kipling, Joyce, Márquez, Angelou, and well, you know the names. I expected that students would arrive early for literature class and leave late for their next class. I expected I'd never have to worry about teaching someone to read—that was for the elementary teachers. I was going to teach *Literature*. Those expectations changed quickly. First, I didn't have students who loved literature. Most of my students didn't even like literature. Second, I didn't have students who could already read. When I didn't get the students I expected, I didn't know what to do.

Twenty years later, I'm still not getting what I expected when it comes to teaching. But I've learned that if I understand students' strengths and have some ideas about how to address their weaknesses, then they'll often give me more than I ever expected.

I've spent the past twenty years learning how to help these secondary students who can't read and don't like to read become better readers. I've worked with students at all grade levels and all ability levels. I've gone back to school to study how to teach reading, and now I see myself as a reading/literature teacher. The teaching of literature and the teaching of reading are integral to one another, so interconnected that separating them seems an abomination. ❞

How can a teacher use a literature anthology with the increasing numbers of students who have serious difficulty reading any text?

❝After many years of working with all types of readers, but especially struggling and reluctant readers, I've learned some things that have helped me reach those students. I've found that struggling readers have difficulty reading for a myriad of reasons. Often they don't know a lot of words, so limited vocabulary keeps them from understanding what they've read. Sometimes they lack decoding ability, so they don't know how to get through big words. Other times, they can call words well, but they don't know how to make sense of what they've read. And sometimes, their distaste for reading makes them think reading is meaningless, so they see no reason for putting any effort into it. As I work with students and address those issues, I keep what I call the ABCDE rules in mind. A look at the diagram below will quickly show you what these rules are. ❞

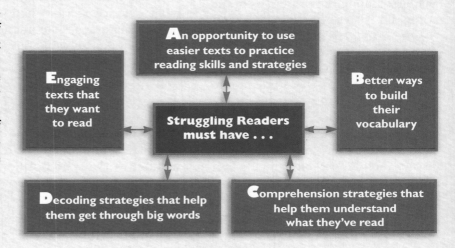

An opportunity to use easier texts to practice reading skills and strategies

Engaging texts that they want to read

Struggling Readers must have . . .

Better ways to build their vocabulary

Decoding strategies that help them get through big words

Comprehension strategies that help them understand what they've read

To help provide this ABCDE rule for struggling readers, what should a literature program include?

> A literature program should help teachers with each of those areas, particularly A, B, C, and E. If publishers want to help, they will have to develop specialized materials that complement the basal text. Here's what we did with the *Reading Skills and Strategies* binder for *Elements of Literature*:

❶ Easier Selections Provide Practice for Skills and Strategies.

We hired a group of professional writers to write easy fiction and nonfiction pieces. These selections, or MiniReads, are short texts written at an easier level than the selections in the literature book. The purpose of the MiniReads is to give students the opportunity to practice decoding skills, comprehension strategies, and vocabulary strategies with a text that is not only easier but engaging as well.

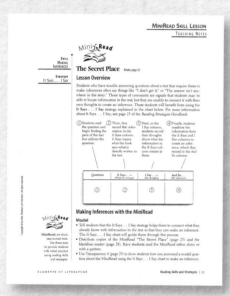

❷ Our MiniRead Lessons Include Modeling.

Each MiniRead includes a complete lesson plan that provides modeling of the skill and strategy. Transparencies help teachers focus students on the strategies. Blackline masters give students a chance to practice the strategies before applying them to selections in the Pupil's Edition.

❸ Reading Skills and Strategies Are Connected to the Selections in *Elements of Literature*.

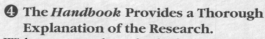

All skills and strategies are *applied* to selections in the anthology. The detailed lesson plans can be used not only with struggling readers, but with all readers.

❹ The *Handbook* Provides a Thorough Explanation of the Research.

Without research to back them up, the lessons would have no foundation. The *Reading Strategies Handbook* includes transcripts from actual classrooms in which the strategies have been tested with struggling readers. The handbook *shows* rather than just *tells* how to initiate specific strategies, what pitfalls to avoid, and how to document progress. Articles about each of the strategies help teachers become more comfortable withusing the strategies with any selection. ”

Reading Matters

Dr. Richard T. Vacca, *Kent State University*

Bringing Literature and Reading Together

Technologically advanced societies like ours value literate behavior and demand that citizens acquire literacy for personal, social, academic, and economic success. The pressure to hold teachers accountable for students' reading development is greater today than at any time in our nation's history. To the extent that texts are an integral part of learning in all content areas, *every* teacher has a role to play in helping students become readers, writers, and oral communicators. Yet the responsibility for teaching literacy usually lies with English teachers and with reading specialists in middle and high schools. English teachers, however, are not reading specialists and shouldn't view their roles as such. Showing students how to use reading strategies in the literature classroom doesn't require the specialized training of a reading specialist. Nor does the development of reading skills and strategies in the context of the literature classroom diminish the teacher's role as a subject matter specialist. It is far more realistic and effective to integrate the skills and strategies that readers actually need. The real value of reading lies in the way it is used. To be literate in literature classrooms, students must learn how to use reading to construct meaning from literary texts. Because literacy use is situational, the most meaningful way for students to develop reading skills and strategies is in the context in which they must be used. A student using reading to find meaning in literature gains confidence in his or her ability to read and to interpret texts.

Scaffolding reading experiences is the key to bringing literature and reading together in the literature classroom. The term *scaffolding* is a metaphor used in teaching and learning to suggest a means by which you help students do what they cannot do at first. In other words, scaffolding reading experiences allows teachers to provide the instructional support and guidance that students need to be successful. Instructional scaffolding allows teachers to support students' efforts to think clearly, critically, and creatively about literary texts *while* showing them how to use skills and strategies that will allow them to read more effectively than if left to their own devices.

Developing Skills and Strategies

Because skills and strategies are best learned through meaningful use, the lesson organization for the literary selections in **Elements of Literature** provides numerous opportunities to scaffold students' exploration and interpretation of literary texts. Each lesson creates an instructional framework that respects the nature of the literary experience while making provisions to scaffold students' use of reading skills and strategies. Instructional scaffolding before reading, for example, demonstrates to students the importance of anticipation, making predictions, raising questions, and other strategies that connect their world to the world of the text.

Students are in a strategic position to learn with literature whenever they use their prior knowledge to construct meaning. Prior knowledge includes the experiences, conceptual understandings, attitudes, values, skills, and strategies the reader brings to a text situation. How readers *activate* prior knowledge is the mechanism by which they connect their world to the world of the text. Prior knowledge, when activated, allows readers to seek, organize, retain, and elaborate meaning. In *Elements of Literature*, features such as *Make the Connection* and *Quickwrites* activate prior knowledge in relation to the issues, problems, conflicts, or themes to be studied through the literary experience. These scaffolds provide students with an imaginative entry into the text by raising expectations, arousing curiosity, and anticipating what is ahead in the literature selection.

Making students aware of *why, how,* and *when* they should use strategies to activate prior knowledge and anticipate content is as important as understanding *what* the strategies are. For example: Why is activating what students already know about a topic through a quickwrite (or any prereading strategy) important? How can students connect what they know to what they are about to read? When should a technique such as quickwrite be used and when shouldn't it? From a strategy-learning perspective, these discussions provide students with a rationale for skill and strategy use and build *procedural knowledge*, which is knowledge about why, how, and what skill and strategy to use.

While readers explore meaning before and during reading, they often need to engage in clarification and elaboration after reading. Postreading questions and activities at the end of each literary selection in *Elements of Literature* create another type of instructional support for students. They help students extend their thinking and evaluate the significance of the literary experience.

In addition to scaffolding reading experiences at the point of use, there are other features of *Elements of Literature* that will help you support and guide students' reading development. For example, the MiniRead lessons in the reading binder, *Reading Skills and Strategies: Reaching Struggling Readers,* are instructional resources that provide *explicit instruction* for students who need additional guidance and support. The MiniRead lessons allow students to share insights and knowledge that they might otherwise never discover. These explicit lessons create a framework that unifies skill and strategy development. They provide methods for struggling readers to become aware of, to use, and to develop control over skills and strategies that can make a difference in their literate lives.

Elements of Literature on the Internet

TO THE STUDENT

Discover more about the stories, poems, and essays in *Elements of Literature* by logging on to the Internet. At **go.hrw.com** we help you complete your homework assignments, learn more about your favorite writers, and find facts that support your ideas and inspire you with new ones. Here's how to log on:

1. Start your Web browser and enter **go.hrw.com** in the location field.

| Back | Forward | Reload | Home | Search |

Location: http://go.hrw.com

2. Note the keyword in your textbook.

 **go.hrw.com**
LE0 10-1

3. In your Web browser, enter the keyword and click on GO.

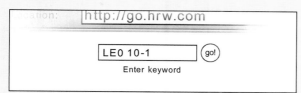

Location: http://go.hrw.com

LE0 10-1 (go!)

Enter keyword

Now that you've arrived, you can peek into the palaces and museums of the world, listen to stories of exploration and discovery, or view fires burning on the ocean floor. As you move through *Elements of Literature,* use the best on-line resources at **go.hrw.com.**

Elements of Literature

The Tragedy of Julius Caesar

William Shakespeare

More About the Writer

Walk to School with Will Shakespeare
Sometimes it seems that Shakespeare lived far away and long ago. Perhaps he did, but only 4,000 miles and only 500 years ago. Through this site you can visit the same buildings Shakespeare might have seen as he walked to school in his hometown of Stratford-on-Avon.

Before You Read: The Tragedy of Julius Caesar, page 774

Law and Chaos
Is a strong government with an active legal system always the sign of an orderly society? Read about the increase in the number of lawyers and lawsuits in Elizabethan England and compare it to our society today. Can you think of factors, other than laws, that contribute to an orderly society?

Literature and Beliefs, page 791

Who's Afraid of a Big Bright Comet?

Enjoy the Internet, but be critical of the information you find there. Always evaluate your sources for credibility, accuracy, timeliness, and possible bias.

Web sites accessed through **go.hrw.com** are reviewed regularly. However, on-line materials change continually and without notice. Holt, Rinehart and Winston cannot ensure the accuracy or appropriateness of materials other than our own. Students, teachers, and guardians should assume responsibility for checking all on-line materials. A full description of Terms of Use can be found at **go.hrw.com.**

1. Read short stories on the themes "Hard Choices"; "Hearts That Love"; "Exiles, Castaways, and Strangers"; and "Breakthroughs"
2. Interpret literary elements, with special emphasis on plot, setting, character, theme, irony and satire, point of view, and symbols
3. Apply a variety of reading strategies, particularly making meanings, or having a dialogue with the text
4. Respond to the literature in a variety of modes
5. Learn and use new words
6. Plan, draft, revise, edit, proof, and publish a persuasive essay and an evaluation
7. Write sentences based on professional models, expand sentences using phrases and clauses
9. Demonstrate the ability to read a science article
10. With a group, formulate and apply a series of steps for resolving conflicts

The Short-Story Collections

There are only two or three human stories, and they go on repeating themselves as fiercely as if they had never happened before.

—Willa Cather

Responding to the Quotation

Tell students that when she refers to "stories," Willa Cather probably means basic human conflicts that recur all over the world from generation to generation. Ask what some of these basic "stories" might be. [Possible responses: young lovers who must overcome the opposition of their parents; coping with the death or suffering of a loved one; overcoming a jealous or envious rival; overcoming the temptations of greed; dealing with the consequences of betrayal.] Then, ask why these stories might seem as if they repeat themselves "fiercely." [Sample answer: Every time an individual experiences a conflict, it feels to that person as if the story is happening for the first time.]

Selection Readability

This Annotated Teacher's Edition provides a summary of each selection in the student book. Following each Summary heading, you will find one, two, or three small icons. These icons indicate, in an approximate sense, the reading level of the selection.

- ■ One icon indicates that the selection is easy.
- ■ ■ Two icons indicate that the selection is on an intermediate reading level.
- ■ ■ ■ Three icons indicate that the selection is challenging.

Olive Hill (1987)
by Frank Romero
(1941–).
Oil on canvas.
Private collection.

Frank Romero (1941–) grew up in California and often portrays urban landscapes in his paintings. A figure in the Chicano art movement, Romero first received recognition as a painter in the 1970s. Like many of Romero's works, *Olive Hill* includes an image of a freeway. He says, "I see the freeways as the arteries of the city, as the lifeblood of the city, because in L.A. you spend so much time in your car. I started to see that the freeways make beautiful links, and they connect places."

Activity. Ask students what strange, mysterious details they see in the painting. You might select a popular song to play while students look at the painting and ask them to jot down in their Writer's Notebook the feelings and ideas that the song and the painting convey to them. What kinds of stories can they imagine taking place in the landscape shown in the painting?

WRITERS ON WRITING

A Conversation with Ray Bradbury. In this interview, a famous science fiction writer describes the writing process he has used to create his award-winning stories.

Ask each student to read the interview and to choose the line he or she considers the most interesting or important. Then, have students read aloud the lines they've chosen and explain their choices. If more than one student has selected the same line, have the class compare and contrast each student's reason for selecting the line.

Reading Skills and Strategies

Responding to the Text

❓ Notice Bradbury's personification of a short story as something that "dances out of your subconscious." Has a creative idea ever come to you this way? [Responses will vary. Some students will have had this kind of imaginative experience, while others may be skeptical.]

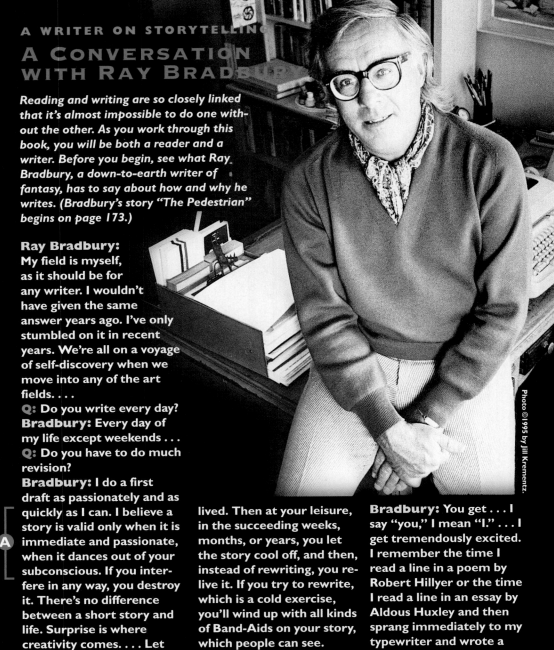

A WRITER ON STORYTELLING

A CONVERSATION WITH RAY BRADBURY

Reading and writing are so closely linked that it's almost impossible to do one without the other. As you work through this book, you will be both a reader and a writer. Before you begin, see what Ray Bradbury, a down-to-earth writer of fantasy, has to say about how and why he writes. (Bradbury's story "The Pedestrian" begins on page 173.)

Ray Bradbury: My field is myself, as it should be for any writer. I wouldn't have given the same answer years ago. I've only stumbled on it in recent years. We're all on a voyage of self-discovery when we move into any of the art fields. . . .

Q: Do you write every day?

Bradbury: Every day of my life except weekends . . .

Q: Do you have to do much revision?

A **Bradbury:** I do a first draft as passionately and as quickly as I can. I believe a story is valid only when it is immediate and passionate, when it dances out of your subconscious. If you interfere in any way, you destroy it. There's no difference between a short story and life. Surprise is where creativity comes. . . . Let your characters have their way. Let your secret life be lived. Then at your leisure, in the succeeding weeks, months, or years, you let the story cool off, and then, instead of rewriting, you relive it. If you try to rewrite, which is a cold exercise, you'll wind up with all kinds of Band-Aids on your story, which people can see.

Q: How do you feel a story coming on?

Bradbury: You get . . . I say "you," I mean "I." . . . I get tremendously excited. I remember the time I read a line in a poem by Robert Hillyer or the time I read a line in an essay by Aldous Huxley and then sprang immediately to my typewriter and wrote a short story. . . .

—*Writer's Digest*, February 1967

Photo ©1995 by Jill Krementz.

2 THE SHORT-STORY COLLECTIONS

Using Students' Strengths

Interpersonal Learners

These students may enjoy role-playing as they explore ideas for a short story. Invite students to base their story on some primary emotion, such as greed, jealousy, or love. Encourage them to use Bradbury's process of letting their ideas "dance" out of their imagination without interference. Appoint one student to record the group's ideas for descriptions and any improvised dialogue. Then, have students individually turn this material into their own short stories.

Intrapersonal Learners

These students may find it interesting to reflect on their own drafting and revising processes for creating a story. First, have them quickwrite one or more ideas for a story, letting their ideas "dance" out of their imagination. Then, they should wait a few days and "relive" their original idea in order to create a final draft. Finally, have them write a paragraph about the experience of composing a story this way. As an extension activity, you might have interpersonal learners and intrapersonal learners compare and contrast their experiences in writing a story.

Reading Skills and Strategies

OBJECTIVES
1. Recognize ways of making meaning from a text
2. Understand how to use context clues to determine a word's meaning

READING A SHORT STORY: MAKING MEANINGS

You might think that reading a story is a passive activity, but something mysterious happens as you read. The words on a page enter your mind and interact with whatever else happens to be there—your experiences, thoughts, memories, hopes, and fears. If a character says, "I had to run away. I had no choice," you might say, "Yeah, I know what that feels like." Another reader, however, may say, "What is he talking about? You always have a choice." We all make our own meaning depending on who we are. Here are some of the ways we do that:

1. **We connect with the text.** We might think, "This reminds me of something," or "I once did that."

2. **We ask questions.** We ask about unfamiliar words, or about what might happen next, or about a character's motivation.

3. **We make predictions.** We may not realize that we are making predictions as we read, but if we've ever been surprised by something in a story, that means we had predicted something else.

4. **We interpret.** We figure out what each part of a story means and how the parts work together to create meaning.

5. **We extend the text.** We extend the meaning of a story to the wider life around us, including other stories, films, and actual life.

6. **We challenge the text.** We might feel that a character is not realistic or that the plot is poor or that we don't like the writing.

HOW TO OWN A WORD

Learning from Context

One strategy we use when we're confronted with an unfamiliar word is the use of **context clues.** That is, we try to get the word's meaning (or a very good idea of it) from the words surrounding the unfamiliar word. We also use the knowledge we already have in our heads.

In the following story, a group of boys approaches some pheasants, but the birds don't "flush." Here is how a reader who is not sure what *flush* means guesses (almost correctly) that the word must mean "to fly away." (It means, in this context, "to fly up suddenly, as if from a hiding place.")

What does *flush* mean?

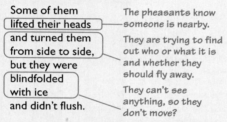

Some of them
lifted their heads — The pheasants know someone is nearby.
and turned them from side to side, — They are trying to find out who or what it is and whether they should fly away.
but they were
blindfolded
with ice — They can't see anything, so they don't move?
and didn't flush.

***Flush* might mean "to fly up or away."**

Extending your store of words. *Flush* is a word with **multiple meanings.** If the context is card playing, *flush* has one meaning. If the context is a display of emotion, it has another meaning. If the context is carpentry, *flush* has yet another meaning. Do you know all three of these meanings?

Apply the strategy on the next page. ▶

Reading Skills and Strategies

This feature focuses on specific strategies that skilled readers use to make meaning from fiction. Explain that skilled readers may use several but not necessarily all of the strategies when reading a selection.

Mini-Lesson:
Making Meanings
Making meanings is not restricted to reading. A similar process helps us make meanings while watching a movie or television show. Identify a specific television program that most of your students watched recently, and use it as an example to explore the process of making meanings. Model some of your internal meaning-making strategies. For example, "I really identified with the mother in that movie" (*connect*); "I couldn't figure out why they kept flashing back to her childhood, and then it suddenly hit me" (*interpret*); "That show made me think about how we treat people with mental illness" (*extend*); "I thought that the ending was unrealistic—that would never happen in real life" (*challenge*).

Mini-Lesson:
How to Own a Word
Write the following sentence from "What Happened During the Ice Storm" on the chalkboard: "The grass seeds looked like little yolks inside gelatin whites." Ask students how they might be able to tell what *gelatin* is, if they do not already know. [Sample answer: Egg whites are like jelly; gelatin might be something that is jellylike.]

Getting Students Involved

Cooperative Learning
Word Clues. Have students work in small groups to come up with a difficult word they think their classmates will not know. One student should read the dictionary entry and explain the word's meaning to the group until they believe they understand how to use the word correctly. Then, have students work together to write a short paragraph containing the unfamiliar word along with context clues, such as synonyms, examples, comparisons, or contrasts. Groups should exchange paragraphs and try to determine the new word's meaning through context. Have each group tell the class what they think the meaning of the word is and explain how they determined the meaning. If a group guesses an incorrect definition, the group that submitted the word should give additional clues before revealing the word's meaning.

Dialogue with the Text

Suggest that students review the Making Meanings strategies and attempt to apply some of those strategies as they read this selection. Explain that the strategies they apply at certain points in the story may be different from those applied by the student reader, Melissa Bender, and that their responses to even the same strategy may differ from Melissa's.

Summary ■ ■

A freezing rain presents some farm boys with a choice involving life and death. The beautiful but deadly rain is relentless, freezing shut the eyes of wild pheasants that farmers will "harvest" with clubs. Without weapons or sacks, the boys also hunt for these helpless birds. After standing over them with uncertainty, one boy covers two pheasants with his coat; the other boys follow suit. They run home coatless, leaving all the birds covered.

The setting functions almost as a character in this story. Its dangerous, glittering atmosphere forces the story's main external conflict. At the story's climax, the boys choose to protect the innocent creatures instead of killing them.

 Reading Skills and Strategies

Making Meanings: Connecting with the Text

❓ Based on what you have experienced or on what you have read about ice storms, what are some of the possible things this story might be about? [Possible responses: damage done to crops, harm to animals, traffic accidents, power outages.]

Resources

Listening
Audio CD Library
For a recording of this selection see the *Audio CD Library:*
• Disc 1, Track 2

They stood looking at each other, each expecting the other to do something.

 Dialogue with the Text

The notes that follow show the thoughts of one reader as she read this story for the first time. For your first reading, cover her responses with a sheet of paper, and write your own responses in your notebook. Then compare your responses with hers.

What Happened During the Ice Storm

Jim Heynen

T4

On their second reading, when students compare their responses with the model, ask them to identify which Making Meanings strategy they used and which ones Melissa Bender used. [Students' strategies will vary. Melissa asked questions ("Why does this winter matter?" "What do pheasants have to do with anything?" and so on); she connected with the text ("I like this imagery." "The eyes freezing over does create a picture" ". . . I don't see a reason for it.")]

Ⓑ Elements of Literature
Imagery
The author uses sensory details to contrast the visual beauty of the ice (*shine, glistened*) with the damage and harm it causes (*broke like glass, thickened, blurred, froze shut*).

Ⓒ Reading Skills and Strategies
Making Meanings:
Making Predictions
? What do you think will happen to the pheasants? Why do you think so? [Some students might correctly predict that the boys will save the pheasants, but many will expect the boys to harm them. The narrator states that the birds are vulnerable and that the adults are killing them. Some students might expect the boys to mimic the adults, whereas others may say the boys will rebel against (or act more humanely than) their fathers.]

Oﾠne winter there was a freezing rain. "How beautiful!" people said when things outside started to shine with ice. But the freezing rain kept coming. Tree branches glistened like glass. Then broke like glass. Ice thickened on the windows until everything outside blurred. Farmers moved their livestock into the barns, and most animals were safe. But not the pheasants. Their eyes froze shut.

Some farmers went ice-skating down the gravel roads with clubs to harvest pheasants that sat helplessly in the roadside ditches. The boys went out into the freezing rain to find pheasants too. They saw dark spots along a fence. Pheasants, all right. Five or six of them. The boys slid their feet along slowly, trying not to break the ice that covered the snow. They slid up close to the pheasants. The pheasants pulled their heads down between their wings. They couldn't tell how easy it was to see them huddled there.

Dialogue with the Text

Why does this winter matter?

Ⓑ I like this imagery.

What do pheasants have to do with anything? But the eyes freezing shut does create a picture.
OK, here are pheasants again, but I still don't see the reason for it. Who are these boys? Friends of the narrator? Bystanders or participants?

Ⓒ

WHAT HAPPENED DURING THE ICE STORM 5

Reaching All Students

Struggling Readers
The skill of carrying on a Dialogue with the Text, or Making Meanings, was introduced on p. 3. You might reassure these students that they can write anything they think of as they read this story—that there is no "right" response when they carry on a dialogue with a text. Every student's response is different and equally valid.

English Language Learners
Explain that this story depicts a rural environment. Work with students to write down words that tell them the story takes place in the country. [*farmers, livestock, barns, pheasants, gravel roads, barbed-wire, grass seeds, fields*] Have them discuss in small groups whether they think the story's events, or something comparable, could happen in an urban environment. Each student should give at least one reason for his or her opinion.

Advanced Learners
Have these students meet with partners to compare their Dialogue with the Text notes. Then, have them read Melissa Bender's final entry on p. 6 and discuss whether they agree that the story's ending is emotionally satisfying but not particularly realistic. Have them discuss why or why not.

Dialogue with the Text

Encourage students to record in their Writer's Notebook their own connection to the characters and events in the selection.

 Reading Skills and Strategies
Making Meanings: Ask Questions

❓ If you didn't know the meaning of the word *flush* in this context, what question would you ask and how would you try to find the meaning of the word? **What might the word *flush* mean?** [Possible question, strategy, and answer: "What does flush mean here?" I'd use context clues. The word might mean "run from under cover" or "run in order to escape."]

Ⓑ **Appreciating Language**
Incomplete Sentences

❓ Notice how the author uses incomplete sentences. How does this affect your interpretation of the scenery and events? [Possible responses: It makes them seem more realistic, as if the author were talking to me directly; it seems a little disjointed—I had to read the fragments twice.]

 Reading Skills and Strategies
Making Meanings: Challenging the Text

❓ Did you feel what the boys did was realistic? Why or why not? [Some students may feel that what the boys did was realistic because some people do indeed have compassion for helpless animals in distress; some students may say the boys behaved unrealistically because some boys in this situation— like their fathers—would have killed the birds for fun or sport.]

Ⓓ **Critical Thinking**
Speculating

❓ How do you think the boys will feel when they get home? [Possible responses: They may feel happy because they have helped the defenseless pheasants; they may feel worried or embarrassed about having to explain what happened to their jackets; they may feel puzzled about what has happened.]

Dialogue with the Text

Ⓐ

These boys are in conflict. Don't they want to kill the pheasants? Why can't they bring themselves to do it?

wow! I can really see this!

Ⓒ

Oh, my gosh! This isn't what I expected. I like this ending better than the boys killing the pheasants. It's not as realistic, but it does have an emotional appeal.

Melissa Bender

—Melissa Bender
Torrance High School
Torrance, California

The boys stood still in the icy rain. Their breath came out in slow puffs of steam. The pheasants' breath came out in quick little white puffs. Some of them lifted their heads and turned them from side to side, but they were blindfolded with ice and didn't flush. The boys had not brought clubs, or sacks, or anything but themselves. They stood over the pheasants, turning their own heads, looking at each other, each expecting the other to do something. To pounce on a pheasant, or to yell "Bang!" Things around them were shining and dripping with icy rain. The barbed-wire fence. The fence posts. The broken stems of grass. Even the grass seeds. The grass seeds looked like little yolks inside gelatin whites. And the pheasants looked like unborn birds glazed in egg white. Ice was hardening on the boys' caps and coats. Soon they would be covered with ice too.

Then one of the boys said, "Shh." He was taking off his coat, the thin layer of ice splintering in flakes as he pulled his arms from the sleeves. But the inside of the coat was dry and warm. He covered two of the crouching pheasants with his coat, rounding the back of it over them like a shell. The other boys did the same. They covered all the helpless pheasants. The small gray hens and the larger brown cocks. Now the boys felt the rain soaking through their shirts and freezing. They ran across the slippery fields, unsure of their footing, the ice clinging to their skin as they made their way toward the blurry lights of the house.

Using Students' Strengths

Visual Learners
Have these students create collages that convey the same mood as the imagery in this story: both the beauty and the potential dangers of winter. Display the collages and ask students to explain why they chose each image. Other students may want to create drawings or paintings of scenes in the story.

Naturalist Learners
Have these students research how pheasants are classified among birds. Ask them to give short talks about pheasants' distinctive physical characteristics, their means of adapting to their habitat, and their place in the food chain.

Collection 1

Hard Choices

Theme

Revelations in Fiction and in Life *Choices are essential in life, and sometimes all of the available options have difficult consequences. It's not surprising that many story plots revolve around a choice and what that choice reveals about the character who makes it. In literature, these moments of decision are moments of truth, revealing a person's deepest values and loyalties. In life and in literature, choices force us to look beyond the decision itself to the kind of person we'd like to be.*

Reading the Anthology

Reaching Struggling Readers

The *Reading Skills and Strategies: Reaching Struggling Readers* binder provides materials coordinated with the Pupil's Edition (see the Collection Planner, p. T6B) to help students who have difficulty reading and comprehending text, or students who are reluctant readers. The binder for tenth grade is organized around sixteen individual skill areas and offers the following options:

- **MiniRead** MiniReads are short, easy texts that give students a chance to practice a particular skill and strategy before reading selections in the Pupil's Edition. Each MiniRead Skill Lesson can be taught independently or used in conjunction with a Selection Skill Lesson.

- **Selection Skill Lessons** Selection Skill Lessons allow students to apply skills introduced in the MiniReads. Each Selection Skill Lesson provides reading instruction and practice specific to a particular piece of literature in the Pupil's Edition.

Reading Beyond the Anthology

Read On

Collection 1 includes an annotated bibliography of books suitable for extended reading. The suggested books are related to works in this collection by theme, by author, or by subject. To preview the Read On for Collection 1, please turn to p. T84.

HRW Library

The *HRW Library* offers novels, plays, and short-story collections for extended reading. Each book in the Library includes one or more major works and thematically related Connections. Each book in the *HRW Library* is also accompanied by a Study Guide that provides teaching suggestions and worksheets. For Collection 1, the following titles are recommended.

A TALE OF TWO CITIES
Charles Dickens
The two cities, of course, are London and Paris. This is the unforgettable story of one man's heroic self-sacrifice for the woman he loves.

THE CHOSEN
Chaim Potok
Despite the disapproval of one father, two boys from different worlds forge a friendship and make choices about their futures. A different kind of "choice" is signaled by the title.

Collection 1 Hard Choices

Resources for this Collection

Note: All resources for this collection are available for preview on the *One-Stop Planner CD-ROM 1 with Test Generator.* All worksheets and blackline masters may be printed from the CD-ROM.

Internet Resources
go.hrw.com LE0 10-1

Selection or Feature	Reading and Literary Skills	Vocabulary, Language, and Grammar

The Cold Equations (p. 8)
Tom Godwin
 	
Connections: Lunar Legacy
from The New York Times (p. 28)
	• *Reading Skills and Strategies: Reaching Struggling Readers*
	  • MiniRead Skill Lesson, p. 1
	  • Selection Skill Lesson, p. 7
	
	• *Graphic Organizers for Active Reading,* Worksheet p. 1
	
	• *Literary Elements:* Transparency 1
	  Worksheet p. 4
		• *Words to Own,* Worksheet p. 1
		
		• *Grammar and Language Links:*
		  Subject-Verb Agreement, Worksheet p. 1
		
		• *Language Workshop CD-ROM,*
		  Subject-Verb Agreement
		
		• *Daily Oral Grammar,*
		  Transparency 1

Elements of Literature: Plot (p. 32)	• *Literary Elements,* Transparency 2	

The Bass, the River, and Sheila Mant (p. 34)
W. D. Wetherell
	• *Reading Skills and Strategies: Reaching Struggling Readers*
	  • MiniRead Skill Lesson, p. 11
	  • Selection Skill Lesson, p. 18
	
	• *Graphic Organizers for Active Reading,* Worksheet p. 2
	
	• *Literary Elements:* Transparency 2
	  Worksheet p. 7
		• *Words to Own,* Worksheet p. 3
		
		• *Grammar and Language Links:*
		  Imagery, Worksheet p. 3
		
		• *Daily Oral Grammar,*
		  Transparency 2

The Book of Sand (p. 43)
Jorge Luis Borges
translated by
Norman Thomas Di Giovanni
	• *Reading Skills and Strategies: Reaching Struggling Readers*
	  • MiniRead Skill Lesson, p. 22
	  • Selection Skill Lesson, p. 29
	
	• *Graphic Organizers for Active Reading,* Worksheet p. 3
		• *Words to Own,* Worksheet p. 4
		
		• *Grammar and Language Links:*
		  Personal Pronouns, Worksheet p. 5
		
		• *Language Workshop CD-ROM,* Pronouns
		
		• *Daily Oral Grammar,*
		  Transparency 3

Elements of Literature: Setting (p. 50)	• *Literary Elements,* Transparency 3	

Boys and Girls (p. 52)
Alice Munro
 	
Connections: Same Song (p. 65)
Pat Mora
	• *Reading Skills and Strategies: Reaching Struggling Readers*
	  • MiniRead Skill Lesson, p. 33
	  • Selection Skill Lesson, p. 40
	
	• *Graphic Organizers for Active Reading,* Worksheet p. 4
		• *Words to Own,* Worksheet p. 5
		
		• *Grammar and Language Links:*
		  Connotations, Worksheet p. 7
		
		• *Daily Oral Grammar,*
		  Transparency 4

Everyday Use (p. 69)
Alice Walker
 	
Connections: In Georgia's Swept Yards, a Dying Tradition (p. 77)
Anne Raver
	• *Reading Skills and Strategies: Reaching Struggling Readers*
	  • MiniRead Skill Lesson, p. 44
	  • Selection Skill Lesson, p. 51
	
	• *Graphic Organizers for Active Reading,* Worksheet p. 5
	
	• *Literary Elements:* Transparency 3
	  Worksheet p. 10
		• *Words to Own,* Worksheet p. 6
		
		• *Grammar and Language Links:*
		  Diction, Worksheet p. 9
		
		• *Daily Oral Grammar,*
		  Transparency 5

Extending the Theme: *from* **Travels with Charley** (p. 81) John Steinbeck	The Extending the Theme feature provides students with an unstructured opportunity to practice reading strategies using a selection that extends the theme of the collection.	
Writer's Workshop: Persuading Through Personal Narrative (p. 85)		
Sentence Workshop: Building from the Basics (p. 91)		• *Workshop Resources,* p. 55

Other Resources for This Collection

- *Cross-Curricular Activities,* p. 1
- *Portfolio Management System,* Introduction to Portfolio Assessment, p. 1
- *Test Generator,* Collection Test

Writing	Listening and Speaking / Viewing and Representing	Assessment
• *Portfolio Management System,* Rubrics for Choices, p. 89	• *Visual Connections:* Videocassette A, Segment 1 • *Audio CD Library,* Disc 1, Track 3 • *Viewing and Representing:* Fine Art Transparency 1 Worksheet p. 4 • *Portfolio Management System,* Rubrics for Choices, p. 89	• *Formal Assessment,* Selection Test, p. 1 • *Standardized Test Preparation,* pp. 10, 12 • *Test Generator (One-Stop Planner CD-ROM)*
		• *Formal Assessment,* Literary Elements Test, p. 11
• *Portfolio Management System,* Rubrics for Choices, p. 91	• *Audio CD Library,* Disc 2, Track 2 • *Portfolio Management System,* Rubrics for Choices, p. 91	• *Formal Assessment,* Selection Test, p. 3 • *Test Generator (One-Stop Planner CD-ROM)*
• *Portfolio Management System,* Rubrics for Choices, p. 92	• *Audio CD Library,* Disc 2, Track 3 • *Portfolio Management System,* Rubrics for Choices, p. 92	• *Formal Assessment,* Selection Test, p. 5 • *Test Generator (One-Stop Planner CD-ROM)*
		• *Formal Assessment,* Literary Elements Test, p. 13
• *Portfolio Management System,* Rubrics for Choices, p. 93	• *Audio CD Library,* Disc 3, Track 2 • *Portfolio Management System,* Rubrics for Choices, p. 93	• *Formal Assessment,* Selection Test, p. 7 • *Standardized Test Preparation,* p. 14 • *Test Generator (One-Stop Planner CD-ROM)*
• *Portfolio Management System,* Rubrics for Choices, p. 95	• *Audio CD Library,* Disc 3, Track 3 • *Viewing and Representing:* Fine Art Transparency 2 Worksheet p. 8 • *Portfolio Management System,* Rubrics for Choices, p. 95	• *Formal Assessment,* Selection Test, p. 9 • *Standardized Test Preparation,* p. 16 • *Test Generator (One-Stop Planner CD-ROM)*
	• *Audio CD Library,* Disc 3, Track 4	

• *Workshop Resources,* p. 1
 • *Writer's Workshop 2 CD-ROM:* Autobiographical Incident, Controversial Issue
	• *Viewing and Representing,* HRW Multimedia Presentation Maker	• *Portfolio Management System*
		  • Prewriting, p. 97
		  • Peer Editing, p. 98
		  • Assessment Rubric, p. 99

 Transparency   CD-ROM Video   Audio CD

Collection 1 Hard Choices

Skills Focus

Selection or Feature	Reading Skills and Strategies	Elements of Literature	Vocabulary/Language/ Grammar	Writing	Listening/ Speaking	Viewing/ Representing
The Cold Equations (p. 8) Tom Godwin	Monitor Your Reading, pp. 8, 29 Summarize a Story, p. 29 Contrast, p. 29	Suspense, pp. 8, 29 Setting, p. 29 Title, p. 29 Images, p. 29	Subject-Verb Agreement, p. 31 Glossary and Dictionary, p. 31	Identify a Problem, p. 30 Write a New Ending for a Story, p. 30 Write a Letter to the Editor, p. 30	Research and Report on Aspects of Technology, p. 30 Prepare and Present a Speech on Space Exploration, p. 30	
Elements of Literature: Plot (p. 32)		Plot, p. 32 • Basic Situation • Conflict, Internal and External • Climax • Resolution				
The Bass, the River, and Sheila Mant (p. 34) W. D. Wetherell	Understand Cause and Effect, pp. 34, 41	Conflict, External and Internal, pp. 34, 41 Title, p. 41 Climax, p. 41	Sensory Images, p. 42 Vocabulary Resource File, p. 42	Identify an Issue, p. 41 Write a Short Narrative, p. 41 Write a Critical Review, p. 41		
The Book of Sand (p. 43) Jorge Luis Borges *translated by* Norman Thomas Di Giovanni	Make Predictions, pp. 43, 48 Identify Main Events, p. 48	Conflicts, p. 43 Resolutions, pp. 43, 48 Setting, p. 48 Events, p. 48 Analogies, p. 48 Character, p. 48	Pronoun Case, p. 49 • Nominative • Objective Prefixes, Suffixes, and Roots, p. 49	Freewrite About a Decision, p. 48 Write a Story Sequel, p. 48 Write an Explanation, p. 48		Illustrate an Explanation, p. 48
Elements of Literature: Setting (p. 50)		Setting, p. 50 • Atmosphere • Time Frame • Verisimilitude • Emotional Effect • Influence on Character				
Boys and Girls (p. 52) Alice Munro	Make Generalizations, pp. 52, 66 Story Map, p. 66	Climax, pp. 52, 66 Conflict, p. 66 Setting, p. 66 Character, p. 66 Resolution, p. 66	Connotation and Denotation, p. 68 Analogy, p. 68	Respond to a Poll, p. 67 Write a New Ending, p. 67 Support an Opinion, p. 67 Write a Response to a Poem, p. 67	Conduct a Debate, p. 67 Research and Report on Gender Roles in the 1940s and 1950s, p. 67	
Everyday Use (p. 69) Alice Walker	Compare and Contrast, pp. 69, 78 Use Context Clues, p. 80	Conflict, pp. 69, 78 Character, p. 78 Setting, p. 78 Title, p. 78	Diction, p. 80 Dialogue, p. 80 Context Clues Diagrams, p. 80	Write an Opinion Statement, p. 79 Write from a Character's Perspective, p. 79 Write an Op-Ed Article, p. 79 Write a Letter to an Author, p. 79		Design a Quilt Reflecting Aspects of Cultural Heritage, p. 79
Extending the Theme: *from* **Travels with Charley** (p. 81) John Steinbeck	Dialogue with the Text, p. 81 Use a Double-Entry Journal, pp. 81, 83	The Extending the Theme feature provides students with an unstructured opportunity to practice reading skills using a selection that extends the theme of the collection.				
Writer's Workshop: Persuading Through Personal Narrative (p. 85)		Chronological Order, p. 86 Sensory Details, p. 86 Dialogue, p. 86		Write a Personal Narrative Supporting an Opinion, pp. 85–90		
Sentence Workshop: Building from the Basics (p. 91)			Subject, p. 91 Verb, p. 91 Complement, p. 91	Revising Sentences Based on Models, p. 91		
Reading for Life: Reading a Science Article (p. 92)	Strategies for Reading a Science Article, p. 92		Use a Dictionary or Glossary, p. 92			Create a Graphic Organizer, p. 92

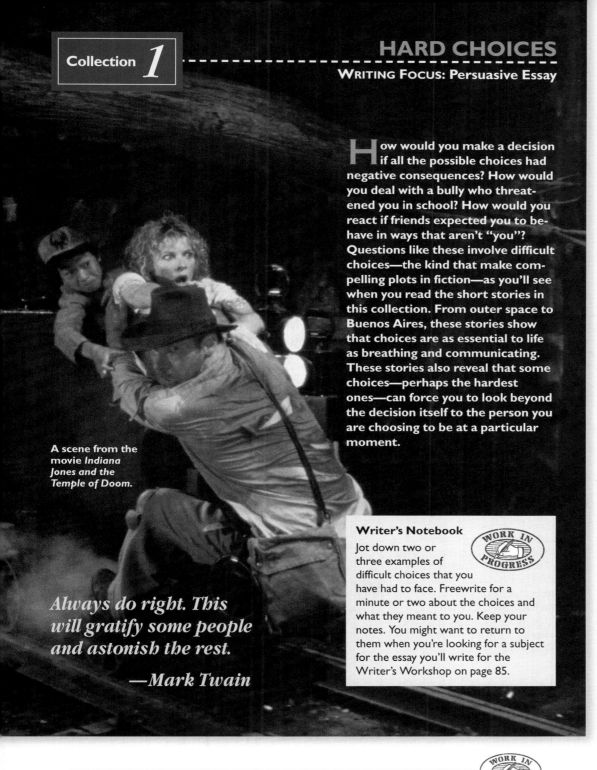

HARD CHOICES

WRITING FOCUS: Persuasive Essay

How would you make a decision if all the possible choices had negative consequences? How would you deal with a bully who threatened you in school? How would you react if friends expected you to behave in ways that aren't "you"? Questions like these involve difficult choices—the kind that make compelling plots in fiction—as you'll see when you read the short stories in this collection. From outer space to Buenos Aires, these stories show that choices are as essential to life as breathing and communicating. These stories also reveal that some choices—perhaps the hardest ones—can force you to look beyond the decision itself to the person you are choosing to be at a particular moment.

A scene from the movie *Indiana Jones and the Temple of Doom.*

Always do right. This will gratify some people and astonish the rest.

—*Mark Twain*

Writer's Notebook

Jot down two or three examples of difficult choices that you have had to face. Freewrite for a minute or two about the choices and what they meant to you. Keep your notes. You might want to return to them when you're looking for a subject for the essay you'll write for the Writer's Workshop on page 85.

OBJECTIVES

1. Read short stories on the theme of "Hard Choices"
2. Interpret literary elements, with special emphasis on plot and setting
3. Apply a variety of reading strategies, particularly Making Meanings
4. Respond to the literature in a variety of modes
5. Learn and use new words
6. Plan, draft, revise, proof, and publish a persuasive essay

Introducing the Theme

Remind students that Indiana Jones, shown in the photo, is an action hero whose hard choices usually involve physical courage. Ask if these are the kind of difficult choices most people encounter in life, or whether choices involving emotional and moral courage are more typical. Encourage a free discussion of ideas on this issue.

Responding to the Quotation

Ask students to explain the humor of Twain's statement and to tell why they do or do not agree with it. [The humor lies in the suggestion that just doing the right thing can be a way of astonishing people, because many people assume the worst of others and expect them to be selfish. Some students may agree with this view of human nature; others may find it too pessimistic.]

Writer's Notebook

Emphasize that the choices they write about should be experiences they're willing to share with their classmates.

Writing Focus: Persuading Through Personal Narrative

The following **Work in Progress** assignments build to a culminating **Writer's Workshop** at the end of the collection.

• The Cold Equations	Finding a topic (p. 30)
• The Bass, the River, and Sheila Mant	Using a personal experience (p. 41)
• The Book of Sand	Writing about a decision (p. 48)
• Boys and Girls	Expressing a view (p. 67)
• Everyday Use	Stating an opinion (p. 79)

Writer's Workshop: Persuasive Writing / Persuading Through Personal Narrative (p. 85)

OBJECTIVES

1. Read and interpret the story
2. Identify suspense in the story
3. Monitor reading: questioning
4. Express understanding through writing, science research/critical thinking, or speaking
5. Identify and use subject-verb agreement
6. Learn and use new words

SKILLS

Literary and Reading
- Identify suspense
- Monitor reading: questioning

Writing
- Collect ideas for a persuasive essay
- Write a new ending
- Evaluate a story in a letter

Speaking/Listening
- Give a speech about the value of space exploration

Grammar/Language
- Identify and use subject-verb agreement

Vocabulary
- Use new words
- Use a glossary and a dictionary

Science
- Research future technology and evaluate a story's accuracy

Viewing/Representing
- Respond to an illustration (ATE)

Planning

- **Block Schedule**
  Block Scheduling Lesson Plans with Pacing Guide
- **Traditional Schedule**
  Lesson Plans Including Strategies for English-Language Learners
- **One-Stop Planner**
  CD-ROM with Test Generator

Make the Connection

No Easy Way Out

No one gets through life without having to make hard decisions. Think of all the choices we have to make in life— as students, parents, friends, teachers, voters, jurors, politicians, lawyers, law enforcers, journalists, scientists, business people, builders, doctors.

Quickwrite

What kinds of choices might we have to make in life that would have difficult consequences—no matter what we decide to do? Freewrite about such a choice. How would you make a decision when faced with such a hard choice?

Elements of Literature

Suspense: What Next?

Suspense can be an important element in stories that force characters to make hard decisions. In literature, as in life, suspense is our uncertainty about future events. It's a feeling of keen tension. We feel that *something* is going to happen to someone we care about, and we fear it may be bad.

As you read this story, think about *why* you feel suspense. What are you afraid will happen?

Suspense is a feeling of anxious curiosity about what is going to happen next in a story.

For more on Suspense, p.1005 see the Handbook of Literary Terms. (p. 995)

Reading Skills and Strategies

Monitoring Your Reading: Questioning

Good readers keep questioning as they read—whether they're reading a detective story or a serious novel. As you read "The Cold Equations," write in your notebook any questions you have about what is going to happen *next*. Can you predict how this suspenseful tale will end? Also note your questions about the characters' actions, their unusual setting, and any passages that strike you as especially important or controversial. You may even have questions about Godwin's science.

 go.hrw.com
LEO 10-1

Preteaching Vocabulary

Words to Own

Have students read the definitions of the Words to Own on pp. 10–26. Then, have them respond to the following questions.

1. Why couldn't a person become *inured* to happiness?
2. Why can't pay cuts be called *increments*?
3. If someone *recoiled* from you, how would you feel?
4. Does the leading actor in a play have the *paramount* role?
5. If a town were *annihilated*, would any people remain?
6. If a decision is *irrevocable*, can it be altered?
7. Would you describe the weather in your locale as *immutable*?
8. What animal might be described as *ponderous*?
9. When might you feel a sense of *apprehension*?
10. Why might a spectacular sunrise be described as *ineffably* beautiful?

The Cold Equations

Tom Godwin

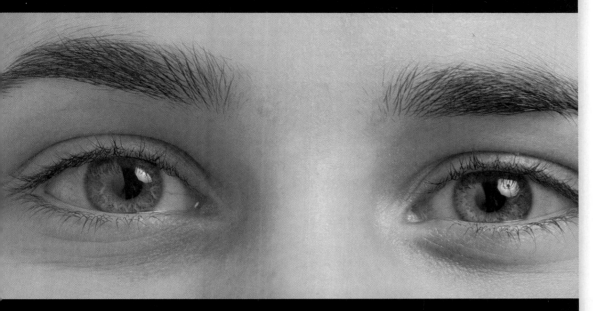

Summary ■ ■

In the year 2178, Barton pilots a space-craft toward the planet Woden, carrying serum for six gravely ill men in an exploration party from Earth. Barton finds evidence of a stowaway and must jettison this person, because the extra weight will deplete the precisely calculated fuel level and cause the craft to crash. The stowaway is eighteen-year-old Marilyn Cross, longing to see her brother on Woden. Torn by her innocence and racing against time, Barton slows fuel use and connects Marilyn with Gerry by radio. Yet he cannot overcome the title's cold equation: either she dies or eight people will die. Marilyn writes letters to her family, briefly speaks with Gerry, enters the airlock, and is blown into space.

Resources

Viewing and Representing
Videocassette A, Segment 1
This *Visual Connections* segment will help students focus on the theme in a vivid, realistic way.

Listening
Audio CD Library
A gripping recording of this story is provided in the *Audio CD Library*:
• Disc 1, Track 3

Viewing and Representing
Fine Art Transparency
A Fine Art Transparency of Robert McCall's painting *Floating City* can be used after students read the story.
• Transparency 1
• Worksheet, p. 4

Elements of Literature
Suspense
For additional instruction on suspense, see *Literary Elements*:
• Transparency 1
• Worksheet, p. 4

It was the law, and there could be no appeal.

He was not alone.
There was nothing to indicate the fact but the white hand of the tiny gauge on the board before him. The control room was empty but for himself; there was no sound other than the murmur of the drives—but the white hand had moved. It had been on zero when the little ship was launched from the *Stardust*; now, an hour later, it had crept up. There was something in the supply closet across the room, it was saying, some kind of a body that radiated heat.
It could be but one kind of a body—a living, human body.

THE COLD EQUATIONS **9**

Resources: Print and Media

Reading
• *Reading Skills and Strategies*
  MiniRead Skill Lesson, p. 1
  Selection Skill Lesson, p. 7
• *Graphic Organizers for Active Reading*, p. 1
• *Words to Own*, p. 1
• *Audio CD Library*, Disc 1, Track 3

Elements of Literature
• *Literary Elements*
  Transparency 1
  Worksheet, p. 4

Writing and Language
• *Daily Oral Grammar*
  Transparency 1
• *Grammar and Language Links*
  Worksheet, p. 1
• *Language Workshop CD-ROM*

Viewing and Representing
• *Viewing and Representing*
  Fine Art Transparency 1
  Fine Art Worksheet p. 4

• *Visual Connections*
  Videocassette A, Segment 1

Assessment
• *Formal Assessment*, p. 1
• *Portfolio Management System*, p. 89
• *Standardized Test Preparation*, pp. 10, 12
• *Test Generator (One-Stop Planner CD-ROM)*

Internet
• go.hrw.com (keyword: LE0 10-1)

A Reading Skills and Strategies

Monitoring Your Reading: Questioning

? What questions occur to you at this point in the story? [Possible responses: Who is in the supply closet? Why does the person have to die? How will the stowaway react when discovered? Will the narrator really kill the stowaway? If so, how?]

B Vocabulary

Jargon

Have students familiar with space science or science fiction explain the meanings of such terms as *interstellar* ("among the stars"), *jettisoned* ("thrown overboard"), *galactic* ("pertaining to a galaxy, especially the Milky Way"), and *hyperspace* ("space of more than three dimensions").

C Elements of Literature

Setting

? When and where is the story set? [The story is set in the future, aboard a small Emergency Dispatch Ship (EDS) that deals with emergencies in frontier space colonies far from Earth.]

D Reading Skills and Strategies

Making Inferences

? What does this passage suggest about the effect of the stowaway on the fuel supply? [There will not be enough fuel with the stowaway on board.]

E Elements of Literature

Suspense

? How does the author build suspense about what will happen to the stowaway? [Sample answer: The author suggests it is too late to alter the situation but does not explain right away what the situation is—except to say that the consequences will be terrible.]

He leaned back in the pilot's chair and drew a deep, slow breath, considering what he would have to do. He was an EDS pilot, <u>inured</u> to the sight of death, long since accustomed to it and to viewing the dying of another man with an objective lack of emotion, and he had no choice in what he must do. There could be no alternative—but it required a few moments of conditioning for even an EDS pilot to prepare himself to walk across the room and coldly, deliberately, take the life of a man he had yet to meet.

He would, of course, do it. It was the law, stated very bluntly and definitely in grim Paragraph L, Section 8, of Interstellar Regulations: *"Any stowaway discovered in an EDS shall be jettisoned immediately following discovery."*

It was the law, and there could be no appeal.

It was a law not of men's choosing but made imperative by the circumstances of the space frontier. Galactic expansion had followed the development of the hyperspace drive, and as men scattered wide across the frontier, there had come the problem of contact with the isolated first colonies and exploration parties. The huge hyperspace cruisers were the product of the combined genius and effort of Earth and were long and expensive in the building. They were not available in such numbers that small colonies could possess them. The cruisers carried the colonists to their new worlds and made periodic visits, running on tight schedules, but they could not stop and turn aside to visit colonies scheduled to be visited at another time; such a delay would destroy their schedule and produce a confusion and uncertainty that would wreck the complex interdependence between old Earth and the new worlds of the frontier.

Some method of delivering supplies or assistance when an emergency occurred on a world not scheduled for a visit had been needed, and the Emergency Dispatch Ships had been the answer. Small and collapsible, they occupied little room in the hold of the cruiser; made of light metal and plastics, they were driven by a small rocket drive that consumed relatively little fuel. Each cruiser carried four EDSs, and when a call for aid was received, the nearest cruiser would drop into normal space long enough to launch an EDS with the needed supplies or personnel, then vanish again as it continued on its course.

The cruisers, powered by nuclear converters, did not use the liquid rocket fuel, but nuclear converters were far too large and complex to permit their installation in the EDSs. The cruisers were forced by necessity to carry a limited amount of bulky rocket fuel, and the fuel was rationed with care, the cruiser's computers determining the exact amount of fuel each EDS would require for its mission. The computers considered the course coordinates, the mass of the EDS, the mass of pilot and cargo; they were very precise and accurate and omitted nothing from their calculations. They could not, however, foresee and allow for the added mass of a stowaway.

The *Stardust* had received the request from one of the exploration parties stationed on Woden, the six men of the party already being stricken with the fever carried by the green kala midges and their own supply of serum destroyed by the tornado that had torn through their camp. The *Stardust* had gone through the usual procedure, dropping into normal space to launch the EDS with the fever serum, then vanishing again in hyperspace. Now, an hour later, the gauge was saying there was something more than the small carton of serum in the supply closet.

He let his eyes rest on the narrow white door of the closet. There, just inside, another man lived and breathed and was beginning to feel assured that discovery of his presence would now be too late for the pilot to alter the situation. It *was* too late; for the man behind the door it was far later than he thought and in a way he would find it terrible to believe.

There could be no alternative. Additional fuel would be used during the hours of deceleration to compensate for the added mass of the stow-

---

WORDS TO OWN

inured (in·yoord') *v.* used as *adj.*: accustomed (to something difficult or painful).

Reaching All Students

Struggling Readers

Monitor Your Reading was introduced on p. 8. For a lesson directly tied to this story that teaches students to monitor their reading by using a strategy called Think-Aloud, see the *Reading Skills and Strategies* binder
- MiniRead Skill Lesson, p. 1
- Selection Skill Lesson, p. 7

English Language Learners

The writer uses a variety of long, complicated sentences, which some students may find difficult to follow, especially when he explains the story's basic conflict in its opening pages. Read these pages aloud to aid in students' comprehension. Encourage them to ask questions about any sentences they do not understand.

Advanced Learners

These students will likely take the lead in examining the author's assumptions, logic, and scientific ideas. Encourage them to share their questions with the class as they read. You might also have them work together on Choices activities 3 or 4 (p. 30), which invite students to challenge the text.

"Come out!" His command was harsh and abrupt above the murmur of the drive.

It seemed he could hear the whisper of a furtive movement inside the closet, then nothing. He visualized the stowaway cowering closer into one corner, suddenly worried by the possible consequences of his act, his self-assurance evaporating.

"I said *out!*"

He heard the stowaway move to obey, and he waited with his eyes alert on the door and his hand near the blaster at his side.

The door opened and the stowaway stepped through it, smiling. "All right—I give up. Now what?"

It was a girl.

He stared without speaking, his hand dropping away from the blaster, and acceptance of what he saw coming like a heavy and unexpected physical blow. The stowaway was not a man—she was a girl in her teens, standing before him in little white gypsy sandals, with the top of her brown, curly head hardly higher than his shoulder, with a faint, sweet scent of perfume coming from her, and her smiling face tilted up so her eyes could look unknowing and unafraid into his as she waited for his answer.

Now what? Had it been asked in the deep, defiant voice of a man, he would have answered it with action, quick and efficient. He would have taken the stowaway's identification disk and ordered him into the air lock. Had the stowaway refused to obey, he would have used the blaster. It would not have taken long; within a minute the body would have been ejected into space—had the stowaway been a man.

He returned to the pilot's chair and motioned her to seat herself on the boxlike bulk of the drive-control units that were set against the wall beside him. She obeyed, his silence making the smile fade into the meek and guilty expression of a pup that has been caught in mischief and knows it must be punished.

WORDS TO OWN

increments (in′krə·mənts) *n.*: small increases.

---

away, infinitesimal increments of fuel that would not be missed until the ship had almost reached its destination. Then, at some distance above the ground that might be as near as a thousand feet or as far as tens of thousands of feet, depending upon the mass of ship and cargo and the preceding period of deceleration, the unmissed increments of fuel would make their absence known; the EDS would expend its last drops of fuel with a sputter and go into whistling free fall. Ship and pilot and stowaway would merge together upon impact as a wreckage of metal and plastic, flesh and blood, driven deep into the soil. The stowaway had signed his own death warrant when he concealed himself on the ship; he could not be permitted to take seven others with him.

He looked again at the telltale white hand, then rose to his feet. What he must do would be unpleasant for both of them; the sooner it was over, the better. He stepped across the control room to stand by the white door.

F **Struggling Readers**
Breaking Down Difficult Text
Some students may need help to understand this difficult and important passage. First, define challenging terms such as *infinitesimal, increments, mass, deceleration,* and *free fall.* Then, help students understand the purpose of deceleration as well as why a small increase in mass can lead to a great increase in demand for fuel.

G **Reading Skills and Strategies**
Identifying Cause and Effect
? Why will the stowaway "take seven others with him" by staying on board? [Barton will die in the crash, too; if Barton dies, he cannot deliver medicine to the six ill space colonists, and they will die.]

H **Reading Skills and Strategies**

Monitoring Your Reading: Questioning
? What questions have arisen in your mind by this point? [Possible responses: Who is the stowaway? Is he or she armed? Will he or she offer resistance or take over the ship?]

I **Critical Thinking**
Determining Author's Purpose
? Why does the author describe the girl's appearance in such detail? [Possible responses: to show that she is defenseless; to create sympathy for her.]

J **Elements of Literature**
Metaphor
? What comparison reinforces the idea that the girl is harmless and unaware of the serious consequences of her actions? [She is compared to a puppy.]

Using Students' Strengths

Mathematical/Logical Learners
Make sure that students understand the implications of the equation. You might encourage them to use a graphic aid illustrating causes and effects as they consider the equation. Or students might use the "If __, then __" grammatical structure to construct sentences explaining the story's basic conflict. For example, "If Marilyn stays on board, then the ship will run out of fuel too soon"; or "If Marilyn is jettisoned, the exploration party will get the medicine they need."

Spatial Learners
To help students understand how the story's setting influences events, have them use tape to mark off a classroom area they think is the size of the EDS. They can then locate places within the defined area where the supply closet, air lock, and instrument console might be.

Reading Skills and Strategies

Monitoring Your Reading: Questioning

Discuss with students questions that might have occurred to them at this point in the story. For example, does it seem surprising that Marilyn would not know the severe penalty for stowing away? Why wasn't the sign warning stowaways worded more strongly?

Struggling Readers

Identifying Pronoun Antecedents

Ask students to identify the antecedents of the pronouns *him, he, it,* and *her* in this paragraph. [*Him* refers to Marilyn's brother, Gerry Cross; *he* refers to Barton, the pilot; *it* refers to the process of cutting the deceleration; and *her* refers to Marilyn, the stowaway.]

Reading Skills and Strategies

Challenging the Text

❓ Is it possible that a ship in which stowaways pose such a risk would be so easy to break into? [Possible responses: No, such a ship would have had much tougher security; yes, because guards would not suspect the motives of an innocent-looking girl like Marilyn.]

English Language Learners

Multiple Meanings

These students may not be familiar with the meanings of the words *model, keep, fine,* and *patch,* as they are used in this paragraph. Make a list of different meanings for each of the words, and point out which meanings are used in the paragraph.

"You still haven't told me," she said. "I'm guilty, so what happens to me now? Do I pay a fine, or what?"

"What are you doing here?" he asked. "Why did you stow away on this EDS?"

"I wanted to see my brother. He's with the government survey crew on Woden and I haven't seen him for ten years, not since he left Earth to go into government survey work."

"What was your destination on the *Stardust*?"

"Mimir. I have a position waiting for me there. My brother has been sending money home all the time to us—my father and mother and me—and he paid for a special course in linguistics I was taking. I graduated sooner than expected and I was offered this job in Mimir. I knew it would be almost a year before Gerry's job was done on Woden so he could come on to Mimir, and that's why I hid in the closet there. There was plenty of room for me and I was willing to pay the fine. There were only the two of us kids—Gerry and I—and I haven't seen him for so long, and I didn't want to wait another year when I could see him now, even though I knew I would be breaking some kind of a regulation when I did it."

I knew I would be breaking some kind of a regulation. In a way, she could not be blamed for her ignorance of the law; she was of Earth and had not realized that the laws of the space frontier must, of necessity, be as hard and relentless as the environment that gave them birth. Yet, to protect such as her from the results of their own ignorance of the frontier, there had been a sign over the door that led to the section of the *Stardust* that housed the EDSs, a sign that was plain for all to see and heed: UNAUTHORIZED PERSONNEL KEEP OUT!

"Does your brother know that you took passage on the *Stardust* for Mimir?"

"Oh, yes. I sent him a spacegram telling him about my graduation and about going to Mimir on the *Stardust* a month before I left Earth. I already knew Mimir was where he would be stationed in a little over a year. He gets a promotion then, and he'll be based on Mimir and not have to stay out a year at a time on field trips, like he does now."

There were two different survey groups on Woden, and he asked, "What is his name?"

"Cross—Gerry Cross. He's in Group Two—that was the way his address read. Do you know him?"

Group One had requested the serum: Group Two was eight thousand miles away, across the Western Sea.

"No, I've never met him," he said, then turned to the control board and cut the deceleration to a fraction of a gravity, knowing as he did so that it could not avert the ultimate end, yet doing the only thing he could do to prolong that ultimate end. The sensation was like that of the ship suddenly dropping, and the girl's involuntary movement of surprise half lifted her from her seat.

"We're going faster now, aren't we?" she asked. "Why are we doing that?"

He told her the truth. "To save fuel for a little while."

"You mean we don't have very much?"

He delayed the answer he must give her so soon to ask, "How did you manage to stow away?"

"I just sort of walked in when no one was looking my way," she said. "I was practicing my Gelanese on the native girl who does the cleaning in the Ship's Supply office when someone came in with an order for supplies for the survey crew on Woden. I slipped into the closet there after the ship was ready to go just before you came in. It was an impulse of the moment to stow away, so I could get to see Gerry—and from the way you keep looking at me so grim, I'm not sure it was a very wise impulse. But I'll be a model criminal—or do I mean prisoner?" She smiled at him again. "I intended to pay for my keep on top of paying the fine. I can cook and I can patch clothes for everyone and I know how to do all kinds of useful things, even a little bit about nursing."

There was one more question to ask:

"Did you know what the supplies were that the survey crew ordered?"

"Why, no. Equipment they needed in their work, I supposed."

Why couldn't she have been a man with

---

12 THE SHORT-STORY COLLECTIONS

Crossing the Curriculum

Social Studies

Ask students to research and create a time line illustrating the efforts of human beings to explore space in the twentieth century. Since this topic is broad, you might divide it into the following segments: early satellites, early flights with astronauts or cosmonauts, flights to the moon, space shuttle missions, communications satellites, and weather satellites.

Science

Invite a group of students to begin a KWL chart on the scientific principles of astronomy or space travel. What do they already know about the topic? What would they like to know? Then ask them to complete the "L" section by researching the answers to their questions, using encyclopedias, science books, and the Internet. You might have the group present their findings in a panel discussion.

Mathematics

To extend their reading, have students research some of the mathematical equations used to compute the effects of gravity. If possible, ask a student gifted in math to teach a lesson on how to apply these formulas.

some ulterior motive? A fugitive from justice hoping to lose himself on a raw new world; an opportunist seeking transportation to the new colonies where he might find golden fleece for the taking; a crackpot with a mission. Perhaps once in his lifetime an EDS pilot would find such a stowaway on his ship—warped men, mean and selfish men, brutal and dangerous men—but never before a smiling, blue-eyed girl who was willing to pay her fine and work for her keep that she might see her brother.

He turned to the board and turned the switch that would signal the *Stardust*. The call would be futile, but he could not, until he had exhausted that one vain hope, seize her and thrust her into the air lock as he would an animal—or a man. The delay, in the meantime, would not be dangerous with the EDS decelerating at fractional gravity.

A voice spoke from the communicator. "*Stardust*. Identify yourself and proceed."

"Barton, EDS 34GII. Emergency. Give me Commander Delhart."

There was a faint confusion of noises as the request went through the proper channels. The girl was watching him, no longer smiling.

"Are you going to order them to come back after me?" she asked.

The communicator clicked and there was the sound of a distant voice saying, "Commander, the EDS requests . . ."

"Are they coming back after me?" she asked again. "Won't I get to see my brother after all?"

"Barton?" The blunt, gruff voice of Commander Delhart came from the communicator. "What's this about an emergency?"

"A stowaway," he answered.

"A stowaway?" There was a slight surprise to the question. "That's rather unusual—but why the 'emergency' call? You discovered him in time, so there should be no appreciable danger, and I presume you've informed Ship's Records so his nearest relatives can be notified."

"That's why I had to call you, first. The stowaway is still aboard and the circumstances are so different—"

"Different?" the commander interrupted, impatience in his voice. "How

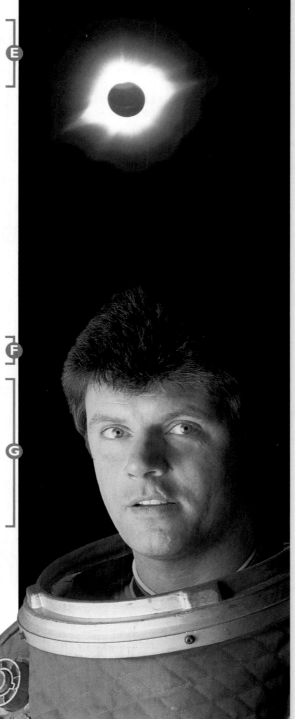

E
F
G

E Literary Connections

Allusion

In Greek mythology, the golden fleece is the wool, made of pure gold, taken from a magical winged ram. The search for the golden fleece was the quest of Jason and the Argonauts, who faced many adventures and tests before finally (with the help of Jason's future wife, Medea) seizing the fleece from the oak tree where it had been nailed.

F Appreciating Language

Subject-Verb Agreement

Ask students why the singular verb *was,* rather than the plural *were,* is used in this sentence. [The subject is the singular noun *confusion.*] Remind students that "there" is never the subject of a sentence; and that subjects never appear in a prepositional phrase.

G Elements of Literature

Suspense

Point out that the author creates suspense in this passage by describing Barton's actions, and the communicator's sounds, without explaining Barton's thoughts. The girl's unanswered questions heighten the suspense. Ask students to share questions that go through their mind as they wait for Barton to explain the situation to Commander Delhart. [Possible responses: Will the Commander take pity on Marilyn and find some way to save her life? Will Barton plead for Marilyn's life? How will Marilyn react to the conversation between Barton and the Commander? Will she find out that she is about to die?]

Using Students' Strengths

Mathematical/Logical Learners

Ask students to research the methods scientists use to compute the distance from Earth to other planets. To help them get started, refer them to a geometry textbook, and tell them the process involves using the distance formula for three dimensions. Ask them to report to the class on their findings and to demonstrate on the chalkboard the mathematics involved.

Naturalist Learners

Encourage these students to help others who might be having difficulty understanding why lack of extra fuel will cause the EDS to crash. [Sample explanation: The added mass (Marilyn's weight) will cause the EDS to use more fuel when it slows down (decelerates), because force will have to be exerted by firing rockets in the direction opposite the one in which the gravity of Woden is pulling the ship. The greater the mass of the EDS, the greater the opposite force will have

to be. Therefore, more fuel will be needed to produce this greater force, and without *any* extra fuel, the EDS must crash if Marilyn remains on board.]

? Are you surprised at how quickly the commander decided he cannot help Marilyn? Do you wonder why he doesn't take time to brainstorm possible ways to save her life? [Responses will vary. Some students might say they do not question the commander's immediate negative reply, because it is based on scientific laws he cannot change. Others might say that people in the past have faced seemingly impossible situations and used their problem-solving skills to find a solution, so people in the technologically advanced future should be able to do the same or better.]

B Struggling Readers

Reading Aloud
To bring this scene to life and help students feel Marilyn's desperate sense of disbelief and horror, have a boy and a girl read the dialogue aloud. If necessary, coach the readers until they can dramatically convey the feeling of the scene.

C Elements of Literature

Simile
? What two comparisons does the author use here to describe Marilyn's appearance? [He says she is "small and limp like a little rag doll" and that her lipstick stands out "like a blood-red cupid's bow."] What impressions of Marilyn do these similes convey? [Possible responses: The first emphasizes how small and helpless Marilyn looks; the second conveys a sense of her as vulnerable, feminine, and eager to appear older than she really is.]

---

can they be different? You know you have a limited supply of fuel; you also know the law as well as I do: 'Any stowaway discovered in an EDS shall be jettisoned immediately following discovery.'"

There was the sound of a sharply indrawn breath from the girl. *"What does he mean?"*

"The stowaway is a girl."

"What?"

"She wanted to see her brother. She's only a kid and she didn't know what she was really doing."

A "I see." All the curtness was gone from the commander's voice. "So you called me in the hope I could do something?" Without waiting for an answer he went on, "I'm sorry—I can do nothing. This cruiser must maintain its schedule; the life of not one person but the lives of many depend on it. I know how you feel but I'm powerless to help you. You'll have to go through with it. I'll have you connected with Ship's Records."

The communicator faded to a faint rustle of sound, and he turned back to the girl. She was leaning forward on the bench, almost rigid, her eyes fixed wide and frightened.

B "What did he mean, to go through with it? To jettison me . . . to go through with it—what did he mean? Not the way it sounded . . . he couldn't have. What did he mean—what did he really mean?"

Her time was too short for the comfort of a lie to be more than a cruelly fleeting delusion.

"He meant it the way it sounded."

"No!" She recoiled from him as though he had struck her, one hand half raised as though to fend him off and stark unwillingness to believe in her eyes.

"It will have to be."

"No! You're joking—you're insane! You can't mean it!"

"I'm sorry." He spoke slowly to her, gently. "I should have told you before—I should have, but I had to do what I could first; I had to call the *Stardust*. You heard what the commander said."

"But you can't—if you make me leave the ship, I'll *die*."

"I know."

She searched his face, and the unwillingness to believe left her eyes, giving way slowly to a look of dazed horror.

"You know?" She spoke the words far apart, numbly and wonderingly.

"I know. It has to be like that."

"You mean it—you really mean it." She sagged back against the wall, small and limp like a little rag doll, and all the protesting and disbelief gone. "You're going to do it—you're going to make me die?"

"I'm sorry," he said again. "You'll never know how sorry I am. It has to be that way and no human in the universe can change it."

C "You're going to make me die and I didn't do anything to die for—I didn't *do* anything——"

He sighed, deep and weary. "I know you didn't, child. I know you didn't."

"EDS." The communicator rapped brisk and metallic. "This is Ship's Records. Give us all information on subject's identification disk."

He got out of his chair to stand over her. She clutched the edge of the seat, her upturned face white under the brown hair and the lipstick standing out like a blood-red cupid's bow.

"Now?"

"I want your identification disk," he said.

She released the edge of the seat and fumbled at the chain that suspended the plastic disk from her neck with fingers that were trembling and awkward. He reached down and unfastened the clasp for her, then returned with the disk to his chair.

"Here's your data, Records: Identification Number T837——"

"One moment," Records interrupted. "This is to be filed on the gray card, of course?"

"Yes."

"And the time of execution?"

"I'll tell you later."

"Later? This is highly irregular; the time of the subject's death is required before——"

He kept the thickness out of his voice with

WORDS TO OWN

recoiled (ri·koild′) *v.*: drew back in fear, surprise, or disgust.

Taking a Second Look

Review: Describing Mental Images
Remind students that readers visualize, or form mental images of, a story by combining descriptions in the text with their own prior knowledge and experience.

Activity
1. Have one or more volunteers read p. 14 aloud, and ask students to note any descriptive details the author provides to help readers picture the scene in their mind. Write these details on the chalkboard.

2. Now ask students if the scene reminds them of any similar moments they have seen in movies or in television dramas. Also, ask if Marilyn or Barton reminds them of any people they know in real life. Invite them to note how descriptions of the actions, words, and appearance of the characters help them make these connections.

3. Then, ask students to close their eyes and visualize the scene as you read it aloud a second time. Finally, have volunteers discuss what they saw as you read and identify which parts of the scene were easiest to visualize.

an effort. "Then we'll do it in a highly irregular manner—you'll hear the disk read first. The subject is a girl and she's listening to everything that's said. Are you capable of understanding that?"

There was a brief, almost shocked silence; then Records said meekly, "Sorry. Go ahead."

He began to read the disk, reading it slowly to delay the inevitable for as long as possible, trying to help her by giving her what little time he could to recover from her first horror and let it resolve into the calm of acceptance and resignation.

"Number T8374 dash Y54. Name, Marilyn Lee Cross. Sex, female. Born July 7, 2160." *She was only eighteen.* "Height, five-three. Weight, a hundred and ten." *Such a slight weight, yet enough to add fatally to the mass of the shell-thin bubble that was an EDS.* "Hair, brown. Eyes, blue. Complexion, light. Blood type O." *Irrelevant data.* "Destination, Port City, Mimir." *Invalid data.*

He finished and said, "I'll call you later," then turned once again to the girl. She was huddled back against the wall, watching him with a look of numb and wondering fascination.

"They're waiting for you to kill me, aren't they? They want me dead, don't they? You and everybody on the cruiser want me dead, don't you?" Then the numbness broke and her voice was that of a frightened and bewildered child. "Everybody wants me dead and I didn't *do* anything. I didn't hurt anyone—I only wanted to see my brother."

"It's not the way you think—it isn't that way at all," he said. "Nobody wants it this way; nobody would ever let it be this way if it was humanly possible to change it."

"Then why is it? I don't understand. Why is it?"

"This ship is carrying kala fever serum to Group One on Woden. Their own supply was destroyed by a tornado. Group Two—the crew your brother is in—is eight thousand miles away across the Western Sea, and their helicopters can't cross it to help Group One. The fever is invariably fatal unless the serum can be had in time, and the six men in Group One will die unless this ship reaches them on schedule. These little ships are always given barely enough fuel to reach their destination, and if you stay aboard, your added weight will cause it to use up all its fuel before it reaches the ground. It will crash then, and you and I will die and so will the six men waiting for the fever serum."

It was a full minute before she spoke, and as she considered his words, the expression of numbness left her eyes.

"Is that it?" she asked at last. "Just that the ship doesn't have enough fuel?"

"Yes."

"I can go alone or I can take seven others with me—is that the way it is?"

"That's the way it is."

"And nobody wants me to have to die?"

"Nobody."

"Then maybe—— Are you sure nothing can be done about it? Wouldn't people help me if they could?"

"Everyone would like to help you, but there is nothing anyone can do. I did the only thing I could do when I called the *Stardust*."

"And it won't come back—but there might be other cruisers, mightn't there? Isn't there any hope at all that there might be someone, somewhere, who could do something to help me?"

She was leaning forward a little in her eagerness as she waited for his answer.

"No."

The word was like the drop of a cold stone and she again leaned back against the wall, the hope and eagerness leaving her face. "You're sure—you *know* you're sure?"

"I'm sure. There are no other cruisers within forty light-years; there is nothing and no one to change things."

She dropped her gaze to her lap and began twisting a pleat of her skirt between her fingers, saying no more as her mind began to adapt itself to the grim knowledge.

It was better so; with the going of all hope would go the fear; with the going of all hope would come resignation. She needed time and she could have so little of it. How much?

D Reading Skills and Strategies
Responding to the Text
❓ How do you feel about Barton and the records clerk as they discuss Marilyn's fate? [Sample response: At first they both seem unfeeling in their exchange of official information, but then Barton launches an emotional defense of Marilyn's feelings, and the clerk responds sympathetically; the exchange humanizes both of them.]

E Appreciating Language
Italics
❓ Why does the author use italics here? [They indicate Barton's thoughts, in contrast to his spoken words.]

F Struggling Readers
Rereading
Some students may remain puzzled about why the EDS ships do not carry even a little extra fuel for emergencies. Encourage them to reread the fifth and sixth paragraphs on p. 10 to help them accept this crucial part of the story's conflict.

G Elements of Literature
Suspense
Point out that Marilyn's desperate questions echo the reader's own at this point in the story; the reader, too, is "leaning forward a little" in eagerness to learn his answer.

H Elements of Literature
Simile
❓ What word from the title is echoed in this comparison? [cold] In what way is Barton's response to Marilyn "like the drop of a cold stone"? [Possible response: His reply is cold, because it offers no comfort; it is like a stone, because it is solid and hard, and spoken with an air of finality.]

I Reading Skills and Strategies
Challenging the Text
❓ Do you agree with the idea conveyed in this sentence? [Sample responses: Yes, because knowledge of one's true fate can help bring acceptance and end a desperate feeling of uncertainty; no, when there is no hope, one's sense of fear and dread can only increase.]

Listening to Music ♪

from *Also sprach Zarathustra* ("Thus Spake Zarathustra") by Richard Strauss, performed by the Chicago Symphony Orchestra

German composer Richard Strauss (1864–1949) accepted the concept of the superman central to the philosophy of Friedrich Nietzsche. *Also sprach Zarathustra* tries to capture musically Nietzsche's idea of the superman. Zarathustra is actually another name for Zoroaster, prophet of a pre-Islamic Persian (Iranian) religion.

Activity
After students read the selection, have them listen to the famous opening of *Also sprach Zarathustra*. Note that the music was made popular in the 1968 film *2001: A Space Odyssey* and has since become almost a cliché for the idea of science-fiction films involving space exploration. Have students explain why they feel the music would or would not be good background music for a film version of "The Cold Equations."

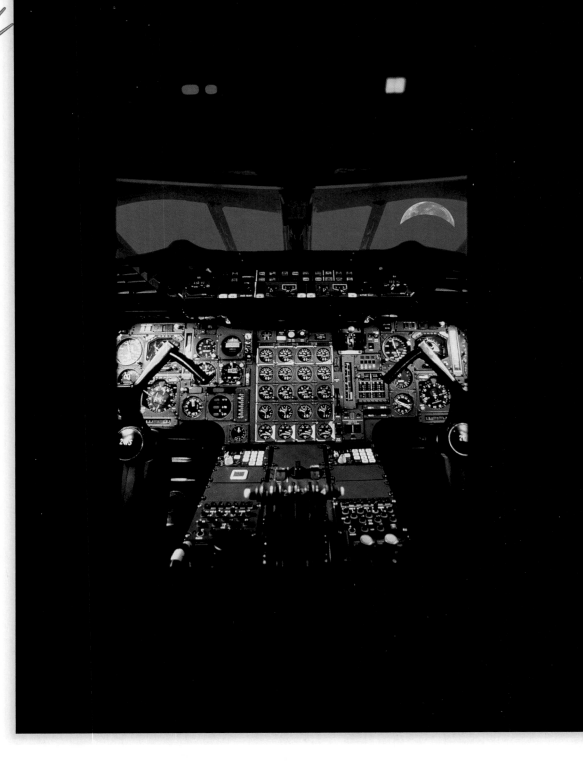

Skill Link

Identifying Subjects and Adjective Phrases

Prepare students for the Subject-Verb Agreement Grammar Link on p. 31 with some practice in finding the subject of a sentence. Tell students that a **prepositional phrase** begins with a preposition and ends with a noun or pronoun that is the object of that preposition. When a prepositional phrase modifies a noun or pronoun, it is called an **adjective phrase.** Adjective phrases can modify the subject of a sentence; however, the object of the preposition can never be the subject.

Activity

Have students identify the subject of each sentence, as well as the adjective phrase or phrases that modify each subject.

1. The memory banks of the computers contain all the necessary data. [banks; of the computers]

2. There are five little segments of metal in the second bank. [segments; of metal, in the second bank]

3. The chronometer on the instrument panel read 18:10. [chronometer; on the instrument panel]

4. A check with Records shows Barton's report. [check; with Records]

The EDSs were not equipped with hull-cooling units; their speed had to be reduced to a moderate level before they entered the atmosphere. They were decelerating at .10 gravity, approaching their destination at a far higher speed than the computers had calculated on. The *Stardust* had been quite near Woden when she launched the EDS; their present velocity was putting them nearer by the second. There would be a critical point, soon to be reached, when he would have to resume deceleration. When he did so, the girl's weight would be multiplied by the gravities of deceleration, would become, suddenly, a factor of <u>paramount</u> importance, the factor the computers had been ignorant of when they determined the amount of fuel the EDS should have. She would have to go when deceleration began; it could be no other way. When would that be—how long could he let her stay?

"How long can I stay?"

He winced involuntarily from the words that were so like an echo of his own thoughts. How long? He didn't know; he would have to ask the ship's computers. Each EDS was given a meager surplus of fuel to compensate for unfavorable conditions within the atmosphere, and relatively little fuel was being consumed for the time being. The memory banks of the computers would still contain all data pertaining to the course set for the EDS; such data would not be erased until the EDS reached its destination. He had only to give the computers the new data—the girl's weight and the exact time at which he had reduced the deceleration to .10.

"Barton." Commander Delhart's voice came abruptly from the communicator as he opened his mouth to call the *Stardust*. "A check with Records shows me you haven't completed your report. Did you reduce the deceleration?"

So the commander knew what he was trying to do.

"I'm decelerating at point ten," he answered. "I cut the deceleration at seventeen fifty and the weight is a hundred and ten. I would like to stay at point ten as long as the computers say I can. Will you give them the question?"

It was contrary to regulations for an EDS pilot

to make any changes in the course or degree of deceleration the computers had set for him, but the commander made no mention of the violation. Neither did he ask the reason for it. It was not necessary for him to ask; he had not become commander of an interstellar cruiser without both intelligence and an understanding of human nature. He said only, "I'll have that given to the computers."

The communicator fell silent and he and the girl waited, neither of them speaking. They would not have to wait long; the computers would give the answer within moments of the asking. The new factors would be fed into the steel maw° of the first bank, and the electrical impulses would go through the complex circuits. Here and there a relay might click, a tiny cog turn over, but it would be essentially the electrical impulses that found the answer; formless, mindless, invisible, determining with utter precision how long the pale girl beside him might live. Then five little segments of metal in the second bank would trip in rapid succession against an inked ribbon and a second steel maw would spit out the slip of paper that bore the answer.

The chronometer on the instrument board read 18:10 when the commander spoke again.

"You will resume deceleration at nineteen ten."

She looked toward the chronometer, then quickly away from it. "Is that when . . . when I go?" she asked. He nodded and she dropped her eyes to her lap again.

"I'll have the course correction given to you," the commander said. "Ordinarily I would never permit anything like this, but I understand your position. There is nothing I can do, other than what I've just done, and you will not deviate from these new instructions. You will complete your report at nineteen ten. Now—here are the course corrections."

°**maw:** huge, all-consuming mouth.

- -

WORDS TO OWN
paramount (par′ə·mount′) *adj.*: supreme; dominant.

- -

THE COLD EQUATIONS 17

Getting Students Involved

Cooperative Learning
Gender Differences. After students have finished reading "The Cold Equations," invite them to work in groups of three to improvise dramatic scenes that might have occurred had the stowaway been an adult man or woman or an adolescent male instead of an adolescent girl. Tell students that their scenes are not intended to be scripted and rehearsed, yet they should strive to convey the emotions and thoughts of the characters.

Encourage students to draw conclusions concerning differences or the lack of differences that might occur if the gender or age of the stowaway were different. Students might discuss, for example, how the other characters and spaceship devices might respond to the stowaway and how the author might change the similes referring to the stowaway.

A Struggling Readers
Summarizing

? What will happen at 19:10? [Barton must begin the process of deceleration, which will increase the effects of Marilyn's weight and use up too much fuel, so she must be jettisoned.]

B Reading Skills and Strategies
Connecting with the Text

? If you were Marilyn, what might be going through your mind as you waited in silence? [Possible responses: I might be trying to understand the logic of what's happening to me; I might be thinking of my family and friends at home; I might be praying for a surprise reprieve or for acceptance of my fate.]

C Critical Thinking
Determining the Author's Purpose

? Why do you think the author states these facts using the abstract terms h, m, and x? [Sample answer: These are mathematical formulas, the "cold equations" of the title, and the author uses abstract mathematical symbols to emphasize this fact.]

D Reading Skills and Strategies

Monitoring Your Reading: Questioning

Ask students if they question Barton's view of the peace and security of life on Earth. Or do they accept his description as a reasonable contrast with life on the space frontier? [Students may feel that Barton's view of life on Earth is oversimplified and much too rosy; some may say that it makes sense for him to remember Earth that way while in the more dangerous world of the space frontier.]

The voice of some unknown technician read them to him, and he wrote them down on the pad clipped to the edge of the control board. There would, he saw, be periods of deceleration when he neared the atmosphere when the deceleration would be five gravities—and at five gravities, one hundred ten pounds would become five hundred fifty pounds.

The technician finished and he terminated the contact with a brief acknowledgment. Then, hesitating a moment, he reached out and shut off the communicator. It was 18:13 and he would have nothing to report until 19:10. In the meantime, it somehow seemed indecent to permit others to hear what she might say in her last hour.

He began to check the instrument readings, going over them with unnecessary slowness. She would have to accept the circumstances, and there was nothing he could do to help her into acceptance; words of sympathy would only delay it.

It was 18:20 when she stirred from her motionlessness and spoke.

"So that's the way it has to be with me?"

He swung around to face her. "You understand now, don't you? No one would ever let it be like this if it could be changed."

"I understand," she said. Some of the color had returned to her face and the lipstick no longer stood out so vividly red. "There isn't enough fuel for me to stay. When I hid on this ship, I got into something I didn't know anything about and now I have to pay for it."

She had violated a man-made law that said KEEP OUT, but the penalty was not for men's making or desire and it was a penalty men could not revoke. A physical law had decreed: *h amount of fuel will power an EDS with a mass of m safely to its destination;* and a second physical law had decreed: *h amount of fuel will not power an EDS with a mass of m plus x safely to its destination.*

EDSs obeyed only physical laws, and no amount of human sympathy for her could alter the second law.

"But I'm afraid. I don't want to die—not now. I want to live, and nobody is doing anything to help me; everybody is letting me go ahead and acting just like nothing was going to happen to me. I'm going to die and nobody *cares*."

"We all do," he said. "I do and the commander does and the clerk in Ship's Records; we all care and each of us did what little he could to help you. It wasn't enough—it was almost nothing—but it was all we could do."

"Not enough fuel—I can understand that," she said, as though she had not heard his own words. "But to have to die for it. *Me* alone . . ."

How hard it must be for her to accept the fact. She had never known danger of death, had never known the environments where the lives of men could be as fragile and fleeting as sea foam tossed against a rocky shore. She belonged on gentle Earth, in that secure and peaceful society where she could be young and gay and laughing with the others of her kind, where life was precious and well guarded and there was always the assurance that tomorrow would come. She belonged in that world of soft winds and a warm sun, music and moonlight and gracious manners, and not on the hard, bleak frontier.

"How did it happen to me so terribly quickly? An hour ago I was on the *Stardust,* going to Mimir. Now the *Stardust* is going on without me and I'm going to die and I'll never see Gerry and Mama and Daddy again—I'll never see anything again."

He hesitated, wondering how he could explain it to her so she would really understand and not feel she had somehow been the victim of a reasonlessly cruel injustice. She did not know what the frontier was like; she thought in terms of safe, secure Earth. Pretty girls were not jettisoned on Earth; there was a law against it. On Earth her plight would have filled the newscasts and a fast black patrol ship would have been racing to her rescue. Everyone, everywhere, would have known of Marilyn Lee Cross, and no effort would have been spared to save her life. But this was not Earth and there were no patrol ships; only the *Stardust,* leaving them behind at many times the speed of light. There was no one to help her; there would be no Marilyn Lee Cross smiling from the newscasts tomorrow. Marilyn Lee Cross would be but

Using Students' Strengths

Interpersonal Learners
Have students imagine that Barton is open to finding a different solution to the problem he and Marilyn face. Ask pairs of students to role-play a brainstorming session between Barton and Marilyn in which they imagine other possible ways out of their dilemma. Have them list every solution they can think of and then evaluate the pros and cons of each one. Can they find one preferable to jettisoning Marilyn?

Intrapersonal Learners
Have students imagine that they are in Marilyn's place. Invite them to write a final reflection that might help them accept the apparently inevitable tragedy to come.

a poignant memory for an EDS pilot and a name on a gray card in Ship's Records.

"It's different here; it's not like back on Earth," he said. "It isn't that no one cares; it's that no one can do anything to help. The frontier is big, and here along its rim the colonies and exploration parties are scattered so thin and far between. On Woden, for example, there are only sixteen men—sixteen men on an entire world. The exploration parties, the survey crews, the little first colonies—they're all fighting alien environments, trying to make a way for those who will follow after. The environments fight back, and those who go first usually make mistakes only once. There is no margin of safety along the rim of the frontier; there can't be until the way is made for the others who will come later, until the new worlds are tamed and settled. Until then men will have to pay the penalty for making mistakes, with no one to help them, because there is no one *to* help them."

"I was going to Mimir," she said. "I didn't know about the frontier; I was only going to Mimir and *it's* safe."

"Mimir is safe, but you left the cruiser that was taking you there."

She was silent for a little while. "It was all so wonderful at first; there was plenty of room for me on this ship and I would be seeing Gerry so soon. I didn't know about the fuel, didn't know what would happen to me. . . ."

Her words trailed away, and he turned his attention to the viewscreen, not wanting to stare at her as she fought her way through the black horror of fear toward the calm gray of acceptance.

Woden was a ball, enshrouded in the blue haze of its atmosphere, swimming in space against the background of star-sprinkled dead blackness. The great mass of Manning's Continent sprawled like a gigantic hourglass in the Eastern Sea, with the western half of the Eastern Continent still visible. There was a thin line of shadow along the right-hand edge of the globe, and the Eastern Continent was disappearing into it as the planet turned on its axis. An hour before, the entire continent had been in view; now a thousand miles of it had gone into the thin edge of shadow and around to the night that lay on the other side of the world. The dark blue spot that was Lotus Lake was approaching the shadow. It was somewhere near the southern edge of the lake that Group Two had their camp. It would be night there soon, and quick behind the coming of night the rotation of Woden on its axis would put Group Two beyond the reach of the ship's radio.

He would have to tell her before it was too late for her to talk to her brother. In a way, it would be better for both of them should they not do so, but it was not for him to decide. To each of them the last words would be something to hold and cherish, something that would cut like the blade of a knife yet would be infinitely precious to remember, she for her own brief moments to live and he for the rest of his life.

He held down the button that would flash the grid lines on the viewscreen and used the known diameter of the planet to estimate the distance the southern tip of Lotus Lake had yet to go until it passed beyond radio range. It was approximately five hundred miles. Five hundred miles; thirty minutes—and the chronometer read 18:30. Allowing for error in estimating, it would not be later than 19:05 that the turning of Woden would cut off her brother's voice.

The first border of the Western continent was already in sight along the left side of the world. Four thousand miles across it lay the shore of the Western Sea and the camp of Group One. It had been in the Western Sea that the tornado had originated, to strike with such fury at the camp and destroy half their prefabricated buildings, including the one that housed the medical supplies. Two days before, the tornado had not existed; it had been no more than great gentle masses of air over the calm Western Sea. Group One had gone about their routine survey work, unaware of the meeting of air masses out at sea, unaware of the force the union was spawning. It had struck their camp without warning—a thundering, roaring de-

E Historical Connections

Space has been described as "the final frontier." Discuss with students the parallels between frontier life in space and frontier life during westward expansion of the United States. [Possible responses: the element of risk; the presence of instant justice and isolation; a sense of excitement and adventure.]

F Reading Skills and Strategies
Responding to the Text

❓ What colors do *you* associate with the horror of fear and the calm of acceptance? Why? [Possible responses: Red goes with horror because it is the color of blood; blue goes with acceptance because it is reassuring, like the sky.]

G English Language Learners
Using Graphic Aids

Make sure these students know what an hourglass is. Ask if any students have used one. Ask them to describe what it does and what it looks like. Explain that the word is used to describe a shape that is large and rounded at the top, narrow in the middle, and large and rounded at the bottom. Encourage one or more volunteers to draw an hourglass on the chalkboard.

H Elements of Literature
Suspense

Ask students what new uncertainties provide suspense at this point in the story. [Possible responses: Will Marilyn be able to talk to her brother before she must die? Will she decide not to talk to him even if there is time? Will he fight to save her life? How will Barton respond to a tearful goodbye between Marilyn and her brother?]

I Reading Skills and Strategies
Identifying Cause and Effect

❓ Why does Godwin take time to describe the origin of this tornado? [The tornado destroyed the medical supplies of the space colonists and made Barton's trip necessary. Had the tornado not occurred, Barton would not be facing his difficult choice. The tornado is another example of the physical world's "cold equations," which have no respect for human life.]

T19

One of the leaders in exploring the "inner space" of the oceans is marine biologist Sylvia Earle, who is known affectionately as "Her Deepness." In the course of more than fifty expeditions, Earle has spent more than six thousand hours undersea. In 1970, Earle led the first team of women aquanauts in a two-week expedition working in an undersea laboratory off the U.S. Virgin Islands. In 1979, she made a solo descent in the submersible *Deep Rover* and walked on the ocean floor 1,250 feet below the surface. Earle is explorer-in-residence for the National Geographic Society, where she is a leader in the Sustainable Seas Expeditions project. Author of the book *Sea Change,* she works to protect the oceans— "the place where the history of life actually can be found, not in fossils but in living creatures that represent life as it has been, perhaps from the beginning of time."

A **Elements of Literature**

Theme

Note that the author repeats the theme of the helplessness of human beings against the laws of nature.

B **Vocabulary Note**

Prefixes

Point out that both vocabulary words in this sentence contain prefixes meaning "not." The prefix *ir-* is used before root words beginning with the letter *r* (*irreversible, irresistible, irresponsible*), whereas the prefix *im-* is used before root words beginning with the letters *m* or *p* (*immodest, immoderate, imprudent, impossible, impervious*).

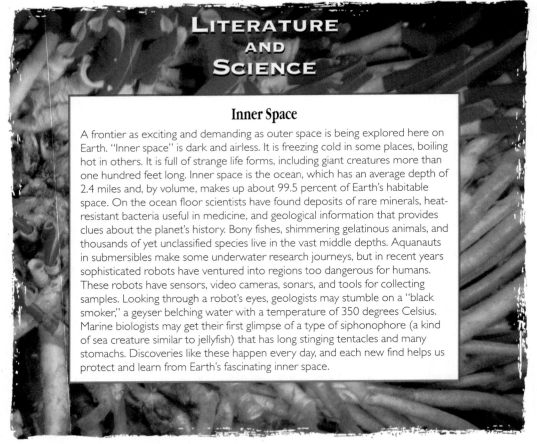

LITERATURE AND SCIENCE

Inner Space

A frontier as exciting and demanding as outer space is being explored here on Earth. "Inner space" is dark and airless. It is freezing cold in some places, boiling hot in others. It is full of strange life forms, including giant creatures more than one hundred feet long. Inner space is the ocean, which has an average depth of 2.4 miles and, by volume, makes up about 99.5 percent of Earth's habitable space. On the ocean floor scientists have found deposits of rare minerals, heat-resistant bacteria useful in medicine, and geological information that provides clues about the planet's history. Bony fishes, shimmering gelatinous animals, and thousands of yet unclassified species live in the vast middle depths. Aquanauts in submersibles make some underwater research journeys, but in recent years sophisticated robots have ventured into regions too dangerous for humans. These robots have sensors, video cameras, sonars, and tools for collecting samples. Looking through a robot's eyes, geologists may stumble on a "black smoker," a geyser belching water with a temperature of 350 degrees Celsius. Marine biologists may get their first glimpse of a type of siphonophore (a kind of sea creature similar to jellyfish) that has long stinging tentacles and many stomachs. Discoveries like these happen every day, and each new find helps us protect and learn from Earth's fascinating inner space.

(Background) Giant tube worms in the Galápagos deep-water vents.

struction that sought to annihilate all that lay before it. It had passed on, leaving the wreckage in its wake. It had destroyed the labor of months and had doomed six men to die and then, as though its task was accomplished, it once more began to resolve into gentle masses of air. But, for all its deadliness, it had destroyed with neither malice nor intent. It had been a blind and mindless force, obeying the laws of nature, and it would have followed the same course with the same fury had men never existed.

Existence required order, and there was order; the laws of nature, irrevocable and immutable. Men could learn to use them, but men could not change them. The circumference of a circle was always pi times the diameter, and no science of man would ever make it otherwise. The combination of chemical A with chemical B under condition C invariably produced reaction D. The law of gravitation was a

WORDS TO OWN

annihilate (ə·nī′ə·lāt′) *v.*: destroy; demolish.
irrevocable (ir·rev′ə·kə·bəl) *adj.*: irreversible; incapable of being canceled or undone.
immutable (im·myō͞ot′ə·bəl) *adj.*: unchangeable; never changing or varying.

Getting Students Involved

Research and Writing: Technology

Suggest that students use available technology such as CD-ROMs, videotape recordings, laser disc recordings, and the Internet to research information about "inner" as well as outer space. Have students focus on a topic and report to the class on that topic. Topics that students might explore include space probes to planets; the building of the first space station; launching and use of the Hubble telescope; the structure and general capability of the space shuttle; deep sea explorations by Sylvia Earle; and the structure and function of specific oceanographic vehicles.

rigid equation, and it made no distinction between the fall of a leaf and the <u>ponderous</u> circling of a binary star system. The nuclear conversion process powered the cruisers that carried men to the stars; the same process in the form of a nova would destroy a world with equal efficiency. The laws *were,* and the universe moved in obedience to them. Along the frontier were arrayed all the forces of nature, and sometimes they destroyed those who were fighting their way outward from Earth. The men of the frontier had long ago learned the bitter futility of cursing the forces that would destroy them, for the forces were blind and deaf; the futility of looking to the heavens for mercy, for the stars of the galaxy swung in their long, long sweep of two hundred million years, as inexorably controlled as they by the laws that knew neither hatred nor compassion. The men of the frontier knew—but how was a girl from Earth to fully understand? *h amount of fuel will not power an EDS with a mass of m plus x safely to its destination*. To him and her brother and parents she was a sweet-faced girl in her teens; to the laws of nature she was *x,* the unwanted factor in a cold equation.

She stirred again on the seat. "Could I write a letter? I want to write to Mama and Daddy. And I'd like to talk to Gerry. Could you let me talk to him over your radio there?"

"I'll try to get him," he said.

He switched on the normal-space transmitter and pressed the signal button. Someone answered the buzzer almost immediately.

"Hello. How's it going with you fellows now—is the EDS on its way?"

"This isn't Group One; this is the EDS," he said. "Is Gerry Cross there?"

"Gerry? He and two others went out in the helicopter this morning and aren't back yet. It's almost sundown, though, and he ought to be back right away—in less than an hour at the most."

"Can you connect me through to the radio in his copter?"

"Huh-uh. It's been out of commission for two months—some printed circuits went haywire

and we can't get any more until the next cruiser stops by. Is it something important—bad news for him, or something?"

"Yes—it's very important. When he comes in, get him to the transmitter as soon as you possibly can."

"I'll do that; I'll have one of the boys waiting at the field with a truck. Is there anything else I can do?"

"No, I guess that's all. Get him there as soon as you can and signal me."

He turned the volume to an inaudible minimum, an act that would not affect the functioning of the signal buzzer, and unclipped the pad of paper from the control board. He tore off the sheet containing his flight instructions and handed the pad to her, together with pencil.

"I'd better write to Gerry too," she said as she took them. "He might not get back to camp in time."

She began to write, her fingers still clumsy and uncertain in the way they handled the pencil, and the top of it trembling a little as she poised it between words. He turned back to the viewscreen, to stare at it without seeing it.

She was a lonely little child trying to say her last goodbye, and she would lay out her heart to them. She would tell them how much she loved them and she would tell them to not feel bad about it, that it was only something that must happen eventually to everyone and she was not afraid. The last would be a lie and it would be there to read between the sprawling, uneven lines: a valiant little lie that would make the hurt all the greater for them.

Her brother was of the frontier and he would understand. He would not hate the EDS pilot for doing nothing to prevent her going; he would know there had been nothing the pilot could do. He would understand, though the understanding would not soften the shock and pain when he learned his sister was gone. But the others, her father and mother—they would not

---

WORDS TO OWN
ponderous (pän′dər·əs) *adj.:* heavy and slow-moving.

C Elements of Literature
Theme
Tell students that this long paragraph conveys the story's theme. Have small groups read the paragraph together and try stating its main idea in their own words. Write their suggestions on the board, and have the class select the clearest, most concise statement of the theme. [Possible responses: The laws of nature are unchangeable and do not play favorites; human beings are helpless in the face of natural laws.]

D Elements of Literature
Suspense
? How does the author draw out the suspense at this point in the story? [It turns out that Gerry is unavailable for about an hour, and Marilyn has only an hour left to live. The reader wonders whether Gerry will return in time to talk to his sister one last time.]

E Reading Skills and Strategies

Monitoring Your Reading: Questioning
Ask students if they find it believable that the radio is broken at the very moment Gerry's sister desperately needs to talk to him. [Possible responses: Yes, because the author has earlier made the point that the space colonies do not receive supplies often, so equipment is likely to break and not get fixed for a long time; no, because a well-run space program would not leave colonists stranded without enough supplies to repair broken equipment.]

F Appreciating Language
Euphemism
? Why does the author use the word *going* instead of the word *dying* here? [Sample answer: Although the meaning is clear, *going* is a less harsh and frightening word than *dying*.]

Ⓐ Reading Skills and Strategies
Speculating
❓ How do you think Marilyn's parents will feel about Barton? [Possible responses: Her parents will not blame him when the situation is explained to them; her parents will be angry at Barton and never accept that her death was necessary.]

Ⓑ Vocabulary Note
Prefixes
Point out that this paragraph contains words with additional prefixes meaning "not" (see p. T20). These include *un-* (*unknowingly*), *in-* (*incapable*), and *il-* (*illogical*). Have students list other words that use each of these prefixes to mean "not." [Possible responses: *unbelieving, indirect, illegal.*]

Ⓒ Elements of Literature
Personification
Point out that the author personifies the pencil by describing it as "whispering." Urge students to explain why this personification is appropriate or effective. [Possible responses: It conveys the quiet of the ship as Marilyn writes and the privacy of her words; it accurately describes the sound of a pencil being used.]

Ⓓ Reading Skills and Strategies
Making Inferences
❓ Why will the letters be important despite not being received until some future time? [Possible responses: They will represent a voice from beyond the grave; they are the family's last communication from their daughter.]

understand. They were of Earth and they would think in the manner of those who had never lived where the safety margin of life was a thin, thin line—and sometimes nothing at all. What would they think of the faceless, unknown pilot who had sent her to her death?

They would hate him with cold and terrible intensity, but it really didn't matter. He would never see them, never know them. He would have only the memories to remind him; only the nights of fear, when a blue-eyed girl in gypsy sandals would come in his dreams to die again. . . .

He scowled at the viewscreen and tried to force his thoughts into less emotional channels. There was nothing he could do to help her. She had unknowingly subjected herself to the penalty of a law that recognized neither innocence nor youth nor beauty, that was incapable of sympathy or leniency. Regret was illogical—and yet, could knowing it to be illogical ever keep it away?

She stopped occasionally, as though trying to find the right words to tell them what she wanted them to know; then the pencil would resume its whispering to the paper. It was 18:37 when she folded the letter in a square and wrote a name on it. She began writing another, twice looking up at the chronometer, as though she feared the black hand might reach its rendezvous before she had finished. It was 18:45 when she folded it as she had done the first letter and wrote a name and address on it.

She held the letters out to him. "Will you take care of these and see that they're enveloped and mailed?"

"Of course." He took them from her hand and placed them in a pocket of his gray uniform shirt.

"These can't be sent off until the next cruiser stops by, and the *Stardust* will have long since told them about me, won't it?" she asked. He nodded and she went on: "That makes the letters not important in one way, but in another way they're very important—to me, and to them."

"I know. I understand, and I'll take care of them."

Getting Students Involved

Cooperative Learning
Word Pictures. The author gives a detailed description of Marilyn but not of the story's other characters. Have students work in groups of three to develop descriptions of what they think Barton, Gerry, and the commander of the *Stardust* might look like. After students have worked for ten minutes, invite one student from each group to share the group's descriptions.

Changing Genres. Have groups of three to five students put together one or more articles for Marilyn's hometown newspaper concerning what has happened to her. They should include at least one photo or sketch to accompany their articles. Some group members could organize and execute the writing; others might handle art and layout.

She glanced at the chronometer, then back to him. "It seems to move faster all the time, doesn't it?"

He said nothing, unable to think of anything to say, and she asked, "Do you think Gerry will come back to camp in time?"

"I think so. They said he should be in right away."

She began to roll the pencil back and forth between her palms. "I hope he does. I feel sick and scared and I want to hear his voice again and maybe I won't feel so alone. I'm a coward and I can't help it."

"No," he said, "you're not a coward. You're afraid, but you're not a coward."

"Is there a difference?"

He nodded. "A lot of difference."

"I feel so alone. I never did feel like this before; like I was all by myself and there was nobody to care what happened to me. Always, before, there were Mama and Daddy there and my friends around me. I had lots of friends, and they had a going-away party for me the night before I left."

Friends and music and laughter for her to remember—and on the viewscreen Lotus Lake was going into the shadow.

"Is it the same with Gerry?" she asked. "I mean, if he should make a mistake, would he have to die for it, all alone and with no one to help him?"

"It's the same with all, along the frontier; it will always be like that so long as there is a frontier."

"Gerry didn't tell us. He said the pay was good, and he sent money home all the time because Daddy's little shop just brought in a bare living, but he didn't tell us it was like this."

"He didn't tell you his work was dangerous?"

"Well—yes. He mentioned that, but we didn't understand. I always thought danger along the frontier was something that was a lot of fun; an exciting adventure, like in the three-D shows." A wan smile touched her face for a moment. "Only it's not, is it? It's not the same at all, because when it's real you can't go home after the show is over."

"No," he said. "No, you can't."

Her glance flicked from the chronometer to the door of the air lock, then down to the pad and pencil she still held. She shifted her position slightly to lay them on the bench beside her, moving one foot out a little. For the first time he saw that she was not wearing Vegan gypsy sandals, but only cheap imitations; the expensive Vegan leather was some kind of grained plastic, the silver buckle was gilded iron, the jewels were colored glass. *Daddy's little shop just brought in a bare living. . . .* She must have left college in her second year, to take the course in linguistics that would enable her to make her own way and help her brother provide for her parents, earning what she could by part-time work after classes were over. Her personal possessions on the *Stardust* would be taken back to her parents—they would neither be of much value nor occupy much storage space on the return voyage.

"Isn't it——" She stopped, and he looked at her questioningly. "Isn't it cold in here?" she asked, almost apologetically. "Doesn't it seem cold to you?"

"Why, yes," he said. He saw by the main temperature gauge that the room was at precisely normal temperature. "Yes, it's colder than it should be."

"I wish Gerry would get back before it's too late. Do you really think he will, and you didn't just say so to make me feel better?"

"I think he will—they said he would be in pretty soon." On the viewscreen Lotus Lake had gone into the shadow but for the thin blue line of its western edge, and it was apparent he had overestimated the time she would have in which to talk to her brother. Reluctantly, he said to her, "His camp will be out of radio range in a few minutes; he's on that part of Woden that's in the shadow"—he indicated the viewscreen—"and the turning of Woden will put him beyond contact. There may not be much time left when he comes in—not much time to talk to him before he fades out. I wish I could do something about it—I would call him right now if I could."

"Not even as much time as I will have to stay?"

"I'm afraid not."

Getting Students Involved

Short Story Writing

After students have read the story, explore the genre of science fiction by asking them to work in groups of four for ten or fifteen minutes, generating ideas for short stories about space travel. Encourage groups to include ideas based on the theme "Hard Choices." Each group should then choose one idea and develop it into an original short story. Volunteers can read their stories to the rest of the class.

E Critical Thinking
Expressing an Opinion
❓ Do you think Barton is correct? Why or why not? [Sample answer: Cowardice usually implies a lack of moral strength to act according to one's principles or an inability to face one's fears. Marilyn fears death, but she faces it with courage and dignity.]

F Elements of Literature
Suspense
❓ Why does the narrator mention this detail about Lotus Lake? [Lotus Lake is the location of Gerry's camp; the fact that it is going into shadow indicates that it will soon be out of radio range. Knowing this fact increases Barton's tension and the reader's sense of suspense: The odds that Marilyn will talk to her brother are decreasing.]

G Elements of Literature
Character
❓ What does Barton's observation of these details add to our understanding of Marilyn? [Sample answers: The details indicate that her family is poor, hardworking, and admirable; we learn more about her background and her determination; she seems more real; we feel more sympathy for her and her family.]

H Reading Skills and Strategies
Drawing Conclusions
❓ Why does Barton agree with Marilyn? [Possible responses: He does not want to upset her further by disagreeing; he realizes why she feels so cold; he is acknowledging the "coldness" of their situation.]

A **Critical Thinking**
Making Judgments

❓ Does Marilyn's decision reinforce or contradict Barton's earlier statement that she is not a coward? [Possible responses: It reinforces his statement, because she shows that she is ready to face her death; it contradicts his statement, because she is too cowardly to continue living once she knows she'll never talk to her brother again.]

B **Reading Skills and Strategies**
Making Generalizations

❓ In your opinion, do most teenagers think the way Marilyn does about her family? Why or why not? [Possible responses: Most teenagers probably take their families for granted until they face a serious situation like the one Marilyn is in; many teenagers appreciate their families and do not take them for granted, even when things are going well.]

C **English Language Learners**
Multiple Meanings

Tell students that when the word *keep* is used before an *-ing* word, it means that the action "continues." Provide examples from your daily experience. [Possible examples: "I keep forgetting to make that phone call"; "It's hard to keep listening when you want a turn to talk."] You might also encourage students to use a dictionary to review other meanings of the word *keep*.

A "Then——" She straightened and looked toward the air lock with pale resolution. "Then I'll go when Gerry passes beyond range. I won't wait any longer after that—I won't have anything to wait for."

Again there was nothing he could say.

"Maybe I shouldn't wait at all. Maybe I'm selfish—maybe it would be better for Gerry if you just told him about it afterward."

There was an unconscious pleading for denial in the way she spoke and he said, "He

wouldn't want you to do that, to not wait for him."

"It's already coming dark where he is, isn't it? There will be all the long night before him, and Mama and Daddy don't know yet that I won't ever be coming back like I promised them I would. I've caused everyone I love to be hurt, haven't I? I didn't want to—I didn't intend to."

"It wasn't your fault," he said. "It wasn't your fault at all. They'll know that. They'll understand."

B "At first I was so afraid to die that I was a coward and thought only of myself. Now I see how selfish I was. The terrible thing about dying like this is not that I'll be gone but that I'll never see them again; never be able to tell them that I didn't take them for granted; never be able to tell them I knew of the sacrifices they made to make my life happier, that I knew all the things

they did for me and that I loved them so much more than I ever told them. I've never told them any of those things. You don't tell them such things when you're young and your life is all before you—you're so afraid of sounding sentimental and silly. But it's so different when you have to die—you wish you had told them while you could, and you wish you could tell them you're sorry for all the little mean things you ever did or said to them. You wish you could tell them that you didn't really mean to ever hurt their feelings and for them to only remember that you always loved them far more than you ever let them know."

"You don't have to tell them that," he said. "They will know—they've always known it."

"Are you sure?" she asked. "How can you be sure? My people are strangers to you."

"Wherever you go, human nature and human hearts are the same."

"And they will know what I want them to know—that I love them?"

"They've always known it, in a way far better than you could ever put in words for them."

C "I keep remembering the things they did for me, and it's the little things they did that seem to be the most important to me, now. Like Gerry—he sent me a bracelet of fire rubies on my sixteenth birthday. It was beautiful—it must have cost him a month's pay. Yet I remember

24 THE SHORT-STORY COLLECTIONS

Skill Link

Compound Subjects

Students will need to identify compound subjects to complete the Grammar Link exercise on p. 31. Remind them that a **compound subject** consists of two or more subjects that are joined by a conjunction and have the same verb. There are two good examples of sentences with compound subjects on p. 24:

a. **Mama** and **Daddy** don't know yet that I won't ever be coming back like I promised them I would.

b. Wherever you go, **human nature** and **human hearts** are the same.

Compound subjects can be joined by the coordinating conjunctions *and* or *or*. They can also

be joined by the correlative conjunctions *either . . . or* and *neither . . . nor*.

Activity

Have students rewrite the two preceding example sentences so that the subjects are joined by *neither . . . nor*. If they need help with subject-verb agreement, refer them to the Grammar Link Mini-Lesson on p. 31.

him more for what he did the night my kitten got run over in the street. I was only six years old and he held me in his arms and wiped away my tears and told me not to cry, that Flossy was gone for just a little while, for just long enough to get herself a new fur coat, and she would be on the foot of my bed the very next morning. I believed him and quit crying and went to sleep dreaming about my kitten coming back. When I woke up the next morning, there was Flossy on the foot of my bed in a brand-new white fur

insides all ruptured and exploded and their lungs out between their teeth and then, a few seconds later, they're all dry and shapeless and horribly ugly. I don't want them to ever think of me as something dead and horrible like that."

"You're their own, their child and their sister. They could never think of you other than the way you would want them to, the way you looked the last time they saw you."

"I'm still afraid," she said. "I can't help it, but I don't want Gerry to know it. If he gets back in

coat, just like he had said she would be. It wasn't until a long time later that Mama told me Gerry had got the pet-shop owner out of bed at four in the morning and, when the man got mad about it, Gerry told him he was either going to go down and sell him the white kitten right then or he'd break his neck."

"It's always the little things you remember people by, all the little things they did because they wanted to do them for you. You've done the same for Gerry and your father and mother; all kinds of things that you've forgotten about, but that they will never forget."

"I hope I have. I would like for them to remember me like that."

"They will."

"I wish——" She swallowed. "The way I'll die—I wish they wouldn't ever think of that. I've read how people look who die in space—their

time, I'm going to act like I'm not afraid at all and——"

The signal buzzer interrupted her, quick and imperative.

"Gerry!" She came to her feet. "It's Gerry now!"

He spun the volume control knob and asked, "Gerry Cross?"

"Yes," her brother answered, an undertone of tenseness to his reply. "The bad news—what is it?"

She answered for him, standing close behind him and leaning down a little toward the communicator, her hand resting small and cold on his shoulder.

"Hello, Gerry." There was only a faint quaver to betray the careful casualness of her voice. "I wanted to see you——"

"Marilyn!" There was sudden and terrible

THE COLD EQUATIONS 25

D **Critical Thinking**
Expressing an Opinion
? Do you think Gerry did the right thing about the kitten? Why or why not? [Possible responses: Gerry handled the incident well by helping his sister feel better; Gerry lied and did not help his sister learn to deal with the reality of loss—moreover, his plan could have backfired if he hadn't been able to find a new kitten in time.]

E **Reading Skills and Strategies**
Monitoring Your Strategies: Questioning
Encourage students to share any questions that arise in their mind as they read this graphic passage. [Possible responses: Are these details accurate? Why does the author include them? Why is Marilyn aware of such details?]

F **Elements of Literature**
Suspense
? What remains unknown in the story, now that it is clear that Marilyn will get a chance to speak to Gerry? [Possible responses: How long will they have to talk? Will Gerry plead for Marilyn's life or threaten Barton? What will Barton and Marilyn do once the conversation is over?]

Assessing Learning

Self-Assessment
Have students evaluate their reading habits by rating themselves on each of the following statements:
  1=rarely   2=sometimes   3=always
_____ **1.** As I'm reading, I ask myself why characters act the way they do.
_____ **2.** As I'm reading, I try to predict what characters will do next.
_____ **3.** As I'm reading, I note words and ideas that interest or puzzle me.
_____ **4.** As I'm reading, I jot down ideas for discussion or writing.
_____ **5.** As I'm reading, I try to notice figures of speech and symbols.

<u>apprehension</u> in the way he spoke her name. "What are you doing on that EDS?"

"I wanted to see you," she said again. "I wanted to see you, so I hid on this ship——"

"You *hid* on it?"

"I'm a stowaway. . . . I didn't know what it would mean——"

"Marilyn!" It was the cry of a man who calls, hopeless and desperate, to someone already and forever gone from him. "What have you done?"

"I . . . it's not——" Then her own composure broke and the cold little hand gripped his shoulder convulsively. "Don't, Gerry—I only wanted to see you; I didn't intend to hurt you. Please, Gerry, don't feel like that——"

Something warm and wet splashed on his wrist, and he slid out of the chair to help her into it and swing the microphone down to her level.

"Don't feel like that. Don't let me go knowing you feel like that——"

The sob she had tried to hold back choked in her throat, and her brother spoke to her. "Don't cry, Marilyn." His voice was suddenly deep and infinitely gentle, with all the pain held out of it. "Don't cry, Sis—you mustn't do that. It's all right, honey—everything is all right."

"I——" Her lower lip quivered and she bit into it. "I didn't want you to feel that way—I just wanted us to say goodbye, because I have to go in a minute."

"Sure—sure. That's the way it'll be, Sis. I didn't mean to sound the way I did." Then his voice changed to a tone of quick and urgent demand. "EDS—have you called the *Stardust*? Did you check with the computers?"

"I called the *Stardust* almost an hour ago. It can't turn back; there are no other cruisers within forty light-years, and there isn't enough fuel."

"Are you sure that the computers had the correct data—sure of everything?"

"Yes—do you think I could ever let it happen if I wasn't sure? I did everything I could do. If there was anything at all I could do now, I would do it."

"He tried to help me, Gerry." Her lower lip

was no longer trembling and the short sleeves of her blouse were wet where she had dried her tears. "No one can help me and I'm not going to cry anymore and everything will be all right with you and Daddy and Mama, won't it?"

"Sure—sure it will. We'll make out fine."

Her brother's words were beginning to come in more faintly, and he turned the volume control to maximum. "He's going out of range," he said to her. "He'll be gone within another minute."

"You're fading out, Gerry," she said. "You're going out of range. I wanted to tell you—but I can't now. We must say goodbye so soon—but maybe I'll see you again. Maybe I'll come to you in your dreams with my hair in braids and crying because the kitten in my arms is dead; maybe I'll be the touch of a breeze that whispers to you as it goes by; maybe I'll be one of those gold-winged larks you told me about, singing my silly head off to you; maybe, at times, I'll be nothing you can see, but you will know I'm there beside you. Think of me like that, Gerry; always like that and not—the other way."

Dimmed to a whisper by the turning of Woden, the answer came back:

"Always like that, Marilyn—always like that and never any other way."

"Our time is up, Gerry—I have to go now. Good——" Her voice broke in midword and her mouth tried to twist into crying. She pressed her hand hard against it and when she spoke again the words came clear and true:

"Goodbye, Gerry."

Faint and <u>ineffably</u> poignant and tender, the last words came from the cold metal of the communicator:

"Goodbye, little sister . . ."

She sat motionless in the hush that followed, as though listening to the shadow-echoes of the words as they died away; then she turned away from the communicator, toward the air lock,

---

WORDS TO OWN

apprehension (ap′rē·hen′shən) *n.*: dread; fear of a future event.
ineffably (in·ef′ə·blē) *adv.*: indescribably; inexpressibly.

Making the Connections

Connecting to the Theme: "Hard Choices"

In this story, Barton has to carry out the rules for jettisoning a stowaway, but he is reluctant to do so. Ask students to discuss in their Writer's Notebook the hard choices he must make. [He can either jettison Marilyn or allow the EDS to crash, causing several people to die. Some students may say that Barton has to follow the rules. Others may say he could have jettisoned something else on board.]

Cultural Connections

In June 1983, Sally Ride became the first American female astronaut to travel in space. In August of that same year, Guion Bluford, Jr., became the first African American astronaut in space. Both astronauts' missions were on the *Challenger* space shuttle and involved pharmaceutical research and the launching of communications satellites. Both astronauts also helped test the shuttle's remote manipulator arm.

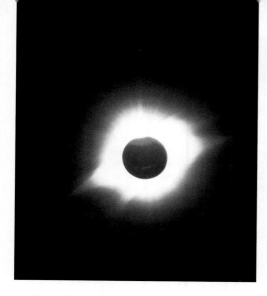

and he pulled down the black lever beside him. The inner door of the air lock slid swiftly open to reveal the bare little cell that was waiting for her, and she walked to it.

She walked with her head up and the brown curls brushing her shoulders, with the white sandals stepping as sure and steady as the fractional gravity would permit and the gilded buckles twinkling with little lights of blue and red and crystal. He let her walk alone and made no move to help her, knowing she would not want it that way. She stepped into the air lock and turned to face him, only the pulse in her throat to betray the wild beating of her heart.

"I'm ready," she said.

He pushed the lever up and the door slid its quick barrier between them, enclosing her in black and utter darkness for her last moments of life. It clicked as it locked in place and he jerked down the red lever. There was a slight waver of the ship as the air gushed from the lock, a vibration to the wall as though something had bumped the outer door in passing; then there was nothing and the ship was dropping true and steady again. He shoved the red lever back to close the door on the empty air lock and turned away, to walk to the pilot's chair with the slow steps of a man old and weary.

Back in the pilot's chair he pressed the signal button of the normal-space transmitter. There was no response; he had expected none. Her brother would have to wait through the night until the turning of Woden permitted contact through Group One.

It was not yet time to resume deceleration, and he waited while the ship dropped endlessly downward with him and the drives purred softly. He saw that the white hand of the supply-closet temperature gauge was on zero. A cold equation had been balanced and he was alone on the ship. Something shapeless and ugly was hurrying ahead of him, going to Woden, where her brother was waiting through the night, but the empty ship still lived for a little while with the presence of the girl who had not known about the forces that killed with neither hatred nor malice. It seemed, almost, that she still sat, small and bewildered and frightened, on the metal box beside him, her words echoing hauntingly clear in the void she had left behind her:

I didn't do anything to die for.... I didn't do anything....

MEET THE WRITER

A Sci-Fi Pioneer

Tom Godwin (1915–1980) lived for many years in various small towns in the Mojave Desert—a harsh environment that the average urbanite or suburbanite might consider as alien as outer space. Godwin began publishing science-fiction stories in magazines in the early 1950s. He also published three novels: *The Survivors; The Space Barbarians*, which describes warfare on the planet Ragnarok; and *Beyond Another Sun*. His best-known work by far, however, is "The Cold Equations."

F **Appreciating Language**
Connotation
The author's use of the word *weary*, rather than *tired*, suggests Barton's feeling of emotional exhaustion or despair.

G **Reading Skills and Strategies**
Monitoring Your Reading: Questioning
? Do you wonder what the "something shapeless and ugly" is? What do you think the author is describing? [Possible responses: Marilyn's dead body; Barton's guilt; the despair her loved ones will feel.]

H **Reading Skills and Strategies**
Challenging the Text
? In your opinion, is this a good way to end this story? Why or why not? [Sample responses: Yes, it's haunting and realistic, and it stays with you; no, it's too depressing—a rescue would have been more exciting.]

Resources ———

Selection Assessment
Formal Assessment
• Selection Test, p. 1
Test Generator (One-Stop Planner)
• CD-ROM

Assessing Learning

Check Test: True–False
1. Instruments on the EDS are able to detect a stowaway. [True]
2. The EDS pilot is in complete control of determining the ship's course. [False]
3. Marilyn knows in advance the consequences of her stowing away. [False]
4. Marilyn comes from a rich family. [False]
5. Marilyn is rescued at the end of the story. [False]

Standardized Test Preparation
For practice with standardized test format specific to this selection, see
• *Standardized Test Preparation*, pp. 10, 12
For practice in proofreading and editing, see
• *Daily Oral Grammar*, Transparency 1

Connections

This *New York Times* editorial looks back at the U.S. moon landing, a direct result of the Cold War, and at NASA's subsequent decline. The U.S. space program has proved more expensive and has produced fewer results than the lunar landing promised. The space program's most important legacy is the image of our planet, fragile and isolated, in outer space.

Ⓐ Historical Connection

The race to the moon began on October 4, 1957, when the Soviet Union launched *Sputnik I,* the first artificial satellite, into orbit. A few months later, on January 31, 1958, the United States launched its first satellite, *Explorer I.* The Soviets put the first astronaut into orbit in April 1961; on July 20, 1969, two American astronauts walked on the moon.

Ⓑ Critical Thinking

Recognizing Persuasive Techniques

Have students point out loaded words (words with strong positive or negative connotations) that the writer uses to contrast NASA's original promise with its later failures. [Words with negative connotations include *blew up, incompetence, shriveled,* and *cling;* words with positive connotations include *omnipotence, venturing,* and *epic.*]

Ⓒ Reading Skills and Strategies

Distinguishing Fact and Opinion

❓ What facts and opinions does the writer use to build the argument about the space program? [Facts:"Automated devices" could have been sent at a "fraction of the cost" of manned flights; space flights have turned out to be "far more expensive" than was originally thought. Opinions:"The moon program, born of Cold War desperation, had nowhere to go after its success"; space flights have proved "far less useful" than originally thought and "difficult to justify."]

Ⓓ Reading Skills and Strategies

Finding the Main Idea

❓ In the writer's opinion, what has been the most important legacy of landing astronauts on the moon? [seeing the Earth as it looks from space and realizing how fragile and isolated our planet is]

Lunar Legacy

Ⓐ When Neil Armstrong set foot on the moon twenty-five years ago today, the nation responded ecstatically. It was not just that American astronauts had beaten Soviet cosmonauts to the moon in the Cold War's most visible symbolic struggle.° Their feat implied that the same combination of heroism, determination, technical wizardry, and managerial genius would soon conquer other worlds and a host of earthly ills as well.

Ⓑ But how fast the dream dissipated! The space agency that put astronauts on the moon later blew up the shuttle Challenger and gained a reputation for in-

° *The Cold War was the state of hostility and the struggle for global dominance between the United States and the Soviet Union. It lasted roughly from the end of World War II, in 1945, until the collapse of the Soviet Union, in 1991. The race to land a person on the moon was one aspect of the Cold War.*

competence rather than omnipotence. Space budgets shriveled. NASA lowered its sights. Instead of venturing onward to Mars, astronauts now cling close to home, working only in low earth orbit. It is as if, critics say, Columbus's epic voyage to the New World had been followed with boat trips around the harbor.

The space agency's fall from grace should not be exaggerated. The mythology of the lunar achievement makes it easy to forget that three astronauts were incinerated in a fire on the launch pad and three others almost lost in an explosion on the way to the moon. But in that race for national supremacy, losses were tolerated that today might prove crippling.

Historians in coming centuries will have to judge whether the moon landing was a "giant leap for mankind," as Mr. Armstrong proclaimed on taking his first step, or merely the most ex-

treme and daring example of an exploit on the order of climbing Mount Everest or reaching the poles. As of now, it has not led to much—a few follow-up landings, a momentary reputation as the world's top technical power, and some genuine scientific gains in determining the moon's age, composition, and likely origin. But more might have been learned at a fraction of the cost by sending an armada of automated devices.

Ⓒ The moon program, born of Cold War desperation, had nowhere to go after its success. Once the Soviets had been vanquished, why run another lap? In subsequent years, space operations have proved far more expensive and far less useful than enthusiasts once imagined, thus difficult to justify without an overriding political goal.

In the end it was the sheer strangeness of the experience—man on the moon!—that caused it to endure in memory with a romance that cannot quite be blown away by hardheaded analysis. Perhaps the most memorable image to emerge from the moon program was that of astronauts bobbing around the lunar surface or planting an American flag.

Ⓓ But a far more important image was the sight of the Earth seen from afar—a radiant blue-and-white sphere, beautiful and vulnerable, shimmering against the dark background of space. The lunar landing that some thought would launch mankind on its way as a spacefaring species instead highlighted the fragility and isolation of home.

—from *The New York Times,*
July 20, 1994

Apollo 11 (7/20/69). Edwin "Buzz" Aldrin, on lunar surface, next to solar-wind composition.

28 THE SHORT-STORY COLLECTIONS

Connecting Across Texts

Connecting to "The Cold Equations"

Both "The Cold Equations" and "Lunar Legacy" examine the grim reality behind the glamour and excitement of space travel. Point out to students that "The Cold Equations" predates the editorial by forty years and predates the moon landing by fifteen years. Godwin obviously viewed space travel as the wave of the future. Ask students to discuss whether they think, in light of the facts and opinions explored in "Lunar Legacy," that commercial space travel will ever be common.

MAKING MEANINGS

First Thoughts

[synthesize]
1. How did you think the story would end? Why?

Shaping Interpretations

[analyze]
2. 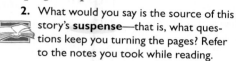 What would you say is the source of this story's **suspense**—that is, what questions keep you turning the pages? Refer to the notes you took while reading.

[contrast]
3. This story **contrasts** life on Earth with life on the space frontier. In what important ways are these **settings** different? Do you find Godwin's space frontier believable? Why or why not?

[evaluate]
4. What do you think is the most important passage in this story, and why?

[analyze]
5. Find the passage toward the middle of the story that explains its **title**. What are the "cold equations"? What other **images** of coldness can you find in the story?

[evaluate]
6. The title of the story seems to imply that the more technology influences our lives, the less room there is for human choice and emotions. How does the story illustrate that idea? Do you agree, or not? Why?

Connecting with the Text

[connect]
7. How believable are Marilyn's choice to stow away and her later responses to her fate? If you were in her situation, how do you think you would react? Be sure to check your Quickwrite notes.

Extending the Text

[analyze]
8. "The Cold Equations" was written in 1954, at a time when technology was far less advanced than it is now. Today we are living in what, to Tom Godwin in 1954, was the future (though not as far in the future as the story is set). Do you think the technological "future" is turning out to be as cold and harsh as Godwin expected? Explain your answer with specific examples from your own experience. You might organize your thoughts in a chart like this:

What Godwin Predicted	Today's Reality

Challenging the Text

[evaluate]
9. The story says on page 11 that Barton would have immediately carried out the regulation to eject the stowaway if it had been a man. What do you think of this attitude?

Reading Check

> **Reading Check**
>
> **Summarize** the main events of this story in a paragraph. Open with a note describing the **setting,** and then tell who the **characters** are and what their **problem** is. Be sure to explain how the problem is resolved.

Sample summary: The story is set on a small Emergency Dispatch Ship in the future. The main character is a spaceship pilot named Barton, who is delivering emergency medical supplies to a frontier space colony. The other important character is Marilyn, a teenage girl who has stowed away on the ship in order to pay a surprise visit to her brother, who is stationed on the space colony Barton is flying to. Marilyn is unaware that the penalty for stowing away on an EDS is extreme and automatic: She must be set adrift to die in space because the EDS has only enough fuel to land one person, the pilot. Barton is forced to let her die—or else both he and Marilyn would die in a crash landing and the six space colonists who are awaiting the shipment of medicine would also die.

MAKING MEANINGS

First Thoughts

1. Some students may say that the story's title gave away its conclusion; others may have predicted a happier ending, based on their own sympathy for the girl, their judgment of Barton's character, or their own sense of justice.

Shaping Interpretations

2. Possible responses: The main question is "Will Marilyn survive?" Others include: "Is the stowaway dangerous?" "Will the computer find a different course of action?" "Will Marilyn get to talk to her brother?" "Will Barton find a way to save Marilyn without hurting anyone else?"

3. The main difference is that the space frontier lacks many resources, including rescue systems, that exist on Earth. Thus, people on the frontier are more likely to confront the hard laws of physics and be unable to act on their compassion. Responses about believability should be supported by reasons.

4. Students may mention the passage detailing the equations, passages of great suspense, when Marilyn begins to accept her imminent death, Barton's efforts to reach Gerry, the siblings' conversation, or the end of the story.

5. "Cold equations" are scientific formulas that cannot be changed, regardless of human emotion. Other images of coldness include comparing the word *no* to a cold stone, the imagined cold hatred of Marilyn's parents for Barton, Marilyn's finding the EDS cold, her cold hand as she grips Barton's shoulder, and the cold metal of the communicator.

6. The fuel supply, predetermined by computers, allows for no changes. Some students may agree that computers and other technology are increasingly controlling our lives, while others may feel that new technology gives us more choices.

Connecting with the Text

7. Some students will say that Marilyn seems unrealistically naive about the rules and consequences of her world and accepting of her impending death. Students' reactions will vary.

Making Meanings answers continue on p. T30.

Extending the Text

8. Sample answer: In contrast to Godwin's predictions, much of today's technology is quite user-friendly. Examples include desktop and laptop computers instead of room-sized models.

Challenging the Text

9. Some students may find Barton's attitude prejudiced against men; others may find it reasonable since a grown man would be more physically threatening.

Grading Timesaver

Rubrics for each Choices assignment appear on p. 89 in the *Portfolio Management System*.

CHOICES: Building Your Portfolio

1. Writer's Notebook With each selection, a Writer's Notebook activity appears as the first option in the Choices section. These brief, work-in-progress assignments build toward the writing assignment presented in the Writer's Workshop at the end of the collection. If students save their work for their Writer's Notebook activities as they move through the collection, they should be able to use some of them as starting points for the workshop.

2. Creative Writing Have students work in groups to brainstorm other plausible endings. To help students visualize the new ending, suggest that they draw a storyboard of the last few paragraphs.

Choices annotations continue at the bottom right.

CHOICES: Building Your Portfolio

Writer's Notebook
1. Collecting Ideas for a Persuasive Essay

Finding a topic.

This story may have made you think about problems or issues such as the

role of technology in our lives or the conflicts involved in obeying difficult rules. With a partner or small group, brainstorm a list of school, local, national, or world problems. These should be debatable issues or situations that you think need fixing. On your list, check off the issues that you've had some personal experience with. You may have worked in a day care center, for example, or helped in a local political campaign. (Save your list for use with the Writer's Workshop on p. 85.)

> **Issues for Persuasive Essay**
>
> Technology—good or bad?
> ✓ Bikes for borrowing
> Teenage violence
> ● Helping the elderly
> ✓ Laws for teenage drivers
> ✓ Medical care for elderly—
>   hard choices
>   (my grandfather)
>   stereotyping

Creative Writing
2. Changing the Ending

You are a researcher in the year 2196. You discover some pages of an ancient textbook containing a short story called "The Cold Equations." However, the final pages are missing. The last bit of text you can read is Marilyn's "I'm ready" on page 27. Write a plausible resolution for the story that is different from the present ending. Suppose you are an optimistic researcher. Is it possible to find a happy ending?

Evaluating a Story
3. Letter to the Editor

For "The Cold Equations" to succeed, the writer must convince us, first, that Marilyn could actually have been able to stow away on the ship, and, second, that Barton had no choice but to eject her. Is the story airtight, or are there leaks in it? Suppose you are reading this story in a magazine, and you want to write a letter to the editor, commenting on its credibility. Write the letter, including specific details to support your evaluation. You might find the notes you took while reading useful.

Science Research/ Critical Thinking
4. Godwin's Science

Godwin imagines a technological future in which space travel is as common as airplane travel is today. Yet he imagines that the EDS will not have the smallest amount of extra fuel for unforeseen emergencies. Is this realistic? Go back to the text to find other aspects of Godwin's technological future. Formulate any questions you have. The notes you took while reading may help. Then, do some research to determine how scientifically accurate Godwin is. You might check the library or up-to-date databases or the Internet. Present your results to the class.

Current Events/ Speaking
5. A Political Decision

Read the editorial about the NASA space program (see **Connections** on page 28), and prepare a two-minute speech offering your view of the value of space exploration. Outline your talk, limiting it to two or three key ideas. At the end, ask your audience for feedback. How compelling were your opinions and your presentation?

---

3. Evaluating a Story To help students who may find it difficult to find leaks in the story, have them focus on other choices Barton might have had for rebalancing the "cold equation": Is there a way that Barton could have removed the excess weight without jettisoning Marilyn?

4. Science Research/Critical Thinking Have students, working in pairs, go back to the story to create a list of scientific points worth checking. Another research possibility is for students to interview local science experts. Have them audiotape or videotape any interviews they conduct.

5. Current Events/Speaking As students read the editorial on p. 28, have them make notes of ideas they agree with, disagree with, or question. Also, have them ask themselves whether the author has left out any important points about space travel. Students can use their notes to find ideas for their speeches.

GRAMMAR LINK — MINI-LESSON

Language Handbook HELP

See Agreement of Subject and Verb, pages 1022-1024.

Technology HELP

See Language Workshop CD-ROM. Key word entry: subject-verb agreement.

They Always Agree—Subject and Verb

Probably the most common error people make in their writing and speaking has to do with subject-verb agreement. The rule is simple: **Singular subjects take singular verbs; plural subjects take plural verbs.** The trick is to find the subject and determine its **number**.

1. The number of the subject is not changed by a phrase following the subject.

   EXAMPLE:

   The <u>dials</u> in the EDS control room <u>were</u> flashing.

2. Singular subjects joined by *or* or *nor* take a singular verb.

   EXAMPLE:

   Neither Barton nor his supervisor <u>wants</u> to carry out the rules.

3. When a singular subject and a plural subject are joined by *or* or *nor,* the verb agrees with the subject nearer the verb.

   EXAMPLE:

   Neither Barton nor his supervisors <u>want</u> to eject the girl.

Try It Out

➤ Identify the subjects below and determine their number. Then decide which verb choice is correct.

1. Marilyn or her brother <u>is/are</u> going to die.

2. Neither Barton nor his supervisors <u>was/were</u> willing to make an exception to the rule.

3. The men on the EDS team <u>is/are</u> obliged to eject Marilyn.

➤ When you proofread your writing, always check the subject of each sentence, and be sure the verb agrees with it in number. There's only one situation in which you can leave such errors uncorrected: when you're writing dialogue for a character who's careless about the rules.

VOCABULARY — HOW TO OWN A WORD

WORD BANK

inured
increments
recoiled
paramount
annihilate
irrevocable
immutable
ponderous
apprehension
ineffably

Meet the Glossary and Check a Dictionary

A **glossary** is a mini-dictionary containing specialized vocabulary that is often included at the back of a textbook. (Your science and history textbooks probably have glossaries.) Become familiar with the glossary in this book (see pages 1065–1073). There you'll find the **pronunciation, part of speech,** and **definition** for each Word to Own as it is used in the selection. Now check a **dictionary** to see what additional information you can discover about each word in the Word Bank. Does the word have other meanings besides those listed in the glossary? Can the word function as a different part of speech? Does the dictionary list any **synonyms** (words that have the same meaning)? Compile all the information you gather, and write an example sentence using each word in the Word Bank.

THE COLD EQUATIONS 31

GRAMMAR LINK

Try It Out

Answers

1. Marilyn, brother (singular), is
2. Barton, supervisors (plural), were
3. men (plural), are

When students write their persuasive essays for the Writing Workshop on p. 85, remind them to proofread for subject-verb agreement. They should first locate the subject or subjects of each sentence. Remind them that the subject is never found in a prepositional phrase.

VOCABULARY

In a dictionary, students might find additional meanings for several of the words. For instance, *recoil* can be used as a noun to mean "the kickback of a gun that has been fired." A college dictionary might include a discussion of the distinctions in meaning among synonyms of *recoil,* such as *shrink, flinch, wince,* and *quail.*

Some dictionaries may note that *ponderous* can also mean "very dull," or that *apprehension* can also mean "arrest or seizure of a criminal" or "the power of understanding."

Resources

Language
- *Grammar and Language Links* Worksheet, p. 1

Vocabulary
- *Words to Own* Worksheet, p. 1

Grammar Link Quick Check

Select the correct verb form from the choices given in parentheses.

1. The calculations of the computer (is, are) taken very seriously. [are]
2. Neither Marilyn nor her brother (has, have) much hope for a rescue. [has]
3. (There's, There are) several reasons Marilyn should have kept to her original plan. [There are]
4. The men on the *Stardust* (wants, want) to help Barton. [want]
5. Neither Barton nor the others (wants, want) Marilyn to die. [want]

Resources ———

Elements of Literature
Plot
For additional instruction on plot, see
Literary Elements:
• Transparency 2

Assessment
Formal Assessment
• Literary Elements Test, p. 11

Elements of Literature

This lesson uses a cartoon and a contemporary version of an old fairy tale to capture students' interest and teach the importance of conflict and complications in making a story compelling. Have volunteers read each section of the essay feature aloud. Give students time to respond to the humorous storyline and to discuss the importance of each plot element.

Elements of Literature

PLOT: The Story's Framework *by* John Leggett

© The New Yorker Collection 1998 Roz Chast from cartoonbank.com. All Rights Reserved.

"What Happened?"

This cartoon is funny, but it actually shows the "nuts and bolts" plot elements of any story. **Plot** is a series of related events—it's what happens between "Once upon a time" and "happily ever after." The plot of a story includes characters who experience some problem or conflict (maybe a dragon), which is solved in some way (maybe by a Superman). A complete story, of course, fills in the interesting details. Let's see how in another example.

A Character with a Problem

Once upon a time, there was a rock star who had been changed into an ugly, deformed wombat by an irate parent.

We've just stated the **basic situation** of a story. We have a main character, and he has a problem.

The wombat, still human behind his claws and fur, was desperately lonely in his mansion. People ran off screaming at the sight of him. Would anyone ever love him?

We've just learned the single most important fact about our character's inner life. He wants love. As you will see, his struggle to win someone's love despite his claws and fur will be the central **conflict** of the story. This conflict is **external** because it involves the beast and another person. The conflict also becomes **internal** as the beast struggles to adjust to people's understandable reactions to his appearance.

The Plot Thickens: Complications

One dark and stormy night, there came a knock at the mansion door. It was a shoehorn salesman, drenched and lost, seeking shelter.

A new factor has been added, which gives the main character a new problem to deal with. This is a **complication**. If it weren't for the beast's worry that the salesman will go hysterical when he sees his host's furry face, the visitor's arrival wouldn't be a problem at all. The beast could simply let him in for the night and let him out the next morning.

Now the beast must deal with a whole chain of

32 THE SHORT-STORY COLLECTIONS

Reaching All Students

Struggling Readers
Have students complete a Story Grammar for "The Cold Equations" with the following sentences:
This story is about _____.
The characters in this story are _____.
The main problem of this story is _____.
The problem ends when _____.
After students have successfully completed these sentences, tie the Story Grammar entries to the plot elements of basic situation and resolution.

English Language Learners
To help these students analyze the elements of plot, have them meet in small groups and tell a familiar folktale or fairy tale from their own cultural background. Once you understand the story, help them identify the basic situation, the complications, the climax, and the resolution of their story.

Advanced Readers
You might have these students work in pairs or small groups to write other humorous or serious models for a story (like the rock star wombat one) to teach the elements of plot. Since the models are really a plot summary, some students may want to actually write their stories. Have them share the completed models or stories with the class.

complications triggered by the visitor's arrival. They include

- the arrival of the salesman's beautiful daughter
- the daughter's terror at the sight of the huge furry wombat
- the daughter's illness, which is cured by the beast, an expert in herbal medicine
- the beast's growing love for the daughter
- the attempts of nearby villagers to free the daughter from the beast

Complications tend to come in a series. Each event is usually linked to what happened before and what happens afterward by bonds of cause and effect. The reader's excitement builds incident by incident as the plot thickens with complications.

The High Point: The Climax

Eventually, the high point of the plot is reached. In our story this might happen when the villagers break down the mansion's doors and try to rescue the daughter (who at this point realizes she loves the wombat for his kind heart and

doesn't want to be rescued, which is another complication). The young woman's change of heart is the **climax** of the plot, the most exciting moment, when something happens that will determine the outcome of the conflict. After the climactic moment comes the **resolution,** when the story is closed.

The now-repentant villagers cheered the wedding of the rock star and his bride. From then on, the shoehorn salesman and the couple lived happily ever after, touring the world and occasionally giving free concerts on the village green.

"Happily Ever After," Sort Of

A good resolution solves the conflict, but especially in modern fiction, it doesn't necessarily solve everything in the characters' lives. The conclusion of a story may even open up new questions, prolonging our pleasure by giving us something to think, talk, and write about after we close the book.

Although "they lived happily ever after" is very gratifying, such an ending can sound unrealistic, except in a fairy tale. A more modern resolution to our story would suggest "they lived happily ever after, sort of" and hint at what's behind the "sort of."

The Most Important Question in Fiction

Not every story depends on a full-fledged plot that marches along as methodically as our example does. Many modern short stories focus not so much on plot as on revelation of character. Such stories often drop us right into the middle of the action at the start.

Even in modern fiction, however, the question "What happens next?" is the single most important question readers ask about stories—and no matter how the world changes or what new media are invented, people will never stop asking it: "And then what happens? And then? And then...?"

> **"W**hat happens next?" is the single most important question readers ask about stories.

ELEMENTS OF LITERATURE: PLOT 33

- After students finish reading the essay, retell the story of "The Cold Equations" (p. 9), leaving out all of the conflict. Suppose that Barton has plenty of fuel. He finds the stowaway and sends her out into space without a second thought. Discuss the effect this lack of conflict has on the story. Then, use a plot diagram like the following:

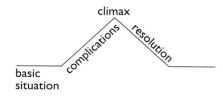

- Using the diagram to guide the class, ask students to identify the plot elements in "The Cold Equations."

Applying the Element

Have students discuss plot elements in other stories and novels they have read recently. You might extend the discussion to plots of traditional fairy tales ("Sleeping Beauty," for example), movies, and TV shows. Ask what kinds of plots they enjoy most—those involving exciting external conflict or those with intense internal conflict. Do they prefer stories with conflicts that are neatly resolved or those in which questions remain at the end? Encourage students to continue their evaluation of plot elements as they read the rest of the stories in the Short Story Collections.

Assessing Learning

Check Test: Short Answer

1. What does the basic situation tell us about the story? [Possible response: who the main character is and what his or her problem is.]

2. What are the two basic types of conflict? [external conflict and internal conflict]

3. What is a complication? [Sample answer: an event that causes a new problem for the main character.]

4. What happens at the climax of a story? [Possible response: The climax is the most exciting moment; something happens that will affect how the story will end.]

5. What happens during the resolution? [Possible responses: The conflict is solved; the story ends.]

OBJECTIVES

1. Read and interpret the story
2. Analyze the narrator's external and internal conflicts
3. Identify causes and effects
4. Express understanding through writing
5. Identify imagery and use imagery in writing
6. Understand and use new words

SKILLS

Literary
• Analyze external and internal conflicts

Reading
• Identify causes and effects

Writing
• Collect ideas for a persuasive essay
• Write a personal narrative
• Write a review

Grammar/Language
• Identify and use imagery

Vocabulary
• Use new words
• Create a Vocabulary Resource File

Planning

• **Traditional Schedule**
  Lesson Plans Including Strategies for English-Language Learners

• **One-Stop Planner**
  CD-ROM with Test Generator

Before You Read

THE BASS, THE RIVER, AND SHEILA MANT

Make the Connection

Fish, or Cut Bait!

This may be a story about a search for love (or a quest for a fish). Consider the problems of a young man who's searching for both—and who will always think about the one that got away.

Quickwrite

Think back to some time when you had to give up one thing for something else. Write down what happened. Did you make the right choice? Do you have some regrets?

Elements of Literature

Conflict Inside and Out

A showdown with another person or a struggle with nature puts us in opposition to something outside of ourselves. That **external conflict** is often the heart of adventure stories or mysteries. The most difficult struggles, however, may be those within us. The **internal conflict** between two sides of our personalities, between competing desires, forces us to choose, and that choice can be agonizing. In this story, a boy is caught up in both external and internal conflicts—watch to see how he deals with them.

In an **external conflict,** a character struggles against an outside force—nature, another person, a machine, or even a whole society. An **internal conflict** takes place when a character struggles mentally to resolve opposing needs, desires, or emotions.

For more on Conflict, see pages 32–33 and the Handbook of Literary Terms.

Reading Skills and Strategies

Understanding Cause and Effect

A **cause** is *why* something happens. An **effect** is the *result* of some event or action. As you read this story, think about the causes behind the narrator's behavior. Think about the effects of the girl's words and actions. Tuning in to cause-and-effect relationships—the "why's" between one moment and the next—can help you understand what happens in a plot, and why it happens.

go.hrw.com
LEO 10-1

Preteaching Vocabulary

Words to Own

Have students meet in groups of three to read the definitions of the Words to Own at the bottom of selection pages. Then, suggest to them that the words might be used to create a good mystery or horror story. Challenge each group to use as many of the words as possible in an original story. If groups need help getting started, suggest an opening sentence such as this one:

The *denizens* of Breakneck Ridge crept *surreptitiously* around the darkened old house.

Have each group read their story aloud, and ask the class to vote for their favorite.

The Bass, the River, and Sheila Mant

W. D. Wetherell

I never made the
same mistake again.

Summary ▪▪

The story's first-person narrator recalls a summer on a New England river when he was fourteen years old and obsessively fished and admired the girl next door, seventeen-year-old Sheila Mant. One day he musters the courage to ask Sheila to a dance and picks her up in his canoe. Not noticing the fishing rod resting on the boat's floor or the line in the water, Sheila declares fishing "dumb." When the boy moves to conceal the rod, a huge bass strikes. The narrator creates suspense by keeping the exciting, hidden fish on the line as beautiful, self-absorbed Sheila chatters away. He faces external conflicts (with the bass and with keeping Sheila ignorant of it) as well as the internal conflict of trying to decide whether he wants Sheila or the bass more. Secretly cutting the fishing line at the story's climax, the narrator chooses romance. The dance, however, is anticlimactic: Sheila leaves with a college boy who drives a sports car. The older, reflective narrator calls the hard choice he made as an adolescent a mistake that he has never repeated.

Resources

Listening
Audio CD Library
This coming-of-age story is brought to life in a recording in the Audio CD Library:
• Disc 2, Track 2

Elements of Literature
Plot
For additional instruction on conflict and plot, see Literary Elements:
• Transparency 2
• Worksheet, p. 7

Resources: Print and Media

Reading
• *Reading Skills and Strategies*
   MiniRead Skill Lesson, p. 11
   Selection Skill Lesson, p. 18
• *Graphic Organizers for Active Reading*, p. 2
• *Words to Own*, p. 3
• *Audio CD Library*
   Disc 2, Track 2

Elements of Literature
• *Literary Elements*
   Transparency 2
   Worksheet, p. 7

Writing and Language
• *Daily Oral Grammar*
   Transparency 2
• *Grammar and Language Links*
   Worksheet, p. 3

Assessment
• *Formal Assessment*, p. 3
• *Portfolio Management System*, p. 91
• *Test Generator (One-Stop Planner CD-ROM)*

Internet
• go.hrw.com (keyword: LE0 10-1)

There was a summer in my life when the only creature that seemed lovelier to me than a largemouth bass was Sheila Mant. I was fourteen. The Mants had rented the cottage next to ours on the river; with their parties, their frantic games of softball, their constant comings and goings, they appeared to me denizens of a brilliant existence. "Too noisy by half," my mother quickly decided, but I would have given anything to be invited to one of their parties, and when my parents went to bed I would sneak through the woods to their hedge and stare enchanted at the candlelit swirl of white dresses and bright, paisley skirts.

Sheila was the middle daughter—at seventeen, all but out of reach. She would spend her days sunbathing on a float my Uncle Sierbert had moored in their cove, and before July was over I had learned all her moods. If she lay flat on the diving board with her hand trailing idly in the water, she was pensive, not to be disturbed. On her side, her head propped up by her arm, she was observant, considering those around her with a look that seemed queenly and severe. Sitting up, arms tucked around her long, suntanned legs, she was approachable, but barely, and it was only in those glorious moments when she stretched herself prior to entering the water that her various suitors found the courage to come near.

These were many. The Dartmouth heavyweight crew would scull[1] by her house on their way upriver, and I think all eight of them must have been in love with her at various times during the summer; the coxswain[2] would curse them through his megaphone, but without effect—there was always a pause in their pace when they passed Sheila's float. I suppose to these jaded twenty-year-olds she seemed the incarnation of innocence and youth, while to me she appeared unutterably suave, the epitome[3] of sophistication. I was on the swim team at school, and to win her attention would do end-

less laps between my house and the Vermont shore, hoping she would notice the beauty of my flutter kick, the power of my crawl. Finishing, I would boost myself up onto our dock and glance casually over toward her, but she was never watching, and the miraculous day she was, I immediately climbed the diving board and did my best tuck and a half for her and continued diving until she had left and the sun went down and my longing was like a madness and I couldn't stop.

It was late August by the time I got up the nerve to ask her out. The tortured will-I's, won't-I's, the agonized indecision over what to say, the false starts toward her house and embarrassed retreats—the details of these have been seared from my memory, and the only part I remember clearly is emerging from the woods toward dusk while they were playing softball on their lawn, as bashful and frightened as a unicorn.

Sheila was stationed halfway between first and second, well outside the infield. She didn't seem surprised to see me—as a matter of fact, she didn't seem to see me at all.

"If you're playing second base, you should move closer," I said.

She turned—I took the full brunt of her long red hair and well-spaced freckles.

"I'm playing outfield," she said, "I don't like the responsibility of having a base."

"Yeah, I can understand that," I said, though I couldn't. "There's a band in Dixford tomorrow night at nine. Want to go?"

One of her brothers sent the ball sailing over the left-fielder's head; she stood and watched it disappear toward the river.

"You have a car?" she said, without looking up.

I played my master stroke. "We'll go by canoe."

I spent all of the following day polishing it. I turned it upside down on our lawn and rubbed

---

1. **scull** (skəl): row, as in a rowboat.
2. **coxswain** (käk′sən): person steering a racing shell and calling out the rhythm of the strokes for the crew.
3. **epitome** (ē·pit′ə·mē): embodiment; one that is representative of a type or class.

WORDS TO OWN

denizens (den′ə·zənz) *n.:* inhabitants or occupants.
pensive (pen′siv) *adj.:* dreamily thoughtful.

Reaching All Students

every inch with Brillo, hosing off the dirt, wiping it with chamois[4] until it gleamed as bright as aluminum ever gleamed. About five, I slid it into the water, arranging cushions near the bow so Sheila could lean on them if she was in one of her pensive moods, propping up my father's transistor radio by the middle thwart[5] so we could have music when we came back. Automatically, without thinking about it, I mounted my Mitchell reel on my Pfleuger spinning rod and stuck it in the stern.

I say automatically, because I never went anywhere that summer without a fishing rod. When I wasn't swimming laps to impress Sheila, I was back in our driveway practicing casts, and when I wasn't practicing casts, I was tying the line to Tosca, our springer spaniel, to test the reel's drag, and when I wasn't doing any of those things, I was fishing the river for bass.

Too nervous to sit at home, I got in the canoe early and started paddling in a huge circle that would get me to Sheila's dock around eight. As automatically as I brought along my rod, I tied on a big Rapala plug, let it down into the water, let out some line, and immediately forgot all about it.

It was already dark by the time I glided up to the Mants' dock. Even by day the river was quiet, most of the summer people preferring Sunapee or one of the other nearby lakes, and at night it was a solitude difficult to believe, a corridor of hidden life that ran between banks like a tunnel. Even the stars were part of it. They weren't as sharp anywhere else; they seemed to have chosen the river as a guide on their slow wheel toward morning, and in the course of the summer's fishing, I had learned all their names.

I was there ten minutes before Sheila appeared. I heard the slam of their screen door first, then saw her in the spotlight as she came slowly down the path. As beautiful as she was on the float, she was even lovelier now—her white dress went perfectly with her hair, and complimented her figure even more than her swimsuit.

4. **chamois** (sham′ē): soft leather used for polishing.
5. **middle thwart**: brace across the middle of a canoe.

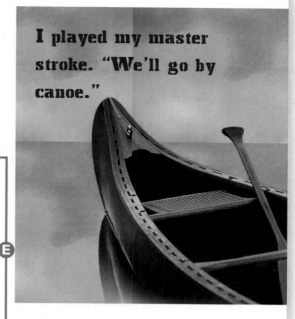

I played my master stroke. "We'll go by canoe."

It was her face that bothered me. It had on its delightful fullness a very dubious expression.

"Look," she said. "I can get Dad's car."

"It's faster this way," I lied. "Parking's tense up there. Hey, it's safe. I won't tip it or anything."

She let herself down reluctantly into the bow. I was glad she wasn't facing me. When her eyes were on me, I felt like diving in the river again from agony and joy.

I pried the canoe away from the dock and started paddling upstream. There was an extra paddle in the bow, but Sheila made no move to pick it up. She took her shoes off and dangled her feet over the side.

Ten minutes went by.

"What kind of band?" she said.

"It's sort of like folk music. You'll like it."

"Eric Caswell's going to be there. He strokes number four."

"No kidding?" I said. I had no idea whom she meant.

WORDS TO OWN
dubious (dōō′bē·əs) *adj.*: doubtful; not sure.

THE BASS, THE RIVER, AND SHEILA MANT **37**

Crossing the Curriculum

T37

"What's that sound?" she said, pointing toward shore.

"Bass. That splashing sound?"

"Over there."

"Yeah, bass. They come into the shallows at night to chase frogs and moths and things. Big largemouths. *Micropterus salmoides*,"[6] I added, showing off.

"I think fishing's dumb," she said, making a face. "I mean, it's boring and all. Definitely dumb."

Now I have spent a great deal of time in the years since wondering why Sheila Mant should come down so hard on fishing. Was her father a fisherman? Her antipathy toward fishing nothing more than normal filial rebellion? Had she tried it once? A messy encounter with worms? It doesn't matter. What does is that at that fragile moment in time I would have given anything not to appear dumb in Sheila's severe and unforgiving eyes.

She hadn't seen my equipment yet. What I *should* have done, of course, was push the

6. *Micropterus salmoides:* the scientific name for a largemouth bass.

"I think fishing's dumb," she said, making a face. "I mean, it's boring and all. Definitely dumb."

canoe in closer to shore and carefully slide the rod into some branches where I could pick it up again in the morning. Failing that, I could have surreptitiously dumped the whole outfit overboard, written off the forty or so dollars as love's tribute. What I actually *did* do was gently lean forward, and slowly, ever so slowly, push the rod back through my legs toward the stern where it would be less conspicuous.

It must have been just exactly what the bass was waiting for. Fish will trail a lure sometimes, trying to make up their mind whether or not to attack, and the slight pause in the plug's speed caused by my adjustment was tantalizing enough to overcome the bass's inhibitions. My rod, safely out of sight at last, bent double. The line, tightly coiled, peeled off the spool with the shrill, tearing zip of a high-speed drill.

Four things occurred to me at once. One, that it was a bass. Two, that it was a big bass. Three, that it was the biggest bass I had ever hooked. Four, that Sheila Mant must not know.

"What was that?" she said, turning half around.

"Uh, what was what?"

"That buzzing noise."

"Bats."

She shuddered, quickly drew her feet back into the canoe. Every instinct I had told me to pick up the rod and strike back at the bass, but there was no need to—it was already solidly hooked. Downstream, an awesome distance downstream, it jumped clear of the water, landing with a concussion heavy enough to ripple the entire river. For a moment, I thought it was gone, but then the rod was bending again, the tip dancing into the water. Slowly, not making

WORDS TO OWN
antipathy (an·ti′pə·thē) *n.:* feeling of hatred; powerful and deep dislike.
filial (fil′ē·əl) *adj.:* pertaining to or due from a son or a daughter.
surreptitiously (sur′əp·tish′əs·lē) *adv.:* stealthily; sneakily.
conspicuous (kən·spik′yoo·əs) *adj.:* obvious or easy to see.
concussion (kən·kush′ən) *n.:* powerful shock or impact.

Using Students' Strengths

Kinesthetic Learners
Before students read the story, ask them to share experiences of being in a canoe or other small boat. How does it feel to float in a small craft? What is the size and shape of a canoe? Students might mark out on the floor the outline of a canoe. As students read the story, you could ask volunteers to act out the narrator's various movements and facial expressions after Sheila criticizes fishing.

Verbal Learners
Ask students to rewrite the story as a magazine article wholly concerned with the fish that got away. In their articles, students should answer all of the 5 W-How questions: Who? What? When? Where? Why? and How? Encourage students to include sensory images in their accounts, and remind them to regard Wetherell's story as a springboard (rather than a blueprint) for their accounts.

any motion that might alert Sheila, I reached down to tighten the drag.

While all this was going on, Sheila had begun talking, and it was a few minutes before I was able to catch up with her train of thought. **E**

"I went to a party there. These fraternity men. Katherine says I could get in there if I wanted. I'm thinking more of UVM or Bennington.[7] Somewhere I can ski." **F**

The bass was slanting toward the rocks on the New Hampshire side by the ruins of Donaldson's boathouse. It had to be an old bass—a young one probably wouldn't have known the rocks were there. I brought the canoe back into the middle of the river, hoping to head it off.

"That's neat," I mumbled. "Skiing. Yeah, I can see that."

"Eric said I have the figure to model, but I thought I should get an education first. I mean, it might be a while before I get started and all. I was thinking of getting my hair styled, more swept back? I mean, Ann-Margret?[8] Like hers, only shorter."

She hesitated. "Are we going backward?"

We were. I had managed to keep the bass in the middle of the river away from the rocks, but it had plenty of room there, and for the first time a chance to exert its full strength. I quickly computed the weight necessary to draw a fully loaded canoe backward—the thought of it made me feel faint.

"It's just the current," I said hoarsely. "No sweat or anything."

I dug in deeper with my paddle. Reassured, Sheila began talking about something else, but all my attention was taken up now with the fish. I could feel its desperation as the water grew shallower. I could sense the extra strain on the line, the frantic way it cut back and forth in the water. I could visualize what it looked like—the gape of its mouth, the flared gills and thick, vertical tail. The bass couldn't have encountered many forces in its long life that it wasn't capable of handling, and the unrelenting tug at its mouth must have been a source of great puzzlement and mounting panic.

Me, I had problems of my own. To get to Dixford, I had to paddle up a sluggish stream that came into the river beneath a covered bridge. There was a shallow sandbar at the mouth of this stream—weeds on one side, rocks on the other. Without doubt, this is where I would lose the fish.

"I have to be careful with my complexion. I tan, but in segments. I can't figure out if it's even worth it. I wouldn't even do it probably. I saw Jackie Kennedy[9] in Boston, and she wasn't tan at all."

Taking a deep breath, I paddled as hard as I could for the middle, deepest part of the bar. I could have threaded the eye of a needle with the canoe, but the pull on the stern threw me off, and I overcompensated—the canoe veered left and scraped bottom. I pushed the paddle down and shoved. A moment of hesitation . . . a moment more. . . . The canoe shot clear into the deeper water of the stream. I immediately looked down at the rod. It was bent in the same tight arc—miraculously, the bass was still on. **G**

The moon was out now. It was low and full enough that its beam shone directly on Sheila there ahead of me in the canoe, washing her in a creamy, <u>luminous</u> glow. I could see the lithe, easy shape of her figure. I could see the way her hair curled down off her shoulders, the proud, alert tilt of her head, and all these things were as a tug on my heart. Not just Sheila, but the aura she carried about her of parties and casual touchings and grace. Behind me, I could feel the strain of the bass, steadier now, growing weaker, and this was another tug on my heart, not just the bass but the beat of the river and the slant of the stars and the smell of the night, until finally it seemed I would be torn apart between longings, split in half. Twenty yards **H** **I**

---

9. **Jackie Kennedy** (1929–1994): First Lady during the administration of President John F. Kennedy; greatly admired by the public for her dignity and sense of style.

---

7. **UVM or Bennington:** University of Vermont or Bennington College, Bennington, Vermont.
8. **Ann-Margret** (1941–   ): movie star, very popular at the time of this story.

WORDS TO OWN
luminous (lo͞o·mə′nəs) *adj.*: glowing; giving off light.

THE BASS, THE RIVER, AND SHEILA MANT **39**

E **Elements of Literature**
Irony
? What is the dramatic irony in this sentence? [The reader knows what Sheila does not: that the narrator is distracted from her self-centered ramblings by his attention to the fish.]

F **Critical Thinking**
Analyzing Character
? What do Sheila's thoughts about choosing a college reveal about her personality? [Possible responses: She is rather shallow; she does not think about academics, only parties and skiing.]

G **Elements of Literature**
External Conflict
? What physical struggle does the narrator face in the story? [He has hooked a large bass that is strong enough to pull the canoe backward. It takes all the narrator's strength to keep the fish on the line and the canoe in the middle of the river, away from rocks and weeds.]

H **Appreciating Language**
Imagery
? Why do you think the writer includes details about Sheila's appearance here? [Sample answer: The details indicate that the narrator's attention is veering away from the bass and back to Sheila. The narrator's internal conflict is intensifying.]

I **Elements of Literature**
Internal Conflict
? What two "tugs" or "longings" make the narrator feel "split in half"? [his longing for Sheila and his longing to catch the bass] According to the narrator, what more general aspects of life do Sheila and the bass represent? [Sheila represents a sophisticated social world the narrator would like to share; the bass represents his longing to be close to nature.]

Making the Connections

Connecting to the Theme: "Hard Choices"
An important insight provided by this story is that even when we make the "wrong" choice, we have the opportunity to learn from our mistake and make better choices in the future. Urge students to consider this idea as they write personal narratives in Choices activity 2 on p. 41.

Cultural Connections
Point out to students that the story's reference to Jackie Kennedy accurately demonstrates the influence she had on fashion in the United States while her husband was President. You may want to discuss with students the roles and influence of important women today. Ask students if they think these roles reflect a change in the way American society views women. You may also want to have students comment on the influence of famous women leaders in other parts of the world.

ahead of us was the road, and once I pulled the canoe up on shore, the bass would be gone, irretrievably gone. If instead I stood up, grabbed the rod, and started pumping, I would have it—as tired as the bass was, there was no chance it could get away. I reached down for the rod, hesitated, looked up to where Sheila was stretching herself lazily toward the sky, her small breasts rising beneath the soft fabric of her dress, and the tug was too much for me, and quicker than it takes to write down, I pulled a penknife from my pocket and cut the line in half.

Ⓐ With a sick, nauseous feeling in my stomach, I saw the rod unbend.

"My legs are sore," Sheila whined. "Are we there yet?"

Through a superhuman effort of self-control, I was able to beach the canoe and help Sheila off. The rest of the night is much foggier. We walked to the fair—there was the smell of popcorn, the sound of guitars. I may have danced once or twice with her, but all I really remember is her coming over to me once the music was done to explain that she would be going home in Eric Caswell's Corvette.

"Okay," I mumbled.

For the first time that night she looked at me, really looked at me.

"You're a funny kid, you know that?"

Funny. Different. Dreamy. Odd. How many times was I to hear that in the years to come, all spoken with the same quizzical, half-accusatory tone Sheila used then. Poor Sheila! Before the month was over, the spell she cast over me was gone, but the memory of that lost bass haunted me all summer and haunts me still. There would be other Sheila Mants in my life, other fish, and though I came close once or twice, it was these secret, hidden tuggings in the night that claimed me, and I never made the same mistake again.

- -

WORDS TO OWN
quizzical (kwiz′i·kəl) *adj.:* puzzled; questioning.

- -

MEET THE WRITER

An Eye for Detail

W. D. Wetherell (1948–   ) lives in New Hampshire. He was born in Mineola, New York, and earned a bachelor's degree at Hofstra University, on Long Island. Like many writers, he has worked at various jobs—he has been a magazine editor, a movie extra, a teacher, a journalist, and a tour guide. Wetherell's works have won numerous awards, including the O. Henry Award, the Drue Heinz Literature Prize, and a fellowship in fiction from the National Endowment for the Arts. "The Bass, the River, and Sheila Mant" won the 1983 PEN Syndicated Fiction Prize. After reading this story, you won't be surprised to learn that Wetherell has also written essays about nature and fishing.

In one essay, he relates a "fish story" with an ending quite different from the one you just read. In the Pacific Northwest, his wife asked him to take a photograph of her and the fish she had caught.

❝ And I did, and as I focused the lens, the fog lifted, and behind her I saw the snowbanks and glacier and cliffs that framed the pond, revealing themselves only now when the moment was perfect. I held the camera steady until the beauty of the water and the woman and the trout came together, then—the moment captured—I crossed over the logs and took my wife by the hand. **❞**

Assessing Learning

Check Test: Short Answers

1. What is the story's setting? [summer on a river in New England]
2. What are the narrator's two passions? [fishing and Sheila Mant]
3. Who else notices Sheila Mant? [the Dartmouth rowing crew, specifically Eric Caswell]
4. Where does the narrator ask Sheila to go with him? [to a dance]
5. At the end of the story, what does Sheila call the narrator? ["a funny kid"]

Standardized Test Preparation

For practice in proofreading and editing, see
• *Daily Oral Grammar,* Transparency 2

MAKING MEANINGS

First Thoughts

[connect]

1. What choice would *you* have made if you had been this narrator?

Shaping Interpretations

[apply]

2. How does the story's **title** suggest all the narrator's **external** and **internal conflicts**? What do you think of the title?

[analyze]

3. What do you think is the story's **climax**?

[synthesize]

4. What mistake has the narrator never repeated? What are the "secret, hidden tuggings in the night" that he mentions?

Challenging the Text

[evaluate]

5. A reader objects to the character of Sheila Mant, saying she is portrayed as a stereotypical "airhead." How would you respond?

[evaluate]

6. Another reader says the boy isn't believable. How would you respond?

Reading Check

Make a cause-and-effect list of the **main events** in this story. The first and last events are listed:

> Narrator asks Sheila out.
>
> ↓
>
> Sheila says he's a funny kid.

CHOICES: Building Your Portfolio

Writer's Notebook

1. Collecting Ideas for a Persuasive Essay

Using an experience. Look back at the issues you listed in your Writer's Notebook for the exercise on page 30. Zero in now on a specific incident related to one of those issues or to another issue of interest to you. Perhaps this story made you think of issues involving dating, or even stereotyping. Jot down all the details you can recall about your experience.

Keep your notes for possible use in the Writer's Workshop on page 85.

Personal Narrative

2. A Choice Effect

Use the experience you wrote about in your Quickwrite as the basis for a narrative about your own experience making a choice. (If you wish, disguise the names in your story.) Tell what you decided, what happened as a result, what you did next, and what the final effect was. Will your narrative be funny, or serious?

Evaluating a Story

3. Thumbs Up? Thumbs Down?

In a review that might be published in a school magazine, tell whether you would recommend this story to other students. Rate the story on a scale from zero (worst) to ten (best). Give at least three reasons for your rating. Think about the believability of the characters and the plot, the story's message, and the story's language.

MAKING MEANINGS

First Thoughts

1. Possible responses: the girl, because there are other fish; the fish, because the girl was not very nice.

Shaping Interpretations

2. It describes his inner conflict of having to decide and his external conflict with the bass and the river. Students may say the title made them curious about the connection among the items; others may prefer a title that more clearly suggests a story about a teenager in love.

3. The narrator decides to cut the line and let the fish get away.

4. Possible responses: Hiding something about himself to prevent someone from looking down on him; choosing a girl over a fish. The tuggings could be a memory of the physical struggle with the fish or of his mental struggle that night.

Challenging the Text

5. Possible responses: Some people really are shallow; the narrator is remembering how he felt about the girl as a teenager; maybe he exaggerated her negative qualities to save face for not winning her over.

6. Possible responses: He seems real, because he shows the real conflict teenagers face between being true to themselves and trying to be attractive to others; the writer's later experiences may have led him to oversimplify this time in his life.

Grading Timesaver

Rubrics for each Choices assignment appear on p. 91 in the *Portfolio Management System*.

Reading Check

Possible list: He polishes the canoe. He paddles to Sheila's house and drops a fishing line in the water. She boards, and they head upstream. She criticizes fishing. He hides the gear, hooks a fish, and struggles secretly against its pull. Realizing he must let the fish go or reveal his pursuit of the fish, he cuts the line. They get to the fair and dance once or twice. After the dance, Sheila says that Eric Caswell will drive her home.

CHOICES: Building Your Portfolio

1.-3. Encourage students to make a cause-effect chart of the main events in their experience. Have students debate their conclusions.

Try It Out
Possible Answers

1. Sample passages: "I took the full brunt of her long red hair and well-spaced freckles"; "... it jumped clear of the water, landing with a concussion heavy enough to ripple the entire river"; "I could sense the extra strain on the line, the frantic way it cut back and forth in the water"; "I could see the way her hair curled down off her shoulders, the proud, alert tilt of her head"; "With a sick, nauseous feeling in my stomach, I saw the rod unbend."

2. Students' descriptions will vary. Sample response: When I read the description of the bass leaping from the water and falling back, I saw and heard a huge splash of water—like a person doing a belly flop—and I saw ripples that rocked the canoe.

VOCABULARY

Students should review definitions of the Words to Own at the bottom of the selection pages. A sample sentence is provided for each word except *denizens*.

- She looked *pensive* as she wrote in her diary.
- His mother was *dubious* that he had already cleaned his room.
- She expressed her *antipathy* for that music group.
- The kittens had a strong *filial* bond with their mother.
- The dog *surreptitiously* snatched a cookie.
- Mustard leaves a *conspicuous* stain.
- The *concussion* from the bomb hitting nearby caused the walls to collapse.
- Their faces look *luminous* in the candlelight.
- The toddler had a *quizzical* expression as she eyed the squirrel.

Resources ———

Language
- *Grammar and Language Links*
  Worksheet, p. 3

Vocabulary
- *Words to Own*
  Worksheet, p. 3

LANGUAGE LINK | MINI-LESSON |

Handbook of Literary Terms
H E L P

See Imagery.

See Me, Hear Me—Using Imagery

An **image** describes something so that we think we can **see, smell, taste, touch,** or **hear** it. Below are three general statements that W. D. Wetherell *could* have used in "The Bass, the River, and Sheila Mant." Following each one is the sentence the author actually wrote. Notice how Wetherell's imagery (underscored) makes each statement come alive.

1. I would look at the dancers moving in the candlelight.

   Wetherell: "I would . . . stare enchanted at the <u>candlelit swirl of white dresses and bright, paisley skirts</u>."

2. The stars seemed to follow the river as morning approached.

   Wetherell: "They [the stars] <u>seemed to have chosen the river as a guide on their slow wheel toward morning</u>."

3. The line came off the spool with a snap.

   Wetherell: "The line, <u>tightly coiled, peeled off the spool with the shrill, tearing zip of a high-speed drill</u>."

Try It Out

1. Find at least four other passages in this story where the writer uses imagery to help you see, hear, smell, taste, or even feel something.

2. Write a detailed description of the mental picture you formed after reading each of Wetherell's passages. Use words that are different from his. Share your mental pictures with your classmates.

A tip for writers: Imagery is a key element in any writing. When you revise your writing, try to bring clarity and vividness to it by adding images that evoke color, sound, taste, smell, or tactile sensations. Remember that imagery is used not only in fiction and poetry but also in historical and scientific writings.

VOCABULARY | HOW TO OWN A WORD |

WORD BANK

denizens
pensive
dubious
antipathy
filial
surreptitiously
conspicuous
concussion
luminous
quizzical

Vocabulary Resource File

By now, you've studied a number of words. You might want to create a Vocabulary Resource File—something you can refer to when you're writing and at a loss for words. Put each entry on an index card. Note the word, its definition, and two or three sentences that show how the word can be used. Make out a card for each word in this Word Bank. The first one is done for you. (The words could also be filed on a computer.)

denizens (noun)

Definition: inhabitants or occupants

Examples:

Whales and octopuses are <u>denizens</u> of the deep.

The rock star entertained the <u>denizens</u> of the discothèque.

My father, mother, brother, and I are the <u>denizens</u> of my house.

Note: A denizen is <u>not</u> a monster. That's what I always thought. It has a monsterlike sound—like a dragon or dinosaur.

Language Link Quick Check

Name the sense to which each of the following images appeals.

1. The kitten's soft, velvety fur. [touch]
2. The sharp scent of onion. [smell]
3. The tart apple. [taste]
4. The shrill alarm clock. [hearing]
5. A tiny scarlet flower. [sight]

Before You Read

THE BOOK OF SAND

Make the Connection

What's Real?

We take for granted that reality is dependable—that gravity will continue to keep us from floating away, that time always moves forward, that an object can exist in only one place at a time. However, what if one of our dependable realities suddenly changed? Jorge Luis Borges loved to play with puzzles and reality. "The Book of Sand," like much of his work, invites you to join in his game.

Quickwrite

Jot down at least two more dependable realities of daily life—things we take for granted, that we expect will never change. Circle one, and briefly describe what you imagine the world would be like if that reality no longer existed, or shifted slightly.

HRW go.hrw.com
LEO 10-1

Elements of Literature

Resolution: So, How Does It End?

In years past, stories were expected to provide us with neat **resolutions** to all their **conflicts**. In these stories, we end up knowing exactly what happens to all the main characters and how the various mysteries and difficulties are untangled. (In French, the resolution of a story is called the *dénouement*, which means "untying of the knot.")

In contrast, many modern stories end right in the midst of the action, and some end by opening up new questions for the reader to consider. Readers who dislike these endings complain that they are "left hanging," but others enjoy the challenge of figuring out for themselves what happens. After all, life itself hardly ever has neat endings.

> The **resolution** comes at the end of a story and reveals the characters' final situation. In modern stories the resolution is often inconclusive or omitted altogether.
>
> *For more on Plot, see pages 32–33 and the Handbook of Literary Terms.*

Reading Skills and Strategies

Making Predictions: Guessing Ahead

Part of the pleasure of reading comes from making predictions about what will happen next. A **prediction** is a type of inference, a guess based on evidence. In a story that presents a mystery or puzzle, we read carefully, looking for clues. We base our predictions on the characters and their situations and on our own experiences and knowledge about life. As a story unfolds, we may adjust our predictions to fit new events and information. Sometimes despite our careful reading, a writer still surprises us. Those are often the stories we remember best.

Preteaching Vocabulary

Words to Own

After students study the definitions of the Words to Own, ask the following questions:

1. Why might a *bibliophile* discuss his collection *pedantically?* [A book collector might be interested in historical and scholarly points casual readers wouldn't understand.]

2. What kinds of *contrivances* do magicians use? [Possible responses: boxes with false bottoms, hidden pockets, invisible strings or openings.]

3. Would you rather have choices that are *infinite* or finite? Why? [Possible response: People have trouble dealing with lack of boundaries or endless choices, so many will prefer ones that are finite.]

4. What might cause a person's *misanthropy?* [Possible responses: mistreatment or lack of understanding as a child; betrayals or cruel, unjust treatment as an adult.]

Summary ■■■

One day a stranger appears at the narrator's door and offers to sell him a rare book he has found in India. The narrator examines the book and finds that it is endless and that it changes every time he looks at it. The narrator buys the book and soon becomes obsessed by it. He cannot sleep, and he isolates himself from other people. Finally, he decides he must rid himself of the monstrous book. He is afraid to destroy it, so he places it on a dusty shelf in the basement of a huge public library, leaving its eventual fate a mystery.

Background

One theorem of mathematics states that between any two points another point can be found. Consequently, on a line segment that has two points, A and B, a third point, C, can be found. Then, between points A and C another point can be found, as well as another point between points C and B. This process of finding points can continue *ad infinitum*. Thus, there are an infinite number of points on any given line segment, indicating that infinity does not necessarily mean a great deal of space. The letters A, B, C, and so on are arbitrary markers for points and are not limited to the twenty-six letters of the alphabet. Once that set of letters is used, another set can be used (A-1, B-1, for example), and there are an infinite number of such sets.

Ⓐ Struggling Readers
Questioning

The first paragraph will intimidate these students—and others as well. Assure students they don't have to understand mathematics to enjoy the story. To help students understand the story, you might read it aloud using the round-robin style, pausing to ask a *5W-How?* question after each paragraph. For example, after the second paragraph, you might ask, "Who is at the door?" This strategy will help these students stay focused on the story.

Ⓑ Historical Connection
The Bible

Explain that the narrator is referring to various translations of the Bible done over many centuries. The Vulgate is a Latin translation begun in A.D. 383. Wycliffe's (or Wyclif's) Bible was the first English translation, completed in 1380, though not printed in its entirety until 1850.

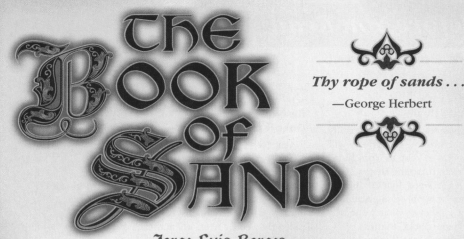

THE BOOK OF SAND

Thy rope of sands . . .
—George Herbert

Jorge Luis Borges
translated by Norman Thomas Di Giovanni

Ⓐ The line is made up of an infinite number of points; the plane, of an infinite number of lines; the volume, of an infinite number of planes; the hypervolume, of an infinite number of volumes. . . . No, unquestionably this is not—*more geometrico*—the best way of beginning my story. To claim that it is true is nowadays the convention of every made-up story. Mine, however, *is* true.

I live alone in a fourth-floor apartment on Belgrano Street, in Buenos Aires. Late one evening, a few months back, I heard a knock at my door. I opened it and a stranger stood there. He was a tall man, with nondescript features—or perhaps it was my myopia[1] that made them seem that way. Dressed in gray and carrying a gray suitcase in his hand, he had an unassuming look about him. I saw at once that he was a foreigner. At first, he struck me as old; only later did I realize that I had been misled by his thin blond hair, which was, in a Scandinavian sort of way, almost white. During the course of our conversation, which was not to last an hour, I found

out that he came from the Orkneys.[2]

I invited him in, pointing to a chair. He paused awhile before speaking. A kind of gloom emanated from him—as it does now from me.

"I sell Bibles," he said.

Somewhat pedantically, I replied, "In Ⓑ this house are several English Bibles, including the first—John Wycliffe's. I also have Cipriano de Valera's, Luther's—which, from a literary viewpoint, is the worst—and a Latin copy of the Vulgate. As you see, it's not exactly Bibles I stand in need of."

After a few moments of silence, he said, "I don't only sell Bibles. I can show you a holy book I came across on the outskirts of Bikaner.[3] It may interest you."

He opened the suitcase and laid the book on a table. It was an octavo volume, bound

2. **Orkneys:** group of islands to the north of Scotland.
3. **Bikaner** (bē·kə·nir′): city in northwest India.

WORDS TO OWN
infinite (in′fə·nit) *adj.*: endless.
pedantically (pi·dant′i·klē) *adv.*: with undue attention to trivial points of scholarship.

1. **myopia** (mī·ō′pē·ə): nearsightedness.

44 THE SHORT-STORY COLLECTIONS

  Resources: Print and Media

Reading
- *Reading Skills and Strategies*
  MiniRead Skill Lesson, p. 22
  Selection Skill Lesson, p. 29
- *Graphic Organizers for Active Reading,* p. 3
- *Words to Own,* p. 4
- *Audio CD Library*
  Disc 2, Track 3

Writing and Language
- *Daily Oral Grammar*
  Transparency 3

- *Grammar and Language Links*
  Worksheet, p. 5
- *Language Workshop CD-ROM*

Assessment
- *Formal Assessment,* p. 5
- *Portfolio Management System,* p. 92
- *Test Generator (One-Stop Planner CD-ROM)*

Internet
- go.hrw.com (keyword: LE0 10-1)

in cloth. There was no doubt that it had passed through many hands. Examining it, I was surprised by its unusual weight. On the spine were the words "Holy Writ" and, below them, "Bombay."

"Nineteenth century, probably," I remarked.

"I don't know," he said. "I've never found out."

I opened the book at random. The script was strange to me. The pages, which were worn and typographically poor, were laid out in double columns, as in a Bible. The text was closely printed, and it was ordered in versicles.[4] In the upper corners of the pages were Arabic numbers. I noticed that one left-hand page bore the number (let us say) 40,514 and the facing right-hand page 999. I turned the leaf; it was numbered with eight digits. It also bore a small illustration, like the kind used in dictionaries—an anchor drawn with pen and ink, as if by a schoolboy's clumsy hand.

It was at this point that the stranger said, "Look at the illustration closely. You'll never see it again."

I noted my place and closed the book. At once, I reopened it. Page by page, in vain, I looked for the illustration of the anchor. "It seems to be a version of Scriptures in some Indian language, is it not?" I said to hide my dismay.

"No," he replied. Then, as if confiding a secret, he lowered his voice. "I acquired the book in a town out on the plain in exchange for a handful of rupees and a Bible. Its owner did not know how to read. I suspect that he saw the Book of Books as a talisman.[5] He was of the lowest caste; nobody but other untouchables could tread his shadow without contamination. He told me his book was called the Book of Sand, because neither the book nor the sand has any beginning or end."

The stranger asked me to find the first page.

I laid my left hand on the cover and, trying to put my thumb on the flyleaf, I opened the book. It was useless. Every time I tried, a number of pages came between the cover and my thumb. It was as if they kept growing from the book.

"Now find the last page."

Again I failed. In a voice that was not mine, I barely managed to stammer, "This can't be."

Still speaking in a low voice, the stranger said, "It can't be, but it *is*. The number of pages in this book is no more or less than infinite. None is the first page, none the last. I don't know why they're numbered in this arbitrary way. Perhaps to suggest that the terms of an infinite series admit any number."

Then, as if he were thinking aloud, he said, "If space is infinite, we may be at any point in space. If time is infinite, we may be at any point in time."

His speculations irritated me. "You are religious, no doubt?" I asked him.

"Yes, I'm a Presbyterian. My conscience is clear. I am reasonably sure of not having cheated the native when I gave him the Word of God in exchange for his devilish book."

I assured him that he had nothing to reproach himself for, and I asked if he were just passing through this part of the world. He replied that he planned to return to his country in a few days. It was then that I learned that he was a Scot from the Orkney Islands. I told him I had a great personal affection for Scotland, through my love of Stevenson and Hume.

"You mean Stevenson and Robbie Burns,"[6] he corrected.

While we spoke, I kept exploring the infinite book. With feigned indifference,

4. **versicles:** short verses.
5. **talisman:** something thought to have special or magical powers; a charm.

6. Robert Louis Stevenson (1850–1894) and Robert Burns (1759–1796) were famous and very popular Scottish writers. David Hume (1711–1776) was a Scottish philosopher.

THE BOOK OF SAND 45

C Struggling Readers
Finding Details
❓ What strange things does the narrator notice about the book immediately? [The pages are not numbered in sequence; the page numbers are very high; he sees an illustration once and then can never find it again.]

D Cultural Connections
The caste system in India originated in ancient times, dividing Hindu society into distinct social ranks based on occupation, descent, and marriage. Untouchables, members of the lowest caste, were formerly forbidden social contact with members of all other castes. The designation was made illegal in India in 1949 and in Pakistan in 1953. Mahatma Gandhi, who led India's fight for independence from Great Britain, referred to untouchables as *Harijans*, "children of God."

E Elements of Literature
Foreshadowing
❓ Why do you think the stranger calls the book "devilish"? What do you think might happen if the narrator buys it? [Possible responses: The book is like no other book because it keeps changing; it seems unnatural and impossible; something bad may happen to the narrator if he buys it.]

Reaching All Students

Struggling Readers
Explain that the narrator of the story is a collector of rare books and that he uses many terms and titles familiar to scholars. These references help reveal his character, but assure students that it's not necessary for them to understand these terms and titles to enjoy the story. Encourage them to skip over unfamiliar terms pertaining to books.

Advanced Learners
This selection is rich in literary allusions, philosophical and mathematical concepts, and the artistic explorations of M. C. Escher. Encourage these students to research ideas and works mentioned in the text and to explore their relationship to Borges' story. Volunteers might give brief oral reports.

T45

A **Reading Skills and Strategies**

Making Predictions

? Do you think the narrator will buy the book? Why or why not? [Yes, because the narrator seems fascinated and puzzled by the book, and because he loves rare books; no, because the narrator finds the mysterious book too frightening.]

B **Literary Connections**

The Thousand and One Nights, also known as the *Arabian Nights' Entertainment,* is a collection of folk tales, narrated by a fictional character named Scheherazade. Night after night she tells her husband a never-ending series of stories in order to postpone her execution. Among the famous tales in this collection are "Ali Baba and the Forty Thieves" and "Sinbad the Sailor."

LITERATURE AND ART

Impossible Worlds: An Artist's View

Dutch graphic artist M.C. Escher (1898–1972) often conjured up strange, "Borges-like" worlds filled with visual puzzles and illusions. What, for example, do you see happening in *Reptiles*? How does the lithograph seem to bring a two-dimensional sketch to life?

Reptiles by M.C. Escher.

I asked, "Do you intend to offer this curiosity to the British Museum?"

"No. I'm offering it to you," he said, and he stipulated a rather high sum for the book.

I answered, in all truthfulness, that such a sum was out of my reach, and I began thinking. After a minute or two, I came up with a scheme.

"I propose a swap," I said. "You got this book for a handful of rupees and a copy of the Bible. I'll offer you the amount of my pension check, which I've just collected, and my black-letter Wycliffe Bible. I inherited it from my ancestors."

"A black-letter Wycliffe!" he murmured.

I went to my bedroom and brought him the money and the book. He turned the leaves and studied the title page with all the fervor of a true <u>bibliophile</u>.

"It's a deal," he said.

It amazed me that he did not haggle. Only later was I to realize that he had entered my house with his mind made up to sell the book. Without counting the money, he put it away.

We talked about India, about Orkney, and about the Norwegian jarls who once ruled it. It was night when the man left. I have not seen him again, nor do I know his name.

I thought of keeping the Book of Sand in the space left on the shelf by the Wycliffe, but in the end I decided to hide it behind the volumes of a broken set of *The Thousand and One Nights.* I went to bed and did not sleep. At three or four in the morning, I turned on the light. I got down the impossible book and leafed through its pages. On one of them I saw engraved a mask. The upper corner of the page carried a number,

---

WORDS TO OWN

bibliophile (bib′lē·ə·fīl′) *n.:* book lover or collector.

Making the Connections

Connecting to the Theme: "Hard Choices"

The narrator's "hard choice" in this selection is a philosophical one—whether to hold on to a puzzle that fascinates him but which has the power to destroy him. The author seems to ask how much uncertainty human beings can live with without losing touch with everyday reality.

which I no longer recall, elevated to the ninth power.

I showed no one my treasure. To the luck of owning it was added the fear of having it stolen, and then the misgiving that it might not truly be infinite. These twin preoccupations intensified my old <u>misanthropy</u>. I had only a few friends left; I now stopped seeing even them. A prisoner of the book, I almost never went out anymore. After studying its frayed spine and covers with a magnifying glass, I rejected the possibility of a <u>contrivance</u> of any sort. The small illustrations, I verified, came two thousand pages apart. I set about listing them alphabetically in a notebook, which I was not long in filling up. Never once was an illustration repeated. At night, in the meager intervals my insomnia granted, I dreamed of the book.

Summer came and went, and I realized that the book was monstrous. What good did it do me to think that I, who looked upon the volume with my eyes, who held it in my hands, was any less monstrous? I felt that the book was a nightmarish object, an obscene thing that affronted and tainted reality itself.

I thought of fire, but I feared that the burning of an infinite book might likewise prove infinite and suffocate the planet with smoke. Somewhere I recalled reading that the best place to hide a leaf is in a forest. Before retirement, I worked on Mexico Street, at the Argentine National Library, which contains nine hundred thousand volumes. I knew that to the right of the entrance a curved staircase leads down into the basement, where books and maps and periodicals are kept. One day I went there and, slipping past a member of the staff and trying not to notice at what height or distance from the door, I lost the Book of Sand on one of the basement's musty shelves.

MEET THE WRITER
Argentine Dreamer

At age six, **Jorge Luis Borges** (hôr´he lōō ēs´ bôr´hes) (1899–1986) knew that he wanted to be a writer, and by nine, he had translated a fairy tale by Oscar Wilde from English into Spanish. Borges learned English from his British grandmother, immersing himself in Edgar Allan Poe's stories and Robert Louis Stevenson's novels. In an autobiographical essay, Borges wrote,

❝If I were asked to name the chief event of my life, I should say my father's library.❞

Like many artists, Borges had a quirky upbringing. His parents were well educated and fairly well off, but they lived in a tough Buenos Aires suburb. Although Borges traveled to Europe with his family during his youth and to the United States and Japan as an adult, he once commented that he had seen little of the world. He suffered from poor eyesight, and after going through a series of grueling cataract operations in his twenties and thirties, he became totally blind in middle age.

Borges wrote as no one had before him— strange playful tales filled with puzzles, games, riddles, and paradoxes. In *The Garden of the Forking Paths* (1941) and *El Aleph* (1949), Borges wrote dreamlike stories that blur fantasy and reality, stories of transparent tigers, infinite houses, and mythical labyrinths.

❝Writing is nothing more than a guided dream,❞ he wrote.

THE BOOK OF SAND **47**

C Reading Skills and Strategies
Making Predictions

❓ Do you think the narrator will keep the book? Why or why not? [Possible responses: Some may say that the narrator is so obsessed he will not be able to let go of the book even if it drives him insane and causes his death; others will predict that the narrator will want to save himself and will find a way to rid himself of it.]

D Elements of Literature
Resolution

❓ Why does the narrator decide to leave the Book of Sand in the musty basement of a library? [He has decided that the book is monstrous, and he hopes that no one will ever find it again, if it is "hidden" among other musty, unused books.] **Do you think his plan will be successful?** [Answers will vary. Many students may be intrigued by the idea of the book's being discovered by another innocent person, which is probably what Borges wants readers to imagine about the never-ending book.]

BROWSING IN THE FILES

A Critic's Comment. Author James Atlas has this to say about Borges' work and life: "Borges dwells in a realm of occult prophecies, apparitions, fantastic episodes.... For Borges, who has been nearly blind since youth, the uncertain border between appearance and reality, the relativity of time, the suspicion that we are living in a dream are more than literary tropes: They are the crucial experiences of a life lived wholly in the imagination."

Assessing Learning

Check Test: True–False
1. A close friend gives the narrator the Book of Sand. [False]
2. The man from the Orkneys says there is a curse on the book. [False]
3. The Book of Sand has no beginning and no end. [True]
4. The Book of Sand changes every time the narrator looks at it. [True]
5. The narrator finally burns the Book of Sand. [False]

Standardized Test Preparation
For practice in proofreading and editing, see
• *Daily Oral Grammar,* Transparency 3

T47

MAKING MEANINGS
• First Thoughts

OBJECTIVES

1. Define setting
2. Recognize that setting contributes to a story's emotional effect
3. Recognize that setting may reveal character or be the major source of external conflict

Resources

Elements of Literature
Setting
For additional instruction on setting, see *Literary Elements*:
• Transparency 3

Assessment
Formal Assessment
• Literary Elements Test, p. 13

Elements of Literature

This feature gives many examples of how important setting (when and where the action takes place) can be in stories. Setting may create an atmosphere, or mood. A character's home setting helps reveal the character; characters may struggle against some aspect of their setting, as in "The Cold Equations."

Elements of Literature

SETTING: Putting Us There *by* John Leggett

All Events Occur Somewhere

It is possible for an interesting story to have no **setting** at all—that is, no indication of when or where the action is set. If the characters and their situation are strong enough, they will hold our attention in empty space, just as a play presented on a bare stage can hold our interest.

But in life all events occur somewhere. Often a story's place and its **atmosphere**—its feeling of gloom or cheer, of beauty or ugliness—affect the characters and the way they lead their lives. Think of how crucial setting would be to a story about a prisoner, or to a story about castaways adrift on the Pacific, or to a story about a high-school graduation in a coal town.

Setting puts us there—it gives us a feeling of being *in* the situation with the characters. If we are in the square of a town in Honduras, we should feel hot, sweaty, and thirsty. We should see how the sun is baking the back of the little burro

> **I**t is this sense of place in fiction that gives us the chance for armchair travel.

tethered at the side of the church. We should smell the *zozo*, the native delicacy of fish heads and banana skins, as it sizzles over the charcoal.

The setting tells us not only *where* we are, but also *when*—it can reveal a **time frame.** If the passing traffic is horse drawn, we can guess we have gone back in time. An inch of new-fallen snow on the porch rail tells us it's winter. If the sun is just up over the pine ridge or if the *Ledger* is being tossed onto the front steps, it is morning.

Setting can be a high school in Texas, the deck of a boat crossing the Atlantic, a winter evening in a New York brownstone. Setting can be a reservation in the American Southwest or a colony on Mars.

Setting can give the story a kind of truth or believability. We call this **verisimilitude** (ver′ə·si·mil′ə·tood′), which means "the appearance of being true to life."

It is this sense of place in fiction that gives us the chance for armchair travel—to visit faraway places without leaving home.

Setting and Our Emotions

A more important function of setting, however, is to contribute to a story's **emotional effect**. We all know that some settings can make us feel gloomy and others can make us feel cheerful. An autumnal setting can increase the sense of loss in a story about a doomed love. A spring setting can give a note of hope to a story of a girl's coming of age.

Here is a description of a rice paddy in Vietnam. How does it make you feel?

. . . his boots sank into the thick paddy water, and he smelled it all around him. He would tell his mother how it smelled: mud and algae and cattle manure and chlorophyll; decay, breeding mosquitoes and leeches as big as mice; the fecund warmth of the paddy waters rising up to his cut knee.

—Tim O'Brien,
"Where Have You Gone,
Charming Billy?" (page 198)

This Vietnam jungle setting is used in another part of the same story to contrast with

Crossing the Curriculum

History and Geography

Tell students that setting plays an important role in the next two stories they will read: "Boys and Girls" by Alice Munro (p. 53) and "Everyday Use" by Alice Walker (p. 70).

"Boys and Girls," which deals with gender roles, is set in rural Canada in the 1940s. Ask students why the historical period may play an important role in the story. [Sample answer: Gender roles were much more rigidly defined in the past than they are today.]

"Everyday Use," the story of an African American family, is set in the rural South in the 1960s. Ask how the time and place of the setting may influence what happens to the characters. [Possible response: During the 1960s the civil rights movement in the South used marches, boycotts, sit-ins, and voter registration drives to fight for equal rights for African Americans, who were asserting a new pride in their heritage. The characters may have been involved in that struggle.]

the young soldier's comforting memories of home in Iowa. The emotional effect of that contrast is shattering.

He was pretending he was a boy again, camping with his father in the midnight summer along the Des Moines River. In the dark, with his eyes pinched shut, he pretended. He pretended that when he opened his eyes, his father would be there by the campfire and they would talk softly about whatever came to mind and then roll into their sleeping bags. . . .

Setting and Characters

Setting also reveals character. We all affect our environment in one way or another, so a writer wishing to portray an untidy Alice will show us the mess in her bedroom—pajamas, hangers, sneakers in a snarl on the floor of her closet, CDs and magazines strewn beneath the unmade bed. We know something about Alice even before we see her.

Here is Jimmy's room with a set of weights in one corner; on the bedside table a copy of the *Guinness Book of World Records;* on the wall, school pennants, photographs of the basketball team, a set of antlers; and hanging from a hook on the closet door, a pair of boxing gloves. How much do we know about Jimmy before he even opens the door?

Here is a house, the home of a very old man whose life is almost over. What does the setting reveal about this character, even before he appears?

The house had only two rooms, but he owned it—the last scrap of the farm that he had sold off years ago. It stood in a hollow of dying trees beside a superhighway in Baltimore County. All it held was a few sticks of furniture, a change of clothes, a skillet, and a set of dishes.

— Anne Tyler,
"With All Flags Flying"
(pages 310–311)

THERE'S NO PLOT.

HE DIDN'T KNOW HOW TO APPRECIATE NATURE.

© The New Yorker Collection 1992 Bruce Eric Kaplan from cartoonbank.com. All Rights Reserved.

Setting as a Character

Though we find that in some stories, setting hardly matters, in others the setting can have all the importance of a major character. We'd find this situation in a story where the main characters are pitted against the setting, such as a story about a polar expedition fighting against the harshness of the arctic tundra. We also find setting assuming the importance of a character in the story "The Cold Equations" (page 9), where the characters are in conflict with their environment—the cold, harsh realities of the space frontier.

> In some stories, setting can have all the importance of a major character.

Mini-Lesson:
Setting
Assign groups of students to read Tim O'Brien's descriptions of settings in Vietnam and Iowa quoted in the feature. Have them discuss the emotional effect of each description.

Then read aloud the section on Setting and Characters. Have students discuss the impression given by each description of a character's room or house. Students may enjoy describing (either in writing or speaking) their own rooms and sharing their descriptions with a partner or small group.
Applying the Element
To help students understand the importance of setting, ask them to consider how changing the setting of "The Bass, the River, and Sheila Mant" (p. 35) would alter the plot. Have students freewrite for several minutes about what would happen to the story if it were set in a different time or place. They should focus not only on logistical changes and the effect on the characters, but also on the effect on the reader. Once students have finished writing, have them share their responses.

Ⓐ **Critical Thinking**
   Classifying
Ask students to think of other examples and situations in which setting is the source of the main character's external conflict. [Possible responses: fighting to survive a natural disaster, such as a flood, an earthquake, or volcano eruption; fighting to survive in a hostile environment, such as a desert or mountaintop.]

Assessing Learning

Self-Assessment: Comprehension
Choose the correct word in parentheses.
1. It is (possible/impossible) to have a story without a setting. [possible]
2. A story's atmosphere is the (weather/feeling) created by the setting. [feeling]
3. Verisimilitude is a kind of (poetry/truth). [truth]
4. Setting contributes to a story's (logical/emotional) effect. [emotional]
5. Setting reveals the time and (place/meaning) of the story's events. [place]

Planning

Before You Read

BOYS AND GIRLS

Make the Connection

Gender Issues

Do you think boys and girls have the same choices in life? Are boys and girls expected to feel and act in different ways? If so, are these expectations based on inborn differences, or are they the result of social customs that can change? Discuss these questions in a group. Note if the boys and girls respond differently from each other.

Quickwrite

In your notebook, record your thoughts about your group discussions on what is expected of boys and girls today. Use a chart like the one below.

Expectations	
Boys	
Girls	

Elements of Literature

The Moment of Truth

You can usually identify the **climax** in a story or movie because it is often marked by a significant action, even a moment of violence. In Shakespeare's *Romeo and Juliet,* for example, the horrifying climax comes right at the end, when

Romeo and Juliet both kill themselves in the underground tomb. At the moment of climax, the conflict in the story is finally resolved.

The climax usually comes near the story's end. It might help to imagine the story as a movie and to listen in your mind for the dramatic crescendo of music at the climax.

> The **climax** of a story is that emotional moment toward the end when something dramatic happens to determine the outcome of the conflict.
>
> *For more on Plot, see pages 32–33 and the Handbook of Literary Terms.*

Reading Skills and Strategies

Making Generalizations

A **generalization** is a broad statement that can be applied to many situations. If you say, "Boys usually like adventure movies, while most girls prefer romances," you are making some generalizations. (Generalizations can be challenged—as those would be!) When you read, you make generalizations by combining what you learn from the text with what you already know. This story about an eleven-year-old girl and her younger brother suggests some generalizations about gender roles. Think about what they are as you read.

go.hrw.com
LEO 10-1

Preteaching Vocabulary

"*Never mind, she's only a girl.*"

Boys and Girls

Alice Munro

My father was a fox farmer. That is, he raised silver foxes, in pens; and in the fall and early winter, when their fur was prime, he killed them and skinned them and sold their pelts to the Hudson's Bay Company or the Montreal Fur Traders. These companies supplied us with heroic calendars to hang, one on each side of the kitchen door. Against a background of cold blue sky and black pine forests and treacherous northern rivers, plumed adventurers planted the flags of England or of France; magnificent savages bent their backs to the portage.[1]

For several weeks before Christmas, my father worked after supper in the cellar of our

---

1. **portage:** carrying of boats and supplies overland from one river or lake to another.

BOYS AND GIRLS 53

Summary ▪ ▪

The unnamed first-person narrator of this story, the daughter of a Canadian fox farmer, remembers events over several years leading up to her adolescence. She enjoys helping her father, though his work is smelly and grisly; she resists both housework and the implications of the word *girl*. Yet after she and her younger brother watch her father shoot an old horse for fox food, she feels less allied with her father and his work. The story's climax occurs when an old but spirited mare makes a run for freedom, and the girl opens a gate, allowing it to escape. When her brother reveals the truth about the incident, the narrator is simultaneously excused and dismissed by her father as "only a girl."

Resources

Listening
Audio CD Library
To help students appreciate the story's dramatic climax, play the recording of "Boys and Girls" provided in the *Audio CD Library*. A recording of Pat Mora's "Same Song" (p. 65) can also be found there:
- Disc 3, Track 2

FROM THE EDITOR'S DESK

Alice Munro once told an interviewer that she wants her stories to "cast a spell," and her vividly remembered stories of childhood do just that. Students particularly enjoy this story because it gives them a chance to talk about gender roles and stereotypes.

Ⓐ English Language Learners
Multiple Meanings
These students may not be familiar with these uses of the words *pen,* meaning "a small enclosure for animals," and *prime,* meaning "of the highest quality."

A Reading Skills and Strategies
Comparing/Contrasting

? How are the narrator's and the mother's feelings about the pelting operation different? [The mother dislikes everything about the operation, especially the smell of the dead foxes, and wishes it didn't occur in her house. The narrator finds the smell "reassuringly seasonal, like the smell of oranges and pine needles," which are pleasant smells.]

B Struggling Readers
Identifying Pronoun Antecedents

? To whom does the pronoun *we* refer? [the narrator and her brother, Laird] What details in the story so far suggest that these two are close? [They sit on the stairs together and watch their father work; they seem to share the same feelings about Henry Bailey.]

C Elements of Literature
Figurative Language

? What figures of speech does the narrator use to describe the wind and the snowdrifts? [She uses a simile, comparing *snowdrifts* to *sleeping whales,* and she personifies the wind by saying that it "harassed us all night."]

D Reading Skills and Strategies
Making Generalizations

? What generalizations can you make about children and fear of the dark? [Possible responses: Children have vivid imaginations about scary things that might lurk in the dark; children tend to make superstitious "rules" to feel safe in situations they fear.]

house. The cellar was whitewashed and lit by a hundred-watt bulb over the worktable. My brother Laird and I sat on the top step and watched. My father removed the pelt inside out from the body of the fox, which looked surprisingly small, mean, and ratlike deprived of its arrogant weight of fur. The naked, slippery bodies were collected in a sack and buried at the dump. One time the hired man, Henry Bailey, had taken a swipe at me with this sack, saying, "Christmas present!" My mother thought that was not funny. In fact she disliked the whole pelting operation—that was what the killing, skinning, and preparation of the furs was called—and wished it did not have to take place in the house. There was the smell. After the pelt had been stretched inside out on a long board, my father scraped away delicately, removing the little clotted webs of blood vessels, the bubbles of fat; the smell of blood and animal fat, with the strong primitive odor of the fox itself, penetrated all parts of the house. I found it reassuringly seasonal, like the smell of oranges and pine needles.

Henry Bailey suffered from bronchial[2] troubles. He would cough and cough until his narrow face turned scarlet and his light-blue, derisive eyes filled up with tears; then he took the lid off the stove and, standing well back, shot out a great clot of phlegm—hsss—straight into the heart of the flames. We admired him for this performance and for his ability to make his stomach growl at will, and for his laughter, which was full of high whistlings and gurglings and involved the whole faulty machinery of his chest. It was sometimes hard to tell what he was laughing at, and always possible that it might be us.

After we had been sent to bed, we could still smell fox and still hear Henry's laugh, but these things, reminders of the warm, safe, brightly lit downstairs world, seemed lost and diminished, floating on the stale, cold air upstairs. We were afraid at night in the winter. We were not afraid of *outside,* though this was the time of year when snowdrifts curled around our house like sleeping whales and the wind harassed us all night, coming up from the buried fields, the frozen swamp, with its old bugbear[3] chorus of threats and misery. We were afraid of *inside,* the room where we slept. At this time the upstairs of our house was not finished. A brick chimney went up one wall. In the middle of the floor was a square hole, with a wooden railing around it; that was where the stairs came up. On the other side of the stairwell were the things that nobody had any use for anymore—a soldiery roll of linoleum standing on end, a wicker baby carriage, a fern basket, china jugs and basins with cracks in them, a picture of the Battle of Balaclava, very sad to look at. I had told Laird, as soon as he was old enough to understand such things, that bats and skeletons lived over there; whenever a man escaped from the county jail, twenty miles away, I imagined that he had somehow let himself in the window and was hiding behind the linoleum. But we had rules to keep us safe. When the light was on, we were safe as long as we did not step off the square of worn carpet which defined our bedroom space; when the light was off, no place was safe but the beds themselves. I had to turn out the light kneeling on the end of my bed and stretching as far as I could to reach the cord.

In the dark we lay on our beds, our narrow

---

3. **bugbear:** frightening. A bugbear is an imaginary creature used to scare children.

---

2. **bronchial** (bräŋ′kē·əl): relating to the major air passageways of the lungs.

WORDS TO OWN
derisive (di·rī′siv) *adj.*: mocking.

Reaching All Students

Struggling Readers
Making Generalizations was introduced on p. 52. For a lesson directly tied to this story that teaches students to make generalizations by using a strategy called It Says . . . I Say, see the *Reading Skills and Strategies* binder
• MiniRead Skill Lesson, p. 33
• Selection Skill Lesson, p. 40

English Language Learners
These students will need help identifying the connotations of many English words. Use the Skill Link activity on p. T56 to give them some practice in identifying synonyms and their shades of meaning.

Advanced Learners
This selection raises a lot of issues regarding the history (and the causes and effects) of gender roles in different historical, cultural, and geographic settings. Encourage students to pursue these issues through the Choices activities or independent research projects of their own.

life rafts, and fixed our eyes on the faint light coming up the stairwell and sang songs. Laird sang "Jingle Bells," which he would sing anytime, whether it was Christmas or not, and I sang "Danny Boy."[4] I loved the sound of my own voice, frail and supplicating, rising in the dark. We could make out the tall frosted shapes of the windows now, gloomy and white. When I came to the part *When I am dead, as dead I well may be*—a fit of shivering caused not by the cold sheets but by pleasurable emotion almost silenced me. *You'll kneel and say an Ave[5] there above me*—what was an Ave? Every day I forgot to find out.

Laird went straight from singing to sleep. I could hear his long, satisfied, bubbly breaths. Now, for the time that remained to me, the most perfectly private and perhaps the best time of the whole day, I arranged myself tightly under the covers and went on with one of the stories I was telling myself from night to night. These stories were about myself, when I had grown a little older; they took place in a world that was recognizably mine, yet one that presented opportunities for courage, boldness, and self-sacrifice, as mine never did. I rescued people from a bombed building (it discouraged me that the real war had gone on so far away from Jubilee). I shot two rabid wolves who were menacing the schoolyard (the teachers cowered terrified at my back). I rode a fine horse spiritedly down the main street of Jubilee, acknowledging the townspeople's gratitude for some yet-to-be-worked-out piece of heroism (nobody ever rode a horse there, except King Billy in the Orangemen's Day[6] parade). There was always riding and shooting in these stories, though I had only been on a horse twice—bareback because we did not own a saddle—and the second time I

had slid right around and dropped under the horse's feet; it had stepped placidly over me. I really was learning to shoot, but I could not hit anything yet, not even tin cans on fence posts.

Alive, the foxes inhabited a world my father made for them. It was surrounded by a high guard fence, like a medieval town, with a gate that was padlocked at night. Along the streets of this town were ranged large, sturdy pens. Each of them had a real door that a man could go through, a wooden ramp along the wire for the foxes to run up and down on, and a kennel—something like a clothes chest with airholes—where they slept and stayed in winter and had their young. There were feeding and watering dishes attached to the wire in such a way that they could be emptied and cleaned from the outside. The dishes were made of old tin cans, and the ramps and kennels of odds and ends of old lumber. Everything was tidy and ingenious; my father was tirelessly inventive and his favorite book in the world was *Robinson Crusoe*.[7] He had fitted a tin drum on a wheelbarrow, for bringing water down to the pens. This was my job in summer, when the foxes had to have water twice a day. Between nine and ten o'clock in the morning, and again after supper, I filled the drum at the pump and trundled it down through the barnyard to the pens, where I parked it, and filled my watering can and went along the streets. Laird came too, with his little cream-and-green gardening can, filled too full and knocking against his legs and slopping water on his canvas shoes. I had the real watering can, my father's, though I could only carry it three-quarters full.

7. ***Robinson Crusoe:*** novel by Daniel Defoe that tells the story of a sailor stranded on an island for twenty-four years. Crusoe survives through skill, cleverness, and hard work.

4. **"Danny Boy":** sad song in the words of an Irish mother whose son is going off to war.
5. **Ave** (ä′vā): prayer in Latin to the Virgin Mary, used in the Roman Catholic Church; it begins with the words "Ave, Maria," meaning "Hail, Mary."
6. **Orangemen's Day:** holiday celebrated by the Orangemen, an Irish Protestant society, on July 12. It marks the defeat in 1690 of the Catholic forces in Ireland by the Protestant English king known as William of Orange.

WORDS TO OWN

supplicating (sup′lə·kāt′iŋ) *v.* used as *adj.*: appealing humbly and earnestly, as if in prayer.
placidly (plas′id·lē) *adv.*: calmly; in an undisturbed way.
ingenious (in·jēn′yəs) *adj.*: made or done in a clever or inventive way.

BOYS AND GIRLS 55

Ⓔ Critical Thinking
Speculating
❓ Why do you think Laird sings "Jingle Bells" all year? [Possible responses: It might be the only song he knows; he might like the cheerful melody; he might like the association of the song with Christmas, traditionally a happy time of year for children.]

Ⓕ Elements of Literature
The Moment of Truth: Climax
❓ The narrator's fantasies foreshadow the decision she makes in the story's climax. What kinds of stories does the narrator tell herself at night? [romantic, adventurous stories in which she performs heroic rescues] What do the stories tell you about what she is yearning for in her life? [She yearns for opportunities to display courage, boldness, and self-sacrifice.]

Ⓖ Reading Skills and Strategies
Making Inferences
❓ How does the narrator seem to feel about her father at this point in the story? [Possible response: She admires his ingenuity in inventing ways to take care of the foxes more efficiently.]

Ⓗ Reading Skills and Strategies
Comparing/Contrasting
❓ How does the narrator contrast the ways she and her younger brother help with the watering? [Laird uses his little toy watering can and does not really help much because he spills so much water. The narrator uses her father's "real" watering can and carries heavy loads.]

Crossing the Curriculum

Social Studies
The pelts of the foxes in this story are made into fur coats and other items of clothing. Some people view this use of animals' fur as valid and important, whereas others protest what they consider the cruelty of fur as fashion. Ask students to research the protest movement against wearing fur and to participate in an informal discussion about opposing opinions on the issue. Students could also write editorials supporting their opinions. Remind editorial writers to support their opinions with facts.

Home Economics
The mother in this story spends much of her time preserving and canning food for the family. Ask students to locate an expert on the processes of preserving and canning food, such as a parent, a home economics teacher, or a county agent, and invite this person to speak to the class.

The foxes all had names, which were printed on a tin plate and hung beside their doors. They were named not when they were born but when they survived the first year's pelting and were added to the breeding stock. Those my father had named were called names like Prince, Bob, Wally, and Betty. Those I had named were called Star or Turk, or Maureen or Diana. Laird named one Maud after a hired girl we had when he was little, one Harold after a boy at school, and one Mexico, he did not say why.

Naming them did not make pets out of them or anything like it. Nobody but my father ever went into the pens, and he had twice had blood poisoning from bites. When I was bringing them their water, they prowled up and down on the paths they had made inside their pens, barking seldom—they saved that for nighttime, when they might get up a chorus of community frenzy—but always watching me, their eyes burning, clear gold, in their pointed, malevolent faces. They were beautiful for their delicate legs and heavy, aristocratic tails and the bright fur sprinkled on dark down their backs—which gave them their name—but especially for their faces, drawn exquisitely sharp in pure hostility, and their golden eyes.

Besides carrying water, I helped my father when he cut the long grass, and the lamb's-quarters and flowering money-musk, that grew between the pens. He cut with the scythe[8] and I raked into piles. Then he took a pitchfork and threw fresh-cut grass all over the top of the pens, to keep the foxes cooler and shade their coats, which were browned by too much sun. My father did not talk to me unless it was about the job we were doing. In this he was quite different from my mother, who, if she was feeling cheerful, would tell me all sorts of things—the name of a dog she had had when she was a little girl, the names of boys she had gone out with later on when she was grown up, and what certain dresses of hers had looked like—she could not imagine now what had become of them. Whatever thoughts and stories my father had

---

8. **scythe** (*sīth*): tool with a long blade set at an angle on a long, curved handle.

were private, and I was shy of him and would never ask him questions. Nevertheless, I worked willingly under his eyes, and with a feeling of pride. One time a feed salesman came down into the pens to talk to him and my father said, "Like to have you meet my new hired man." I turned away and raked furiously, red in the face with pleasure.

"Could of fooled me," said the salesman. "I thought it was only a girl."

After the grass was cut, it seemed suddenly much later in the year. I walked on stubble in the earlier evening, aware of the reddening skies, the entering silences, of fall. When I wheeled the tank out of the gate and put the padlock on, it was almost dark. One night at this time I saw my mother and father standing talking on the little rise of ground we called the gangway, in front of the barn. My father had just come from the meathouse; he had his stiff bloody apron on and a pail of cut-up meat in his hand.

It was an odd thing to see my mother down at the barn. She did not often come out of the house unless it was to do something—hang out the wash or dig potatoes in the garden. She looked out of place, with her bare lumpy legs, not touched by the sun, her apron still on and damp across the stomach from the supper dishes. Her hair was tied up in a kerchief, wisps of it falling out. She would tie her hair up like this in the morning, saying she did not have time to do it properly, and it would stay tied up all day. It was true, too; she really did not have time. These days our back porch was piled with baskets of peaches and grapes and pears, bought in town, and onions and tomatoes and cucumbers grown at home, all waiting to be made into jelly and jam and preserves, pickles and chili sauce. In the kitchen there was a fire in the stove all day, jars clinked in boiling water, sometimes a cheesecloth bag was strung on a pole between two chairs, straining blue-black grape pulp for jelly. I was given jobs to do and I would sit at the table peeling peaches that had been soaked in the hot water, or cutting up onions, my eyes smarting and streaming. As soon as I was done, I ran out of the house, try-

---

Skill Link

ing to get out of earshot before my mother thought of what she wanted me to do next. I hated the hot, dark kitchen in summer, the green blinds and the flypapers, the same old oilcloth table and wavy mirror and bumpy linoleum. My mother was too tired and preoccupied to talk to me; she had no heart to tell about the Normal School Graduation Dance; sweat trickled over her face and she was always counting under her breath, pointing at jars, dumping cups of sugar. It seemed to me that work in the house was endless, dreary, and peculiarly depressing; work done out of doors, and in my father's service, was ritualistically[9] important.

I wheeled the tank up to the barn, where it was kept, and I heard my mother saying, "Wait till Laird gets a little bigger, then you'll have a real help."

What my father said I did not hear. I was pleased by the way he stood listening, politely as he would to a salesman or a stranger, but with an air of wanting to get on with his real work. I felt my mother had no business down here, and

9. **ritualistically:** as if it were a rite, or ceremony.

I wanted him to feel the same way. What did she mean about Laird? He was no help to anybody. Where was he now? Swinging himself sick on the swing, going around in circles, or trying to catch caterpillars. He never once stayed with me till I was finished.

"And then I can use her more in the house," I heard my mother say. She had a dead-quiet, regretful way of talking about me that always made me uneasy. "I just get my back turned and she runs off. It's not like I had a girl in the family at all."

I went and sat on a feed bag in the corner of the barn, not wanting to appear when this conversation was going on. My mother, I felt, was not to be trusted. She was kinder than my father and more easily fooled, but you could not depend on her, and the real reasons for the things she said and did were not to be known. She loved me, and she sat up late at night making a dress of the difficult style I wanted, for me to wear when school started, but she was also my enemy. She was always plotting. She was plotting now to get me to stay in the house more, although she knew I hated it (*because* she knew I hated it) and keep me from working for my father. It seemed to me she would do this simply

BOYS AND GIRLS **57**

Professional Notes

Critical Comment: Family Values

Writer Bharati Mukherjee has summarized the world of Munro's fiction in the following way: "Family loyalty is the primary virtue, and for a daughter—often, in the earlier stories, a bright adolescent with artistic pretensions—the only escape is through education, not marriage. The family, knowing that to educate is to relinquish, would rather a daughter marry a neighborhood lout than leave the hometown. 'Who do you think you are?' is the family's cruelest reprimand.

In Munro country, grim homogeneity is layered over with superstition, ignorance, rectitude, and diligence. To not know one's place—and worse, to want to change it, to try to move up—constitutes prideful rebellion."

Invite students to explain how well they think this description fits the world of "Boys and Girls" and whether they think any of these attitudes still exist today.

E **Cultural Connections**

A normal school (from the French *école normale*) trained high school graduates to become teachers. The program usually lasted two years and chiefly trained elementary school teachers.

F **Critical Thinking**

Extending the Text

? Do you think work outside of the house is generally considered more important than work inside the house, or housework? Explain. [Students may say that even though everyone depends on someone's cooking and cleaning to guarantee survival, health, and comfort, this kind of work tends to be devalued as less important than "careers" outside the home.]

G **Elements of Literature**

The Moment of Truth: Climax

Ultimately, the climax of the story involves the narrator's shift in allegiance from her father's to her mother's world. At this point in the story, however, she still sees herself allied with her father against her mother's plans.

H **Reading Skills and Strategies**

Making Inferences

? What attitude toward the narrator does the mother's comment imply? [Possible responses: She is unhappy about her daughter's lack of interest in housework or lack of commitment to helping her; she may be jealous or resentful that her husband gets more help and loyalty from the children than she does.]

I **Critical Thinking**

Analyzing

? What positive and negative characteristics does the narrator see in her mother? [Sample answer: Her mother is kind and loving and makes sacrifices for her, but the narrator believes she is unreliable because she seems to have plans and schemes to limit her daughter's freedom.] Why does the narrator prefer the relationship she has with her father? [Sample answer: She believes her father is more dependable, and she understands him better.]

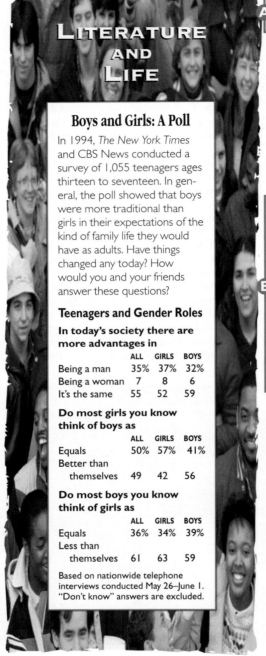

LITERATURE AND LIFE

Boys and Girls: A Poll

In 1994, *The New York Times* and CBS News conducted a survey of 1,055 teenagers ages thirteen to seventeen. In general, the poll showed that boys were more traditional than girls in their expectations of the kind of family life they would have as adults. Have things changed any today? How would you and your friends answer these questions?

Teenagers and Gender Roles

In today's society there are more advantages in

	ALL	GIRLS	BOYS
Being a man	35%	37%	32%
Being a woman	7	8	6
It's the same	55	52	59

Do most girls you know think of boys as

	ALL	GIRLS	BOYS
Equals	50%	57%	41%
Better than themselves	49	42	56

Do most boys you know think of girls as

	ALL	GIRLS	BOYS
Equals	36%	34%	39%
Less than themselves	61	63	59

Based on nationwide telephone interviews conducted May 26–June 1. "Don't know" answers are excluded.

out of perversity and to try her power. It did not occur to me that she could be lonely, or jealous. No grown-up could be; they were too fortunate. I sat and kicked my heels monotonously against a feed bag, raising dust, and did not come out till she was gone.

At any rate, I did not expect my father to pay any attention to what she said. Who could imagine Laird doing my work—Laird remembering the padlock and cleaning out the watering dishes with a leaf on the end of the stick, or even wheeling the tank without its tumbling over? It showed how little my mother knew about the way things really were.

I have forgotten to say what the foxes were fed. My father's bloody apron reminded me. They were fed horsemeat. At this time most farmers still kept horses, and when a horse got too old to work, or broke a leg, or got down and would not get up, as they sometimes did, the owner would call my father, and he and Henry went out to the farm in the truck. Usually they shot and butchered the horse there, paying the farmer from five to twelve dollars. If they had already too much meat on hand, they would bring the horse back alive and keep it for a few days or weeks in our stable, until the meat was needed. After the war the farmers were buying tractors and gradually getting rid of horses altogether, so it sometimes happened that we got a good healthy horse that there was just no use for anymore. If this happened in the winter, we might keep the horse in our stable till spring, for we had plenty of hay, and if there was a lot of snow—and the plow did not always get our road cleared—it was convenient to be able to go to town with a horse and cutter.[10]

The winter I was eleven years old, we had two horses in the stable. We did not know what

10. **cutter:** small, light sleigh, usually drawn by one horse.

WORDS TO OWN

perversity (pər·vur'sə·tē) *n.:* stubborn opposition or contrariness.

Taking a Second Look

names they had had before, so we called them Mack and Flora. Mack was an old black workhorse, sooty and indifferent. Flora was a sorrel mare,[11] a driver. We took them both out in the cutter. Mack was slow and easy to handle. Flora was given to fits of violent alarm, veering at cars and even at other horses, but we loved her speed and high stepping, her general air of gallantry and abandon. On Saturdays we went down to the stable, and as soon as we opened the door on its cozy, animal-smelling darkness, Flora threw up her head, rolled her eyes, whinnied despairingly, and pulled herself through a crisis of nerves on the spot. It was not safe to go into her stall; she would kick.

This winter also I began to hear a great deal more on the theme my mother had sounded when she had been talking in front of the barn. I no longer felt safe. It seemed that in the minds of the people around me there was a steady undercurrent of thought, not to be deflected, on this one subject. The word *girl* had formerly seemed to me innocent and unburdened, like the word *child;* now it appeared that it was no such thing. A girl was not, as I had supposed, simply what I was; it was what I had to become. It was a definition, always touched with emphasis, with <u>reproach</u> and disappointment. Also it was a joke on me. Once Laird and I were fighting, and for the first time ever I had to use all my strength against him; even so, he caught and pinned my arm for a moment, really hurting me. Henry saw this and laughed, saying, "Oh, that there Laird's gonna show you, one of these days!" Laird was getting a lot bigger. But I was getting bigger too.

My grandmother came to stay with us for a few weeks and I heard other things. "Girls don't slam doors like that." "Girls keep their knees together when they sit down." And worse still, when I asked some questions, "That's none of girls' business." I continued to slam the doors and sit as awkwardly as possible, thinking that by such measures I kept myself free.

When spring came, the horses were let out in the barnyard. Mack stood against the barn wall

11. **sorrel mare:** reddish-brown female horse.

trying to scratch his neck and haunches, but Flora trotted up and down and reared at the fences, clattering her hooves against the rails. Snow drifts dwindled quickly, revealing the hard gray-and-brown earth, the familiar rise and fall of the ground, plain and bare after the fantastic landscape of winter. There was a great feeling of opening out, of release. We just wore rubbers now, over our shoes; our feet felt ridiculously light. One Saturday we went out to the stable and found all the doors open, letting in the unaccustomed sunlight and fresh air. Henry was there, just idling around looking at his collection of calendars, which were tacked up behind the stalls in a part of the stable my mother had probably never seen.

"Come to say goodbye to your old friend Mack?" Henry said. "Here, you give him a taste of oats." He poured some oats into Laird's cupped hands and Laird went to feed Mack. Mack's teeth were in bad shape. He ate very slowly, patiently shifting the oats around in his mouth, trying to find a stump of a molar to grind it on. "Poor old Mack," said Henry mournfully. "When a horse's teeth's gone, he's gone. That's about the way."

"Are you going to shoot him today?" I said. Mack and Flora had been in the stable so long I had almost forgotten they were going to be shot.

Henry didn't answer me. Instead he started to sing in a high, trembly, mocking-sorrowful voice, *Oh, there's no more work, for poor Uncle Ned, he's gone where the good folks go.* Mack's thick, blackish tongue worked <u>diligently</u> at Laird's hand. I went out before the song was ended and sat down on the gangway.

I had never seen them shoot a horse, but I knew where it was done. Last summer Laird and I had come upon a horse's entrails before they were buried. We had thought it was a big black

---

WORDS TO OWN

reproach (ri·prōch') *n.:* blame; expression of disapproval.
diligently (dil'ə·jənt·lē) *adv.:* in a steady, careful, and hard-working manner.

Getting Students Involved

Cooperative Learning

Tableau. Have students work in groups to choose a scene from the story to enact in a tableau. Group members can choose characters in the scene and plan how to portray these characters' involvement in the scene's events. As the scene is enacted for the class, you can choose a moment to stop the action: Actors should freeze in the characters' positions at that

instant. The group leader (who does not play a character) explains the scene to the class and moves within the scene to tap each character on the shoulder. When the character is tapped, the student playing the character tells what the character is thinking. Students may incorporate dialogue from the story as they explain their characters.

C Struggling Readers
Summarizing
❓ How would you summarize the differences between the male horse Mack and the female horse Flora? [Possible responses: Mack is slow and easygoing; Flora is fast, emotional, and unpredictable.]

D Critical Thinking
Interpreting
❓ What does the narrator mean when she says, "I no longer felt safe"? [Possible responses: Though she is not in physical danger, she fears she may lose the freedom she has enjoyed while working with her father; she feels her parents are joining together to force her into a more restricted feminine role; she fears growing up.]

E Cultural Connections
Connotations
The word *girl* has had different connotations for different groups of people in America and Canada over the past fifty years. For many years, women of all ages were referred to as *girls;* the word was intended to convey positive associations of youth, innocence, and attractiveness. In the 1960s feminists and others proclaimed that the word *women* was the more respectful term for adult females. Many women, however, especially African American women, address close friends affectionately as "girls." Some young women today refer to themselves as "grr-ls," giving the word a roaring fierceness. You might encourage students to interview people of different ages and cultural backgrounds to find out what positive or negative associations they have with the words *girl, woman, lady,* and *gal.*

F Reading Skills and Strategies
Making Generalizations
Ask students what generalizations people make today about how boys and girls should behave. Have them complete the following sentences independently. Then, have them compare and discuss their responses in small groups or with the whole class:
• Girls should always/never _____.
• Boys should always/never _____.

T59

A Reading Skills and Strategies

Making Inferences

❓ Why does the narrator feel ashamed? [Possible responses: She has gotten her brother to watch; she now feels her father's work is brutal, and she no longer wants to be associated with it.]

B Appreciating Language

Style

❓ Notice the series of participles (verb forms that end in -ing) in this passage. What -ing words and phrases does the author use to describe the actions of the horse? [running free, running, whinnying, going up on her hind legs, prancing and threatening like a horse in a Western movie] How does the narrator feel about the horse's actions? [She finds them exciting and admirable.]

C Elements of Literature

The Moment of Truth: Climax

This is the story's climax: going against her father, the narrator lets the horse run away.

D Critical Thinking

Analyzing Motivation

❓ What are some possible reasons the narrator lets Flora escape? [Sample responses: She wants to express her rebellion; she feels sorry for the horse; she feels that she does not want to be responsible for activities that make her feel ashamed.]

E Elements of Literature

Symbolism

❓ What do you think the horse symbolizes to the narrator? [The horse might symbolize freedom and passion for living. The horse running for her life might symbolize the narrator's struggle to avoid having others decide her fate.]

Mack kicked his legs in the air. I did not have any great feeling of horror and opposition, such as a city child might have had; I was too used to seeing the death of animals as a necessity by which we lived. Yet I felt a little ashamed, and there was a new wariness, a sense of holding off, in my attitude to my father and his work.

It was a fine day, and we were going around the yard picking up tree branches that had been torn off in winter storms. This was something we had been told to do, and also we wanted to use them to make a teepee. We heard Flora whinny, and then my father's voice and Henry's shouting, and we ran down to the barnyard to see what was going on.

The stable door was open. Henry had just brought Flora out, and she had broken away from him. She was running free in the barnyard, from one end to the other. We climbed up on the fence. It was exciting to see her running, whinnying, going up on her hind legs, prancing and threatening like a horse in a Western movie, an unbroken ranch horse, though she was just an old driver, an old sorrel mare. My father and Henry ran after her and tried to grab the dangling halter. They tried to work her into a corner, and they had almost succeeded when she made a run between them, wild-eyed, and disappeared around the corner of the barn. We heard the rails clatter down as she got over the fence, and Henry yelled, "She's into the field now!"

That meant she was in the long L-shaped field that ran up by the house. If she got around the center, heading toward the lane, the gate was open; the truck had been driven into the field this morning. My father shouted to me, because I was on the other side of the fence, nearest the lane, "Go shut the gate!"

I could run very fast. I ran across the garden, past the tree where our swing was hung, and jumped across a ditch into the lane. There was the open gate. She had not got out; I could not see her up on the road; she must have run to the other end of the field. The gate was heavy. I lifted it out of the gravel and carried it across the roadway. I had it halfway across when she

came in sight, galloping straight toward me. There was just time to get the chain on. Laird came scrambling through the ditch to help me.

Instead of shutting the gate, I opened it as wide as I could. I did not make any decision to do this; it was just what I did. Flora never slowed down; she galloped straight past me, and Laird jumped up and down, yelling, "Shut it, shut it!" even after it was too late. My father and Henry appeared in the field a moment too late to see what I had done. They only saw Flora heading for the township road. They would think I had not got there in time.

They did not waste any time asking about it. They went back to the barn and got the gun and the knives they used, and put these in the truck; then they turned the truck around and came bouncing up the field toward us. Laird called to them, "Let me go too, let me go too!" and Henry stopped the truck and they took him in. I shut the gate after they were all gone.

I supposed Laird would tell. I wondered what would happen to me. I had never disobeyed my father before, and I could not understand why I had done it. Flora would not really get away. They would catch up with her in the truck. Or if they did not catch her this morning, somebody would see her and telephone us this afternoon or tomorrow. There was no wild country here for her to run to, only farms. What was more, my father had paid for her, we needed the meat to feed the foxes, we needed the foxes to make our living. All I had done was make more work for my father, who worked hard enough already. And when my father found out about it, he was not going to trust me anymore; he would know that I was not entirely on his side. I was on Flora's side, and that made me no use to anybody, not even to her. Just the same, I did not regret it; when she came running at me and I held the gate open, that was the only thing I could do.

I went back to the house, and my mother said, "What's all the commotion?" I told her that Flora had kicked down the fence and got away. "Your poor father," she said, "now he'll have to go chasing over the countryside. Well, there

Using Students' Strengths

Interpersonal Learners

In small groups, have students discuss the pros and cons of both rebellion and conformity. When is it appropriate or healthy to rebel against the expectations of others? When is it appropriate to conform to the expectations of friends, family, or society? After their discussion, have students make a list of at least three generalizations on which they can agree.

Kinesthetic Learners

The story ends with the family at the dinner table. Ask pairs of students to role-play a conversation between Laird and the narrator as they are washing the dishes after dinner. The conversation should focus on what took place at the table, and each actor should try to portray the personality of the character.

isn't any use planning dinner before one." She put up the ironing board. I wanted to tell her but thought better of it and went upstairs and sat on my bed.

Lately I had been trying to make my part of the room fancy, spreading the bed with old lace curtains and fixing myself a dressing table with some leftovers of cretonne[13] for a skirt. I planned to put up some kind of barricade between my bed and Laird's, to keep my section separate from his. In the sunlight, the lace curtains were just dusty rags. We did not sing at night anymore. One night when I was singing, Laird said, "You sound silly," and I went right on but the next night I did not start. There was not so much need to anyway; we were no longer afraid. We knew it was just old furniture over there, old jumble and confusion. We did not keep to the rules. I still stayed awake after Laird

13. **cretonne** (krē·tän′): heavy printed cotton or linen cloth, named after Creton, a village in Normandy, France.

was asleep and told myself stories, but even in those stories something different was happening, mysterious alterations took place. A story might start off in the old way, with a spectacular danger, a fire or wild animals, and for a while I might rescue people; then things would change around, and instead, somebody would be rescuing me. It might be a boy from our class at school or even Mr. Campbell, our teacher, who tickled girls under the arms. And at this point the story concerned itself at great length with what I looked like—how long my hair was and what kind of dress I had on; by the time I had these details worked out, the real excitement of the story was lost.

It was later than one o'clock when the truck came back. The tarpaulin was over the back, which meant there was meat in it. My mother had to heat dinner up all over again. Henry and my father had changed from their bloody overalls into ordinary working overalls in the barn,

BOYS AND GIRLS 63

Making the Connections

Connecting to the Theme: "Hard Choices"

The narrator makes what appears to be a split-second decision to open the gate for Flora to escape. Actually, many events in the story lead to her decision. Ask students to explore why this was, in fact, a "hard choice" for the narrator. [Students may mention the narrator's respect for her father, her knowledge that the horse flesh was needed to feed the foxes, which were needed to support the family.]

Cultural Connections: Gender Stereotyping

A discussion of gender stereotyping will naturally evolve from this story. While students may not have faced the extreme limitations that the narrator does, ask them if the expression "She's only a girl" is ever used today, and what it means or implies. Keep in mind that students from different cultural backgrounds may face different gender expectations.

A Critical Thinking

Interpreting

? Why do you think Laird shows off the blood on his arm? [Sample responses: to prove he did more than just watch; to prove he's a man; to make his story about Flora more exciting.]

B Reading Skills and Strategies

Drawing Conclusions

? How has the children's relationship with each other and with their father changed since the story's climax? [Laird has gained power over his sister because he has participated in the killing and slaughtering of Flora; he is now more closely allied with their father than the narrator is; the narrator's act of independence has created distance between her and her brother and father.]

C Reading Skills and Strategies

Drawing Conclusions

? What do you think the father's comment reveals about his attitude toward women? [Possible response: He thinks women are not as strong, tough-minded, logical, or dependable as men.]

Resources

Selection Assessment
Formal Assessment
• Selection Test, p. 7
Test Generator (One-Stop Planner)
• CD-ROM

BROWSING IN THE FILES

About the Author. In an interview, Alice Munro described how she tries to combine past and present in her stories: "I'm very interested in the present, in the culture as it is right now, but I always want to tie it in to what I remember. Anyone my age has seen a lot of change in social attitudes, in the fabric of the culture that surrounds people's lives. I'm interested in how that affects people, I want to skip around in time."

A and they washed their arms and necks and faces at the sink and splashed water on their hair and combed it. Laird lifted his arm to show off a streak of blood. "We shot old Flora," he said, "and cut her up in fifty pieces."

"Well, I don't want to hear about it," my mother said. "And don't come to my table like that."

My father made him go and wash the blood off.

We sat down and my father said grace and Henry pasted his chewing gum on the end of his fork, the way he always did; when he took it off, he would have us admire the pattern. We began to pass the bowls of steaming, overcooked vegetables. Laird looked across the table at me and said proudly, distinctly, B "Anyway, it was her fault Flora got away."

"What?" my father said.

"She could of shut the gate and she didn't. She just open' it up and Flora run out."

"Is that right?" my father said.

Everybody at the table was looking at me. I nodded, swallowing food with great difficulty. To my shame, tears flooded my eyes.

My father made a curt sound of disgust. "What did you do that for?"

I did not answer. I put down my fork and waited to be sent from the table, still not looking up.

But this did not happen. For some time nobody said anything; then Laird said matter-of-factly, "She's crying."

C "Never mind," my father said. He spoke with resignation, even good humor, the words which absolved and dismissed me for good. "She's only a girl," he said.

I didn't protest that, even in my heart. Maybe it was true.

WORDS TO OWN

absolved (ab·zälvd') *v.:* freed from guilt, blame, or responsibility.

MEET THE WRITER

Soul of a Story

For **Alice Munro** (1931–) a story is like a house. "I've got to make, I've got to build up, a house, a story to fit around the indescribable 'feeling' that is like the soul of a story." An important part of the "house" Munro builds is the details. "I'm very, very excited by what you might call the surface of life, and it must be that this seems to me meaningful in a way I can't analyze or describe."

The details of many of Munro's stories are drawn from her childhood in rural Ontario and British Columbia in Canada. She started writing when she was about fourteen or fifteen, and earlier than that she made up stories all the time. Her stories focus on ordinary lives. Her heroines are usually young girls or women who discover the uneasiness of adolescence, the tension that can exist within families, the impermanence of human relationships. "Boys and Girls" is from her first collection of stories, *Dance of the Happy Shades*. Asked why she writes only short stories, not novels, Munro said this:

Photo © 1994 by Jill Krementz.

❝ I never intended to be a short-story writer. I started writing them because I didn't have time to write anything else—I had three children. And then I got used to writing stories, so I saw my material that way, and now I don't think I'll ever write a novel. . . . There's a kind of tension that if I'm getting a story right I can feel right away, and I don't feel that when I try to write a novel. I kind of want a moment that's explosive, and I want everything gathered into that. ❞

Assessing Learning

Check Test: True–False

1. The narrator's father raises and kills foxes for their fur. [True]
2. Some of the foxes on the farm are looked upon as pets. [False]
3. The narrator likes to help her father do farm work. [True]
4. The narrator watches her father shoot a horse. [True]
5. The narrator does everything she can to keep Flora from escaping. [False]

Standardized Test Preparation

For practice with standardized test format specific to this selection, see
• *Standardized Test Preparation,* p. 14

For practice in proofreading and editing, see
• *Daily Oral Grammar,* Transparency 4

Same Song

Pat Mora

While my sixteen-year-old son sleeps,
my twelve-year-old daughter
stumbles into the bathroom at six a.m.
plugs in the curling iron
5 squeezes into faded jeans
curls her hair carefully
strokes Aztec Blue shadow on her eyelids
smoothes Frosted Mauve blusher on her cheeks
outlines her mouth in Neon Pink
10 peers into the mirror, mirror on the wall
frowns at her face, her eyes, her skin,
not fair.

At night this daughter
stumbles off to bed at nine
15 eyes half-shut while my son
jogs a mile in the cold dark
then lifts weights in the garage
curls and bench presses
expanding biceps, triceps, pectorals,
20 one-handed push-ups, one hundred sit-ups
peers into that mirror, mirror and frowns too.

for Libby

Connections

The speaker in this poem describes the early morning beauty ritual of her twelve-year-old daughter, while her sixteen-year-old son sleeps. At night, the daughter goes early to bed while the son jogs and then lifts weights. Both are critical of their appearance.

Ⓐ Critical Thinking
Analyzing Details
❓ Why does the poet include so many specific details of her daughter's morning beauty routine? What effect do these details have on readers? [Sample answer: The details show how extensive, carefully planned, and important the ritual is. Naming the makeup colors brings the scene vividly to life for readers.]

Ⓑ Elements of Literature
Allusion
Make sure students catch this allusion to the fairy tale "Snow White," in which the wicked queen daily asks her magic mirror, "Mirror, mirror, on the wall—who's the fairest of them all?" Every day the mirror answers that the queen is the fairest, until one day Snow White becomes more beautiful than the queen, and the mirror tells her so.

Ⓒ Reading Skills and Strategies
Comparing/Contrasting
❓ How is the son's routine different from the daughter's? How is it similar? [Sample answer: It is different in that it takes place at night and involves building his strength rather than making his face look beautiful with makeup. It is similar in that he is trying to live up to an ideal of how an attractive person of his gender should look, and he is disappointed with the results when he looks in the mirror.]

Connecting Across Texts

Connecting with "Boys and Girls"
Like the short story "Boys and Girls," this poem focuses on gender-based standards and expectations for boys and girls. Munro's story focuses on work, family relationships, and a struggle for freedom. Mora's poem focuses on standards of appearance for both sexes and how hard boys and girls work to meet them. Have students discuss these questions: Are boys and girls expected to meet equally tough standards when it comes to their appearance? Do you think both sexes feel equally compelled to try to meet those standards in order to be accepted and feel good about themselves?

MAKING MEANINGS

First Thoughts

1. Some students may agree with the father and think the girl's reaction is typical. Others may disagree and think she should have asserted herself in reply.

Shaping Interpretations

2. The mother expects the girl to conform to traditional female behavior; the girl thinks that her mother is trying to prevent her from being herself.

3. She likes being outdoors and thinks his work is more important.

4. Possible responses: She is less interested in "men's work"; she feels a little ashamed and wary, perhaps because she thinks she would never want to do the brutal thing her father has done.

5. **Before:** not concerned about appearance, dominates brother, daydreams of being heroic, does not think about boys, fearful of the unfinished bedroom. **After:** more concerned with appearance, notes brother's strength, daydreams of being rescued, interested in boys, decorates her room.

6. Possible responses: She values freedom and compassion; she no longer feels she's "one of the boys."

Connecting with the Text

7. Possible generalizations from **story:** Girls are more compassionate than boys; boys accept the cruel necessities of life; boys are expected not to show their feelings; most people eventually accept the gender roles society assigns to them. Possible generalizations from **poll:** Men and women have the same advantages in today's society; girls think of boys as equals; boys think they are better than girls; girls know that boys think of girls as less than boys.

8. Possible responses: Girls today have more role and career opportunities than in the past; girls are still expected to be soft-spoken, less active, less brave, and more self-sacrificing than boys.

   In "The Cold Equations" Barton did not want to enforce a harsh penalty on a girl but would have had no trouble jettisoning a man. Students may say some people today feel the same way about capital punishment for women and sending women into battle.

T66

MAKING MEANINGS

First Thoughts

[connect]

1. Two important things happen at the end. How did you feel when the narrator's father dismissed her as "only a girl"? How did you feel about the girl's reaction?

Shaping Interpretations

[analyze]

2. One of the **conflicts** in the story takes place between the narrator and her mother. What does the mother expect of her daughter? Why does the narrator feel that her mother is her "enemy"?

[interpret]

3. Why does the girl find her father's work more interesting than her mother's?

[analyze]

4. After the girl watches her father shoot Mack, how does her attitude toward men's work change? How would you account for this change?

[analyze]

5. What other changes does the girl experience after the shooting incident? Try listing them on a chart like this one.

Girl's Attitude Toward	Before Mack Dies	After Mack Dies
her appearance		
her brother		
her daydreams		
boys her age		
her bedroom		

[analyze]

6. Another **conflict** in this story takes place in the girl's mind. What do you think the girl has decided when she says, "I was on Flora's side"?

Connecting with the Text

[synthesize]

7. What **generalizations** about boys and girls could you make based on this story? What generalizations could you make based on the poll on page 58?

[synthesize]

8. In your own experience, are the roles of girls and boys (or men and women) as distinct as they are in the rural Canada of this story? Refer to your own Quickwrite notes and to the poll results on page 58. Discuss your opinions with your group. Is there agreement or disagreement? You might also consider Barton's attitudes in "The Cold Equations" (page 9).

Challenging the Text

[evaluate]

9. Do you like the way Alice Munro ended the story, or do you wish something else had happened? Explain.

66 THE SHORT-STORY COLLECTIONS

Challenging the Text

9. Some students may dislike the ending because of the father's dismissal of the girl; they may wish that the girl had kept fighting her family's expectations; others may like the ending because it seems realistic.

Reading Check
Basic situation/setting: a family living on a fox farm in rural Canada. **Main character:** narrator, an eleven-year-old girl. **Her problem:** Her mother tries to force her into a traditional female role; she prefers her father's work. **Main events/complications:** her mother's efforts to get her to do "women's work"; the killing of Mack; her father's decision to kill Flora. **Climax:** She lets Flora escape. **Resolution:** Her father dismisses her action because she is "only a girl."

CHOICES: Building Your Portfolio

Writer's Notebook

1. Collecting Ideas for a Persuasive Essay

What's your view?

Look at the poll on page 58. How would you answer these questions about men's and women's roles? (You might tally your classmates' answers and compare the results with the percentages given on page 58.) Look also at your Quickwrite notes. Then, in your notebook, freewrite about one or more experiences that helped shape your ideas about the roles of women and men. Keep your notes for the Writer's Workshop on page 85.

Issue: Stereotyped Roles

Incident: The time I signed up for a car repair class & I was the only girl—20 guys. They all laughed—thought girls can't do anything mechanical till I proved I could.

Critical Thinking/Speaking

2. A Debate

Conduct a debate on this proposition: Boys' and girls' roles should be very distinct in our society. To prepare for the debate, divide the class into two teams, one to support and one to refute this proposition. Each side should first meet to assemble **evidence** and **arguments** and then engage the other side in a formal debate.

Creative Writing

3. Changing the Ending

Write a different ending, in which the narrator does protest her father's dismissal of her as just a girl. If she voices her protest, what does she say to her father? If she protests only in her heart, what does she think and feel? Read your new ending aloud to the class, and compare it with other revised endings.

Supporting an Opinion

4. Real Men Don't . . .

How have gender roles changed since Alice Munro wrote this story in the 1960s, and what do you think of the changes? What's it like for a man today? In a brief essay, express your views, using facts, examples, and anecdotes to support your opinions.

Creative Writing

5. Same Song?

Imagine that the narrator of "Boys and Girls" has read the poem "Same Song" (see **Connections** on page 65). How would she respond to that poem? (For that matter, how do *you* respond to it?) Would she agree with the portrayal of the son and daughter in the poem? Answer these questions in a creative medium of your choice. For example, the girl might write a diary entry or a letter to the daughter in the poem, or the girl might reply in a poem of her own.

Research/Viewing

6. The Way We Were

Look backward—sample the **media** (TV shows, movies, and magazines) of the 1940s and 1950s to see what they reveal about men's and women's roles in the "good old days." Watch some vintage TV (reruns of *I Love Lucy* are still shown), and rent some movie classics (such as *The Best Years of Our Lives*). Survey the advertisements in old copies of *Life, Saturday Evening Post,* and other magazines if you can find them in a library. Based on your research, what generalizations can you make about men's and women's roles in America during the 1940s and 1950s?

Rubrics for each Choices assignment appear on p. 93 in the *Portfolio Management System.*

CHOICES: Building Your Portfolio

1. **Writer's Notebook**   Before students freewrite about experiences that shaped their attitudes, suggest that they think about experiences at home, at school, at places of worship, on the playground, in organized sports, and in clubs made up of girls or boys.
2. **Critical Thinking/Speaking**   Before students debate, review any general guidelines for debates that might be appropriate.
3. **Creative Writing**   Have students work in pairs to brainstorm different ways in which the narrator could have protested her father's dismissal of her. Students may prefer to write their revised endings as a dialogue between the girl and her father.
4. **Supporting an Opinion**   To collect anecdotes about male roles, suggest students interview their fathers, older brothers, or other relatives, as well as male teachers. To collect examples and facts, students can search for news stories about gender roles, using the Internet or the *Readers' Guide to Periodical Literature.*
5. **Creative Writing**   Before students decide on a creative response to the poem, have them summarize how the son and the daughter are portrayed in the poem, as well as how Munro's narrator's attitudes change from the beginning to the end of the story.
6. **Research/Viewing**   The whole class might enjoy this activity. Divide the class into groups and assign each group an area to explore—TV, movies, or magazine ads. Other movie classics students might view include *Kitty Foyle, The Philadelphia Story, Suspicion, Mildred Pierce, A Letter to Three Wives, All About Eve, A Streetcar Named Desire, The Country Girl,* and *Marty.*

LANGUAGE LINK

Tell students that connotations play an important role in persuasive writing. In persuasive writing, writers use words with positive connotations to bolster their own point of view, and they use words with negative connotations to attack their opponents' point of view.

Try It Out
Possible Answers

1. *Ratlike* has negative connotations; it suggests something sneaky, vile, and dirty.
2. Since *kittenlike* has positive connotations, I would probably object to skinning a fox that is *kittenlike*.
3. *Arrogant* has negative connotations; it suggests the fox is boastful and too self-important.
4. *Proud* has positive connotations; it suggests the fox has a right to feel proud of its fur.

VOCABULARY

(See p. T1019 for a more in-depth treatment of analogies.)

1. perversity
2. placidly
3. absolved
4. remote
5. reproach
6. ingenious
7. derisive
8. supplicating
9. diligently
10. negligently

Resources

Language
• *Grammar and Language Links* Worksheet, p. 7

Vocabulary
• *Words to Own* Worksheet, p. 5

LANGUAGE LINK   `MINI-LESSON`

Handbook of Literary Terms HELP

See Connotations.

Connotations—How Words Can Make You Feel

The narrator in "Boys and Girls" discovers that a familiar word has shades of meaning she had not been aware of before:

> "The word *girl* had formerly seemed to me innocent and unburdened, like the word *child*; now it appeared that it was no such thing. A girl was not, as I had supposed, simply what I was; it was what I had to become. It was a definition, always touched with emphasis, with reproach and disappointment."

The narrator learns that the word *girl* suggests more than its strict literal dictionary meaning, or **denotation.** She learns that *girl* also carries a whole range of **connotations,** or emotional associations.

To help you choose the descriptive word with just the right shade of meaning, you may want to invent word chains like the ones that follow, which show a progression from negative to positive connotations.

miserly → cheap → thrifty
immature → childish → young

Try It Out

Think about the connotations of the underlined words in this passage from the story:

> My father removed the pelt inside out from the body of the fox, which looked surprisingly small, mean, and <u>ratlike</u> deprived of its <u>arrogant</u> weight of fur.

1. What are the connotations of *ratlike*?
2. How would you feel about the fox's being skinned if it had been described as *kittenlike*?
3. What are the connotations of *arrogant*?
4. How would you feel if the writer had used *proud* instead?

VOCABULARY   `HOW TO OWN A WORD`

WORD BANK	Analogies: Matching Relationships
derisive	In an **analogy** two pairs of words have the same relationship. They may be antonyms or synonyms, for example, or they may share some other relationship. Work with a partner to complete each analogy with a word from the Word Bank. The first one has been done as an example.
supplicating	
placidly	
ingenious	
perversity	
reproach	
diligently	
negligently	
remote	
absolved	

1. *Darkness* is to *light* as <u>perversity</u> is to *compliance.*
2. *Slowly* is to *quickly* as _____ is to *nervously.*
3. *Relieved* is to *worry* as _____ is to *blame.*
4. *Powerful* is to *mighty* as _____ is to *distant.*
5. *Praise* is to *approval* as _____ is to *disapproval.*
6. *Strong* is to *weightlifter* as _____ is to *inventor.*
7. *Tired* is to *exhausted* as _____ is to *mocking.*
8. *Commanding* is to *ordering* as _____ is to *appealing.*
9. *Cautiously* is to *recklessly* as _____ is to *lazily.*
10. *Casually* is to *informally* as _____ is to *carelessly.*

68 THE SHORT-STORY COLLECTIONS

Language Link Quick Check

Tell whether the underlined word has positive or negative connotations.

1. "the <u>stale</u>, cold air upstairs" [negative]
2. "the teachers <u>cowered</u> terrified at my back" [negative]
3. "Everything was tidy and <u>ingenious</u>." [positive]
4. "her bare <u>lumpy</u> legs" [negative]
5. "There was a great feeling of opening out, of <u>release</u>." [positive]

T68

Before You Read

EVERYDAY USE

Make the Connection

Generation Clashes

To parents the new generation's choices often seem strange or wrong. To children the older generation often seems stuck in the past.

"Everyday Use" takes place in the rural South during the 1960s, when values and ways of life were changing rapidly. In this story, an African American mother is living an old-fashioned farm life with one of her daughters. When her other daughter visits, with new values and a new boyfriend, the mother must make a choice.

Quickwrite

Many families have traditions or heirlooms that are handed down to the younger generation. Do you have any in your family? Jot down your feelings about maintaining traditions and continuity in a family.

Elements of Literature

Conflict: Blocked Desires

It is the **conflict** in a story that stirs our emotions. If the conflict hooks our interest, it creates suspense and makes us want to read on.

Conflict often occurs when a character's desires are blocked in some way. Conflicts that stir our emotions can be big and dramatic, or they can be as quiet as the question of what to do with an old quilt.

> **C**onflict is a struggle that usually occurs when the main character's desires are blocked in some way.
>
> *For more on Conflict, see pages 32–33 and the Handbook of Literary Terms.*

Reading Skills and Strategies

Comparing and Contrasting Characters

Maggie and Dee are the two adult sisters in this story. Much of the conflict in the story arises because the sisters are separated by wide differences in appearance, education, values, and personalities. As you read, **compare and contrast** the sisters. Track any shifting feelings and sympathies you may have for one sister or the other.

go.hrw.com
LEO 10-1

OBJECTIVES

1. Read and interpret the story
2. Identify and analyze the story's conflict
3. Compare and contrast characters
4. Express understanding through writing or art
5. Identify and use informal diction in writing a dialogue
6. Use new words

SKILLS

Literary
- Identify and analyze conflict

Reading
- Compare and contrast characters

Writing
- Collect ideas for a persuasive essay
- Tell the story from a different point of view
- Write an op-ed article
- Write a letter to the author

Grammar/Language
- Identify and use informal diction in writing a dialogue

Vocabulary
- Use new words
- Diagram context clues

Art
- Design a quilt

Planning

- **Block Schedule**
  Block Scheduling Lesson Plans with Pacing Guide

- **Traditional Schedule**
  Lesson Plans Including Strategies for English-Language Learners

- **One-Stop Planner**
  CD-ROM with Test Generator

Preteaching Vocabulary

Words to Own

Divide the class into groups and have them study the definitions of the Words to Own at the bottom of selection pages. Then, ask each group to choose one of the words and plan how to act it out for a game of charades. Members of the group may try out different methods and then choose the one they like best. The group can choose one member to perform their charade for the class.

Summary ■ ■

The story, set in the rural South in the 1960s, is told from the point of view of a mother awaiting a visit from Dee, her "successful" daughter. Dee, who has adopted African dress and an African name, comes home with a man to visit her mother and her sister Maggie. Maggie is physically and emotionally scarred from a long-ago house fire—revealed in flashbacks. Dee, still disdainful of her family's old-fashioned way of life, asks for old family possessions, which she sees as exotic. Mama balks at letting Dee take two quilts promised to Maggie. Indignant, Dee says that Maggie will ruin the quilts with "everyday use" and that her mother and sister just don't understand their heritage.

Background

During the 1960s many African Americans took part in the Black Pride movement, which grew out of political action for civil rights. It was a time of rediscovering African roots and taking pride in African styles of clothing, art, language, music, and religion.

Ⓐ Cultural Connections

See the Connections article "In Georgia's Swept Yards, a Dying Tradition" on p. 77.

Ⓑ Reading Skills and Strategies

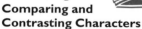

Comparing and Contrasting Characters

❓ What differences between the sisters are clear from the beginning of the story? [Possible responses: Maggie is nervous and shy, ashamed of her burn scars; she is envious of Dee's success; Maggie has stayed home with her mother, while Dee lives away from home.]

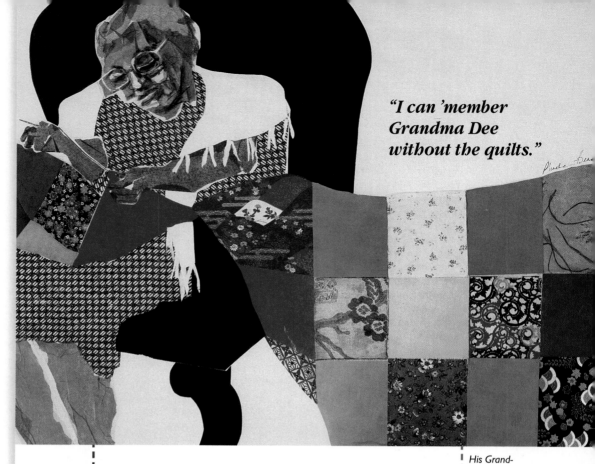

"I can 'member Grandma Dee without the quilts."

His Grandmother's Quilt (1988) by Phoebe Beasley (1943–   ). Collage.
Courtesy of the artist.

Everyday Use

For Your Grandmama   **Alice Walker**

Ⓐ I will wait for her in the yard that Maggie and I made so clean and wavy yesterday afternoon. A yard like this is more comfortable than most people know. It is not just a yard. It is like an extended living room. When the hard clay is swept clean as a floor and the fine sand around the edges lined with tiny, irregular grooves, anyone can come and sit and look up into the elm tree and wait for the breezes that never come inside the house.

Ⓑ Maggie will be nervous until after her sister goes: She will stand hopelessly in corners, homely and ashamed of the burn scars down her arms and legs, eyeing her sister with a mixture of envy and awe.

70 THE SHORT-STORY COLLECTIONS

Resources: Print and Media

Reading
- *Reading Skills and Strategies*
    MiniRead Skill Lesson, p. 44
    Selection Skill Lesson, p. 51
- *Graphic Organizers for Active Reading,* p. 5
- *Words to Own,* p. 6
- *Audio CD Library*
    Disc 3, Track 3

Elements of Literature
- *Literary Elements*
    Transparency 3

Worksheet, p. 10

Writing and Language
- *Daily Oral Grammar*
    Transparency 5
- *Grammar and Language Links*
    Worksheet, p. 9

Viewing and Representing
- *Viewing and Representing*
    Fine Art Transparency 2
    Fine Art Worksheet, p. 8

Assessment
- *Formal Assessment,* p. 9
- *Portfolio Management System,* p. 95
- *Standardized Test Preparation,* p. 16
- *Test Generator (One-Stop Planner CD-ROM)*

Internet
- go.hrw.com (keyword: LE0 10-1)

She thinks her sister had held life always in the palm of one hand, that "no" is a word the world never learned to say to her.

You've no doubt seen those TV shows where the child who has "made it" is confronted, as a surprise, by her own mother and father, tottering in weakly from backstage. (A pleasant surprise, of course: What would they do if parent and child came on the show only to curse out and insult each other?) On TV mother and child embrace and smile into each other's faces. Sometimes the mother and father weep; the child wraps them in her arms and leans across the table to tell how she would not have made it without their help. I have seen these programs.

Sometimes I dream a dream in which Dee and I are suddenly brought together on a TV program of this sort. Out of a dark and soft-seated limousine I am ushered into a bright room filled with many people. There I meet a smiling, gray, sporty man like Johnny Carson who shakes my hand and tells me what a fine girl I have. Then we are on the stage, and Dee is embracing me with tears in her eyes. She pins on my dress a large orchid, even though she had told me once that she thinks orchids are tacky flowers.

In real life I am a large, big-boned woman with rough, man-working hands. In the winter I wear flannel nightgowns to bed and overalls during the day. I can kill and clean a hog as mercilessly as a man. My fat keeps me hot in zero weather. I can work outside all day, breaking ice to get water for washing; I can eat pork liver cooked over the open fire minutes after it comes steaming from the hog. One winter I knocked a bull calf straight in the brain between the eyes with a sledgehammer and had the meat hung up to chill before nightfall. But of course all this does not show on television. I am the way my daughter would want me to be: a hundred pounds lighter, my skin like an uncooked barley pancake. My hair glistens in the hot bright lights. Johnny Carson has much to do to keep up with my quick and witty tongue.

But that is a mistake. I know even before I wake up. Who ever knew a Johnson with a quick tongue? Who can even imagine me looking a strange white man in the eye? It seems to me I have talked to them always with one foot raised in flight, with my head turned in whichever way is farthest from them. Dee, though. She would always look anyone in the eye. Hesitation was no part of her nature.

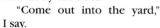

"How do I look, Mama?" Maggie says, showing just enough of her thin body enveloped in pink skirt and red blouse for me to know she's there, almost hidden by the door.

"Come out into the yard," I say.

Have you ever seen a lame animal, perhaps a dog run over by some careless person rich enough to own a car, sidle up to someone who is ignorant enough to be kind to him? That is the way my Maggie walks. She has been like this, chin on chest, eyes on ground, feet in shuffle, ever since the fire that burned the other house to the ground.

Dee is lighter than Maggie, with nicer hair and a fuller figure. She's a woman now, though sometimes I forget. How long ago was it that the other house burned? Ten, twelve years? Sometimes I can still hear the flames and feel Maggie's arms sticking to me, her hair smoking and her dress falling off her in little black papery flakes. Her eyes seemed stretched open, blazed open by the flames reflected in them. And Dee. I see her standing off under the sweet gum tree she used to dig gum out of, a look of concentration on her face as she watched the last dingy gray board of the house fall in toward the red-hot brick chimney. Why don't you do a dance around the ashes? I'd wanted to ask her. She had hated the house that much.

I used to think she hated Maggie, too. But that was before we raised the money, the church and me, to send her to Augusta to

---

EVERYDAY USE **71**

Resources

Listening
Audio CD Library
Students will hear the characters' diction and family conflicts come to life on the *Audio CD Library* recording.
• Disc 3, Track 3

Viewing and Representing
Fine Art Transparency
A Fine Art Transparency of Faith Ringgold's #4 *The Sunflowers Quilting Bee at Arles* can be used after students have read the story.
• Transparency 2
• Worksheet, p. 8

Elements of Literature
Setting
For additional instruction on setting and its role in this story, see *Literary Elements:*
• Transparency 3
• Worksheet, p. 10

C Elements of Literature
Conflict
? What conflict exists between the sisters even before Dee arrives? [Maggie envies Dee's success and considers herself inferior to Dee; she thinks that Dee has always gotten everything she wanted.]

D Elements of Literature
Flashback
? Why do you think the writer includes this flashback? [Possible responses: It explains how Maggie got her burn scars; it reveals Dee's aloof character, her hatred of the old house.]

E Reading Skills and Strategies
Comparing and Contrasting Characters
? What does this passage reveal about the narrator's feelings about her two daughters? [She seems much closer to Maggie than she is to Dee.]

Reaching All Students

Struggling Readers
Comparing and Contrasting was introduced on page 69. For a lesson directly tied to this story that teaches students to make generalizations by using a strategy called Semantic Differential Scales, see the *Reading Skills and Strategies* binder
• MiniRead Skill Lesson, p. 44
• Selection Skill Lesson, p. 51

English Language Learners
These students may need background on the civil rights and Black Pride movements to understand why Dee has changed her name, adopted a new style of dress, and speaks a foreign language to her own mother.

Advanced Learners
The character of Dee is sometimes difficult to sympathize with, but challenge these students to speculate on the feelings that may motivate her behavior and her insensitivity to her mother and sister. Do they see any hope for Dee to become a more compassionate person? Why or why not?

school. She used to read to us without pity, forcing words, lies, other folks' habits, whole lives upon us two, sitting trapped and ignorant underneath her voice. She washed us in a river of make-believe, burned us with a lot of knowledge we didn't necessarily need to know. Pressed us to her with the serious ways she read, to shove us away at just the moment, like dimwits, we seemed about to understand.

Dee wanted nice things. A yellow organdy dress to wear to her graduation from high school; black pumps to match a green suit she'd made from an old suit somebody gave me. She was determined to stare down any disaster in her efforts. Her eyelids would not flicker for minutes at a time. Often I fought off the temptation to shake her. At sixteen she had a style of her own: and knew what style was.

I never had an education myself. After second grade the school closed down. Don't ask me why: In 1927 colored asked fewer questions than they do now. Sometimes Maggie reads to me. She stumbles along good-naturedly but can't see well. She knows she is not bright. Like good looks and money, quickness passed her by. She will marry John Thomas (who has mossy teeth in an earnest face), and then I'll be free to sit here and I guess just sing church songs to myself. Although I never was a good singer. Never could carry a tune. I was always better at a man's job. I used to love to milk till I was hooked in the side in '49. Cows are soothing and slow and don't bother you, unless you try to milk them the wrong way.

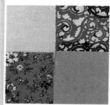

I have deliberately turned my back on the house. It is three rooms, just like the one that burned, except the roof is tin; they don't make shingle roofs anymore. There are no real windows, just some holes cut in the sides, like the portholes in a ship, but not round and not square, with rawhide holding the shutters up on the outside. This house is in a pasture, too, like the other one. No doubt when Dee sees it she will want to tear it down. She wrote me once that

no matter where we "choose" to live, she will manage to come see us. But she will never bring her friends. Maggie and I thought about this and Maggie asked me, "Mama, when did Dee ever *have* any friends?"

She had a few. <u>Furtive</u> boys in pink shirts hanging about on washday after school. Nervous girls who never laughed. Impressed with her, they worshiped the well-turned phrase, the cute shape, the scalding humor that erupted like bubbles in lye. She read to them.

When she was courting Jimmy T, she didn't have much time to pay to us but turned all her faultfinding power on him. He *flew* to marry a cheap city girl from a family of ignorant, flashy people. She hardly had time to recompose herself.

When she comes, I will meet—but there they are!

Maggie attempts to make a dash for the house, in her shuffling way, but I stay her with my hand. "Come back here," I say. And she stops and tries to dig a well in the sand with her toe.

It is hard to see them clearly through the strong sun. But even the first glimpse of leg out of the car tells me it is Dee. Her feet were always neat looking, as if God himself shaped them with a certain style. From the other side of the car comes a short, stocky man. Hair is all over his head a foot long and hanging from his chin like a kinky mule tail. I hear Maggie suck in her breath. "Uhnnnh" is what it sounds like. Like when you see the wriggling end of a snake just in front of your foot on the road. "Uhnnnh."

Dee next. A dress down to the ground, in this hot weather. A dress so loud it hurts my eyes. There are yellows and oranges enough to throw back the light of the sun. I feel my whole face warming from the heat waves it throws out. Earrings gold, too, and hanging down to her shoulders. Bracelets dangling and making noises when she moves her arm up to shake the folds

WORDS TO OWN
furtive (fʉr′tiv) *adj.*: acting as if trying not to be seen. *Furtive* also means "done secretly."

Using Students' Strengths

Interpersonal Learners
After students have finished reading the story, remind them of the everyday objects referred to in the story. Ask pairs of students to interview someone who lived through the 1930s or 1940s. Their questions should focus on objects once common in the home that are rarely seen or used today. Ask the pairs to present brief oral reports or to create visual displays from their findings. Be sure they obtain permission from parents, guardians, and interviewees.

Intrapersonal Learners
Invite students to reflect on an object that pertains to some aspect of their own cultural heritage. Have them write about the object's significance to their family and to themselves personally.

of the dress out of her armpits. The dress is loose and flows, and as she walks closer, I like it. I hear Maggie go "Uhnnnh" again. It is her sister's hair. It stands straight up like the wool on a sheep. It is black as night and around the edges are two long pigtails that rope about like small lizards disappearing behind her ears.

"Wa-su-zo-Tean-o!" she says, coming on in that gliding way the dress makes her move. The short, stocky fellow with the hair to his navel is all grinning, and he follows up with "Asalamalakim,[1] my mother and sister!" He moves to hug Maggie but she falls back, right up against the back of my chair. I feel her trembling there, and when I look up I see the perspiration falling off her chin.

"Don't get up," says Dee. Since I am stout, it takes something of a push. You can see me trying to move a second or two before I make it. She turns, showing white heels through her sandals, and goes back to the car. Out she peeks next with a Polaroid. She stoops down quickly and lines up picture after picture of me sitting there in front of the house with Maggie <u>cowering</u> behind me. She never takes a shot without making sure the house is included. When a cow comes nibbling around in the edge of the yard, she snaps it and me and Maggie *and* the house. Then she puts the Polaroid in the back seat of the car and comes up and kisses me on the forehead.

Meanwhile, Asalamalakim is going through motions with Maggie's hand. Maggie's hand is as limp as a fish, and probably as cold, despite the sweat, and she keeps trying to pull it back. It looks like Asalamalakim wants to shake hands but wants to do it fancy. Or maybe he don't know how people shake hands. Anyhow, he soon gives up on Maggie.

"Well," I say. "Dee."

"No, Mama," she says. "Not 'Dee,' Wangero Leewanika Kemanjo!"

1. **Asalamalakim:** Asalaam aleikum (ä·sə·läm′ ä·lā′koom′), greeting used by Muslims meaning "peace to you."

"What happened to 'Dee'?" I wanted to know.

"She's dead," Wangero said. "I couldn't bear it any longer, being named after the people who oppress me."

"You know as well as me you was named after your aunt Dicie," I said. Dicie is my sister. She named Dee. We called her "Big Dee" after Dee was born.

"But who was *she* named after?" asked Wangero.

"I guess after Grandma Dee," I said.

"And who was she named after?" asked Wangero.

"Her mother," I said, and saw Wangero was getting tired. "That's about as far back as I can trace it," I said. Though, in fact, I probably could have carried it back beyond the Civil War through the branches.

"Well," said Asalamalakim, "there you are."

"Uhnnnh," I heard Maggie say.

"There I was not," I said, "before 'Dicie' cropped up in our family, so why should I try to trace it that far back?"

He just stood there grinning, looking down on me like somebody inspecting a Model A car. Every once in a while he and Wangero sent eye signals over my head.

"How do you pronounce this name?" I asked.

"You don't have to call me by it if you don't want to," said Wangero.

"Why shouldn't I?" I asked. "If that's what you want us to call you, we'll call you."

"I know it might sound awkward at first," said Wangero.

"I'll get used to it," I said. "Ream it out again."

Well, soon we got the name out of the way. Asalamalakim had a name twice as long and three times as hard. After I tripped over it two or three times, he told me to just call him Hakim-a-barber. I wanted to ask him was he a barber, but I didn't really think he was, so I didn't ask.

WORDS TO OWN

cowering (kou′ər·iŋ) v. used as *adj.*: drawing back or huddling in fear.

G H I J

G Elements of Literature
Irony
Asalamalakim is a greeting, not the man's name. Mrs. Johnson knows the difference but uses the term as his name in mild mockery of his appearance and mannerisms.

H Critical Thinking
Expressing an Opinion
? Which name do you think better reflects Dee's heritage? Why? [Sample responses: Dee, because it is the name her family gave her, and she was named after her aunt; Wangero, because she chose it to honor her African heritage.]

I Appreciating Language
Diction
The colloquial expression "cropped up" sounds natural in Mama's dialogue because that is how many people speak.

J English Language Learners
Historical Terms
These students may not recognize the term "Model A car." Tell them that Model A was the name of one of the first cars ever produced by Henry Ford; very few remain. Mama is saying that Hakim-a-barber is looking at her as if she were some kind of rare antique, hopelessly out of date.

Getting Students Involved

Cooperative Learning
Describing Characters. Divide the class into several groups, and assign one of the four characters to each group. Allow the groups six or seven minutes to list as many adjectives as they can that describe the personality of their character. Students should review the story for quotations that support their choices. When time is up, let the groups that have the same character collaborate to produce a master list of adjectives for that character. After five minutes, ask one member of each group to report to the rest of the class.

Creating Dialogue
After the Visit. Let students work with a partner to role-play the characters of Dee and Hakim-a-barber as they drive home after their visit to Dee's family. The dialogue that occurs should be in keeping with the personalities and attitudes of the two characters and should reflect the conflicts they have just experienced. After the partners have finished their dialogues, put them in groups of three or four to compare their interpretations of the characters.

Ⓐ Cultural Connections
Soul Food
The lunch consists of items that today would be called "soul food"—food that is traditional within African American culture. Collards are a green vegetable similar to cabbage or spinach; chitlins, or chitterlings, are prepared from the intestines of pigs; corn bread is made from corn meal.

Ⓑ English Language Learners
Slang
The expression "talk a blue streak" means to talk quickly and at length. It may have come from comparing fast things to a streak of lightning.

Ⓒ Struggling Readers
Finding Details
❓ What detail tells you that Mama and Maggie are still using the churn to make butter? [The churn has milk in it that has turned to clabber, a stage in the making of butter.]

Ⓓ Reading Skills and Strategies
Comparing and Contrasting Characters
❓ What differences can you notice between Dee and Maggie as they talk about the churn? [Maggie speaks shyly and remembers the family history of the churn. Dee thinks of the churn as something she can take apart and make artistic.]

Ⓔ Cultural Connections
Quilt Patterns
Lone Star and Walk Around the Mountain are two traditional quilt patterns. Students should be able to find pictures of them in books about quilting.

Ⓕ Elements of Literature
Conflict
❓ Why does Maggie slam the door when she hears Dee ask for the quilts? [Possible responses: She assumes that Dee will get her way, just as she did with the churn; that Dee will simply take whatever she wants, and Mama will not stop her. Maggie is afraid to express her anger directly to Dee, so slamming a door from the distance is the only way she can express it.]

"You must belong to those beef-cattle peoples down the road," I said. They said "Asalamalakim" when they met you, too, but they didn't shake hands. Always too busy: feeding the cattle, fixing the fences, putting up salt-lick shelters, throwing down hay. When the white folks poisoned some of the herd, the men stayed up all night with rifles in their hands. I walked a mile and a half just to see the sight.

Hakim-a-barber said, "I accept some of their doctrines, but farming and raising cattle is not my style." (They didn't tell me, and I didn't ask, whether Wangero—Dee—had really gone and married him.)

Ⓐ We sat down to eat and right away he said he didn't eat collards, and pork was unclean. Wangero, though, went on through the chitlins and corn bread, the greens, and everything else.
Ⓑ She talked a blue streak over the sweet potatoes. Everything delighted her. Even the fact that we still used the benches her daddy made for the table when we couldn't afford to buy chairs.

"Oh, Mama!" she cried. Then turned to Hakim-a-barber. "I never knew how lovely these benches are. You can feel the rump prints," she said, running her hands underneath her and along the bench. Then she gave a sigh, and her hand closed over Grandma Dee's butter dish. "That's it!" she said. "I knew there was something I wanted to ask you if I could have." She jumped up from the table and went over in the corner where the churn stood, the milk in it clabber[2] by now. She looked at the churn and looked at it.

Ⓒ "This churn top is what I need," she said. "Didn't Uncle Buddy whittle it out of a tree you all used to have?"

"Yes," I said.

"Uh huh," she said happily. "And I want the dasher,[3] too."

"Uncle Buddy whittle that, too?" asked the barber.

Dee (Wangero) looked up at me.

Ⓓ "Aunt Dee's first husband whittled the dash,"

2. **clabber:** thickly curdled sour milk.
3. **dasher:** pole that stirs the milk in a churn.

---

said Maggie so low you almost couldn't hear her. "His name was Henry, but they called him Stash."

"Maggie's brain is like an elephant's," Wangero said, laughing. "I can use the churn top as a centerpiece for the alcove table," she said, sliding a plate over the churn, "and I'll think of something artistic to do with the dasher."

When she finished wrapping the dasher, the handle stuck out. I took it for a moment in my hands. You didn't even have to look close to see where hands pushing the dasher up and down to make butter had left a kind of sink in the wood. In fact, there were a lot of small sinks; you could see where thumbs and fingers had sunk into the wood. It was beautiful light-yellow wood, from a tree that grew in the yard where Big Dee and Stash had lived.

After dinner Dee (Wangero) went to the trunk at the foot of my bed and started rifling through it. Maggie hung back in the kitchen over the dishpan. Out came Wangero with two quilts. They had been pieced by Grandma Dee, and then Big Dee and me had hung them on the quilt frames on the front porch and quilted
Ⓔ them. One was in the Lone Star pattern. The other was Walk Around the Mountain. In both of them were scraps of dresses Grandma Dee had worn fifty and more years ago. Bits and pieces of Grandpa Jarrell's paisley shirts. And one teeny faded blue piece, about the size of a penny matchbox, that was from Great Grandpa Ezra's uniform that he wore in the Civil War.

"Mama," Wangero said sweet as a bird. "Can I
Ⓕ have these old quilts?"

I heard something fall in the kitchen, and a minute later the kitchen door slammed.

"Why don't you take one or two of the others?" I asked. "These old things was just done by me and Big Dee from some tops your grandma pieced before she died."

"No," said Wangero. "I don't want those.

WORDS TO OWN
doctrines (däk′trinz) *n.:* principles; teachings; beliefs.
rifling (rī′flin) *v.* used as *n.:* searching thoroughly or in a rough manner.

Crossing the Curriculum

Social Studies
Dee's clothing, hairstyle, and interest in African names and languages represent elements of the Black Pride movement of the 1960s. Have students research the origins of this movement and how it functioned in relation to the civil rights movement. Students might use an encyclopedia, newspaper and magazine articles, biographies of civil rights leaders, and interviews with adults who lived through this period.

Art
Invite someone who is skilled in quilt making to come to class to explain and demonstrate how quilts are made. If possible, have two or three quilts on display during the presentation. Have the expert explain the significance of the pattern of each quilt. If actual quilts are not available, find library books that show quilt designs and explain their significance. Students can use what they learn when they design their own quilts for Choices activity 5 on p. 79.

They are stitched around the borders by machine."

"That'll make them last better," I said.

"That's not the point," said Wangero. "These are all pieces of dresses Grandma used to wear. She did all this stitching by hand. Imagine!" She held the quilts securely in her arms, stroking them.

"Some of the pieces, like those lavender ones, come from old clothes her mother handed down to her," I said, moving up to touch the quilts. Dee (Wangero) moved back just enough so that I couldn't reach the quilts. They already belonged to her.

"Imagine!" she breathed again, clutching them closely to her bosom.

"The truth is," I said, "I promised to give them quilts to Maggie, for when she marries John Thomas."

She gasped like a bee had stung her.

"Maggie can't appreciate these quilts!" she said. "She'd probably be backward enough to put them to everyday use."

"I reckon she would," I said. "God knows I been saving 'em for long enough with nobody using 'em. I hope she will!" I didn't want to bring up how I had offered Dee (Wangero) a quilt when she went away to college. Then she had told me they were old-fashioned, out of style. G

"But they're *priceless*!" she was saying now, furiously; for she has a temper. "Maggie would put them on the bed and in five years they'd be in rags. Less than that!"

"She can always make some more," I said. "Maggie knows how to quilt."

Dee (Wangero) looked at me with hatred. "You just will not understand. The point is *these* quilts, these quilts!"

"Well," I said, stumped. "What would *you* do with them?"

"Hang them," she said. As if that was the only thing you *could* do with quilts.

Maggie by now was standing in the door. I could almost hear the sound her feet made as they scraped over each other.

"She can have them, Mama," she said, like somebody used to never winning anything or H

having anything reserved for her. "I can 'member Grandma Dee without the quilts."

I looked at her hard. She had filled her bottom lip with checkerberry snuff, and it gave her face a kind of dopey, hangdog look. It was Grandma Dee and Big Dee who taught her how to quilt herself. She stood there with her scarred hands hidden in the folds of her skirt. She looked at her sister with something like fear, but she wasn't mad at her. This was Maggie's portion. This was the way she knew God to work.

When I looked at her like that, something hit me in the top of my head and ran down to the soles of my feet. Just like when I'm in church and the spirit of God touches me and I get happy and shout. I did something I never had done

before: hugged Maggie to me, then dragged her on into the room, snatched the quilts out of Miss Wangero's hands, and dumped them into Maggie's lap. Maggie just sat there on my bed with her mouth open. I

"Take one or two of the others," I said to Dee.

But she turned without a word and went out to Hakim-a-barber.

"You just don't understand," she said, as Maggie and I came out to the car.

"What don't I understand?" I wanted to know.

"Your heritage," she said. And then she turned to Maggie, kissed her, and said, "You ought to try to make something of yourself, too, Maggie. It's really a new day for us. But from the way you and Mama still live, you'd never know it." J

She put on some sunglasses that hid everything above the tip of her nose and her chin.

Maggie smiled, maybe at the sunglasses. But a real smile, not scared. After we watched the car dust settle, I asked Maggie to bring me a dip of snuff. And then the two of us sat there just enjoying, until it was time to go in the house and go to bed.

EVERYDAY USE 75

G **Elements of Literature**
Conflict
? Besides the question of who is entitled to the quilts, what other issue surrounds the quilts? [Dee and Mama argue over how the quilts should be used. Dee thinks they should be hung on a wall and preserved; Mama and Maggie plan to put the quilts to the "everyday use" they were intended for.]

H **Critical Thinking**
Extending the Text
? Why do you think some people, like Maggie, do not fight for what is rightfully theirs? [Possible responses: They might not feel entitled; they are afraid of people with stronger wills and prefer to avoid conflict; they may feel that peace is more important than getting what they want.]

I **Reading Skills and Strategies**
Drawing Conclusions
? Based on this passage, what do you think Mama wants to accomplish by giving the quilts to Maggie? [Possible responses: She wants Maggie to feel loved and entitled; she wants Maggie to know that she will fight Dee to protect Maggie's rights.]

J **Advanced Learners**
Have these students analyze how Dee's statements about heritage are ironic, or contradictory. [Sample response: She accuses her mother of not appreciating her heritage, while also criticizing her for maintaining the family's traditional way of life; Mama and Maggie appreciate their heritage by living it and putting it to "everyday use," while Dee wants to leave the old ways behind and preserve them only as artifacts on a wall.]

Resources ————

Selection Assessment
Formal Assessment
• Selection Test, p. 9
Test Generator (One-Stop Planner)
• CD-ROM

Making the Connections

Connecting to the Theme: "Hard Choices"
In "Everyday Use" Mrs. Johnson makes the hard choice of standing up to Dee and giving the quilts to Maggie. Have students discuss the effect this choice is likely to have on Mama's relationship with Dee in the future. [Responses will vary. Some students may feel it will have no effect and that Dee will continue to try to get

everything she wants. Others may feel that the choice redefines their relationship and that Mama will be more in control in the future.]

Cultural Connections
Dee left behind the cultural world of her family when she went away to college and left the rural setting in which she grew up. Children of

immigrants will relate to issues that arise when children become educated and assimilated into a culture very different from the one their parents know. Have students discuss—in general—ways that families deal with issues of preserving their heritage and cultural traditions versus assimilating into the broader culture.

Alice Walker and her daughter, Rebecca.

MEET THE WRITER

Out of Eatonton

Alice Walker (1944–   ), shown above with her daughter, Rebecca, was born in the small town of Eatonton, Georgia, the youngest of eight children. Her father was a sharecropper, and her mother worked as a maid. When she was eight years old, Walker was blinded in one eye by a shot from a BB gun. The resulting scar tissue made her painfully shy and self-conscious, and she spent her free time alone outdoors, reading and writing stories. With the aid of a scholarship for handicapped students, she attended Spelman College, a college for African American women in Atlanta.

Women have always played an important role in Walker's life. She has said that she grew up believing there was absolutely nothing her mother couldn't do once she set her mind to it. So when the women's movement came along, she said that she was delighted because she felt they were trying to go where her mother was and where she had always assumed she would go.

Walker's third novel, *The Color Purple,* won the Pulitzer Prize for fiction in 1983 and was made into a popular movie. Walker has been a contributing editor of *Ms.* magazine and has been active in both the women's movement and the civil rights movement.

Walker has published short stories, poems, essays, and novels, so it comes as a surprise to learn that she never intended to be a writer.

❝ I just kind of found myself doing it. I remember wanting to be a scientist, wanting to be a pianist, wanting to be a painter. But all the while I was wanting to be these other things, I was writing. We were really poor, and writing was about the cheapest thing to do. You know, I feel amazed that I have been able to do exactly what I wanted to do. ❞

Assessing Learning

Check Test: Short Answers

1. In Mama's dream, where does she imagine meeting Dee? [on a TV show]
2. Why did Mama not go to school beyond second grade? [because the school closed]
3. When Dee takes photos, what structure does she include in every one? [the house]
4. What does Dee plan to do with the churn top? [use it as a centerpiece on a table]
5. Why didn't Dee take a quilt to college? [She said they were old fashioned.]

Standardized Test Preparation

For practice with standardized test format specific to this selection, see
• *Standardized Test Preparation,* p. 16
For practice in proofreading and editing, see
• *Daily Oral Grammar,* Transparency 5

In Georgia's Swept Yards, a Dying Tradition

ANNE RAVER

ATHENS, Ga.—Mismatched pots of begonias and petunias hang from old porches that could use some work. Painted chicken feeders blossom with zinnias and red salvia. These yards have no grass—because they are swept clean with a broom made of dogwood branches gathered in the woods.

They don't look like much at first glance. But hidden in their unconscious design are traces of West Africa and the emergence of a hard-won independence.

Blacks here, descendants of slaves brought, mainly from West Africa, to work the cotton fields in Georgia's hard clay, are carrying on the traditions that their ancestors brought from the Gold Coast°—everything from cooking and washing outdoors to sharing the latest gossip under a shade tree. But these yards and the life they hold are fast disappearing, as the people who have long tended them grow old and their children move on.

The swept yard was the most important "room" of the household, the heart of the home. Slave quarters were cramped and hot. So you washed and cooked outside, and when the meal was over, everything could be swept into the fire.

Sixteen years ago, when Richard Westmacott, an Englishman, came to Athens to teach landscape architecture at the University of Georgia, he and his wife, Jean, moved into an abandoned pre–Civil War house in rural Ogle-

° The Gold Coast is a former British colony in western Africa, now an independent country called Ghana.

thorpe County, about twenty miles east of town. In visiting the gardens of his neighbors, he realized that what the local people took for granted was the embodiment of a fast-disappearing culture.

"I have no doubt that the swept yard did come from Africa—and then was adopted by white folks," said Mr. Westmacott, whose book, *African-American Gardens and Yards in the Rural South,* was published last year by the University of Tennessee. "Almost everybody had swept yards, including the plantations, which were swept by slaves or servants."

Mr. Westmacott's book, which examines the traditions and folk art of these black gardeners, is the result of his travels through rural Georgia, Alabama, and South Carolina. His photographs capture a society that is fast disappearing, as children move to the cities for work and buy their vegetables at the supermarket. His book also includes photographs of villages in West Africa, taken at the turn of the century and preserved in British archives, that show striking similarities to the swept yards of the South.

Swept yards are so familiar to some that they have become invisible.

When Mr. Westmacott asked why they swept their yards, gardeners simply said that their mothers and grandmothers did it that way.

"It comes from way back," said Dell Appling, sitting on an old glider under some oak trees brought from the woods and "set out" years ago. "My mother—she was ninety when she passed—would sweep the yard with a brush broom we made out of dogwood."

—from *The New York Times,* August 8, 1993

Yard-sweeping near Lodge, South Carolina.

Photo by Richard Westmacott

Connections

This *New York Times* article discusses the origin of Georgia's traditional swept yards. An English landscape architect has traced their origin to West Africa, specifically to the Gold Coast, now Ghana. Confined to cramped quarters, enslaved West Africans in America made the yard the most important room of their homes. They swept the yard with dogwood branches, a tradition that still continues, although it is fast disappearing.

Ⓐ Reading Skills and Strategies
Drawing Conclusions
❓ Why do you think the children abandon the tradition of swept yards when they move on? [Possible responses: A swept yard is too much trouble to maintain; they would feel out of place with swept yards in the areas they move to; the children want to forget traditions associated with the poverty of their youth.]

Ⓑ Critical Thinking
Speculating
❓ Why might an English landscape architect notice the significance of swept yards? [Possible responses: As a foreigner, he took nothing for granted, as local people might. Also, as a landscape architect, he was trained in the symbolic, as well as the practical, aspects of landscape design.]

Ⓒ Cultural Connections
Preserving Traditions
Swept yards are being preserved in places like Westville, a living history museum of life in a Georgia village in the 1850s. Westville is near Lumpkin, in southwest Georgia.

Connecting Across Texts

Connecting to "Everyday Use"
Much of "Everyday Use" is set outdoors in the Johnsons' swept yard. Although the swept yard is only mentioned in the first paragraph of the story, it is as much a part of the cultural heritage of the family as the handmade quilts and the butter churn. This article from *The New York Times* demonstrates that practices like sweeping the yards, which the Johnsons consider a matter of "everyday use," have deep historical and cultural roots. Have students discuss other such traditions with which they are familiar.

MAKING MEANINGS

First Thoughts

1. Possible responses: Maggie, who is the underdog and was promised the quilts; Dee, who will appreciate their artistic value.

Shaping Interpretations

2. Some will say Mama is the main character and that her desire to see Maggie treated fairly is blocked by Dee. Others may say Dee is the main character and that her desire to preserve relics of her heritage is blocked by Mama, who will not let her have the quilts. The conflict is both external and internal.

3. Dee has "made it," that is, become successful, because she is educated, apparently affluent, and self-assured.

4. The most significant similarity is that they share the same family history, cultural background, and memories. Their most compelling difference is that Dee is very assertive, while Maggie is shy.

5. Responses will vary. Yes, Mama does not understand the monetary or artistic value of preserving the quilts and other objects. However, she and Maggie understand the importance of preserving their family heritage; they feel pride in and love for their objects of "everyday use."

6. Possible response: Mama changes by the end of the story because she stands up to Dee in favor of Maggie.

7. Possible responses: The dedication may have been written to her own daughter or as a reminder to all people to cherish the heritages passed on by their grandmothers, who made beautiful things for "everyday use."

Extending the Text

8. Possible responses: Maggie will probably be married to John Thomas and caring for their children. Mama will probably be living where she is. Dee might be a highly successful person, still earnest about her causes.

9. Possible responses: Similar problems could arise whenever one sibling is more successful than another; whenever some siblings have opportunities for getting an education and entering a broader world than the rest of the family has known; when family members disagree about the best way to preserve their heritage; when family members fight over treasured heirlooms.

MAKING MEANINGS

First Thoughts

[connect]

1. Which character did you side with in the conflict over the quilts, and why?

Shaping Interpretations

[analyze]

2. What do you think is the source of the **conflict** in this story? Consider:
   - Which **character** sets the action in motion?
   - Which of her desires are blocked?
   - Who or what is blocking them?
   - Is the battle **external** or **internal** or both?

[interpret]

3. Dee is referred to as the child who has "made it." What do you think that means, and what signs tell you that she has "made it"?

[analyze]

4. Use a diagram like the one on the right to **compare and contrast** Dee and Maggie. What is the most significant thing they have in common? What is their most compelling difference?

[evaluate]

5. Near the end of the story, Dee accuses Mama of not understanding their African American heritage. Do you agree or disagree with Dee, and why?

[interpret]

6. Has any character changed by the end of the story? Go back to the text and find details to support your answer.

[synthesize]

7. Why do you think Alice Walker dedicated her story "For Your Grandmama"?

Extending the Text

[synthesize]

8. What do you think each of these three women will be doing ten years after the story ends?

[connect]

9. This story takes place in a very particular **setting** and a very particular **culture**. Talk about whether or not the problems faced by this family could be experienced by any family, anywhere.

Challenging the Text

[evaluate]

10. Do you think Alice Walker chose the right narrator for her story? How would the story differ if Dee or Maggie were telling it, instead of Mama? (What would we know that we don't know now?)

78 THE SHORT-STORY COLLECTIONS

Reading Check

a. According to Mama, how is Dee different from her and from Maggie?

b. How would Maggie and Dee use the quilts differently?

c. When she was a child, something terrible happened to Maggie. What was it?

d. How did the mother choose to resolve the **conflict** over the quilts?

e. Find the passage in the text that explains the **title**.

Churn (1935–1942), rendering by Lelah Nelson. Watercolor, pen and ink, and graphite on paperboard (18¹⁄₁₆˝ × 11¾˝).

Index of American Design, ©1998 Board of Trustees, National Gallery of Art, Washington, D.C.

Challenging the Text

10. Possible responses: Mama is a good narrator because she has keen insight about her two children that neither one has about herself or about her sister. Dee might be tempted to tell the story as an example of her mother's ignorance and backwardness. Maggie might be tempted to tell it as a victory over Dee.

Reading Check

a. Aside from a different physical appearance, Dee is educated and rejects her family's traditional way of life.

b. Maggie would use them on beds; Dee would display them as works of art.

c. She was badly burned in a house fire.

d. She keeps her promise to give Maggie the quilts; she offers Dee other quilts.

e. This passage appears in the middle of the first column on p. 75, in Dee's speech.

CHOICES: Building Your Portfolio

Writer's Notebook

1. Collecting Ideas for a Persuasive Essay

Taking a stand. It isn't always easy to make up your mind about a complex issue or problem, but it's a good idea to practice taking a stand. For an issue you've been thinking about in this collection or an issue that this story may have inspired, make up your mind about what you think is right. Then, in a single sentence, state your **opinion**. To **persuade** someone that you're right, think of a personal experience or firsthand observation related to the issue. Jot down your notes and save them for the Writer's Workshop on page 85.

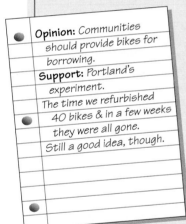

Opinion: Communities should provide bikes for borrowing.

Support: Portland's experiment.

The time we refurbished 40 bikes & in a few weeks they were all gone.

Still a good idea, though.

Creative Writing

2. What Does Maggie Say?

Let Maggie narrate the climactic scene in her own voice. Start on page 74, at the moment Wangero/Dee says, "Can I have these old quilts?" Why does Maggie offer Dee the quilts? How does she feel when Mama dumps them on her lap? Why does she smile at the end?

Editorial Writing

3. Preserving Through Writing

Many newspapers today have opposite their main editorial page an op-ed page, which contains signed essays on topics of special interest. Write an **op-ed article** about something important in your family heritage. It might be a holiday, a recipe, a traditional style of clothing, or a way of fixing your yard (see **Connections** on page 77). Elaborate in your essay by adding a few vivid descriptive details. Share your op-ed article with classmates by reading it aloud.

Supporting an Opinion

4. Dear Author

Alice Walker once said that she gathers up the historical and psychological threads of the lives of her ancestors, and in writing about their lives, she feels the joy of continuity. Do you think all people find joy in continuity—in looking back at the lives of their ancestors? Write a **letter** to Walker agreeing or disagreeing with this idea.

Art/Culture

5. Design a Quilt

Quilts have been designed to commemorate bicentennials, historical events, family histories, and so on, as well as to honor people who have died from AIDS. Design a quilt that reflects an aspect or aspects of your **cultural heritage**. Write a brief explanation of why you chose the various elements of your design and how each reflects your cultural heritage.

The AIDS quilt in Washington, D.C.

Grading Timesaver

Rubrics for each Choices assignment appear on p. 95 in the *Portfolio Management System*.

CHOICES: Building Your Portfolio

1. **Writer's Notebook** Before students take a stand, encourage them to list the pros and cons of each side and then decide which side carries more weight, in their opinion.

2. **Creative Writing** To help students get an idea of how Maggie would react to Mama's giving her the quilts, have them complete a character map of her characteristics and behavior, using details from the story. The map could appear as follows:

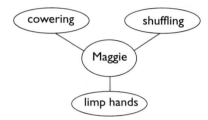

3. **Editorial Writing** If students prefer not to write about a family tradition, have them brainstorm for traditions shared as a nation or by cultures they find interesting. Students might begin by looking through a calendar and noting significant dates.

4. **Supporting an Opinion** To get students started, have them list reasons people might or might not enjoy looking back at their ancestors' lives. Students should review their lists for the strongest points and include them as support for the opinions in their letters. Tell students to state their opinions clearly at the outset of their letters.

5. **Art/Culture** Have students consider the following aspects of cultural heritage and how they might be represented in a quilt: objects handed down from one generation to the next, food, holidays and other celebrations, traditions, stories and sayings.

LANGUAGE LINK

When revising dialogue for a piece of writing, students may read their dialogue to a partner. The partner should offer suggestions for how to make the dialogue sound more natural. Students could also record their dialogue and play it back, listening for areas where improvements could be made.

Possible Answers

1. Answers may vary. Most students will infer that the word indicates the word used by Mama's generation. Others may say it indicates her lack of education or awareness.

2. Hakim-a-barber seems educated, sophisticated, and well informed. The other way of saying the statement would make him seem uneducated and unsophisticated.

VOCABULARY

Help students begin this activity by modeling a context diagram for the word *doctrines*.

Hakim-a-barber accepts the group's doctrines.	Their doctrines are contrasted with their physical actions.	Doctrines are probably teachings or beliefs held by the group.

Remind students that in determining a word's meaning from context, they should also include what they know from their own experience.

Resources ━━━

Language
- *Grammar and Language Links* Worksheet, p. 9

Vocabulary
- *Words to Own* Worksheet, p. 6

LANGUAGE LINK   MINI-LESSON

Handbook of Literary Terms
H E L P

See Diction.

Diction—Finding the Right Word

Diction is **word choice.** Whether you say "diction" or "word choice" is a matter of diction—or word choice. Diction can be formal ("remove yourself") or informal ("get a move on"). Diction can be plain ("clothes") or fancy ("apparel").

Here are two sentences from "Everyday Use." Note the underlined words.

1. "In 1927 <u>colored</u> asked fewer questions than they do now."

What does it suggest to you that Mama says "colored," not "African Americans" or "black people"?

2. "Hakim-a-barber said, '<u>I accept some of their doctrines, but farming and raising cattle is not my style.</u>'"

What impression of Hakim-a-barber do you get from his diction? How would he seem different if he'd said, "I hear that stuff they're saying, but I ain't no sodbuster"?

A Tip for Writers

In your own writing, especially in a personal narrative, you will probably use **dialogue.** To sound natural, the diction you use in dialogue must reflect how that person would really speak. Many people pronounce words carelessly and often speak in fragments. They sometimes use colorful expressions (as when Mama remarks "Ream it out again" instead of "Say it again"). Spoken language doesn't sound like a formal essay, although Hakim-a-barber's comes close. Always read your dialogue aloud. Practice rewriting it until it sounds like real speech.

VOCABULARY   HOW TO OWN A WORD

WORD BANK
sidle
furtive
cowering
doctrines
rifling

Diagraming Context

The diagram below shows how one reader figured out the meaning of *sidle* by using **context clues.** After noting this reader's strategies, locate the other words at the left as they appear in the story, and make a context diagram for each word.

"Have you ever seen (a lame animal,) perhaps a dog run over by some careless person rich enough to own a car, (sidle) up to someone who is ignorant enough (to be kind to him)?"

A lame dog might not walk straight.

Sidle might mean "move sideways." (It sounds like *side*.)

The dog wants someone to be nice to him, so *sidle* also probably means he's begging for attention, sort of pitifully.

Language Link Quick Check

Answer "yes" or "no" regarding whether Mrs. Johnson (Mama) would be likely to use the sentence in conversation. Be prepared to support your answers.

1. I am utterly amazed at Dee's audacity. [no]
2. Maggie's my baby. [yes]
3. Dee, you want everything you see. [yes]
4. These quilts are an authentic representation of our cultural heritage. [no]
5. I find Dee's current fascination with the trappings of African culture quite encouraging. [no]

from Travels with Charley

John Steinbeck

I moved the cross hairs to the breast of the animal and pushed the safety.

Background

Every journey to a new place is also a journey toward oneself. In 1960, John Steinbeck took his aged poodle, Charley, and set out to "discover" America in a homemade camper he named Rocinante (after the run-down horse that carried the Spanish "knight" Don Quixote on his quests; see page 577). *Travels with Charley* is the book Steinbeck wrote about his travels. In this excerpt, a desert creature presents Steinbeck with a choice between public issues and private ones.

Reading Skills and Strategies

Dialogue with the Text

As you read this selection, be alert for sentences, phrases, or words that strike you, that make you stop and think or see something more clearly. Copy the passages in the left column of a two-column sheet. (If you'd rather not interrupt your reading, note the location of the passage so that you can return to it after you've finished.) Here is what this **double-entry journal** would look like:

Passages	My Comments

go.hrw.com
LEO 10-1

Extending the Theme

In this nonfiction excerpt, Steinbeck watches two coyotes—magnified through his rifle's telescope sight. They are an easy shot, yet Steinbeck hesitates. He presents his choice as an internal conflict: his "good citizen" vermin-killing side versus his "old and lazy" noninterfering side. When he decides not to kill the coyotes, he recalls the Chinese belief that a person who saves a life is responsible for it. Leaving dog food for the coyotes, he concludes that the world is a delicate web of relationships.

Background

Coyotes are carnivorous members of the dog family. They can be distinguished from wolves by their narrower nose pads and longer ears. Originally coyotes were found only in the back country of Mexico and the southwestern United States. Recently, however, their range has expanded as far north as Alaska and east to the Atlantic. Coyotes will eat almost anything, including domestic animals, and have become pests in some areas.

Reading Skills and Strategies

A Dialogue with the Text

To help students get started on their double-entry journals, ask them to pay special attention to sensory details, colorful adjectives, and precise verbs.

Making the Connections

Connecting to the Theme: "Hard Choices"

Each main character in the selections in this collection faces a hard choice. The choices these characters make are influenced by a variety of factors, including societal expectations and personal convictions. In choosing to spare the lives of two coyotes, Steinbeck acknowledges that he is going against public opinion and

his own conditioning and training. He seems motivated by a respect for the two living creatures and an acknowledgment of their right to live.

Refer students to "What Happened During the Ice Storm" (p. 4). Have them compare and contrast the two narratives. [Possible responses:

Steinbeck makes his choice as an adult with a full range of experience and learning; the boys' decision is made early in life, perhaps out of innocence. Steinbeck and the boys act against popular opinion and out of a respect for living creatures. The boys probably don't feel responsible for the birds they saved.]

T81

READ ON

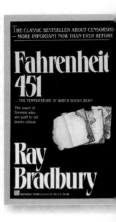

Burning Books

In Ray Bradbury's world of *Fahrenheit 451* (Ballantine), the censors have taken over. People can read only books that the state approves, and any unauthorized books are burned by "firemen." (Paper catches fire at 451 degrees Fahrenheit.) Then one fireman questions what he's doing. . . .

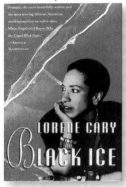

Questions of Identity

In her autobiography, *Black Ice* (Knopf), Lorene Cary tells of the choices she had to make when she moved from her African American neighborhood in Philadelphia to an elite prep school in New Hampshire. Cary learns a hard lesson—how difficult it is to succeed without seeming to reject her heritage.

Sand, Sand, Everywhere

Frank Herbert's classic science fiction novel *Dune* (Berkley) takes place on a strange desert planet. There the colonizers must decide how to deal with unusual life forms called sandworms, which produce a substance that turns humans into bizarre creatures.

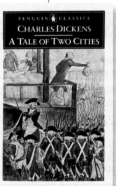

"It Is a Far, Far Better Thing . . ."

Charles Dickens's *A Tale of Two Cities* takes place during the French Revolution. Its sweeping action shifts between England and France. The novel contains everything—love, death, bloodshed, heroism, and villainy. The choice made by one character at the end is often quoted when people talk of heroic sacrifice. (This title is available in the HRW Library.)

Finding Their Own Way

In *The Chosen* by Chaim Potok (1929–   ), Danny Saunders and Reuven Malter, both Orthodox Jews, become friends after Danny's line drive to first base injures Reuven's eye. Danny's father expects his son to follow in his footsteps as a Hasidic rabbi, but Danny has other ideas. The boys' friendship survives obstacles as both struggle to find their own way in life. The 1981 movie version stars Rod Steiger and Robby Benson.

from Travels with Charley

John Steinbeck

I moved the cross hairs to the breast of the animal and pushed the safety.

Background

Every journey to a new place is also a journey toward oneself. In 1960, John Steinbeck took his aged poodle, Charley, and set out to "discover" America in a homemade camper he named Rocinante (after the run-down horse that carried the Spanish "knight" Don Quixote on his quests; see page 577). *Travels with Charley* is the book Steinbeck wrote about his travels. In this excerpt, a desert creature presents Steinbeck with a choice between public issues and private ones.

Reading Skills and Strategies

Dialogue with the Text

As you read this selection, be alert for sentences, phrases, or words that strike you, that make you stop and think or see something more clearly. Copy the passages in the left column of a two-column sheet. (If you'd rather not interrupt your reading, note the location of the passage so that you can return to it after you've finished.) Here is what this **double-entry journal** would look like:

Passages	My Comments

go.hrw.com
LEO 10-1

Extending the Theme

In this nonfiction excerpt, Steinbeck watches two coyotes—magnified through his rifle's telescope sight. They are an easy shot, yet Steinbeck hesitates. He presents his choice as an internal conflict: his "good citizen" vermin-killing side versus his "old and lazy" noninterfering side. When he decides not to kill the coyotes, he recalls the Chinese belief that a person who saves a life is responsible for it. Leaving dog food for the coyotes, he concludes that the world is a delicate web of relationships.

Background

Coyotes are carnivorous members of the dog family. They can be distinguished from wolves by their narrower nose pads and longer ears. Originally coyotes were found only in the back country of Mexico and the southwestern United States. Recently, however, their range has expanded as far north as Alaska and east to the Atlantic. Coyotes will eat almost anything, including domestic animals, and have become pests in some areas.

Ⓐ Reading Skills and Strategies
A Dialogue with the Text
To help students get started on their double-entry journals, ask them to pay special attention to sensory details, colorful adjectives, and precise verbs.

Making the Connections

Connecting to the Theme: "Hard Choices"

Each main character in the selections in this collection faces a hard choice. The choices these characters make are influenced by a variety of factors, including societal expectations and personal convictions. In choosing to spare the lives of two coyotes, Steinbeck acknowledges that he is going against public opinion and

his own conditioning and training. He seems motivated by a respect for the two living creatures and an acknowledgment of their right to live.

Refer students to "What Happened During the Ice Storm" (p. 4). Have them compare and contrast the two narratives. [Possible responses:

Steinbeck makes his choice as an adult with a full range of experience and learning; the boys' decision is made early in life, perhaps out of innocence. Steinbeck and the boys act against popular opinion and out of a respect for living creatures. The boys probably don't feel responsible for the birds they saved.]

Ⓐ bout fifty yards away two coyotes stood watching me, their tawny coats blending with sand and sun. I knew that with any quick or suspicious movement of mine they could drift into invisibility. With the most casual slowness I reached down my new rifle from its sling over my bed—the .222, with its bitter little high-speed, long-range stings. Very slowly I brought the rifle up. Perhaps in the shade of my house I was half hidden by the blinding light outside. The little rifle has a beautiful telescope sight with a wide field. The coyotes had not moved.

I got both of them in the field of my telescope, and the glass brought them very close. Their tongues lolled out so that they seemed to smile mockingly. They were favored animals, not starved but well furred, the golden hair tempered with black guard hairs. Their little lemon-yellow eyes were plainly visible in the glass. I moved the cross hairs to the breast of the right-hand animal and pushed the safety. My elbows on the table steadied the gun. The cross hairs lay unmoving on the brisket.[1] And then the coyote sat down like a dog and its right paw came up to scratch the right shoulder.

My finger was reluctant to touch the trigger. I must be getting very old and my ancient conditioning worn thin. Coyotes are vermin. They steal chickens. They thin the ranks of quail and all other game birds. They must be killed. They are the enemy. My first shot would drop the sitting beast, and the other would whirl to fade away. I might very well pull him down with a running shot because I am a good rifleman.

And I did not fire. My training said, "Shoot!" and my age replied, "There isn't a chicken within thirty miles, and if there are any, they aren't my chickens. And this waterless place is not quail country. No, these boys are keeping their figures with kangaroo rats and jack rabbits, and that's vermin eat vermin. Why should I interfere?"

"Kill them," my training said. "Everyone kills them. It's a public service." My finger moved to the trigger. The cross was steady on the breast just below the panting tongue. I could imagine

the splash and jar of angry steel, the leap and struggle until the torn heart failed, and then, not too long later, the shadow of a buzzard, and another. By that time I would be long gone—out of the desert and across the Colorado River. And beside the sagebrush there would be a naked, eyeless skull, a few picked bones, a spot of black dried blood, and a few rags of golden fur.

I guess I'm too old and too lazy to be a good citizen. The second coyote stood sidewise to my rifle. I moved the cross hairs to his shoulder and held steady. There was no question of miss-

---

1. **brisket:** chest.

Crossing the Curriculum

Social Studies
In many parts of the United States, there are currently heated debates about efforts to preserve wild animals, such as wolves and bears, that some people consider pests. Have students research these issues in periodicals, explain the hard choices involved in the debate, and decide which side of the issue to support. Have them list at least three good reasons for their decision.

Folklore
Old Man Coyote plays a major role in Native American myths. Coyote is a trickster hero who easily transforms himself into human or animal form. Have students research some of the hundreds of coyote myths and read aloud or retell several to the class.

ing with that rifle at that range. I owned both animals. Their lives were mine. I put the safety on and laid the rifle on the table. Without the telescope they were not so intimately close. The hot blast of light tousled the air to shimmering.

Then I remembered something I heard long ago that I hope is true. It was unwritten law in China, so my informant told me, that when one man saved another's life, he became responsible for that life to the end of its existence. For, having interfered with a course of events, the sav-

ior could not escape his responsibility. And that has always made good sense to me.

Now I had a token responsibility for two live and healthy coyotes. In the delicate world of relationships, we are tied together for all time. I opened two cans of dog food and left them as a votive.[2]

2. **votive:** something offered to fulfill a vow or pledge or in thanks. In some churches, votive candles are lit in thanksgiving for answered prayers.

FINDING COMMON GROUND

Now that you've finished reading, go back to the passages you noted in your **double-entry journal.** Reflect for a few minutes, and then fill out the column labeled "My Comments." Do you agree or disagree with these passages? Did they make you see or feel something in a new way?

Form groups of three or four, and discuss the Steinbeck piece, using these approaches:

1. Discuss your journal entries. You might have each member read one passage and comment on it. Did other members of the group notice the same passage? Did you react similarly to it? Be sure each person has a chance to share at least one entry.

2. Move on to wider issues. Steinbeck doesn't directly comment on public issues, but he leaves plenty of room for them between the lines. In your groups talk about the public issues this desert narrative raises:

   - How do you think Steinbeck felt about nature, civilization, and progress?

   - How do you feel about the choices he made?

   - What range of views do you find in your group?

   - What impression did this selection give you of the man who wrote it?

3. Share your group's responses and conclusions with the entire class. Do you find agreement, or are some issues still controversial?

E Struggling Readers
Paraphrasing
? What do you think the author means when he says, "I owned both animals. Their lives were mine"? [Sample answer: He has taken aim at the coyotes with his rifle and is sure he will hit them if he shoots. He has the power of deciding whether they will live or die.]

F Reading Skills and Strategies

Dialogue with the Text
? What do you think about this "unwritten law"? If you saved someone's life, do you think you would feel responsible for that life forever? Explain. [Possible responses: Yes, because by intervening I have altered that person's fate forever; no, I have already done that person a great service and have no further obligation.]

Finding Common Ground

As its name suggests, this feature encourages students to explore issues related to the theme of the selection and to discover areas of agreement through lively discussion. As you move from group to group, you might find the following questions useful in stimulating discussion.

1. **Does Steinbeck feel that the coyotes have rights?** [He seems to. He points out that the two coyotes do not pose a threat to either chickens or quail, so there is no good reason for killing them.]

2. **How would you express Steinbeck's view of the coyotes in your own words?** [Possible response: He seems to believe that the civilized world does not appreciate the coyotes' beauty and their right to exist as part of the balance of nature.]

3. **Is Steinbeck convinced that ridding the desert of coyotes would be real progress?** [Apparently not. He thinks coyotes serve a purpose in the balance of nature, and that killing them all would not be true progress.]

Assessing Learning

Check Test: True–False
1. The coyotes run when Steinbeck first picks up his rifle. [False]
2. He steadies his gun by leaning on a table. [True]
3. Coyotes steal chickens and kill game birds, such as quail. [True]
4. Steinbeck knows that there is a chicken farm nearby. [False]
5. He finally shoots the coyotes. [False]

Observation Assessment
Complete the following statements for each group by checking the descriptor that applies.
1. Students refer to journal entries.
___ Often ___ Sometimes ____ Seldom
2. Students participate by either speaking or listening.
___ Often ___ Sometimes ____ Seldom
3. Students move beyond the selection to consider wider issues.
___ Often ___ Sometimes ___ Seldom

READ ON

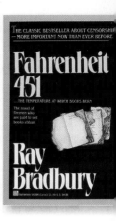

Burning Books

In Ray Bradbury's world of *Fahrenheit 451* (Ballantine), the censors have taken over. People can read only books that the state approves, and any unauthorized books are burned by "firemen." (Paper catches fire at 451 degrees Fahrenheit.) Then one fireman questions what he's doing. . . .

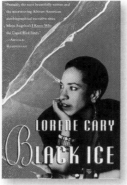

Questions of Identity

In her autobiography, *Black Ice* (Knopf), Lorene Cary tells of the choices she had to make when she moved from her African American neighborhood in Philadelphia to an elite prep school in New Hampshire. Cary learns a hard lesson—how difficult it is to succeed without seeming to reject her heritage.

Sand, Sand, Everywhere

Frank Herbert's classic science fiction novel *Dune* (Berkley) takes place on a strange desert planet. There the colonizers must decide how to deal with unusual life forms called sandworms, which produce a substance that turns humans into bizarre creatures.

"It Is a Far, Far Better Thing . . ."

Charles Dickens's *A Tale of Two Cities* takes place during the French Revolution. Its sweeping action shifts between England and France. The novel contains everything—love, death, bloodshed, heroism, and villainy. The choice made by one character at the end is often quoted when people talk of heroic sacrifice. (This title is available in the HRW Library.)

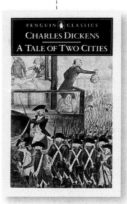

Finding Their Own Way

In *The Chosen* by Chaim Potok (1929–   ), Danny Saunders and Reuven Malter, both Orthodox Jews, become friends after Danny's line drive to first base injures Reuven's eye. Danny's father expects his son to follow in his footsteps as a Hasidic rabbi, but Danny has other ideas. The boys' friendship survives obstacles as both struggle to find their own way in life. The 1981 movie version stars Rod Steiger and Robby Benson.

84 THE SHORT-STORY COLLECTIONS

BUILDING YOUR PORTFOLIO
Writer's Workshop

PERSUASIVE WRITING
PERSUADING THROUGH PERSONAL NARRATIVE

You often share with friends stories about hilarious, exciting, or upsetting things that happened in your life. Occasionally you might tell your real-life stories to **persuade** someone, as in the following examples:

- a college application essay designed to convince an admissions committee that you'd be a good student
- a job interview where you hope your story will convince an employer that you'd be the best person for the job
- a letter to the editor that expresses your opinion on an issue

In this Writer's Workshop you'll use a **personal narrative** in an essay to support your opinion on an issue. You'll be saying, in effect, "Here's what I think about this issue. I feel strongly about the issue because this is what happened to me."

Prewriting

1. Choose Your Issue

Check your Writer's Notebook entries for this collection. If you haven't settled on a topic yet, review the stories to see what ideas they suggest. (See the notepad on the right.) Do you still have no topic? Skim a newspaper or newsmagazine, or watch a TV news program. You might choose a problem or issue (something you think needs fixing) in your own community or school. Make sure you choose a topic with which you've had some personal experience.

2. State Your Opinion

The first—and sometimes the hardest—thing to do is to take a stand on an issue. So that you can base your opinion solidly on facts, you might read a little, ask questions, and talk to people who know something about the issue. For **background information** for your essay, do some research. Then, write an **opinion statement,** a single sentence that expresses your opinion clearly—for example, "Recent advances in technology have made our lives better."

Technology HELP

See Writer's Workshop 2 CD-ROM. Assignments: Controversial Issue; Autobiographical Incident.

ASSIGNMENT

Write an essay stating your opinion about a problem, a situation, or an issue. Support your opinion with a personal narrative.

AIM

To persuade.

AUDIENCE

Your teacher and classmates; readers of a school or local newspaper; a group with power to act on your ideas.

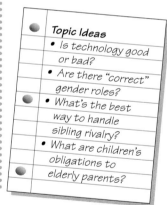

Topic Ideas
- Is technology good or bad?
- Are there "correct" gender roles?
- What's the best way to handle sibling rivalry?
- What are children's obligations to elderly parents?

WRITER'S WORKSHOP 85

Teaching the Writer's Workshop

Prewriting

Have students use the techniques suggested on pp. 85–86 (or any others with which they may be comfortable) to generate ideas.

Try It Out
Possible Answers

1. On the breezy spring day, a freckled and bespectacled student sat at the neighborhood park with two senior citizens who were using their laptops to teach her the ins and outs of the Internet.

2. Along the buzzing highway, a woman and two children—all armored in blaze orange safety vests—picked up litter cast-off by thoughtless motorists.

3. Instead of sleeping in on student holidays, I read to eager-eyed children at the neighborhood daycare center where I spent my preschool days.

My "Story"/Experience

Last summer worked with three friends painting and repairing dozens of bikes

Touch—beating sun, feel of sandpaper on rusty bikes

Sight—neon orange paint, splashes on clothes and driveway, grease on hands and arms

Sounds—Lots of laughter, boombox playing

Try It Out

Elaborate each of the following statements by adding details that would create a vivid picture for readers.

1. A student sat with two senior citizens at a computer.
2. A woman and two children picked up litter.
3. I read to children at a day-care center.

---

3. Tell Your Story

Now, focus on the story part of your essay, the **personal narrative** that relates your experience to the issue. You might write about a one-time experience (helping to clean up a trash-filled vacant lot) or an experience that stretched over many weeks (a summer working in a nursing home). The Student Model on page 88 summarizes an experience that took place over several months.

When you tell a story, you generally use **chronological order,** relating events in the order in which they happened. List the main events of your story. You might try putting them on a time line to be sure they're in the correct order.

Then, make some notes about how you felt and what you thought about your experience. What did you learn from the experience that might interest others? How, exactly, does your experience relate to the issue?

4. Elaborate: Pile on the Details

Instead of writing about "a school on East Elm Street," help your readers see the school: "the crumbling red-brick school with the dirty windows and broken steps on East Elm Street." Try sitting patiently for a few minutes, perhaps with your eyes closed, and picturing where your experience took place. Remember everything that you can: Who was there? What did the place look like? Try to capture **sensory details:** the sights, sounds, smells, tastes, and touch sensations of your experience. These details will help make the experience come alive for your readers.

Dialogue is another sure-fire way to add interest to your narrative. Were important things said? Write them down just as the people said them. It's important to make dialogue as true to life as possible.

5. Call to Action: What to Do?

You've stated an opinion and told your story. A good way to end a persuasive essay is with a **call to action,** a clear statement of what you want your audience to do. You might ask your readers to join an organization, write a letter, or contribute to a cause you support.

EXAMPLE
Make your voice heard, and send your views to your state representatives. Find their addresses on your state government's Web site.

Using Students' Strengths

Auditory Learners

Students might benefit from telling their stories to one or more classmates who could write down the key details as they listen. The classmates can then give the details back to the speaker for use in his or her writing. Students can help the storyteller by asking questions that will provide many and varied details for the writer to use. If possible, allow every student to serve as both a storyteller and listener.

Visual/Kinesthetic

Have students each create a collage series with magazine/newspaper pictures depicting the issue of their persuasive essay. Students might want to add captions to their series as needed to help convey meaning.

Drafting

1. Organize!

You have two main choices for organizing your essay. Either one will work effectively. First, to intrigue your reader, you can tell your personal narrative at the start and save your opinion statement for the end, as in the Student Model on page 88. Second, you can start out with the issue and your opinion statement and end with your personal narrative, as in the brief **outline** at the right. (For more about outlining, see page 334.)

Decide how you'll tell your narrative, too. The most obvious way to tell a story—and it's a solid, traditional way—is to begin with the earliest event, go on to the second event, and proceed in **chronological order** to the last event. "What Happened During the Ice Storm" (page 4) is an example of a story that is narrated chronologically.

Another way to organize your narrative is to begin with an exciting moment right in the middle of the action—*in medias res* ("into the midst of things") is the Latin term. "The Cold Equations" (page 9), for instance, begins with that great sentence telling you that the space pilot is not alone; then the story **flashes back** to explain his mission.

> EXAMPLES
>
> **Beginning at the beginning.** First I checked out the project with the Scout Master, and then I began to check around to find out where I could get abandoned and decrepit bikes that could be repaired.
>
> **Beginning in the middle.** With a great sense of accomplishment, I stepped back, splashed in orange, to admire the first freshly painted bike.

2. Use Your Own Voice

The experience happened to you, not to someone else, so write about it in your own words, the way you think about it or the way you would discuss it with a friend. Don't even try to write like Edgar Allan Poe or Alice Walker or another famous writer. Avoid difficult words and long, complicated sentences. Find your own voice, and express yourself clearly and directly (a good rule for every kind of writing).

> EXAMPLES
>
> **Artificial voice.** Bicycles of highly intense hues are logistically situated in vehicular retainers and at the shoulders of thoroughfares for all persons in the population to employ.
>
> **Authentic voice.** Brightly colored bicycles are placed in bike racks and alongside streets for anyone to use.

Outline for a Persuasive Personal Narrative

I. Introduction
  A. Opinion statement
  B. Background information (if needed)
II. Personal narrative (elaborated with sensory details, maybe dialogue)
  A. What happened
    1. When and where
    2. Who
  B. Thoughts and feelings
III. Conclusion
  A. Call to action
  B. Restatement of opinion or summary of experience

Language/Grammar Link
H E L P

Subject-verb agreement: page 31. Imagery: page 42. Pronouns: page 49. Connotations: page 68. Diction: page 80.

Communications Handbook
H E L P

See Checking Your Comprehension.

Drafting

Before students begin to write, have them study the Student Model provided on pp. 88–89.

To help students organize their drafts, have them create time lines of the events they want to depict in their narratives. Once students have their ideas placed on the time line, they can determine where the points of their persuasive argument may effectively fit into the structure of their narratives.

Remind students to use double spacing when they write their drafts. They should also leave extra space in the right margin. These blank spaces will be used for comments and editing marks.

Reaching All Students

Struggling Writers

Using personal narrative within a persuasive essay can build students' self-esteem because it makes them realize that, in addition to facts and opinions from "experts," their own experiences are important. Encourage students to take themselves and their experiences seriously as subject matter for their writing. If students have a hard time expressing the connection between their personal experience and the issue they are discussing, work with them individually to help them make these connections.

Read and discuss the model with students, focusing on questions such as the following:

? What is the issue being argued by the author? Does this issue have two sides? Are both presented?

? At what point does the author introduce his thesis?

? What types of details does the author provide to help you visualize the event?

? Is the "call to action" clear and effective? Why or why not?

? What techniques does this writer use that you might incorporate into your paper?

A TEST OF HONOR

Are trustworthiness and the spirit of sharing still alive in our cities? Last June, as an Eagle Scout candidate with Troop 87 in Syracuse, I began a project that suggested some answers to that question.

Intriguing question as opener. Personal narrative begins.

I created a "community bicycle" program in our city, inspired by newspaper reports about such projects elsewhere. Attaining the Eagle Scout rank, the highest in Boy Scouting, requires a public service project, and I hoped I could create something that would have long-term success.

Community biking has existed in Europe for decades and has recently been transplanted to the United States. Brightly colored bicycles are placed in bike racks and alongside streets for anyone to use. The riders are asked to leave the bicycles for others when they are done.

Background information.

The benefits can be substantial. The bicycles provide an alternative to short-range trips by car, reducing automobile exhaust. And bicycling improves the fitness of the rider.

Persuasive argument: the benefits of bicycling. Personal narrative resumes.

Once I explained my idea, the local Kiwanis and Rotary Clubs donated fifty used, sometimes mangled bicycles. Volunteers from the Boy Scouts and Kiwanis put hundreds of hours into refurbishing as many of these bicycles as possible, painting them fluorescent orange and attaching tags explaining the concept. In the end, we had thirty-five working bicycles downtown and at Syracuse University.

Descriptive details.

Three months later, there appear to be just seven or eight in use. As far as I can tell, the rest have been stolen.

I had hoped that the bright orange and the fact that the bicycles were almost worthless would deter theft, but apparently some people aren't too selective—in fact, the downtown bikes started disappearing within hours of being distributed.

Was my project a failure? Was I surprised, disappointed, angry?

Questions introduce writer's thoughts on experience.

I tell myself that the project was never intended to be anything more than an experiment, and that you can't call an experiment a failure simply because it did not produce the results you wanted. Still, I had hoped for better in a community that has always seemed warm, helpful, and generous. Syracuse has always shown the kind of good will that would make a bike project successful.

In fact, my esteem for our city has actually increased because of the cooperation and support I received from so many parts of the community. Yet the experience has made me acutely aware of the "bad apple" effect—it took only a few people

Persuasive argument: increase in writer's esteem for city.

Crossing the Curriculum

Art

Bring to class art reproductions (such as Goya's *The Third of May, 1808,* Delacroix's *The Massacre at Chios,* or Diego Rivera's *The Exploiters*) and discuss with students how the paintings convey information about events, thoughts, and feelings. Ask students to write about the paintings as though they were one of the artists telling about the experience that led to the creation of the artwork.

History

Much written history consists of personal narratives of battles, political campaigns, and other events. Students are probably familiar with the first-person narratives found in the diaries of Anne Frank and Zlata Filipovic of Sarajevo. These writings may have effectively influenced the students' views of history by making the events more personal. Ask students to find a newspaper or magazine article that reports factual information about an important event. Then, ask them to rewrite the article as though they were participants in the event, turning it into a personal narrative.

in a city of 300,000 to sink this project.

So how can community bicycle programs work? Some smaller towns, like Telluride, Colorado, have had success, but in larger cities the answer has often been no. In Portland, Oregon, and Boulder, Colorado, many community bikes have done a vanishing act, sometimes within weeks of their introduction. As a Portland police officer said, "It didn't take people long to figure out that a free bike is a free bike."

Perhaps we should adopt a more American version of the community bike program, with controlled sign-out and deposit points. The spirit wouldn't be the same, but maybe we've asked too much of the honor system.

Topic sentence as question.

Factual information.

Quotation.

Call to action.

—Owen Robinson
Corcoran High School
Syracuse, New York

Evaluating and Revising

1. Self-Evaluation

In a personal narrative, it's easy to fall into the trap of beginning too many sentences with *I*. ("I did this" and "I did that" and "I think" . . .) If you find more than two sentences in a row that begin with that pushy little word, rewrite at least one of the sentences. While you're revising, check to see that you've varied the length, beginnings, and structure of the sentences. Try reading your essay aloud, listening for awkward repetitions and sentences that sound like a thrumming, choppy march.

2. Peer Evaluation

Don't just give criticism: Point out passages that work for you, and tell why they impressed you. Is the essay clear? You should not have to question what issue is being discussed, what the writer thinks, and how the personal narrative relates to that issue. Is the narrative part of the essay deadly dull (so dull that it makes you wonder, "Who cares?"), or is it intriguing?

GRAMMAR INVADERS

"It's a new concept in teaching machines. You get 50 points for every grammatical error you blast away!"

GLASBERGEN   © Randy Glasbergen

■ *Evaluation Criteria*

A good persuasive personal narrative

1. *clearly states the writer's opinion on an issue*

2. *gives the readers background information, if needed*

3. *relates a personal narrative (a series of related events) that supports the writer's opinion*

4. *elaborates the personal narrative with specific sensory language*

5. *ends with a call to action or a restatement of the writer's views*

Evaluating and Revising

Have students use the Evaluation Criteria provided here to review their drafts and determine needed revisions.

To help students check for descriptive details and a clear narrative, have them highlight in different colors words that indicate sensory details and words that show the chronological sequence of events.

Then, have students consider whether or not there are sufficient highlighted words to accomplish the writer's purpose.

Students should also evaluate the sentence structure in their narratives. If they find their sentence patterns repetitive and need help in adding variety, refer them to the Sentence Workshop on p. 91. This workshop contains modeling strategies and examples for varying sentence structure.

Getting Students Involved

Cooperative Learning

Have students create **detail charts.** Working in small groups, students create charts of details they might include in their personal narratives. Other students provide spontaneous questions and feedback after reviewing the chart.

Who or What?	Details
Events	
People	
Places	
Thoughts and Feelings	

Proofreading

Have students proofread their own paper first and then exchange it with another student. For this assignment, remind students to be particularly careful of spelling errors. If time permits, the final copy should be put aside for at least a day before it is proofread for the final time by the author.

Remind students that proofreading to eliminate errors will help their readers take their ideas more seriously.

Publishing

Have students review the possibilities described on p. 90 and select an appropriate forum for their work.

Reflecting

Encourage students to reflect on how they felt about the process of composing a persuasive essay. Have students answer these questions and include their answers in their portfolios, attached to their narratives:

1. I had the most trouble
   _____.

2. The easiest part of the writing was
   _____.

3. I'm adding this to my portfolio because
   _____.

4. The next time I write a persuasive essay with a personal narrative I will
   _____.

Resources ───────

Peer Editing Forms and Rubrics
Portfolio Management System, p. 98

Revision Transparencies
Workshop Resources, p. 1

Grading Timesaver

Rubrics for this Writer's Workshop assignment appear on p. 99 of the *Portfolio Management System*.

Sentence Workshop
H E L P

Sentence modeling: page 91.

Proofreading Tips

- If a word looks funny to you or you're not sure how to spell it, check the spelling in a dictionary (or with a spelling checker if you're using a computer).

- Keep a **proofreading log** (a special notebook or section of a notebook) in which you record all the grammar, usage, and spelling mistakes you've made. Review your log right before you start revising.

Communications Handbook
H E L P

See Proofreaders' Marks.

Revision Model

	Peer Comments
I created a "community bicycle"	
~~inspired~~ program in our city, ~~I got the idea~~	Too many sentences start with I.
by ~~reading~~ newspaper reports about	
~~such~~ ~~community bicycle~~ projects ~~in other~~	Can you avoid repetition?
elsewhere. Attaining the ~~countries and in other cities. I hope~~	
rank, the highest in Boy Scouting, requires ~~to become an~~ Eagle Scout. ~~I need to do~~	What's an Eagle Scout?
a public service project, and ~~I sure hoped I~~	Tighten wording and combine sentences?
could create something ~~successful~~ that	
have long-term success. would ~~last a long time.~~	

Publishing Tips

Share your essay with an audience; don't keep it to yourself.

- Send it as a letter to the editor of your school or local newspaper.

- Some local TV and radio stations give audiences a chance to air their views on important issues. Find out where and to whom you can send your essay.

- Post it on a Web site that publishes students' writing. Ask your librarian to help you find the relevant World Wide Web addresses.

- Convert your essay to a brief persuasive speech (or read it aloud). Ask for permission to present the speech to an appropriate body—perhaps the student council, school board, city government, or a local civic organization.

Sentence Workshop

OBJECTIVES
1. Recognize basic sentence structure as subject, verb, and complement
2. Use sentence models in order to learn sentence structure
3. Improve basic structures through elaboration

SENTENCE MODELING: BUILDING FROM THE BASICS

The best way to learn to write well is to read widely. In this lesson, see how much you can learn about sentence building by modeling some sentences after the sentences of famous writers.

Although the sentences below sound varied, they all have the same basic structure: subject, verb, and complement. The writers have elaborated on these basic sentences with additional chunks of meaning. The basic sentence parts are underlined. Other chunks of meaning are set off by slashes.

1. "Back in the pilot's chair / <u>he pressed the signal button</u> / of the normal-space transmitter."

   —Tom Godwin, "The Cold Equations" (page 27)

2. "<u>She held the quilts securely</u> / in her arms, / stroking them."

   —Alice Walker, "Everyday Use" (page 75)

Here are sentences modeled after those above:

1. From the glider plane / <u>I saw a patchwork quilt</u> / of autumn colors.

2. <u>He took the rudder quickly</u> / with one turn, / regaining course.

Writer's Workshop Follow-up: Revision

The shaping and reshaping of sentences is done largely during revision. Look back at the essay you wrote for the Writer's Workshop (page 85). Have you built up your basic sentences in a variety of ways? Can you improve any of your sentences by elaborating on your basic structure the way the professionals do? Always read your work aloud (or try to hear it in your mind) to see if your sentences sound right.

Language Handbook HELP

See Sentence Structure, page 1038.

Try It Out

Underline the basic sentence in each of the following professional models, and set off the added chunks of meaning with slash marks.

1. "The boys slid their feet along slowly, trying not to break the ice that covered the snow."

   —Jim Heynen, "What Happened During the Ice Storm" (page 5)

2. "Instead of shutting the gate, I opened it as wide as I could."

   —Alice Munro, "Boys and Girls" (page 62)

3. "In real life I am a large, big-boned woman with rough, man-working hands."

   —Alice Walker, "Everyday Use" (page 71)

Now write three sentences of your own on any subject, imitating the pattern of elaboration in each of the preceding models. Exchange your work for a partner's, and use underscoring and slash marks to see if the sentences follow the models.

Resources

Workshop Resources
Worksheet, p. 55

Try It Out
Possible Answers
1. "<u>The boys slid their feet</u>/along slowly,/trying not to break the ice/that covered the snow."
2. "Instead of shutting the gate,/<u>I opened it</u>/as wide as I could."
3. "In real life/<u>I am a large, big-boned woman</u>/with rough, man-working hands."
4. <u>The graduates threw their caps</u>/up joyously,/helping to lighten the seriousness/that marked the occasion.
5. Rather than keeping the money,/<u>he spent it</u>/as quickly as he could.
6. On TV/<u>she plays a brilliant, hard-working doctor</u>/with a tough, no-nonsense attitude.

Assessing Learning

Quick Check: Basic Sentences

For the following sentences, underline the sentence division containing the basic sentence.
1. Along the way,/we heard stories/about the old days.
2. Since we had warned her/of the possible risks,/we felt little sympathy.
3. The smallest children edged closer/to have a good look/at the litter of kittens.
4. Though they could not identify the driver,/the witnesses were sure/of the make/of the car.
5. Rain still fell/in the valley/after the sun had come out/in the highlands.

Standardized Test Preparation

For practice with standardized test prompts and formats, see
• *Standardized Test Preparation*, pp. 124, 132

OBJECTIVES
1. Develop strategies for reading scientific articles
2. Recognize the main idea of an article
3. Paraphrase and summarize the information from an article
4. Evaluate a writer's credibility and the reliability of his or her information

Teaching the Lesson

Explain that by applying specific strategies, students can evaluate information in a scientific article and understand difficult terms and concepts in the article.

Using the Strategies

Possible Answers

1. An author is not cited for this article. The article comes from an encyclopedia on a CD-ROM. The information is copyrighted 1993–1996.

2. Humans would be unable to breathe in space because outer space contains neither air nor oxygen.

3. The term might mean that air is withdrawn from something so quickly that the object explodes. You could check the meaning in the glossary of a book about space, in a dictionary, or in an encyclopedia.

4. Summary: The article describes several reasons why humans would be unable to survive in outer space without protection, including lack of air and oxygen, extreme temperatures, and radiation. The article also explains that spacecraft must be designed to withstand some of the same harmful elements that can affect humans.

5. Possible questions: What advances have been made in protecting humans from the harmful conditions of space since this article was published? How is ozone depletion affecting Earth?

6. The information is reliable because the copyright holder probably had the article written by an expert and checked against other sources.

Reading for Life

Reading a Science Article

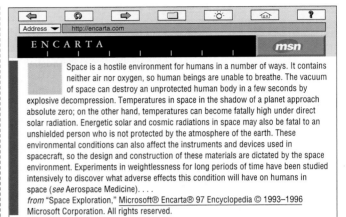

Situation

After reading "The Cold Equations," you want to research problems of space travel. Here are strategies to follow when you read scientific articles.

Strategies

Note the article's source.
- Does the author seem to be qualified in the field?
- Is the article dated or current?

Skim the entire article to get an overview.
- Read **headings** and notice words in **boldface** or *italic* type. Read the first sentence of each paragraph, which may give you the main ideas.

Read the article carefully.
- With a difficult text, read slowly; stop to **summarize** or **paraphrase** information.
- When you don't understand something, make a note of it in the form of a question. Then **reread** the sentence or paragraph. Your comprehension improves the more you reread.
- If you don't understand a sentence, break it down into its core parts—**subject** and **verb.**
- Look for **context clues** that can help you understand unfamiliar words.

Space is a hostile environment for humans in a number of ways. It contains neither air nor oxygen, so human beings are unable to breathe. The vacuum of space can destroy an unprotected human body in a few seconds by explosive decompression. Temperatures in space in the shadow of a planet approach absolute zero; on the other hand, temperatures can become fatally high under direct solar radiation. Energetic solar and cosmic radiations in space may also be fatal to an unshielded person who is not protected by the atmosphere of the earth. These environmental conditions can also affect the instruments and devices used in spacecraft, so the design and construction of these materials are dictated by the space environment. Experiments in weightlessness for long periods of time have been studied intensively to discover what adverse effects this condition will have on humans in space (*see* Aerospace Medicine). . . .

from "Space Exploration," Microsoft® Encarta® 97 Encyclopedia © 1993–1996 Microsoft Corporation. All rights reserved.

- Use a **dictionary** or **glossary** to look up words that remain unclear to you.
- Create a **graphic organizer,** such as an outline, word map, or chart, to help you understand the article.

Review the article.
- After carefully reading the article once, review its key points, using your notes and graphic organizer.
- Ask yourself: What is the main idea in this article?

Using the Strategies

1. Is an author cited for the above article? Where did the article come from? What is its date?

2. According to this paragraph, why would humans be unable to breathe in space?

3. What do you think the phrase "explosive decompression" means? How could you check the meaning?

4. Summarize, paraphrase, or outline this paragraph.

5. List any questions you have after reading the paragraph.

6. Do you think this information is reliable? Why or why not?

Extending the Strategies

Which of these strategies would be most useful and most important in reading science textbooks?

Reaching All Students

Struggling Readers

You may wish to prepare graphic organizers in advance for readers you anticipate will have difficulty in creating appropriate forms to use with this strategy.

Advanced Readers

Have students find two or more articles on the same aspect of space exploration. Ask students to compare the articles, indicating similarities and differences between the writers' qualifications, which articles are more current, whether or not the authors assume the same audience, and which author's information seems more reliable and why.

Collection 2

Hearts That Love

Theme

Love's Many Forms *The power of love is a theme that has persisted through all of literature, from the earliest epics to the newest short stories and novels. As the stories in this collection show, love can be the cause of conflict, and it can be the power that resolves our problems. Don't expect only romantic love here: These stories deal also with parental love, friendship, and kindness.*

Reading the Anthology

Reaching Struggling Readers

The *Reading Skills and Strategies: Reaching Struggling Readers* binder provides materials coordinated with the Pupil's Edition (see the Collection Planner, p. T92B) to help students who have difficulty reading and comprehending text, or students who are reluctant readers. The binder for tenth grade is organized around sixteen individual skill areas and offers the following options:

- **MiniRead** MiniReads are short, easy texts that give students a chance to practice a particular skill and strategy before reading selections in the Pupil's Edition. Each MiniRead Skill Lesson can be taught independently or used in conjunction with a Selection Skill Lesson.

- **Selection Skill Lessons** Selection Skill Lessons allow students to apply skills introduced in the MiniReads. Each Selection Skill Lesson provides reading instruction and practice specific to a particular piece of literature in the Pupil's Edition.

Reading Beyond the Anthology

Read On Collection 2 includes an annotated bibliography of books suitable for extended reading. The suggested books are related to works in this collection by theme, by author, or by subject. To preview the Read On for Collection 2, please turn to p. T163.

HRW Library The *HRW Library* offers novels, plays, and short-story collections for extended reading. Each book in the Library includes one or more major works and thematically related Connections. Each book in the *HRW Library* is also accompanied by a Study Guide that provides teaching suggestions and worksheets. For Collection 2, the following titles are recommended.

WUTHERING HEIGHTS
Emily Brontë
One of the great love stories of all time, this novel shows how the passion of Heathcliff destroys his beloved Catherine.

GREAT EXPECTATIONS
Charles Dickens
Pip, whose expectations form the narrative of this wonderful novel, loves his haughty Estella through years of misfortune and disappointment.

Collection 2 Hearts That Love

Resources for this Collection

Note: All resources for this collection are available for preview on the *One-Stop Planner CD-ROM 1 with Test Generator.* All worksheets and blackline masters may be printed from the CD-ROM.

Selection or Feature	Reading and Literary Skills	Vocabulary, Language, and Grammar

Two Kinds (p. 94)
Amy Tan
 	
Connections: Melting Pot Still Bubbles at IS 237 (p. 105)
Charisse Jones
	• *Reading Skills and Strategies: Reaching Struggling Readers*
	  • MiniRead Skill Lesson, p. 55
	  • Selection Skill Lesson, p. 62
	• *Graphic Organizers for Active Reading*, Worksheet p. 6
	• *Literary Elements:* Transparency 4
	Worksheet p. 13
		• *Words to Own*, Worksheet p. 7
		• *Grammar and Language Links:*
		Dialogue, Worksheet p. 11
		• *Language Workshop CD-ROM,* Dialogue
		• *Daily Oral Grammar,*
		Transparency 6

Elements of Literature: **Character** (p. 110)	• *Literary Elements,* Transparency 4	
Geraldo No Last Name (p. 112) Sandra Cisneros **Connections: Hello Papa, . . .** (p. 116) Patricia Zarate	• *Graphic Organizers for Active Reading*, Worksheet p. 7 • *Literary Elements:* Transparency 5 Worksheet p. 16	• *Daily Oral Grammar,* Transparency 7
The First Seven Years (p. 119) Bernard Malamud **Connections: Jacob and Rachel** (p. 128) *from* New English Bible	• *Graphic Organizers for Active Reading*, Worksheet p. 8	• *Words to Own*, Worksheet p. 8 • *Grammar and Language Links:* Dialect, Worksheet p. 13 • *Daily Oral Grammar,* Transparency 8

Distillation (p. 132)
Hugo Martinez-Serros
 	
Connections: Powder (p. 141)
Tobias Wolff
	• *Reading Skills and Strategies: Reaching Struggling Readers*
	  • MiniRead Skill Lesson, p. 66
	  • Selection Skill Lesson, p. 73
	• *Graphic Organizers for Active Reading*, Worksheet p. 9
		• *Words to Own*, Worksheet p. 9
		• *Grammar and Language Links:*
		Verbs, Worksheet p. 15
		• *Language Workshop CD-ROM,*
		Verbs and Adverbs
		• *Daily Oral Grammar,*
		Transparency 9

Life Is Sweet at Kumansenu (p. 146) Abioseh Nicol	• *Graphic Organizers for Active Reading*, Worksheet p. 10	• *Words to Own*, Worksheet p. 10 • *Grammar and Language Links:* Adverbs, Worksheet p. 17 • *Language Workshop CD-ROM,* Verbs and Adverbs • *Daily Oral Grammar,* Transparency 10
Extending the Theme: Lessons of **Love** *from* **Silent Dancing** (p. 157) Judith Ortiz Cofer	The Extending the Theme feature provides students with an unstructured opportunity to practice reading strategies using a selection that extends the theme of the collection.	
Writer's Workshop: Analyzing a **Character** (p. 164)		
Sentence Workshop: **Using Adjectives and** **Adverbs** (p. 169)		• *Workshop Resources*, p. 57 • *Language Workshop CD-ROM,* Expanding Sentences

Other Resources for this Collection

- *Cross-Curricular Activities,* p. 2
- *Portfolio Management System,* Introduction to Portfolio Assessment, p. 1
- *Test Generator,* Collection Test 💿

Writing	Listening and Speaking Viewing and Representing	Assessment
• *Portfolio Management System,* Rubrics for Choices, p. 100	• *Visual Connections:* Videocassette A, Segment 2 📼 • *Audio CD Library,* Disc 4, Track 2 🎧 • *Portfolio Management System,* Rubrics for Choices, p. 100	• *Formal Assessment,* Selection Test, p. 15 • *Standardized Test Preparation,* p. 18 • *Test Generator (One-Stop Planner CD-ROM)* 💿
		• *Formal Assessment,* Literary Elements Test, p. 24
• *Portfolio Management System,* Rubrics for Choices, p. 101	• *Portfolio Management System,* Rubrics for Choices, p. 101	• *Formal Assessment,* Selection Test, p. 17 • *Standardized Test Preparation,* p. 20 • *Test Generator (One-Stop Planner CD-ROM)* 💿
• *Portfolio Management System,* Rubrics for Choices, p. 103	• *Audio CD Library,* Disc 4, Track 3 🎧 • *Viewing and Representing:* Fine Art Transparency 3 Worksheet p. 12 • *Portfolio Management System,* Rubrics for Choices, p. 103	• *Formal Assessment,* Selection Test, p. 18 • *Test Generator (One-Stop Planner CD-ROM)* 💿
• *Portfolio Management System,* Rubrics for Choices, p. 104	• *Audio CD Library,* Disc 5, Track 2 🎧 • *Portfolio Management System,* Rubrics for Choices, p. 104	• *Formal Assessment,* Selection Test, p. 20 • *Test Generator (One-Stop Planner CD-ROM)* 💿
• *Portfolio Management System,* Rubrics for Choices, p. 105	• *Audio CD Library,* Disc 5, Track 3 🎧 • *Viewing and Representing:* Fine Art Transparency 4 Worksheet p. 16 • *Portfolio Management System,* Rubrics for Choices, p. 105	• *Formal Assessment,* Selection Test, p. 22 • *Standardized Test Preparation,* pp. 22, 24 • *Test Generator (One-Stop Planner CD-ROM)* 💿
	• *Audio CD Library,* Disc 5, Track 4 🎧	

• *Workshop Resources,* p. 7	• *Viewing and Representing,* HRW Multimedia Presentation Maker	• *Portfolio Management System*
		  • Prewriting, p. 106
		  • Peer Editing, p. 107
		  • Assessment Rubric, p. 108

 **Transparency**   **CD-ROM**   **Video**   **Audio CD**

Collection Planner

Selection or Feature	Reading Skills and Strategies	Elements of Literature	Vocabulary/Language/Grammar	Writing	Listening/Speaking	Viewing/Representing
Two Kinds (p. 94) Amy Tan	Make Inferences, pp. 94, 107	Motivation, pp. 94, 107 Character, p. 107 Resolution, p. 107 Conflict, p. 107 Title, p. 107	Dialogue, p. 109 Context Clues, p. 109	Determine a Character's Motivation, p. 108 Describe a Character, p. 108	Role-Play a Conversation, p. 108 Write a Letter to the Editor, p. 108 Read a Scene Aloud, p. 109	
Elements of Literature: Character (p. 110)		Character, p. 110 • Direct and Indirect Characterization • Round vs. Flat • Stock • Motivation				
Geraldo No Last Name (p. 112) Sandra Cisneros	Monitor Your Reading with Questions, pp. 112, 117 Retell a Story, p. 117 Make Inferences, p. 117	Style, pp. 112, 118 Character, p. 117 Direct and Indirect Characterization, p. 118		Write a Poem, p. 118	Present an Oral Interpretation, p. 118	Use a Cluster Diagram, p. 118 Create a Collage, p. 118 Create a Database, p. 118
The First Seven Years (p. 119) Bernard Malamud	Compare and Contrast, pp. 119, 129 Use a Story Map, p. 129	Protagonist, pp. 119, 129 Antagonist, pp. 119, 129 Foreshadow, p. 129 Character, p. 129 Point of View, p. 130	Dialect, p. 131 Syntax, p. 131 Word Charts, p. 131 Dictionary, p. 131 Root Words, p. 131	Identify Change in a Character, p. 130 Rewrite a Key Event from Another Character's Point of View, p. 130 Predict Events, p. 130	Research and Present an Informal Speech on Immigrant Life, p. 130	
Distillation (p. 132) Hugo Martinez-Serros	Establish a Purpose for Reading, pp. 132, 143 • Enjoy • Discover • Interpret	Dynamic and Static Characters, pp. 132, 143 Protagonist, p. 143 Sensory Details, p. 143 Title, p. 143 Conflict, p. 143	Vivid Verbs, p. 145 Identify Meanings, p. 145	Identify Character Traits, p. 144 Write a Story, p. 144 Write a Reflective Essay, p. 144	Prepare and Present a Speech Analyzing Quest Elements in the Story, p. 144	Create a Map Based on Story Details, p. 144 Prepare Visuals for a Speech, p. 144
Life Is Sweet at Kumansenu (p. 146) Abioseh Nicol	Compare Cultures, pp. 146, 154	Foreshadow, pp. 146, 154 Message, p. 154 Character, p. 155 • Credible • Round/Flat • Stereotype/Stock • Dynamic/Static	Adverbs, p. 156 Semantic Mapping, p. 156	Evaluate a Character, p. 155 Make Notes on a Culture, p. 155	Prepare and Present an Informal Speech, p. 155	Create a Diorama, p. 155
Extending the Theme: Lessons of Love from **Silent Dancing** (p. 158) Judith Ortiz Cofer	Dialogue with the Text, p. 158 Keep a Double-Entry Journal, pp. 158, 162 Summarize a Story, p. 162	Title, p. 162	The Extending the Theme feature provides students with an unstructured opportunity to practice reading skills using a selection that extends the theme of the collection.			
Writer's Workshop: Analyzing a Character (p. 164)		Methods of Characterization, p. 165		Write an Essay Analyzing a Fictional Character, pp. 164–168		
Sentence Workshop: Using Adjectives and Adverbs (p. 169)			Adjectives and Adverbs, p. 169	Expanding Sentences Using Modifiers, p. 169		
Reading for Life: Reading a Map (p. 170)	Types of Maps, p. 170 Map Features, p. 170					Interpreting a Map, p. 170

Skills Focus

HEARTS THAT LOVE

Collection 2

WRITING FOCUS: Analyzing a Character

L ove—we think about it, sing about it, dream about it, lose sleep worrying about it. When we don't have it, we search for it; when we discover it, we don't know what to do with it; when we have it, we fear losing it. It's a constant source of pleasure and pain, but we can't predict from one minute to the next which it's going to be today. It takes on many shapes and many disguises: We love our parents, our brothers and sisters, our boyfriends and girlfriends, our cats and dogs, our comfortable shoes, and our baseball gloves. Love—it's a short word, easy to spell, difficult to define, impossible to live without.

Where there is great love, there are always miracles.
—*Willa Cather*

Writer's Notebook

In the stories, novels, and plays that you've read over the past few years, which characters do you remember best? Were they involved in a search for love, or did they struggle to find something else? List the names of the fictional characters who stick in your memory—because you either liked them or thought them horrible. Save your notes. You may want to write about one of these characters in the Writer's Workshop on page 164.

La Verbena (1992) by Nick Quijano (1953–   ). Gouache on paper (30″ × 22″).

Collection of Dorothy and Phillip Zaro, New York.

Writing Focus: Analyzing a Character

The following **Work in Progress** assignments build to a culminating **Writer's Workshop** at the end of the collection.

• Two Kinds	Analyzing motives (p. 108)
• Geraldo No Last Name	Finding character clues (p. 118)
• The First Seven Years	Analyzing a character's changes (p. 130)
• Distillation	Analyzing character traits (p. 144)
• Life Is Sweet at Kumansenu	Evaluating a character (p. 155)

Writer's Workshop: Expository Writing / Analyzing a Character (p. 164)

OBJECTIVES

1. Read short stories on the theme "Hearts That Love"
2. Interpret literary elements with special emphasis on character
3. Apply a variety of reading strategies
4. Respond to the literature in a variety of modes
5. Learn and use new words
6. Plan, draft, revise, proof, and publish an expository essay analyzing a character
7. Demonstrate the ability to read a map

Responding to the Quotation

❓ In the quotation, what do you think Willa Cather means by "miracles"? [Possible responses: acts that seem beyond human strength; extraordinary, wondrous, or mysterious events.]

RESPONDING TO THE ART

Nick Quijano (1953–   ) evokes young love in *La Verbena.* His medium is *gouache,* opaque water colors. Other paintings by Quijano appear on pp. 114 and 117. **Activity.** The Spanish title means "The County Fair" or "The Night Festival." Ask students to list details that support the title, and to discuss the mood evoked by the background details. [Possible responses: Details include a Ferris wheel, a roller coaster, a merry-go-round, and other rides; the mood is festive, celebratory, exciting.]

Writer's Notebook

Encourage students to include characters from stories in Collection 1 as well as characters from works they have previously read, such as Scout in *To Kill a Mockingbird,* or the title characters from *Romeo and Juliet.* Have students add a brief note after each name, giving the reason they remember the character—for example, "a real villain" or "I identified with her."

OBJECTIVES
1. Read and interpret the story
2. Interpret motivation
3. Make inferences about character
4. Express understanding through writing and role playing
5. Identify dialogue and read aloud a scene from the story
6. Understand and use new words

SKILLS

Literary
- Interpret motivation

Reading
- Make inferences about character

Writing
- Make notes on the motivation of a character
- Write a character sketch
- Write a letter supporting an opinion

Speaking/Listening
- Role-play a conversation between characters

Grammar/Language
- Identify dialogue and read aloud a scene from the story

Vocabulary
- Understand and use new words

Viewing/Representing
- Respond to fine art (ATE)

Planning

- **Block Schedule**
  Block Scheduling Lesson Plans with Pacing Guide
- **Traditional Schedule**
  Lesson Plans Including Strategies for English-Language Learners
- **One-Stop Planner**
  CD-ROM with Test Generator

Before You Read

TWO KINDS

Make the Connection

Sometimes It Hurts to Love

Have you ever wondered why our biggest conflicts are often with the people we love the most? In this story about a Chinese immigrant mother and her American-born daughter, conflicts arise from differences in culture. They also arise from a more common source—the differing views of parent and child on how the child should live her life and what her goals should be.

Quickwrite

Write two or three sentences describing what you'd like to be doing in ten years and what you think other people would want you to be doing. You needn't show your writing to anyone.

Elements of Literature

Motivation

When actors get parts in a play, they ask themselves and the director, "Why do I do this?" and "Why do I say this?" What they're asking about is **motivation,** or the reasons for their character's behavior. Understanding motivation is important for anyone—actor or writer—who wants to create a convincing character.

> **M**otivation is a person's reasons for doing something or for feeling a certain way.
>
> *For more on Motivation, see page 111.*

Reading Skills and Strategies

Making Inferences About Character

To understand a character's motivation, you must make **inferences,** or intelligent guesses. You base your inferences on clues from the text— you think about the character's actions and words and you observe how others react to the character. Using these clues—and your own life experiences with people— think about what motivates both Jing-mei and her mother in this story.

HRW go.hrw.com
LEO 10-2

Shadows at 687 (1988) by Flo Oy Wong (1938–   ). Graphite drawing on paper (20¼″ × 17½″).

Courtesy of Allison Kale Chop.

Preteaching Vocabulary

Words to Own

Have students work in pairs to locate, pronounce, discuss, and use in original sentences the ten Words to Own that appear at the bottom of the selection pages. Then, have partners match each word with the best synonym in the lettered column. Students should consult a dictionary as necessary and discuss reasons for their choices. Finally, compare answers in a class discussion. Review the meanings of words still causing confusion, and call for examples of their use in sentences.

[i] betrayal	a. child genius
[f] dawdled	b. without energy
[d] discordant	c. fascinating
[h] fiasco	d. clashing
[e] lamented	e. mourned
[b] listlessly	f. wasted time
[c] mesmerizing	g. afflicted
[j] nonchalantly	h. complete failure
[a] prodigy	i. treachery
[g] stricken	j. casually

Two Kinds

Amy Tan

My mother believed you could be anything you wanted to be in America. You could open a restaurant. You could work for the government and get good retirement. You could buy a house with almost no money down. You could become rich. You could become instantly famous.

"Of course you can be <u>prodigy</u>, too," my mother told me when I was nine. "You can be best anything. What does Auntie Lindo know? Her daughter, she is only best tricky."

America was where all my mother's hopes lay. She had come here in 1949 after losing everything in China: her mother and father, her family home, her first husband, and two daughters, twin baby girls. But she never looked back with regret. There were so many ways for things to get better.

A

We didn't immediately pick the right kind of prodigy. At first my mother thought I could be a Chinese Shirley Temple.[1] We'd watch Shirley's old movies on TV as though they were training films. My mother would poke my arm and say, "Ni kan"—You watch. And I would see Shirley tapping her

---

1. **Shirley Temple** (1928–): child movie star who was popular during the 1930s. Mothers all across the United States tried to set their daughters' hair to look like Shirley Temple's sausage curls.

WORDS TO OWN

prodigy (präd′ə·jē) *n.:* child of highly unusual talent or genius.

TWO KINDS **95**

Summary ■ ■

In "Two Kinds," Jing-mei, the American-born daughter of Chinese immigrants, tells how her mother relentlessly drove her to become a prodigy. At first motivated to win her parents' approval, Jing-mei becomes angry and demoralized after failing at several "talents." Unconvinced, her mother settles on piano lessons, but Jing-mei doesn't apply herself and disgraces herself and her family at a talent show. In the story's climax, her mother demands further practice, but Jing-mei angrily rebels. As Jing-mei grows older, she clings to the right to fail. But now, at age thirty, she gratefully accepts the family piano as a peace offering from her mother.

Resources

Viewing and Representing
Videocassette A, Segment 2
The *Visual Connections* segment "Chinese Americans: Culture and Contributions" provides helpful background for "Two Kinds."

Listening
Audio CD Library
An engaging recording of "Two Kinds" is provided in the *Audio CD Library*:
- Disc 4, Track 2

Elements of Literature
Character: The Actors in a Story
For additional instruction on character, see *Literary Elements*:
- Transparency 4
- Worksheet, p. 13

A **Historical Connections**

After a long and bloody civil war, the Communists, led by Mao Tse-tung, defeated the Nationalists in 1949 and established the People's Republic of China.

Resources: Print and Media

Reading
- *Reading Skills and Strategies*
   MiniRead Skill Lesson, p. 55
   Selection Skill Lesson, p. 62
- *Graphic Organizers for Active Reading*, p. 6
- *Words to Own*, p. 7
- *Audio CD Library*
   Disc 4, Track 2

Elements of Literature
- *Literary Elements*
   Transparency 4
   Worksheet, p. 13

Writing and Language
- *Daily Oral Grammar*
   Transparency 6
- *Grammar and Language Links*
   Worksheet, p. 11
- *Language Workshop CD-ROM*

Viewing and Representing
- *Visual Connections*
   Videocassette A, Segment 2

Assessment
- *Formal Assessment*, p. 15
- *Portfolio Management System*, p. 100
- *Standardized Test Preparation*, p. 18
- *Test Generator (One-Stop Planner CD-ROM)*

Internet
- go.hrw.com (keyword: LE0 10-2)

Appreciating Language
Dialect

Point out to students that the mother came from China as an adult and speaks English as a second language. Tan represents the mother's dialect of English by leaving out certain words—such as the subject *You* in her final sentence here, and the articles *a* and *the* in the second paragraph on p. 95.

B **Cultural Connections**

Note that Peter Pan is the title character of a popular (1904) play by James M. Barrie. A Peter Pan haircut seems appropriate for a girl because the role of Peter, "the boy who wouldn't grow up," is traditionally played by a young woman.

C **Elements of Literature**
Allusion

❓ What do these allusions reveal about the daughter's initial expectations? [Possible responses: She feels special, even exalted, as she pictures how wonderful she might become; she expects great fame and wondrous achievements.]

D **Elements of Literature**
Motivation

❓ What motivates Jing-mei to try to become the prodigy her mother wants? [Possible responses: The desire for her parents' unconditional love and approval; fear of being reproached for being ordinary.]

E **Reading Skills and Strategies**

Making Inferences about Character

❓ What does this passage tell you about the character of the mother? What details support your interpretation? [Possible responses: She is energetic and hardworking, as shown by her cleaning houses and still spending time with her daughter; she is inventive and creative, as shown by the tests she devises; she seems to want to be very American, as shown by the piles of magazines.]

---

feet, or singing a sailor song, or pursing her lips into a very round O while saying, "Oh my goodness."

A "Ni kan," said my mother as Shirley's eyes flooded with tears. "You already know how. Don't need talent for crying!"

Soon after my mother got this idea about Shirley Temple, she took me to a beauty training school in the Mission district and put me in the hands of a student who could barely hold the scissors without shaking. Instead of getting big fat curls, I emerged with an uneven mass of crinkly black fuzz. My mother dragged me off to the bathroom and tried to wet down my hair.

B "You look like Negro Chinese," she lamented, as if I had done this on purpose.

The instructor of the beauty training school had to lop off these soggy clumps to make my hair even again. "Peter Pan is very popular these days," the instructor assured my mother. I now had hair the length of a boy's, with straight-across bangs that hung at a slant two inches above my eyebrows. I liked the haircut and it made me actually look forward to my future fame.

In fact, in the beginning, I was just as excited as my mother, maybe even more so. I pictured this prodigy part of me as many different images, trying each one on for size. I was a dainty ballerina girl standing by the curtains, waiting to hear the right music that would send me floating on my tiptoes. I was like the Christ child lifted out of the straw manger, crying with holy in-

C dignity. I was Cinderella stepping from her pumpkin carriage with sparkly cartoon music filling the air.

In all of my imaginings, I was filled with a sense that I would soon become *perfect.*

D My mother and father would adore me. I would be beyond reproach. I would never feel the need to sulk for anything.

But sometimes the prodigy in me became impatient. "If you don't hurry up and get me out of here, I'm disappearing for

---

good," it warned. "And then you'll always be nothing."

E Every night after dinner, my mother and I would sit at the Formica kitchen table. She would present new tests, taking her examples from stories of amazing children she had read in *Ripley's Believe It or Not,* or *Good Housekeeping, Reader's Digest,* and a dozen other magazines she kept in a pile in our bathroom. My mother got these magazines from people whose houses she cleaned. And since she cleaned many houses each week, we had a great assortment. She would look through them all, searching for stories about remarkable children.

The first night she brought out a story about a three-year-old boy who knew the capitals of all the states and even most of the European countries. A teacher was quoted as saying the little boy could also pronounce the names of the foreign cities correctly.

"What's the capital of Finland?" my mother asked me, looking at the magazine story.

All I knew was the capital of California, because Sacramento was the name of the street we lived on in Chinatown. "Nairobi!"[2] I guessed, saying the most foreign word I could think of. She checked to see if that was possibly one way to pronounce "Helsinki" before showing me the answer.

The tests got harder—multiplying numbers in my head, finding the queen of hearts in a deck of cards, trying to stand on my head without using my hands, predicting the daily temperatures in Los Angeles, New York, and London.

One night I had to look at a page from the Bible for three minutes and then report

2. **Nairobi** (nī·rō′bē): capital of Kenya, a nation in Africa.

Reaching All Students

Struggling Readers
Making Inferences was introduced on p. 94. For a lesson directly tied to this story that teaches students to make inferences by using a strategy called It Says . . . I Say, see the *Reading Skills and Strategies* binder:
• MiniRead Skill Lesson, p. 55
• Selection Skill Lesson, p. 62

English Language Learners
Help these students with allusions to aspects of American culture, such as the popularity of Shirley Temple movies. Additionally, you might give English language learners practice by having them convert some of the mother's English dialect to Standard English:
• Of course you can be [a] prodigy, too.
• Who ask[ed] you [to] be [a] genius?
• Our problem worser [is worse] than yours.
• Turn off [the] TV.
• [It's] too late [to] change this.

Advanced Learners
Encourage students to imagine how the attitudes of Jing-mei's mother may influence Jing-mei when she rears her own children. Have them create a chart in which they take notes on the mother's attitudes and speculate on Jing-mei's adult attitudes toward schoolwork, competition in sports, music lessons, and watching television.

everything I could remember. "Now Jehoshaphat had riches and honor in abundance and . . . that's all I remember, Ma," I said.

And after seeing my mother's disappointed face once again, something inside of me began to die. I hated the tests, the raised hopes and failed expectations. Before going to bed that night, I looked in the mirror above the bathroom sink and when I saw only my face staring back—and that it would always be this ordinary face—I began to cry. Such a sad, ugly girl! I made high-pitched noises like a crazed animal, trying to scratch out the face in the mirror.

And then I saw what seemed to be the prodigy side of me—because I had never seen that face before. I looked at my reflection, blinking so I could see more clearly. The girl staring back at me was angry, powerful. This girl and I were the same. I had new thoughts, willful thoughts, or rather thoughts filled with lots of won'ts. I won't let her change me, I promised myself. I won't be what I'm not.

So now, on nights when my mother presented her tests, I performed listlessly, my head propped on one arm. I pretended to be bored. And I was. I got so bored I started counting the bellows of the foghorns out on the bay while my mother drilled me in other areas. The sound was comforting and reminded me of the cow jumping over the moon. And the next day, I played a game with myself, seeing if my mother would give up on me before eight bellows. After a while I usually counted only one, maybe two bellows at most. At last she was beginning to give up hope.

Two or three months had gone by without any mention of my being a prodigy again. And then one day my mother was watching *The Ed Sullivan Show* on TV. The TV was old and the sound kept shorting out. Every time my mother got halfway up from the sofa to adjust the set, the sound would go back on and Ed would be talking. As soon as she sat down, Ed would go silent again. She got up, the TV broke into loud piano music. She sat down. Silence. Up and down, back and forth, quiet and loud. It was like a stiff embraceless dance between her and the TV set. Finally she stood by the set with her hand on the sound dial.

She seemed entranced by the music, a little frenzied piano piece with this <u>mesmerizing</u> quality, sort of quick passages and then teasing, lilting ones before it returned to the quick, playful parts.

"Ni kan," my mother said, calling me over with hurried hand gestures. "Look here."

I could see why my mother was fascinated by the music. It was being pounded out by a little Chinese girl, about nine years old, with a Peter Pan haircut. The girl had the sauciness of a Shirley Temple. She was proudly modest like a proper Chinese child. And she also did this fancy sweep of a curtsy, so that the fluffy skirt of her white dress cascaded slowly to the floor like the petals of a large carnation.

In spite of these warning signs, I wasn't worried. Our family had no piano and we couldn't afford to buy one, let alone reams[3] of sheet music and piano lessons. So I could be generous in my comments when my mother bad-mouthed the little girl on TV.

"Play note right, but doesn't sound good! No singing sound," complained my mother.

3. **reams:** here, great amount. A ream of paper is about five hundred sheets.

WORDS TO OWN

listlessly (list′lis·lē) *adv.*: without energy or interest.

mesmerizing (mez′mər·īz′iŋ) *v.* used as *adj.*: spellbinding; hypnotic; fascinating.

F Reading Skills and Strategies
Making Inferences about Character
❓ What change does this discovery indicate has taken place in the speaker? [Possible responses: She has gone from enjoying her mother's attention to resenting it; she has seen another, darker, more rebellious side of herself.]

G Cultural Connections
Some students may not know about the history of *The Ed Sullivan Show*. This variety show was one of the most popular American television programs of the 1960s. It is credited with first presenting the Beatles in the United States and with giving rock and roll musician Elvis Presley his first wide exposure on national television.

H Elements of Literature
Simile
❓ What mental image does this simile create? [Possible response: The mother extends her arms to her "partner," the television set, as she moves back and forth across the floor.]

I Reading Skills and Strategies
Making Predictions
❓ What do you predict will happen after the mother has seen this particular child perform on *The Ed Sullivan Show?* [Possible responses: The mother will have her daughter take piano lessons; the daughter may learn the piano but have no particular talent for it.]

Crossing the Curriculum

World History
Ask students to work in groups to research the conflict and events that preceded the establishment of the People's Republic of China in 1949. Ask them to note how these events may have motivated Jing-mei's mother to emigrate to the United States. Groups might present their findings through oral reports or visual displays.

Geography
The story includes several references to its San Francisco setting, such as Sacramento Street in Chinatown (p. 96) and "foghorns out on the bay" (p. 97). Have students obtain a San Francisco city map or guidebook and locate all places referred to in the story. They might also identify and discuss the city's distinctive geographical features—its hills, its location in relation to the Pacific Ocean, San Francisco Bay, and the Golden Gate and other bridges.

Music
Ask interested students to select piano passages representative of the composers Grieg, Beethoven, and Schumann. Then have them compile a short audiotape, play it for the class, and explain the challenges faced by a beginning pianist in learning such works. Other students might research and report to the class on Beethoven's life and the effect of his deafness (mentioned on p. 98) on his career.

"What are you picking on her for?" I said carelessly. "She's pretty good. Maybe she's not the best, but she's trying hard." I knew almost immediately I would be sorry I said that.

"Just like you," she said. "Not the best. Because you not trying." She gave a little huff as she let go of the sound dial and sat down on the sofa.

The little Chinese girl sat down also to play an encore of "Anitra's Dance" by Grieg.[4] I remember the song, because later on I had to learn how to play it.

Three days after watching *The Ed Sullivan Show,* my mother told me what my schedule would be for piano lessons and piano practice. She had talked to Mr. Chong, who lived on the first floor of our apartment building. Mr. Chong was a retired piano teacher, and my mother had traded housecleaning services for weekly lessons and a piano for me to practice on every day, two hours a day, from four until six.

When my mother told me this, I felt as though I had been sent to hell. I whined and then kicked my foot a little when I couldn't stand it anymore.

"Why don't you like me the way I am? I'm *not* a genius! I can't play the piano. And even if I could, I wouldn't go on TV if you paid me a million dollars!" I cried.

My mother slapped me. "Who ask you be genius?" she shouted. "Only ask you be your best. For you sake. You think I want you be genius? Hnnh! What for! Who ask you!"

"So ungrateful," I heard her mutter in Chinese. "If she had as much talent as she has temper, she would be famous now."

Mr. Chong, whom I secretly nicknamed

---

4. **Grieg** (grēg): Edvard Grieg (1843–1907), Norwegian composer; "Anitra's Dance" is from his *Peer Gynt Suite.*

Old Chong, was very strange, always tapping his fingers to the silent music of an invisible orchestra. He looked ancient in my eyes. He had lost most of the hair on top of his head and he wore thick glasses and had eyes that always looked tired and sleepy. But he must have been younger than I thought, since he lived with his mother and was not yet married.

I met Old Lady Chong once and that was enough. She had this peculiar smell like a baby that had done something in its pants. And her fingers felt like a dead person's, like an old peach I once found in the back of the refrigerator; the skin just slid off the meat when I picked it up.

I soon found out why Old Chong had retired from teaching piano. He was deaf. "Like Beethoven!" he shouted to me. "We're both listening only in our head!" And he would start to conduct his frantic silent sonatas.

Our lessons went like this. He would open the book and point to different things, explaining their purpose: "Key! Treble! Bass! No sharps or flats! So this is C major! Listen now and play after me!"

And then he would play the C scale a few times, a simple chord, and then, as if inspired by an old, unreachable itch, he gradually added more notes and running trills and a pounding bass until the music was really something quite grand.

I would play after him, the simple scale, the simple chord, and then I just played some nonsense that sounded like a cat running up and down on top of garbage cans. Old Chong smiled and applauded and then said, "Very good! But now you must learn to keep time!"

So that's how I discovered that Old Chong's eyes were too slow to keep up with the wrong notes I was playing. He went through the motions in half-time. To help me keep rhythm, he stood behind me,

---

Using Students' Strengths

Kinesthetic Learners

Help students understand aspects of the story by having them act out movements described in the text. For example, on p. 97 the narrator describes her mother's movements between the TV set and her chair as "a stiff embraceless dance." Ask volunteers to figure out what this looks like and to demonstrate it for the class.

Auditory Learners

Ask students to role-play the mother and Auntie Lindo bragging about their children. Have pairs of students begin with the passage on pp. 99–100 and improvise additional comments and complaints. As partners practice for a class presentation, they should refine where they will raise or lower their voices, pause for suspense, or slow down for emphasis.

Interpersonal Learners

Have these students explore in greater depth the mother-daughter relationship depicted in the story. Introduce a new situation, such as Jing-mei's messy room, and have them work in pairs to write a dialogue between Jing-mei and her mother about cleaning the room. For help with writing dialogue, refer students to the Language Link feature on p. 109.

Wiping the Table (1985) by Flo Oy Wong (1938–   ). Graphite drawing on paper (17⅜″ × 20⅛″).

pushing down on my right shoulder for every beat. He balanced pennies on top of my wrists so I would keep them still as I slowly played scales and arpeggios.[5] He had me curve my hand around an apple and keep that shape when playing chords. He marched stiffly to show me how to make each finger dance up and down, staccato,[6] like an obedient little soldier.

He taught me all these things, and that was how I also learned I could be lazy and get away with mistakes, lots of mistakes. If

---

5. **arpeggios** (är·pej'ōz): chords whose notes are played quickly one after another, rather than at the same time.
6. **staccato** (stə·kät'ō): with clear-cut breaks between notes.

I hit the wrong notes because I hadn't practiced enough, I never corrected myself. I just kept playing in rhythm. And Old Chong kept conducting his own private reverie.

So maybe I never really gave myself a fair chance. I did pick up the basics pretty quickly, and I might have become a good pianist at that young age. But I was so determined not to try, not to be anybody different, that I learned to play only the most earsplitting preludes, the most <u>discordant</u> hymns.

Over the next year, I practiced like this, dutifully in my own way. And then one day I heard my mother and her friend Lindo Jong both talking in a loud bragging tone of voice so others could hear. It was after church, and I was leaning against the brick wall, wearing a dress with stiff white petticoats. Auntie Lindo's daughter, Waverly, who was about my age, was standing farther down the wall, about five feet away. We had grown up together and shared all the closeness of two sisters squabbling over crayons and dolls. In other words, for the most part, we hated each other. I thought she was snotty. Waverly Jong had gained a certain amount of fame as "Chinatown's Littlest Chinese Chess Champion."

"She bring home too many trophy," <u>lamented</u> Auntie Lindo that Sunday. "All day she play chess. All day I have no time do nothing but dust off her winnings." She threw a scolding look at Waverly, who pretended not to see her.

"You lucky you don't have this problem," said Auntie Lindo with a sigh to my mother.

And my mother squared her shoulders

WORDS TO OWN

discordant (dis·kord″nt) *adj.*: clashing; not in harmony.
lamented (lə·ment′id) *v.*: said with regret or sorrow. *Lamented* also means "mourned or grieved for" or "regretted deeply."

TWO KINDS **99**

Getting Students Involved

T99

A Reading Skills and Strategies

Making Inferences about Character

❓ What does this detail reveal about Jing-mei's parents? [Possible response: They are frugal, hardworking, and dedicated to doing what they believe will help their daughter.]

B Elements of Literature

Irony

❓ What is ironic about Jing-mei's daydreams? [She resents that her mother does not let her be herself, yet she daydreams about wanting to be someone else.]

C Reading Skills and Strategies

Making Inferences about Character

❓ What do these details add to your understanding of Jing-mei's parents and their expectations about her performance? [Possible responses: They are so proud of their daughter that they invite all their friends to the talent show; they expect her to perform well.]

D Reading Skills and Strategies

Comparing/Contrasting

❓ How do Jing-mei's expectations before she plays the Schumann piece contrast with what actually happens? [She feels certain she will perform so well she could be invited to *The Ed Sullivan Show*. In actuality, she plays one wrong note after another and can't correct herself.] **How do her *feelings* before she plays contrast with her *feelings* afterward?** [She goes from feeling excited and confident to feeling horrified.]

---

and bragged: "Our problem worser than yours. If we ask Jing-mei wash dish, she hear nothing but music. It's like you can't stop this natural talent."

And right then, I was determined to put a stop to her foolish pride.

A few weeks later, Old Chong and my mother conspired to have me play in a talent show which would be held in the church hall. By then, my parents had saved up enough to buy me a secondhand piano, a black Wurlitzer spinet with a scarred bench. It was the showpiece of our living room.

For the talent show, I was to play a piece called "Pleading Child" from Schumann's[7] *Scenes from Childhood*. It was a simple, moody piece that sounded more difficult than it was. I was supposed to memorize the whole thing, playing the repeat parts twice to make the piece sound longer. But I dawdled over it, playing a few bars and then cheating, looking up to see what notes followed. I never really listened to what I was playing. I daydreamed about being somewhere else, about being someone else.

The part I liked to practice best was the fancy curtsy: right foot out, touch the rose on the carpet with a pointed foot, sweep to the side, left leg bends, look up and smile.

My parents invited all the couples from the Joy Luck Club[8] to witness my debut. Auntie Lindo and Uncle Tin were there. Waverly and her two older brothers had also come. The first two rows were filled with children both younger and older than I was. The littlest ones got to go first. They recited simple nursery rhymes, squawked

---

7. **Schumann:** Robert Schumann (1810–1856), German composer.
8. **Joy Luck Club:** social club to which Jing-mei's mother and three other Chinese mothers belong.

---

out tunes on miniature violins, twirled Hula-Hoops, pranced in pink ballet tutus, and when they bowed or curtsied, the audience would sigh in unison, "Awww," and then clap enthusiastically.

When my turn came, I was very confident. I remember my childish excitement. It was as if I knew, without a doubt, that the prodigy side of me really did exist. I had no fear whatsoever, no nervousness. I remember thinking to myself, This is it! This is it! I looked out over the audience, at my mother's blank face, my father's yawn, Auntie Lindo's stiff-lipped smile, Waverly's sulky expression. I had on a white dress layered with sheets of lace, and a pink bow in my Peter Pan haircut. As I sat down I envisioned people jumping to their feet and Ed Sullivan rushing up to introduce me to everyone on TV.

And I started to play. It was so beautiful. I was so caught up in how lovely I looked that at first I didn't worry how I would sound. So it was a surprise to me when I hit the first wrong note and I realized something didn't sound quite right. And then I hit another, and another followed that. A chill started at the top of my head and began to trickle down. Yet I couldn't stop playing, as though my hands were bewitched. I kept thinking my fingers would adjust themselves back, like a train switching to the right track. I played this strange jumble through two repeats, the sour notes staying with me all the way to the end.

When I stood up, I discovered my legs were shaking. Maybe I had just been nervous and the audience, like Old Chong, had seen me go through the right motions and had not heard anything wrong at all. I swept my right foot out, went down on my knee, looked up and smiled. The room was

---

WORDS TO OWN

dawdled (dôd′'ld) *v.*: wasted time; lingered.

Skill Link

Understanding Dialogue

Experienced story writers often tell beginners, "Show, don't tell!" One way to *show* meaning instead of *telling* it directly is through dialogue. Consider the following narrative:

Jack sat reading the newspaper at the kitchen table, not really conscious of the sound of the shower running. When the phone rang, he continued to read until he heard his wife call out, "I'm in the shower!" Accustomed to their "shorthand," he knew she was really asking him to take the call. Being a considerate

man, he shouted back to her, "I'll get it, Flo!"

A more experienced writer might *show* the very same things through dialogue:

Jack was reading the newspaper at the kitchen table when the phone rang.

"I'm in the shower!" Flo shouted.

"I'll get it, honey," Jack replied.

Notice that the second version allows the reader to infer the couple's affection (through *honey*) and their "shorthand" method of communication.

Activity

Have students brainstorm other situations in which dialogue carries unstated meaning. They might begin with situations that arise at home, and proceed to others that involve school, sports, or activities like shopping. Then, have pairs of students create brief dialogues and read them aloud. Encourage the rest of the class to infer the situations and unstated meanings.

quiet, except for Old Chong, who was beaming and shouting, "Bravo! Bravo! Well done!" But then I saw my mother's face, her stricken face. The audience clapped weakly, and as I walked back to my chair, with my whole face quivering as I tried not to cry, I heard a little boy whisper loudly to his mother, "That was awful," and the mother whispered back, "Well, she certainly tried."

And now I realized how many people were in the audience, the whole world it seemed. I was aware of eyes burning into my back. I felt the shame of my mother and father as they sat stiffly throughout the rest of the show.

We could have escaped during intermission. Pride and some strange sense of honor must have anchored my parents to their chairs. And so we watched it all: the eighteen-year-old boy with a fake mustache who did a magic show and juggled flaming hoops while riding a unicycle. The breasted girl with white makeup who sang from *Madama Butterfly*[9] and got honorable mention. And the eleven-year-old boy who won first prize playing a tricky violin song that sounded like a busy bee.

After the show, the Hsus, the Jongs, and the St. Clairs from the Joy Luck Club came up to my mother and father.

"Lots of talented kids," Auntie Lindo said vaguely, smiling broadly.

"That was somethin' else," said my father, and I wondered if he was referring to me in a humorous way, or whether he even remembered what I had done.

Waverly looked at me and shrugged her shoulders. "You aren't a genius like me," she said matter-of-factly. And if I hadn't felt so bad, I would have pulled her braids and punched her stomach.

But my mother's expression was what devastated me: a quiet, blank look that said

9. *Madama Butterfly:* opera by the Italian composer Giacomo Puccini.

she had lost everything. I felt the same way, and it seemed as if everybody were now coming up, like gawkers at the scene of an accident, to see what parts were actually missing. When we got on the bus to go home, my father was humming the busy-bee tune and my mother was silent. I kept thinking she wanted to wait until we got home before shouting at me. But when my father unlocked the door to our apartment, my mother walked in and then went to the back, into the bedroom. No accusations. No blame. And in a way, I felt disappointed. I had been waiting for her to start shouting, so I could shout back and cry and blame her for all my misery.

I assumed my talent-show fiasco meant I never had to play the piano again. But two days later, after school, my mother came out of the kitchen and saw me watching TV.

"Four clock," she reminded me as if it were any other day. I was stunned, as though she were asking me to go through the talent-show torture again. I wedged myself more tightly in front of the TV.

"Turn off TV," she called from the kitchen five minutes later.

I didn't budge. And then I decided. I didn't have to do what my mother said anymore. I wasn't her slave. This wasn't China. I had listened to her before and look what happened. She was the stupid one.

She came out from the kitchen and stood in the arched entryway of the living room. "Four clock," she said once again, louder.

WORDS TO OWN

stricken (strik′ən) *adj.:* heartbroken; affected by or suffering from something painful or distressing.
fiasco (fē·äs′kō) *n.:* complete failure.

? What is ironic about the way Mr. Chong cheers Jing-mei's performance? [Because he is deaf, he has no idea how badly she performed; he was simply watching her hands move on the keys.]

F **Elements of Literature**
 Motivation

? What do you think of Jing-mei's interpretation of her parents' reasons for sitting through the rest of the show? [Possible response: She is probably right since they would not want to let others know how embarrassed they feel by getting up and leaving.] Why do you think Jing-mei remains anchored to her own chair? [Possible responses: She doesn't dare embarrass herself or her parents any further by leaving; she is so shocked by her poor performance that she is too numb to think of taking any kind of action.]

G **Critical Thinking**
 Extending the Text

? Who do you think is more to blame for Jing-mei's misery—her mother or herself? Explain. [Possible responses: Her mother, because she pressures Jing-mei too much; Jing-mei, because she doesn't really try to learn the piano.]

H **Critical Thinking**
 Challenging the Text

? What is illogical about Jing-mei's thinking? [Possible responses: There is no reason to think her parents would treat her any differently if they lived in China; obeying your parents is not akin to being a slave.]

Getting Students Involved

Cooperative Learning
Jigsaw Sharing. Have students discuss the story in groups of four for ten minutes. Each member should concentrate on one of the following elements of literature: motivation, setting, conflict, and suspense. All members should help each other jot down incidents or details from the story that relate to the assigned

elements. After ten minutes, ask students who worked on the same element to form new groups to compare their findings. After ten minutes, ask students to return to their original groups to share new insights they have gained from the members of other groups.

Enrichment
What's in a Name. As students read, have them note the point in the story where the title is explained (p. 102). After students have finished the story, have them write in their notebooks a brief explanation of why they think the title is appropriate to the story. If they do not find the title appropriate, have them suggest a new title and explain why they chose it. Have students share their responses with the class.

? What do you think of Jing-mei's behavior? [Sample responses: She is throwing a tantrum like a baby; she is right to stand up to her mother, but she doesn't have to yell and scream.]

B Elements of Literature

Motivation

? In this stunning climax to the mother-daughter confrontation, what do you think is Jing-mei's motivation for cruelly referring to her mother's dead babies? [Possible response: She deliberately says the most hurtful thing she can imagine in order to push her mother to "the breaking point."]

C English Language Learners

Word Choice

Explain to English language learners that "Alakazam" is a nonsense word used by magicians to introduce something amazing.

"I'm not going to play anymore," I said nonchalantly. "Why should I? I'm not a genius."

She walked over and stood in front of the TV. I saw her chest was heaving up and down in an angry way.

"No!" I said, and I now felt stronger, as if my true self had finally emerged. So this was what had been inside me all along.

"No! I won't!" I screamed.

She yanked me by the arm, pulled me off the floor, snapped off the TV. She was frighteningly strong, half pulling, half carrying me toward the piano as I kicked the throw rugs under my feet. She lifted me up and onto the hard bench. I was sobbing by now, looking at her bitterly. Her chest was heaving even more and her mouth was open, smiling crazily, as if she were pleased I was crying.

"You want me to be someone that I'm not!" I sobbed. "I'll never be the kind of daughter you want me to be!"

"Only two kinds of daughters," she shouted in Chinese. "Those who are obedient and those who follow their own mind! Only one kind of daughter can live in this house. Obedient daughter!"

"Then I wish I wasn't your daughter. I wish you weren't my mother," I shouted. As I said these things, I got scared. It felt like worms and toads and slimy things crawling out of my chest, but it also felt good, as if this awful side of me had surfaced, at last.

"Too late change this," said my mother shrilly.

And I could sense her anger rising to its breaking point. I wanted to see it spill over. And that's when I remembered the babies she had lost in China, the ones we never talked about. "Then I wish I'd never been born!" I shouted. "I wish I were dead! Like them."

It was as if I had said the magic words. Alakazam!—and her face went blank, her

---

Mom, Pop, Me (1984) by Flo Oy Wong (1938–   ). Graphite drawing on paper (19¼" × 15½").

Courtesy of the Artist.

---

mouth closed, her arms went slack, and she backed out of the room, stunned, as if she were blowing away like a small brown leaf, thin, brittle, lifeless.

It was not the only disappointment my mother felt in me. In the years that followed, I failed her so many times, each time asserting my own will, my right to fall short of expectations. I didn't get straight A's. I didn't become class president. I didn't get into Stanford.[10] I dropped out of college.

For unlike my mother, I did not believe I

10. **Stanford:** high-ranking university in Stanford, California.

WORDS TO OWN

nonchalantly (nän′shə·länt′lē) *adv.:* without interest or concern; indifferently.

Taking a Second Look

Review: Comparing and Contrasting Characters

Comparing characters means identifying ways in which they are similar; contrasting them means identifying ways in which they differ. Within a story, writers sometimes create contrasting characters in order to make both characters stand out more sharply. You can see such a contrast in "Two Kinds" between the non-achieving Jing-mei and the prize-winning Waverly. One can also compare and contrast characters across stories.

For example, you can compare and contrast Jing-mei's mother in "Two Kinds" with the mother who narrates "Everyday Use" (p. 70).

Activity

From stories students have read so far, have them select two characters who have something in common. Then, have them construct a chart to help organize their thinking about the two characters. The chart should show ways in

which the characters are similar, and ways in which they differ. Encourage students to focus on traits such as gender, age, motives, personality, style of speech, and appearance. Finally, students should present their findings to the class in a format of their choice: essay, poster, collage, a pair of bumper stickers, or anything else that demonstrates the two characters' similarities and differences.

could be anything I wanted to be. I could only be me. **D**

And for all those years, we never talked about the disaster at the recital or my terrible accusations afterward at the piano bench. All that remained unchecked, like a betrayal that was now unspeakable. So I never found a way to ask her why she had hoped for something so large that failure was inevitable.

And even worse, I never asked her what frightened me the most: Why had she given up hope? **E**

For after our struggle at the piano, she never mentioned my playing again. The lessons stopped. The lid to the piano was closed, shutting out the dust, my misery, and her dreams.

So she surprised me. A few years ago, she offered to give me the piano, for my thirtieth birthday. I had not played in all those years. I saw the offer as a sign of forgiveness, a tremendous burden removed.

"Are you sure?" I asked shyly. "I mean, won't you and Dad miss it?"

"No, this your piano," she said firmly. "Always your piano. You only one can play."

"Well, I probably can't play anymore," I said. "It's been years."

"You pick up fast," said my mother, as if she knew this was certain. "You have natural talent. You could been genius if you want to."

"No, I couldn't."

"You just not trying," said my mother. And she was neither angry nor sad. She said it as if to announce a fact that could never be disproved. "Take it," she said. **F**

But I didn't at first. It was enough that she had offered it to me. And after that, every time I saw it in my parents' living room, standing in front of the bay windows, it made me feel proud, as if it were a shiny trophy I had won back.

Last week I sent a tuner over to my parents' apartment and had the piano reconditioned, for purely sentimental reasons. My mother had died a few months before, and I had been getting things in order for my father, a little bit at a time. I put the jewelry in special silk pouches. The sweaters she had knitted in yellow, pink, bright orange—all the colors I hated—I put those in mothproof boxes. I found some old Chinese silk dresses, the kind with little slits up the sides. I rubbed the old silk against my skin, then wrapped them in tissue and decided to take them home with me.

After I had the piano tuned, I opened the lid and touched the keys. It sounded even richer than I remembered. Really, it was a very good piano. Inside the bench were the same exercise notes with handwritten scales, the same secondhand music books with their covers held together with yellow tape.

I opened up the Schumann book to the dark little piece I had played at the recital. It was on the left-hand side of the page, "Pleading Child." It looked more difficult than I remembered. I played a few bars, surprised at how easily the notes came back to me.

And for the first time, or so it seemed, I noticed the piece on the right-hand side. It was called "Perfectly Contented." I tried to play this one as well. It had a lighter melody but the same flowing rhythm and turned out to be quite easy. "Pleading Child" was shorter but slower; "Perfectly Contented" was longer but faster. And after I played them both a few times, I realized they were two halves of the same song. **G**

WORDS TO OWN

betrayal (bē·trā′əl) *n.*: failure to fulfill another's hopes. *Betrayal* also means "act of disloyalty" or "deception."

D **Appreciating Language**
Multiple Meanings
Jing-mei's mother uses the word *be* in the sense of *become*. She means that Jing-mei can achieve any goal she sets for herself. Jing-mei uses *be* in a more existential way, referring to her essential personhood. She means that she cannot change her fundamental character traits.

E **Critical Thinking**
Interpreting
? Why do you think Jing-mei feels frightened? [Possible responses: Maybe she doubts that her mother loves her; maybe she thinks she knows the answer and is afraid to hear it.]

F **Elements of Literature**
Plot
? How is the mother-daughter conflict resolved? [The mother and daughter learn to accept each other as individuals with different expectations.]

G **Reading Skills and Strategies**
Making Inferences about Character
? What does Jing-mei imply in the last sentence? [Possible responses: She seems to imply that discontented pleading must come before a state of contentment—both are part of the natural condition of being human; just as she had overlooked "Perfectly Contented," so people often overlook positive aspects of their lives and focus instead on the negative parts.]

Resources ———
Selection Assessment
Formal Assessment
• Selection Test, p. 15
Test Generator (One-Stop Planner)
• CD-ROM

Making the Connections

Connecting to the Theme: "Hearts That Love"

One way Jing-mei's mother expresses her love for her daughter is by wanting her daughter to achieve success in areas that are closed to herself. However, Jing-mei does not feel the same need for success as her mother, and she takes her mother's efforts as interference in her life. In the end, mother and daughter arrive at an uneasy truce, but Jing-mei apparently bears a measure of guilt for having failed to fulfill her mother's expectations. Ask students to describe in their Writer's Notebook how they think Jing-mei's mother feels when Jing-mei fails to make A's and when she drops out of college. [Possible response: Most students will probably believe that the mother is disappointed and frustrated at her daughter's failure to live up to her capabilities.]

Cultural Connections

Chinese immigrants first came to the United States because of the California Gold Rush in 1849. These immigrants were instrumental in helping to build America's first transcontinental railroad. Chinese Americans now live in communities throughout the country (with the greatest concentration in California), and many large cities boast a Chinatown.

BROWSING IN THE FILES

About the Author. On publication of Tan's third novel, *The Hundred Secret Senses*, interviewer Sarah Lyall noted that Tan "has an American practicality, but her life has been so marked by quirks of fate that she has gradually come to believe, as her Chinese mother does, that there are things in the world that can't be explained rationally." Thus, Tan sees that some of her dreams have come true; yet (on the negative side) she suffers from "mechanical difficulties." Like the character Kwan in her third novel, when Tan is around, TV sets and television cameras inexplicably go haywire.

A Critic's Comment. The *San Francisco Chronicle* characterized Tan's *The Joy Luck Club* with these words: "What it is to be American, and a woman, mother, daughter, lover, wife, sister and friend— these are the troubling, loving alliances and affiliations that Tan molds into the sixteen intricate interlocking stories that constitute this remarkable first novel."

WRITERS ON WRITING

Amy Tan notes how exciting unexpected personal discoveries found during the writing process can be: "You can come up with structures and ideas at first, but it's what you stumble across without self-consciousness that's new, exciting, and much more honest. These things are within you, in your life's experience and the way you perceive the world."

MEET THE WRITER
Many Englishes

Amy Tan (1952–) says that she grew up with several Englishes. The Englishes were primarily American English and Chinese English. Tan was born in Oakland, California, two and a half years after her parents fled China's Communist revolution and settled in the United States. Although Tan's parents had wanted her to become a surgeon, with piano as a hobby, she got a master's degree in linguistics instead. Her first short story, written at a writers' workshop in 1985, was eventually published in *Seventeen*.

At the request of a literary agent, Tan next drafted a proposal for a novel based on the lives of four Chinese mothers and their American daughters. Then Tan left on a trip to China with her own mother, who had just recovered from a serious illness.

When she returned, Tan was amazed to find that her agent had obtained a sizable advance for a novel she hadn't even written yet. She immediately devoted herself full-time to writing *The Joy Luck Club*—a collection of related stories told from the points of view of four mothers and four daughters.

"When I wrote these stories, it was as much a discovery to me as to any reader reading them for the first time," Tan has said. "Things would surprise me. I would sit there laughing and I would say, 'Oh you're kidding!' It was like people telling me the stories, and I would write them down as fast as I could." Published in 1989 to rave reviews, *The Joy Luck Club* became an instant bestseller. In 1993, it was made into a movie.

Afraid of bombing after the huge success of *The Joy Luck Club,* Tan agonized over her second novel, *The Kitchen God's Wife* (1991).

In writing that book, she says, she "had to fight for every single character, every image, every word." She needn't have worried. The novel, the story of a woman's harrowing life in pre-Communist China, was another block-buster.

Here is what Tan says about being a writer who knows two cultures:

66 I am a writer. I am fascinated by language in daily life. I spend a great deal of my time thinking about the power of language—the way it can evoke an emotion, a visual image, a complex idea, or a simple truth. Language is the tool of my trade. And I use them all—all the Englishes I grew up with. 99

104 THE SHORT-STORY COLLECTIONS

Assessing Learning

Peer Assessment: Group Work

Have students rate the performance of their work and discussion groups on the following basis: A=Always, S=Sometimes, N=Never

____**1.** The group gets to work right away.

____**2.** The group stays focused on the assignment.

____**3.** Group members contribute equally.

____**4.** Group members listen attentively to what others have to say.

____**5.** Group members complete the assignment.

Check Test: True-False

1. Jing-mei's mother devises tests to discover her daughter's talents. [True]

2. A television show gives the mother the idea that Jing-mei should play piano. [True]

3. Jing-mei's performance during the talent show is a tremendous success. [False]

4. Jing-mei hurts her mother in an argument after the talent show. [True]

5. Jing-mei sells the family piano after her mother dies. [False]

Standardized Test Preparation

For practice with standardized test format specific to this selection, see

• *Standardized Test Preparation,* p. 18

For practice in proofreading and editing, see

• *Daily Oral Grammar,* Transparency 6

Melting Pot Still Bubbles at IS 237 Ⓐ

CHARISSE JONES

In parts of her India, it would not have been proper, this friendship between a young man and a young woman, says Nitu Singh. But here, in the United States, she believes it is necessary.

She is sixteen, and in less than two years has graduated quickly from one level to the next in the school's English-as-a-second-language program. He, Jatinder Singh, fifteen, has been here two months and speaks no English. Their bond is the Punjabi language and their shared understanding of what it is like to be new in a foreign country.

"He needs help, so I help him," she said. "I treat him like my brother." Ⓑ

The school that has brought Nitu and Jatinder together, Intermediate School 237, the Rachel L. Carson School, at a quiet intersection in Flushing, Queens, is a modern brick building that is among the most diverse schools in New York City. Its students fill the hallways with the accents of El Salvador, Taiwan, and Pakistan and go home to households where mothers scold and comfort them in Spanish, Mandarin, and Urdu.

To wander the halls of IS 237 is to see the baby steps and giant strides of young people wrestling Ⓒ with assimilation and ethnic pride, with change and acceptance.

"A lot of them are terrified," said Rosiland Tseng, who has been a guidance counselor at IS 237 for six years. "They're also very confused about the system, like changing the classrooms. They don't understand."

At the school, one approach has been a buddy system that pairs newcomers with immigrants who have been here longer. Ⓓ

The buddies are often in the same classes, their interdependence evolving into friendship.

Opening a Universe

Nitu helped Jatinder decipher the mystery of a combination lock on his locker, showing him as many as fifteen times how to unlock it until he got it right. She explained Ⓔ to him that here children are fed

(continued on next page)

Part of the diverse student population of IS 237.

TWO KINDS 105

Connecting Across Texts

Like Amy Tan, Jing-mei, the protagonist of "Two Kinds," was born in the United States and grew up in an exclusively Chinese culture until she entered school. Therefore, Jing-mei could probably understand some of the adjustments the students in this news feature face. Have students work in groups to write letters from Jing-mei, offering advice to the students described in the article. (Students should look back through "Two Kinds" to find clues to what Jing-mei might say to the students at IS 237.) Additionally, take advantage of the first-hand expertise of any students in your classroom who have immigrated to the United States and learned English as a second language. Ask them to contribute any insights they are willing to share.

Connections

In this *New York Times* article, the writer interviews multi-ethnic students at Intermediate School 237 in Flushing, Queens. The school's buddy system pairs new immigrants with students who have been in America for some time. Students from different countries talk about their experiences adapting to new customs and feeling excluded from groups. Parent-child conflict has always accompanied cultural adaptation, a historian notes. The school's guidance counselor mentions other school-related problems that newcomers and their parents must deal with.

Ⓐ **English Language Learners**
Abbreviation
Point out to students that the letters *I*, *S*, are pronounced separately rather than as the word *is*, because they stand for the words *Intermediate School*.

Ⓑ **Cultural Connections**
❓ In some cultures the marriages of young people are arranged by their parents. What effect do you think this tradition might have on teenagers' social lives here in America? [Possible responses: Teenagers are probably allowed to do things only in groups or as chaperoned couples. Note that some students might come from groups where marriages are still arranged.]

Ⓒ **Reading Skills and Strategies**
Making Inferences
❓ What conflict is implied in this paragraph? [Possible response: internal conflict between the students' native cultures and their adopted U.S. culture.]

Ⓓ **Reading Skills and Strategies**
Responding to the Text
❓ What advantages do you see in this buddy system? [Possible responses: A new student would have an instant friend; the buddy system lets a newcomer learn from someone who knows exactly the kinds of things he or she will find strange.]

Ⓔ **Cultural Connections**
❓ What is the advantage of having all students eat together in the school cafeteria? [Possible responses: Food is an important part of culture, and sharing it fosters community; the practice introduces students to American foods.]

Critical Thinking

Challenging the Text

? Do you agree with Lisa Hou that fitting in doesn't matter? Explain. [Possible responses: No, because your peers are constantly judging you, and you have to fit in if you want to have friends; yes, because true friends like you for yourself, and you shouldn't worry about what other people think.]

B ## Reading Skills and Strategies

Finding Cause and Effect

? What are some things that might cause conflict between parents and children in this situation? [Possible responses: Parents might not understand how important it is for their children to wear certain kinds of clothes and listen to certain kinds of music in order to fit in; parents might be afraid that their children will lose touch with their native culture.]

Connections

Melting Pot Still Bubbles at IS 237

Students working with a puzzle of the United States.

(continued from previous page) in a cafeteria, instead of bringing their own food from home.

In a classroom recently, Nitu sat next to Jatinder quietly helping him piece together a puzzle of the United States. She smiled when he uttered the states' names correctly, and provided friendship when he felt different and alone.

The Start Is Bumpy

The first days are the hardest, the children say, filled with the noise of a language not understood, the strangeness of customs never before encountered.

"I felt excluded from the group," Lisa Hou, fourteen, remembered, "because you look different, because you don't dress the way they do. I wanted to be a part of them. Back home I never had this kind of problem."

That was nearly four years ago, when she first came from Taiwan. Now, she says, fitting in no longer matters. "I don't really care. I can't change the way I look."

But minutes earlier, as she tried to describe the taunts she had endured, her words got lost in tears.

Many immigrant children are initiated into the youthful mores° of American culture the painful way, compelled to get hip in a hurry to stop the insults that come from sporting no-name sneakers and speaking English with a heavy accent.

° **mores** (môr′ēz′): here, customs and habits.

Cultural adaptation, and the pain that often comes with it, has always been part of the immigrant experience, said Dr. Stephan F. Brumberg, a historian and author. Another is conflict between children and parents.

"There are the problems that arise between generations," he said, "parents who come of age in one cultural, linguistic setting who are raising children in a different one. It's an unavoidable tension, and it's something that people who emigrate probably don't really foresee: that they're going to raise aliens."

Often it is the school's guidance counselors who must try to bridge the widening gulf between children and parents. Mrs. Tseng said that some immigrant children feel overwhelmed by the academic expectations their parents hold for them, as well as the clash of cultures. Parents may also be confused about how to deal with their children but feel it is improper to ask others for advice, especially school officials, whom they were often taught in their homelands to obey and fear.

Must Get Involved

"The parents often feel they're not supposed to be active in the schools because the school authorities know best," she said. "They don't understand that's part of the process, to get involved."

Programs are also in place for the children, who, once the newness has passed, still often face reminders that they are not originally from here.

The most vivid reminder is language. Luis Figueroa, fourteen, born in Peru, has lived in the United States for six years. He speaks English with ease and wears the teenage uniform: sweat shirt, bluejeans, and sneakers.

Still, there are moments he'll be sitting in class, and it will happen. "You read a book," he said, "and you always see a word that you don't know."

—from *The New York Times*

Listening to Music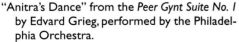

"Anitra's Dance" from the *Peer Gynt Suite No. 1* by Edvard Grieg, performed by the Philadelphia Orchestra.

"Pleading Child" from *Kinderszenen (Scenes from Childhood)* by Robert Schumann, performed by Vladimir Horowitz.

Norway's greatest composer, Edvard Grieg (grēg) (1843–1907) wrote his best-known work at the request of another Norwegian giant, the playwright Henrik Ibsen. In 1874 Ibsen came to Grieg seeking incidental music for his fantasy drama *Peer Gynt*. That music, which Grieg later adapted into two orchestral suites, includes the hugely famous "Morning," "Åse's Death," and "In the Hall of the Mountain King," as well as "Anitra's Dance." German composer Robert Schumann (1810–1856) is best known for his piano pieces, in part because his wife Clara, a noted pianist, won fame playing them all over Europe. A remark of Clara's was the inspiration of Schumann's *Kinderszenen,* which presents thirteen musical "scenes" from childhood.

Activity

After students read "Two Kinds," play the two pieces of music, noting that both are mentioned in the selection. Have students contrast the moods of the two compositions.

Applying the Element
A good way to help students understand the methods of indirect characterization is to have them create a fictional character of their own. Assign students to groups of five. First, have the group select the kind of character they wish to create—a talented athlete, for example, or an ideal politician—and then list the traits they want the character to possess. Next, group members should write passages that reveal characterization indirectly, as in the examples on p. 110. Student #1 contributes a description of the character's appearance; student #2 contributes typical actions, and so on. Then, have the group read and polish each other's statements and arrange the passages in the order they prefer. Finally, have a reader from each group present their character to the class by reading their passages aloud.

Resources

Assessment
Formal Assessment
• Literary Element Test, p. 24

---

round characters. A **flat character** is like a paper doll, with only one surface. Such a character has only one or two key personality traits and can be described in a single sentence. A **round character**, on the other hand, cannot be summed up so neatly. A round character is fleshed out. He or she is more complex—there are more sides to this character's personality, more dimensions.

In good fiction, flat characters are included for a reason: Too many round characters would be distracting. Most works of fiction, particularly short stories, require a certain number of flat characters to get the story told.

Stock Characters: Off the Shelf

The problem with second-rate fiction is that even the main characters are flat characters. These flat characters found in inferior fiction are often also stock characters. A **stock character** is a person who fits our preconceived notions about a type (a typical old man, a typical teenager, a typical detective, a typical politician).

Stock characters have no individuality; there are dozens just like them on the shelf.

You know stock characters on sight (they exist on TV and in the movies, too): the mad scientist, the nerdy intellectual, the tough guy with the soft heart, the poor little rich girl.

It is their predictability that makes these stock characters so stale. We've met them all before in countless other stories, and we know that the writer has simply taken them off the shelf (or out of the "stockroom") and set them in motion by winding each character's key. We know that real people aren't like this—real people are endlessly complex and never wholly predictable. What fascinates and delights us in fiction is the portrayal of characters who somehow manage to confound our expectations yet still seem true to life.

What's the Motivation?

One of the ways a writer rounds out a character is to show us what **motivates**, or moves, that person to act as he or she does. Unless we understand why an otherwise dutiful daughter suddenly lashes out at

her mother, her behavior will strike us as inconsistent and unbelievable. But once we recognize the need she is trying to satisfy (say, to punish someone—anyone she can get her hands on—for the way her boyfriend has neglected her), her behavior begins to make sense, and she is no longer the two-dimensional "dutiful daughter." She seems like a real person—someone who is usually kind but who is also capable (as all of us are) of cruelty.

Writers do not often state a character's motives directly. ("She screamed at her mother because Bill hadn't called in two weeks.") Instead, they imply what those motives are—maybe even scatter clues throughout the story—and trust their readers to make intelligent guesses about why their characters act as they do.

Trying to understand the motivation of characters in literature can be as puzzling and satisfying as it is in real life. While we may know that real people surprise us with their behavior, we also know that there are reasons for what they do. In real life we may never find out what those reasons are. In fiction we do.

Using Students' Strengths

Kinesthetic Learners
To help students understand the methods of indirect characterization, you might have them practice with study cards. Provide envelopes (marked with each of the five methods listed on p. 110) and a stack of index cards containing a series of examples of the methods of indirect characterization. Shuffle the cards and ask students to read each one. Have them work in pairs or groups to decide which method is being used, and to sort the cards into the appropriate envelopes.

Auditory/Musical Learners
Ask students to find or invent melodies that can be used as musical themes for four or five stock characters of their choice, either those described on p. 111 or others they recognize from fiction, film, and television. Have students provide a list of the stock characters portrayed and play the melodies (without naming the character evoked by each one). Challenge other students to match the stock characters with the melodies.

Visual Learners
Using characters from several stories of your choice from Collection 1 or 2, have students work in pairs to make lists of round and flat characters. After pairs have completed their work, have students compare lists, discuss their reasons for any differences in designation, and re-evaluate whether those characters are mostly flat or round.

Planning

Before You Read

GERALDO NO LAST NAME

Make the Connection

We Are All One

There are billions of people on this planet, and each one is in some ways just like you and me, with a history and a need to love and share life. But unexpected things happen, and sometimes we lose a link to a person who might have become important to us.

Quickwrite

Make some notes about someone you met briefly whom you wish you could have known better. Jot down details about how you met the person and why you remember him or her.

go.hrw.com
LEO 10-2

Elements of Literature

Style: The Personal Stamp

Just as no two people in the world have the same fingerprints, so does everyone have a unique style. Your **style** is your own mode of expression. The way you dress is a style. So is the way you shape your sentences. Are they short and simple or long and complicated? When you read your writing aloud, does it have the rhythm of poetry, or does it sound plain and direct? Some writers' styles are so famous that people can read a single sentence and know they are reading, for example, Ernest Hemingway. A Cisneros story has that kind of distinctive style. Listen for it.

> **S**tyle is the particular way that writers use language to express themselves and their ideas.

Reading Skills and Strategies

Monitoring Your Reading: Questioning

Good readers ask **questions** as they read—perhaps about unfamiliar vocabulary, a confusing description, or a character's behavior. Good writers, like Cisneros, sometimes invite questions by purposely leaving some things unanswered.

Resources: Print and Media

Geraldo No Last Name

Sandra Cisneros

An accident, don't you know. Hit and run.

She met him at a dance. Pretty too, and young. Said he worked in a restaurant, but she can't remember which one. Geraldo. That's all. Green pants and Saturday shirt. Geraldo. That's what he told her.

Summary ■

In this very brief story, or **vignette,** a young Mexican American woman named Marin meets a man named Geraldo at a dance. She is the last to see him before he is struck by a hit-and-run driver. He is alive when taken to the hospital but dies without regaining consciousness. Because Geraldo spoke only Spanish, carried no identification, and didn't mention his last name, Marin cannot help the hospital staff or police identify him. Moreover, she cannot explain her motivation for maintaining a long vigil in the emergency room. This story is about love but not necessarily romantic love. Marin's love for Geraldo seems to be part of a love we feel for all of our fellow human beings, especially those in unfortunate situations; this kind of love might also be called kindness, affection, caring, even neighborliness.

Resources ————

Elements of Literature
Style: The Personal Stamp
For additional instruction on style, see *Literary Elements:*
*   Transparency 5
*   Worksheet, p. 16

Reading Skills and Strategies
Monitor
Strategies: Questioning
❓ From reading this short paragraph, what questions do you have about the two characters? [Possible questions: Who is "she"? What kind of dance was it? Why did she learn so little about Geraldo? Is something going to happen to him?]

Reaching All Students

Struggling Readers
Monitoring Your Reading was introduced on p. 112. One good strategy to use with this skill is Think-Aloud. For information on using this strategy, see p. 135 in the *Reading Strategies Handbook* in the front of the *Reading Skills and Strategies* binder.

English Language Learners
Have students work in pairs to retell the story from Marin's point of view. Work with them to create "I" statements based on the story—for example, "I am Marin. I am_____. I enjoy _____." Then, ask student pairs to retell Marin's story in a mode of their choice, such as a monologue, a dialogue with a hospital clerk or reporter, a letter to a friend, or even an art work.

Advanced Learners
Ask students to research how someone can immigrate legally from Mexico to the United States; how a legal immigrant can become a U.S. citizen; the penalties for undocumented (illegal) immigration; and the rights of illegal aliens. Have students work in groups to create informational posters based on their findings.

And how was she to know she'd be the last one to see him alive. An accident, don't you know. Hit and run. Marin, she goes to all those dances. Uptown. Logan. Embassy. Palmer. Aragon. Fontana. The manor. She likes to dance. She knows how to do cumbias and salsas and rancheras even. And he was just someone she danced with. Somebody she met that night. That's right.

El Club (1990) by Nick Quijano (1953–   ). Gouache on paper (22″ × 30″).

Permanent Collection, Puerto Rico Tourism Museum, Old San Juan, Puerto Rico.

That's the story. That's what she said again and again. Once to the hospital people and twice to the police. No address. No name. Nothing in his pockets. Ain't it a shame.

Only Marin can't explain why it mattered, the hours and hours, for somebody she didn't even know. The hospital emergency room. Nobody but an intern working all alone. And maybe if the surgeon would've come, maybe if he hadn't lost so much blood, if the surgeon had only come, they would know who to notify and where.

Connecting Across Texts

But what difference does it make? He wasn't anything to her. He wasn't her boyfriend or anything like that. Just another brazer[1] who didn't speak English. Just another wetback.[2] You know the kind. The ones who always look ashamed. And what was she doing out at 3:00 A.M. anyway? Marin who was sent home with her coat and some aspirin. How does she explain?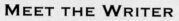

She met him at a dance. Geraldo in his shiny shirt and green pants. Geraldo going to a dance.

What does it matter?

They never saw the kitchenettes. They never knew about the two-room flats[3] and sleeping rooms he rented, the weekly money orders sent home, the currency exchange. How could they?

His name was Geraldo. And his home is in another country. The ones he left behind are far away, will wonder, shrug, remember. Geraldo—he went north . . . we never heard from him again.

1. **brazer** (brā′zer): Americanization of the Spanish word *bracero*, used in the United States to refer to a Mexican laborer allowed into the United States temporarily to work.
2. **wetback:** offensive term for a Mexican laborer who illegally enters the United States, often by swimming or wading the Rio Grande.
3. **flats:** apartments.

MEET THE WRITER
Unforgettable as a First Kiss

Sandra Cisneros (1954–   ) spent her childhood moving back and forth between Chicago, where she was born, and Mexico, where her father was born. She currently lives in San Antonio, Texas.

Cisneros's first full-length work, *The House on Mango Street,* appeared in 1984. The narrator of this series of connected stories is a lively and thoughtful girl named Esperanza. (Her name means "hope" in Spanish.) Cisneros has also published collections of her poetry, including *My Wicked Wicked Ways* (1987), and another collection of stories, *Woman Hollering Creek* (1991). One critic has said that her stories "invite us into the souls of characters as unforgettable as a first kiss."

Cisneros did not find her unique voice as a writer until she attended the Writers' Workshop at the University of Iowa.

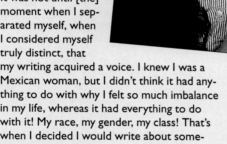

66 Everyone seemed to have some communal knowledge which I did not have. It was not until [the] moment when I separated myself, when I considered myself truly distinct, that my writing acquired a voice. I knew I was a Mexican woman, but I didn't think it had anything to do with why I felt so much imbalance in my life, whereas it had everything to do with it! My race, my gender, my class! That's when I decided I would write about something my classmates couldn't write about. 99

D Elements of Literature
Style
? In which phrases does the author especially seem to be imitating the rhythm and phrasing of Marin's speech? [Possible responses: "or anything like that," "Just another," "You know the kind."]

E Reading Skills and Strategies
Making Inferences
? From where is Marin sent home "with her coat and some aspirin"? [The hospital] How do you know? [The previous paragraph places her there for "hours and hours."] Why is she given aspirin? [Sample answer: All the stress and the late night hour have given her a headache.]

F Elements of Literature
Style
? The narrator is no longer speaking in Marin's "voice," but rather as an omniscient author able to reveal that Geraldo was a real person with real responsibilities. In what specific ways does the style change? [The sentences are complete, not fragments; the style is more formal and less conversational.]

Resources ———
Selection Assessment
Formal Assessment
• Selection Test, p. 17
Test Generator (One-Stop Planner)
• CD-ROM

Making the Connections

Connecting to the Theme: "Hearts That Love"
Have students write in their notebooks how the theme of "Hearts That Love" is reflected in "Geraldo No Last Name." [Possible response: Some students might point out that Marin's willingness to stay with Geraldo after the accident is an act of love, even though she does not know him and is not in love with him.] **After students have recorded their thoughts,** ask volunteers to share their observations with the class.

Cultural Connections: "Latin American Dance"
The story mentions three dances that Marin likes to do—cumbias, salsas, and rancheras. If any of your students know these dances, allow them to describe or even demonstrate them for the class.

Connections

This is an actual letter a young woman wrote to her family in Guadalajara, Mexico. (Have students notice the date and place she is writing from.) She left without her parents' permission and wants to reassure them that she is safe. She is staying with acquaintances, looking for work, and going to mass. She tells them that she plans to return home and to school after a few months and asks them to trust her and to write to her.

A Reading Skills and Strategies
Making Inferences

❓ What does the phrase "in spite of everything" imply about the situation with Patricia's parents? [Possible responses: Her parents have suffered some misfortune; she has done something to hurt them or upset them.]

B Elements of Literature
Motivation

❓ Why do you think Patricia's parents might have refused to let her go to the United States? [Possible responses: They considered her too young or the United States too dangerous; they worried about what might happen to her if she entered the United States illegally.]

C Critical Thinking
Hypothesizing

❓ Why do you think Patricia includes the postscript about going to mass? [She wants to reassure them that she is keeping up with the religious practices they taught her to value.]

RESPONDING TO THE ART

Los Bailadores, the title of the painting on p. 117, translates into English as *The Dancers.* Other works by **Nick Quijano** appear on pp. 93 and 114.

Activity. Ask students if the art reflects their mental images of Marin and Geraldo, and to explain their thinking.

T116

 A LETTER HOME

Ventura, CA
February 27, 1981

José Zarate and Family
Guadalajara, Mexico

A Hello Papa, Mama, brothers and sisters,
    I hope this finds you very well in spite of everything.
    By now you will have found out I'm in the United States (California) and you will be asking yourselves what I'm doing here.
    Before anything I want to ask you to have a lot of trust in me. I came with the desire to work here a few months in order to gather a little money.
    I have great faith that it's going to go very well for me, and this is important. Here everything is different from Mexico, but I assure you I'm never going to forget anything I learned from you!!
    I remember you a lot and this is going to be decisive in my behavior. <u>I am not going to fail you! Of that I assure you!!</u>
    When I arrived in the U.S. Wednesday morning I had two addresses of people I could head for. One is of Panchi and his sisters. The other address is that of some married friends of mine, which was the one I opted for, and I'm sure that if you knew them you'd quit worrying. They're Mexican. They have two daughters, little ones. They work mornings. Someone takes care of the girls. Meanwhile I'm alone in the house until 4 P.M., when they return, and since it's different here, people don't go out into the street then. I've gone with them downtown and to look for work.
B   Papa, Mama, I consider it very important that you trust me. I know that with the way I did things you may distrust me, but I knew you were never going to let me do it. I'm going to behave myself very well! I'm going to go to my aunt Cuca and if she offers me her house I'll stay. I already spoke with her and she told me yes, to go to her house, I have her address and phone number. I also have the address of my uncle Felipe in case I need it.
    I just want to work a few months and return to you to continue in school.
    I want you to be calm. My being alone right now is going to help me a lot to start being responsible for myself.
    I'm going to write constantly to tell you how it's going with me.
    I hope you also write me, even if it is to box my ears. Until soon.

Loving you all,
Patricia Zarate

C Just now we went to mass at a church called La Asunción de Maria. It was a bilingual mass with mariachi.

Connecting Across Texts

Connecting with "Geraldo No Last Name"

It is possible to imagine that Geraldo of "Geraldo No Last Name" could have written a similar letter home when he first arrived in the United States. A particularly revealing aspect of Patricia Zarate's letter is what she implies, throughout the letter, about her parents' attitudes toward her going to the United States on her own—in effect, running away from home.

  Ask students to work in small groups to write one of the following letters. Allow students who choose the second or third option to make up details not provided in "Geraldo No Last Name," such as the surname of Geraldo's family, the family's attitude toward his move, and his early experiences in the United States.

- A letter from the Zarate family to Patricia
- A letter from Geraldo to his family
- A letter from Geraldo's family to Geraldo

MAKING MEANINGS

First Thoughts

[analyze]

1. There's a lot we don't know when we finish reading Cisneros's sketch. Write down questions that you think are left unanswered. Be sure to share your questions, and some of their possible answers, with other readers.

Shaping Interpretations

[interpret]

2. At the end of this little sketch, Cisneros says "they" never saw certain aspects of Geraldo's life. Who are "they"?

[interpret]

3. After Geraldo dies, Marin says she can't understand why their meeting mattered, why she spent so many hours in the hospital waiting room. Why do you think she keeps thinking about the meeting and wondering what it meant?

[infer]

4. Exactly what do you know about the **character** of Geraldo? What **inferences,** or guesses, can you make about the kind of person he was?

[evaluate]

5. Do you think this story is about love? Talk about your responses in class.

Connecting with the Text

[connect]

6. Look back at your Quickwrite notes. Are there any similarities between the "brief encounter" you described and the one in the story? Explain.

[respond]

7. Review the letter from a young woman who has immigrated to California from Mexico (see *Connections* on page 116). How does her letter home affect your responses to Geraldo's story?

Extending the Text

[speculate]

8. Geraldo has no identification papers and may be an illegal immigrant. In what other ways can people become lost in our society? How might that happen, and to whom?

Los Bailadores (1990) by Nick Quijano (1953–   ). Gouache on paper (6½″ × 6½″).

Collection Marc Briller, New York.

> ### Reading Check
> Retell the events of this story to a classmate, as you imagine Marin told them to the police.

GERALDO NO LAST NAME 117

MAKING MEANINGS

First Thoughts

1. Sample responses: Does Geraldo have a family? Probably, since he sent money home. Does he have friends? Perhaps not, or someone would know his last name. How will his family in Mexico react when they no longer hear from him or receive money orders? Someone might begin an investigation. What will happen to his belongings? The police might locate his family through the money orders, and send them his belongings.

Shaping Interpretations

2. Possible responses: the police, the hospital staff, or society in general.

3. Possibly Marin felt that nobody should be left alone in such dire circumstances. Possibly she was attracted to Geraldo more than she realized.

4. He worked and enjoyed dancing and socializing. Students might infer that he was a responsible person and felt obligations toward his family, that he was willing to put up with poor living conditions to save money, and that he was faithful in helping his family.

5. Sample responses: It is not a romantic story, but it is a story of love in the sense that one person shows concern for another. It is a love story, and Marin falls in love with Geraldo without consciously realizing it.

Connecting with the Text

6. Answers will vary, but many may reveal the existence of regrets, unanswered questions, or musings about what might have been.

7. Some students' responses may not change; other students might realize that Geraldo was not completely alone—he had people who cared about him back home.

Extending the Text

8. Someone could run away. Someone could deliberately move without leaving a forwarding address.

> ### Reading Check
> Narratives will vary but should include these major details: Geraldo and Marin meet at a dance; she does not know his last name or the name of the restaurant where he works; Geraldo is injured by a hit-and-run driver; she waits at the hospital but no surgeon comes; Geraldo dies.

Assessing Learning

Check Test: Short Answers

1. Where does Geraldo work? [at a restaurant]

2. Where does Marin meet Geraldo? [at a dance]

3. Who is on duty in the emergency room? [an intern working alone]

4. What kind of doctor does Marin think might have been able to save Geraldo? [a surgeon]

5. Where is Geraldo's family? ["in another country," probably Mexico]

Standardized Test Preparation

For practice with standardized test format specific to this selection, see

• *Standardized Test Preparation*, p. 20

For practice in proofreading and editing, see

• *Daily Oral Grammar*, Transparency 7

Rubrics for each Choices assignment appear on p. 101 in the *Portfolio Management System*.

CHOICES: Building Your Portfolio

1. **Writer's Notebook** Students should identify Cisneros's clues as indirect characterization. Nowhere in the story does Cisneros describe Geraldo's character directly.

2. **Creative Writing** Remind students that their poems do not need to rhyme or follow any particular metrical pattern. Students should refer to the story for clues to how Marin might respond. As an alternative to completing the poem, visual learners might wish to create a collage instead. First, have them fill in the blank lines after the prompts, and then ask them to translate their responses into the visual form of a collage.

3. **Oral Interpretation** Have students practice their oral readings using either an audio or a video recorder. Students should first read through the story several times silently, focusing on how each sentence should sound.

4. **Art** Even though the story gives few details about Geraldo's appearance, encourage students to reread the story carefully and to jot down the physical details that are presented. Students should also note information in the text from which they can infer details of his appearance. For this activity, you may wish to allow auditory and musical learners to substitute composing a song about Geraldo. They can use a familiar melody or create a new one for their song. They may share their lyrics only or perform their songs for the class.

5. **Research/Social Studies** Allow students to work in small groups on the data base about Mexican immigrants. When their work has been completed, students may donate it to the school library so that others can make use of their research.

CHOICES: Building Your Portfolio

Writer's Notebook
1. Collecting Ideas for a Character Analysis

Finding the clues. Although we never meet Geraldo, we have an impression of the kind of person he was. How has Sandra Cisneros managed to create a character in less than two pages? (Does she use **direct** or **indirect characterization,** or some combination of both?) Look back at "Geraldo No Last Name" to find the clues that help you to know Geraldo. Then, fill in a cluster diagram like the one below. Save your notes for possible use in the Writer's Workshop on page 164.

Opposite: *Miguel El Coreógrafo* (1991) by Margaret Garcia (1951–   ). Oil on wood (24″ × 24″).

Courtesy of Nancy Thomas and Kevin Goff.

Creative Writing
2. Healing Words

Imagine that you are Marin and you have just come home from the hospital on the night Geraldo died. Express your thoughts and feelings in a **poem** by finishing these lines:

I am _____ .

I wonder _____ .

I hear _____ .

I see _____ .

I wish _____ .

I am _____ .

Art
4. Creating a Portrait

Using details from the story, as well as your own imagination, draw a portrait of Geraldo, or create a **collage** of images and words that suggest his life or personality. When you share your artwork with your classmates, be prepared to explain why you presented Geraldo as you did.

Cluster diagram:
- appearance
- actions
- traits
- Geraldo
- what other characters say about him
- what no one knows about him

Oral Interpretation
3. Hearing a Style

Present an **oral interpretation** of the story. Decide how you should use your voice to emphasize Cisneros's unusual **style.** Think of when you should pause, read slowly, read quickly, and raise or lower your voice. Ask your audience for feedback. (For help, see the Speaking and Listening Workshop on pages 750–751.)

Research/Social Studies
5. Database

Create a database containing statistical information about Mexican immigration to the United States. First, decide where you will find your data. The Internet would be a good source, particularly a U.S. government site. You might concentrate on numbers, quotas, areas where immigrants live, typical jobs, wages. Be sure to include some of your information in a graph or table.

118 THE SHORT-STORY COLLECTIONS

Before You Read

THE FIRST SEVEN YEARS

Make the Connection

The Many Faces of Love

Love can blossom in the most unexpected places. People who seem totally unsuited sometimes fall in love, and those who appear well matched often leave each other cold. The seeming illogic of love is an age-old subject.

Quickwrite

How do you think most people feel when someone tries to arrange a date for them—or even find them a husband or wife? Jot down your feelings about this practice of matchmaking. You might want to use a pro and con chart.

Pros	Cons

Elements of Literature

The Protagonist: The Main Character

Most stories have a main character, called the **protagonist,** on whom our attention focuses. Usually, but not always, the protagonist is admirable and likable, the sort of person we identify with. It is also possible to have a protagonist who is not very nice at all. In a good

(Background pp. 119 and 120) Victoria and Albert Museum, London/Art Resource, NY

story, the protagonist is a real, complicated human being, with just enough strengths, weaknesses, and contradictions to remind us of ourselves.

As a rule, the story's action begins when this main character wants something and sets out to get it. (The **antagonist** is the character or force that comes into conflict with the protagonist. Just as the protagonist is rarely all good, the antagonist is rarely all bad.)

> The **protagonist** is the main character, usually the one who sets the action in motion.
>
> *For more on Protagonist, see the Handbook of Literary Terms.*

Reading Skills and Strategies

Comparing and Contrasting Characters

Some stories are built around characters who present dramatic contrasts—in appearance, perhaps, or in values, or in actions or speech. Malamud has created two very different characters in this story. As you read (or in your rereading), track the characteristics of both Sobel and Max—do they also have qualities in common?

Background

In "The First Seven Years," love finds its way, almost unnoticed, into a poor shoemaker's shop in New York City in the 1950s. Feld, the old shoemaker, is a Jewish immigrant who came to America from Poland years before.

go.hrw.com
LEO 10-2

Facial Features from *The World of Sholom Aleichem* (1953) by Ben Shahn (1898–1969). Pen and ink (8⅞″ × 5⅞″).

Gift of Robert and Carol Straus, 1963. © Estate of Ben Shahn/Licensed by VAGA, New York, NY.

Preteaching Vocabulary

Words To Own

Have students read the Words to Own on pp. 120–127. Then discuss the following scenarios to reinforce understanding of the words.

1. What if your *reverie* could become a reality?
2. What if you could *discern* what others were thinking?
3. What if ninety percent of a country's population were *illiterate*?
4. What if you found out that your best friend was *unscrupulous*?
5. What if apple trees were *profuse* in your backyard?
6. What if everyone felt that human life was *sanctified*?
7. What if somebody you like did something you found *repugnant*?
8. What if you discovered that you were *deft* at every athletic feat you undertook?
9. What if you turned *pallid* every time someone called your name?
10. What if everyone gave you *devious* answers?

Summary ▪▪

The story immediately introduces the four main characters and sets the stage for their conflicts. The protagonist is Feld, a Polish immigrant who owns a shoe-repair shop; it is his mind that the reader enters in the third-person limited narration. Feld's nineteen-year-old daughter, Miriam, has disappointed him by working rather than attending college, but she loves to read and discuss literature with thirty-five-year-old Sobel, a Polish refugee and Feld's trusted assistant of five years. When "college boy" Max enters the store, Feld asks him to call Miriam, and Sobel leaves in a rage—a foreshadowing of his passion for her. Miriam rejects Max, and Feld's distress is compounded by a new worker's thievery and a heart attack. Finally he begs Sobel to return; Sobel will do so only if he can marry Miriam. Feld mourns his dreams for her but asks only that Sobel wait two years before proposing. Sobel immediately returns to work.

The story's many kinds of love *agape* include parental, romantic, silent, sacrificial, and philosophical—the love of wisdom for its own sake. The title alludes to the Biblical story of Jacob, who worked seven years for his love, Rachel.

Background

Before students read the story, tell them about these aspects of the Eastern European Jewish immigrant community: the strong patriarchal family structure, the tradition of arranged marriages, and the emphasis on education as the key to a better future. What other cultures do they know that emphasize the same values?

Resources

Listening
Audio CD Library
A recording of this story is provided in the *Audio CD Library*:
• Disc 4, Track 3

Viewing and Representing
Fine Arts Transparency
A Fine Art transparency of *The Birthday* by Marc Chagall complements the stories of this collection, especially "The First Seven Years." See the *Viewing and Representing Transparencies and Worksheets:*
• Transparency 3
• Worksheet, p. 12

The First Seven Years

Bernard Malamud

"She will never marry a man so old and ugly like you."

Full Figure with Cane, Dressed in Long Coat and Large Brimmed Flat Hat from *The World of Sholom Aleichem* (1953) by Ben Shahn (1898–1969). Pen and ink (9" × 5¹⁵⁄₁₆").

Gift of Robert and Carol Straus, 1963. © Estate of Ben Shahn/Licensed by VAGA, New York, NY.

Ⓐ

F eld, the shoemaker, was annoyed that his helper, Sobel, was so insensitive to his reverie that he wouldn't for a minute cease his fanatic pounding at the other bench. He gave him a look, but Sobel's bald head was bent over the last[1] as he worked, and he didn't notice. The shoemaker shrugged and continued to peer through the partly frosted window at the nearsighted haze of falling February snow. Neither the shifting white blur outside nor the sudden deep remembrance of the snowy Polish village where he had wasted his youth could turn his thoughts from Max the college boy (a constant visitor in the mind since early that morning when Feld saw him trudging through the snowdrifts on his way to school), whom he so much respected because of the

1. **last:** wooden or metal model of a foot on which a shoemaker makes or repairs shoes.

WORDS TO OWN
reverie (rev'ər·ē) *n.*: daydreaming; state of being absorbed in thought.

 — ── *Resources: Print and Media* ──

Reading
• *Graphic Organizers for Active Reading*, p. 8
• *Words to Own*, p. 8
• *Audio CD Library*
  Disc 4, Track 3

Writing and Language
• *Daily Oral Grammar*
  Transparency 8
• *Grammar and Language Links*
  Worksheet, p. 13

Viewing and Representing
• *Viewing and Representing*
  Fine Art Transparency 3
  Fine Art Worksheet, p. 12

Assessment
• *Formal Assessment*, p. 18
• *Portfolio Management System*, p. 103
• *Test Generator (One-Stop Planner CD-ROM)*

Internet
• go.hrw.com (keyword: LE0 10-2)

sacrifices he had made throughout the years—in winter or direst heat—to further his education. An old wish returned to haunt the shoemaker: that he had had a son instead of a daughter; but this blew away in the snow, for Feld, if anything, was a practical man. Yet he could not help but contrast the diligence of the boy, who was a peddler's son, with Miriam's unconcern for an education. True, she was always with a book in her hand, yet when the opportunity arose for a college education, she had said no, she would rather find a job. He had begged her to go, pointing out how many fathers could not afford to send their children to college, but she said she wanted to be independent. As for education, what was it, she asked, but books, which Sobel, who diligently read the classics, would as usual advise her on. Her answer greatly grieved her father.

A figure emerged from the snow and the door opened. At the counter the man withdrew from a wet paper bag a pair of battered shoes for repair. Who he was, the shoemaker for a moment had no idea; then his heart trembled as he realized, before he had thoroughly discerned the face, that Max himself was standing there, embarrassedly explaining what he wanted done to his old shoes. Though Feld listened eagerly, he couldn't hear a word, for the opportunity that had burst upon him was deafening.

He couldn't exactly recall when the thought had occurred to him, because it was clear he had more than once considered suggesting to the boy that he go out with Miriam. But he had not dared speak, for if Max said no, how would he face him again? Or suppose Miriam, who harped so often on independence, blew up in anger and shouted at him for his meddling? Still, the chance was too good to let by: All it meant was an introduction. They might long ago have become friends had they happened to meet somewhere; therefore was it not his duty—an obligation—to bring them together, nothing more, a harmless connivance to replace an accidental encounter in the subway, let's say, or a mutual friend's introduction in the street? Just let him once see and talk to her and he would for sure be interested. As for Miriam, what possible harm

for a working girl in an office, who met only loudmouthed salesmen and illiterate shipping clerks, to make the acquaintance of a fine scholarly boy? Maybe he would awaken in her a desire to go to college; if not—the shoemaker's mind at last came to grips with the truth—let her marry an educated man and live a better life.

When Max finished describing what he wanted done to his shoes, Feld marked them, both with enormous holes in the soles which he pretended not to notice, with large white-chalk X's, and the rubber heels, thinned to the nails, he marked with O's, though it troubled him he might have mixed up the letters. Max inquired the price, and the shoemaker cleared his throat and asked the boy, above Sobel's insistent hammering, would he please step through the side door there into the hall. Though surprised, Max did as the shoemaker requested, and Feld went in after him. For a minute they were both silent, because Sobel had stopped banging, and it seemed they understood neither was to say anything until the noise began again. When it did, loudly, the shoemaker quickly told Max why he had asked to talk to him.

"Ever since you went to high school," he said in the dimly lit hallway, "I watched you in the morning go to the subway to school, and I said always to myself, this is a fine boy that he wants so much an education."

"Thanks," Max said, nervously alert. He was tall and grotesquely thin, with sharply cut features, particularly a beaklike nose. He was wearing a loose, long, slushy overcoat that hung down to his ankles, looking like a rug draped over his bony shoulders, and a soggy old brown hat, as battered as the shoes he had brought in.

"I am a businessman," the shoemaker abruptly said to conceal his embarrassment, "so I will explain you right away why I talk to you. I have a girl, my daughter Miriam—she is nineteen—a very nice girl and also so pretty that everybody

----

WORDS TO OWN

discerned (di·zurnd') v.: recognized; perceived.
illiterate (il·lit'ər·it) adj.: ignorant; uneducated; not knowing how to read or write.

Ⓐ Reading Skills and Strategies
Comparing and Contrasting Characters
❓ What four characters are introduced in the first paragraph of the story? Give a phrase to identify each. [Feld, the shoemaker; Sobel, his helper; Max, the college boy; Miriam, Feld's daughter] What contrasts can you already see between Sobel and Max? [Sobel is bald, so he must be older than Max; Feld seems to respect "college boy" Max more than he does his helper, Sobel.] How does Feld mentally compare and contrast Miriam, Max, and Sobel? [Miriam and Sobel read the classics and work instead of going to college; Max is earning a degree.]

Ⓑ Reading Skills and Strategies
Finding the Main Idea
❓ Why does Feld want his daughter to marry a college-educated man? [He wants her to have a "better life."]

Ⓒ Appreciating Language
Dialect
Both Feld and Sobel speak English well, but their syntax throughout the story indicates that English is not their first language. This use of dialect builds richer, more developed characters.

Ⓓ Critical Thinking
Analyzing
❓ What does this description of Max suggest about his character? [It suggests that he does not care about material things like clothes, or that he is poor and cannot afford better clothing; his main concerns are intellectual.] How does the description connect with the drawing by Ben Shahn on p. 120? [The drawing shows a person wearing a "soggy hat" and a long overcoat.]

Reaching All Students

Struggling Readers
Comparing and Contrasting was introduced on p. 119. One good strategy to use with comparing and contrasting characters is Semantic Differential Scales. Create a scale to compare the characters Feld and Sobel at the beginning and at the end of the story. For information on using this strategy see p. 93 in the *Reading Strategies Handbook* in the *Reading Skills and Strategies* binder.

English Language Learners
Ask these students to focus on the character of Sobel as they read the story. They should take notes on how they think he feels when Max first visits the shop, when he learns that Feld wants Max to date Miriam, when he storms out of the shop, when he spends time alone in his room, and when Feld tells him that he is old and ugly. What advice would they give Sobel at these moments?

Advanced Learners
After these students have read the story, have them work in small groups to select what they consider to be the most important passage in the story. Each group should reach a consensus about its choice and present the passage to the class. Every member of each group should be prepared to explain why the particular passage was chosen.

A Critical Thinking

Expressing an Opinion

? What do you think of Max's request for a picture of Miriam? [Possible responses: It makes him seem shallow; it seems appropriate, since he has never met her; he seems to care more about her looks than her mind or character.]

B Critical Thinking

Extending the Text

? How do you think Miriam would feel about Max's lukewarm attitude toward meeting her? [Possible responses: She might accept the situation as the way things are done in her culture; she might be annoyed that her father wants her to date someone who seems to have little interest in meeting her.]

C Elements of Literature

Motivation

? Sobel's noisiness becomes "violent clanging" just before he breaks the last and storms out of the shop. Why do you think he acts this way? [Possible responses: He is upset about a private matter; he doesn't like Feld's meddling with Miriam's life; he fears that Miriam will stop asking him for advice on classic books if she starts dating a college man; he has feelings for Miriam himself.]

D Elements of Literature

Protagonist and Antagonist

? A conflict is clearly developing between Feld and Sobel. Which man is the protagonist and which is the antagonist? Why? [Feld is the protagonist because the story is told from his point of view and because he is the one whose desire for something sets things in motion.]

E Reading Skills and Strategies

Comparing and Contrasting Characters

? How does Sobel compare with Max in age, appearance, and ambition? [Sobel is older than Max, bald, and apparently uninterested in career advancement.] What else does this passage tell you about Sobel's personality or character? [He is sensitive to good literature; he is a fast learner; he is a skilled worker.]

looks on her when she passes by in the street. She is smart, always with a book, and I thought to myself that a boy like you, an educated boy—I thought maybe you will be interested sometime to meet a girl like this." He laughed a bit when he had finished and was tempted to say more but had the good sense not to.

Max stared down like a hawk. For an uncomfortable second he was silent; then he asked, "Did you say nineteen?"

"Yes."

"Would it be all right to inquire if you have a picture of her?"

"Just a minute." The shoemaker went into the store and hastily returned with a snapshot that Max held up to the light.

"She's all right," he said.

Feld waited.

"And is she sensible—not the flighty kind?"

"She is very sensible."

After another short pause, Max said it was OK with him if he met her.

"Here is my telephone," said the shoemaker, hurriedly handing him a slip of paper. "Call her up. She comes home from work six o'clock."

Max folded the paper and tucked it away into his worn leather wallet.

"About the shoes," he said. "How much did you say they will cost me?"

"Don't worry about the price."

"I just like to have an idea."

"A dollar—dollar fifty. A dollar fifty," the shoemaker said.

At once he felt bad, for he usually charged two twenty-five for this kind of job. Either he should have asked the regular price or done the work for nothing.

Later, as he entered the store, he was startled by a violent clanging and looked up to see Sobel pounding with all his might upon the naked last. It broke, the iron striking the floor and jumping with a thump against the wall, but before the enraged shoemaker could cry out, the assistant had torn his hat and coat from the hook and rushed out into the snow.

So Feld, who had looked forward to anticipating how it would go with his daughter

and Max, instead had a great worry on his mind. Without his temperamental helper he was a lost man, especially since it was years now that he had carried the store alone. The shoemaker had for an age suffered from a heart condition that threatened collapse if he dared exert himself. Five years ago, after an attack, it had appeared as though he would have either to sacrifice his business upon the auction block and live on a pittance thereafter or put himself at the mercy of some <u>unscrupulous</u> employee who would in the end probably ruin him. But just at the moment of his darkest despair, this Polish refugee, Sobel, appeared one night from the street and begged for work. He was a stocky man, poorly dressed, with a bald head that had once been blond, a severely plain face, and soft blue eyes prone to tears over the sad books he read, a young man but old—no one would have guessed thirty. Though he confessed he knew nothing of shoemaking, he said he was apt and would work for a very little if Feld taught him the trade. Thinking that with, after all, a landsman,[2] he would have less to fear than from a complete stranger, Feld took him on, and within six weeks the refugee rebuilt as good a shoe as he and not long thereafter expertly ran the business for the thoroughly relieved shoemaker.

Feld could trust him with anything and did, frequently going home after an hour or two at the store, leaving all the money in the till, knowing Sobel would guard every cent of it. The amazing thing was that he demanded so little. His wants were few; in money he wasn't interested—in nothing but books, it seemed—which he one by one lent to Miriam, together with his <u>profuse</u>, queer written comments, manufactured during his lonely rooming house evenings, thick pads of commentary which the

2. **landsman** (länts'mən): fellow Jew originally from the same local area in Eastern Europe.

WORDS TO OWN

unscrupulous (un·skrōō'pyə·ləs) *adj.:* not restrained by ideas of right and wrong.
profuse (prō·fyōōs') *adj.:* plentiful; given freely.

Getting Students Involved

Cooperative Learning

Matchmaking. At this point in the story, Feld is convinced that Sobel is an uneducated man who is unworthy of his daughter. Have students of different ability levels work in groups of four or five to create lists of: (a) attributes a father might want his daughter's fiancé to possess; (b) attributes a young woman might desire in a husband; (c) facts known about Max and Sobel so far; (d) facts about Max and Sobel that Feld may be overlooking. When groups have completed their lists, have them reach consensus on whether Sobel or Max seems the better match for Miriam and provide reasons for their conclusions. They should then go on to predict how they think the story will actually develop.

Inside Looking Out (1953) by Ben Shahn (1898–1969). Casein (17″ × 15″).

The Butler Institute of American Art, Youngstown, Ohio. © Estate of Ben Shahn/Licensed by VAGA, New York, NY.

shoemaker peered at and twitched his shoulders over as his daughter, from her fourteenth year, read page by sanctified page, as if the word of God were inscribed on them. To protect Sobel, Feld himself had to see that he received more than he asked for. Yet his conscience bothered him for not insisting that the assistant accept a better wage than he was getting, though Feld had honestly told him he could earn a handsome salary if he worked elsewhere or maybe opened a place of his own. But the assistant answered, somewhat ungraciously, that he was not interested in going elsewhere, and though Feld frequently asked himself—what keeps him here? why does he stay?—he finally answered it that the man, no doubt because of his terrible experiences as a refugee, was afraid of the world.

After the incident with the broken last, angered by Sobel's behavior, the shoemaker decided to let him stew for a week in the rooming house, although his own strength was taxed dangerously and the business suffered. However, after several sharp, nagging warnings from both his wife and daughter, he went finally in search of Sobel, as he had once before, quite recently, when over some fancied slight—Feld had merely asked him not to give Miriam so

G -

WORDS TO OWN

sanctified (saŋk′tə·fīd′) *adj.*: blessed; made holy.

THE FIRST SEVEN YEARS 123

Crossing the Curriculum

Art

To help students explore the effect of setting on the events of a story, have them work in small groups to produce murals of Feld's shoe shop. They may need to make a field visit to a shoe repair shop to see the kinds of equipment shoe shops still contain, such as lasts and sewing machines. The murals might show Sobel working at his bench and Feld talking with a customer. Have groups display their finished work in the classroom.

Social Studies

Both Feld and Sobel are Jewish immigrants from Poland. Ask students to research Jewish immigration from Eastern Europe during the first fifty years of the twentieth century. Then, based on their findings, small groups can produce a narrative or short play that includes information about why these immigrants came to America, where they settled, and the kinds of work they found.

F **Reading Skills and Strategies**

Making Inferences

? What inferences can you draw about Sobel and Miriam, and the relationship they have established? [Possible responses: Both are interested in literary classics; Sobel shows respect for Miriam's mind by writing detailed commentaries for her; Miriam shows respect for Sobel's mind by treating his words as if they were sacred scripture; their friendship may be far deeper than anyone else realizes.]

G **Critical Thinking**

Evaluating an Interpretation

? Is Feld correct in his interpretation of why Sobel stays with him? [Sample answer: No—Sobel stays because his relationship with Miriam matters deeply to him, and it is unlikely that Feld would allow him to continue the relationship if he worked somewhere else.]

RESPONDING TO THE ART

Ben Shahn (1898–1969) was an immigrant to the United States, like Feld and Sobel in Malamud's story. Born in Lithuania, Shahn was eight when his family emigrated to New York City. He worked as a lithographer's apprentice while earning his high school diploma at night and later studied art. His early drawings and paintings supported social or political causes, but in the 1950s his work turned more reflective. **Activity.** Begin by asking students to describe what they see in the painting and to speculate on what it reveals about the girl. Have them consider the title. [An old fashioned bureau mirror reflects a girl seated in front of a bare-looking window, where she can look out when she pauses in her writing. The sewing machine might suggest that she sews for a living. The title suggests isolation, perhaps longing.] Then, have students comment on how the painting reflects the character of Miriam. [It shows a girl who seems quiet, young, and studious in a very modest setting. Like Miriam, she seems to have dreams.]

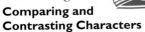
many books to read, because her eyes were strained and red—the assistant had left the place in a huff, an incident which, as usual, came to nothing, for he had returned after the shoemaker had talked to him, and taken his seat at the bench. But this time, after Feld had plodded through the snow to Sobel's house—he had thought of sending Miriam but the idea became repugnant to him—the burly landlady at the door informed him in a nasal voice that Sobel was not at home, and though Feld knew this was a nasty lie, for where had the refugee to go? still, for some reason he was not completely sure of—it may have been the cold and his fatigue—he decided not to insist on seeing him. Instead he went home and hired a new helper.

Having settled the matter, though not entirely to his satisfaction, for he had much more to do than before and so, for example, could no longer lie late in bed mornings, because he had to get up to open the store for the new assistant, a speechless, dark man with an irritating rasp as he worked, whom he would not trust with the key, as he had Sobel. Furthermore, this one, though able to do a fair repair job, knew nothing of grades of leather or prices, so Feld had to make his own purchases; and every night at closing time it was necessary to count the money in the till and lock up. However, he was not dissatisfied, for he lived much in his thoughts of Max and Miriam. The college boy had called her, and they had arranged a meeting for this coming Friday night. The shoemaker would personally have preferred Saturday, which he felt would make it a date of the first magnitude, but he learned Friday was Miriam's choice, so he said nothing. The day of the week did not matter. What mattered was the aftermath. Would they like each other and want to be friends? He sighed at all the time that would have to go by before he knew for sure. Often he was tempted to talk to Miriam about the boy, to ask whether she thought she would like his type—he had told her only that he considered Max a nice boy and had suggested he call her—but the one time he tried she snapped at him—justly—how should she know?

At last Friday came. Feld was not feeling par-

ticularly well, so he stayed in bed, and Mrs. Feld thought it better to remain in the bedroom with him when Max called. Miriam received the boy, and her parents could hear their voices, his throaty one, as they talked. Just before leaving, Miriam brought Max to the bedroom door, and he stood there a minute, a tall, slightly hunched figure wearing a thick, droopy suit and apparently at ease as he greeted the shoemaker and his wife, which was surely a good sign. And Miriam, although she had worked all day, looked fresh and pretty. She was a large-framed girl with a well-shaped body, and she had a fine open face and soft hair. They made, Feld thought, a first-class couple.

Miriam returned after 11:30. Her mother was already asleep, but the shoemaker got out of bed and, after locating his bathrobe, went into the kitchen, where Miriam, to his surprise, sat at the table, reading.

"So, where did you go?" Feld asked pleasantly.

"For a walk," she said, not looking up.

"I advised him," Feld said, clearing his throat, "he shouldn't spend so much money."

"I didn't care."

The shoemaker boiled up some water for tea and sat down at the table with a cupful and a thick slice of lemon.

"So how," he sighed after a sip, "did you enjoy?"

"It was all right."

He was silent. She must have sensed his disappointment, for she added, "You can't really tell much the first time."

"You will see him again?"

Turning a page, she said that Max had asked for another date.

"For when?"

"Saturday."

"So what did you say?"

"What did I say?" she asked, delaying for a moment—"I said yes."

Afterward she inquired about Sobel, and

WORDS TO OWN

repugnant (ri·pug′nənt) *adj.*: distasteful; offensive.

Skill Link

Feld, without exactly knowing why, said the assistant had got another job. Miriam said nothing more and began to read. The shoemaker's conscience did not trouble him; he was satisfied with the Saturday date.

During the week, by placing here and there a <u>deft</u> question, he managed to get from Miriam some information about Max. It surprised him to learn that the boy was not studying to be either a doctor or lawyer but was taking a business course leading to a degree in accountancy. Feld was a little disappointed because he thought of accountants as bookkeepers and would have preferred a "higher profession." However, it was not long before he had investigated the subject and discovered that certified public accountants were highly respected people, so he was thoroughly content as Saturday approached. But because Saturday was a busy day, he was much in the store and therefore did not see Max when he came to call for Miriam. From his wife he learned there had been nothing especially revealing about their meeting. Max had rung the bell and Miriam had got her coat and left with him—nothing more. Feld did not probe, for his wife was not particularly observant. Instead, he waited up for Miriam with a newspaper on his lap, which he scarcely looked at, so lost was he in thinking of the future. He awoke to find her in the room with him, tiredly removing her hat. Greeting her, he was suddenly inexplicably afraid to ask anything about the evening. But since she volunteered nothing, he was at last forced to inquire how she had enjoyed herself. Miriam began something noncommittal but apparently changed her mind, for she said after a minute, "I was bored."

When Feld had sufficiently recovered from his anguished disappointment to ask why, she answered without hesitation, "Because he's nothing more than a materialist."

"What means this word?"

"He has no soul. He's only interested in things."

He considered her statement for a long time but then asked, "Will you see him again?"

"He didn't ask."

"Suppose he will ask you?"

"I won't see him."

He did not argue; however, as the days went by, he hoped increasingly she would change her mind. He wished the boy would telephone, because he was sure there was more to him than Miriam, with her inexperienced eye, could discern. But Max didn't call. As a matter of fact he took a different route to school, no longer passing the shoemaker's store, and Feld was deeply hurt.

Then one afternoon Max came in and asked for his shoes. The shoemaker took them down from the shelf where he had placed them, apart from the other pairs. He had done the work himself, and the soles and heels were well built and firm. The shoes had been highly polished and somehow looked better than new. Max's Adam's apple went up once when he saw them, and his eyes had little lights in them.

"How much?" he asked, without directly looking at the shoemaker.

"Like I told you before," Feld answered sadly. "One dollar fifty cents."

Max handed him two crumpled bills and received in return a newly minted silver half-dollar.

He left. Miriam had not been mentioned. That night the shoemaker discovered that his new assistant had been all the while stealing from him, and he suffered a heart attack.

Though the attack was very mild, he lay in bed for three weeks. Miriam spoke of going for Sobel, but sick as he was, Feld rose in wrath against the idea. Yet in his heart he knew there was no other way, and the first weary day back in the shop thoroughly convinced him, so that night after supper he dragged himself to Sobel's rooming house.

He toiled up the stairs, though he knew it was bad for him, and at the top knocked at the door. Sobel opened it and the shoemaker entered. The room was a small, poor one, with a single window facing the street. It contained a

---

WORDS TO OWN

deft *adj.*: skillful in a quick and sure way.

E **Critical Thinking**
Analyzing Motivation
? Why do you think Feld lies to Miriam about Sobel? [Possible responses: He feels guilty for the way he treated Sobel; he does not want Miriam to feel sympathetic toward Sobel.]

F **English Language Learners**
Dialect
Point out to English language learners that instead of "he was much in the store," a native English speaker would say something like "he was in the store many hours," "he worked long hours," or "he was in the store a lot." Malamud uses the word order of Feld's dialect because the story is told from Feld's point of view.

G **Critical Thinking**
Analyzing Motivation
? What makes Feld afraid to ask Miriam about her evening? [Possible responses: Miriam's body language and facial expression may suggest that the date was not a success; if she is not interested in Max, the still-hopeful Feld doesn't want to know yet.]

H **Reading Skills and Strategies**
Making Inferences
? What qualities does Miriam imply that she wants in a boyfriend? [She wants someone who has intellectual interests, such as literature, art, music, and philosophical ideas.]

I **Critical Thinking**
Cause and Effect
? Is there a cause-and-effect connection between Feld's heart attack and the other two significant events of the day—Max's coming for his shoes and Feld's discovery that his assistant has been stealing from him? [Sample responses: Yes, both events are highly stressful for a man with a weak heart; no, the heart attack was bound to happen sometime, and the timing is pure coincidence.]

Resources ———

Selection Assessment
Formal Assessment
• Selection Test, p. 18
Test Generator (One-Stop Planner)
• CD-ROM

Taking a Second Look

Review: Protagonist and Antagonist
The protagonist, or main character, is usually the one who sets the action in motion. The antagonist is the character or force who comes into conflict with the protagonist. Additional discussion of protagonist and antagonist appears in the *Handbook of Literary Terms* (under Protagonist) on p. 1003.

Activities
Have students review the information on pp. 119 and 1003 and list characteristics that help the reader identify protagonist and antagonist.

Encourage students to reconsider the question of the protagonist and antagonist in Malamud's story. Invite them to give their reasons for naming Feld the protagonist and Sobel the antagonist. (If some students still see Sobel as protagonist because his leaving the shop causes Feld to come to him, help them understand that Feld's desire to see his daughter married to a college graduate sets the plot into motion earlier and causes Sobel to leave in the first place.)

Ⓐ Elements of Literature

Conflict

❓ How does this scene at last reveal the internal conflict that has been tearing Sobel apart? [It makes clear his long-term love for Miriam.] **How does it also contribute to an external conflict between Sobel and Feld?** [Feld wants someone "better" than Sobel for his daughter's husband.]

---

narrow cot, a low table, and several stacks of books piled haphazardly around on the floor along the wall, which made him think how queer Sobel was, to be uneducated and read so much. He had once asked him, Sobel, why you read so much? and the assistant could not answer him. Did you ever study in a college someplace? he had asked, but Sobel shook his head. He read, he said, to know. But to know what, the shoemaker demanded, and to know, why? Sobel never explained, which proved he read much because he was queer.

Feld sat down to recover his breath. The assistant was resting on his bed with his heavy back to the wall. His shirt and trousers were clean, and his stubby fingers, away from the shoemaker's bench, were strangely _pallid_. His face was thin and pale, as if he had been shut in this room since the day he had bolted from the store.

"So when you will come back to work?" Feld asked him.

To his surprise, Sobel burst out, "Never."

Jumping up, he strode over to the window that looked out upon the miserable street. "Why should I come back?" he cried.

"I will raise your wages."

"Who cares for your wages!"

The shoemaker, knowing he didn't care, was at a loss what else to say.

"What do you want from me, Sobel?"

"Nothing."

"I always treated you like you was my son."

Sobel vehemently denied it. "So why you look for strange boys in the street they should go out with Miriam? Why you don't think of me?"

The shoemaker's hands and feet turned freezing cold. His voice became so hoarse he couldn't speak. At last he cleared his throat and croaked, "So what has my daughter got to do with a shoemaker thirty-five years old who works for me?"

"Why do you think I worked so long for you?" Sobel cried out. "For the stingy wages I sacrificed five years of my life so you could have to eat and drink and where to sleep?"

"Then for what?" shouted the shoemaker.

"For Miriam," he blurted—"for her."

The shoemaker, after a time, managed to say, "I pay wages in cash, Sobel," and lapsed into silence. Though he was seething with excitement, his mind was coldly clear, and he had to admit to himself he had sensed all along that Sobel felt this way. He had never so much as thought it consciously, but he had felt it and was afraid.

"Miriam knows?" he muttered hoarsely.

"She knows."

"You told her?"

"No."

"Then how does she know?"

WORDS TO OWN

pallid (pal′id) *adj.*: pale; lacking in color.

Making the Connections

Connecting to the Theme: "Hearts That Love"

In this story, Feld loves his daughter enough to want a future for her that is socially and economically better than that of a shoemaker's wife. However, the college boy with the good prospects doesn't love Miriam, and she doesn't love him. It is Sobel the shoemaker who loves Miriam—enough to dedicate years of his life to earning the opportunity to marry her. The implication throughout the story is that Sobel could do better for himself educationally and economically, yet he is content to read simply "to know" and willing to accept low wages in order to stay near Miriam until he can ask her to marry him.

You might have students discuss which man's love for Miriam they find easier to understand, and why; and whose they find more admirable, and why.

When he was once asked about writing, Malamud said this:

> 66 You write by sitting down and writing. There's no particular time or place—you suit yourself, your nature. How one works, assuming he's disciplined, doesn't matter. If he or she is not disciplined, no sympathetic magic will help. The trick is to make time—not steal it—and produce the fiction. If the stories come, you get them written, you're on the right track. Eventually everyone learns his or her own best way. The real mystery to crack is you. 99

"How does she know?" Sobel said. "Because she knows. She knows who I am and what is in my heart."

Feld had a sudden insight. In some <u>devious</u> way, with his books and commentary, Sobel had given Miriam to understand that he loved her. The shoemaker felt a terrible anger at him for his deceit.

"Sobel, you are crazy," he said bitterly. "She will never marry a man so old and ugly like you."

Sobel turned black with rage. He cursed the shoemaker, but then, though he trembled to hold it in, his eyes filled with tears and he broke into deep sobs. With his back to Feld, he stood at the window, fists clenched, and his shoulders shook with his choked sobbing.

Watching him, the shoemaker's anger dimin-

ished. His teeth were on edge with pity for the man, and his eyes grew moist. How strange and sad that a refugee, a grown man, bald and old with his miseries, who had by the skin of his teeth escaped Hitler's incinerators,[3] should fall in love, when he had got to America, with a girl less than half his age. Day after day, for five years he had sat at his bench, cutting and hammering away, waiting for the girl to become a woman, unable to ease his heart with speech, knowing no protest but desperation.

"Ugly I didn't mean," he said half aloud.

Then he realized that what he had called ugly was not Sobel but Miriam's life if she married him. He felt for his daughter a strange and gripping sorrow, as if she were already Sobel's bride, the wife, after all, of a shoemaker, and had in her life no more than her mother had had. And all his dreams for her—why he had slaved and destroyed his heart with anxiety and labor—all these dreams of a better life were dead.

The room was quiet. Sobel was standing by the window reading, and it was curious that when he read, he looked young.

"She is only nineteen," Feld said brokenly. "This is too young yet to get married. Don't ask her for two years more, till she is twenty-one; then you can talk to her."

Sobel didn't answer. Feld rose and left. He went slowly down the stairs, but once outside, though it was an icy night and the crisp falling snow whitened the street, he walked with a stronger stride.

But the next morning, when the shoemaker arrived, heavy-hearted, to open the store, he saw he needn't have come, for his assistant was already seated at the last, pounding leather for his love.

---

3. **Hitler's incinerators:** the furnaces in which the Nazis burned the bodies of Jews and other people whom they murdered in the death camps during World War II.

WORDS TO OWN

devious (dē'vē·əs) *adj.*: roundabout; indirect. *Devious* also means "deceitful."

B Elements of Literature
Theme
One interpretation of the theme of this story is that enduring a long period of suffering is possible if a person is deeply in love. This idea is exemplified by Sobel's willingness to work another two years, for a total of seven, before even asking Miriam if she will marry him.

C Elements of Literature
Protagonist
❓ What goal of Feld's set the plot into motion? [his desire to see Miriam make a marriage that would give her a secure future] How does this passage of text demonstrate the depth of his love for his daughter? [He is willing to sacrifice his idea of a good future for her if Sobel is the man she wants to marry.]

D Reading Skills and Strategies
Responding to the Text
❓ Do you think Sobel makes the right decision? Why or why not? [Possible responses: Yes, because he really loves Miriam and believes that this is the only way he will be able to marry her; no, because he has no guarantee that Miriam will marry him even if he stays.]

Assessing Learning

Check Test: True–False
1. Feld sees Max for the first time when Max brings a pair of shoes into the shop. [False]
2. Max wants to see a picture of Miriam before he agrees to ask her out. [True]
3. Feld finds Sobel extremely trustworthy. [True]
4. Sobel welcomes Feld on Feld's first visit to Sobel's rooming house. [False]
5. Feld finally agrees to let Sobel talk to Miriam about marriage if he will wait two more years. [True]

Self-Assessment
Reading
Have students rate themselves on the following items, using a scale from 1 to 5, with 1 meaning "little" and 5 meaning "great":
____1. Amount of attention I pay while reading
____2. Effort I make to predict events while reading
____3. My ability to re-tell the events of the story

Standardized Test Preparation
For practice in proofreading and editing, see
• *Daily Oral Grammar,* Transparency 8

A Reading Skills and Strategies

Responding to the Text

❓ How do you react to the idea of a father bartering his daughter this way? [Sample response: Maybe it was all right in Biblical times, since those were the cultural standards of the time, but it isn't acceptable today.]

B Critical Thinking

Challenging the Text

❓ Do you think Laban is justified in tricking Jacob? Why or why not? [Yes, Laban has tradition on his side, and Jacob should have known; no, Laban breaks his agreement with Jacob—if Laban wanted Leah to be married first, he should have said so.]

C Elements of Literature

Metaphor

❓ To what does the speaker compare himself? [a moth drawn to the flame of the girl's beauty]

MAKING MEANINGS

First Thoughts

1. Possible responses: Sobel will marry Miriam because they have already established a deep friendship and Miriam loves every word that comes from Sobel's pen; Sobel will not marry Miriam because he will never be brave enough to ask her. Sobel could identify with the speaker of the poem because he talks about books with Miriam instead of directly telling her how much he loves her.

Shaping Interpretations

2. Some students will have suspected Sobel's love from his earliest loud hammering; most will guess when he breaks the last and bolts from the shop. Other clues include his willingness to work for so long for so little and the extensive book notes he writes for Miriam.

3. Miriam shows her independence by working in an office and sharing books with Sobel instead of attending college. She respects her father but will not violate her own principles for his sake. She can be blunt and show her temper.

(Answers continue on p. T129)

T128

Jacob and Rachel

The title of Malamud's story is an allusion to the Biblical story of Jacob and Rachel, which follows. As a young man, Jacob was sent by his father to his uncle Laban to marry one of Laban's daughters. Jacob stayed with Laban and worked for him for many years.

Laban said to Jacob, "Why should you work for me for nothing simply because you are my kinsman? Tell me what your wages ought to be." Now Laban had two daughters: The elder was called Leah, and the younger, Rachel. Leah was dull-eyed, but Rachel was graceful and beautiful. Jacob had fallen in love with Rachel, and he said, "I will work seven years for your younger daughter, Rachel." Laban replied, "It is better that I should give her to you than to anyone else. Stay with me."

So Jacob worked seven years for Rachel, and they seemed like a few days because he loved her. Then Jacob said to Laban, "I have served my time. Give me my wife so that we may sleep together."

So Laban gathered all the men of the place together and gave a feast. In the evening he took his daughter Leah and brought her to Jacob, and Jacob slept with her. . . . But when morning came, Jacob saw that it was Leah° and said to Laban, "What have you done to me? Did I not work for Rachel? Why have you deceived me?" Laban answered, "In our country it is not right to give the younger sister in marriage before the elder. Go through with the seven days' feast for the elder, and the younger shall be given you in return for a further seven years' work." Jacob agreed and completed the seven days for Leah.

Then Laban gave Jacob his daughter Rachel as wife; . . . [Jacob] loved her rather than Leah, and he worked for Laban for a further seven years.

—Genesis 29:15–30, New English Bible

° The deception was possible probably because Leah wore a veil.

Jacob and Rachel (c. 1830) by William Dyce (1806–1864). Oil on canvas.

I Wish I Had Said . . .

I wish I had said . . .
Your beauty is like a light,
And I am drawn to it,
Fluttering by its flame.
5 I wish I had said . . .
Your body is to die for,
And I long to be martyred.
Yes, I wish I had said . . .
Your smile melts through
10 My heart, leaving only
Your warmth. Oh, how
I wish I had said . . .
Your translucent eyes
Send your soul to my heart,
15 Forcing it to beat again.
Yes, that is what I wish
I had said, but,
With confounded cowardice,
All I said was . . .
20 Hello, with a smile,
And I passed you by.

—Christian O'Connor
Gonzaga College High School
Washington, D.C.

Connecting Across Texts

Jacob and Rachel. Malamud's story directly parallels the Biblical story of Jacob and Rachel. Like Jacob, Sobel is willing to work seven years to marry the woman he loves; he shows endurance and courage in overcoming obstacles to attain true love. However, Jacob must first marry an older sister and then work another seven years for his true love; Sobel has no older sister to worry about, but he is confronted by Feld's reluctance to allow them to marry right away.

I Wish I Had Said . . . Like the speaker of this poem, Sobel loves Miriam from a distance. Instead of expressing his love for her, he continues to work for her father at an inadequate wage, to recommend books to her, and to spend a great deal of time writing commentaries on the books for her. Ask students to compare and contrast further the speaker of the poem and Sobel. Why do both hesitate to speak their love? What might they fear?

MAKING MEANINGS

First Thoughts

[speculate]

1. Do you think Sobel will eventually marry Miriam? Why, or why not? Would Sobel identify with the speaker of the poem on page 128? Why, or why not?

Shaping Interpretations

[predict]

2. At what point in the story did you realize that Sobel is in love with Miriam? What clues in the text do you think **foreshadow** Sobel's secret?

[analyze]

3. How would you describe Miriam's **character**, in view of what she says and does? Did any of Miriam's actions surprise you? Talk about your response to Miriam.

[compare and contrast]

4. Use a circle diagram like the one at the right to **compare and contrast** the **characters** of Max and Sobel. List each man's individual qualities. In the shaded area, list the qualities they share. Which man do you think would make Miriam happier, and why? (On the other hand, do you feel that neither is a good match for Miriam?)

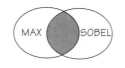

[evaluate]

5. This story is about parental as well as romantic love. What do you think of the way Feld shows his love for his daughter? Despite the differences in culture, do you think Feld resembles the mother in "Two Kinds" (see page 95)? Why?

[analyze]

6. Suppose you were directing this story for a TV production. Whom would you focus on as the **protagonist,** and why? Who would be his or her **antagonist**? How would the production differ depending on who the protagonist was?

Connecting with the Text

[connect]

7. How do you feel about arranged dates and about arranged marriages such as the one Feld wanted for his daughter? (Did this story affect the views you expressed in your Quickwrite notes?)

Extending the Text

[compare and contrast]

8. This story is set in a specific **culture** that may be very different from yours. What can you learn about that culture from the text? Could these events take place in any other culture, including your own? Talk about your thoughts on this issue of culture and its influence on our lives.

[connect]

9. Read the Biblical account of Jacob and Rachel (see *Connections* on page 128). What parallels and what important differences do you see between the Biblical story and Malamud's? Do you think the kind of love shown by Jacob and Sobel is believable? Why, or why not?

THE FIRST SEVEN YEARS 129

Reading Check

Plot a **story map** to review the main elements of this story.

Setting	
Characters	
Their wants	
What blocks their wants	
Main events	
Climax	
Resolution	

(Answers continued from p.T128)

4. Sample answers: **Max**—about Miriam's age, attending college, materialistic, interested in getting ahead, sees education as job training, impatient for success. **Sobel**—considerably older than Miriam, patient, genuinely interested in intellectual life for the pleasure ideas bring, spiritual. **Both**—eligible bachelors, not very handsome, strong feelings and desires (but for different things). Sobel possesses more of the qualities that Miriam herself has identified as important to her.

5. Some students may admire Feld's desire to help his daughter; others may see him as meddling. Both Feld and Jing-mei's mother want what they consider best for their daughters; both daughters resent the interference.

6. Feld is the protagonist because his goals for Miriam set the story in motion. Sobel is the antagonist. Making Sobel the protagonist for a television version would mean changing the point of view and emphasizing different events and conversations. We might not learn so much about Feld's problems, for example.

Connecting with the Text

7. Some students might agree to go on an arranged date or agree to an arranged marriage to please whoever arranged it or to meet someone new. Others might dislike the whole idea, preferring to choose their own dates or spouses.

Extending the Text

8. Possible responses: Students may mention the emphasis on marriage for women and the value placed on education. Students will probably agree that the events of the story could occur in many, but not all, cultures.

9. The main parallel is Jacob's and Sobel's working seven years to marry the women they love. The stories differ in that Feld cannot deceive Sobel by giving him an older daughter first, since Miriam is his only child. Still, the "first" in the title of the story suggests that Sobel, like Jacob, might end up waiting longer than seven years to marry Miriam. Some students will find love like Jacob's and Sobel's believable; others will say that no one would wait that long.

Reading Check

Setting: A shoe shop in New York City in the 1950s (Sobel escaped Hitler's incinerators)
Characters: Feld, Sobel, Max, Miriam, Mrs. Feld, and the new assistant
Their wants: Feld wants Max and Miriam to marry each other. Sobel wants to marry Miriam. Miriam wants to be independent.
What blocks their wants: Max and Miriam do not like each other. Feld does not want Miriam to marry Sobel.

Main events: Feld talks to Max about meeting his daughter. Sobel overhears this conversation and storms out of the shop. Miriam is bored during her dates with Max. The new assistant steals from Feld. Feld has a mild heart attack. His wife and daughter urge him to go to Sobel.
Climax: Feld visits Sobel to ask him to return to work; he finds out that Sobel loves Miriam.
Resolution: Feld agrees to allow Sobel to propose to Miriam in two years' time. Sobel returns to work.

T129

Rubrics for each Choices assignment appear on p. 103 in the *Portfolio Management System*.

CHOICES: Building Your Portfolio

1. **Writer's Notebook** Students may find that Feld is the only character who really changes in "The First Seven Years." Remind students to save their work. They may use it as prewriting for the Writer's Workshop on p. 164.

2. **Creative Writing** As students work on this activity, encourage them to listen mentally to Miriam's voice as they imagine it, and then to try to capture that voice in writing. They might also try speaking aloud in her voice to see how natural their phrasing sounds. They should note that, unlike her father, Miriam speaks standard English, not a dialect.

3. **Creative Writing** Encourage students to think through this assignment in terms of what they know about both Sobel and Miriam. Remind them that people do not often make drastic, surprising changes in their lives. Have students share their predictions in small groups or with the class as a whole.

4. **Research/Social Studies** Remind students that pictures, charts, and other visual aids can help focus the attention of their audience and leave them with strong mental images. Encourage students to find or make visual aids that enrich the content of their talks, and to use these visuals as they make their presentations.

CHOICES: Building Your Portfolio

Writer's Notebook

1. Collecting Ideas for a Character Analysis

How do they change, and why? A good strategy to use for analyzing a character is to identify how the character changes—from your first glimpse of the person at the story's beginning to your last look at him or her at the end. Select a character from "The First Seven Years" or from another story, and take notes on how he or she changes in the course of the story. What does your character learn or discover by the story's end?

How have the character's feelings changed? What has caused this change? Be sure you assess the change—is it believable? Save your notes for possible use in the Writer's Workshop on page 164.

Creative Writing

2. What Does Miriam Think?

Rewrite any key event in this story from Miriam's **point of view.** Miriam might describe one of her dates with Max or report a conversation with Feld or describe her feelings for Sobel. Write as "I," as Miriam. You may want to write a **journal entry** or a **letter.** If you write a journal entry, be sure to make up a date. If you write a letter, make it clear whom Miriam is writing to. Read aloud your interpretations of Miriam's feelings, and respond to your classmates' interpretations. Are there differences of opinion?

Creative Writing

3. "When two years had passed . . ."

The ending of this love story is not entirely clear. Sobel appears to be willing to wait for two more years before asking Miriam to marry him. In two years, though, many things can change. In a paragraph, tell what you think might happen to Miriam and Sobel in the next two years.

Research/Social Studies

4. Reporting on an Immigrant Culture

Although Malamud does not locate this story specifically on the Lower East Side, his characters could have been among the millions of Eastern European Jewish immigrants who lived in this poor neighborhood in New York City in the early and middle years of the twentieth century. Using your library, the Internet, and electronic databases, prepare a brief **informal talk** on Jewish immigrant life in New York City. After you gather your data, you'll have to narrow your focus to a manageable topic. Be sure to tell what you learned from Malamud's text. Ask your audience for feedback. Was your presentation clear and focused?

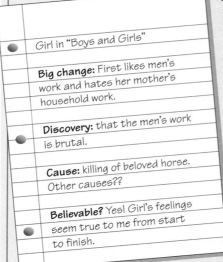

Girl in "Boys and Girls"

Big change: First likes men's work and hates her mother's household work.

Discovery: that the men's work is brutal.

Cause: killing of beloved horse. Other causes??

Believable? Yes! Girl's feelings seem true to me from start to finish.

Using Students' Strengths

Auditory Learners
Before they begin Choice 2, students may benefit from improvising a monologue using Miriam's "voice." They can tape record their monologue and play it back to check whether or not their phrasing and ideas sound like Miriam's. Alternatively, they might practice speaking as Miriam in front of a mirror.

Kinesthetic/Spatial Learners
For Choice 4, students may enjoy building models of apartments, synagogues, neighborhood stores, schools, settlement houses, and other structures that were important to Jewish immigrants. Students can use these models in their presentations and leave them on display in the classroom.

LANGUAGE LINK   MINI-LESSON

Handbook of Literary Terms HELP

See Dialect.

Dialect—How We Speak

A **dialect** is a form of a language spoken in a specific region (Maine, Appalachia, Brooklyn) or by a particular group of people. For example, if you pronounce *Mary, marry,* and *merry* exactly the same way, you are probably from the Midwest. If you are from the Northeast, you probably pronounce each word differently.

Besides differences in pronunciation, dialects are distinguished by differences in vocabulary and **syntax** (the way words are organized in a sentence). The dialect of a particular ethnic group usually contains traces of the syntax of the group's native language.

A Russian immigrant might omit the definite article *the* and the indefinite article *a* because in Russian those forms do not exist. ("He has big house in country.")

A French-speaking Haitian immigrant might add unnecessary articles because articles are used more often in French than in English. ("Do you know where is the Fifth Avenue?")

In "The First Seven Years," Feld and Sobel speak the English dialect of their ethnic group—Polish Jews whose native languages are Polish and Yiddish.

Try It Out

Find at least five examples in this story in which a character uses **syntax** that is not Standard English syntax. Rewrite these passages in Standard English. What does the use of Standard English change about the character?

A tip for writers: When you write dialogue, try to make it sound like your characters' real speech. When you reproduce dialect, you must try to make the speech sound authentic, but you must also avoid seeming to mock the characters. Malamud writes accurate dialect without ever seeming to belittle his characters.

VOCABULARY   HOW TO OWN A WORD

WORD BANK

reverie
discerned
illiterate
unscrupulous
profuse
sanctified
repugnant
deft
pallid
devious

Word Charts: All You Need to Know

Work with a partner or small group to make a chart of basic information about each word in the Word Bank. You will have to use a **dictionary.** Hint: If you can't find a word's origin, try looking up the **root word** (*scruple* instead of *unscrupulous,* for example).

discerned
• **Meaning:** "recognized"; "perceived" • **Origin:** Latin *dis-,* "apart," and *cernere,* "to separate" • **Related words:** *discernible* and *discerning* (adj.); *discernibly* (adv.); *discernment* (n.) • **Examples (things that can be discerned):** *light, colors, smells, tastes, cold,* or *heat;* when a friend is upset; when someone is frightened

THE FIRST SEVEN YEARS **131**

Language Link Quick Check

Have students give full answers to the following questions.

1. What is a dialect? [A dialect is a form of a language spoken in a specific region or by a particular group of people.]
2. Besides pronunciation, how are dialects distinguished from one another? [differences in vocabulary and syntax, or word order]
3. How does a group's native language influence its dialect? [The dialect usually contains traces of the syntax of the original language.]
4. How might Russian-speaking and French-speaking immigrants differ with respect to using articles? [The Russian speaker might omit *the* and *a* because they do not exist in Russian; the French speaker might add unnecessary articles because French uses more articles than English.]

LANGUAGE LINK

Try It Out
Possible Answers

1. ". . . this is a fine boy that he wants so much an education." [This is a fine boy who wants an education so much.]
2. ". . . so I will explain you right away." [So I will explain it to you right away.]
3. "I thought maybe you will be interested sometime to meet a girl like this." [I thought you might be interested in meeting a girl like this sometime.]
4. "What means this word?" [What does this word mean?]
5. "Ugly I didn't mean." [I didn't mean ugly.]

VOCABULARY

Possible Answers

1. *reverie* daydreaming; French *rever,* to roam; no other parts of speech; losing track of time while staring at the sea
2. *illiterate* uneducated, unable to read or write; Latin *il-,* not, *literatus,* literate; *illiteracy* (n.), *illiterately* (adv.); unable to read a menu
3. *unscrupulous* not restrained by ideas of right and wrong; Latin *un-,* not, *scrupus,* sharp stone; *scruples* (n.), *unscrupulously* (adv.); shoplifting
4. *profuse* plentiful, abundant; Latin *pro-,* forth, *fundere,* to pour; *profusely* (adv.), *profusion* (n.); colors in a flower show
5. *sanctified* blessed, made holy; Latin *sanctus,* sacred, *facere,* to make; *sanctuary* (n.), *sanctifier* (n.); Bible
6. *repugnant* distasteful, offensive; Latin *re-,* back or against, *pugnare,* to fight; *repugnance* (n.), *repugnantly* (adv.); chewing with mouth open
7. *deft* skillful, in a quick and sure way; Middle English *defte; deftly* (adv.), *deftness* (n.); making a graceful dance step
8. *pallid* pale; Latin *pallidus,* pale; *pallidly* (adv.), *pallidness* (n.); face of someone in shock
9. *devious* roundabout, indirect; Latin *de-,* off, from, and *via,* road; *deviously* (adv.), *deviousness* (n.); telling half-truths

Resources ———

Language
• *Grammar and Language Links* Worksheet, p. 13

Vocabulary
• *Words to Own,* Worksheet, p. 8

OBJECTIVES

1. Read and interpret the story
2. Analyze dynamic and static characters
3. Establish purpose for reading
4. Express understanding through writing, critical thinking/speaking, or drawing
5. Identify lively verbs and use them in writing
6. Understand and use new words

SKILLS

Literary
• Analyze dynamic and static characters

Reading
• Establish purpose for reading

Writing
• Analyze a character
• Use sensory details in a story
• Write a reflection on love

Speaking/Listening
• Present an analysis of a quest

Grammar/Language
• Identify and use lively verbs

Vocabulary
• Understand and use new words

Art
• Create a map of a journey

Viewing/Representing
• Respond to the art (ATE)

Planning

• **Block Schedule**
  Block Scheduling Lesson Plans with Pacing Guide

• **Traditional Schedule**
  Lesson Plans Including Strategies for English-Language Learners

• **One-Stop Planner**
  CD-ROM with Test Generator

Before You Read

DISTILLATION

Make the Connection

The Power of Love

We all remember days from our childhood that made a special and lasting impression on us. The narrator of "Distillation" recalls one such day—a particular Saturday when he recognized suddenly the force of his father's love.

Distillation is a chemical process in which the essence of a substance is separated from impurities. Keep that definition in mind as you read the story, which is set in a poor Chicago neighborhood in the 1930s.

Quickwrite

Think back on your childhood, and remember a special day when you came to understand someone close to you. Write briefly about the day and your feelings.

Elements of Literature

Characters Who Change

Life changes people. We have victories and defeats and disappointments. Characters in stories change, too, or we wouldn't be much interested in their lives. Characters who change in significant ways are **dynamic characters.** By the end of the story, they have usually come to some new understanding, made some important decision, or taken a crucial action. Such a change often provides a clue to a story's meaning. **Static characters,** those who change less significantly, or not at all, are usually background figures.

> **D**ynamic characters undergo change as a result of the story's action. **Static characters** do not change—they remain the same throughout the story.

For more on Character, see pages 110–111 and the Handbook of Literary Terms.

Reading Skills and Strategies

Establishing a Purpose for Reading

Maybe you're not consciously aware of it, but you usually have a **purpose** when you sit down to read. If you're reading fiction, you might simply want to **enjoy** getting caught up in a "good read" and appreciating a writer's style. You might read to **discover** another time and place and characters different from yourself. Sometimes, you might have a deeper purpose for reading—you might want to gain some insight into life and people. When you read for this purpose, you **interpret** a writer's message or a character's complex motivation. Often, when reading fiction, you combine all three purposes. Try it as you read "Distillation."

 go.hrw.com
LE0 10-2

Resources: Print and Media

Reading
• *Reading Skills and Strategies*
  MiniRead Skill Lesson, p. 66
  Selection Skill Lesson, p. 73
• *Graphic Organizers for Active Reading,* p. 9
• *Words to Own,* p. 9
• *Audio CD Library*
  Disc 5, Track 2

Writing and Language
• *Daily Oral Grammar*

Transparency 9
• *Grammar and Language Links*
  Worksheet, p. 15
• *Language Workshop CD-ROM*

Assessment
• *Formal Assessment,* p. 20
• *Portfolio Management System,* p. 104
• *Test Generator (One-Stop Planner CD-ROM)*

Internet
• go.hrw.com (keyword: LE0 10-2)

DISTILLATION

Hugo Martinez-Serros

One day alone remains--a day so different from the rest that I cannot forget it.

Summary ▪ ▪

This is a classic quest story, but the heroic journey is a father's weekly trip to the Chicago dump with his four young sons. As a poor family of Mexican Americans in the 1930s, they sort through garbage for edible and usable items. The youngest son (five at that time) chronicles in first-person narration his father's arduous, exhilarating feat of pulling a wagon bearing his sons through hazardous Chicago crossings and over a mountainous bridge. At the dump, the family is caught in a terrifying hailstorm. The father spreads a tarp over his back and shields his sons from the hail with his body as he comforts them with his voice. Back home, the sight of his father's bruised and welted body sparks an epiphany in the narrator, who suddenly recognizes his father's great love for his family. This insight is one of the possible "distillations" of the title and evidence of the dynamic character of the narrator.

As the adult narrator makes explicit, the telling of the story is his own act of love. Using both mythic imagery and Biblical allusion, he renders his father as a superhuman giant.

Resources

Listening
Audio CD Library
A gripping recording of "Distillation" is provided in the *Audio CD Library:*
• Disc 5, Track 2

Preteaching Vocabulary

Words To Own
Have students work in pairs to discuss the Words to Own on pp. 134–140. Then have them choose the best word to complete each of the following sentences about a game-show competition.

abated	myriad
eclipsed	spoils
galvanized	taut
glower	tentative
livid	zenith

1. The tension never [abated] during the exciting show.
2. Possible answers sometimes seemed [myriad], but the judges would accept only one.
3. Clues within the questions often [galvanized] a competitor to answer quickly.
4. One question was so difficult that nobody risked even a [tentative] response.
5. Once, the defending champion was so tense that the muscles in her neck grew [taut].
6. Applause at her correct answer marked the [zenith] of the competition.
7. Her final score was so high that it [eclipsed] the scores of the runners-up.
8. The last-place contestant scowled and [glowered] at everyone.
9. He was so badly injured that his skin looked blotched and [livid] .
10. The fabulous [spoils] awarded to the winner included a dream vacation for two.

A Reading Skills and Strategies

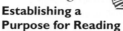

Establishing a Purpose for Reading

? After reading the first paragraph, what questions immediately pop into your mind? [Possible responses: Who is "he"? What is the "it" he does on Saturdays? Who are "we"? Why does one Saturday stand out in the narrator's memory?] Point out to students that answering questions that arise in their minds is essential to fulfilling reading— regardless of whether their purpose is enjoyment, discovering other people and places, or interpreting a writer's message or a character's motivation.

B Elements of Literature

Characterization

? What does this paragraph suggest about the father's character and personality? [Sample answer: He is rather strict, and can be rough and impatient.]

C Appreciating Language

Metaphor

? To what does the speaker compare the day? [a vast blue balloon] the sunlight? [the air inflating the balloon]

A He went on Saturdays because it was the best day. He did it for years and we, his sons, were his helpers. And yet one day alone remains, that single distant Saturday—a day so different from the rest that I cannot forget it:

Friday night I was in bed by nine. It would take us about an hour to get there, and we had to leave by eight the following morning to arrive just before the first tall trucks. All day the trucks would come and go, all day until five in the afternoon. My father wanted to get there before anyone else. He wanted to look it all over and then swoop down on the best places. There the spoils would go to the quickest hands, and we would work in swift thrusts, following his example, obeying the gestures and words he used to direct us.

B That Saturday morning my father waited impatiently for us, his piercing whistles shrilling his annoyance at our delay. Anxious for us, my mother pushed us through the door as she grazed us with her lips. My father was flicking at his fingers with a rag and turned sharply to glower at us. I saw fresh grease on the hubs of the big iron wheels that supported the weight of his massive wagon, its great wooden bed and sides fixed on heavy steel axletrees.[1] He spoke harshly to us, for we had kept him waiting and he was angry: "What took you so long? ¡Vámonos!"[2]

He had already lowered the wagon's sides. Now, grasping us at the armpits, he picked us up and set us in beside the burlap sacks and a bag of food, starting with me, the youngest, and following the order of our ages—five, six and a half, eight, and eleven. He handed us a gallon jug of water and then pulled the guayín[3] through the door in the backyard fence, easing it out into the alley by the very long shaft that was its handle, like some vaguely familiar giant gently drawing a ship by its prow.

Yawning in the warmth of May, I leaned back, like my brothers, in anticipation of the joys of a

1. **axletrees:** bars connecting the opposite wheels of a wagon.
2. **Vámonos** (vä′mô·nôs): Spanish for "Let's go."
3. **guayín** (gwä·yēn′): Spanish dialect term for a wagon that can be pulled by a person.

C crossing that would reach almost the full length of the longest line that could be drawn in the world as I knew it. That world, dense and more durable than a name, extended just beyond South Chicago. The day, a vast blue balloon stretched to its limits by a great flood of light, contained us and invited our blinking eyes to examine all that it enveloped.

The fastest route led us down alleys, away from pedestrians, cars, trucks, and wide horse-drawn wagons that plied the streets. The alleys, always familiar, seemed somehow new in the morning light that gleamed on piles of garbage and everywhere flashed slivers of rainbows in beads of moisture. Garbage men used shovels to clear away these piles. What garbage cans there were stood sheltered against walls and fences or lay fallen in heaps of refuse. Through the unpaved alleys we went, over black earth hard packed and inlaid with myriad fragments of glass that sparkled in the morning radiance. Ahead of us rats scattered, fleeing the noise and bulk that moved toward them. Stray dogs, poking their noses into piles, did not retreat at our approach. Sunlight and shadows mottled my vision as the wagon rolled past trees, poles, fences, garages, sheds. My father moved in and out of the light, in and out of the shadows. On clotheslines, threadbare garments waved and swelled. Without slowing down, my father navigated around potholes, and these sudden maneuvers shook loose squeals and laughter as our bodies swayed.

At 86th Street he had to leave the alleys to continue south. There the steel mills and train yards suddenly closed in on us. We rattled over the railroad crossing at Burley Avenue, a busy, noisy pass, and this made me stiffen and press my palms against my ears. For one block Burley

---

WORDS TO OWN

spoils *n.*: loot; goods gotten through special effort. Here, *spoils* can also be seen as a reference to spoiled food.
glower (glou′ər) *v.*: glare; stare angrily.
myriad (mir′ē·əd) *adj.*: countless or of a highly varied nature.

Reaching All Students

Struggling Readers
Establishing a Purpose for Reading was introduced on p. 132. For a lesson directly tied to this story that teaches students to establish a purpose by using a strategy called Anticipation Guides, see the Reading Skills and Strategies binder:
• MiniRead Skill Lesson, p. 66
• Selection Skill Lesson, p. 73

English Language Learners
You might wish to divide the story into sections and assign each section to a small group of students. Ask groups to select words that are not in their active vocabularies and to try to figure out their meanings from context clues. Challenging words include *flicking, prow, slivers, coursing, veered, labyrinth, smoldering, ponderous, scudded, sheared, bawling,* and *welts.* Have groups combine lists to create a master list on the chalkboard.

Advanced Learners
Ask these students to work in small groups to develop questions that could serve as the basis of a class discussion of the story. Have a representative from each group write the group's questions on the board. Then, have the whole group of advanced learners select the ten best questions to address each of the following areas: plot, theme, symbolism, character, and tone. Two questions should be devoted to each literary element.

Avenue was a corridor—the only one for some distance around—that allowed movement north and south. At 89th Street my father followed a southwesterly course, going faster and faster, farther and farther from the steel mills, moving beyond the commercial area into a zone where the houses looked more and more expensive and the lawns grew thicker and greener. Already there were many flowers here, but no noise and few children, and there were no alleys. As my father rushed through these neighborhoods, we fell silent. I was baffled by the absence of garbage, and my eyes searched for an explanation that was to remain hidden from me for years.

At the end of a street that advanced between rows of brick bungalows stood the tunnel. We entered it and I tensed, at once exhilarated and alarmed by the wagon's din, frightened by the sudden darkness yet braving it because my father was there. A long time passed before we reached midpoint, where I feared everything would cave in on us. Then slowly my father's silhouette, pillarlike, filled the space ahead of me, growing larger and larger as we approached the light. Beyond the tunnel there were no houses, and we emerged into the radiance of 95th Street and Torrence Avenue.

There, stopping for the traffic that raced along 95th Street, my father quickly harnessed himself to the wagon with the double rope that was coiled around its prowlike handle. He was safe in this rude harness, for he could loosen it instantly and drop back alongside the great vehicle to brake it if the need arose. Now he pulled his wagon into Torrence Avenue, and his legs pumped, hard at first, and then they let up and soon he was running. Torrence Avenue, broad and well paved, shone like still water, and he ran smoothly, with long strides, at about three quarters of his top speed. We were smiling now, and we saw the smile on his face when he looked back over his shoulder. Breathing easily, he ran before us, and I watched his effortless movement forward. I felt a sudden keen desire to be just like him and for an instant found it difficult to breathe. To our right was a green expanse—trees, wildflowers, grasses, and a

bountiful variety of weeds—like a green sea extending to the horizon. Torrence Avenue now curved gently to the left for a half block and farther ahead gradually straightened along a stretch of several blocks, flanked on the left by a high fence and a long dense row of poplars. As my father navigated out of the curve we urged him on.

"Faster, Pa, faster! ¡Más rápido!"

"Come on, Pa, you c'n go faster'n that!"

"Pa, as fast as you c'n go, Pa, as fast as you c'n go!"

"Like a car, Pa, like a car!"

The prow shot forward, chasing my father as he reached top speed, and the craft darted into the straight lane that would take us to 103rd Street. My heart unleashed and racing, I looked up into the row of trees at the shoreline, saw swift islets[4] of blue sky coursing brightly through the green current of foliage. Along the shoreline my father's pace gradually slowed until he seemed to be moving at half speed. Whenever he glanced backward, we saw sweat trickling down his forehead and following the line of his eyebrows to join the streamlets running from his temples. Beads of perspiration swelled at his hairline and slid down his neck into the blue denim shirt, which deepened to a dolphin color. Far beyond the fence, their smoking stacks thrust into the sky, the steel mills took on the appearance of enormous, dark, steam-driven vessels.

At 103rd Street my father veered due west. Ahead of us, at a distance of several blocks, loomed the 103rd Street Bridge. All his pacing had led to this, was a limbering up for this ascent. Many yards before the street rose, my father began to increase his speed with every stride. He did it gradually, never slackening, for the wagon was heavy and accelerated slowly. I placed the gallon jug of water between my legs and tightened them around it as he reached full speed just before storming the incline. He started up unfalteringly, tenaciously, with short, rapid steps and his body bent forward, his natural reaction to the exaggerated resistance sud-

4. **islets** (ī'lits): very small islands.

DISTILLATION 135

D Reading Skills and Strategies
Making Inferences
❓ Why is there an absence of garbage in this neighborhood? [This wealthy neighborhood is better maintained than the area where the narrator lives.]

E Elements of Literature
Characterization
❓ What does the father's smile add to your earlier characterization of him? [Possible responses: He is a strong man who enjoys the physical exertion and time spent with his sons; he may be less rough or strict than he seemed at first.]

F Reading Skills and Strategies
Drawing Conclusions
❓ Why do you think the narrator feels a keen desire to be like his father at this moment? [Possible responses: He is impressed with his father's joy and strength; he realizes how hard his father works for his family; he catches a glimpse of his father's love.]

G Vocabulary
Deriving Meaning from Context
❓ How can you deduce that the Spanish phrase ¡Más rápido! means "faster"? [Its position indicates that it is a repeat of the English "Faster!"]

H English Language Learners
Contractions
Point out to these students that the author contracts "can" and "faster than" to "c'n" and "faster'n" to approximate the boys' pronunciation.

I Appreciating Language
Metaphor
❓ To what does the narrator compare the sky and the foliage? [He compares the patches of blue sky to small islands, and the foliage of trees, passing overhead, to the flowing water of a stream.]

Using Students' Strengths

Visual/Kinesthetic Learners
Some students may have difficulty visualizing the wagon, the garbage dump, and other details or settings in the story. Read the descriptive passages aloud, and ask students to describe the objects or scenes in their own words. Allow students to use classroom objects to set up a model that will help them understand the arrangement of wagon, shack, and so on as the story proceeds.

Auditory/Musical Learners
Invite students to choose a paragraph that describes the hailstorm near the end of the story. Have them prepare an oral reading that communicates the atmosphere they think the author intended to create. Urge them to practice, considering where they will pause for suspense, raise or lower their voices, or slow down for emphasis. Videotape the readings so that students can see their facial expressions, gestures, and body language in a playback of the performance.

A denly offered by the wagon. From a point high in the sky the pavement poured down on us. Immediately my father was drenched in sweat. His face, in profile now on the left, now on the right, became twisted with exertion while his broad back grew to twice its size under the strain. **B** We held our breath, maintained a fragile silence, and did not move, our bodies taut from participation in his struggle. All the way up we lost speed by degrees. His breathing grew heavy, labored. His legs slowed, seeking now to recover with more powerful thrusts what they had lost with a diminished number of strokes. His jaw tightened, his head fell, sometimes he closed his eyes, and we could see his tortured face as his arms swung desperately at some invisible opponent, and still he went up, up, up.

When the pavement leveled off, he yielded for a moment, broke into a smile, and then, summoning reserves from the labyrinth of his will, lunged forward furiously, as if galvanized by his victory, and reached full speed at the moment the wagon began to descend. Miraculously, he freed himself from the harness, turned the shaft back into the wagon, and jumped on. Winking at us, he fell to his knees and leaned hard on the shaft. He was happy, wildly happy, and saw that we were too, and he laughed without restraint. **C** "Miren, vean, look around you!" he shouted to us.

We were at the summit and the world fell away from us far into the horizon. To the east, steel mills, granaries, railroad yards, a profusion of industrial plants; to the north and south, prairies, trees, some houses; to the west, main arteries, more plants, the great smoking heaps of the city dump, and, farther still, houses and a green sweep of trees that extended as far as the eye saw. **D** Years have changed this area in many ways, but that landscape, like a photo negative, glows in memory's light.

We had churned up the mountainous wave of the bridge, and now, as we coasted down ever faster, we screeched and I could feel my body pucker. Our excitement was different now. It came of expectancy, of the certain knowledge that we would soon be sailing. We were safe with our incomparable pilot, but we howled with nervous delight as we picked up speed. Down, down, straight down we fell, and then the guayín righted itself and my stomach shot forward, threatening for a fraction of a second to move beyond its body.

When the wagon finally came to a stop, my father got down. Again he harnessed himself to it and pulled us onward. He moved with haste but did not run. Looking into the immense blue dome above us, we knew our journey would soon end and we began to shift uneasily, anticipating our arrival. With cupped hands we covered our faces and grew silent while the wheels **E** beneath us seemed to clack-clack louder and louder each time they passed over the pavement lines. At the divided highway my father turned south. We would be there in minutes.

The wagon stopped. We dropped our hands, exposing our faces, and climbed down. The full stink of decomposing garbage, fused to that of slow-burning trash, struck us. Before us was the city dump—a great raw sore **F** on the landscape, a leprous[5] tract oozing flames and smoldering, hellish grounds columned in smoke and grown tumid across years. Fragments of glass, metal, wood, lay everywhere, some of them menacingly jagged where they had not been driven into the earth by the wheels of the ponderous trucks.

My father had learned that the dump yielded more and better on Saturdays. Truckloads of spoiled produce were dumped that day, truckloads from warehouses, markets, stores, truckloads of stale or damaged food. We would spend the entire day here, gathering, searching, sifting, digging, following the trucks' shifting centers of activity.

Along a network of roads that crisscrossed the dumping grounds, trucks lumbered to and fro, grinding forward over ruts, jerking back-

5. **leprous:** diseased; covered with sores, as in leprosy.

WORDS TO OWN
taut (tôt) *adj.:* tightly stretched; tense.
galvanized (gal′və·nīzd′) *v.:* stimulated; excited.

ward, all of them rocking from side to side. My father took some burlap sacks, scanned the area, and pointed to the site where we would work. He went toward it quickly, followed by my oldest brothers. Lázaro and I stationed the wagon beyond reach of the clumsy vehicles that were already dumping and then made our way to the site. We started to work on a huge pile of deteriorating fruit, picking only what a paring knife would later make edible.

After several trips to the wagon, my father and brothers moved on to other piles. My job was to stay and guard the wagon, neatly arranging all that went into it. When I remembered, I took the jug of water and buried it in the earth to keep it cool. Eager for their company, I waited for my brothers to return with their newest finds.

From where I stood guard, I could see my father and brothers hurrying toward a truck that had just arrived. It was rumbling toward a dump area just beyond me. The men on that high, wobbly truck were pointing, nodding, waving—gestures signaling my father and brothers to follow because they carried a rich load. Directed by a man who advanced slowly and seemed to walk on his knees, the truck waded into a heap of garbage, dumped its cargo to the whir of a hydraulic mechanism, and was pulling out as my father and brothers drew close enough to express their gratitude with a slight movement of their heads.

Now my father waved to me. It was a call to join them before others arrived. As I started toward them, my brother Lázaro foundered on a spongy mass, fell through it, and disappeared. I stopped in my tracks, stunned. "Buried," I whispered, "he's buried!" My father saw him fall, bolted to his side, and thundered a command, "Alzate, Lázaro, get up, get up!" and in seconds he had raised him. Unsteady on his feet, Lázaro shook himself off like a wet dog and then brushed away scabs of rotting stuff that clung to him. Suddenly the stench of decay, the idea of grabbing something that might crumble into muck, the thought of losing my footing in all that garbage, filled me with terror. On tentative feet I went forward cautiously, expecting the

ground to give way beneath me. My steps were becoming steady when one of them set off a long, frenzied squeak. A rat sprang from under my foot and retreated grudgingly, black eyes unblinking, sharp teeth flashing beneath bristly whiskers, long tail stiffly trailing its fat body. I did not move until my father's shrill whistle roused me; then he called me in an angry voice and I moved on.

Working in silence, we gathered what we wanted from that mound. Now and again the sun's oppressive heat was dimmed by clouds that seemed to come from nowhere, bringing us relief.

By noon the sky was overcast. We pulled the wagon away from the dumping area and sat on the ground to eat what we had brought from home. By then the stench no longer bothered us. My father handed us bean and potato tacos that were still warm. Hunger made them exquisite, and I sat there chewing slowly, deliberately, making them last, too happy to say anything. We shared the jug of water, bits of damp earth clinging to our hands after we set it down.

Before us was the coming and going of trucks, the movement of men, rats scurrying everywhere, some dogs, and just beyond us, under a tentlike tarp, a big gas-powered pump that was used to drain water from that whole area, which flooded easily in a heavy rain. Behind us was a tiny shack, crudely assembled with cardboard, wood, and sheet metal, home of the dump's only dweller, Uñas. He was nowhere in sight, but my mind saw him—a monstrous dung beetle[6] rolling balls endlessly, determination on his pockmarked face, jaws in constant motion and his hands thrashing

6. **dung beetle:** beetle that lives in and feeds on animal waste, or dung. The dung beetle lays its egg in a large ball of dung, which it rolls along and finally buries in the ground.

WORDS TO OWN

tentative (ten′tə·tiv) adj.: uncertain; hesitant. *Tentative* also means "not definite or final."

G

ⓖ Reading Skills and Strategies
Drawing Conclusions

❓ Why is the narrator given the task of guarding the wagon? [Possible responses: To shoo away rats and deter thieves; perhaps it is simply an important-sounding task assigned to him because he is too small to help forage for useful items.]

ⓗ Literary Connections

The name *Lázaro* is Lazarus in English. In the Bible (John 11:1-44), Lazarus, a friend of Jesus, dies and is buried in a tomb. Four days later Jesus calls out, "Lazarus, come forth!" and Lazarus is raised from the dead. The Spanish *Alzate* helps evoke the allusion because it is stronger than "get up," meaning rather "raise yourself" or "lift yourself up."

ⓘ Reading Skills and Strategies
Drawing Conclusions

❓ Why do you think the narrator is so happy at this moment? [Possible responses: He is struck with complete contentment at the chance to rest and eat; or he suddenly feels the warmth of being with his father and brothers.]

Skill Link

Word Choice: Lively Verbs

Lively verbs give readers a clear picture of the action involved in a scene, as in "*swoop down on* the best places" instead of the colorless "*go to* the best places." Have students circle each use of *go* or *say* in the sentences below, and then replace each verb with a stronger or more colorful verb that fits the context. Sample responses are given in brackets.

1. Every Saturday we go [hurry, travel] to the city dump together.

2. When we are late getting started my father says [scolds, demands], "What took you so long?"

3. The cart goes [bumps, bounces, rolls] down the streets, pulled by my father.

4. At 103rd Street my father goes [turns, veers] west.

5. Next we go [climb, creep, inch] up the mountainous bridge.

6. When Lázaro falls into the garbage, my father says [shouts, thunders], "Lift up!"

7. Trucks go [lumber, rumble] back and forth across the dump all day.

8. Big black clouds go [roll, scud, tumble] across the sky.

9. During the storm my father says [croons, murmurs], "You're safe, you're safe with me."

10. Afterward we go [wade, splash] through a foot of water.

nervously, searching the grounds with a frenzy unleashed by the appearance of intruders.

By 12:30 the sky's blue was completely eclipsed. Above us an ugly gray was pressing down the sky, flattening it by degrees. My father stood up and looked hard at the sky as he spun on his heel. The temperature dropped abruptly and a strong wind rose, blowing paper, cans, boxes, and other objects across the grounds in all directions. He issued orders rapidly: "¡Pronto! Block the wheels and cover the wagon with the lona! Tie it down!" Then he took a sack and hurried off to a heap he had been eyeing while we ate.

We leaped forward, the two youngest scurrying in search of something to anchor the wheels with, while the two eldest raised the wagon's sides and unfolded the tarp my father had designed for such an emergency. The wheels blocked, we turned to help our brothers. We had seen our father tie down the tarp many times. We pulled it taut over the wagon and carefully drew the ends down and under, tying securely the lengths of rope that hung from its edges.

Huddled around the wagon, we watched the day grow darker. Big black clouds, their outlines clearly visible, scudded across the sky. It was cold and we shivered in our shirt sleeves. Now the wind blew with such force that it lifted things and flung them into spasmodic flight. We moved in together and bent down to shield and anchor ourselves. Frightened, we held our silence and pressed in closer until one of us, pointing, gasped, "Look! No one's out there! No one! Jus' look! We're all alone!"

A bolt of lightning ripped the sky and a horrendous explosion followed. Terror gripped us and we began to wail. The clouds dumped their load of huge, cold drops. And suddenly my father appeared in the distance. He looked tiny as he ran, flailing his arms, unable to shout over the sound of wind and water. He was waving us into the shack and we obeyed at once. Inside, cowed by the roar outside and pressing together, we trembled as we waited for him. He had almost reached us when the wind sheared off the roof. Part of one side was blown away as the first small pebbles of ice began to fall. He was shouting as he ran, "Salgan, come out, come out!"

We tumbled out, arms extended as we groped toward him, clutched his legs when he reached us and pulled us away seconds before the wind leveled what remained of the shack. A knot of arms and legs, we stumbled to the wagon. There was no shelter for hundreds of yards around and we could not see more than several yards in front of us. The rain slashed down, diminished, and hail fell with increasing density as the size of the spheres grew. Now we cried out with pain as white marbles struck us. My father's head pitched furiously and he bellowed with authority, "¡Cállense! Be still! Don't move from here! I'll be right back, ahorita vuelvo!"

In seconds he was back, dragging behind him the huge tarp he had torn from the pump, moving unflinchingly under the cold jawbreakers[7] that were pummeling us. With a powerful jerk he pulled it up his back and over his head, held out his arms like wings, and we instinctively darted under. The growing force of the hailstorm crashed down on him. Thrashing desperately under the tarp, we found his legs and clung to them. I crawled between them. We could not stop bawling.

Once more he roared over the din. "There's nothing to fear! ¡Nada! You're safe with me, you know that, ya lo saben!" And then little by little he lowered his voice until he seemed to be whispering, "I would never let anything harm you, nunca, nunca. Ya, cállense, cállense ya. Cálmense, be still, you're safe, seguros, you're with me, with Papá. It's going to end now, very soon, very soon, it'll end, you'll see, ya verán, ya verán. Be still, be still, you're with me, with me. Ya, ya, cállense. . . ."

---

7. **jawbreakers:** round, very hard candies. The writer is comparing the hail to these candies.

- -

WORDS TO OWN

eclipsed (i·klipst′) *v.*: covered over; darkened. *Eclipsed* also means "outshone" or "surpassed."

- -

Crossing the Curriculum

Art

Have a group of three or four students create a mural of several scenes in the story to help the class appreciate its visual aspects. Display the mural in the classroom, and have a representative from the group explain to the class what the mural shows.

Science

To help students cultivate their knowledge of weather, invite a science teacher or local meteorologist to explain to the class how and why hailstorms occur. If a guest speaker is not available, ask interested students to research the phenomenon of hail and explain it to the class.

Health

To help students plan for grocery shopping, have them find out how long it takes for fruits and vegetables to become inedible. Also have them find out about the kinds of illnesses people can get from eating spoiled food. Have them design and present a poster that displays their findings.

Spanish

Ask students to list all of the Spanish words and phrases they find in the story. Bring several Spanish dictionaries to class, and have them look up the words on their lists. If some of your students speak Spanish, ask them to explain nuances not made clear by the dictionaries, and to teach the class the proper pronunciations.

CÁLLENSE
Ya

RESPONDING TO THE ART

Ask students what they see in this illustration. [The illustration is an abstract image of the father holding the tarp over his children as hail falls from the sky.]

Activity. Have students list key moments or events from the story and select one of them to illustrate. Let them use any medium they wish, such as drawing, painting, or collage. Students might work individually, in pairs, or in small groups.

Bent forward, he held fast, undaunted, fixed to the ground, and we tried to cast off our terror. Huddled under the wings of that spreading giant, we saw the storm release its savagery, hurl spheres of ice like missiles shot from slings. They came straight down, so dense that we could see only a few feet beyond us. Gradually the storm abated, and we watched the spheres bounce with great elasticity from hard surfaces, carom when they collided, spring from the wagon's tarp like golf balls dropped on black-topped streets. When it stopped hailing, the ground lay hidden under a vast white beaded quilt. At a distance from us and down, the highway was a string of stationary vehicles with their lights on. Repeatedly, bright bolts of lightning tore the sky from zenith to horizon and set off detonations that seemed to come from deep in the earth. At last the rain let up. My father straightened himself, rose to his full height, and we emerged from the tarp as it slid from his shoulders. He ordered us with a movement of his head and eyes, and as he calmly flexed his arms, the four of us struggled to cover the damaged pump with his great canvas mantle.

His unexpected "¡Vámonos!" filled us with joy and we prepared to leave. Hail and water were cleared from the wagon's cover. My brothers and I dug through the ice to free the wheels, and when my father took up the handle and pulled, we pushed from behind with all our might, slipping, falling, rising, moving the wagon forward by inches, slowly gaining a little speed, and finally holding at a steady walk to keep from losing control. Where the road met the highway, we waded through more than a foot of water and threw our shoulders into the wagon to shove it over the last bump. Long columns of stalled cars lined the highway as drivers examined dents and shattered or broken windows and windshields. We went home in a dense silence, my father steering and pulling in front, we propelling from behind.

Entering the yard from the alley, we unloaded the wagon without delay. While

---

WORDS TO OWN

abated (ə·bāt′id) *v.:* let up; lessened; decreased.
zenith (zē′nith) *n.:* point directly overhead in the sky; highest point.

DISTILLATION 139

G **Literary Connection**

In the phrase *that spreading giant,* the father acquires almost mythic stature. He is reminiscent of Atlas in Greek mythology, a Titan (giant deity) who held the heavens on his shoulders.

H **English Language Learners**
Word Choice

Point out to these students that the word *carom* evokes action like that of billiard balls bouncing off each other.

I **Critical Thinking**
Interpreting the Text

❓ Why are the boys silent on the way home? [Possible responses: Everyone is still shocked and dazed by the noise and power of the storm; they are thinking about what their father just did for them.]

Assessing Learning

Check Test: Short Answer

1. What does the father use to carry the food home from the dump? [a wagon that he must pull]
2. What baffles the narrator about the neighborhoods with the more expensive houses? [He sees no garbage.]
3. When does the father jump on the wagon? [when they swoop down the descending side of a steep bridge]
4. What scares the narrator when he steps on it at the dump? [a rat]
5. Why does the narrator go into the bathroom when his father is bathing? [to get gauze and tape because one of his brothers has cut himself]

Standardized Test Preparation

For practice in proofreading and editing, see
• *Daily Oral Grammar,* Transparency 9

A Reading Skills and Strategies
Making Inferences
? Why are the boys so eager to talk now? [Possible response: They are overwhelmed with relief and need to release their earlier tension; they are reliving the storm in order to come to an understanding of what they experienced.]

B Elements of Literature
Symbolism
The wounds that the father sustains in protecting his children reinforce the Christian symbolism in the earlier reference to Lazarus. Like Jesus, who was beaten and then stretched on a cross, the father suffers a severe beating as he stretches out his arms, sacrificing himself to protect his children.

C Critical Thinking
Hypothesizing
? What might the narrator mean by "full knowledge"? [Possible responses: As an adult, he now understands how unselfishly his father loved his children; he may mean that he now knows his father was a hero.]

D Elements of Literature
Dynamic and Static Characters
? Is the character of the narrator dynamic or static? Explain your reasoning. [Sample answer: The narrator is dynamic because his knowledge of and attitudes toward his father change during the story.]

Resources
Selection Assessment
Formal Assessment
• Selection Test, p. 20
Test Generator (One-Stop Planner)
• CD-ROM

---

my father worked his wagon into the coal shed and locked the door, my brothers and I carried the sacks up to our second-floor flat. It was almost four when we finished emptying the sacks on newspapers spread on the kitchen floor. There we began to pare while my mother, scrubbing carefully, washed in the sink. We chattered furiously, my brothers and I, safe now from the danger outside.

Lázaro brought the knife down on the orange, the orange slipped from his hand, and the blade cut the tip of his thumb. He held his thumb in his fist and I got up to bring him gauze and tape from the bathroom. I knew my father would let me in even if he had already started to bathe.

Some object fallen between the bathroom door and its frame had kept it ajar, but he did not hear me approach. I froze. He was standing naked beside a heap of clothes, running his hands over his arms and shoulders, his fingertips pausing to examine more closely. His back and arms were a mass of ugly welts, livid flesh that had been flailed again and again until the veins beneath the skin had broken. His arms dropped to his sides and I thought I saw him shudder. Suddenly he seemed to grow, to swell, to fill the bathroom with his great mass. Then he threw his head back, shaking his black mane, smiled, stepped into the bathtub, and immersed himself in the water. Without knowing why, I waited a moment before timidly entering—even as I have paused all these years, and pause still, in full knowledge now, before entering that distant Saturday.

WORDS TO OWN
livid (liv'id) *adj.*: bruised; black-and-blue.

MEET THE WRITER
Celebrating Survival
Hugo Martinez-Serros (1930–   ) is a native of South Chicago where most of his stories take place. His characters, like his Mexican-born parents, are generally newcomers to a harsh urban environment that challenges their capacity to survive. Yet their stories are full of joy, and their ultimate triumph is reflected in the title of the book from which "Distillation" comes: *The Last Laugh and Other Stories* (1988).

Martinez-Serros became a professor of Spanish American literature at Lawrence University in Appleton, Wisconsin. He says that "Distillation" is fundamentally a true story and that he is the narrator.

66 What I wanted to achieve in the story was the five-year-old's vision of a man who is both near and far. Near because he is his father, a familiar and intimate figure, with all that this implies; far because he is larger than life, heroic, a miracle worker . . . profoundly unlike the child. In a number of senses, 'Distillation' is the story of a journey—a journey into the past, to the 103rd Street bridge, to the city dump, into the father's character. 99

Making the Connections

Connecting to the Theme: "Hearts That Love"
"Distillation" dramatically illustrates the theme "Hearts That Love" by describing a father who puts aside his own safety and comfort in order to protect his children from harm. He does this without a second thought, or a moment's regret, or a complaint about his injuries. When the narrator sees his father's welts and wounds at the end of the story, he realizes how unselfishly his father has acted, and thereby sees his father's love for him in a new light.

Powder · Tobias Wolff Ⓐ

Just before Christmas my father took me skiing at Mount Baker. He'd had to fight for the privilege of my company, because my mother was still angry with him for sneaking me into a nightclub during our last visit, to see Thelonious Monk.[1]

He wouldn't give up. He promised, hand on heart, to take good care of me and have me home for dinner on Christmas Eve, and she relented. But as we were checking out of the lodge Ⓑ that morning it began to snow, and in this snow he observed some quality that made it necessary for us to get in one last run. We got in several last runs. He was indifferent to my fretting. Snow whirled around us in bitter, blinding squalls, hissing like sand, and still we skied. As the lift bore us to the peak yet again, my father looked at his watch and said, "Criminey. This'll have to be a fast one."

By now I couldn't see the trail. There was no point in trying. I stuck to him like white on rice Ⓒ and did what he did and somehow made it to the bottom without sailing off a cliff. We returned our skis and my father put chains on the Austin-Healy while I swayed from foot to foot, clapping my mittens and wishing I were home. I could see everything. The green tablecloth, the plates with the holly pattern, the red candles waiting to be lit.

We passed a diner on our way out. "You want some soup?" my father asked. I shook my head. "Buck up," he said. "I'll get you there. Right, doctor?"

I was supposed to say, "Right, doctor," but I didn't say anything.

A state trooper waved us down outside the resort. A pair of sawhorses were blocking the road. The trooper came up to our car and bent down to my father's window. His face was bleached by the cold. Snowflakes clung to his eyebrows and to the fur trim of his jacket and cap.

"Don't tell me," my father said.

The trooper told him. The road was closed. It might get cleared, it might not. Storm took everyone by surprise. So much, so fast. Hard to get people moving. Christmas Eve. What can you do?

My father said, "Look. We're talking about four, five inches. I've taken this car through worse than that."

The trooper straightened up, boots creaking. His face was out of sight but I could hear him. "The road is closed."

My father sat with both hands on the wheel, rubbing the wood with his thumbs. He looked at the barricade for a long time. He seemed to be trying to master the idea of it. Then he thanked the trooper, and with a weird, old-maidy show of caution turned the car around. "Your mother will never forgive me for this," he said.

"We should have left before," I said. "Doctor."

He didn't speak to me again until we were both in a booth at the diner, waiting for our burgers. "She won't forgive me," he said. "Do you understand? Never."

"I guess," I said, but no guesswork was required; she wouldn't forgive him.

"I can't let that happen." He bent toward me. "I'll tell you what I want. I want us to be together again. Is that what you want?"

I wasn't sure, but I said, "Yes, sir."

He bumped my chin with his knuckles. "That's all I needed to hear."

When we finished eating he went to the pay phone in the back of the diner, then joined me in the booth again. I figured he'd called my mother, but he didn't give a report. He sipped at his coffee and stared out the window at the empty road. "Come on!" When the trooper's car went past, lights flashing, he got up and dropped some money on the check. "Okay. *Vámonos.*"[2]

---

1. **Thelonious Monk** (1920–1982): American jazz musician, famed as a pianist and composer; one of the creators of the "bop" style of jazz.

2. **Vámonos** (vä′mô·nôs): Spanish for "Let's go."

Connecting Across Texts

Connecting with "Distillation"

The father in "Powder" brings his son safely through a storm to his mother's house. Yet this father is different from the father in "Distillation." Students may wish or need to spend some time discussing the characters of the fathers and the complex relationships that can develop between parents and children when one parent has custody and the other has only visiting rights. Again as in "Distillation," the story reflects, for the son, a moment of epiphany—a day when, despite his ability to see his father's faults and limitations clearly, he loves his father for who he is.

The wind had died. The snow was falling straight down, less of it now; lighter. We drove away from the resort, right up to the barricade. "Move it," my father told me. When I looked at him he said, "What are you waiting for?" I got out and dragged one of the sawhorses aside, then pushed it back after he drove through. When I got inside the car, he said, "Now you're an accomplice. We go down together." He put the car in gear and looked at me. "Joke, doctor."

"Funny, doctor."

Down the first long stretch I watched the road behind us, to see if the trooper was on our tail. The barricade vanished. Then there was nothing but snow: snow on the road, snow kicking up from the chains, snow on the trees, snow in the sky; and our trail in the snow. I faced around and had a shock. The lie of the road behind us had been marked by our own tracks, but there were no tracks ahead of us. My father was breaking virgin snow between a line of tall trees. He was humming "Stars Fell on Alabama." I felt snow brush along the floorboards under my feet. To keep my hands from shaking I clamped them between my knees.

My father grunted in a thoughtful way and said, "Don't ever try this yourself."

"I won't."

"That's what you say now, but someday you'll get your license and then you'll think you can do anything. Only you won't be able to do this. You need, I don't know—a certain instinct."

"Maybe I have it."

"You don't. You have your strong points, but not . . . you know. I only mention it because I don't want you to get the idea this is something just anybody can do. I'm a great driver. That's not a virtue, okay? It's just a fact, and one you should be aware of. Of course you have to give the old heap some credit, too—there aren't many cars I'd try this with. Listen!"

I listened. I heard the slap of the chains, the stiff, jerky rasp of the wipers, the purr of the engine. It really did purr. The car was almost new. My father couldn't afford it, and kept promising to sell it, but here it was.

I said, "Where do you think that policeman went to?"

"Are you warm enough?" He reached over and cranked up the blower. Then he turned off the wipers. We didn't need them. The clouds had brightened. A few sparse, feathery flakes drifted into our slipstream and were swept away. We left the trees and entered a broad field of snow that ran level for a while and then tilted sharply downward. Orange stakes had been planted at intervals in two parallel lines and my father ran a course between them, though they were far enough apart to leave considerable doubt in my mind as to where exactly the road lay. He was humming again, doing little scat riffs around the melody.

"Okay then. What are my strong points?"

"Don't get me started," he said. "It'd take all day."

"Oh, right. Name one."

"Easy. You always think ahead."

True. I always thought ahead. I was a boy who kept his clothes on numbered hangers to ensure proper rotation. I bothered my teachers for homework assignments far ahead of their due dates so I could make up schedules. I thought ahead, and that was why I knew that there would be other troopers waiting for us at the end of our ride, if we got there. What I did not know was that my father would wheedle and plead his way past them—he didn't sing "O Tannenbaum" but just about—and get me home for dinner, buying a little more time before my mother decided to make the split final. I knew we'd get caught; I was resigned to it. And maybe for this reason I stopped moping and began to enjoy myself.

Why not? This was one for the books. Like being in a speedboat, only better. You can't go downhill in a boat. And it was all ours. And it kept coming, the laden trees, the unbroken surface of snow, the sudden white vistas. Here and there I saw hints of the road, ditches, fences, stakes, but not so many that I could have found my way. But then I didn't have to. My father in his forty-eighth year, rumpled, kind, bankrupt of honor, flushed with certainty. He was a great driver. All persuasion, no coercion. Such subtlety at the wheel, such tactful pedalwork. I actually trusted him. And the best was yet to come—switchbacks and hairpins impossible to describe. Except maybe to say this: If you haven't driven fresh powder, you haven't driven.

MAKING MEANINGS

MAKING MEANINGS

First Thoughts

[evaluate]

1. How did your three **purposes—discover, interpret, enjoy**—come into play as you read "Distillation"? Which ended up being strongest for you? Why?

Shaping Interpretations

[respond]

2. How did you feel about the father during the scene in the dump and the final scene in the bathroom? How do you think his sons felt about him?

[evaluate]

3. The writer says on page 140 that he wanted to share his vision of a father who was "larger than life, heroic, a miracle worker." What details did he use to create this sense of the father? Do you think he succeeded? (Be sure to reread the part where the father saves Lázaro from being buried alive.)

[analyze]

4. The writer says that the landscape of the dump glows in his memory "like a photo negative." List all the **sensory details** that make that landscape vivid to you. What is the overall feeling you get for the dump?

[analyze]

5. Think about the character of the narrator. Is he a **dynamic** or **static** character—does he change or grow or discover anything in the course of the story? Go back to the text, and find passages to support your interpretation.

[apply]

6. The word *distillation* is defined on page 132. How could this term apply to this story? What do you think of it as a **title**?

[interpret]

7. How is love displayed in this story? Consider:
   - the father's actions during the journey and at the dump
   - the father's words
   - the sons' feelings for their father

Connecting with the Text

[infer]

8. Why do you suppose the narrator still pauses before thinking back upon that long-ago Saturday? Are his feelings at all like those you described in your Quickwrite notes? Explain.

Extending the Text

[connect]

9. What connections can you find or feel between "Powder" (see *Connections* on pages 141–142) and this story?

DISTILLATION 143

Reading Check

a. Which character in "Distillation" is the **protagonist**? (If you think there is more than one possibility, consider which character you focus on and which one sets the action in motion.)

b. Explain what the protagonist **wants.**

c. List the **actions** the protagonist takes to get what he or she wants.

d. What **obstacles** does the protagonist have to overcome to get what he wants?

e. Explain how the main **conflict** is finally resolved.

Reading Check
a. The father is the protagonist.
b. The father wants to gather food for his family and to protect his children from the hailstorm.
c. The father pulls the cart (carrying his sons) to the dump, organizes the food gathering, saves Lázaro from sinking into the rotting garbage, protects his children by covering them with his own body and the tarp, and leads them home again.

d. He pulls a heavy cart for miles (both before and after a day's scavenging work), mounts the tremendously steep incline to a bridge, and endures the pain of the hailstones.
e. The conflict of nature versus human beings is resolved when the father sacrifices his own comfort and safety to save his children from the storm.

MAKING MEANINGS
First Thoughts

1. Responses will vary; many students will say that ultimately they read with all three purposes in mind.

Shaping Interpretations

2. Possibilities include admiration, pity, and amazement. Some students may feel that except for the narrator, the sons do not fully appreciate what their father endures for them.

3. Details include the father's almost superhuman strength when he pulls the wagon, his power when he commands Lázaro to rise from the garbage, his heroism in shielding his sons with the tarp, and his love for his sons. Most students will probably feel the writer succeeds in sharing his vision.

4. Sensory details include smells of decomposing garbage and burning trash and sights and sounds of dogs and rats. Some students will find the dump interesting or scary; others will find it disgusting.

5. The narrator is dynamic. He realizes the dump is dangerous; he discovers the depth of his father's love. Supporting passages include especially the final page of the story.

6. Possible response: The episode distills everyday concerns and reveals the extent of the father's heroism and self-sacrifice. Some students may find the title too abstract, whereas others will consider it appropriate.

7. Actions: The father works hard to provide for his family and protect his sons from the storm. Words: He tells his children he will let nothing hurt them. Sons' feelings: They look forward to Saturdays and they love and respect their father.

Connecting with the Text

8. Possible response: His feelings are so deep that he feels choked up. Students should explain why these feelings do or do not resemble those in their Quickwrite notes.

Extending the Text

9. Possible response: Both stories involve the fathers keeping the sons safe. Both stories are about the power of love.

Rubrics for each Choices assignment appear on p. 104 in the *Portfolio Management System.*

CHOICES:
Building Your Portfolio

WORK IN PROGRESS

1. **Writer's Notebook** Circulate among students as they work, checking their charts for supporting evidence. Encourage students to go back over the story to find supporting words, actions, thoughts, and others' responses. Remind students to save their work. They may use it as prewriting for the Writer's Workshop on p. 164.

2. **Creative Writing** After they have completed a rough draft of their narratives, have students read the Grammar Link (p. 145) on lively verbs. Ask them to revise their draft, using lively, action verbs.

3. **Reflective Essay** Have students make a list of supporting incidents, words, or phrases from the story before they write their essay. Also, discuss with them the concept of "miracle," and how it can apply to the fathers' almost superhuman feats in "Distillation" and "Powder."

4. **Drawing** Students might find it useful to create a chronology of the plot to make sure they understand the sequence of places mentioned. The chronology can be a simple list. Remind students that their maps need not be drawn perfectly to scale.

5. **Critical Thinking/Speaking** Point out to students that this assignment requires them to do two things: present information on the quest pattern and show how "Distillation" fits the pattern. Students may want to find additional information about the quest pattern in reference books before they begin this assignment.

CHOICES: Building Your Portfolio

Writer's Notebook
1. Collecting Ideas for a Character Analysis

Collecting evidence for elaboration. For the *WORK IN PROGRESS* Writer's Workshop on page 164, you may want to analyze one of the characters in this story: the father, the son who tells the story, or the mother, who is largely behind the scenes. Pick one of these characters, and jot down all the **character traits,** or special personal qualities, you see in that character. Then, think about how you arrived at these traits. Skim the story, looking for passages that support the traits you've identified. Focus on the character's **words, actions,** and **thoughts.** Look also for **how other people respond** to the character. Use a chart like the one in column I to collect details that reveal certain character traits. Save your notes.

Character: Father in "Powder"

Traits	Evidence
Loving	Fights to see son

Creative Writing
2. "One day . . ."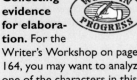

We come to understand the father in "Distillation" by watching his actions and observing how they affect his sons. Tell your own story about a special day when you came to understand someone close to you. Refer to your Quickwrite notes, and describe

- who the person was
- what happened that day
- what you realized about the person
- how the day affected you

To make your story come alive, elaborate with sensory details and dialogue.

Reflective Essay
3. "Where there is great love . . ."

Look back at the quotation by Willa Cather on page 93. Write a reflection on how you think "Distillation" and "Powder" connect with Cather's statement about great love and miracles. Elaborate on your ideas with specific incidents from each story.

Drawing
4. Mapping the Journey

Create a **map** that traces the route the narrator and his family took to the garbage dump. Be sure to check the text closely so you can indicate all the streets and landmarks mentioned by the narrator. Illustrate the map with sights the family saw as they made their perilous journey.

Critical Thinking/Speaking
5. A Modern Quest

The heroic quest is an age-old pattern in narrative fiction. Work with a partner to see if this modern story conforms to the quest pattern. To gather your information, complete a chart like the one below; it is filled in with details from Homer's great **epic** the *Odyssey.* When you've finished your chart, prepare a presentation of your findings to the class. You might even illustrate your talk with pictures of old and new quest stories (from the *Odyssey* to *Indiana Jones*).

The *Odyssey*	
Hero	warrior
Companions	fellow warriors
Journey	sea voyage
Perils	monsters, storms
Purpose	return home

Using Students' Strengths

Kinesthetic Learners
For Choice 1, students might find it useful to dramatize or pantomime actions they feel are significant in revealing the personality of the character they have chosen. After the dramatization or pantomime, students can then describe in words what they acted out. Some students may find it helpful to videotape and then review the enactment before doing their writing.

Interpersonal Learners
For Choice 5, encourage students to make their presentations interactive with their audience by including questions, games, or other rhetorical devices to help listeners explore the quest pattern and see how it is used in "Distillation."

Verbs Make It Vivid

Language Handbook HELP

See Verbs, pages 1021 and 1026-1028.

MARTINEZ-SERROS'S VIVID VERBS

swoop
glower
dart
thrust
lunge
churn
howl
fling
chatter
freeze

Notice how the **verbs** in the following sentence from "Distillation" give a clear picture of the mother's actions:

"Anxious for us, my mother pushed us through the door as she grazed us with her lips."

The mother's actions would be less vivid if tamer verbs had been used:

Anxious for us, my mother moved us through the door as she touched us with her lips.

Sometimes the use of a particular verb is significant. For example, on page 137, when little Lázaro is buried in the muck in the dump, the father thunders out "Alzate!" In Spanish, *alzar* means "to raise; to lift up." For many readers, this verb will bring to mind the raising from the dead of another Lazarus in the Gospels. (If the father had used the verb *subir*, the feeling would have been different. *Subir* means just "to get up.")

Try It Out

1. Look through "Distillation" for at least ten examples of lively verbs that describe precisely what characters are doing. (Find verbs different from those in the list at left.) Make a list of these words in your journal.

2. Here are five tame, overused verbs. Brainstorm a list of vivid, lively verbs that would make each action much more specific: *go, say, walk, look, move.*

➤ Take out a writing assignment you're working on—perhaps from this collection. Circle or highlight weak verbs that could be replaced with more vivid, precise verbs. You might keep a list of "verbs I like" in your notebook for reference and inspiration.

VOCABULARY   HOW TO OWN A WORD

WORD BANK

spoils
glower
myriad
taut
galvanized
tentative
eclipsed
abated
zenith
livid

Which Word?

Work with a partner to choose the correct word.
1. Which word describes a suddenly energized person?
2. Which word names the highest point in the sky overhead?
3. Which word describes skin that is discolored and bruised?
4. Which word tells what a cloud did to a patch of sunlight?
5. Which word describes a hesitant or unsure movement?
6. Which word is another name for loot or booty?
7. Which word tells what a downpour did when it let up?
8. Which word tells what people do when they look at you angrily?
9. Which word applies to a rope that is tightly stretched?
10. Which word refers to a great variety of people or things?

DISTILLATION   145

GRAMMAR LINK

Try It Out
Possible Answers

1. A sampling of the many lively verbs students can find includes *grazed, flicking, gleamed, sparkled, scattered, mottled, rattled, raced, pumped, navigated.*
2. Possible answers for each verb:
   a. *go:* march, advance, roll, wade
   b. *say:* announce, proclaim, remark, mumble
   c. *walk:* saunter, stroll, limp, shuffle, prance, stalk, plod, trudge, scramble
   d. *look:* gaze, stare, gawk, watch, glance, view
   e. *move:* stir, shift, transfer, budge, yank, push, pull

First, have students circle weak verbs in a piece of current writing. Then, have them use a thesaurus to look up three synonyms for each weak verb and include one of these replacements if it fits the context.

VOCABULARY

Answers
1. galvanized
2. zenith
3. livid
4. eclipsed
5. tentative
6. spoils
7. abated
8. glower
9. taut
10. myriad

Resources ————————

Grammar
• *Grammar and Language Links* Worksheet, p. 15

Vocabulary
• *Words to Own,* Worksheet, p. 9

Grammar Link Quick Check

Have students select the lively verb or verbs in each of the following sentences.
1. My older brother galloped to the yard, crossing in front of the wagon my father was pulling. [galloped]
2. After they criticized her cooking, Mama slapped the food on their plates and stalked away. [slapped, stalked]
3. When my father called for our attention, the eyes of every child in the family flashed in his direction. [flashed]
4. Unaware of the traffic, my little brother ambled out into the middle of the street. [ambled]
5. Fiery red welts spotted my father's back. [spotted]

OBJECTIVES

1. Read and interpret the story
2. Identify foreshadowing
3. Compare cultures
4. Express understanding through writing, culture/anthropology, comparing and contrasting/ speaking, or art
5. Identify adverbs and use adverbs in writing
6. Understand and use new words

SKILLS

Literary
- Identify foreshadowing

Reading
- Compare cultures

Writing
- Analyze a character

Speaking/Listening
- Orally compare and contrast cultures

Grammar/Language
- Identify and use adverbs

Vocabulary
- Understand and use new words

Culture/Anthropology
- Write field notes on a Nigerian village

Art
- Create a diorama

Viewing/Representing
- Respond to fine art (ATE)

Planning

- **Block Schedule**
  Block Scheduling Lesson Plans with Pacing Guide

- **Traditional Schedule**
  Lesson Plans Including Strategies for English-Language Learners

- **One-Stop Planner**
  CD-ROM with Test Generator

Before You Read

LIFE IS SWEET AT KUMANSENU

Make the Connection

Love Is Sweet

The love between parent and child is one of the most powerful of all human bonds. In this story, the love of a mother and a son overcomes barriers that most people would say were insurmountable on this earth.

Quickwrite

Have you heard about the woman who lifted a car to save her child who was trapped underneath? Do you know of anyone who has done the "undoable" for love? Just how strong is the power of love? Freewrite for several minutes.

Elements of Literature

Foreshadowing: Finding the Clues

Sometimes a story's ending takes us completely by surprise. Sometimes we can predict a surprise ending (if we read carefully) because the writer has dropped clues into the text. These clues **foreshadow**, or hint at, future events. Part of our pleasure at the end of such a story is seeing how many clues we noticed—and how many details make sense to us only when the story is over.

Foreshadowing is the use of clues that hint at what is going to happen later in a story.

For more on Foreshadowing, see the Handbook of Literary Terms.

Reading Skills and Strategies

Comparing Cultures

Because this story is set in a culture very different from the one you live in, you may be puzzled by the way Bola and her West African family live and think. We quickly spot how people are different from us, but we may take for granted the characteristics that we all share. As you read "Life Is Sweet at Kumansenu," note details and questions you have about Bola and her family. Notice also feelings shared by families everywhere: love, grief, and hope.

Background

The story's characters—an old woman, Bola; her grown son, Meji; and his young daughter, Asi—are members of an extended Yoruba family. They live in a rural area in Nigeria, a West African country that was once a colony of Britain. Although many people in Bola's village have converted to Islam or Christianity, they have not abandoned their traditional African beliefs. (See Literature and Culture on page 150.) Almost every aspect of their everyday lives is affected by a strong belief in a spirit world.

go.hrw.com
LEO 10-2

Preteaching Vocabulary

Words To Own

The Words to Own for this selection are *plaintive* (p. 148), *cajoled* (p. 151), *diffuse* (p. 152), and *complacent* (p. 152). Have students work in small groups and use dictionaries to describe the relationships they discover among the words in each of the following sets.

1. *plaintive, plaintiff, complain, complainant* [Possible response: Besides sharing the element *plain*, all of the words have something to do with grief or with bringing a grievance to court.]
2. *cajole, jolly* [Possible response: Both can be used as verbs that mean to use a good-humored approach to coax someone into a better mood or an action.]
3. *diffuse, confused, suffused* [Possible response: Besides sharing the element *fuse*, they deal in some way with mixed, scattered, or different components.]
4. *complacent, placate, pleasant, pleasure* [Possible response: The first two share the root *plac*, and the last two share *pleas*. They all have something to do with being pleased.]

"Let us enjoy each other. . . .
Life is too short."

Life Is Sweet at
Kumansenu

Abioseh Nicol

The sea and the wet sand to one side of it; green
tropical forest on the other; above it, the slow,
tumbling clouds. The clean, round, blinding disk of
sun and the blue sky covered and surrounded the
small African village, Kumansenu.

147

Summary ■■

This modern ghost story, set in a rural
West African village, reveals a heart
that loves even after death. The widow
Bola (the focus of the third-person
limited narration) bore six sons who
died. However, she and the magician
Musa believe that the six were actually
one child, whose spirit returned repeatedly to torment Bola. To prevent the
spirit from returning, Musa advised her
to mangle the sixth corpse, but she
refused. Instead, she made a mark on
the corpse with a sharp stick. She then
bore a seventh son, Meji, who bears
the same mark on his body; he is now
thirty and a clerk in the city. Asi, Meji's
young daughter, lives with Bola.

One Friday, Meji appears unexpectedly. He refuses a celebratory party
and insists on being alone with his
mother and daughter. Many details
foreshadow trouble or mystery: a scarf
always around his neck, his hoarseness,
his not eating or casting a shadow, the
smell of decay in the room. At the
climax of the story Meji disappears on
a Sunday, bidding Bola good-bye with
the words, "Life is sweet . . . thank you."
That afternoon Bola learns that Meji
had died the past Friday of a broken
neck. The villagers don't believe that
she and Asi saw him, even though Asi
demonstrates foreknowledge of a gift
brought only that day by her mother.

Love of life and love between parent
and child are both themes of the story.
At the end, Musa chastises Bola for not
mutilating her sixth dead child, but she
responds she is glad she didn't, for life
is sweet and she is glad she gave her
child a chance to come back.

Resources

Listening
Audio CD Library
A recording of this story is provided in
the *Audio CD Library:*
• Disc 5, Track 3

Viewing and Representing
Fine Art Transparency
A Fine Art transparency of *Balinese
Landscape* by Miguel Covarrubias helps
students understand scenes of village
life. See the *Viewing and Representing
Transparencies and Worksheets:*
• Transparency 4
• Worksheet, p. 16

Resources: Print and Media

Reading
• *Graphic Organizer for Active Reading,* p. 10
• *Words to Own,* p. 10
• *Audio CD Library*
    Disc 5, Track 3

Writing and Language
• *Daily Oral Grammar*
    Transparency 10
• *Grammar and Language Links*
    Worksheet, p. 17
• *Language Workshop* CD-ROM

Viewing and Representing
• *Viewing and Representing*
    Fine Art Transparency 4
    Fine Art Worksheet, p. 16

Assessment
• *Formal Assessment,* p. 22
• *Portfolio Management System,* p. 105
• *Standardized Test Preparation,* pp. 22, 24
• *Test Generator (One-Stop Planner CD-ROM)*

Internet
• go.hrw.com (keyword: LE0 10-2)

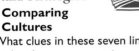

A Reading Skills and Strategies

Comparing Cultures

? What clues in these seven lines immediately suggest a setting outside the United States? [the mud houses, corrugated zinc roofs, cocoa, influence of traders, palm-oil stew]

B Critical Thinking

Speculating

? What does Bola's ability to count in English suggest about the economy of the area? [Sample answer: English is the language of the market, of commerce. One reason for this might be that different peoples in the area speak different African languages, so they have learned some English for use in the marketplace.]

C Reading Skills and Strategies

Comparing Cultures

? In Bola's culture, what do people believe when a woman bears one child after another, and all of these children die? [The same spirit keeps returning; all of the children are really the same person.] **What might be the scientific reason for the deaths of these children?** [They are all different children, and some genetic condition, birth defect, disease, or nutrition problem caused their deaths.] **Why do you think Bola refused to mutilate the body of her sixth dead child?** [Perhaps, as a mother, she could not stand to see even the corpse of a child hurt. She wanted the child to return.]

A A few square mud houses with roofs like helmets were here thatched, and there covered with corrugated zinc,[1] where the prosperity of cocoa and trading had touched the head of the family.

The widow Bola stirred her palm-oil stew and thought of nothing in particular. She chewed a kola nut rhythmically with her strong toothless jaws, and soon unconsciously she was chewing in rhythm with the skipping of Asi, her grandaughter. She looked idly at Asi, as the seven-year-old brought the twisted palm-leaf rope smartly over her head and jumped over it, counting in English each time the rope struck the ground and churned up a little red dust. Bola herself did not understand English well, but she could easily count up to twenty in English, for market purposes. Asi shouted, "Six," and then said, "Nine, ten." Bola called out that after six came seven. "And I should know," she sighed. Although now she was old and her womb and breasts were withered, there was a time when she bore children regularly, every two years. Six times she had borne a boy child and six times they had died. Some had swollen up and with weak, <u>plaintive</u> cries had faded away. Others had shuddered in sudden convulsions, with burning skins, and had rolled up their eyes and died. They had all died; or rather he had died, Bola thought, because she knew it

Batik by women of Burkina Faso, West Africa.

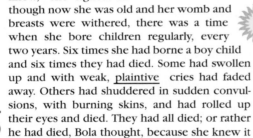

was one child all the time whose spirit had crept up restlessly into her womb to be born and mock her. The sixth time, Musa, the village magician whom time had now transformed into a respectable Muslim, had advised her and her husband to break the bones of the quiet little corpse and mangle it so that it could not come back to torment them alive again. But she had held on to the child and refused to let them mutilate it. Secretly, she had marked it with a sharp pointed stick at the left buttock before it was wrapped in a mat and taken away. When at the seventh time she had borne a son and the purification ceremonies had taken place, she had turned it surreptitiously to see whether the mark was there. It was. She showed it to the old woman who was the midwife[2] and asked her what it was, and she had forced herself to believe that it was an accidental scratch made while the child was being scrubbed with herbs to remove placental[3] 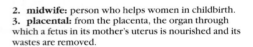 blood. But this child had stayed. Meji, he had been called. And he was now thirty years of age and a second-class clerk in government offices in a town ninety miles away. Asi, his daughter, had been left with her to do the

---

2. **midwife:** person who helps women in childbirth.
3. **placental:** from the placenta, the organ through which a fetus in its mother's uterus is nourished and its wastes are removed.

WORDS TO OWN

plaintive (plān′tiv) *adj.*: sad; expressing sorrow.

---

1. **corrugated zinc:** sheets made partially of zinc, a metal, that have been shaped into parallel ridges.

Reaching All Students

Struggling Readers

To help students become active readers, have them take notes on details that are not clear on first reading—for example, Meji's casting no shadow. Tell them that such details can be clues to a story's outcome. Students should predict the meaning of each mysterious detail that they record. After they have finished reading, have them check their predictions.

English Language Learners

These students may understand the story more easily by listening to an oral reading of it. It may also be helpful to have these students visualize the events in sequence. To do so, have them make a horizontal list (a timetable), with arrows indicating how each event leads into the next. For example, Meji's return might be followed by his resting overnight and then taking Asi for a walk the next day.

Advanced Learners

Ask students first to review the story from Bola's perspective and list the details she witnesses in chronological order. Second, have them review the story from Mr. Addai's perspective, listing "actual" events as he understands them. Then, have students discuss which account a newspaper would more likely accept as true. Using the appropriate list, they can write a news story, incorporating elements from the other list to add interest and contrast.

things an old woman wanted a small child for: to run and take messages to the neighbors, to fetch a cup of water from the earthenware pot in the kitchen, to sleep with her, and to be fondled.

She threw the washed and squeezed cassava leaves into the red, boiling stew, putting in a finger's pinch of salt, and then went indoors, carefully stepping over the threshold, to look for the dried red pepper. She found it and then dropped it, leaning against the wall with a little cry. He turned around from the window and looked at her with a twisted half smile of love and sadness. In his short-sleeved, open-necked white shirt and gray gabardine trousers, gold wristwatch, and brown suede shoes, he looked like the picture in African magazines of a handsome clerk who would get to the top because he ate the correct food or regularly took the correct laxative, which was being advertised. His skin was grayish brown and he had a large red handkerchief tied round his neck.

"Meji, God be praised," Bola cried. "You gave me quite a turn. My heart is weak and I can no longer take surprises. When did you come? How did you come? By truck, by fishing boat? And how did you come into the house? The front door was locked. There are so many thieves nowadays. I'm so glad to see you, so glad," she mumbled and wept, leaning against his breast.

Meji's voice was hoarse, and he said, "I'm glad to see you too, Mother," rubbing her back affectionately.

Asi ran in and cried, "Papa, Papa," and was rewarded with a lift and a hug.

"Never mind how I came, Mother," Meji said, laughing. "I'm here, and that's all that matters."

"We must make a feast, we must

have a big feast. I must tell the neighbors at once. Asi, run this very minute to Mr. Addai, the catechist,[4] and tell him your papa is home. Then to Mami Gbera to ask her for extra provisions, and to Pa Babole for drummers and musicians . . ."

"Stop," said Meji, raising his hand. "This is all quite unnecessary. I don't want to see *anyone,* no one at all. I wish to rest quietly and completely. No one is to know I'm here."

Bola looked very crestfallen. She was so proud of Meji and wanted to show him off. The village would never forgive her for concealing such an important visitor. Meji must have sensed this because he held her shoulder comfortingly and said, "They will know soon enough. Let us enjoy each other, all three of us, this time. Life is too short."

Bola turned to Asi, picked up the packet of pepper, and told her to go and drop a little into the boiling pot outside, taking care not to go too near the fire or play with it. After the child had gone, Bola said to her son, "Are you in trouble? Is it the police?"

He shook his head. "No," he said, "it's just that I like returning to you. There will always be this bond of love and affection between us, and I don't wish to share it with others. It is our private affair and that is why I've left my daughter with you." He ended up irrelevantly, "Girls somehow seem to stay with relations longer."

4. **catechist** (kat′ə·kist′): person who teaches the principles of a religion through questions and answers.

Skill Link

Adverbs

An **adverb** is a word that modifies a verb, an adjective, or another adverb. An adverb shows *how, where, when,* or *to what extent* (how much, how long) an action is performed.

Activity

To complete each sentence, have students choose the best adverb from the indicated category. Sample answers are given; some may vary.

HOW	carefully, energetically, slowly
WHERE	ahead, behind, outside
WHEN	afterward, early, late
EXTENT	always, ever, fully, never, often

1. (HOW) Bola [carefully] added a precise amount of pepper to the stew.
2. (HOW) Excited by her father's visit, Asi skipped rope [energetically].
3. (WHERE) Bola always did her cooking [outside].

4. (WHEN) Meji and Asi left the house [early].
5. (WHEN) Having promised to say nothing about Meji's visit, Bola went off to the market [afterward].
6. (EXTENT) "I will [always] love you," Meji told Bola.
7. (EXTENT) "No one will [ever] know that I came," said Meji.

Ⓐ Elements of Literature

Foreshadowing

❓ **What signs does Bola notice that indicate something odd or mysterious is going on?** [Meji is pale, keeps scraping his throat, and feels cold to her touch.] **What seems odd in Meji's response to Bola?** [He says that he is extremely tired because he has traveled very far that day. A ninety-mile trip would not be that taxing by bus, truck or boat; a normal person could not travel so far on foot in a day.]

Ⓑ Critical Thinking

Analyzing Details

❓ **What additional clues show that there is something very strange about Meji?** [He casts no shadow, his watch stopped at noon, and he jokes that his head would fall off if he didn't wear a neckerchief.] **What are you beginning to suspect about Meji and his visit?** [Possible responses: He is a ghost or spirit; he died in some way that injured his neck.]

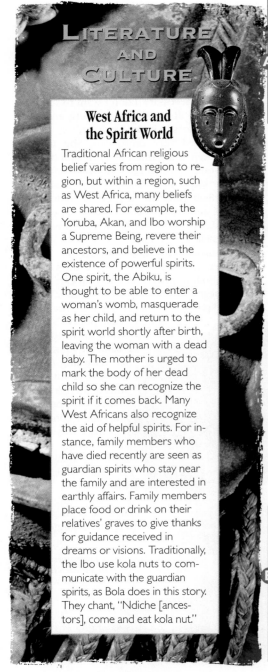

LITERATURE AND CULTURE

West Africa and the Spirit World

Traditional African religious belief varies from region to region, but within a region, such as West Africa, many beliefs are shared. For example, the Yoruba, Akan, and Ibo worship a Supreme Being, revere their ancestors, and believe in the existence of powerful spirits. One spirit, the Abiku, is thought to be able to enter a woman's womb, masquerade as her child, and return to the spirit world shortly after birth, leaving the woman with a dead baby. The mother is urged to mark the body of her dead child so she can recognize the spirit if it comes back. Many West Africans also recognize the aid of helpful spirits. For instance, family members who have died recently are seen as guardian spirits who stay near the family and are interested in earthly affairs. Family members place food or drink on their relatives' graves to give thanks for guidance received in dreams or visions. Traditionally, the Ibo use kola nuts to communicate with the guardian spirits, as Bola does in this story. They chant, "Ndiche [ancestors], come and eat kola nut."

150 THE SHORT-STORY COLLECTIONS

"And don't I know it," said Bola. "But you look pale," she continued, "and you keep scraping your throat. Are you ill?" She laid her hand on his brow. "And you're cold, too."

"It's the cold, wet wind," he said, a little harshly. "I'll go and rest now if you can open and dust my room for me. I'm feeling very tired. Very tired indeed. I've traveled very far today, and it has not been an easy journey."

"Of course, my son, of course," Bola replied, bustling away hurriedly but happily.

Meji slept all afternoon till evening, and his mother brought his food to his room and, later, took the empty basins away. Then he slept again till morning.

The next day, Saturday, was a busy one, and after further promising Meji that she would tell no one he was about, Bola went off to market. Meji took Asi for a long walk through a deserted path and up into the hills. She was delighted. They climbed high until they could see the village below in front of them, and the sea in the distance, and the boats with their wide white sails. Soon the sun had passed its zenith and was halfway toward the west. Asi had eaten all the food, the dried fish and the flat tapioca pancakes and the oranges. Her father said he wasn't hungry, and this had made the day perfect for Asi, who had chattered, eaten, and then played with her father's fountain pen and other things from his pocket. They soon left for home because he had promised that they would be back before dark; he had carried her down some steep boulders and she had held on to his shoulders because he had said his neck hurt so and she must not touch it. She had said, "Papa, I can see behind you and you haven't got a shadow. Why?"

He had then turned her around facing the sun. Since she was getting drowsy, she had started asking questions, and her father had joked with her and humored her. "Papa, why has your watch stopped at twelve o'clock?" "Because the world ends at noon." Asi had chuckled at that. "Papa, why do you wear a scarf always around your neck?" "Because my head would fall off if I didn't." She had laughed out loud at

---

Getting Students Involved

that. But soon she had fallen asleep as he bore her homeward.

Just before nightfall, with his mother dressed in her best, they had all three, at her urgent request, gone to his father's grave, taking a secret route and avoiding the main village. It was a small cemetery, not more than twenty years or so old, started when the Rural Health Department had insisted that no more burials were to take place in the back yard of households. Bola took a bottle of wine and a glass and four split halves of kola, each a half sphere, two red and two white. They reached the graveside and she poured some wine into the glass.

Then she spoke to her dead husband softly and caressingly. She had brought his son to see him, she said. This son whom God had given success, to the confusion and discomfiture of their enemies. Here he was, a man with a pensionable clerk's job and not a poor farmer, a fisherman, or a simple mechanic. All the years of their married life, people had said she was a witch because her children had died young. But this boy of theirs had shown that she was a good woman. Let her husband answer her now, to show that he was listening. She threw the four kola nuts up into the air and they fell onto the grave. Three fell with the flat face upward and one with its flat face downward. She picked them up again and conversed with him once more and threw the kola nuts up again. But still there was an odd one or sometimes two.

They did not fall with all four faces up, or with all four faces down, to show that he was listening and was pleased. She spoke endear-

Batik by women of Burkina Faso, West Africa.

ingly, she cajoled, she spoke severely. But all to no avail. She then asked Meji to perform. He crouched by the graveside and whispered. Then he threw the kola nuts and they rolled a little, Bola following them eagerly with her sharp old eyes. They all ended up face downward. Meji emptied the glass of wine on the grave and then said that he felt nearer his father at that moment than he had ever done before in his life. **D**

It was sundown, and they all three went back silently home in the short twilight. That night, going outside the house toward her son's window, she had found, to her sick disappointment, that he had been throwing all the cooked food away out there. She did not mention this when she went to say good night, but she did sniff and say that there was a smell of decay in the room. Meji said that he thought there was a dead rat up in the rafters, and he would clear it away after she had gone to bed. **E**

That night it rained heavily, and sheet lightning turned the darkness into brief silver daylight for one or two seconds at a time. Then the darkness **F** again and the rain. Bola woke soon after midnight and thought she could hear knocking. She went to Meji's room to ask him to open the door, but he wasn't there. She thought he had gone out for a while and had been locked out by mistake. She opened **G**

WORDS TO OWN

cajoled (kə·jōld') v.: coaxed with flattery, soothing words, or promises.

LIFE IS SWEET AT KUMANSENU **151**

RESPONDING TO THE ART

Batik, used by many cultures around the world, is a colorful method of dyeing cloth. The dyes are usually made from plants and minerals native to the region. To make a batik, one first applies wax with a stylus or a brush to create an image or pattern. This wax repels the dye, so that the image or pattern stands out against the colored background. Batik often features stylized designs or abstract patterns, but the ones on pp. 148 and 151 show details of daily family life in a West African village. You might invite a local artist or art teacher to demonstrate the process of making a batik.

Activity. You might ask students to design a T-shirt that shows a daily activity they value. Or have them compare the batik on p. 148 with the painting *Proletarian* by Gordon Samstag, p. 509 [women stooping over to work].

C Reading Skills and Strategies

Comparing Cultures

❓ What other beliefs or strategies (from any culture) related to contacting the dead do you know about? [Possible responses: use of a Ouija board; channeling through a medium at a seance.]

D Critical Thinking

Speculating

❓ Why do you think Meji has never "felt nearer" to his father than at this moment? [Students who have already concluded Meji is dead may say that he is with his father; others may suggest that he is experiencing an emotional connection because of the visit to the grave.]

E F G Elements of Literature

Foreshadowing

❓ What new oddities do these passages add to your list? [Meji does not need food, his room smells of decay, and he can disappear quietly.] How do you explain them? [Some students will already have figured out that Meji is dead. Others may suggest that he is seriously ill.]

Crossing the Curriculum

Geography

To help students visualize the setting, bring an up-to-date map of Africa to class. Ask students to look up Africa in an encyclopedia or atlas and to draw or construct a relief or economic map, emphasizing West Africa and Nigeria.

Home Economics

Food is a crucial part of any culture, and it plays an important part in this story. Ask students to research the kinds of food people eat in northwestern Africa. If possible, ask students to cook for the class dishes that are native to the region.

Foreign Language

The word *cola* comes from *kola,* a West African term for a tree. It is one of a number of English words from the native languages of Africa. Have students locate the origin and meaning of the following words: *banjo* [Kimbundu, stringed instrument], *chimpanzee* [Kongo, humanlike ape], *dashiki* [Yoruba, colorful pullover garment], *gumbo* [Bantu, thick soup], *impala* [Zulu, antelope], *mamba* [Zulu, black snake], *marimba* [Bantu, xylophone], *okra* [Ibo, vegetable], *tote* [Gullah and Krio, carry], *zombie* [Kongo, walking dead person].

A Elements of Literature

Foreshadowing

? What clues confirm your growing suspicion that Bola and Asi have been visited by a ghost? [The rain does not wet Meji; he is grateful for "a chance" to visit Bola; he speaks of leaving with a sense of finality.]

B Reading Skills and Strategies

Predicting

? From the tone of Mr. Addai's Biblical-sounding remark, what message do you expect him to deliver? [Sample answer: Someone has died.]

C D Elements of Literature

Foreshadowing

? Which clues that you noted earlier are explained by this news? [Meji's grayish skin, his failure to eat, lack of a shadow, stopped watch, odor of decay, and use of a neckerchief]

E Reading Skills and Strategies

Drawing Conclusions

? Why does the crowd tell Asi to hush? [Possible responses: The news is gruesome and they don't want Asi to upset Bola further; Asi shouts out disrespectfully.]

F Critical Thinking

Interpreting

? Why does Asi's mother, Meji's wife, tremble "with fear"? [Possible responses: Something very mysterious is occurring; Asi knows something she cannot possibly know in any natural way.]

---

the door quickly, holding an oil lamp upward. He stood on the veranda, curiously unwet, and refused to come in.

"I have to go away," he said hoarsely, coughing.

"Do come in," she said.

"No," he said, "I have to go, but I wanted to thank you for giving me a chance."

"What nonsense is this?" she said. "Come in out of the rain."

"I did not think I should leave without thanking you."

The rain fell hard, the door creaked, and the wind whistled.

"Life is sweet, Mother dear, goodbye, and thank you."

He turned around and started running. There was a sudden diffuse flash of silent lightning, and she saw that the yard was empty.

She went back heavily and fell into a restless sleep. Before she slept, she said to herself that she must see Mr. Addai next morning, Sunday, or better still, Monday, and tell him about all this, in case Meji was in trouble. She hoped Meji would not be annoyed. He was such a good son.

But it was Mr. Addai who came instead, on Sunday afternoon, quiet and grave, and met Bola sitting on an old stool in the veranda, dressing Asi's hair in tight, thin plaits.

Mr. Addai sat down and, looking away, he said, "The Lord giveth and the Lord taketh away." Soon half the village was sitting around the veranda and in the yard.

"But I tell you, he was here on Friday and left Sunday morning," Bola said. "He couldn't have died on Friday."

Bola had just recovered from a fainting fit after being told of her son's death in town. His wife, Asi's mother, had come with the news, bringing some of his property. She said Meji had died instantly at noon on Friday and had been buried on Saturday at sundown. They would have brought him to Kumansenu for burial. He had always wished that. But they could not do so in time, as bodies did not last more than a day in the hot season, and there were no trucks available for hire.

"He was here, he was here," Bola said, rubbing her forehead and weeping.

Asi sat by quietly. Mr. Addai said comfortingly, "Hush, hush, he couldn't have been, because no one in the village saw him."

"He said we were to tell no one," Bola said.

The crowd smiled above Bola's head and shook their heads. "Poor woman," someone said, "she is beside herself with grief."

"He died on Friday," Mrs. Meji repeated, crying. "He was in the office and he pulled up the window to look out and call the messenger. Then the sash broke. The window fell, broke his neck, and the sharp edge almost cut his head off; they say he died at once."

"My papa had a scarf around his neck," Asi shouted suddenly.

"Hush," said the crowd.

Mrs. Meji dipped her hand into her bosom and produced a small gold locket and put it around Asi's neck, to quiet her.

"Your papa had this made last week for your Christmas present. You may as well have it now."

Asi played with it and pulled it this way and that.

"Be careful, child," Mr. Addai said, "it is your father's last gift."

"I was trying to remember how he showed me yesterday to open it," Asi said.

"You have never seen it before," Mrs. Meji said sharply, trembling with fear mingled with anger.

She took the locket and tried to open it.

"Let me have it," said the village goldsmith, and he tried whispering magic words of incantation. Then he said, defeated, "It must be poor-quality gold; it has rusted. I need tools to open it."

"I remember now," Asi said in the flat, complacent voice of childhood.

The crowd gathered around quietly, and

WORDS TO OWN

diffuse (di·fyōos') *adj.:* not focused; scattered.
complacent (kəm·plā'sənt) *adj.:* self-satisfied; smug.

Assessing Learning

Observation Assessment

Self-Assessment

Have students answer these questions.

1. Did you read the story carefully?
2. Did you take notes while you read?
3. Did you try to predict how the story would end?
4. Did you look up words you did not know and could not figure out from context?
5. Did you try to form a mental picture of the characters and events of the story?

Check Test: True–False

1. Bola lives alone. [False]
2. Meji's quiet arrival startles Bola. [True]
3. Meji takes Asi on a long walk on Saturday. [True]
4. Bola notices an odor of decay in Meji's bedroom. [True]
5. Asi is able to open a locket that even the goldsmith cannot open. [True]

Standardized Test Preparation

For practice with standardized test format specific to this selection, see

• *Standardized Test Preparation*, pp. 22, 24

For practice in proofreading and editing, see

• *Daily Oral Grammar*, Transparency 10

the setting sun glinted on the soft red African gold of the dangling trinket. The goldsmith handed the locket over to Asi and asked in a loud whisper, "How did he open it?"

"Like so," Asi said and pressed a secret catch. It flew open and she spelled out gravely the word inside, "A-S-I."

The silence continued.

"His neck, poor boy," Bola said a little wildly. "That is why he could not eat the lovely meals I cooked for him."

Mr. Addai announced a service of intercession after vespers[5] that evening. The crowd began to leave quietly.

Musa, the magician, was one of the last to leave. He was now very old and bent. In times of grave calamity, it was known that even Mr. Addai did not raise objection to his being consulted.

He bent over further and whispered in Bola's ear, "You should have had his bones broken and mangled thirty-one years ago when he went for the sixth time, and then he would not have come back to mock you all these years by pretending to be alive. I told you so. But you women are naughty and stubborn."

Bola stood up, her black face held high, her eyes terrible with maternal rage and pride.

"I am glad I did not," she said, "and that is why he came back specially to thank me before he went for good."

She clutched Asi to her. "I am glad I gave him the opportunity to come back, for life is sweet. I do not expect you to understand why I did so. After all, you are only a man."

---

5. **service of intercession after vespers:** A service of intercession consists of prayers on behalf of someone. Vespers is an evening service.

MEET THE WRITER
The Real Africa

Abioseh Nicol (1924–1994) was born in Sierra Leone, a small country in western Africa. He was educated in Sierra Leone and Nigeria and later at Cambridge University in England, where he did research in biochemistry. When he returned to Africa in the 1960s, Nicol decided to write about his own people because "most of those who wrote about us seldom gave any nobility to their African characters." His poems and stories are usually set in rural villages, where he felt the true heart and spirit of Africa survive. In this story, the real Africa is found in the indomitable, life-affirming character of the old woman, Bola.

Making the Connections

Connecting to the Theme:
"Hearts That Love"

In this story, both Meji and Bola have hearts that love. Meji wants to see his mother one last time before he departs, and Bola is very concerned about her son's welfare. In fact, Bola has already proved her love years before the story begins by refusing to permit the remains of her sixth baby to be mutilated, even though it meant going against the advice of the magician and the practices of her people. In this story, love is stronger than death.

Cultural Connections

Although the setting may be unfamiliar to most students, the feelings that Bola, Meji, and Asi have for one another are universal. Ask students to comment in their Writer's Notebooks on how Bola's reaction to Meji's visit would be similar to the reaction of most reunited family members anywhere. [Possible response: Bola is proud of Meji and wants to show him off to her neighbors. She is concerned about his health. She wants to make sure he has plenty of his favorite foods to eat.]

Try It Out
Possible Answers
1. Some students may say that deleting the adverbs does not affect their picture of the action. Others may say that the picture loses vividness and precision.
2. Possible replacements:"idly": *carefully, closely, eagerly;* "smartly": *quickly, slowly.* Adverbs can change the meaning of a sentence completely.
3. Answers will vary. Possible responses: *rhythmically, unconsciously, well, easily, regularly, hurriedly, caressingly, endearingly, hoarsely,* and *gravely.* Help students to see that adverbs should be used sparingly so that they enhance passages that can be made more vivid, but do not distract from the basic meaning of the sentence.

VOCABULARY

Answers
1. *cajoled*—Definition: coaxed with flattery, soothing words, or promises. Synonyms: flattered, coaxed. Examples: a mother coaxing her child to go to bed, or someone persuading a friend to attend a certain party
2. *diffuse*—Definition: not focused, scattered. Synonyms: dispersed, strewn. Examples: seeds blown by the wind, or rambling words that do not focus on a topic
3. *complacent*—Definition: self-satisfied, smug. Synonyms: content, satisfied. Examples: a person who is not very ambitious, or a person whose prediction has proven correct

Resources

Grammar
• *Grammar and Language Links* Worksheet, p. 17

Vocabulary
• *Words to Own,* Worksheet, p. 10

GRAMMAR LINK MINI-LESSON

Making Motion Pictures—Adverbs

Language Handbook HELP

See Adverbs, page 1031.

A modifier makes the meaning of another word more specific. An **adverb** modifies a verb, an adjective, or another adverb. Look at some specific meanings or shades of meaning adverbs can give to the verb *eats.*

In all these examples, the adverb specifies *how* the eating is done.

eats <u>sloppily</u>	eats <u>constantly</u>
eats <u>neatly</u>	eats <u>daintily</u>
eats <u>fast</u>	eats <u>well</u>

The adverbs in the following sentence from Nicol's story show *how* two actions are performed. Adverbs can also tell *where, when,* and *to what extent* (*how long, how much*).

> "She looked <u>idly</u> at Asi, as the seven-year-old brought the twisted palm-leaf rope <u>smartly</u> over her head. . . ."

Try It Out
1. Delete the adverbs from Nicol's sentence at the left. What happens to your picture of the actions?
2. Substitute another adverb for each one in Nicol's sentence. How can adverbs change the meaning of the sentence?
3. Find five other adverbs in the story that show how an action is performed.

➤ Take out a piece of writing you are working on now or your notes about a character you might analyze for the Writer's Workshop on page 164. What adverbs could you add to help your readers visualize precisely how actions are performed?

VOCABULARY HOW TO OWN A WORD

WORD BANK
plaintive
cajoled
diffuse
complacent

Semantic Mapping

Working out a simple map or chart like the one here can help you own new or challenging words.

Make a **semantic map** like this for the other words from the Word Bank. Before you work out your maps, be sure to locate the word in the story to see how it is used.

plaintive
|
DEFINITION
"sad, expressing sorrow"
|
SYNONYMS
sad, mournful
|
EXAMPLES
the coo-coo cry of the dove
the wail of the blues singer

156 THE SHORT-STORY COLLECTIONS

Grammar Link Quick Check

Have students identify the adverbs in the following sentences.
1. Bola could count quickly from one to twenty in English. [quickly]
2. Asi longingly eyed the locket that the village goldsmith cradled delicately between his fingers. [longingly, delicately]
3. The village magician eagerly offered Bola advice to prevent the death of her next child. [eagerly]
4. Meji told Asi that she hiked well for a child of her age. [well]
5. Meji rapidly left the village after bidding his mother farewell. [rapidly]

EXTENDING *the theme*

AN AUTOBIOGRAPHY

I had chosen to love a boy who was out of my reach.

Vistas from the Barrio (1985) by Pedro Villarini (1933–   ).
Oil on canvas (38″ × 36″).   *Courtesy of the artist.*

Extending the Theme

In this autobiographical narrative, Cofer recalls the "sweet agony" of her first crush. A freshman at a Catholic school in New Jersey, she secretly loves a boy who is out of reach, but that doesn't deter her from contriving ways to catch glimpses of him. After a school drama production, he intercepts her for a kiss—her first—and then vanishes. After several painful weeks, she concludes that the kiss was for him a mere trophy.

Cofer reflects that love, never simple, is at once a psychological battle, a physical "salute to life," and "the greatest prize of all."

RESPONDING TO THE ART
Pedro Villarini (1933–   ) creates an ethnic neighborhood that springs colorfully to life. The mood of the painting is one of happiness and prosperity.
Activity. You might ask students to work in small groups to create a portrait of their own neighborhood or of ethnic neighborhoods in their own or in another city. Students can combine magazine photos, photographs, drawings, and text, or work in any medium they choose.

Reaching All Students

Struggling Readers
Help students focus attention on the text by suggesting that they look for answers to questions as they read. The double-entry journal suggested on p. 158 can serve this purpose, or students can use the questions in Finding Common Ground on p. 162 as a guide. If they do the latter, they should read the questions before reading the story and refer to them periodically to keep them in mind.

English Language Learners
Because Cofer's sentence structure is complex and her narrator makes many allusions, English language learners may need help in breaking down the text. You might pair them with more advanced readers and have partners break each paragraph into its component ideas until students feel able to continue on their own. Or you might have them listen to the selection in the *Audio CD Library,* focusing their attention on the selection's general meaning and events before having them read.

Advanced Learners
These students might enjoy compiling a list of the narrator's many references to religion, literature, art, and history—allusions ranging from Sophocles and Euripides to the Renaissance artist Michelangelo. They should then explain how each allusion connects with the narration and what the allusions add to the text.

Background

Ask students to think about a first love that they are familiar with through reading or some other experience. Then, invite them to jot down five words that come to mind to describe this first love. Collect the slips of paper and read some of the word lists without identifying who wrote them. If any words come up several times, ask students to discuss why this description of first love might be common.

A Reading Skills and Strategies

Predicting

❓ Based on what the narrator tells you in this first sentence, what do you think will happen? [Possible responses: She might make a fool of herself trying to get the boy's attention; she might actually end up dating him.]

B Elements of Literature

Conflict

❓ Identify the conflicts implied in these sentences? [The speaker's internal conflict over her love for the boy; the external conflict caused by the differences between them]

C Elements of Literature

Irony

❓ What makes this encounter ironic? [The circumstances are extremely ordinary and unromantic, yet the speaker is thrilled beyond belief.]

Resources

Listening

Audio CD Library

A recording of this selection is provided in the *Audio CD Library:*
• Disc 5, Track 4

Lessons of Love

from **Silent Dancing**

Judith Ortiz Cofer

Background

First love—we yearn for it, but sometimes, when it finally comes, we can barely stand it. It's no surprise, then, that stories of first love are often mixtures of happiness, sadness, and foolishness.

This selection is from an autobiography about a young Puerto Rican girl whose family lives in the city of Paterson, New Jersey. The girl goes to a Catholic school.

Reading Skills and Strategies

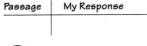

Dialogue with the Text

Keep a **double-entry journal** as you read this true story. In the first column, note passages that you think are especially good (maybe they tap into your own experience), or passages that you disagree with. Write your response to each passage in the second column.

Passage	My Response

go.hrw.com
LE0 10-2

A I fell in love, or my hormones awakened from their long slumber in my body, and suddenly the goal of my days was focused on one thing: to catch a glimpse of my secret love. And it had to remain secret, because I had, of course, in the great tradition of tragic romance, chosen to love a boy who was totally out of my reach. He was not Puerto Rican; he was Italian and rich. He was also an older man. He was a senior at the high school when I came in as a freshman. I first saw him in the hall, leaning casually on a wall that was the border line between girlside and boyside for underclassmen. He looked extraordinarily like a young Marlon Brando—down to the ironic little smile. The total of what I **B** knew about the boy who starred in every one of my awkward fantasies was this: that he was the nephew of the man who owned the supermarket on my block; that he often had parties at his parents' beautiful home in the suburbs, which I would hear about; that this family had money (which came to our school in many ways); and that—this fact made my knees weak—he worked at the store near my apartment building on weekends and in the summer.

My mother could not understand why I became so eager to be the one sent out on her endless errands. I pounced on every opportunity from Friday to late Saturday afternoon to go after eggs, cigarettes, milk (I tried to drink as much of it as possible, although I hated the stuff)—the staple items that she would order from the "American" store.

Week after week I wandered up and down the aisles, taking furtive glances at the stock room in the back, breathlessly hoping to see my prince. Not that I had a plan. I felt like a pilgrim waiting for a glimpse of Mecca.[1] I did not expect him to notice me. It was sweet agony.

C One day I did see him. Dressed in a white outfit, like a surgeon: white pants and shirt, white cap, and (gross sight, but not to my love-glazed eyes) blood-smeared butcher's apron. He was help-

---

1. **Mecca:** birthplace, in what is now Saudi Arabia, of Mohammed, the prophet who founded the Muslim religion. Mecca is a holy city for Muslims, who are strongly encouraged by their religion to make a pilgrimage there.

Using Students' Strengths

Auditory Learners

Some students may need to hear all or part of the selection read aloud in order to grasp its tone. Read the first paragraph aloud, emphasizing the ironic tone, and ask students to describe the speaker's attitude. Lead them toward an understanding of the irony implicit in almost every line. If they can then read the next three or four paragraphs silently and understand the irony, let them continue. If not, resume reading aloud.

Interpersonal Learners

Have interpersonal learners role-play a newspaper column for the lovelorn. Working in pairs, one partner can be the narrator, who writes to the newspaper when she feels devastated about moving to Puerto Rico for six months. The other student can be the columnist, who replies to her letter with frank advice. Encourage students to think of other situations (the boy complains the girl is stalking him; the mother complains her daughter is acting weird; and so on).

ing to drag a side of beef into the freezer storage area of the store. I must have stood there like an idiot, because I remember that he did see me; he even spoke to me! I could have died. I think he said, "Excuse me," and smiled vaguely in my direction.

After that, I *willed* occasions to go to the supermarket. I watched my mother's pack of cigarettes empty ever so slowly. I wanted her to smoke them fast. I drank milk and forced it on my brother (although a second glass for him had to be bought with my share of Fig Newton cookies, which we both liked, but we were restricted to one row each). I gave my cookies up for love, and watched my mother smoke her L&M's with so little enthusiasm that I thought that she might be cutting down on her smoking or maybe even giving up the habit. At this crucial time!

I thought I had kept my lonely romance a secret. Often I cried hot tears on my pillow for the things that kept us apart. In my mind there was no doubt that he would never notice me (and that is why I felt free to stare at him—I was invisible). He could not see me because I was a skinny Puerto Rican girl, a freshman who did not belong to any group he associated with.

At the end of the year I found out that I had not been invisible. I learned one little lesson about human nature—adulation[2] leaves a scent, one that we are all equipped to recognize, and no matter how insignificant the source, we seek it.

In June the nuns at our school would always arrange for some cultural extravaganza. In my freshman year it was a Roman banquet. We had been studying Greek drama (as a prelude to Church history—it was at a fast clip that we galloped through Sophocles and Euripides[3] toward the early Christian martyrs), and our young, energetic Sister Agnes was in the mood for spectacle. She ordered the entire student body (it was a small group of under three hundred students) to have our mothers make us togas[4] out of

2. **adulation** (a'jōō·lā'shən): intense admiration.
3. **Sophocles** (säf'ə·klēz') **and Euripides** (yoo·rip'ə·dēz'): Greek writers of tragic dramas in the fifth century B.C.
4. **togas** (tō'gəz): loose one-piece robes worn by citizens of ancient Rome.

sheets. She handed out a pattern on mimeo pages fresh out of the machine. I remember the intense smell of the alcohol on the sheets of paper and how almost everyone in the auditorium brought theirs to their noses and inhaled deeply—mimeographed handouts were the school-day buzz that the new Xerox generation of kids is missing out on. Then, as the last couple of weeks of school dragged on, the city of Paterson becoming a concrete oven and us wilting in our uncomfortable uniforms, we labored like frantic Roman slaves to build a splendid banquet hall in our small auditorium. Sister Agnes wanted a raised dais where the host and hostess would be regally enthroned.

She had already chosen our Senator and Lady from among our ranks. The Lady was to be a beautiful new student named Sophia, a recent Polish immigrant, whose English was still practically unintelligible, but whose features, classically perfect without a trace of makeup, enthralled us. Everyone talked about her gold hair cascading past her waist, and her voice, which could carry a note right up to heaven in choir. The nuns wanted her for God. They kept saying that she had a vocation.[5] We just looked at her in awe, and the boys seemed afraid of her. She just smiled and did as she was told. I don't know what she thought of it all. The main privilege of beauty is that others will do almost everything for you, including thinking.

Her partner was to be our best basketball player, a tall, red-haired senior whose family sent its many offspring to our school. Together, Sophia and her Senator looked like the best combination of immigrant genes our community could produce. It did not occur to me to ask then whether anything but their physical beauty qualified them for the starring roles in our production. I had the highest average in the Church history class, but I was given the part of one of many "Roman citizens." I was to sit in front of the plastic fruit and recite a greeting in Latin along with the rest of the school when our hosts came into the hall and took their places on their throne.

5. **vocation:** divine call to enter the religious life (here, to be a nun).

D Elements of Literature
Irony

❓ What is ironic about the narrator's comments on her mother's smoking? [Under ordinary circumstances, most people—including the narrator—would be delighted if a smoker cuts back or quits.]

E Elements of Literature
Suspense

❓ How does this paragraph create suspense? [It makes the reader want to know what event occurred and what the speaker learned from it.]

F Elements of Literature
Flashback

❓ What purpose does this flashback serve? [Possible responses: It gives a general date for the experience; it amuses readers old enough to remember a similar experience.]

G English Language Learners
Idiom

Tell English language learners that the expression *wanted her for God* means that the nuns wanted the girl to join their religious order and devote her life to the service of God through the church.

H Critical Thinking
Recognizing Bias

❓ What does the narrator seem to think of people who are exceptionally good looking? [They cannot think for themselves.] Do you think the narrator really believes this, or is she just using humorous overstatement? [Possible response: The kernel of envy in the statement suggests that part of her may really think good-looking people have no intelligence, but since the overall tone of the selection is ironic, she may also be going for humor here.]

I Reading Skills and Strategies
Responding to the Text

❓ Does this passage ring true to you? Have you ever felt that people were too quick to judge others by their looks? [Many students will be able to think of instances when attractive people received preference. Most will feel that appearance alone is not a reliable guide to character.]

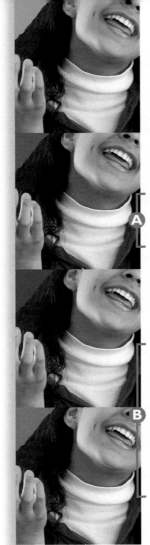

Ⓐ Appreciating Language

Figurative Language

❓ What does the speaker imply by "a peasant woman with a golden needle"? [Sample answer: She knows her mother has many fine qualities and skills, but at this moment she would trade all of them for her being able to sew a wonderful Roman toga.]

Ⓑ Critical Thinking

Connecting with the Text

❓ Do you think other people have these kinds of feelings about themselves? In your answer, give examples from movies, television shows, or books. [Sample response: Almost everyone feels this way at one time or another. For example, students may mention Maggie in Alice Walker's "Everyday Use."]

Ⓒ Elements of Literature

Allusions

The Fates are three goddesses in Greek mythology who control every phase of human destiny: birth, life itself, and death. "Nubian slaves" refers to people from Nubia, a region in northern Africa, held in slavery by the Romans.

Ⓓ Reading Skills and Strategies

Making Inferences

❓ Where in this passage do you find an example of the self-mockery of an older person looking back in time? ["How did I survive the killing power" suggests that the narrator is now laughing gently at the extremes of infatuation she once felt.]

On the night of our banquet, my father escorted me in my toga to the door of our school. I felt foolish in my awkwardly draped sheet (blouse and skirt required underneath). My mother had no great skill as a seamstress. The best she could do was hem a skirt or a pair of pants. That night I would have traded her for a peasant woman with a golden needle. I saw other Roman ladies emerging from their parents' cars looking authentic in sheets of material that folded over their bodies like the garments on a statue by Michelangelo.[6] How did they do it? How was it that I always got it just slightly wrong, and worse, I believed that other people were just too polite to mention it. "The poor little Puerto Rican girl," I could hear them thinking. But in reality, I must have been my worst critic, self-conscious as I was.

Soon, we were all sitting at our circle of tables joined together around the dais. Sophia glittered like a golden statue. Her smile was beatific:[7] a perfect, silent Roman lady. Her Senator looked uncomfortable, glancing around at his buddies, perhaps waiting for the ridicule that he would surely get in the locker room later. The nuns in their black habits stood in the background watching us. What were they supposed to be, the Fates? Nubian slaves? The dancing girls did their modest little dance to tinny music from their finger cymbals; then the speeches were made. Then the grape juice "wine" was raised in a toast to the Roman Empire we all knew would fall within the week—before finals, anyway.

All during the program I had been in a state of controlled hysteria. My secret love sat across the room from me looking supremely bored. I watched his every move, taking him in gluttonously. I relished the shadow of his eyelashes on his ruddy cheeks, his pouty lips smirking sarcastically at the ridiculous sight of our little play. Once he slumped down on his chair, and our sergeant-at-arms nun came over and tapped him sharply on his shoulder. He drew himself up slowly, with disdain. I loved his rebellious spirit. I believed myself still invisible to him in my "nothing" status as I looked upon my beloved. But toward the end of the evening, as we stood chanting our farewells in Latin, he looked straight across the room and into my eyes! How did I survive the killing power of those dark pupils? I trembled in a new way. I was not cold—I was burning! Yet I shook from the inside out, feeling lightheaded, dizzy.

The room began to empty and I headed for the girls' lavatory. I wanted to relish the miracle in silence. I did not think for a minute that anything more would follow. I was satisfied with the enormous favor of a look from my beloved. I took my time, knowing that my father would be waiting outside for me, impatient, perhaps glowing in the dark in his phosphorescent[8] white Navy uniform. The others would ride home. I would walk home with my father, both of us in costume. I wanted as few witnesses as possible. When I could no longer hear the crowds in the hallway, I emerged from the bathroom, still under the spell of those mesmerizing eyes.

The lights had been turned off in the hallway, and all I could see was the lighted stairwell, at the bottom of which a nun would be stationed. My father would be waiting just outside. I nearly

---

6. **Michelangelo** (mī′kəl·an′jə·lō′) (1475–1564): Italian sculptor, painter, architect, and poet.
7. **beatific** (bē′ə·tif′ik): angelic; displaying delight or kindliness.
8. **phosphorescent** (fäs′fə·res′ənt): giving off light; glowing.

Assessing Learning

Observation Assessment

As students discuss the story, take note of the following behaviors, rating each student *High, Medium,* or *Low* for each:

1. The student appears to be engaged in the discussion.
2. The student volunteers to make comments.
3. The student appears to listen to the comments of others.

Check Test: Short Answers

1. Where does the narrator hope her mother will send her on errands? [to the local grocery store where the boy she has a crush on works]
2. What kind of "cultural extravaganza" does the school stage in June? [a Roman banquet]
3. What role does the narrator play in the school production? [She is one of many ordinary Roman citizens.]
4. What happens in the school hallway after the production? [The boy she loves kisses her.]
5. Where is the family scheduled to move once school is out for the summer? [to the narrator's grandmother's house in Puerto Rico]

screamed when I felt someone grab me by the waist. But my mouth was quickly covered by someone else's mouth. I was being kissed. My first kiss and I could not even tell who it was. I pulled away to see that face not two inches away from mine. It was he. He smiled down at me. Did I have a silly expression on my face? My glasses felt crooked on my nose. I was unable to move or to speak. More gently, he lifted my chin and touched his lips to mine. This time I did not forget to enjoy it. Then, like the phantom lover that he was, he walked away into the darkened corridor and disappeared.

I don't know how long I stood there. My body was changing right there in the hallway of a Catholic school. My cells were tuning up like musicians in an orchestra, and my heart was a chorus. It was an opera I was composing, and I wanted to stand very still and just listen. But of course, I heard my father's voice talking to the nun. I was in trouble if he had had to ask about me. I hurried down the stairs, making up a story on the way about feeling sick. That would explain my flushed face and it would buy me a little privacy when I got home.

The next day Father announced at the breakfast table that he was leaving on a six-month tour of Europe with the Navy in a few weeks and that at the end of the school year my mother, my brother, and I would be sent to Puerto Rico to stay for half a year at Mamá's (my mother's mother) house. I was devastated. This was the usual routine for us. We had always gone to Mamá's to stay when Father was away for long periods. But this year it was different for me. I was in love, and . . . my heart knocked against my bony chest at this thought . . . he loved me too? I broke into sobs and left the table.

In the next week I discovered the inexorable truth about parents. They can actually carry on with their plans right through tears, threats, and the awful spectacle of a teenager's broken heart. My father left me to my mother, who impassively packed while I explained over and over that I was at a crucial time in my studies and that if I left my entire life would be ruined. All she would say was, "You are an intelligent girl, you'll catch up." Her head was filled with visions of

casa[9] and family reunions, long gossip sessions with her mamá and sisters. What did she care that I was losing my one chance at true love?

In the meantime I tried desperately to see him. I thought he would look for me too. But the few times I saw him in the hallway, he was always rushing away. It would be long weeks of confusion and pain before I realized that the kiss was nothing but a little trophy for his ego. He had no interest in me other than as his adorer. He was flattered by my silent worship of him, and he had *bestowed* a kiss on me to please himself and to fan the flames. I learned a lesson about the battle of the sexes then that I have never forgotten: The object is not always to win, but most times simply to keep your opponent (synonymous at times with "the loved one") guessing.

But this is too cynical a view to sustain in the face of that overwhelming rush of emotion that is first love. And in thinking back about my own experience with it, I can be objective only to the point where I recall how sweet the anguish was, how caught up in the moment I felt, and how every nerve in my body was involved in this salute to life. Later, much later, after what seemed like an eternity of dragging the weight of unrequited love around with me, I learned to make myself visible and to relish the little battles required to win the greatest prize of all. And much later, I read and understood Camus's[10] statement about the subject that concerns both adolescent and philosopher alike: If love were easy, life would be too simple.

9. **casa** (kä′sä): Spanish for "house" or "home."
10. **Camus** (ka·mōō′): Albert Camus (1913–1960), French writer and philosopher.

Making the Connections

Connecting to the Theme: "Hearts That Love"
The author opens this section of her autobiography with the words, "I fell in love. . . ." As her story progresses, readers learn that she now realizes her love was really a crush or infatuation, but at the time it seemed very real to her.

First, ask students to write several sentences about the nature of infatuation. Then, ask students to write a definition of love in one or two sentences. Write some of these on the board in two columns. Using the students' definitions as a starting point, have the class reach a consensus on definitions of both infatuation and love. Conclude by discussing the importance of being able to distinguish the two.

Cultural Connections
This narrative is the story of what happens to a Puerto Rican girl during her freshman year in a multi-ethnic Catholic high school in the United States. Her experience is hardly limited to that context, however. As students will have sensed when they connected this story with the collection theme, the dizzying experience of a first crush occurs in every culture. Discuss with students how different cultures allow young people to express or realize that experience.

FINDING COMMON GROUND

As its name suggests, this feature requires students to engage in lively discussion in order to discover areas of agreement about something related to the theme of the collection, "Hearts That Love," and about issues in the selection itself.

Possible Responses

1. The main events are as follows: Judith falls in love with an older boy, who is out of her reach and who works in a grocery store in her neighborhood. She is eager to run errands to the store. One day she sees the boy dragging a side of beef out of a freezer; he sees her and speaks to her, and she is embarrassed. Later, both she and the boy are in a school production of a Roman banquet. After the production he catches her in the hall and surprises her with a kiss. The next morning she learns that her family will move to Puerto Rico and live there while her father is away in the Navy for six months. The story ends with Judith's reflections about what she learned about relationships between men and women from the incident.

2. Responses about the most important image, passage, event, or idea will vary. Some students may feel that the kiss is the most important event. Others may think the boy's pulling the frozen side of beef across the grocery store floor is important because the event marks the first time he notices Judith.

3. Responses will vary. Many students will probably find the story believable, but some might think the kiss in the darkened hallway a bit far-fetched. Most students will recognize that the author's feelings are universal.

4. Responses will vary. Many students will feel that the most important lesson she learned is not to fall in love too quickly, and to base her love on more important qualities than a person's looks.

MEET THE WRITER

Tracing Family Lives

Judith Ortiz Cofer (1952–   ) travels between two cultures. She was born in Puerto Rico and began her visits to the mainland when she was four. When her father, a career Navy man, was overseas, his family returned to Puerto Rico; when he sailed back to the States, his family rejoined him in Paterson, New Jersey. Judith Ortiz Cofer has said,

66 My first language was Spanish. It was a challenge not only to learn English, but to master it enough to teach it and—the ultimate goal—to write poetry in it. 99

She has published poetry; a novel, *The Line of the Sun* (1989); a book of personal essays, *Silent Dancing* (1990); a collection of prose and poetry called *The Latin Deli* (1993); and *An Island like You: Stories of the Barrio* (1995).

66 My family is one of the main topics of my poetry," she has said. "In tracing their lives, I discover more about mine. 99

FINDING COMMON GROUND

You are going to be working with a partner and talking about your responses to this story of first love and first rejection. Before you meet with your partner, make notes responding to these questions:

1. What did you see happening in the text? **Summarize** the main events of the story in your notes.

2. As you look back on your **double-entry journal,** decide what was the central focus for you. In other words, what was the most important image, event, or idea in the text? Why do you think so?

3. This is a true story. How believable do you find the girl's experiences with love? Are her feelings specific to her particular culture, or are they universal feelings?

4. Be sure to talk about the **title**. What lessons of love did the girl learn?

Now you are ready to share your notes with your partner. How do your responses differ? Does your understanding of the text change as you talk about it? What agreements can you reach about the text?

READ ON

A Friendship like No Other

John and Lorraine, high school students, take turns telling "the truth and nothing but the truth" about Mr. Angelo Pignati, whom they nickname the Pigman. What starts as a telephone prank turns into a friendship that changes all their lives. *The Pigman* (HarperCollins), Paul Zindel's enormously popular novel, revolutionized young adult fiction when it appeared in 1968. (The book is available in the HRW Library.) The sequel, *The Pigman's Legacy,* continues John and Lorraine's story.

Father and Son

The father and son in August Wilson's 1987 Pulitzer Prize–winning play *Fences* (New American Library) have conflicting dreams for the boy's future. Excluded from the major leagues because of his race, the father finds it difficult to encourage his son's ball-playing ambitions.

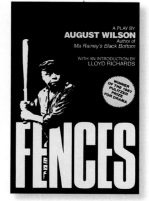

Love Is the Glue

The teenage daughter of Appalachian sharecroppers, Mary Call Luther struggles to keep her brothers and sisters together after both parents die. You won't forget *Where the Lilies Bloom* (Lippincott) by Vera and Bill Cleaver.

Learning to Love Herself

Steven Spielberg's 1985 film of Alice Walker's Pulitzer Prize–winning novel, *The Color Purple* (Harcourt Brace), stars Whoopi Goldberg and Oprah Winfrey. The movie focuses on an African American woman who must overcome a tragic personal history and the legacy of slavery before she can take pride in who she is.

Writer's Workshop

ASSIGNMENT

Write an essay analyzing a fictional character in a short story, novel, movie, or TV show.

AIM

To use critical thinking skills; to give information.

AUDIENCE

Your teacher, classmates, or a friend.

A Box of Traits	
sociable	taciturn
playful	withdrawn
talkative	morose
stable	erratic
prudent	reckless
sensitive	insensitive
altruistic	self-centered
caring	manipulative
optimistic	pessimistic
hard-working	slothful

I don't have a very clear idea of who the characters are until they start talking.
—Joan Didion

EXPOSITORY WRITING
ANALYZING A CHARACTER

According to the writer W. Somerset Maugham, "You can never know enough about your characters." He was speaking as the *creator* of fictional characters—but the same can also be said for the reader. The more we know about the characters in a work of fiction, the more we understand its meaning.

In this workshop, you'll write an essay analyzing a fictional character. When you **analyze** something, you examine it closely to see how it works. You take it apart as if it were a puzzle or a machine, and try to discover how all its separate elements are put together and how each piece connects to the whole. When you analyze a fictional character, you do the same thing. You closely examine all the ways the writer reveals that character's nature or personality. Then, you put all these details back together again to create a portrait of what the character is like.

Prewriting

1. Choose a Character

Look back over the entries in your Writer's
Notebook to see if you've already found a character you'd like to examine more closely. If you're having trouble deciding on one, consider the characters in novels, movies, or TV shows you've enjoyed. Try to find someone who seems particularly real or complex or mysterious to you. The stronger your feelings about the character, the better.

2. Gather Information

Once you've chosen a character, review the work, looking for details that reveal information about that character. As you take notes, think about these questions:

• **Does the writer show or tell?** What does the writer *tell* us directly about the character? What does the writer reveal indirectly by describing, or *showing*, the character's **appearance, speech, thoughts,** and **actions**? What can we infer by observing **how other characters respond** to that person?

 Resources: Print and Media

Writing and Language
• *Portfolio Management System*
  Prewriting, p. 106
  Peer Editing, p. 107
  Assessment Rubric, p. 108

• *Workshop Resources*
  Revision Strategy Teaching Notes, p. 7
  Revision Strategy Transparencies 4, 5, 6

The history of the written word is rich and time

Once upon a time

Page

- **What's the personality?** From all the evidence you've noted, what would you say are the character's main **traits,** or personal qualities? Is he or she a **flat**—even a **stock**—character who exhibits only one or two personality traits? Is this a **round,** complex character with a many-sided personality?

- **Does the character change?** Is the character **static,** basically remaining the same throughout the story? Is he or she **dynamic,** changing in some significant way—by learning or realizing something, making an important decision, or taking some key action? If so, describe the change. Is it predictable, or did it surprise you in some way?

- **What motivates the character?** What are the reasons for the character's behavior? (If you're not sure, think about what the character wants or needs.) Do you find the motivation believable, or does it seem unrealistic or flimsy?

- **What's the character's role?** Is the character the **protagonist,** the person whose conflict sets the plot in motion?

3. Develop a Thesis Statement

Narrow your focus to three or four key points, and write a **thesis statement** that sums up your **main idea** about this character. Consider the approaches on the next page.

Data Bank for Analyzing a Character
Appearance
Speech
Thoughts
Actions
Main traits
How others respond
Motivation
Change(s)?
Protagonist?

Thesis Statement

In "Geraldo No Last Name," the sheer beauty of Sandra Cisneros's description of the character Marin is enthralling, while at the same time keeping Marin distant from us.

"O.K., so I dig a hole and put the bone in the hole. But what's my motivation for burying it?"

Introducing the Writer's Workshop

Write the names of several characters from popular television programs on the chalkboard and lead students through a discussion of them in terms of the questions under Gather Information, pp. 164–165. Lead students to understand that we analyze and make judgments about characters in short stories in the same way we do for characters on television.

Teaching the Writer's Workshop

Prewriting

- Suggest that students think of three characters from short stories in this collection and freewrite about them. Then they can exchange their ideas about these characters with a partner.

- Look at A Box of Traits on p. 164. Have students identify the overall character of each list of words. Which list is positive, which negative? Which word is the most negative? Discuss with students the denotative and connotative properties of words using the following examples: (1) straw-colored, yellow, tow-headed, blonde; (2) thrifty, cheap, frugal, responsible. Caution students to read carefully for verbal clues to character.

Getting Students Involved

Cooperative Learning

Students might find it helpful to form partnerships with other students who have read the same stories but have chosen different characters to analyze.

Partners can serve as sounding boards from the beginning to the end of the writing process, from brainstorming to proofreading. Their familiarity with the stories will enable them to offer each other additional insights and ideas.

Drafting

- Have students read and discuss the Student Model on p. 167 before beginning their drafts.
- Remind students to use only every other line when they write their drafts. They should also leave extra space in the right margin. These blank spaces will be used for comments and editing marks.
- Also explain to students that while using quotations as supporting details is good, quotations cannot stand alone. Writers must comment on the quotations they use to show how these quotations support their main points.

Try It Out
Possible Answers

1. Feld wants Miriam to marry an educated man who can provide a better life for her. When he discovers that Max is studying accounting, he satisfies himself that certified public accountants are respected professionals. When Sobel tells him he reads to know, Feld asks him what he wants to know.

2. Despite her thinking that what happened makes no difference, that Geraldo meant nothing to her, she can't help thinking about his life—where he lived, the money he sent home to his family, the currency exchange he used, and his family's reaction when they don't hear from him again.

Language/Grammar Link
H E L P

Dialogue: page 109.
Dialect: page 131.
Vivid verbs: page 145.
Adverbs: page 156.

Try It Out

When you **elaborate** on a **topic sentence** in a character analysis, you provide specific evidence from the story: dialogue, descriptive passages, interaction between characters, specific incidents.

1. How would you support the generalization that Feld in "The First Seven Years" is "a practical man"?

2. What evidence would you cite to show that Marin in "Geraldo No Last Name" is changed by the story's events?

Language Handbook
H E L P

Using quotation marks: pages 1054–1056.

Sentence Workshop
H E L P

Using adjectives and adverbs: page 169.

- Summarize the character's most important traits.
- Identify the character's change or discovery.
- Explain why the character is or is not the protagonist.

4. Organize Your Ideas

Think about the clearest order in which to present your three or four key points. (Each point will serve as the **topic sentence** for a paragraph in the body of your essay.) The Student Model, for example, arranges key points in this sequence: method of characterization, some character traits, the character's relationship with another character. Play around with several possibilities, and start an **outline** (see pages 334 and 450) showing your key points.

5. Elaborate: Back Up Your Ideas with Evidence

Now, fill in your outline with the strongest evidence to elaborate your topic sentences:

- **direct quotations** from the story
- references to **specific actions** and **dialogue**
- **specific adjectives** to describe the character's traits
- **comparisons** with other characters in the story or in other literary works

Drafting

You've already done a lot of planning, but there's still time to refocus your thesis or even discover new ideas during the writing process. You can either begin with your introduction or skip it for now and start with the body of your essay. Just get your thoughts down in writing—you can revise and polish later. Here are the three basic parts of your essay.

- **Introduction.** Your first paragraph should draw readers into your topic and present your **thesis statement.** Identify both the story (author and title) and the character you're analyzing.

- **Body.** You've already outlined the body of your essay and written a topic sentence for each paragraph. Now, turn your supporting details into complete sentences. Refer to specific events, descriptions, and dialogue to back up your generalizations about the character. Try to include direct quotations from the story. When you describe the character, choose specific and vivid adjectives that give the reader a clear picture.

- **Conclusion.** In your last paragraph, restate your thesis and add a final comment about the character or the meaning of the story as a whole. If possible, end with a dramatic clincher sentence, as in the Student Model.

Reaching All Students

Struggling Writers

Encourage students who have difficulty in analyzing character to make a list of all other characters in the story and determine how they seemed to feel about the character selected for analysis.

Next to the word or phrase describing the other characters' feelings, have the writer give examples that show how these feelings were demonstrated in the story. In a sense, the student writer is taking a straw poll within the story's world to determine if the character being analyzed is likable, honest, a leader, etc. The results of this poll may suggest an approach to analyzing the character.

"Geraldo No Last Name"

Sandra Cisneros has a way with words that is un-paralleled in her ability to grasp the essence of a character. In "Geraldo No Last Name," the sheer beauty of her description of the character Marin is enthralling, while at the same time keeping Marin distant from us.

Identifies author, title, and character
Thesis statement

Her description may seem meager at first glance (Cisneros says so little about her characters), but after reading the story, you discover that her descrip-tion is bursting with insight. Marin is drawn as one might see her in one night. Cisneros lets you know that she is a stranger, not about to share dark secrets and wishes, a simple person.

Topic sentence: indirect characterization

Marin is just a girl who likes to have fun, twenty-something, vivacious and slightly materialistic while remaining innocent to life's tragedies. She doesn't realize that what exists can be gone in seconds, and reasons that were always so obvious cannot be explained. She went looking for a good time and was "sent home with her coat and some aspirin." She is not familiar with death, and the death of this stranger has left her confused.

Topic sentence: Marin's charac-ter traits (vivid adjectives)

How Marin changes—what she learns

Elaboration: quotation from the story

Geraldo is just as much a stranger to Marin as she is to the reader: "Just another brazer who didn't speak English. Just another wetback." Her relationship with him may seem cold at first, but as the experience unfolds, you find his hold on her is strong. She will not forget him. He has touched her, perhaps not in life, but most certainly in death, and this unexpected experience will change her outlook.

Topic sentence: Marin's relation-ship with Geraldo

By the conclusion of the story, Marin knows that Geraldo will forever remain a question unanswered. She knows then that she cannot change that; she cannot make it better; she can only accept its reality.

Clincher sentence

—Alicia Weaver
Communications Arts High
School
San Antonio, Texas

Using the Model

- On the first reading of the model, focus students' attention on the placement of the thesis statement and the arrangement of supporting statements.
- After students have completed their first drafts, you may wish to examine the structure of the model with them again. Write an outline of the model on the chalkboard. Include the thesis sentence, the three topic sen-tences, and the primary support-ing details. Then, have students outline their own essays in the same way to see if they have clear theses, topic sentences, and supporting details.

Reaching All Students

Advanced Learners

Have students think of characters in other works of literature or in real life who compare and/or contrast significantly with the characters they have just analyzed. Then have them create a chart or some other visual that would illus-trate the similarities and/or differences in the two characters.

Evaluating and Revising

Have students use the Evaluation Criteria provided here to review their drafts and determine needed revisions.

Proofreading

Have students proofread their own papers first and then exchange them with other students. For this assignment, remind students that the critical spelling words would include characters' names, details of setting, and major points of plot. Have them review and verify the spelling of this critical vocabulary.

If time permits, the final copy should be put aside for at least a day before it is proofread for the final time by the author.

Publishing

Have students work with their classmates to combine their essays into a gallery of characters from the short story collection just completed. Suggest that they illustrate their book with sketches of the characters and incidents from the stories.

Reflecting

Have students write brief reflections on one or more of the following: the most helpful prewriting technique, the most troublesome part of the drafting stage, and the best part of their final drafts.

Resources

Peer Editing Forms and Rubrics
• *Portfolio Management System*, p. 107.

Revision Transparencies
• *Workshop Resources*, p. 7

Grading Timesaver

Rubrics for this Writer's Workshop assignment appear on p. 108 of the *Portfolio Management System*.

T168

■ *Evaluation Criteria*

A good character analysis

1. *identifies the character, title, and author in the introduction*

2. *includes a thesis statement that sums up the main ideas*

3. *presents at least three main ideas about the character*

4. *supports each main idea with specific evidence from the story*

5. *ends by restating the thesis*

Proofreading Tip

A good way to catch mistakes is to slow yourself down by pointing to every word and punctuation mark with a pencil.

Communications Handbook
HELP

See Proofreaders' Marks.

Publishing Tips

• If several students have analyzed the same character, collect your essays into a booklet: "All About . . ."

• If your school has a Web site, see if you can post your work on the student page.

Evaluating and Revising

1. Self-Evaluation

Read your essay aloud, looking for ways to eliminate wordiness, improve transitions, and sharpen your language. Consider adding words like *first, second, finally, because,* and *however* to clarify connections among ideas. Pay particular attention to replacing overused adjectives and adverbs with more vivid modifiers.

2. Peer Review

Try this experiment: Read your thesis statement aloud to a partner without identifying the character, story, or author. If your classmate can't guess the character, try making your thesis statement more specific. Then exchange drafts. Make comments about your partner's essay, focusing on the evaluation criteria at the left. Offer suggestions for how he or she might improve the essay, but also provide positive feedback about the paper's strengths.

Revision Model

	Peer Comments
~~The author~~ Sandra Cisneros has a way with words	*Identify author and story.*
that is unparalleled in her ability to grasp the essence of a character. In "Geraldo No Last Name," ~~her story~~ the sheer beauty of her	
description of the character ^Marin is	*Who is the character?*
enthralling, while ~~distant~~ keeping Marin distant from us at the same time.	*This is confusing.*
Her description may seem meager at (Cisneros says so little about her characters) first glance, but after reading the	*What do you mean here?*
story, you discover that ~~they are~~ her description is bursting with insight.	*Who is "they"?*

Sentence Workshop

OBJECTIVES
1. Expand sentences using adjectives and adverbs
2. Use elaboration to limit or sharpen meaning

EXPANDING SENTENCES: USING ADJECTIVES AND ADVERBS

Read the following sentences, which have been adapted from the stories in this collection.

1. He was wearing an overcoat that hung down to his ankles.

2. A rat sprang from under my feet and retreated.

3. The disk of sun and the sky covered and surrounded the village.

Now read the sentences as their writers wrote them. Notice how the underlined words help you to imagine more concretely and in greater detail the ideas, objects, and events described.

1. "He was wearing a <u>loose</u>, <u>long</u>, <u>slushy</u> overcoat that hung down to his ankles. . . ."

   —Bernard Malamud, "The First Seven Years" (page 121)

2. "A rat sprang from under my foot and retreated <u>grudgingly</u>. . . ."

   —Hugo Martinez-Serros, "Distillation" (page 137)

3. "The <u>clean</u>, <u>round</u>, <u>blinding</u> disk of sun and the <u>blue</u> sky covered and surrounded the <u>small</u> <u>African</u> village. . . ."

   —Abioseh Nicol, "Life Is Sweet at Kumansenu" (page 147)

In the first group, each sentence is a plain statement. In the second group, the underlined words are **adjectives** and **adverbs**, words that *modify* other words. Modifiers are used to elaborate—they limit or sharpen the meanings of other words.

Writer's Workshop Follow-up: Revision

Exchange drafts with a partner when you revise your work. Ask for reactions to your descriptions. If your partner calls for more specific details and sensory images, try expanding your sentences by using precise, vivid adjectives and adverbs. Remember that adjectives tell *What kind? Which one? How many?* Adverbs tell *How? How often? To what extent?*

Language Handbook
HELP

See Using Modifiers, pages 1031–1033.

Technology
HELP

See Language Workshop CD-ROM. Key word entry: expanding sentences.

Try It Out

1. Looking at How Modifiers Work

With a small group, look back at the stories in this collection. Copy at least five sentences that you think contain modifiers that give you vivid pictures of people and places—of their appearance and actions. Find at least two modifiers that establish a mood or emotional tone—words that make you feel positively or negatively about a character or place or thing.

2. Using Modifiers

Go back to the first three numbered sentences opposite. Use new modifiers to elaborate on the sentences to give them a different mood or tone. How many variations can you think of for each sentence? Be sure to compare your results in your group.

Resources ───────

Workshop Resources
• Worksheet, p. 57
Language Workshop CD-ROM
• Expanding Sentences

Try It Out
Possible Answers
1. • "And she also did this <u>fancy</u> sweep of a curtsy so that the <u>fluffy</u> skirt of her <u>white</u> dress cascaded <u>slowly</u> to the floor like the petals of a <u>large</u> carnation." (from "Two Kinds")
   • ". . .Miriam brought Max to the bedroom door, and he stood there a minute, a <u>tall</u>, <u>slightly hunched</u> figure wearing a <u>thick</u>, <u>droopy</u> suit and <u>apparently</u> at ease as he greeted the shoemaker and his wife. . . ." (from "The First Seven Years")
   • "He started up <u>unfalteringly</u>, <u>tenaciously</u>, with <u>short</u>, <u>rapid</u> steps and his body bent <u>forward</u>. . . ." (from "Distillation")
   • "She went back <u>heavily</u> and fell into a <u>restless</u> sleep." (from "Life is Sweet at Kumansenu")
   • "He looked <u>extraordinarily</u> like a <u>young</u> Marlon Brando—down to the <u>ironic</u> <u>little</u> smile." (from "Lessons of Love")
2. • *tight, uncomfortable, stuffy* overcoat
   • retreated *hastily*
   • *hazy, oval, dim* disk; *overcast* sky; *rural, Nigerian* village.

Assessing Learning

Quick Check: Expanding Sentences

Expand each of the following sentences by adding an adjective and an adverb to each. (A possible answer follows each sentence.)

1. Jing-mei's mother wanted her to practice the piano. [Jing-mei's *assertive* mother *desperately* wanted her to practice the piano.]
2. Marin believed that a surgeon could have saved Geraldo's life. [Marin believed *absolutely* that a *first-rate* surgeon could have saved Geraldo's life.]
3. Feld, the shoemaker, toiled to establish his shoe repair shop. [Feld, the *immigrant* shoemaker, toiled *furiously* to establish his shoe repair shop.]
4. The father protected his children from the hail by holding a tarp over them. [The father *courageously* protected his *terrified* children from the hail by holding a tarp over them.]
5. Bola felt concern for her son when she discovered he was not eating the meals she prepared for him. [Bola felt *deep* concern for her son when she *suddenly* discovered he was not eating the meals she prepared for him.]

OBJECTIVES
1. Read a map
2. Understand the different types of maps
3. Learn to use map features

Teaching the Lesson

Explain to students that reading maps is something they will often do as they look beyond their own home, state, and country. From floor plans of complex buildings to geographical features of unfamiliar territories, maps help people find their way by addressing spatial information and relationships. Remind students that there are different kinds of maps, and show them examples and features of the types already listed, which may be found in your school library.

In addition, you may want to have them construct their own map or experience a challenging orientation exercise that makes use of a map.

Using the Strategies

Possible Answers

1. Eighty-sixth Street does not appear on the map, but students can guess its whereabouts. Torrence Avenue meets 95th Street on the bottom right-hand corner of the map.
2. Answers will vary but may include: Sears Tower, Museum of African American History, and University of Chicago.
3. Answers will vary, but the main road is Interstate 90/94.
4. From Midway Airport, it's about 9 miles to the Sears Tower, traveling in a NE direction.

Reading for Life

Reading a Map

Situation

After reading "Distillation" (page 133), you want to see a map of the area in which the story takes place, South Chicago. To find the correct map and to read it, apply the strategies below.

Strategies

Understand the different types of maps.

- A **physical map** uses colors and shadings to show an area's natural landscape, including landforms and elevation.

- A **political map** shows political units, such as nations, states, capitals, and major cities.

- A **special purpose map** presents specific information. For example, a **road map** shows the system of roadways in an area, as well as campsites, parks, airports, and other places of special interest.

Learn to use map features.

- The **compass rose** indicates direction: north, south, east, and west. In most maps north is at the top.

- The **distance scale** relates distances on the map to actual distances.

- Many maps also have a **legend**, or **key**, that explains special symbols on the map.

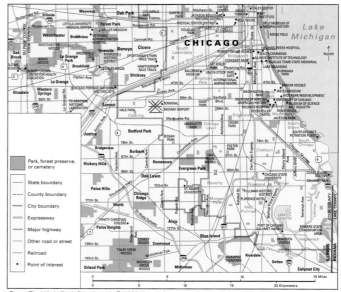

From *The World Book Encyclopedia* © 1998 World Book, Inc. By permission of the publisher.

- A map may also have a **locator map**, a secondary map that shows the relationship of the area in the main map to a larger area.

Using the Strategies

1. Using the map above, can you locate these places mentioned in the story: 86th Street, 95th Street, Torrence Avenue?

2. Which points of interest might you want to visit in Chicago?

3. If you were driving into Chicago from the south, what road could you take to get to the Sears Tower?

4. About how far, and in which direction, would you have to drive to get from Midway Airport to the Sears Tower?

Extending the Strategies

Locate a road map of your town, city, or state. List three of the area's major roads and the directions they take. Could you use the map if you wanted to take a camping trip?

Crossing the Curriculum

Interdisciplinary Studies

Have students bring in textbooks from other disciplines that contain maps. Have each student select a map and present it to the class. The presenter should explain the map's title and purpose, its type, and any special features of coloration or design.

Collection 3

Exiles, Castaways, and Strangers

Theme

Characters at Odds In ironic literature, characters are often isolated and set adrift from the support of a community. The world these characters move in is often limited. Heroes are rare in these stories. Students should recognize some of the motifs in these stories from popular movies and novels.

Reading the Anthology

Reaching Struggling Readers

The *Reading Skills and Strategies: Reaching Struggling Readers* binder provides materials coordinated with the Pupil's Edition (see the Collection Planner, p. T170B) to help students who have difficulty reading and comprehending text, or students who are reluctant readers. The binder for tenth grade is organized around sixteen individual skill areas and offers the following options:

- **Mini Read** MiniReads are short, easy texts that give students a chance to practice a particular skill and strategy before reading selections in the Pupil's Edition. Each MiniRead Skill Lesson can be taught independently or used in conjunction with a Selection Skill Lesson.

- **Selection Skill Lessons** Selection Skill Lessons allow students to apply skills introduced in the MiniReads. Each Selection Skill Lesson provides reading instruction and practice specific to a particular piece of literature in the Pupil's Edition.

Reading Beyond the Anthology

Read On Collection 3 includes an annotated bibliography of books suitable for extended reading. The suggested books are related to works in this collection by theme, by author, or by subject. To preview the Read On for Collection 3, please turn to p. T239.

HRW Library The *HRW Library* offers novels, plays, and short-story collections for extended reading. Each book in the Library includes one or more major works and thematically related Connections. Each book in the *HRW Library* is also accompanied by a Study Guide that provides teaching suggestions and worksheets. For Collection 3, the following titles are recommended.

JANE EYRE
Charlotte Brontë
Jane is a penniless orphan sent to live with cruel relatives. When she goes out into the world, she finds work as a governess for a brooding man who seems to be as lonely and isolated as she is.

READINGS IN WORLD LITERATURE
Great stories often involve characters tested by isolation or exile: Ruth, who, for the sake of love, becomes a stranger in a strange land; Achilles, whose wrath isolates him; and Don Quijote, whose dreams make him the subject of ridicule.

Collection 3 Exiles, Castaways, and Strangers

Resources for this Collection

Note: All resources for this collection are available for preview on the *One-Stop Planner CD-ROM 1 with Test Generator*. All worksheets and blackline masters may be printed from the CD-ROM.

Internet Resources
go.hrw.com LE0 10-3

Collection Planner

Selection or Feature	Reading and Literary Skills	Vocabulary, Language, and Grammar

The Pedestrian (p. 172)
Ray Bradbury
	• *Reading Skills and Strategies: Reaching Struggling Readers*
	  • MiniRead Skill Lesson, p. 77
	  • Selection Skill Lesson, p. 84
	• *Graphic Organizers for Active Reading*, Worksheet p. 11
		• *Words to Own*, Worksheet p. 11
		• *Grammar and Language Links:* Prepositions, Worksheet p. 19
		• *Language Workshop CD-ROM*, Prepositions
		• *Daily Oral Grammar*, Transparency 11

Elements of Literature: Theme (p. 182)	• *Literary Elements*, Transparency 6	

Liberty
Julia Alvarez (p. 184)
 	
Connections: Havana Journal: A Sentimental Journey to la Casa of Childhood (p. 191)
Mirta Ojito
	• *Reading Skills and Strategies: Reaching Struggling Readers*
	  • MiniRead Skill Lesson, p. 88
	  • Selection Skill Lesson, p. 94
	• *Graphic Organizers for Active Reading*, Worksheet p. 12
		• *Words to Own*, Worksheet p. 12
		• *Grammar and Language Links:* Pronouns, Worksheet p. 21
		• *Language Workshop CD-ROM*, Pronouns
		• *Daily Oral Grammar*, Transparency 12

Elements of Literature: Irony and Satire (p. 194)	• *Literary Elements*, Transparency 7	
Where Have You Gone, Charming Billy? (p. 196) Tim O'Brien **Connections: The Friendship Only Lasted a Few Seconds** (p. 205) Lily Lee Adams	• *Graphic Organizers for Active Reading*, Worksheet p. 13 • *Literary Elements:* Transparency 6 Worksheet p. 19	• *Words to Own*, Worksheet p. 13 • *Grammar and Language Links:* Clauses, Worksheet p. 23 • *Language Workshop CD-ROM*, Independent and Subordinate Clauses • *Daily Oral Grammar*, Transparency 13
The Bet (p. 209) Anton Chekhov *translated by* Constance Garnett	• *Graphic Organizers for Active Reading*, Worksheet p. 14 • *Literary Elements:* Transparency 7 Worksheet p. 22	• *Words to Own*, Worksheet p. 14 • *Grammar and Language Links:* Voice, Worksheet p. 25 • *Language Workshop CD-ROM*, Voice • *Daily Oral Grammar*, Transparency 14

A Very Old Man with Enormous Wings (p. 222)
Gabriel García Márquez
translated by Gregory Rabassa
 	
Connections: Sonnet for Heaven Below (p. 231)
Jack Agüeros
	• *Reading Skills and Strategies: Reaching Struggling Readers*
	  • MiniRead Skill Lesson, p. 98
	  • Selection Skill Lesson, p. 105
	• *Graphic Organizers for Active Reading*, Worksheet p. 15
		• *Words to Own*, Worksheet p. 16
		• *Grammar and Language Links:* Adjective Clauses, Worksheet p. 27
		• *Language Workshop CD-ROM*, Types of Subordinate Clauses
		• *Daily Oral Grammar*, Transparency 15

Extending the Theme: You Are Now Entering the Human Heart (p. 235) Janet Frame	The Extending the Theme feature provides students with an unstructured opportunity to practice reading strategies using a selection that extends the theme of the collection.	
Writer's Workshop: Analyzing a Story (p. 240)		
Sentence Workshop: Using Phrases (p. 245)		• *Workshop Resources*, p. 59 • *Language Workshop CD-ROM*, Combining Sentences

Other Resources for this Collection

- *Cross-Curricular Activities,* p. 3
- *Portfolio Management System,* Introduction to Portfolio Assessment, p. 1
- *Test Generator,* Collection Test 💿

Writing	Listening and Speaking Viewing and Representing	Assessment
• *Portfolio Management System,* Rubrics for Choices, p. 109	• *Audio CD Library,* 🎧 Disc 6, Track 2 • *Viewing and Representing:* 📽 Fine Art Transparency 5 Worksheet p. 20 • *Portfolio Management System,* Rubrics for Choices, p. 109	• *Formal Assessment,* Selection Test, p. 26 • *Test Generator (One-Stop Planner CD-ROM)* 💿
		• *Formal Assessment,* Literary Elements Test, p. 36
• *Portfolio Management System,* Rubrics for Choices, p. 111	• *Portfolio Management System,* Rubrics for Choices, p. 111	• *Formal Assessment,* Selection Test, p. 28 • *Standardized Test Preparation,* p. 26 • *Test Generator (One-Stop Planner CD-ROM)* 💿
		• *Formal Assessment,* Literary Elements Test, p. 38
• *Portfolio Management System,* Rubrics for Choices, p. 112	• *Visual Connections:* Videocassette A, Segment 3 📼 • *Audio CD Library,* 🎧 Disc 7, Tracks 2, 3 • *Portfolio Management System,* Rubrics for Choices, p. 112	• *Formal Assessment,* Selection Test, p. 30 • *Standardized Test Preparation,* p. 28 • *Test Generator (One-Stop Planner CD-ROM)* 💿
• *Portfolio Management System,* Rubrics for Choices, p. 114	• *Audio CD Library,* 🎧 Disc 7, Track 4 • *Portfolio Management System,* Rubrics for Choices, p. 114	• *Formal Assessment,* Selection Test, p. 32 • *Standardized Test Preparation,* p. 30 • *Test Generator (One-Stop Planner CD-ROM)* 💿
• *Portfolio Management System,* Rubrics for Choices, p. 115	• *Audio CD Library,* 🎧 Disc 7, Track 5 • *Portfolio Management System,* Rubrics for Choices, p. 115	• *Formal Assessment,* Selection Test, p. 34 • *Test Generator (One-Stop Planner CD-ROM)* 💿
	• *Audio CD Library,* 🎧 Disc 7, Track 6	

• *Workshop Resources,* p. 13
 • *Writer's Workshop 2 CD-ROM,* Interpretation 💿
	• *Viewing and Representing,* HRW Multimedia Presentation Maker	• *Portfolio Management System*
		  • Prewriting, p. 117
		  • Peer Editing, p. 118
		  • Assessment Rubric, p. 119

Collection Planner

Transparency CD-ROM Video 🎧 Audio CD

T170C

Collection 3 Exiles, Castaways, and Strangers
Skills Focus

Selection or Feature	Reading Skills and Strategies	Elements of Literature	Vocabulary/Language/Grammar	Writing	Listening/Speaking	Viewing/Representing
The Pedestrian (p. 172) Ray Bradbury	Identify the Writer's Purpose, pp. 172, 179	Setting, pp. 172, 179 Mood, pp. 172, 180 Atmosphere, pp. 172, 180 Foreshadow, p. 179	Connotation and Denotation, p. 181 Context Clues, p. 181	Freewrite on a Topic, p. 180 Write a Dialogue, p. 180 Write a Brief Essay Comparing and Contrasting Views of Technology, p. 180	Act Out a Scene, p. 180 Stage a Panel Discussion, p. 180 Summarize and Evaluate a Speaker's Performance, p. 180	Create a Stage Set, p. 180
Elements of Literature: Theme (p. 182)		Theme, p. 182				
Liberty (p. 184) Julia Alvarez	Connecting Literature to Current Events, pp. 184, 192 Create a Story Map, p. 192	Tone, pp. 184, 192 Theme, p. 192 Conflict, p. 192 Main Events, p. 192 Climax, p. 192	Pronoun and Antecedent Agreement, p. 193 Ambiguous Pronoun References, p. 193 Thesaurus, p. 193 Synonym, p. 193	Write a Sequel Using a Different Point of View, p. 192	Research and Present a Report on Immigration, p. 192	
Elements of Literature: Irony and Satire (p. 194)		Irony, p. 194 • Verbal • Sarcasm • Situational • Dramatic Satire, p. 195				
Where Have you Gone, Charming Billy? (p. 196) Tim O'Brien	Understand Historical Context, pp. 196, 206	Theme and Character, pp. 196, 206 Irony, p. 206 Quest, p. 206	Sensory Images, p. 208 Meaning Maps, p. 208	Gather Details About a Character, p. 207 Write About a Childhood Experience, p. 207 Write an Essay Supporting an Opinion, p. 207	Retell a Story from the Point of View of a News Correspondent, p. 206 Collect Oral Histories, p. 207	Create Graphics Based on a Database, p. 207
The Bet (p. 209) Anton Chekhov *translated by* Constance Garnett	Make Inferences About Theme, p. 209 Identify Key Passages, p. 209	Ambiguity, p. 209 Theme, pp. 209, 219, 220 Motivation, p. 219	Active and Passive Voice of Verbs, p. 221 Use New Words, p. 221	Write a Sentence Expressing the Theme of a Story, p. 220 Write a Dialogue, p. 220 Write a Reflective Essay, p. 220	Enact a Scene, p. 220 Hold a Round-Table Discussion, p. 220	Summarize Events Using a Time Line, p. 219
A Very Old Man with Enormous Wings (p. 222) Gabriel García Márquez *translated by* Gregory Rabassa	Appreciate a Writer's Craft, pp. 222, 232	Magic Realism, pp. 222, 232 Irony, p. 232 Satire, p. 232 Image, p. 232 Symbol, p. 232 Setting, p. 233	Imagery, p. 234 Word Roots, p. 234 Part of Speech, p. 234 Suffix, p. 234	Make Notes About Setting, p. 233 Write a Letter, p. 233 Write a Fantastic Story, p. 233		Evaluate Illustrations, p. 233 Make a Drawing, Sculpture, or Collage, p. 233
Extending the Theme: You Are Now Entering the Human Heart (p. 235) Janet Frame	The Extending the Theme feature provides students with the unstructured opportunity to practice reading strategies using a selection that extends the theme of the collection.					
Writer's Workshop: Analyzing a Story (p. 240)		Plot, p. 240 Character, p. 240 Setting, p. 240 Tone, p. 240 Theme, p. 240		Write an Essay Analyzing a Short Story, pp. 240–244		
Sentence Workshop: Using Phrases (p. 245)			Prepositional, Verbal, and Appositive Phrases, p. 245	Combining Sentences Using Phrases, p. 245		
Reading for Life: Evaluating a Documentary (p. 246)					Determine Purpose, p. 246 Assess Credibility, p. 246	

I been a wanderin'
Early and late,
New York City
To the Golden Gate,
An' it looks like
I'm never gonna cease
my wanderin'.

—American folk song

Where do I belong? What makes me feel at home? Writers have explored these questions by creating characters who have found their rightful homes or who are searching for answers to who they are and how they want to live. Perhaps you've felt a sense of peace with your life, or perhaps you've experienced uncertainty when you moved to a new neighborhood. If you've had experiences like these, you'll understand the characters in this collection. Like most of us at one time or another, they are trying to find their way to a place of peace, happiness, and freedom. They are searching for "home."

Writer's Notebook

You're backpacking alone for a week—high in the mountains or deep in a tropical forest. You won't have TV, e-mail, or a phone. What kinds of stories would you take along to read? List some of your favorite stories and some that you've disliked. Save your lists for possible use in the workshop on page 240.

Responding to the Quotation

❓ What does this photograph and the quotation, from a song popular in the 1960s, say about the theme "Exiles, Castaways, and Strangers"? [Sample response: People who live as exiles, castaways, and strangers are not always people cast off or excluded by society. Sometimes, they are simply people, like Thoreau perhaps, who choose to go their own way to experience solitude, for one reason or another.]

Writer's Notebook

The purpose of this assignment is to get students thinking about the kinds of stories they most enjoy—and those they most definitely do not like. Other assignments in this collection will help them with other prewriting activities in preparation for the Workshop on analyzing a story at the end of the collection.

Writing Focus: Analyzing a Story

The following **Work in Progress** assignments build to a culminating **Writer's Workshop** at the end of the collection.

OBJECTIVES

1. Read and interpret the story
2. Describe the setting and atmosphere of the story
3. Recognize the author's point of view and purpose
4. Express understanding through various modes
5. Identify connotations and use connotative words in writing
6. Understand and use new words
7. Use context clues

SKILLS

Literary
- Describe setting and atmosphere

Reading
- Identify the author's purpose

Writing
- Analyze a story
- Write and act out a sequel to the story

Speaking/Listening
- Debate expectations for future society

Grammar/Language
- Understand and use connotative language

Vocabulary
- Use new words

Art
- Draw or build a model of a stage set

Viewing/Representing
- Analyze a painting's mood (ATE)
- Compare paintings (ATE)

Planning

- **Block Schedule**
  Block Scheduling Lesson Plans with Pacing Guide

- **Traditional Schedule**
  Lesson Plans Including Strategies for English-Language Learners

- **One-Stop Planner**
  CD-ROM with Test Generator

Before You Read

THE PEDESTRIAN

Make the Connection

What's It All About?

Have you ever finished reading a story or sat through a whole movie and then asked, "What was that all about?" Some stories can leave us with more questions than answers. Yet often those stories can provide us with the most enjoyable kind of discussion—talking to others about what our questions are and what we think the answers might be.

Quickwrite

What questions do you have about what life will be like in the year 2053? Write them down and save your notes.

Elements of Literature

Setting and Atmosphere

Writers can use the setting of a story to create an atmosphere—a **mood** or very subtle emotional overtone that can strongly affect our feelings. Settings can be used to suggest freedom, community, and peace. Settings can also be used to suggest control, isolation, and anxiety. See what atmosphere you sense in Bradbury's very first paragraph.

The **setting** of a story establishes the time and place of the action. Setting can be used to establish a **mood,** or **atmosphere,** and to suggest the writer's particular worldview.

For more on Setting, see pages 50–51 and the Handbook of Literary Terms.

Reading Skills and Strategies

Does the Writer Have a Purpose?

Many fiction writers, poets, and dramatists have no **purpose** when they sit down to write other than to share a feeling or an experience, to re-create a whole world of their own making. Ray Bradbury, however, is the kind of fiction writer who often writes for another purpose. Like many nonfiction writers, Bradbury tries to persuade us to agree with his attitude, or viewpoint, on some issue. To discover a writer's attitude, you must read closely. Take notes as you read (or on a second reading). Look for **key passages** that directly express opinions. Watch for **loaded words.** Bradbury's comparison of the city to a graveyard in the second paragraph should immediately send off signals.

Background

In the early 1950s Ray Bradbury was a young man living in Southern California. He did not know how to drive, and he liked walking around his suburban neighborhood at night. Even back then, such behavior was so rare that one time the police stopped and questioned him. If an innocent walk could seem so suspicious in mid-twentieth-century America, Bradbury wondered how it might be viewed in a future society. Then he wrote this story.

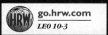
go.hrw.com
LEO 10-3

172

Preteaching Vocabulary

Words to Own

Have students review the Words to Own at the bottom of the selection pages. They should work in pairs and ask each other a question about each new word. ("When a tide is ebbing, is it coming in or going out?") Then, have them fill in the blanks in the following sentences with one of the words.

1. Because the tide was _____, the beach seemed to be getting wider. [ebbing]

2. He did not begin to _____ feelings of loneliness until his close friend moved away. [manifest]

3. Do you agree that violence is _____ behavior that is no longer useful in society? [regressive]

4. She wrote with _____ energy; some days working eight hours or more and other days lacking energy even to begin. [intermittent]

A metallic voice called to him: "Stand still. Stay where you are!"

The Pedestrian

Ray Bradbury

Freeway Interchange (1982) by Wayne Thiebaud. Oil on canvas.
Courtesy of Allan Stone Gallery, New York City.

To enter out into that silence that was the city at eight o'clock of a misty evening in November, to put your feet upon that buckling concrete walk, to step over grassy seams and make your way, hands in pockets, through the silences, that was what Mr. Leonard Mead most dearly loved to do. He would stand upon the corner of an intersection and peer down long moonlit avenues of sidewalk in four directions, deciding which way to go, but it really made no difference; he was alone in this world of A.D. 2053, or as good as alone, and with a final decision made, a path selected, he would stride off, sending patterns of frosty air before him like the smoke of a cigar.

THE PEDESTRIAN 173

Summary ▪▪

This story's setting is an urban landscape in the year 2053. On a cold November night, Leonard Mead takes a walk alone through the city, as he has habitually done for ten years. He meets no one. The city is rigidly controlled and barren: tomblike homes where everyone watches TV; dog "squads" that harass walkers; freeways that are totally deserted at night; three million people, one police car, and no crime. Almost back home, Mead is stopped and interrogated by a robotic police car. Because he is exhibiting aberrant behavior as a pedestrian, he is driven away to the "Psychiatric Center for Research on Regressive Tendencies."

RESPONDING TO THE ART

Wayne Thiebaud (1920–   ) is a realist painter known for his urban landscapes and his paintings of ordinary objects. About his painting process he says, "For me, realist painting is an alive confrontation. If you stare at an object, as you do when you paint, there is no point at which you can stop learning things about it. You can just look and look, and if you really are a realist painter, you finally realize that what you are doing is a tremendous amount of adoption, adaptation, and change."

Activity. Have students talk about whether this painting suggests community or isolation. What mood does the painting create for them? (It could be ominous. Note how the freeway cuts up the city.) You might have students compare *Freeway Interchange* with Frank Romero's painting *Olive Hill* (see pp. xxiv–1).

Resources: Print and Media

Reading
- *Reading Skills and Strategies*
  MiniRead Skill Lesson, p. 77
  Selection Skill Lesson, p. 84
- *Graphic Organizers for Active Reading*, p. 11
- *Words to Own*, p. 11
- *Audio CD Library*
  Disc 6, Track 2

Writing and Language
- *Daily Oral Grammar*
  Transparency 11
- *Grammar and Language Links*
  Worksheet, p. 19
- *Language Workshop CD-ROM*

Viewing and Representing
- *Viewing and Representing*
  Fine Art Transparency 5
  Fine Art Worksheet, p. 20

Assessment
- *Formal Assessment*, p. 26
- *Portfolio Management System*, p. 109
- *Test Generator (One-Stop Planner CD-ROM)*

Internet
- go.hrw.com (keyword: LE0 10-3)

Resources

Listening
Audio CD Library
A richly atmospheric reading of the story appears in the *Audio CD Library:*
• Disc 6, Track 2

Viewing and Representing
Fine Art Transparency
The Fine Art transparency of Gregory Manchess's *Safe Neighborhood* might be used as a writing prompt after students have finished reading the selection. See the *Viewing and Representing Transparencies and Worksheets:*
• Transparency 5
• Worksheet, p. 20

FROM THE EDITOR'S DESK

We videotaped some classes of students discussing this story. We expected them to be outraged by the fact that Leonard Mead is stopped for simply walking through his neighborhood. But some of the students surprised us. They thought he shouldn't have been out by himself at night in the first place—he looked suspicious, they said, and the police were right to stop and question him.

Ⓐ Elements of Literature

Setting and Atmosphere
❓ What details reveal the setting and create an atmosphere for the story?
[The setting is a silent city of the future. Key phrases include "To enter out into that silence" (p. 173) and "this world of A.D. 2053" (p. 173). The atmosphere is ominous and dark. Key words and phrases include "graveyard," "gray phantoms," and "whisperings and murmurs."]

Sometimes he would walk for hours and miles and return only at midnight to his house. And on his way he would see the cottages and homes with their dark windows, and it was not unequal to walking through a graveyard where only the faintest glimmers of firefly light appeared in flickers behind the windows. Sudden gray phantoms seemed to manifest upon inner room walls where a curtain was still undrawn against the night, or there were whisperings and murmurs where a window in a tomblike building was still open.

Mr. Leonard Mead would pause, cock his head, listen, look, and march on, his feet making no noise on the lumpy walk. For long ago he had wisely changed to sneakers when strolling at night, because the dogs in intermittent squads would parallel his journey with barkings if he wore hard heels, and lights might click on and faces appear and an entire street be startled by the passing of a lone figure, himself, in the early November evening.

On this particular evening he began his journey in a westerly direction, toward the hidden sea. There was a good crystal frost in the air; it cut the nose and made the lungs blaze like a Christmas tree inside; you could feel the cold light going on and off, all the branches filled with invisible snow. He listened to the faint push of his soft shoes through autumn leaves with satisfaction and whistled a cold, quiet whistle between his teeth, occasionally picking up a leaf as he passed, examining its skeletal pattern in the infrequent lamplights as he went on, smelling its rusty smell.

"Hello, in there," he whispered to every house on every side as he moved. "What's up tonight on Channel 4, Channel 7, Channel 9? Where are the cowboys rushing, and do I see the United States Cavalry over the next hill to the rescue?"

The street was silent and long and empty, with only his shadow moving like the shadow of a hawk in midcountry. If he closed his eyes and stood very still, frozen, he could imagine himself upon the center of a plain, a wintry, windless Arizona desert with no house in a thousand miles, and only dry riverbeds, the streets, for company.

"What is it now?" he asked the houses, noticing his wristwatch. "Eight-thirty P.M.? Time for a dozen assorted murders? A quiz? A revue? A comedian falling off the stage?"

Was that a murmur of laughter from within a moon-white house? He hesitated but went on when nothing more happened. He stumbled over a particularly uneven section of sidewalk. The cement was vanishing under flowers and grass. In ten years of walking by night or day, for thousands of miles, he had never met another person walking, not one in all that time.

He came to a cloverleaf intersection which stood silent where two main highways crossed the town. During the day it was a thunderous surge of cars, the gas stations open, a great insect rustling, and a ceaseless jockeying for position as the scarab beetles,[1] a faint incense puttering from their exhausts, skimmed homeward to the far directions. But now these highways, too, were like streams in a dry season, all stone and bed and moon radiance.

He turned back on a side street, circling around toward his home. He was within a block of his destination when the lone car turned a corner quite suddenly and flashed a fierce white cone of light upon him. He stood entranced, not unlike a night moth, stunned by the illumination and then drawn toward it.

A metallic voice called to him:
"Stand still. Stay where you are! Don't move!"
He halted.

---

1. scarab beetles: stout-bodied, brilliantly colored beetles. Bradbury is using the term as a metaphor for automobiles.

WORDS TO OWN

manifest (man′ə·fest′) *v.:* appear; become evident. *Manifest* also means "show" or "reveal."
intermittent (in′tər·mit″nt) *adj.:* appearing or occurring from time to time.

---

174 THE SHORT-STORY COLLECTIONS

Reaching All Students

Struggling Readers
Determining Author's Purpose is introduced as a reading skill on p. 172. For a lesson directly tied to this story that teaches students to determine purpose by using a strategy called Sketch to Stretch, see the *Reading Skills and Strategies* binder:
• MiniRead Skill Lesson, p. 77
• Selection Skill Lesson, p. 84

English Language Learners
Identify and explain some of the concrete images in the opening paragraph on p. 173. Explain that these images help establish the setting and atmosphere. Urge students to look for similar images as they read and to discuss them with English-proficient students. For additional strategies for English language learners, see
• *Lesson Plans Including Strategies for English-Language Learners*

Advanced Learners
Point out that the protagonist, Leonard Mead, gets into trouble for doing a quite ordinary thing. Ask students to consider these questions as they read: Why does society, through the police, regard Mead's actions as a threat? Can people get into trouble in today's world by doing such innocent things?

"Put up your hands!"

"But——" he said.

"Your hands up! Or we'll shoot!"

The police, of course, but what a rare, incredible thing; in a city of three million, there was only *one* police car left, wasn't that correct? Ever since a year ago, 2052, the election year, the force had been cut down from three cars to one. Crime was ebbing; there was no need now for the police, save for this one lone car wandering and wandering the empty streets.

"Your name?" said the police car in a metallic whisper. He couldn't see the men in it for the bright light in his eyes.

"Leonard Mead," he said.

"Speak up!"

"Leonard Mead!"

"Business or profession?"

"I guess you'd call me a writer."

"No profession," said the police car, as if talking to itself. The light held him fixed, like a museum specimen, needle thrust through chest.

"You might say that," said Mr. Mead. He hadn't written in years. Magazines and books didn't sell anymore. Everything went on in the tomblike houses at night now, he thought, continuing his fancy. The tombs, ill-lit by television light, where the people sat like the dead, the gray or multicolored lights touching their faces, but never really touching them.

"No profession," said the phonograph voice, hissing. "What are you doing out?"

"Walking," said Leonard Mead.

WORDS TO OWN

ebbing *v.*: lessening or weakening. The ebb is the flow of water away from the land as the tide falls.

B Reading Skills and Strategies

Author's Point of View and Purpose

? What is Bradbury's purpose in having the police say writing is "No profession." [Possible response: He is stressing that in this society, creativity is not recognized or appreciated.] What is Bradbury's stance, or point of view? [Possible response: Society has gone wrong when writers are not respected.]

C Elements of Literature

Setting and Atmosphere

? What words in this passage suggest deadness? [*tomblike houses, tombs ill-lit, people sat like the dead, gray . . . lights*]

RESPONDING TO THE ART

James Doolin creates a surreal feeling in his paintings by a process called "staging." He finds that night landscapes are ideal vehicles for making staged spaces. In creating the paintings, he positions lights to suit a specific color and purpose—for example to play "warm" places off "cool" places, "near" areas off "far" areas, and so on. The result is a theatricality the artist finds very satisfying.

Activity. Have students compare *Highway Patrol* with Wayne Thiebaud's *Freeway Interchange* on p. 173. [Sample response: One views highways from a distance; the other is a view from inside a vehicle.] Ask them if they find any strange details in *Highway Patrol*. [There is no driver.]

Highway Patrol (1986) by James Doolin. Oil on canvas.

Courtesy of Koplin Gallery, Los Angeles, California.

THE PEDESTRIAN 175

Crossing the Curriculum

Science

The earliest computers depended upon punch cards, which were cards punched in specific places to record information. These cards were used somewhat like floppy disks: information could be both read from and saved on the punch cards. Ask interested students to investigate this older computer technology and to tell how it is used in the story.

Health

The benefits of exercise, and in particular of walking, are well documented, and yet in this futuristic society, people do little but stare at television during their time off. What health problems would result from this lifestyle? What could be the long-term effects on society as a whole? Do you think Bradbury's prediction of a couch-potato society in the future is realistic?

Assessing Learning

Self-Assessment

After they finish the story, have students complete the following statements to assess their writing skills.

1. The thing I did best in connection with my writing assignments for this story is_____.

2. The thing I most need to work on in my writing is_____.

"Walking!"

"Just walking," he said simply, but his face felt cold.

"Walking, just walking, walking?"

"Yes, sir."

"Walking where? For what?"

"Walking for air. Walking to *see*."

"Your address!"

"Eleven South Saint James Street."

"And there is air *in* your house, you have an air *conditioner,* Mr. Mead?"

"Yes."

"And you have a viewing screen in your house to see with?"

"No."

"No?" There was a crackling quiet that in itself was an accusation.

"Are you married, Mr. Mead?"

"No."

"Not married," said the police voice behind the fiery beam. The moon was high and clear among the stars and the houses were gray and silent.

"Nobody wanted me," said Leonard Mead with a smile.

"Don't speak unless you're spoken to!"

Leonard Mead waited in the cold night.

"Just *walking,* Mr. Mead?"

"Yes."

"But you haven't explained for what purpose."

"I explained: for air, and to see, and just to walk."

"Have you done this often?"

"Every night for years."

The police car sat in the center of the street with its radio throat faintly humming.

"Well, Mr. Mead," it said.

"Is that all?" he asked politely.

"Yes," said the voice. "Here." There was a sigh, a pop. The back door of the police car sprang wide. "Get in."

"Wait a minute, I haven't done anything!"

"Get in."

"I protest!"

"Mr. Mead."

He walked like a man suddenly drunk. As he passed the front window of the car, he looked in. As he had expected, there was no one in the front seat, no one in the car at all.

"Get in."

He put his hand to the door and peered into the back seat, which was a little cell, a little black jail with bars. It smelled of riveted² steel. It smelled of harsh antiseptic; it smelled too clean and hard and metallic. There was nothing soft there.

"Now, if you had a wife to give you an alibi," said the iron voice. "But——"

"Where are you taking me?"

The car hesitated, or rather gave a faint, whirring click, as if information, somewhere, was dropping card by punch-slotted card under electric eyes. "To the Psychiatric Center for Research on Regressive Tendencies."

He got in. The door shut with a soft thud. The police car rolled through the night avenues, flashing its dim lights ahead.

They passed one house on one street a moment later, one house in an entire city of houses that were dark, but this one particular house had all of its electric lights brightly lit, every window a loud yellow illumination, square and warm in the cool darkness.

"That's *my* house," said Leonard Mead.

No one answered him.

The car moved down the empty riverbed streets and off away, leaving the empty streets with the empty sidewalks and no sound and no motion all the rest of the chill November night.

---

2. **riveted** (riv′it·id): held together by rivets (metal bolts or pins).

WORDS TO OWN

regressive (ri·gres′iv) *adj.*: moving backward or returning to an earlier or less advanced condition.

Making the Connections

Connecting to the Theme: "Exiles, Castaways, and Strangers"

When students have finished reading the story, discuss how it relates to the theme of this collection. You might begin by asking if Mead is an exile, a castaway, or a stranger. [Possible answers: He is an exile in that his own society doesn't accept him; he is a castaway in that his philosophy and values are not taken seriously; he is a stranger in that he and his neighbors do not interact.]

Cultural Connections

People in the United States don't walk much anymore, depending instead on 136 million cars (in 1995). Ask students to speculate on how this dependence on the automobile has affected our society. Students should consider malls vs. small shopping centers; the need for highways; taxes; pollution; built-in obsolescence; financial costs to families; deaths from traffic accidents; and so on. Be sure students consider advantages as well.

MEET THE WRITER
The Man with the Child Inside

Ray Bradbury (1920–) calls himself "that special freak—the man with the child inside who remembers all." Bradbury was born in Waukegan, Illinois, and began writing when he was seven.

Bradbury sees himself as a "magic realist" (see page 222) and as a disciple of Edgar Allan Poe (see page 302). He says that his lifelong hatred of thought control grows out of his sympathy for his ancestor Mary Bradbury, who was tried as a witch in seventeenth-century Salem, Massachusetts. Here is how his imagination grew:

66 When I was three my mother snuck me in and out of movies two or three times a week. My first film was Lon Chaney in *The Hunchback of Notre Dame*. I suffered permanent curvature of the spine and of my imagination that day a long time ago in 1923. From that hour on, I knew a kindred and wonderfully grotesque compatriot of the dark when I saw one. . . .

I was in love, then, with monsters and skeletons and circuses and carnivals and dinosaurs and at last, the red planet, Mars.

From these primitive bricks I have built a life and a career. By my staying in love with all of these amazing things, all of the good things in my existence have come about.

In other words, I was *not* embarrassed at circuses. Some people are. Circuses are loud, vulgar, and smell in the sun. By the time many people are fourteen or fifteen, they have been divested of their loves, their ancient and intuitive tastes, one by one, until when they reach maturity there is no fun left, no zest, no gusto, no flavor. Others have criticized, and they have criticized themselves, into embarrassment. When the circus pulls in at five of a dark cold summer morn, and the calliope sounds, they do not rise and run, they turn in their sleep, and life passes by.

I did rise and run. . . . 99

Books by Bradbury

The Martian Chronicles (Bantam), about early settlers on Mars.
Fahrenheit 451 (Ballantine), about a future society that burns books.
Dandelion Wine (Bantam), about a young boy with special mental powers.

THE PEDESTRIAN 177

BROWSING IN THE FILES

About the Author. Ray Bradbury considers himself a storyteller who tells cautionary tales—tales to alert people to the dangers in the world around them. Most people think of cautionary tales as being warnings to children who behave badly; however, Bradbury's stories usually warn people about the dangers of technology.

A Critic's Comment. Some reviewers have criticized Bradbury for creating unimaginative plots and characterizations. Orson Scott Card explains, however, that "It is not the characters he expects you to identify with. Rather, he means to capture you in his own voice, expects you to see through his eyes. And his eyes see, not the cliché plot, but the whole meaning of the events; not the scenes or the individual people, but yourself and your own fears and your own family and the answer, at last, to the isolation that seemed inevitable to you."

WRITERS ON WRITING

Bradbury often begins his stories by thinking of the characters he wants to write about. "You can't have 'plot' and 'setting' really, until you have a character who wants something with all his heart," he says. "The character, on his way to getting what he wants, be it love, survival, or destruction, will write your story for you."

Assessing Learning

Check Test: True-False
1. Leonard Mead prefers television to walking. [False]
2. Homes in the city display bright lights at night. [False]
3. No one is in the patrol car. [True]
4. Mead stops and talks to people along his route. [False]
5. The desire to see the world and breathe fresh air is considered unnatural in the city. [True]

Standardized Test Preparation
For practice with proofreading and editing specific to this selection, see
• *Daily Oral Grammar,* Transparency 11

A "cybertripper" describes his experiences in virtual reality. He experiences the beauty of fresh, unspoiled nature—a forest, a tropical forest, a cleansing rainstorm. He feels peace. He has no sense of time. His senses are alive to the natural world. Then the batteries run out and he must return to the real world, which he describes as a nightmare of steel, rust, crowds, and pollution.

Virtuality

Time passes, yet I am oblivious to it, forgetting that such a thing exists. Where I am, there is no time, no sense of minutes or hours. Days could be passing, but I do not care.

Where I am, there is beauty.

I stroll through a forest, a place that puts my mind at ease and comforts my soul. Massive trees tower above, their leaves creating a canopy that shields me from the bright sun. The forest is cool and crisp and damp; the smell of moist earth greets my nose. The wind whispers gently and rustles the trees, sounding like a calm ocean breaking on a shore. Serenity.

My stomach hungers and craves food. I ignore it, for I am now appreciating a tropical forest cleansed from an early morning rain, millions of droplets glittering like diamonds on the thick vegetation. There is a strong connection with the beginning of things here; I feel primal wonderment as humidity masks my face. I see a light haze hanging over the valleys and mountains of this prehistoric setting. The jungle is like a multifaceted gem, where myriad species mingle under the mysterious trees. The air, although hot, is clean.

My mouth thirsts for water; but it is a vague sensation now, and I do not pay much attention to it. Because where I am, there is nature and purity. I look up and think of rain and suddenly behold a thunderstorm. The sky darkens and heavy drops of rain shower the earth, like shards of a mirror falling from the heavens and reflecting the world about them. Fierce lightning shatters the dark sky, and I watch in child-like awe, staring in reverence at the electrified claw ripping the cosmos. The storm is not frightening; it cleanses this paradise.

I had a nightmare once about a world of steel and rust, of crowded buildings and slime-covered streets. It was a place where people dwell under a gray blanket of smog, where each intake of breath is like inhaling toxins, and the rain falling from the sky is greasy and oily and burns the skin. But here the world is fresh and clean, cool and crisp.

Where I am, there is such a thing as peace.

And it is all real; I can see the beauty and hear the sounds and feel what there is to be felt. In my nightmare, nature is dead. But I am awake, and here it is alive, and this is reality for me.

Then I stand on a grassy field where bright dandelions lie like flecks of sunlight, and I feel a cool breeze brushing by me, and . . .

There is an angry buzzing, an ugly mechanical sound, and my heart aches because I know where I really am and I fear being reminded. Bright white words flash across my field of vision: YOUR VIRTUAL WORLD MUST END NOW

No! It isn't virtual, it's real! No!

BATTERIES ARE OUT OF POWER

No! Please . . .

TIME TO RETURN TO REALITY

The visions of the nature-worlds fade and go black, and I take off the headset, trembling. My stomach aches for food, my mouth thirsts; days might have passed. The headset, called Virtuality Gear, provides computerized images which look real and perfect. The gear provides sensory stimuli: fantasy sight, sound, touch. I despair because I am out of the terribly expensive batteries which are the keys to my paradise. And I am reminded that I am just one of the growing number of cybertrippers, people who flee to the fantasy worlds Virtuality Gear gives them.

—Brian Trusiewicz
Sacred Heart High School
Waterbury, Connecticut

Connecting Across Texts

Connecting with "The Pedestrian"

In some senses, both Bradbury and the student writer have written about alienation: Leonard Mead is alienated from his conformist society, in which television controls people's lives; the narrator of "Virtuality" is alienated from a world he describes as filthy, polluted, and destructive.

Ask students to comment on each writer's point of view. What arguments can they make to challenge each story's message? Note that in each story, technology plays a key role. It is a villain in Bradbury's story and a savior in "Virtuality."

MAKING MEANINGS

MAKING MEANINGS

First Thoughts

1. Possible responses: How was Leonard punished? Did he ever get out? Did he conform? What was your purpose in writing this story?

Shaping Interpretations

2. Possible response: He wants to warn people about addiction to technology, of giving up thinking for themselves, of alienating themselves from the natural world. Supporting details include the graveyard-like neighborhood, the lack of respect for writing as a profession, and the dehumanized police.

3. Possible response: People may have gradually become so mind-dead from watching television that they lost their liberties without realizing it.

4. Crime and homelessness have disappeared. Leonard misses the freedom to walk without being questioned.

5. Possible answers: Automated police cars can stop and arrest people; television keeps people occupied after work. Bradbury could be saying that people should be careful that their inventions do not control them. One supporting passage is marked *C* on p. 175.

Connecting with the Text

6. Answers will vary. You might ask how much time a day they themselves spend watching television vs. being outdoors. Student responses to whether they go walking at night now will vary; they should give specific reasons.

Extending the Text

7. Possible responses: Bradbury was right about the growth of technology and how it has affected people—they don't walk much and are often glued to their televisions. He was wrong because crime has not been eliminated and the police cannot arrest someone without due process. Most city streets are still filled with people at night.

Challenging the Text

8. Possible responses: He's too pessimistic because television and computers have brought a great deal of information into the home. He's not too pessimistic because people do spend hours watching television and using computers instead of getting exercise or doing things with other people.

First Thoughts

[respond]

1. What question would you like to ask Bradbury?

Shaping Interpretations

[infer]

2. What do you think Bradbury's **purpose** was in writing this story? Cite details from the story to support your opinion.

[analyze]

3. Bradbury doesn't tell us directly what has happened to cause the strange situation in this story. What do you guess has caused this severe limitation on individual freedom?

[synthesize]

4. Which of today's problems seem to have been eliminated from Leonard Mead's society? What does Leonard miss that we still enjoy today?

[infer]

5. How is technology used to control Leonard's world? What point about technology and its power do you think Bradbury is making? What key words or phrases or events in the story support your interpretation?

Reading Check

a. What ominous fact about this future society is **foreshadowed** at once by the "buckling concrete walk" in the first paragraph? As the story develops, what else are you told about the **setting** of "The Pedestrian"?

b. Find the sentences and phrases that at first suggest that Leonard Mead is the only person living in this setting in A.D. 2053. Find the passage that reveals that there are other living people in this setting.

c. Leonard Mead is the only human character in the story. Who, or what, appears to be in charge of this future world?

d. Explain Leonard Mead's "regressive tendencies."

e. Describe the police automaton's response when Mead says he is a writer.

Connecting with the Text

[speculate]

6. If you lived in the same time and place as Leonard, do you think you would go walking outside at night or stay inside as Leonard's neighbors do? Do you go walking on the streets at night where you live? Why or why not?

Extending the Text

[compare]

7. In 1951, when "The Pedestrian" was published, it was read as a prediction of the future. Now that we are closer to 2053, **compare** Bradbury's vision of the future with today's reality. In what ways was he wrong or right?

Challenging the Text

[criticize]

8. Do you think Bradbury is too pessimistic about technology? Support your opinion with details from the text and from the real world.

Reading Check

a. The disrepair of the sidewalk suggests that nobody besides Mead walks anymore. The setting includes deserted streets, dark houses, and a deserted highway.

b. The second sentence on p. 173 suggests Leonard is alone. Phrases include "dark windows" and "gray phantoms." The passage that reveals he is not alone appears on p. 174 and begins with "Mr. Leonard Mead would pause, cock his head ..."

c. Students may say that machines are in charge, or that a small group or a single leader is running things through machines.

d. Mead continues to do things that were done before technology changed society: he walks, he does not watch television, and he writes.

e. The automated car describes Mead as unemployed.

Grading Timesaver

Rubrics for each assignment appear on p. 109 in the *Portfolio Management System*.

CHOICES:
Building Your Portfolio

1. **Writer's Notebook** Remind students to save their work from these Writer's Notebook activities; their work will be helpful when they do the Writing Workshop at the end of the collection.

2. **Creative Writing/Performing** Suggest that students begin with an impromptu role-playing of the scene in order to develop ideas. Encourage students to read lines of dialogue aloud to each other as they write, to see if the lines sound realistic and natural.

3. **Speaking and Listening** Urge students to spend time thinking about the questions before participating in the panel discussion. They might try freewriting answers to the questions.

4. **Drawing or Model Building** Suggest that students begin by either sketching the set or by writing words or phrases to describe it.

5. **Comparing and Contrasting Texts** Have students create a compare-and-contrast chart to help them organize their comparisons.

CHOICES: Building Your Portfolio

Writer's Notebook
1. Collecting Ideas for Analyzing a Story

Finding a topic. In the Writer's Workshop on page 240, you'll analyze a short story. Your first task will be to find a topic—a story to focus on. Skim through the short-story collections in this book, and take a quick look at the stories you've read so far. Make a list of the stories you really liked and another of those you disliked. Be sure to include "The Pedestrian" on one of your lists. Now, freewrite for several minutes about one story and what you either liked or disliked about its plot, theme, characters, or language. Save your notes.

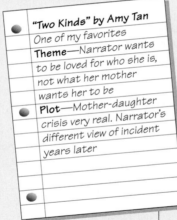

- "Two Kinds" by Amy Tan
  One of my favorites
  Theme—Narrator wants to be loved for who she is, not what her mother wants her to be
- Plot—Mother-daughter crisis very real. Narrator's different view of incident years later

Creative Writing / Performing
2. Continuing the Story

Imagine what happens when Leonard arrives at the Psychiatric Center for Research on Regressive Tendencies. Write a **dialogue** that he might have with the authorities there. Decide whether the researchers are humans or robots. How might Leonard try to explain his way of life? What might the authorities decide to do about him? With a group, act out the sequel to Leonard's story. If you like, wear costumes that suggest the **mood,** or **atmosphere,** of the story as you sense it.

Speaking and Listening
3. Debating the Future

Form a panel, and discuss what you think society will actually be like in the year 2053. Will technology isolate us from one another, as "The Pedestrian" suggests, or will technology be a force for good? Will the individual citizen be freer or less free? How do you think the technology described in "Virtuality" (page 178) might affect the future? As a class, be sure to check your

Quickwrite notes for other questions. Before you start, assign a moderator and establish rules for the panel. At the end of the discussion, each person in the audience should prepare a **summary** of the panel's views and an **evaluation** of the participants' performances.

Drawing or Model Building
4. Creating a Stage Set

Ray Bradbury has dramatized many of his stories for the stage and television. Suppose you were the set designer for a TV adaptation of "The Pedestrian." Draw or build a model of a set for the play. Go back to the text, and use Bradbury's own descriptions of the **setting** as the basis for your design. Display your drawing or model to the class, and be prepared to explain the reasons for your design decisions.

Comparing and Contrasting Texts
5. Future Tech

Think about the use of technology in "The Pedestrian" and "The Cold Equations" (page 9). What similarities and differences can you find? Write a brief essay in which you **compare** and **contrast** the way the two stories view technology.

180 THE SHORT-STORY COLLECTIONS

Using Students' Strengths

Naturalist Learners
For Choice 4, urge these students to think about the environment of the setting—the natural nighttime sights, sounds, and smells. Have them consider which of these they would include and how they can bring this natural environment alive in their set. They might incorporate some ideas into their models or drawings and list others, such as sounds, on a separate sheet of paper.

Auditory/Musical Learners
Encourage these students to identify music that will accompany the performance of the sequel developed for Choice 2 or that could accompany a dramatization of the story for the stage set for Choice 4. Students might play a recording or perform the music, if they have the skill. Have students explain why they chose the music.

LANGUAGE LINK   `MINI-LESSON`

**Handbook of
Literary
Terms
HELP**

*See Conno-
tations.*

The Power of Connotations

As you know, certain words have emotional overtones, or **connotations,** that go beyond their literal meanings, or **denotations.** Consider the difference between the two words in the following pairs:

> unusual / odd
> young / immature
> proud / smug
> assertive / pushy
> frugal / stingy

In each pair, the first word has more positive connotations than the second word has. We might use the first word to describe ourselves but the second word to describe someone else. In fact, the British philosopher Bertrand Russell once gave a classic example of the different connotations of words: "I am firm. You are obstinate. He is a pigheaded fool."

Here are some passages from "The Pedestrian" that describe the **setting** by using words with powerful connotations.

1. "And on his way he would see the cottages and homes with their dark windows, and it was not unequal to walking through a graveyard. . . ."

2. "Sudden gray phantoms seemed to manifest upon inner room walls . . . , or there were whisperings and murmurs where a window in a tomblike building was still open."

3. "It [the inside of the car] smelled of harsh antiseptic; it smelled too clean and hard and metallic. There was nothing soft there."

Try It Out

➤ Write down what you think is the strongest word or phrase in each numbered passage below. Then, describe briefly what the word or phrase suggests to you or how it makes you feel.

➤ Rewrite each passage with words that have more positive connotations. The graveyard, for example, could become a sleepy village.

VOCABULARY   `HOW TO OWN A WORD`

WORD BANK

*manifest
intermittent
ebbing
regressive*

Using Context Clues

Explain what each underlined word means, and point out the context clues that help you guess the meaning. Then, go back to Bradbury's story, and see if you can find context clues for the same underlined words. Write down any context clues that you find.

1. Passengers' anger is quick to <u>manifest</u> when flights are canceled.
2. Today's forecast is for cloudy weather and <u>intermittent</u> showers.
3. Pet ownership shows no signs of <u>ebbing</u>; the sale of pet foods and pet-related products continues to increase.
4. Temper tantrums and whining are <u>regressive</u> behaviors in adults.

THE PEDESTRIAN 181

Language Link Quick Check

Change the underlined word in each sentence to give the sentence a more positive connotation.

1. The car stopped and shined a <u>fierce</u> light on Mr. Mead. [intense]
2. Mr. Mead saw a <u>smelly</u> flower on his walk. [fragrant]
3. Mr. Mead was in a <u>brooding</u> mood. [reflective]
4. The rules of this society were <u>tyrannical</u>. [strict]
5. The automated police officer was <u>curt</u>. [direct]

LANGUAGE LINK

Have students choose a piece of writing from their portfolios and revise it by circling vague words and replacing them with words that have more fitting and vivid connotations.

Try It Out
Possible Answers

1. "Graveyard": suggests death, isolation. "And on his way he would see the cottages and homes with their dark windows, and it was not unequal to walking through a quiet forest."
2. "Gray phantoms"; "tomblike building": suggest abandonment, death, nothingness. "Sudden soft images seemed to manifest upon inner room walls . . . , or there were whisperings and murmurs where a window in a cozy home was still open."
3. "Harsh antiseptic"; "hard"; "metallic": suggest something unpleasant, cold, sterile. "It smelled of cleanliness; it smelled clean and shiny and gleaming. There was nothing soiled there."

VOCABULARY

1. "Become evident." Clues: anger, quick, when flights are canceled. Clues in story: "phantoms," "inner room walls," "curtain was still undrawn."
2. "Occurring from time to time." Clues: forecast, cloudy weather. Clues in story: "squads," "parallel his journey with barkings."
3. "Lessening." Clues: sale of pet foods and pet-related products continues to increase. Clues in story: "no need now for police."
4. "Returning to an earlier condition." Clues: temper tantrums, whining, behaviors in adults. Clues in story: general context suggesting Mead's behavior is no longer typical.

Resources ━━━━━━

Language
• *Grammar and Language Links* Worksheet, p. 19

Vocabulary
• *Words to Own,* Worksheet, p. 11

OBJECTIVES
1. Understand the definition of theme
2. Recognize and interpret aspects of a selection that relate to its theme
3. State a theme in a complete sentence

Resources

Elements of Literature
Theme
For additional instruction on theme, see *Literary Elements:*
• Transparency 6

Elements of Literature

This lesson provides a detailed discussion of theme, defining it and explaining what it is and what it is not.

Mini-Lesson:
Theme
You might use this Mini-Lesson after students have read pp. 182–183.

• First, review the definition of theme with the class. Emphasize that theme is not what the story is about, but what the story means. Remind students that they will find clues to theme by considering how the protagonist changes or what he or she learns during the story.

• Next, list several popular movies or familiar television episodes on the chalkboard. Choose one as an example and work with the class to develop a theme statement.

• Have students work in groups of three or four to prepare a theme statement for each of the remaining movies or TV episodes.

• Have the groups compare and contrast their theme statements in class discussion. Invite groups to explain how they arrived at their statements. Emphasize that no two theme statements will be exactly the same.

THEME: The Story's Meaning and Roots

I once read a student's story that was full of action—a pair of mountain climbers were about to plunge down a ravine, a skier was schussing into peril, and a killer was waiting in the valley below. Despite all this action and intrigue, the story was boring to read because it was impossible to tell what the student writer meant by it. As it turned out, the student didn't know either. The story had no theme.

A story's characters and events take on significance only when we recognize what they mean to us. In other words, all the elements of a good story must add up to a **theme**—some idea or insight about human life and human nature that gives meaning to the story.

The Writer's Worldview

Theme can also reveal the writer's whole view of life, of how the world works—or fails to work.

Suppose, for example, that a writer has a heroine work diligently at her job in the fish cannery and be rewarded by a two-dollar-an-hour raise and a trip to Vancouver. We recog-nize this writer's world as demanding but fair, a place where human beings have some control over their destiny. Suppose another writer takes this same heroine and has her fired for her pains. As she leaves for home, she even finds that her bicycle has been stolen. We recognize in this story another kind of world—a barren world swept by cold and indifferent winds.

What Do We Mean by Theme?

The story's theme is really its roots. Theme is unseen and usually unstated, yet it is vital. It gives meaning to the story's characters and events, and at the same time it reveals the writer's own personal attitude toward the world, toward how people should behave and how they actually do behave. If we like the writer's view of the world, we may well come back for more; we may even adopt the writer's attitude as our own. But if that view of the world is one we don't accept as "true," we probably will stop reading that writer altogether.

We do not have to accept every theme, but we should not simply condemn or dismiss a story because we disagree with its theme. A writer's view of the world or of human nature may be different from our own, but it may be worthwhile to explore that viewpoint anyway. It is always interesting to learn how other people see the world.

> Theme is unseen and usually unstated, yet it is vital.

Theme is neither the story's plot (what happens) nor the story's subject (which might be boxing or prospecting for gold). Rather, theme is an idea; it is what the writer means by everything he or she has set down. A story's theme may give us insight into some aspect of life that we have never really thought about before, or it may make us understand something we always knew but never realized we knew.

Reaching All Students

Struggling Readers
Unlike setting and character, which usually have at least some explicit explanation in the text, theme can be very subtle and may pose a frustrating puzzle to many readers. Repeated modeling of how to discover a theme using very short stories may help students. You may want to emphasize the distinction between theme and moral, different ways of stating the same theme, and multiple themes in a single story.

Advanced Learners
Challenge students to select a short story they have written and to evaluate it for theme. Have them begin by writing a statement of the theme. You might encourage them to work with a peer reviewer to discuss how the story develops the theme. Then, ask them to identify specific ways to strengthen the story's theme.

by John Leggett

Discovering a Story's Theme

Often a writer's theme cannot be stated easily or completely. (Remember that the writer has had to write the whole story to get that theme across to us.) After we have read a story, we may feel that we understand what it is about, and yet for some reason we cannot put our feeling into words. The story has struck us as true—it has touched our emotions on some profound, wordless level—but still we cannot state the truth it has revealed to us.

The attempt to put a story's theme into words can often help us understand the story more fully—it can reveal aspects of the story that we may have ignored. It is one thing to understand *what has happened* in a story, but it is quite another thing to understand *what those events mean.* Here are some general guidelines for discovering a story's theme:

1. A theme may be stated in a single sentence, or a full essay may be required to do it justice. But we must use at least one complete sen- tence to state a theme. In other words, a theme must be a statement about the subject of the story, rather than a phrase such as "the rewards of old age." (Some- times you can reword this type of phrase to form a sentence: "Old age can be a time of great satisfaction.")

> **I**t is one thing to understand *what has happened* in a story, but it is quite another thing to understand *what those events mean.*

2. A theme is not the same as a moral, which is a rule of conduct. A work of serious fiction is not a sermon in- tended to teach us how to live better or more suc- cessful lives. One critic has said that, in getting at a story's theme, we should ask ourselves "What does this story reveal?" rather than "What does this story teach?" Thus, it is usually a mistake to reduce a theme (at least a serious writer's theme) to a familiar saying or cliché, such as "Crime doesn't pay" or "The course of true love never did run smooth." A theme is usually a much more complex and original reve- lation about life.

3. One of the best ways to discover a story's theme is to ask how the protagonist has *changed* during the course of the story. Often, what this character has learned about life is the truth the writer also wants to reveal to the reader.

4. There is no one correct way to state the theme of a story. If there are twenty- five students in your English class, for instance, you will have twenty-five distinct ways of putting a story's central insight into words. You may also have several different ideas about what the story's major theme is.

> **"**To produce a mighty book, you must choose a mighty theme.**"**
>
> —Herman Melville

Applying the Element

Ask students to work individually to apply what they've learned about theme by answering these questions about "The Pedestrian."

- **What is the subject of "The Pedes- trian"?** [Possible response: Technology and how it affects one man.]
- **Does Mr. Mead change or discover something in the course of the story?** [Sample answer: He learns that his eccentric view of technology is not socially acceptable, that he is going to be punished for having an imagination, for not accepting technology as oth- ers have, and for taking walks at night.]
- **What is the theme of the story?** [Possible response: Technology offers many benefits, but if it is allowed to get out of control, it can result in a loss of imagination, an indifference to the natural world, and a loss of indi- vidual freedom.]

As students read the remaining stories in this collection, remind them to look for evidence of the theme.

Resources

Assessment
Formal Assessment
- Literary Elements Test, p. 36

Using Students' Strengths

Visual Learners

Point out that all works of art convey some kind of meaning, or theme. Have students work in small groups to come up with statements of the themes they find in several works of art. They might select the fine art used in one of the sto- ries in this collection. Remind them that a theme must be stated in at least one sentence.

Kinesthetic Learners

Ask students how the movement and gestures of the human body can express theme or mean- ing in a dance, a play, or a pantomime. Have them work in pairs or small groups to select a play or dance and state its theme as they inter- pret it. You might encourage groups to provide a demonstration for the class.

OBJECTIVES

1. Read and interpret the story
2. Identify and analyze tone
3. Connect literature to current events
4. Express understanding through writing, history, and research
5. Identify pronoun antecedents and use clear pronoun references
6. Understand and use new words
7. Use a thesaurus to find synonyms

SKILLS

Literary
• Identify tone

Reading
• Understand connections to current events

Writing
• Analyze a story
• Write a story

Grammar/Language
• Identify pronoun antecedents and use pronoun references clearly

Vocabulary
• Use new words

Planning

• **Block Schedule**
Block Scheduling Lesson Plans with Pacing Guide

• **Traditional Schedule**
Lesson Plans Including Strategies for English-Language Learners

• **One-Stop Planner**
CD-ROM with Test Generator

Before You Read

LIBERTY

Make the Connection

Leaving It All Behind

Whether you love where you live or long to be somewhere different, moving is a jolt. Loading the last box, seeing the rooms bare, taking one last look at your neighborhood—memories flood in. If you've ever moved, you know how it feels to ache for the familiar. If you haven't, look around. What would break your heart to leave behind?

Quickwrite

Imagine that your family is leaving home because you're in great danger. You must leave *now*, and there's no chance of return. You can take with you only one special belonging. What will it be? List your top three choices. Then quickwrite about what you'd miss most about your home.

Elements of Literature

Tone: Revealing Attitude

"Don't take that tone with me!" When you speak, your voice reveals how you feel. Through their choice of words and details, writers also convey a **tone**—their attitude or feelings about a subject or character. When Alvarez describes two men in dark glasses "crouched" behind a hedge and behaving cruelly to a dog, we feel a sinister tone. The tone would be quite different if the men were friendly dog lovers. Tone is also influenced by the choice of narrator—an innocent, bewildered child conveys one tone; a worldly-wise adult would convey something very different.

> **Tone** is the attitude a writer takes toward a subject, a character, or the reader.
> *For more on Tone, see the Handbook of Literary Terms.*

Reading Skills and Strategies

Connecting Literature to Current Events

Journalists aren't the only writers who deal with what's happening in the real world. Today, many fiction writers base their stories on actual events. In "Liberty," Alvarez tells a story that could be in today's newspaper. Yet through the fiction writer's craft, Alvarez is able to pull us into these events in an intensely personal way.

When you read a story like "Liberty," you have to read between the lines to discover parallels between the story and actual events. Be on your toes as you read this story. The child narrator can tell us only what she sees and feels.

Background

In recent decades, many people have emigrated from the Dominican Republic (Julia Alvarez's childhood home) and other Caribbean and Latin American countries. They may have left their homelands because of political oppression, war, or harsh living conditions. Like immigrants throughout America's history, they've come to the United States for that precious gift of liberty.

go.hrw.com
LEO 10-3

Preteaching Vocabulary

Words to Own

Have students work in small groups to review the Words to Own. You might suggest that they play charades, pantomiming the meaning of each word as other team members guess the word. Then, use the following sentences to reinforce students' understanding of the words.

1. The small child was so _____ that even her sister could not keep up with her. [hyperactive]

2. No _____ to take proper care of the puppy were needed; she never forgot to feed it or give it water. [admonitions]

3. When the child's puppy ran away, she was _____, crying incessantly. [inconsolable]

4. She _____ her teeth tightly in anger when we told her the puppy might not return. [clenched]

5. She did not _____ to pick out another puppy to replace it for a long time. [elect]

LIBERTY

Julia Alvarez

P api came home with a dog whose kind we had never seen before. A black-and-white-speckled electric current of energy. It was a special breed with papers, like a person with a birth certificate. Mami just kept staring at the puppy with a cross look on her face. "It looks like a mess!" she said. "Take it back."

"Mami, it is a gift!" Papi shook his head. It would be an insult to Mister Victor, who had given us the dog. The American consul[1] wanted to thank us for all we'd done for him since he'd been assigned to our country.

"If he wanted to thank us, he'd give us our visas," Mami grumbled. For a while now, my parents had been talking about going to the United States so Papi could return to school. I couldn't understand why a grown-up who could do whatever he wanted would elect to go back to a place I so much wanted to get out of.

> *"We will call him Liberty. Life, liberty, and the pursuit of happiness."*

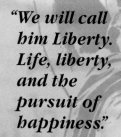

1. American consul: person appointed by the United States government to represent American interests and provide assistance to Americans living in a foreign country.

- - - - - - - - - - - - - - - - - - -
WORDS TO OWN
elect (ē·lekt′): v.: choose.
- - - - - - - - - - - - - - - - - - -

 Resources: Print and Media

Reading
- *Reading Skills and Strategies*
  - MiniRead Skill Lesson, p. 88
  - Selection Skill Lesson, p. 94
- *Graphic Organizer for Active Reading,* p. 12
- *Words to Own,* p. 12

Writing and Language
- *Daily Oral Grammar*
  - Transparency 12

- *Grammar and Language Links*
  - Worksheets, p. 21
- *Language Workshop* CD-ROM

Assessment
- *Formal Assessment,* p. 28
- *Portfolio Management System,* p. 111
- *Standardized Test Preparation,* p. 26
- *Test Generator (One-Stop Planner* CD-ROM)

Internet
- go.hrw.com (keyword: LE0 10-3)

Summary ■ ■

The story's setting is not named, but it is clear at once that the father is trying to get visas so that the family can leave for the U.S.A. We know that there is some trouble because the parents get a "scared" look when they talk of leaving. One day, the narrator's father brings home a puppy, a gift from the American consul, and the narrator falls in love with it. The father names the dog Liberty. After a run-in with the narrator's mother, Mami, the narrator takes Liberty to his pen, but the dog breaks free and runs to a hiding place in the front yard, where he and the narrator are grabbed by strangers. They are released, and the narrator reports the trouble to her parents. The consul then becomes an almost constant companion of the family. Soon after, surveillance wires are discovered in the house. One morning, Mami tells her daughters that the family will leave for the United States that evening. Liberty cannot go, and the narrator is inconsolable. Just before leaving, the narrator releases Liberty from his pen, and, making a heartbreaking decision, but one she hopes will save her beloved dog, she kicks him to chase him away. She is afraid that the men watching the house will hurt Liberty if they find him.

Background

The story is fiction. Although the setting is not named, the story probably takes place in the Dominican Republic, where Alvarez lived her first ten years, until her family was forced to go into exile because of her father's opposition to the dictator, Rafael Trujillo. Trujillo first gained power in the Dominican Republic in 1930 and ran the country until 1961, when he was assassinated. During his reign, people had few civil liberties, and the secret police kept a lid on all opposition.

A Reading Skills and Strategies

Connecting Literature to Current Events

❓ How does this family's need for visas connect to real-world events you've heard or read about? [Students should mention people who have left their countries because of oppression.]

B Elements of Literature

Tone: Revealing Attitude

❓ How does the tone expressed by Mami compare to the tone expressed by Papi? [Mami's tone is one of anger and irritability. Papi's is one of good humor, delight, and enjoyment.] **What evidence of tone do you find?** [Possible answers: Mami shakes her head; the narrator says Mami has enough to do caring for children; Mami wants to call the dog Trouble; she kicks it. Papi defends it as a "well-behaved" and "American" dog and says it is a "lucky sign."]

C English Language Learners

Word Meanings

Discuss the terms *tomboy* (a word formed with *Tom*, a boy's name, which means "a girl who acts like a boy"); *live wire* (slang meaning "an energetic person"); *trouble maker* (which means "someone who continually causes trouble"); and *drive Mami to drink* (an idiom meaning "upset Mami").

A On their faces when they talked of leaving there was a scared look I also couldn't understand.

"Those visas will come soon," Papi promised. **B** But Mami just kept shaking her head about the dog. She had enough with four girls to take on puppies, too. Papi explained that the dog would stay at the end of the yard in a pen. He would not be allowed in the house. He would not be pooping in Mami's orchid garden. He would not be barking until late at night. "A well-behaved dog," Papi concluded. "An American dog."

The little black-and-white puppy yanked at Papi's trouser cuff with his mouth. "What shall we call you?" Papi asked him.

"Trouble," Mami suggested, kicking the puppy away. He had left Papi's trousers to come slobber on her leg.

"We will call him Liberty. Life, liberty, and the pursuit of happiness." Papi quoted the U.S.A Constitution. "Eh, Liberty, you are a lucky sign!"

Liberty barked his little toy barks and all us kids laughed. "Trouble." Mami kept shaking her head as she walked away. Liberty trotted behind her as if he agreed that that was the better name for him.

Mami was right, too—Liberty turned out to be trouble. He ate all of Mami's orchids, and that little <u>hyperactive</u> baton of a tail knocked things off the low coffee table whenever Liberty climbed on the couch to leave his footprints in among the flower prints. He tore up Mami's garden looking for buried treasure. Mami screamed at Liberty and stamped her foot. "Perro sin vergüenza!"[2] But Liberty just barked back at her.

"He doesn't understand Spanish," Papi said lamely. "Maybe if you correct him in English, he'll behave better!"

Mami turned on him, her slipper still in midair. Her face looked as if she'd light into him after she was done with Liberty. "Let him go be a pet in his own country if he wants instructions in English!" In recent weeks, Mami had changed her tune about going to the United States. She wanted to stay in her own country. She didn't want Mister Victor coming around our house

and going off into the study with Papi to talk over important things in low, worried voices.

"All liberty involves sacrifice," Papi said in a careful voice. Liberty gave a few perky barks as if he agreed with that.

Mami glared at Papi. "I told you I don't want trouble—" She was going to say more, but her eye fell on me and she stopped herself. "Why aren't you with the others?" she scolded. It was as if I had been the one who had dug up her lily bulbs.

C The truth was that after Liberty arrived, I never played with the others. It was as if I had found my double in another species. I had always been the tomboy, the live wire, the trouble-maker, the one who was going to drive Mami to drink, the one she was going to give away to the Haitians. While the sisters dressed pretty and stayed clean in the playroom, I was out roaming the world looking for trouble. And now I had found someone to share my adventures.

"I'll take Liberty back to his pen," I offered. There was something I had figured out that Liberty had yet to learn: when to get out of Mami's way.

She didn't say yes and she didn't say no. She seemed distracted, as if something else was on her mind. As I led Liberty away by his collar, I could see her talking to Papi. Suddenly she started to cry, and Papi held her.

"It's okay," I consoled Liberty. "Mami doesn't mean it. She really does love you. She's just nervous." It was what my father always said when Mami scolded me harshly.

At the back of the property stood Liberty's pen—a chain-link fence around a dirt square at the center of which stood a doghouse. Papi had built it when Liberty first came, a cute little house, but then he painted it a putrid green that reminded me of all the vegetables I didn't like. It was always a job to get Liberty to go into that pen.

Sure enough, as soon as he saw where we were headed, he took off, barking, toward the

---

2. **"Perro sin vergüenza!"** (per′rō sēn ver·gwen′sä): Spanish for "shameless dog."

WORDS TO OWN

hyperactive (hī′pər·ak′tiv) *adj.:* abnormally active; very lively.

186 THE SHORT-STORY COLLECTIONS

Reaching All Students

Struggling Readers

Connecting Literature to Current Events was introduced on p. 185. For a lesson directly tied to this story that teaches students to connect literature to current events by using a strategy called Say Something, see the *Reading Skills and Strategies* binder:
• MiniRead Skill Lesson, p. 88
• Selection Skill Lesson, p. 94

English Language Learners

Read the passage from the Declaration of Independence that includes the phrase "Life, Liberty, and the pursuit of Happiness." Invite students to discuss the meaning of this passage and why it is significant for the family in this story and for people in the United States and other countries. For additional strategies to supplement instruction for these students, see
• *Lesson Plans Including Strategies for English-Language Learners*

Advanced Learners

Point out that the word *liberty* is used repeatedly in the story. Ask students to analyze its use each time. They might begin by thinking about these questions: What is the meaning of *liberty* in each context? Does it sometimes have more than one meaning? What meaning or meanings does it have in the title?

house, then swerved to the front yard to our favorite spot. It was a grassy knoll surrounded by a tall hibiscus hedge. At the center stood a tall, shady samán tree. From there, no one could see you up at the house. Whenever I did something wrong, this was where I hid out until the punishment winds blew over. That was where Liberty headed, and I was fast behind on his trail.

Inside the clearing I stopped short. Two strange men in dark glasses were crouched behind the hedge. The fat one had seized Liberty by the collar and was pulling so hard on it that poor Liberty was almost standing on his hind legs. When he saw me, Liberty began to bark, and the man holding him gave him a yank on the collar that made me sick to my stomach. I began to back away, but the other man grabbed my arm. "Not so fast," he said. Two little scared faces—my own—looked down at me from his glasses.

"I came for my dog," I said, on the verge of tears.

"Good thing you found him," the man said. "Give the young lady her dog," he ordered his friend, and then he turned to me. "You haven't seen us, you understand?"

I didn't understand. It was usually I who was the one lying and grown-ups telling me to tell the truth. But I nodded, relieved when the man released my arm and Liberty was back in my hands.

"It's okay, Liberty." I embraced him when I put him back in his pen. He was as sad as I was. We had both had a hard time with Mami, but this was the first time we'd come across mean and scary people. The fat man had almost broken Liberty's neck, and the other one had left his fingerprints on my arm. After I locked up the pen, I watched Liberty wander back slowly to his house and actually go inside, turn around, and stick his little head out the door. He'd always avoided that ugly doghouse before. I walked back to my own house, head down, to find my parents and tell them what I had seen.

Overnight, it seemed, Mister Victor moved in. He ate all his meals with us, stayed 'til late, and when he had to leave, someone from the embassy was left behind "to keep an eye on things." Now, when Papi and Mister Victor talked or when the *tíos*[3] came over, they all went down to the back of the property near Liberty's pen to talk. Mami had found some wires in the study, behind the portrait of Papi's great-grandmother fanning herself with a painted fan. The wires ran behind a screen and then out a window, where there was a little box with lots of other wires coming from different parts of the house.[4]

Mami explained that it was no longer safe to talk in the house about certain things. But the only way you knew what things those were was when Mami leveled her eyes on you as if she were pressing the off button on your mouth. She did this every time I asked her what was going on.

"Nothing," she said stiffly, and then she urged me to go outside and play. Forgotten were the admonitions to go study or I would flunk out of fifth grade. To go take a bath or the *microbios*[5] might kill me. To drink my milk or I would grow up stunted and with no teeth. Mami seemed absent and tense and always in tears. Papi was right—she was too nervous, poor thing.

I myself was enjoying a heyday of liberty. Several times I even got away with having one of Mister Victor's Coca-Colas for breakfast instead of my boiled milk with a beaten egg, which Liberty was able to enjoy instead.

"You love that dog, don't you?" Mister Victor asked me one day. He was standing by the pen with Papi waiting for the uncles. He had a funny accent that sounded like someone making fun of Spanish when he spoke it.

I ran Liberty through some of the little tricks I had taught him, and Mister Victor laughed. His face was full of freckles—so that it looked as if he and Liberty were kin. I had the impression that God had spilled a lot of his colors when he was making American things.

---

3. *tíos* (tē'ōs): Spanish for "uncles."
4. **little box . . . house:** probably refers to a device used to listen in secretly on conversations in the house.
5. *microbios* (mē·krō'bē·ōs): Spanish for "germs."

WORDS TO OWN
admonitions (ad'mə·nish'ənz) *n.*: scoldings; warnings.

D Critical Thinking
Speculating
❓ Who might these men be? [Possible responses: bodyguards; government agents who are keeping the family under surveillance.]

E Appreciating Language
Pronoun Antecedents
Read aloud the passage beginning with "The fat man had almost broken Liberty's neck...." As you read, substitute a pronoun for each noun referring to a person or the dog. Point out to students that the meaning of the passage is garbled because the pronoun references are unclear. Then, reread the passage as it is written. Explain to students that they will learn more about using clear pronoun references in their writing in the Grammar Link on p. 193.

F Elements of Literature
Character
❓ What do you learn about Mami from this passage? [Sample answer: She is worried and trying to keep the fact from her daughter.] **How does the author give us this information?** [Sample answer: The author uses what the mother says, her body language, and the narrator's description of her. She ordinarily is very attentive in caring for her daughter.]

Taking a Second Look

Review: Establishing a Purpose
Remind students that they may have many purposes in reading a selection, including discovering new information, interpreting the characters' motives, or enjoying the story. Establishing a purpose *before* reading helps readers understand and appreciate the text better and enables them to evaluate it and have a deeper response to it.

Activities
1. Before students begin reading, ask them to think about the title of the story. Ask them: What does the title suggest about the subject and theme of the story? Then, have them page through the story and look at the pictures. You might have them read the opening paragraph. Ask them to write a statement of what they expect this story to be about.

2. Have students write five questions about things that they would like to learn in the story before they read. Suggest that they write questions beginning with *who, what, when, where, why,* and *how.* As students read the story, have them answer the questions they wrote. Encourage them to write and answer more questions as they read.

Soon the uncles arrived and the men set to talking. I wandered into the pen and sat beside Liberty with my back to the house and listened. The men were speaking in English, and I had picked up enough of it at school and in my parents' conversations to make out most of what was being said. They were planning some hunting expedition for a goat with guns to be delivered by Mister Charlie. Papi was going to have to leave the goat to the others because his tennis shoes were missing. Though I understood the words—or thought I did—none of it made sense. I knew my father did not own a pair of tennis shoes, we didn't know a Mister Charlie, and who ever heard of hunting a goat?

As Liberty and I sat there with the sun baking the tops of our heads, I had this sense that the world as I knew it was about to end. The image of the two men in mirror glasses flashed through my head. So as not to think about them, I put my arm around Liberty and buried my face in his neck.

Late one morning Mami gave my sisters and me the news. Our visa had come. Mister Victor had arranged everything, and that very night we were going to the United States of America! Wasn't that wonderful! She flashed us a bright smile, as if someone were taking her picture.

We stood together watching her, alarmed at this performance of happiness when really she looked like she wanted to cry. All morning aunts had been stopping by and planting big kisses on our foreheads and holding our faces in their hands and asking us to promise we would be very good. Until now, we hadn't a clue why they were so worked up.

Mami kept smiling her company smile. She had a little job for each of us to do. There would not be room in our bags for everything. We were to pick the one toy we wanted to take with us to the United States.

I didn't even have to think twice about my choice. It had suddenly dawned on me we were leaving, and that meant leaving *everything* behind. "I want to take Liberty."

Mami started shaking her head no. We could not take a dog into the United States of America. That was not allowed.

"Please," I begged with all my might. "Please, please, Mami, please." Repetition sometimes worked—each time you said the word, it was like giving a little push to the yes that was having a hard time rolling out of her mouth.

"I said no!" The bright smile on Mami's face had grown dimmer and dimmer. *"N-O."* She spelled it out for me in case I was confusing no with another word like yes. "I said a toy, and I mean a toy."

I burst into tears. I was not going to the United States unless I could take Liberty! Mami shook me by the shoulders and asked me between clenched teeth if I didn't understand we had to go to the United States or else. But all I could understand was that a world without Liberty would break my heart. I was inconsolable. Mami began to cry.

Tía[6] Mimi took me aside. She had gone to school in the States and always had her nose in a book. In spite of her poor taste in how to spend her free time, I still loved her because she had smart things to say. Like telling Mami that punishment was not the way to make kids behave. "I'm going to tell you a little secret," she offered now. "You're going to find liberty when you get to the United States."

"Really?" I asked.

She hesitated a minute, and then she gave me a quick nod. "You'll see what I mean," she said. And then, giving me a pat on the butt, she added, "Come on, let's go pack. How about taking that wonderful book I got you on the Arabian Nights?"

Late in the night someone comes in and shakes us awake. "It's time!"

Half asleep, we put on our clothes, hands helping our arms to go into the right

6. **Tía** (tē′ä): Spanish for "aunt."

WORDS TO OWN

clenched (klench′t) v.: tightly closed.
inconsolable (in′kən·sōl′ə·bəl) adj.: unable to be comforted; brokenhearted.

Using Students' Strengths

San Antonio de Oriente (1957) by José Antonio Velasquez. Oil on canvas (27″ x 37″).

E Elements of Literature
Tone: Revealing Attitude
? What is the narrator's tone? [fearful] How does the author reveal the narrator's tone? [The author uses images of unnecessary violence done to familiar objects in the home.]

F Elements of Literature
Character
? Is the narrator a flat character or a round character? Explain. [Her character is round. Possible explanation: The narrator is naive because she is a child, but she has complex desires and motives, as evidenced in this passage, in which she recognizes the danger that Liberty is in and is capable of taking the tough actions necessary to save his life.]

sleeves, buttoning us up, running a comb through our hair.

We were put to sleep hours earlier because the plane had not come in.

But now it's time.

"Go sit by the door," we are ordered, as the hands, the many hands that now seem to be in control, finish with us. We file out of the bedroom, one by one, and go sit on the bench where packages are set down when Mami comes in from shopping. There is much rushing around. Mister Victor comes by and pats us on the head like dogs. "We'll have to wait a few more minutes," he says.

In that wait, one sister has to go to the bathroom. Another wants a drink of water. I am left sitting with my baby sister, who is dozing with her head on my shoulder. I lay her head down on the bench and slip out.

Through the dark patio down the path to the back of the yard I go. Every now and then a strange figure flashes by. I have said good-bye to Liberty a dozen times already, but there is something else I have left to do.

Sitting on the bench, I had an image again of those two men in mirror glasses. After we are gone, they come onto the property. They smash the picture of Papi's great-grandmother fanning herself. They knock over the things on the coffee table as if they don't know any better. They throw the flowered cushions on the floor. They smash the windows. And then they come to the back of the property and they find Liberty.

Quickly, because I hear calling from the big house, I slip open the door of the pen. Liberty is all over me, wagging his tail so it beats against my legs, jumping up and licking my face.

"Get away!" I order sharply, in a voice he is not used to hearing from me. I begin walking back to the house, not looking around so as not

LIBERTY 189

Making the Connections

Connecting to the Theme: "Exiles, Castaways, and Strangers"

When students have finished reading the story, guide a discussion of how the theme of this story connects to the theme of the collection. Ask students to discuss these questions: Are all the family members going into exile for the same reason? Do they each have the same attitude toward their exile? You might also point out that Liberty is also going into exile; he has been cast away by the narrator and sent to live among strangers. Invite students to compare and contrast the collection theme as it is developed in this story with how it is developed in "The Pedestrian." Who are the exiles? Why are the characters going into exile? Are they also castaways? strangers? What are the characters giving up? Do they have a choice about going into exile?

Cultural Connections

Point out that many people from numerous cultures throughout history have gone into exile. There have been various reasons, including political unrest, prejudice or other injustice, and a desire for improved economic and social opportunities. Remind students that many people who came to America were originally exiles, castaways, and strangers. Invite volunteers to talk about the reasons their families came to the United States.

Elements of Literature
Tone: Revealing Attitude

❓ What is the tone of this final paragraph? [Possible responses: hopeful; optimistic; uncertain; sad.]

Resources ───────

Selection Assessment
Formal Assessment
• Selection Test, p. 28
Test Generator (One-Stop Planner)
• CD-ROM

BROWSING IN THE FILES

About the Author. Julia Alvarez was born in New York City, so she is officially a U.S. citizen by birth. She lived in the U.S. just three weeks, however, before her family moved back to the Dominican Republic, where she lived for the next ten years. While there, her father became involved in a plot to unseat the Dominican dictator, Rafael Trujillo. When the plot failed, the family had to flee back to the U.S.

A Critic's Comment. Critic Ilan Stavans observes: "In the current wave of Latina novelists she [Alvarez] strikes me as … the one listening most closely to the subtleties of her own artistic call. She stands apart stylistically, a psychological novelist who uses language skillfully to depict complex inner lives for her fictional creations."

Writers on Writing. "I am a Dominican, hyphen, American," Alvarez comments. "As a fiction writer, I find that the most exciting things happen in the realm of that hyphen, the place where two worlds collide or blend together."

---

to encourage him. I want him to run away before the gangsters come.

He doesn't understand and keeps following me. Finally I have to resort to Mami's techniques. I kick him, softly at first, but then, when he keeps tagging behind me, I kick him hard. He whimpers and dashes away toward the front yard, disappearing in areas of darkness, then reappearing when he passes through lighted areas. At the front of the house, instead of turning toward our secret place, he keeps on going straight down the drive, through the big gates, to the world out there.

He will beat me to the United States is what I am thinking as I head back to the house. I will find Liberty there, like Tía Mimi says. But I already sense it is a different kind of liberty my aunt means. All I can do is hope that when we come back—as Mami has promised we will— my Liberty will be waiting for me here.

MEET THE WRITER

"Magic Happened in My Life"

When **Julia Alvarez** (1950–   ) says, "I write stories for different reasons," she means it. Like the girl in "Liberty," she knows political terror and exile firsthand, for her family fled from the Dominican Republic when she was ten. Alvarez says she "can't shut up" about important human events. One of her novels, *In the Time of the Butterflies* (1994), is based on the true story of the 1960 murders of the three Mirabal sisters, wives of political prisoners in her homeland.

Some of her fiction, she says, is "like cupping my hands around a moth" to save it, and some stories she writes to keep her heart from breaking.

❝ I think of myself at ten years old, newly arrived in this country, feeling out of place, feeling that I would never belong in this world. … And then, magic happened in my life. … An English teacher asked us to write little stories about ourselves. I began to put into words some of what my life had been like in the Dominican Republic. Stories about my gang of cousins and the smell of mangoes and the iridescent, vibrating green of hummingbirds. Since it was my own little world I was making with words, I could put what I wanted in it. … I could save what I didn't want to lose— memories and smells and sounds, things too precious to put anywhere else. ❞

Julia Alvarez teaches English at Middlebury College in Vermont, yet having two cultures and two languages is still central to her world and writing. Two novels (*How the García Girls Lost Their Accents,* 1991, and *¡Yo!,* 1997) follow four sisters who grow up in America speaking "Spanglish," a mixture of Spanish and English.

❝ No matter what my motive is when I begin, I end up understanding myself and the world around me much better. I think that's why I like being a writer: with each revision, the world gets clearer and, ironically, though writing is so solitary, people get closer, more real. ❞

190 **THE SHORT-STORY COLLECTIONS**

Assessing Learning

Check Test: True-False
1. The story is about a young girl and a dog named Trouble. [False]
2. The narrator's mother doesn't like the dog. [True]
3. Government agents wearing sunglasses are keeping an eye on the narrator's family. [True]
4. Government agents arrest the family and force them to go into exile in the United States. [False]
5. Before she leaves, the narrator frees the dog from his pen and drives him away. [True]

Standardized Test Preparation
For practice with standardized test format specific to this selection, see
• *Standardized Test Preparation,* p. 26

Written for a newspaper, this article is based on a journal the writer kept during a visit to Cuba, her childhood home.

HAVANA JOURNAL

A Sentimental Journey to la Casa of Childhood

MIRTA OJITO

HAVANA, Feb. 1—This is the moment when, in my dreams, I begin to cry. And yet, I'm strangely calm as I go up the stairs to the apartment of my childhood in Santos Suárez, the only place that, after all these years, I still refer to as la casa, home.

I am holding a pen and a reporter's notebook in my hand and, as I always do when I am working, I count the steps: 20. In my memory, there were only 16. The staircase seems narrower than I remember, the ceiling lower.

Perhaps I have grown taller, perhaps my whims have widened with age and pregnancy. I am buying mental time, distracting my mind from what I am certain will be a shock.

After 17 years and 8 months, I have returned to Cuba as a reporter. I am here to cover the visit of Pope John Paul II,° not to cry at the sight of a chipped, old tile on the floor.

The last time I went down these steps I was 16 years old and a police car was waiting for me and my family downstairs. They had come to tell us that my uncle, like thousands of other Cuban exiles who had returned to Cuba to claim

°*visit of Pope John Paul II:* John Paul II's visit to Cuba, from January 21 to 25, 1998, was the first by a pope to this island nation. It drew an unprecedented number of foreign reporters.

their relatives, waited at the port of Mariel to take us to Miami in a leased shrimp boat.

It was May 7, 1980, the first days of what became known as the Mariel boat lift, the period from April to September 1980 when more than 125,000 Cubans left the island for the United States.

That day I left my house in a hurry. The police gave us 10 minutes to get ready and pack the few personal items we were allowed to take: an extra set of clothing, some pictures, toothbrushes. Everything else, from my books to my dolls and my parents' wedding china, remained behind. There were dishes in the sink and food in the refrigerator. My underwear in a drawer and my mother's sewing machine open for work.

Since then, I have often thought about this house, remembering every detail, every curve and tile and squeaky sound. The green walls of the living room, the view from the balcony, the feel of the cold tiles under my bare feet, the sound of my father's key in the keyhole and the muffled noise from the old refrigerator in the kitchen.

A stranger opens the door and I tell her who I am and what I want. "I used to live here," I say. "I'd like to take a look."

Surprisingly, she knows my name. She asks if I am the older or the younger child who used to live in the house. I say I am the older as I look over her head. Straight into my past. My home remains practically as we left it, seemingly frozen

in time, like much of Cuba today....

This is a strange feeling. I knew I would face my childhood by coming here, but I never expected to relive it as I am doing now. I go out to the balcony and then, as if on cue, I hear someone calling out my childhood nickname, "Mirtica! Mirtica!"

For a moment, I do not know who is calling or even if the call is real. It sounds like my mother calling me for dinner. But it is the neighbor from the corner who looked up from her terrace and somehow recognized me. I wave faintly. I want to stay in this apartment for a long time. I want to be left alone. But I cannot. It is no longer my home.

The Jiménez family now lives in the house. He is a truck driver, just as my father was. They have a 15-year-old son who sleeps on a sofa bed in the living room, just as my sister and I did. The Government gave them the apartment a few months after we left. Their own house, nearby, had been badly damaged in a hurricane....

Had I stayed, would I have talked to a returning neighbor the way they talk to me? They tell me about the sadness of their lives, their husbands, their lovers, their misguided children, their ungrateful relatives, their never-ending litany of needs: bread, toilet paper, underwear, freedom....

After a second visit to the apartment, I leave. And I leave exactly the way I left almost 18 years ago, profoundly sad, surrounded by friends and neighbors, people glad that I remembered them, unselfish people who are happy that I left and live better than they do.

Who says that Cubans are divided by politics or even by an ocean? In Enamorados Street, at the foot of a small hill called San Julio, my home and my people remain.

—from *The New York Times*
February 3, 1998

Connections

In this *New York Times* article, Mirta Ojito describes her return to her childhood home in Cuba after 17 years. Note that the account is called a "journal," indicating that it reflects the entries Ojito made in her journal during the visit to Havana. Keeping a journal allowed the writer to record conversations and impressions that might have been difficult to recollect.

A **Reading Skills and Strategies**
Connecting with the Text
❓ How would you feel if, after being away for many years, you revisited the childhood home that you fondly remember? [Possible answers: apprehensive that the home will not be as you remember it; nostalgic over the memories; sad about all that has happened since.]

B **Critical Thinking**
Expressing an Opinion
❓ Do you think the reporter would talk to a returning neighbor in the same way that the neighbor talks with her? Why or why not? [Possible answer: Yes, because if she had stayed in Cuba, she might be like this person, eager to welcome a former neighbor, and share stories with her.]

C **Critical Thinking**
Making Judgments
❓ Do you think the reporter regrets having left her home in Cuba? Explain. [Most students will say that she does not regret it. It was her first home, so she misses it, and she probably regrets being separated from the country and culture of her birth. However, she recognizes the opportunities that she has been given as a result of leaving Cuba for the United States.]

Connecting Across Texts

Connecting with "Liberty"
Invite students to compare and contrast this news article with "Liberty." You might stimulate discussion by asking students to tell how the two main characters—the narrator and the reporter—are alike and different. How is the reporter's departure from Cuba similar to and different from the narrator's departure from her home in "Liberty"? How do you think

the reporter responded to her new home in the United States when she first arrived? Would the narrator of "Liberty" have felt the same or different? After growing up in the United States, do you think the narrator in "Liberty" would respond similarly to the opportunity to revisit her childhood home?

You might encourage interested students to investigate the political conditions in Cuba in 1980 and compare them with those in the Dominican Republic around 1960. Have them explain what political conditions caused people to leave their homes and go into exile.

MAKING MEANINGS

First Thoughts

1. The family members are being spied on. Evidently, the government is suspicious of their actions.

Shaping Interpretations

2. Possible response: The family members face a dilemma: they can become exiles and have liberty, or they can stay but sacrifice their liberty.

3. The narrator's understanding of what is happening is limited. Her naive attitude contributes to the tone of innocence, bewilderment, desperation, and fear.

Extending the Text

4. Students should draw parallels between their own experiences and Ojita's.

5. Possible answers: escape from political unrest, war, injustice, oppression, poverty, and lack of economic opportunity.

Grading Timesaver

Rubrics for each Choices assignment appear on p. 111 in the *Portfolio Management System.*

CHOICES: Building Your Portfolio

1. **Writer's Notebook** You might allow students to work in small groups to respond to the questions.

2. **History/Research** Students might divide responsibility for research and combine their results.

3. **Creative Writing** To stimulate ideas, suggest that students try asking "What if?" questions.

T192

MAKING MEANINGS

First Thoughts

[respond]

1. What is really happening in this story? Read between the lines (the hidden wires, the American consul's visits, etc.), and explain the family's situation.

Shaping Interpretations

[interpret]

2. The word *liberty* is central to this story—it's the title, the dog's name, and an important concept throughout. Explain how the story's **theme,** or insight about life, relates to liberty.

[analyze]

3. Does the narrator understand what is happening to her family? How does her attitude contribute to the **tone** of the story? Think of three words you could use to describe the tone.

Extending the Text

[compare and contrast]

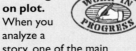

4. If you've ever had to leave a home, what do you miss most about it? Did you ever return to it, as Mirta Ojita did when she visited Havana (see ***Connections*** on page 191)? **Compare** your experiences with hers.

[connect]

5. Check recent news reports about people immigrating to the United States today. What are their reasons for wanting to live in the United States?

Reading Check

Sketch a map that shows the story's **setting.** Include the following: (a) the house, (b) the dog pen, (c) the grassy knoll and hedge, (d) the drive and big gates. Then make a map legend, identifying the important **events** that occur at each location.

CHOICES: Building Your Portfolio

Writer's Notebook

1. Collecting Ideas for Analyzing a Story

Focusing on plot. When you analyze a story, one of the main elements to consider is plot. Think about the plot of "Liberty" or of another story you've read, and jot down notes on your reactions to these questions: What is the cause of the **conflict,** and how is it resolved? What are the **main events?** Do they create suspense? When does the **climax** occur? Save your notes for the Writer's Workshop on page 240.

History/Research

2. Newcomers to America

With a small group, brainstorm questions you'd like to research about the history of American immigration. To answer the questions you've raised, explore various sources, including electronic databases and the Internet. You might, instead, trace your family's history, researching when and why relatives came to America and where they settled. Choose from a variety of media (maps, photos, oral or written reports) to present your information to classmates.

Creative Writing

3. Liberty's Tale

What happens to Liberty? Take up the little dog's story after he goes through the gate. You might want to tell the story from Liberty's point of view, using the pronoun "I." Tell what happens next and how you (Liberty) are feeling.

Reading Check

Maps and legends will vary. A sample is given.

Legend

a. House
- Wires are discovered behind portrait.
- Narrator learns she can't take Liberty with her.

b. Dog pen
- Narrator overhears plans of Papi, Mister Victor, and uncles.
- Narrator frees Liberty and kicks him.

c. Grassy knoll and hedge
- Two strangers grab Liberty and narrator.

d. Drive and gates
- Liberty leaves through the gates.

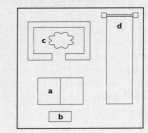

GRAMMAR LINK   MINI-LESSON

Language Handbook HELP

Clear Pronoun Reference: page 1031.

Technology HELP

See Language Workshop CD-ROM. Key word entry: pronouns.

Who's Who? Making Pronouns Clear

Have you ever discovered, partway through a conversation, that you and a friend were talking about two different people? **Unclear pronoun reference,** a common mistake, causes misunderstandings. *You* always know whom you're referring to when you say *he, she,* or *they,* but your readers or listeners may have someone else in mind.

A **pronoun** should refer clearly to its **antecedent** (the noun or pronoun to which the pronoun refers). Avoid unclear, or **ambiguous,** pronoun references, which occur when a pronoun can refer to either of two antecedents. Usually, you can pin down your meaning by replacing the pronoun with the noun to which it refers.

UNCLEAR	Papi and Mister Victor both talk to Liberty, but *he* speaks Spanish with an accent.
CLEAR	Papi and Mister Victor both talk to Liberty, but Mister Victor speaks Spanish with an accent.
CLEAR	Papi and Mister Victor, who speaks Spanish with an accent, both talk to Liberty.

Try It Out

➤ Reword the following sentences to correct the unclear pronoun references. You may reword the sentences any way you want.

1. Papi brought home a puppy, and he caused a lot of trouble.
2. When Liberty and the strange man with the sunglasses saw me, he looked frightened.
3. All morning aunts stopped by to kiss the sisters because they were leaving for America.
4. Tía Mimi said that Mami was upset, and she had a secret.

VOCABULARY   HOW TO OWN A WORD

WORD BANK

elect
hyperactive
admonitions
clenched
inconsolable

Using a Thesaurus to Find Synonyms

A **synonym** is a word that has the same, or nearly the same, meaning as another word. To find synonyms, writers use a **thesaurus,** either in book or electronic form.

Most thesauruses list synonyms based on a word's different shades of meaning. You might want to look at all the synonyms and follow the cross-references given until you find the exact meaning you want to convey.

This chart shows how one student used a thesaurus to find synonyms for *admonitions*. Make a thesaurus chart for synonyms for the other four words in the Word Bank.

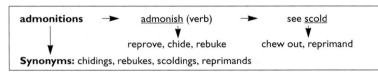

admonitions → admonish (verb) → see scold

reprove, chide, rebuke   chew out, reprimand

Synonyms: chidings, rebukes, scoldings, reprimands

GRAMMAR LINK

Ask students to select a piece of writing from their portfolio and analyze their pronoun references. Have them identify and correct any unclear references.

Try It Out
Possible Answers

1. Papi brought home a puppy, and the dog caused a lot of trouble.
2. Liberty looked frightened when he and the strange man with the sunglasses saw me.
3. All morning aunts stopped by to kiss the sisters because the children were leaving for America.
4. Tía Mimi said that Mami was upset because of a secret Mami had.

VOCABULARY

Sample answers are given.
elect   synonyms: choose, pick, go with, opt for
hyperactive   synonyms: overactive, hyper, frenetic, hyperkinetic
clenched   clench (verb) grasp, grip, hold onto; synonyms: grasping viselike, gripping, tenacious
inconsolable   console (verb) comfort, relieve, soothe; synonyms: disconsolate, comfortless, forlorn, heartsick

Resources ───────

Language
• *Grammar and Language Links* Worksheet, p. 21

Vocabulary
• *Words to Own,* Worksheet, p. 12

Grammar Link Quick Check

Replace each ambiguous pronoun reference in the following sentences with a specific noun. [Possible responses follow.]

1. Mami and Tía Mimi tried to console the narrator, but she couldn't get her to listen. [*she* replaced by either *Mami* or *Tía Mimi*]
2. Even though Mister Victor and Papi agreed on the best time to leave, he kept worrying about the decision. [*he* replaced by either *Mister Victor* or *Papi*]
3. Papi laughed at Liberty's antics when he ran after him. [*he* replaced by *Papi* or *Liberty* and/or *him* replaced by *Papi* or *Liberty*]
4. The stranger grabbed Liberty's collar, and he growled. [*he* replaced by *Liberty*]
5. The narrator and her sister waited on the bench, and after a moment she fell asleep. [*she* replaced by *the narrator* or *her sister*]

Resources

Elements of Literature
Irony and Satire
For additional instruction on irony and satire, see *Literary Elements*:
• Transparency 7

Elements of Literature

This lesson guides students to an understanding of the different types and purposes of irony and satire.
Mini-Lesson:
Irony and Satire
After students have read pp. 194–195, use this Mini-Lesson to clarify and reinforce their understanding of irony and satire.

• Invite students to give examples of irony and satire from books and stories they have read or from movies, plays, or television programs they have seen.

• Point out that irony requires the participation of the reader. Ask students: What is the role of the reader when a writer uses verbal, situational, or dramatic irony?
[Possible responses: Verbal irony must be recognized by the reader because it says the opposite of what it means. Situational irony depends on the reader's having expectations that are not met. Dramatic irony works by creating a team of the writer and the reader, both of whom know more than the characters.]

IRONY AND SATIRE: The Might of the Word

Three Types of Irony

Irony, in its original Greek sense, means acting ignorant in order to make fun of a person or to expose the truth about a situation. We see this very old kind of irony still at work today when a story or movie shows a shrewd farmer pretending to be dumb in order to make fun of a city slicker. But *irony* has also come to have far broader meanings.

We find three kinds of irony in stories, each of them involving some kind of contrast between expectation and reality. **Verbal irony**—the simplest kind—is being used when someone *says* one thing but *means* the opposite.

If we say "You sure can pick 'em" to the man whose team finished last, we are using verbal irony. A parent uses verbal irony when she looks up from the string of D's on Willie's report card and says "It is certainly gratifying to find you are getting so much out of your education."

If the speaker goes on to use words in a particularly harsh and cruel way, we see the use of **sarcasm.** Sarcasm is intended to wound, to bite in a hurtful way.

Someone looking at Willie's report card would be sarcastic if he said "I've seen shirts with higher IQs than yours."

Situational irony is much more important to the story-teller than other kinds of irony are: It describes an occurrence that is not just surprising; it is *contrary* to what we expected. In an ironic situation, what actually happens is so contrary to our expectations that it seems to mock human intentions and the confidence with which we plan our futures. The ironic possibility that this haughty rich man will come begging from us tomorrow or that this girl who is dreading tonight's party will meet her future husband there keeps our lives interesting. Of course, it does the same for our fiction.

An example of situational irony would be found in a story that told how, after years of searching and after many bloody quarrels over the treasure map, the characters discover the treasure chest and find that it is full of old bottle caps.

A classic example of situational irony is found in the myth of King Midas. This greedy king wishes for a golden touch, but when his wish is granted, something unexpected happens: Midas can no longer eat because even his food turns to gold when he touches it. The golden touch has brought him not only riches, but misery, even death, as well.

Dramatic irony is the kind of irony that occurs when *we* know what is in store for a character but the character does not know. This is called dramatic irony because it's so often used on stage.

Jean arranges a surprise party for Fred's birthday, and all his friends are hiding behind the curtains waiting for him to arrive home. When Fred, looking haggard, calls into an apparently empty hall "Hello? Jean? Anybody home? Boy, am I *tired*!" we recognize dramatic irony. Our sense that the exhausted Fred is soon going to be astonished by a happy-birthday chorus heightens our interest in Fred (we wonder if he'll just fall to the floor).

Dramatic irony adds to our enjoyment of a story because it mimics life, which is forever pulling surprises on us.

Irony of all kinds is somehow enormously satisfying,

Reaching All Students

Struggling Readers
Bring a selection of editorial cartoons or comic strips to class. Have students work in groups to identify and discuss the use of irony and satire. Ask them to begin by responding to these questions: What kind of irony is it? What is being satirized? What must the reader understand in order to appreciate the irony?

English Language Learners
Invite these students to share examples of irony and satire from their first culture. Discuss the examples to ensure that the students understand the characteristics of irony and satire. For additional strategies to supplement instruction for English language learners, see
• *Lesson Plans Including Strategies for English-Language Learners*

Advanced Learners
Challenge students to select a social or political situation and write a brief essay, story, or poem that satirizes it. Remind them that in order for it to be effective, satire must be recognized by its audience, so they should think carefully about who their readers are and what these readers know about the issue. Encourage students to submit their satires to their school or local newspapers or to publish them in an appropriate forum on the Internet.

by John Leggett

perhaps because we know instinctively that our carefully laid plans and ambitions and strivings often come to little, whereas good luck (or bad) often finds unlikely targets.

> Irony is enormously satisfying, perhaps because we know instinctively that our carefully laid plans and ambitions and strivings often come to little.

Satire: A Social Purpose

Satire is a close relative of irony and often uses irony to accomplish its purpose. **Satire** is any writing that uses ridicule with the intention of bringing about social reform. The satirist wants to expose and eliminate human stupidity and wickedness. Greed, injustice, cruelty, and deceit are all targets of the satirist.

Jonathan Swift's novel *Gulliver's Travels* is often read by children, but it is really one of the most stinging satires in the English language. The story mocks people in early eighteenth-century England who thought their nation was the most civilized on earth. George Orwell's novel *Animal Farm* is another famous satire, one that uses barnyard animals to mock the way people abuse political power.

Comedians on television use satire all the time, often to make fun of themselves. The long-running television show *M*A*S*H* used satire to make us laugh (and cry) at the insanity of war.

Ironic and satiric writing can be humorous. It can lay bare a weakness or a pretense, and it can also invite laughter at someone's expense. Irony and satire may sometimes sting. They may sometimes be cruel in purpose and in effect, but it would be a mistake to ignore them.

Whenever you hear the ancient claim that "the pen is mightier than the sword," think of irony and satire. A pen (or computer) that uses irony or satire can even become a sword, and it can be taken up in a good cause. Irony and satire can hold up to us the mirror of art and reveal our own faults and foolishnesses. They can make us aware of all the ways in which we humans persuade ourselves that we are righteous and right-minded—when, in fact, we just may be dead wrong.

Complete Peace

ELEMENTS OF LITERATURE: IRONY AND SATIRE 195

Applying the Element

- Invite students to think back about "Liberty" and to cite examples of irony and satire. Get them started by asking these questions: **What is ironic about the behavior of the dog just after the family chooses the name Liberty rather than Trouble?** [Possible responses: The dog trots behind Mami, who wanted to name him Trouble; the dog gets into a lot of trouble.] **What kind of irony is the narrator using when she describes herself as "the one who was going to drive Mami to drink"? Explain.** [This is sarcasm because it is exaggerated and harsh.] **How does the dog's name turn out to be ironic for the narrator?** [In order for her to have her liberty in the United States, she must give up her dog Liberty.]

- Ask students to work in groups and to identify and discuss examples of irony and satire in stories they have read in *Elements of Literature*. Have groups share their results in class discussion.

- Challenge students to look for additional instances of irony and satire as they read the remaining stories in this collection. You might have them keep a list of examples that can be shared after students finish reading each selection.

Resources ———

Assessment
Formal Assessment
- Literary Elements Test, p. 38

Using Students' Strengths

Visual Learners
Divide students into groups, and have each group create a cartoon or comic strip to illustrate satire, verbal irony, situational irony, and dramatic irony. Groups should provide captions. Allow students to display their cartoons and comic strips and discuss how the illustrations function as satire and irony.

Kinesthetic Learners
Pantomime offers wonderful opportunities to study dramatic and situational irony and satire. Challenge students to work individually or in pairs to create a pantomime that uses irony and satire to comment on a current political or social issue.

T195

OBJECTIVES

1. Read and interpret the story
2. Identify and analyze character and theme
3. Connect literature to historical context
4. Express understanding through creative writing, critical thinking, history/research, graphic organizers, or speaking/listening
5. Identify imagery and use imagery in writing
6. Understand and use new words

SKILLS

Literary
- Identify theme and character

Reading
- Understand historical context

Writing
- Analyze a story
- Write about a personal memory
- Write an essay

Speaking/Listening
- Collect oral histories

Grammar/Language
- Understand and use imagery

Vocabulary
- Use new words

Art
- Create graphics

Planning

- **Traditional Schedule**
  Lesson Plans Including Strategies for English-Language Learners
- **One-Stop Planner**
  CD-ROM with Test Generator

Before You Read

WHERE HAVE YOU GONE, CHARMING BILLY?

Make the Connection

What Does This All Mean?

The Vietnam War divided America with particular bitterness. Some of those who served in Vietnam have asked what it all meant. Although this war had a profound effect on our nation, few people have written fiction about Vietnam. Tim O'Brien, who served in Vietnam, is an exception. In the story that follows, he focuses on one soldier's feelings during his initiation into combat.

Quickwrite

Have you ever been in a frightening situation—an accident, a flood, a bad fight, maybe even war? What did you do to make yourself feel better? Write down a few notes about your experience. If you don't want to write about yourself, write about someone you know.

go.hrw.com
LEO 10-3

Elements of Literature

Theme and Character

The subject of this story is clearly war, but the story's **theme** is much more complex. One way of getting at the theme of any story is to look at how the main character changes in the course of the story, or at what he or she has learned by the story's end. Often, what this character has discovered about life is the truth the writer wants to reveal to us, too.

> **W**hat the main **character** learns in the course of a story often leads us to the story's **theme**.
>
> *For more on Theme, see pages 182–183 and the Handbook of Literary Terms.*

Reading Skills and Strategies

Understanding Historical Context

"Where Have You Gone, Charming Billy?" re-creates in harrowing detail a young soldier's fears on his first night in the field. To appreciate some of the details in the story, you need to understand its **historical context,** the war in Vietnam. There were no "front lines" in Vietnam, and fighting took the form of unexpected guerrilla skirmishes. From moment to moment, Paul doesn't know what to expect—from his strange surroundings or from his own heart. Nor do we.

Before you read, review with a partner some of the facts you know about the war in Vietnam. You might also want to read Tim O'Brien's note on the war on page 204.

He was pretending

196 THE SHORT-STORY COLLECTIONS

Preteaching Vocabulary

Words to Own

Have students work in pairs to review the two Words to Own that appear in the selection. One student might make up a question about one of the words. The other student could answer the question. Then, have students answer the following questions. Note that more than one answer is possible.

1. Which of these places could be described as <u>fecund</u>? [c]
   a. parking lot
   b. sand dune
   c. marsh

2. If you were driving, which of these situations would you want to <u>skirt</u>? [a,b,c]
   a. traffic jam
   b. flooded street
   c. parade

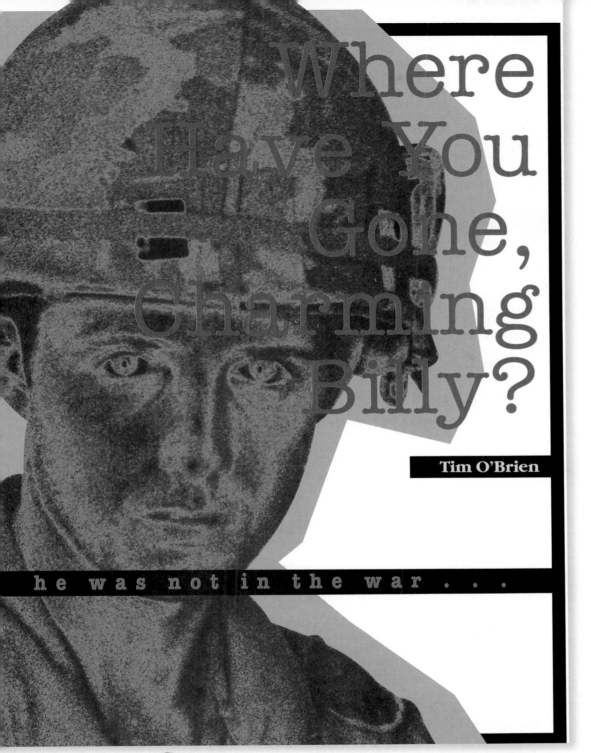

Where Have You Gone, Charming Billy?

Tim O'Brien

he was not in the war . . .

Summary ■■

The story is told from a limited third-person viewpoint, focusing on Paul Berlin's mental struggle to conquer his terrors in Vietnam. After his first day in the war (during which he watched Billy Boy Watkins die of a heart attack), Paul Berlin is on a tense night march to the sea. To quell his fear, he thinks about home, his childhood, and his father. Flashbacks reveal the details of Billy Boy's death: After a mine blows off his foot, Billy's fear brings on a heart attack. In further ironic ignominy, his body later falls from the helicopter lifting it and is fished from a rice paddy by his platoon, who sing the children's song of the title. As he remembers these events, Paul cracks: He giggles so hysterically that another soldier must smother him into silence so the noise does not draw the Vietcong to their position. The patrol finally gets to the sea, their objective, but Paul's fear remains.

Background

You might first send students to the database on p. 200. The U.S. involvement in the war in Vietnam developed after Vietnam became a divided nation with a Communist North Vietnam and a non-Communist South Vietnam. American policy was to support nations fighting Communism. At first, U.S. involvement was limited to military advisors and supplies, but in 1965, President Johnson sent troops to Vietnam. By 1969, 540,000 American troops were in Vietnam. The U.S. fought the war with two basic strategies: heavy bombing of North Vietnam and ground missions that sought to destroy Communist strongholds in South Vietnam. The patrol in this story is on one of these ground missions.

Resources: Print and Media

Reading
- *Graphic Organizer for Active Reading*, p. 13
- *Words to Own*, p. 13
- *Audio CD Library*
  Disc 7, Track 2

Elements of Literature
- *Literary Elements*
  Transparency 6
  Worksheet, p. 19

Writing and Language
- *Daily Oral Grammar*
  Transparency 13
- *Grammar and Language Links*
  Worksheet, p. 23
- *Language Workshop CD-ROM*

Viewing and Representing
- *Visual Connections*
  Videocassette A, Segment 3

Assessment
- *Formal Assessment*, p. 30
- *Portfolio Management System*, p. 112
- *Standardized Test Preparation*, p. 28
- *Test Generator* (One-Stop Planner CD-ROM)

Internet
- go.hrw.com (keyword: LE0 10-3)

Ⓐ Reading Skills and Strategies

Understanding Historical Context

❓ Read O'Brien's comments on his experience during the Vietnam War on p. 204. Why does the other soldier speak so harshly to Paul Berlin? [The soldier knows his survival depends partly on Berlin. He doesn't want Berlin making mistakes.]

The platoon of twenty-six soldiers moved slowly in the dark, single file, not talking. One by one, like sheep in a dream, they passed through the hedgerow, crossed quietly over a meadow, and came down to the rice paddy. There they stopped. Their leader knelt down, motioning with his hand, and one by one the other soldiers squatted in the shadows, vanishing in the primitive stealth of warfare. For a long time they did not move. Except for the sounds of their breathing, the twenty-six men were very quiet: some of them excited by the adventure, some of them afraid, some of them exhausted from the long night march, some of them looking forward to reaching the sea, where they would be safe. At the rear of the column, Private First Class Paul Berlin lay quietly with his forehead resting on the black plastic stock of his rifle, his eyes closed. He was pretending he was not in the war, pretending he had not watched Billy Boy Watkins die of a heart attack that afternoon. He was pretending he was a boy again, camping with his father in the midnight summer along the Des Moines River. In the dark, with his eyes pinched shut, he pretended. He pretended that when he opened his eyes, his father would be there by the campfire and they would talk softly about whatever came to mind and then roll into their sleeping bags, and that later they'd wake up and it would be morning and there would not be a war, and that Billy Boy Watkins had not died of a heart attack that afternoon. He pretended he was not a soldier.

In the morning, when they reached the sea, it would be better. The hot afternoon would be over, he would bathe in the sea, and he would forget how frightened he had been on his first day at the war. The second day would not be so bad. He would learn.

There was a sound beside him, a movement, and then a breathed "Hey!"

Ⓐ He opened his eyes, shivering as if emerging from a deep nightmare.

"Hey!" a shadow whispered. "We're *moving.* Get up."

"Okay."

"You sleepin', or something?"

"No." He could not make out the soldier's face. With clumsy, concrete hands he clawed for his rifle, found it, found his helmet.

The soldier shadow grunted. "You got a lot to learn, buddy. I'd shoot you if I thought you was sleepin'. Let's go."

Private First Class Paul Berlin blinked.

Ahead of him, silhouetted against the sky, he saw the string of soldiers wading into the flat paddy, the black outline of their shoulders and packs and weapons. He was comfortable. He did not want to move. But he was afraid, for it was his first night at the war, so he hurried to catch up, stumbling once, scraping his knee, groping as though blind; his boots sank into the thick paddy water, and he smelled it all around him. He would tell his mother how it smelled: mud and algae and cattle manure and chlorophyll;[1] decay, breeding mosquitoes and leeches as big as mice; the fecund warmth of the paddy waters rising up to his cut knee. But he would not tell how frightened he had been.

Once they reached the sea, things would be better. They would have their rear guarded by three thousand miles of ocean, and they would swim and dive into the breakers and hunt crayfish and smell the salt, and they would be safe.

He followed the shadow of the man in front of him. It was a clear night. Already the Southern Cross[2] was out. And other stars he could not yet name—soon, he thought, he would learn their names. And puffy night clouds. There was not yet a moon. Wading through the paddy, his boots made sleepy, sloshing sounds, like a lull-

---

1. **chlorophyll** (klôr′ə·fil′): green substance found in plant cells.
2. **Southern Cross:** constellation, or group of stars, in the Southern Hemisphere.

WORDS TO OWN
fecund (fē′kənd) *adj.*: fertile; producing abundantly.

Reaching All Students

Struggling Readers
Because of the fantasy sequences and flashbacks, some students may have difficulty following the sequence of events in this story. Encourage students to create a time line of events as they read. Suggest that they indicate when the events told in the flashback occurred as well as when the flashback occurs within the story. For additional strategies, see the *Reading Strategies Handbook* in the *Reading Skills and Strategies* binder.

English Language Learners
Many of these students will not have developed a vocabulary that includes the military terms used in this story, such as *machine gun, breech, muzzle,* and *ammunition.* You might encourage them to maintain a list of unfamiliar terms to discuss and learn. For additional strategies to supplement instruction for English language learners, see
• *Lesson Plans Including Strategies for English-Language Learners*

Advanced Learners
Point out that this story paints a graphic picture of one soldier's first day facing the terrors of night patrol in the Vietnam jungle. Ask students to consider these questions as they read: How do soldiers learn to live with such intense fear? What long-term effects might this kind of experience leave with soldiers? Students might discuss the conditions called *combat fatigue,* or *shell shock,* and *post-traumatic stress disorder.*

aby, and he tried not to think. Though he was afraid, he now knew that fear came in many degrees and types and peculiar categories, and he knew that his fear now was not so bad as it had been in the hot afternoon, when poor Billy Boy Watkins got killed by a heart attack. His fear now was diffuse and unformed: ghosts in the tree line, nighttime fears of a child, a boogeyman in the closet that his father would open to show empty, saying, "See? Nothing there, champ. Now you can sleep." In the afternoon it had been worse: The fear had been bundled and

reached the sea,

tight and he'd been on his hands and knees, crawling like an insect, an ant escaping a giant's footsteps, and thinking nothing, brain flopping like wet cement in a mixer, not thinking at all, watching while Billy Boy Watkins died.

Now, as he stepped out of the paddy onto a narrow dirt path, now the fear was mostly the fear of being so terribly afraid again.

He tried not to think.

There were tricks he'd learned to keep from thinking. Counting: He counted his steps, concentrating on the numbers, pretending that the steps were dollar bills and that each step through the night made him richer and richer, so that soon he would become a wealthy man, and he kept counting and considered the ways he might spend the money after the war and what he would do. He would look his father in the eye and shrug and say, "It was pretty bad at first, but I learned a lot and I got used to it."

it would be better.

Then he would tell his father the story of Billy Boy Watkins. But he would never let on how frightened he had been. "Not so bad," he would say instead, making his father feel proud.

Songs, another trick to stop from thinking: *Where have you gone, Billy Boy, Billy Boy, oh, where have you gone, charming Billy? I have gone to seek a wife, she's the joy of my life, but she's a young thing and cannot leave her mother,* and other songs that he sang in his thoughts as he walked toward the sea. And when he reached the sea, he would dig a deep

hole in the sand and he would sleep like the high clouds and he would not be afraid anymore.

The moon came out. Pale and shrunken to the size of a dime.

The helmet was heavy on his head. In the morning he would adjust the leather binding. He would clean his rifle, too. Even though he had been frightened to shoot it during the hot afternoon, he would carefully clean the breech and the muzzle and the ammunition so that next time he would be ready and not so afraid. In the morning, when they reached the sea, he would begin to make friends with some of the other soldiers. He would learn their names and laugh at their jokes. Then when the war was over, he would have war buddies, and he would write to them once in a while and exchange memories.

Walking, sleeping in his walking, he felt better. He watched the moon come higher.

Once they <u>skirted</u> a sleeping village. The smells again—straw, cattle, mildew. The men were quiet. On the far side of the village, buried in the dark smells, a dog barked. The column stopped until the barking died away; then they marched fast away from the village, through a graveyard filled with conical-shaped burial mounds and tiny altars made of clay and stone. The graveyard had a perfumy smell. A nice place to spend the night, he thought. The mounds would make fine battlements, and the smell was nice and the place was quiet. But they went on, passing through a hedgerow and across another paddy and east toward the sea.

He walked carefully. He remembered what he'd been taught: Stay off the center of the path, for that was where the land mines and booby traps were planted, where stupid and lazy soldiers like to walk. Stay alert, he'd been taught.

WORDS TO OWN

skirted v.: passed around rather than through. *Skirted* also means "missed narrowly" or "avoided."

WHERE HAVE YOU GONE, CHARMING BILLY? 199

B **English Language Learners**
Allusions
Be sure students know what a cement mixer is, and how it turns and turns, each turn flopping and mixing the wet materials that will be cement. The image suggests a rather terrifying cycle of "not thinking."

C **Elements of Literature**
Theme and Character
? Based on what you've learned about the character so far, what do you predict the theme of this story will be? [Possible response: It will have something to do with fear, and fear of fear.]

D **Advanced Learners**
Tone
? How does the tone differ here? [The tone here is optimistic and controlled. It appears that Paul is struggling to hold on to this view.]

E **Reading Skills and Strategies**
Understanding Historical Context
Most Vietnamese are Buddhist and Taoist. Buddhists burn incense during religious ceremonies and in honor of their ancestors. The "perfumy" smell Paul notices is probably incense burned at the clay-and-stone altars in the graveyard.

Skill Link

Using Imagery
Imagery is the use of details that evoke sensory experiences. Writers use imagery to help readers experience a scene as if at first hand. Focus on a paragraph from the text, and have students identify the images and the senses appealed to (sight, hearing, smell, taste, and touch). Be sure to have them notice details they may supply from their own imagination.

Activity
Have students use imagery in writing a short passage about an experience of their own. They should try to include images that appeal to all five of the senses.

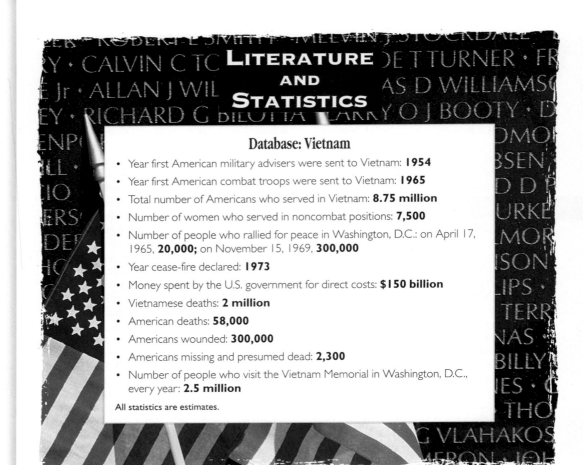

LITERATURE AND STATISTICS

Database: Vietnam

- Year first American military advisers were sent to Vietnam: **1954**
- Year first American combat troops were sent to Vietnam: **1965**
- Total number of Americans who served in Vietnam: **8.75 million**
- Number of women who served in noncombat positions: **7,500**
- Number of people who rallied for peace in Washington, D.C.: on April 17, 1965, **20,000;** on November 15, 1969, **300,000**
- Year cease-fire declared: **1973**
- Money spent by the U.S. government for direct costs: **$150 billion**
- Vietnamese deaths: **2 million**
- American deaths: **58,000**
- Americans wounded: **300,000**
- Americans missing and presumed dead: **2,300**
- Number of people who visit the Vietnam Memorial in Washington, D.C., every year: **2.5 million**

All statistics are estimates.

Better alert than inert. Ag·ile, mo·bile, hos·tile. He wished he'd paid better attention to the training. He could not remember what they'd said about how to stop being afraid; they hadn't given any lessons in courage—not that he could remember—and they hadn't mentioned how Billy Boy Watkins would die of a heart attack, his face turning pale and the veins popping out.

Private First Class Paul Berlin walked carefully.

Stretching ahead of him like dark beads on an invisible chain, the string of shadow soldiers whose names he did not yet know moved with the silence and slow grace of smoke. Now and again moonlight was reflected off a machine gun or a wristwatch. But mostly the soldiers were quiet and hidden and faraway-seeming in a peaceful night, strangers on a long street, and

B e t t e r   a l e r t   t h a n   i n e r t.

he felt quite separate from them, as if trailing behind like the caboose on a night train, pulled along by inertia,[3] sleepwalking, an afterthought to the war.

So he walked carefully, counting his steps.

3. **inertia** (in·ur′shə): tendency to remain either at rest or in motion.

200 THE SHORT-STORY COLLECTIONS

Crossing the Curriculum

Geography

Although most of the action during the Vietnam War took place in North and South Vietnam, the war spilled over into neighboring countries. Ask students to do research to identify other countries involved in the conflict and to locate them on a map of Southeast Asia. You might also ask students to locate the boundary that formerly existed between North and South Vietnam, the capitals of those two countries, and the location of major conflicts.

History

The United States became involved in Vietnam in 1954, but the Vietnamese began a struggle against foreign domination much earlier. Have students investigate the complex history of what was first known as the Indochina War, its causes, and the events that led to American involvement. You might have students work together to do research and then to plan and present a multimedia explication of the war to the class.

Listening to Music

"Billy Boy" (traditional), performed by the Jones Brothers & Log Cabin Boys

Activity

Point out that the song is usually identified as a children's song. Have students discuss why Tim O'Brien might have chosen it for this story. You may also want to have students make up additional lyrics that reflect an event or mood from the story.

When he had counted to 3,485, the column stopped.

One by one the soldiers knelt or squatted down.

The grass along the path was wet. Private First Class Paul Berlin lay back and turned his head so that he could lick at the dew with his eyes closed, another trick to forget the war. He might have slept. "I *wasn't* afraid," he was screaming or dreaming, facing his father's stern eyes. "I wasn't afraid," he was saying. When he opened his eyes, a soldier was sitting beside him, quietly chewing a stick of Doublemint gum.

"You sleepin' again?" the soldier whispered.

"No," said Private First Class Paul Berlin. "Hell, no."

The soldier grunted, chewing his gum. Then he twisted the cap off his canteen, took a swallow, and handed it through the dark.

"Take some," he whispered.

"Thanks."

"You're the new guy?"

"Yes." He did not want to admit it, being new to the war.

The soldier grunted and handed him a stick of gum. "Chew it quiet—OK? Don't blow no bubbles or nothing."

"Thanks. I won't." He could not make out the man's face in the shadows.

They sat still and Private First Class Paul Berlin chewed the gum until all the sugars were gone; then the soldier said, "Bad day today, buddy."

Private First Class Paul Berlin nodded wisely, but he did not speak.

"Don't think it's always so bad," the soldier whispered. "I don't wanna scare you. You'll get

used to it soon enough. . . . They been fighting wars a long time, and you get used to it."

"Yeah."

"You will."

They were quiet awhile. And the night was quiet, no crickets or birds, and it was hard to imagine it was truly a war. He searched for the soldier's face but could not find it. It did not

matter much. Even if he saw the fellow's face, he would not know the name; and even if he knew the name, it would not matter much.

"Haven't got the time?" the soldier whispered.

"No."

"Rats. . . . Don't matter, really. Goes faster if you don't know the time, anyhow."

"Sure."

"What's your name, buddy?"

"Paul."

"Nice to meet ya," he said, and in the dark beside the path, they shook hands. "Mine's Toby. Everybody calls me Buffalo, though." The soldier's hand was strangely warm and soft. But it was a very big hand. "Sometimes they just call me Buff," he said.

And again they were quiet. They lay in the grass and waited. The moon was very high now and very bright, and they were waiting for cloud cover. The soldier suddenly snorted.

"What is it?"

"Nothin'," he said, but then he snorted again. "A bloody *heart attack*!" the soldier said. "Can't get over it—old Billy Boy croaking from a lousy heart attack. . . . A heart attack—can you believe it?"

The idea of it made Private First Class Paul Berlin smile. He couldn't help it.

"Ever hear of such a thing?"

"Not till now," said Private First Class Paul Berlin, still smiling.

"Me neither," said the soldier in the dark. "Gawd, dying of a heart attack. Didn't know him, did you."

"No."

"Tough as nails."

"Yeah."

Ag-ile, mo-bile, hos-tile.

"And what happens? A heart attack. Can you imagine it?"

"Yes," said Private First Class Paul Berlin. He wanted to laugh. "I can imagine it." And he imagined it clearly. He giggled—he couldn't help it. He imagined Billy's father opening the telegram: SORRY TO INFORM YOU THAT YOUR SON BILLY BOY WAS YESTERDAY SCARED TO DEATH IN AC-

WHERE HAVE YOU GONE, CHARMING BILLY? 201

C Elements of Literature

Character and Theme

❓ According to this passage, what is Paul anxious about? [He seems to fear his father's "stern" eyes, perhaps accusing his son of cowardice—as if fear is a sign of cowardice.]

D Reading Skills and Strategies

Drawing Conclusions

❓ Why do you think the soldier's name and what he looks like are not important to Paul? [Possible response: Paul is wary of intimacy because the man might be killed.]

E English Language Learners

Idioms and Slang

"Got the time?" is an idiom meaning "What time is it?" Notice in the text below that the word *croaking* is used as slang to mean "dying." English language learners might also need help with the word *bloody* in the same paragraph. Explain that it is a British slang intensifier, like the word *very*. (In England *bloody* is considered vulgar.)

Using Students' Strengths

Interpersonal Learners

After students have read the story, have them work in pairs to study the two characters Paul and Toby. Have one student portray Paul and the other portray Toby. They should improvise a dialogue, in character, for five minutes. When students have completed their dialogue, have them describe the conflicts their characters are experiencing.

Visual Learners

Students could create a piece of artwork, such as a sketch, collage, or painting, that expresses Paul's emotional state at several points during the story. Have them display their work and explain the images they have chosen to illustrate Paul's emotions.

Auditory/Musical Learners

Have students select appropriate music for each scene to accompany a dramatic reading of the story. Students should explain why each piece of music is appropriate for each scene.

A Elements of Literature
Imagery

? This long single sentence contains a series of events linked by *and*, with imagery that helps us experience the terrifying scene almost as if we were there ourselves. What images does the writer use? What senses does each image evoke? ["hissed," sound; "giggling," sound; "drinking Coca-Cola from bright-red aluminum cans," sight, taste, touch; "it made a tiny little sound—*poof,*" sound; "his foot lying behind him, most of it still in the boot," sight.] Note the terrible understatement in the last five lines.

B English Language Learners
Idioms

"Scared stiff" is an idiom suggesting the paralysis that sometimes accompanies intense fear. (Note also that this is not a full sentence.) Watch how the term "scared stiff" is repeated in the story, especially after Billy Boy literally has been scared to death.

C Elements of Literature
Conflict

? What two conflicts are going on here? Are they internal or external conflicts? [Possible response: the conflict between the soldier and Paul, which is external, and the conflict within Paul as he tries to stifle his hysteria, which is internal.]

TION IN THE REPUBLIC OF VIETNAM, VALIANTLY SUCCUMBING TO A HEART ATTACK SUFFERED WHILE UNDER ENORMOUS STRESS, AND IT IS WITH GREATEST SYMPATHY THAT . . . He giggled again. He rolled onto his belly and pressed his face into his arms. His body was shaking with giggles.

The big soldier hissed at him to shut up, but he could not stop giggling and remembering the hot afternoon, and poor Billy Boy, and how they'd been drinking Coca-Cola from bright-red aluminum cans, and how they'd started on the day's march, and how a little while later poor Billy Boy stepped on the mine, and how it made a tiny little sound—*poof*—and how Billy Boy stood there with his mouth wide open, looking down at where his foot had been blown off, and how finally Billy Boy sat down very casually, not saying a word, with his foot lying behind him, most of it still in the boot.

He giggled louder—he could not stop. He bit his arm, trying to stifle it, but remembering: "War's over, Billy," the men had said in consolation, but Billy Boy got scared and started crying and said he was about to die. "Nonsense," the medic said, Doc Peret, but Billy Boy kept bawling, tightening up, his face going pale and transparent and his veins popping out. Scared stiff. Even when Doc Peret stuck him with morphine, Billy Boy kept crying.

"Shut up!" the big soldier hissed, but Private First Class Paul Berlin could not stop. Giggling and remembering, he covered his mouth. His eyes stung, remembering how it was when Billy Boy died of fright.

"Shut up!"

But he could not stop giggling, the same way Billy Boy could not stop bawling that afternoon.

Afterward Doc Peret had explained: "You see, Billy Boy really died of a heart attack. He was scared he was gonna die—so scared he had himself a heart attack—and that's what really killed him. I seen it before."

So they wrapped Billy in a plastic poncho, his eyes still wide open and scared stiff, and they carried him over the meadow to a rice paddy, and then when the Medevac helicopter arrived, they carried him through the paddy and put him aboard, and the mortar rounds were falling everywhere, and the helicopter pulled up, and Billy Boy came tumbling out, falling slowly and then faster, and the paddy water sprayed up as if Billy Boy had just executed a long and dangerous dive, as if trying to escape Graves Registration, where he would be tagged and sent home under a flag, dead of a heart attack.

"Shut up!" the soldier hissed, but Paul Berlin could not stop giggling, remembering: scared to death.

Later they waded in after him, probing for Billy Boy with their rifle butts, elegantly and del-

Where have you

oh, where have you gone,

Getting Students Involved

Cooperative Learning
Storyboard. Have students work in groups of four or five to create a storyboard for the selection. Each group should appoint a recorder to take notes. Have groups identify which scenes should be included and then decide how to organize the flashbacks and daydream sequences. Have students divide responsibility for creating the panels and assembling the storyboard. Groups should display their storyboards, and discuss similarities and differences.

Enrichment Activity
Character Interview. Have students work in small groups to conduct interviews with Paul, Toby, or Billy Boy about his war experiences. Have each group list questions for the soldier to answer. Groups should then exchange questions and provide the soldier's responses. Answers should be consistent with what is known about the characters. Groups might select representatives to enact the interview for the class.

Assessing Learning

Observation Assessment
Use the following criteria to assess students' responses to the story:

A = Always   S = Sometimes   R = Rarely

Characteristic	Date	Rating
Asks questions to clarify understanding		
Shares interpretations		
Uses text to evaluate personal views		
Challenges text		

moon move, or the clouds moving across the moon. Wounded in action, dead of fright. A fine war story. He would tell it to his father, how Billy Boy had been scared to death, never letting on . . . He could not stop.

The soldier smothered him. He tried to fight back, but he was weak from the giggles.

The moon was under the clouds and the column was moving. The soldier helped him up. "You OK now, buddy?"

"Sure."

"What was so bloody funny?"

"Nothing."

"You can get killed, laughing that way."

"I know. I know that."

"You got to stay calm, buddy." The soldier handed him his rifle. "Half the battle, just staying calm. You'll get better at it," he said. "Come on, now."

He turned away and Private First Class Paul Berlin hurried after him. He was still shivering.

He would do better once he reached the sea, he thought, still smiling a little. A funny war story that he would tell to his father, how Billy Boy Watkins was scared to death. A good joke. But even when he smelled salt and heard the sea, he could not stop being afraid.

icately probing for Billy Boy in the stinking paddy, singing—some of them—*Where have you gone, Billy Boy, Billy Boy, oh, where have you gone, charming Billy?* Then they found him. Green and covered with algae, his eyes still wide open and scared stiff, dead of a heart attack suffered while——

"Shut up!" the soldier said loudly, shaking him.

But Private First Class Paul Berlin could not stop. The giggles were caught in his throat, drowning him in his own laughter: scared to death like Billy Boy.

Giggling, lying on his back, he saw the

WHERE HAVE YOU GONE, CHARMING BILLY? 203

Critical Thinking
Interpreting
? Why do the soldiers sing? [Possible response: Singing is a way of alleviating the tension and stress of this horrible event.]

Elements of Literature
Theme and Character
? What is the principal conflict in this story? [the conflict within Paul to master his fear] What has Paul learned about war? [The fear is constant; he won't get over it.] Note the recurring mention of his father.

Resources
Selection Assessment
Formal Assessment
• Selection Test, p. 30
Test Generator (One-Stop Planner)
• CD-ROM

Making the Connections

Connecting to the Theme:
"Exiles, Castaways, and Strangers"
When students have finished reading the story, guide a discussion of the theme. Point out that the title of the collection stresses the different ways in which individuals can feel isolated. Certainly, Paul Berlin fits this description. He is new to his patrol, "the new guy," a stranger.

He doesn't know his fellow soldiers, and his situation and surroundings are alien to him. He feels like a castaway or exile, sent off to Vietnam by his own country. He is cut off and longs for his father and home.

Cultural Connections
Students from other cultures may have different perspectives on war. Classroom discussion might include issues that go beyond O'Brien's story, perhaps the unrest the Vietnam War caused around the world, or the purpose and value of war in general and in solving specific conflicts.

MEET THE WRITER

The Power of the Heart

It was the Vietnam War that made **Tim O'Brien** (1946–   ) a writer. He was drafted immediately after graduating from Macalester College in St. Paul, Minnesota, in 1968. He then spent two years as an infantry-man in Vietnam.

When he returned from Vietnam, O'Brien used his imagination to cope with memories of the war. Many of his stories are told from the point of view of a young soldier named Paul Berlin. These stories eventually grew into a novel called *Going After Cacciato,* which won the National Book Award in 1979. "Where Have You Gone, Charming Billy?" was used, with some changes, as Chapter 31 of the novel.

In 1990, O'Brien published *The Things They Carried,* referring to the burdens, both material and emotional, carried by the American soldiers in Vietnam—the M-16 rifles, the comic books, the flak jackets, and the fear. In 1994, he published *In the Lake of the Woods,* another novel about his persistent theme—the lingering memory of Vietnam. The following account is from *If I Die in a Combat Zone, Box Me Up and Ship Me Home.* Mad Mark was the platoon leader.

❝ One of the most persistent and appalling thoughts which lumbers through your mind as you walk through Vietnam at night is the fear of getting lost, of becoming detached from the others, of spending the night alone in that frightening and haunted countryside. It was dark. We walked in a single file, perhaps three yards apart. Mad Mark took us along a crazy, wavering course. We veered off the road, through clumps of trees, through tangles of bamboo and grass, zigzagging through grave-yards of dead Vietnamese who lay there under conical mounds of dirt and clay. The man to the front and the man to the rear were the only holds on security and sanity. We followed the man in front like a blind man after his dog, like Dante following Virgil through the Inferno, and we prayed that the man had not lost his way, that he hadn't lost contact with the man to his front. We tensed the muscles around our eyeballs and peered straight ahead. We hurt ourselves staring at the man's back. We strained. We dared not look away for fear the man might fade and dis-sipate and turn into absent shadow. Some-times, when the jungle closed in, we reached out to him, touched his shirt.

The man to the front is civilization. He is the United States of America and every friend you have ever known; he is Erik and blond girls and a mother and a father. He is your life, and he is your altar and God combined. And, for the man stumbling along behind you, you alone are his torch. ❞

Assessing Learning

Check Test: True-False
1. Paul Berlin is in his first day of combat. [True]
2. Billy Boy dies of loss of blood after he steps on a land mine. [False]
3. Paul focuses on reaching the sea. [True]
4. Toby offers Paul advice on how to be a good soldier. [True]
5. By the end of the story, Paul has overcome his fear. [False]

Standardized Test Preparation
For practice with standardized test format specific to this selection, see
• *Standardized Test Preparation,* p. 28

For centuries, women have gone to war, but their contributions have rarely been acknowledged. Lily Lee Adams was one of the thousands of women who cared for wounded and dying soldiers in Vietnam. She served with the Army Nurse Corps at the Twelfth Evacuation Hospital in Cu Chi from 1969 to 1970.

The Friendship Only Lasted a Few Seconds

Lily Lee Adams

> He said "Mom,"
> And I responded
> And became her.   **A**
> I never lied
> 5 to him.
> And I couldn't
> Explain that to others.
> I got all and more back.
> But the friendship
> 10 Only lasted a few seconds.   **B**
>
> And he called me Mary.   **C**
> I wished she could
> Be there for him.
> I felt I was in   **D**
> 15 Second place,
> But I did the
> Best I could
> And the friendship
> Only lasted a few seconds.
>
> 20 And he told me,
> "I don't believe this,
> I'm dying for nothing."
> Then he died.
> Again, the friendship
> 25 Only lasted a few seconds.

> How can the World
> Understand any of this?
> How can I keep the   **E**
> World from forgetting?
> 30 After all the friendship
> Only lasted a few seconds.

Vietnam Women's Memorial in Washington, D.C.

WHERE HAVE YOU GONE, CHARMING BILLY? 205

Connecting Across Texts

MAKING MEANINGS

First Thoughts

1. Possible responses: I didn't understand how he could laugh at Billy's death. I understood his reaction; he was under stress and couldn't control his emotions. He was hysterical with fear.

Shaping Interpretations

2. The use of the song is ironic because its cheery tone contrasts with the horror of Billy's death. (The song is about a boy who goes to seek a wife, "but she's a young thing and cannot leave her mother.")

3. It is ironic that Billy dies from fear, not from his terrible wound. It is ironic that instead of being taken away with dignity, his body falls from the helicopter.

4. He has discovered that war is terrifying, unfair, brutal, and indifferent to individual life. He has also discovered that he can be made hysterical with fear. Possible themes: "War is hell." Fear can be as destructive as the cause of the fear.

5. He expects the sea to bring him safety and an end to fear. Instead, his fear is still with him.

6. He is an outsider in Vietnam and in the army, where he is the "new guy." He is exiled from his family and home. In a year, he might be hardened and able to control his fear; or, he might be home and in emotional trouble; or, he might be dead.

Connecting with the Text

7. Answers will vary. Some will prefer a more heroic treatment. Others will appreciate the honesty.

8. It emphasizes the fragility of life, the need for contact, the fear of dying.

Extending the Text

9. Sample answer: Like the movie *Born on the Fourth of July* (1989), also about Vietnam, Paul's story focuses on the brutal reality of war. Unlike *Saving Private Ryan* (1998), about World War II, it does not have a hero or victory.

MAKING MEANINGS

First Thoughts

[respond]

1. What was your reaction to Paul's uncontrolled giggling at the story's end?

Shaping Interpretations

[interpret]

2. On page 199 the writer quotes a bit of the children's song that gives the story its title. (If you don't know the rest of this song, see if you can find someone who does.) What is **ironic** about the author's use of this particular song in a war story?

[analyze]

3. There is a central **irony** in warfare, which has to do with the fact that soldiers kill people they do not even know. What is ironic about how Billy Boy dies? about how his body is removed?

[synthesize]

4. What do you think Paul has discovered about war and about himself on his first day of combat? What **theme,** or central idea, relating to war have you become aware of by sharing Paul's experiences?

[interpret]

5. In a sense, this is a story about a hero's journey, which often takes the form of a **quest**—a search for something of great value. What is it that Paul expects to find at the sea, the end point of his journey? Ironically, what does he find instead?

[predict]

6. In what ways is Paul an exile and an outsider? What do you imagine Paul will be like a year after this story ends?

Connecting with the Text

[respond]

7. How do you feel about the way this writer has treated the subject of war?

[synthesize]

 8. Look back at the poem written by a nurse in Vietnam (see *Connections* on page 205). How does it affect your understanding of O'Brien's story and of the Vietnam War?

Extending the Text

[apply]

 9. Think about the story's **historical context.** How does Paul's story resemble other war stories you have read or war movies you have seen? How is it different?

Reading Check

Tell the story of Billy Boy's death to a partner, as you imagine a war correspondent might report it on the nightly news. Tell **what** happened, **whom** it happened to, **where** it happened, **when** it happened, **why** it happened, and **how** it happened.

Reading Check

Possible news report: In Vietnam today, William Watkins died of a heart attack after experiencing severe trauma to his lower extremities as a result of a land mine that detonated in his vicinity. His body was evacuated by helicopter to be returned home to his family.

CHOICES: Building Your Portfolio

Writer's Notebook

1. Collecting Ideas for Analyzing a Story

Focusing on character.  Now that you've met Paul Berlin, what can you say about him as a fictional character? In many stories, we come to know characters so well that we make **inferences** about why they behave the way they do and **predict** what they'll do next. Use a chart like the one below to gather details about Paul Berlin or a character in another story from Collections 1 to 3. Save your notes for the Writer's Workshop on page 240.

Character: Father in "Distillation"

Traits: hard-working, strong, brave, loving

Actions/speeches reveal character: saves Lazaro; shelters children from hail

What character wants: to feed family, protect children

What others think: narrator sees father's strength/courage

How character changes: doesn't really change—narrator's perception changes

---

Creative Writing

2. Happy Memories?

Paul Berlin pulls a happy childhood experience out of his memory to help him when he feels afraid. Recall an experience from your childhood that makes you feel happy or one that triggers other feelings. (Refer to your Quickwrite notes.) Write about that experience, recapturing its sights, sounds, and other sensory details. Include your thoughts about what the experience might reveal about life or even about the sources of joy or pain.

Supporting an Opinion

3. Why War?

War is a recurring subject in literature and film. Why do you think writers and moviemakers so often choose war as their subject? Write an essay proposing answers to this question. To support your opinion, give reasons why people *write* about war and its violence and why others *read* about it. At the end of your essay, explain how war stories like this one affect *you*.

History/Research

4. I Remember . . .

Suppose you are a historian who wants to collect firsthand data on the Vietnam era. Work with a partner to collect **oral histories** about the war years. Before you conduct an interview, be sure you make a list of the questions you want to ask your subject. You might want to record your interviews on audiotape, or even videotape the session. You'll have to decide on the final format you want your oral histories to take: Will you present them on audiotape, videotape, or in print?

Visual Literacy

5. Words into Graphics

Sometimes graphics communicate information more directly than words. Use the information on page 200 to create one or more graphics. You might make a **time line** of events or a **bar graph** or **pie graph** of the numbers of casualties. What other kinds of graphics can you create using the information given?

Grading Timesaver

Rubrics for each Choices assignment appear on p. 112 in the *Portfolio Management System*.

CHOICES: Building Your Portfolio

1. **Writer's Notebook** You might suggest that students freewrite or create a cluster diagram to develop ideas about their character.
2. **Creative Writing** Suggest that students create a chart like the following one to generate sensory details.

Senses	Details
Sight	
Sound	
Smell	
Touch	
Taste	

3. **Supporting an Opinion** Allow students to meet in small groups to discuss the questions before they begin writing.
4. **History/Research** Students might compile their oral histories into a documentary. The presentations could combine video- and audiotaped recordings with their own narrative that ties the recordings together.
5. **Visual Literacy** Have students meet as a group to compare their work and to discuss the advantages of each type of graphic.

LANGUAGE LINK

The point of the exercise suggested in the third paragraph is to help students realize how their own imaginations work with a writer's to re-create a scene. The writer needs only to supply a few details, and our own imaginations will at once provide the rest. (You might review the essay on setting on pp. 50–51.) The use of our own imaginations as we read is an important concept that should be stressed over and over again.

Try It Out
Possible Answers

(1) The description of the soldiers in the rice paddy (first paragraph, column 1, p. 198); senses—sight, hearing, touch. (2) The description of soldiers in the rice paddy (paragraph beginning "Ahead of him," column 2, p. 198); senses—sight, touch, smell. (3) Description of the "sleeping village" (paragraph beginning "Once they skirted," column 2, p. 199); senses—smell, hearing, sight. (4) Description of Billy's death (first paragraph, column 1, p. 202); senses—hearing, touch, sight, taste. (5) Description of Billy's body falling from the helicopter (last paragraph, column 1, p. 202); senses—touch, sight, sound.

VOCABULARY

The questions are important in this exercise. Possibilities:
Skirted: What situations would you want to *skirt*? (traffic jam, sensitive issue, danger) What places on earth could be called *fecund*? (swamps, marshes, rice paddies) What places are the opposite of *fecund*? (parched field, paved road, desert)

Resources ———————————

LANGUAGE LINK `MINI-LESSON`

Imagery Puts Us There

Handbook of Literary Terms
H E L P

See Imagery.

Image comes from the Latin word *imago,* which means "copy." In a sense, an **image** is a copy of a sensory experience—a **sight**, a **sound**, a **smell**, a **taste**, or a **touch**.

For example, we read that Paul pretends he is a boy again, camping with his dad "in the midnight summer along the Des Moines River." He imagines "that when he opened his eyes, his father would be there by the campfire and they would talk softly about whatever came to mind and then roll into their sleeping bags." We can share Paul's remembered experience here because O'Brien gives us images of sight (a campfire in the darkness), of sound (talking quietly), and of touch (rolling into the softness of a sleeping bag on the hard ground).

To see how the right images can prompt your own imagination to supply all kinds of other details, describe to a partner exactly what *you* think that campsite was like. How different are your imagined pictures of Paul's memory?

Try It Out

➤Look back through the story, and write down at least five passages that use images that help you share the sights, smells, and sounds of Paul's journey. Identify the senses to which each image appeals.

➤Look carefully at your own descriptive passages. Ask: Have I made my people and settings real? Have I told how they looked, smelled, tasted, sounded, or felt?

VOCABULARY `HOW TO OWN A WORD`

WORD BANK
fecund
skirted

Meaning Maps

On page 200, Tim O'Brien uses the word *inertia* to describe a feeling of being pulled as if by a train. *Inertia* is a hard word to use. Many people think of it only as laziness or inactivity. The dictionary calls it the "tendency of an object in motion to keep moving in the same direction or of an object at rest to remain at rest, unless the object is affected by another force." Look at the meaning map one person made to understand this tough but important word.

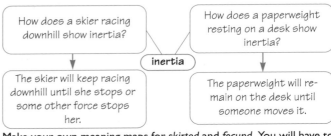

Make your own meaning maps for *skirted* and *fecund*. You will have to think of your own questions and answers.

Language Link Quick Check

Identify the senses to which the following images appeal. [Answers may vary.]

1. The soldiers walked through the crackling leaves. [hearing, touch, sight]

2. Paul clicked off the safety on his rifle. [hearing]

3. The mist hung low. [sight, touch]

4. The soldier tasted the gritty, muddy water. [taste, touch]

5. His injured leg throbbed. [touch]

Before You Read

THE BET

Make the Connection

The Search for Meaning

Would you give up all human company for years to win an amazing fortune? A character in this famous Russian story bets that he can do it, and his voluntary solitude raises some big questions—for him and for readers.

Quickwrite

Think about a time when you chose to be alone for a while. Maybe you needed to study to pass a test, or you may have wanted to be alone to think about an important decision. Jot down the details of your experience. What did you learn from your solitude?

Elements of Literature

Ambiguity: More Than One Meaning?

The **theme,** or overall meaning, of a story is almost never stated directly by the writer in any one place in the text. In fact, few writers want to reduce the meaning of their stories to *one* fixed and final statement. Instead, writers expect readers to make their own meaning after looking at the complex interplay of all the elements in the story. Because readers bring their own values and experiences to the reading of any text, individual interpretations are bound to differ.

Some interpretations even go beyond what the writer consciously intended the story to mean. "The Bet" is a striking example of a story that raises more questions than it answers. Its theme is particularly **ambiguous,** or open to a variety of interpretations.

> The **theme,** or overall meaning, of a story is **ambiguous** when the elements that make up the story are open to many interpretations. *For more on Theme, see pages 182–183 and the Handbook of Literary Terms.*

Reading Skills and Strategies

Making Inferences About Theme

How would you go about determining the theme of a story? You'll need to make **inferences,** or guesses based on clues in the story: You'll look at the title, at whether the characters change, and at what they learn. You'll look, too, for **key passages** that seem to hint at the author's message. In "The Bet," for example, the lawyer's letter certainly merits a careful look.

(HRW) go.hrw.com
LE0 10-3

THE BET **209**

Preteaching Vocabulary

Summary ■ ■ ■

Set in Russia in 1885, this story begins with a flashback. An elderly banker remembers a dinner-party argument fifteen years earlier concerning the relative humaneness of capital punishment versus life imprisonment. When a young lawyer claimed he would choose the latter, the banker bet him two million he couldn't stay in solitary confinement for five years. The lawyer took the bet, boasting he could do it for fifteen years. Since then, the lawyer has been confined in the banker's lodge. He can have books, wine, music, and other things, but cannot see or talk to anyone. We learn about his confinement: his solace in music; his loneliness, stoicism, dissipation, hysteria, ecstasy in learning, religious study, and disjointed reading. Now, fifteen years later, the banker is about to lose his bet, which will bankrupt him. On the eve of the prisoner's release, the banker wants to kill him. Entering the lodge, he finds the eerie, emaciated man asleep before a letter renouncing the money, all earthly pleasures, and even wisdom. Overjoyed but ashamed, the banker quietly leaves. Later, the prisoner slips away, forfeiting the wager, and the banker locks up the letter.

Ⓐ English Language Learners
Using Context Clues
❓ What context clues suggest the meaning of the phrase *capital punishment?* ["Death penalty" is mentioned in the following sentence.]

"The death penalty is more humane than imprisonment for life."

The Verandah at Liselund (detail) (1916) by Peter Ilsted. Oil on canvas.
Courtesy of Adelson Galleries, New York.

The Bet

Anton Chekhov
translated by Constance Garnett

1

It was a dark autumn night. The old banker was walking up and down his study and remembering how, fifteen years before, he had given a party one autumn evening. There had been many clever men there, and there had been interesting conversations. Among other things, they had talked of capital punishment. The majority of the guests, among whom were many journalists and intellectual men, disapproved of the death penalty. They considered that form of punishment out of date, immoral, and unsuitable for Christian states.[1] In the opinion of some of them, the death penalty ought to be replaced everywhere by imprisonment for life.

"I don't agree with you," said their host, the banker. "I have not tried either the death penalty or imprisonment for life, but if one may judge a priori,[2] the death penalty is more

1. **Christian states:** countries in which Christianity is the main religion.
2. **a priori** (ā′prī·ôr′ī): here, on the basis of theory rather than experience.

Portrait of the Painter Konstantin Alekseevich Korovin (1891) by Valentin Serov. Oil on canvas. Tretiakov Gallery, Moscow, Russia.
Scala/Art Resource, New York.

Resources: Print and Media

Reading
- *Graphic Organizers for Active Reading,* p. 14
- *Words to Own,* p. 14
- *Audio CD Library*
  Disc 7, Track 4

Elements of Literature
- *Literary Elements*
  Transparency 7
  Worksheet, p. 22

Writing and Language
- *Daily Oral Grammar*
  Transparency 14
- *Grammar and Language Links*
  Worksheet, p. 25
- *Language Workshop CD-ROM*

Assessment
- *Formal Assessment,* p. 32
- *Portfolio Management System,* p. 114
- *Standardized Test Preparation,* p. 30
- *Test Generator (One-Stop Planner CD-ROM)*

Internet
- go.hrw.com (keyword: LE0 10-3)

Resources

Listening
Audio CD Library
A gripping recording of the story appears in the *Audio CD Library:*
- Disc 7, Track 4

Elements of Literature
Irony
For additional instruction on irony, see *Literary Elements:*
- Transparency 7
- Worksheet, p. 22

FROM THE EDITOR'S DESK
Chekhov often wrote about exiles and strangers. In this famous story, the character's exile is self-imposed. Though the story is challenging, teachers have told us that it is a classroom favorite.

RESPONDING TO THE ART
Valentin Serov (1865–1911) was primarily a portraitist who paid homage in this portrait to Konstantin Alekseevich Korovin (1863–1939), a Russian scene painter.
Activity. Ask students what draws their attention in this painting. What colors do they see, and what mood do the colors create? What characteristics of the sitter are suggested by the portrait? What details in the portrait suggest that the sitter is an artist?

Reaching All Students

Struggling Readers
Making Inferences About Theme is introduced as a reading skill on p. 209. One good strategy to use with making inferences about theme is Save the Last Word for Me. For information on using this strategy, see p. 77 in the *Reading Strategies Handbook* in the front of the *Reading Skills and Strategies* binder.

English Language Learners
Point out that the two main characters in the story are educated and middle class; the banker is wealthy. Only a very small number of people in Russia were so privileged. The language Chekhov uses reflects the characters' level of education. Note also that Chekhov makes numerous references to aspects of their lifestyle, such as musical talent, literacy, wine, and books.

Advanced Learners
Ask students to read the anecdote on p. 218 in which Chekhov expresses his understanding of the meaning of life by comparing it to a carrot. Then, have students analyze this story and consider the question of whether it reinforces or contradicts Chekhov's carrot statement.

A Elements of Literature

Ambiguous Theme

? Based on this early passage, what do you think the story's theme will be? [Possible responses: The death penalty is immoral. Life always has value, even under the worst circumstances. People often make decisions affecting their entire lives without giving it much thought. Passion can destroy lives.]

B Critical Thinking

Extending the Text

? Do you think such a bet would ever be carried out in real life? [Possible answers: No, no one would ever voluntarily accept imprisonment. Yes, some people want money badly enough that they would do anything for it, even give up years of their lives.]

C Critical Thinking

Analyzing

? How has the banker's view of the bet changed? [The banker now thinks that the bet cannot prove what it was intended to prove, and he has trouble seeing the point of it all. He believes it was a mistake for everyone.]

D Elements of Literature

Conflict

? Although the plot appears simple on the surface, it is complicated by the conflicts between and within characters. What conflicts have you identified so far? Are they internal or external? [the external conflict between the banker and the young lawyer; the internal conflict within the banker over the capriciousness of the bet; the prisoner's internal conflict as he confronts his confinement and loneliness]

moral and more humane than imprisonment for life. Capital punishment kills a man at once, but lifelong imprisonment kills him slowly. Which executioner is the more humane, he who kills you in a few minutes or he who drags the life out of you in the course of many years?"

"Both are equally immoral," observed one of the guests, "for they both have the same object—to take away life. The state is not God. It has not the right to take away what it cannot restore when it wants to."

Among the guests was a young lawyer, a young man of five-and-twenty. When he was asked his opinion, he said: "The death sentence and the life sentence are equally immoral, but if I had to choose between the death penalty and imprisonment for life, I would certainly choose the second. To live anyhow is better than not at all."

A lively discussion arose. The banker, who was younger and more nervous in those days, was suddenly carried away by excitement; he struck the table with his fist and shouted at the young man: "It's not true! I'll bet you two million you wouldn't stay in solitary confinement for five years."

"If you mean that in earnest," said the young man, "I'll take the bet, but I would stay not five, but fifteen years."

"Fifteen? Done!" cried the banker. "Gentlemen, I stake two million!"

"Agreed! You stake your millions and I stake my freedom!" said the young man.

And this wild, senseless bet was carried out! The banker, spoiled and frivolous, with millions beyond his reckoning, was delighted at the bet. At supper he made fun of the young man and said: "Think better of it, young man, while there is still time. To me two million is a trifle, but you are losing three or four of the best years of your life. I say three or four, because you won't stay longer. Don't forget either, you unhappy man, that voluntary confinement is a great deal harder to bear than compulsory. The thought that you have the right to step out in liberty at any moment will poison your whole existence in prison. I am sorry for you."

And now the banker, walking to and fro, remembered all this and asked himself: "What was the object of that bet? What is the good of that man's losing fifteen years of his life and my throwing away two million? Can it prove that the death penalty is better or worse than imprisonment for life? No, no. It was all nonsensical and meaningless. On my part it was the caprice of a pampered man, and on his part simple greed for money. . . ."

Then he remembered what followed that evening. It was decided that the young man should spend the years of his captivity under the strictest supervision in one of the lodges in the banker's garden. It was agreed that for fifteen years he should not be free to cross the threshold of the lodge, to see human beings, to hear the human voice, or to receive letters and newspapers. He was allowed to have a musical instrument and books and was allowed to write letters, to drink wine, and to smoke. By the terms of the agreement, the only relations he could have with the outer world were by a little window made purposely for that object. He might have anything he wanted—books, music, wine, and so on—in any quantity he desired, by writing an order, but could receive them only through the window. The agreement provided for every detail and every trifle that would make his imprisonment strictly solitary, and bound the young man to stay there *exactly* fifteen years, beginning from twelve o'clock of November 14, 1870, and ending at twelve o'clock of November 14, 1885. The slightest attempt on his part to break the conditions, if only two minutes before the end, released the banker from the obligation to pay him two million.

For the first year of his confinement, as far as one could judge from his brief notes, the prisoner suffered severely from loneliness and depression. The sounds of the piano could be heard continually day and night from his lodge. He refused wine and tobacco. Wine, he wrote, excites the desires, and desires are the worst foes of the prisoner; and besides, nothing could

WORDS TO OWN

compulsory (kəm·pul'sə·rē) *adj.:* required; enforced.
caprice (kə·prēs') *n.:* sudden notion or desire.

Using Students' Strengths

Visual Learners

To help students follow the sequence of events, suggest that they create a time line beginning with the evening of the argument and proceeding through the imprisonment to the end of the story. Then, have students retell in their own words the major events of the story in chronological order.

Interpersonal Learners

Have students discuss how the lawyer changes during the story. Then, have them work in pairs to prepare an interview that demonstrates the prisoner's state of mind at a particular point in the narrative. One student should take the role of the prisoner, the other that of the interviewer. Ask them to present the interview to the class.

Intrapersonal Learners

Have students imagine themselves in the lawyer's situation and write a diary entry for one day of their imprisonment. They might choose any time during the confinement and describe how they spent the day, what they read, what music they played, what they thought, how they felt, and what their plans are for the next day.

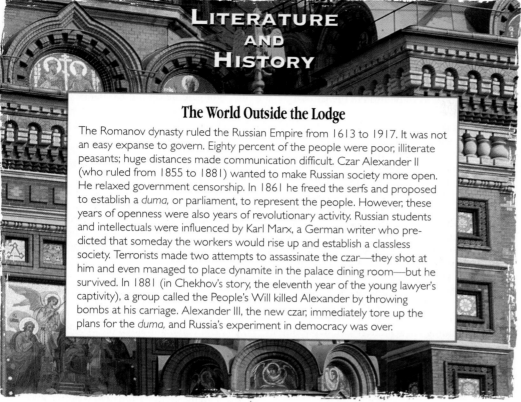

The World Outside the Lodge

The Romanov dynasty ruled the Russian Empire from 1613 to 1917. It was not an easy expanse to govern. Eighty percent of the people were poor, illiterate peasants; huge distances made communication difficult. Czar Alexander II (who ruled from 1855 to 1881) wanted to make Russian society more open. He relaxed government censorship. In 1861 he freed the serfs and proposed to establish a *duma,* or parliament, to represent the people. However, these years of openness were also years of revolutionary activity. Russian students and intellectuals were influenced by Karl Marx, a German writer who predicted that someday the workers would rise up and establish a classless society. Terrorists made two attempts to assassinate the czar—they shot at him and even managed to place dynamite in the palace dining room—but he survived. In 1881 (in Chekhov's story, the eleventh year of the young lawyer's captivity), a group called the People's Will killed Alexander by throwing bombs at his carriage. Alexander III, the new czar, immediately tore up the plans for the *duma,* and Russia's experiment in democracy was over.

be more dreary than drinking good wine and seeing no one. And tobacco spoiled the air of his room. In the first year the books he sent for were principally of a light character—novels with a complicated love plot, sensational and fantastic stories, and so on.

In the second year the piano was silent in the lodge, and the prisoner asked only for the classics. In the fifth year music was <u>audible</u> again, and the prisoner asked for wine. Those who watched him through the window said that all that year he spent doing nothing but eating and drinking and lying on his bed, frequently yawning and talking angrily to himself. He did not read books. Sometimes at night he would sit down to write; he would spend hours writing and in the morning tear up all that he had written. More than once he could be heard crying.

In the second half of the sixth year the prisoner began <u>zealously</u> studying languages, philosophy, and history. He threw himself eagerly into these studies—so much so that the banker had enough to do to get him the books he ordered. In the course of four years, some six hundred volumes were procured at his request. It was during this period that the banker received the following letter from his prisoner:

"My dear Jailer, I write you these lines in six languages. Show them to people who know the languages. Let them read them. If they find not one mistake, I implore you to fire a shot in the

WORDS TO OWN
audible (ô′də·bəl) *adj.*: capable of being heard.
zealously (zel′əs·lē) *adv.*: fervently; devotedly.

THE BET 213

Crossing the Curriculum

A **Vocabulary Note**

The Prefix in-

Point out the word *indiscriminately* and explain that this word is constructed using the prefix *in-*, which means "not," "no," or "without." Since *discriminately* means "making careful choices," *indiscriminately* means "without making careful choices." Then, explain that the prefix *in-* takes different forms when it precedes different consonants. The word *impolite*, for example, includes the *im-* form of the prefix.

B **Struggling Readers**

Finding Sequence of Events

? Most of the events in the story have been told in a flashback up to this point. When did the events occur? [over the past fifteen years] When did the flashback begin? [in the second sentence of the story on p. 210] In this paragraph the story moves back into the present.

C **Reading Skills and Strategies**

Make Inferences About Theme

? Does this passage change your prediction of what the story's theme might be? Explain. [Possible response: It implies that freedom doesn't necessarily make life valuable. The banker was free and wasted his fortune and is now reduced to wanting to commit murder. The prisoner has made good use of his time, even though he was not free.]

garden. That shot will show me that my efforts have not been thrown away. The geniuses of all ages and of all lands speak different languages, but the same flame burns in them all. Oh, if you only knew what unearthly happiness my soul feels now from being able to understand them!" The prisoner's desire was fulfilled. The banker ordered two shots to be fired in the garden.

Then, after the tenth year, the prisoner sat immovably at the table and read nothing but the Gospels. It seemed strange to the banker that a man who in four years had mastered six hundred learned volumes should waste nearly a year over one thin book easy of comprehension. Theology[3] and histories of religion followed the Gospels.

A In the last two years of his confinement, the prisoner read an immense quantity of books quite <u>indiscriminately</u>. At one time he was busy with the natural sciences; then he would ask for Byron[4] or Shakespeare. There were notes in which he demanded at the same time books on chemistry, and a manual of medicine, and a novel, and some treatise on philosophy or theology. His reading suggested a man swimming in the sea among the wreckage of his ship and trying to save his life by greedily clutching first at one spar[5] and then at another.

2

B The old banker remembered all this and thought: "Tomorrow at twelve o'clock he will regain his freedom. By our arrangement I ought to pay him two million. If I do pay him, it is all over with me: I shall be utterly ruined."

C Fifteen years before, his millions had been beyond his reckoning; now he was afraid to ask himself which were greater, his debts or his assets. Desperate gambling on the Stock Exchange, wild speculation, and the excitability which he could not get over even in advancing years had by degrees led to the decline of his

---

3. **theology** (thē·äl′ə·jē): the study of religious teachings concerning God and God's relation to the world.
4. **Byron:** George Gordon Byron (1788–1824), known as Lord Byron, English Romantic poet.
5. **spar:** pole that supports or extends a ship's sail.

214 THE SHORT-STORY COLLECTIONS

---

fortune, and the proud, fearless, self-confident millionaire had become a banker of middling rank, trembling at every rise and fall in his investments. "Cursed bet!" muttered the old man, clutching his head in despair. "Why didn't the man die? He is only forty now. He will take my last penny from me, he will marry, will enjoy life, will gamble on the Exchange, while I shall look at him with envy like a beggar and hear from him every day the same sentence: 'I am indebted to you for the happiness of my life; let me help you!' No, it is too much! The one means of being saved from bankruptcy and disgrace is the death of that man!"

It struck three o'clock. The banker listened; everyone was asleep in the house, and nothing could be heard outside but the rustling of the chilled trees. Trying to make no noise, he took from a fireproof safe the key of the door which had not been opened for fifteen years, put on his overcoat, and went out of the house.

It was dark and cold in the garden. Rain was falling. A damp, cutting wind was racing about the garden, howling and giving the trees no rest. The banker strained his eyes but could see neither the earth nor the white statues, nor the lodge, nor the trees. Going to the spot where the lodge stood, he twice called the watchman. No answer followed. Evidently the watchman had sought shelter from the weather and was now asleep somewhere either in the kitchen or in the greenhouse.

"If I had the pluck to carry out my intention," thought the old man, "suspicion would fall first upon the watchman."

He felt in the darkness for the steps and the door and went into the entry of the lodge. Then he groped his way into a little passage and lighted a match. There was not a soul there. There was a bedstead with no bedding on it, and in the corner there was a dark cast-iron stove. The seals on the door leading to the prisoner's rooms were intact.

WORDS TO OWN

indiscriminately (in′di·skrim′i·nit·lē) *adv.*: without making careful choices or distinctions; randomly.

Skill Link

Recognizing Verbs

Use the following activity to evaluate students' ability to identify verbs and as preparation for the Grammar Link Mini-Lesson on active and passive verbs on p. 221. Remind students that a verb is a word that shows an action or expresses a state of being. A sentence must contain one verb and may have several. (For reference see the *Language Handbook* at the back

of this text.) Have students identify the verbs in each of the following sentences. (Verbs are underlined.)
1. The old banker <u>strides</u> back and forth as he <u>thinks</u> back about the argument that first night.
2. He <u>realizes</u> that it <u>was</u> a foolish mistake <u>to</u>

have <u>made</u> the bet, and <u>wonders</u> what he <u>can do</u> now.
3. Meanwhile, the prisoner <u>sits</u> up late and <u>ponders</u> what <u>will</u> <u>happen</u> tomorrow.
4. He no longer <u>cares</u> if he <u>wins</u> the bet or not.
5. The watchman <u>had</u> <u>deserted</u> his post outside the lodge.

When the match went out, the old man, trembling with emotion, peeped through the little window. A candle was burning dimly in the prisoner's room. He was sitting at the table. Nothing could be seen but his back, the hair on his head, and his hands. Open books were lying on the table, on the two easy chairs, and on the carpet near the table.

Five minutes passed and the prisoner did not once stir. Fifteen years' imprisonment had taught him to sit still. The banker tapped at the window with his finger, and the prisoner made no movement whatever in response. Then the banker cautiously broke the seals off the door and put the key in the keyhole. The rusty lock gave a grating sound and the door creaked. The banker expected to hear at once footsteps and a cry of astonishment, but three minutes passed and it was as quiet as ever in the room. He made up his mind to go in.

At the table a man unlike ordinary people was sitting motionless. He was a skeleton with the skin drawn tight over his bones, with long curls like a woman's, and a shaggy beard. His face was yellow with an earthy tint in it, his cheeks were hollow, his back long and narrow, and the hand on which his shaggy head was propped was so thin and delicate that it was dreadful to look at it. His hair was already streaked with silver, and seeing his emaciated, aged-looking face, no one would have believed that he was only forty. He was asleep. . . . In front of his bowed head there lay on the table a sheet of paper, on which there was something written in fine handwriting.

"Poor creature!" thought the banker, "he is asleep and most likely dreaming of the millions. And I have only to take this half-dead man, throw him on the bed, stifle him a little with the pillow, and the most conscientious expert would find no sign of a violent death. But let us first read what he has written here. . . ."

The banker took the page from the table and read as follows:

"Tomorrow at twelve o'clock I regain my freedom and the right to associate with other men, but before I leave this room and see the sunshine, I think it necessary to say a few words to you. With a clear conscience I tell you, as before God, who beholds me, that I despise freedom and life and health and all that in your books is called the good things of the world.

"For fifteen years I have been intently studying earthly life. It is true I have not seen the earth or men, but in your books I have drunk fragrant wine, I have sung songs, I have hunted stags and wild boars in the forests, I have loved women. . . . Beauties as ethereal as clouds, created by the magic of your poets and geniuses, have visited me at night and have whispered in my ears wonderful tales that have set my brain in a whirl. In your books I have climbed to the peaks of Elburz and Mont Blanc,[6] and from there I have seen the sun rise and have watched it at evening flood the sky, the ocean, and the mountaintops with gold and crimson. I have watched from there the lightning flashing over my head and cleaving the storm clouds. I have seen green forests, fields, rivers, lakes, towns. I have heard the singing of the sirens,[7] and the strains of the shepherds' pipes; I have touched the wings of comely devils who flew down to converse with me of God. . . . In your books I have flung myself into the bottomless pit, performed miracles, slain, burned towns, preached new religions, conquered whole kingdoms. . . .

"Your books have given me wisdom. All that the unresting thought of man has created in the ages is compressed into a small compass in my brain. I know that I am wiser than all of you.

"And I despise your books, I despise wisdom and the blessings of this world. It is all worthless, fleeting, illusory, and deceptive, like a mirage. You may be proud, wise, and fine, but

---

6. **Elburz** (el·boorz′) **and Mont Blanc** (mōn blän′): Elburz is a mountain range in northern Iran; Mont Blanc, in France, is the highest mountain in the Alps.

7. **sirens:** in Greek mythology, partly human female creatures who lived on an island and lured sailors to their death with their beautiful singing.

WORDS TO OWN

ethereal (ē·thir′ē·əl) *adj.*: light and delicate; unearthly.
cleaving (klēv′iŋ) *v.* used as *adj.*: splitting.
illusory (i·lo͞o′sə·rē) *adj.*: not real; based on false ideas.

THE BET **215**

Taking a Second Look

T215

A Critical Thinking

Extending the Text

❓ Do you think the prisoner would have felt this way if he had not been imprisoned? [Possible answers: Yes, because he seems to be idealistic and eventually he would have come to this conclusion. No, he reached this opinion only after fifteen years of solitary confinement.]

B Reading Skills and Strategies

Making Inferences About Theme

❓ What does this letter imply about the theme of the story? [Possible response: One aspect of the theme is that all of our accomplishments on earth are of little value.]

C Elements of Literature

Ambiguous Theme

❓ Does leaving the theme ambiguous strengthen or weaken the story? Explain. [Possible answers: It strengthens it because readers can dig deep into the story; an easy analysis isn't as interesting as a tough one. It makes the story weaker because it's too hard to know what the writer really means.]

D Advanced Learners

Philosophy of Life

❓ Why does the banker lock up the prisoner's letter in a fireproof safe? [Possible responses: The banker keeps it for evidence because he doesn't completely believe the prisoner's renunciation. He hides it away because he is ashamed of what the prisoner asserts and doesn't want others to know it.]

Resources

Selection Assessment

Formal Assessment
• Selection Test, p. 32.

Test Generator (One-Stop Planner)
• CD-ROM

"You have lost your reason and taken the wrong path."

death will wipe you off the face of the earth as though you were no more than mice burrowing under the floor, and your <u>posterity</u>, your history, your immortal geniuses will burn or freeze together with the earthly globe.

A "You have lost your reason and taken the wrong path. You have taken lies for truth and hideousness for beauty. You would marvel if, owing to strange events of some sort, frogs and lizards suddenly grew on apple and orange trees instead of fruit or if roses began to smell like a sweating horse; so I marvel at you who exchange heaven for earth. I don't want to understand you.

B "To prove to you in action how I despise all that you live by, I <u>renounce</u> the two million of which I once dreamed as of paradise and which now I despise. To deprive myself of the right to the money, I shall go out from here five minutes before the time fixed and so break the compact. . . ."

C When the banker had read this, he laid the page on the table, kissed the strange man on the head, and went out of the lodge, weeping. At no other time, even when he had lost heavily on the Stock Exchange, had he felt so great a contempt for himself. When he got home, he lay on his bed, but his tears and emotion kept him for hours from sleeping.

D Next morning the watchmen ran in with pale faces and told him they had seen the man who lived in the lodge climb out of the window into the garden, go to the gate, and disappear. The banker went at once with the servants to the lodge and made sure of the flight of his prisoner. To avoid arousing unnecessary talk, he took from the table the writing in which the millions were renounced and, when he got home, locked it up in the fireproof safe.

WORDS TO OWN

posterity (päs·ter′ə·tē) *n.*: descendants or all future generations.
renounce (ri·nouns′) *v.*: give up, especially by formal statement; reject.

The Verandah at Liselund (1916) by Peter Ilsted. Oil on canvas.

Courtesy of Adelson Galleries, New York.

Assessing Learning

Observation Assessment

Use the following criteria to assess students' written or oral responses to literature.

Key: A = always S = sometimes
      R = rarely N = never

Characteristic	Rating
Shows enjoyment of and involvement with literature	
Makes personal and universal connections to literature	
Gets beyond "I like/dislike" the literature	
Interprets the literature, giving evidence of multiple meanings	
Discusses author's control of elements in creating the literature	

THE BET **217**

RESPONDING TO THE ART

Peter Ilsted (1861–1933) was a member of the Danish "Copenhagen Interior School." Through his use of soft and muted colors, Ilsted explores the various ways that light changes throughout the day. As in *The Verandah at Liselund,* his work evokes a quiet and sometimes mysterious feeling. Many of his paintings and his well-known prints explore family life in Copenhagen.

Activity. You might ask students what they think of when they see a photo or painting of an open window. What mood do they sense in this painting? What details contribute to the mood? (Note how the canvas can be seen through the paint, and how that provides an interesting texture to the picture.)

Making the Connections

Connecting to the Theme: "Exiles, Castaways, and Strangers"

The theme of this collection reverberates throughout "The Bet." The young lawyer voluntarily places himself in exile when he accepts imprisonment. He becomes a castaway, lost to the society in which he had lived. When he repudiates books, society, wisdom, and knowledge at the end of the story, he still remains outside of society as an exile. Invite students to discuss the idea of voluntary exile. Do people in real life ever willingly go into exile? Why? How do the lawyer's choices compare to the choices made by characters in other stories in this collection?

Cultural Connections

Different cultures have different views of solitude. Some cultures see it as a useful strategy for personal well-being, while others view it as antisocial behavior or as a method of punishment. Invite students to explore the meanings of solitude in various cultures. How could a different view of solitude affect the outcome of this story?

T217

BROWSING IN THE FILES

About the Author. Although Chekhov addressed alienation in his writing, his actions indicate that humanity was of great importance to him. For example, during the later years in his life, he organized relief efforts for a cholera epidemic and famine. He also sought to improve the prison conditions in his country. His book *The Island of Sakhalin,* his only work of nonfiction, describes conditions at a remote Siberian prison.

A Critic's Comment. The English writer W. Somerset Maugham commented about Chekhov's characters: "His people are shadowy; but . . . though lacking the fine distinction of personality they have a common humanity. I despair of making myself clear when I say that they strike me less as persons than as human beings. Each one is as it were a part of everyone else, and the hurt that one does to another is bearable because in a way it is hurt that he does to himself. And because they are shadowy they remain secret. We understand them as little as we understand ourselves."

Writers on Writing. Chekhov once explained why readers are sometimes puzzled by his writing. "You confuse two things: solving a problem and stating a problem correctly. It is only the second that is obligatory for the artist." He then concludes, "My business is only to be talented, i.e., to be able to distinguish between important and unimportant statements, to be able to illuminate the characters and speak their language."

MEET THE WRITER
Master of Ironies

Anton Chekhov (1860–1904) was the grandson of a Russian serf—this means that his grandfather was a farm laborer who could be bought and sold with the land he worked. Eventually Chekhov's grandfather succeeded in purchasing his freedom and raising a family as a free man. Chekhov's father tried to move up the economic ladder by running a general store in a small town in southern Russia, but he did not prosper. The young Anton, trying in his turn to better himself, won a scholarship to medical school. While he was studying in Moscow, his father went bankrupt, and Chekhov had to support his parents, four brothers, and a sister. He managed to do this and stay in school by writing stories and sketches for humor magazines. These short, light pieces, published under an assumed name, earned Chekhov a popular following, a steady income, and an opportunity to develop as a writer. After receiving his medical degree, he practiced medicine for a short time only. He chose to continue writing instead. By the time he was in his thirties, Chekhov was recognized as a serious writer and was wealthy enough to purchase a country estate, an unexpected achievement for the grandson of a serf. In the last years of his short life, knowing he was dying from tuberculosis, Chekhov wrote five full-length plays, all dealing in some way with the theme of loss. Four of them are considered masterpieces of realistic drama: *The Sea Gull, Uncle*

Anton Chekhov and Leo Tolstoy.

Anton Chekhov in Yalta at the beginning of the 1900s.

Vanya, The Three Sisters, and *The Cherry Orchard.* Chekhov died tragically young, when he was only forty-four years old. The critic V. S. Pritchett says that the stories are Chekhov's life, tunes that his Russia put into his head.

66 'What is the meaning of life?' Olga [his wife] once asked in a letter . . . Chekhov replied: 'It is like asking what a carrot is. A carrot is a carrot and nothing more is known.' 99

Anton Chekhov reads his play *The Sea Gull* to the actors of the Art Theater.

Assessing Learning

Check Test: True-False

1. The young lawyer agrees to stay in confinement for five years. [False]
2. During his imprisonment, the lawyer reads hundreds of books. [True]
3. The banker decides to kill the lawyer to avoid paying him. [True]
4. Just before he would collect his winnings, the lawyer purposely loses the bet. [True]
5. At the end of the story, the banker gives the money for the bet to the poor. [False]

Standardized Test Preparation

For practice with standardized test format specific to this selection, see
- *Standardized Test Preparation,* p. 30

MAKING MEANINGS

MAKING MEANINGS

First Thoughts

[respond]

1. Who do you think won the bet, and what did he win? Compare answers with your classmates.

Shaping Interpretations

[analyze]

2. Imagine you are a psychologist observing the lawyer periodically during his confinement. Write a year-by-year **summary** of how he spends his time and what his emotional state appears to be. Use a **time line.**

```
Year 1                          Year 2
|_____|_____
is lonely, depressed            stops playing piano
reads escapist fiction
plays piano
refuses wine, tobacco
```

[evaluate]

3. After making the bet, the banker tells himself that "greed for money" was the lawyer's **motivation** for betting. Do you agree or disagree? Look for evidence in the text to support your view.

[conclude]

4. For fifteen years, the lawyer lives in exile. How does this experience affect him? How do your Quickwrite responses compare with his experience?

[synthesize]

5. Looking back, the banker believes he took the bet on "the caprice of a pampered man." How does he feel about himself at the end of the fifteen years? What do you think this reveals about Chekhov's view of what is important in life?

[evaluate]

6. Identify what *you* think is the story's most important passage. How would *you* interpret the story's **theme**? Discuss your statement of theme with other readers. Are several thematic focuses possible?

Connecting with the Text

[connect]

7. At the story's end, would you rather be the banker or the lawyer? Why?

Extending the Text

[interpret]

8. Russian history has been a long and troubled search for freedom. (See the article on page 213.) How do you think the political problems in the last years of the czar's reign might have influenced Chekhov's—and his characters'—ideas on freedom, materialism, and personal sacrifice?

[generalize]

9. Do you believe there is such a thing as "internal freedom"—the kind of freedom the lawyer comes to know in prison? Think of people imprisoned for their beliefs. Are they freer than their jailers? If so, how?

THE BET 219

Reading Check

a. Explain the terms of the bet.

b. At the end of fifteen years, what has happened to the banker?

c. After the same period, what has happened to the lawyer?

d. Why does the banker go to the lodge on the last night of the lawyer's captivity?

e. What decision does the lawyer announce in a letter, and why?

Reading Check

a. The banker bet the lawyer two million that he could not stay imprisoned without contact with the outside world for fifteen years.

b. He is deeply in debt and will be ruined if he pays off the bet to the lawyer.

c. He has studied and learned many things but is emotionally withdrawn and physically changed.

d. He plans to murder the lawyer.

e. He will violate the terms of the bet in order to show how much he despises money and all the things that other people see as important.

First Thoughts

1. Possible responses: Both won—the banker got to keep his money, and the lawyer gained wisdom and knowledge. Both lost—the lawyer lost his ability to relate to humanity, and the banker lost his self-respect.

Shaping Interpretations

2. Students' time lines will vary, but they should be supported by details from the text and should include statements about the prisoner's activities and state of mind.

3. Possible responses: Disagree—the lawyer offers to stay three times longer than the banker demands. Agree—in his letter he says he once dreamed of the money as paradise.

4. He has become alienated from other people, his health has deteriorated, he has gained knowledge, and he believes earthly pursuits are without value. Comparisons will vary.

5. He feels ashamed but is trying to protect himself from criticism. Perhaps Chekhov is showing what some people will do for money, or the value of self-respect.

6. There are many important passages. Possible themes: Freedom and social interaction are essential human needs. Earthly accomplishments are worthless in the face of death.

Connecting with the Text

7. Possible responses: The banker, because the lawyer has lost contact with humanity. The lawyer, because the banker is greedy and heartless. Neither, since both have extreme views.

Extending the Text

8. Possible answer: They may have caused him to reassess the meaning of freedom and material possessions.

9. Possible responses: Yes, no one can take internal freedom away. No, internal freedom is incomplete without the ability to move about in the world. Some students may say that people imprisoned for their beliefs are freer than their jailers because they have achieved a moral or spiritual freedom which transcends physical freedom. Other students may disagree, saying that imprisonment limits action on behalf of one's beliefs.

T219

Rubrics for each Choices assignment appear on p. 114 in the *Portfolio Management System*.

CHOICES:
Building Your Portfolio

1. **Writer's Notebook** Emphasize to students that the theme is not usually what the writer says about the subject, but what he or she thinks about it. They should be wary of taking the words of any character as a statement of theme. Remind students to save their work. It may be useful for prewriting for the Writer's Workshop at the end of this collection.

2. **Creative Writing/Dramatizing** You might suggest that students generate ideas for their written dialogue by having an extemporaneous conversation between the lawyer and a stranger. Have them discuss their dialogue and take notes of their ideas.

3. **Writing a Reflective Essay** Encourage students to close their eyes and visualize how they would fill one day of their confinement.

4. **Speaking and Listening** Encourage groups to use a chart, like the one that follows, to guide the discussion and record their ideas.

Lawyer's Views	Agree/ Disagree	Reasons

CHOICES: Building Your Portfolio

Writer's Notebook
1. Collecting Ideas for Analyzing a Story

Focusing on theme.
But what does it all *mean*? In a single sentence, try to express the **theme** of "The Bet" or of another story you've read in Collections 1 to 3. Use the chart below to help you. Remember:

• The theme expresses a general insight about human life or human nature.

• No single statement of theme is "correct."

• A story may have more than one theme.

Save your notes for the Writer's Workshop on page 240.

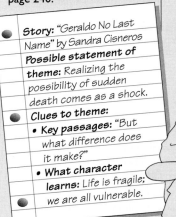

○ **Story:** *"Geraldo No Last Name" by Sandra Cisneros*
Possible statement of theme: *Realizing the possibility of sudden death comes as a shock.*
○ **Clues to theme:**
• **Key passages:** *"But what difference does it make?"*
• **What character learns:** *Life is fragile; we are all vulnerable.*
○

Creative Writing/ Dramatizing
2. Famous First Words

Suppose the fleeing lawyer finds himself at a village inn some distance from the lodge, among a group of strangers. He hasn't spoken to anyone in fifteen years, but he decides to confide his feelings to a stranger. Write a **dialogue** for the lawyer's first conversation as a "free" man. Work with a partner to develop the character of the confidant. How that person reacts to the lawyer will depend on his or her own background and values. Rehearse your **scene,** and present it to your class or group.

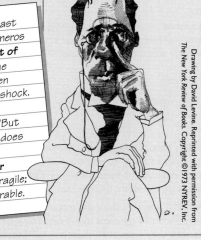

Anton Chekhov.

Drawing by David Levine. Reprinted with permission from The New York Review of Books. Copyright © 1973 NYREV, Inc.

Reflective Essay
3. Home Alone

Imagine yourself in the lawyer's place: What would you do if you were confined alone for one year? The rules include no human contact, no exit, no TV or radio, no VCR, no phone, no computer. You can ask for books, hobby supplies, musical instruments, and exercise equipment. Write a brief essay, telling how you imagine you'd spend 365 days (the lawyer spent 15 times that) alone. It seems unimaginable, but think about it. How *would* you spend the time?

Speaking and Listening
4. Philosophy of Life

In Chekhov's story, the lawyer's letter to his "jailer" is quite specific about his philosophy of life—what he considers important and unimportant and what freedom means to him. In a small group, read the letter, and then hold a **round-table discussion** of the lawyer's views. Choose a discussion leader who will make sure that all who speak offer reasons and examples to support their views. At the close of the discussion, prepare a **summary** for the class of the group's responses to the lawyer's philosophy.

Getting Students Involved

Enrichment
Chekhov's Views. Invite interested students who are working on Choice 4 to investigate Anton Chekhov's own philosophy of life. Have them meet as a group and compare the lawyer's views with those of Chekhov. Would Chekhov agree with this character?

Enrichment
Sequel. Challenge students who are working on Choice 2 to take the task one step further. Have them imagine a conversation that takes place one year after the lawyer has left his prison. Through the dialogue, have students examine what the lawyer has been doing, how he has survived, and how he now regards his fifteen years imprisonment and his decision to forfeit the two million.

GRAMMAR LINK

Active or Passive? Pick the Right Voice

Language Handbook
HELP

See Passive Voice, page 1028.

Technology HELP

See Language Workshop CD-ROM. Key word entry: voice.

Verbs that express action can be in the **active** or **passive voice.**

ACTIVE "At supper he made fun of the young man. . . ."
[The action is done *by* the subject, *he*.]

PASSIVE At supper the young man was made fun of.
[The action is done *to* the subject, *the young man*. The doer of the action is not even mentioned.]

In this story, Chekhov usually uses the active voice, but he moves to the passive voice more frequently after the lawyer becomes a prisoner. The passive voice emphasizes the lawyer's decreased ability to act for himself.

"He was allowed to have a musical instrument and books. . . ."

Try It Out

Find a paragraph in which Chekhov uses verbs in the passive voice. Make a list of the subjects and their passive verbs. How could you rephrase each sentence so that it uses an active verb?

A tip for writers: Writers and speakers often use the passive voice to conceal the person who performs the action. You might say "The machine was left on" instead of "Karl left the machine on" to save Karl's feelings or to hide the fact that Karl was responsible.

When you revise your own writing, circle your verbs, and notice the voice of each one. Be sure you use the passive voice only when you have a specific reason to downplay or conceal the doer of the action.

VOCABULARY   HOW TO OWN A WORD

WORD BANK	Yes or No?
compulsory	Be sure that you justify your answers to these questions.
caprice	1. If attendance is compulsory, are you free to stay home?
audible	2. Is a caprice something you think about for weeks?
zealously	3. Is a herd of elephants usually audible?
indiscriminately	4. Are you likely to act zealously when you believe in a cause?
ethereal	5. If you speak indiscriminately, might you regret it later?
cleaving	6. Would you call the music that comes from a harp ethereal?
illusory	7. If lightning is cleaving the clouds, are the clouds being separated?
posterity	8. Can you rely on illusory promises?
renounce	9. Do you look to posterity for help with current problems?
	10. If you renounce a bad habit, do you intend to stop it?

THE BET 221

GRAMMAR LINK

Have students review a piece of writing from their portfolios for examples of passive voice, circling the forms of *be* and the main verbs. Students should try to replace the passive verb phrases with active phrases.

Try It Out
Possible Answers
Students' selection and revisions of paragraphs will vary. Example: "More than once he could be heard crying" could be changed to "More than once they heard him crying."

VOCABULARY
Possible Answers
1. No, because *compulsory* means "required."
2. No, because *caprice* means "a sudden desire."
3. Yes, because they make a lot of noise when they move around.
4. Yes, because you are passionately devoted to it.
5. Yes, if you hurt someone's feelings. No, it depends on what is said and to whom it is said.
6. Yes, because harp music is delicate. No, because the sound is irritating.
7. Yes, because *cleaving* means "splitting."
8. No, because *illusory* means "not real."
9. No, because you cannot afford to wait that long, nor do you know whether or not help will be available.
10. Yes, because *renounce* means "to give up."

Resources ————

Language
• *Grammar and Language Links* Worksheet, p. 25

Vocabulary
• *Words to Own*, Worksheet, p. 14

Grammar Link Quick Check

Underline the verb in each sentence and indicate whether the verb is active or passive.
1. In 1890, Chekhov visited Siberia. [*visited*, active]
2. On his trip to Italy and France shortly thereafter, he was accompanied by a friend and the friend's son. [*was accompanied*, passive]
3. In the early years of the twentieth century, Chekhov made frequent trips around Russia. [*made*, active]
4. He was welcomed everywhere. [*was welcomed*, passive]
5. Chekhov was impressed by his visit to Ceylon. [*was impressed*, passive]

OBJECTIVES

1. Read and interpret the story
2. Recognize elements of magic realism in the story
3. Read to appreciate the writer's craft
4. Express understanding through writing or art
5. Identify imagery and find examples in the story
6. Understand and use new words

SKILLS

Literary
- Identify characteristics of magic realism

Reading
- Appreciate the writer's craft

Writing
- Collect notes for a story analysis
- Write a letter
- Write a fantastic story

Grammar/Language
- Identify imagery

Vocabulary
- Use new words

Art
- Draw, sculpt, or make a collage of the old man with wings

Viewing/Representing
- Write in various modes, using photographs as a springboard (ATE)

Planning

- **Block Schedule**
  Block Scheduling Lesson Plans with Pacing Guide

- **Traditional Schedule**
  Lesson Plans Including Strategies for English-Language Learners

- **One-Stop Planner**
  CD-ROM with Test Generator

Before You Read

A VERY OLD MAN WITH ENORMOUS WINGS

Make the Connection

The Strange Visits the Familiar

This story hangs on that intriguing hook of *What if?* What if one day an old man with huge, bug-infested wings dropped out of the sky into your backyard? How would people respond to this "miracle"? How would the "angel" himself feel?

Quickwrite

Brainstorm a list of characters from myth and legend who have wings. What happens to each of those characters? Then brainstorm a list of modern stories or movies in which an alien visits the ordinary world. What usually happens to those strangers visiting a strange land?

Elements of Literature

Magic Realism

Like many contemporary South American writers, García Márquez writes a kind of fiction called **magic realism**. This style of writing is characterized by elements of fantasy (often borrowed from mythology) that are casually inserted into the most earthy, realistic settings. The magic realists often suspend the usual laws of nature. In using this bizarre mixture of the commonplace and the outlandish, the magic realists can force us to think about our fixed notions of "reality" and "normality."

> **M**agic realism is a style of fiction associated with modern Latin American writers, in which fantasy and reality are casually combined, with humorous and thought-provoking results.

Reading Skills and Strategies

Appreciating a Writer's Craft

One of the great pleasures of reading is appreciating how talented writers work—creating captivating images, unforgettable characters, edge-of-your-seat suspense. As you read this story by García Márquez, notice the way he tosses together the offbeat, the homely, and the sublime into that strange mix known as **magic realism.** Notice, too, his startling combinations of images, and be aware of the things they help you to see. Try to decide why some of his images seem funny, some sad, and some—appropriately enough—magical.

 go.hrw.com
LEO 10-3

The illustrations with this story were created by the artist Sergio Bustamante and the photographer Clint Clemens.

Preteaching Vocabulary

Words to Own

Have students review the Words to Own and then list two possible answers for each question.

1. What might cause a <u>stench</u> in a vacant lot?
2. How could you be <u>impeded</u> by wings?
3. What would you do if a millionaire became <u>magnanimous</u> toward you?
4. What would happen if <u>reverence</u> for tradition were abandoned?
5. What might happen if your senator were <u>frivolous</u>?
6. What might happen if parents ignored their children's <u>impertinences</u>?
7. What would happen to an <u>ingenuous</u> person in a bargaining situation?
8. What would happen if you didn't use <u>prudence</u> in budgeting your money?
9. What kind of <u>cataclysms</u> might occur in your town?
10. What <u>providential</u> things do you wish for?

A flesh-and-blood angel was held captive in Pelayo's house.

A Very Old Man with Enormous WINGS

Gabriel García Márquez
translated by Gregory Rabassa

A Tale for Children

On the third day of rain they had killed so many crabs inside the house that Pelayo had to

A VERY OLD MAN WITH ENORMOUS WINGS 223

Summary ▪▪

One night when Pelayo and Elisenda's baby is very ill, they discover an elderly, dirty, pitiful winged man in their courtyard. Because of his dialect and "sailor's voice," they guess he's a castaway, but a neighbor claims he's an angel sent for the child. The couple lock him in a chicken coop, the child recovers, the villagers come to gawk at and torment the creature, and the priest begins an interminable investigation into his angelic authenticity. Meanwhile, Pelayo and Elisenda become rich by charging admission to see the angel. Although bizarre miracles occur, the angel eventually loses his audience to a traveling spider-woman. The angel, now a nuisance, roams through Pelayo and Elisenda's new house until both he and the child, who has reached school age, become ill. Recovered, he begins to grow new feathers and sing sea chanteys. One day, he flaps awkwardly away.

Background

"A Very Old Man with Enormous Wings" was published with six other stories in a book called *The Incredible and Sad Story of Innocent Eréndira and Her Heartless Grandmother*. Critics have noted that this volume marks a transition for Gabriel García Márquez from his most famous novel, *One Hundred Years of Solitude,* to his later novels. In this story collection, Márquez seems to be responding to his still-new celebrity status. This story about the old man, and other stories in the volume, hint at his discomfort with fame. All the stories deal with public figures, and some, like the old angel in this story, would rather escape that public exposure altogether.

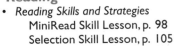

Resources: Print and Media

Reading
- *Reading Skills and Strategies*
    MiniRead Skill Lesson, p. 98
    Selection Skill Lesson, p. 105
- *Graphic Organizers for Active Reading,* p. 15
- *Words to Own,* p. 16

Writing and Language
- *Daily Oral Grammar*
    Transparency 15
- *Grammar and Language Links*
    Worksheet, p. 27
- *Language Workshop* CD-ROM

Assessment
- *Formal Assessment,* p. 34
- *Portfolio Management System,* p. 115
- *Test Generator (One-Stop Planner* CD-ROM)

Internet
- go.hrw.com (keyword: LE0 10-3)

A Elements of Literature

Magic Realism

? What elements of magic realism do you find in this paragraph? [Up to the final phrase, the paragraph describes common people and events in an ordinary place, using everyday speech. Into this setting a fantastic element, the wings, is casually introduced.]

B Reading Skills and Strategies

Appreciating a Writer's Craft

? How does this description make you feel about the angel? [Sample answers: sorry, sympathetic, sad.] How does the writer evoke this response? [He places the angel in a degrading situation, which contrasts with the pure, clean, ethereal conditions in which we expect to find an angel.]

cross his drenched courtyard and throw them into the sea, because the newborn child had a temperature all night and they thought it was due to the <u>stench</u>. The world had been sad since Tuesday. Sea and sky were a single ash-gray thing, and the sands of the beach, which on March nights glimmered like powdered light, had become a stew of mud and rotten shellfish. The light was so weak at noon that when Pelayo was coming back to the house after throwing away the crabs, it was hard for him to see what it was that was moving and groaning in the rear of the courtyard. He had to go very close to see that it was an old man, a very old man, lying face down in the mud, who, in spite of his tremendous efforts, couldn't get up, <u>impeded</u> by his enormous wings.

Frightened by that nightmare, Pelayo ran to get Elisenda, his wife, who was putting compresses on the sick child, and he took her to the rear of the courtyard. They both looked at the fallen body with mute stupor. He was dressed like a ragpicker. There were only a few faded hairs left on his bald skull and very few teeth in his mouth, and his pitiful condition of a drenched great-grandfather had taken away any sense of grandeur he might have had. His huge buzzard wings, dirty and half plucked, were forever entangled in the mud. They looked at him so long and so closely that Pelayo and Elisenda very soon overcame their surprise and in the end found him familiar. Then they dared speak to him, and he answered in an incomprehensible dialect with a strong sailor's voice. That was how they skipped over the inconvenience of the wings and quite intelligently concluded that he was a lonely castaway from some foreign ship wrecked by the storm. And yet, they called in a neighbor woman who knew everything about life and death to see him, and all she needed was one look to show them their mistake.

"He's an angel," she told them. "He must have been coming for the child, but the poor fellow is so old that the rain knocked him down."

On the following day everyone knew that a flesh-and-blood angel was held captive in Pelayo's house. Against the judgment of the wise neighbor woman, for whom angels in those times were the fugitive survivors of a celestial conspiracy,[1] they did not have the heart to club him to death. Pelayo watched over him all afternoon from the kitchen, armed with his bailiff's[2] club, and before going to bed, he dragged him out of the mud and locked him up with the hens in the wire chicken coop. In the middle of the night, when the rain stopped, Pelayo and Elisenda were still killing crabs. A short time afterward the child woke up without a fever and with a desire to eat. Then they felt <u>magnanimous</u> and decided to put the angel on a raft with fresh water and provisions for three days and leave him to his fate on the high seas. But when they went out into the courtyard with the first light of dawn, they found the whole neighborhood in front of the chicken coop having fun with the angel, without the slightest <u>reverence</u>, tossing him things to eat through the openings in the wire as if he weren't a supernatural creature but a circus animal.

Father Gonzaga arrived before seven o'clock, alarmed at the strange news. By that time onlookers less <u>frivolous</u> than those at dawn had already arrived and they were making all kinds of conjectures concerning the captive's future. The simplest among them thought that he should be named mayor of the world. Others of sterner mind felt that he should be promoted to the rank of five-star general in order to win all wars. Some visionaries hoped that he could be

1. **celestial conspiracy:** According to the Book of Revelation in the Bible (12:7–9), Satan originally was an angel who led a rebellion in Heaven. As a result, he and his followers, called the fallen angels, were cast out of Heaven.
2. **bailiff's:** A bailiff is a minor local official.

WORDS TO OWN

stench *n.:* offensive smell.
impeded (im·pēd′id) *v.* used as *adj.:* held back or blocked, as by an obstacle.
magnanimous (mag·nan′ə·məs) *adj.:* generous; noble.
reverence (rev′ər·əns) *n.:* attitude or display of deep respect.
frivolous (friv′ə·ləs) *adj.:* not properly serious; silly. *Frivolous* also means "of little value or importance."

Reaching All Students

Struggling Readers

Appreciating a Writer's Craft is introduced on p. 222 as a reading skill for this story. For a lesson directly tied to this story that teaches students to appreciate a writer's craft by using a strategy called Read, Rate, Reread, see the *Reading Skills and Strategies* binder:
• MiniRead Skill Lesson, p. 98
• Selection Skill Lesson, p. 105

English Language Learners

To help students grasp the irony of the story, they'll have to understand how the old man with wings completely contradicts the conventional images of angels in Western literature and art. You might bring in reproductions of paintings (for example by Renaissance Italian painters) and even discuss the use of angels in current television shows and movies.

Advanced Learners

As students read the story, have them think about how the photographs connect to the story. How do the images by themselves suggest magic realism? What could be the photographer's purpose in combining reality and fantasy?

put to stud in order to implant on earth a race of winged wise men who could take charge of the universe. But Father Gonzaga, before becoming a priest, had been a robust woodcutter. Standing by the wire, he reviewed his catechism[3] in an instant and asked them to open the door so that he could take a close look at that pitiful man who looked more like a huge decrepit hen among the fascinated chickens. He was lying in a corner drying his open wings in the sunlight among the fruit peels and breakfast leftovers that the early risers had thrown him. Alien to the impertinences of the world, he only lifted his antiquarian[4] eyes and murmured something in his dialect when Father Gonzaga went into

C

the chicken coop and said good morning to him in Latin. The parish priest had his first suspicion of an impostor when he saw that he did not understand the language of God or know how to greet His ministers. Then he noticed that seen close up, he was much too human: He had an unbearable smell of the outdoors, the back side of his wings was strewn with parasites[5] and his main feathers had been mistreated by terrestrial winds, and nothing about him measured up to the proud dignity of angels. Then he came out of the chicken coop and in a brief sermon warned the curious against the risks of being ingenuous. He reminded them that the devil had the bad habit of making use of carnival

3. **catechism** (katʹə·kizʹəm): book of religious principles consisting of a series of questions and answers.
4. **antiquarian** (anʹti·kwerʹē·ən): ancient.
5. **parasites:** plants or animals that live on or in other living things, on which they feed.

tricks in order to confuse the unwary. He argued that if wings were not the essential element in determining the difference between a hawk and an airplane, they were even less so in the recognition of angels. Nevertheless, he promised to write a letter to his bishop so that the latter would write to his primate[6] so that the latter would write to the Supreme Pontiff[7] in order to get the final verdict from the highest courts.

His prudence fell on sterile hearts. The news of the captive angel spread with such rapidity that after a few hours the courtyard had the bustle of a marketplace, and they had to call in troops with fixed bayonets to disperse the mob that was about to knock the house down.

Elisenda, her spine all twisted from sweeping up so much marketplace trash, then got the idea of fencing in the yard and charging five cents admission to see the angel.

The curious came from far away. A traveling carnival arrived with a flying acrobat, who buzzed over the crowd several times, but no one paid any attention to him because his wings

D
E

6. **primate** (prīʹmit): archbishop or highest-ranking bishop in an area.
7. **Supreme Pontiff:** pope, head of the Roman Catholic Church.

WORDS TO OWN

impertinences (im·pʉrtʹn·ən·siz) *n.*: insults; disrespectful acts or remarks.
ingenuous (in·jenʹyōō·əs) *adj.*: trusting; innocent; tending to believe too readily.
prudence (prōōdʹns) *n.*: cautiousness; sound judgment.

A VERY OLD MAN WITH ENORMOUS WINGS   225

C Struggling Readers
Identifying Pronoun Antecedents

In these sentences, the pronoun *he* is used repeatedly to refer to both Father Gonzaga and the old man. The use of *he* in "He was lying in a corner" may be confusing. Does the pronoun refer to the priest or the angel? Students can clarify the pronoun reference by replacing "He" with "The old man" or "The angel."

D Elements of Literature
Magic Realism

❓ What senses are appealed to in this description of the angel? [sound, smell, sight] What details that are not normally linked are placed together in these images? [angel "wings" that are "strewn with parasites"]

E Reading Skills and Strategies
Responding to the Text

❓ What do you think of Elisenda's decision? [Sample responses: She has worked hard and needs the money. It is cruel to put the man on display. Elisenda is merely following the entrepreneur tradition of making money when you can.]

Skill Link

Multiple Meanings
The word *race* in the first line on this page is one of many words in English that have multiple meanings. Ask students to look up *race* in the dictionary and find the definition that fits its use in this sentence. How many meanings does *race* have? [at least 20] Ask students to find other words on this page that have multiple meanings.

Activity
Have students look up in the dictionary each of the underlined words that follow and write its meaning as used in the sentence. Then, have them write other sentences, using each word in another sense. Have students compare their sentences.

1. The tired angel couldn't <u>lift</u> his wings.
2. The angel wanted to be <u>left</u> alone.
3. Who could <u>grudge</u> the angel a place to <u>stay</u>?
4. The angel did not <u>bear</u> up <u>well</u> under <u>close</u> inspection.

RESPONDING TO THE ART

Clint Clemens traveled to Mexico to take photographs of **Sergio Bustamante's** fantastic sculptures for a book collaboration. Be sure students notice how Bustamante has combined disparate elements to form unexpected compositions.

Sergio Bustamante was born in Mexico and has lived for many years in Guadalajara. He was trained as an architect but found the profession too restricting. He started making sculptures by experimenting with papier mâché, and later he began working in bronze and ceramic. His pieces, which include creatures, humans, and a mixture of both, are surreal, whimsical, and vibrant with life.

Activity. Ask students to write a fairy tale or myth based on the man-snail on pp. 222–223. They could write a speech for the ostrich in the picture on p. 225. They could describe the scene on p. 228 from the tree's point of view, or write a news report based on the photograph on p. 229. They could also write a story set in a village where all these strange creatures have appeared.

Using Students' Strengths

Verbal Learners

Students who like to work with words may want to try imitating García Márquez's style. You might suggest that they write a story of their own using magic realism or that they expand on Márquez's story, perhaps following the flight of the old man and narrating what happens to him in his next landing.

Visual Learners

This story is so rich visually that these students should have a great deal of fun with it. Ask students to imagine that the story is being made into a film, and they have to create a storyboard for it. Since the story is magic realism, they can use special effects and other nonrealistic techniques to depict the characters and their setting.

Kinesthetic Learners

Have students work in a group and transform the story into a dramatic performance. They might write dialogue and present the story as a play, they might have a narrator tell the story as others act it out, or they might present the entire story in mime. Be sure their works are performed before an audience.

were not those of an angel but, rather, those of a sidereal[8] bat. The most unfortunate invalids on earth came in search of health: a poor woman who since childhood had been counting her heartbeats and had run out of numbers; a Portuguese man who couldn't sleep because the noise of the stars disturbed him; a sleepwalker who got up at night to undo the things he had done while awake; and many others with less serious ailments. In the midst of that shipwreck disorder that made the earth tremble, Pelayo and Elisenda were happy with fatigue, for in less than a week they had crammed their rooms with

money and the line of pilgrims waiting their turn to enter still reached beyond the horizon.

The angel was the only one who took no part in his own act. He spent his time trying to get comfortable in his borrowed nest, befuddled by the hellish heat of the oil lamps and sacramental candles that had been placed along the wire. At first they tried to make him eat some mothballs, which, according to the wisdom of the wise neighbor woman, were the food prescribed for angels. But he turned them down, just as he turned down the papal[9] lunches that the penitents brought him, and they never found out whether it was because he was an angel or because he was an old man that in the end he ate nothing but eggplant mush. His only supernatural virtue seemed to be patience. Especially during the first days, when the hens pecked at him, searching for stellar parasites that proliferated in his wings, and the cripples pulled out feathers to touch their defective parts with, and even the most merciful

8. **sidereal** (sī·dir′ē·əl): of the stars.
9. **papal** (pā′pəl): here, fit for the pope.

threw stones at him, trying to get him to rise so they could see him standing. The only time they succeeded in arousing him was when they burned his side with an iron for branding steers, for he had been motionless for so many hours that they thought he was dead. He awoke with a start, ranting in his hermetic[10] language and with tears in his eyes, and he flapped his wings a couple of times, which brought on a whirlwind of chicken dung and lunar dust and a gale of panic that did not seem to be of this world. Although many thought that his reaction had been one not of rage but of pain, from then on they were careful not to annoy him, because the majority understood that his passivity was not that of a hero taking his ease but that of a cataclysm in repose.

Father Gonzaga held back the crowd's frivolity with formulas of maidservant inspiration while awaiting the arrival of a final judgment on the nature of the captive. But the mail from Rome showed no sense of urgency. They spent their time finding out if the prisoner had a navel, if his dialect had any connection with Aramaic,[11] how many times he could fit on the head of a pin, or whether he wasn't just a Norwegian with wings. Those meager letters might have come and gone until the end of time if a providential event had not put an end to the priest's tribulations.

10. **hermetic:** difficult to understand; mysterious.
11. **Aramaic** (ar′ə·mā′ik): ancient Middle Eastern language spoken by Jesus and his disciples.

WORDS TO OWN
cataclysm (kat′ə·kliz′əm) *n.:* disaster; sudden, violent event.
providential (präv′ə·den′shəl) *adj.:* fortunate; like something caused by a divine act.

A VERY OLD MAN WITH ENORMOUS WINGS **227**

A Elements of Literature
Magic Realism
❓ What elements of magic realism do you find here? [the fact that an angel makes a nest, the notion that angels eat mothballs, and the casual acceptance of the reality of all of this]

B Reading Skills and Strategies

Appreciating a Writer's Craft
❓ How do you respond to this image of the chickens pecking at the angel's wings? [Sample answers: by laughing; by feeling sad or uncomfortable; with surprise.]

C Elements of Literature
Character
❓ What can you conclude about the character of the angel? [Sample response: He's not angry or dangerous but uninterested in the crowds and in their petty curiosity. He feels physical pain when the crowd brands him. He weeps. He is patient.]

D Reading Skills and Strategies

Appreciating a Writer's Craft
❓ In a few words, Márquez characterizes the angel. What would a "cataclysm in repose" be like? [Possible response: dangerous, powerful, like a sleeping volcano.] It's an interesting oxymoron.

E Cultural Connections
Allusions
These questions are being asked to determine if the stranger is an angel. A navel indicates that a person has been born from a mother. In medieval times, theologians debated how many angels would fit on the head of a pin. Note the final down-to-earth suggestion: maybe he's "just a Norwegian with wings"! Márquez is satirizing some of the heated theological disputes of past eras here.

Getting Students Involved

Cooperative Learning
Have students work in small groups to produce an advertising promotion campaign that Pelayo and Elisenda could use to make people aware of the angel and to encourage them to pay to see him.

Enrichment Activity
"A Very Old Man with Enormous Wings" appeared in a book of short stories called *The Incredible and Sad Story of Innocent Eréndira and Her Heartless Grandmother,* in which it is paired with "The Handsomest Drowned Man in the World." Both stories are subtitled "A Tale for Children." Have students find this second story in the library (it is also in *Leaf Storm and Other Stories*) and then hold a panel discussion to compare it with the fallen-angel story.

It so happened that during those days, among so many other carnival attractions, there arrived in town the traveling show of the woman who had been changed into a spider for having disobeyed her parents. The admission to see her was not only less than the admission to see the

angel, but people were permitted to ask her all manner of questions about her absurd state and to examine her up and down so that no one would ever doubt the truth of her horror. She was a frightful tarantula the size of a ram and with the head of a sad maiden. What was most heart-rending, however, was not her outlandish shape but the sincere affliction with which she recounted the details of her misfortune. While still practically a child, she had sneaked out of her parents' house to go to a dance, and while she was coming back through the woods after having danced all night without permission, a fearful thunderclap rent the sky in two and through the crack came the lightning bolt of brimstone[12] that changed her into a spider. Her only nourishment came from the meatballs that charitable souls chose to toss into her mouth. A spectacle like that, full of so much human truth and with such a fearful lesson, was bound to defeat without even trying that of a haughty angel who scarcely deigned to look at mortals. Besides, the few miracles attributed to the angel

showed a certain mental disorder, like the blind man who didn't recover his sight but grew three new teeth, or the paralytic who didn't get to walk but almost won the lottery, or the leper whose sores sprouted sunflowers. Those consolation miracles, which were more like mocking fun, had already ruined the angel's reputation when the woman who had been changed into a spider finally crushed him completely. That was how Father Gonzaga was cured forever of his insomnia and Pelayo's courtyard went back to being as empty as during the time it had rained for three days and crabs walked through the bedrooms.

The owners of the house had no reason to lament. With the money they saved they built a two-story mansion with balconies and gardens and high netting so that crabs wouldn't get in during the winter, and with iron bars on the windows so that angels wouldn't get in. Pelayo also set up a rabbit warren close to town and gave up his job as bailiff for good, and Elisenda bought some satin pumps with high heels and many dresses of iridescent silk, the kind worn on Sunday by the most desirable women in those times. The chicken coop was the only thing that didn't receive any attention. If they washed it down with creolin and burned tears of myrrh[13] inside it every so often, it was not in

---

12. **brimstone:** sulfur, a pale-yellow element that burns with a blue flame and a suffocating odor.

13. **myrrh** (mur): sweet-smelling substance used in making perfume.

---

homage to the angel but to drive away the dung-heap stench that still hung everywhere like a ghost and was turning the new house into an old one. At first, when the child learned to walk, they were careful that he not get too close to the chicken coop. But then they began to lose their fears and got used to the smell, and before the child got his second teeth, he'd gone inside the chicken coop to play, where the wires were falling apart. The angel was no less standoffish with him than with other mortals, but he tolerated the most ingenious infamies[14] with the patience of a dog who had no illusions. They both came down with chickenpox at the same time. The doctor who took care of the child couldn't resist the temptation to listen to the angel's heart, and he found so much whistling in the heart and so many sounds in his kidneys that it seemed impossible for him to be alive. What surprised him most, however, was the logic of his wings. They seemed so natural on that completely human organism that he **E** couldn't understand why other men didn't have them too.

When the child began school, it had been some time since the sun and rain had caused the collapse of the chicken coop. The angel went dragging himself about here and there like a **F** stray dying man. They would drive him out of the bedroom with a broom and a moment later find him in the kitchen. He seemed to be in so many places at the same time that they grew to think that he'd been duplicated, that he was re-producing himself all through the house, and the exasperated and unhinged Elisenda shouted that it was awful living in that hell full of angels. He could scarcely eat and his antiquarian eyes had also become so foggy that he went about bumping into posts. All he had left were the bare cannulae[15] of his last feathers. Pelayo threw a blanket over him and extended him the charity of letting him sleep in the shed, and only then did they notice that he had a temperature at night and was delirious with the tongue twisters of an old Norwegian. That was one of the few times they became alarmed, for they thought he was going to die and not even the **G** wise neighbor woman had been able to tell them what to do with dead angels.

And yet he not only survived his worst winter but seemed improved with the first sunny days. He remained motionless for several days in the farthest corner of the courtyard,

14. **infamies:** here, disrespectful acts; insults.

15. **cannulae** (kan′yōō·lē′): tubes.

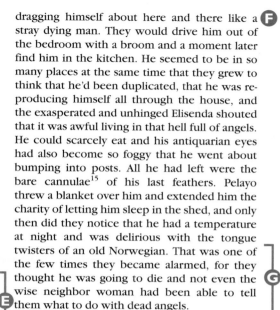

A VERY OLD MAN WITH ENORMOUS WINGS **229**

E **Elements of Literature**
Magic Realism
? How do the doctor's findings suggest a rethinking of our fixed ideas about reality? [He finds the wings perfectly logical and natural and wonders why everyone doesn't have them.]

F **English Language Learners**
Idioms
"Here and there" is an idiom meaning "to various places."

G **Elements of Literature**
Paradox
Notice the paradox here—angels are usually immortal. Elisenda and Pelayo are not upset by the thought of the old man dying; they just don't know what to do with deceased angels.

Making the Connections

Connecting to the Theme:
"Exiles, Castaways, and Strangers"
When students have finished the story, discuss its link to the collection theme. It has all the ingredients described in the theme title. The old man with wings is certainly a castaway. His body has failed him, stranding him among total strangers in an isolated village in a strange land.

He is, moreover, an exile, or at least he must feel like one. No one—angels or winged Norwegians—comes to look for him. He's on his own and only escapes when his feathers regrow, giving him the ability to move on or to return to wherever he came from.

A Reading Skills and Strategies
Responding to the Text

? What do you think of the way the story ends? [Answers will vary. Some will think it's sad. Some will laugh at the "senile vulture." Some will be very dissatisfied because they still don't know who the old man is.]

Resources

Selection Assessment
Formal Assessment
• Selection Test, p. 34.
Test Generator (One-Stop Planner)
• CD-ROM

BROWSING IN THE FILES

About the Author. Gabriel García Márquez began making up stories while very young. "My earliest recollection is of drawing 'comics,'" he said, "and I realize now that this may have been because I couldn't yet write. I've always tried to find ways of telling stories and I've stuck to literature as the most accessible. But I think my vocation is not so much to be a writer as a story-teller."

A Critic's Comment. Critic Regina Janes, among others, has noted that an essential element in the delight created by the story is the contrast between our perceptions of what angels are like and García Márquez's angel who talks like a sailor, is smelly and parasite-ridden, and is not very good at flying.

where no one would see him, and at the beginning of December some large, stiff feathers began to grow on his wings, the feathers of a scarecrow, which looked more like another misfortune of decrepitude. But he must have known the reason for those changes, for he was quite careful that no one should notice them, that no one should hear the sea chanteys[16] that he sometimes sang under the stars. One morning Elisenda was cutting some bunches of onions for lunch when a wind that seemed to come from the high seas blew into the kitchen. Then she went to the window and caught the **A** angel in his first attempts at flight. They were so clumsy that his fingernails opened a furrow in the vegetable patch and he was on the point of knocking the shed down with the ungainly flapping that slipped on the light and couldn't get a grip on the air. But he did manage to gain altitude. Elisenda let out a sigh of relief, for herself and for him, when she saw him pass over the last houses, holding himself up in some way with the risky flapping of a senile vulture. She kept watching him even when she was through cutting the onions and she kept on watching until it was no longer possible for her to see him, because then he was no longer an annoyance in her life but an imaginary dot on the horizon of the sea.

16. **chanteys** (shan′tēz): songs sung by sailors to set a rhythm for their work.

MEET THE WRITER

Memory's Magician

Gabriel García Márquez (1928–   ) sets much of his fiction in the imaginary town of Macondo, which in many ways resembles the sleepy, decaying, backwater town of Aracataca, Colombia, where he was born. Because his parents were poor, young Gabriel was raised by his maternal grandparents, in a large old house crowded with relatives and relics of the family's past. His grandmother told him tales of ancestors, spirits, and ghosts; and his grandfather, a retired colonel (whom García Márquez has called "the most important figure of my life"), spoke continually of a past so vivid that it became as real to the young boy as the present.

After studying law and working abroad as a journalist for many years, García Márquez became an international celebrity with the publication of his novel *One Hundred Years of Solitude* (1967). This epic masterpiece tells the comic and tragic saga of seven generations of Macondo's founding family. The Chilean poet Pablo Neruda called the novel "the greatest revelation in the Spanish language since *Don Quixote*." García Márquez won the Nobel Prize for literature in 1982.

He says this about writing when you are young:

❝ When you are young, you write almost—well, every writer is different, I'm talking about myself—almost like writing a poem. You write on impulses and inspiration. You have so much inspiration that you are not concerned with technique. You just see what comes out, without worrying much about what you are going to say and how. On the other hand, later, you know exactly what you are going to say and what you want to say. And you have a lot to tell. Even if all of your life you continue to tell about your childhood, later you are better able to interpret it, or at least interpret it in a different way. ❞

230 THE SHORT-STORY COLLECTIONS

Assessing Learning

Check Test: True-False
1. The townspeople treat the man with wings with respect because they believe he is an angel. [False]
2. The people finally lose interest in the man with wings. [True]
3. Pelayo and Elisenda resent the presence of the man with wings in their new mansion. [True]

4. The doctor discovers that the man's wings are pasted on. [False]
5. The man with wings eventually sprouts new feathers and flies away. [True]

Standardized Test Preparation
For practice with proofreading and editing specific to this selection, see
• *Daily Oral Grammar,* Transparency 15

*Like Gabriel García Márquez, Jack Agüeros transforms ordinary realities with a touch of fantasy. In this poem he presents a startling vision of the homeless people who use the subways of New York City for shelter. Agüeros roots his images in the everyday through realistic details—references to Calcutta, a city in India where hundreds of thousands live on the streets, and the Gowanus Canal, a polluted body of water in Brooklyn, New York. But he also includes an **allusion** to Macondo, an imaginary village that is the setting for much of García Márquez's fiction.*

Sonnet for Heaven Below

Jack Agüeros

No, it wasn't Macondo, and it wasn't Calcutta in time past.
But subway magic turned the tunnels into Beautyrest mattresses
And plenty of God's children started sleeping there. Some
Were actually Angels fatigued from long hours and no pay.

5   This is an aside, but I have to alert you. Angels run
Around, don't shave or bathe; acid rain fractures their
Feathers, and french fries and coca cola corrupt
The color of their skin and make them sing hoarsely.
The gossamer shoes so perfect for kicking clouds
10 Stain and tear on the concrete and in the hard light
Of the city they start to look like abandoned barges
Foundering in the cancerous waters of the Gowanus Canal.

Shabby gossamer shoes always arouse the derision of smart New Yorkers.
Mercifully, Angels aren't tourists, so they are spared total disdain.

A VERY OLD MAN WITH ENORMOUS WINGS 231

Connections

This sonnet is about the homeless people who sleep in New York City subways—or who used to. Be sure students read the italicized headnote before they read the poem. In his first line, Agüeros alludes to two famous practitioners of magic realism: García Márquez, whose stories are set in the fictional town of Macondo, and Salman Rushdie, who writes about India. Agüeros also alludes to the technique of magic realism when he says that magic has turned the subway tunnels into mattresses. The "Angels" that sleep in the subway tunnels are tired from trying to survive on long hours and no pay. Like the old man with wings, these Angels are not what you think of as angelic: They don't shave or bathe; they eat food that discolors their skin; their gossamer shoes tear on the concrete. In the last two lines the poet notes, almost as an aside, that the Angels' "shabby gossamer shoes" are looked down on by smart New Yorkers, but the Angels are spared New Yorkers' total disdain since they are not tourists.

Resources

Listening
Audio CD Library
A recording of this sonnet is provided in the Audio CD Library:
• Disc 7, Track 5

Connecting Across Texts

Connecting with "A Very Old Man with Enormous Wings"
Guide a discussion comparing "Sonnet for Heaven Below" with "A Very Old Man with Enormous Wings." How are the angels in the two pieces similar and different? [The angels in both pieces are earthy and even downtrodden. None are pure, clean, and ethereal. The angel in the story does have wings and eventually flies; we're not sure the subway angels fly, but the speaker does refer to their fractured feathers.]

What elements of magic realism do you find in the two pieces? [Both pieces include many ordinary, realistic details that are casually blended with magical elements, including the angels, subways turned into Beautyrest mattresses, and gossamer shoes.] How do the speaker of the poem and the narrator of the story feel about their angels? [They describe them in ways that arouse our sympathies and pity. Most readers will

identify with the poor angels and not with the disdainful New Yorkers or the self-centered villagers who are so indifferent to the miracle in their midst.]

MAKING MEANINGS

First Thoughts

1. Possible responses: Who or what is this old man with wings? Is he really an angel?

Shaping Interpretations

2. Description of angels will vary. In art representations, most are dazzlingly beautiful, and ethereal. This man has a body, does not seem immortal, has lice, can feel pain, speaks some "hermetic" language, and sings sea chanteys. He is compared with a chicken, a buzzard, a hen, and a senile vulture.

3. Possible responses: Lack of humility or compassion; selfishness; gullibility; suspiciousness; fickleness; ignorance.

4. Sample examples: the existence of a flesh-and-blood angel; the miracles; the story of the spider-woman. Possible images: the description of the old man in the chicken coop, the angel's response to the branding iron, the spider-woman.

5. Possible responses: His actions give few clues to either a divine or evil origin. He might be mythical, but there is little evidence. He has many human qualities, which suggests he is not from another universe.

6. It certainly has a deeper meaning. It may mean that when we meet something unusual we may try to make the situation fit our expectations rather than accepting it as it is. It may mean that even when the miraculous falls into our backyard, we won't recognize it.

Connecting with the Text

7. Students' responses will vary. Some will say it connects with their emotions, imagination, and intellect.

Extending the Text

8. They are alike in that they suffer as humans do. Agüeros seems to be talking about people, whereas García Márquez's angel has supernatural qualities. Unlike García Márquez's angel, Agüeros's angels do not have another place where they belong. Both New Yorkers and the townspeople in García Márquez's story treat their angels with contempt, indifference, annoyance.

9. It would depend on what they saw and on how the alien acted. They might call the police, paramedics, and news media. Think of the movie *E.T.*

MAKING MEANINGS

First Thoughts

[respond]
1. What is the first question you'd like to ask García Márquez? What is your second question?

Shaping Interpretations

[speculate]
2. If an angel did come to Earth, what would you expect it to look like? How is this old man **ironically** unlike an angel?

[analyze]
3. What human shortcomings might García Márquez be **satirizing** in this story? Consider:
   - How do Pelayo and Elisenda treat the old man?
   - Why does Father Gonzaga suspect the old man is not an angel?
   - How do people react to the "spectacles" of the angel and the spider-woman?

[identify]

4. What details in this story are examples of **magic realism**? Which of García Márquez's **images** did you find most startling and memorable?

[interpret]

5. Do you think the old man is a divine figure or an evil one? Are there any other explanations for his identity? Did he fall into our world from the world of myth, or is he an alien from another universe that is full of winged persons? (Check your Quickwrite notes.)

[evaluate]
6. Do you think this story is intended merely to amuse and astonish us, or does it mean something deeper? Consider:
   - Does the old man **symbolize** the miracles we wish for but are unable to accept when they happen?
   - Does the old man **symbolize** the artist, who is often mocked and misunderstood by other people and whose imagination longs to soar?

Connecting with the Text

[connect]
7. Great literature, whether realistic or fantastic, connects to our hearts, imaginations, or minds. Did this story connect with you at all? Elaborate.

Extending the Text

[compare]
8. How are the "angels" described in "Sonnet for Heaven Below" (see *Connections* on page 231) similar to the very old man with enormous wings? Do "smart New Yorkers" treat these angels the way the townspeople in the story treat the old man?

[extend]
9. How do you suppose people in your community would act if an angel or another alien or being fell into someone's backyard?

Reading Check

a. The townspeople draw various conclusions about who, or rather what, the winged old man is. What do Pelayo and Elisenda think he is? What does their know-it-all neighbor think? and Father Gonzaga?

b. How does the old man change the lives of Pelayo and Elisenda?

c. What miracles are attributed to the old man?

d. What happens when a new novelty, the spider-woman, comes to town?

Reading Check

a. Pelayo and Elisenda conclude that he is a cast-away, shipwrecked by a storm. The neighbor thinks he is an angel. Father Gonzaga fears he may be a fraud.

b. Pelayo and Elisenda charge admission to see him. The money helps them build a mansion and live well.

c. A blind man grows three new teeth, a person who cannot walk almost wins the lottery, and a person with leprosy sprouts sunflowers from the sores.

d. People lose interest in the angel.

CHOICES: Building Your Portfolio

Writer's Notebook

1. Collecting Ideas for Analyzing a Story

Focusing on setting.
García Márquez writes fantasy, but he is also very earthy. Look back at the first paragraph, and list the details that help you see, touch, smell, and hear his rainy **setting**. Collect notes about the setting of Márquez's story or another story in this book. Comb through your story carefully to find all the details you can about setting. Is the setting crucial to the action—could the story happen anyplace else? Save your notes for the Writer's Workshop assignment on page 240.

Creative Writing

2. The Angel Talks

The old man talks, but the townspeople do not understand his language. What do you imagine is going through the old man's mind as he patiently endures the indignities of the chicken coop? Write a **letter** to Pelayo and Elisenda that the old man might have written just before flying away. Include details about his true home, the reason he strayed into the yard, how human life looked from his perspective, and where he is heading now. Write in the first person, using *I*.

Viewing/Critical Writing

3. What Do You See?

Look carefully at the illustrations that accompany this story. How appropriate do you think they are? What do you see happening in each illustration? Write a brief essay in which you describe these illustrations and evaluate their use for this story. How did you respond to them?

Creative Writing

4. Be a Magic Realist

Perhaps the old man in the story is Daedalus, the craftsman in Greek mythology who made himself wings to escape from prison. Write a **fantastic story** of your own about another person from folklore, mythology, or popular culture who falls into the actual world. You might consider these possibilities:

- Hercules, the strongest teenager in the world, enrolls at your school.
- A fairy godmother visits a poor girl in New York City.
- King Arthur is elected president.
- A dragon asks to be admitted to the zoo.

Art

5. A Different Angel

All kinds of angels have become popular lately, but García Márquez's angel is different. Make a **drawing** or **sculpture** or **collage** of this old man with enormous wings. Follow the description of his appearance in the story, but also feel free to add details of your own. Arrange a class display of your angel illustrations, perhaps using lines from the story as **captions.**

Handwritten note:

Setting in "Where Have You Gone, Charming Billy?"
Place/time frame
Vietnam sometime between 1965 and 1973

Details of setting:
- "mosquitoes and leeches as big as mice"
- "thick paddy water"

Character's feelings about setting:
He hates the smells, decay, mosquitoes—most of all the danger.

Crucial to story: Setting presents character with part of his problems.

A VERY OLD MAN WITH ENORMOUS WINGS 233

Grading Timesaver

Rubrics for each Choices assignment appear on p. 115 in the *Portfolio Management System*.

CHOICES: Building Your Portfolio

1. **Writer's Notebook**   Remind students that the setting includes time as well as place. It can also include customs, food, leisure activities, religion, etc.
2. **Creative Writing**   Point out that the content of their letter will depend in part on who or what they think the old man is and what his purpose has been. Suggest they spend a few minutes freewriting before beginning their letter.
3. **Viewing/Critical Writing**   You might allow students to meet in small groups of two or three to discuss their responses to the pictures. Have them write their essays individually.
4. **Creative Writing**   Remind students that they need not use a humorous tone for their stories. Provide time for students to do some research before writing their stories.
5. **Art**   Students who are skilled with design software might create a computer-generated image of the angel.

Using Students' Strengths

Visual Learners
As an alternative to Choice 2, you might have your visual learners imagine that the angel was an artist. Ask them to draw the sketches he might have left behind to express his feelings about the humans with whom he lived. Cartoons are also a possibility.

Interpersonal Learners
For Choice 4, students could work in groups and write their story as a play.

Language Link

Try It Out

Possible Answers

1. All appeal to sight; 1 and 3 may also appeal to smell and 2 and 5 to touch.
2. Glimmering sands and powdered light/mud and rotten shellfish; stellar/parasites; chicken dung/lunar dust; miracles/mental disorder; sores/sunflowers
3. There are many answers. Have students read their favorites aloud.

Vocabulary

Sample Answers

stench, n.; root: Old English *stincan,* "to stink"; related words: none

impeded, v.; root: Latin *impedire,* "to entangle"; related word: *impediment,* n.

magnanimous, adj.; root: Latin *magnanimus,* "great mind"; related words: *magnanimity,* n. *magnificent,* adj., *magnate,* n.

reverence, n.; root: Latin *reverentia,* "feeling of awe"; related words: *revere,* v.; *reverend,* n.; *reverent,* adj.

frivolous, adj.; root: Latin *frivolus,* "silly"; related word: *frivolity,* n.

impertinences, n.; root: Latin *impertinens,* "not to hold"; related words: *impertinent,* adj., *pertain,* v.

ingenuous, adj.; root: Latin *ingenuus,* "naive, honest"; related words: *ingenuity,* n.; *ingénue,* n.

prudence, n.; root: Latin *prudens,* "wise, foreseeing"; related words: *prudential,* adj.; *prudent,* adj.

cataclysm, n.; root: Greek *kataklysmos,* "deluge"; related word: *cataclysmic,* adj.

providential, adj.; root: Latin *providens,* "to foresee"; related words: *providence,* n.; *provident,* adj.

Resources

Language

- *Grammar and Language Links* Worksheet, p. 27

Vocabulary

- *Words to Own,* Worksheet, p. 16

Language Link — MINI-LESSON

Come to Your Senses: Images of a Magic Realist

Handbook of Literary Terms HELP

See Imagery.

Imagery is language that appeals directly to the senses and the imagination. Most images are visual—that is, they appeal to our sense of sight—but images may also appeal to our senses of sound, smell, touch, and taste. In addition to sensory appeal, García Márquez's imagery frequently has another interesting quality: It brings together experiences or details that are usually separate or in opposition.

1. ". . . the sands of the beach, which on March nights glimmered like powdered light, had become a stew of mud and rotten shellfish."
2. ". . . hens pecked at him, searching for stellar parasites that proliferated in his wings. . . ."
3. ". . . a whirlwind of chicken dung and lunar dust . . ."
4. ". . . the few miracles attributed to the angel showed a certain mental disorder, like the blind man who didn't recover his sight but grew three new teeth. . . ."
5. ". . . whose sores sprouted sunflowers."

Try It Out

Examine the passages quoted opposite and García Márquez's unusual images:

1. To which senses do the images appeal?
2. Where do you find opposing images or experiences?
3. Look back at the story, and find three other examples of García Márquez's imagery that you think are especially unusual or funny or unexpected.

A tip for writers: Be aware of the world around you. Add descriptive observations to your notebook from time to time so that you build up a kind of image bank.

Vocabulary — HOW TO OWN A WORD

Word Bank

stench
impeded
magnanimous
reverence
frivolous
impertinences
ingenuous
prudence
cataclysm
providential

Roots and Relations

Using a dictionary, find the **root** and **part of speech** of each word in the Word Bank. Then, look for **related forms** and their parts of speech. (Some of the words have many related forms; one word has none.) Note that adding or changing a **suffix** often changes a word's part of speech. Summarize your findings in a graphic like the one below for the word *impeded.*

adj.

adv.

word root
Latin *impedire,*
"to entangle"

v.
impeded

n.
impediment

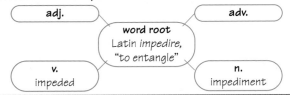

Language Link Quick Check

Identify the images in the following sentences (they are underscored here). Answers might vary slightly.

1. Pelayo crossed his <u>drenched</u> <u>courtyard</u>.
2. Sea and sky were a <u>single</u> <u>ash-gray</u> <u>thing</u>.
3. The sands were like <u>powdered</u> <u>light</u>.
4. He was dressed like a <u>ragpicker</u>.
5. He had <u>huge</u> <u>buzzard</u> <u>wings</u>.

Think of a time
when you had to
go through an experience
that you feared, but you
thought you absolutely
had to avoid showing your
fear. Write a few notes
about how you felt about
the experience later.

go.hrw.com
HRW
LEO 10-3

EXTENDING
the theme
A PERSONAL ESSAY

*She just managed to
drag the fear from her eyes . . .*

You Are Now Entering
the Human Heart

Janet Frame

I looked at the notice. I wondered if I had time before my train left Philadelphia for Baltimore in one hour. The heart, ceiling high, occupied one corner of the large exhibition hall, and from wherever you stood in the hall, you could hear it beating, *thum-thump-thum-thump*. It was a popular exhibit, and sometimes, when there were too many children about, the entrance had to be roped off, as the children loved to race up and down the blood vessels and match their cries to the heart's beating. I could see that

the heart had already been punished for the day—the floor of the blood vessel was worn and dusty, the chamber walls were covered with marks, and the notice "You Are Now Taking the Path of a Blood Cell Through the Human Heart" hung askew. I wanted to see more of the Franklin Institute and the Natural Science Museum across the street, but a journey through the human heart would be fascinating. Did I have time?

Later. First, I would go across the street to

YOU ARE NOW ENTERING THE HUMAN HEART 235

OBJECTIVES
• Find thematic connections
  across genres and across
  cultures
• Discuss the essay and its theme
• Evaluate discussion

Extending the Theme

In this personal essay, Janet Frame narrates an unsettling experience that takes place in a Philadelphia museum. The narrator wants to see an exhibit of a huge human heart, which one can actually walk through, but she decides to go first across the street to the Natural Science Museum. There, she observes an elementary school class being taught to respect snakes. As a demonstration, a museum attendant drapes a grass snake around the neck of the teacher. The teacher is terrified but tries to hide it. When the snake moves its head toward her face, however, the teacher loses her composure, throws the snake to the floor, and rushes across the room where she shrinks, embarrassed, into a chair. She has lost the respect of her students. The narrator cannot watch any longer and hurries off to catch her train. She need not take the journey through the great artificial heart; she has seen the real human heart cruelly exposed.

Reaching All Students

Struggling Readers
To help sudents formulate Frame's main idea, you might want to apply a strategy called Most Important Word for this essay. See *Reading Strategies Handbook* in the front of the *Reading Skills and Strategies* binder.

English Language Learners
Janet Frame uses unusual constructions in her writing that may confuse some students. For example, she sometimes uses incomplete sentences and occasionally uses sentences such as "I saw her fear," as though fear were a concrete noun. You may want to read the story aloud with these students, discussing any syntactical issues or other questions that arise.

Advanced Learners
Point out that situations that isolate us as exiles, castaways, and strangers are often thrust upon us out of the blue. As they read this selection, ask students to think of examples from the news of real-life situations in which someone is suddenly jerked out of a perfectly normal, comfortable situation and isolated. Have them discuss how these situations parallel the one described in this essay. Who is the exile— the teacher, the narrator, or both?

A English Language Learners

Supplying Missing Words

❓ This paragraph features three incomplete sentences. Which are incomplete? [the second, third, and fourth] How would you reword the sentences to make them complete? [Possible responses: I saw more children sitting in rows on canvas chairs. The children were from an elementary class from a city school, under the control of an elderly teacher. A museum attendant held a basket, and all eyes gazed at it.]

B Elements of Literature

Metaphor

❓ What is the light compared with? [The words *blinked* and *hooded* suggest a snake.]

C Reading Skills and Strategies

Predicting

❓ What do you think Miss Aitcheson will do? [Possible responses: Throw off the snake and run. Enjoy the experience after she realizes that the snake is not going to hurt her.]

D Elements of Literature

Tone

❓ How has the author's tone changed as she tells this story? [The tone has changed from a direct, matter-of-fact reporting of events to sympathy for the teacher (and perhaps identification with her) and contempt for the snake handler.]

---

the Hall of North America, among the bear and the bison, and catch up on American flora and fauna.°

I made my way to the Hall. More children, sitting in rows on canvas chairs. An elementary class from a city school, under the control of an elderly teacher. A museum attendant holding a basket, and all eyes gazing at the basket.

"Oh," I said. "Is this a private lesson? Is it all right for me to be here?"

The attendant was brisk. "Surely. We're having a lesson in snake handling," he said. "It's something new. Get the children young and teach them that every snake they meet is not to be killed. People seem to think that every snake has to be knocked on the head. So we're getting them young and teaching them."

"May I watch?" I said.

"Surely. This is a common grass snake. No harm, no harm at all. Teach the children to learn the feel of them, to lose their fear."

He turned to the teacher. "Now, Miss—Mrs.——" he said.

"Miss Aitcheson."

He lowered his voice. "The best way to get through to the children is to start with teacher," he said to Miss Aitcheson. "If they see you're not afraid, then they won't be."

She must be near retiring age, I thought. A city woman. Never handled a snake in her life. Her face was pale. She just managed to drag the fear from her eyes to some place in their depths, where it lurked like a dark stain. Surely the attendant and the children noticed?

"It's harmless," the attendant said. He'd worked with snakes for years.

Miss Aitcheson, I thought again. A city woman born and bred. All snakes were creatures to kill, to be protected from, alike the rattler, the copperhead, king snake, grass snake—venom and victims. Were there not places in the South where you couldn't go into the streets for fear of the rattlesnakes?

Her eyes faced the lighted exit. I saw her fear. The exit light blinked, hooded. The children, none of whom had ever touched a live snake,

° **flora and fauna:** plants and animals.

were sitting hushed, waiting for the drama to begin; one or two looked afraid as the attendant withdrew a green snake about three feet long from the basket and with a swift movement, before the teacher could protest, draped it around her neck and stepped back, admiring and satisfied.

"There," he said to the class. "Your teacher has a snake around her neck and she's not afraid."

Miss Aitcheson stood rigid; she seemed to be holding her breath.

"Teacher's not afraid, are you?" the attendant persisted. He leaned forward, pronouncing judgment on her, while she suddenly jerked her head and lifted her hands in panic to get rid of the snake. Then, seeing the children watching her, she whispered, "No, I'm not afraid. Of course not." She looked around her.

"Of course not," she repeated sharply.

I could see her defeat and helplessness. The attendant seemed unaware, as if his perception had grown a reptilian covering. What did she care for the campaign for the preservation and welfare of copperheads and rattlers and common grass snakes? What did she care about someday walking through the woods or the desert and deciding between killing a snake and setting it free, as if there would be time to decide, when her journey to and from school in downtown Philadelphia held enough danger to occupy her? In two years or so, she'd retire and be in that apartment by herself and no doorman, and everyone knew what happened then, and how she'd be afraid to answer the door and to walk after dark and carry her pocketbook in the street. There was enough to think about without learning to handle and love the snakes, harmless and otherwise, by having them draped around her neck for everyone, including the children—most of all the children—to witness the outbreak of her fear.

"See, Miss Aitcheson's touching the snake. She's not afraid of it at all."

As everyone watched, she touched the snake. Her fingers recoiled. She touched it again.

"See, she's not afraid. Miss Aitcheson can

Using Students' Strengths

Verbal Learners

After students have read the essay, ask them to select a character, such as the teacher, one of the children, or the museum attendant. Have students assume the role of the character and write a diary entry describing and responding to what happened that day in the museum.

Naturalist Learners

Ask students to analyze what the museum attendant did wrong and to suggest how the presentation could have been handled. Suggest they start with these questions: Were the attendant's motives in teaching about snakes wrong? What was wrong with his methods? What should people know about snakes? How should they be instructed? Have students prepare a lesson plan for teaching about snakes.

Intrapersonal Learners

Ask students to analyze the character of the teacher, the museum attendant, the narrator, and the children as the events unfold. In their analysis, students should answer these questions: What are the characters thinking and feeling? What will be the long-term effects of this event on the characters?

stand there with a beautiful snake around her neck and touch it and stroke it and not be afraid."

The faces of the children were full of admiration for the teacher's bravery, and yet there was a cruelly persistent tension; they were waiting, waiting.

"We have to learn to love snakes," the attendant said. "Would someone like to come out and stroke teacher's snake?"

Silence.

One shamefaced boy came forward. He stood petrified in front of the teacher.

"Touch it," the attendant urged. "It's a friendly snake. Teacher's wearing it around her neck and she's not afraid."

The boy darted his hand forward, resting it lightly on the snake, and immediately withdrew his hand. Then he ran to his seat. The children shrieked with glee.

"He's afraid," someone said. "He's afraid of the snake."

The attendant soothed. "We have to get used to them, you know. Grown-ups are not afraid of them, but we can understand that when you're small, you might be afraid, and that's why we want you to learn to love them. Isn't that right, Miss Aitcheson? Isn't that right? Now, who else is going to be brave enough to touch teacher's snake?"

Two girls came out. They stood hand in hand side by side and stared at the snake and then at Miss Aitcheson.

I wondered when the torture would end. The 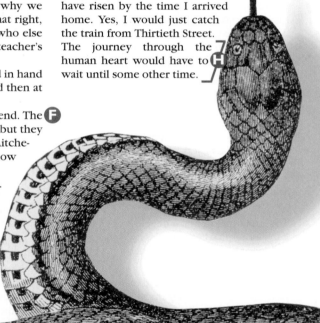 two little girls did not touch the snake, but they smiled at it and spoke to it, and Miss Aitcheson smiled at them and whispered how brave they were.

"Just a minute," the attendant said. "There's really no need to be brave. It's not a question of bravery. The snake is absolutely *harmless*. Where's the bravery when the snake is harmless?"

Suddenly the snake moved around to face Miss Aitcheson and thrust its flat head toward her cheek. She gave a scream, flung up her hands, and tore the snake from her throat and

threw it on the floor, and, rushing across the room, she collapsed into a chair beside the Bear Cabinet.

I didn't feel I should watch any longer. Some of the children began to laugh, some to cry. The attendant picked up the snake and nursed it. Miss Aitcheson, recovering, sat helplessly exposed by the small piece of useless torture. It was not her fault she was city bred, her eyes tried to tell us. She looked at the children, trying in some way to force their admiration and respect; they were shut against her. She was evicted from them and from herself and even from her own fear-infested tomorrow, because she could not promise to love and preserve what she feared. She had nowhere, at that moment, but the small canvas chair by the Bear Cabinet of the Natural Science Museum.

I looked at my watch. If I hurried, I would catch the train from Thirtieth Street. There would be no time to make the journey through the human heart. I hurried out of the museum. It was freezing cold. The icebreakers would be at work on the Delaware and the Susquehanna; the mist would have risen by the time I arrived home. Yes, I would just catch the train from Thirtieth Street. The journey through the human heart would have to wait until some other time.

E Reading Skills and Strategies
Making Inferences
? What are the children waiting for? [Possible answer: They are waiting for Miss Aitcheson to show fear.]

F Struggling Readers
Questioning
? What question might you ask about this sentence? [Possible question: What torture is taking place?] **What's the answer?** [Miss Aitcheson is being tortured by being forced to act brave while the snake crawls over her.]

G Critical Thinking
Making Connections
? How is Miss Aitcheson like Paul Berlin in "Where Have You Gone, Charming Billy?" [Both characters are forced to confront their fears, although Miss Aitcheson has the freedom to flee.]

H Elements of Literature
Irony
? What is ironic about this statement? [While the narrator did not get to view the artificial human heart, she did journey through a real human heart and witnessed Miss Aitcheson's fear and humiliation.]

Making the Connections

Connecting to the Theme: "Exiles, Castaways, and Strangers"
Discuss how this essay develops the theme of the collection. The teacher, who is the head of the group at the beginning, becomes exiled because the fear that comes over her when the snake is placed around her neck turns her students away. Her display of panic pushes her into exile. The children are "shut against her" and she is "evicted from them and from herself."

Cultural Connections
A Universal Fear? The narrator sympathizes with Miss Aitcheson in part because she is a "city woman" whose upbringing and culture, she thinks, have made her fear snakes. Ask students if fear of snakes is universal, or if snakes are totally accepted by some people and some cultures. How would they have responded in Miss Aitcheson's place?

FINDING COMMON GROUND

This feature should stimulate classroom discussion about the essay and its connection to the theme of this collection. Have students begin by recording their responses to these questions in their reading notes.

1. Possible question: How can someone enter the human heart?

2. Possible reason: The question connects the title with the ending.

3. Have students share these questions. Invite the class to try to answer some of them.

4. Possible responses: Yes, the teacher becomes an exile the moment the snake is placed around her neck. She becomes a stranger and a castaway to her students, who are used to seeing her in control.

5. Students should find that the discussion leads them to see new elements that they did not previously notice.

MEET THE WRITER

Shy

Janet Frame (1924–   ) was raised in the little town of Oamaru, New Zealand, and as a young woman she trained for a career as a teacher. Her life story, told in three volumes—*To the Island* (1982), *An Angel at My Table* (1984), and *The Envoy from Mirror City* (1985)—reads like a horror story. (Her autobiography was made into the movie *An Angel at My Table* in 1990.) Extremely shy as a child, Frame lived for a time with her aunt and her dying uncle in a cottage where there was not enough space, food, or heat. Her two beloved sisters accidentally drowned. Though she "delighted in the children at school and in teaching," Frame was so shy that she could not face the inspection needed to earn her teaching certificate.

When she sought help for her painful timidity, Frame became the victim of a devastating mistaken diagnosis. She was labeled "schizophrenic" and shipped off to a psychiatric ward. For the next eight years she was in and out of mental institutions. Eight years of her life were needlessly lost.

Through all the horror of those years, she never forgot her childhood dream to be recognized "as a true poet." When a New Zealand writer offered her an army hut in which to live and write, she accepted and began her first novel. Eventually, doctors concluded that Frame was not mentally ill; what's more, she never had been.

Though she still lives in New Zealand, Frame has traveled in America and worked at two famous writers' retreats, the Yaddo Foundation and the MacDowell Colony. "You Are Now Entering the Human Heart," an essay about an experience she had in Philadelphia, first appeared in *The New Yorker* magazine.

At last Janet Frame has realized her dream: The shy young woman who spent eight years cruelly shut away is now New Zealand's preeminent writer.

FINDING COMMON GROUND

"You Are Now Entering the Human Heart" is an essay, a piece of personal writing in which the writer explores a subject and reflects on what it means. Essays can begin in many ways. Some writers get their ideas from questions: Why are people sometimes so cruel? What did the death of my little calf mean to me? What is friendship?

1. This essay explores how people deal with fear. If the writer had begun this essay with a question, what do you think that question would have been?

2. Write down the question, and then jot down your reasons for thinking that it could have been the starting point for the essay.

3. Check your Quickwrite notes. Do they raise other questions about how people deal with fear?

4. The writer, of course, didn't write her essay so that it could fit into this book in a collection called "Exiles, Castaways, and Strangers." Jot down your response to these questions: Does this essay fit here? Why, or why not?

5. In class, talk over all your questions, their answers, and your feelings about the essay's fit in this collection. After your discussion, think again about your own responses: Did the discussion add anything to your understanding of the essay?

238 THE SHORT-STORY COLLECTIONS

Assessing Learning

Check Test: True-False

1. The essay is about a visit to a huge artificial heart exhibit. [False]

2. The museum attendant is speaking to a group of elementary school students. [True]

3. Miss Aitcheson volunteers to help the attendant give the demonstration. [False]

4. After the snake is placed around Miss Aitcheson's neck, she panics. [True]

5. Because the children are also scared, they sympathize with their teacher's fear. [False]

READ ON

The Other Side of the Mirror

Lewis Carroll's *Alice in Wonderland* presents *Alice's Adventures in Wonderland* and *Through the Looking-Glass.* Young Alice literally falls into another world and finds herself at times out of her depth with talking cats, flamingoes, and mad royalty. Available in many editions, these tales are presented with explanations in *The Annotated Alice* (Clarkson N. Potter), with an introduction and notes by Martin Gardner.

On a Desert Island with Uh-Oh . . .

Schoolboys find themselves on an island that has no grown-ups. Such freedom seems ideal . . . until the boys find that, even without the grown-ups who seem to cause so much trouble, they are perfectly capable of reinventing trouble—they don't even need models. William Golding's novel *Lord of the Flies* begins as an adventure story and explodes into a parable about the human conscience.

Don't Open That Door!

Charlotte Brontë's *Jane Eyre* has all the elements of a great adventure story—an orphan banished to a grim boarding school, a mysterious estate ruled by a more mysterious owner, a desperate cross-country journey, and a locked room that contains a dreadful secret. Try the book (available in the HRW Library) or the 1996 movie (starring William Hurt).

Troubled Teens in the '60s

The Outsiders, Francis Ford Coppola's 1983 movie version of S. E. Hinton's best-selling novel (1967), is set in Oklahoma during the 1960s. Hinton was only 16 when she began writing her novel about troubled teenagers. Howell, the narrator, likes poetry and *Gone with the Wind* but gets caught up in violence and gang rivalry. Tom Cruise, Matt Dillon, and Patrick Swayze star in the movie; S. E. Hinton, the author, appears briefly as a nurse.

READ ON

These Read On selections have been chosen for their appropriateness to the collection theme "Exiles, Castaways, and Strangers."

Portfolio Assessment Options

The following projects can help you evaluate and assess your students' reading accomplishments outside class. The projects themselves, or videotapes or photographs of the projects, can be included in students' portfolios.

- **Compare the Book and the Movie** Each of the three novels has been adapted for the motion picture screen. Suggest that students view a videotape of their selection and write an essay comparing the book with its film version. (Note that the 1990 movie version of *Lord of the Flies* is R-rated.) In their essay, students should note similarities and differences in setting, characterization, scenes, and dialogue. Students should end their essay with an evaluation of how well the film version conveys the content of the novel.

- **Create Your Own Adventure Story** Have students write a story in book or hypertext form in which the readers have the option of choosing their own adventure, based on the setting, characters, and scenes in the novel. Each page or screen of the adventure story should allow readers to choose action that would lead to different consequences.

- **Dramatization** Encourage pairs or small groups of students to prepare a dramatic presentation of a scene from the book. Students should identify the scene, script the dialogue and stage directions, rehearse (adding costumes and scenery, if they wish), and present the scene to the class, preceded by an introduction describing the context of the scene in relation to the events in the book.

BUILDING YOUR PORTFOLIO
Writer's Workshop

Technology HELP

See Writer's Workshop 2 CD-ROM. *Assignment: Interpretation.*

ASSIGNMENT

Write an essay analyzing one of the short stories in this book or another story of your choice.

AIM

To think critically; to inform.

AUDIENCE

Your teacher and your classmates.

EXPOSITORY WRITING
ANALYZING A STORY

You can often find out how a device like an old clock or a small motor works by taking it apart and seeing how it's put together. When you **analyze** a work of literature, you examine its literary elements and try to figure out how they interact to create meaning. In this workshop, you'll write an essay analyzing one of the stories you've read. You'll focus on three or four elements—such as **plot, character, setting, tone,** or **theme**—and discuss how they work together to create the story's meaning.

Prewriting

1. Choose a Story

Look through your Writer's Notebook for notes you've made on stories in this collection and in the first two collections. Choose a story that you feel strongly about —one you either love or hate. Is there one that stands out in your memory, maybe because it surprised you or touched your emotions or challenged your thinking?

2. Do a Close Reading

Reread your story two or three times, and take notes (perhaps in the form of a chart). You need to do two things: focus on the important literary elements and step back to look at the story as a whole. Think about these questions as you read:

- **Plot.** What **conflict** sets the plot in motion? Is it external or internal or both? Is the plot suspenseful? Does the writer use **foreshadowing** to hint at what will happen? What is the story's **climax**? Is the **resolution** satisfying? Is it **ambiguous** (open to more than one interpretation)?

- **Character.** Who are the story's main characters, and how does the writer reveal their natures? Who is the **protagonist**? What **motivates** these characters? Do they change, and if so, how? What do they learn during the story? Are their actions, motives, changes, and discoveries believable?

240 THE SHORT-STORY COLLECTIONS

Resources: Print and Media

Writing and Language
- *Portfolio Management System*
  - Prewriting, p. 117
  - Peer Editing, p. 118
  - Assessment Rubric, p. 119

- *Workshop Resources*
  - Revision Strategy Teaching Notes, p. 13
  - Revision Strategy Transparencies 7, 8, 9
- *Writer's Workshop 2 CD-ROM*
  - Interpretation

The history
of the written
word is rich and
Once upon a time

- **Setting.** Where and when does the story take place? Does the setting reveal anything about the characters? Is it central to the conflict (as in "Trap of Gold," p. 249)? Does it evoke a **mood,** or **atmosphere**?

- **Tone.** How would you describe the writer's attitude, and how is it revealed? Does **irony** or **satire** play an important role in the story?

- **Theme.** What central insight into life or human nature does the story reveal? Is the theme stated **directly,** or do you have to piece together clues to find the story's meaning? What do you think of the theme? Do you agree with it? Is it important? overused? **ambiguous**?

"Two Kinds" by Amy Tan (page 95)		
Element	Examples	Importance in Story
Plot/ conflict	External conflict: mother wants Jing-mei to be a prodigy; Jing-mei fails, then rebels.	Crucial to story's theme.
Character	Jing-mei: strong-willed, angry; wants her mother's approval; sees her mother differently at the end.	Character of Jing-mei is well developed (we know her thoughts & feelings); so is that of her mother. Characters very memorable and believable.
Setting	Chinatown, somewhere in U.S.	Cultural conflict important to theme. But not Chinatown itself.
Theme	Universal: Love between mother and daughter goes beyond their differences and conflicts.	Most important.

3. State Your Main Ideas

Look over your notes, and decide which elements play the biggest role in revealing the story's meaning. Try to state your

Try It Out

With a partner, try filling in one or two rows of a chart of literary elements. Here are some ideas:

1. Make a character row for "Everyday Use" (page 70) or "Distillation" (page 133).

2. Make a theme row for "Boys and Girls" (page 53) or "Liberty" (page 185).

Introducing the Writer's Workshop

List the elements of prose fiction on the board and have students rank them for importance in their own reading. Do they most often choose stories by setting, by plot, by mood, or by character?

See if students can give examples of short stories or novels that had intricate plots, vivid settings, or fleshed-out characters. How does the element of pacing enter into the mix? How does the combination of many elements work together to make a compelling read?

Teaching the Writer's Workshop

Prewriting

Remind students to select a short story to which they have a strong reaction—positive or negative. Ask students to think about the reasons for their reactions. Do they find the plot compelling or dull? Are the characters believable? Are they likable? Can the students visualize the setting as the author has described it? Have students quickwrite their impressions for a few minutes.

Now, have students organize their notes into a simple chart like the one on this page. Have students use the techniques suggested on pp. 240-241 to generate ideas as they prepare to write their first drafts. Remind students that their aim is to analyze, not to summarize, the short story.

Reaching All Students

English Language Learners

Encourage speakers of other languages to use the language that is most comfortable for them in prewriting. If they choose their original language for prewriting, allow them to write their first draft this way, too. Then, have them select two paragraphs from their essay (the introduction and one other) to put into standard English. Allow them to complete their entire essay in English as a portfolio option.

Drafting

- Before they begin to write their drafts, have students read and study the Student Model on p. 243. Use the analytical comments provided in the margin and in the *Teacher's Edition* as a focus for discussion.
- Discuss the patterns of organization listed on this page and have students identify their uses in the Student Model. What is the most basic pattern seen in the model? [chronological order]
- Review all of the prewriting steps with students, but place particular emphasis on the methods of elaboration explored on this page. Students should be aware that one aspect of evaluation will be how well they support their analysis with specific details and evidence from the story.

Language/Grammar Link
HELP

Connotations: page 181.
Pronoun reference: page 193.
Imagery: pages 208 and 234.
Active and passive verbs: page 221.

Sentence Workshop
HELP

Combining sentences: page 245.

Patterns of Organization

- In your essay as a whole (and in a paragraph about theme or character), you might organize your ideas in **order of importance** (from most to least important or vice versa).
- In a paragraph summarizing the plot, it makes more sense to use **chronological order** (the order in which events occur).
- In a paragraph about setting, you might use **spatial order** (in which objects are described from left to right, near to far, and so on).

---

main idea about each element in one or two sentences; you'll use these later to write **topic sentences.** Here is the Student Model writer's main idea about Jing-mei's **character:**

MAIN IDEA: Jing-mei is not a quiet, obedient daughter, but rather a strong-willed and frustrated child. She is caught between her mother's expectations and a growing anger inside herself.

Now, try drafting a **thesis statement** that sums up your ideas about your story. (You may need to make several drafts before you settle on a wording.) Here is the student writer's thesis statement:

THESIS STATEMENT: "Two Kinds" by Amy Tan gives insight into the relationship between a Chinese mother and her Chinese American daughter.

4. Elaborate: Back It Up

Don't worry if your analysis of a story differs from a classmate's; there is no one correct analysis of any story. Just be sure to back up your statements with specific details and examples from the story. Here are some types of supporting evidence you can use to **elaborate** on your topic sentences:

- references to specific events in the story
- descriptions of character traits with details to support them
- details describing the setting
- quotations from the story (not too many, though, so that your essay won't sound choppy)
- comparisons with other stories

Drafting
1. Start Writing

You've got notes, topic sentences, and a thesis statement—everything you need in order to begin writing. Now, start supporting each topic sentence with evidence. In your **introduction,** identify the title and author of your story and present your **thesis statement.** In the **body,** elaborate on three or four main ideas. In your **conclusion,** restate the thesis and perhaps add a final comment. You may want to begin by drafting your introduction, or you may prefer to begin with the body.

2. Don't Summarize—Analyze!

As you write, make sure you are truly *analyzing* the story. Don't just summarize the plot, string together quotations, and present your immediate reactions to the story. Your purpose is to reveal a level of meaning your readers may have missed. Assume that they've read the story—but not as closely as you have.

242 THE SHORT-STORY COLLECTIONS

Using Students' Strengths

Interpersonal Learners

When pairing or grouping students for writing activities, rather than merely creating groups with mixed ability levels, you might also group students who enjoy writing with students who are motivated by working in groups. This might allow the students to build on sharing an enthusiasm for the assignment as well as the prospect of working on it together, thus inspiring their peers within the group.

"TWO KINDS" BY AMY TAN

"Two Kinds" by Amy Tan gives insight into the relationship between a Chinese mother and her Chinese American daughter. Jing-mei, the narrator and main character, now grown, is recalling childhood memories of her mother after her mother's death. As a child, Jing-mei is constantly pushed by her mother to be a prodigy. Tired of not being accepted for her true self, Jing-mei rebels by not even trying at anything anymore. The story's resounding theme is that the love between mother and daughter goes beyond their differences and problems.

Thesis statement.

Statement of the story's theme.

Because the story is told by Jing-mei, we know her thoughts and feelings. She is not a quiet, obedient daughter, but rather a strong-willed and frustrated child. She is caught between the pressure, on the one hand, of her mother's expectations and her own hopes of being something great and, on the other hand, a growing anger inside that multiplies with each new failure. One day, when looking in the mirror, Jing-mei discovers that "the girl staring back at me was angry, powerful. This girl and I were the same." That is when she decides never to let her mother change her, and she constantly attempts to fail. Thus begins the conflict between the two.

Topic sentence.

Character and motivation.

Quotation from the text.
Conflict.

Throughout the story, the mother finds new ways of testing Jing-mei through different talents she has discovered in magazines; and, of course, Jing-mei never succeeds. Finally, when her mother has almost given up all hope, she sees a young Chinese girl playing the piano on the <u>Ed Sullivan Show</u>. She works out a way for Jing-mei to get lessons, but the girl tries her best <u>not</u> to learn anything.

References to events in the story.

At the end of the story, Jing-mei is looking through her mother's things after her mother's death. She keeps the sweaters her mother made that she hated to wear and gets the piano tuned just for reminiscing. This shows how much she loved her mother, despite the fact that they could never see eye to eye. These actions all portray the story's theme of family ties: that the love between a mother and daughter cannot be spoiled by their differences.

Resolution reinforces theme.

I think this story teaches people not to take for granted those that they love. The relationship between Jing-mei and her mother is parallel to many mother-daughter relationships everywhere. The author's powerful writing and well-developed characters allow us to learn a lot from the events in the story.

Personal response to story and restatement of thesis.

—Elisabeth Kristof
Austin High School
Austin, Texas

After students have completed their drafts, they may benefit from another look at the Student Model. Have students ask themselves the following questions:

❓ What important elements does the writer include in her first paragraph?

❓ What conflicts does the writer examine?

❓ How convincing is the writer's summary of the plot? Is there enough information to give me a good idea of what the story is about?

❓ How convincing are the writer's interpretations of events in the story?

❓ How well does the writer express her personal response? Is it interesting? Does it connect with the story's theme?

❓ What techniques does the writer use that I can apply in my writing?

Using Students' Strengths

Auditory Learners

Students might benefit from explaining the concept of their essays to a partner who will listen and write down the key details. The writer will benefit from hearing which details struck the listener as important in the planned development of the analysis.

Evaluating and Revising

- Students should use Evaluation Criteria in self-evaluation and peer editing.
- Students should not write on their partners' papers. Comments should be made on another sheet of paper or on self-sticking notes.
- Encourage students to look for sentences that could be combined by using phrases. Students should refer to the Sentence Workshop on p. 245 for guidance.

Proofreading

Have students proofread their own papers first and then exchange them with another student. For this assignment, remind students to be particularly careful to use the present tense correctly.

Students might also want to isolate what types of errors they are looking for when they proofread a peer's paper. For example, in one pass they could focus on errors in grammar, in another pass on usage, and in another on mechanics and spelling.

Publishing

Students might want to publish their essays in the school literary magazine or in an appropriate journal.

Reflecting

If students are adding their expository essays to their portfolios, they might also include answers to the following questions:

1. How did my writing increase my understanding of the work that I selected?
2. What problems did I have understanding the literary work and how did I solve them?
3. What, if anything, will I do differently the next time I write an expository essay?

■ *Evaluation Criteria*

A good analysis of a story

1. *gives the story's title and author and presents a thesis statement in the introduction*

2. *discusses three or four literary elements*

3. *provides evidence (such as quotations and details from the text) to support main ideas*

4. *includes transitional expressions*

5. *concludes by restating the thesis*

Proofreading Tip

If you're writing with a computer, use the spelling checker to check for words you often misspell.

Communications Handbook
H E L P

See Proofreaders' Marks.

Publishing Tip

Share your literary analysis by reading it aloud to your class or reading group or by posting it on your school's Web site.

Evaluating and Revising

1. Self-Evaluation

Reread your draft to make sure that questions and references to the story fit smoothly into your sentences. Pay particular attention to the flow of ideas. You may need to add transitional words or phrases (such as *first, second, finally, in addition, although,* or *as a result*) to signal where you're going and to show how your ideas are related. If your writing sounds choppy, consider combining sentences or paraphrasing some of your quotations.

2. Peer Review

Exchange drafts with a partner, and give him or her suggestions for revision. Focus on the evaluation criteria at the left, but also point out unnecessary or overused words, irrelevant or unconvincing evidence, and confusing or awkward transitions. Be sure to give your partner positive feedback as well.

Revision Model

	Peer Comments
At the end of the story, Jing-mei is looking through her	When is this happening?
after her mother's death mother's things. She keeps the	
sweaters her mother made that she	
and gets the piano tuned just for reminiscing hated to wear. This shows how much	Mention other actions.
she loved her mother, despite the	
fact that they could never see eye to	
eye. These actions all portray the	
that story's theme of family ties: the love	You need to state the theme more fully.
cannot be spoiled by their differences between a mother and daughter.	

Getting Students Involved

Cooperative Learning

Some students may feel that once they receive feedback on their essay, the work is no longer their own. One way to emphasize that a collaborative effort can still represent an individual writer's thoughts would be to ask some professional writers to talk about the difference between collaborative work and work that is created by one person but is edited by others. For example, you could invite journalists from a local newspaper to discuss the roles of the writer, assigning editor, copy editor, page design editor, etc.

Sentence Workshop

COMBINING SENTENCES: USING PHRASES

Read the following passage aloud. How does it sound?

> He turned back. He was on a side street. He was circling around. He circled toward his home.

To most readers, this series of short sentences, all beginning with "He," will sound choppy and monotonous. See how Ray Bradbury combined the short, choppy sentences into one smooth sentence by using **phrases**. The phrases are marked off by slash marks.

> "He turned back / on a side street, / circling around / toward his home."
>
> —Ray Bradbury, "The Pedestrian" (page 174)

Phrases are groups of words that do not have both subjects and verbs. Commonly used phrases include **prepositional phrases**, **verbal phrases**, and **appositive phrases**.

Here are two other sentences from the stories in this collection. The phrases are marked off by slash marks. How could each of these passages be written as two or more short sentences?

> "On the far side / of the village, / buried in the dark smells, / a dog barked."
>
> —Tim O'Brien, "Where Have You Gone, Charming Billy?" (page 199)

> "He was lying / in a corner / drying his open wings / in the sunlight / among the fruit peels and breakfast leftovers. . . . "
>
> —Gabriel García Márquez, "A Very Old Man with Enormous Wings" (page 225)

Writer's Workshop Follow-up: Revision

Do an oral reading of the essay you wrote for the Writer's Workshop on page 240. In the reading, listen for passages that sound choppy or awkward. Underline these passages, and see if you can improve them by combining sentences. Look for ideas that can be put into phrases that answer the questions *which one? what kind? where? when? how? why?*

Language Handbook HELP

See Phrases, pages 1034–1036.

Technology HELP

See Language Workshop CD-ROM. Key word entry: combining sentences.

Try It Out

Combining with phrases. Combine each of the following series of short, choppy sentences into a single, smooth sentence by using phrases. To test your revised sentences, look at the text on the page indicated in parentheses to see how the professional writer used phrases to combine the same series of ideas.

1. Private First Class Paul Berlin lay quietly. He was at the rear of the column. His forehead rested on his rifle. His rifle had a black plastic stock. He closed his eyes. (page 198)

2. He was a skeleton. The skin was drawn tight over his bones. His long curls were like a woman's. He had a shaggy beard. (page 215)

OBJECTIVES
1. Use phrases to combine short, choppy sentences
2. Identify phrases within a sentence
3. Identify some kinds of phrases: prepositional, verbal, appositive

Resources

Workshop Resources
• Worksheet, p. 59
Language Workshop CD-ROM
• Combining Phrases

Mini-Lesson: Combining Sentences
After explaining the three types of phrases and reviewing their characteristics, ask students to identify each phrase in the sample sentences from stories in this collection. Discuss the cues that help students determine which type of phrase each is. Then, have them complete the Try It Out exercise before they reread and revise their own work from the Writer's Workshop on p. 240.

Try It Out
Possible Answers
1. Private First Class Paul Berlin lay quietly at the rear of the column with his forehead resting on the black plastic stock of his rifle, his eyes closed.
2. He was a skeleton with the skin drawn tight over his bones, long curls like a woman's, and a shaggy beard.

Assessing Learning

Quick Check: Combining Sentences
Combine each of the following sets of sentences by using phrases. [Answers will vary.]
1. The house was painted yellow. The house was by the pond. [The house by the pond was painted yellow.]
2. The bus was speeding. The bus was going down the highway. [The bus was speeding down the highway.]

3. Elena is well known for her paella. Paella is a Spanish dish. [Elena is well known for her paella, a Spanish dish.]
4. Jemma describes the conflict between two cultures. She does this as she writes fictional tales. [Writing fictional tales, Jemma describes the conflict between two cultures.]

T245

Reading for Life

Evaluating a Documentary

Teaching the Lesson

Explain that being able to evaluate a documentary helps students become more astute viewers not only of documentaries, but of docudramas and films based on true stories. Ask students to name documentaries that they've seen recently and to describe what they learned from them. Ask whether they pursued information about the topic in other sources such as reference books and other nonfiction books.

Using the Strategies

You may want to assign individuals, pairs, or small groups to view a documentary and apply the strategies outlined in this lesson. Suggest that students inquire at the school media center, school library, or their local library for documentaries on videocassette. Encourage students to share their evaluations.

Resource

Viewing and Representing
HRW Multimedia Presentation Maker

Students may wish to use the *Multimedia Presentation Maker* to create their own documentary of information about the Vietnam War.

Situation

After reading Tim O'Brien's story on page 197, you want to know more about the war in Vietnam. At your local video store, you find a documentary film about this controversial war. Here are strategies you can use to evaluate any documentary.

Strategies

Understand the purpose of a documentary.

• A documentary is now called a kind of "nonfiction." As such, a documentary is designed to present actual people and events in a factual way. You may not realize it, but a documentary, like print nonfiction, also presents a point of view. Indeed, two different documentaries may present dramatically opposing views of the same subject.

Assess its credibility.

• **Investigate the source of the documentary.** First, find out who directed and produced it. Ask yourself if the filmmakers have a special interest in presenting a particular point of view. Then, make sure that what you're watching is a true documentary, not a "docudrama." In a **docudrama,** for example, you're likely to see film of the Roman legions marching off to

Part of the film credits for the IMAX documentary *Everest* (1998). A MacGillivray Freeman Film. Greg MacGillivray, producer and director.

Carthage. In that case, of course, you would *know* you're not watching a documentary. But other docudramas are more subtle. You must be alert and read the credits carefully.

• **Who is narrating the documentary, and what are his or her qualifications?** Is the narrator associated with any particular political viewpoint?

• **Keep in mind what you already know.** A good documentary should add to your knowledge of the subject. It may even be persuasive enough to change your thinking about it. Use your prior knowledge to evaluate the depth and seriousness of the documentary's coverage.

• **Check the facts.** Use outside reference sources to check any new information you discover in the documen-

tary, particularly any information that strikes you as questionable.

• **Be aware of how the filmmaker has used visual and sound techniques to convey a message, and perhaps to manipulate your emotions.** Documentaries are usually intended to persuade their audiences to accept a particular point of view. Film clips of actual events and people can be edited and sequenced to affect the audience in a certain way. Watch the way the filmmaker juxtaposes images. Listen carefully to the narrator's tone of voice and to music and other sound effects that accompany the film. Do they create a certain mood or effect?

Using the Strategies

Apply these strategies to a documentary currently on TV.

Reaching All Students

English Language Learners
It might be informative and interesting for students to seek a foreign-made documentary about the Vietnam war. The students could identify the documentary's point of view and assess the credibility of the information. If the documentary is presented in the native language of an English language learner in the class, it might be interesting to have the student practice his or her English vocabulary and explain the content of the documentary to the rest of the class.

Advanced Learners
Have students research the accuracy of facts in the documentary and support their findings with newspaper articles and periodicals. It may be of interest to have students analyze the visual and audio presentation of facts in the documentary and offer opinions on the appropriateness of the filmmaker's presentation. Students might then assemble their own mini-documentary on the Vietnam War by using photos, recordings, and articles uncovered during their research.

Collection 4

Breakthroughs

Theme

Turning Points *We all face turning points—moments when we make decisions or face our problems in ways that change our lives forever. In just such moments of truth, the characters in this collection's stories break through to new levels of understanding. The "breakthrough" in a story is often the moment that also clarifies the story's theme—it is the moment in which the character makes that key discovery about life that is the essence of theme.*

Reading the Anthology

Reaching Struggling Readers

The *Reading Skills and Strategies: Reaching Struggling Readers* binder provides materials coordinated with the Pupil's Edition (see the Collection Planner, p. T246B) to help students who have difficulty reading and comprehending text, or students who are reluctant readers. The binder for tenth grade is organized around sixteen individual skill areas and offers the following options:

- 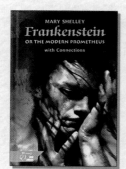 **MiniReads** are short, easy texts that give students a chance to practice a particular skill and strategy before reading selections in the Pupil's Edition. Each MiniRead Skill Lesson can be taught independently or used in conjunction with a Selection Skill Lesson.

- **Selection Skill Lessons** Selection Skill Lessons allow students to apply skills introduced in the MiniReads. Each Selection Skill Lesson provides reading instruction and practice specific to a particular piece of literature in the Pupil's Edition.

Reading Beyond the Anthology

Read On

Collection 4 includes an annotated bibliography of books suitable for extended reading. The suggested books are related to works in this collection by theme, by author, or by subject. To preview the Read On for Collection 4, please turn to p. T327.

HRW Library

The *HRW Library* offers novels, plays, and short-story collections for extended reading. Each book in the Library includes one or more major works and thematically related Connections. Each book in the *HRW Library* is also accompanied by a Study Guide that provides teaching suggestions and worksheets. For Collection 4, the following titles are recommended.

FRANKENSTEIN
Mary Shelley
The breakthrough is Dr. Frankenstein's discovery of the secret of imparting life to inanimate matter—and the unspeakable horror that results.

THE YEARLING
Marjorie Kinnan Rawlings
An enduring American classic, this story of Jody and his fawn reveals a young boy's discoveries about responsibility, love, and family in the course of a year.

Collection 4 Breakthroughs

Resources for this Collection

Note: All resources for this collection are available for preview on the *One-Stop Planner CD-ROM 1 with Test Generator.* All worksheets and blackline masters may be printed from the CD-ROM.

Internet Resources
go.hrw.com LE0 10-4

Selection or Feature	Reading and Literary Skills	Vocabulary, Language, and Grammar

Trap of Gold (p. 248)
Louis L'Amour
 	
Connections: "It is Wonderful!"
from **Diary of the discovery of the tomb of Tutankhamen** (p. 258)
Howard Carter
	• *Reading Skills and Strategies: Reaching Struggling Readers*
	  • MiniRead Skill Lesson, p. 111
	  • Selection Skill Lesson, p. 119
	• *Graphic Organizers for Active Reading*, Worksheet p. 16
		• *Words to Own*, Worksheet p. 17
		• *Grammar and Language Links:* Comparisons, Worksheet p. 29
		• *Language Workshop CD-ROM*, Using Comparative and Superlative Forms
		• *Daily Oral Grammar*, Transparency 16

Elements of Literature: Point of View (p. 262)	• *Literary Elements*, Transparency 8	

By the Waters of Babylon (p. 264)
Stephen Vincent Benét
	• *Reading Skills and Strategies: Reaching Struggling Readers*
	  • MiniRead Skill Lesson, p. 124
	  • Selection Skill Lesson, p. 131
	• *Graphic Organizers for Active Reading*, Worksheet p. 17
	• *Literary Elements:* Transparency 8
	Worksheet p. 25
		• *Grammar and Language Links:* Subjects, Worksheet p. 31
		• *Language Workshop CD-ROM*, Subject-Verb Agreement
		• *Daily Oral Grammar*, Transparency 17

Through the Tunnel (p. 276) Doris Lessing	• *Graphic Organizers for Active Reading*, Worksheet p. 18	• *Words to Own*, Worksheet p. 18 • *Grammar and Language Links:* Participles, Worksheet p. 33 • *Language Workshop CD-ROM*, Participles • *Daily Oral Grammar*, Transparency 18

The Pit and the Pendulum (p. 288)
Edgar Allan Poe
	• *Reading Skills and Strategies: Reaching Struggling Readers*
	  • MiniRead Skill Lesson, p. 135
	  • Selection Skill Lesson, p. 142
	• *Graphic Organizers for Active Reading*, Worksheet p. 19
	• *Literary Elements:* Transparency 9
	Worksheet p. 28
		• *Words to Own*, Worksheet p. 19
		• *Grammar and Language Links:* Repetition, Worksheet p. 35
		• *Daily Oral Grammar*, Transparency 19

Elements of Literature: Symbols (p. 306)	• *Literary Elements*, Transparency 9	
With All Flags Flying (p. 308) Anne Tyler **Connections: Señora X No More** (p. 317) Pat Mora	• *Graphic Organizers for Active Reading*, Worksheet p. 20	• *Words to Own*, Worksheet p. 20 • *Grammar and Language Links:* Verbs, Worksheet p. 37 • *Language Workshop CD-ROM*, Verbs and Adverbs • *Daily Oral Grammar*, Transparency 20
Extending the Theme: By Any Other Name (p. 321) Santha Rama Rau	The Extending the Theme feature provides students with an unstructured opportunity to practice reading strategies using a selection that extends the theme of the collection.	
Writer's Workshop: Evaluating a Story or Movie (p. 328)		
Sentence Workshop: Using Coordination (p. 333)		• *Workshop Resources*, p. 61 • *Language Workshop CD-ROM*, Combining Sentences
Learning for Life: Conflict Resolution (p. 335)		

Other Resources for this Collection

- *Cross-Curricular Activities*, p. 4
- *Portfolio Management System,* Introduction to Portfolio Assessment, p. 1
- *Formal Assessment,* Genre Test, p. 54
- *Test Generator,* Collection Test 🔘

Writing	Listening and Speaking / Viewing and Representing	Assessment
• *Portfolio Management System,* Rubrics for Choices, p. 120	• *Audio CD Library,* 🎧 Disc 8, Track 2 • *Viewing and Representing:* Fine Art Transparency 6; Worksheet p. 24 📇 • *Portfolio Management System,* Rubrics for Choices, p. 120	• *Formal Assessment,* Selection Test, p. 40 • *Standardized Test Preparation,* pp. 32, 34 • *Test Generator (One-Stop Planner CD-ROM)* 🔘
		• *Formal Assessment,* Literary Elements Test, p. 50
• *Portfolio Management System,* Rubrics for Choices, p. 121	• *Audio CD Library,* 🎧 Disc 8, Track 3 • *Portfolio Management System,* Rubrics for Choices, p. 121	• *Formal Assessment,* Selection Test, p. 42 • *Test Generator (One-Stop Planner CD-ROM)* 🔘
• *Portfolio Management System,* Rubrics for Choices, p. 123	• *Audio CD Library,* 🎧 Disc 9, Track 2 • *Portfolio Management System,* Rubrics for Choices, p. 123	• *Formal Assessment,* Selection Test, p. 44 • *Standardized Test Preparation,* p. 36 • *Test Generator (One-Stop Planner CD-ROM)* 🔘
• *Portfolio Management System,* Rubrics for Choices, p. 124	• *Visual Connections:* Videocassette A, Segment 4 📼 • *Audio CD Library,* 🎧 Disc 9, Track 3 • *Portfolio Management System,* Rubrics for Choices, p. 124	• *Formal Assessment,* Selection Test, p. 46 • *Standardized Test Preparation,* pp. 38, 40 • *Test Generator (One-Stop Planner CD-ROM)* 🔘
		• *Formal Assessment,* Literary Elements Test, p. 52
• *Portfolio Management System,* Rubrics for Choices, p. 126	• *Audio CD Library,* 🎧 Disc 10, Track 2 • *Viewing and Representing:* Fine Art Transparency 7; Worksheet p. 28 📇 • *Portfolio Management System,* Rubrics for Choices, p. 126	• *Formal Assessment,* Selection Test, p. 48 • *Test Generator (One-Stop Planner CD-ROM)* 🔘
	• *Audio CD Library,* 🎧 Disc 10, Track 3	• *Standardized Test Preparation,* p. 42

• *Workshop Resources,* p. 19
 • *Writer's Workshop 2 CD-ROM,* Evaluation 🔘
	• *Viewing and Representing,* HRW Multimedia Presentation Maker	• *Portfolio Management System*
		  • Prewriting, p. 127
		  • Peer Editing, p. 128
		  • Assessment Rubric, p. 129

		• *Portfolio Management System,* Rubrics, p. 130

 Transparency   CD-ROM   Video   Audio CD

T246C

Collection Planner

Collection 4 Breakthroughs

Skills Focus

Selection or Feature	Reading Skills and Strategies	Elements of Literature	Vocabulary/Language/Grammar	Writing	Listening/Speaking	Viewing/Representing
Trap of Gold (p. 248) Louis L'Amour	Chronological Order, pp. 248, 259	Setting, pp. 248, 259 Antagonist, pp. 248, 259 Suspense, pp. 248, 259 Point of View, p. 259	Comparisons and Analogies, p. 261 Synonyms and Antonyms, p. 261	Develop Criteria for Evaluating a Story, p. 260 Write a New Ending, p. 260 Report on Basic Plots in the News, p. 260	Research and Prepare an Oral Report, p. 260	Create Story Maps, p. 260
Elements of Literature: Point of View (p. 262)		Point of View, p. 262 • Omniscient • First Person • Third-Person Limited				
By the Waters of Babylon (p. 264) Stephen Vincent Benét	Draw Conclusions, pp. 264, 273 Summarize Main Events, p. 273	Fantasy, p. 264 First-Person Point of View, pp. 264, 273 Allusion, pp. 264, 273	Inverted Order, p. 275 Prefix, p. 275 Suffix, p. 275	Evaluate an Author's Craft, p. 274 Write a Prequel, p. 274	Research and Present an Oral Report, p. 274	Compare and Contrast a Film and a Story, p. 274 Prepare Visuals for an Oral Report, p. 274
Through the Tunnel (p. 276) Doris Lessing	Monitor Your Reading, pp. 276, 285	Omniscient Point of View, pp. 276, 285 Theme, p. 285 Suspense, p. 285	Participles and Participial Phrases, p. 287 Analogies, p. 287	Gather Evidence to Support an Opinion, p. 286 Write a Brief Essay Analyzing Setting, p. 286	Retell the Events in a Story from Another Point of View, p. 285 Prepare and Present a Dramatic Reading, p. 286	Create a Collage, p. 286
The Pit and the Pendulum (p. 288) Edgar Allan Poe	Summarize, pp. 288, 303	Symbolic Meaning, pp. 288, 303 Setting, p. 303 Image, p. 303	Rhythm, Repetition, and Sound Effects, p. 305 Alliteration, p. 305 Context Clues, p. 305	State an Evaluation Opinion, p. 304 Update a Story, p. 304 Write a Poem in Response to a Story, p. 304	Research and Prepare an Oral Report, p. 304	Draw or Paint Images That Suggest the Setting, p. 304
Elements of Literature: Symbols (p. 306)		Public Symbols, p. 306 Figurative Language, p. 307 Theme, p. 307				
With All Flags Flying (p. 308) Anne Tyler	Compare and Contrast Themes, pp. 308, 318	Third-Person Limited Point of View, p. 308 Motives, p. 318 Character, p. 318 Title, p. 318	Vigorous Verbs, p. 320 Word Maps, p. 320	Compare and Evaluate Two Stories, p. 319 Support an Opinion, p. 319 Write a Scene from Another Character's Perspective, p. 319		Draw a Setting, p. 319
Extending the Theme: By Any Other Name (p. 321) Santha Rama Rau	The Extending the Theme feature provides students with an unstructured opportunity to practice reading strategies using a selection that extends the theme of the collection.					
Writer's Workshop: Evaluating a Story or Movie (p. 328)				Write an Evaluation of a Story or Movie, pp. 328–332		
Sentence Workshop: Using Coordination (p. 333)			Coordinating Conjunctions, p. 333 Compound Sentences, p. 333	Combine Sentences Using Coordination, p. 333		
Reading for Life: Scanning, Skimming, Note Taking, and Outlining (p. 334)	Use Prereading and Reading Strategies to Improve Comprehension, p. 334					
Learning for Life: Conflict Resolution (p. 335)		Conflict, p. 335			Role-Play the Resolution of a Conflict, p. 335 Prepare and Present Short Radio Broadcasts, p. 335	Create a Poster Campaign, p. 335

BREAKTHROUGHS

WRITING FOCUS: Evaluating a Story or Movie

First you're a child, then you become an adolescent, then an adult. You may start out poor and become rich—or vice versa. You may start out foolish and become wise. Your life may be full of strife, but with effort or luck it becomes peaceful. You may be lonely and then find companionship. You may be sick and break through to health. You may be in a trap and suddenly find yourself free. All of us can probably think of break-throughs we would like to make in our lives and of ones we've already made. In some respects, most fiction is about break-throughs—maybe that's because we long so deeply for that lucky break, for those changes that will transform our lives.

I had been my whole life a bell, and never knew it until at that moment I was lifted and struck.
—Annie Dillard

Collection of Barry C. Scheck and Lawrence A. Vogelman.

Willie Mays (1978) (detail) by Ron Cohen. Acrylic and oil on canvas.

Writer's Notebook

WORK IN PROGRESS

What makes a story good? Write down all the factors that, for you, make a good story. (You may want to work with a partner.) Write freely now. You'll focus on these criteria for good storytelling and add to them as you read the stories in this collection. Save your notes for the Writer's Workshop on page 328.

247

OBJECTIVES

1. Read short stories on the theme "Breakthroughs"
2. Interpret literary elements used in the literature with special emphasis on point of view and symbols
3. Apply a variety of reading strategies to the literature
4. Respond to the literature in a variety of modes
5. Learn and use new words
6. Plan, draft, revise, proof, and publish an evaluation of a story or movie
7. Demonstrate the ability to use skimming, scanning, note taking, and outlining
8. Explore through a variety of media the process of conflict resolution

Responding to the Quotation

❓ What does this quotation say about breakthroughs? [The potential to do something can exist unknown in people; however, until they are challenged, people may not know what they can do.]

RESPONDING TO THE ART

Ronald M. Cohen is known for his large-scale paintings of people, such as *Willie Mays*. His paintings almost always focus on male subjects.

A New York baseball legend, Willie Mays (b. 1931) was one of the most exciting players in baseball history. For most of his career, he played center field for the New York Giants (later of San Francisco). Mays was a sensational fielder, a crack batter, and a daring base runner. His career batting average was .302. Mays is a member of the National Baseball Hall of Fame.

Activity. Ask students what kind of "breakthroughs" can take place in sports. Consider not only the physical "breakthroughs" that can take place in the course of a game (touchdowns, home runs, tie-breakers, and so on) but the psychological "breakthroughs" that might be experienced by both players and fans.

Writing Focus: Evaluating a Story or Movie

WORK IN PROGRESS

The following **Work in Progress** assignments build to a culminating **Writer's Workshop** at the end of the collection.

- Trap of Gold   Developing criteria (p. 260)
- By the Waters of Babylon   Evaluating the author's craft (p. 274)
- Through the Tunnel   Gathering evidence (p. 286)
- The Pit and the Pendulum   Stating an opinion (p. 304)
- With All Flags Flying   Comparing works (p. 319)

Writer's Workshop: Persuasive Writing / Evaluating a Story or Movie (p. 328)

OBJECTIVES
1. Read and interpret the story
2. Analyze the story's setting
3. Recognize chronological order
4. Express understanding through creative writing or research/oral report
5. Identify comparisons and use such comparisons in writing
6. Understand and use new words
7. Identify synonyms and antonyms

SKILLS
Literary
• Analyze setting

Reading
• Recognize chronological order

Writing
• Make an evaluation
• Write a new ending to the story
• Make a story map

Speaking/Listening
• Give a brief oral report

Grammar/Language
• Use comparisons

Vocabulary
• Use new words

Viewing/Representing
• Write a detailed description (ATE)

Planning

• **Traditional Schedule**
Lesson Plans Including Strategies for English-Language Learners

• **One-Stop Planner**
CD-ROM with Test Generator

Before You Read

TRAP OF GOLD

Make the Connection

Risky Business

In making decisions, we weigh the pros and cons: If I do this, what are the risks? What are the benefits?

Wetherton, the hero of this Western story, makes his own analysis of risks and benefits as he takes one chance after another—and moves us to the edge of our seats. How far will this prospector go to get rich?

Quickwrite

There's an old saying: Money makes the world go round. Is it true? Does money drive *your* actions? How much would you risk for a hundred dollars? a million? How much would tempt you to risk your life? Freewrite about the power of money and the risks people take to get it.

Elements of Literature

Setting as Antagonist

Louis L'Amour knew his West well. The **setting** he creates in this story is meticulously described, often in the specialized vocabulary of geology and mining. In this story, in fact, L'Amour has given the setting a major role. The mountain is Wetherton's **antagonist.** It is this mountain that the hero is struggling against. Try to visualize the setting so you can understand how, little by little, it is threatening to become Wetherton's tomb.

> **S**etting is the time and place in which a story's action occurs. At times, setting can even assume the role of **antagonist** in a story.
>
> *For more on Setting, see pages 50–51 and the Handbook of Literary Terms.*

Reading Skills and Strategies

Chronological Order

Most narratives, whether fiction or nonfiction, follow **chronological order**—that is, they show events unfolding in sequence over time. In "Trap of Gold," each moment might be the main character's last, so the use of chronological order is particularly effective in building **suspense.** As you look for words signaling the passage of time, notice too how the setting is very subtly changing as the minutes tick by.

go.hrw.com
LE0 10-4

Preteaching Vocabulary

Words to Own

Have students work in pairs and read the Words to Own at the bottom of the selection pages. Have them take turns creating a sentence using each word. Then use the following questions to reinforce students' understanding of the words. **(1)** How can both a cloth and a person be *abrasive?* **(2)** Where would you go if you were feeling *contemplative?* Why? **(3)** How might a student be *deluded* about his or her popularity? **(4)** What *portals* have you passed through today? **(5)** What do some streets have as an *impediment* to speeding cars? **(6)** How might a headache be *alleviated?* **(7)** What is an *inevitable* season after winter? **(8)** Name three things someone might keep in a *cache.* **(9)** What emotions might you feel when you have a sense of *foreboding?* **(10)** What is an *untenable* excuse for being absent from school?

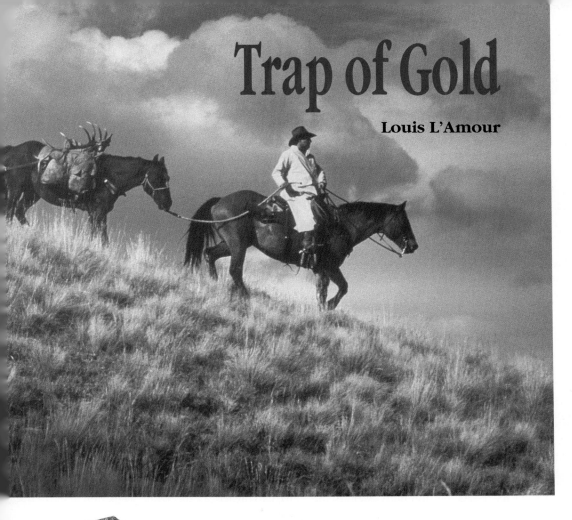

Trap of Gold

Louis L'Amour

Background

In the United States, the first "gold rush" occurred in California in 1849. Tens of thousands of prospectors panned for gold, and many found it. Subsequent gold rushes drew many thousands more to places like Gold Hill, Colorado (1859), Deadwood, South Dakota (1876), Tombstone, Arizona (1877), and Nome, Alaska (1899). Prospectors wandered valleys and mountains with picks, shovels, and gold pans, following instinct—and rumors—and relying on both luck and experience.

Summary ■■

Several "traps" of gold exist in this story: a prospector's greed, his recklessness, and the dangerous setting in which he discovers gold. In a mountainous desert far from home, Wetherton finds an enormous vein of gold, but he must chip it from a huge granite batholith that could collapse on him at any moment.

He resolves to work deliberately, never to forget the danger, and to resist the temptation for "a little more." Briefly, the desire for more gold overpowers his reason, but he breaks through his greed and says, "No more." In a hasty exit from the mountain cave, he narrowly escapes death.

Resources

Listening
Audio CD Library
A dramatic reading of "Trap of Gold" is provided in the Audio CD Library:
• Disc 8, Track 2

Viewing and Representing
Fine Art Transparency
A fine art transparency of *Sunset in the Yosemite Valley* by Albert Bierstadt can be used to stimulate a discussion in which students compare and contrast wilderness as it is depicted in the painting and in "Trap of Gold." See the *Viewing and Representing* booklet:
• Transparency 6
• Worksheet, p. 24

Enormous wealth was here for the taking.

Wetherton had been three months out of Horsehead before he found his first color.[1] At first it was a few scattered grains taken from the base of an alluvial fan[2] where millions of tons of sand and silt had washed down from a chain of rugged peaks; yet the gold was ragged under the magnifying glass.

1. **color:** here, trace of gold.
2. **alluvial fan:** fan-shaped deposit of soil or sand.

Resources: Print and Media

Reading
• *Reading Skills and Strategies*
    MiniRead Skill Lesson, p. 111
    Selection Skill Lesson, p. 119
• *Graphic Organizers for Active Reading*, p. 16
• *Words to Own*, p. 17
• *Audio CD Library*
    Disc 8, Track 2

Writing and Language
• *Daily Oral Grammar*
    Transparency 16
• *Grammar and Language Links*
    Worksheet, p. 29
• *Language Workshop CD-ROM*

Viewing and Representing
• *Viewing and Representing*
    Fine Art Transparency 6

Fine Art Worksheet, p. 24

Assessment
• *Formal Assessment*, p. 40
• *Portfolio Management System*, p. 120
• *Standardized Test Preparation*, pp. 32, 34
• *Test Generator (One-Stop Planner CD-ROM)*

Internet
• go.hrw.com (keyword: *LEO 10-4*)

T249

A Elements of Literature

Setting as Antagonist

These paragraphs are dense with details about the setting that will play a crucial part in Wetherton's struggle. Help students clarify the overall scene by illustrating it in a diagram on the board. In the foreground, you might show Wetherton's camp and burros. Above this, you could picture "the wash that skirted the base of the mountain." This *wash* or "fan" is "a half-mile across" and is shaped like a wide V (with the point toward the mountain). L'Amour writes that the point "lay between two towering upthrusts of granite." These granite columns rise more than two thousand feet, and it is behind them at that altitude that Wetherton will do his difficult work.

Gold that has carried any distance becomes worn and polished by the <u>abrasive</u> action of the accompanying rocks and sand, so this could not have been carried far. With caution born of harsh experience, he seated himself and lighted his pipe, yet excitement was strong within him.

A <u>contemplative</u> man by nature, experience had taught him how a man may be <u>deluded</u> by hope, yet all his instincts told him the source of the gold was somewhere on the mountain above. It could have come down the wash that skirted the base of the mountain, but the ragged condition of the gold made that impossible.

The base of the fan was a half-mile across and hundreds of feet thick, built of silt and sand washed down by centuries of erosion among the higher peaks. The point of the wide V of the fan lay between two towering upthrusts of granite, but from where Wetherton sat he could see that the actual source of the fan lay much higher.

Wetherton made camp near a tiny spring west of the fan, then picketed his burros and began his climb. When he was well over two thousand feet higher, he stopped, resting again, and while resting he dry-panned some of the silt. Surprisingly, there were more than a few grains of gold even in that first pan, so he continued his climb and passed at last between the towering <u>portals</u> of the granite columns.

Above this natural gate were three smaller alluvial fans that joined at the gate to pour into the greater fan below. Dry-panning two of these brought no results, but the third, even by the relatively poor method of dry-panning, showed a dozen colors, all of good size.

The head of this fan lay in a gigantic crack in a granitic[3] upthrust that resembled a fantastic ruin. Pausing to catch his breath, his gaze wandered along the base of this upthrust, and right before him the crumbling granite was slashed with a vein of quartz that was literally laced with gold!

Struggling nearer through the loose sand, his heart pounding more from excitement than

3. **granitic** (grə·nit′ik): made of granite, a very hard rock.

250 THE SHORT-STORY COLLECTIONS

---

from altitude and exertion, he came to an abrupt stop. The band of quartz was six feet wide, and that six feet was cobwebbed with gold.

It was unbelievable, but here it was.

Yet even in this moment of success, something about the beetling[4] cliff stopped him from going forward. His innate caution took hold, and he drew back to examine it at greater length. Wary of what he saw, he circled the batholith[5] and then climbed to the ridge behind it, from which he could look down upon the roof. What he saw from there left him dry-mouthed and jittery.

The granitic upthrust was obviously a part of a much older range, one that had weathered and worn, suffered from shock and twisting until finally this tower of granite had been violently upthrust, leaving it standing, a shaky ruin among younger and sturdier peaks. In the process the rock had been shattered and riven by mighty forces until it had become a miner's horror. Wetherton stared, fascinated by the prospect. With enormous wealth here for the taking, every ounce must be taken at the risk of life.

One stick of powder might bring the whole crumbling mass down in a heap, and it loomed all of three hundred feet above its base in the fan. The roof of the batholith was riven with gigantic cracks, literally seamed with breaks, like the wall of an ancient building that has remained standing after heavy bombing. Walking back to the base of the tower, Wetherton found he could actually break loose chunks of the quartz with his fingers.

4. **beetling:** projecting; jutting out.
5. **batholith** (bath′ō·lith′): large, deeply embedded mass of rock.

WORDS TO OWN

abrasive (ə·brā′siv) *adj.*: scraping; rubbing; wearing away. *Abrasive* also means "irritating" or "harsh."
contemplative (kən·tem′plə·tiv′) *adj.*: thoughtful.
deluded (di·lo̅o̅d′id) *v.*: misled; fooled; deceived.
portals (pôrt′′lz) *n.*: doorways or gates, especially large, impressive ones.

Reaching All Students

Struggling Readers

Analyzing Chronological Order was introduced on p. 248. For a lesson directly tied to this story that teaches students to analyze chronological order by using a strategy called Story Impressions, see the *Reading Skills and Strategies* binder:
• MiniRead Skill Lesson, p. 111
• Selection Skill Lesson, p. 119

English Language Learners

Pair English language learners with more able English speakers to find pictures from geology books (or other reference books) that illustrate the specialized vocabulary used in the story. Students may then photocopy or sketch these pictures in order to create a classroom reference.

For additional strategies to supplement instruction for these students, see
• *Lesson Plans Including Strategies for English-Language Learners*

Advanced Learners

As students read this story, ask them to recall other fiction or nonfiction stories they have read that feature a search for treasure. Do these treasure hunts seem to have any characteristics in common? What qualities, if any, do the treasure hunters share?

The vein itself lay on the downhill side and at the very base. The outer wall of the upthrust was sharply tilted, so that a man working at the vein would be cutting his way into the very foundations of the tower, and any single blow of the pick might bring the whole mass down upon him. Furthermore, if the rock did fall, the vein would be hopelessly buried under thousands of tons of rock and lost without the expenditure of much more capital than he could command. And at this moment Wetherton's total of money in hand amounted to slightly less than forty dollars.

Thirty yards from the face he seated himself upon the sand and filled his pipe once more. A man might take tons out of there without trouble, and yet it might collapse at the first blow. Yet he knew he had no choice. He needed money, and it lay here before him. Even if he were at first successful, there were two things he must avoid. The first was tolerance of danger

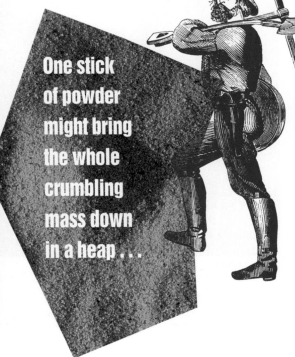

One stick of powder might bring the whole crumbling mass down in a heap . . .

that might bring carelessness; the second, that urge to go back for that "little bit more" that could kill him.

It was well into the afternoon and he had not eaten, yet he was not hungry. He circled the batholith, studying it from every angle, only to reach the conclusion that his first estimate had been correct. The only way to get at the gold was to go into the very shadow of the leaning wall and attack it at its base, digging it out by main strength. From where he stood, it seemed ridiculous that a mere man with a pick could topple that mass of rock, yet he knew how delicate such a balance could be.

The tower was situated on what might be described as the military crest of the ridge, and the alluvial fan sloped steeply away from its lower side, steeper than a steep stairway. The top of the leaning wall overshadowed the top of the fan, and if it started to crumble and a man had warning, he might run to the north with a bare chance of escape. The soft sand in which he must run would be an <u>impediment</u>, but that could be <u>alleviated</u> by making a walk from flat rocks sunken into the sand.

It was dusk when he returned to his camp. Deliberately, he had not permitted himself to begin work, not by so much as a sample. He must be deliberate in all his actions, and never for a second should he forget the mass that towered above him. A split second of hesitation when the crash came—and he accepted it as <u>inevitable</u>—would mean burial under tons of crumbled rock.

The following morning he picketed his burros on a small meadow near the spring, cleaned the spring itself, and prepared a lunch. Then he

WORDS TO OWN

impediment (im·ped′ə·mənt) *n.:* obstacle; something that slows or prevents movement or progress.
alleviated (ə·lē′vē·āt′id) *v.:* reduced; made easier to bear or deal with.
inevitable (in·ev′i·tə·bəl) *adj.:* certain to happen; unavoidable.

B

B Critical Thinking
Challenging the Text
❓ Why does Wetherton feel he has "no choice"? [He needs money.] Do you agree that he has no choice? Why or why not? [Some students may feel that Wetherton's reasoning is sound, whereas others may say that another individual would choose to forego this kind of danger, despite his or her poverty.]

C Struggling Readers
Visualizing
Discuss the setting with students, helping them understand technical terms such as *alluvial fan, batholith,* and *granitic.* Encourage students to make a detailed sketch of this crest so they can more easily visualize it.

D Reading Skills and Strategies

Chronological Order
Have students summarize in chronological order the events that have occurred so far. [Wetherton finds color in an alluvial fan. He camps and then traces the gold to a rock tower. He studies the tower, sits and thinks about it, and then walks around it. He returns to camp.] You might create a time line for the story on the chalkboard. Guide students in adding events to the time line as they continue reading.

E Historical Connections
Explain that burros—also called donkeys—were commonly used by miners because they are durable animals that can carry heavy loads and that require minimal care. Burros are related to horses, but are not to be confused with mules (the offspring of mated burros and horses).

Crossing the Curriculum

Geography
Although depicted as generally flat, hot, and dry regions, all deserts are not alike. They support a variety of animal and plant life and feature a wide range of landforms. There are about 500,000 square miles of deserts in North America. Have students use appropriate reference materials to locate these deserts.

Science
Gold is found in many places—in ocean water, rocks, even in ordinary soil. In most cases, however, the gold is too sparse to extract. When found in a concentrated form, it is extracted by mining. Have students investigate various mining processes. They might develop diagrams and other graphics to illustrate their findings.

A Elements of Literature

Setting as Antagonist

? Which of Wetherton's actions suggest that he recognizes the mountain crest as an antagonist? [Possible responses: He has repeatedly inspected the batholith from every angle, sat and thought over his options, planned an escape route and built a walk of flat rocks, delayed setting to work, and resolved to be deliberate in all his actions. Finally, he sets to work with great care.]

B Critical Thinking

Analyzing Style

Draw students' attention to the way L'Amour alternates passages of close description of physical actions with passages in which he describes ideas and background information. Explain that one effect of this alternating style is to build suspense by delaying the development and resolution of the chain of actions and events. Here L'Amour builds suspense by taking time to explain the risks and to spell out the reasons that Wetherton faces them. Ask students to be alert to other examples of this technique in the story.

C Reading Skills and Strategies

Chronological Order

? Which words give clues that help readers follow the chronology of these events? [*after* and *until*] What other clues to chronology can you find on this page? [Possible answers: *finally, when, by daybreak,* and *first day's work.*]

D Appreciating Language

Style

Before reading aloud the paragraph, point out that L'Amour wastes few words. His word choice and sentence structure are typically simple, direct, and workmanlike. Here, each straightforward sentence is packed with information.

---

removed his shirt, drew on a pair of gloves, and walked to the face of the cliff. Yet even then he did not begin, knowing that upon this habit of care and deliberation might depend not only his success in the venture, but life itself. He gathered flat stones and began building his walk. "When you start moving," he told himself, "you'll have to be fast."

Finally, and with infinite care, he began tapping at the quartz, enlarging cracks with the pick, removing fragments, then prying loose whole chunks. He did not swing the pick, but used it as a lever. The quartz was rotten, and a man might obtain a considerable amount by this method of picking or even pulling with the hands. When he had a sack filled with the richest quartz, he carried it over his path to a safe place beyond the shadow of the tower. Returning, he tamped[6] a few more flat rocks into his path and began on the second sack. He worked with greater care than was, perhaps, essential. He was not and had never been a gambling man.

In the present operation he was taking a careful calculated risk in which every eventuality had been weighed and judged. He needed the money and he intended to have it; he had a good idea of his chances of success, but he knew that his gravest danger was to become too greedy, too much engrossed in his task.

Dragging the two sacks down the hill, he found a flat block of stone and with a single jack proceeded to break up the quartz. It was a slow and a hard job, but he had no better means of extracting the gold. After breaking or crushing the quartz, much of the gold could be separated by a knife blade, for it was amazingly concentrated. With water from the spring, Wetherton panned the remainder until it was too dark to see.

Out of his blankets by daybreak, he ate breakfast and completed the extraction of the gold. At a rough estimate, his first day's work would run to four hundred dollars. He made a <u>cache</u> for the gold sack and took the now empty ore sacks and climbed back to the tower.

6. **tamped:** packed down.

252 THE SHORT-STORY COLLECTIONS

Shiprock (1994) by P. A. Nisbet. Oil on canvas.

WORDS TO OWN

cache (kash) *n.:* safe place for storing or hiding things. *Cache* may also refer to anything stored or hidden in such a place.

Taking a Second Look

Review: Making Inferences About Character

Remind students that an inference is an intelligent guess about something or someone based on evidence. An inference gives new information that is not presented directly by the writer. To draw inferences about a character, students should look at descriptions of the character's appearance and at the way he or she thinks and acts.

Activities

1. Have students create a profile of Wetherton as they read. They should record facts and details the author provides about the character. Then, have them analyze this information to make inferences about his character.

2. Ask students to read the selection in pairs. Have them stop after every page and discuss what they believe to be true about Wetherton, citing evidence to support their statements.

Courtesy of the artist.

E Elements of Literature
Imagery
❓ What image does the author use to convey Wetherton's sense of readiness and pleasure in pursuing the gold? [The author says Wetherton ". . . liked the feel of the pick in his hands."]

F Critical Thinking
Determining Author's Purpose or Slant
❓ Why do you think L'Amour decides to introduce and name Wetherton's wife (Laura) and son (Tommy)? [Sample responses: He wants to give readers a better understanding of Wetherton and justify why the prospector is taking the risks; he wants to give us more characters to care about.]

The air was clear and fresh, the sun warm after the chill of night, and he liked the feel of **E** the pick in his hands.

Laura and Tommy awaited him back in Horsehead, and if he was killed here, there was small **F** chance they would ever know what had become of him. But he did not intend to be killed. The gold he was extracting from this rock was for them, and not for himself.

It would mean an easier life in a larger town,

TRAP OF GOLD 253

Getting Students Involved

Cooperative Learning
Strange Behavior. Point out that Wetherton gambles for gold with his life. He acts "unlike himself" when he gets carried away with greed and excitement. Have students work in small groups to brainstorm other situations in which people change because of money. (Students might mention the behavior of people who suddenly become wealthy or of people who are so desperate they take to cheating or stealing.) Have groups discuss the similarities and differences between Wetherton and the people the groups mention. Have each group designate a recorder to chart these similarities and differences. After students complete their group discussions, ask each group to share the most interesting comparisons with the class.

Writing Activity
Newspaper Stories. Have students work in groups to create stories and advertisements that might appear in the local Horsehead newspaper, regarding the possibility of finding gold in the area. Students' work could be displayed on a bulletin board or in a newsletter or newspaper format. Their newspapers might include a headline story, editorials, classified ads, an advice column, a travel story, and one or more mining or travel ads.

a home of their own and the things to make the home a woman desires, and it meant an education for Tommy. For himself, all he needed was the thought of that home to return to, his wife and son—and the desert itself. And one was as necessary to him as the other.

The desert would be the death of him. He had been told that many times and did not need to be told, for few men knew the desert as he did. The desert was to him what an orchestra is to a fine conductor, what the human body is to a surgeon. It was his work, his life, and the thing he knew best. He always smiled when he looked first into the desert as he started a new trip. Would this be it?

The morning drew on, and he continued to work with an even-paced swing of the pick, a careful filling of the sack. The gold showed bright and beautiful in the crystalline quartz,

The desert would be the death of him. He had been told that many times . . .

which was so much more beautiful than the gold itself. From time to time as the morning drew on, he paused to rest and to breathe deeply of the fresh, clear air. Deliberately, he refused to hurry.

For nineteen days he worked tirelessly, eight hours a day at first, then lessening his hours to seven, and then to six. Wetherton did not explain to himself why he did this, but he realized it was becoming increasingly difficult to stay on the job. Again and again he would walk away from the rock face on one excuse or another, and each time he would begin to feel his scalp prickle, his steps grow quicker, and each time he returned more reluctantly.

Three times, beginning on the thirteenth, again on the seventeenth, and finally on the nineteenth day, he heard movement within the tower. Whether that whispering in the rock was normal he did not know. Such a natural movement might have been going on for centuries. He only knew that it happened now, and each time it happened, a cold chill went along his spine.

His work had cut a deep notch at the base of the tower, such a notch as a man might make in felling a tree, but wider and deeper. The sacks of gold, too, were increasing. They now numbered seven, and their total would, he believed, amount to more than five thousand dollars—probably nearer to six thousand. As he cut deeper into the rock, the vein was growing richer.

He worked on his knees now. The vein had slanted downward as he cut into the base of the tower and he was all of nine feet into the rock with the great mass of it above him. If that rock gave way while he was working, he would be crushed in an instant with no chance of escape.

Nevertheless, he continued.

The change in the rock tower was not the only change, for he had lost weight and he no longer slept well. On the night of the twentieth day he decided he had six thousand dollars and his goal would be ten thousand. And the following day the rock was the richest ever! As if to tantalize him into working on and on, the deeper he cut, the richer the ore became. By nightfall of that day he had taken out more than a thousand dollars.

Now the lust of the gold was getting into him, taking him by the throat. He was fascinated by the danger of the tower as well as the desire for the gold. Three more days to go—could he leave it then? He looked again at the tower and felt a peculiar sense of foreboding, a feeling that here he was to die, that he would never escape. Was it his imagination, or had the outer wall leaned a little more?

On the morning of the twenty-second day he climbed the fan over a path that use had built into a series of continuous steps. He had never counted those steps, but there must have been over a thousand of them. Dropping his canteen into a shaded hollow and pick in hand, he started for the tower.

The forward tilt *did* seem somewhat more than before. Or was it the light? The crack that ran behind the outer wall seemed to have widened, and when he examined it more closely, he found a small pile of freshly run silt near the bottom of the crack. So it had moved!

Wetherton hesitated, staring at the rock with wary attention. He was a fool to go back in there again. Seven thousand dollars was more than he had ever had in his life before, yet in the next few hours he could take out at least a thousand dollars more, and in the next three days he could easily have the ten thousand he had set for his goal.

He walked to the opening, dropped to his knees, and crawled into the narrowing, flat-roofed hole. No sooner was he inside than fear climbed up into his throat. He felt trapped, stifled, but he fought down the mounting panic and began to work. His first blows were so frightened and feeble that nothing came loose. Yet when he did get started, he began to work with a feverish intensity that was wholly unlike him.

When he slowed and then stopped to fill his sack, he was gasping for breath, but despite his hurry the sack was not quite full. Reluctantly, he lifted his pick again, but before he could strike a blow, the gigantic mass above him seemed to creak like something tired and old. A deep shud-der went through the colossal pile and then a deep grinding that turned him sick with horror. All his plans for instant flight were frozen, and it was not until the groaning ceased that he realized he was lying on his back, breathless with fear and expectancy. Slowly, he edged his way into the air and walked, fighting the desire to run, away from the rock.

When he stopped near his canteen, he was wringing with cold sweat and trembling in every muscle. He sat down on the rock and fought for control. It was not until some twenty minutes had passed that he could trust himself to get to his feet.

Despite his experience, he knew that if he did not go back now, he would never go. He had out but one sack for the day and wanted another. Circling the batholith, he examined the widening crack, endeavoring again, for the third time, to find another means of access to the vein.

The tilt of the outer wall was obvious, and it could stand no more without toppling. It was possible that by cutting into the wall of the column and striking down, he might tap the vein at a safer point. Yet this added blow at the foundation would bring the tower nearer to collapse and render his other hole untenable. Even this new attempt would not be safe, although immeasurably more secure than the hole he had left. Hesitating, he looked back at the hole.

Once more? The ore was now fabulously rich, and the few pounds he needed to complete the sack he could get in just a little while. He stared at the black and undoubtedly narrower hole, then looked up at the leaning wall. He picked up his pick and, his mouth dry, started back, drawn by a fascination that was beyond all reason.

His heart pounding, he dropped to his knees at the tunnel face. The air seemed stifling and

---

WORDS TO OWN

foreboding (fôr·bōd'iŋ) n.: feeling that something bad is about to happen.
untenable (un·ten'ə·bəl) adj.: incapable of being defended, maintained, or occupied.

E **Reading Skills and Strategies**
Making Predictions
Have a student volunteer read aloud this paragraph, and then ask students to write a prediction about what will happen. Encourage them to share their ideas and to tell which details from the story support their predictions. [Some students may predict that the tower will collapse, killing Wetherton; others may predict that he will escape the falling tower; still others may predict that he will leave before the tower falls. Possible supporting details include his failure to observe his own rules; his lust for the gold and fascination with danger; the changes in the tower; and his resolve not to become greedy or to forget the danger.]

F **Reading Skills and Strategies**

Chronological Order
? How has the rock tower changed? [It has become more threatening: The crack is much wider, and the rock is making noises and leaning precariously.]

G **Critical Thinking**
Speculating
? Why do you think that Wetherton, who has been so careful and deliberate, begins to work in such a frenzy? [Possible responses: He has become obsessed with lust for gold; his fear has driven him to rush forward and take less care.]

H **Elements of Literature**
Setting as Antagonist
? What words indicate that L'Amour once again is using personification to bring the mountain to life as Wetherton's antagonist? [The words *tired, shudder,* and *groaning* personify the mountain.]

Crossing the Curriculum

Art
Have students find and bring to class examples of Western art that explore themes such as rugged individualism, people versus nature, the majesty of nature, and the lure of the West. You might suggest that they begin with reproductions of paintings and sculptures by Frederic Remington. Additionally, you might encourage students to compose a rough draft of a creative story or poem based on the artwork they bring to class.

Science/Social Studies
Have students work in pairs to research and write short reports on some aspect of gold—its properties, why it is considered a precious metal, how it is mined today, or its role in major historical events, such as nineteenth century gold rushes or the exploration of the American West.

Debate
Have students consider the ways in which Wetherton might be considered "responsible"—both in his profession and to his family. Then have them consider ways in which he might be deemed "irresponsible." Have small teams of students debate their opinions, using evidence from the text to back up their ideas.

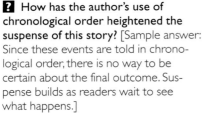
he could feel his scalp tingling, but once he started to crawl, it was better. The face where he now worked was at least sixteen feet from the tunnel mouth. Pick in hand, he began to wedge chunks from their seat. The going seemed harder now, and the chunks did not come loose so easily. Above him the tower made no sound. The crushing weight was now something tangible. He could almost feel it growing, increasing with every move of his. The mountain seemed resting on his shoulder, crushing the air from his lungs.

Suddenly he stopped. His sack almost full, he stopped and lay very still, staring up at the bulk of the rock above him.

No.

He would go no further. Now he would quit. Not another sackful. Not another pound. He would go out now. He would go down the mountain without a backward look, and he would keep going. His wife waiting at home, little Tommy, who would run gladly to meet him—these were too much to gamble.

With the decision came peace, came certainty. He sighed deeply, and relaxed, and then it seemed to him that every muscle in his body had been knotted with strain. He turned on his side and with great deliberation gathered his lantern, his sack, his hand-pick.

A He had won. He had defeated the crumbling tower; he had defeated his own greed. He backed easily, without the caution that had marked his earlier movements in the cave. His blind, trusting foot found the projecting rock, a **B** piece of quartz that stuck out from the rough-hewn wall.

The blow was too weak, too feeble to have brought forth the reaction that followed. The rock seemed to quiver like the flesh of a beast when stabbed; a queer vibration went through that ancient rock, then a deep, gasping sigh.

He had waited too long!

Fear came swiftly in upon him, crowding him, while his body twisted, contracting into the smallest possible space. He tried to will his muscles to move beneath the growing sounds that vibrated through the passage. The whis-

pers of the rock grew into a terrible groan, and there was a rattle of pebbles. Then silence.

The silence was more horrifying than the **C** sound. Somehow he was crawling, even as he expected the avalanche of gold to bury him. Abruptly, his feet were in the open. He was out.

He ran without stopping, but behind him he heard a growing roar that he couldn't outrace. When he knew from the slope of the land that he must be safe from falling rock, he fell to his knees. He turned and looked back. The muted, roaring sound, like thunder beyond mountains, continued, but there was no visible change in the tower. Suddenly, as he watched, the whole rock formation seemed to shift and tip. The movement lasted only seconds, but before the tons of rock had found their new equilibrium, his tunnel and the area around it had utterly vanished from sight.

D When he could finally stand, Wetherton gathered up his sack of ore and his canteen. The wind was cool upon his face as he walked away; and he did not look back again.

The rock seemed to quiver like the flesh of a beast when stabbed . . .

Making the Connections

Connecting to the Theme: "Breakthroughs"

This selection provides opportunities to discuss the theme "Breakthroughs" from several perspectives. Wetherton is down to his last forty dollars when he discovers gold, and he must overcome his fear and risk everything to mine the gold. As he works the mine, he breaks through his greed for more gold. Invite students to compare these breakthroughs to those made by characters in other stories, novels, and nonfiction.

Cultural Connections

Students from cultures outside the United States may need further explanation of the "Western" genre. Explain that it is a type of American romance that appears in literature, television, and film. Typically set in the mid- to late nineteenth century, Westerns feature idealized heroes fighting for justice. You might direct students to such authors as Zane Grey, Owen Wister, and Larry McMurtry as well as to films such as *Shane* and *Stagecoach*.

MEET THE WRITER

Best of the West

66 I feel like a midwife to a thousand stories that have to be told and never would be unless I told . . . not the lives of generals and public men, but of all those buried in anonymous graves who suffered to build this country. 99

Louis L'Amour (1908–1988) may not have told a thousand stories in his lifetime, but since his death, the seventy novels and four hundred short stories that he did publish have continued to sell widely.

L'Amour, a fifteenth-generation American, was born in Jamestown, North Dakota. He was fascinated by stories about his pioneer ancestors, who included sod busters, trappers, cavalrymen, and cowboys.

After dropping out of school at fifteen, L'Amour traveled throughout the West, working as a fruit picker, lumberjack, miner, and elephant handler. Later he went to sea and spent time in the Far East. During World War II, he told Western tales to his fellow servicemen. Encouraged by their enthusiastic response, he began writing down some of his stories and publishing them.

An avid reader and researcher on the history of the Old West, L'Amour took pride in the accuracy and realism of his stories. "I don't just tell you that a forty-niner panned for gold," L'Amour asserted. "I tell you exactly how he panned for gold."

This comment by writer Louise Erdrich might have been made about "Trap of Gold": "The best parts of Mr. L'Amour's novels are the tight spots in which we find our hero—bushwhacked, surrounded, hanging over deep chasms, enslaved, defying no-good cowards who have somehow got him in their thrall."

BROWSING IN THE FILES

About the Author. Many people do not realize that early in his career, Louis L'Amour wrote poetry and stories about the Far East. He also wrote sports and detective stories. Well-researched Western novels were L'Amour's specialty, however. At the time of his death in 1988, he had gathered so many historical details that he was able to leave outlines for fifty more novels!

A Critic's Comment. The critic Michael T. Marsden made these observations about L'Amour's place in American literature: "*Popular Western fiction has strong ties to the oral tradition in American culture. In his works, L'Amour clearly considers himself to be in the tradition of the oral storyteller. . . .*"

WRITERS ON WRITING

Louis L'Amour was often asked about the possible limitations of writing within a very specific fictional genre. He commented: "There's no difference in the Western novel and any other novel. . . . A Western starts with a beginning and it goes to an end. It's a story about people, and that's the important thing to always remember. Every story is about people—people against the canvas of their times."

Assessing Learning

Check Test: Questions and Answers

1. What are the two temptations Wetherton must avoid? [carelessness and greed]
2. What does Wetherton do to aid his escape in case the tower crumbles? [He lays down a path of flat rocks.]
3. Who are Laura and Tommy? [Wetherton's wife and son]
4. What causes the rock to shift and fall? [Wetherton accidentally kicks a piece of projecting quartz; or the rock has been shifting all along, and he stays past the breaking point.]
5. What does Wetherton <u>not</u> do after escaping? [He doesn't look back.]

Standardized Test Preparation

For practice with standardized test format specific to this selection, see
• *Standardized Test Preparation*, pp. 32, 34
For practice in proofreading and editing, see
• *Daily Oral Grammar*, Transparency 16

This excerpt from the famous diary of Howard Carter (1873–1939), co-discoverer of the tomb of the young King Tutankhamen, conveys the suspense and awe of a fabulous discovery. Tutankhamen was king of ancient Egypt from about 1347 to 1339 B.C. Until 1922 his tomb in the lonely Valley of the Kings had been untouched, except for some grave robbers who probably got into the tomb shortly after burial. King Tut, as he has become known, died young. Some suspect he was murdered, since his burial appears to have been hasty. As the tombs of Pharaohs go, Tut's was not lavish, though it contained incredible treasure: a coffin of solid gold, gold statues, and Tut's gold and lapis funeral mask, shown opposite.

Ⓐ Struggling Readers

Breaking Down Difficult Text
Help students break down this difficult sentence by focusing on vocabulary, sentence structure, and context. Explain that *procured* means "obtained" or "gotten"; *telltale* means "a person who tells secrets" or "a device that indicates something secret"; *subterranean* means "underground"; and *excavation* means "a hole made by digging." After students are more comfortable with these words, draw their attention to the structure of the sentence. Point out that the words following the dash give more information about the candles. Help them understand that excavators use candles much as miners have used canaries in the past—to detect the presence of toxic gases inside an underground compartment.

Ⓑ Critical Thinking

Analyzing
❓ How does Carter create suspense? [He describes the process of uncovering the treasure slowly, step-by-step, in chronological order. He describes the scene while emphasizing what he can't see or doesn't know, leaving the reader with questions to be resolved.]

Gold has lured people to mountains, deserts, and even ancient tombs. For centuries, stories circulated about fabulous treasures buried in Egypt in the tombs of the pharaohs. In 1922, Howard Carter, a British Egyptologist working with Lord Carnarvon, uncovered the tomb of the young King Tutankhamen. In this excerpt from his diary, Carter describes his entry down into the tomb's antechamber.

"It Is Wonderful!"

Sunday, November 26, 1922
Feverishly we cleared away the remaining last scraps of rubbish on the floor of the passage before the doorway, until we had only the clean, sealed doorway before us, in which, after making preliminary notes, we made a tiny breach in the top left-hand corner to see what was beyond. . . . Candles were procured—the all-important telltale for foul gases when opening an ancient subterranean excavation. I widened the breach and by means of the candle looked in. . . .

As soon as one's eyes became accustomed to the glimmer of the light, the interior of the chamber gradually loomed before one, with its strange and wonderful medley of extraordinary and beautiful objects heaped upon one another.

There was naturally short suspense for those present who could not see. When Lord Carnarvon said to me "Can you see anything?" I replied to him, "Yes, it is wonderful!" I then with precaution made the hole sufficiently large for both of us to see. . . . Our sensations and astonishment are difficult to describe as the better light revealed to us the marvelous collection of treasures: two strange ebony-black effigies of a king, gold sandaled, bearing staff and mace, loomed out from the cloak of darkness; gilded couches in strange forms, lion-headed, Hathor-headed, and beast infernal; exquisitely painted, inlaid, and ornamental caskets; flowers, alabaster vases, some beautifully executed of lotus and papyrus device; strange black shrines with a gilded monster snake appearing from within; quite ordinary-looking white chests; finely carved chairs; a golden inlaid throne; a heap of large, curious white oviform boxes; beneath our very eyes, on the threshold, a lovely lotiform wishing cup in translucent alabaster; stools of all shapes and design, of both common and rare materials; and lastly a confusion of overturned parts of chariots glinting with gold, peering from amongst which was a manikin. The first impressions . . . suggested the property room of an opera of a vanished civilization.

Our sensations were bewildering and full of strange emotion. We questioned one another as to the meaning of it all. Was it a tomb or merely a cache? A sealed doorway between the two sentinel statues proved there was more beyond, and with the numerous cartouches bearing the name of Tutankhamen on most of the objects before us, there was little doubt that there, behind, was the grave of that pharaoh.

—from Howard Carter's diary of the discovery of the tomb of Tutankhamen

Tutankhamen's funerary mask. Gold, lapis, and carnelian (height 8⅞").

258 THE SHORT-STORY COLLECTIONS

Connecting Across Texts

Connecting with "Trap of Gold"
Guide a discussion of how this diary excerpt connects to L'Amour's short story. You might ask students to compare the two men—Wetherton and Carter—and their two breakthroughs. [Both are searching for fabulous treasure. Both have become obsessed with the quest (though that is not clear in the extract from Carter's diary). Both are in danger: Wetherton is in danger of being crushed by the rock; Carter is in danger of foul gases. Carter would also feel some trepidation because traditionally it was believed that anyone who tampered with the tombs would be cursed.]

First Thoughts

[opinion]

1. In "Trap of Gold," there's no dialogue, no confrontation between a hero and a villain. Does the story hold your attention anyway? Why?

Shaping Interpretations

[identify]

2. Find the moments in the story when the writer makes you think Wetherton will fail in his quest. L'Amour said that writers, to heighten **suspense**, should refer to sights, sounds, and smells. What passages help you to *feel* Wetherton's physical responses to his ordeal?

[analyze]

3. Find at least three images that make the **setting** of the story—the tower of granite—seem like a human **antagonist.** Is the tower characterized as evil, as good, or as something else? Find details that support your answer.

[synthesize]

4. Suppose Wetherton himself were telling the story. How would this change in **point of view** affect the impact of the story—particularly the element of suspense?

[infer]

5. On one level, the **title** refers to a real rock formation. What else is the "trap of gold"?

[interpret]

6. What breakthroughs take place in this story?

Connecting with the Text

[connect]

7. What do you find especially horrifying about Wetherton's situation? What deep-seated human fears do you think are aroused by this particular setting?

Extending the Text

[connect]

8. What people in real life have taken extraordinary risks to get money? Tell how the "trap of gold" affected them. For help, refer to your Quickwrite notes.

Challenging the Text

[evaluate]

9. The story briefly mentions Wetherton's wife and son, Laura and Tommy. Would you have been less sympathetic if the writer had let you assume that Wetherton wanted the money just for himself? Or do you think that the information about Wetherton's family is corny and manipulative? Defend your opinion to another reader.

Reading Check

L'Amour builds **suspense** by gradually "paying out" information about Wetherton's progress toward his goal.

a. Make a numbered list in **chronological order** of all the actions Wetherton takes once he decides to mine the gold.

b. What is the purpose of each of these actions?

Reading Check

a. (1) He circles the batholith and studies it. (2) He returns to camp. (3) He builds a walk. (4) He carefully removes rock. (5) He takes bags of rocks to camp and extracts the gold. (6) He returns to the mine for nineteen days. (7) He decides that ten thousand dollars is his goal. (8) He observes silt, indicating the rock has moved. (9) He begins mining feverishly. (10) After the rock shudders, he crawls from the hole. (11) He circles the mine, looking for another place to dig. (12) He goes back into the hole and digs. (13) He decides to quit. (14) He crawls out, kicking a rock along the way, and runs to safety. (15) He looks back and watches the tower collapse. (16) He leaves without looking back.

b. Actions 1–6, 8, 10, and 13–14 build suspense and show Wetherton's cautious nature. Actions 7, 9, and 11–12 create suspense as they show that he is struggling with his own greed.

First Thoughts

1. Most students will say it holds their interest because the mountain is as compelling an antagonist as a human or animal character would be.

Shaping Interpretations

2. Students might cite the time Wetherton believes he hears the rocks whispering (p. 254) or when he thinks it is too late to escape before the tower collapses (p. 256).

3. Most evidence suggests that the granite tower is an evil antagonist— for example, a number of images support the depiction of a battle. Students might mention descriptions of the tower looking like a building after a bombing and Wetherton's *attacking* the wall as he digs for gold.

4. Possible answers: First-person point of view might make the story less suspenseful by removing the third-person narrator's objective descriptions, which support the suspense; it might add to the story's impact by showing Wetherton's innermost thoughts.

5. The "trap" is also Wetherton's obsession with going back for more gold, even though he knows how risky this will be.

6. Possible answers: Wetherton discovers the gold he has long been seeking; he realizes his wife and son are more important than gold; having decided more gold is not worth further risk, he leaves in time.

Connecting with the Text

7. Wetherton risks being buried alive. Many people fear being in an enclosed place and unable to breathe.

Extending the Text

8. Sample answer: Some people have gambled on risky investments and caused the collapse of banks. Obviously, they did not escape the trap of gold.

Challenging the Text

9. Possible answer: The mention of Tommy and Laura makes Wetherton seem more human, showing that something matters to him besides gold. Without this information, the reader would be less inclined to identify with him as he takes even greater risks.

Rubrics for each Choices assignment appear on p. 120 in the *Portfolio Management System*.

CHOICES:
Building Your Portfolio

1. **Writer's Notebook** With each selection, a Writer's Notebook activity appears as the first option in the Choices section. These brief, work-in-progress assignments build toward the writing assignment presented in the Writer's Workshop at the end of the collection. If students save their work for their Writer's Notebook activities as they move through the collection, they should be able to use some of them as starting points for the workshop.

   Be sure students work in groups to establish their criteria. If they need help in recalling the elements of a short story, refer them to the essays on the Elements of Literature on pp. 32, 50, 110, 182. Encourage students to keep adding to their criteria as they move through the stories in this Collection. If they do that, they should have solid lists of criteria by the time they are ready for the assignment in the Writer's Workshop on p. 328.

2. **Creative Writing** Suggest that students spend two or three minutes freewriting about the new ending before beginning their story ending. When they begin writing, remind them to think about sensory details: sight, sound, smell, feel, and taste.

3. **Creative Writing** You might model the process by reading one or two newspaper articles to students and discussing possible story plots based on the articles. Create a story map on the chalkboard for one article.

4. **Research/Oral Report** Encourage students to think of creative ways to present their findings. You might suggest incorporating a dramatic narrative into the report, including quotations by treasure hunters, and using graphic organizers.

CHOICES: Building Your Portfolio

Writer's Notebook
1. Collecting Ideas for an Evaluation

Developing criteria. When you make a critical judgment about a story (as you will be doing in the Writer's Workshop on page 328), you need to know what your standards, or criteria, are. Work with a small group to develop a list of criteria for just one story element. For example, what makes a good **character** in fiction? an exciting **plot**? an interesting **setting**? Then apply your criteria to that one element in "Trap of Gold." You may want to evaluate the story element by rating it from 1 to 4, with 1 being least effective and 4 practically perfect.

Creative Writing
2. The Trap Wins

Rewrite the ending of "Trap of Gold," beginning with the line "He had waited too long!" on page 256. Suppose this line turned out to be literally true. What would happen to Wetherton? Write a **new ending** in which the trap of gold wins the struggle.

Creative Writing
3. Plotting the News

L'Amour said: "All stories fall into certain patterns of behavior which we call plots. Plots are nothing but a constantly recurring human situation, patterns of behavior. It's my belief that 90 percent of all fiction is based on just twelve to eighteen plots, and you can find them in any metropolitan newspaper in any given week."

Test this statement. Look in a major newspaper or in a national newsmagazine and see if you can find at least three news stories that could provide material for fiction. Write a report on your research in which you make a **story map** outlining a **plot** for each news story. Use an outline like this:

Basic Situation	
Characters	
Their problems	
Complications	
Resolution	
Setting	

Research/Oral Report
4. The Quest for Gold

Howard Carter's diary (see *Connections* on page 258) records his feelings at unearthing the long-buried treasure of Tutankhamen. The quest for treasure has captivated gold diggers throughout history. See what exciting facts you can discover, using print and Internet sources, about the topic below that most interests you. Present your findings in a brief oral report. Try to make your audience feel the thrill of "gold fever"!

- the gold rush of 1849
- Egyptian tomb caches
- sunken treasures

Evaluation of Setting
"Trap of Gold"

Criteria	Ratings
Makes me feel I'm there.	4
Is part of the conflict.	4
Reveals character.	1
Could not be changed without greatly altering the story.	4
Creates an emotional effect or atmosphere.	4
Helps me learn something about a place.	2

LANGUAGE LINK [MINI-LESSON]

Using Comparisons and Analogies to Clarify

Handbook of Literary Terms
HELP

See Analogy, Metaphor, Simile.

To help us understand and visualize what's happening in "The Trap of Gold," L'Amour does something that good writers do instinctively: He takes a little time to make a **comparison** or an **analogy** between the new thing and something his readers are likely to recognize. (For a definition of analogy, see the Handbook of Literary Terms.) Most times the comparisons are explicit: L'Amour will say *how* one thing is like something else. Sometimes the comparison is made by a single word. In the sentences from "Trap of Gold" that follow, what comparisons and analogies help you understand the complex setting?

1. "The band of quartz was six feet wide, and that six feet was cobwebbed with gold."

2. "The roof of the batholith was riven with gigantic cracks, literally seamed with breaks, like the wall of an ancient building that has remained standing after heavy bombing."

3. ". . . the alluvial fan sloped steeply away from its lower side, steeper than a steep stairway."

4. ". . . the gigantic mass above him seemed to creak like something tired and old."

Try It Out

The best writers use **comparisons** and **analogies** (a type of comparison) to help readers understand complex ideas or structures. The discoverers of DNA, for example, described their discovery as a double helix (or spiral). A biology textbook helped students visualize DNA by comparing it to a twisted ladder. Think of something you know well and want to help someone else understand. It could be a car, a scientific experiment, even a hairstyle. Using a comparison, write a brief description so that someone totally unfamiliar with your subject can understand it.

VOCABULARY [HOW TO OWN A WORD]

WORD BANK
abrasive
contemplative
deluded
portals
impediment
alleviated
inevitable
cache
foreboding
untenable

Identifying Synonyms and Antonyms

In items 1–5, choose the *best* **synonym** (word that has the same, or a similar, meaning). In items 6–10, choose the *best* **antonym** (word that has an opposite meaning). This exercise format will give you practice for taking standardized tests.

1. IMPEDIMENT: (a) obstacle (b) aid (c) illness (d) law
2. DELUDED: (a) guided (b) bribed (c) lessened (d) misled
3. PORTALS: (a) harbors (b) cracks (c) doorways (d) tunnels
4. CACHE: (a) storage place (b) paper money (c) coins (d) sacks
5. FOREBODING: (a) luck (b) ending (c) beginning (d) prediction
6. INEVITABLE: (a) destined (b) avoidable (c) easy (d) careless
7. ABRASIVE: (a) harsh (b) irritating (c) soothing (d) angry
8. CONTEMPLATIVE: (a) unthinking (b) careful (c) alert (d) mad
9. UNTENABLE: (a) legible (b) defensible (c) empty (d) busy
10. ALLEVIATED: (a) cried (b) worsened (c) raised (d) improved

TRAP OF GOLD 261

LANGUAGE LINK

Ask students to choose a piece of writing from their portfolio and to circle any concept, object, or procedure that might be unfamiliar to the reader. Suggest that they make a quick word-association graphic or pictorial sketch to help them think of suitable comparisons.

Comparisons in the story:
1. The presence of gold in the quartz is compared with a cobweb.
2. The cracked roof of the batholith is compared with the wall of a building that's been bombed.
3. The slope of the fan is compared with the steep slope of a stairway.
4. The sound of the rock above him is compared to the creaking of something (animal?) tired and old.

Try It Out
Possible Answers
Descriptions will vary. Be sure that students have compared an unfamiliar object to a familiar one. Sample response: In the 1960s, a teenager's music collection consisted of 45-rpm records. A 45-rpm record looks like a seven-inch black CD with a large hole in the middle.

VOCABULARY
1. (a) obstacle
2. (d) misled
3. (c) doorways
4. (a) storage place
5. (d) prediction
6. (b) avoidable
7. (c) soothing
8. (a) unthinking
9. (b) defensible
10. (b) worsened

Resources
Language
• *Grammar and Language Links* Worksheet, p. 29

Vocabulary
• *Words to Own* Worksheet, p. 17

Language Link Quick Check

Identify the comparisons in each sentence.
1. "The rock seemed to quiver like the flesh of a beast when stabbed." [rock; quivering flesh]
2. "His work had cut a deep notch at the base of the tower, such a notch as a man might make in felling a tree, but wider and deeper." [notch in the rock; cut in a tree]
3. "Now the lust of the gold was getting into him, taking him by the throat." [his desire; something strangling him]
4. "The desert was to him what an orchestra is to a fine conductor, what the human body is to a surgeon." [his knowledge of the desert; a conductor's knowledge of an orchestra, a surgeon's knowledge of the human body]
5. ". . . this tower of granite had been violently upthrust, leaving it standing, a shaky ruin among younger and sturdier peaks." [rock—a very old person among the young; rock—a crumbling building]

Resources

Elements of Literature
Point of View
For additional instruction on Point of View, see *Literary Elements:*
- Transparency 8

Elements of Literature
This lesson discusses how point of view affects both the telling of a story and the way a reader understands and responds to the story.

Mini-Lesson:
Point of View
Invite volunteers to use the first-person point of view to relate a scene involving more than one character. The scene might be from a story, novel, television program, film, or from a student's life. After this telling, have the class answer and discuss these questions:
- How much does this narrator know about the motives and feelings of the characters?
- What information might this narrator be withholding or unaware of?
- Can you trust this narrator to tell you what he or she knows? Why or why not?

Repeat the activity for the omniscient and the third-person limited points of view.

Elements of Literature

POINT OF VIEW: The Story's Voice *by* John Leggett

Point of view—the vantage point from which a writer tells a story—has a more powerful effect than you might imagine.

The Omniscient Point of View: Know It All

The traditional vantage point for storytelling, the one you are probably most familiar with, is the omniscient point of view.

Omniscient means "all-knowing." The **omniscient narrator** is a godlike observer who knows everything that is going on in the story and who can see into each character's heart and mind. This storyteller is outside the story's action altogether.

A newly married pair had boarded this coach at San Antonio. The man's face was reddened from many days in the wind and sun, and a direct result of his new black clothes was that his brick-colored hands were constantly performing in a most conscious fashion. From time to time he looked down respectfully at his attire. He sat with a hand on each knee, like a man waiting in a barber's shop. The glances he devoted to other passengers were furtive and shy.

The bride was not pretty, nor was she very young. She wore a dress of blue cashmere, with small reservations of velvet here and there, and with steel buttons abounding. She continually twisted her head to regard her puff sleeves, very stiff, straight, and high. They embarrassed her.

—Stephen Crane, "The Bride Comes to Yellow Sky"

The omniscient narrator can tell us as much—or as little—as the writer of the story permits. This narrator may tell us what all—or only some—of the characters are thinking, feeling, and observing. This narrator may comment on the meaning of the story or make asides about the story's characters or events.

The First-Person Point of View: "I" Speaks

At the opposite extreme from the omniscient point of view is the first-person point of view. In stories told in the **first person,** an "I" tells the story. This "I" also participates in the action (though possibly taking a very minor role). The omniscient point of view gives us the impression that we are standing nearby, watching and listening but with unusual insight into the events and the characters. The first-person point of view, on the other hand, lets us feel that we are being addressed directly by one of the characters or even that we have taken on the identity of one of the characters. Suppose Stephen Crane had let us hear the bride herself tell the story:

We boarded the Pullman car at San Antonio and sat stiffly in the plush seat, barely touching. First time on a train for me, but I was so nervous I didn't notice anything except that my new husband seemed ill at ease. Did he regret our marriage already? I felt myself falling in love with his shyness.

The first-person point of view presents only what the "I" character can see, hear, and know. This point of view also tells only what the "I" character chooses to tell. Consequently, we must always keep in mind that a first-person narrator may or may not be objective, reliable, honest—or even terribly perceptive about what's going on in the story. We must always ask ourselves how much the writer of the

Using Students' Strengths

Verbal Learners
Ask students to work in pairs as storytellers. One student can retell the story of "Trap of Gold" or make up a story. After a minute or so, the other student calls out a new point of view and retells the events from that angle. Students can continue alternating versions of the story in this way. Advise them to be on the alert for lapses in maintaining the point of view.

Visual Learners
To help students understand point of view, invite them to take photographs or make drawings of a scene from several different angles. For instance, they could photograph people exiting a bus from the point of view of a person still seated on the bus, of a person waiting to board the bus, and of a person watching the scene from an armchair near a window overlooking the bus stop. How does the information in each image differ?

story is allowing the narrator to know and understand—and how much the writer agrees with the narrator's perspective on life. In fact, the whole point of a story told from the first-person point of view may lie in the contrast between what the narrator tells us and what the writer allows us to understand in spite of the narrator.

> In choosing a point of view, the writer must consider how much information to tell the reader and how much to withhold.

The Third-Person Limited Point of View: Zooming In

Between the two extremes of the omniscient and first-person points of view lies the third-person limited point of view. Here the story is told by an outside observer speaking in the **third person** (like the godlike narrator of the omniscient point of view). But this narrator views the action only from the vantage point of a sin-

gle character in the story. It is as if the narrator were standing alongside this one character and recording only his or her thoughts, perceptions, and feelings. Chances are that this narrator will tell us more than that character would be able to tell us (or might choose to tell us) if he or she were narrating the story. (This point of view is called third-person because the narrator never refers to himself or herself as "I." The third-person pronouns are used to refer to all characters.) Suppose Crane had decided to have a third-person limited narrator tell us the story of the bride. Now he might zoom in on the husband:

> He was a working man—a sheriff—and dressed in a new suit for the first time in his life. His face was like a map—full of lines from exposure to the sun. He was terrified of what he'd done—married a woman he hardly knew—but pleased with himself. He was also pleased with his bride's quiet ways. He knew that what faced her in Yellow Sky would be anything but quiet.

In choosing a point of view, the writer must consider how

much information to tell the reader and how much to withhold. And in reading a story, we might ask ourselves, "How would this story have been different if it had been told by someone else?"

What Is the Point of View?

Whenever you read a work of fiction, you should ask yourself five important questions about its point of view:

1. Who is telling the story?

2. How much does this narrator know and understand?

3. How much does this narrator want me to know?

4. How would the story be different if someone else were telling it?

5. Can I trust this narrator?

Reprinted from The Saturday Evening Post.

Applying the Element

Ask students to apply their knowledge of point of view by answering these questions about "Trap of Gold."

- **What is the point of view?** [third-person limited] **How do you know?** [The story tells about Wetherton's thoughts and actions, but he himself is not speaking to the reader. The narrator does not make judgments about the character or suggest a meaning for the story.]

- **What kinds of changes would you expect in the story if the point of view were omniscient?** [The narrator might have made value judgments about Wetherton's actions. For example, the narrator might have said, "How foolish Wetherton was to go back for another sackful!" An omniscient narrator also might have told about other people's attempts to mine the gold.]

- **How would the story be different if told from the first-person point of view?** [The story would be basically the same, but Wetherton would tell it using the pronouns *I* and *me*. However, the outcome of the story would not be a surprise because if Wetherton had been killed, he could not have told the story. Additionally, the reader would probably learn some of Wetherton's private thoughts.]

Have students meet in small groups and answer the questions in "What Is the Point of View?" regarding a novel or short story that they enjoyed.

Resources

Assessment
Formal Assessment
- Literary Elements Test, p. 50

Getting Students Involved

Cooperative Learning
Have students work in small groups to write three different versions of a scene in which Wetherton arrives home. Laura and Tommy have been waiting for him, and he has the money and his memories. One version of the scene should be a continuation of the third-person limited point of view. The second version should be a first-person account, and the third version should be from the omniscient point of view.

Discussion Activity
Have students work in a small group to analyze two or three stories that are told from the first-person or third-person limited point of view. Have students compare and contrast the stories' narrators. Does each have the same degree of knowledge and insights into the action, the characters, and the outcome of events? How trustworthy is each narrator? What, if anything, can readers tell about the narrator from what he or she doesn't say?

Before You Read

BY THE WATERS OF BABYLON

Make the Connection

What Is This Place?

Part of the fun of reading a **fantasy** comes from imagining the invented setting and culture. In this fantasy story you'll accompany John, the narrator, as he tries to understand his world, his people's past, and their myths. Sharpen your detecting powers—you'll need them to solve the puzzle of this story.

Quickwrite

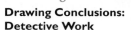

Think back thousands of years. Can whole civilizations disappear? Which ones have? Using what you know of world history, jot down some questions you have about a civilization so long gone that only faint traces of it remain.

Elements of Literature

First-Person Point of View

When a story is told from the **first-person point of view,** two important things happen. First, we share immediately in the narrator's experience and feelings. Second, we know *only* what the narrator knows. All we learn about the story's events and the other characters comes from the narrator's observations. Writers often choose the first-person point of view to create a sense of intimacy, as if the narrator is a friend talking directly to us. Benét uses this point of view to limit our knowledge—we know only what the narrator tells us as he makes his journey to the Place of the Gods.

> A story written in the **first-person point of view** is told by a character who refers to himself or herself as "I."
>
> *For more on Point of View, see pages 262–263 and the Handbook of Literary Terms.*

Reading Skills and Strategies

Drawing Conclusions: Detective Work

When you read mystery stories and other stories that present a puzzle, as "By the Waters of Babylon" does, you must act like a detective. You must look for clues and **draw conclusions** about what certain details in the story mean. As you read this story, be especially alert to clues about the setting. Read carefully the descriptions of objects and places. Think about what the narrator and writer may *not* be telling you. Then throw into the mix your own experience and knowledge as you try to solve the story's puzzles. Remember: like a detective, you'll have to keep monitoring and revising your conclusions as new clues surface.

Background

The title of this story is an **allusion** to Psalm 137 in the Bible. The psalm tells of the Israelites' great sorrow over the destruction of their Temple in Jerusalem (Zion) and their enslavement in the land of Babylon. The psalm begins:

> *By the waters of Babylon, there we sat down and wept, when we remembered Zion.*

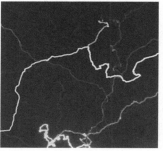

go.hrw.com
LEO 10-4

BY THE WATERS OF BABYLON

Stephen Vincent Benét

At night, I would lie awake and listen to the wind—it seemed to me that it was the voice of the gods.

The north and the west and the south are good hunting ground, but it is forbidden to go east. It is forbidden to go to any of the Dead Places except to search for metal, and then he who touches the metal must be a priest or the son of a priest. Afterward, both the man and the metal must be purified. These are the rules and the laws; they are well made. It is forbidden to cross the great river and look upon the place that was the Place of the Gods—this is most strictly forbidden. We do not even say its name though we know its name. It is there that spirits live, and demons—it is there that there are the ashes of the Great Burning. These things are forbidden—they have been forbidden since the beginning of time.

My father is a priest; I am the son of a priest. I have been in the Dead Places near us, with my father—at first, I was afraid.

Summary ■ ■

The narrator is the son of a priest, and he visits the Dead Places with his father to collect metal. Only priests and sons of priests can go to these places. When he gets older, he tells his father he must go on a journey. His father approves and oversees a purification ceremony for his son. During the ceremony the narrator tells about his dream of the Dead Place and the gods. He goes on his journey, crosses a river on a raft, and enters the Place of the Gods, a great city of tall buildings, all in ruins. He is chased by dogs that do not fear him, and escapes into a tall building, where he stays the night. He is amazed at the mysterious things he finds. During the night, he feels the spirits of the gods drawing him out of his body, and he sees the city when it was still alive, filled with lights, chariots, and people. Then he witnesses the destruction of the city in the Great Burning. The next morning he finds the body of the god who lived in the place where he slept. He realizes that the god was a man. The narrator then returns home. His father acknowledges his son's achievement and observes that truth must come out little by little. The narrator promises that when he is chief priest, he will take his people to the Place of the Gods to begin building again.

Resources ——

Listening
Audio CD Library
A riveting audio recording of this story can be found in the *Audio CD Library:*
• Disc 8, Track 3

Resources: Print and Media

Reading
• *Reading Skills and Strategies*
    MiniRead Skill Lesson, p. 124
    Selection Skill Lesson, p. 131
• *Graphic Organizers for Active Reading*, p. 17
• *Audio CD Library*
    Disc 8, Track 3

Elements of Literature
• *Literary Elements*
    Transparency 8
    Worksheet, p. 25

Writing and Language
• *Daily Oral Grammar*
    Transparency 17
• *Grammar and Language Links*
    Worksheet, p. 31
• *Language Workshop CD-ROM*

Assessment
• *Formal Assessment*, p. 42
• *Portfolio Management System*, p. 121
• *Test Generator (One-Stop Planner CD-ROM)*

Internet
• go.hrw.com (keyword: *LEO 10-4*)

A Elements of Literature

First-Person Point of View

❓ How do you know this narrative is told from the first-person point of view? [The narrator uses the pronoun *I*, and we see all the events through his eyes. We know only what the narrator knows.]

B Reading Skills and Strategies

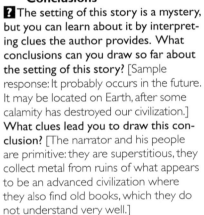

Drawing Conclusions

❓ The setting of this story is a mystery, but you can learn about it by interpreting clues the author provides. What conclusions can you draw so far about the setting of this story? [Sample response: It probably occurs in the future. It may be located on Earth, after some calamity has destroyed our civilization.]
What clues lead you to draw this conclusion? [The narrator and his people are primitive: they are superstitious, they collect metal from ruins of what appears to be an advanced civilization where they also find old books, which they do not understand very well.]

When my father went into the house to search for the metal, I stood by the door and my heart felt small and weak. It was a dead man's house, a spirit house. It did not have the smell of man, though there were old bones in a corner. But it is not fitting that a priest's son should show fear. I looked at the bones in the shadow and kept my voice still.

Then my father came out with the metal—a good, strong piece. He looked at me with both eyes but I had not run away. He gave me the metal to hold—I took it and did not die. So he knew that I was truly his son and would be a priest in my time. That was when I was very young—nevertheless, my brothers would not have done it, though they are good hunters. After that, they gave me the good piece of meat and the warm corner by the fire. My father watched over me—he was glad that I should be a priest. But when I boasted or wept without a reason, he punished me more strictly than my brothers. That was right.

After a time, I myself was allowed to go into the dead houses and search for metal. So I learned the ways of those houses—and if I saw bones, I was no longer afraid. The bones are light and old—sometimes they will fall into dust if you touch them. But that is a great sin.

I was taught the chants and the spells—I was taught how to stop blood from a wound and many secrets. A priest must know many secrets—that was what my father said. If the hunters think we do all things by chants and spells, they may believe so—it does not hurt them. I was taught how to read in the old books and how to make the old writings—that was hard and took a long time. My knowledge made me happy—it was like a fire in my heart. Most of all, I liked to hear of the Old Days and the stories of the gods. I asked myself many questions that I could not answer, but it was good to ask them. At night, I would lie awake and listen to the wind—it seemed to me that it was the voice of the gods as they flew through the air.

We are not ignorant like the Forest People—our women spin wool on the wheel, our priests wear a white robe. We do not eat grubs from the tree, we have not forgotten the old writings, although they are hard to understand. Nevertheless, my knowledge and my lack of knowledge burned in me—I wished to know more. When I was a man at last, I came to my father and said, "It is time for me to go on my journey. Give me your leave."

He looked at me for a long time, stroking his beard, then he said at last, "Yes. It is time." That night, in the house of the priesthood, I asked for and received purification. My body hurt but my spirit was a cool stone. It was my father himself who questioned me about my dreams.

He bade me look into the smoke of the fire and see—I saw and told what I saw. It was what I have always seen—a river, and, beyond it, a great Dead Place and in it the gods walking. I have always thought about that. His eyes were stern when I told him—he was no longer my father but a priest. He said, "This is a strong dream."

"It is mine," I said, while the smoke waved and my head felt light. They were singing the Star song in the outer chamber and it was like the buzzing of bees in my head.

He asked me how the gods were dressed and I told him how they were dressed. We know how they were dressed from the book, but I saw them as if they were before me. When I had finished, he threw the sticks three times and studied them as they fell.

"This is a very strong dream," he said. "It may eat you up."

"I am not afraid," I said and looked at him with both eyes. My voice sounded thin in my ears but that was because of the smoke.

He touched me on the breast and the forehead. He gave me the bow and the three arrows.

"Take them," he said. "It is forbidden to travel east. It is forbidden to cross the river. It is forbidden to go to the Place of the Gods. All these things are forbidden."

"All these things are forbidden," I said, but it was my voice that spoke and not my spirit. He looked at me again.

Reaching All Students

Struggling Readers

Drawing Conclusions was introduced on p. 264. For a lesson directly tied to this story that teaches students to draw conclusions by using a strategy called Sketch to Stretch, see the *Reading Skills and Strategies* binder.
• MiniRead Skill Lesson, p. 124
• Selection Skill Lesson, p. 131

English Language Learners

Point out that this story includes many references to chants, spells, and religious beliefs and practices. Explain that these are fictional but based on types of traditions that are common in many cultures. Invite students to look for similarities within their own cultures. For additional strategies to supplement instruction for English language learners, see
• *Lesson Plans Including Strategies for English-Language Learners*

Advanced Learners

Tell students that stories such as this one are sometimes called apocalyptic literature: writing that deals with cataclysmic events that end civilization. Some stories by Edgar Allan Poe, H. P. Lovecraft, and Nathaniel Hawthorne fit this description. Invite students to meet as a group and brainstorm stories they've read or films they've seen that deal with this topic. Ask, "What characteristics are shared by these stories?"

"My son," he said. "Once I had young dreams. If your dreams do not eat you up, you may be a great priest. If they eat you, you are still my son. Now go on your journey."

I went fasting, as is the law. My body hurt but not my heart. When the dawn came, I was out of sight of the village. I prayed and purified myself, waiting for a sign. The sign was an eagle. It flew east.

Sometimes signs are sent by bad spirits. I waited again on the flat rock, fasting, taking no food. I was very still—I could feel the sky above me and the earth beneath. I waited till the sun was beginning to sink. Then three deer passed in the valley, going east—they did not wind[1] me or see me. There was a white fawn with them—a very great sign.

I followed them, at a distance, waiting for what would happen. My heart was troubled about going east, yet I knew that I must go. My head hummed with my fasting—I did not even see the panther spring upon the white fawn. But, before I knew it, the bow was in my hand. I shouted and the panther lifted his head from the fawn. It is not easy to kill a panther with one arrow but the arrow went through his eye and into his brain. He died as he tried to spring—he rolled over, tearing at the ground. Then I knew I was meant to go east—I knew that was my journey. When the night came, I made my fire and roasted meat.

It is eight suns' journey to the east and a man passes by many Dead Places. The Forest People are afraid of them but I am not. Once I made my fire on the edge of a Dead Place at night and, next morning, in the dead house, I found a good knife, little rusted. That was small to what came afterward but it made my heart feel big. Always when I looked for game, it was in front of my arrow, and twice I passed hunting parties of the Forest People without their knowing. So I knew my magic was strong and my journey clean, in spite of the law.

Toward the setting of the eighth sun, I came to the banks of the great river. It was half a day's

1. **wind** (wind): detect the scent of.

journey after I had left the god-road—we do not use the god-roads now, for they are falling apart into great blocks of stone, and the forest is safer going. A long way off, I had seen the water through trees but the trees were thick. At last, I came out upon an open place at the top of a cliff. There was the great river below, like a giant in the sun. It is very long, very wide. It could eat all the streams we know and still be thirsty. Its name is Ou-dis-sun, the Sacred, the Long. No man of my tribe had seen it, not even my father, the priest. It was magic and I prayed.

Then I raised my eyes and looked south. It was there, the Place of the Gods.

How can I tell what it was like—you do not know. It was there, in the red light, and they were too big to be houses. It was there with the red light upon it, mighty and ruined. I knew that in another moment the gods would see me. I covered my eyes with my hands and crept back into the forest.

Surely, that was enough to do, and live. Surely it was enough to spend the night upon the cliff. The Forest People themselves do not come near. Yet, all through the night, I knew that I should have to cross the river and walk in the places of the gods, although the gods ate me up. My magic did not help me at all and yet there was a fire in my bowels, a fire in my mind. When the sun rose, I thought, "My journey has been clean. Now I will go home from my journey." But, even as I thought so, I knew I could not. If I went to the Place of the Gods, I would surely die, but, if I did not go, I could never be at peace with my spirit again. It is better to lose one's life than one's spirit, if one is a priest and the son of a priest.

Nevertheless, as I made the raft, the tears ran out of my eyes. The Forest People could have killed me without fight, if they had come upon me then, but they did not come. When the raft was made, I said the sayings for the dead and painted myself for death. My heart was cold as a frog and my knees like water, but the burning in my mind would not let me have peace. As I pushed the raft from the shore, I began my death song—I had the right. It was a fine song.

C Appreciating Language
Style
❓ Listen as the passage is read aloud. The story is written in a very simple, spare style. Many of the sentences are simple sentences. The clauses are short, using few words. How does this style complement the depiction of the character? [The character is an innocent, unsophisticated, slightly educated person. The style of the writing echoes the way such a person might speak and think.]

D English Language Learners
Reading Elliptical Constructions
Explain that this sentence contains an elliptical construction: "my journey clean." The verb *was* is missing; the reader must fill in this word to make sense of the meaning.

E Elements of Literature
Conflict
❓ Two kinds of conflict are internal and external. What kind of conflict is described in this paragraph? Explain. [The narrator struggles with an internal conflict: his fear of visiting the Place of the Gods.] This story includes many conflicts of both types. Look for further examples as you read.

Taking a Second Look

Review: Monitoring Strategies: Questioning
Encourage students to monitor their understanding as they read by asking themselves questions, such as What are these Dead Places? Why is it forbidden to enter the Dead Places? What does the father mean by "Truth is a hard deer to hunt"? Everything in the text can be questioned. Suggest that students reread to find answers, or keep the question in mind and look for answers as they read on.

Activities
1. Model the process of questioning by reading a page of the story aloud. Pause occasionally to ask questions about setting, vocabulary, figurative language, and so on. Discuss your method of finding the answers.
2. Ask students to read a page to themselves and to write questions and answers. Invite volunteers to share their questions and to explain how they found the answers and what evidence supports their answers.
3. Ask students to read the story aloud in pairs or small groups. Have them pause periodically and take turns asking questions and discussing their answers.

A Elements of Literature

First-Person Point of View

? The first-person point of view can provide intimate insights into the emotions and thinking of the narrator. What information would be lost in this passage if it were told in the third person by another narrator? [Readers would probably not learn that the young man is very afraid and feels "small and naked as a new-hatched bird," for example.]

B Elements of Literature

Conflict

? What is the conflict described in this passage? [a conflict between the narrator and the river] Is it an internal or external conflict? Explain. [It is an external conflict that occurs between the narrator and an outside force.]

C Reading Skills and Strategies

Drawing Conclusions

The writer has given many clues to the setting. Challenge students to identify the following places and events: Great Burning, the Bitter Water, the river, the Place of the Gods. You might ask them to write down their conclusions at this time. Tell them to look for more clues as they read and to revise their conclusions when they find new evidence.

D Struggling Readers

Questioning

? Remember to pause and ask yourself questions whenever you read something you don't understand or that doesn't make sense to you. What does the writer mean in saying "my skin ready for danger"? [Possible response: His skin was prickling as sometimes happens when we feel fear.]

"I am John, son of John," I sang. *"My people are the Hill People. They are the men.*
I go into the Dead Places but I am not slain.
I take the metal from the Dead Places but I am not blasted.
I travel upon the god-roads and am not afraid. E-yah! I have killed the panther, I have killed the fawn!
E-yah! I have come to the great river. No man has come there before.
It is forbidden to go east, but I have gone, forbidden to go on the great river, but I am there.
Open your hearts, you spirits, and hear my song. Now I go to the Place of the Gods, I shall not return.
My body is painted for death and my limbs weak, but my heart is big as I go to the Place of the Gods!"

All the same, when I came to the Place of the Gods, I was afraid, afraid. The current of the great river is very strong—it gripped my raft with its hands. That was magic, for the river itself is wide and calm. I could feel evil spirits about me, in the bright morning; I could feel their breath on my neck as I was swept down the stream. Never have I been so much alone—I tried to think of my knowledge, but it was a squirrel's heap of winter nuts. There was no strength in my knowledge anymore and I felt small and naked as a new-hatched bird—alone upon the great river, the servant of the gods.

Yet, after a while, my eyes were opened and I saw. I saw both banks of the river—I saw that once there had been god-roads across it, though now they were broken and fallen like broken vines. Very great they were, and wonderful and broken—broken in the time of the Great Burning when the fire fell out of the sky. And always the current took me nearer to the Place of the Gods, and the huge ruins rose before my eyes.

I do not know the customs of rivers—we are the People of the Hills. I tried to guide my raft with the pole but it spun around. I thought the river meant to take me past the Place of the

Gods and out into the Bitter Water of the legends. I grew angry then—my heart felt strong. I said aloud, "I am a priest and the son of a priest!" The gods heard me—they showed me how to paddle with the pole on one side of the raft. The current changed itself—I drew near to the Place of the Gods.

When I was very near, my raft struck and turned over. I can swim in our lakes—I swam to the shore. There was a great spike of rusted metal sticking out into the river—I hauled myself up upon it and sat there, panting. I had saved my bow and two arrows and the knife I found in the Dead Place but that was all. My raft went whirling downstream toward the Bitter Water. I looked after it, and thought if it had trod me under, at least I would be safely dead. Nevertheless, when I had dried my bowstring and restrung it, I walked forward to the Place of the Gods.

It felt like ground underfoot; it did not burn me. It is not true what some of the tales say, that the ground there burns forever, for I have been there. Here and there were the marks and stains of the Great Burning, on the ruins, that is true. But they were old marks and old stains. It is not true either, what some of our priests say, that it is an island covered with fogs and enchantments. It is not. It is a great Dead Place—greater than any Dead Place we know. Everywhere in it there are god-roads, though most are cracked and broken. Everywhere there are the ruins of the high towers of the gods.

How shall I tell what I saw? I went carefully, my strung bow in my hand, my skin ready for danger. There should have been the wailings of spirits and the shrieks of demons, but there were not. It was very silent and sunny where I had landed—the wind and the rain and the birds that drop seeds had done their work—the grass grew in the cracks of the broken stone. It is a fair island—no wonder the gods built there. If I had come there, a god, I also would have built.

How shall I tell what I saw? The towers are not all broken—here and there one still stands, like a great tree in a forest, and the birds nest high. But the towers themselves look blind, for the gods are

---

Using Students' Strengths

Verbal Learners

Ask students to imagine that many years have passed. The narrator is now old and has been the chief priest for a long time. Has he fulfilled his plans for his people and for visiting the Place of the Gods? Have students imagine themselves as the narrator who is now telling this story. Have students develop the tale for oral storytelling. They might work together or individually. Have them tell their stories to the class.

Naturalist Learners

Invite students to work as a group and prepare an analysis of the natural environment in which this story takes place. They might begin by studying the region's geography and present-day environment and then extrapolating what the area would be like if allowed to return to natural vegetation. Encourage students to develop a multi-media approach to organizing and presenting their findings to the class.

Visual Learners

Invite students to work as a group to prepare a mural showing the Place of the Gods that is visited by the narrator. Encourage them to study the skyline and architecture of New York and to imagine how it would look after the Great Burning and the passage of many years. Students might present their cityscape as the narrator first saw it after crossing the river, or later, as he viewed it from the window of the apartment.

gone. I saw a fish-hawk, catching fish in the river. I saw a little dance of white butterflies over a great heap of broken stones and columns. I went there and looked about me—there was a carved stone with cut-letters, broken in half. I can read letters but I could not understand these. They said UBTREAS. There was also the shattered image of a man or a god. It had been made of white stone and he wore his hair tied back like a woman's. His name was ASHING, as I read on the cracked half of a stone. I thought it wise to pray to ASHING, though I do not know that god.

How shall I tell what I saw? There was no smell of man left, on stone or metal. Nor were there many trees in that wilderness of stone. There are many pigeons, nesting and dropping in the towers—the gods must have loved them, or, perhaps, they used them for sacrifices. There are wild cats that roam the god-roads, green-eyed, unafraid of man. At night they wail like demons but they are not demons. The wild dogs are more dangerous, for they hunt in a pack, but them I did not meet till later. Everywhere there are the carved stones, carved with magical numbers or words.

I went north—I did not try to hide myself. When a god or a demon saw me, then I would die, but meanwhile I was no longer afraid. My hunger for knowledge burned in me—there was so much that I could not understand. After a while, I knew that my belly was hungry. I could have hunted for my meat, but I did not hunt. It is known that the gods did not hunt as we do—they got their food from enchanted boxes and jars. Sometimes these are still found in the Dead Places—once, when I was a child and foolish, I opened such a jar and tasted it and found the food sweet. But my father found out and punished me for it strictly, for, often, that food is death. Now, though, I had long gone past what was forbidden, and I entered the likeliest towers, looking for the food of the gods.

I found it at last in the ruins of a great temple in the midcity. A mighty temple it must have been, for the roof was painted like the sky at night with its stars—that much I could see, though the colors were faint and dim. It went down into great caves and tunnels—perhaps they kept their slaves there. But when I started to climb down, I heard the squeaking of rats, so

I did not go—rats are unclean, and there must have been many tribes of them, from the squeaking. But near there, I found food, in the heart of a ruin, behind a door that still opened. I ate only the fruits from the jars—they had a very sweet taste. There was drink, too, in bottles of glass—the drink of the gods was strong and made my head swim. After I had eaten and drunk, I slept on the top of a stone, my bow at my side.

When I woke, the sun was low. Looking down from where I lay, I saw a dog sitting on his haunches. His tongue was hanging out of his mouth; he looked as if he were laughing. He was a big dog, with a gray-brown coat, as big as a wolf. I sprang up and shouted at him but he did not move—he just sat there as if he were laughing. I did not like that. When I reached for a stone to throw, he moved swiftly out of the way of the stone. He was not afraid of me; he looked at me as if I were meat. No doubt I could have killed him with an arrow, but I did not know if there were others. Moreover, night was falling.

I looked about me—not far away there was a great, broken god-road, leading north. The towers were high enough, but not so high, and while many of the dead houses were wrecked, there were some that stood. I went toward this god-road, keeping to the heights of the ruins, while the dog followed. When I had reached the god-road, I saw that there were others behind him. If I had slept later, they would have come upon me asleep and torn out my throat. As it was, they were sure enough of me; they did not hurry. When I went into the dead house, they kept watch at the entrance—doubtless they thought they would have a fine hunt. But a dog cannot open a door and I knew, from the books, that the gods did not like to live on the ground but on high.

I had just found a door I could open when the dogs decided to rush. Ha! They were surprised when I shut the door in their faces—it was a good door, of strong metal. I could hear their foolish

BY THE WATERS OF BABYLON 269

E Reading Skills and Strategies
Drawing Conclusions
❓ Who does the statue represent? [George Washington] **What clues lead you to this conclusion?** [Washington wore his hair long, and tied back "like a woman's." The inscription is "ASHING," which is what might be left of the name Washington on the cracked half of the stone.]

F Appreciating Language
Inverted Order
❓ We ordinarily expect to find the subject of a sentence at the beginning of a sentence, followed by a verb, but that sometimes isn't the case. There are many examples of inverted word order in this story. Which of the sentences in this paragraph have inverted order? [The first five sentences and the last sentence.] Find the subjects of these sentences. You'll learn more about inverted word order in the Grammar Link on p. 275.

G Critical Thinking
Challenging the Text
❓ What do you think of this confrontation with the dog? Is it realistic? [Sample answer: It is realistic. Dogs that have learned to live independently of humans and who may not even have seen humans would revert to their wild state as predators. They would have no reason to fear humans and would consider them prey.]

Crossing the Curriculum

History
Although this story is fiction, there have been occasions when atomic blasts and nuclear disasters have devastated a city or a region: Hiroshima and Nagasaki, Japan, during World War II and the explosion at the nuclear power plant in Chernobyl, Ukraine, in 1986. Invite interested students to investigate one of these events. What brought it about? What have been the short-term and long-term effects? Could such a disaster happen again?

Science
The narrator and his people are survivors of what must have been a world-wide calamity resulting from atomic or nuclear war. Invite students to investigate effects of such an event. How does a nuclear blast affect people? Who might survive? How? What effect would it have on the food supply, drinking water, communications? How long would the site of a nuclear blast remain uninhabitable?

Social Studies
Many movies have been made and science fiction and nonfiction books written about the aftermath of a cataclysmic disaster and how people would survive and rebuild their society. Invite students to investigate some of these theories and prepare their own scenario for the recovery of civilization after such a disaster.

A Critical Thinking

Speculating

? What is the "long small chamber"? [Possible answer: the hallway.] **What is the bronze door?** [Possible answer: the door to the elevator.]

B Elements of Literature

First-Person Point of View

Review with students one characteristic of the first-person point of view: readers know directly what the narrator knows and feels. Point out that as this story progresses, most readers actually do know more about what the narrator sees than he does. Ask students to tell why this happens. [Possible response: Clues in the story indicate that the narrator is exploring what used to be an Earth civilization which includes artifacts that people today would recognize.]

C Reading Skills and Strategies

Connecting with the Text

? How would you have felt if you had been in the narrator's place? [Many students will share the narrator's feelings of uneasiness and fear. Some may say they would have been too excited to sleep. Others may say they would have enjoyed the chance to stay in such a fascinating place.]

---

baying beyond it but I did not stop to answer them. I was in darkness—I found stairs and climbed. There were many stairs, turning around till my head was dizzy. At the top was another door—I found the knob and opened it. I was in a long small chamber—on one side of it was a bronze door that could not be opened, for it had no handle. Perhaps there was a magic word to open it but I did not have the word. I turned to the door in the opposite side of the wall. The lock of it was broken and I opened it and went in.

Within, there was a place of great riches. The god who lived there must have been a powerful god. The first room was a small anteroom—I waited there for some time, telling the spirits of the place that I came in peace and not as a robber. When it seemed to me that they had had time to hear me, I went on. Ah, what riches! Few, even, of the windows had been broken—it was all as it had been. The great windows that looked over the city had not been broken at all though they were dusty and streaked with many years. There were coverings on the floors, the colors not greatly faded, and the chairs were soft and deep. There were pictures upon the walls, very strange, very wonderful—I remember one of a bunch of flowers in a jar—if you came close to it, you could see nothing but bits of color, but if you stood away from it, the flowers might have been picked yesterday. It made my heart feel strange to look at this picture—and to look at the figure of a bird, in some hard clay, on a table and see it so like our birds. Everywhere there were books and writings, many in tongues that I could not read. The god who lived there must have been a wise god and full of knowledge. I felt I had right there, as I sought knowledge also.

Nevertheless, it was strange. There was a washing-place but no water—perhaps the gods washed in air. There was a cooking-place but no wood, and though there was a machine to cook food, there was no place to put fire in it. Nor were there candles or lamps—there were things that looked like lamps but they had neither oil nor wick. All these things were magic, but I touched them and lived—the magic had gone out of them.

Let me tell one thing to show. In the washing-place, a thing said "Hot" but it was not hot to the touch—another thing said "Cold" but it was not cold. This must have been a strong magic but the magic was gone. I do not understand—they had ways—I wish that I knew.

It was close and dry and dusty in their house of the gods. I have said the magic was gone but that is not true—it had gone from the magic things but it had not gone from the place. I felt the spirits about me, weighing upon me. Nor had I ever slept in a Dead Place before—and yet, tonight, I must sleep there. When I thought of it, my tongue felt dry in my throat, in spite of my wish for knowledge. Almost I would have gone down again and faced the dogs, but I did not.

I had not gone through all the rooms when the darkness fell. When it fell, I went back to the big room looking over the city and made fire. There was a place to make fire and a box with wood in it, though I do not think they cooked there. I wrapped myself in a floor-covering and slept in front of the fire—I was very tired.

Now I tell what is very strong magic. I woke in the midst of the night. When I woke, the fire had gone out and I was cold. It seemed to me that all around me there were whisperings and voices. I closed my eyes to shut them out. Some will say that I slept again, but I do not think that I slept. I could feel the spirits drawing my spirit out of my body as a fish is drawn on a line.

Why should I lie about it? I am a priest and the son of a priest. If there are spirits, as they say, in the small Dead Places near us, what spirits must there not be in that great Place of the Gods? And would not they wish to speak? After such long years? I know that I felt myself drawn as a fish is drawn on a line. I had stepped out of my body—I could see my body asleep in front of the cold fire, but it was not I. I was drawn to look out upon the city of the gods.

It should have been dark, for it was night, but it was not dark. Everywhere there were lights—lines of light—circles and blurs of light—ten thousand torches would not have been the

---

Assessing Learning

Self-Assessment

To enable students to successfully assess their understanding of the story, ask them to create a story map like the one shown for the following scenes. In each box, they should write a brief summary of the scene.

Visit to the dead house with his father

His purification and dream

His journey

The river crossing

The Place of the Gods

same. The sky itself was alight—you could barely see the stars for the glow in the sky. I thought to myself, "This is strong magic," and trembled. There was a roaring in my ears like the rushing of rivers. Then my eyes grew used to the light and my ears to the sound. I knew that I was seeing the city as it had been when the gods were alive.

That was a sight indeed—yes, that was a sight: I could not have seen it in the body—my body would have died. Everywhere went the gods, on foot and in chariots—there were gods beyond number and counting and their chariots blocked the streets. They had turned night to day for their pleasure—they did not sleep with the sun. The noise of their coming and going was the noise of many waters. It was magic what they could do— it was magic what they did.

I looked out of another window—the great vines of their bridges were mended and the god-roads went east and west. Restless, restless were the gods, and always in motion! They burrowed tunnels under rivers—they flew in the air. With unbelievable tools they did giant works—no part of the earth was safe from them, for, if they wished for a thing, they summoned it from the other side of the world. And always, as they labored and rested, as they feasted and made love, there was a drum in their ears—the pulse of the giant city, beating and beating like a man's heart.

Were they happy? What is happiness to the gods? They were great, they were mighty, they were wonderful and terrible. As I looked upon them and their magic, I felt like a child—but a little more, it seemed to me, and they would pull down the moon from the sky. I saw them with wisdom beyond wisdom and knowledge beyond knowledge. And yet not all they did was well done—even I could see that—and yet their wisdom could not but grow until all was peace.

Then I saw their fate come upon them and that was terrible past speech. It came upon them as they walked the streets of their city. I have been in the fights with the Forest People—I have seen men die. But this was not like that. When gods war with gods, they use weapons we do not know. It was fire falling out of the sky and a mist that poisoned. It was the time of the Great Burning and the Destruction. They ran about like ants in the streets of their city—poor gods, poor gods! Then the towers began to fall. A few escaped—yes, a few. The legends tell it. But, even after the city had become a Dead Place, for many years the poison was still in the ground. I saw it happen, I saw the last of them die. It was darkness over the broken city and I wept.

All this, I saw. I saw it as I have told it, though not in the body. When I woke in the morning, I was hungry, but I did not think first of my hunger, for my heart was perplexed and confused. I knew the reason for the Dead Places but I did not see why it had happened. It seemed to me it should not have happened, with all the magic they had. I went through the house looking for an answer. There was so much in the house I could not understand—and yet I am a priest and the son of a priest. It was like being on one side of the great river, at night, with no light to show the way.

Then I saw the dead god. He was sitting in his chair, by the window, in a room I had not entered before and, for the first moment, I thought that he was alive. Then I saw the skin on the back of his hand—it was like dry leather. The room was shut, hot and dry—no doubt that had kept him as he was. At first I was afraid to approach him—then the fear left me. He was sitting looking out over the city—he was dressed in the clothes of the gods. His age was neither young nor old— I could not tell his age. But there was wisdom in his face and great sadness. You could see that he would have not run away. He had sat at his window, watching his city die—then he himself had died. But it is better to lose one's life than one's spirit—and you could see from the face that his spirit had not been lost. I knew that, if I touched him, he would fall into dust—and yet, there was something unconquered in the face.

That is all of my story, for then I knew he was a man—I knew then that they had been men, neither gods nor demons. It is a great knowledge,

---

D Struggling Readers

Summarizing

Have students pause in their reading and paraphrase what is happening in this episode. [The narrator may have fallen asleep. He is dreaming or having a vision of the living city the way it appeared before it was destroyed.]

E Reading Skills and Strategies

Drawing Conclusions

❓ What has happened to the city? [It was destroyed by a weapon of mass destruction, such as a nuclear weapon.] **What clues helped you draw this conclusion?** [The narrator describes it as a war unlike any known in his primitive society. It came out of the sky (by rocket) and had a mist that poisoned the city (fallout) and remained toxic for many years.]

F Critical Thinking

Making Connections

❓ Why do you think the author titled this story "By the Waters of Babylon"? [It occurs beside a large river and tells of the destruction of a great civilization and of the narrator's sorrow at the loss of all the knowledge and brilliance of that dead society.]

G Advanced Learners

Comparing Literature

Invite students to compare the characteristics of this story with other stories or movies that tell of the end of civilization.

Making the Connections

Connecting to the Theme: "Breakthroughs"

After students have finished reading the selection, guide a discussion of how the collection theme is developed in this story. The narrator's breakthrough in reaching the Place of the Gods and returning safely home is obvious. Students, however, should recognize that the greatest breakthrough is the narrator's recognition that the gods were only humans and that their knowledge was accessible to him and his people. Invite students to suggest other stories, movies, or actual events in which important breakthroughs have been the gaining of knowledge.

Cultural Connections

Most cultures have stories, folk tales, legends, and myths about the destruction of civilization and its ultimate survival. Invite students to share such stories from their cultures. As an extension, encourage students to learn about the stories of another culture relating to this topic. They might do library or Internet research, or they might interview friends and relatives.

A Reading Skills and Strategies

Drawing Conclusions

Invite students to share the conclusions they have drawn about the setting of this story and their evidence for those conclusions. How many identified the city as New York?

Resources

Selection Assessment
Formal Assessment
• Selection Test, p. 42.
Test Generator (One-Stop Planner)
• CD-ROM

BROWSING IN THE FILES

About the Author. Born in Bethlehem, Pennsylvania, Stephen Vincent Benét was steeped in military and American history from his childhood on. As a youth, Benét attended a military academy, and he read widely in military history. His writing naturally shaped itself to these roots. Besides poetry and short stories, Benét wrote five novels and two short opera librettos. At the time of his death, he was writing an epic about the American West. He finished the first volume, *Western Star,* for which he was posthumously awarded the 1944 Pulitzer Prize.

A Critic's Comment. A critic in *Forum and Century* has commented, "Stephen Vincent Benét's distinction . . . is in his ability to create characters that have the fundamental human qualities and the fixed destinies of people in a folk tale."

---

hard to tell and believe. They were men—they went a dark road, but they were men. I had no fear after that—I had no fear going home, though twice I fought off the dogs and I was hunted for two days by the Forest People. When I saw my father again, I prayed and was purified. He touched my lips and my breast, he said, "You went away a boy. You come back a man and a priest." I said, "Father, they were men! I have been in the Place of the Gods and seen it! Now slay me, if it is the law—but still I know they were men."

He looked at me out of both eyes. He said, "The law is not always the same shape—you have done what you have done. I could not have done it my time, but you come after me. Tell!"

I told and he listened. After that, I wished to tell all the people but he showed me otherwise. He said, "Truth is a hard deer to hunt. If you eat too much truth at once, you may die of the truth. It was not idly that our fathers forbade the Dead Places." He was right—it is better the truth should come little by little. I have learned

that, being a priest. Perhaps, in the old days, they ate knowledge too fast.

Nevertheless, we make a beginning. It is not for the metal alone we go to the Dead Places now—there are the books and the writings. They are hard to learn. And the magic tools are broken—but we can look at them and wonder. At least, we make a beginning. And, when I am chief priest we shall go beyond the great river. We shall go to the Place of the Gods—the place newyork—not one man but a company. We shall look for the images of the gods and find the god ASHING and the others—the gods Lincoln and Biltmore[2] and Moses.[3] But they were men who built the city, not gods or demons. They were men. I remember the dead man's face. They were men who were here before us. We must build again.

2. Biltmore: New York City hotel.
3. Moses: Robert Moses (1888–1981): New York City public official who oversaw many large construction projects, such as bridges and public buildings.

MEET THE WRITER

Mr. American History

Stephen Vincent Benét (1898–1943) found many of his subjects in American history, folklore, and legend. *John Brown's Body* (1928), a book-length narrative poem about the fiery abolitionist who led an attack on Harpers Ferry in 1859 and was hanged for treason, won him the Pulitzer Prize for poetry. According to one biographer, Benét "wrote short stories for money and poetry for love."

Despite his preference for poetry, some of Benét's stories have remained his best-known works. "The Devil and Daniel Webster," a fantasy about the great American orator, has been remade several times for the stage, radio, and television. "By the Waters of Babylon," another well-known fantasy, first appeared as "The Place of the Gods" in the *Saturday Evening Post* in July 1937. Benét later changed its title.

Emphasizing the importance of clear style, Benét advised one young writer: 66 Don't use four adjectives when one will do. Don't use five long words to say, 'We were happy.' 'It rained.' 'It was dark.' Write of the simple things simply. 99

Assessing Learning

Check Test: True-False
1. The narrator's father is a priest, and he enters the dead houses to find metal. [True]
2. The narrator is guided on his way to the Place of the Gods by the Forest People. [False]
3. The narrator nearly dies while crossing the river. [True]

4. A man living in the Place of the Gods tells the narrator about the Great Burning that ended civilization. [False]
5. The narrator decides he will someday take his people back to the Place of the Gods. [True]

Standardized Test Preparation
For practice in proofreading and editing, see
• *Daily Oral Grammar,* Transparency 17

T272

MAKING MEANINGS

First Thoughts

[respond]

1. Does John's story make you feel encouraged or discouraged about humanity? Why? Compare your responses with those of other classmates.

Shaping Interpretations

[respond]

2. At what point in the story did you first begin to guess what the Place of the Gods was?

[infer]

3. To understand what is really happening in this story, you have to **draw conclusions** based on the writer's clues and your own experience and knowledge. What do you think John is really seeing (and how are you able to tell) when he describes each of the items below? (You might want to work with a group to solve these puzzles.)

   - the Great Burning
   - Ou-dis-sun
   - the statue of a man named ASHING
   - the temple in mid-city with a roof painted like the sky at night
   - the caves and tunnels where John thinks the gods kept their slaves

[analyze]

4. Find a place in the story where John achieves a breakthrough, and explain what he discovers. How does the **first-person point of view** help you appreciate his breakthrough?

[interpret]

5. The background on page 264 explains the Biblical **allusion** in the story's **title**. Now that you have read the story, explain how the words of the psalm connect with Benét's story.

Connecting with the Text

[interpret]

6. Near the end of the story, John says, "Perhaps in the old days, they ate knowledge too fast." What do you think he means? Are we "eating knowledge too fast" today? Explain.

Extending the Text

[extend]

7. Benét wrote this story in 1937, before the first atom bomb was invented. World War II and the Cold War are over now. Do Benét's warnings about the complete destruction of a civilization still have relevance today? Why?

Challenging the Text

[evaluate]

8. Do you think Benét made the secret of the Place of the Gods too easy to guess, or too hard, or were the clues just difficult enough? Explain.

> ### Reading Check
>
> Imagine that you are John, the narrator, telling the Hill People about your journey to the Place of the Gods. Briefly **summarize** the **main events** of your journey, either orally or in writing. Explain why you went and what you learned.

Reading Check

Main events include: purification ceremony and dream; sighting of the eagle, which is corroborated by seeing the three deer and the white fawn and by his killing the panther; discovery of the knife in the Dead Place; crossing the river; the statue of ASHING; being chased by the dogs; exploring the apartment; vision of the destruction of the city; realization that the dead man was not a god. The narrator went on the journey to gain knowledge. What he learns is that the Place of the Gods was not occupied by gods but by humans. He believes that the knowledge of these humans can be regained to help his own people.

MAKING MEANINGS

First Thoughts

1. Possible responses: Encouraged because people survived, gained wisdom, and are beginning to rebuild; discouraged because civilization and culture were totally destroyed, leaving behind little with which to rebuild.

Shaping Interpretations

2. Possible answers include these clues: the river "Ou-dis-sun," p. 267; the "huge ruins," p. 268; the "great Dead Place—greater than any Dead Place we know," p. 268; "ASHING," p. 269.

3. Sample answers: The Great Burning—nuclear war; Ou-dis-sun—Hudson River; statue of ASHING—George Washington; temple—Grand Central Station; caves and tunnels—subway system

4. Sample answer: The narrator discovers the man in the apartment is not a god. The first-person point of view helps us see his emotional and intellectual response.

5. John, like the singer of the psalm, is sitting beside a river, mourning the loss of a great city.

Connecting with the Text

6. Possible answer: They gained knowledge too quickly and easily but didn't learn to use it wisely. Some students will say we eat knowledge too fast today; others will say we cannot learn too much.

Extending the Text

7. Possible answer: Yes, because there is still no end to the threat of nuclear war.

Challenging the Text

8. Most students will have guessed the setting and will think the clues were easy or just difficult enough. Some students may lack sufficient knowledge of New York and will have found the clues insufficient.

Grading Timesaver

Rubrics for each assignment appear on p. 121 in the *Portfolio Management System*.

CHOICES: Building Your Portfolio

1. **Writer's Notebook** As a class, you might have students brainstorm a list of story elements that students can consider in their freewriting. Tell students to save their notes; they might be useful for prewriting of their evaluations.
2. **Creative Writing** If students have difficulty coming up with plot ideas, suggest they pose What if? questions. What if the man was like John? What if he knew the end was coming? What if people ignored his warnings?
3. **Visual Literacy/Comparing** Encourage students to form a discussion group to analyze the movie.
4. **Research/History** Urge students to use the Internet to locate information on their topics.
5. **Art** Suggest that students freewrite about each setting for two minutes to generate ideas for their sketches.

CHOICES: Building Your Portfolio

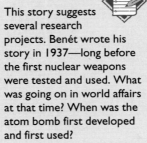

Writer's Notebook

1. Collecting Ideas for an Evaluation

Evaluating the author's craft. In your Writer's Notebook, freewrite your initial reactions to the way "By the Waters of Babylon" is written (or you might want to focus on the craft of another story in these collections). Did you find the plot and the ending believable? Is there anything in the story that doesn't make sense? Did the writer use description effectively, to help you feel you were "there"? In your Writer's Notebook, jot down your evaluation of the author's craft. Save your notes for possible use with the Writer's Workshop assignment on page 328.

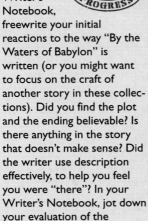

"The Pedestrian"
by Ray Bradbury

One of my favorite stories because of its language. Spooky setting. Great descriptions (some good comparisons).

Creative Writing

2. Babylon II?

What had happened to the city that John calls the Place of the Gods? Write a **prequel**, a story of the events that led up to "By the Waters of Babylon." You might write your story from the **first-person point of view** of the man John finds "sitting looking out over the city." Or you might write the story in the form of the man's last journal entries.

If you prefer, write a **sequel** to "By the Waters of Babylon," telling what happens after Benét's ending. Project the story several years into the future. What has become of John and his people?

Visual Literacy/ Comparing

3. The Apes Rule

Find and rent the science fiction movie classic *Planet of the Apes* (1968), starring Kim Hunter, Charlton Heston, and Roddy McDowall. How is the aftermath of nuclear war portrayed in the movie? Write a comparison of the movie and Benét's story. Consider **plot, characters, theme,** and how the **setting** is revealed.

Research/History

4. Into the Past

This story suggests several research projects. Benét wrote his story in 1937—long before the first nuclear weapons were tested and used. What was going on in world affairs at that time? When was the atom bomb first developed and first used?

You might want to focus on another long-gone civilization, such as those below:

- ancient Egypt
- the kingdom of Mali
- the kingdom of the Incas
- the people of Mesa Verde

First, brainstorm a list of questions you have about the period you'll focus on. Then, research your topic. Choose a presentation medium, such as a **time line, oral report,** or **photo essay,** and present your findings to your class.

Art

5. Designing the Place of the Gods

Suppose you are the **set designer** for a stage or screen adaptation of "By the Waters of Babylon." Sketch designs for at least two scenes, possibly including the Hill People's village, the forest, the view overlooking the Place of the Gods, and various parts of the ruined city.

Getting Students Involved

Cooperative Learning
Babylon—Take One. As an extension of Choice 5, invite students to write and stage one scene from the screen adaptation of the story. Students should divide up responsibility. They should select one person to serve as producer. He or she will oversee the entire production.

Other students should be assigned to add costumes for the narrator and his father, the Hill People, and Forest People. Urge them to select music to accompany their screen adaptations. Have students rehearse, perform, and videotape their production.

Enrichment
Challenge students to work in groups and to create models of the sets they design for Choice 5. Have students present their models to the class.

Inverted Order: Subjects Ahead

Language Handbook HELP

See Agreement of Subject and Verb: pages 1022–1024.

Technology HELP

See Language Workshop CD-ROM. *Key word entry:* subject-verb agreement.

As you know, singular subjects take singular verbs and plural subjects take plural verbs. The rule is easy, but finding the subject can be hard.

For example, some sentences or parts of sentences use **inverted order**—that is, the subject follows the verb. Inverted order is often used in questions and in sentences or clauses that begin with the word *here* or *there.* (Sometimes a sentence in inverted order will begin with a phrase or an adjective or adverb.) In the following examples from "By the Waters of Babylon," the subject is under-scored once and the verb twice.

1. "<u>Were</u> <u>they</u> happy?"
2. "There <u>was</u> a white <u>fawn</u> with them— a very great sign."
3. "Restless, restless <u>were</u> the <u>gods</u>, and always in motion!"

Try It Out

➤ For each sentence, first find the subject and determine whether it is singular or plural. Then choose the verb that agrees with the subject. It will help to turn the inverted sentence into normal subject-verb-complement order. Thus, to decide whether to use <u>was</u> or <u>were</u> in the sentence "Was/were they happy?" you should turn the sentence around: "They <u>were</u> happy."

1. Here (lie, lies) our future.
2. Why (is, are) John on his journey?
3. There (was, were) coverings on the floor.
4. From hard journeys (come, comes) new breakthroughs.
5. Where (was, were) the dogs?

VOCABULARY   HOW TO OWN A WORD

Clues to Word Meaning: Prefixes and Suffixes

Just a few letters tacked onto the beginning of a word (a **prefix**) or the end of a word (a **suffix**) change its meaning and often its part of speech. When you find an unfamiliar word, look for prefixes and suffixes that provide clues to how the **root,** the base meaning of the word, changes. Do a word chart like the one at right for each word from "By the Waters of Babylon" in the Word Bank below. If you need help with the meaning of a prefix or suffix, check a dictionary.

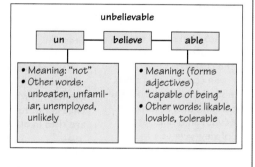

unbelievable

| un | believe | able |

- Meaning: "not"
- Other words: unbeaten, unfamiliar, unemployed, unlikely

- Meaning: (forms adjectives) "capable of being"
- Other words: likable, lovable, tolerable

WORD BANK

enchantments • destruction • forehead • restrung • anteroom

BY THE WATERS OF BABYLON 275

Ask students to select a piece of writing from their portfolios and review it for sentences with inverted word order. In each case, have them identify the subject and check for subject-verb agreement.

Try It Out
1. lies
2. is
3. were
4. come
5. were

VOCABULARY

Students should present their answers in chart form. Some answers will vary. Sample answers: *enchantments*—en- (Meaning: "in" or "into"; Other words: enclose, encounter, engage), chant, -ment (Meaning: "state, condition"; Other words: bewilderment, contentment); *destruction*—de- (Meaning: "down"; Other words: detest, devote, deter), struct, -ion (Meaning: forms nouns, "the result of"; Other words: construction, correction, formation); *forehead*—fore- (Meaning: "the front part of"; Other words: foreword, forearm, foreground), head; *restrung*— re- (Meaning: "over again"; Other words: repeat, restate, review), strung; *anteroom*—ante- (Meaning: "before"; Other words: antecedent, antedate, ante-Victorian), room.

Resources ———

Language
- *Grammar and Language Links* Worksheet, p. 31

Grammar Link Quick Check

Proofread these sentences for problems with subject-verb agreement. Change the verb to agree with the subject in sentences that are incorrect. (Not all sentences have errors.)

1. Does the narrator and his father agree that he should go on the journey? [Do the narrator and his father agree that he should go on the journey?]
2. Here in the dead place are two windows overlooking the city. [Correct]
3. There is many buildings still standing. [There are many buildings still standing.]
4. Was the narrator and his people afraid to visit the Place of the Gods? [Were the narrator and his people afraid to visit the Place of the Gods?]
5. There are several good reasons for the narrator to return home. [Correct]

1. Read and interpret the story
2. Identify and analyze the omniscient point of view
3. Monitor reading through using resources
4. Express understanding through writing, art, or listening/speaking
5. Identify participles and use such participles in writing
6. Understand and use new words
7. Understand and use analogies

SKILLS

Literary
- Understand the omniscient point of view
- Monitor reading through using resources

Writing
- Evaluate a story element
- Analyze setting

Speaking/Listening
- Make an audio recording of a dramatic reading

Grammar/Language
- Identify and use participles

Vocabulary
- Understand and use new words

Art
- Make a collage

Planning

- **Block Schedule**
  Block Scheduling Lesson Plans with Pacing Guide

- **Traditional Schedule**
  Lesson Plans Including Strategies for English-Language Learners

- **One-Stop Planner**
  CD-ROM with Test Generator

Before You Read

THROUGH THE TUNNEL

Make the Connection

A Need to Prove Yourself

Sometimes you need to prove yourself. Maybe you want so badly to play on the basketball team that you spend nights shooting baskets in the park. Maybe you practice alone for hours to learn a new dance. If what you want really matters to you, you'll endure tedium and possibly suffer physical pain to make the breakthrough—to accomplish your goal.

Quickwrite

Freewrite about a time you committed yourself to achieving something. What did you have to go through to get it? How did you feel at the end?

Elements of Literature

Knowing It All: Omniscient Point of View

An **omniscient**, or all-knowing, narrator can reveal the private thoughts and motives of all the characters and sometimes even comment on them. Unlike stories written from the first-person point of view, stories with an omniscient point of view give us a more reliable perspective. We know we are in the hands of an all-knowing narrator, and we trust that voice.

> **I**n a story told from the **omniscient point of view,** the narrator is an all-knowing observer who can reveal the thoughts and feelings of all the characters.
>
> *For more on Point of View, see pages 262–263 and the Handbook of Literary Terms.*

Reading Skills and Strategies

Monitoring Your Reading: Using Resources

Many selections in this book have **resources** to enrich your reading. This story has the usual footnotes and photographs, but it also has a special feature called Literature and Anthropology (page 283), which provides information on initiation rites. This information should invite you to look beneath the surface of this story about a young English boy and consider the ways in which his experience connects with coming-of-age rites in other cultures.

go.hrw.com
LE0 10-4

Water surged into his mouth; he choked, sank, came up.

Preteaching Vocabulary

Words to Own

Have students work in pairs to read the Words to Own at the bottom of the selection pages. One student pronounces the word, the other reads the definition. Then, have each student use the word in a sentence. Reinforce students' understanding of the words by having them fill in the blanks in the following sentences with one of the words.

1. He was lonely and asked with _____ if he could come to the party. [supplication]

2. The fish was _____, barely a quarter of an inch long. [minute]

3. She was _____ when he said that it was a counterfeit bill. [incredulous]

4. A sense of _____ came over him when he broke his grandmother's dish. [contrition]

5. She was _____ about who he was, what he did, and where he came from. [inquisitive]

Through the Tunnel

Doris Lessing

Going to the shore on the first morning of the vacation, the young English boy stopped at a turning of the path and looked down at a wild and rocky bay and then over to the crowded beach he knew so well from other years. His mother walked on in front of him,

Background

This story takes place at an unnamed seaside resort frequented by English tourists. This resort could be located on the Mediterranean Sea, perhaps along the coast of France or North Africa.

Summary ■ ■

The protagonist of this initiation story is Jerry, a young British boy who is vacationing on a foreign coast with his widowed mother. The omniscient narrator offers psychological insight into both characters: Jerry longs to go to the "wild and rocky bay" but is uncomfortable leaving his mother on the "safe" beach; she worries about his encountering danger but worries more about babying him. At the bay, Jerry is blissful when older local boys let him swim with them. He's terrified, though, as they swim through an underwater tunnel in the rock. When he clowns childishly instead of following their lead, the boys leave. Jerry is determined to swim the tunnel. Suspense builds as he practices and prepares obsessively, enduring physical trauma (nosebleeds) as he increases his ability to hold his breath for longer periods of time. Suspense peaks in Jerry's climactic swim through the dark, dangerous tunnel. After his breakthrough, Jerry feels no more need of the boys' approval or of the bay as a testing ground.

Resources

Listening
Audio CD Library
A vivid reading of the story appears in the *Audio CD Library:*
• Disc 9, Track 2

Resources: Print and Media

Reading
• *Graphic Organizers for Active Reading,* p. 18
• *Words to Own,* p. 18
• *Audio CD Library*
    Disc 9, Track 2

Writing and Language
• *Daily Oral Grammar*
    Transparency 18
• *Grammar and Language Links*
    Worksheet, p. 33

• *Language Workshop CD-ROM*

Assessment
• *Formal Assessment,* p. 44
• *Portfolio Management System,* p. 123
• *Standardized Test Preparation,* p. 36
• *Test Generator (One-Stop Planner CD-ROM)*

Internet
• go.hrw.com (keyword: LE0 10-4)

A Elements of Literature

Omniscient Point of View

❓ How do you know that this story is told by an omniscient narrator? [It is written in the third-person; the narrator plays no part in the story but describes what each character is thinking and feeling.] What descriptions in this passage indicate this omniscient viewpoint? [the mother's worry about her son; Jerry's familiarity with his mother's smile; Jerry's feeling of contrition; Jerry's thoughts of the safe beach]

B Elements of Literature

Conflict

Point out that the omniscient narrator can express internal conflicts in more than one character. Here Jerry is in conflict about whether to strike off on his own; his mother struggles to provide Jerry with both protection and independence.

---

carrying a bright striped bag in one hand. Her other arm, swinging loose, was very white in the sun. The boy watched that white naked arm and turned his eyes, which had a frown behind them, toward the bay and back again to his mother. When she felt he was not with her, she swung around. "Oh, there you are, Jerry!" she said. She looked impatient, then smiled. "Why, darling, would you rather not come with me? Would you rather——" She frowned, conscientiously worrying over what amusements he might secretly be longing for, which she had been too busy or too careless to imagine. He was very familiar with that anxious, apologetic smile. Contrition sent him running after her. And yet, as he ran, he looked back over his shoulder at the wild bay; and all morning, as he played on the safe beach, he was thinking of it.

Next morning, when it was time for the routine of swimming and sunbathing, his mother said, "Are you tired of the usual beach, Jerry? Would you like to go somewhere else?"

"Oh, no!" he said quickly, smiling at her out of that unfailing impulse of contrition—a sort of chivalry. Yet, walking down the path with her, he blurted out, "I'd like to go and have a look at those rocks down there."

She gave the idea her attention. It was a wild-looking place, and there was no one there, but she said, "Of course, Jerry. When you've had enough, come to the big beach. Or just go straight back to the villa, if you like." She walked away, that bare arm, now slightly reddened from yesterday's sun, swinging. And he almost ran after her again, feeling it unbearable that she should go by herself, but he did not.

She was thinking, Of course he's old enough to be safe without me. Have I been keeping him too close? He mustn't feel he ought to be with me. I must be careful.

He was an only child, eleven years old. She was a widow. She was determined to be neither possessive nor lacking in devotion. She went worrying off to her beach.

As for Jerry, once he saw that his mother had gained her beach, he began the steep descent to the bay. From where he was, high up among red-brown rocks, it was a scoop of moving bluish green fringed with white. As he went lower, he saw that it spread among small promontories and inlets of rough, sharp rock, and the crisping, lapping surface showed stains of purple and darker blue. Finally, as he ran sliding and scraping down the last few yards, he saw an edge of white surf and the shallow, luminous movement of water over white sand and, beyond that, a solid, heavy blue.

He ran straight into the water and began swimming. He was a good swimmer. He went out fast over the gleaming sand, over a middle region where rocks lay like discolored monsters under the surface, and then he was in the real sea—a warm sea where irregular cold currents from the deep water shocked his limbs.

When he was so far out that he could look back not only on the little bay but past the promontory that was between it and the big beach, he floated on the buoyant surface and looked for his mother. There she was, a speck of yellow under an umbrella that looked like a slice of orange peel. He swam back to shore, relieved at being sure she was there, but all at once very lonely.

On the edge of a small cape that marked the side of the bay away from the promontory was a loose scatter of rocks. Above them, some boys were stripping off their clothes. They came running, naked, down to the rocks. The English boy swam toward them but kept his distance at a stone's throw. They were of that coast; all of them were burned smooth dark brown and speaking a language he did not understand. To be with them, of them, was a craving that filled his whole body. He swam a little closer; they turned and watched him with narrowed, alert dark eyes. Then one smiled and waved. It was enough. In a minute, he had swum in and was on the rocks beside them, smiling with a desperate, nervous supplication. They shouted

---

WORDS TO OWN

contrition (kən·trish′ən) *n.*: regret or sense of guilt at having done wrong.

supplication (sup′lə·kā′shən) *n.*: humble appeal or request.

Reaching All Students

Struggling Readers

To help students with this selection, use the Somebody Wanted But So strategy. Students create a chart with four headings: "Somebody," "Wanted," "But," and "So." As students read the selection, they pause to fill in the appropriate information. The categories provide a framework for identifying and summarizing plot developments. For help in applying this strategy, see the *Reading Strategies Handbook,* p. 111 in the *Reading Skills and Strategies* binder.

English Language Learners

Lessing uses words and phrases that reflect the characters' social status and Englishness. Discuss the fact that in parts of Europe, a *villa* is a large vacation house. Certain phrases that reflect the mother's education and upper-middle class status and manner include: "Why darling, would you rather not come with me?"; "worrying off to her beach"; "gained her beach"; "She gave the idea her attention"; and "He mustn't feel he ought to be with me."

Advanced Learners

Ask students to identify some of the dangers that anyone might face when swimming alone in the ocean, even if the person is a "good" swimmer. Students can research information about tides, ocean currents, and undertow, as well as potentially harmful animals such as eels and sharks.

cheerful greetings at him; and then, as he preserved his nervous, uncomprehending smile, they understood that he was a foreigner strayed from his own beach, and they proceeded to forget him. But he was happy. He was with them.

They began diving again and again from a high point into a well of blue sea between rough, pointed rocks. After they had dived and come up, they swam around, hauled themselves up, and waited their turn to dive again. They were big boys—men, to Jerry. He dived, and they watched him; and when he swam around to take his place, they made way for him. He felt he was accepted and he dived again, carefully, proud of himself.

Soon the biggest of the boys poised himself, shot down into the water, and did not come up. The others stood about, watching. Jerry, after waiting for the sleek brown head to appear, let out a yell of warning; they looked at him idly and turned their eyes back toward the water. After a long time, the boy came up on the other side of a big dark rock, letting the air out of his lungs in a sputtering gasp and a shout of triumph. Immediately the rest of them dived in. One moment, the morning seemed full of chattering boys; the next, the air and the surface of the water were empty. But through the heavy blue, dark shapes could be seen moving and groping.

Jerry dived, shot past the school of underwater swimmers, saw a black wall of rock looming at him, touched it, and bobbed up at once to the surface, where the wall was a low barrier he could see across. There was no one visible; under him, in the water, the dim shapes of the swimmers had disappeared. Then one and then another of the boys came up on the far side of the barrier of rock, and he understood that they had swum through some gap or hole in it. He plunged down again. He could see nothing through the stinging salt water but the blank rock. When he came up, the boys were all on the diving

rock, preparing to attempt the feat again. And now, in a panic of failure, he yelled up, in English, "Look at me! Look!" and he began splashing and kicking in the water like a foolish dog.

They looked down gravely, frowning. He knew the frown. At moments of failure, when he clowned to claim his mother's attention, it was with just this grave, embarrassed inspection that she rewarded him. Through his hot shame, feeling the pleading grin on his face like a scar that he could never remove, he looked up at the group of big brown boys on the rock and shouted, "Bonjour! Merci! Au revoir! Monsieur, monsieur!"[1] while he hooked his fingers round his ears and waggled them.

Water surged into his mouth; he choked, sank, came up. The rock, lately weighted with boys, seemed to rear up out of the water as their weight was removed. They were flying down

1. **Bonjour! Merci! Au revoir! Monsieur, monsieur!:** French for "Hello! Thank you! Goodbye! Mr., Mr.!"—probably the only French words Jerry knows.

279

C Elements of Literature

Setting

? One function of setting is to create atmosphere. What atmosphere does Lessing create with the following expressions: "big dark rock," "heavy blue, dark shapes," "black wall of rock looming at him," and "blank rock"? [Students may suggest that the words create a frightening, forbidding atmosphere.]

D Critical Thinking

Interpreting

? Why is it so important for Jerry to have the older boys' approval? [Possible responses: He is lonely and wants to be accepted by these older boys as an equal; he wants to change from being a child to being an adolescent.]

E Reading Skills and Strategies

Monitoring Your Reading: Using Resources

? How does the footnote in this passage help you to understand that Jerry, out of frustration, is trying to attract the boys' attention. [Sample answer: The footnote reveals that the words Jerry shouts in French are absurd when run together like this.]

Getting Students Involved

Cooperative Learning

Dangerous Breakthroughs. After students have read the story, discuss the role of danger in making personal breakthroughs. Point out that many adventurers, such as mountain climbers and Arctic travelers, risk everything for the exhilaration of testing themselves to the limits and surviving. Provide time for students to do research about such a real-life adventurer. Then ask students to meet in groups of three or four

to share their research findings and to discuss the motives and accomplishments of individuals who take great risks. One group member should take notes as the group considers these questions: Do these kinds of people always achieve breakthroughs? How are their breakthroughs similar to, and different from, Jerry's breakthrough? Groups can then share their conclusions in a general class discussion.

Writing Activity

A Different Perspective. Ask students to think about how "Through the Tunnel" would be different if it were told from the first-person point of view by either Jerry or his mother. Discuss the question in class. Then challenge students to rewrite one scene from the story from the first-person point of view.

Making Inferences

? Why do the older boys leave? [Jerry is acting like a child; he has not passed the test of performing and acting like one of them.]

B Elements of Literature

Setting

In this passage, Lessing contrasts the mother's landscape with Jerry's landscape. In the former, she uses colors; in the latter, she personifies the boulders and uses another metaphor to describe the rock. Ask students to identify specific words that create this contrast and to tell what effect is created. [Words and phrases for the mother's landscape are *yellow spot* and *orange umbrella*; for Jerry's landscape, *fanged and angry boulders,* and *wall of rock.* One setting might be described as cheerful; the other, menacing.]

C Elements of Literature

Omniscient Point of View

? This description of Jerry is not flattering. How might it be different if Jerry were the narrator of the story? [Possible responses: The description would be more positive and understanding; Jerry might say he urgently needed the goggles to achieve his goal.]

D Struggling Readers

Finding Details

? What details does the writer provide to help you visualize the scene in the water? [Details include the "clean, shining white sand, rippled firm and hard," "two grayish shapes," "a water dance," "swimming in flaked silver," and the rock that is "black, tufted lightly with greenish weed."]

---

past him now, into the water; the air was full of falling bodies. Then the rock was empty in the hot sunlight. He counted one, two, three . . .

At fifty, he was terrified. They must all be drowning beneath him, in the watery caves of the rock! At a hundred, he stared around him at the empty hillside, wondering if he should yell for help. He counted faster, faster, to hurry them up, to bring them to the surface quickly, to drown them quickly—anything rather than the terror of counting on and on into the blue emptiness of the morning. And then, at a hundred and sixty, the water beyond the rock was full of boys blowing like brown whales. They swam back to the shore without a look at him.

He climbed back to the diving rock and sat down, feeling the hot roughness of it under his thighs. The boys were gathering up their bits of clothing and running off along the shore to another promontory. They were leaving to get away from him. He cried openly, fists in his eyes. There was no one to see him, and he cried himself out.

It seemed to him that a long time had passed, and he swam out to where he could see his mother. Yes, she was still there, a yellow spot under an orange umbrella. He swam back to the big rock, climbed up, and dived into the blue pool among the fanged and angry boulders. Down he went, until he touched the wall of rock again. But the salt was so painful in his eyes that he could not see.

He came to the surface, swam to shore, and went back to the villa to wait for his mother. Soon she walked slowly up the path, swinging her striped bag, the flushed, naked arm dangling beside her. "I want some swimming goggles," he panted, defiant and beseeching.

She gave him a patient, inquisitive look as she said casually, "Well, of course, darling."

But now, now, now! He must have them this minute, and no other time. He nagged and pestered until she went with him to a shop. As soon as she had bought the goggles, he grabbed them from her hand as if she were going to claim them for herself, and was off, running down the steep path to the bay.

Jerry swam out to the big barrier rock, ad-

justed the goggles, and dived. The impact of the water broke the rubber-enclosed vacuum, and the goggles came loose. He understood that he must swim down to the base of the rock from the surface of the water. He fixed the goggles tight and firm, filled his lungs, and floated, face down, on the water. Now he could see. It was as if he had eyes of a different kind—fish eyes that showed everything clear and delicate and wavering in the bright water.

Under him, six or seven feet down, was a floor of perfectly clean, shining white sand, rippled firm and hard by the tides. Two grayish shapes steered there, like long, rounded pieces of wood or slate. They were fish. He saw them nose toward each other, poise motionless, make a dart forward, swerve off, and come around again. It was like a water dance. A few inches above them the water sparkled as if sequins were dropping through it. Fish again—myriads of minute fish, the length of his fingernail— were drifting through the water, and in a moment he could feel the innumerable tiny touches of them against his limbs. It was like swimming in flaked silver. The great rock the big boys had swum through rose sheer out of the white sand—black, tufted lightly with greenish weed. He could see no gap in it. He swam down to its base.

Again and again he rose, took a big chestful of air, and went down. Again and again he groped over the surface of the rock, feeling it, almost hugging it in the desperate need to find the entrance. And then, once, while he was clinging to the black wall, his knees came up and he shot his feet out forward and they met no obstacle. He had found the hole.

He gained the surface, clambered about the stones that littered the barrier rock until he found a big one, and with this in his arms, let himself down over the side of the rock. He dropped, with the weight, straight to the sandy floor. Clinging tight to the anchor of stone, he

---

WORDS TO OWN

inquisitive (in·kwiz′ə·tiv) *adj.*: questioning; curious.
minute (mī·nōōt′) *adj.*: small; tiny.

Taking a Second Look

Review: Establishing a Purpose

Remind students that readers should have a reason or motive for reading, such as to gather information, to discover something new, or simply to enjoy it. By setting a purpose, readers will gain a better understanding of a text and have a greater appreciation of what they have read.

Activities

1. Before students begin reading, ask them to think about the title and to examine the pictures. Have volunteers tell what they think they might discover while reading the story. What do they think is the most apt purpose for reading this story?

2. Ask students to write questions they would like to have answered by the story. Suggest they think about *who, what, when, where, why,* and *how* questions. As they read, have them write the answers they find.

3. Have students explain how they might regard technical information about diving and about an unnamed setting if their purpose is to enjoy the story. How would their approach change if their purpose is to gather information?

lay on his side and looked in under the dark shelf at the place where his feet had gone. He could see the hole. It was an irregular, dark gap; but he could not see deep into it. He let go of his anchor, clung with his hands to the edges of the hole, and tried to push himself in.

He got his head in, found his shoulders jammed, moved them in sidewise, and was inside as far as his wrist. He could see nothing ahead. Something soft and clammy touched his mouth; he saw a dark frond moving against the grayish rock, and panic filled him. He thought of octopuses, of clinging weed. He pushed himself out backward and caught a glimpse, as he retreated, of a harmless tentacle of seaweed drifting in the mouth of the tunnel. But it was enough. He reached the sunlight, swam to shore, and lay on the diving rock. He looked down into the blue well of water. He knew he must find his way through that cave, or hole, or tunnel, and out the other side.

First, he thought, he must learn to control his breathing. He let himself down into the water with another big stone in his arms, so that he could lie effortlessly on the bottom of the sea. He counted. One, two, three. He counted steadily. He could hear the movement of blood in his chest. Fifty-one, fifty-two. . . . His chest was hurting. He let go of the rock and went up into the air. He saw that the sun was low. He rushed to the villa and found his mother at her supper. She said only, "Did you enjoy yourself?" and he said, "Yes."

All night the boy dreamed of the water-filled cave in the rock, and as soon as breakfast was over, he went to the bay.

That night, his nose bled badly. For hours he had been underwater, learning to hold his breath, and now he felt weak and dizzy. His mother said, "I shouldn't overdo things, darling, if I were you."

That day and the next, Jerry exercised his lungs as if everything, the whole of his life, all that he would become, depended upon it. Again his nose bled at night, and his mother insisted on his coming with her the next day. It was a torment to him to waste a day of his careful self-training, but he stayed with her on that

other beach, which now seemed a place for small children, a place where his mother might lie safe in the sun. It was not his beach.

He did not ask for permission, on the following day, to go to his beach. He went, before his mother could consider the complicated rights and wrongs of the matter. A day's rest, he discovered, had improved his count by ten. The big boys had made the passage while he counted a hundred and sixty. He had been counting fast, in his fright. Probably now, if he tried, he could get through that long tunnel, but he was not going to try yet. A curious, most unchildlike persistence, a controlled impatience, made him wait. In the meantime, he lay underwater on the white sand, littered now by stones he had brought down from the upper air, and studied the entrance to the tunnel. He knew every jut and corner of it, as far as it was possible to see. It was as if he already felt its sharpness about his shoulders.

He sat by the clock in the villa, when his mother was not near, and checked his time. He was incredulous and then proud to find he could hold his breath without strain for two minutes. The words "two minutes," authorized by the clock, brought close the adventure that was so necessary to him.

In another four days, his mother said casually one morning, they must go home. On the day before they left, he would do it. He would do it if it killed him, he said defiantly to himself. But two days before they were to leave—a day of triumph when he increased his count by fifteen— his nose bled so badly that he turned dizzy and had to lie limply over the big rock like a bit of seaweed, watching the thick red blood flow onto the rock and trickle slowly down to the sea. He was frightened. Supposing he turned dizzy in the tunnel? Supposing he died there, trapped? Supposing—his head went around, in the hot sun, and he almost gave up. He thought he would return to the house and lie down, and

---

WORDS TO OWN

incredulous (in·krej′ōō·ləs) *adj.*: disbelieving; skeptical.

THROUGH THE TUNNEL **281**

E **Elements of Literature**
Symbol
On p. 280, draw students' attention to the image of the dark hole in the underwater rock. Point out that holes are frequently used to signify the unknown, danger, fear, and birth.

F **Appreciating Language**
Participles
Draw attention to the phrase *clinging weed* and ask students how the word *clinging* functions in relation to *weed*. [It is an adjective modifying *weed*.] Explain that *clinging* is a participle— a verb form that functions as an adjective. Ask students to find other participles on the page. Students will learn more about using participles in the Grammar Link on p. 287.

G **Elements of Literature**
Symbol
❓ In addition to *hole*, Lessing uses the words *cave* and *tunnel* to characterize the place Jerry must go through. What might his journey mean on a symbolic level? [the journey from boyhood to manhood; a psychological breakthrough]

H **Critical Thinking**
Speculating
❓ Why doesn't Jerry tell his mother what he is trying to do? [Possible answers: He is afraid she will tell him to stop; he is afraid of worrying her; he is acting on his own and for himself.]

I **Vocabulary Note**
The Prefix per-
Explain that the word *persistence* is composed of the prefix *per-*, ("through") and the Latin root *sistere* ("to cause to stand"). *Persistence*, therefore, means "standing through or enduring." Ask students to list additional words formed with the prefix *per-*. [Sample answers: *permit, permeate, permanent, perjury, perfect,* and *perspective.*]

Using Students' Strengths

Auditory/Musical Learners
Ask students to work in pairs to select a scene from the story and to select music to accompany it. First, have them discuss the scene, analyzing its mood and setting as well as the actions and emotions of any characters. Then, have students choose or compose appropriate music to accompany the passage. Invite them to present to the class a reading of the scene with musical accompaniment.

Logical/Mathematical Learners
Ask students to investigate how fast people of different abilities and ages might swim underwater in two minutes. Then, based on Jerry's ability to hold his breath for about two minutes, determine about how far he swims under water. Students might check and compare endurance records in a source such as the *Guinness Book of Records*.

Visual Learners
Invite students to create a diagram, map, or drawing of the setting of the story. They should include each major component of the setting, such as the safe beach, the promontory, the rocks near the "unsafe" beach, and the underwater rocks. Suggest students label setting features and display the illustrations for the class.

Style

Point out the author's use of parallel structures, repetition, and rhythm. You might want to have the passage read aloud (perhaps more than once). Then, ask students to describe the effects of these stylistic elements. [Sample answer: These elements give the passage a heightened sense of drama and importance.]

B Elements of Literature

Imagery

Point out how Lessing uses imagery related to the sense of touch to describe Jerry's physical ordeal.

C Struggling Readers

Finding Details

Suggest that students focus on details of what is happening to Jerry's body and how he uses his body under water. Ask students to make notes in two columns labeled "What Happens to Jerry" and "What Jerry Does." Afterward, have students summarize the scene.

next summer, perhaps, when he had another year's growth in him—then he would go through the hole.

But even after he had made the decision, or thought he had, he found himself sitting up on the rock and looking down into the water; and he knew that now, this moment, when his nose had only just stopped bleeding, when his head was still sore and throbbing—this was the moment when he would try. If he did not do it now, he never would. He was trembling with fear that he would not go; and he was trembling with horror at the long, long tunnel under the rock, under the sea. Even in the open sunlight, the barrier rock seemed very wide and very heavy; tons of rock pressed down on where he would go. If he died there, he would lie until one day—perhaps not before next year—those big boys would swim into it and find it blocked.

He put on his goggles, fitted them tight, tested the vacuum. His hands were shaking. Then he chose the biggest stone he could carry and slipped over the edge of the rock until half of him was in the cool enclosing water and half in the hot sun. He looked up once at the empty sky, filled his lungs once, twice, and then sank fast to the bottom with the stone. He let it go and began to count. He took the edges of the hole in his hands and drew himself into it, wriggling his shoulders in sidewise as he remembered he must, kicking himself along with his feet.

Soon he was clear inside. He was in a small rock-bound hole filled with yellowish-gray water. The water was pushing him up against the roof. The roof was sharp and pained his back. He pulled himself along with his hands—fast, fast—and used his legs as levers. His head knocked against something; a sharp pain dizzied him. Fifty, fifty-one, fifty-two . . . He was without light, and the water seemed to press upon him with the weight of rock. Seventy-one, seventy-two . . . There was no strain on his lungs. He felt like an inflated balloon, his lungs were so light and easy, but his head was pulsing.

He was being continually pressed against the sharp roof, which felt slimy as well as sharp. Again he thought of octopuses, and wondered if the tunnel might be filled with weed that could tangle him. He gave himself a panicky, convulsive kick forward, ducked his head, and swam. His feet and hands moved freely, as if in open water. The hole must have widened out. He thought he must be swimming fast, and he was frightened of banging his head if the tunnel narrowed.

A hundred, a hundred and one . . . The water paled. Victory filled him. His lungs were beginning to hurt. A few more strokes and he would be out. He was counting wildly; he said a hundred and fifteen and then, a long time later, a hundred and fifteen again. The water was a clear jewel-green all around him. Then he saw, above his head, a crack running up through the rock. Sunlight was falling through it, showing the clean, dark rock of the tunnel, a single mussel[2] shell, and darkness ahead.

He was at the end of what he could do. He looked up at the crack as if it were filled with air and not water, as if he could put his mouth to it to draw in air. A hundred and fifteen, he heard himself say inside his head—but he had said that long ago. He must go on into the blackness ahead, or he would drown. His head was swelling, his lungs cracking. A hundred and fifteen, a hundred and fifteen, pounded through his head, and he feebly clutched at rocks in the dark, pulling himself forward, leaving the brief space of sunlit water behind. He felt he was dying. He was no longer quite conscious. He struggled on in the darkness between lapses into unconsciousness. An immense, swelling pain filled his head, and then the darkness cracked with an explosion of green light. His hands, groping forward, met nothing; and his feet, kicking back, propelled him out into the open sea.

He drifted to the surface, his face turned up to the air. He was gasping like a fish. He felt he would sink now and drown; he could not swim the few feet back to the rock. Then he was clutching it and pulling himself up onto it. He lay face down, gasping. He could see nothing

---

2. **mussel:** shellfish, similar to a clam or an oyster, that attaches itself to rocks.

Crossing the Curriculum

Health

Jerry enjoys swimming, and clearly he's good at it. Have interested students work in a group to research the advantages of swimming as part of a fitness program. Have other groups research the advantages of various other sports. Each group should then create a chart illustrating the health benefits of their sport. The class can then rank the different sports in terms of how good each is for a person's health.

Social Studies

Tell students that diving without the benefit of oxygen tanks is called breath-hold diving. Whereas most people can dive 30–40 feet under water, some skilled divers have dived for two minutes to depths of 100 feet. Invite interested students to investigate and report on breath-hold diving. They might research its history, techniques, and records, as well as the people who do it for a living.

Science

Underwater tunnels, caves, and other rock formations are not unusual. Invite interested students to research information on how these natural features are created. Students might write a short report and include diagrams illustrating the process.

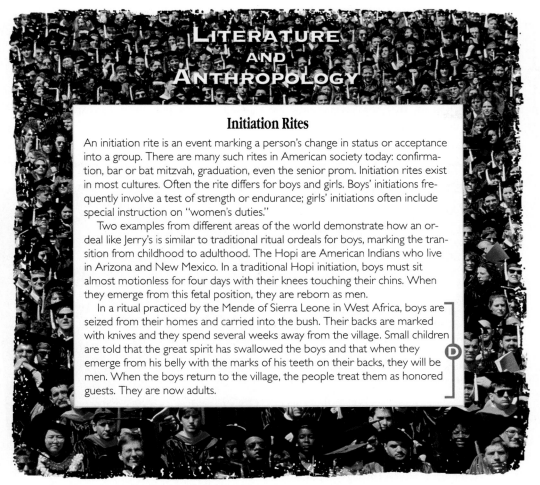

LITERATURE AND ANTHROPOLOGY

Initiation Rites

An initiation rite is an event marking a person's change in status or acceptance into a group. There are many such rites in American society today: confirmation, bar or bat mitzvah, graduation, even the senior prom. Initiation rites exist in most cultures. Often the rite differs for boys and girls. Boys' initiations frequently involve a test of strength or endurance; girls' initiations often include special instruction on "women's duties."

Two examples from different areas of the world demonstrate how an ordeal like Jerry's is similar to traditional ritual ordeals for boys, marking the transition from childhood to adulthood. The Hopi are American Indians who live in Arizona and New Mexico. In a traditional Hopi initiation, boys must sit almost motionless for four days with their knees touching their chins. When they emerge from this fetal position, they are reborn as men.

In a ritual practiced by the Mende of Sierra Leone in West Africa, boys are seized from their homes and carried into the bush. Their backs are marked with knives and they spend several weeks away from the village. Small children are told that the great spirit has swallowed the boys and that when they emerge from his belly with the marks of his teeth on their backs, they will be men. When the boys return to the village, the people treat them as honored guests. They are now adults.

D

---

but a red-veined, clotted dark. His eyes must have burst, he thought; they were full of blood. He tore off his goggles and a gout[3] of blood went into the sea. His nose was bleeding, and the blood had filled the goggles.

He scooped up handfuls of water from the cool, salty sea, to splash on his face, and did not know whether it was blood or salt water he tasted. After a time, his heart quieted, his eyes cleared, and he sat up. He could see the local boys diving and playing half a mile away. He did

3. **gout:** large glob.

not want them. He wanted nothing but to get back home and lie down.

In a short while, Jerry swam to shore and climbed slowly up the path to the villa. He flung himself on his bed and slept, waking at the sound of feet on the path outside. His mother was coming back. He rushed to the bathroom, thinking she must not see his face with bloodstains, or tearstains, on it. He came out of the bathroom and met her as she walked into the villa, smiling, her eyes lighting up.

"Have a nice morning?" she asked, laying her hand on his warm brown shoulder a moment.

E

THROUGH THE TUNNEL **283**

LITERATURE AND ANTHROPOLOGY

Have students investigate an initiation rite that interests them. Emphasize that initiation rites can be found in all cultures and even within individual families. Students might enjoy finding out more about a religious rite such as baptism, confirmation, bar or bat mitzvah, or a cultural rite. Suggest that students consider how these rites of initiation compare and contrast with more ordinary rites of passage, such as getting a driver's license or graduating from high school.

D **Reading Skills and Strategies**

Monitoring Your Reading: Using Resources

? How are Jerry's efforts to swim through the tunnel like the formal rituals described in this feature? [Jerry must pass a test to move on to the next stage of development—adulthood. He prepares for the ordeal, undergoes suffering, and returns wounded but successful.]

E **English Language Learners**

Understanding Idioms

Explain that the idiom *lighting up* means that her eyes are becoming cheerful and animated.

Making the Connections

Connecting to the Theme: "Breakthroughs"

After students have finished reading the selection, discuss the theme "Breakthroughs." Point out that the theme is first touched on in the title, "Through the Tunnel," which suggests a passage into something new—a breakthrough. During the story, Jerry makes several break-

throughs: He learns to hold his breath for two minutes; he overcomes his fear; he swims through the tunnel; he achieves the self-confidence that allows him to emerge into a more independent stage of his life.

Cultural Connections

When the boys find out that Jerry comes from another country and cannot speak their language, they dismiss his presence. As "Through the Tunnel" shows, language plays an important role in cultural identity, and it is not unusual for one group to exclude others because of language differences. Ask students to suggest ways that people speaking different languages can feel less isolated from one another.

A Advanced Students

 What effect does Lessing's use of a third-person omniscient narrator have on your final reaction to Jerry's triumph at the conclusion of the story? How might your reaction have changed had she used a first-person narrator?
[Sample answer: A reader can see clearly both Jerry's sense of accomplishment and his mother's growing confidence in her parenting skills. If Jerry had narrated, a reader might have a more emotional response; and if Jerry's mother had narrated, the reader might feel first concern and then relief.]

Resources

Selection Assessment
Formal Assessment
• Selection Test, p. 44
Test Generator (One-Stop Planner)
• CD-ROM

BROWSING IN THE FILES

About the Author. During her long career, Doris Lessing has moved from social realism to science fiction. Many of her early writings are autobiographical, including her series of novels, *Children of Violence* (1952–1969), which focuses on the growth of Martha Quest, a woman who questions racism and class divisions. Asked about the source of her characters, Lessing has said, "Some people I write about come out of my life. Some, well, I don't know where they come from. They just spring from my own consciousness, perhaps the subconscious, and I'm surprised as they emerge. This is one of the excitements about writing. Someone says something, drops a phrase, and later you find that phrase turning into a character in a story, or a single, isolated, insignificant incident becomes the germ of a plot."

"Oh, yes, thank you," he said.

"You look a bit pale." And then, sharp and anxious, "How did you bang your head?"

"Oh, just banged it," he told her.

A She looked at him closely. He was strained; his eyes were glazed-looking. She was worried. And then she said to herself, Oh, don't fuss! Nothing can happen. He can swim like a fish.

They sat down to lunch together.

"Mummy," he said, "I can stay underwater for two minutes—three minutes, at least." It came bursting out of him.

"Can you, darling?" she said. "Well, I shouldn't overdo it. I don't think you ought to swim anymore today."

She was ready for a battle of wills, but he gave in at once. It was no longer of the least importance to go to the bay.

MEET THE WRITER
Out of Africa

Doris Lessing (1919–   ) was born in Persia (now Iran), where her British father was in charge of a bank. When she was five, her father, growing tired of the corruption around him and longing for a freer life, moved the family to a three-thousand-acre farm in Southern Rhodesia (now Zimbabwe). Life was extremely hard there. The farm's thirty to fifty African laborers lived in mud huts with no sanitation. Lessing's mother was homesick for England and often ill; her impulsive father was increasingly unpredictable. The nearest neighbor was miles away. Lessing has described this childhood as "hellishly lonely." She has also acknowledged the advantage of such a childhood: Lacking company, she enriched her mind by reading classic European and American literature.

At the age of fifteen, Lessing quit school and went to work in Salisbury, the capital of Rhodesia, first as a nursemaid and then as a stenographer and telephone operator. Salisbury had a white population of about ten thousand and a larger black population that Lessing discovered "didn't count." During this period of her life, she became involved in radical politics, and she was twice married and twice divorced. In 1949, with her two-year-old son and the manuscript of her first novel, *The Grass Is Singing,* she fulfilled a lifelong wish by immigrating to England. The novel, about the complex relationship between a white farm wife and her African servant, was published in 1950, one of the earliest treatments in fiction of Africa's racial problems. From then on, Lessing supported herself by her writing. Her powerful stories and novels are among the most admired writings of our day.

Lessing admits she writes to be "an instrument of change."

❝ It is not merely a question of preventing evil, but of strengthening a vision of good which may defeat the evil. **❞**

284 THE SHORT-STORY COLLECTIONS

Assessing Learning

Check Test: Questions and Answers
1. Who is the protagonist? [Jerry, an eleven-year-old English boy]
2. Where is the story set? [along the coast of a foreign country, where Jerry and his mother stay at a villa near a beach]
3. How does Jerry reach the underwater tunnel? [by using rocks as anchors]
4. What piece of equipment does Jerry need for his adventure? [swimming goggles]
5. To whom does Jerry brag about finally swimming through the tunnel? [no one]

Standardized Test Preparation
For practice with standardized test format specific to this selection, see
• *Standardized Test Preparation,* p. 36
For practice in proofreading and editing, see
• *Daily Oral Grammar,* Transparency 18

MAKING MEANINGS

First Thoughts

[respond]

1. Is Jerry crazy to risk his life, or does he get something important out of his ordeal? Talk about your responses.

Shaping Interpretations

[interpret]

2. Why do you think it is so important to Jerry to be with the boys on the wild beach?

[summarize]

3. What physical and mental "tortures" does Jerry go through, first as he prepares for his ordeal and then as he swims through the tunnel?

[interpret]

4. A ticking clock is usually good for creating **suspense**. How does this story use a "ticking clock" to increase our anxiety?

[identify]

5. What breakthroughs has Jerry achieved by the story's end? Consider:
   - his conquest of the tunnel
   - his feelings about himself
   - his dependence on his mother

[infer]

6. What do you think is the main focus of this story—in other words, what would you say is its **theme**? Consider:
   - what the swim through the tunnel means to Jerry
   - why Jerry no longer feels he has to go to the bay

[classify]

7. Read carefully the information provided in Literature and Anthropology on page 283. Do you think Jerry's experience can be viewed as an initiation rite? What similarities and differences can you find between his experience and the coming-of-age rites in other cultures?

[apply]

8. Check the text to see what you learn about the thoughts and feelings of Jerry's mother. How would the story be different if she, rather than the **omniscient narrator,** were telling it?

Connecting with the Text

[connect]

9. What details about Jerry's swim through the tunnel were most vivid and terrifying to you?

Challenging the Text

[connect]

10. Have you ever taken great risks to prove yourself? (Check your Quickwrite notes.) Do you find it convincing that Jerry takes such a risk and survives? Explain.

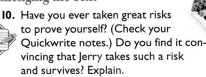

> ### Reading Check
> Retell the **main events** of this story as Jerry might tell them to his best friend back home when he returns from vacation or later in life to his own son.

Reading Check
Students should retell the main events in the first person, beginning with Jerry's experience with the older boys and his discovery of the tunnel. Accounts should include his use of rocks to reach the sea floor; his acquisition of the goggles; his self-training, which causes his nose to bleed; his decision to make the attempt; and major details of his extended swim through the tunnel. It should conclude with his meeting with his mother back at the villa.

MAKING MEANINGS

First Thoughts

1. Possible responses: Yes, Jerry is crazy to risk his life for a minor feat; no, going through the tunnel is important for building his self-esteem.

Shaping Interpretations

2. Possible response: Jerry wants friends and a life apart from his mother.

3. While training, he experiences dizziness, nosebleeds, and fear. As he swims through the tunnel, he worries about octopuses, banging his head, and dying.

4. Jerry can hold his breath for only 135 seconds. He counts to 115 with no end to the tunnel in sight. As time ticks down, his fear mounts, and so does the reader's.

5. Jerry makes it through the tunnel; he feels good about himself and is less dependent upon his mother because he has proved to himself that he's strong and self-sufficient.

6. Possible theme: Sometimes we take on challenges to prove something to ourselves, and it doesn't matter if anyone else sees or knows about it.

7. Sample answer: Yes, it qualifies as an initiation rite. Jerry goes through the same kinds of intense preparation, introspection, and trials as do others who make a transition. Unlike the others, Jerry's rite of passage is not public, and he gets no public acclaim or new status.

8. Possible answer: The story would be very different because she does not observe his underwater ordeal. The story would focus on her concerns about whether she is giving Jerry too much (or too little) freedom and about his health.

Connecting with the Text

9. Sample answer: The sunlight coming through the crack with only darkness ahead and Jerry's body being pushed upward against the rocks.

Challenging the Text

10. Possible answer: Jerry's survival is believable because he is an excellent swimmer and has prepared himself for the adventure.

Grading Timesaver

Rubrics for each assignment appear on p. 123 in the *Portfolio Management System*.

CHOICES:
Building Your Portfolio

1. **Writer's Notebook** A Writer's Notebook activity appears as the first option in the Choices section with each selection. These brief, work-in-progress assignments build toward the writing assignment presented in the Writer's Workshop at the end of the collection. If students save their work for their Writer's Notebook activities as they move through the collection, they should be able to use some of them as starting points for the workshop. Other elements students might evaluate are character (did they care about Jerry?), setting (did they understand the setting? could they visualize it?), language (did the English expressions bother them?), details in the plot (did anything puzzle them? were questions left unanswered?). Encourage honesty, but the criteria should be very clear.

2. **Analyzing Setting** You might allow students to meet in small groups to discuss the significance of the settings. Then have each student take one of the settings and find quotations that support the group's analysis.

3. **Art** Have students work in groups and brainstorm ideas about what kind of mood the collage should evoke. Encourage students to think about how different colors, textures, and images might evoke different moods.

4. **Speaking and Listening** Have students describe how they will handle the dialogue. You might suggest that they practice by reading aloud passages to each other and providing each other with feedback on such aspects as reading speed, enunciation, loudness, and how the reader's voice might change to reflect different events or moods.

CHOICES: Building Your Portfolio

Writer's Notebook
1. Collecting Ideas for an Evaluation

Gathering evidence.

Although your evaluation of a story begins with your reactions to it, you need to look closely at the aspects of the text that evoked those responses. Make an evaluation of just one story element in "Through the Tunnel." Look for evidence in the text to support your judgment. You may want to record your evidence in a chart like the one here.

Story Element: Plot	
Evaluation	**Evidence**
Very suspenseful; made me really think Jerry would drown.	"He felt he was dying. He was no longer quite conscious. He struggled on in the dark-ness...." (page 282)
	Blood. (page 283)

Analyzing Setting
2. Settings and Deep Meanings

Write a brief essay analyzing the significance of three settings in the story: the wild bay, the safe beach, and the tunnel. Tell what you think each setting represents to Jerry. Also consider this question: Could the passage through the tunnel be seen as either a birth or a death? Support your analysis and elaborate with direct references to details in the story.

Art
3. A Collage of the Wild Bay

A collage is an arrangement of images (photographs, magazine art, drawings), words, and other objects (sand, shells, stones, and so forth) glued to a surface. Make a collage called "The Wild Bay." Find words from the text that can go with your images. What mood do you want to convey in your collage?

Speaking and Listening
4. Stories "To Go"

National Public Radio often features short stories read aloud by writers or by actors. Many people like to listen to these stories as they travel by car—it's a good way to learn something new and to get where you are going at the same time. Record "Through the Tunnel" as if for National Public Radio. Use no sound effects—only your own voice. You'll have to practice reading aloud before you do your taping. (For help, see the Speaking and Listening Workshop on **oral interpretation,** pages 750–751.) Be sure to begin by giving the title of the story and its author. Present your tape to someone who enjoys listening to stories while driving.

GRAMMAR LINK MINI-LESSON

Language Handbook HELP

See Participles, pages 1034–1035.

Technology HELP

See Language Workshop CD-ROM. Key word entry: participles.

Powerful Participles

Participles are verb forms that can be used as adjectives to modify nouns and pronouns: hang-ing head, spotted foot, running water. Present participles always end in *-ing*, and most past participles end in *-ed* or *-d*. Because they combine the action of verbs and the descriptive power of adjectives, participles can create vivid pictures in just a few words. Look at how Doris Lessing uses participles in the following items:

1. "He could see nothing through the stinging salt water but the blank rock."

2. "It was like swimming in flaked silver."

Participial phrases are participles with all their complements and modifiers.

1. "Her other arm, swinging loose, was very white in the sun."

2. "He was in a small rock-bound hole filled with yellowish-gray water."

An introductory participial phrase is followed by a comma to prevent confusion.

> Swinging loose her other arm was very white in the sun. [confusing]

> Swinging loose, her other arm was very white in the sun. [clear]

Try It Out

Write five sentences about "Through the Tunnel," using one of the following participles in each sentence. Be sure you use the participle as an adjective.

lapping	rippled
diving	glittered
clinging	

Now, write five more sentences, using the same participles in phrases. Compare your sentences with a partner's.

Tips for writers: You can tighten your writing with participles. Whenever you have long, cumbersome sentences, see if there's a clause that can be reduced to a participle or participial phrase.

VOCABULARY HOW TO OWN A WORD

WORD BANK
contrition
supplication
inquisitive
minute
incredulous

Analogies: Make It Complete

In an **analogy** the words in one pair relate to each other in the same way as the words in a second pair. For example, a pair of words could be synonyms or antonyms, or one word could describe a char-acteristic of the other or be a part of the other. Work with a partner to fill in each blank below with the word from the Word Bank that completes the analogy. Here, analogies are written out. Sometimes they are written like this: *huge : elephant ::* _____ *: gnat*

1. *Huge* is to *elephant* as _____ is to *gnat.*
2. *Sadness* is to *mourning* as _____ is to *regretting.*
3. *Secure* is to *safe* as _____ is to *curious.*
4. *Needy* is to *beggar* as _____ is to *skeptic.*
5. *Whisper* is to *shout* as _____ is to *demand.*

GRAMMAR LINK

Have students review a piece of writing from their portfolio in order to iden-tify participles and participial phrases they have used. Invite them to locate places where they might add participial phrases to enrich the descriptive power of their writing.

Try It Out
Possible Answers

1. The lapping waves edged up to the rocks. Lapping against the rocks, the water looked cool and inviting.
2. The diving boy sprang from the rock. Diving from the high rocks, the boys disappeared into the water.
3. Jerry was afraid of the clinging sea-weed. Clinging to the heavy rock, Jerry reached the bottom quickly.
4. The fish swam above the rippled bottom. Jerry swam to the bottom and touched the sand rippled by the tides.
5. The surface of the sun-glittered water caught his eye. Having glittered the rock surface with brilliance through the afternoon, the sun gradually sank in the west.

VOCABULARY

(See p. T1019 for a more in-depth treatment of analogies.)
1. minute
2. contrition
3. inquisitive
4. incredulous
5. supplication

Resources

Language
• *Grammar and Language Links* Work-sheet, p. 33

Vocabulary
• *Words to Own* Worksheet, p. 18

Grammar Link Quick Check

Revise the following sentences. Maintain the meaning, but use a participle or a participial phrase in place of a verb.

Example: The leaf fluttered in the breeze and gently fell to Earth.

Revision: Fluttering in the breeze, the leaf gently fell to Earth.

1. The fish swam under the reef and looked for food. [Looking for food, the fish swam under the reef.]

2. The divers jumped from the rock and streaked into the water. [Jumping from the rock, the divers streaked into the water.]

3. His mother called to him and wondered if he was all right. [Calling to him, his mother won-dered if he was all right.]

4. The seaweed brushed against his leg, and it seemed to be an octopus. [Brushing against his leg, the seaweed seemed to be an octopus.]

Before You Read

THE PIT AND THE PENDULUM

Make the Connection

Our Deepest Fears

Here is Poe's horrifying story of confinement in a prison cell during the Spanish Inquisition. Poe's story uses a grotesque form of torture that stirs our deepest fears.

Quickwrite

What things arouse your fears? Freewrite for a few minutes about some of your fears and the feelings and images you associate with them.

Reading Skills and Strategies

Summarizing

When you read long stories, it helps to stop at key points and sum up what is happening. Try this strategy with Poe's horror story. You'll find the symbol 📖 at certain points in the story. Stop at these points, and **summarize** what has just happened. Focus on the main events or on the narrator's last crisis. If you need to, go back and reread certain sections to be sure you have understood what has happened.

go.hrw.com
LEO 10-4

Elements of Literature

Symbolic Meaning: More Than a Scare

When we read, we often sense that a story means more than what happens on the surface. For instance, if a young woman in a story is in serious conflict with her parents over her earrings, we should suspect that those earrings represent something more important to her—perhaps freedom or maturity. One of the pleasures of reading lies in thinking about symbols.

What elements in Poe's story could be symbolically significant? What might they mean?

> The **symbolic meaning** of a story emerges from an overall interpretation of the story's individual symbols.
>
> *For more on Symbol, see pages 306–307 and the Handbook of Literary Terms.*

Background

The purpose of the Spanish Inquisition was to punish people who were suspected of not being true believers in the Christian faith.

Poe may have gotten his idea for this story from a book by Juan Antonio Llorente. Poe read a review of this book, which contains the following passage:

". . . the Inquisition was thrown open, in 1820, by the orders of the Cortes of Madrid. Twenty-one prisoners were found in it . . . . Some had been confined three years, some a longer period, and not one knew perfectly the nature of the crime of which he was accused. One of these prisoners had been condemned and was to have suffered on the following day. His punishment was to be death by the Pendulum. The method of thus destroying the victim is as follows: The condemned is fastened in a groove, upon a table, on his back; suspended above him is a Pendulum, the edge of which is sharp, and it is so constructed as to become longer with every movement. The wretch sees this implement of destruction swinging to and fro above him, and every moment the keen edge approaching nearer and nearer."

288 THE SHORT-STORY COLLECTIONS

Preteaching Vocabulary

Words to Own

On the chalkboard, write the Words to Own, which appear at the bottom of the selection pages. Then, ask a student volunteer to provide a definition of one of the words (but without *saying* the word). Challenge other students to identify the defined word and then to devise a sentence using it. Reinforce students' understanding of the words by having them complete the following analogies with them.

1. [insuperable] : unbeatable :: brilliant : bright
2. [ponders] : considers :: data : information
3. [lucid] : unclear :: accept : reject
4. peaceful : [tumultuous] :: calm : nervous
5. invisible : [imperceptible] :: weep : cry
6. [prostrate] : upright :: ordinary : unique
7. weak : [potent] :: love : hate
8. [lethargy] : vigor :: horror : joy
9. light : dark :: distance : [proximity]
10. deep : shallow :: faced : [averted]

Any horror but this!

The Pit and the Pendulum

Edgar Allan Poe

Background

Although torture is today outlawed throughout the world, it still occurs. Torture has been used for at least two thousand years, since the governments of ancient Greece and Rome used it to obtain confessions or to otherwise punish alleged wrong doers. It occurred during the Spanish Inquisition (1478–1834) and during the witch trials in colonial America. In the United States, the Eighth Amendment to the Constitution essentially prohibits torture by forbidding cruel and unusual punishment.

Summary ■■■

In this famous horror story, the first-person narrator is a condemned prisoner in the final days of the Spanish Inquisition. In a pitch-dark dungeon, he narrowly escapes a mortal fall into a pit. Awaking from a drugged sleep, he finds himself bound to a frame with a razor-sharp pendulum descending toward him. He rubs meat scraps on his bindings so that rats will eat through them. As he rolls free, the red hot dungeon walls begin to move inward, forcing him toward the pit. Suddenly, the prisoner is rescued by General Lasalle of the French army.

Ⓐ Critical Thinking
Hypothesizing
Ask students to consider what might happen in a horror story that involves a pit and a pendulum. Have them write down their responses, which can be discussed after reading this tale.

 Resources: Print and Media

Reading
- *Reading Skills and Strategies*
  MiniRead Skill Lesson, p. 135
  Selection Skill Lesson, p. 142
- *Graphic Organizers for Active Reading*, p. 19
- *Words to Own*, p. 19
- *Audio CD Library*
  Disc 9, Track 3

Elements of Literature
- *Literary Elements*
  Transparency 9

Worksheet, p. 28
Writing and Language
- *Daily Oral Grammar*
  Transparency 19
- *Grammar and Language Links*
  Worksheet, p. 35

Viewing and Representing
- *Visual Connections*
  Videocassette A, Segment 4

Assessment
- *Formal Assessment*, p. 46
- *Portfolio Management System*, p. 124
- *Standardized Test Preparation*, p. 38, 40
- *Test Generator (One-Stop Planner CD-ROM)*

Internet
- go.hrw.com (keyword: *LEO 10-4*)

Viewing and Representing

Videocassette A, Segment 4
"Thrills and Chills: Edgar Allan Poe."
Available in Spanish and English.
The *Visual Connections* segment presents
a biography of Poe.
For full lesson plans and worksheets, see
the *Visual Connections Teacher's Manual.*

Listening
Audio CD Library
A chilling reading of the story appears
in the *Audio CD Library:*
• Disc 9, Track 3

Elements of Literature
**Symbols: Signs of Something
More**
For additional instruction on symbols,
see *Literary Elements:*
• Transparency 9
• Worksheet, p. 28

Ⓐ Critical Thinking
Analyzing Point of View
❓ Notice the first-person narration.
What basic assumption can be made
about the story's outcome, due to this
point of view? [The narrator survives
this ordeal.]

Ⓑ Elements of Literature
Symbolic Meaning
❓ Poe's narrator describes the
emotional effect of seeing the candles
literally, symbolically, and then literally
again. What do candles symbolize
for the narrator? [At first they seemed
to be angels who might save him; then
they became "meaningless specters."]

Ⓐ I was sick—sick unto death with that long agony; and when they at length unbound me, and I was permitted to sit, I felt that my senses were leaving me. The sentence—the dread sentence of death—was the last of distinct accentuation which reached my ears. After that, the sound of the Inquisitorial voices seemed merged in one dreamy, indeterminate hum. It conveyed to my soul the idea of *revolution*[1]—perhaps from its association in fancy[2] with the burr of a mill wheel. This only for a brief period, for presently I heard no more. Yet for a while, I saw—but with how terrible an exaggeration! I saw the lips of the black-robed judges. They appeared to me white—whiter than the sheet upon which I trace these words—and thin even to grotesqueness; thin with the intensity of their expression of firmness—of immovable resolution—of stern contempt of human torture. I saw that the decrees of what to me was Fate were still issuing from those lips. I saw them writhe with a deadly locution.[3] I saw them fashion the syllables of my name; and I shuddered because no sound succeeded.[4] I saw, too, for a few moments of delirious horror, the soft and nearly <u>imperceptible</u> waving of the sable draperies which enwrapped the walls of the apartment. And then my vision fell upon the

Ⓑ seven tall candles upon the table. At first they wore the aspect of charity and seemed white, slender angels who would save me; but then, all at once, there came a most deadly nausea over my spirit, and I felt every fiber in my frame thrill as if I had touched the wire of a galvanic battery, while the angel forms became meaningless specters, with heads of flame, and I saw that from them there would be no help. And then there stole into my fancy, like a rich musical note, the thought of what sweet rest there must be in the grave. The thought came gently and stealthily, and it seemed long before it attained full appreciation; but just as my spirit came at length properly to feel and entertain it, the fig-

1. **revolution:** here, rotation; turning motion.
2. **fancy:** here, imagination.
3. **locution** (lō·kyoo'shən): utterance; statement.
4. **succeeded:** here, followed.

ures of the judges vanished, as if magically, from before me; the tall candles sank into nothingness! Their flames went out utterly; the blackness of darkness supervened; all sensations appeared swallowed up in a mad rushing descent, as of the soul into Hades. Then silence, and stillness, and night were the universe.

I had swooned;[5] but still will not say that all of consciousness was lost. What of it there remained I will not attempt to define, or even to describe; yet all was not lost. In the deepest slumber—no! In delirium—no! In a swoon—no! In death—no! Even in the grave all *is not* lost. Else there is no immortality for man. Arousing from the most profound of slumbers, we break the gossamer web of *some* dream. Yet in a second afterward (so frail may that web have been), we remember not that we have dreamed. In the return to life from the swoon, there are two stages: first, that of the sense of mental or spiritual; second, that of the sense of physical existence. It seems probable that if, upon reaching the second stage, we could recall the impressions of the first, we should find these impressions eloquent in memories of the gulf beyond. And that gulf is—what? How at least shall we distinguish its shadows from those of the tomb? But if the impressions of what I have termed the first stage are not, at will, recalled, yet, after long interval, do they not come unbidden, while we marvel whence they come? He who has never swooned is not he who finds strange palaces and wildly familiar faces in coals that glow; is not he who beholds floating in midair the sad visions that the many may not view; is not he who <u>ponders</u> over the perfume of some novel flower; is not he whose brain grows bewildered with the meaning of some musical cadence which has never before arrested his attention.

5. **swooned:** fainted.

WORDS TO OWN
imperceptible (im'pər·sep'tə·bəl) *adj.*: not clear or
  obvious to the senses or the mind; too slight or
  gradual to be noticeable.
ponders (pän'dərz) *v.*: thinks deeply.

Reaching All Students

Struggling Readers
Summarizing was introduced on page 288. For a lesson directly tied to this story that teaches students to summarize by using a strategy called Somebody Wanted But So, see the *Reading Skills and Strategies* binder:
• MiniRead Skill Lesson, p. 135
• Selection Skill Lesson, p. 142

English Language Learners
These students may find this selection challenging because of the archaic vocabulary, the complex sentence structure, and the imagery. You may want to pair these students with more accomplished English speakers. For additional strategies to supplement instruction for English language learners, see
• *Lesson Plans Including Strategies for English-Language Learners*

Advanced Learners
Point out to students that Poe was an innovator whose influence may surpass his literary output. He is often cited as the creator of two literary genres—the mystery (or detective) story and the horror story. Invite students to investigate the characteristics of these two genres and to then look for telltale signs of these types of works as they read.

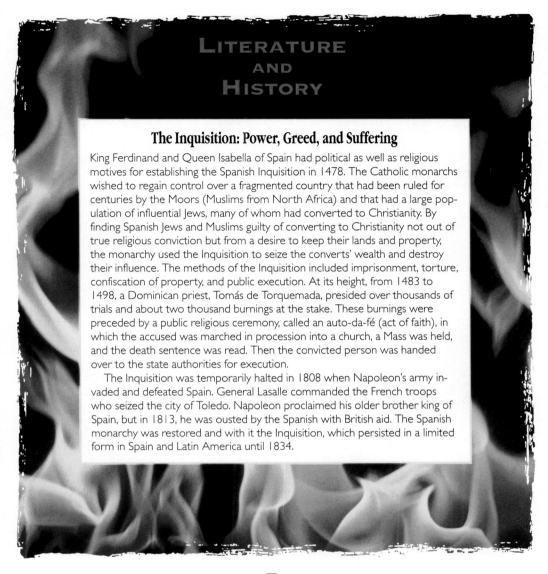

LITERATURE AND HISTORY

The Inquisition: Power, Greed, and Suffering

King Ferdinand and Queen Isabella of Spain had political as well as religious motives for establishing the Spanish Inquisition in 1478. The Catholic monarchs wished to regain control over a fragmented country that had been ruled for centuries by the Moors (Muslims from North Africa) and that had a large population of influential Jews, many of whom had converted to Christianity. By finding Spanish Jews and Muslims guilty of converting to Christianity not out of true religious conviction but from a desire to keep their lands and property, the monarchy used the Inquisition to seize the converts' wealth and destroy their influence. The methods of the Inquisition included imprisonment, torture, confiscation of property, and public execution. At its height, from 1483 to 1498, a Dominican priest, Tomás de Torquemada, presided over thousands of trials and about two thousand burnings at the stake. These burnings were preceded by a public religious ceremony, called an auto-da-fé (act of faith), in which the accused was marched in procession into a church, a Mass was held, and the death sentence was read. Then the convicted person was handed over to the state authorities for execution.

The Inquisition was temporarily halted in 1808 when Napoleon's army invaded and defeated Spain. General Lasalle commanded the French troops who seized the city of Toledo. Napoleon proclaimed his older brother king of Spain, but in 1813, he was ousted by the Spanish with British aid. The Spanish monarchy was restored and with it the Inquisition, which persisted in a limited form in Spain and Latin America until 1834.

Amid frequent and thoughtful endeavors to remember, amid earnest struggles to regather some token of the state of seeming nothingness into which my soul had lapsed, there have been moments when I have dreamed of success; there have been brief, very brief, periods when I have conjured up remembrances which the lucid reason of a later epoch assures me could have had reference only to that condition of

C **WORDS TO OWN**
lucid (lo͞o′sid) *adj.*: clearheaded; not confused. *Lucid* also means "understandable" or "bright and shining."

Crossing the Curriculum

El Greco (1541–1614) was one of the great original painters of the sixteenth century. Born in Greece, El Greco spent the last decades of his life in Toledo, Spain, where "The Pit and the Pendulum" takes place. El Greco's interest in the movements of nature and the human body combine with his use of light and brilliant colors to create a ghostly feeling in many of his paintings. Well known for his portraits, he painted only two landscapes during his long career, *View of Toledo* and *View and Plan of Toledo*. Both paintings show the urban landscape of the early seventeenth century.

Activity. Ask students to identify Toledo on a map of Spain and to locate pictures of Toledo today. Then, ask them to list the differences and similarities between El Greco's *View of Toledo* and pictures in a travel book. As a further activity, have students compare El Greco's urban landscape with Wayne Thiebaud's *Freeway Interchange* on p. 173.

Ⓐ Appreciating Language
Rhythm and Repetition

❓ What is the effect of the repetition of the word *down*? [Possible answers: At this point, such repetition seems heavy and frightening; this repetition hints at the depths into the earth where the dungeon is located.] Students will learn more about rhythm and repetition in the Language Link on p. 305.

View of Toledo (1608) by El Greco. Oil on canvas.

The Metropolitan Museum of Art, H. O. Havemeyer Collection, Bequest of Mrs. H. O. Havemeyer, 1929 (29.100.6)
Photograph (c)1992 The Metropolitan Museum of Art.

Ⓐ seeming unconsciousness. These shadows of memory tell, indistinctly, of tall figures that lifted and bore me in silence down—down—still down—till a hideous dizziness oppressed me at the mere idea of the interminableness of the descent. They tell also of a vague horror at my heart, on account of that heart's unnatural stillness. Then comes a sense of sudden motion-

292 THE SHORT-STORY COLLECTIONS

Using Student's Strengths

Auditory/Musical Learners
Ask students to work together to create sound effects to accompany specific parts of the story. Students might begin by looking for the sound imagery Poe includes in the text. They can add more sounds to suggest the setting and events in the story. Have students present parts of the play with narration and sound effects. Students may also record the narration and sound effects and play the recording for the class.

Visual Learners
Invite students to work as a group to build a model of the setting or create a diagram of it. Have them look for specific details about the size and general shape of the room, the location of the pit and of the pendulum, the images on the walls, and other details given by the author. Encourage them to build or draw it to scale, using the narrator's estimates of size.

Interpersonal Learners
Invite students to imagine that the narrator is on a speaking tour to talk about his experiences and to speak out against the Inquisition. Have students play the role of the narrator. They might work as a group and divide up the talk. For example, one student might tell about the horror of discovering the pit; another might discuss the injustices of the Inquisition. Students might include a question-and-answer session to involve their audience.

lessness throughout all things; as if those who bore me (a ghastly train!) had outrun, in their descent, the limits of the limitless, and paused from the wearisomeness of their toil. After this I call to mind flatness and dampness; and then all is *madness*—the madness of a memory which busies itself among forbidden things.

Very suddenly there came back to my soul motion and sound—the tumultuous motion of the heart and, in my ears, the sound of its beating. Then a pause in which all is blank. Then again sound, and motion, and touch—a tingling sensation pervading my frame. Then the mere consciousness of existence, without thought—a condition which lasted long. Then, very suddenly, *thought,* and shuddering terror, and earnest endeavor to comprehend my true state. Then a strong desire to lapse into insensibility. Then a rushing revival of soul and a successful effort to move. And now a full memory of the trial, of the judges, of the sable draperies, of the sentence, of the sickness, of the swoon. Then entire forgetfulness of all that followed; of all that a later day and much earnestness of endeavor have enabled me vaguely to recall.

So far, I had not opened my eyes. I felt that I lay upon my back, unbound. I reached out my hand, and it fell heavily upon something damp and hard. There I suffered[6] it to remain for many minutes, while I strove to imagine where and *what* I could be. I longed, yet dared not, to employ my vision. I dreaded the first glance at objects around me. It was not that I feared to look upon things horrible, but that I grew aghast lest there should be *nothing* to see. At length, with a wild desperation at heart, I quickly unclosed my eyes. My worst thoughts, then, were confirmed. The blackness of eternal night encompassed me. I struggled for breath. The intensity of the darkness seemed to oppress and stifle me. The atmosphere was intolerably close. I still lay quietly, and made effort to exercise my reason. I brought to mind the Inquisitorial proceedings and attempted from that point to deduce my real condition. The sentence had passed; and it appeared to me that a very long

6. **suffered:** here, allowed; tolerated.

interval of time had since elapsed. Yet not for a moment did I suppose myself actually dead. Such a supposition, notwithstanding what we read in fiction, is altogether inconsistent with real existence—but where and in what state was I? The condemned to death, I knew, perished usually at the autos-da-fé, and one of these had been held on the very night of the day of my trial. Had I been remanded to my dungeon, to await the next sacrifice, which would not take place for many months? This I at once saw could not be. Victims had been in immediate demand. Moreover, my dungeon, as well as all the condemned cells at Toledo, had stone floors, and light was not altogether excluded.

A fearful idea now suddenly drove the blood in torrents upon my heart, and for a brief period I once more relapsed into insensibility. Upon recovering, I at once started to my feet, trembling convulsively in every fiber. I thrust my arms wildly above and around me in all directions. I felt nothing; yet dreaded to move a step, lest I should be impeded by the walls of a *tomb.* Perspiration burst from every pore and stood in cold, big beads upon my forehead. The agony of suspense grew at length intolerable, and I cautiously moved forward, with my arms extended and my eyes straining from their sockets in the hope of catching some faint ray of light. I proceeded for many paces; but still all was blackness and vacancy. I breathed more freely. It seemed evident that mine was not, at least, the most hideous of fates.

And now, as I still continued to step cautiously onward, there came thronging upon my recollection a thousand vague rumors of the horrors of Toledo. Of the dungeons there had been strange things narrated—fables I had always deemed them—but yet strange, and too ghastly to repeat, save in a whisper. Was I left to perish of starvation in the subterranean world of darkness; or what fate, perhaps even more

---

WORDS TO OWN

tumultuous (tōō·mul′chōō·əs) *adj.:* violent; greatly agitated or disturbed. *Tumultuous* also means "wild, noisy, and confused."

THE PIT AND THE PENDULUM 293

fearful, awaited me? That the result would be death, and a death of more than customary bitterness, I knew too well the character of my judges to doubt. The mode and the hour were all that occupied or distracted me.

In the confusion attending my fall, I did not immediately apprehend a somewhat startling circumstance . . .

My outstretched hands at length encountered some solid obstruction. It was a wall, seemingly of stone masonry—very smooth, slimy, and cold. I followed it up, stepping with all the careful distrust with which certain antique narratives had inspired me. This process, however, afforded me no means of ascertaining the dimensions of my dungeon, as I might make its circuit and return to the point whence I set out without being aware of the fact, so perfectly uniform seemed the wall. I therefore sought the knife which had been in my pocket when led into the Inquisitorial chamber, but it was gone; my clothes had been exchanged for a wrapper of coarse serge. I had thought of forcing the blade in some minute crevice of the masonry, so as to identify my point of departure. The difficulty, nevertheless, was but trivial; although, in the disorder of my fancy, it seemed at first insuperable. I tore a part of the hem from the robe and placed the fragment at full length and at right angles to the wall. In groping my way around the prison, I could not fail to encounter this rag upon completing the circuit. So, at least, I thought; but I had not counted upon the extent of the dungeon, or upon my own weakness. The ground was moist and slippery. I staggered onward for some time, when I stumbled and fell. My excessive fatigue induced me to remain prostrate; and sleep soon overtook me as I lay.

Upon awaking and stretching forth an arm, I found beside me a loaf and a pitcher with water. I was too much exhausted to reflect upon this

circumstance, but ate and drank with avidity.[7] Shortly afterward, I resumed my tour around the prison and, with much toil, came at last upon the fragment of the serge. Up to the period when I fell, I had counted fifty-two paces, and upon resuming my walk, I had counted forty-eight more—when I arrived at the rag. There were in all, then, a hundred paces; and, admitting two paces to the yard, I presumed the dungeon to be fifty yards in circuit. I had met, however, with many angles in the wall, and thus I could form no guess at the shape of the vault, for vault I could not help supposing it to be.

I had little object—certainly no hope—in these researches; but a vague curiosity prompted me to continue them. Quitting the wall, I resolved to cross the area of the enclosure. At first, I proceeded with extreme caution, for the floor, although seemingly of solid material, was treacherous with slime. At length, however, I took courage and did not hesitate to step firmly—endeavoring to cross in as direct a line as possible. I had advanced some ten or twelve paces in this manner when the remnant of the torn hem of my robe became entangled between my legs. I stepped on it and fell violently on my face.

In the confusion attending my fall, I did not immediately apprehend a somewhat startling circumstance, which yet, in a few seconds afterward and while I still lay prostrate, arrested my attention. It was this—my chin rested upon the floor of the prison, but my lips and the upper portion of my head, although seemingly at a less elevation than the chin, touched nothing. At the same time, my forehead seemed bathed in a clammy vapor, and the peculiar smell of decayed fungus arose to my nostrils. I put forward my arm, and shuddered to find that I had fallen

7. **avidity** (ə·vid′ə·tē): great eagerness.

WORDS TO OWN

insuperable (in·soo′pər·ə·bəl) *adj.*: incapable of being overcome or passed over.
prostrate (präs′trāt′) *adj.*: lying flat. *Prostrate* also means "helpless; overcome" or "lying with the face downward to show devotion or submission."

Crossing the Curriculum

Art

Have students study the painting by El Greco that appears on p. 292 and describe the atmosphere the artist creates. Students should consider the ways in which the painting relates to the atmosphere of Poe's story. Have them write a short essay in which they compare and contrast the painting and the story.

Health

The narrator's great fear after first awakening is that he has been placed alive in a tomb. Poe himself was preoccupied with the possibility of being buried alive; the theme appears in other stories of his and is the subject of his tale "The Premature Burial." At one time, people were, in fact, sometimes buried alive. Scientifically accurate methods for determining death had not been devised, and on rare occasions a person

who was merely unconscious was mistaken for dead. One practical purpose of the funeral wake was to provide an opportunity for friends and family to watch for signs of life. Invite interested students to investigate and report on the medical definition of death. Students might also report on the implications of the definition for the patient, the patient's family, and the public—for example, in regard to organ donations.

at the very brink of a circular pit, whose extent, of course, I had no means of ascertaining at the moment. Groping about the masonry just below the margin, I succeeded in dislodging a small fragment and let it fall into the abyss. For many seconds I hearkened to its reverberations as it dashed against the sides of the chasm in its descent; at length, there was a sullen plunge into water, succeeded by loud echoes. At the same moment, there came a sound resembling the quick opening and as rapid closing of a door overhead, while a faint gleam of light flashed suddenly through the gloom and as suddenly faded away.

I saw clearly the doom which had been prepared for me, and congratulated myself upon the timely accident by which I had escaped. Another step before my fall, and the world had seen me no more. And the death just avoided was of that very character which I had regarded as fabulous and frivolous in the tales respecting the Inquisition. To the victims of its tyranny, there was the choice of death with its direst physical agonies or death with its most hideous moral horrors. I had been reserved for the latter. By long suffering, my nerves had been unstrung, until I trembled at the sound of my own voice and had become in every respect a fitting subject for the species of torture which awaited me.

Shaking in every limb, I groped my way back to the wall; resolving there to perish rather than risk the terrors of the wells, of which my imagination now pictured many in various positions about the dungeon. In other conditions of mind, I might have had courage to end my misery at once, by a plunge into one of these abysses; but now I was the veriest[8] of cowards. Neither could I forget what I had read of these pits—that the *sudden* extinction of life formed no part of their most horrible plan.

Agitation of spirit kept me awake for many long hours, but at length I again slumbered. Upon arousing, I found by my side, as before, a loaf and a pitcher of water. A burning thirst consumed me, and I emptied the vessel at a draft. It must have been drugged; for scarcely had I

8. **veriest** (ver′ē·ist): greatest.

A scene from "The Pit and the Pendulum," illustrated by Arthur Rackham.

drunk before I became irresistibly drowsy. A deep sleep fell upon me—a sleep like that of death. How long it lasted of course I know not; but when, once again, I unclosed my eyes, the objects around me were visible. By a wild, sulfurous luster,[9] the origin of which I could not at first determine, I was enabled to see the extent and aspect of the prison.

In its size I had been greatly mistaken. The whole circuit of its walls did not exceed twenty-five yards. For some minutes this fact occasioned me a world of vain trouble; vain indeed, for what could be of less importance, under the terrible circumstances which environed me, than the mere dimensions of my dungeon? But

9. **sulfurous** (sul′fər·əs) **luster:** glow like that of burning sulfur, which produces a blue flame. The word *sulfurous* is also used to mean "suggesting the fires of hell."

THE PIT AND THE PENDULUM 295

D Elements of Literature

Symbolic Meaning

❓ How does the falling piece of stone serve as a symbol for the narrator's fate? [The stone falls at length into a deep pit, which is what might have happened to the narrator if he had not tripped.]

E Reading Skills and Strategies

Summarizing

❓ What has happened to the narrator since he awakened in the dungeon? [He has opened his eyes and found himself in complete darkness. He fears he is in a tomb, but he finds that he is in a prison. While trying to measure the dungeon, he narrowly misses falling into a pit. He resolves not to explore further.]

Getting Students Involved

Cooperative Learning

News from the Pit. Have small mixed-ability groups prepare a news story about the narrator's imprisonment. Students should first brainstorm key story events, then assume individual tasks such as illustrator, writer, editor, and announcer. Encourage groups to present their news feature stories to the class.

Writing Activity

Have students write an updated version of the story. You might conduct a class brainstorming session for modern situations, such as a prisoner-of-war scenario. Students could then work in pairs to plot and write their own updated stories. Each pair should produce a finished story.

Ⓐ Reading Skills and Strategies
Making Inferences
? Why might the narrator be so interested in the minute details of his cell? [Possible responses: He is trying to keep his mind busy as a way of staying sane; he is still hopeful that he'll find a way out.]

Ⓑ Elements of Literature
Setting
? Now that the narrator sees his surroundings more clearly, what impact does the setting have on him? [Possible answer: He is even more horrified by the images and devices he sees.]

Ⓒ Vocabulary Note
The Prefix con-
? The word *convolutions* is formed by joining the prefix *con-* ("together") and the Latin root *volvere* ("to roll"). A *convolution,* therefore, is something that is "rolled together." The prefixes *col-, com-,* and *cor-* also mean "together." What are some other words formed with the prefixes *con- col-, com-, and cor-?* [Sample answers: construction, convulsion, convene, collapse, colleague, compile, composite, correspond, correct.]

Ⓓ English Language Learners
Breaking Down Difficult Text
Explain to students that one reason Poe's style is difficult is because he often uses unusual or archaic words and word order. Have students work in pairs to break down this sentence into three simple sentences. [I looked up at it. It was right over me. I thought I saw it moving.]

Ⓐ my soul took a wild interest in trifles, and I busied myself in endeavors to account for the error I had committed in my measurement. The truth at length flashed upon me. In my first attempt at exploration I had counted fifty-two paces, up to the period when I fell; I must then have been within a pace or two of the fragment of serge; in fact, I had nearly performed the circuit of the vault. I then slept, and upon awaking, I must have returned upon my steps—thus supposing the circuit nearly double what it actually was. My confusion of mind prevented me from observing that I began my tour with the wall to the left and ended it with the wall to the right.

Ⓑ I had been deceived, too, in respect to the shape of the enclosure. In feeling my way I had found many angles and thus deduced an idea of great irregularity; so <u>potent</u> is the effect of total darkness upon one arousing from <u>lethargy</u> or sleep! The angles were simply those of a few slight depressions, or niches, at odd intervals. The general shape of the prison was square. What I had taken for masonry seemed now to be iron, or some other metal, in huge plates, whose sutures or joints occasioned the depression. The entire surface of this metallic enclosure was rudely daubed[10] in all the hideous and repulsive devices to which the charnel[11] superstition of the monks has given rise. The figures of fiends in aspects of menace, with skeleton forms, and other, more really fearful images, overspread and disfigured the walls. I observed that the outlines of these monstrosities were sufficiently distinct, but that the colors seemed faded and blurred, as if from the effects of a damp atmosphere. I now noticed the floor, too, which was of stone. In the center yawned the circular pit from whose jaws I had escaped; but it was the only one in the dungeon.

All this I saw indistinctly and by much effort; for my personal condition had been greatly changed during slumber. I now lay upon my back, and at full length, on a species of low framework of wood. To this I was securely

---

10. **daubed:** painted crudely or unskillfully.
11. **charnel:** suggestive of death. A charnel house is a building or place where bones or bodies are deposited.

Ⓒ bound by a long strap resembling a surcingle.[12] It passed in many convolutions about my limbs and body, leaving at liberty only my head, and my left arm to such extent that I could, by dint of much exertion, supply myself with food from an earthen dish which lay by my side on the floor. I saw, to my horror, that the pitcher had been removed. I say to my horror, for I was consumed with intolerable thirst. This thirst it appeared to be the design of my persecutors to stimulate—for the food in the dish was meat pungently seasoned.

In the center yawned the circular pit from whose jaws I had escaped . . .

Looking upward, I surveyed the ceiling of my prison. It was some thirty or forty feet overhead and constructed much as the side walls. In one of its panels a very singular figure riveted my whole attention. It was the painted figure of Time as he is commonly represented, save[13] that, in lieu of[14] a scythe, he held what, at a casual glance, I supposed to be the pictured image of a huge pendulum, such as we see on antique clocks. There was something, however, in the appearance of this machine which caused me Ⓓ to regard it more attentively. While I gazed directly upward at it (for its position was immediately over my own), I fancied that I saw it in motion. In an instant afterward the fancy was confirmed. Its sweep was brief and of course slow. I watched it for some minutes somewhat

---

12. **surcingle** (sur'sin'gəl): strap passed around a horse's body to bind on a saddle or a pack.
13. **save:** here, except.
14. **in lieu** (loo) **of:** instead of.

WORDS TO OWN
potent (pōt''nt) *adj.*: powerful or effective.
lethargy (leth'ər·jē) *n.*: abnormal drowsiness. *Lethargy* also means "great lack of energy; dull or indifferent state."

Taking a Second Look

Review: Cause and Effect
Review cause and effect with students, reminding them that a cause is what makes something happen and an effect is the result. On p. 295, for example, the narrator is thirsty (cause), so he drinks water (effect). The water has been drugged (cause), so he falls asleep (effect). Remind students that some causes may have more than one effect, and some effects may have more than one cause.

Activities
1. As students read the selection, have them list specific causes and corresponding effects. When they finish reading, have them meet in groups and compare the causes and effects they have identified.
2. Ask students to discuss how cause-and-effect relationships affect the plot. What major causes and effects govern the character's situation and actions?

in fear, but more in wonder. Wearied at length with observing its dull movement, I turned my eyes upon the other objects in the cell.

A slight noise attracted my notice, and looking to the floor, I saw several enormous rats traversing it. They had issued from the well which lay just within view to my right. Even then, while I gazed, they came up in troops, hurriedly, with ravenous eyes, allured by the scent of the meat. From this it required much effort and attention to scare them away.

It might have been half an hour, perhaps even an hour (for I could take but imperfect note of time), before I again cast my eyes upward. What I then saw confounded and amazed me. The sweep of the pendulum had increased in extent by nearly a yard. As a natural consequence its velocity was also much greater. But what mainly disturbed me was the idea that it had perceptibly *descended.* I now observed—with what horror it is needless to say—that its nether extremity[15] was formed of a crescent of glittering steel, about a foot in length from horn to horn; the horns upward, and the under edge evidently as keen as that of a razor. Like a razor also, it seemed massy and heavy, tapering from the edge into a solid and broad structure above. It was appended to a weighty rod of brass, and the whole *hissed* as it swung through the air.

I could no longer doubt the doom prepared for me by monkish ingenuity in torture. My cognizance[16] of the pit had become known to the Inquisitorial agents—*the pit,* whose horrors had been destined for so bold a recusant[17] as myself—*the pit,* typical of hell and regarded by rumor as the ultima Thule[18] of all their punishments. The plunge into this pit I had avoided by the merest of accidents, and I knew that surprise, or entrapment into torment, formed an important portion of all the grotesquerie of these dungeon deaths. Having failed to fall, it was no part of the demon plan to hurl me into

the abyss, and thus (there being no alternative) a different and a milder destruction awaited me. Milder! I half smiled in my agony as I thought of such application of such a term.

What boots it[19] to tell of the long, long hours of horror more than mortal, during which I counted the rushing vibrations of the steel! Inch by inch—line by line—with a descent only appreciable at intervals that seemed ages—down and still down it came! Days passed—it might have been that many days passed—ere it swept so closely over me as to fan me with its acrid breath. The odor of the sharp steel forced itself into my nostrils. I prayed—I wearied heaven with my prayer for its more speedy descent. I grew frantically mad and struggled to force myself upward against the sweep of the fearful scimitar.[20] And then I fell suddenly calm and lay smiling at the glittering death, as a child at some rare bauble.

There was another interval of utter insensibility; it was brief; for, upon again lapsing into life, there had been no perceptible descent in the pendulum. But it might have been long—for I knew there were demons who took note of my swoon and who could have arrested the vibration at pleasure. Upon my recovery, too, I felt very—oh! inexpressibly—sick and weak, as if through long inanition.[21] Even amid the agonies of that period, the human nature craved food. With painful effort I outstretched my left arm as far as my bonds permitted and took possession of the small remnant which had been spared me by the rats. As I put a portion of it within my lips, there rushed to my mind a half-formed thought of joy—of hope. Yet what business had *I* with hope? It was, as I say, a half-formed thought—man has many such, which are never completed. I felt that it was of joy—of hope; but I felt also that it had perished in its formation. In vain I struggled to perfect—to regain it. Long suffering had nearly annihilated all my ordinary powers of mind. I was an imbecile—an idiot.

---

15. **nether** (ne*th*′ər) **extremity:** lower end.
16. **cognizance** (käg′nə·zəns): awareness.
17. **recusant** (rek′yoo·zənt): person who refuses to obey an established authority.
18. **ultima Thule** (ul′ti·mə thoo͞′lē): most extreme. The term is Latin for "northernmost region of the world."

19. **what boots it:** of what use is it.
20. **scimitar** (sim′ə·tər): sword with a curved blade, used mainly by Arabs and Turks.
21. **inanition** (in′ə·nish′ən): weakness from lack of food.

THE PIT AND THE PENDULUM **297**

E Reading Skills and Strategies
Summarizing
? What has happened since the narrator discovered the pit and crawled back to the wall, vowing not to move again? [He lies awake many hours but then falls asleep. Awaking, he finds bread and water. The water has been drugged, and he falls into a deep sleep after drinking it. When he awakes, he is bound to a platform and can view his dungeon. Above him, he observes a painted figure of Time with a moving pendulum. He then discovers rats, attracted by his food, coming from the pit.]

F Elements of Literature
Setting
The *period* of a pendulum is the time it takes for the device's weight to pass back and forth over the path that the pendulum travels. The length of the period is relative to the length of the pendulum's swing.

G Vocabulary Note
Multiple Meanings
Point out to students that here the word *typical* means "symbolic, archetypal."

H English Language Learners
Archaic Language
The phrase *What boots it* means "of what use is it," and the word *ere* means "before." Explain that these terms are archaic, or no longer in popular use. Ask students to look up *boots* and *ere* in the dictionary, and point out to them how the dictionary identifies them as archaic. Remind students that Poe's story was written in the early 1840s.

I Elements of Literature
Symbolic Meaning
? What symbol does Poe use to describe the narrator's tormentors? [He calls them demons.]

Crossing the Curriculum

Social Studies/History
Before 1700 it was rare that criminals were sent to prison. Offenders might be fined or sentenced to death, depending on the crime. Prisons such as the Tower of London and the Bastille were for traitors and other political enemies. Have students research the history of prisons and prison reform. Students might focus on changes in prison conditions or on punishable crimes.

Science
Dutchman Christian Huygens invented the first clock to use a pendulum in the mid-1600s, although both pendulums and clocks had been in existence well before then. Huygens' goal was to develop a clock that would stay accurate onboard a ship. Challenge students to research and report on the invention of the mechanical clock in the Middle Ages or on subsequent developments in clock design.

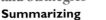
The vibration of the pendulum was at right angles to my length. I saw that the crescent was designed to cross the region of the heart. It would fray the serge of my robe—it would return and repeat its operations—again—and again. Notwithstanding its terrifically wide sweep (some thirty feet or more) and the hissing vigor of its descent, sufficient to sunder these very walls of iron, still the fraying of my robe would be all that, for several minutes, it would accomplish. And at this thought I paused. I dared not go further than this reflection. I dwelt upon it with a pertinacity²² of attention—as if, in so dwelling, I could arrest²³ *here* the descent of the steel. I forced myself to ponder upon the sound of the crescent as it should pass across the garment—upon the peculiar thrilling sensation which the friction of cloth produces on the nerves. I pondered upon all this frivolity until my teeth were on edge.

Down—steadily down it crept. I took a frenzied pleasure in contrasting its downward with its lateral velocity. To the right—to the left—far and wide—with the shriek of a damned spirit! to my heart, with the stealthy pace of the tiger! I alternately laughed and howled, as the one or the other idea grew predominant.

Down—certainly, relentlessly down! It vibrated within three inches of my bosom! I struggled violently—furiously—to free my left arm. This was free only from the elbow to the hand. I could reach the latter, from the platter beside me, to my mouth, with great effort, but no farther. Could I have broken the fastenings above the elbow, I would have seized and attempted to arrest the pendulum. I might as well have attempted to arrest an avalanche!

Down—still unceasingly—still inevitably down! I gasped and struggled at each vibration. I shrunk convulsively at its every sweep. My eyes followed its outward or upward whorls with the eagerness of the most unmeaning despair; they closed themselves spasmodically at the descent, although death would have been a relief, oh, how unspeakable! Still I quivered in

every nerve to think how slight a sinking of the machinery would precipitate that keen, glistening ax upon my bosom. It was *hope* that prompted the nerve to quiver—the frame to shrink. It was *hope*—the hope that triumphs on the rack—that whispers to the death-condemned even in the dungeons of the Inquisition.

I saw that some ten or twelve vibrations would bring the steel in actual contact with my robe, and with this observation there suddenly came over my spirit all the keen, collected calmness of despair. For the first time during many hours—or perhaps days—I *thought*. It now occurred to me that the bandage, or surcingle, which enveloped me, was *unique*. I was tied by no separate cord. The first stroke of the razor-like crescent athwart any portion of the band would so detach it that it might be unwound from my person by means of my left hand. But how fearful, in that case, the proximity of the steel! The result of the slightest struggle, how deadly! Was it likely, moreover, that the minions²⁴ of the torturer had not foreseen and provided for this possibility? Was it probable that the bandage crossed my bosom in the track of the pendulum? Dreading to find my faint and, as it seemed, my last hope frustrated, I so far elevated my head as to obtain a distinct view of my breast. The surcingle enveloped my limbs and body close in all directions—*save in the path of the destroying crescent.*

Scarcely had I dropped my head back into its original position when there flashed upon my mind what I cannot better describe than as the unformed half of that idea of deliverance to which I had previously alluded, and of which a moiety²⁵ only floated indeterminately through my brain when I raised food to my burning lips. The whole thought was now present—feeble, scarcely sane, scarcely definite—but still entire. I proceeded at once, with the nervous energy of despair, to attempt its execution.

---

24. **minions:** servants; followers.
25. **moiety** (moi′ə·tē): part.

WORDS TO OWN

proximity (präks·im′ə·tē) *n.:* nearness.

---

22. **pertinacity** (pʉr′tə·nas′ə·tē): stubborn persistence.
23. **arrest:** here, stop.

Skill Link

Alliteration

Explain to students that **alliteration** is the repetition of consonant sounds. Usually these repeated sounds occur at the beginning of words, though they can occur anywhere. Help students understand that alliteration contributes to the rhythm of literary language. Have students identify the alliteration in the following sentences from this page.

Activity

1. I saw that the crescent was designed to cross the region of the heart.
2. It would fray the serge of my robe—it would return and repeat its operations—again—and again.
3. Down—steadily down it crept.
4. Still I quivered in every nerve to think

how slight a sinking of the machinery would precipitate that keen, glistening ax upon my bosom.

Then have students write five original sentences that contain alliteration. Volunteers might read aloud their sentences. Ask other students to identify the alliteration.

A scene from "The Pit and the Pendulum," illustrated by John Byam Shaw.

RESPONDING TO THE ART

John Byam Shaw (1872–1919) illustrated numerous books with watercolors and drawings. Influenced by the composition and intense use of color of the Pre-Raphaelites, Shaw was known for his romantic flair. In his later work, he enjoyed painting allegories that combined realistic details with images of fantasy. **Activity.** Have students compare the styles of the illustrations in other stories by Edgar Allan Poe. Then, ask students to illustrate a scene from the story, using watercolors, drawings, or collage techniques with photographs from magazines and newspapers.

Connecting Across Texts

Connecting with "Trap of Gold"

Have students compare "The Pit and the Pendulum" and "Trap of Gold" in a class discussion. Stimulate discussion with questions such as: **How are the characters alike?** [Both appear to be deliberate, thoughtful, diligent, and very careful men. Both are trapped, although in different ways, and both narrowly escape death.] **How is suspense developed in the two stories?** [In both, it slowly builds with the authors' precise elaboration of details. The chronological development of the plot and slow, almost minute-to-minute description of events add to the suspense.] **Which do you find more suspenseful? Why?** [Students should give reasons for their responses.]

For many hours the immediate vicinity of the low framework upon which I lay had been literally swarming with rats. They were wild, bold, ravenous—their red eyes glaring upon me as if they waited but for motionlessness on my part to make me their prey. "To what food," I thought, "have they been accustomed in the well?"

> **I knew that in more than one place it must be already severed. With a more than human resolution I lay still.**

They had devoured, in spite of all my efforts to prevent them, all but a small remnant of the contents of the dish. I had fallen into a habitual seesaw or wave of the hand about the platter; and, at length, the unconscious uniformity of the movement deprived it of effect. In their voracity, the vermin frequently fastened their sharp fangs in my fingers. With the particles of the oily and spicy viand which now remained, I thoroughly rubbed the bandage wherever I could reach it; then, raising my hand from the floor, I lay breathlessly still.

A At first, the ravenous animals were startled and terrified at the change—at the cessation of movement. They shrank alarmedly back; many sought the well. But this was only for a moment. I had not counted in vain upon their voracity. Observing that I remained without motion, one or two of the boldest leaped upon the framework and smelled at the surcingle. This seemed the signal for a general rush. Forth from the well they hurried in fresh troops. They clung to the wood—they overran it and leaped in hundreds upon my person. The measured movement of the pendulum disturbed them not at all. Avoiding its strokes, they busied themselves with the anointed bandage. They pressed—they swarmed upon me in ever accumulating heaps. They writhed upon my throat; their cold lips sought my own; I was half stifled by their thronging pressure; disgust for which the world has no name swelled my bosom and chilled, with a heavy clamminess, my heart. Yet one minute, and I felt that the struggle would be over. Plainly I perceived the loosening of the bandage. I knew that in more than one place it must be already severed. With a more than human resolution I lay *still.*

Nor had I erred in my calculations—nor had I endured in vain. I at length felt that I was *free.* The surcingle hung in ribbons from my body. But the stroke of the pendulum already pressed upon my bosom. It had divided the serge of the robe. It had cut through the linen beneath. Twice again it swung, and a sharp sense of pain shot through every nerve. But the moment of escape had arrived. At a wave of my hand my deliverers hurried tumultuously away. With a steady movement—cautious, sidelong, shrinking, and slow—I slid from the embrace of the bandage and beyond the reach of the scimitar. **B** For the moment, at least, *I was free.*

Free!—and in the grasp of the Inquisition! I had scarcely stepped from my wooden bed of horror upon the stone floor of the prison when the motion of the hellish machine ceased, and I beheld it drawn up, by some invisible force, through the ceiling. This was a lesson which I took desperately to heart. My every motion was undoubtedly watched. Free!—I had but escaped death in one form of agony to be delivered **C** unto worse than death in some other. With that thought I rolled my eyes nervously around on the barriers of iron that hemmed me in. Something unusual—some change which at first I could not appreciate distinctly—it was obvious, had taken place in the apartment. For many minutes of a dreamy and trembling abstraction, I busied myself in vain, unconnected conjecture. During this period, I became aware, for the first time, of the origin of the sulfurous light which illumined the cell. It proceeded from a fissure, about half an inch in width, extending entirely around the prison at the base of the walls, which thus appeared, and were, completely separated from the floor. I endeavored, **D** but of course in vain, to look through the aperture.

As I arose from the attempt, the mystery of the alteration in the chamber broke at once

Assessing Learning

upon my understanding. I had observed that, although the outlines of the figures upon the walls were sufficiently distinct, yet the colors seemed blurred and indefinite. These colors had now assumed and were momentarily assuming, a startling and most intense brilliance that gave to the spectral and fiendish portraitures an aspect that might have thrilled even firmer nerves than my own. Demon eyes, of a wild and ghastly vivacity, glared upon me in a thousand directions where none had been visible before, and gleamed with the lurid luster of a fire that I could not force my imagination to regard as unreal.

Unreal!—even while I breathed, there came to my nostrils the breath of the vapor of heated iron! A suffocating odor pervaded the prison! A deeper glow settled each moment in the eyes that glared at my agonies! A richer tint of crimson diffused itself over the pictured horrors of blood. I panted! I gasped for breath! There could be no doubt of the design of my tormenters—oh! most unrelenting! oh! most demoniac of men! I shrank from the glowing metal to the center of the cell. Amid the thought of the fiery destruction that impended, the idea of the coolness of the well came over my soul like balm. I rushed to its deadly brink. I threw my straining vision below. The glare from the enkindled roof illumined its inmost recesses. Yet for a wild moment did my spirit refuse to comprehend the meaning of what I saw. At length it forced—it wrestled its way into my soul—it burned itself in upon my shuddering reason.—Oh! for a voice to speak!—oh! horror!—oh! any horror but this! With a shriek, I rushed from the margin and buried my face in my hands—weeping bitterly.

The heat rapidly increased, and once again I looked up, shuddering as with a fit of the ague.[26] There had been a second change in the cell—and now the change was obviously in the *form*. As before, it was in vain that I at first endeavored to appreciate or understand what was taking place. But not long was I left in doubt. The Inquisitorial vengeance had been hurried by my twofold escape, and there was to be no more dallying with the King of Terrors. The room had been square. I saw that two of its iron angles were now acute[27]—two, consequently, obtuse.[28] The fearful difference quickly increased with a low rumbling or moaning sound. In an instant the apartment had shifted its form into that of a lozenge.[29] But the alteration stopped not here—I neither hoped nor desired it to stop. I could have clasped the red walls to my bosom as a garment of eternal peace. "Death," I said, "any death but that of the pit!" Fool! Might I not have known that *into the pit* it was the object of the burning iron to urge me? Could I resist its glow? Or if even that, could I withstand its pressure? And now, flatter and flatter grew the lozenge, with a rapidity that left me no time for contemplation. Its center, and of course its greatest width, came just over the yawning gulf. I shrank back—but the closing walls pressed me resistlessly onward. At length, for my seared and writhing body, there was no longer an inch of foothold on the firm floor of the prison. I struggled no more, but the agony of my soul found vent in one loud, long, and final scream of despair. I felt that I tottered upon the brink—I <u>averted</u> my eyes—— 📖

There was a discordant hum of human voices! There was a loud blast as of many trumpets! There was a harsh grating as of a thousand thunders! The fiery walls rushed back! An outstretched arm caught my own as I fell, fainting, into the abyss. It was that of General Lasalle. The French army had entered Toledo. The Inquisition was in the hands of its enemies. 📖

---

27. acute (ə·kyoōt′): of less than 90 degrees.
28. obtuse (äb·toōs′): of more than 90 degrees and less than 180 degrees.
29. lozenge (läz′ənj): diamond shape.

WORDS TO OWN

averted (ə·vʉrt′id) *v*.: turned away. *Averted* also means "prevented."

---

26. ague (ā′gyōō′): chills.

Making the Connections

MEET THE WRITER

Nightmare Worlds

Edgar Allan Poe (1809–1849) was a moody, sensitive person whose stories and poems dwell on the supernatural and on crime, torture, premature burial, and death. His writing, which brought him little comfort or security, reflects the dark, nightmare side of the imagination.

Poe's stormy personal history began when his father deserted his mother, a popular young actress, who died in 1811 in a theatrical rooming house in Richmond, Virginia, just before Edgar was three years old.

A wealthy, childless couple, the Allans of Richmond, took him in and gave him a good education, expecting him to take over John Allan's business eventually. Edgar wanted to be a writer, though, not a businessman. This disagreement and John Allan's persistent refusal to adopt Edgar legally led to frequent fights. By the time he was twenty-one, Poe and John Allan had severed all connections, and Poe had entered upon a hectic, full-time literary career, working for a number of periodicals in Baltimore and New York.

In 1836, Poe married his thirteen-year-old cousin, Virginia Clemm. Although a drinking problem often led him into destructive fights with other writers and critics, Poe managed somehow to keep his household together. In 1845, he sold his poem "The Raven" to a newspaper for about fifteen dollars. "The Raven" was soon on everyone's lips, as popular as a top-ten song hit is today.

Poe was to know no peace, however. Virginia had already fallen victim to that plague of nineteenth-century life, tuberculosis. In 1847, she died, and Poe's loneliness and drinking increased. On October 3, 1849, when he was only forty years old, Poe was found, disoriented and suffering from exposure, at a tavern in rainy, windswept Baltimore. He died in a Baltimore hospital, from unspecified causes, three days later.

Poe, a meticulous writer who was devoted to his craft, invented two genres: the mystery story and the horror story. Both forms have flourished ever since.

More Murder and Mayhem by Poe

"The Murders in the Rue Morgue"

"The Gold-Bug"

"The Masque of the Red Death"

"Hop-Frog"

Assessing Learning

Check Test: Questions and Answers

1. Give a brief description of the judges. [blackrobed, stern, and with thin, white lips]
2. What does the narrator use to mark his place as he tries to determine the dimensions of his cell? [a piece of cloth he tears from the hem of his robe]
3. What benefit comes from the narrator's fall? [He discovers the pit.]
4. What is painted on the ceiling of the dungeon? [the figure of Time]
5. How does the narrator get the rats to help him? [He rubs his bindings with oily food so that the rats will eat through them and free him.]

Standardized Test Preparation

For practice with standardized test format specific to this selection, see
- *Standardized Test Preparation*, pp. 38, 40

For practice in proofreading and editing, see
- *Daily Oral Grammar*, Transparency 19

MAKING MEANINGS

First Thoughts

1. What **image** in this horror story do you think you will remember longest? Why?

Shaping Interpretations

2. Probably the scariest aspect of this story is its **setting**. List all its horrible details. Did any of these horrors connect with your own fears? (Check your Quickwrite notes.)

3. On one level, this is the story of a man tortured by the Inquisition. However, some critics read it on another level, as the story of a man who dies, almost loses his soul to Hell, and is rescued at the end by God. See if the story "works" if it is read **symbolically** with this interpretation. Consider:

   - The man, above all, fears falling into the pit. What could the pit symbolize?

   - What does a pendulum suggest to you, and what does an old man with a scythe represent? What connection might there be between these symbols and the scythe on the pendulum in this story?

   - Rats are often used as symbols of death, decay, and the lower world. How does the prisoner's response to these rats—especially when they crawl all over him—suggest that he might see them in this way?

   - What sounds are usually associated with Judgment Day at the end of the world? Do you hear these sounds at the story's end?

   Do you think this symbolic reading makes sense, or is it stretching the meaning of a "simple" horror story? Explain.

Challenging the Text

4. Did General Lasalle's arrival seem an exceptionally lucky coincidence to you? If so, did the last-minute rescue lessen the story's credibility or your enjoyment of it? Explain your responses.

Reading Check

Refer back to the **summaries** you made while reading the story. They should help you answer the following questions:

a. Find the details at the start that suggest that the prisoner's experience might be part of a dream or a lapse into madness.

b. When the narrator first regains consciousness, what "most hideous of fates" does he think the Inquisition has planned for him? How does he discover the truth?

c. When he wakens from a drugged sleep, the narrator discovers that he is in a second and even worse crisis. What new torture does he face? How does he escape?

d. What third crisis does he face when he has scarcely stepped from his "bed of horror"?

e. What sensational breakthrough occurs at the end?

MAKING MEANINGS

First Thoughts

1. Possible answers: the pit, the rats, the pendulum, burning walls. Students will probably conclude that each is described with frightening detail.

Shaping Interpretations

2. Sample responses: blackness, silence, tomblike enclosure, circular pit, smell of decay, rats, pendulum with a razor-sharp edge, walls that move, fire; students may connect any of these elements with their own fears.

3. A symbolic interpretation seems valid because it gives depth to a story that clearly includes symbols.
   - Death or hell
   - A pendulum suggests time, and the old man suggests the Grim Reaper (death); these symbols and the scythe on the pendulum suggest time is running out; the Grim Reaper is about to claim the man, and the pendulum is the agent of death.
   - He feels chilled and disgusted by them.
   - Sounds of wailing and fear, trumpet blasts. The story records sounds of discordant human voices, trumpets blaring, and thunder.

   Many students may feel the symbolic interpretation is plausible but prefer to read the story as a simple horror tale.

Challenging the Text

4. Some students might say they expected the prisoner to be saved, because the story was written in the first person from the narrator's memory of events. Other students might feel that the story ended too suddenly and was not believable.

Reading Check

a. The narrator says he was sick, his senses were leaving him. He doesn't hear the sentencing and everything became a "dreamy" hum in his ears. He had the idea that everything was revolving, and then he heard nothing. He has visions of grotesqueness and sees the candles as angels.

b. He thinks he is buried alive in a tomb. He moves about and discovers it is a dungeon.

c. He is tied to a platform with a razor-sharp pendulum slowly descending upon him. He rubs meat on his bindings and the rats chew through the bindings, releasing him.

d. The walls become fiery hot and begin moving toward him, forcing him into the pit.

e. General Lasalle has captured the prison and reversed the movement of the walls. He grabs the narrator as he is falling into the pit.

Grading Timesaver

Rubrics for each assignment appear on p. 124 in the *Portfolio Management System*.

CHOICES:
Building Your Portfolio

1. **Writer's Notebook**   Before students begin writing, you might lead a brief class discussion, summarizing the plot, setting, point of view, and theme of the selection. Remind students to save their work; it might be useful when they begin the Writer's Workshop on p. 328.
2. **Creative Writing**   Consider allowing students to work in pairs to complete the chart but have them write their paragraphs independently.
3. **Research/Report**   As students list questions, remind them to think about the five *W*'s and *H*: *Who? What? When? Where? Why?* and *How?*
4. **Art and Symbolism**   Encourage students to think about the images painted on the walls and ceiling of the dungeon and about the attitudes and beliefs of the Inquisitors and the narrator.
5. **Creative Writing**   Suggest that students pair up with peer editors and provide reactions to each other's work-in-progress.

CHOICES: Building Your Portfolio

Writer's Notebook
1. Collecting Ideas for an Evaluation

Stating your opinion. Evaluations (you'll write one for the Writer's Workshop on page 328) usually begin by identifying the subject of the evaluation and stating the writer's opinion. The evaluation then goes on to offer reasons for the opinion. Write a one-sentence evaluation statement in which you state your opinion of Poe's story or another story in this book. You may want to focus on a single element of the story: plot, setting, point of view, theme.

> Edgar Allan Poe creates an atmosphere of terror in his story "The Pit and the Pendulum" by creating a setting that brings out our worst fears—of being eaten alive by rats or being entombed alive.

Creative Writing
2. Updating the Story

"The Pit and the Pendulum" is a famous psychological horror story. Do you think the story has relevance to events that could take place today? In a paragraph or two, tell how you would update the story but maintain its basic plot. Filling out the following chart might help you organize your ideas.

	Poe Story	Updated Story
Setting (when and where?)		
Protagonist (what is his or her crime?)		
Punishment		
Opponents or jailers		
Rescuers		

Research/Report
3. Digging Deeper

For a brief **oral report**, tell how you'd research one of the three topics below, using both print and Internet sources. List questions you have about the topic, and cite the sources that should help you unearth the answers. Be sure to tell how you evaluated the reliability of your sources, especially if they are from the Internet.
- the Spanish Inquisition
- the Moors in Spain during the Middle Ages
- El Greco (artist, see page 292)

Art and Symbolism
4. Looking into the Pit

On page 301, the narrator rushes to the pit's brink. You are never told what he sees there. Draw or paint the images that you imagine meet his eye. As you visualize the pit, recall what you think it symbolizes.

Creative Writing
5. Poems for Poe

Respond to Poe's story in a poem. Your poem could be any one of a number of types. It might express your reactions and feelings after reading "The Pit and the Pendulum." It might be about one of your own personal fears. You might even address your poem directly to Poe. If you want a real challenge, either alone or with a small group, try rewriting "The Pit and the Pendulum" in the form of a story-poem. Read a few of Poe's famous poems like "The Raven" before you begin. For the ultimate challenge, make your poem imitate Poe's haunting rhythm and rhymes.

LANGUAGE LINK · MINI-LESSON

The Effect of Rhythm and Repetition

Handbook of Literary Terms HELP

See Alliteration and Rhythm.

Poe paid as much attention to the sound of his words as he did to their sense. Skillful use of **rhythm, repetition,** and other **sound effects** reinforces the emotional effect of his story. In the following passage, note how the repetition of words and consonants and the slow, steady rhythm of the long sentences reflect the relentless, downward movement of the blade.

> "Inch by inch—line by line—with a descent only appreciable at intervals that seemed ages—down and still down it came! Days passed—it might have been that many days passed—ere it swept so closely over me as to fan me with its acrid breath."

The repetition of consonant sounds, usually at the beginnings of words, is called **alliteration**. Poe uses alliteration for sound effects. Notice in the sentence below how the swishing, hissing s sounds reproduce the hissing sound of the blade as it swings over the prisoner.

> "With a steady movement—cautious, sidelong, shrinking, and slow—I slid from the embrace of the bandage and beyond the reach of the scimitar."

Try It Out

Working with a group, select passages from the story for oral reading. Look for passages that contain especially good sound effects and rhythmical qualities. An excellent passage begins on page 298 with "The vibration of the pendulum" and ends on page 298 with "dungeons of the Inquisition."

VOCABULARY · HOW TO OWN A WORD

WORD BANK

imperceptible
ponders
lucid
tumultuous
insuperable
prostrate
potent
lethargy
proximity
averted

Using Context Clues

Justify your response to each numbered item below. Then, indicate the **context clues** in each sentence that gave you hints to the meaning of each underlined word. After you've done that, go back to Poe's story and see if you can find context clues for each of the same underlined words. Write down any context clues that you find in the story.

1. Why would simple, lucid instructions help someone who ponders over how to operate a videocassette recorder?
2. A mystery movie's sound track begins faintly with an almost imperceptible noise quickly followed by tumultuous sounds. Suggest examples for each type of sound.
3. Explain why a woman averted her eyes for protection in the proximity of a blinding flash of light.
4. Why might desperate people facing an insuperable enemy prostrate themselves on the ground?
5. Name three potent smells that would rouse you from a couch potato's lethargy.

THE PIT AND THE PENDULUM 305

LANGUAGE LINK

Have students reread a descriptive piece from their portfolio to find places where they can use alliteration. Their alliterations should repeat a consonant sound two or three times.

Try It Out

When students read the suggested passage, they should emphasize the repetition of the word *down*. They should also note that the s sounds in the passage mimic the sound of the pendulum. The many d sounds may remind them of the narrator's impending doom.

VOCABULARY

1. Clear instructions would be helpful to a person trying to operate a recorder. Clues: "simple" and "how to operate."
2. A quiet creak of a floorboard followed by rapid gunfire and screaming. Clues: "faintly" and "followed by . . . sounds."
3. The woman turned her eyes away from the flash to avoid temporary blindness. Clues: "for protection" and "blinding flash of light."
4. When people confront an enemy that can't be overcome, it might be best to lie down in submission. Clues: "desperate" and "on the ground."
5. I would rouse myself from drowsiness if I smelled smoke, gas, or rotten eggs. Clues: "smells," "rouse," and "couch potato's."

Resources ———

Language
- *Grammar and Language Links* Worksheet, p. 35

Vocabulary
- *Words to Own* Worksheet, p. 19

Language Link Quick Check

For practice with repetition and alliteration read the passages below and answer the questions that follow.

1. "But what mainly disturbed me was the idea that it had perceptibly *descended*." (p. 297) What is the effect of the repetition of the d sound? [It reminds the reader of the downward movement of the pendulum.]
2. "My cognizance of the pit had become known to the Inquisitorial agents—*the pit,* whose horrors had been destined for so bold a recusant as myself—*the pit,* typical of hell and regarded by rumor as the ultima Thule of all their punishments. The plunge into this pit I had avoided . . . " (p. 297)
   - What is the effect of the repetition of the word *pit?* [It increases the importance of the pit.]
   - What words other than *pit* have the p sound? [*typical, punishments, plunge*]

Resources ———————

Elements of Literature
Symbols
For additional instruction on symbols, see *Literary Elements:*
• Transparency 9

Elements of Literature
This feature defines symbols and describes how they work. The discussion advises readers on how to identify symbols and addresses the question of why writers use symbols.

Mini-Lesson
Symbols: Signs of Something More
After students have read pp. 306–307, use this mini-lesson to clarify and reinforce their understanding of symbols.

• Ask students to define *symbol*. [an object, a setting, an event, an animal, or a person that stands for something other than itself] **Invite students to give examples of symbols.** [Examples include an eagle, apple pie, a heart, a yellow ribbon, the Olympic rings, the Statue of Liberty, a red cross.] **Ask students to discuss the meanings of some of these symbols.**

(Mini-Lesson continues on p.T307)

SYMBOLS: Signs of Something More

Our everyday lives are heaped with symbols. The ring on your finger, though actually a piece of metal with a stone in it, may also be a symbol of something less concrete. For you it may symbolize love, calling to mind the special person who saved for months to buy it for you.

> The ring on your finger, though actually a piece of metal with a stone in it, may also be a symbol of something less concrete.

There are many symbols in our culture that we know and recognize at once. We automatically make the associations suggested by a cross, a six-pointed star, a crown, a skull and crossbones, a clenched fist, the Stars and Stripes, and a dove with an olive branch. These commonly accepted symbols are **public symbols**.

Symbols in Literature: Making Associations

Writers of fiction, poetry, and drama create new, personal symbols in their work. Some literary symbols, like the great white whale in *Moby-Dick* and like that stubborn spot of blood on Lady Macbeth's hand, become so widely known that eventually they too become a part of our public stockpile of symbols.

In literature, a **symbol** is an object, a setting, an event, an animal, or even a person that functions in a story the way you'd expect it to but, more important, also stands for something more than itself, usually for something abstract. The white whale in *Moby-Dick* is a very real white whale in the novel, and Captain Ahab spends the whole book chasing it. But certain passages in that novel make clear to us that this whale is also associated with the mystery of evil in the world. That is how symbols work—by association. Most people associate the color green with new life, and therefore with hope. In some cultures, the color white is associated with innocence and purity; in others, white is a color of death. We usually associate gardens with joy and wastelands with futility and despair. We associate winter with sterility and spring with fertility. We associate cooing doves with peace and pecking ravens with death, but these are associations, not equations.

A symbol isn't just a sign with one specific meaning. The picture of a cigarette in a circle with a line drawn diagonally through it is a sign meaning, precisely and specifically, "No Smoking." The white whale, on the other hand, doesn't mean, precisely and specifically, "the mystery of evil." Instead, the associations suggested by the writer, made by the characters in the story, and ultimately made by the reader evoke images of evil (and perhaps other elements), suggest aspects of the darker side of life, and hint at possible ways of seeing and thinking about the events portrayed.

> That is how symbols work—by association.

Symbols invite the reader to participate in making sense of the text by building on the associations and connections that the symbols suggest.

Reaching All Students

Struggling Readers
Suggest that students pause when they think they recognize a symbol in a piece of literature but are unsure of its meaning. They can use free association to list the ideas and emotional responses they associate with the symbolic object. Suggest that students evaluate their responses. Do any of these responses make sense in the context of the literature?

English Language Learners
Because students with limited English skills may not have command of the connotations of words, they may have difficulty with verbal symbols. These students may also lack the familiarity with Western culture that would enable them to readily recognize public symbols. Spend extra time to help these students discuss symbols that appear in selections. You might also acquaint students with a dictionary of symbols.

Advanced Learners
Tell students that the Symbolists were a group of poets who were influenced by Edgar Allan Poe and Charles Baudelaire. The Symbolists believed that the ultimate purpose of art was to express personal emotions. To accomplish this, they relied upon dense and often very private symbols and metaphors. Invite students to read and interpret poems by Mallarmé, Verlaine, or Rimbaud.

by John Leggett

Is It a Symbol?

However, you must be careful not to start looking for symbols in everything you read: They won't be there. Here are some guidelines to follow when you sense that a story is operating on a symbolic level:

1. Symbols are often visual.

2. When some event or object or setting is used as a symbol in a story, you will usually find that the writer has given it a great deal of emphasis. Often it reappears throughout the story. In a story called "The Scarlet Ibis" by James Hurst, a rare bird dies because it has strayed out of its natural tropical setting. The scarlet ibis, which symbolizes the special delicacy and beauty of the narrator's younger brother, is mentioned many times in the story and even is used as the title.

3. A symbol in literature is a form of **figurative language**. Like a metaphor, a symbol is something that is identified with something else that is *very different* from it but that shares some quality. When you are thinking about whether

"I don't know. What do you think it is?"
Reprinted from The Saturday Evening Post.

something is used symbolically, ask yourself this: Does this item also stand for something essentially different from itself? Think of "The Scarlet Ibis" again. The beautiful, fragile ibis functions as a real bird in the story (it actually falls into the family's yard), but it also functions as a symbol of the frail, little boy and his unusual nature.

4. A symbol usually has something to do with a story's **theme**. When we think about the ibis, we realize that the death of the exotic bird points to the fact that the little brother also died because he could not survive in a world in which he was an outsider.

Why Use Symbols?

Why do writers use symbols? Why don't they just come out

and tell us directly what they want to say?

One answer is that people are born symbol makers. It seems to be part of our nature. Even in the earliest paintings and writings, we find symbols. Think of all those mysterious markings on the walls of caves. Think of the owl used in ancient Greek art to symbolize the great goddess of wisdom, Athena. Think of our language itself, which uses sounds to symbolize certain abstract and concrete things in the world.

In some sense, we never fully exhaust the significance of the great symbols. For example, critics have written whole books to explain *Moby-Dick,* yet probably no one is certain that the meaning of that white whale has been fully explored.

You may not be able to articulate fully what a symbol means. But you will find that the symbol, if it is powerful and well chosen, will speak forcefully to your emotions and to your imagination. You may also find that you will remember and think about the symbol long after you have forgotten other parts of the story's plot.

ELEMENTS OF LITERATURE: SYMBOLS **307**

(Continued from p. T306)

- Divide students into groups of three or four to discuss and provide answers to the following questions:

1. What do the beach and the wild bay symbolize to Jerry in "Through the Tunnel"? [beach—safety, childhood; bay—danger, adulthood]

2. What does the tunnel symbolize in the same story? [the passage from childhood to adulthood]

3. What two things might the vein of gold represent to Wetherton in the "Trap of Gold"? [Sample responses: security, greed.]

4. What symbols can you think of to represent yourself? Make sure you can fully explain why this object represents you—or a part of you. [Reponses will vary.]

Applying the Element

Edgar Allan Poe uses many symbols to build up layers of meaning in "The Pit and the Pendulum."

- Invite students to work individually to review "The Pit and the Pendulum" and to list all the symbols they can find. Then have them work in pairs to compare and evaluate their lists. Have them apply John Leggett's guidelines for identifying symbols and produce a final list of symbols.

- Have paired students interpret the symbols on their list and explain how the symbols contribute to the meaning of the story. Encourage them to consider whether the symbols create a story within the story. Have students share their symbolic interpretations in a class discussion.

Resources —————

Assessment
Formal Assessment
- Literary Elements Test, p. 52

Using Students' Strengths

Visual Learners

Explain to students that some European families once had coats of arms that symbolized the qualities or experiences for which the family wanted to be recognized. Have students design a coat of arms for their family. Students might divide the shield into several parts, each part representing a particular trait or quality. Allow student volunteers to explain their family shields to the rest of the class.

Auditory/Musical Learners

Invite students to choose music that symbolizes who they are. Encourage students to choose an instrumental passage (rather than one with lyrics) to represent themselves. Offer them the opportunity to share and explain the significance of their selections.

1. Read and interpret the story
2. Identify third-person limited point of view
3. Compare and contrast themes
4. Express understanding through writing or drawing
5. Identify and use vivid verbs
6. Understand and use new words
7. Use word mapping

SKILLS

Literary
- Identify and analyze the third-person limited point of view

Reading
- Compare and contrast themes

Writing
- Write an evaluation statement
- Write a description to reveal character
- Write an opinion
- Write a scene for the story

Grammar/Language
- Use vivid verbs

Vocabulary
- Use new words

Art
- Draw a description to reveal character

Viewing/Representing
- Describe a memory (ATE)
- Write and perform a dialogue (ATE)
- Compare paintings (ATE)
- Compare the mood in ads with the mood in a painting (ATE)

Planning

- **Block Schedule**
  Block Scheduling Lesson Plans with Pacing Guide

- **Traditional Schedule**
  Lesson Plans Including Strategies for English-Language Learners

- **One-Stop Planner**
  CD-ROM with Test Generator

Before You Read

WITH ALL FLAGS FLYING

Make the Connection

I Did It My Way

Old age is different from what it used to be. Years ago older people tended to stay with their adult children. Below are some generalizations about old age. Talk about them with a partner. Do you share these opinions?

- Older people have lost their interest in adventure.

- Most older people prefer to live with their families.

- The worst thing about old age is failing health.

- Older people do not want someone else to make decisions for them.

Quickwrite

Take notes on your talk with your partner, and record your thoughts on this subject of old age.

go.hrw.com
LEO 10-4

Elements of Literature

Third-Person Limited Point of View

Like the omniscient narrator, the narrator of a story written from the **third-person limited point of view** stands outside the action and refers to all the characters by name or as "he" or "she." Unlike the omniscient narrator, however, this narrator zooms in on the thoughts, actions, and feelings of only *one* character. We almost never know what the other people are thinking. This point of view is popular with modern writers because it combines the possibilities of the omniscient point of view with the intense, personal focus of first-person narration.

> **A** story told from the **third-person limited point of view** focuses on the experiences and thoughts of one character.
>
> *For more on Point of View, see pages 262–263 and the Handbook of Literary Terms.*

Reading Skills and Strategies

Comparing and Contrasting Themes

The **theme** is the central idea or insight in a literary work. When you read works about similar subjects, you can **compare and contrast** their themes by looking for similarities and differences in the views of life they present. Each of the following two selections—the story, "With All Flags Flying," and the *Connections* poem, "Señora X No More"—presents a view of independence. Consider what these views have in common and how they differ.

Frank Murphy and His Family (1980) by Catherine Murphy. Oil on canvas.

Courtesy Lennon Weinberg, Inc., New York.

Preteaching Vocabulary

Words to Own

Have students work in pairs to review the Words to Own, which appear at the bottom of the selection pages. Have one student give the definition and the other identify the word and provide a sample sentence. Then have them change roles. Finally, have them look up the etymologies of *telescoped* and *chronic* and answer the following questions based on these etymologies.

1. How might events in a story, play, movie, or TV show be *telescoped*? [Possible response: Events that occurred in the past are brought quickly forward and condensed into one scene or image.]

2. What is the difference between a *chronic* illness (such as earaches and arthritis) and one that is not chronic (such as mumps)? [Chronic illnesses keep occurring over a long period of time, whereas illnesses that are not chronic occur only once in a while.]

*He had chosen long ago what kind of old
age he would have . . .*

With All Flags Flying

Anne Tyler

309

Summary ▪ ▪

Because of declining health, Mr. Carpenter, a fiercely independent eighty-two-year-old widower, decides he can no longer live alone. He locks his house and goes to his daughter's home with plans to enter a nursing home. His whole family urges him to remain with them, but not wanting to be a burden, he remains adamant in his plans. At the nursing home, Mr. Carpenter expresses pride in not being a burden and in not weakly craving his family's love. His new roommate asks why Mr. Carpenter worries about being a burden if he does not long for love.

RESPONDING TO THE ART

Catherine Murphy (1946–   ) paints in a realist and sometimes super realist style. In her recent work, she paints found objects and scenes, focusing on the surfaces and how the surface reflects the passage of time.

Activity. Ask students to describe a memory that this painting reminds them of. You might have students write and perform a dialogue between the people in the painting. Ask students to compare this portrait with Florence Flo Oy Wong's family drawing, *Mom, Pop, Me* on p. 102.

Ⓐ Appreciating Language
Idioms

Point out that the story's title is also a naval expression. It alludes to a situation in which the commander of a ship under attack refuses to signify surrender by furling the ship's flags. Instead, the ship would hold its position "with all flags flying."

Resources: Print and Media

Reading
- *Graphic Organizers for Active Reading*, p. 20
- *Words to Own*, p. 20
- *Audio CD Library*
  Disc 10, Track 2

Writing and Language
- *Daily Oral Grammar*
  Transparency 20
- *Grammar and Language Links*
  Worksheet, p. 37
- *Language Workshop CD-ROM*

Viewing and Representing
- *Viewing and Representing*
  Fine Art Transparency 7
  Fine Art Worksheet, p. 28

Assessment
- *Formal Assessment*, p. 48
- *Portfolio Management System*, p. 126
- *Test Generator (One-Stop Planner CD-ROM)*

Internet
- go.hrw.com (keyword: *LEO 10-4*)

Listening
Audio CD Library
A reading of the story appears in the *Audio CD Library:*
- Disc 10, Track 2

Viewing and Representing
Fine Art Transparency
A fine art transparency of Philomé Obin's *Autoportrait* might be used as a postreading writing prompt.
- Transparency 7
- Worksheet, p. 28

RESPONDING TO THE ART

The American artist **Tom Blackwell** (1938–) uses images of everyday objects to show the fragility of nature and the power of urban society. He often prepares his canvases by covering them with a dark undercoat of paint, over which he applies light colors. This painting is an example of super realism, a genre in the visual arts in which objects are rendered so realistically that they appear as clearly as an image in a photograph.
Activity. Have students bring in newspaper or magazine advertisements for motorcycles and ask them to compare the mood in the ads with the mood in this painting.

Ⓐ Critical Thinking
Interpreting
❓ How might bones seem watery? What does this description suggest about the way the man feels? [Sample answer: His bones might feel too limp to support him, as if they were filled with water rather than marrow. The description suggests that the man feels weak.]

Gary's Chopper (1972) by Tom Blackwell. Oil on canvas.
Courtesy Louis K. Meisel Gallery, New York.

Ⓦeakness was what got him in the end. He had been expecting something more definite—chest pains, a stroke, arthritis—but it was only weakness that put a finish to his living alone. A numbness in his head, an airy feeling when he walked. A wateriness in his bones that made it an effort to pick up his coffee cup in the morning. He waited some days for it to go away, but it never did. And meanwhile the dust piled up in corners; the refrigerator wheezed and creaked for want of defrosting. Weeds grew around his rosebushes.

He was awake and dressed at six o'clock on a Saturday morning, with the patchwork quilt pulled up neatly over the mattress. From the kitchen cabinet he took a hunk of bread and two Fig Newtons, which he dropped into a paper bag. He was wearing a brown suit that he had bought on sale in 1944, a white T-shirt, and copper-toed work boots. Those and his other set of underwear, which he put in the paper bag along with a razor, were all the clothes he took with him. Then he rolled down the top of the bag and stuck it under his arm, and stood in the middle of the kitchen, staring around him for a moment.

The house had only two rooms, but he owned it—the last scrap of the farm that he had

310 THE SHORT-STORY COLLECTIONS

Reaching All Students

Struggling Readers
Students can take advantage of the stops in the story to summarize what they've just read. Each time students read the end of a section, have them create as much of a Somebody Wanted But So chart as possible. For more information on this strategy, see the *Reading Strategies Handbook,* p. 111 in the *Reading Skills and Strategies* binder.

English Language Learners
Explain some of the phrases on pp. 310 and 311, including "Fig Newtons" (p. 310), "patchwork quilt" (p. 310), "hollow" (p. 311—meaning "a small sheltered valley"), "sticks of furniture" (p. 311—meaning "unadorned, simple, spare pieces of furniture"), "Whereabouts did you plan on going?" (p. 311—meaning "Where are you going?"), and "I'll drop you off" (p. 311—meaning "I'll stop and let you off at your destination").

Advanced Learners
Have students think about the title and look at the illustrations in the story. Then ask them to read the first two paragraphs of the selection. Based on these clues, challenge them to write a prediction of what the main character will do—or what will happen to him.

sold off years ago. It stood in a hollow of dying trees beside a superhighway in Baltimore County. All it held was a few sticks of furniture, a change of clothes, a skillet, and a set of dishes. Also odds and ends, which disturbed him. If his inventory was complete, he would have to include six clothespins, a salt and a pepper shaker, a broken-toothed comb, a cheap ball-point pen—oh, on and on, past logical numbers. Why should he be so cluttered? He was eighty-two years old. He had grown from an infant owning nothing to a family man with a wife, five children, everyday and Sunday china, and a thousand appurtenances,° down at last to solitary old age and the bare essentials again, but not bare enough to suit him. Only what he needed surrounded him. Was it possible he needed so much?

Now he had the brown paper bag; that was all. It was the one satisfaction in a day he had been dreading for years.

He left the house without another glance, heading up the steep bank toward the superhighway. The bank was covered with small, crawling weeds planted especially by young men with scientific training in how to prevent soil erosion. Twice his knees buckled. He had to sit and rest, bracing himself against the slope of the bank. The scientific weeds, seen from close up, looked straggly and gnarled. He sifted dry earth through his fingers without thinking, concentrating only on steadying his breath and calming the twitching muscles in his legs.

Once on the superhighway, which was fairly level, he could walk for longer stretches of time. He kept his head down and his fingers clenched tight upon the paper bag, which was growing limp and damp now. Sweat rolled down the back of his neck, fell in drops from his temples. When he had been walking maybe half an hour, he had to sit down again for a rest. A black motorcycle buzzed up from behind and stopped a few feet away from him. The driver was young and shabby, with hair so long that it drizzled out beneath the back of his helmet.

°**appurtenances:** items that go with other things but are not strictly necessary.

"Give you a lift, if you like," he said. "You going somewhere?"

"Just into Baltimore."

"Hop on."

He shifted the paper bag to the space beneath his arm, put on the white helmet he was handed, and climbed on behind the driver. For safety he took a clutch of the boy's shirt, tightly at first, and then more loosely when he saw there was no danger. Except for the helmet, he was perfectly comfortable. He felt his face cooling and stiffening in the wind, his body learning to lean gracefully with the tilt of the motorcycle as it swooped from lane to lane. It was a fine way to spend his last free day.

Half an hour later they were on the outskirts of Baltimore, stopped at the first traffic light. The boy turned his head and shouted, "Whereabouts did you plan on going?"

"I'm visiting my daughter, on Belvedere near Charles Street."

"I'll drop you off, then," the boy said. "I'm passing right by there."

The light changed, the motor roared. Now that they were in traffic, he felt more conspicuous, but not in a bad way. People in their automobiles seemed sealed in, overprotected; men in large trucks must envy the way the motorcycle looped in and out, hornetlike, stripped to the bare essentials of a motor and two wheels. By tugs at the boy's shirt and single words shouted into the wind, he directed him to his daughter's house, but he was sorry to have the ride over so quickly.

His daughter had married a salesman and lived in a plain, square stone house that the old man approved of. There were sneakers and a football in the front yard, signs of a large, happy family. A bicycle lay in the driveway. The motorcycle stopped just inches from it. "Here we are," the boy said.

"Well, I surely do thank you."

He climbed off, fearing for one second that his legs would give way beneath him and spoil everything that had gone before. But no, they held steady. He took off the helmet and handed

WITH ALL FLAGS FLYING **311**

B **Critical Thinking**
Making Connections
? How does the man's view of material possessions compare to your own? [Most students will not relate to the man's attitude, but some may admire his Spartan approach.]

C **Reading Skills and Strategies**
Responding to the Text
? What is unexpected about the behavior of the motorcyclist and the elderly man? [The motorcyclist offers a ride to the elderly man, and the man accepts and enjoys it.]

D **Elements of Literature**
Third-Person Limited Point of View
? How does this passage demonstrate the author's use of the third-person limited point of view? [The narrator is not in the story but knows what the man is thinking and feeling. However, the narrator provides no information about the younger man's thoughts and feelings.]

Crossing the Curriculum

Health
Have students research and give reports on the care of older people in their community. You may wish to encourage students to interview people who are knowledgeable in this field, such as public and private social workers, nursing home administrators, doctors, and other caregivers. Students can then incorporate some of the information from the interviews into their reports. Encourage students to present graphs or charts of any statistical information they gather.

Social Studies
The population of the United States is becoming steadily older, with a growing portion of the total population in the over-65 age group. Challenge interested students to investigate the consequences of the aging of the American population. How will this condition affect students as they enter the work force and begin to raise families? You might share the following data.

- In 1996, 12.8 percent of the population, or 33.9 million adults, were 65 and older.
- At 65, people can expect to live an additional 17.7 years.
- In 2030, 20 percent of the population, or 70 million adults, will be 65 and older.

it to the boy, who waved and roared off. It was a really magnificent roar, ear-dazzling. He turned toward the house, beaming in spite of himself, with his head feeling cool and light now that the helmet was gone. And there was his daughter on the front porch, laughing. "Daddy, what on *earth*?" she said. "Have you turned into a teeny-bopper?" Whatever that was. She came rushing down the steps to hug him—a plump, happy-looking woman in an apron. She was getting on toward fifty now. Her hands were like her mother's, swollen and veined. Gray had started dusting her hair.

"You never *told* us," she said. "Did you ride all this way on a motorcycle? Oh, why didn't you find a telephone and call? I would have come. How long can you stay for?"

"Now . . ." he said, starting toward the house. He was thinking of the best way to put it. "I came to a decision. I won't be living alone anymore. I want to go to an old folks' home. That's what I *want*," he said, stopping on the grass so she would be sure to get it clear. "I don't want to live with you—I want an old folks' home." Then he was afraid he had worded it too strongly. "It's nice *visiting* you, of course," he said.

"Why, Daddy, you know we always asked you to come and live with us."

"I know that, but I decided on an old folks' home."

"We couldn't do that. We won't even talk about it."

"Clara, my mind is made up."

Then in the doorway a new thought hit her, and she suddenly turned around. "Are you sick?" she said. "You always said you would live alone as long as health allowed."

"I'm not up to that anymore," he said.

"What is it? Are you having some kind of pain?"

"I just decided, that's all," he said. "What I *will* rely on you for is the arrangements with the home. I know it's a trouble."

"We'll talk about that later," Clara said. And she firmed the corners of her mouth exactly the way her mother used to do when she hadn't won an argument but wasn't planning to lose it yet either.

In the kitchen he had a glass of milk, good and cold, and the hunk of bread and the two Fig Newtons from his paper bag. Clara wanted to make him a big breakfast, but there was no sense wasting what he had brought. He munched on the dry bread and washed it down with milk, meanwhile staring at the Fig Newtons, which lay on the smoothed-out bag. They were the worse for their ride—squashed and pathetic looking, the edges worn down and crumbling. They seemed to have come from somewhere long ago and far away. "Here, now, we've got cookies I baked only yesterday," Clara said; but he said, "No, no," and ate the Fig Newtons, whose warmth on his tongue filled him with a vague, sad feeling deeper than homesickness. "In my house," he said, "I left things a little messy. I hate to ask it of you, but I didn't manage to straighten up any."

"Don't even think about it," Clara said. "I'll take out a suitcase tomorrow and clean everything up. I'll bring it all back."

"I don't want it. Take it to the poor people."

"Don't want any of it? But, Daddy——"

He didn't try explaining it to her. He finished his lunch in silence and then let her lead him upstairs to the guest room.

Clara had five boys and a girl, the oldest twenty. During the morning as they passed one by one through the house on their way to other places, they heard of his arrival and trooped up to see him. They were fine children, all of them, but it was the girl he enjoyed the most. Francie. She was only thirteen, too young yet to know how to hide what she felt. And what she felt was always about love, it seemed: whom she just loved, who she hoped loved her back. Who was just a darling. Had thirteen-year-olds been so aware of love in the old days? He didn't know and didn't care; all he had to do with Francie was sit smiling in an armchair and listen. There was a new boy in the neighborhood who walked his English sheep dog past her yard every morning, looking toward her house. Was it because of her, or did the dog just like to go that way? When he telephoned her brother Donnie, was he hoping for her to answer? And when she did answer, did he want her to talk a

---

Using Students' Strengths

Verbal Learners

Explain to students that loaded words are words that contain strong emotional connotations. Anne Tyler uses them effectively to convey the emotions of the man in the story. As students read, have them identify and list these loaded words, using a chart like the one shown to record their results. In the first column, they should write the loaded words. In the second column, they should write the attitude or emotions the word conveys.

"Loaded" word	Attitude or Emotion
dreaded	fear
wince	discomfort

Auditory/Musical Learners

Have students listen to songs that relate to the themes of aging, change, transitions, and breakthroughs in life. As a starting point, you may want to play a recording of the Beatles' "Eleanor Rigby" or "She's Leaving Home," or Simon and Garfunkel's "Old Friends." Ask students to bring recordings of other songs that relate to these themes. Have them compare and contrast the messages in the songs with those of the story.

minute or to hand the receiver straight to Donnie? But what would she say to him, anyway? Oh, all her questions had to do with where she might find love, and everything she said made the old man wince and love her more. She left in the middle of a sentence, knocking against a doorknob as she flew from the room, an unlovable-looking tangle of blond hair and braces and scrapes and Band-Aids. After she was gone, the room seemed too empty, as if she had accidentally torn part of it away in her flight.

Getting into an old folks' home was hard. Not only because of lack of good homes, high expenses, waiting lists; it was harder yet to talk his family into letting him go. His son-in-law argued with him every evening, his round, kind face anxious and questioning across the supper table. "Is it that you think you're not welcome here? You are, you know. You were one of the reasons we bought this big house." His grandchildren, when they talked to him, had a kind of urgency in their voices, as if they were trying to impress him with their acceptance of him. His other daughters called long-distance from all across the country and begged him to come to them if he wouldn't stay with Clara. They had room, or they would make room; he had no idea what homes for the aged were like these days. To all of them he gave the same answer: "I've made my decision." He was proud of them for asking, though. All his children had turned out so well, every last one of them. They were good, strong women with happy families, and they had never given him a moment's worry. He was luckier than he had a right to be. He had felt lucky all his life, dangerously lucky, cursed by luck; it had seemed some disaster must be waiting to even things up. But the luck had held. When his wife died, it was at a late age, sparing her the pain she would have had to face, and his life had continued in its steady, reasonable pattern with no more sorrow than any other man's. His final lot was to weaken, to crumble, and to die—only a secret disaster, not the one he had been expecting.

He walked two blocks daily, fighting off the weakness. He shelled peas for Clara and mended little household articles, which gave him an excuse to sit. Nobody noticed how he arranged to climb the stairs only once a day, at bedtime. When he had empty time, he chose a chair without rockers, one that would not be a symbol of age and weariness and lack of work. He rose every morning at six and stayed in his room a full hour, giving his legs enough warning to face the day ahead. Never once did he disgrace himself by falling down in front of people. He dropped nothing more important than a spoon or a fork.

Meanwhile the wheels were turning; his name was on a waiting list. Not that that meant anything, Clara said. "When it comes right down to driving you out there, I just won't let you go," she told him. "But I'm hoping you won't carry things that far. Daddy, won't you put a stop to this foolishness?"

He hardly listened. He had chosen long ago what kind of old age he would have; everyone does. Most, he thought, were weak and chose to be loved at any cost. He had seen women turn soft and sad, anxious to please, and had watched with pity and impatience their losing battles. And he had once known a schoolteacher, no weakling at all, who said straight out that when she grew old, she would finally eat all she wanted and grow fat without worry. He admired that—a simple plan, dependent upon no one. "I'll sit in an armchair," she had said, "with a ladies' magazine in my lap and a box of homemade fudge on the lamp stand. I'll get as fat as I like and nobody will give a hang." The schoolteacher was thin and pale, with a kind of stooped, sloping figure that was popular at the time. He had lost track of her long ago, but he liked to think that she had kept her word. He imagined her fifty years later, cozy and fat in a puffy chair, with one hand moving constantly between her mouth and the candy plate. If she had died young or changed her mind or put off her eating till another decade, he didn't want to hear about it.

WITH ALL FLAGS FLYING **313**

E Reading Skills and Strategies
Making Inferences
? Why do you think the man winces?
[Possible responses: He finds it hard to relate to Francie's teenage concerns, yet he feels genuine love and concern for her; he feels the conflict of love for Francie at a time when he is trying to disentangle himself from his family; he believes that Francie's attitude leaves her open to being hurt.]

F Critical Thinking
Analyzing Character
Perhaps the man's lifelong good luck explains his fear of needing other people. Unlike those who have experienced disasters or whose children have needed their help, he has not had a chance to learn that need does not necessarily destroy love.

G Reading Skills and Strategies
Comparing and Contrasting Themes
The man is working hard to maintain his image as an independent person who does not need softness or love from his family. Encourage students to compare and contrast this theme with the theme of another story, movie, or television show with which they are familiar. Encourage students to describe how the main characters and themes are alike and different.

H English Language Learners
Interpreting Idioms
Identify the phrase "the wheels were turning" as an idiom and explain that it means that actions were being taken.

I Advanced Learners
? How might the man, too, be seen as choosing "to be loved at any cost"?
[Sample answer: The man's cost is different from that of the "soft and sad" and "anxious to please." He may feel that his family will stop loving him if he becomes a burden to them, so he is willing to deny his need for them—to go to a nursing home—to retain their love.]

Taking a Second Look

Review: Making Generalizations
Remind students that a generalization is a type of inference in which readers combine information in the text with what they already know to make a judgment that goes beyond the text. It is a general statement based on specific facts. For example, based on the actions of the man's family and on personal experience, someone could make the generalization that families usually want their older relatives to live with them.

Activities
1. After students read "With All Flags Flying," have them make generalizations about how American families deal with the issue of aging parents. Have them cite data and experience on which they base their generalizations.
2. Have groups discuss these questions: How are generalizations useful? What are the dangers of making generalizations?

He had chosen independence. Nothing else had even occurred to him. He had lived to himself, existed on less money than his family would ever guess, raised his own vegetables, and refused all gifts but an occasional tin of coffee. And now he would sign himself into the old folks' home and enter on his own two feet, relying on the impersonal care of nurses and cleaning women. He could have chosen to die alone of neglect, but for his daughters that would have been a burden too—a different kind of burden, much worse. He was sensible enough to see that.

Meanwhile, all he had to do was to look as busy as possible in a chair without rockers and hold fast against his family. Oh, they gave him no peace. Some of their attacks were obvious—the arguments with his son-in-law over the supper table—and some were subtle; you had to be on your guard every minute for those. Francie, for instance, asking him questions about what she called the "olden days." Inviting him to sink unnoticing into doddering reminiscence. "Did I see Granny ever? I don't remember her. Did she like me? What kind of person was she?" He stood his ground, gave monosyllabic answers. It was easier than he had expected. For him, middle age tempted up more memories. Nowadays events had telescoped. The separate agonies and worries—the long, hard births of each of his children, the youngest daughter's chronic childhood earaches, his wife's last illness—were smoothed now into a single, summing-up sentence: He was a widowed farmer with five daughters, all married, twenty grandchildren, and three great-grandchildren. "Your grandmother was a fine woman," he told Francie; "just fine." Then he shut up.

Francie, not knowing that she had been spared, sulked and peeled a strip of sunburned skin from her nose.

Clara cried all the way to the home. She was the one who was driving; it made him nervous. One of her hands on the steering wheel held a balled-up tissue, which she had stopped using. She let tears run unchecked down her face and drove jerkily, with a great deal of brake slamming and gear gnashing.

"Clara, I wish you wouldn't take on so," he told her. "There's no need to be sad over *me*."

"I'm not sad so much as mad," Clara said. "I feel like this is something you're doing *to* me, just throwing away what I give. Oh, why do you have to be so stubborn? It's still not too late to change your mind."

The old man kept silent. On his right sat Francie, chewing a thumbnail and scowling out the window, her usual self except for the unexplainable presence of her other hand in his, tight as wire. Periodically she muttered a number; she was counting red convertibles and had been for days. When she reached a hundred, the next boy she saw would be her true love.

He figured that was probably the reason she had come on this trip—a greater exposure to red convertibles.

Whatever happened to DeSotos? Didn't there used to be a car called a roadster?

They parked in the U-shaped driveway in front of the home, under the shade of a poplar tree. If he had had his way, he would have arrived by motorcycle, but he made the best of it—picked up his underwear sack from between his feet, climbed the front steps ramrod straight. They were met by a smiling woman in blue who had to check his name on a file and ask more questions. He made sure to give all the answers himself, overriding Clara when necessary. Meanwhile Francie spun on one squeaky sneaker heel and examined the hall, a cavernous, polished square with old-fashioned parlors on either side of it. A few old people were on the plush couches, and a nurse sat idle beside a lady in a wheelchair.

They went up a creaking elevator to the second floor and down a long, dark corridor deadened by carpeting. The lady in blue, still carry-

---

WORDS TO OWN
telescoped (tel′ə·skōpt′) v.: slid or collapsed into one another, like the sections of a collapsible telescope.
chronic (krän′ik) adj.: constant; lasting a long time or recurring often.

---

ing a sheaf of files, knocked at number 213. Then she flung the door open on a narrow green room flooded with sunlight.

"Mr. Pond," she said, "this is Mr. Carpenter. I hope you'll get on well together."

Mr. Pond was one of those men who run to fat and baldness in old age. He sat in a rocking chair with a gilt-edged Bible on his knees.

"How-do," he said. "Mighty nice to meet you."

They shook hands cautiously, with the women ringing them like mothers asking their children to play nicely with each other. "Ordinarily I sleep in the bed by the window," said Mr. Pond, "but I don't hold it in much importance. You can take your pick."

"Anything will do," the old man said.

Clara was dry-eyed now. She looked frightened.

"You'd best be getting on back now," he told her. "Don't you worry about me. I'll let you know," he said, suddenly generous now that he had won, "if there is anything I need."

Clara nodded and kissed his cheek. Francie kept her face turned away, but she hugged him tightly, and then she looked up at him as she stepped back. Her eyebrows were tilted as if she were about to ask him one of her questions. Was it her the boy with the sheep dog came for? Did he care when she answered the telephone?

They left, shutting the door with a gentle click. The old man made a great business out of settling his underwear and razor in a bureau drawer, smoothing out the paper bag and folding it, placing it in the next drawer down.

"Didn't bring much," said Mr. Pond, one thumb marking his page in the Bible.

"I don't need much."

"Go on—take the bed by the window. You'll feel better after a while."

"I *wanted* to come," the old man said.

"That there window is a front one. If you look out, you can see your folks leave."

He slid between the bed and the window and looked out. No reason not to. Clara and Francie were just climbing into the car, the sun lacquering the tops of their heads. Clara was blowing her nose with a dot of tissue.

"*Now* they cry," said Mr. Pond, although he had not risen to look out himself. "Later they'll buy themselves a milkshake to celebrate."

"I wanted to come. I made them bring me."

"And so they did. *I* didn't want to come. My son wanted to put me here—his wife was expecting. And so he did. It all works out the same in the end."

"Well, I could have stayed with one of my daughters," the old man said, "but I'm not like some I have known. Hanging around making burdens of themselves, hoping to be loved. Not me."

"If you don't care about being loved," said Mr. Pond, "how come it would bother you to be a burden?"

Then he opened the Bible again, at the place where his thumb had been all the time, and went back to reading.

The old man sat on the edge of the bed, watching the tail of Clara's car flash as sharp and hard as a jewel around the bend of the road. Then, with nobody to watch that mattered, he let his shoulders slump and eased himself out of his suit coat, which he folded over the foot of the bed. He slid his suspenders down and let them dangle at his waist. He took off his copper-toed work boots and set them on the floor neatly side by side. And although it was only noon, he lay down full-length on top of the bedspread. Whiskery lines ran across the plaster of the ceiling high above him. There was a crackling sound in the mattress when he moved; it must be covered with something waterproof.

The tiredness in his head was as vague and restless as anger; the weakness in his knees made him feel as if he had just finished some exhausting exercise. He lay watching the plaster cracks settle themselves into pictures, listening to the silent, neuter voice in his mind form the words he had grown accustomed to hearing now: Let me not give in at the end. Let me continue gracefully till the moment of my defeat. Let Lollie Simpson be alive somewhere even as I lie on my bed; let her be eating homemade fudge in an overstuffed armchair and growing fatter and fatter and fatter.

F Critical Thinking
Expressing an Opinion
? Do you think the man is right about the questions Francie seems ready to ask? Explain. [Sample answer: No, she may want to ask if he will change his mind. He misjudges her intent in order to protect himself from feeling her love.]

G Reading Skills and Strategies
Comparing and Contrasting Themes
? What connection is Mr. Pond making between being loved and being a burden? [Possible responses: Someone who did not want to be loved would not worry about being a burden to others; people who want love from others should not be afraid to express their need for love or for help.]

H Struggling Readers
Pronoun Antecedents
? Since both Mr. Pond and Mr. Carpenter are present in this scene, readers must be attentive to clarifying pronoun antecedents. What is the antecedent of *he* in the clause "he opened the Bible again"? [Mr. Pond] Who lets "his shoulders slump" in the following paragraph? [Mr. Carpenter]

Resources
Selection Assessment
Formal Assessment
• Selection Test, p. 48
Test Generator (One-Stop Planner)
• CD-ROM

Making the Connections

Connecting to the Theme: "Breakthroughs"
When students have finished reading the selection, guide a discussion of how it relates to the theme of this collection. You may want to emphasize that the story illustrates that not all breakthroughs are positive or truly desirable. In the face of his weakening physical condition, Mr. Carpenter wishes to remain independent of his family's loving care. He makes a breakthrough by making the transition from his own home to a nursing home. Yet he misses a potential breakthrough into the warmth of his own family's love.

Cultural Connections: The Elderly
If your class is culturally diverse, you may wish to have student volunteers discuss the ways in which older people are regarded and treated in their original cultures. If this is not practical in your class, have students choose a culture and research and report on how the elderly are treated by society and within the family in that culture.

MEET THE WRITER

Still Just Writing

One time a friend made the mistake of asking **Anne Tyler** (1941–   ), "Have you found work yet? Or are you still just writing?"

Anne Tyler was born in a Quaker community in Minneapolis, Minnesota, and grew up in Raleigh, North Carolina. She graduated from high school at sixteen and from Duke University at nineteen. Her first novel, written when she was twenty-two, has been followed by a steady stream of other novels and stories.

Anne Tyler's perceptions about the lives of ordinary people have won her widespread praise. One critic sees a kind of innocence in her view of life, a sense of wonder at all the crazy things in the world, and an abiding affection for her own flaky characters.

Some of Tyler's popular novels include *Dinner at the Homesick Restaurant* (1982); *The Accidental Tourist* (1985), which was made into a movie; *Breathing Lessons* (1988), which won a Pulitzer Prize; *Saint Maybe* (1991); and *A Patchwork Planet* (1998).

Here is an excerpt from an essay by Anne Tyler, written in response to that friend's question about her writing. Titled "Still Just Writing," the essay examines her life as a writer:

66 I think I was born with the impression that what happened in books was much more reasonable, and interesting, and *real,* in some ways, than what happened in life. I hated childhood and spent it sitting behind a book waiting for adulthood to arrive. When I ran out of books, I made up my own. At night, when I couldn't sleep, I made up stories in the dark. Most of my plots involved girls going

west in covered wagons. I was truly furious that I'd been born too late to go west in a covered wagon. . . .

I spent my adolescence planning to be an artist, not a writer. After all, books had to be about major events, and none had ever happened to me. All I knew were tobacco workers stringing the leaves I handed them and talking up a storm. Then I found a book of Eudora Welty's short stories in the high school library. She was writing about Edna Earle, who was so slow-witted she could sit all day just pondering how the tail of the *C* got through the loop of the *L* on the Coca-Cola sign. Why, I knew Edna Earle. You mean you could *write* about such people? I have always meant to send Eudora Welty a thank-you note, but I imagine she would find it a little strange. . . . 99

Señora X No More

Pat Mora

Straight as a nun I sit.
My fingers foolish before paper and pen
hide in my palms. I hear the slow, accented echo
　　　How are yu? I ahm fine. How are yu?
5　of the other women who clutch notebooks
and blush at their stiff lips resisting
sounds that float gracefully as
bubbles from their children's mouths.
My teacher bends over me, gently squeezes
10　my shoulders, the squeeze I give my sons,
hands louder than words.
She slides her arms around me:
a warm shawl, lifts my left arm
onto the cold, lined paper.
15　"*Señora,* don't let it slip away," she says
and opens the ugly, soap-wrinkled fingers
of my right hand with a pen like I pry open
the lips of a stubborn grandchild.
My hand cramps around the thin hardness.
20　"Let it breathe," says this woman who knows
my hand and tongue knot, but she guides
and I dig the tip of my pen into that white.
I carve my crooked name, and again at night
until my hand and arm are sore,
25　I carve my crooked name,
my name.

WITH ALL FLAGS FLYING 317

Connections

"Señora X No More" is a poem about an immigrant woman learning to read and write. *Señora* indicates her Hispanic heritage, and *X* refers to the fact that she has always had to use an X to sign her name because she is illiterate.

Ⓐ Critical Thinking
Analyzing the Title
❓ From the title and picture, what do you think the poem will be about? [Sample answer: A Hispanic woman who never learned to write is learning to do so.]

Ⓑ Cultural Connections
❓ These lines point out some difficulties that people, especially adults, face in learning to speak a second language. Why are some words misspelled in l. 4? [to emphasize the accent of the women in the class]

Ⓒ Reading Skills and Strategies

Comparing and Contrasting Themes
❓ The theme is the central idea or insight of a literary work. How would you state the theme of this poem? [Possible theme statement: Acquiring a skill or making a change is hard work but can give a person a sense of pride and accomplishment.] **How does this theme relate to the theme of "With All Flags Flying"?** [Sample answer: The two themes are similar because both selections express the idea of making change and becoming independent. They are different because Señora X is embracing many new possibilities, while Mr. Carpenter is closing off possibilities.]

Connecting Across Texts

Connecting with "With All Flags Flying"
After students have read Pat Mora's poem, "Señora X No More," have them discuss these questions:
• What breakthrough is the subject or protagonist making?
• Why is this breakthrough necessary?
• Why is this breakthrough difficult?

Then, ask students to answer the same questions about Mr. Carpenter in "With All Flags Flying." Have students compare and contrast the protagonists in the two pieces and their approaches to making their breakthroughs. [Sample answer: Both selections involve a character who wants to be independent; however, the thrust of the independence

is in opposite directions. The poem's speaker, an immigrant, wishes to learn to write so that she can enter society as an independent person. Mr. Carpenter, on the other hand, wants to leave his family, remaining a person who does not depend on his children for help.]

MAKING MEANINGS

First Thoughts

1. Some students may feel that the man is acting selfishly; some may feel that he is acting unselfishly. Some students may admire the man's strength and independence.

Shaping Interpretations

2. Like a ship "with all flags flying," the man is proud of his independence and doesn't want to lose it.

3. Sample response: Francie reminds him of the past when his daughters were growing up. She brings out a feeling of love that he tries to hide, for fear of losing his resolve.

4. Sample response: Because he is also elderly, Mr. Pond relates to Mr. Carpenter's situation. He makes the dilemma clear by pointing out that the issue is not only about independence, but also about love.

5. To Mr. Carpenter, Lollie represents the ideal of how one should grow old. "Flying her flags" in her case means eating what she wants without worrying about consequences.

6. Possible responses: The man was able to remain independent as he imagines Lollie Simpson does, so it was a triumph for him; the man got what he wanted, but the victory was hollow.

Connecting with the Text

7. Many students will express surprise at the man's need for independence. Others will identify with his need for independence.

Extending the Text

8. The speaker in "Señora X No More" is learning English in order to be independent, but she appreciates help along the way. Mr. Carpenter in "With All Flags Flying" also values his independence, but he almost invariably spurns help. He knows that real independence is no longer possible but clings to the little he has.

Challenging the Text

9. Most students will not feel upbeat about the story. Despite his victory, the man's life seems sad, lonely, and largely hopeless.

T318

MAKING MEANINGS

First Thoughts

[connect]

1. How did you feel about the old man's decision in "With All Flags Flying"?

Shaping Interpretations

[interpret]

2. This story's **title** describes a ship proudly displaying all the flags and pennants that proclaim its national identity. How does the title relate to the old man and what he wants?

[analyze]

3. Why do you think the writer put the **character** Francie in the story? What does she bring out in the old man?

[analyze]

4. Why do you think the writer put the **character** Mr. Pond in the story? What does Mr. Pond help to make clear about the old man?

[interpret]

5. At the end of the story, the old man is thinking of Lollie Simpson eating fudge. What does Lollie represent to the old man? How does she relate to the story's **title**?

[respond]

6. Do you see the story's outcome as a victorious breakthrough for the old man or as something less triumphant and clear-cut? Explain.

Connecting with the Text

[connect]

7. Refer to the discussion about old age that you had with a partner before beginning this story. Did the story affect any of your feelings about old age? Review your opinions (see your Quickwrite notes), and see how you feel now.

Extending the Text

[compare and contrast]

8. "With All Flags Flying" and "Señora X No More" (see **Connections** on page 317) express different attitudes about independence. **Compare and contrast** the **themes,** or the views about independence, in these two works.

Challenging the Text

[connect]

9. Do you think this is an upbeat story, or did it leave you with other feelings? How do you think the writer wants you to feel at the story's end?

> **Reading Check**
>
> **a.** Why has the old man made this decision—what are his **motives**?
>
> **b.** What do his children want the old man to do?
>
> **c.** Describe the journey the old man makes to his daughter's home.
>
> **d.** What other journey does the old man make, and how does it **contrast** with the first one?

Reading Check

a. He wants to be independent rather than dependent and a burden on his family.

b. They want him to move in with one of them.

c. He begins by walking, but then he is picked up by a young motorcyclist who takes him to his daughter's house.

d. His second journey is to the retirement home. The unexpected motorcycle ride made the first journey exhilarating; the second journey with Clara and Francie is emotional and sad.

CHOICES: Building Your Portfolio

Writer's Notebook

1. Collecting Ideas for an Evaluation

Comparing works. Many reviewers, in evaluating a literary work, compare that work with another work that has a similar theme or similar characters or a similar plot. In the evaluation you'll write for the Writer's Workshop on page 328, you might want to compare the work you're writing about to some other work. The notebook page below shows notes for a comparison of the old man in Tyler's story with the father in Anderson's play *I Never Sang for My Father* (page 636).

Look back at the stories you've read, and choose one that you think has ele-ments you can compare with elements of "With All Flags Flying." List all the similarities and differences you can think of. Then, state your evaluation.

Writing or Drawing

2. Setting Can Reveal Character

On page 310, Tyler reveals something about the old man's character simply by describing his house: "The house had only two rooms, but he owned it. . . ." Reread her description, and then characterize an older person you know by describing his or her surroundings. You can use words or pictures. Be sure to include specific objects that suggest their owner's personality and way of life—as Tyler mentions six clothespins, a broken-toothed comb, and a cheap ballpoint pen.

Supporting an Opinion

3. Doing the Right Thing?

How do you feel about the old man in this story? Do you consider him heroic for wanting to end his life "with all flags flying," or do you think he has made a serious mistake in hurting his children? In a paragraph, give your opinion of the old man's actions, and elaborate with reasons *why* you feel as you do. Does he do the right thing—and for whom?

Creative Writing

4. What Are They Feeling?

When Clara drives her father to the nursing home, she says to him, "I'm not sad so much as mad . . . I feel like this is something you're doing *to* me, just throwing away what I give." Because the story is told from the **third-person limited point of view** of the old man, we know what Clara says, but we never know her thoughts. What do you imagine Clara is thinking and feeling on the way home? Would she share her feelings with Francie? For that matter, what are Francie's thoughts and feelings? Write the going-home scene. Use either the **first-person point of view,** with Clara as the narrator, or the **omniscient point of view,** and analyze what is going on with both Clara and Francie.

Characters
Tyler's "old man"
Anderson's Tom Garrison

Similarities
Both in failing health.

Differences
The old man doesn't ask his kids for anything. Garrison wants his son to take care of him.

Evaluation
I like the old man better, but Garrison is probably more realistic.

Grading Timesaver

Rubrics for each assignment appear on p. 126 in the *Portfolio Management System*.

CHOICES: Building Your Portfolio

1. **Writer's Notebook** Have students brainstorm a list of stories and poems that have similarities to "With All Flags Flying." Remind students to save their work; it might be useful when they begin the Writer's Workshop on p. 328.

2. **Writing or Drawing** Encourage students to make a cluster diagram with the person's name and the setting in the middle. Then have them complete the cluster by writing details about the setting in the surrounding circles.

3. **Supporting an Opinion** Suggest that students analyze the issue by first listing possible reasons that Mr. Carpenter's decision was the *right* one and then listing possible reasons why it was the *wrong* one.

4. **Creative Writing** Students might consider the following questions before writing their scene.
   - Are Clara's words motivated by guilt or love? Are these feelings that she would share with Francie?
   - How does Francie feel about her grandfather? Would she share these feelings with her mother?

Getting Students Involved

Cooperative Learning

Carpenter Clusters. Have the class brainstorm a list of Mr. Carpenter's character traits. Then, have students form groups of four or five to work together to produce a cluster diagram like the one shown at right. Group members might divide the traits equally among themselves and search the text for supporting evidence. Have groups rejoin the class and share their profiles.

Writing Activity

Another View. Have students select a portion of the story that reveals Mr. Carpenter's interactions with Francie. Challenge students to rewrite the section from Francie's point of view. They should write in the first-person, expressing her ideas and feelings about what is happening to her grandfather.

GRAMMAR LINK

Have students look for vivid verbs in a piece of writing from their portfolio. Suggest that they circle all verbs and choose several to replace with more precise or vivid verbs.

Try It Out
Possible Answers
1. A black motorcycle roared up from behind and stopped a few feet away from him.
2. The driver was young and shabby, with hair so long that it cascaded out beneath the back of his helmet.

VOCABULARY

Diagrams will vary. When students finish the activity, they should conclude that *telescoped* means "compressed" and *chronic* means "constant or recurring."

Resources

Language
• *Grammar and Language Links* Worksheet, p. 37

Vocabulary
• *Words to Own* Worksheet, p. 20

GRAMMAR LINK   MINI-LESSON

• Verbs Add Vigor

TYLER'S VIVID VERBS

creak
buckle
loop
munch
tear
sulk
peel
spin
flash
slump

How can you make your writing strong and vivid and inventive? One of the most influential books ever written about the art of composition gives this advice:

> Write with nouns and verbs, not with adjectives and adverbs. The adjective hasn't been built that can pull a weak or inaccurate noun out of a tight place. This is not to disparage adjectives and adverbs; they are indispensable parts of speech. . . . In general, however, it is nouns and verbs, not their assistants, that give good writing its toughness and color.
>
> —William Strunk, Jr., and E. B. White, *The Elements of Style*

Anne Tyler makes good use of verbs. For example, in the first paragraph of the story, she says, ". . . the refrigerator wheezed and creaked for want of defrosting." Consider how diluted her description would have been if she had merely said, ". . . the refrigerator made noises for want of defrosting." In the following sentences, Tyler's tough and colorful verbs are underscored.

1. "A black motorcycle <u>buzzed</u> up from behind and stopped a few feet away from him."
2. "The driver was young and shabby, with hair so long that it <u>drizzled</u> out beneath the back of his helmet."

Try It Out

➤ Rewrite each numbered sentence so that it has a similar meaning but a different tough, colorful verb.
➤ When you revise your own writing, check your verbs. If you are continually repeating verbs like *do, say,* or *go,* replace them with more specific, vivid verbs.

A tip for writers: Using too many tough, vivid verbs will result in what is called overwriting. The key is balance, and that's a skill you learn by wide reading and by practice.

VOCABULARY   HOW TO OWN A WORD

WORD BANK •

telescoped
chronic

Word Mapping: What Do You Know About a Word?

When you read a new or unfamiliar word, find out how much you know about the word. Look at the **word map** for *wheeze.* (On page 310, a refrigerator wheezed.) Make word maps for the two words in the Word Bank. You'll need to create your own questions and answers.

When do people wheeze?
• with a cold
• with asthma

wheeze

Why would a refrigerator wheeze?
• wearing out
• old
• used too much

How does a wheeze sound?
• rasping, breathy
• rattling, whistling

320 THE SHORT-STORY COLLECTIONS

Grammar Link Quick Check

Rewrite the sentences below, replacing the underlined verbs with more vivid verbs. Sample answers are provided in brackets.

1. The man <u>walked</u> slowly along the highway. [tottered]
2. The traffic <u>passed</u> by him, and the horns <u>sounded</u> in his ears. [whizzed; blared]
3. The young man on the motorcycle <u>saw</u> the older man sitting beside the road and <u>came</u> to a stop. [spotted; screeched]
4. The motorcycle <u>got</u> back onto the highway and <u>made</u> its way through the traffic. [zoomed; angled]
5. The wind <u>blew</u> past the older man's ears, and he <u>held</u> to the young man's shirt with all his might. [howled; clung]

EXTENDING *the theme*

AN AUTOBIOGRAPHY

Quickwrite

How important is a person's name? Suppose that someone suddenly took your name away, and from then on you were referred to only by a seven-digit number: 5831680. How would that affect you? Quickwrite your response in two or three sentences.

Background

At the time this account takes place, educated natives of India were expected to learn English in addition to their own native languages. (Hindi, Urdu, and Gujarati are just a few of the many languages spoken in India.) The headmistress of the type of school in the essay was white and British. Many of the students were also white and British, from families of British civil servants sent to India as colonial rulers.

The title of the essay is from William Shakespeare's *Romeo and Juliet*. Juliet is wishing that her beloved Romeo's surname, Montague, were some other name because the Montagues are sworn enemies of her family. "What's in a name?" she asks. "That which we call a rose/By any other name would smell as sweet."

go.hrw.com
LEO 10-4

By Any Other Name

Santha Rama Rau

Santha Rama Rau (right), her older sister Premila, and their dog in Simla, in India, 1927.

BY ANY OTHER NAME 321

Reaching All Students

Struggling Readers

This selection includes a large number of unfamiliar words and phrases, both English and Hindi. You might want to present this story through oral reading, which will provide opportunities for frequent pauses to discuss vocabulary and concepts.

English Language Learners

You might discuss the position occupied by British citizens in India at the time of this story. Point out that many British citizens, like the headmistress, lived in India for years and considered it home, yet they didn't adopt Indian customs. In fact, they implanted British culture on Indian soil. The author, for example, speaks British English and her family displays British colonial culture, as when her ayah wakes her for "tea."

OBJECTIVES

1. Read an autobiography
2. Identify cultural conflicts
3. Find thematic connections across genres
4. Appreciate oral history

Planning

- **Block Schedule**
  Block Scheduling Lesson Plans with Pacing Guide

Extending the Theme

As a small girl of five and a half, Santha is sent off to the Anglo-Indian school with her sister, Premila, who's eight. The English headmistress cannot pronounce their names, so she gives them English names: Pamela and Cynthia. The English school is new to Santha, but she accepts it easily because she is now Cynthia and does not feel personally involved with this Cynthia's activities. On the first day of the second week, Premila marches into Santha's classroom and orders her to bring her things and to come home with her immediately. When they arrive home, Premila explains that all the Indian children were made to sit with a vacant desk in between because, the teacher said, Indians cheat. Premila says she thinks they shouldn't go back. Mother agrees, but hopes that Santha doesn't understand. Santha does but isn't bothered about it because it all happened to that other girl, Cynthia.

Background

British influence in India began in the seventeenth century, and direct control began in the nineteenth century. Despite rebellions and organized independence movements, the British maintained control until 1947 when India was granted independence. In the 1920s, when this story takes place, the British colonial government remained firmly in control but had already begun making concessions to Indian demands for independence.

Resources 🎧

Listening

Audio CD Library

A reading of this selection appears in the *Audio CD Library*

• Disc 10, Track 3

Ⓐ Reading Skills and Strategies

Responding to the Text

Invite volunteers to tell how they felt on their first day of school or their first day in a new school. Then, invite students to describe how the two girls may be feeling.

Ⓑ Elements of Literature

Irony

❓ What is ironic about the head-mistress's inability to pronounce the girls' names? [She had been in India long enough to develop this skill.]

Ⓒ Vocabulary

Context Clues

❓ This selection includes many English and Indian terms that may be unfamiliar. Context clues will often provide hints to the meanings of these words. Notice the word *intimidated*. What clues to the word's meaning can you find? [Sister is "less easily intimidated" and keeps "stubborn silence." Santha says "'Thank you,' in a very tiny voice."] What may be the meaning of the word? [made afraid]

Ⓓ English Language Learners

Paraphrasing

Explain that *insular* has two meanings and both apply here. It means "isolated from one's surroundings as on an island" and it means "narrow-minded." Ask students to paraphrase this adage, or saying. [Sample answer: Just as a dog's tail is naturally curly and can't be made straight even by burying it for seven years, a Britisher comes from an island and is naturally narrow-minded. He can't be changed even if you take him away from his home for a lifetime.]

"Suppose we give you pretty English names . . ."

Ⓐ At the Anglo-Indian day school in Zorinabad to which my sister and I were sent when she was eight and I was five and a half, they changed our names. On the first day of school, a hot, windless morning of a north Indian September, we stood in the headmistress's study, and she said, "Now you're the *new* girls. What are your names?"

My sister answered for us. "I am Premila, and she"—nodding in my direction—"is Santha."

Ⓑ The headmistress had been in India, I suppose, fifteen years or so, but she still smiled her helpless inability to cope with Indian names. Her rimless half-glasses glittered, and the precarious bun on the top of her head trembled as she shook her head. "Oh, my dears, those are much too hard for me. Suppose we give you pretty English names. Wouldn't that be more jolly? Let's see, now—Pamela for you, I think." She shrugged in a baffled way at my sister. "That's as close as I can get. And for *you*," she said to me, "how about Cynthia? Isn't that nice?"

Ⓒ My sister was always less easily intimidated than I was, and while she kept a stubborn silence, I said "Thank you," in a very tiny voice.

We had been sent to that school because my father, among his responsibilities as an officer of the civil service, had a tour of duty to perform

322 THE SHORT-STORY COLLECTIONS

Ⓓ in the villages around that steamy little provincial town, where he had his headquarters at that time. He used to make his shorter inspection tours on horseback, and a week before, in the stale heat of a typically postmonsoon[1] day, we had waved goodbye to him and a little procession—an assistant, a secretary, two bearers, and the man to look after the bedding rolls and luggage. They rode away through our large garden, still bright green from the rains, and we turned back into the twilight of the house and the sound of fans whispering in every room.

Up to then, my mother had refused to send Premila to school in the British-run establishments of that time, because, she used to say, "You can bury a dog's tail for seven years and it still comes out curly, and you can take a Britisher away from his home for a lifetime and he still remains insular." The examinations and degrees from entirely Indian schools were not, in those days, considered valid. In my case, the question had never come up and probably never would have come up if Mother's extraordinary good health had not broken down. For the first time in my life, she was not able to continue the lessons she had been giving us every morning. So our Hindi[2] books were put away, the stories of the Lord Krishna[3] as a little boy were left in midair, and we were sent to the Anglo-Indian school.

That first day at school is still, when I think of it, a remarkable one. At that age, if one's name is changed, one develops a curious form of dual personality. I remember having a certain detached and disbelieving concern in the actions of "Cynthia," but certainly no responsibility. Accordingly, I followed the thin, erect back of the headmistress down the veranda to my classroom, feeling, at most, a passing interest in what was going to happen to me in this strange, new atmosphere of School.

---

1. **postmonsoon:** after the monsoon, or seasonal heavy rains.
2. **Hindi:** official language of India.
3. **Lord Krishna:** in the Hindu religion, human form taken by the god Vishnu. Many Hindu stories recount episodes in the life of Krishna.

Taking a Second Look

Review: Cause and Effect

Point out that many of the events in "By Any Other Name" are part of a cause-and-effect sequence. Remind students that a cause is what makes something happen and an effect is the result. Santha and Premila attend the Anglo-Indian school (effect) because their mother is sick (cause), and the other events flow from this cause.

Activities

1. Suggest that students create a cause-and-effect chart modeled on the one below. Have groups compare their charts.

Mother becomes ill

↓

Santha and Premila attend Anglo-Indian school

↓   ↓

2. Ask students to discuss how cause-and-effect relationships affect the plot. Are all of the events governed by causes and effects?

The building was Indian in design, with wide verandas opening onto a central courtyard, but Indian verandas are usually whitewashed, with stone floors. These, in the tradition of British schools, were painted dark brown and had matting on the floors. It gave a feeling of extra intensity to the heat.

I suppose there were about a dozen Indian children in the school—which contained perhaps forty children in all—and four of them were in my class. They were all sitting at the back of the room, and I went to join them. I sat next to a small, solemn girl, who didn't smile at me. She had long, glossy black braids and wore a cotton dress, but she still kept on her Indian jewelry—a gold chain around her neck, thin gold bracelets, and tiny ruby studs in her ears. Like most Indian children, she had a rim of black kohl[4] around her eyes. The cotton dress should have looked strange, but all I could think of was that I should ask my mother if I couldn't wear a dress to school, too, instead of my Indian clothes.

I can't remember too much about the proceedings in class that day, except for the beginning. The teacher pointed to me and asked me to stand up. "Now, dear, tell the class your name."

I said nothing.

"Come along," she said, frowning slightly. "What's your name, dear?"

"I don't know," I said, finally.

The English children in the front of the class—there were about eight or ten of them—giggled and twisted around in their chairs to look at me. I sat down quickly and opened my eyes very wide, hoping in that way to dry them off. The little girl with the braids put out her hand and very lightly touched my arm. She still didn't smile.

Most of that morning I was rather bored. I looked briefly at the children's drawings pinned to the wall, and then concentrated on a lizard clinging to the ledge of the high, barred window behind the teacher's head. Occasionally it would shoot out its long yellow tongue for a fly,

and then it would rest, with its eyes closed and its belly palpitating, as though it were swallowing several times quickly. The lessons were mostly concerned with reading and writing and simple numbers—things that my mother had already taught me—and I paid very little attention. The teacher wrote on the easel-blackboard words like "bat" and "cat," which seemed babyish to me; only "apple" was new and incomprehensible.

When it was time for the lunch recess, I followed the girl with braids out onto the veranda. There the children from the other classes were assembled. I saw Premila at once and ran over to her, as she had charge of our lunchbox. The children were all opening packages and sitting down to eat sandwiches. Premila and I were the only ones who had Indian food—thin wheat chapatis,[5] some vegetable curry, and a bottle of buttermilk. Premila thrust half of it into my hand and whispered fiercely that I should go and sit with my class, because that was what the others seemed to be doing.

The enormous black eyes of the little Indian girl from my class looked at my food longingly, so I offered her some. But she only shook her head and plowed her way solemnly through her sandwiches.

I was very sleepy after lunch, because at home we always took a siesta. It was usually a pleasant time of day, with the bedroom darkened against the harsh afternoon sun, the drifting off into sleep with the sound of Mother's voice reading a story in one's mind, and, finally, the shrill, fussy voice of the ayah[6] waking one for tea.

At school, we rested for a short time on low, folding cots on the veranda, and then we were expected to play games. During the hot part of the afternoon we played indoors, and after the shadows had begun to lengthen and the slight breeze of the evening had come up, we moved outside to the wide courtyard.

I had never really grasped the system of competitive games. At home, whenever we played

5. **chapatis** (chə·pät′ēz): thin, flat bread.
6. **ayah** (ä′yə): Indian term for "nanny" or "maid."

E Reading Skills and Strategies
Drawing Conclusions
❓ What conclusions can you draw about the relationship between the English and Indian students? [They don't mix much: the English sit in front and the Indians in the back.]

F Elements of Literature
Irony
❓ What is ironic about Santha's class? [Her Indian mother has already taught her more difficult English words than she is being taught in this British school.]

G Elements of Literature
Character
Ask students what they know about Premila's character thus far. [Sample responses: She's a responsible older sister, not easily intimidated by people, and wants to be accepted by others.] You might point out that there are some seeming paradoxes in Premila's character. On the one hand she's stubborn and independent; on the other, she wants to fit in. Invite students to discuss whether or not real people's personalities include such paradoxes.

H Cultural Connection
Tea
Tea is an enormously popular drink in India, which today is the world's largest tea producer. Having "tea" is an English custom. It is really a meal in late afternoon and consists of strong tea along with light foods such as cookies, cake, and sandwiches.

Crossing the Curriculum

History

This story takes place at a time in Indian history when the surge toward independence was gathering momentum but still had many years to go before realization. Invite students to investigate the politics and social movements of this time. Were Premila's independence and ethnic pride and her mother's firm support for her actions typical or unusual for this time? Have students share their findings in an oral report.

Geography

Rama Rau describes the hot September afternoons in school and the long walk home. Ask students to locate Zorinabad on a map of India and then investigate the climate, vegetation, and geography of this region. Have students work together to produce an oral report that describes the region and compares it to students' own region.

Architecture

Ask students to create an illustration of an Indian home like the one that Rama Rau lived in with her parents. Students should begin by researching the architecture of colonial Indian homes. Then, using clues from the story, they should create a drawing, or series of drawings, that show what the house and grounds might have looked like.

tag or guessing games, I was always allowed to "win"—"because," Mother used to tell Premila, "she is the youngest, and we have to allow for that." I had often heard her say it, and it seemed quite reasonable to me, but the result was that I had no clear idea of what "winning" meant.

When we played twos-and-threes[7] that afternoon at school, in accordance with my training I let one of the small English boys catch me but was naturally rather puzzled when the other children did not return the courtesy. I ran about for what seemed like hours without ever catching anyone, until it was time for school to close. Much later I learned that my attitude was called "not being a good sport," and I stopped allowing myself to be caught, but it was not for years that I really learned the spirit of the thing.

7. **twos-and-threes:** game similar to tag.

When I saw our car come up to the school gate, I broke away from my classmates and rushed toward it yelling, "Ayah! Ayah!" It seemed like an eternity since I had seen her that morning—a wizened, affectionate figure in her white cotton sari,[8] giving me dozens of urgent and useless instructions on how to be a good girl at school. Premila followed more sedately, and she told me on the way home never to do that again in front of the other children.

When we got home, we went straight to Mother's high, white room to have tea with her, and I immediately climbed onto the bed and bounced gently up and down on the springs. Mother asked how we had liked our first day in

8. **sari** (sä′rē): long piece of cloth wrapped around the body. One end forms a skirt. The other end goes across the chest and over one shoulder.

Connecting Across Texts

Connecting with "Through the Tunnel"
After students have completed reading "By Any Other Name," invite them to compare the story with Doris Lessing's story, "Through the Tunnel." Point out that both stories involve young people who are making discoveries about the adult world that they will soon be part of. You might stimulate discussion by asking students to respond to these questions, first about one story and then about the other.

• What breakthrough is the character making?
• Is this breakthrough necessary or avoidable? Explain.
• How will this breakthrough prepare the character for adult life?
• In later life, do you think the character will look back on the experience as positive or negative?

school. I was so pleased to be home and to have left that peculiar Cynthia behind that I had nothing whatever to say about school, except to ask what "apple" meant. But Premila told Mother about the classes, and added that in her class they had weekly tests to see if they had learned their lessons well.

I asked, "What's a test?"

Premila said, "You're too small to have them. You won't have them in your class for donkey's years."[9] She had learned the expression that day and was using it for the first time. We all laughed enormously at her wit. She also told Mother, in an aside, that we should take sandwiches to school the next day. Not, she said, that *she* minded. But they would be simpler for me to handle.

That whole lovely evening I didn't think about school at all. I sprinted barefoot across the lawns with my favorite playmate, the cook's son, to the stream at the end of the garden. We quarreled in our usual way, waded in the tepid water under the lime trees, and waited for the night to bring out the smell of the jasmine.[10] I listened with fascination to his stories of ghosts and demons, until I was too frightened to cross the garden alone in the semidarkness. The ayah found me, shouted at the cook's son, scolded me, hurried me in to supper—it was an entirely usual, wonderful evening.

It was a week later, the day of Premila's first test, that our lives changed rather abruptly. I was sitting at the back of my class, in my usual inattentive way, only half listening to the teacher. I had started a rather guarded friendship with the girl with the braids, whose name turned out to be Nalini (Nancy in school). The three other Indian children were already fast friends. Even at that age, it was apparent to all of us that friendship with the English or Anglo-Indian children was out of the question. Occasionally, during the class, my new friend and I would draw pictures and show them to each other secretly.

The door opened sharply and Premila marched in. At first, the teacher smiled at her in a kindly and encouraging way and said, "Now, you're little Cynthia's sister?"

Premila didn't even look at her. She stood with her feet planted firmly apart and her shoulders rigid and addressed herself directly to me. "Get up," she said. "We're going home."

I didn't know what had happened, but I was aware that it was a crisis of some sort. I rose obediently and started to walk toward my sister.

"Bring your pencils and your notebook," she said.

I went back for them, and together we left the room. The teacher started to say something just as Premila closed the door, but we didn't wait to hear what it was.

In complete silence we left the school grounds and started to walk home. Then I asked Premila what the matter was. All she would say was, "We're going home for good."

It was a very tiring walk for a child of five and a half, and I dragged along behind Premila with my pencils growing sticky in my hand. I can still remember looking at the dusty hedges and the tangles of thorns in the ditches by the side of the road, smelling the faint fragrance from the eucalyptus trees, and wondering whether we would ever reach home. Occasionally a horse-drawn tonga[11] passed us, and the women, in their pink or green silks, stared at Premila and me trudging along on the side of the road. A few coolies[12] and a line of women carrying baskets of vegetables on their heads smiled at us. But it was nearing their hottest time of day, and the road was almost deserted. I walked more and more slowly, and shouted to Premila, from time to time, "Wait for me!" with increasing peevishness. She spoke to me only once, and that was to tell me to carry my notebook on my head, because of the sun.

9. **donkey's years:** expression meaning "a very long time."
10. **jasmine:** (jaz′min): tropical plant with fragrant flowers.

11. **tonga:** two-wheeled carriage.
12. **coolies:** unskilled laborers.

B Elements of Literature
Character
❓ Do you think Premila's real motivation for requesting sandwiches is because it will be easier for Santha to eat? Explain. [Most students will infer from this request and from what they have already learned about Premila that she wants the sandwiches so that they will both be eating the same kinds of food as everyone else. She wants to fit in.]

C Appreciating Language
Style
Explain that Rama Rau learned British English, and her style of writing incorporates British stylistic idiosyncrasies. For example, her style is somewhat formal, even though she's writing about herself as an unsophisticated child. Also, she uses terms such as *rather* (in this paragraph) and phrases such as "laughed *enormously*" and "*lovely* evening" (the second and third paragraphs of the first column), which are typically British word choices.

Making the Connections

Connecting to the Theme: "Breakthroughs"
Guide students in a discussion of the theme "Breakthroughs" as it relates to this selection. One breakthrough occurs when Premila leaves school, taking Santha with her, because she won't accept discrimination. Her stand is supported by her mother, who keeps the girls at home, refusing to allow her daughters' self-worth to be quashed. Santha achieves a breakthrough of a somewhat different kind. She knows what Premila and her mother are talking about—racism—but she is able to put it aside because, after all, it happened to Cynthia, not her.

Cultural Connections
Point out that the small rebellion described in this selection mirrors the greater rebellion occurring in India during this period. Led by Mohandas Gandhi, the Indians used nonviolent disobedience to fight for independence. (One facet of this rebellion was a refusal to attend English schools.) Invite students to draw parallels with the American civil rights movement and the nonviolent demonstrations of the 1950s and 1960s.

Ask students to compare and contrast Premila with the character of the elderly man in "With All Flags Flying." [Possible responses: Similarities—both are strong, highly independent characters who are fiercely determined to preserve their dignity. Differences—Premila acts out of a sense of fairness, the old man out of pride and fear of losing his family's love.]

BROWSING IN THE FILES

About the Author. Rama Rau first moved to the United States in 1941 and received her bachelor's degree from Wellesley College. She has produced works in many genres, from cookbooks to a stage adaptation of E. M. Forster's *A Passage to India*. She has attained her greatest success, however, in writing travel books. According to one critic, Rama Rau is skilled in "transcribing life to paper in terms of people, their talk, their manners and customs."

FINDING COMMON GROUND

This feature allows students to plan and prepare for a wide-ranging discussion of issues relating to the theme of breakthroughs, to the significance of names, and to other issues relating to this selection. You may want to divide students into small discussion groups for this activity. Have groups select a leader to keep the discussion on topic and to make sure all questions are covered.

When we got to our house, the ayah was just taking a tray of lunch into Mother's room. She immediately started a long, worried questioning about what are you children doing back here at this hour of the day.

Mother looked very startled and very concerned and asked Premila what had happened.

A Premila said, "We had our test today, and She made me and the other Indians sit at the back of the room, with a desk between each one."

Mother said, "Why was that, darling?"

"She said it was because Indians cheat," Premila added. "So I don't think we should go back to that school."

Mother looked very distant and was silent a long time. At last she said, "Of course not, darling." She sounded displeased.

MEET THE WRITER
A Stranger in Her Own Land

Santha Rama Rau (1923–   ) was born into one of India's most influential families but has spent most of her life in other lands. Her father was a knighted diplomat, her mother a social reformer. Santha Rama Rau made her first trip to England at the age of six and returned for a much longer stay when she was eleven. In 1939, as war was breaking out in Europe, Lady Rama Rau took her two daughters back to India for safety. Feeling somewhat like an outsider, Santha made a conscious effort to reorient herself to her homeland and her extended family. In 1947, she witnessed the turmoil of India's independence from Britain. Five years later, she married an American and settled in New York City.

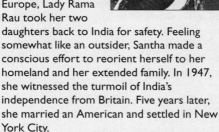

We all shared the curry she was having for lunch, and afterward I was sent off to the beautifully familiar bedroom for my siesta. I could hear Mother and Premila talking through the open door.

Mother said, "Do you suppose she understood all that?"

Premila said, "I shouldn't think so. She's a baby."

Mother said, "Well, I hope it won't bother her."

Of course, they were both wrong. I understood it perfectly, and I remember it all very clearly. But I put it happily away, because it had all happened to a girl called Cynthia, and I never was really particularly interested in her.

FINDING COMMON GROUND

With a small group of classmates, compare the notes you made for your Quickwrite, and talk about the importance of getting a person's name right. Use your notes to come up with ideas for a group discussion of Santha Rama Rau's experiences. If you need more questions to stimulate discussion, you might try these:

1. Describe the breakthroughs in this selection. Who do you think made them, and why are the breakthroughs important?

2. What would you have done if you had been in Premila's situation? What would you have done as her parent?

3. What does this autobiographical excerpt say about the nature of prejudice? Do you think events like the ones Rau described are happening in other settings today? Explain.

Assessing Learning

Check Test: Questions and Answers

1. **Why must Premila and Santha go to the Anglo-Indian school?** [Their mother has become ill and can no longer teach them at home.]

2. **How do the two girls get the names of Pamela and Cynthia?** [The headmistress gives them these names because she can't pronounce their Indian names.]

3. **Why doesn't Santha pay more attention in class?** [She is bored; her mother has already taught her all the things being studied in class.]

4. **Why does Premila take Santha out of school?** [Premila's teacher separated the Indians during a test and said that Indians cheat. Premila wouldn't accept the discrimination.]

5. **Why isn't Santha upset by the events that occurred at the school?** [It all happened to Cynthia, Santha's school name. Santha regards Cynthia as someone else.]

Standardized Test Preparation

For practice with standardized test format specific to this selection, see

• *Standardized Test Preparation,* p. 42

READ ON

A Country Divided

Cry, the Beloved Country by Alan Paton (Scribner) is one of the great novels of this century, a touching story of two fathers and their sons, one father a Zulu pastor and the other a white planter. The story takes place in South Africa before that tragic country granted equality to all its people. The 1995 movie, filmed in South Africa, stars James Earl Jones and Richard Harris.

So Near and Yet So Far

In *Teaching a Stone to Talk* (Harper Colophon), Annie Dillard once again takes a journey through different places and cultures, recording the shock and amazement of her meetings with people and creatures, plants and landscapes. From Ecuador to the Galápagos Islands to Tinker Creek, Dillard shares her discoveries about life and living on our planet.

Tiny? Yes . . . Dangerous? Yes!

For a true story that even Stephen King said was one of the most horrifying things he'd ever read, get *The Hot Zone* by Richard Preston (Random House). This nonfiction chiller focuses on a deadly new virus that nearly escaped from a laboratory in Reston, Virginia.

Hidden Memories

Incidents in the Life of a Slave Girl by Harriet A. Jacobs (Harvard) is a moving firsthand account of slavery told by a woman who became a fugitive in 1835 and hid for nearly seven years in a tiny crawl space above a storehouse in her grandmother's home in Edenton, North Carolina.

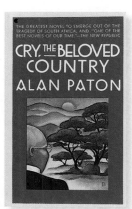

MAIN OBJECTIVE

Write an evaluation of a story or movie

PROCESS OBJECTIVES

1. Use appropriate prewriting techniques to identify and develop a topic
2. Create a first draft
3. Use Evaluation Criteria as a basis for determining revision strategies
4. Revise the first draft incorporating suggestions generated by self- or peer evaluation
5. Proofread and correct errors
6. Create a final draft
7. Choose an appropriate method of publication
8. Reflect on progress as a writer

Planning

- **Block Schedule**
  Block Scheduling Lesson Plans with Pacing Guide
- **One-Stop Planner**
  CD-ROM with Test Generator

Introducing the Writer's Workshop

Have students bring to class the section of a newspaper or popular magazine in which movies are reviewed. Read aloud a short review, and discuss with students which elements are necessary to even a basic review: title, type of movie (western, terror, thriller, etc.), the criteria being used to formulate the evaluation, and the opinion of the critic. Then, have students examine the reviews they have brought to class, looking for answers to questions such as the following:

- Is a plot summary an adequate movie review? Why or why not?
- Are humor and/or sarcasm appropriate in a review? Why or why not?
- What should an effective review do? Does the review you selected meet those standards?

Technology HELP

See Writer's Workshop 2 CD-ROM. *Assignment: Evaluation.*

ASSIGNMENT

Write an evaluation of a story or movie.

AIM

To persuade; to inform.

AUDIENCE

Your teacher, classmates, friends, or family; readers of a school newspaper. (You choose.)

PERSUASIVE WRITING

EVALUATING A STORY OR MOVIE

When you **evaluate** something, you give your opinion or judgment about its value. If a friend asked you what you thought of a movie, you might say, "Well, the acting was great, but the plot had a lot of holes in it." That's an evaluation. If you then pointed out some of those holes, you'd be supporting your evaluation with specific evidence.

Some people get paid to make precisely this sort of evaluation—and to convince others to accept their judgment. Even if you don't become a movie critic or book reviewer, you'll often have to evaluate something: a college you might attend, a car you might buy, a job you might take, a politician you might vote for. Be sure your evaluation is based on solid evidence and specific standards.

Prewriting

1. Review Your Writer's Notebook

In your notebook entries for this collection, you've explored several techniques for evaluating a short story. You may already have decided on a subject from working through these exercises.

WORK IN PROGRESS

2. Choose a Work to Evaluate

One way to find a topic is to quickwrite a list of stories or movies that you remember well. Circle the works that seem to create the strongest feeling or the most vivid images for you—it doesn't matter if those feelings and images are positive or negative. You may sometimes write best about something you dislike. The important thing is to write about a work that you respond to strongly.

3. Decide What's Important

Because you won't have the time or space to discuss every aspect of the work you are evaluating, you'll need to select a few key elements and focus on those. If you're evaluating one of the short stories in this collection, look back at your notebook for help.

 Resources: Print and Media

Writing and Language
- *Portfolio Management System*
  - Prewriting, p. 127
  - Peer Editing, p. 128
  - Assessment Rubric, p. 129

- *Workshop Resources*
  - Revision Strategy Teaching Notes, p. 19
  - Revision Strategy Transparencies 10, 11
- *Writer's Workshop 2 CD-ROM*
  - Evaluation

Teaching the Writer's Workshop

Prewriting

To help students plan, review the elements that are commonly used to evaluate a work.

- Story or novel: title, characters, setting, plot, theme, important symbols, diction, etc.
- Movie or videotape: Most of the above plus acting, direction, cinematography, soundtrack, and special effects.

You may wish to require that students write down and rank their evaluation criteria (Prewriting step 4) before beginning to write their reviews.

4. Think About Your Standards

To make a judgment on the worth of something, you must have **criteria,** or standards, to measure it by. The more specific your standards, the easier it is to make an evaluation and to give good reasons for your judgment. When you develop your criteria, ask yourself questions like these:

- What makes a mystery story a good mystery?
- What makes a novel hard to put down?
- What's the best fantasy movie I've ever seen? the worst?

5. Review the Work

If possible, read the story or see the movie again, jotting down notes on aspects that seem particularly praiseworthy or problematic. Consider making a **double-entry journal** like the one below. In the left column, make notes on passages or elements from the work; in the right column, record your responses.

Notes for "The Pit and the Pendulum"

Passage	My Response
Setting: "For many hours the immediate vicinity of the low framework upon which I lay had been literally swarming with rats. They were wild, bold, ravenous—their red eyes glaring upon me. . . ."	Great description. I can really see this. Visual details good and weird. "Ravenous" suggests they're going to nibble at the prisoner.

6. Develop Your Evaluation Statement

Try writing an **evaluation statement** that expresses your overall opinion of the work. Go back over your notes and the work itself, and decide on the **main idea** that you'd like readers to get from your evaluation. Write it down in one sentence. You may need to write several versions of this statement until you come up with the best possible wording. Since an evaluation is an opinion, be prepared to back it up with evidence from the work.

> **Evaluation Statements**
>
> Despite its clichéd characters and corny dialogue, James Cameron's Titanic is a masterpiece that's worth every penny of the $200 million it cost to produce.
>
> The short story "Trap of Gold" by Louis L'Amour is more than an exciting Western; it's a heart-stopping psychological struggle.

Getting Students Involved

Cooperative Learning

Teams of Critics. Students can work in groups of four to develop an evaluation of a work. Students choose three elements suitable for a particular work. For example, symbol, point of view, and character are appropriate for "Through the Tunnel." Have each of the three students evaluate one of the elements. The fourth student writes the introduction and conclusion of the review. Students can then work as a team, presenting their own sections of the evaluation to the class.

Drafting

- Before students begin their initial drafts, read and discuss the Student Model on pp. 330–331.
- Students may use a two-column chart to develop their ideas about the creative elements they wish to discuss in their reviews. In the first column of the chart, they should list what was effective about the element; in the second column, what was ineffective.
- Remind students to use only every other line when they write their drafts. They should also leave extra space in the right margin for comments and editing marks.

Try It Out
Possible Answers
1. Students' answers will vary but may include any of the elements listed in the Prewriting tips on pp. 328–329.
2. Student answers will vary, but may include statements like the following if evaluating a story/movie title: "After [reading/watching] this [story/movie], it was hard to understand how the title and the [story/movie] connected."

Using the Model

Have students read the model and use the side-column annotations to identify key elements of the review. Then, you may wish to discuss the review further, using questions such as these to focus the discussion:

? Go back through the review and pull out all plot references. How are these references different from a plot summary?

? Do you agree that this is a favorable review? If you had never seen the movie, would you want to go? Why or why not?

? Go back through the review and locate personal information given the reader by the critic. How does this information help you determine the writer's evaluation criteria and objectivity?

Try It Out
For the story or movie you're evaluating—
1. List the three or four key elements you'll focus on in your essay.
2. Then, to elaborate, list at least one example that supports your evaluation of each element. *Be specific.*

Sentence Workshop
H E L P

Combining sentences: page 333.

Language / Grammar Link
H E L P

Comparisons and analogies to clarify: page 261. Subject-verb agreement: page 275. Participles: page 287. Rhythm and repetition: page 305. Verbs: page 320.

Student Model

Drafting

1. Introductory Paragraphs

Start with an attention grabber: a funny comment, an intriguing quotation, or a personal anecdote (as in the Student Model below). Include your thesis statement in the introduction as well as some basic information about the work. (For a story, identify the title and author; for a movie, give the title and names of the director and major actors.) Then tell just enough of the plot to get your readers interested, without spoiling any surprises.

2. Elaborate: Be Specific and Concrete

It's a good idea to focus your evaluation on three or four key elements of the work. Be direct and honest. If you really think something is excellent or awful, say so—as long as you can back up your statement. Support your opinions with detailed, concrete **examples,** such as this one from the Student Model: ". . . the mechanical contraptions of rubber and steel seem more lifelike than their flesh and blood adversaries." **Comparisons** provide another kind of specific support. If you say the hero in a thriller is unbelievable, compare him to a stronger, more credible hero in another thriller.

3. Wrap It Up

End your evaluation by summing up or restating your main ideas and overall opinion of the work. You might choose to add a final thought or response that brings your evaluation to a definite close.

JURASSIC PARK

Remember when your parents would take you to the Natural History Museum as a kid? I'd always rush past the other animal exhibits and go straight to my favorite section: the dinosaurs. Even though they had been reduced to mere skeletons, the extinct beasts still captivated me.

In *Jurassic Park,* Steven Spielberg has taken those dusty bone formations and, with a lot of imagination and a little computer technology, transformed them into the majestic creatures of yesteryear.

In the movie, genetic engineering is the magic wand that makes dinosaurs walk the earth again. Based on the novel by

Writer draws readers in with a personal anecdote and expression of feeling.

Gives title and director and states his view of the film's major achievement.

Reaching All Students

Struggling Writers
To help students evaluate a movie, suggest that they work in a specific order:
1. Select a film they either loved or hated.
2. Identify at least two or three supporting reasons for their response, and rank their reasons in order of importance.
3. Determine which elements of literature are linked to their most important reasons. (For example, a student who says that the hero was a jerk would be commenting on character. A student who says the ending was unbelievable would be commenting on plot resolution.) Before students begin to draft, work with them to discuss whether or how specific elements are related. For example, is the ending unbelievable *because* we think the hero is a jerk who wouldn't know how to defuse the bomb or scale the side of an icy mountain? This discussion may help students to generate basic themes for their reviews.

Michael Crichton (who also wrote the screenplay), *Jurassic Park* creates a world that is only a short step from the present. An idealistic, Santa-like billionaire (Richard Attenborough) discovers a way to create dinosaurs by obtaining DNA from the blood of prehistoric mosquitoes preserved in amber. The dino DNA is then used to create a good number and variety of dinosaurs.

Summarizes the plot without giving away surprises and identifies the major characters and actors.

The full-grown reptiles are then placed in a kind of island zoo called Jurassic Park. The park needs scientific approval before it can open, so the owner invites a paleontologist (Sam Neill), a biologist (Laura Dern), and a sarcastic mathematician (Jeff Goldblum) to check things out. He also brings along his two grandchildren so they can see the fun. As luck would have it, though, the dinosaurs escape their enclosure and begin to wreak havoc on the island.

Like Jurassic Park's proprietor, Steven Spielberg spared no expense on his pets. Over sixty million dollars and two years of preproduction supposedly went into the project. Unfortunately, Spielberg was having such great fun with his lizard pals that he all but forgot about the film's human characters. As a result, the mechanical contraptions of rubber and steel seem more lifelike than their flesh and blood adversaries.

Evaluates the work: weighs weaknesses against strengths.

The character development in *Jurassic Park* is give-and-take—Crichton gives us a little character insight, and Spielberg takes it away to make room for the dinos. Neill and Dern supposedly have a romantic interest, but their time together on screen is less than that of the opening credits. Dern delivers some token feminist lines, but she never gets to build on them. Attenborough does well as the whimsical, disillusioned billionaire, but the best lines he gets are about a flea circus.

Gives specific examples of the film's poor character development.

Children, be warned—*Barney* this ain't. *Jurassic Park* is very intense and suspenseful at times. There are no friendly, singing lizards or frolicking youngsters here. In fact, it is the children who go through the most suffering in this movie; getting electrocuted, crushed, chased, sneezed on, and kicked are only a few of their misfortunes.

Uses a comparison. A good technique in a critical evaluation.

No bones about it, *Jurassic Park* is a monster thriller to rival *Jaws*. Although character development is virtually extinct and the ending is left wide open, Spielberg is finally back doing what he does best—making great films that charge to the edges of the imagination.

Restates evaluation: essentially favorable.

—Matthew Harry
Westlake High School
Westlake, Ohio

First appeared in *Merlyn's Pen: The National Magazines of Student Writing.*

Crossing the Curriculum

Fine Arts

Students who are studying art, music, or dance might prefer to evaluate a work from their field of interest. Remind them that they need to set up their criteria for evaluation before they begin to write. When they turn in their evaluation, have them supply you with a picture of the artwork, an audiotape of the music, or a videotape of the dance.

Reaching All Students

Advanced Learners

Students might like to compare a novel and its cinematic counterpart. The films of many famous novels are now available at video stores. Have students select a film based on a novel and write a review determining how faithfully the movie has interpreted the writer's vision. Caution students to avoid selecting books based on movie scripts because these "novelizations" are virtual clones of the films.

Evaluating and Revising

- Students should use the Evaluation Criteria for self-evaluation and peer review. Point out the peer comments in the revision model.
- To check for their use of supporting details, students can use a highlighter to mark their evaluation statement. Then they can use a second color to mark the supporting facts.
- Students should check their sentence structure. If they find that they used many short, choppy sentences, they might want to combine sentences. Refer them to the Sentence Workshop on p. 333. This workshop contains modeling strategies and examples for combining sentences through coordination. Students may also wish to examine the various sentence structures that are used in the Student Model on pp. 330–331.

Proofreading
Have students proofread their own papers first and then exchange with another student. For this assignment, remind students to be particularly careful of double-checking all titles and names for correct capitalization, punctuation, and spelling.

Publishing
Students may post their reviews electronically on your school's Web page, on an electronic mailing list, or on a Usenet Internet group. Ask the Internet community for feedback. You may want to preview any news activity that you suggest to students. Because these resources are sometimes public forums, their content can be unpredictable.

Reflecting
Have students write and date a brief reflection for their portfolio. Encourage students to reflect on how what they have learned about literary elements is applicable to discussing and evaluating other forms of art.

Resources ———

Peer Editing Forms and Rubrics
- *Portfolio Management System,* p. 128.

Revision Transparencies
- *Workshop Resources,* p. 19

■ *Evaluation Criteria*

A good evaluation

1. *identifies and summarizes the work*

2. *makes its evaluation statement clear*

3. *offers specific supporting evidence*

4. *sums up or restates its evaluation in the conclusion*

Proofreading Tip

Double-check all titles and names for correct capitalization, punctuation, and spelling.

Communications Handbook HELP

See Proofreaders' Marks.

Publishing Tip

Submit your evaluation to your school or local newspaper. Send or e-mail it to a magazine of student writing, such as *Merlyn's Pen.*

Evaluating and Revising

1. Self-Evaluation
Go over your draft to make sure you haven't used overworked and empty adjectives such as *great, unique, terrific,* and *terrible.* Also be on the lookout for short, choppy sentences that could be combined for a smoother flow.

2. Peer Review
If possible, give your evaluation to at least one classmate who is familiar with your subject and one who is not. Ask your readers to consider these questions:
- If you're familiar with the subject, does the summary in the review match your memory of the work?
- Does the evaluation make you think about the work in a new way or challenge your previous opinions?
- If you're unfamiliar with the subject, does the evaluation give you a clear idea of what the work is about?
- Does the evaluation help you decide if you would like to read (or see) the work?
- Does the evaluation present evidence to convince you to accept the writer's opinions?

Revision Model

	Peer Comments
Based on the novel by Michael	
Crichton (who also wrote the screen-	
play), *Jurassic Park* creates an ~~a world that is only a short step from the present. An idealistic, Santa-like~~ ~~almost familiar world. A~~ billionaire	How is the film's world almost familiar? Be more specific.
(Richard Attenborough) discovers a	This character sounds interesting. Add more descriptive details.
way to create dinosaurs by obtaining	
DNA from the blood of prehistoric preserved in amber mosquitoes.	Where did he get the prehistoric mosquitoes?

Grading Timesaver

Rubrics for this Writer's Workshop assignment appear on p. 129 of the *Portfolio Management System.*

Sentence Workshop

COMBINING SENTENCES: USING COORDINATION

Read the following passage aloud.

CHOPPY   Clara nodded and kissed his cheek. Francie kept her face turned away. She hugged him tightly. Then she looked up at him as she stepped back.

To most readers, these sentences sound childish—choppy and repetitive. Look at how a professional writer combined these sentences. Read this passage aloud to see if it sounds smoother.

REVISED   Clara nodded and kissed his cheek. Francie kept her face turned away, *but* she hugged him tightly, *and* then she looked up at him as she stepped back.

—Anne Tyler, "With All Flags Flying" (page 315)

The **coordinating conjunctions** (*and, or, but, for, nor, so, yet*) can help you avoid a monotonous series of simple sentences that repeat the same subject or the same verb. They can also help you create **compound sentences** by connecting one or more simple sentences.

There are many ways that sentences can be combined using coordination. Can you think of another way of revising the choppy passage above?

Writer's Workshop Follow-up: Revision

When you are revising the draft of your evaluation for the Writer's Workshop on page 328, read your sentences aloud to hear the way they sound. Underline your subjects once and your verbs twice. Have you unnecessarily repeated subjects or verbs in strings of short sentences? Can you combine any of these short sentences into one sentence?

Pay attention to your peer reviewer's comments. Often another pair of eyes can spot problems that the writer doesn't notice.

Language Handbook HELP

See Coordinating Conjunctions: page 1021; Compound Sentences: page 1040.

Technology HELP

See Language Workshop CD-ROM. Key word entry: combining sentences.

Try It Out

Act as an editor, and use coordinating conjunctions to make the following passages smoother and more varied. Look for places where you can create compound subjects or verbs or compound sentences.

1. Wetherton made camp near a tiny spring west of the fan. Then he picketed his burros. He began his climb.

2. The impact of the water broke the rubber-enclosed vacuum. The goggles came loose.

3. He took off his copper-toed work boots. He set them on the floor neatly, side by side.

4. Jerry ran after his mother. He looked back over his shoulder at the bay. He thought about it all morning.

SENTENCE WORKSHOP 333

Try It Out
Possible Answers
1. Wetherton made camp near a tiny spring west of the fan, picketed his burros, and began his climb.
2. The impact of the water broke the rubber-enclosed vacuum, and the goggles came loose.
3. He took off his copper-toed work boots and set them on the floor neatly, side by side.
4. Jerry ran after his mother, but he looked back over his shoulder at the bay and thought about it all morning.

Assessing Learning

Quick Check: Combining Sentences
Use a coordinating conjunction to combine each of the following sentences.
1. Jerry dived into the water. Then he turned around. He headed to shore. [Jerry dived into the water, but then he turned around and headed to shore.]
2. After Dad died, Jean felt that life would never seem ordinary again. Her brothers felt the same way. [After Dad died, Jean and her brothers felt that life would never seem ordinary again.]

3. The old man did not want to be a burden. He had seen too many children resent their fathers. [The old man did not want to be a burden, for he had seen too many children resent their fathers.]
4. Wetherton scrambled up the rocks. He looked for veins of gold. He looked for bits of gold dust. [Wetherton scrambled up the rocks and looked for veins of gold or bits of gold dust.]

5. The walls of the room moved inward. They forced the prisoner to the edge of the pit. [The walls of the room moved inward and forced the prisoner to the edge of the pit.]

Teaching the Lesson

Explain that previewing, scanning, skimming, note-taking, and outlining help students recognize the structure and master the content of various kinds of texts.

Using the Strategies

Possible Answers

1. The three main parts are: Symbols in Literature: Making Associations; Is It a Symbol?; Why Use Symbols?

2. Symbols in our culture are: a ring; a cross; a six-pointed star; a crown; a skull and crossbones; a clenched fist; the Stars and Stripes; a dove with an olive branch.

3. Definition: a symbol is an object, a setting, an event, an animal, or even a person that functions in a story the way you'd expect it to but, more important, also stands for something more than itself, usually for something abstract. The word *symbol* in boldfaced type signals where to find the definition.

4. III. Is It a Symbol?
   A. Is often visual
   B. Receives emphasis
   C. Is a form of figurative language—identified with something that is very different from itself
   D. Relates to story's theme
   IV. Why Use Symbols?
   A. Symbols are part of human nature
      1. Cave paintings and writings
      2. Owl in ancient Greece, symbol of Athena
      3. Language uses sounds to symbolize things
   B. Great symbols are of inexhaustible significance
   C. Powerful symbols speak to the emotions and imagination

Situation

You and a friend have just read "Trap of Gold" (see page 249). You think that the treacherous gold-filled rock has symbolic meaning, and your teacher has asked you to present your viewpoint to the class. To help clarify your thinking, you decide to reread and outline the Elements of Literature essay on symbols (see pages 306–307).

Strategies

Preview the material.

• Notice any headings, boxed information, or boldfaced terms. These will help you concentrate on the most important points.

Pace yourself.

• Whenever you read, you should adjust your reading rate to serve your purpose.

• **Scanning** is rapidly searching for key words and then checking the context to make sure you've found what you were looking for.

• **Skimming** is reading quickly to identify main ideas.

• **Close reading** is reading slowly and carefully enough to understand the words and think about their implications.

Take notes in an outline.

• An outline reveals the basic organization of a text: The

Symbols: Signs of Something More

I. Symbols in everyday life
   A. Personal symbols
   B. Public symbols
      1. Examples: flag, cross, doves, clenched fist
      2. Images with commonly accepted associations
II. Symbols in literature
   A. Function on a concrete level but also mean something more
   B. Are created by associations
      1. Colors have associations
      2. Seasons have associations
   C. Have multiple meanings

entries list the ideas in order, and the indentations show the relative importance of the ideas.

Use formal outline structure.

• Use Roman numerals for main topics.

• Use letters and numbers for the subtopics, in the order shown in the sample. (The sample also shows how to capitalize and indent entries.)

• Never use just one subtopic; use either two (or more) or none at all.

• Use parallel grammatical forms for parallel entries. For example, if the first item in a group is a verb, make the others verbs as well.

Using the Strategies

1. Refer to the essay on pages 306–307. What are the three main parts of the essay?

2. Scan the first column of the essay to find examples of symbols in our culture.

3. Scan the essay to find the definition of symbol. (What signals you that this definition is found in column 2?)

4. Complete the topic outline shown here for this essay.

Extending the Strategies

Use the strategies here to read and outline another Elements of Literature essay in this book, or use an outline to review a selection in Collection 6.

Getting Students Involved

Have students outline a movie or book review from a professional and/or entertainment magazine. Encourage them to discuss in small groups whether the outlines indicate any similarities or differences in the structure of articles written for the same purpose but for different audiences.

Learning for Life

Conflict Resolution

OBJECTIVES

1. Identify conflict resolution strategies
2. Identify commonly experienced conflicts
3. Make presentations depicting resolution techniques for the identified conflicts

Problem

Stories derive their power from **conflict,** opposing forces that create tension and cause action. Conflict may be necessary in stories, but it can cause serious problems in real life. The ability to defuse conflicts and to arrive at fair and reasonable solutions is one of the most valuable social skills that you can learn.

Project

Identify a series of steps that can be used to resolve conflicts fairly.

Preparation

1. With a group of classmates, decide on a first step to take in resolving a conflict. This normally includes identifying the parties involved in the conflict and their opposing positions.

2. Continue listing all of the steps needed to resolve a conflict. Another important one might be to get both sides to agree to discuss their dispute before a peer mediator. Note that a **mediator** (a person who listens objectively to both sides of the disagreement) can often help two opposing sides reach a peaceful settlement.

3. Choose a familiar conflict, and test each step you've listed.

4. With your group, evaluate how well your steps work to resolve a conflict.

Procedure

1. Draw up a list of common conflicts that students face in daily life. For example, one student complains that another student is spreading rumors about him.

2. Adapt the list of steps you drew up to fit each specific conflict.

Presentation

Use one of the following formats (or another that your teacher approves):

1. Role-Play

Role-play the resolution of one of the conflicts you listed. Invite comments from the audience, and discuss the issues raised. If possible, have members of the audience take turns trying out some of the conflict-resolution steps on their own. Discuss how well the steps seem to work.

2. Poster Campaign

Create a poster campaign about conflict resolution for your school. List each step in a shortened form. For example:

- Listen without interrupting.

- No name-calling.

Illustrate the steps or create logos or symbols for conflict resolution.

3. Radio Broadcasts

Using your school's public-address system or in-school TV channel, plan and air a series of short programs that illustrate conflict resolution. For each program, write a script that shows conflict-resolution in action. Be sure to include two opposing sides and a mediator. As part of your broadcasts, tell students how they can find out more about conflict resolution.

Processing

What did you learn from this project about the process of managing and resolving conflicts? How important is the idea of **compromise** (each side giving in a little to reach an agreement) in the resolution of a conflict? Write a brief reflection for your portfolio.

Resources

Viewing and Representing
HRW Multimedia
Presentation Maker
Students may wish to use the *Multimedia Presentation Maker* to present the main points of their solutions.

Grading Timesaver

Rubrics for this Learning for Life project appear on p. 130 of the *Portfolio Management System.*

Developing Workplace Competencies

Preparation	Procedure	Presentation
• Works on teams	• Acquires data	• Uses resources well
• Teaches others	• Interprets information	• Makes decisions
• Leads others	• Communicates ideas	• Selects equipment
• Evaluates data	• Exhibits sociability	• Applies technology
• Solves problems		

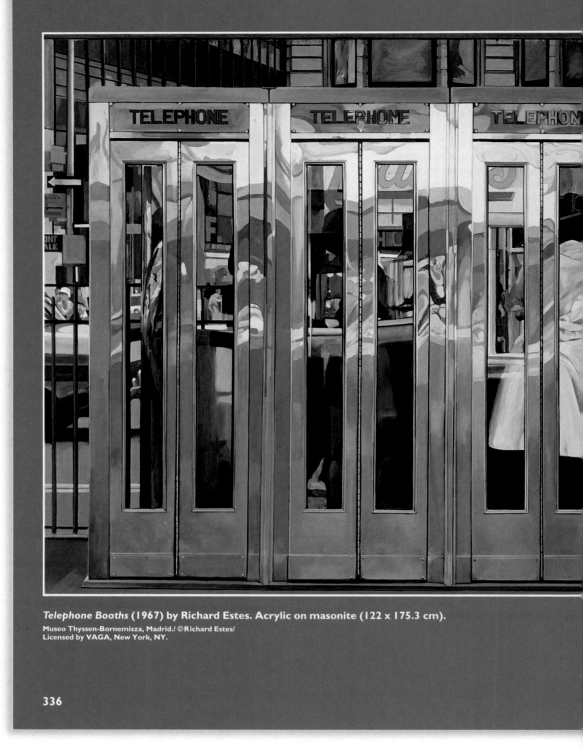

Telephone Booths (1967) by Richard Estes. Acrylic on masonite (122 x 175.3 cm).

Museo Thyssen-Bornemisza, Madrid./ ©Richard Estes/ Licensed by VAGA, New York, NY.

336

Selection Readability

This Annotated Teacher's Edition provides a summary of each selection in the student book. Following each Summary heading, you will find one, two, or three small icons. These icons indicate, in an approximate sense, the reading level of the selection.

■ One icon indicates that the selection is easy.

■ ■ Two icons indicate that the selection is on an intermediate reading level.

■ ■ ■ Three icons indicate that the selection is challenging.

The Nonfiction Collections

If you want to write what the world is about, you have to write details . . . real life is in the dishes. Real life is pushing strollers up the street, folding T-shirts, the alarm clock going off early and you dropping into bed exhausted every night. That's real life.

—Anna Quindlen

337

A CONVERSATION WITH BARRY LOPEZ

Ⓐ Reading Skills and Strategies

Connecting with the Text

Lopez speaks of times when individuals forget about themselves because they are totally caught up in a setting or an event. You might have students, in pairs, take turns telling each other about times in their lives when they temporarily escaped their own personalities because they were fascinated by situations or scenes they were witnessing. Remind students to choose incidents that they do not mind sharing with others.

As you read through this unit, you'll sample the variety, the range, and the power of nonfiction. Listen as Barry Lopez talks about the nonfiction writer's role and responsibility to readers. (You'll read Lopez's report "A Presentation of Whales" on page 434.)

Barry Lopez: I'm conscious of trying to clarify, to make the language work beautifully, and of the reader's needs—how easy is it going to be for the reader to follow, or how can the reader be brought into the scene without violating the scene or violating the reader. By violating the reader I mean making the reader feel like an outsider, choosing a kind of vocabulary or a tone of voice that makes the reader feel uncomfortable or unwelcome. I always mean for a reader to feel welcome in a place. . . .

Q: It's interesting that you think of yourself as an intermediary because in so much of the writing, you seem to disappear, you remove even yourself from being a possible obstacle between the reader and the setting.

Lopez: I try. It's a curious thing to do, in a way. When the reader comes to a writer's work, he or she should sense, very quickly I think, the presence of a distinct personality. Someone with a certain ethical, moral, and artistic dimension. And insofar as that writer is a worthy illuminator of the world for the reader, he or she continues to read the writer's work. Writing is really an extraordinary act of self-assertion. You put down on paper the way you understand the world. But for me there must be a point where the reader loses sight of the writer, where he gains another understanding, a vision of what lies before the writer; so that by the time the reader finishes a book or an essay, he's really thinking about his own thoughts with regard to that subject, or that place, or that set of events and not so much about the writer's. . . .

Q: In a *Publishers Weekly* interview, you said that the Alaskan landscape pulls you "up and out of yourself, and you feel yourself extending into the landscape." Is that feeling of being in harmony with the universe possible to maintain when you come back into the normal routines of life?

Lopez: It's a bit like being in love. When you're in the presence of the beloved, you can't imagine any other moment. But then day-to-day life impinges, the person you love recedes, and you find yourself concentrating on something utterly different. But there is still this very strong attachment in the heart which has to do with memory and longing. I don't think a sense of awe or respect for a particular place diminishes as much as it becomes an isolated memory. Part of the function of literature for me is to rekindle memory and make it part of the present, to compress time. There is a certain amount of ordinary chaos in the human spirit, inside the human mind. I think literature helps to clear that chaos.

Reaching All Students

English Language Learners

Ask these students to focus on the final question and answer in the conversation. First, introduce the terms *landscape* and *rekindle.* Then, invite students to describe landscapes that they love. Lead them in a close reading of the text, and point out that Lopez compares loving a landscape to loving a person: a "strong attachment in the heart which has to do with memory and longing." Highlight Lopez's idea that nonfiction literature can rekindle such attachments. Finally, ask students to list and describe works of literature, art, and music that rekindle their feelings for the landscapes they love. Then, have them classify the literary works as fiction or nonfiction.

Reading Skills and Strategies

OBJECTIVES
1. Identify strategies for reading nonfiction
2. Use word mapping to define words precisely

READING NONFICTION

When you read nonfiction, you interact with the text in some of the same ways you interact with a story or a poem. You may also have a specific purpose in mind—perhaps you are looking for information, or you want to think about a point of view the text offers on an issue that concerns you.

Here are some of the ways we interact with a nonfiction text:

1. **We connect with the text.** We might think, "This is just like Tonya's mother's childhood in Russia," or "I felt this way when I saw the Vietnam Veterans Memorial in Washington."

2. **We ask about the writer.** Careful readers don't believe everything that's printed. We need to evaluate the writer's qualifications and credibility. We need to know the writer's motivation and purpose for writing.

3. **We try to determine if the piece is based on factual evidence or subjective responses.** We evaluate as we read, separating facts from opinions. "Why should I believe you?" is a good question to ask when the writer hands you an opinion.

4. **We interpret.** We figure out the messages the writer is sending us.

5. **We extend the text.** We take the information we're looking for and use it; or we go in search of more information; or we decide that we agree with an argument and take sides accordingly, perhaps even taking action on the issue.

6. **We challenge the text.** We decide how we feel about the writer's main idea. We may find evidence inadequate, an argument faulty, or the writer biased.

HOW TO OWN A WORD

Word Mapping: Pinning Down Meanings

Sometimes you can figure out the meaning of a word from its **context**. Sometimes you can't. Consider this sentence from "R.M.S. Titanic" (page 396):

> "An officer's fist flies out; three shots are fired in the air, and the panic is *quelled*. . . . "

Do things get worse, or better? In this case, you have to refer to a dictionary. Here's how one reader went on to make a **word map** to pin down the precise meaning of *quelled*.

> *Quelled* means "calmed," "quieted," or "subdued."

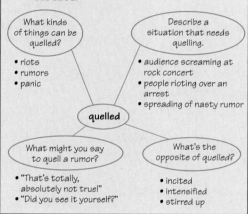

Apply the strategy on the next page. ➡

Reading Skills and Strategies

This feature explains reading strategies for interacting with a nonfiction text. In the accompanying selection, students have the opportunity to practice the strategies immediately, using new material.

Mini-Lesson:
Reading Nonfiction
To give students practice interacting with nonfiction, you might read aloud a brief personal anecdote, such as a humorous incident or a frightening experience. Have students quickwrite their first responses to the anecdote. Then, encourage students to compare their responses and to classify them according to the six ways of interacting listed in this Mini-Lesson.

Mini-Lesson:
How to Own a Word
To give students practice with word mapping, bring in newspapers and news magazines. Have each student select a medium-length article to read, scanning for three words the meaning of which he or she is unsure. Tell students to list the words. Then, divide the class into small groups, and direct groups to create word maps for at least one word from each group member's list.

Reaching All Students

Struggling Readers

Give students the following six questions, one for each of the six ways of interacting with a nonfiction text. Encourage students to apply and answer each question after reading Gary Soto's "The Wrestlers" on pp. 340–342.

1. What experiences in my life does this selection remind me of?
2. What does the writer's main purpose seem to be?
3. What makes this selection believable or unbelievable for me?
4. What unstated messages does the writer seem to be sending?
5. How might this selection apply to my life?
6. How effective do I consider this selection, and why?

Dialogue with the Text

Explain that the side notes in this selection were written by a student who applied some of the strategies presented on p. 339 as she read "The Wrestlers." Point out that she also applied other strategies not included on p. 339.

Summary ■ ■

Fresno, California, in the 1960s is the setting of this autobiographical essay. In his recollections of demoralizing wrestling matches, aimless drives around town, and a dramatic car-crash film in driver's ed, Gary Soto captures the boredom, loneliness, and anxiety of a teen who defines himself primarily as what he is not: not a jock, not popular with girls, not committed to school, not sure what he wants. The essay's meandering structure and veiled suggestions of themes mirror the narrator's uncertainty. A series of death images, as graduation looms, hints at the magnitude of coming changes.

Ⓐ Reading Skills and Strategies
Dialogue with the Text
Soto really makes you feel the physical hurt—"fingerprints still pressed in my arm"—and the humiliation—a stronger opponent "with a grin on his face"—of a wrestling match.

Ⓑ Elements of Literature
Theme
Invite students to decide, as they read further, if one theme of this essay might be losing before you get started.

RESPONDING TO THE ART

Los Angeles-born **Frank Romero** (1941–   ), whose painting adorns the border of this spread (see p. 342), is a pioneering artist/social activist. His paintings and murals feature broad, energetic brush strokes and upbeat, fanciful urban images.
Activity. You might point out that everyone has spent time "just driving around" and ask students to speculate about why it's satisfying. What is the "mood" of Romero's cars? [humorous, playful—the cars look like toys]

T340

READING SKILLS AND STRATEGIES

I suddenly realized life was getting shorter . . .

The Wrestlers
Gary Soto

Dialogue with the Text

Don't look yet! Before you begin reading "The Wrestlers," cover the student's responses in the side column with a piece of paper. As you read, jot down your own responses. Then, when you're done, compare your responses to the story with this reader's responses.

Who is telling this story?

Why wasn't the coach upset?

Who is "I"?

It hurt to be pinned in twelve seconds in a nonleague wrestling match, especially at the end of the 1960s when, except for a few dads and moms and the three regulars with faces like punched-in paper bags, the bleachers were empty of spectators. It hurt to stand under the shower looking at fingerprints still pressed in my arm where my opponent, whose name was Bloodworth, gripped, yanked, and with a grin on his face threw me on my back. The guy next to me had fingerprints around his wrists and arm. Another guy was red around his chest. His eyes were also red. We lost by plenty that night, but coach wasn't too mad. He beat his clipboard against his khaki thigh and joked, "You were a bunch of fishes," by which he meant that we were an easy catch. He pretended to be upset, but we knew that it was the beginning of the season and there was still hope.

I showered and dressed. My best friend Scott was waiting in his Ford Galaxy. He was throwing corn nuts into his mouth, churning beautifully on the taste of salt and roasted nuts. I told him that corn nuts were not good for him, and he asked how that could be, because they tasted good. That night we drove around for a while before he dropped me off at my house and asked me for a quarter. "Gas don't come free," he said. "It costs money when you lose before you get started."

340 THE NONFICTION COLLECTIONS

Reaching All Students

Struggling Readers
Go over the first one or two paragraphs as a group, with each student reading a sentence aloud. Invite students to predict what will happen in the rest of the selection. Have them record their predictions and modify them as they read the remaining paragraphs independently. Then, lead a class discussion in which students share their original predictions and their ideas of what the essay actually is about.

English Language Learners
Some students might need explanations of wrestling/sports jargon (to be pinned, nonleague, bleachers, mats) and of references to pop culture (Ford Galaxy, corn nuts, *Bonanza, Gunsmoke,* Pep-Boys, crew cuts).

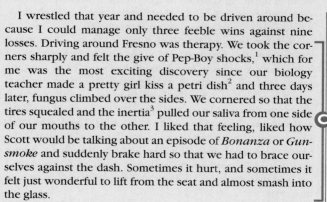

I wrestled that year and needed to be driven around because I could manage only three feeble wins against nine losses. Driving around Fresno was therapy. We took the corners sharply and felt the give of Pep-Boy shocks,[1] which for me was the most exciting discovery since our biology teacher made a pretty girl kiss a petri dish[2] and three days later, fungus climbed over the sides. We cornered so that the tires squealed and the inertia[3] pulled our saliva from one side of our mouths to the other. I liked that feeling, liked how Scott would be talking about an episode of *Bonanza* or *Gunsmoke* and suddenly brake hard so that we had to brace ourselves against the dash. Sometimes it hurt, and sometimes it felt just wonderful to lift from the seat and almost smash into the glass.

I had taken driver's ed from my coach, and on the second day of class he said, "Don't be scared but you're gonna see some punks getting killed." The film was called something like *Red Asphalt* or *Blood on the Pavement,* but I remember a narrator with a crew cut and a neck as thick as a canned ham. When he spoke while holding up a tennis shoe, the muscles in his neck jumped around. He said, "The boy who wore this sneaker is dead." He held it up, and the camera moved in close on the high-top, then flashed to a freeway accident as dramatic music started along with the title credits.

It could have been my sneaker because, like the dead kid, I liked high-tops. It could have been Scott's or any other boy's. The film was meant to scare us, but most of the boys enjoyed it. The girls looked away when the film showed six seconds of a car wreck from different angles. The sound of metal and glass breaking made us listen up. It stopped us from chewing our gum or slipping a corn nut into the inside of our cheeks. Then all was quiet. A bird pumped his tail and chirped on a chain-link fence. The narrator came back on. He was stand-

1. **Pep-Boy shocks:** shock absorbers from Pep-Boys, a national chain of automobile-parts stores.
2. **petri** (pē′trē) **dish:** shallow glass dish in which microorganisms are grown.
3. **inertia** (in·ur′shə): in physics, the tendency of something that is at rest to remain at rest and something that is in motion to remain in motion.

Dialogue with the Text

Why did Scott and "I" drive around before going home?

Why did the girl have to kiss the petri dish?

Why were the boys driving in this manner?

I feel this film will help teach students the dangers of driving.

Were these students actually getting an understanding of the real moral of this film?

THE WRESTLERS **341**

Reaching All Students

Advanced Learners

After they read the selection, invite these students to take the role of Soto at his high school reunion twenty years later. Direct students to write speeches, in Soto's voice, explaining to former classmates and teachers how the experiences recounted in "The Wrestlers" affected him as a person and as the writer he has become. Advise students to review "The Wrestlers" carefully for details and implications to use in their speeches.

Dialogue with the Text

Ask students to identify reading strategies Sara Hunter has used so far. [Possible responses: interpreting ("Why wasn't the coach upset?" "Why did Scott and 'I' drive around before going home?"); identifying point of view ("Who is telling this story?" "Who is 'I'?"); extending the text ("I feel this film will help teach students the dangers of driving."); ascertaining facts ("Were these students actually getting an understanding of the real moral of this film?").]

C Reading Skills and Strategies
Dialogue with the Text
❓ Soto is writing about his impressions, feelings, and thoughts. Why does he use proper nouns like *Fresno, Pep-Boy,* and the titles of old TV series? [Possible answers: to help you visualize things; to make the writing seem more realistic and believable.]

D Reading Skills and Strategies
Connecting with the Text
❓ Have you ever seen this type of film? Did it (or do you imagine it would) motivate you to drive more carefully? Explain. [Possible responses: Yes, because the dangers are real and death is permanent; no, because knowing the film is intended to shock makes it less effective.]

Dialogue with the Text

Encourage students to express their own opinions about the writer's main idea. Do they agree or disagree with Sara Hunter? Why?

Ⓐ Reading Skills and Strategies
Making Inferences

❓ What connections might the narrator be implying between events in his junior year and events in his senior year? [Possible responses: that what he realized in his junior year made him feel lonelier and more desperate during his senior year; that he was going in circles both years, doing the same thing, although for slightly different reasons]

Ⓑ Reading Skills and Strategies
Dialogue with the Text

❓ This essay is about much more than wrestling in a literal sense. How does Soto imply that most people are wrestling with problems? [Possible response: Even the coach, the dean, and the teacher seem to be wrestling with their limitations or anxieties.]

Ⓒ Reading Skills and Strategies
Making Inferences

❓ The 1960s was a decade of war and assassinations. How might the attitude of the piece connect to the time period of its setting? [Possible responses: Maybe that's why this piece seems so downbeat—the narrator harps on things like loneliness and death and doesn't seem to recall any good times; this last paragraph suggests that big changes are on the way, in the narrator's life and in society.]

Dialogue with the Text

What does all of this have to do with wrestling?

How was this wrestler comparing the film with wrestling?

Chicano Lowrider (1993) by Frank Romero. Oil on paper (30" × 40").
Courtesy Frank Romero.

I feel this story is about different struggles adolescents go through during high school. It lets others know that when the going gets tough, the tough get tougher. People should never give up.

Sara Hunter

— Sara Hunter
Southeast High School
Bradenton, Florida

---

ing on the shoulder of a freeway, his tie whipping in the wind of traffic. He warned us that during a head-on collision, your clothes rip off: shirts, skirts, shoes, the whole works—naked as you were born, only you were dead.

I recalled Bloodworth pinning me in twelve seconds and suddenly realized life was getting shorter: A car wreck could kill you in six seconds. It was tough luck—only half the time for the kids in the film. I watched the film, then watched coach laugh along with the boys and turn on the overhead lights, jumble the dimes and quarters in his deep pockets, and slap his clipboard against his thigh. His neck was thick like the narrator's. His hair was a little longer and shiny as the black industrial shoes on his feet. Right in driver's ed, among the idiot boys smelling of sunflower seeds and corn nuts, I realized that wrestlers went on to do more than slam people into mats.

I was a junior that year. During my senior year I was so lonely that I needed to drive around Fresno. Scott was at the wheel, more lonely than me, more desperate because a girl said no, then yes, then finally no again to a Halloween date. It was no for both of us. We had no choice but to drive around corners, the centrifugal force[4] pulling us one way, then another. We had no choice but to throw bottles from the car and sneer at old drivers in long cars.

We often parked at the levee[5] and looked at the water. I said things like, "Scott, I think I've lived before," or, "Scotty, do you ever feel that someone is gripping your shoulder and when you turn around, no one is there? It's spooky." I could still feel Bloodworth's grip on my arm, and would feel it for years.

I didn't like high school. Coach knew only so many words. The dean's hand trembled when he touched doorknobs. Our teacher kept repeating that a noun was a person, place, or thing. She stood at the blackboard, lipstick overrunning her mouth, and said for the thousandth time: Elvis is a noun. Fresno is a noun. Elvis's guitar is also a noun.

The water in the canal was quick as a windblown cloud. The 1960s were coming to an end, and the first of the great rock stars were beginning to die. We were dying to leave home, by car, thumb, or on water, racing west to where the sun went down.

---

4. centrifugal (sen·trif′yōō·gəl) **force:** force that tends to pull something outward when it is rotating rapidly.
5. levee (lev′ē): artificial river bank, built to prevent flooding.

Using Students' Strengths

Spatial/Visual Learners

Invite interested students to sketch a series of key images from the essay and to share their sketches with the class. Have them explain why they chose each image and why they portrayed it as they did.

Naturalist Learners

The levee and the canal are important places for the narrator and Scott. Challenge students to learn more about the Fresno area of California's San Joaquin Valley, including geography, natural vegetation, agriculture, and the canal system. Then, ask these students to present information that will help the class envision the landscapes through which Soto and his friend drive so often.

Auditory/Musical Learners

Invite students to prepare a presentation of appropriate music from the 1960s to complement Soto's essay. Have students tape their musical selections and play them in conjunction with an oral reading of the essay. They might use the music as background, or they might alternate musical selections with segments of the essay.

Collection 5

Becoming Myself

Theme

Finding Our Identity *These selections are autobiographies, the literary form that most consistently and probingly searches for identity. Autobiographies today, as your students will see from these pieces, use all the elements of fiction to portray their characters, create suspense, describe conflict, and, in many cases, give us the gift of laughter.*

Reading the Anthology

Reaching Struggling Readers

The *Reading Skills and Strategies: Reaching Struggling Readers* binder includes a Reading Strategies Handbook that offers concrete suggestions for helping students who have difficulty reading and comprehending text, or students who are reluctant readers. When a specific strategy is most appropriate for a selection, a correlation to the Handbook is provided at the bottom of the teacher's page under the head Struggling Readers. This head may also be used to introduce additional ideas for helping students read challenging texts.

Reading Beyond the Anthology

Read On Collection 5 includes an annotated bibliography of books suitable for extended reading. The suggested books are related to works in this collection by theme, by author, or by subject. To preview the Read On for Collection 5, please turn to p. T379.

HRW Library The *HRW Library* offers novels, plays, and short-story collections for extended reading. Each book in the Library includes one or more major works and thematically related Connections. Each book in the *HRW Library* is also accompanied by a Study Guide that provides teaching suggestions and worksheets. For Collection 5, the following titles are recommended.

PYGMALION
George Bernard Shaw
Eliza Doolittle, who sells flowers in the street, is rescued by a speech teacher and trained to speak like a lady—and so she is accepted as one, in this satiric, humorous play that ridicules the snobbery of Victorian England.

JANE EYRE
Charlotte Brontë
Jane endures a cruel childhood and an inhuman boarding school before she finds her independence as a governess. But she doesn't discover her true self until she falls in love—with a very inappropriate man. (This novel is also recommended for Collection 3, Exiles, Castaways, and Strangers.)

Resources for this Collection

Internet Resources
go.hrw.com LE0 10-5

Note: All resources for this collection are available for preview on the *One-Stop Planner CD-ROM 1 with Test Generator.* All worksheets and blackline masters may be printed from the CD-ROM.

Selection or Feature	Reading and Literary Skills	Vocabulary, Language, and Grammar
Hair *from* **The Autobiography of Malcolm X** (p. 344) Malcolm X *with* Alex Haley	• *Graphic Organizers for Active Reading,* Worksheet p. 21 • *Literary Elements:* Transparency 10 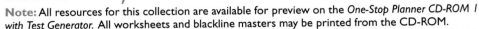 Worksheet p. 31	• *Words to Own,* Worksheet p. 21 • *Grammar and Language Links:* Pronouns, Worksheet p. 39 • *Language Workshop CD-ROM,* Pronouns • *Daily Oral Grammar,* Transparency 21
Elements of Literature Autobiography (p. 353)	• *Literary Elements,* Transparency 10	
It Can't Be Helped *from* **Farewell to Manzanar** (p. 354) Jeanne Wakatsuki Houston *and* James Houston **Connections: Nisei Daughter: The Second Generation** (p. 360) Rose Furuya Hawkins	• *Graphic Organizers for Active Reading,* Worksheet p. 22	• *Words to Own,* Worksheet p. 22 • *Grammar and Language Links:* Capitalization, Worksheet p. 41 • *Language Workshop CD-ROM,* Nouns • *Daily Oral Grammar,* Transparency 22
Typhoid Fever *from* **Angela's Ashes** (p. 365) Frank McCourt **Connections: The Education of Frank McCourt** (p. 372) Barbara Sande Dimmitt	• *Graphic Organizers for Active Reading,* Worksheet p. 23	• *Words to Own,* Worksheet p. 23 • *Grammar and Language Links:* Antecedents, Worksheet p. 43 • *Language Workshop CD-ROM,* Run-on Sentences • *Daily Oral Grammar,* Transparency 23
Extending the Theme: Theme for English B (p. 376) Langston Hughes	The Extending the Theme feature provides students with an unstructured opportunity to practice reading strategies using a selection that extends the theme of the collection.	
Writer's Workshop: Autobiographical Incident (p. 380)		
Sentence Workshop: Using Subordination (p. 385)		• *Workshop Resources,* p. 63 • *Language Workshop CD-ROM,* Combining Sentences

Other Resources for this Collection

- *Cross-Curricular Activities,* p. 5
- *Portfolio Management System,* Introduction to Portfolio Assessment, p. 1
- *Test Generator,* Collection Test

Writing	Listening and Speaking Viewing and Representing	Assessment
• *Portfolio Management System,* Rubrics for Choices, p. 131	• *Visual Connections:* Videocassette A, Segment 5 • *Audio CD Library,* Disc 11, Track 3  • *Portfolio Management System,* Rubrics for Choices, p. 131	• *Formal Assessment,* Selection Test, p. 59 • *Standardized Test Preparation,* p. 44 • *Test Generator (One-Stop Planner CD-ROM)*
		• *Formal Assessment,* Literary Elements Test, p. 65
• *Portfolio Management System,* Rubrics for Choices, p. 132	• *Audio CD Library,* Disc 11, Tracks 4, 5  • *Viewing and Representing:* Fine Art Transparency 8 Worksheet p. 32 • *Portfolio Management System,* Rubrics for Choices, p. 132	• *Formal Assessment,* Selection Test, p. 61 • *Test Generator (One-Stop Planner CD-ROM)*
• *Portfolio Management System,* Rubrics for Choices, p. 134	• *Audio CD Library,* Disc 11, Track 6  • *Portfolio Management System,* Rubrics for Choices, p. 134	• *Formal Assessment,* Selection Test, p. 63 • *Standardized Test Preparation,* p. 46 • *Test Generator (One-Stop Planner CD-ROM)*
	• *Audio CD Library,* Disc 11, Track 7 	

• *Workshop Resources,* p. 23
 • *Writer's Workshop 2 CD-ROM,* Autobiographical Incident
	• *Viewing and Representing,* HRW Multimedia Presentation Maker	• *Portfolio Management System*
		   • Prewriting, p. 135
		   • Peer Editing, p. 136
		   • Assessment Rubric, p. 137

Collection Planner

 Transparency   CD-ROM   Video    Audio CD

Skills Focus

Selection or Feature	Reading Skills and Strategies	Elements of Literature	Vocabulary/Language/Grammar	Writing	Listening/Speaking	Viewing/Representing
Hair *from* **The Autobiography of Malcolm X** (p. 344) Malcolm X *with* Alex Haley	Make Inferences About Tone, pp. 344, 350 Summarize, p. 350	Tone, pp. 344, 350	Tone, p. 352 Diction, p. 352 Etymology, p. 352 Word Roots, p. 352	Collect Ideas, p. 351	Research and Report on an African American Artist, p. 351 Research and Report on Word Origins, p. 351	Create Illustrations of Historic Hairstyles, p. 351
Elements of Literature: Autobiography (p. 353)		Autobiography, p. 353 Biography, p. 353				
It Can't Be Helped *from* **Farewell to Manzanar** (p. 354) Jeanne Wakatsuki Houston and James Houston	Chronological Order, pp. 354, 362 Infer, p. 362	Anecdote, p. 354 Biography, p. 354 Autobiography, p. 354 Setting, p. 362 Point of View, p. 362 Title, p. 362 Tone, pp. 362–363	Specific and Proper Nouns, p. 364 Prefixes, p. 364 Suffixes, p. 364 Etymology, p. 364	Take Notes on an Incident, p. 363 Research and Write a Report on Japanese Internment Camps, p. 363	Stage a Debate, p. 363 Prepare and Present a Reading, p. 363	Use a Map, p. 363 Research and Report on Japanese Wood-blocks, p. 363
Typhoid Fever *from* **Angela's Ashes** (p. 365) Frank McCourt	Evaluate Credibility, pp. 365, 374 Summarize, p. 374	Comic Relief, pp. 365, 374	Voice and the Conventions of Punctuation, p. 375 Antonyms, p. 375 Synonyms, p. 375	Recall Details to Enrich Writing, p. 374 Write a Personal Essay, p. 374	Plan, Practice, and Present an Oral Interpretation, p. 374	Create a Cause-and-Effect Chart, p. 374
Extending the Theme: Theme for English B (p. 376) Langston Hughes		Tone, p. 378	The Extending the Theme feature provides students with an unstructured opportunity to practice reading skills using a selection that extends the theme of the collection.			
Writer's Workshop: Autobiographical Incident (p. 380)				Write an Autobiographical Incident, pp. 380–384		
Sentence Workshop: Using Subordination (p. 385)			Subordinating Conjunctions, p. 385 Subordinate Clauses, p. 385	Combine Choppy Sentences Using Subordinate Clauses, p. 385		
Reading for Life: Reading a Text-book (p. 386)	Identify Text Organizers and Other Features, p. 386 Skim to Overview Contents, p. 386					

Collection **5**

BECOMING MYSELF

WRITING FOCUS: Autobiographical Incident

> *Something in me strives to connect with the past. Not my past, but another's past. An ancestral past. And so, after all, it is my past.*
>
> —*Karen Cooper*

If someone asked "Who are you?" how would you answer? Maybe you'd give your name, age, where you live, a description of your family. That's hardly the whole story, though. So much goes into making up "who you are"—the complete, total story of your life till now.

The three writers in this collection have looked at their lives and found they had stories to tell. From a hairy experience in Boston to a Japanese American internment camp in the desert to a fever hospital in Ireland—these writers have looked at their experiences and tried to get in touch with "who they were." As you read these autobiographies (literally, "self-life-writings"), see what they say to you about that interesting process of becoming yourself.

Writer's Notebook
In your Writer's Notebook, freewrite about the first experience that comes to your mind when you think: **What has helped make me the person I am right now?** Your writing is yours to share with others or to keep for your eyes alone.

OBJECTIVES

1. Read essays on the theme "Becoming Myself"
2. Interpret literary elements used in the essays, with special emphasis on autobiography
3. Apply a variety of reading strategies to the essays
4. Respond to the essays in a variety of modes
5. Learn and use new words
6. Plan, draft, revise, edit, proof, and publish an autobiographical incident
7. Develop skill in sentence variety
8. Develop skill in reading a textbook

Responding to the Quotation

Activity. Ask students how learning of another person's past can have meaning for them. [Sample response: It can spark insights and make one more self-aware.]

Writer's Notebook
Allow volunteers to read their responses aloud. Then, advise students to save their notes for possible use in the Writer's Workshop on p. 380.

RESPONDING TO THE ART

Point out that the illustration depicts a person whose head and arms are in deep shadow.
Activity. Ask students how the figure might illustrate the "ancestral past." [Sample responses: Viewers can imagine any facial features on the figure, so it could be anyone's ancestor; farming is a key to the development of all human civilization.]

Writing Focus: Autobiographical Incident

The following **Work in Progress** assignments build to a culminating **Writer's Workshop** at the end of the collection.

- Hair — Finding an experience (p. 351)
- It Can't Be Helped — Exploring a personal experience (p. 363)
- Typhoid Fever — Making an incident come alive (p. 374)

Writer's Workshop: Narrative Writing / Autobiographical Incident (p. 380)

OBJECTIVES

1. Read and interpret the autobiography
2. Analyze tone
3. Make inferences about tone
4. Express understanding through writing, research and art history, language study, or drawing and research
5. Identify and use tone in writing
6. Understand and use new words
7. Map word roots

SKILLS

Literary, Reading, Writing
- Analyze tone
- Make inferences about tone
- Take notes on a meaningful experience

Grammar/Language
- Identify and use tone
- Report on American slang

Vocabulary
- Use new words
- Map word roots

Research/Art History
- Research and report on an African American artist

Drawing/Research
- Research and sketch hairstyles

Viewing/Representing
- Analyze use of color and composition (ATE)
- Analyze mood and message (ATE)

Planning

- **Block Schedule**
  Block Scheduling Lesson Plans with Pacing Guide
- **Traditional Schedule**
  Lesson Plans Including Strategies for English-Language Learners
- **One-Stop Planner**
  CD-ROM with Test Generator

Before You Read

HAIR

Make the Connection

Everyone Does It

Maybe it's baggy shorts, a baseball cap worn backward, and one earring. The way we choose to look is one way we express who we are. The problem is that sometimes we conform to what is in fashion, instead of daring to be ourselves.

Quickwrite

Brainstorm in class to make a list of some of the fashions in hair, clothing, music, and dancing that are "in" at your school and some that are "out." In your notebook, jot down very quickly how you yourself feel about pressures to conform to what's "in" and to reject what's "out."

Elements of Literature

"Hearing" Tones

"I like your hair." Say this sentence aloud three times so that it communicates three attitudes: "I really do like your hair." "I know I'm supposed to say something nice about your hair, so I'm saying it." "I can't stand your hair, and I want you to feel foolish about it." The person with the hair can infer your meaning from listening to the tone of your voice.

Tone is the writer's attitude toward the audience, the subject, or a character.

For more on Tone, see the Handbook of Literary Terms.

Reading Skills and Strategies

Making Inferences about Tone

When you read, you can't hear the tone of the speaker's or narrator's voice. Writers have to rely on word choice and details to communicate their **tone,** or attitude toward their subjects. Readers must then piece together these clues to **infer,** or make an intelligent guess about, the writer's feelings. What tones do you hear in "Hair"?

Background

For many young African American men in the 1940s, a zoot suit and conked hair were cool. A zoot suit was a big, baggy suit with wide, padded shoulders, an extra-long jacket, and pants that narrowed at the ankle. Conked hair was straightened with congolene—a mixture of harsh lye, potatoes, eggs, and soap. In this excerpt from his autobiography, Malcolm X writes about his first conk and how it made him feel. At this point, Malcolm was living in the Roxbury section of Boston.

go.hrw.com
LEO 10-5

Malcolm X, then Malcolm Little (top row, third from right), as a fourth-grader in Lansing, Michigan.

Preteaching Vocabulary

Words to Own

Have students, working in pairs, read the definitions of the Words to Own at the bottom of p. 347. To enhance students' comprehension of the words, use the following exercise.

Imagine that you are a counselor and your partner is a client in trouble (or vice versa). With your partner, take turns role-playing the counselor and the client in the following scenarios.

1. You use the word <u>self-degradation</u> to talk to a student about drug use.
2. You use the word <u>multitude</u> as you persuade a sixth-grader that she is unique.
3. You use the word <u>violate</u> as you warn an adult about the need to obey the law.
4. You use the word <u>mutilate</u> to talk to a client about excessive body piercing.

THEN MY HEAD CAUGHT FIRE.

HAIR

from **The Autobiography of Malcolm X**

Malcolm X with Alex Haley

Shorty soon decided that my hair was finally long enough to be conked. He had promised to school me in how to beat the barbershops' three- and four-dollar price by making up congolene and then conking ourselves.

The teenage Malcolm, whose reddish hair gave him his nickname, "Big Red."

Summary ■ ■

Malcolm X recalls his first "conk," or hair-straightening, performed by his friend Shorty, using a caustic home-made congolene. In the last two paragraphs, however, Malcolm X castigates his youthful self and all other "brain-washed" black Americans who violate their bodies to conform to racist standards of attractiveness.

Resources

Viewing and Representing
Videocassette A, Segment 5
"The Power of Learning: Malcolm X"
Available in English and Spanish.
This biography shows how education transformed Malcolm X's life. For full lesson plans and worksheets, see the *Visual Connections Teacher's Manual.*

Listening
Audio CD Library
An interesting recording of this autobiography is included in the *Audio CD Library:*
• Disc 11, Track 3

Elements of Literature
Autobiography
For additional instruction on autobiography, see *Literary Elements:*
• Transparency 10
• Worksheet, p. 31

A Elements of Literature
Tone
Have students read the first sentence aloud three times, each time in a different tone of voice: happy, sad, and angry. Then, have them read the first three paragraphs silently. Ask them to decide which tone of voice best fits the writing tone they "hear." [happy, because Malcolm is proud to be getting his first conk]

Resources: Print and Media

Reading
• *Graphic Organizers for Active Reading,* p. 21
• *Words to Own,* p. 21
• *Audio CD Library*
    Disc 11, Track 3

Elements of Literature
• *Literary Elements*
    Transparency 10
    Worksheet, p. 31

Writing and Language
• *Daily Oral Grammar*
    Transparency 21
• *Grammar and Language Links*
    Worksheet, p. 39

Viewing and Representing
• *Visual Connections*
    Videocassette A, Segment 5

Assessment
• *Formal Assessment,* p. 59
• *Portfolio Management System,* p. 131
• *Standardized Test Preparation,* p. 44
• *Test Generator (One-Stop Planner CD-ROM)*

Internet
• go.hrw.com (keyword: LE0 10-5)

Ⓐ Elements of Literature

Tone

❓ Which details show you the attitude of Malcolm X, as a young man, toward his first conk? [Possible answers: his careful attention to all the specifics, his proud grin.] **What word would you use to define his attitude?** [Possible responses: *eager; happy; upbeat; proud; naive.*]

Ⓑ Reading Skills and Strategies

Making Inferences about Tone

❓ Point out the use of colloquial language, such as *glop, real fast, damn right,* and *it burns bad.* What tone is created by these informal words and phrases? Explain your answer. [Possible responses: The tone is comic—the words make Malcolm and Shorty sound a bit like sitcom characters; the tone is straightforward—the words sound relaxed and realistic, but not unusual.]

Barber Shop (1946) by Jacob Lawrence (1917–). Gouache on paper (21⅛″ × 29⅜″). (1975.15)
The Toledo Museum of Art, Toledo, Ohio. Purchased with funds from the Libbey Endowment. Gift of Edward Drummond Libbey. Courtesy of the artist and Francine Seders Gallery, Seattle, Washington.

Ⓐ I took the little list of ingredients he had printed out for me and went to a grocery store, where I got a can of Red Devil lye, two eggs, and two medium-sized white potatoes. Then at a drugstore near the poolroom, I asked for a large jar of Vaseline, a large bar of soap, a large-toothed comb and a fine-toothed comb, one of those rubber hoses with a metal sprayhead, a rubber apron, and a pair of gloves.

"Going to lay on that first conk?" the drugstore man asked me. I proudly told him, grinning, "Right!"

Shorty paid six dollars a week for a room in his cousin's shabby apartment. His cousin wasn't at home. "It's like the pad's mine, he spends so much time with his woman," Shorty said. "Now, you watch me—"

He peeled the potatoes and thin-sliced them into a quart-sized Mason fruit jar, then started stirring them with a wooden spoon as he gradually poured in a little over half the can of lye. "Never use a metal spoon; the lye will turn it black," he told me.

Ⓑ A jellylike, starchy-looking glop resulted from

346 THE NONFICTION COLLECTIONS

Reaching All Students

Struggling Readers

Making Inferences About Tone was introduced on p. 344. One good strategy to use with this selection is Say Something. For information on using this strategy, see p. 85 in the *Reading Strategies Handbook* in front of the *Reading Skills and Strategies* binder.

English Language Learners

Students unfamiliar with American culture may need explanations of the terms *Vaseline* and *pad* (home) and, on p. 347, *homeboy* (a friend from one's own neighborhood) and *brainwashed.* For additional strategies for engaging English language learners with the literature, see
• *Lesson Plans Including Strategies for English-Language Learners*

Advanced Learners

To give an added dimension to the selection, you might have these students read the first chapter of *The Autobiography of Malcolm X.* Encourage them to speculate about how the experiences recounted in that chapter (entitled "Nightmare") might have contributed to the attitudes that Malcolm X reveals in the final paragraph of "Hair."

the lye and potatoes, and Shorty broke in the two eggs, stirring real fast—his own conk and dark face bent down close. The congolene turned pale yellowish. "Feel the jar," Shorty said. I cupped my hand against the outside and snatched it away. "Damn right, it's hot, that's the lye," he said. "So you know it's going to burn when I comb it in—it burns *bad*. But the longer you can stand it, the straighter the hair."

He made me sit down, and he tied the string of the new rubber apron tightly around my neck and combed up my bush of hair. Then, from the big Vaseline jar, he took a handful and massaged it hard all through my hair and into the scalp. He also thickly Vaselined my neck, ears, and forehead. "When I get to washing out your head, be sure to tell me anywhere you feel any little stinging," Shorty warned me, washing his hands, then pulling on the rubber gloves and tying on his own rubber apron. "You always got to remember that any congolene left in burns a sore into your head."

The congolene just felt warm when Shorty started combing it in. But then my head caught fire.

I gritted my teeth and tried to pull the sides of the kitchen table together. The comb felt as if it was raking my skin off.

My eyes watered, my nose was running. I couldn't stand it any longer; I bolted to the washbasin. I was cursing Shorty with every name I could think of when he got the spray going and started soap-lathering my head.

He lathered and spray-rinsed, lathered and spray-rinsed, maybe ten or twelve times, each time gradually closing the hot-water faucet, until the rinse was cold, and that helped some.

"You feel any stinging spots?"

"No," I managed to say. My knees were trembling.

"Sit back down, then. I think we got it all out OK."

The flame came back as Shorty, with a thick towel, started drying my head, rubbing hard. *"Easy, man, easy!"* I kept shouting.

"The first time's always worst. You get used to it better before long. You took it real good, homeboy. You got a good conk."

When Shorty let me stand up and see in the mirror, my hair hung down in limp, damp strings. My scalp still flamed, but not as badly; I could bear it. He draped the towel around my shoulders, over my rubber apron, and began again Vaselining my hair.

I could feel him combing, straight back, first the big comb, then the fine-toothed one.

Then he was using a razor, very delicately, on the back of my neck. Then, finally, shaping the sideburns.

My first view in the mirror blotted out the hurting. I'd seen some pretty conks, but when it's the first time, on your *own* head, the transformation, after the lifetime of kinks, is staggering.

The mirror reflected Shorty behind me. We both were grinning and sweating. And on top of my head was this thick, smooth sheen of shining red hair—real red—as straight as any white man's.

How ridiculous I was! Stupid enough to stand there simply lost in admiration of my hair now looking "white," reflected in the mirror in Shorty's room. I vowed that I'd never again be without a conk, and I never was for many years.

This was my first really big step toward self-degradation: when I endured all of that pain, literally burning my flesh to have it look like a white man's hair. I had joined that multitude of Negro men and women in America who are brainwashed into believing that the black people are "inferior"—and white people "superior"—that they will even violate and mutilate their God-created bodies to try to look "pretty" by white standards.

C Reading Skills and Strategies

Making Inferences about Tone

? Which of Shorty's words imply a tone of concern and warmth for the narrator? [Sample responses: his question about "any stinging spots"; his encouragement: "The first time's always worst. You get used to it. . . . You took it real good, homeboy."]

D Appreciating Language

Tone

? To demonstrate how diction affects tone, have students imagine that the word *staggering* is replaced with *amazing*. What happens to the tone? [Possible response: It becomes lighter.]

E Critical Thinking

Connecting with the Text

? Have you known anyone willing to experience pain for vanity's sake? Did the outcome justify the pain? [Students might give examples of people they know, such as a friend who had several piercings and said it was worth it or a relative who got a tattoo and later regretted it.]

Resources ————

Selection Assessment
Formal Assessment
• Selection Test, p. 59
Test Generator (One-Stop Planner)
• CD-ROM

Getting Students Involved

Cooperative Learning

Becoming Himself. Until his death, Malcolm X continued to evaluate and change his assumptions and actions. Put students in groups of three to learn more about this remarkable leader. Assign each group a decade of Malcolm X's life. Then, direct one member of each group to locate information. Have a second member read it and dictate notes to a third. Ask each group to present its findings to the class.

Making the Connections

Connecting to the Theme: "Becoming Myself"

Malcolm X reveals who he is by recalling an attempt to become who he was not. Though he was pleased with his first conk and had many more, he later sees it as a "step toward self-degradation." This excerpt from his autobiography does not specify how or why he changed his views. Clearly, however, for Malcolm X, becoming oneself begins with respecting oneself and one's heritage.

MEET THE WRITER

A Charismatic Leader

Malcolm X (1925–1965) changed his life and then lost it. One of the most influential African American leaders of the twentieth century, Malcolm wrote an autobiography that has become a modern classic.

Malcolm's father, a Baptist minister active in Marcus Garvey's Universal Negro Improvement Association, died when Malcolm was six, reportedly pushed under a streetcar by white racists. His mother suffered an emotional breakdown and spent twenty-six years in a mental hospital.

At sixteen, Malcolm moved to Boston to live with his half-sister. A life of hustling and burglary landed him in prison from 1946 to 1952, and there he changed his life. He read hundreds of books, starting with the letter *A* in a dictionary ("People don't realize how a man's whole life can be changed by one book," he said), and joined the weekly prison debates.

66 Standing up and speaking before an audience was a thing that throughout my previous life never would have crossed my mind. But I will tell you that, right there, in the prison, debating, speaking to a crowd, was as exhilarating to me as the discovery of knowledge through reading had been. Standing up there, the faces looking up at me, things in my head coming out of my mouth, while my brain searched for the next best thing to follow what I was saying, and if I could sway them to my side by handling it right, then I had won the debate—once my feet got wet, I was gone on debating. 99

Malcolm had converted to the Muslim faith in prison and after his release became the most popular, charismatic preacher in the Nation of Islam movement. He abandoned his

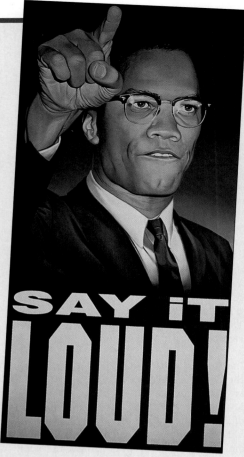

Award-winning oil painting of Malcolm X (1993) by Victor Zavala, a student at California State University at Fullerton, California.

"slave name" and took the surname "X," a letter that in algebra stands for the unknown.

In 1963, after openly challenging the movement's leader, Elijah Muhammad, Malcolm was suspended from the Black Muslim ministry. On February 21, 1965, just as he was about to speak in the Audubon Ballroom in New York City, he was shot and killed.

Assessing Learning

Check Test: True-False
"Hair"
1. Shorty decides when Malcolm's hair should be conked. [True]
2. Malcolm buys all the congolene ingredients at a drugstore. [False]
3. Cold water eases the conking pain. [True]
4. Conking curls Malcolm's hair. [False]
5. The adult Malcolm X looks back at his young self with pride. [False]

Standardized Test Preparation
For practice with standardized test format specific to this selection, see
• *Standardized Test Preparation,* p. 44
For practice in proofreading and editing, see
• *Daily Oral Grammar,* Transparency 21

Barber shop sign (oil on board) in Burkina Faso, a West African country.

A "Piercing" Issue

"C'mon, Jen," they leered, an outstretched hand clutching onto a gleaming needle poised to plunge into my skin at any minute. "Everybody's doin' it."

"NO," I shouted vehemently, shaking my head and glaring at the so-called friends surrounding me. "I won't do it. I'm not giving in to you guys or to all this peer pressure."

My best friend finally collapsed onto a nearby couch, holding her hands up in exasperation and staring at me as if I were some lunatic.

"For Pete's sake, Jenny," she cried. "We're not asking you to do drugs or anything! All we want to do is to pierce your stupid ears!"

All right, so maybe I am acting a bit paranoid **Ⓐ** about pierced ears. Maybe my friends are right when they say that a high school female has to have her ears pierced; that it is some sort of un-

official tradition spreading throughout both genders of our society even as we speak. Maybe men really are attracted to dangling objects hanging from lobes of the skin and that when I become an old maid with no man, I will finally give in to the peer pressure and have my ears punched through. Maybe, maybe, maybe . . .

In a world where insecurity is the norm and **Ⓑ** where "Maybe" is the obsolete answer for so many questions, it is reassuring to know that I have made a decision based on what I know is right for me. Rather than allowing the conforming roles of society to dominate my entire life, I have stood up for myself and won.

Won? How could something so obscure as unblemished earlobes be considered a victory when the world is filled with issues that concern our lives more intensely, such as abortion, politics, and drugs? Have I nothing better to do than stand in front of a mirror and say to myself, "Boy, Jenny, you sure are brave not to have your ears pierced"?

The fact of the matter is, there are very serious issues that we as intelligent people must face every day. With each issue, we must make some sort of decision that will change our lives some way or another. When making such life-altering decisions, how will we know that we have made the correct choice for ourselves, without having someone else cloud our opinions?

For me, all I have to do is glance at the mirror and see my plain, boring earlobes. That glance will always tell me that since I was able to make one decision based on my personal beliefs, I can make a thousand more and know that each and every one was made by me, not by a conforming society.

Maybe I'm just trying to be a pseudo-intellectual nonconformist. Maybe I'm writing this just to impress you with my essay-writing abilities. Maybe it's time to look in the mirror again.

—Jennifer Yu
Warren Township High School
Gurnee, Illlinois

HAIR 349

Student to Student

A student explores underlying issues and potential ramifications of her refusal to have her ears pierced.

Ⓐ Reading Skills and Strategies
Responding to the Text
❓ What is your opinion of ear piercing? Why? [Possible responses: It's harmless—in fact, in some cultures it's a standard procedure done in infancy; it's unsettling to see people with holes bored in their ears; it's practical; it's attractive.]

Ⓑ Elements of Literature
Tone
❓ Compare the tone of these two paragraphs. What differences in tone do you detect? [Possible responses: The paragraph before the break sounds humorous, and the following paragraph sounds serious; the paragraph before the break sounds uncertain, and the following paragraph sounds very firm.]

RESPONDING TO THE ART

Activity. Invite students to compare the amount and type of facial detail in this "primitivist" portrait, in Victor Zavala's photo-realist portrait on p. 348, and in the painting by Jacob Lawrence (who was once considered a primitivist) on p. 346. [Sample response: Zavala uses a great deal of detail to create a realistic likeness; Lawrence uses minimal detail, suggesting expressions with only a few sharp lines; the primitivist barber shop sign falls between the two.]

Connecting Across Texts

Connecting with "Hair"

In both "Hair" and "A 'Piercing' Issue," social pressures create turning points in young peoples' lives, ultimately adding to their self-knowledge. The narrators of both selections feel pressure to conform. The narrator of "Hair" succumbs to the pressure and later regrets his decision. The narrator of "A 'Piercing' Issue" resists the pressure and later takes pride in her decision. Both narrators present their experiences as autobiographical incidents embodying lessons for themselves and for others.

MAKING MEANINGS

First Thoughts

1. Possible responses: *conk,* because it's the subject of the incident and it evokes the racist standards that Malcolm X opposes; *How ridiculous I was,* because it marks a surprising change of tone and sums up Malcolm X's reflections.

Shaping Interpretations

2. Sample responses: He finds it degrading to subject oneself to pain and possible injury out of shame over one's natural looks; he finds it degrading to unthinkingly accept racist standards of attractiveness.

3. Possible response: His tone is angry, bitter, critical. Words/passages: *How ridiculous I was; stupid; self-degradation; brainwashed; superior/inferior; violate and mutilate their God-created bodies to try to look "pretty" by white standards.*

4. Possible responses: He might say that being true to yourself starts with respecting yourself; he might call conking an outward sign of being untrue to yourself; he might point out that it's hard to be true to yourself when you've been taught that you're inferior.

Connecting with the Text

5. Possible responses: These pressures could cause anxiety; confusion about identity; embarrassment; physical danger; problems later in life. Students may also note that these pressures can provide chances to think independently and evaluate social mores—as Malcolm X does.

Extending the Text

6. Possible responses: Focusing on their own strengths; treating themselves well; standing up for their beliefs; helping others.

MAKING MEANINGS

First Thoughts

[connect]

1. What do you think is the most important—or powerful—word or phrase in Malcolm's story? Why?

Shaping Interpretations

[interpret]

2. Why do you think Malcolm feels that conking his hair is a step toward self-degradation?

[infer]

3. What would you **infer** about Malcolm's **tone** at the end of this selection? (List words or passages that help establish the tone.)

[synthesize]

4. In William Shakespeare's play *Hamlet,* a father gives this advice to his son: "This above all: to thine own self be true, and it must follow, as the night the day, thou canst not then be false to any man." What do you think Malcolm would say about this advice?

Connecting with the Text

[analyze]

5. Get together with a small group to talk about the pressures to conform—to be like everyone else—that young people face today. What could happen as a result of these pressures? Be sure to check your Quickwrite notes and refer to the student essay "A Piercing Issue" on page 349.

Extending the Text

[evaluate]

6. Malcolm talks about behavior that leads toward self-degradation. What, on the other hand, do you think gives people a sense of self-respect or self-esteem?

Shorty (played by Spike Lee) and Malcolm X (Denzel Washington) wearing zoot suits in a scene from Spike Lee's movie *Malcolm X* (1992).

Reading Check

Malcolm (the narrator) wants to have his hair "conked" by his friend Shorty, who will do it more cheaply than the barber will. Shorty makes up a batch of lye-based congolene and applies it to Malcolm's head. It burns intolerably but straightens Malcolm's hair. Both men are pleased. Malcolm, however, realizes later that this was his first big step toward self-degradation. Wanting hair like a white person's, and enduring pain to get it, was foolish and degrading, a blind conformity to racist social standards.

CHOICES: Building Your Portfolio

Writer's Notebook

1. Collecting Ideas for an Autobiographical Incident

Finding an experience.

Think of an experience you remember vividly, one that had a mighty impact on you and that you're willing to share with others. Maybe you'll want to talk about your experiences with pressures to conform to the "in" fashions you listed in the Quickwrite before you started reading "Hair." Maybe you'll want to start by making lists (Five Incidents I'd Rather Forget; Three Triumphs). Take notes about your experience to see if it will give you enough material to develop into an autobiographical incident (see the Writer's Work-

shop on page 380). Check the experience that interests you most.

Research/Art History

2. Creative Giants

During the 1940s, the African American communities in Harlem, Chicago, and Los Angeles were wellsprings of artistic creativity. Research the life and work of one of the following artists (or others you discover):

Music: Duke Ellington, Count Basie, Charlie Parker, Dizzy Gillespie

Dance: Katherine Dunham

Painting: Romare Bearden, Jacob Lawrence

Literature: Gwendolyn Brooks, Langston Hughes, Richard Wright

Share with your class the results of your research as well as samples (recordings, writing, reproductions) of the artist's work.

Language Study

3. Where *Hip* Was Invented

Many words that later entered mainstream English slang were used by African Americans during the era when "Hair" takes place. Report on the **origins** of *hip, cool, dig, cat, jive, pad,* and *homeboy.* You'll find these words in a dictionary of American slang.

Drawing/Research

4. Hair Through the Ages

Look up pictures of hairstyles throughout the course of history. Draw four or five of them, and write an informative caption for each. Some possible examples: conked hair; the pageboy; the Afro; cornrows; long hippie hair; punk hair; the crewcut, ponytail, and ducktail; powdered wigs; the squash-blossom hairstyle of the Hopis.

Four Times I Felt Scared
- Losing my brother in the mall.
- Being in Carey's car when she hit a tree.
- ✓ My first debate tournament, only girl.
- When my dad lost his job.

Young, unmarried Hopi women once signaled their eligibility by wearing their hair in maiden's (also called squash-blossom) whorls. Now this traditional hairstyle is worn only on special occasions.

Rubrics for each Choices assignment appear on p. 131 in the *Portfolio Management System.*

CHOICES: Building Your Portfolio

1. **Writer's Notebook** Other possible list headings might include Personal Firsts, Eye-Openers, Passages to Maturity, or Mysterious Experiences.
2. **Research/Art History** Encourage students to use the school library and to ask the librarian for assistance in locating resources, either in hard copy or on-line. Students might also consider other artists like the writer Dorothy West or the painter William Johnson.
3. **Language Study** To extend the assignment, you might suggest that students interview a linguistics professor at a nearby university, asking the following questions:
   - How does slang originate?
   - Why does language change from generation to generation?
   - How does culture affect language?
   Students might conduct their interviews in person, by mail, or via telephone or e-mail.
4. **Drawing/Research** As an alternative to drawing, interested students might find current magazines from which they can clip photos of the hairstyles listed. Direct them to *Natural History, Smithsonian, National Geographic,* and *Arizona Highways,* as well as contemporary fashion magazines. Encourage students to use their pictures and captions in posters or in bulletin-board displays.

Using Students' Strengths

Kinesthetic Learners
Invite students to play Tone Charades. Each student is assigned a segment of "Hair" or "A 'Piercing' Issue." The student then uses posture, motions, gestures, and facial expressions to indicate the tone that he or she finds in the segment. Students in the audience try to guess the word or attitude.

Visual Learners
Direct students to create collages showing their own standards of attractiveness. Have them choose (or sketch), cut out, and arrange images of clothing styles, hairstyles, and activities that reflect their tastes and identities. Ask them to present their collages and briefly explain their choices.

LANGUAGE LINK

Try It Out
Possible Answers

1. ominous; It was quiet on the street—sadly, morbidly quiet. (mournful)
2. cynical; That's the kind of rotten lie I'd expect from that back-stabbing girl. (angry)
3. romantic; We met on an unseasonably stormy night that foreshadowed our disastrous relationship. (critical)

VOCABULARY

Possible Answers

1. *self-degradation* (degradation)—Roots: Latin *de-* + *gradus*; Roots' meanings: down + step; Word's meaning: reduction of one's own worth or dignity; Sample sentence: Too much self-criticism can become a form of self-degradation.
2. *violate*—Root: Latin *vis*; Root's meaning: force; Word's meaning: to harm, break, or desecrate; Sample sentence: To violate a truce is dishonorable.
3. *mutilate*—Root: Latin *mutilus*; Root's meaning: maimed; Word's meaning: to damage severely or irreparably; Sample sentence: Many an untrained singer has mutilated "The Star-Spangled Banner."

Resources

Language
• *Grammar and Language Links,* Worksheet, p. 39

Vocabulary
• *Words to Own,* Worksheet, p. 21

LANGUAGE LINK   MINI-LESSON

Handbook of Literary Terms
HELP

See Connotations.

Watch Your Tone

In written communication, **tone** is conveyed by word choice, or **diction.** See how a change in a single word can change the tone of each of Malcolm's sentences below:

1. "How ridiculous I was!" [Change the word *ridiculous* to *humorous.* What happens to the tone?]
2. "I had joined that multitude of Negro men and women in America who are brainwashed into believing that the black people are 'inferior.' . . ." [Change *brainwashed* to *persuaded.* What happens to the tone?]
3. "A jellylike, starchy-looking glop resulted from the lye and potatoes, . . ." [Change *glop* to *mixture.* What happens to the tone?]

Try It Out

First read each of the following sentences aloud to a partner. Then, find a word from the list below that describes its tone. Finally, reword each sentence to create a different tone. Express basically the same idea, but say it differently. Compare your rewritten sentences.

1. It was quiet on the street—deathly, eerily quiet.
2. That's the kind of answer I'd expect from the likes of her.
3. We met on a wild, wonderful night that shaped my life.

A BOX OF TONES

angry	comic	humorous	mocking	romantic
awed	critical	ironic	mournful	sarcastic
bitter	cynical	loving	ominous	sympathetic

VOCABULARY   HOW TO OWN A WORD

WORD BANK
self-degradation
multitude
violate
mutilate

Mapping a Word's Roots

Every word has a **root,** the part of the word that carries its core meaning. You can discover each word's root by checking its **etymology,** or **origin,** in a dictionary. (Since etymologies trace a word's history backward in time, the oldest known root is the one mentioned last.) Create a word map like the one below for each of the other words in the Word Bank.

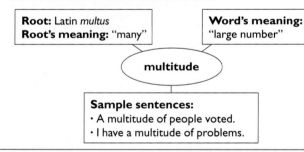

Root: Latin *multus*
Root's meaning: "many"

Word's meaning: "large number"

multitude

Sample sentences:
· A multitude of people voted.
· I have a multitude of problems.

Language Link Quick Check

Choose words from A Box of Tones to describe the tone of each statement below.
(Possible responses are provided.)

1. Your hair is so dreamy; I adore its iridescent sheen. [romantic, loving]
2. Wow—how terrific looking! [awed]
3. Oh, yeah, conking is a laugh a minute, and it feels just wonderful. [ironic, mocking, sarcastic]
4. The outrageous social pressures to conform are ill-conceived and insulting. [angry, critical]
5. ". . . I do not expect to live long enough to read this book in its finished form. . . . I know that societies often have killed the people who have helped to change those societies."
—Malcolm X, in *The Autobiography of Malcolm X* [bitter, cynical, ominous]

Elements of Literature

OBJECTIVES
1. Identify elements of literature in autobiography
2. Recognize the characteristics of an effective autobiography

AUTOBIOGRAPHY: Written Memory *by* Janet Burroway

"It is not true that we have only one life to live," said the linguist S. I. Hayakawa. "If we can read, we can live as many more lives and as many kinds as we wish."

One way we can "live more lives" is by reading **biographies**—stories of people's lives that are written by other people. The best biographies are well researched and objective.

Another way we can enter a person's life is by reading an **autobiography**—someone's personal account of his or her own life.

Many biographies and autobiographies read just like novels—they contain suspense, characters, settings, even plot (the events of the person's life).

If a biography or autobiography is well told, we may even experience "the shock of recognition" as we find something of ourselves in a stranger's life story.

Often, the most interesting autobiographies are the most honest. The writers of these works don't seek to glorify or glamorize or justify themselves; nor do they flinch from reporting that they are less than perfect. They try to tell the truth.

Honesty is difficult. Some writers would never attempt autobiography. "It does no good to write autobiographical fiction," warns fiction writer Toni Cade Bambara, "cause the minute this book hits the stand here comes your mama screamin how could you. . . ."

What We Remember: "Facts" and "Truth"

Writer Harry Crews has said: "What has been most significant in my life had all taken place by the time I was six years old." Crews is stating his strong personal sense of something that most scientists acknowledge as a fact: The preschool years are the "formative" years, and most traits of our character are in place before we reach the age of five.

What an autobiographer remembers about those years is likely to be faulty from the standpoint of absolute fact. What most of us remember most accurately is the significance things had for us, which is something that only *we* can know and judge. Memory has this in common with autobiography (which is, after all, simply written memory): that the

facts may be distorted or misremembered, but the significance of these facts is what we make of them.

Living Like a Writer

Here is how writer Ray Bradbury (see his story on page 173) uses images from his past to help him write:

. . . I was gathering images all of my life, storing them away, and forgetting them. Somehow I had to send myself back, with words as catalysts, to open the memories and see what they had to offer.

So, from the age of twenty-four to thirty-six hardly a day passed when I didn't stroll myself across a recollection of my grandparents' northern Illinois grass, hoping to come across some old half-burnt firecracker, a rusted toy, or a fragment of letter written to myself in some young year, hoping to contact the older person I became, to remind him of his past, his life, his people, his joys, and his drenching sorrows.

Your own life will provide rich background for the Writer's Workshop on page 380.

Reaching All Students

Advanced Learners

Direct students to use the information they have read in this lesson on autobiography to design and lay out a book jacket for one selection in this collection. The text should include several brief, catchy blurbs highlighting the elements that make the selection a strong piece of autobiographical writing. Students can either create a jacket illustration or use type and color to make the design.

Resources

Elements of Literature
Autobiography
For additional instruction on autobiography, see *Literary Elements:*
• Transparency 10
Assessment
Formal Assessment
• Literary Elements Test, p. 65

Elements of Literature

This lesson defines biography and autobiography and discusses characteristics of effective biographical and autobiographical writing.

Mini-Lesson: Autobiography
To reinforce students' understanding of the Mini-Lesson, stress these three points about autobiographical writing:
• It is made memorable by some of the same literary elements that make fiction memorable (character, suspense, setting, plot).
• It is most effective when it shows the author's personal weaknesses as well as strengths.
• It gains meaning when the author not only recalls events, but also explores their significance in his or her life.

Applying the Element
Ask students to reread "Hair," pp. 345–347, with these points in mind. Point out that the last two paragraphs explore the significance of conking in Malcolm's life. Then, challenge students to identify setting, plot, suspense, and techniques of characterization (direct and indirect) in "Hair." Ask which personal strengths and weaknesses Malcolm reveals. As students read the other autobiographical writings in this collection, invite them to use the three points in the Mini-Lesson as criteria for evaluation.

Before You Read

IT CAN'T BE HELPED

Make the Connection
Insiders and Outsiders

In what groups do you feel like an "insider"—safe, comfortable, free to be yourself? If you're like most people, in other groups you probably feel like an "outsider"—uncomfortable and ill at ease. That's because groups tend to set up invisible boundaries to keep insiders in and outsiders out. Sometimes these boundaries are actual walls or fences.

Quickwrite

Meet with a partner and share your knowledge and feelings about Japanese American internment camps in the United States during World War II. (See the Background on this page.) Then, as a class, exchange your ideas. Take notes on what you've learned from the quick-sharing.

 go.hrw.com
LEO 10-5

Elements of Literature
Anecdotes: Mini-Stories

Real life doesn't have a clear plot. We go from day to day, incident to incident, sometimes feeling that our experiences are only casually connected. That's why **biographies** and **autobiographies** are often sprinkled with **anecdotes**—very brief stories about their subjects that make some point, told in capsule form.

Anecdotes can provide a welcome change of pace. They can also reveal something important about the real-life characters or events. "Hair" (page 345) could be called an anecdote. Look for anecdotes as you read "It Can't Be Helped."

> An **anecdote** is a very brief story, often one that makes a special point.

Reading Skills and Strategies

Chronological Order

Events in **chronological order** follow a time sequence: this happened, then this, then this. When you read something structured in chronological order, look for transitions that signal when time is moving forward. Watch also for other important changes as time passes. For example, note the changes in setting in "It Can't Be Helped" as Jeanne's family moves several times within a few months.

Background

In this autobiographical excerpt, a woman remembers what it was like to be a Japanese American on the coast of California during World War II. Executive Order 9066, signed by President Roosevelt in February 1942, ordered all Japanese Americans to leave coastal areas and go to relocation camps inland because many government officials worried that people of Japanese ancestry would cooperate with the Japanese government if there were an invasion. Manzanar was one of ten such camps. It opened in 1942 in a desert near California's eastern Sierras.

We went because the government ordered us to.

354

Preteaching Vocabulary

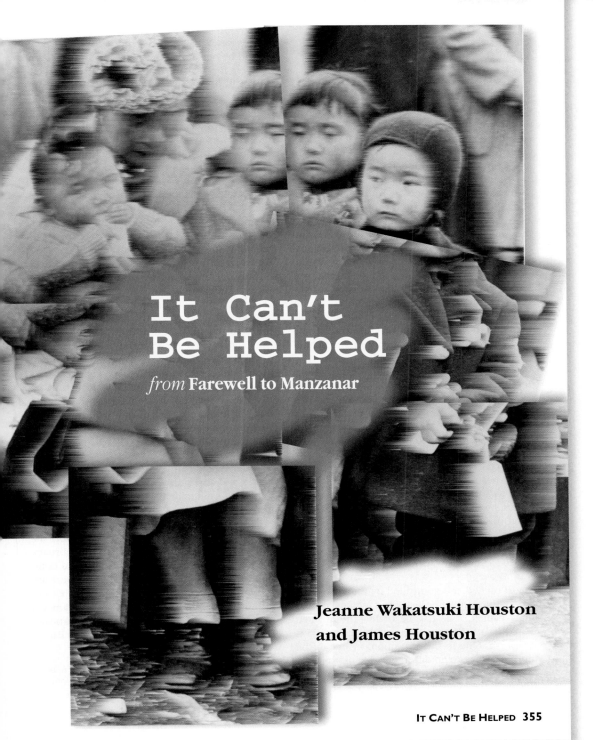

It Can't Be Helped

from **Farewell to Manzanar**

Jeanne Wakatsuki Houston and James Houston

Summary ■ ■

This autobiographical excerpt, set in California during World War II, opens with the arrest of Jeanne Wakatsuki's father and traces the family's "relocation" to Manzanar internment camp. The phrase *Shikata ga nai* ("It can't be helped") sets the tone of deepening resignation as anti-Japanese sentiment and government edicts force the family into steadily deteriorating living conditions. Jeanne, age seven, has her own issues: finding that she, who fears "Orientals," is herself "Oriental"; witnessing her mother's despair and rage; and, ironically, savoring the adventure of the bus trip to the barren, windswept relocation camp, Manzanar.

Background

The Wakatsukis were among 120,000 people—almost the entire Japanese American population of the West Coast—forced to spend World War II in prisonlike internment camps. Roughly two-thirds of the internees, including Mrs. Wakatsuki and her children, were American citizens, born and raised in the United States. (Ironically, Mr. Wakatsuki, arrested as an "enemy alien," had in fact severed all ties with Japan when he emigrated in 1904. He had been denied U.S. citizenship for almost 40 years because of his race.) The few internees who filed legal protests citing abridgment of civil rights lost their cases. In the camps, substandard living conditions took the lives of many. Survivors lost homes, businesses, cars, and any other possessions left behind. Not until 1988 did the government admit to having violated internees' rights.

IT CAN'T BE HELPED **355**

Resources: Print and Media

Reading
- *Graphic Organizers for Active Reading*, p. 22
- *Words to Own*, p. 22
- *Audio CD Library*
    Disc 11, Tracks 4, 5

Writing and Language
- *Daily Oral Grammar*
    Transparency 22

- *Grammar and Language Links*
    Worksheet, p. 41
- *Language Workshop CD-ROM*

Viewing and Representing
- *Viewing and Representing*
    Fine Art Transparency 8
    Fine Art Worksheet, p. 32

Assessment
- *Formal Assessment*, p. 61
- *Portfolio Management System*, p. 132
- *Test Generator (One-Stop Planner CD-ROM)*

Internet
- go.hrw.com (keyword: LE0 10-5)

Resources

Listening
Audio CD Library
A recording of "It Can't Be Helped" is included in the *Audio CD Library*:
• Disc 11, Track 4

Viewing and Representing
Fine Art Transparency
A Fine Art transparency of Dom Lee's *Baseball Saved Us* can be used with this selection. See the *Viewing and Representing Transparencies and Worksheets*:
• Transparency 8
• Worksheet, p. 32

Ⓐ Reading Skills and Strategies
Chronological Order
❓ Which words and phrases help to clarify the order of events in these paragraphs? [Sample answers: *In December of 1941; soon; When I was born; Later; until they picked him up; with him gone; now; once the war began.*]

Ⓑ Elements of Literature
Anecdote
❓ What might this anecdote show about Jeanne's sense of identity? [Possible responses: She identifies with whites; she doesn't have a sense of her own Asian identity.]

Ⓒ Elements of Literature
Tone
❓ Assess the tone of this sentence. What does it suggest about the narrator's attitude toward the navy's decision? [Sample response: The tone is of ironic disapproval. The narrator has established that the Terminal Islanders are hard-working, low-income families, American-born as she and most of her family are—hardly a "dangerous" group.]

In December of 1941 Papa's disappearance didn't bother me nearly so much as the world I soon found myself in.

Ⓐ He had been a jack-of-all-trades. When I was born, he was farming near Inglewood. Later, when he started fishing, we moved to Ocean Park, near Santa Monica, and until they picked him up, that's where we lived, in a big frame house with a brick fireplace, a block back from the beach. We were the only Japanese family in the neighborhood. Papa liked it that way. He didn't want to be labeled or grouped by anyone. But with him gone and no way of knowing what to expect, my mother moved all of us down to Terminal Island. Woody already lived there, and one of my older sisters had married a Terminal Island boy. Mama's first concern now was to keep the family together; and once the war began, she felt safer there than isolated racially in Ocean Park. But for me, at age seven, the island was a country as foreign as India or Arabia would have been. It was the first time I had lived among other Japanese, or gone to school with them, and I was terrified all the time.

This was partly Papa's fault. One of his threats to keep us younger kids in line was "I'm going to sell you to the Chinaman." When I had entered kindergarten two years earlier, I was the only Oriental in the class. They sat me next to a Caucasian girl who happened to have very slanted eyes. I looked at her and began to scream, certain Papa had sold me out at last. My fear of her ran so deep I could not speak of it, even to Mama, couldn't explain why I was screaming. For two weeks I had nightmares about this girl, until the teachers finally moved me to the other side of the room. And it was still with me, this fear of Oriental faces, when we moved to Terminal Island.

Ⓑ In those days it was a company town, a ghetto owned and controlled by the canneries. The men went after fish, and whenever the boats came back—day or night—the women would be called to process the catch while it was fresh. One in the afternoon or four in the morning, it made no difference. My mother had to go to work right after we moved there. I can still hear the whistle—two toots for French's,

three for Van Camp's—and she and Chizu would be out of bed in the middle of the night, heading for the cannery.

The house we lived in was nothing more than a shack, a barracks with single plank walls and rough wooden floors, like the cheapest kind of migrant workers' housing. The people around us were hard-working, boisterous, a little proud of their nickname, *yo-go-re*, which meant literally uncouth one, or roughneck, or dead-end kid. They not only spoke Japanese exclusively, they spoke a dialect peculiar to Kyushu, where their families had come from in Japan, a rough, fisherman's language, full of oaths and insults. Instead of saying *ba-ka-ta-re*, a common insult meaning stupid, Terminal Islanders would say *ba-ka-ya-ro*, a coarser and exclusively masculine use of the word, which implies gross stupidity. They would swagger and pick on outsiders and persecute anyone who didn't speak as they did. That was what made my own time there so hateful. I had never spoken anything but English, and the other kids in the second grade despised me for it. They were tough and mean, like ghetto kids anywhere. Each day after school I dreaded their ambush. My brother Kiyo, three years older, would wait for me at the door, where we would decide whether to run straight home together, or split up, or try a new and unexpected route.

None of these kids ever actually attacked. It was the threat that frightened us, their fearful looks, and the noises they would make, like miniature samurai,[1] in a language we couldn't understand.

At the time it seemed we had been living under this reign of fear for years. In fact, we lived there about two months. Late in February the navy decided to clear Terminal Island completely. Even though most of us were American-born, it was dangerous having that many Orientals so close to the Long Beach Naval Station, on the opposite end of the island. We had known something like this was coming. But, like Papa's

---

1. **samurai** (sam′ə·rī′): soldiers who worked for noblemen in Japan between the twelfth and nineteenth centuries.

356 THE NONFICTION COLLECTIONS

Reaching All Students

Struggling Readers
Chronological Order was introduced on p. 354. One good strategy to use analyzing chronological ordering is Story Impressions. For information on using this strategy, see p. 119 in the *Reading Strategies Handbook* in front of the *Reading Skills and Strategies* binder.

English Language Learners
The Terminal Island children hate Jeanne for not speaking Japanese. Invite these students to compare their own experiences as language learners. Students may have met with help or ridicule; they may recall experiences they found funny, frightening, or enlightening.
For strategies for engaging English language learners with the literature, see:
• *Lesson Plans Including Strategies for English-Language Learners*

arrest, not much could be done ahead of time. There were four of us kids still young enough to be living with Mama, plus Granny, her mother, sixty-five then, speaking no English, and nearly blind. Mama didn't know where else she could get work, and we had nowhere else to move *to*. On February 25 the choice was made for us. We were given forty-eight hours to clear out.

The secondhand dealers had been prowling around for weeks, like wolves, offering humiliating prices for goods and furniture they knew many of us would have to sell sooner or later. Mama had left all but her most valuable possessions in Ocean Park, simply because she had nowhere to put them. She had brought along her pottery, her silver, heirlooms like the kimonos[2] Granny had brought from Japan, tea sets, lacquered tables, and one fine old set of china, blue and white porcelain, almost <u>translucent</u>. On the day we were leaving, Woody's car was so crammed with boxes and luggage and kids we had just run out of room. Mama had to sell this china.

One of the dealers offered her fifteen dollars for it. She said it was a full setting for twelve and worth at least two hundred. He said fifteen was his top price. Mama started to quiver. Her eyes blazed up at him. She had been packing all night and trying to calm down Granny, who didn't understand why we were moving again and what all the rush was about. Mama's nerves were shot, and now navy jeeps were patrolling the streets. She didn't say another word. She just glared at this man, all the rage and frustration channeled at him through her eyes.

He watched her for a moment and said he was sure he couldn't pay more than seventeen fifty for that china. She reached into the red velvet case, took out a dinner plate, and hurled it at the floor right in front of his feet.

The man leaped back shouting, "Hey! Hey, don't do that! Those are valuable dishes!"

Mama took out another dinner plate and hurled it at the floor, then another and another, never moving, never opening her mouth, just

quivering and glaring at the retreating dealer, with tears streaming down her cheeks. He finally turned and scuttled out the door, heading for the next house. When he was gone, she stood there smashing cups and bowls and platters until the whole set lay in scattered blue and white fragments across the wooden floor.

The American Friends Service[3] helped us find a small house in Boyle Heights, another minority ghetto, in downtown Los Angeles, now inhabited briefly by a few hundred Terminal Island refugees. Executive Order 9066 had been signed by President Roosevelt, giving the War Department authority to define military areas in the western states and to exclude from them anyone who might threaten the war effort. There was a lot of talk about internment, or moving inland, or something like that in store for all Japanese Americans. I remember my brothers sitting around the table talking very intently about what we were going to do, how we would keep the family together. They had seen how quickly Papa was removed, and they knew now that he would not be back for quite a while. Just before leaving Terminal Island Mama had received her first letter, from Bismarck, North Dakota. He had been imprisoned at Fort Lincoln, in an all-male camp for enemy aliens.

Papa had been the patriarch. He had always decided everything in the family. With him gone, my brothers, like councilors in the absence of a chief, worried about what should be done. The <u>ironic</u> thing is, there wasn't much left to decide. These were mainly days of quiet, desperate waiting for what seemed at the time to be <u>inevitable</u>. There is a phrase the Japanese use

---

3. **American Friends Service:** American Friends Service Committee, a Quaker organization formed in 1917 to aid victims of war.

- -

WORDS TO OWN
translucent (trans·lōō′sənt) *adj.:* partially transparent.
ironic (ī·rän′ik) *adj.:* opposite of what is expected.
inevitable (in·ev′i·tə·bəl) *adj.:* unavoidable; certain to happen.

- -

2. **kimonos** (kə·mō′nəz): traditional Japanese robes with wide sleeves and a sash.

IT CAN'T BE HELPED 357

Getting Students Involved

Cooperative Learning
The Play's the Thing.   Have students work in groups of five to script and present dramatic scenes based on anecdotes in "It Can't Be Helped." Tell each group to meet, choose an anecdote from the selection, and rough out the scene before scripting begins. Then, designate three members of each group to share the task of writing dialogue and stage directions, while the other two share the task of creating an annotated cast of characters, writing an introduction and descriptions of setting, and gathering props. Give groups time to practice their scenes before presenting them to the class. Afterwards, invite students to compare and contrast the original anecdotes and the dramatic scenes. Direct them to consider effect as well as content.

A Reading Skills and Strategies

Chronological Order

? How do the writers use verb tenses to show the order of events in this paragraph? [Sample answer: They use the past perfect tense—"had been"—to write about Ocean Park and the simple past tense—"felt"—to write about Boyle Heights.]

B Appreciating Language

Proper Nouns

? List the five proper nouns in this passage. [Los Angeles, Mama, Washington, April, Greyhound] If the common noun *bus* were substituted for the proper noun *Greyhound,* how might the effect of the passage change? [Possible responses: The passage would be less specific; the bus and driver might be harder to visualize clearly; the passage might sound less realistic.]

C Elements of Literature

Anecdote

? The brief anecdote of the dust storm introduces Jeanne's first impressions of Manzanar. What does it reveal about the area? [Possible responses: It's sandy, windy, harsh, exposed, desolate; it's not the kind of "camp" that a child might have expected.]

---

in such situations, when something difficult must be endured. You would hear the older heads, the issei,[4] telling others very quietly, *"Shikata ga nai"* (It cannot be helped). *"Shikata ga nai"* (It must be done).

A Mama and Woody went to work packing celery for a Japanese produce dealer. Kiyo and my sister May and I enrolled in the local school, and what sticks in my memory from those few weeks is the teacher—not her looks, her remoteness. In Ocean Park my teacher had been a kind, grandmotherly woman who used to sail with us in Papa's boat from time to time and who wept the day we had to leave. In Boyle Heights the teacher felt cold and distant. I was confused by all the moving and was having trouble with the classwork, but she would never help me out. She would have nothing to do with me.

This was the first time I had felt outright hostility from a Caucasian. Looking back, it is easy enough to explain. Public attitudes toward the Japanese in California were shifting rapidly. In the first few months of the Pacific war, America was on the run. Tolerance had turned to distrust and irrational fear. The hundred-year-old tradition of anti-Orientalism on the West Coast soon resurfaced, more vicious than ever. Its result became clear about a month later, when we were told to make our third and final move.

The name Manzanar meant nothing to us when we left Boyle Heights. We didn't know where it was or what it was. We went because the government ordered us to. And, in the case of my older brothers and sisters, we went with a certain amount of relief. They had all heard stories of Japanese homes being attacked, of beatings in the streets of California towns. They were as frightened of the Caucasians as Caucasians were of us. Moving, under what appeared to be government protection, to an area less directly threatened by the war seemed not such a bad idea at all. For some it actually sounded like a fine adventure.

---

4. **issei** (ē'sā'): Japanese for "first generation," referring to Japanese who immigrated to the United States after 1907 but were not allowed to become citizens until 1952.

B Our pickup point was a Buddhist church in Los Angeles. It was very early, and misty, when we got there with our luggage. Mama had bought heavy coats for all of us. She grew up in eastern Washington and knew that anywhere inland in early April would be cold. I was proud of my new coat, and I remember sitting on a duffel bag trying to be friendly with the Greyhound driver. I smiled at him. He didn't smile back. He was befriending no one. Someone tied a numbered tag to my collar and to the duffel bag (each family was given a number, and that became our official designation until the camps were closed), someone else passed out box lunches for the trip, and we climbed aboard.

I had never been outside Los Angeles County, never traveled more than ten miles from the coast, had never even ridden on a bus. I was full of excitement, the way any kid would be, and wanted to look out the window. But for the first few hours the shades were drawn. Around me other people played cards, read magazines, dozed, waiting. I settled back, waiting too, and finally fell asleep. The bus felt very secure to me. Almost half its passengers were immediate relatives. Mama and my older brothers had succeeded in keeping most of us together, on the same bus, headed for the same camp. I didn't realize until much later what a job that was. The strategy had been, first, to have everyone living in the same district when the evacuation began, and then to get all of us included under the same family number, even though names had been changed by marriage. Many families weren't as lucky as ours and suffered months of anguish while trying to arrange transfers from one camp to another.

C We rode all day. By the time we reached our destination, the shades were up. It was late afternoon. The first thing I saw was a yellow swirl across a blurred, reddish setting sun. The bus was being pelted by what sounded like splattering rain. It wasn't rain. This was my first look at something I would soon know very well, a billowing flurry of dust and sand churned up by the wind through Owens Valley.

We drove past a barbed-wire fence, through a gate, and into an open space where trunks and

---

Using Students' Strengths

Interpersonal Learners

Invite a guest speaker who has been confined during a war to share his or her experiences with students. As preparation for the visit, encourage students to review "It Can't Be Helped" and to list questions for the guest speaker. (For example, students might ask what qualities helped the speaker to endure confinement.) Afterwards, have students compare/contrast the speaker's experiences with those in "It Can't Be Helped."

Kinesthetic Learners

Invite students to create a board game called "Journey to Manzanar," based on Jeanne's experiences between December 1941 and April 1942. Tell students to have players begin in Ocean Park and follow the course that Jeanne and her family took, but to introduce variables that could affect the outcome of the journey. Suggest historical research to determine what these variables and their effects might be.

Naturalist Learners

Encourage interested students to learn more about the Owens Valley and Manzanar and to present their findings to the class. Direct them to look for information about geographic features, climate, soil types, native and cultivated plants, and natural history. Have them speculate about how the attributes of the area might affect Jeanne and her family during the three years they spend in Manzanar.

sacks and packages had been dumped from the baggage trucks that drove out ahead of us. I could see a few tents set up, the first rows of black barracks, and beyond them, blurred by sand, rows of barracks that seemed to spread for miles across this plain. People were sitting on cartons or milling around, with their backs to the wind, waiting to see which friends or relatives might be on this bus. As we approached, they turned or stood up, and some moved toward us expectantly. But inside the bus no one stirred. No one waved or spoke. They just stared out the windows, ominously silent. I didn't understand this. Hadn't we finally arrived, our whole family intact? I opened a window, leaned out, and yelled happily. "Hey! This whole bus is full of Wakatsukis!"

Outside, the greeters smiled. Inside there was an explosion of laughter, hysterical, tension-breaking laughter that left my brothers choking and whacking each other across the shoulders.

WORDS TO OWN
ominously (äm′ə·nəs·lē) *adv.:* in a way that suggests something bad is going to happen.
intact (in·takt′) *adj.:* kept together; not broken up.

MEET THE WRITERS

An Innocent Victim

Jeanne Wakatsuki Houston (1934–   ) kept her feelings about her World War II internment largely bottled up until the age of thirty-seven, when she and her husband, **James D. Houston** (1933–   ), wrote *Farewell to Manzanar* (1974). Until then, she said in an interview, she had felt "sullied" by the experience, even though she had been an innocent victim. "You feel you must have *done* something. You feel you are part of the act."

Writing about Manzanar, she explained, was a way of "coming to terms" with the impact of the experience on her whole life:

“ We began with a tape recorder and an old 1944 yearbook put together at Manzanar High School. It documented the entire camp scene—the graduating seniors, the guard towers, the Judo pavilion, the creeks I used to wade in, my family's barracks. As the photos brought that world back, I began to dredge up feelings that had lain submerged since the forties. I began to make connections I had previously been afraid to see. . . . But this is not political history. It is a story, or a web of stories—my own, my father's, my family's—tracing a few paths, out of the multitude of paths that led up to and away from the experience of the internment. ”

IT CAN'T BE HELPED **359**

Assessing Learning

Check Test: Short Answer
1. How old is the narrator? [seven]
2. Where and when is the selection set? [Southern California during World War II]
3. Why isn't Jeanne's father with the family? [He has been imprisoned as an enemy alien.]
4. Why does the family move repeatedly? [Anti-Japanese sentiment is growing.]
5. What is the family's final destination? [Manzanar internment camp]

Standardized Test Preparation
For practice in proofreading and editing, see
• *Daily Oral Grammar,* Transparency 22

D ### Historical Connections

The Manzanar barracks, covered in black tar paper, consisted of single rooms for entire families. Sand blew in between cracks in the uninsulated plank walls and floors. There were no kitchens or bathrooms; internees ate in a mess hall and used group toilets with no stalls or privacy.

E ### Elements of Literature
Anecdote
❓ What does this final anecdote show about Jeanne as a seven-year-old? [Possible responses: She is spirited; she is naively optimistic; she has initiative and confidence.]

Resources

Selection Assessment
Formal Assessment
• Selection Test, p. 61
Test Generator (One-Stop Planner)
• CD-ROM

BROWSING IN THE FILES

About the Authors. Jeanne Wakatsuki Houston did not leave Manzanar until she was eleven. The Wakatsukis resettled in San Jose, California, where she completed high school and college and worked with troubled youths. She returned to Manzanar for the first time, accompanied by her husband and their three young children, shortly before beginning her autobiography. There the Houstons found crumbling cement foundations, blowing sand, rusted barbed wire, and a white obelisk in memory of the dead. James D. Houston, born in San Francisco, is an author of fiction, nonfiction, and screenplays and a teacher of writing. Much of his subject matter is drawn from West Coast people and places.

GRAMMAR LINK

This mini-lesson will help students to choose effective nouns when they are writing their autobiographical incidents.

Try It Out
Possible Answers
1. <u>The teen</u> in the <u>convertible</u> blasted <u>a rap</u> as he drove along.
2. For <u>Hanukkah, my aunts, uncles, and cousins</u> get together at <u>Grandma Alice's</u> house in <u>Detroit</u>.
3. <u>The Crossfires</u> trounced <u>the Cyclones</u> in the <u>Lake County Finals</u>.

VOCABULARY
Possible Answers
1. translucent: trans-, through; transparent, transfix, transit
2. ironic: -ic, having the quality of; tragic, moronic, idyllic
3. inevitable: in-, not; insane, insufferable, insincere
4. ominously: -ly, in a manner; firmly, happily, swiftly
5. intact: in-, not; intemperate, indecisive, inimitable

Resources ——————

Language
• *Grammar and Language Links* Worksheet, p. 41

Vocabulary
• *Words to Own,* Worksheet, p. 22

GRAMMAR LINK `MINI-LESSON`

Language Handbook
H E L P

See Capitalizing Proper Nouns, page 1047.

Technology
H E L P

See Language Workshop CD-ROM. Key word entry: nouns.

Specific and Proper Nouns

Nouns can be classified as specific or general, proper or common. You can always tell a **proper noun**—it's capitalized and names a particular person, place, or thing.

General	Specific	Proper
building	factory	French's
place	relocation camp	Manzanar
relative	sister	May

There are pluses and minuses to using proper nouns and very specific nouns in writing. A plus is that a proper noun can make your description more specific. A minus is that a proper noun can make a description so specific that readers unfamiliar with the reference can't identify it.

For instance, the very specific description "Number 2 train to 241st Street" conjures up an exact image for residents of New York City, but a reader elsewhere might appreciate the general term "subway train."

Try It Out

Replace the underscored nouns and phrases with specific or proper nouns, and compare the two versions. Which creates a clearer picture for the reader?

1. <u>The boy</u> in the <u>car</u> blasted <u>a song</u> as he drove along.

2. For <u>the holiday, a lot of relatives</u> get together at my <u>relative's</u> house in <u>the city</u>.

3. <u>The soccer team</u> trounced <u>another team</u> in the <u>tournament</u>.

A tip for writers: In deciding when to use proper nouns and specific nouns, ask yourself: "Will my readers understand this reference?" Overuse of proper nouns can confuse readers.

VOCABULARY `HOW TO OWN A WORD`

WORD BANK

translucent
ironic
inevitable
ominously
intact

Beginnings and Endings: Prefixes and Suffixes

Some **prefixes** (word parts added before a root) and **suffixes** (word parts added after a root) have several meanings. Using the chart below, decide which meaning is used in each Word Bank word. (Check a dictionary's **etymology** for help.) Then, with a partner, list other words containing these prefixes and suffixes.

Prefixes	Suffixes
trans- across, over, above and beyond, through **in-** in, within, not, no	**-ly** *(forms adverbs or adjectives):* in a manner or direction, like, characteristic of **-ic** *(forms adjectives or nouns):* dealing with, having the quality of; person or thing showing

---

Grammar Link Quick Check

Identify each noun as common or proper. Capitalize each proper noun.
1. roosevelt [proper; R]
2. country [common]
3. buddhism [proper; B]
4. ocean [common]

5. cannery [common]
6. church [common]
7. van camp's [proper; V, C]
8. owens valley [proper; O, V]
9. desert [common]
10. coca-cola [proper; C, C]

Before You Read

TYPHOID FEVER

Make the Connection

Remembering Myself

Think about it: you have years of stories in your life already. What do you remember from your early life that is important or unusual or funny? It might be a memory of a visit someplace. It might be a memory of a house you lived in. It might even be a memory of a time when you were sick.

Quickwrite

Take some notes on a childhood memory. Try to remember the event from a child's point of view. Ideas might come to you if you begin something like this: "I am seven years old . . ." or "I'm in a playground . . . ." Save your notes.

Elements of Literature

Comic Relief: Horror and Hilarity

Cracking a joke when everyone is tense can provide a terrific relief. That's exactly what **comic relief** does in literature: it eases emotional tension. A humorous character, scene, or bit of dialogue adds variety and keeps tragedy from being overwhelming. Mixing comedy with sadness is lifelike, too, because in the cycles of our life

experiences, laughter and joy often give way to sadness, which in turn gives way once again to laughter and joy. As you read "Typhoid Fever," look for examples where a comic remark makes a sad situation easier to bear—at least for a moment.

> A humorous incident or speech in a serious literary work provides **comic relief.**

Reading Skills and Strategies

Evaluating Credibility: Testing/Trusting Memory

"People are always asking, how does he remember so much," McCourt told an interviewer, "and how much is an Irish storyteller's embroidery?"

Credibility means "believ-ability." How can you judge the credibility of an autobiography? (Some people are now calling this kind of writing "faction"—suggesting that it's a combination of "fact" and "fiction.") Can adults remember exact conversations and events that took place when they were ten years old? Is factual accuracy important, or is it the significance of an event that's of greater interest? Keep all these questions in mind as you read "Typhoid Fever." Does it ring true to you? Could any of the story's facts be checked out?

Background

Angela's Ashes is Frank McCourt's gritty, moving memoir of growing up poor in Limerick, Ireland, in the 1930s and '40s. Frank's family lived in a filthy, overcrowded slum. Bacterial diseases such as typhoid fever and diphtheria were common everywhere, but especially in poor neighborhoods.

Typhoid fever, caused by contaminated food or water, wastes the whole body. Diphtheria, spread by contact with others, starts as a sore throat and can end in suffocation. Because both infections spread easily, sick people are quarantined. In Ireland they were isolated in "fever hospitals." Most of these hospitals were run by the Catholic Church and staffed by nuns. Frank McCourt caught typhoid fever at the age of ten, on the day of his Confirmation. He was sent to a fever hospital.

go.hrw.com
LEO 10-5

Planning

- **Block Schedule**
  Block Scheduling Lesson Plans with Pacing Guide
- **Traditional Schedule**
  Lesson Plans Including Strategies for English-Language Learners
- **One-Stop Planner**
  CD-ROM with Test Generator

Preteaching Vocabulary

Words to Own

Have students work in small groups to read the Words to Own and their definitions at the bottom of pp. 368 and 371. Have group members also play charades with the words, taking turns to act out the meaning of a vocabulary word while others guess which word it is. Then, to ensure familiarity with the words, have groups answer the following questions:

1. How might a toddler be <u>induced</u> to pick up his or her toys?
2. What might make a batch of hot sauce more <u>potent</u>?
3. How might a letter carrier feel about a <u>torrent</u> of junk mail?
4. If a neighbor's kittens are <u>clamoring</u> for attention, what are they doing?

Summary ▪ ▪

In the voice of himself as a ten-year-old, Frank McCourt recalls recovering from typhoid in a Limerick hospital. Allusions to Ireland's struggle against British oppression add to the chill of the hospital's grim rules (no laughing, no singing, no talking to other patients) and of the McCourts' poverty. Against the bleakness, young Frank savors the delights of language: Patricia, the dying girl in the next room, whispers comic impressions of nuns and nurses and recites from the ballad "The Highwayman"; the illiterate orderly Seamus sings pub songs on the sly and "carries poems in his head"; and, in a smuggled book, a line from Shakespeare feels to the boy "like having jewels in my mouth."

Resources ──────

Listening
Audio CD Library
A recording of this selection is included in the *Audio CD Library:*
• Disc 11, Track 6

Ⓐ Elements of Literature
Comic Relief
Point out to students that the selection has opened on a somber note: the narrator is bedridden with typhoid, bewildered, in isolation in a hospital where, he says, "they stick needles in me." In this setting, his fellow patient's breezy "Yoo hoo, are you there, typhoid boy?" sounds almost like a sitcom. However, anyone who knows Ireland and its people will recognize the absolute exactness of McCourt's dialogue.

Ⓑ Historical Connections
Frankie was given a transfusion of blood donated by soldiers stationed in a garrison in Limerick.

TYPHOID FEVER

from **Angela's Ashes**
Frank McCourt

Yoo hoo, are you there, typhoid boy?

The room next to me is empty till one morning a girl's voice says, Yoo hoo, who's there?

I'm not sure if she's talking to me or someone in the room beyond.

Yoo hoo, boy with the typhoid, are you awake?

I am.

Are you better?

I am.

Well, why are you here?

I don't know. I'm still in the bed. They stick needles in me and give me medicine.

What do you look like?

I wonder, What kind of a question is that? I don't know what to tell her.

Ⓐ Yoo hoo, are you there, typhoid boy?

I am.

What's your name?

Frank.

That's a good name. My name is Patricia Madigan. How old are you?

Ten.

Oh. She sounds disappointed.

But I'll be eleven in August, next month.

Well, that's better than ten. I'll be fourteen in September. Do you want to know why I'm in the Fever Hospital?

I do.

I have diphtheria and something else.

What's something else?

They don't know. They think I have a disease from foreign parts because my father used to be in Africa. I nearly died. Are you going to tell me what you look like?

I have black hair.

You and millions.

I have brown eyes with bits of green that's called hazel.

You and thousands.

Ⓑ I have stitches on the back of my right hand and my two feet where they put in the soldier's blood.

Oh, did they?

They did.

You won't be able to stop marching and saluting.

There's a swish of habit and click of beads and then Sister Rita's voice. Now, now, what's this? There's to be no talking between two rooms especially when it's a boy and a girl. Do you hear me, Patricia?

Resources: Print and Media ──────

Reading
• *Graphic Organizers for Active Reading*, p. 23
• *Words to Own*, p. 23
• *Audio CD Library*
  Disc 11, Track 6

Writing and Language
• *Daily Oral Grammar*
  Transparency 23
• *Grammar and Language Links*
  Worksheet, p. 43

• *Language Workshop CD-ROM*

Assessment
• *Formal Assessment*, p. 63
• *Portfolio Management System*, p. 134
• *Standardized Test Preparation*, p. 46
• *Test Generator (One-Stop Planner CD-ROM)*

Internet
• go.hrw.com (keyword: LE0 10-5)

I do, Sister.

Do you hear me, Francis?

I do, Sister.

You could be giving thanks for your two remarkable recoveries. You could be saying the rosary.[1] You could be reading *The Little Messenger of the Sacred Heart*[2] that's beside your beds. Don't let me come back and find you talking.

She comes into my room and wags her finger at me. Especially you, Francis, after thousands of boys prayed for you at the Confraternity.[3] Give thanks, Francis, give thanks.

She leaves and there's silence for awhile. Then Patricia whispers, Give thanks, Francis, give thanks, and say your rosary, Francis, and I laugh so hard a nurse runs in to see if I'm all right. She's a very stern nurse from the County Kerry and she frightens me. What's this, Francis? Laughing? What is there to laugh about? Are you and that Madigan girl talking? I'll report you to Sister Rita. There's to be no laughing for you could be doing serious damage to your internal apparatus.

She plods out and Patricia whispers again in a heavy Kerry accent, No laughing, Francis, you could be doin' serious damage to your internal apparatus. Say your rosary, Francis, and pray for your internal apparatus.

Mam visits me on Thursdays. I'd like to see my father, too, but I'm out of danger, crisis time is over, and I'm allowed only one visitor. Besides, she says, he's back at work at Rank's Flour Mills and please God this job will last a while with the war on and the English desperate for flour. She brings me a chocolate bar and

1. **rosary:** group of prayers that Roman Catholics recite while holding a string of beads.
2. *The Little Messenger of the Sacred Heart:* religious publication for children.
3. **Confraternity:** here, a religious organization made up of nonclergy, or lay people.

that proves Dad is working. She could never afford it on the dole.[4] He sends me notes. He tells me my brothers are all praying for me, that I should be a good boy, obey the doctors, the nuns, the nurses, and don't forget to say my prayers. He's sure St. Jude pulled me through the crisis because he's the patron saint of desperate cases and I was indeed a desperate case.

Patricia says she has two books by her bed. One is a poetry book and that's the one she loves. The other is a short history of England and do I want it? She gives it to Seamus, the man who mops the floors every day, and he brings it to me. He says, I'm not supposed to be bringing anything from a dipteria room to a typhoid room with all the germs flying around and hiding between the pages and if you ever catch dipteria on top of the typhoid they'll know and I'll lose my good job and be out on the street singing patriotic songs with a tin cup in my hand, which I could easily do because there isn't a song ever written about Ireland's sufferings I don't know and a few songs about the joy of whiskey too.

Oh, yes, he knows Roddy McCorley. He'll sing it for me right enough but he's barely into the first verse when the Kerry nurse rushes in. What's this, Seamus? Singing? Of all the people in this hospital you should know the rules against singing. I have a good mind to report you to Sister Rita.

Ah, don't do that, nurse.

Very well, Seamus. I'll let it go this one time. You know the singing could lead to a relapse in these patients.

When she leaves he whispers he'll teach me a few songs because singing is good for passing the time when you're by yourself in a

4. **dole:** government payment to the unemployed; also, money or food given to those in need.

C Cultural Connection
Although County Kerry lies less than fifty miles southwest of the city of Limerick, the Kerry accent differs from that of Limerick.

D Historical Connection
In Europe, World War II lasted from 1939 to 1945. England, heavily bombed and forced to divert almost all its resources to the war effort, suffered severe food shortages.

E Elements of Literature
Comic Relief

? McCourt abruptly introduces the colorful and humorous Seamus (shā'mus). For what sad situation might he be providing comic relief? [Possible responses: young Frank's longing for his father; the McCourts' poverty; the seriousness of young Frank's illness.]

F Reading Skills and Strategies

Evaluating Credibility

? How credible do you consider McCourt's recollection of the hospital rules about laughing and singing? Explain. [Possible responses: He was very young and may not recall the rules exactly. However, given what we know of child-behavior standards and the probable strictness of Irish Catholic nuns in the 1940s, the recollection may be very credible.]

Reaching All Students

Struggling Readers
Students confused by McCourt's stream-of-consciousness style and lack of punctuation may find the selection easy to follow if they read it aloud with members of a group. Invite them to try Popcorn Reading, with each student reading aloud for as long as he or she feels comfortable, then saying "Popcorn!" and naming another student to take over.

English Language Learners
Let these students know that McCourt's writing voice follows Irish speech patterns, rather than the patterns of standard American English. Point out, on p. 369, that the words *boy* and *you* are spelled *by* and *ye* to reflect the pronunciation of the nurse's regional accent. For additional strategies for engaging English language learners with the literature, see
• *Lesson Plans Including Strategies for English-Language Learners*

Advanced Learners
After these students have read the selection, invite them to list lines of literature that feel to them "like having jewels in [their] mouth." Encourage them to check lines of which they are unsure, and remind them to include favorite lines from McCourt's memoir. Then, guide them in analyzing elements that make the lines appealing: sound effects, imagery, diction, balance, and so on.

T367

A Appreciating Language
Voice

❓ How does McCourt re-create the voice—the speaking style, viewpoint, and quirks—of a ten-year-old boy? [He uses rambling sentences strung together with *and*; he has the narrator call Seamus "an old man of forty."]

B Historical Connections

King Henry VIII (1491–1547), famous for his six wives, initiated England's historic breach with the Roman Catholic church in order to divorce Catherine of Aragon (1485–1536) because she bore him no sons. Cardinal Wolsey had tried to have the marriage invalidated by the Roman Catholic pope. Catherine did manage to escape beheading; two of Henry's other wives were less fortunate.

C Reading Skills and Strategies
Drawing Conclusions

❓ What do the narrator's thoughts here reveal about him? [Sample responses: He recognizes the quality of Shakespeare's work though he is only ten years old; he loves words and language; he likes to read. The thoughts seem to point to the teacher and writer Frankie is one day to become.]

D Literary Connections

"The Owl and the Pussycat" is a famous nonsense poem by the English humorist and illustrator Edward Lear (1812–1888).

E Literary Connections

"The Highwayman" by Alfred Noyes has been a popular poem in the classroom both in McCourt's youth and today. Be sure to go over footnote 5 with students and tell them the highwayman's love is named Bess.

---

typhoid room. He says Patricia is a lovely girl the way she often gives him sweets from the parcel her mother sends every fortnight. He stops mopping the floor and calls to Patricia in the next room, I was telling Frankie you're a lovely girl, Patricia, and she says, You're a lovely man, Seamus. He smiles because he's an old man of forty and he never had children but the ones he can talk to here in the Fever Hospital. He says, Here's the book, Frankie. Isn't it a great pity you have to be reading all about England after all they did to us, that there isn't a history of Ireland to be had in this hospital.

The book tells me all about King Alfred and William the Conqueror and all the kings and queens down to Edward, who had to wait forever for his mother, Victoria, to die before he could be king. The book has the first bit of Shakespeare I ever read.

> *I do believe, <u>induced</u> by <u>potent</u>*
>   *circumstances,*
> *That thou art mine enemy.*

The history writer says this is what Catherine, who is a wife of Henry the Eighth, says to Cardinal Wolsey, who is trying to have her head cut off. I don't know what it means and I don't care because it's Shakespeare and it's like having jewels in my mouth when I say the words. If I had a whole book of Shakespeare they could keep me in the hospital for a year.

Patricia says she doesn't know what induced means or potent circumstances and she doesn't care about Shakespeare, she has her poetry book and she reads to me from beyond the wall a poem about an owl and a pussycat that went to sea in a green boat with honey and money and it makes no sense and when I say that Patricia gets huffy and says that's the last poem she'll ever read to me. She says I'm always reciting the lines from Shakespeare and they make no sense either. Seamus stops mopping again and tells us we shouldn't be fighting over poetry because we'll have enough to fight about when we grow up and get married. Patricia says she's sorry and I'm sorry too so she reads me part of another

poem[5] which I have to remember so I can say it back to her early in the morning or late at night when there are no nuns or nurses about,

> *The wind was a <u>torrent</u> of darkness among*
>   *the gusty trees,*
> *The moon was a ghostly galleon tossed*
>   *upon cloudy seas,*
> *The road was a ribbon of moonlight over*
>   *the purple moor,*
> *And the highwayman came riding—*
>   *Riding—riding—*
> *The highwayman came riding, up to the*
>   *old inn door.*
>
> *He'd a French cocked-hat on his forehead, a*
>   *bunch of lace at his chin,*
> *A coat of the claret velvet, and breeches of*
>   *brown doeskin,*
> *They fitted with never a wrinkle. His boots*
>   *were up to the thigh.*
> *And he rode with a jeweled twinkle,*
>   *His pistol butts a-twinkle,*
> *His rapier hilt a-twinkle, under the jeweled*
>   *sky.*

Every day I can't wait for the doctors and nurses to leave me alone so I can learn a new verse from Patricia and find out what's happening to the highwayman and the landlord's red-lipped daughter. I love the poem because it's exciting and almost as good as my two lines of Shakespeare. The redcoats are after the highwayman because they know he told her, I'll come to thee by moonlight, though hell should bar the way.

---

5. **part . . . poem:** reference is to the poem "The Highwayman" by British poet Alfred Noyes (1880–1958). The poem is based on a true story about a highwayman who falls in love with an innkeeper's daughter in 18th-century England. Highwaymen, who robbed rich stagecoaches, were at that time popular, romantic figures.

WORDS TO OWN

induced (in·do̅o̅st′) v.: persuaded; led on.
potent (pōt′'nt) adj.: powerful; convincing.
torrent (tôr′ənt) n.: violent, forceful rush.

Listening to Music

"(Young) Roddy McCorley" (Traditional)
   Lyrics by Ethna Carberry, performed by the Clancy Brothers and Tommy Makem

The poetic lyrics of the famous Irish rebel song "Roddy McCorley" pay tribute to an Irish hero of the Wolfe Tone Rebellion of 1798, one of many unsuccessful Irish rebellions against British rule. Captured while attempting to wrest the Irish town of Antrim from British control, McCorley was hanged at nearby Toome Bridge, on the banks of the River Bann.

Activity

After students read the selection from *Angela's Ashes*, tell them you are going to play the song that Seamus sings in the selection. Explain that it is one of many songs of Irish rebellion against British rule, and provide students with details from the background provided. Then, after you play the song, ask what singing such a song suggests about Seamus's character. [Possible responses: He is sentimental, patriotic, anti-British, verbal, musical, and admiring of rebellious spirits.]

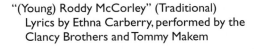

I'd love to do that myself, come by moonlight for Patricia in the next room not giving a hoot though hell should bar the way. She's ready to read the last few verses when in comes the nurse from Kerry shouting at her, shouting at me, I told ye there was to be no talking between rooms. Dipthteria is never allowed to talk to typhoid and visa versa. I warned ye. And she calls out, Seamus, take this one. Take the by. Sister Rita said one more word out of him and upstairs with him. We gave ye a warning to stop the blathering but ye wouldn't. Take the by, Seamus, take him.

Ah, now, nurse, sure isn't he harmless. 'Tis only a bit o' poetry.

Take that by, Seamus, take him at once.

He bends over me and whispers, Ah, I'm sorry, Frankie. Here's your English history book. He slips the book under my shirt and lifts me from the bed. He whispers that I'm a feather. I try to see Patricia when we pass through her room but all I can make out is a blur of dark head on a pillow.

Sister Rita stops us in the hall to tell me I'm a great disappointment to her, that she expected me to be a good boy after what God had done for me, after all the prayers said by hundreds of boys at the Confraternity, after all the care from the nuns and nurses of the Fever Hospital, after the way they let my mother and father in to see me, a thing rarely allowed, and this is how I repaid them lying in the bed reciting silly poetry back and forth with Patricia Madigan knowing very well there was a ban on all talk between typhoid and diphtheria. She says I'll have plenty of time to reflect on my sins in the big ward upstairs and I should beg God's forgiveness for my disobedience reciting a pagan English poem about a thief on a horse and a maiden with red lips who commits a terrible sin when I could have been praying or reading the life of a saint. She made it her business to read that poem so she did and I'd be well advised to tell the priest in confession.

The Kerry nurse follows us upstairs gasping and holding on to the banister. She tells me I better not get the notion she'll be running up to this part of the world every time I have a little pain or a twinge.

There are twenty beds in the ward, all white, all empty. The nurse tells Seamus put me at the far end of the ward against the wall to make sure I don't talk to anyone who might be passing the door, which is very unlikely since there isn't another soul on this whole floor. She tells Seamus this was the fever ward during the Great Famine[6] long ago and only God knows how many died here brought in too late for anything but a wash before they were buried and there are stories of cries and moans in the far reaches of the night. She says 'twould break your heart to think of what the English did to us, that if they didn't put the blight on the potato they didn't do much to take it off. No pity. No feeling at all for the people that died in this very ward, children suffering and dying here while the English feasted on roast beef and guzzled the best of wine in their big houses, little children with their mouths all green from trying to eat the grass in the fields beyond, God bless us and save us and guard us from future famines.

Seamus says 'twas a terrible thing indeed and he wouldn't want to be walking these halls in the dark with all the little green mouths gaping at him. The nurse takes my temperature, 'Tis up a bit, have a good sleep for yourself now that you're away from the chatter with Patricia Madigan below who will never know a gray hair.

She shakes her head at Seamus and he gives her a sad shake back.

Nurses and nuns never think you know what they're talking about. If you're ten going on eleven you're supposed to be simple like my uncle Pat Sheehan who was dropped on his head. You can't ask questions. You can't show you understand what the nurse said about Patricia Madigan, that she's going to die, and you can't show you want to cry over this girl who taught you a lovely poem which the nun says is bad.

6. **Great Famine:** refers to the great famine in Ireland in 1845–1847, when failed potato crops resulted in the starvation and death of about one million people.

F Reading Skills and Strategies
Evaluating Credibility
❓ Does the description of the nurse's reaction seem credible to you? Why or why not? [Possible responses: Yes, since it's already been shown that talking is forbidden and that the nurse is a grouch; no—Frankie's perceptions may be off, since he's afraid of the nurse.]

G Cultural Connection
The woman in the poem commits suicide, which was seen as a mortal sin in the eyes of the Roman Catholic church.

H Elements of Literature
Comic Relief
❓ Which remarks in this paragraph seem a little humorous and help to ease for a moment the emotional tension of this scene? [Possible responses: "…which is very unlikely since there isn't another soul on this whole floor"; "…if they didn't put the blight on the potato they didn't do much to take it off"; the nurse, who shows no compassion and sensitivity to a child, judging the English as having "No pity. No feeling at all…."] **What sad situation do these remarks offset?** [Possible responses: the neglect and loneliness that Frankie now must face.]

I Historical Connection
Blight, a plant disease, caused the failure of Ireland's potato crops during the Great Famine of 1845–1847.

Crossing the Curriculum

Science
Have interested students report on typhoid fever and diphtheria. They might consider causes, symptoms, and transmission; they also might compare current prevention, treatment, and worldwide incidence with those in 1940.

Social Studies
Invite students to research the roots of Ireland's struggle against England and to report their findings to the class.

Making the Connections

Connecting to the Theme: "Becoming Myself"
The narrator of "Typhoid Fever" has many names: He is "typhoid boy" to Patricia, Frank to himself, Francis to the nun and nurse, Frankie to Seamus, and "our little soldier" to his doctors. His Irish heritage, his religion, and his family's economic status all figure in his identity. Still, beneath the roles and labels is a child as bewildered as young Jeanne Wakatsuki in "It Can't Be Helped," undergoing as intense an ordeal.

Paradoxically, as he endures physical illness, cruelty, poverty, isolation, fear, and sorrow, he also discovers what delights him most. He finds joy in language, from pub songs to Shakespeare. Knowing the adult McCourt to be a prizewinning author, readers can infer that this piece of self-discovery will offer young Frank lifelong pleasure.

A Appreciating Language
Voice
? Which words and phrases help to give an idea of Seamus's voice? [Possible responses: "right oul' witch"; "not bloody likely"; "when you're what? ten going on eleven?"; "never heard the likes of it."]

B Elements of Literature
Comic Relief
? What sad situation does this faintly mocking tone introduce? [Patricia's death]

C Reading Skills and Strategies
Making Inferences
? Does young Frank really see "people in the nineteen beds"? [He imagines them so vividly that it's as bad as seeing them.] What does this passage show about the way his punishment affects him? [It's a torment to him; he's terrified.]

D Critical Thinking
Interpreting
? Children can respond in various ways to adversity. They may become resentful, mistrustful, withdrawn, compassionate, courageous, or resilient. Explain which, if any, of these personality traits you see in young Frankie. [Possible answers: compassion (for Patricia); courage (in his determination to walk); resilience (in his memorizing literature as a source of comfort).]

A The nurse tells Seamus she has to go and he's to sweep the lint from under my bed and mop up a bit around the ward. Seamus tells me she's a right oul' witch for running to Sister Rita and complaining about the poem going between the two rooms, that you can't catch a disease from a poem unless it's love ha ha and that's not bloody likely when you're what? ten going on eleven? He never heard the likes of it, a little fella shifted upstairs for saying a poem and he has a good mind to go to the *Limerick Leader* and tell them print the whole thing except he has this job and he'd lose it if ever Sister Rita found out. Anyway, Frankie, you'll be outa here one of these fine days and you can read all the poetry you want though I don't know about Patricia below, I don't know about Patricia, God help us.

B He knows about Patricia in two days because she got out of the bed to go to the lavatory when she was supposed to use a bedpan and collapsed and died in the lavatory. Seamus is mopping the floor and there are tears on his cheeks and he's saying, 'Tis a dirty rotten thing to die in a lavatory when you're lovely in yourself. She told me she was sorry she had you reciting that poem and getting you shifted from the room, Frankie. She said 'twas all her fault.

It wasn't, Seamus.

I know and didn't I tell her that.

Patricia is gone and I'll never know what happened to the highwayman and Bess, the landlord's daughter. I ask Seamus but he doesn't know any poetry at all especially English poetry. He knew an Irish poem once but it was about fairies and had no sign of a highwayman in it. Still he'll ask the men in his local pub where there's always someone reciting something and he'll bring it back to me. Won't I be busy meanwhile reading my short history of England and finding out all about their perfidy.[7] That's what Seamus says, perfidy, and I don't know

7. **perfidy** (pur′fə·dē): treachery; betrayal.

what it means and he doesn't know what it means but if it's something the English do it must be terrible.

He comes three times a week to mop the floor and the nurse is there every morning to take my temperature and pulse. The doctor listens to my chest with the thing hanging from his neck. They all say, And how's our little soldier today? A girl with a blue dress brings meals three times a day and never talks to me. Seamus says she's not right in the head so don't say a word to her.

The July days are long and I fear the dark. There are only two ceiling lights in the ward and they're switched off when the tea tray is taken away and the nurse gives me pills. The nurse tells me go to sleep but I can't because I see people in the nineteen beds in the ward all dying and green around their mouths where they tried to eat grass and moaning for soup Protestant soup any soup and I cover my face with the pillow hoping they won't come and stand around the bed clawing at me and howling for bits of the chocolate bar my mother brought last week.

No, she didn't bring it. She had to send it in because I can't have any more visitors. Sister Rita tells me a visit to the Fever Hospital is a privilege and after my bad behavior with Patricia Madigan and that poem I can't have the privilege anymore. She says I'll be going home in a few weeks and my job is to concentrate on getting better and learn to walk again after being in bed for six weeks and I can get out of bed tomorrow after breakfast. I don't know why she says I have to learn how to walk when I've been walking since I was a baby but when the nurse stands me by the side of the bed I fall to the floor and the nurse laughs, See, you're a baby again.

D I practice walking from bed to bed back and forth back and forth. I don't want to be a baby. I don't want to be in this empty ward with no Patricia and no highwayman and no red-lipped landlord's daughter. I don't want the ghosts of

---

Taking a Second Look

Review: Chronological Order
Remind students that writers clarify the order of events by using time-related words and phrases and by changing verb tenses. For example, to show the order of events in "Typhoid Fever," McCourt uses words and phrases such as *when*, *as soon as*, and *after*. For events that took place before the time of Frankie's hospitalization, he shifts from the present tense to the past tense (as in the nurse's recounting of the Great Famine on p. 369).

Activities
1. Reread the first half of the first column on p. 369, down to "...a blur of dark head on a pillow." Which words or phrases clarify the order of events? ["when in comes ..."; "when we pass through her room ..."]
2. Reread the paragraph on p. 369 that begins, "There are twenty beds ...." How does McCourt show that the Great Famine took place at an earlier time? [He shifts to the past tense; he uses the phrase *long ago*.]

children with green mouths pointing bony fingers at me and <u>clamoring</u> for bits of my chocolate bar.

Seamus says a man in his pub knew all the verses of the highwayman poem and it has a very sad end. Would I like him to say it because he never learned how to read and he had to carry the poem in his head? He stands in the middle of the ward leaning on his mop and recites,

> Tlot-tlot, *in the frosty silence!* Tlot-tlot *in the echoing night!*
> *Nearer he came and nearer! Her face was like a light!*
> *Her eyes grew wide for a moment; she drew one last deep breath,*
> *Then her fingers moved in the moonlight,*
> *Her musket shattered the moonlight,*
> *Shattered her breast in the moonlight and warned him—with her death.*

He hears the shot and escapes but when he learns at dawn how Bess died he goes into a rage and returns for revenge only to be shot down by the redcoats.

> *Blood-red were his spurs in the golden noon; wine-red was his velvet coat,*
> *When they shot him down on the highway,*
> *Down like a dog on the highway,*
> *And he lay in his blood on the highway,*
> *with a bunch of lace at his throat.*

Seamus wipes his sleeve across his face and sniffles. He says, There was no call at all to shift you up here away from Patricia when you didn't even know what happened to the highwayman and Bess. 'Tis a very sad story and when I said it to my wife she wouldn't stop crying the whole night till we went to bed. She said there was no call for them redcoats to shoot that highwayman, they are responsible for half the troubles of the world and they never had any pity on the Irish, either. Now if you want to know any more poems, Frankie, tell me and I'll get them from the pub and bring 'em back in my head.

WORDS TO OWN

clamoring (klam′ər·iŋ) *v.*: crying out; asking.

Resources

Selection Assessment
Formal Assessment
- Selection Test, p. 63
Test Generator (One-Stop Planner)
- CD-ROM

MEET THE WRITER
"We Were Street Kids"

Frank McCourt (1930–   ), who regards himself as more a New Yorker than an Irishman, was born in Brooklyn, New York, the first child of Irish immigrants. When Frank was four, the McCourts made a bad decision and moved back to Ireland, where they lived in worse conditions than the ones they had fled in Brooklyn. Eventually, Frank's father abandoned his wife, Angela, and their three surviving children.

Frank McCourt moved back to New York City at age nineteen. Ten years later he began teaching writing to high school students. Encouraged by his students to write about his own experiences (see *Connections* on page 372), McCourt finally published his first book, *Angela's Ashes,* when he was sixty-six. The book dominated best-seller lists and won a 1997 Pulitzer Prize.

When he was asked how he found such humor in his poverty-stricken childhood, McCourt replied: 66 When you have nothing—no TV, no radio, no music—you have only the language. So you use it. We were street kids—we saw the absurdity and laughed at it. And we were fools; we were always dreaming. Bacon and eggs—we dreamed of that. 99

Assessing Learning

Check Test: True-False

1. Young Frank catches typhoid fever from Patricia. [False]
2. Seamus smuggles a book to him. [True]
3. In the Fever Hospital, no laughing or singing is allowed. [True]
4. Young Frank's family visits every day. [False]
5. Frank never finds out what happens to the highwayman in the poem. [False]

Standardized Test Preparation

For practice with standardized test format specific to this selection, see
- *Standardized Test Preparation,* p. 46

For practice in proofreading and editing, see
- *Daily Oral Grammar,* Transparency 23

Connections

This biographical article links McCourt's years as a high school English teacher to the writing of his first book, when he was in his sixties. McCourt coached his high school students to "Find your own voice and dance your own dance." Before he could take his own advice, however, he had to battle insecurities created by a childhood of poverty and abandonment. His students guided him with their questions and inspired him with the courage and candor of their writing.

A Reading Skills and Strategies

Evaluating Credibility

(Note: See Browsing in the Files, p. T373.)

? Dimmitt describes McCourt's thoughts. Where might she have found this information? How could you check its accuracy? [Possible responses: She might have found her information by interviewing McCourt, by reading letters he wrote, or by talking with friends in whom he had confided. The information could be checked by asking McCourt.]

B Critical Thinking

Responding to the Text

? Do you think people without high school diplomas should be allowed to enroll in universities? Why or why not? [Possible responses: No, because it's unfair to those who work hard for their diplomas; yes, because a diploma isn't the only indicator of intelligence or ability.]

The Education of Frank McCourt   Barbara Sande Dimmitt

"Yo, Teach!" a voice boomed. Frank McCourt scanned the adolescents in his classroom. It was the fall of 1970 and his first week of teaching at Seward Park High School, which sat in the midst of dilapidated tenement buildings on Manhattan's Lower East Side. McCourt located the speaker and nodded. "You talk funny," the student said. "Where ya from?"

"Ireland," McCourt replied. With more than ten years of teaching experience under his belt, this kind of interrogation no longer surprised him. But one question in particular still made him squirm: "Where'd you go to high school?" someone else asked.

A *If I tell them the truth, they'll feel superior to me,* McCourt thought. *They'll throw it in my face.* Most of all, he feared an accusation he'd heard before—from himself: *You come from nothing, so you are nothing.*

But McCourt's heart whispered another possibility: maybe these kids are yearning for a way of figuring out this new teacher. *Am I willing to risk being humiliated in the classroom to find out?*

"Come on, tell us! Where'd you go to high school?"

"I never did," McCourt replied.

"Did you get thrown out?"

I was right, the teacher thought. *They're curious.* McCourt explained he'd left school after the eighth grade to take a job.

"How'd you get to be a teacher, then?" they asked.

"When I came to America," he began, "I dreamed bigger dreams. I loved reading and writing, and teaching was the most exalted profession I could imagine. I was unloading sides of beef down on the docks when I **B** decided enough was enough. By then I'd done a lot of reading on my own, so I persuaded New York University to enroll me."

McCourt wasn't surprised that this story fasci-nated his students. Theirs wasn't the kind of poverty McCourt had known; they had electricity and food. But he recognized the telltale signs of need in some of his students' threadbare clothes, and sensed the bitter shame and hopelessness he knew all too well. If recounting his own experiences would jolt these kids out of their defeatism so he could teach them something, that's what he would do.

A born storyteller, McCourt drew from a repertoire of accounts about his youth. His students would listen, spellbound by the gritty details, drawn by something more powerful than curiosity. He'd look from face to face, recognizing a bit of himself in each sober gaze.

Since humor had been the McCourts' weapon against life's miseries in Limerick, he used it to describe those days. "Dinner usually was bread and tea," he told the students. "Mam used to say, 'We've got our balanced diet: a solid and a liquid. What more could we want?'"

The students roared with laughter. . . .

One day McCourt lugged a tape recorder to class. "We're going to work on writing. Each of you will tell a story into this," he announced. McCourt then transcribed the stories. One boy described the time he was climbing down a fire escape past an open window when an awful smell hit him. "There was a body in the bed," McCourt typed. "The corpse was all juicy and swollen."

McCourt handed back the essay the next day. "See? You're a writer!"

"I was just talking," the boy protested. "I didn't write this."

"Yes, you did. These words came out of your head. They helped me understand something that was important to you. That's what writing's about. Now, learn to do it on paper." The boy's shoulders squared with pride.

The incident reminded McCourt of something that had happened at college. A creative-writing

---

Getting Students Involved

Cooperative Learning

New Voice, New View.   After students finish reading "Typhoid Fever," divide the class into groups of three. Instruct each group to rewrite a part of the selection from the point of view of a character other than Frankie. Suggest that each group begin by choosing a section to retell and a character from whose point of view it will be told. Then, have the group choose one member to ad-lib the section aloud in the character of the new narrator. A second group member should record and a third member should transcribe the retelling. Next, direct members of the group to work together to revise its version, and then write up and edit the final draft. Finally, have groups take turns reading their final drafts to the class, with every member of the group participating. Members should decide in advance who will read various parts of the draft, and everyone should practice her or his presentation.

professor had asked him to describe an object from his childhood. McCourt chose the decrepit bed he and his brothers had shared. He wrote of their being scratched by the stiff stuffing protruding from the mattress and of ending up jumbled together in the sagging center with fleas leaping all over their bodies. The professor gave McCourt an A, and asked him to read the essay to the class.

"No!" McCourt said, recoiling at the thought. But for the first time, he began to see his sordid childhood, with all the miseries, betrayals, and longings that tormented him still, as a worthy topic. *Maybe that's what I was born to put on the page,* he thought.

While teaching, McCourt wrote occasional articles for newspapers and magazines. But his major effort, a memoir of 150 pages that he churned out in 1966, remained unfinished. Now he leafed through his students' transcribed essays. They lacked polish, but somehow they worked in a way his writing didn't. *I'm trying to teach these kids to write,* he thought, *yet I haven't found the secret myself.*

The bell rang in the faculty lounge at Stuyvesant High School in Manhattan. When McCourt began teaching at the prestigious public high school in 1972, he joked that he'd finally made it to paradise. . . .

The bits and pieces that bubbled into his consciousness enlivened the stories he told in class. "Everyone has a story to tell," he said. "Write about what you know with conviction, from the heart. Dig deep," he urged. "Find your own voice and dance your own dance!"

On Fridays the students read their compositions aloud. To draw them out, McCourt would read excerpts from his duffel bag full of notebooks. "You had such an interesting childhood, Mr. McCourt," they said. "Why don't you write a book?" They threw his own words back at him: "It sounds like there's more to that story; dig deeper. . . ."

McCourt was past fifty and painfully aware of the passage of time. But despite his growing frustration at his unfinished book, he never tired of his students' work.

Over the years some talented writers passed through McCourt's popular classes. Laurie

Gwen Shapiro, whose first novel will be published in the spring, was one of them. He decided she was coasting along on her technical skills. "You're capable of much more," McCourt told her. "Try writing something that's meaningful to you for a change."

Near the end of the semester, McCourt laid an essay—graded 100—on Laurie's desk. "If Laurie is willing to read her essay," he announced to the class, "I think we'll all benefit."

Laurie began to read a portrait of love clouded by anger and shame. She told of her father, partially paralyzed, and of resenting his inability to play with her or help her ride a bicycle. The paper shook in her trembling hands, and McCourt understood all too well what it cost her to continue. She also admitted she was embarrassed by her father's limp. The words, McCourt knew, were torn straight from her soul.

When Laurie finished, with tears streaming down her face, the students broke into applause. McCourt looked around the room, his own vision blurred.

These young people have been giving you lessons in courage, he thought. *When will you dare as mightily as they?*

It was October 1994. Frank McCourt, now retired, sat down and read his book's new opening, which he had written a few days before and still found satisfying. But many blank pages lay before him. *What if I never get it right?* he wondered grimly.

He stared at the logs glowing in the fireplace and could almost hear students' voices from years past, some angry, some defeated, others confused and seeking guidance. "It's no good, Mr. McCourt. I don't have what it takes."

Then Frank McCourt, author, heard the steadying tones of Frank McCourt, teacher: *Of course you do. Dig deeper. Find your own voice and dance your own dance.*

He scribbled a few lines. "I'm in a playground on Classon Avenue in Brooklyn with my brother Malachy. He's two, I'm three. We're on the seesaw." In the innocent voice of an unprotected child who could neither comprehend nor control the world around him, Frank McCourt told his tale of poverty and abandonment.

—from *Reader's Digest,* November 1997

BROWSING IN THE FILES

About the Writer. For her biographical article, journalist Barbara Sande Dimmitt (1947–   ) spent hours interviewing not only Frank McCourt but also many of his former students. The man "is a quote a minute," she recalls. He's "just impossible to capture in one place."

Writers on Writing. "[Writing is] a blast," says Dimmitt, "—except for the first draft. Don't speak to me when I'm working on that. Revising is like playing in a sandbox, building castles . . . but for the first draft, it's as if you have to give birth to each individual grain of sand."

C Literary Connections

Laurie Gwen Shapiro's *The Unexpected Salami* was published in May 1998. Frank McCourt might have been pleased to see one critic's comment that Shapiro's prose "marches along smartly to its own arrhythmic, offbeat beat."

D Critical Thinking

Making Connections

? How would you compare the adult Frank McCourt with the young Frankie of "Typhoid Fever"? [Possible responses: Both seem fearful, yet determined; both love language; the adult McCourt seems more interested in helping others; the adult McCourt seems less brave, though he finally did dare to write his book.]

Connecting Across Texts

Connecting with "Typhoid Fever"

Whereas "Typhoid Fever" offers a first-person glimpse into McCourt's childhood, "The Education of Frank McCourt" provides a look at the adult he became. Dimmitt's essay reveals the strengths McCourt developed as well as the scars left by his childhood ordeals. McCourt became a creative and compassionate teacher whose sense of humor never left him. He was able to learn from his students as well as to teach them, so that ultimately he could develop the talent underlying the love of language he discovered as a ten-year-old in Limerick's Fever Hospital. Becoming oneself, this essay suggests, does not stop when one reaches eighteen or twenty-one or even fifty or sixty; rather, it is a lifelong process.

MAKING MEANINGS

First Thoughts

1. Students may cite Patricia's death, Frankie's removal to the empty ward, the anecdote of the starving Irish children, or Sister Rita's spiteful ban on visits from Frankie's mother.

Shaping Interpretations

2. Possible examples: Patricia's mimicking the nurse; the character of Seamus; Frankie's "review" of "The Owl and the Pussycat"; the nurse's urging Frankie to "have a good sleep for yourself" after her allusions to ghosts and to Patricia's death; Seamus's wife's grief over "The Highwayman." Some may find the blend of comedy and sorrow true to life; others may say that comedy makes sorrow more bearable for readers and perhaps for the writer; still others may find the comedy inappropriate.

3. Possible responses: He learns that he can endure a lot; that literature, especially poetry, can give him comfort and strength; that he loves Shakespeare; that his sense of humor is a boon.

Challenging the Text

4. Possible responses: Yes, the nurse and nun are not credible characters— they are one-sided and their actions seem unlikely, bordering (by today's standards) on abuse; yes, Frankie's "seeing" ghosts of starving children proves that the writer blends fact and fantasy; yes, it's implausible that he could remember so much specific dialogue after so many years; no, the work is a credible look at Frankie's inner reality.

Grading Timesaver

Rubrics for each Choices assignment appear on p. 134 in the *Portfolio Management System*.

MAKING MEANINGS

First Thoughts

[connect]

1. In your opinion, what was the saddest or most shocking episode in Frankie's story?

Shaping Interpretations

[interpret]

2. The Kerry nurse asks sharply, "What is there to laugh about?" Find two examples of **comic relief** in McCourt's memoir. How do you feel about the use of comedy in such a sad story?

[apply]

3. What do you think young Frankie discovered about himself in the hospital? Be sure to consider the role that language, and especially poetry, plays in this story.

Challenging the Text

[evaluate]

4. McCourt's mother called one of his stories "a pack of lies," but one reviewer says *Angela's Ashes* is "a truth-teller's work." Using examples from "Typhoid Fever," discuss the writer's **credibility**. Do you think parts of the story sound as if they were made-up?

Reading Check

Briefly **summarize** the **main events** in McCourt's story by answering the questions in the **cause-and-effect** chart below:

> Why are the children in the hospital?

> Why is Frankie moved to another floor?

> What happens to each child?

CHOICES: Building Your Portfolio

Writer's Notebook

1. Collecting Ideas for an Autobiographical Incident

Putting us there. Frank McCourt puts us right inside a young boy's head, right in his Fever Hospital bed, right in the midst of a pack of colorful characters. Whatever past event you use for the Writer's Workshop on page 380, make it "come alive." Choose an incident—perhaps from your Quickwrite notes or your Writer's Notebook. Jot down notes answering these questions: Who was there? What did people say? How did you feel? Did anything comical happen? Help the reader enter your scene.

Creative Response

2. My Reading Experience

"The Highwayman" played an important role in Frankie's young life. What novel, poem, or story do you remember from your childhood? Why did it mean so much to you? Write a brief personal essay about your reading memory.

Oral Interpretation

3. Live from Limerick!

"Typhoid Fever" is full of voices: Frankie, Patricia, Sister Rita, the Kerry nurse, Seamus, even Seamus's wife. It has singing and poetry recitations. With a group, plan, practice, and present an oral interpretation of part of "Typhoid Fever." Try to include some of the parts with "The Highwayman." (For help, see the Speaking and Listening Workshop on pages 750–751.)

CHOICES: Building Your Portfolio

1. **Writer's Notebook** Students might try using the voice of their younger selves, as McCourt does.

2. **Creative Response** Encourage students to recall material read, recited, or sung to them.

3. **Oral Interpretation** Remind students to let their voices show the characters' personalities.

Reading Check

Top box:	Frankie is recovering from typhoid, Patricia from diphtheria and a mysterious "something else."
Middle box:	Frankie is moved as punishment for talking with Patricia.
Bottom box:	Patricia dies; Frankie is terrified and lonely, but he gains strength and survives.

LANGUAGE LINK   MINI-LESSON

Voice—A Bit o' Poetry

Language Handbook HELP

See Run-on Sentences, page 1042.

Technology HELP

See Language Workshop CD-ROM. Key word entry: run-on sentences.

Frank McCourt repeatedly told his students, "Find your own voice" (see **Connections** on page 372). When McCourt found *his* voice, his memoirs took off. The voice he found was that of an innocent child, talking in a stream-of-consciousness style with a child's personal quirks and dialect. McCourt decided not to use standard punctuation and quotation marks because he wanted us to sense that we are overhearing someone's thoughts. To appreciate the effect, read these passages aloud.

1. "Patricia says she doesn't know what induced means or potent circumstances and she doesn't care about Shakespeare, she has her poetry book and she reads to me from beyond the wall a poem about an owl and a pussycat that went to sea in a green boat with honey and money and it makes no sense and when I say that Patricia gets huffy and says that's the last poem she'll ever read to me."

2. "We gave ye a warning to stop the blathering but ye wouldn't. Take the by, Seamus, take him.
   Ah, now, nurse, sure isn't he harmless. 'Tis only a bit o' poetry."

> **Try It Out**
>
> ► **Cleaning Up the Style.**
> Suppose you are a very diligent editor in the publishing house that has accepted McCourt's manuscript. Your job is to "clean up" his style, to make it conform to accepted formal usage. Correct the passages opposite. Correct spellings and punctuate sentences for clarity and correctness. Compare your edited manuscripts in class. What has happened to Frankie's voice?

VOCABULARY   HOW TO OWN A WORD

WORD BANK
induced
potent
torrent
clamoring

Antonyms: Just the Opposite

An **antonym** is a word that has the opposite, or nearly opposite, meaning of another word. Choose the best antonym for each word in capital letters. This exercise format will give you practice for taking standardized tests. Remember, you're looking for the best antonym— not **synonym** (word with the same meaning).

1. INDUCED: (a) persuaded (b) attempted (c) increased (d) discouraged
2. POTENT: (a) impossible (b) weak (c) strong (d) safe
3. TORRENT: (a) trickle (b) flood (c) law (d) tornado
4. CLAMORING: (a) creating (b) whispering (c) opening (d) studying

---

LANGUAGE LINK

Try It Out
Possible Responses

1. Patricia says she doesn't know what <u>induced</u> means, or <u>potent</u> <u>circumstances</u>, and she doesn't care about Shakespeare. She has her poetry book. From beyond the wall, she reads me a poem about an owl and a pussycat that went to sea in a green boat with honey and money. It makes no sense. When I say so, she gets huffy and says, "That's the last poem I'll ever read to you!"

2. "We gave you a warning to stop blathering, but you wouldn't. Take the boy, Seamus; take him." "Ah, now, Nurse, surely he's harmless. It's only a bit of poetry."

Some students may find the edited versions clearer; others may find them flatter and missing the voice of the child.

VOCABULARY

Answers

1. (d) discouraged
2. (b) weak
3. (a) trickle
4. (b) whispering

Resources ————

Language
• *Grammar and Language Links,* Worksheet, p. 43

Vocabulary
• *Words to Own,* Worksheet p. 23

Language Link Quick Check

To show you understand voice, choose the correct answers.

1. The term *voice* in literature refers to
   a. personal opinions expressed by the narrator.
   b. a blend of style, point of view, and personal quirks.
   c. usage of personal pronouns.

2. Frank McCourt's voice in "Typhoid Fever" is
   a. that of an innocent child.
   b. that of an illiterate janitor.
   c. that of a humorous teacher.

3. McCourt helps readers to "hear" his voice by
   a. using diacritical marks to show pronunciation.
   b. including an audiotape with his book.
   c. avoiding standard punctuation and quotation marks.

(Answers: 1. b; 2. a; 3. c)

OBJECTIVES

1. Find thematic connections across genres
2. Generate relevant and interesting questions for discussion
3. Recognize distinctive and shared characteristics of cultures through reading and discussion

Extending the Theme

This lyric poem is the speaker's response to a college assignment to write one page that will "come out of you" and "be true." In informal free verse, he presents facts and feelings about himself, "the only colored student in my class." He speaks of the gulf between himself and his white instructor and points out these truths: They're both Americans, they're both part of each other, they're both learning from each other—but neither one is wholly "free."

Ⓐ Critical Thinking
Challenging the Text
❓ Do you agree that any writing that comes "out of you" is "true"? Explain. [Possible responses: Yes, if *true* means "in keeping with your personality and values"; no, if *true* means "objectively accurate."]

Ⓑ English Language Learners
Tell students that Winston-Salem and Durham are cities in North Carolina and that in many cities the Y, or YMCA, offers no-frills, low-cost rooms to rent. Explain that living at the Y suggests that the speaker is a newcomer to the area and that he has little money.

Ⓒ Elements of Literature
Personification
❓ The speaker personifies Harlem. What sounds from Harlem might he hear? What might those sounds "say"? [Possible responses: He might hear traffic, vendors, footsteps, children at play, arguments, laughter, music. These sounds might "say" that Harlem is a vibrant place.]

Background

The speaker in this poem is an African American student at Columbia University in New York City—the college on the hill above Harlem. Hughes was a student there for a year. As you read, think about how well—or badly—the poem fulfills the instructor's assignment.

Quickwrite

If you were given the same assignment ("Go home and write a page tonight. And let that page come out of you. . . ."), what would you say? Quickwrite whatever comes to your mind in response. You don't have to write a whole paper or a poem!

go.hrw.com
LEO 10-5

Theme for English B

Langston Hughes

The instructor said,

   Go home and write
   a page tonight.
   And let that page come out of you—
   then, it will be true.

5 Ⓐ

I wonder if it's that simple?
I am twenty-two, colored, born in Winston-Salem.
I went to school there, then Durham, then here
to this college on the hill above Harlem.
10 Ⓑ I am the only colored student in my class.
The steps from the hill lead down into Harlem,
through a park, then I cross St. Nicholas,
Eighth Avenue, Seventh, and I come to the Y,
the Harlem Branch Y, where I take the elevator
15 up to my room, sit down, and write this page:

It's not easy to know what is true for you or me
at twenty-two, my age. But I guess I'm what
Ⓒ I feel and see and hear. Harlem, I hear you:
hear you, hear me—we two—you, me, talk on this page.
20 (I hear New York, too.) Me—who?

Well, I like to eat, sleep, drink, and be in love.
I like to work, read, learn, and understand life.
I like a pipe for a Christmas present,
Ⓓ or records—Bessie,° bop, or Bach.

25 I guess being colored doesn't make me *not* like
the same things other folks like who are other races.
So will my page be colored that I write?
Being me, it will not be white.
But it will be

---

24. Bessie: Bessie Smith (1898–1937), a jazz and blues singer.

Listening to Music 🎵

"Careless Love Blues" (Traditional) and "St. Louis Blues" by W. C. Handy, performed by Bessie Smith
"Cubano-Be, Cubano-Bop" by Dizzy Gillespie and George Russell, performed by Dizzy Gillespie
Brandenburg Concerto No. 2 by Johann Sebastian Bach, performed by the Berlin Philharmonic Orchestra

Bessie Smith (1894–1937) was nicknamed "Empress of the Blues," having had many hit recordings in the 1920s. Bop, short for be-bop, was a new form of jazz that emerged in the 1940s. Johann Sebastian Bach (1685–1750) was one of the greatest composers of western classical music.

Activity
Have students listen to the selections after reading the poem. Ask how hearing examples of the music mentioned in l. 24 helped them understand more about the poem's speaker and his tastes.

Rooftops (No. 1, This Is Harlem) (1942–1943) by Jacob Lawrence. Gouache on paper (14⅜″ × 21⅞″).

Hirshhorn Museum and Sculpture Garden/Smithsonian Institution. Gift of Joseph H. Hirshhorn, 1966. Photographer Lee Stalsworth. (66.2921). Courtesy of the artist and the Francine Seders Gallery, Seattle, Washington.

30   a part of you, instructor.
       You are white—
       yet a part of me, as I am a part of you.
       That's American.
       Sometimes perhaps you don't want to be a part of me.
35   Nor do I often want to be a part of you.
       But we are, that's true!
       As I learn from you,
       I guess you learn from me—
       although you're older—and white—
40   and somewhat more free.

       This is my page for English B.

E

D Cultural Connections

"Bach" is German classical composer Johann Sebastian Bach (1685–1750). The combined reference to Bessie Smith, Bach, and bop (a form of jazz) illustrates Hughes's eclectic tastes in music.

E Critical Thinking

Evaluating

❓ Do you think Hughes's message would be communicated more effectively if the entire poem rhymed, as these lines do? Explain. [Possible responses: Yes, because rhyme makes a poem striking and easy to remember; no, because its sound patterns are as free-form and unique as its setting and the self that Hughes is exploring.]

RESPONDING TO THE ART

Social realist **Jacob Lawrence** grew up in Harlem during the Harlem Renaissance.

Activity. Point out that Langston Hughes uses contrasts and varying "angles"—ways of looking at things—to arrive at a tentative sense of unity. Where does Lawrence use contrasts and varying angles? Does *Rooftops* give you a sense of unity or disunity— or some other feeling?

Resources

Listening
Audio CD Library
A vibrant recording of this poem is included in the *Audio CD Library:*
• Disc 11, Track 7

Making the Connections

Connecting to the Theme: "Becoming Myself"

In "Theme for English B," Langston Hughes makes it clear that the self is anything but "simple." He explores the self as interconnecting with many things and people. Like Malcolm X and Jeanne Wakatsuki Houston, Hughes understands that ethnic heritage plays a crucial role in the development of a person's self-image. Hughes also sees, as does Frank McCourt, the powerful influence of economics on who we become. In ll. 16–20, the poet uses direct statement, personification, repetition, and an accumulation of personal pronouns to introduce his broad image of the self. In the last stanza, he directly expresses his view that every one of us is, for better and for worse, a part of everyone else.

BROWSING IN THE FILES

Writers on Writing. In his autobiography, *The Big Sea,* Hughes describes the birth of a poem: "No doubt I changed a few words the next day, or maybe crossed out a line or two. But there are seldom many changes in my poems, once they're down. Generally, the first two or three lines come to me from something I'm thinking about, or looking at, or doing, and the rest of the poem (if there is to be a poem) flows from those first few lines, usually right away. If there is a chance to put the poem down then, I write it down. If not, I try to remember it until I get to a pencil and paper; for poems are like rainbows: they escape you quickly."

RESPONDING TO THE ART

German-born **Winold Reiss** gained fame for his pastel portraits of the Blackfoot Indians, showing their customs and history.
Activity. Ask students what images in the art suggest images from "Theme for English B."

FINDING COMMON GROUND

As its name suggests, this feature requires students, through lively discussion, to discover areas of agreement about something related to tone and issues in the literature.

1. Encourage volunteers to read their Quickwrites aloud.
2. Remind students that tone is a reflection of the writer's attitude. You might have groups work toward statements of the subject of "Theme for English B." They can then explore the poet's attitude toward the subject.

MEET THE WRITER
Discovery

Langston Hughes (1902–1967) was a struggling young writer, working as a busboy in an expensive Washington, D.C., hotel restaurant. One day Hughes heard that Vachel Lindsay, a famous American poet, was going to dine in the hotel that night and then give a reading of his poems. In his autobiography, Hughes describes what happened:

66 I wanted very much to hear him read his poems, but I knew they did not admit colored people to the auditorium. That afternoon, I wrote out three of my poems, 'Jazzonia,' 'Negro Dancers,' and 'The Weary Blues,' on some pieces of paper and put them in the pocket of my white busboy's coat. In the evening when Mr. Lindsay came down to dinner, quickly I laid them beside his plate and went away, afraid to say anything to so famous a poet. . . . I looked back once and saw Mr. Lindsay reading the poems as I picked up a tray of dirty dishes from a side table and started for the dumbwaiter. The next morning on my way to work, as usual I bought a paper—and there I read that Vachel Lindsay had discovered a Negro busboy poet! At the hotel the reporters were already waiting for me. 99

For more about Hughes's life and poetry, see page 510.

Langston Hughes (c. 1925) by Winold Reiss (1886–1953). Pastel on artist board (30 1/16" × 21 5/8").

National Portrait Gallery, Smithsonian Institution / Art Resource, NY.

FINDING COMMON GROUND

Meet with a small group of classmates and decide on your agenda: Which questions and responses to the poem do you want to discuss? What issues has the poem raised in your group? Be sure to cover two topics: (1) How does your own Quickwrite compare with the poem? and (2) What is the **tone** of the poem?

When all groups have finished talking about the poem, each group should assign a spokesperson to summarize for the whole class what that group discovered about the poem. Do you find any consensus?

Assessing Learning

Self-Assessment
Give students a scale of 1 (never) through 5 (always) to assess their interaction with the poem or other texts in Collection 5.

_____ I make personal connections.
_____ I use context clues or dictionaries to determine meanings of unfamiliar words.
_____ I make predictions and ask questions.
_____ I consider the author's purpose and try to determine the central idea or theme.
_____ I pay attention to the tone and diction of literary language.

READ ON

A Hero?

"Whether I shall turn out to be the hero of my own life, or whether that station will be held by anybody else, these pages must show." Thus opens *David Copperfield* by Charles Dickens (available in several paperback editions). Of all his wonderful novels, this story of Davy's coming of age, beginning with the cruelty he endured as a child, is the one that Dickens loved the best.

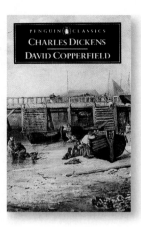

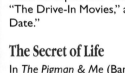

Growing Up Despite It All

Gary Soto's *A Summer Life* (University Press of New England) tells what it was like growing up Chicano in Fresno, California. In a series of funny and touching essays, Soto focuses on topics like "The Shirt," "The Haircut," "The Drive-In Movies," and "The Computer Date."

The Secret of Life

In *The Pigman & Me* (Bantam), writer Paul Zindel describes the funny-sad teenage year he spent in Staten Island, New York. In Zindel's autobiography, you'll meet Nonno Frankie, the real-life neighbor and friend who inspired Zindel's prize-winning first novel *The Pigman.* You'll also discover the secret of life, according to the pigman.

Beautiful, Haunting Africa

The extraordinary adventures of a childhood in Kenya are recounted in Elspeth Huxley's *The Flame Trees of Thika* (Penguin). A version of the story, with its haunting images of Africa, was serialized on television.

Writer's Workshop

Technology HELP

See Writer's Workshop 2 CD-ROM. *Assignment: Autobiographical Incident.*

ASSIGNMENT

Write about an autobiographical incident you remember vividly.

AIM

To express yourself; to reflect on the significance of an experience.

AUDIENCE

Your teacher and classmates; a relative or friend.

NARRATIVE WRITING

AUTOBIOGRAPHICAL INCIDENT

CALVIN AND HOBBES © 1989 Watterson. Reprinted with permission of UNIVERSAL PRESS SYNDICATE. All rights reserved.

If Calvin wrote an account of one of his exploits, he'd be writing a special kind of narrative—an **autobiographical incident,** a true story about a particular incident in the writer's life. In this workshop, you'll face the same challenges and solve the same problems that Malcolm X, Jeanne Wakatsuki Houston, and Frank McCourt did: how to express your feelings about something that happened to you and how to make that story interest your readers.

Prewriting

1. Tell a Single Story

In your Writer's Notebook, you've made some notes about one or more autobiographical incidents that are important to you. Continue with one of those incidents or brainstorm to find a new incident.

Try to choose something that happened in a few hours or in a single day. A time-limited incident (as in Malcolm X's "Hair," which happened in one afternoon) has more intensity than one that extends over a long period.

If you're stuck on finding a topic, preview some possibilities with your writing group—using a sentence or two for each incident—and ask which one they'd most like to read about. You might try thinking about these possibilities: a triumph, a failure, a challenge, friends, bullies, a family story, love, loss, standing up for a cause.

380 THE NONFICTION COLLECTIONS

  Resources: Print and Media

Writing and Language
• *Portfolio Management System*
Prewriting, p. 135
Peer Editing, p. 136
Assessment Rubric, p. 137

• *Workshop Resources*
Revision Strategy Teaching Notes, p. 23
Revision Strategy Transparencies 12, 13
• *Writer's Workshop 2 CD-ROM*
Autobiographical Incident

2. Elaborate: Dig for Details

Imagine yourself reliving the incident, and take notes on these essentials. A cluster diagram will help you gather ideas.

- **Context (setting):** Where and when did the incident happen? How old were you? Who was there besides you?

- **Events:** List your main events in chronological order (the order in which they happened). Do you need to add a flashback to explain something that happened in the past?

- **Sensory details:** Help your readers see the characters and places in your story. Record details of sights, smells, sounds, tastes, touch, and movement.

- **Dialogue/Monologue:** What did people say? What did you say to yourself?

Start Here: The Raw Material of Autobiography

Your own memories: What do you recall immediately (the bare bones)? What details do you recall as you dig deeper?

Other people's memories: What do others who were present tell you about the same incident? (What do you suppose Shorty would have written about Malcolm X's first conk?)

Photographs, home movies, videotapes: These "frozen moments" may jog your memory.

Journals, letters, souvenirs: Explore these sources for additional details.

A visit to the place where your story happened—even in memory (see Bradbury's experience on page 353).

---

3. Tell What the Incident Means to You

What did you learn from the incident? What do you think and feel about it now, and what did you think and feel when it happened? (Look back at page 347 for Malcolm X's powerful reflection on the significance of his first conk.) Plan to conclude your autobiographical incident as Malcolm X does, with a paragraph or two on the significance of your incident. Try a quickwrite (like the sample on the right) or a cluster diagram to discover how you feel about the incident and what you learned from it.

Try It Out

Elaborate by adding descriptive details of sight, sound, smell, taste, or touch (texture, temperature) to each statement. Add as many sentences to each statement as you wish.

1. We lived in a small town.
2. I saw my dog run into the street.
3. They were talking in the next room.

- ● I learned how much I enjoy working with young children. Admire their tremendous energy & eagerness to learn. They're curious about
- ● everything. What happens to them later? Tutoring was fun. Felt important. Made me think I might want to be a teacher—la profesora—especially of
- ● young kids.

- Think of a humorous, poignant, or dramatic event that has happened to you, and tell it to your class as if you were telling the anecdote to friends. Then, have students each select a partner and tell a story from their lives. *Remind students to choose an anecdote they would not mind sharing with others.* After the first student ends his or her story, have the partner also share an anecdote.

- Next, have partners identify the most memorable part of the story told to them. These are the sections of the stories that the teller will want to retain and expand in initial drafts.

Prewriting

Suggest prewriting techniques such as imaging and freewriting. Each student might brainstorm a list of potential facts and ideas to include in either the narrative or descriptive portions of the autobiographical incident: sights, sounds, tastes, smells, textures, action, thoughts, and conversation.

Have students review the information on elaboration (Prewriting 2), and look closely at the ideas they have assembled. How can these impressions be made more vivid and memorable for the reader?

Try It Out
Possible Answers
Answers will vary but might include details like the following:

1. We lived in a small New England factory town, constantly coated with a haze made of sea mist and smoke from the mills.

2. I saw my tiny, wriggling puppy escape my brother's grasp and run into the flooded street just as the power lines came down, hissing and sparking in the swirling water.

3. The costumed dancers, their backs turned from the orchestra, were talking in muffled tones in the next room of the club.

Reaching All Students

Struggling Writers

Students who have difficulty putting their thoughts on paper might tape-record their incident as they relate it to a friend. Listeners should ask questions that clarify the flow of the narrative and prompt the writer to add interesting details.

English Language Learners

Stimulate students' ideas for autobiographical incidents by watching old episodes of *The Wonder Years, Brooklyn Bridge,* or similar programs in which common childhood events become monumental occurrences. After students have viewed an episode, have them discuss the perspective of the narrator, the use of dialogue and monologue, and the event portrayed. Perhaps students will identify events in their lives that would make good episodes of a TV program and serve as the basis of their autobiographical incident.

T381

Drafting

- Before beginning to draft their papers, students should have read and discussed the Student Model.
- The first draft is simply the written version of the oral story students just shared with their partner. Remind students that the most important purpose of this initial draft is to get the whole story written down; it can be improved upon later.
- Remind students to use only every other line when they write their drafts. They should also leave extra space in the right margin. These blank spaces will be used for comments and editing marks.

Using the Model

Read the Student Model (pp. 382–383) with students and be certain they understand the points made in the side-column annotations. Then, discuss the model using questions such as the following:

? What questions does the opening sentence suggest to you? [What kind of teacher has the writer always wanted? Will she succeed? What is she likely to learn from this experience?]

? What one word best describes the writer's experiences as reported in the first paragraph? [shock, dismay, reality]

? Which image in the essay do you find most memorable? [Possible responses: the Incredible Hulk emerging; tennis shoes squealing like brakes.]

? What images or other details would you add to this first draft? [perhaps a metaphor describing the speaker's dismay at the unruliness of the students or one illustrating her relief at the abrupt braking of the sneakers]

Language/Grammar Link
H E L P

Tone: page 352. Specific and proper nouns: page 364. Voice: page 375.

A well-known writer got collared by a university student, who asked, "Do you think I could be a writer?"

"Well," the writer said, "I don't know. . . . Do you like sentences?"

The writer could see the student's amazement. Sentences? Do I like sentences? I am twenty years old and do I like sentences? If he had liked sentences, of course, he could begin, like a joyful painter I knew. I asked him how he came to be a painter. He said, "I liked the smell of paint."

—Annie Dillard

Drafting

Before you start writing, think about the **tone** you'll use. Are you telling a humorous incident? an ironic one? Choose words and details that let the reader know—or guess—how you felt about the incident when it happened and how you feel about it now.

Draft your autobiographical incident in a single sitting. It doesn't have to be perfect; just get it down on paper. Once you've thought of an attention-grabbing beginning (dialogue, a startling statement, a description of the setting), dive right into the action. Elaborate with sensory details, comparisons, and dialogue—everything that makes a narrative interesting to read.

Student Model

LA PROFESORA

I was to spend an hour each Tuesday afternoon with five second-graders and have the chance to be the kind of teacher I always wanted to have. I was relatively calm that first day when I met those five smiling, little angels; I figured, how hard could it be? They quietly and obediently followed me down the long hall to our new classroom, and I thought to myself, "No problem!" But the instant I opened the door, I knew I was wrong. They nearly knocked me over in a mad rush to get to one of the two teacher's chairs in the room. They did not emerge from their shells gradually but broke out of them the way the Incredible Hulk bursts out of his clothes. Well, only fifty-eight minutes and twenty-two seconds left.

That second week I knew I would have to face the ultimate test. I had no choice; I had to address and effectively deal with the age-old elementary school problem: running in the halls. If I did not, I could not be a successful teacher. They knew where the room was, and they knew that whoever got there first would get the big chair in which all little

This is Spanish for "The Teacher." The title creates interest, makes us wonder why the Spanish.

Sets up the context of the incident. The writer reveals her thoughts. A hint at what the problem/conflict will be.

Good comparison—the writer uses humor well.

Time-limited incident begins here. She is very specific here about the conflict.

Crossing the Curriculum

Music

Have interested students choose musical selections that express the same emotions developed in their essays. Students could record brief pieces of music from various works to accompany an oral reading of their essay. (Remind students of the copyright laws governing the fair use of protected material for educational purposes.)

children dream of sitting. We met in the cafeteria, and when all five were there, I took a deep breath and began to speak those fateful words. "I think it's time . . . "—the sprinters lined up and prepared for the race of their lives—" . . . to go."

Uses dialogue.

Then they were off! I knew at once that the usual "Don't run!" was futile, and so I resorted to Plan B: "¡Caminen Uds.! ¡Más despacio!"

Spanish: "Walk! More slowly!"

Their miniature Nikes came to a screeching halt. They turned around, panting, and Matthew, the spokesperson, asked, "What does that mean?" I breathed a sigh of relief.

Sensory details: sound.

"I'll only tell you if you wait for me." They waited. Luckily for me their curiosity had gotten the best of them. Those five little children had so much energy and such an eagerness to learn; all I had to do was channel it in the right direction. Although it can be quite a challenge sometimes and I am always exhausted when I leave, I cherish every moment I spend with them. At four o'clock every week when little Calvin wraps himself around my legs and asks hopefully, "Can we come back tomorrow?" I see the excitement dancing in their eyes and I wonder where the time has gone.

Tells how the problem was resolved.

Significance— her thoughts and feelings about the incident.

A powerful ending.

I wish we could, Calvin.

—Melissa Wafer
Half Hollow Hills High School
Dix Hills, New York

"There's someone here to see you, Howard. He said to mention a pet goldfish you flushed down the toilet when you were six years old."

Reprinted from *The Saturday Evening Post.*

**Sentence Workshop
H E L P**

Using subordination: page 385.

Some Autobiographical Incidents

Each of these essays focuses on an autobiograpical incident. Do the titles give you any ideas for your own essay topic?

- "The Night the Bed Fell" by James Thurber
- "Looking for Work" by Gary Soto
- "Only Daughter" by Sandra Cisneros
- "In the Kitchen" by Henry Louis Gates

WRITER'S WORKSHOP 383

Crossing the Curriculum

Social Studies
Research. Students may wish to study autobiographical incidents from other time periods (Civil War, World War II, etc.) or countries (China, Israel, Lebanon, etc.) The Internet is a valuable source for historical material documenting the lives of people in troubled times. Students might share samples with the class to demonstrate the universality of human experience.

Art
Viewing and Representing. Students who are artistically gifted may wish to draw a cartoon that takes a humorous perspective on their autobiographical moment. Have students examine the sample provided above and then create their own cartoon. Students with a good idea but limited talent may wish to share a project with a more artistically gifted student.

Evaluating and Revising

Have students use the Evaluation Criteria provided here to review their drafts and determine needed revisions. In particular, ask students to state in one word or phrase what emotion they intended to convey. Then, ask students to highlight the passages that provoke this feeling. If students cannot find passages to highlight, have them consider whether their narrative development is at fault.

Publishing

Students might make copies of their essays for family members or friends involved in the incident described. Students might want to add photos or illustrations to the copy. If students use a computerized presentation, they could scan pictures or create graphics to accompany the narratives.

Reflecting

Before students include essays in their portfolios, have them date their papers and attach a reflection answering the following questions.

1. How did I structure my essay? Did I work in chronological order or use flashbacks? Did this choice work well? Why or why not?
2. Which sensory image in my paper brings the moment most clearly back to mind?

Resources ———

Peer Editing Forms and Rubrics
• *Portfolio Management System,* p. 136.

Revision Transparencies
• *Workshop Resources,* p. 23

Grading Timesaver

Rubrics for this Writer's Workshop assignment appear on p. 137 of the *Portfolio Management System.*

■ *Evaluation Criteria*

A good autobiographical incident

1. *narrates a time-limited incident*
2. *has an attention-grabbing beginning, sensory details, and dialogue*
3. *has an easy-to-follow sequence of events (usually in chronological order)*
4. *explains the incident's significance to the writer*

Proofreading Tip

As you proofread, slow your reading down by pointing to every word and punctuation mark.

Communications Handbook HELP

See Proofreaders' Marks.

Publishing Tip

Illustrate your essay, put it in a binder or folder, and give it to a friend or relative who experienced the incident with you.

Evaluating and Revising

1. Self-evaluation

To give your autobiographical incident the appeal of a good story, try the following:

• **Add** more specific details and dialogue.
• **Subtract** (cut) details that wander off the subject.
• **Replace** vague or overused words with more precise or more original ones.

2. Peer Review

Once you've done some early-round revision on your own, share your draft with your writing group. Ask them if the sequence of events is clear.

Revision Model

> Then they were off!
> ~~They ran down the hall again,~~ I
>
> knew at once that the usual "Don't
>
> run!" was futile, and so I resorted to
>
> Plan B: "¡Caminen Uds.! ¡Más despacio!"
> ~~another solution and yelled at them~~
>
> ~~in Spanish.~~
>
> Their miniature Nikes came to a screeching halt.
> They stopped running. They
>
> , and
> turned around, panting.
>
> the spokesperson,
> Matthew, ~~one of the boys I was~~
>
> , "What does that mean?"
> ~~tutoring, asked me what I meant.~~ I
>
> breathed a sigh of relief.

Peer Comments

Can you make this a little livelier? Fix run-on sentence.

What exactly did you say to them?

Add some sensory details?

Choppy—combine some sentences here.

Use dialogue.

Sentence Workshop

OBJECTIVES

1. Identify the function of the subordinate clause
2. Combine sentences using subordinate clauses

Language Handbook
H E L P

See Subordinate Clause,
page 1037.

Technology
H E L P

See Language Workshop
CD-ROM. *Key word entry:*
combining sentences.

COMBINING SENTENCES: USING SUBORDINATION

When you combine sentences using **subordinating conjunctions** (see the list below), the ideas aren't equal. A **subordinate clause** adds to the meaning of the main clause. In the sentences that follow, the subordinate clauses (underscored) tell *when* or *why* the action in the main clause takes place:

CHOPPY   Shorty started combing the congolene in. It just felt warm.

COMBINED   "The congolene just felt warm <u>when Shorty started combing it in.</u>"

                              —Malcolm X, "Hair" (page 347)

CHOPPY   He was farming near Inglewood. I was born at that time.

COMBINED   "<u>When I was born</u>, he was farming near Inglewood."

           — Jeanne Wakatsuki Houston and James Houston, "It Can't Be Helped" (page 356)

CHOPPY   They think I have a disease from foreign parts. My father used to be in Africa.

COMBINED   "They think I have a disease from foreign parts <u>because my father used to be in Africa.</u>"

           — Frank McCourt, "Typhoid Fever" (page 366)

A BOX OF SUBORDINATING CONJUNCTIONS

after	because	so that	whenever
although	before	unless	where
as	if	until	wherever
as if	since	when	while

Writer's Workshop Follow-up: Revising

Read aloud your autobiographical incident or, better, have someone read it aloud to you. Listen for choppy sentences. See if your writing sounds smoother when the choppy sentences are combined using a subordinate clause. You should also notice that your meaning is more specific.

Try It Out

Combine the following sentences by turning one of the sentences into a subordinate clause. You might experiment with different subordinating conjunctions to see how the emphasis of your sentence can change. You might also experiment with placing your subordinate clause in different positions in the sentence.

1. I was cursing Shorty with every name I could think of. He got the spray going and started soap-lathering my head.

2. Shorty let me stand up and see in the mirror. My hair hung down in limp, damp strings.

3. I love the poem. It's exciting and almost as good as my two lines of Shakespeare.

4. It was very early, and misty. We got there with our luggage.

Resources ⎯⎯⎯⎯

Workshop Resources
• Worksheet, p. 63

Language Workshop CD-ROM
• Combining Sentences

Try It Out
Possible Answers

1. Although I was cursing Shorty with every name I could think of, he got the spray going and started soap-lathering my head.

2. Shorty let me stand up and see in the mirror where my hair hung down in limp, damp strings.

3. I love the poem because it's exciting and almost as good as my two lines of Shakespeare.

4. It was very early, and misty, when we got there with our luggage.

SENTENCE WORKSHOP 385

Assessing Learning

Quick Check: Using Subordination

In the sentences below, underline the subordinating conjunction twice, and underline the subordinate clause it introduces once.

1. <u>Although</u> <u>he got his hair conked as a young man,</u> Malcolm X later argued that conking his hair was an act of self-degradation.

2. Langston Hughes gave his poem to a famous writer <u>so that</u> <u>his work might receive some degree of recognition.</u>

3. The mother did not send her children to British schools <u>until</u> <u>she was simply too sick to teach them herself.</u>

4. <u>When</u> <u>they sent my family to an internment camp in California,</u> I was simply too young to understand that something horrible was happening.

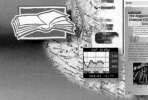

OBJECTIVES
1. Read a textbook
2. Identify text organizers
   - table of contents
   - special features
   - overviews and reviews
   - boldfaced text
   - graphic organizers
   - index

Teaching the Lesson

Discuss with students some of the features of their textbooks that they find helpful. Ask students to identify features with which they would like to become more familiar. Explain that recognizing and learning to use text organizers can help students enhance their reading skills.

Using the Strategies

Possible Answers
1. Three: (1) American Isolationism and the European War; (2) Rallying Round the Flag; (3) Internment of Japanese Americans: Patriotism's Dark Side
2. February 1942. (This information is in the time line.) Japanese Americans were interned because it was feared they would cooperate with the Japanese government. (This information is in the Chapter Overview.)
3. Answers will vary. Students may want to know why the government suspected that Japanese Americans would be traitors or why the government decided on internment in 1942 instead of earlier or later.

Reading for Life

Reading a Textbook

Situation

After reading a firsthand account of Japanese internment camps in "It Can't Be Helped," you want to see how the subject is treated in an American history textbook. Try these strategies to help you read a textbook.

Strategies

Identify the text organizers and other helpful features.
- Review the **table of contents** to see what is covered in the book and how the text is organized.
- Note **special features,** such as primary sources. You should find these listed in the table of contents.
- Does the book supply chapter **overviews** and **reviews**?
- Look for important terms in **boldfaced** type.
- Note **charts** and other **graphic organizers,** such as time lines, maps, and graphs.
- Review photographs and illustrations and their captions.
- At the back of the book, look for an **index**. If you are researching a particular subject, check the index to see how well the topic is covered.

Chapter Outline
1 American Isolationism and the European War
2 Rallying Round the Flag
3 Internment of Japanese Americans: Patriotism's Dark Side

TIME LINE			
September 1939 War begins in Europe	**June 1940** France falls; Aerial Battle of Britain begins	**December 1941** Japanese attack Pearl Harbor naval base	**February 1942** Roosevelt orders internment of Japanese Americans

Chapter Overview
In the late 1930s, the **isolationist movement** drew support from many Americans, who believed that the war looming in Europe was none of their country's concern. However, with the fall of France and the Battle of Britain, more and more Americans began to feel that U.S. entry into the war was only a matter of time. The Japanese attack on Pearl Harbor propelled the country into a war many had come to see as inevitable.

The sacrifices demanded by the war effort were made in a spirit of patriotism. However, one group of Americans was required to sacrifice more than any others: Japanese Americans living on the West Coast were ordered to report to **relocation camps** for fear they would cooperate with the Japanese government.

Study the material.
- Scan chapter headings and subheadings. Then, **skim** the content to get an overview.
- Make a list of questions you want answered.
- Next, **read slowly** to note important information and to find the answers to your questions.

Using the Strategies
1. How many subsections are in the chapter shown here, and what are they?

2. When did President Roosevelt order the internment of Japanese Americans and why? Where did you find these pieces of information?

3. List two questions about the internment of Japanese Americans you expect the textbook to answer.

Extending the Strategies

If you wanted to compare the treatment of Japanese American internment in different textbooks, how would you go about it?

Reaching All Students

Advanced Learners
Students may wish to investigate a second, related topic, such as Nazi concentration camps or Japanese prisoner-of-war camps. Have students find historical sources covering this period and use the strategies listed on p. 386 to investigate the topic. Then, have students report back to the class on their findings.

Collection 6

Being There!

Theme

Eyewitness Reports *The best nonfiction writers today—like the ones represented here—use the devices of fiction to create powerful, unforgettable pictures of places, events, and people, from the distant past to the present.*

Reading the Anthology

Reaching Struggling Readers

The *Reading Skills and Strategies: Reaching Struggling Readers* binder provides materials coordinated with the Pupil's Edition (see the Collection Planner, p. T386B) to help students who have difficulty reading and comprehending text, or students who are reluctant readers. The binder for tenth grade is organized around sixteen individual skill areas and offers the following options:

- **MiniRead** MiniReads are short, easy texts that give students a chance to practice a particular skill and strategy before reading selections in the Pupil's Edition. Each MiniRead Skill Lesson can be taught independently or used in conjunction with a Selection Skill Lesson.

- **Selection Skill Lessons** Selection Skill Lessons allow students to apply skills introduced in the MiniReads. Each Selection Skill Lesson provides reading instruction and practice specific to a particular piece of literature in the Pupil's Edition.

Reading Beyond the Anthology

Read On Collection 6 includes an annotated bibliography of books suitable for extended reading. The suggested books are related to works in this collection by theme, by author, or by subject. To preview the Read On for Collection 6, please turn to p. T447.

HRW Library The *HRW Library* offers novels, plays, works of nonfiction, and short-story collections for extended reading. Each book in the Library includes one or more major works and thematically related Connections. Each book in the *HRW Library* is also accompanied by a Study Guide that provides teaching suggestions and worksheets. For Collection 6, the following titles are recommended.

NEVER CRY WOLF
Farley Mowat
Stay with a writer as he makes a home (of sorts) with Arctic wolves. You will experience bitter cold, you will know what it is like to eat mice, and you will learn from the animals—right along with Mowat.

NIGHT
Elie Wiesel
The writer's personal memories of the Holocaust are a best-selling testament to hope and a tribute to his beloved family, who perished at the hands of the Nazis.

Collection 6 Being There!

Resources for this Collection

Note: All resources for this collection are available for preview on the *One-Stop Planner CD-ROM 1 with Test Generator.* All worksheets and blackline masters may be printed from the CD-ROM.

Internet Resources
go.hrw.com LE0 10-6

Selection or Feature	Reading and Literary Skills	Vocabulary, Language, and Grammar

R.M.S. Titanic (p. 388)
Hanson W. Baldwin
Connections:
• **A Fireman's Story** (p. 404)
Harry Senior
• **From a Lifeboat** (p. 405)
Mrs. D. H. Bishop
	• *Reading Skills and Strategies: Reaching Struggling Readers*
	  • MiniRead Skill Lesson, p. 146
	  • Selection Skill Lesson, p. 154
	• *Graphic Organizers for Active Reading,*
	Worksheet p. 24
	• *Literary Elements:* Transparency 11
	Worksheet p. 34
		• *Words to Own,* Worksheet p. 24
		• *Grammar and Language Links:*
		Misplaced Modifiers, Worksheet p. 45
		• *Language Workshop CD-ROM,*
		Misplaced or Dangling Modifiers
		• *Daily Oral Grammar,*
		Transparency 24

No News from Auschwitz (p. 409) A. M. Rosenthal **Connections: The Butterfly** (p. 414) Pavel Friedmann	• *Graphic Organizers for Active Reading,* Worksheet p. 25 • *Literary Elements:* Transparency 12 Worksheet p. 37	• *Daily Oral Grammar,* Transparency 25
Elements of Literature: Essays and History (p. 416)	• *Literary Elements,* Transparency 11	
from **Into Thin Air** (p. 418) Jon Krakauer	• *Graphic Organizers for Active Reading,* Worksheet p. 26	• *Words to Own,* Worksheet p. 25 • *Grammar and Language Links:* Noun Clauses, Worksheet p. 47 • *Language Workshop CD-ROM,* Types of Subordinate Clauses • *Daily Oral Grammar,* Transparency 26
A Presentation of Whales (p. 433) Barry Lopez	• *Graphic Organizers for Active Reading,* Worksheet p. 27 • *Literary Elements:* Transparency 11 Worksheet p. 34	• *Words to Own,* Worksheet p. 26 • *Grammar and Language Links:* Adverb Clauses, Worksheet p. 49 • *Language Workshop CD-ROM,* Types of Subordinate Clauses • *Daily Oral Grammar,* Transparency 27
Extending the Theme: A Storm in the Mountains (p. 445) Aleksandr Solzhenitsyn *translated by* Michael Glenny	The Extending the Theme feature provides students with an unstructured opportunity to practice reading strategies using a selection that extends the theme of the collection.	
Writer's Workshop: Research Paper (p. 448)		
Sentence Workshop: Correcting Run-on Sentences (p. 453)		• *Workshop Resources,* p. 65 • *Language Workshop CD-ROM,* Run-on Sentences

Collection Planner

Other Resources for this Collection

- *Cross-Curricular Activities,* p. 6
- *Portfolio Management System,* Introduction to Portfolio Assessment, p. 1
- *Test Generator,* Collection Test

Writing	Listening and Speaking Viewing and Representing	Assessment
• *Portfolio Management System,* Rubrics for Choices, p. 138	• *Visual Connections:* Videocassette A, Segment 6 • *Audio CD Library,* Disc 12, Track 2 • *Portfolio Management System,* Rubrics for Choices, p. 138	• *Formal Assessment,* Selection Test, p. 66 • *Standardized Test Preparation,* pp. 48, 50 • *Test Generator (One-Stop Planner CD-ROM)*
• *Portfolio Management System,* Rubrics for Choices, p. 140	• *Audio CD Library,* Disc 12, Track 3 • *Portfolio Management System,* Rubrics for Choices, p. 140	• *Formal Assessment,* Selection Test, p. 68 • *Test Generator (One-Stop Planner CD-ROM)*
		• *Formal Assessment,* Literary Elements Test, p. 74
• *Portfolio Management System,* Rubrics for Choices, p. 141	• *Audio CD Library,* Disc 13, Track 2 • *Portfolio Management System,* Rubrics for Choices, p. 141	• *Formal Assessment,* Selection Test, p. 70 • *Standardized Test Preparation,* p. 52 • *Test Generator (One-Stop Planner CD-ROM)*
• *Portfolio Management System,* Rubrics for Choices, p. 143	• *Audio CD Library,* Disc 14, Track 2 • *Viewing and Representing:* Fine Art Transparency 9 Worksheet p. 36 • *Portfolio Management System,* Rubrics for Choices, p. 143	• *Formal Assessment,* Selection Test, p. 72 • *Standardized Test Preparation,* p. 54 • *Test Generator (One-Stop Planner CD-ROM)*
	• *Audio CD Library,* Disc 14, Track 3	
• *Workshop Resources,* p. 27 • *Writer's Workshop 2 CD-ROM,* Informative Report	• *Viewing and Representing,* HRW Multimedia Presentation Maker	• *Portfolio Management System* • Prewriting, p. 144 • Peer Editing, p. 145 • Assessment Rubric, p. 146

Collection Planner

 Transparency   CD-ROM   Video   Audio CD

Collection 6 Being There!

Skills Focus

Selection or Feature	Reading Skills and Strategies	Elements of Literature	Vocabulary/Language/ Grammar	Writing	Listening/ Speaking	Viewing/ Representing
R.M.S. Titanic (p. 388) Hanson W. Baldwin	Use Text Organizers, pp. 389, 406 Infer, p. 406	Irony, pp. 389, 406 • Dramatic • Situational Objective and Subjective, p. 406 Mood, p. 406 Repetition, p. 406 Characters, p. 408 Dialogue, p. 408 Quotations, p. 408	Combining Narration and Exposition, p. 408 Semantic Features Chart, p. 408	List Questions for Research, p. 407 Write a Summary, p. 407 Compare Responses to a Review, p. 407	Role-Play a Senate Investigation, p. 407	Illustrate a Scene from a Story, p. 407
No News from Auschwitz (p. 409) A. M. Rosenthal	Dialogue with the Text, pp. 409, 415	Objective and Subjective Writing, pp. 409, 415 Irony, p. 415		Identify Research Sources, p. 415 Write an Essay Supporting an Opinion, p. 415		Create a Visual Memorial for a Historic Event, p. 415
Elements of Literature: Essays and History (p. 416)		Essay, p. 416 Personal Essay, p. 416 History and Journalism, p. 416 • Fact • Opinion Informative Articles, p. 416				
Into Thin Air (p. 418) Jon Krakauer	Understand Cause and Effect, pp. 418, 430 Cause-and-Effect Diagram, p. 430 Identify Main Events, p. 430	Imagery, p. 418 Sensory Details, pp. 418, 430–431 Suspense, p. 430	Technical Vocabulary/Jargon, p. 432 Context Clues, p. 432 Analogies, p. 432	Take Research Notes, p. 431 Write a Descriptive Essay, p. 431	Stage a Debate, p. 431 Research and Present an Oral Report, p. 431	Write a Movie Script for a Scene from a Story, p. 431
A Presentation of Whales (p. 433) Barry Lopez	Dialogue with the Text, pp. 433, 443 Use a KWL Chart, pp. 433, 443	Chronological Order, pp. 433, 443	Topic Sentences, p. 444 Main Idea, p. 444 Synonyms and Antonyms, p. 444	Make an Outline, p. 443 Write an Extended Analogy, p. 443		Make a Time Line of Events, p. 443
Extending the Theme: A Storm in the Mountains (p. 445) Aleksandr Solzhenitsyn *translated by* Michael Glenny	Compare and Contrast, p. 446	Prose Poem, p. 446	The Extending the Theme feature provides students with an unstructured opportunity to practice reading skills using a selection that extends the theme of the collection.			
Writer's Workshop: Research Paper (p. 448)	Primary and Secondary Sources, p. 448		Documenting Sources, p. 449	Write a Research Paper Using Information from Several Sources, pp. 448–452		
Sentence Workshop: Correcting Run-on Sentences (p. 453)			Run-on Sentences, p. 453	Revise Run-on Sentences, p. 453		
Reading for Life: Evaluating the Credibility of Sources: Print and Nonprint (p. 454)	Evaluate Sources, p. 454 • Credentials • Medium • Timeliness					

BEING THERE!

WRITING FOCUS: Research Paper

Right now you have access to more information about the past and present than people have ever had. In print, on television, by computer, you can witness history being made and find out almost anything you want to know about the past.

The writers represented in this collection make you an eyewitness to events aboard the *Titanic* one icy night in 1912 and to the horrors of Auschwitz in 1944. A reporter's story of his involvement in a tragic climbing expedition on Mt. Everest gives literal meaning to the term *cliffhanger,* and a report about beached whales puts you on a stench-filled, windswept beach in Oregon.

The reports in this collection are examples of nonfiction at its best—they capture our imagination and, like other kinds of literature, help us share experiences we would otherwise never have.

My ambition was to embrace those general qualities that Ernest Hemingway, a former newspaperman, once said should be present in all good books: "the good and the bad, the ecstasy, the remorse and sorrow, the people and the places and how the weather was."

—*Pete Hamill*

Writer's Notebook

Think of some famous people you'd like to interview or an event you wish you could have witnessed. In your Writer's Notebook, list five or six people or events that you'd like to know more about. Then, rank your choices. Keep your list. Reviewing it may help you choose a topic for the research paper you'll write for the Writer's Workshop on page 448.

Writing Focus: Research Paper

The following **Work in Progress** assignments build to a culminating **Writer's Workshop** at the end of the collection.

- R.M.S. Titanic   Listing questions (p. 407)
- No News from Auschwitz   Exploring sources (p. 415)
- Into Thin Air   Taking notes (p. 431)
- A Presentation of Whales   Organizing information (p. 443)

Writer's Workshop: Expository Writing / Research Paper (p. 448)

Introducing the Theme

Invite students to share any experiences they have had as eyewitnesses to exciting events or as visitors to historic sites. Encourage students to explore differences between seeing such events or places on TV and actually being there. Explain that writers in Collection 6 focus on "big events," combining research and careful craft to create the sense of "being there." Ask what a written report can communicate about these events and places that a broadcast report cannot.

Responding to the Quotation

Although Ernest Hemingway is a famous fiction writer, he is also known for his reportorial style. Ask students if they agree that moral issues, emotions, and the weather are at the heart of nonfiction, or are they only part of the picture? [Possible responses: Many students will say that these are important but that facts, chronology, and cause-and-effect analysis are important, too.]

Writer's Notebook

Encourage students to consider present-day people and events, as well as historical ones. Remind them that they will write best about subjects that touch them personally in some way. Let volunteers read their lists aloud.

OBJECTIVES

1. Read and interpret the article
2. Identify and analyze irony
3. Use text organizers, such as headings
4. Express understanding through writing, role-playing, or art
5. Identify narration and exposition and locate examples of author's narrative techniques
6. Understand and use new words
7. Create and use semantic features charts

SKILLS

Literary and Reading
- Read and interpret the article
- Identify and analyze irony
- Use text organizers, such as headings

Writing
- List possible questions to explore in a research paper
- Write a summary of the selection
- Write a response to a film review

Speaking/Listening/Performing
- Role-play a Senate hearing on the *Titanic* disaster

Grammar/Language
- Identify narration and exposition and locate examples of author's narrative techniques

Vocabulary
- Create and use semantic features charts

Art
- Create a visual representation of a disaster

Viewing/Representing
- Analyze the use of composition, line, and color to convey emotion (ATE)

Before You Read

R.M.S. TITANIC

Make the Connection

Facing Disaster

This account of the sinking of the *Titanic* will remind you of other disaster stories. Reporters present such catastrophes in several ways. The worst writers aim for sensational effects to such an extent that their accounts wind up becoming not only sentimental but also inaccurate. Other writers strive for a more objective rendition of the facts. Still others fictionalize the event, presenting made-up

details. What stance does Baldwin strike immediately in his first paragraph?

Quickwrite

Choose any kind of disaster—a sinking ship, a raging tornado, a flood, an avalanche. Put yourself there. Write briefly about how you'd feel and what you'd do. Save your notes.

WHITE STAR LINE

ROYAL AND UNITED STATES
MAIL STEAMERS
LIVERPOOL·NEW YORK
LIVERPOOL·BOSTON
NEW YORK·MEDITERRANEAN
BOSTON·MEDITERRANEAN

The *Titanic's* captain, E. C. Smith.

go.hrw.com
LE0 10-6

Elements of Literature

Expect the Unexpected

Irony shows us what we all know —that we can't control everything that happens in our lives, much as we may want to or try.

The passengers on the *Titanic*, including the great ship's builders and its financial backers, believed that they were on an unsinkable ship. In that confidence or arrogance lies one of the great ironies of twentieth-century technology.

The Titans were ancient Greek gods depicted as possessing enormous size and incredible strength. For eons they reigned supreme in the universe, according to Greek mythology. Perhaps those who named the ship *Titanic* did not know that even the legendary Titans did not rule forever.

In **dramatic irony**, the reader knows something important that the characters don't know. In **situational irony**, what happens is the opposite of what is expected to happen or should have happened.

For more on Irony, see pages 194–195 and the Handbook of Literary Terms.

Out of the darkness she came, a vast, dim, white, monstrous shape . . .

Reading Skills and Strategies

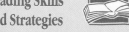

Using Text Organizers

If you have seen the film *Titanic*, you know that this great tragedy involved a complex series of actions occurring within a few hours. In writing this account of the disaster, Hanson Baldwin used the **headings I–V** as **text organizers** to divide that complicated rush of events. Each numbered part covers a different stage in the tragedy. Other, less obvious organizers are notations of the minutes ticking by in part II. These reminders build up suspense and help you keep stark track of the unfolding disaster.

The *Titanic*, underwater 375 miles southeast of Newfoundland, in summer 1991.

R.M.S. TITANIC **389**

The *Titanic*: Research Goes On
Titanic buffs may notice that Captain Smith's initials appear in the selection as E. C., when in fact they were E. J. Since Baldwin first wrote this landmark article in 1934, public fascination with the *Titanic* disaster has continued to grow, and more information seems to come out all the time. As a result, some of the details Baldwin reports may now be considered questionable or even incorrect. Students may want to analyze some of this new information and compare it to Baldwin's article by doing the Choices activity (Collecting Ideas for a Research Paper) on page 407, by scanning Internet sites, or by reading any new book on the topic.

Planning

- **Block Schedule**
  Block Scheduling Lesson Plans with Pacing Guide
- **Traditional Schedule**
  Lesson Plans Including Strategies for English-Language Learners
- **One-Stop Planner**
  CD-ROM with Test Generator

Preteaching Vocabulary

Words to Own

Have students, working in pairs, read the definitions of the Words to Own at the bottom of the selection pages. To familiarize students with the words, have volunteers write the two columns of words on the board, then ask students to match each word in the left column to its closest synonym in the right column.

1. superlative [c]
2. ascertain [d]
3. corroborated [e]
4. quelled [b]
5. poised [a]
6. perfunctory [f]
7. garbled [g]
8. recriminations [j]
9. pertinent [h]
10. vainly [i]

a. ready
b. subdued
c. excellent
d. determine
e. supported
f. unconcerned
g. confused
h. related
i. unsuccessfully
j. reproaches

Summary ■ ■

Baldwin's magazine article about the sinking of the *Titanic* begins as the ship sets sail for New York from Southampton, England, and ends with official investigations of the catastrophe. Intervening are the first unheeded iceberg alerts, the collision at about 11:40 P.M. Sunday (the fifth day), the captain's certainty of doom, passengers' disbelief, the confused lifeboat loading, the total sinking at 2:20 A.M. Monday, the first rescues near dawn, and the 711 survivors' arrival Thursday in New York—to a crowd of 30,000. Baldwin's thorough research results in strong, clear exposition, while his skillful narrative technique—highlighting dramatic and situational ironies—makes for compelling reading.

Resources

Viewing and Representing
Videocassette A, Segment 6
This segment focuses on the sinking of the *Titanic*. For lesson plans and worksheets, see the *Visual Connections Teacher's Manual.*

Listening
Audio CD Library
A recording of this article is included in the *Audio CD Library:*
• Disc 12, Track 2

Elements of Literature
Essays and History
For additional instruction on essays and history, see *Literary Elements:*
• Transparency 11
• Worksheet, p. 34

R.M.S. Titanic

Hanson W. Baldwin

390 THE NONFICTION COLLECTIONS

 Resources: Print and Media

Reading
• *Reading Skills and Strategies*
   MiniRead Skill Lesson, p. 146
   Selection Skill Lesson, p. 154
• *Graphic Organizers for Active Reading*, p. 24
• *Words to Own*, p. 24
• *Audio CD Library,*
   Disc 12, Track 2

Elements of Literature
• *Literary Elements*
   Transparency 11
   Worksheet, p. 34

Writing and Language
• *Daily Oral Grammar*
   Transparency 24
• *Grammar and Language Links*
   Worksheet, p. 45
• *Language Workshop CD-ROM*

Viewing and Representing
• *Visual Connections*
   Videocassette A, Segment 6

Assessment
• *Formal Assessment*, p. 66
• *Portfolio Management System*, p. 138
• *Standardized Test Preparation*, pp. 48, 50
• *Test Generator (One-Stop Planner CD-ROM)*

Internet
• go.hrw.com (keyword: LE0 10-6)

Background

In 1912 William Howard Taft was President; ragtime was a hot craze in music; the radio (called "the wireless") and telegraph were high-tech; steam still powered most engines; and the only way to get from Europe to America was by boat.

Ⓐ Reading Skills and Strategies

Using Text Organizers

Emphasize to students that Baldwin organizes his text not only by providing Roman-numeral headings and repeated references to times and dates but also by leaving extra space between certain paragraphs. Readers can use these markers to identify the stages of the tragedy.

Ⓑ Elements of Literature

Irony

? In light of what we know about the fate of the *Titanic,* how does this description create dramatic irony? [Sample answers: Words such as *fair, bright, fresh,* and *strong* belie the disaster to come; readers know that the *Titanic* will turn out not to be so "strong"; her birth may have been "slow," but readers know that her death will be fast.]

I

The White Star liner *Titanic,* largest ship the world had ever known, sailed from Southampton on her maiden voyage to New York on April 10, 1912. The paint on her strakes[1] was fair and bright; she was fresh from Harland and Wolff's Belfast yards, strong in the strength of her forty-six thousand tons of steel, bent, hammered, shaped, and riveted through the three years of her slow birth.

1. **strakes:** single lines of metal plating extending the whole length of a ship.

Reaching All Students

Struggling Readers

Using Text Organizers was introduced on p. 389. For a lesson directly tied to this selection that teaches students to use text organizers with a strategy called Logographic Cues, see the *Reading Skills and Strategies* binder:
• MiniRead Skill Lesson, p. 146
• Selection Skill Lesson, p. 154

English Language Learners

Before students begin reading, sketch a ship on the board and label parts: *bow, stern, hull, keel, deck, portholes, crow's nest, funnels, hold.* Also, label *fore, aft, port,* and *starboard.* Have students apply the terms to the illustration on pp. 390–391.

For strategies for engaging English language learners with the literature, see
• *Lesson Plans Including Strategies for English-Language Learners*

Advanced Learners

After students finish reading, invite them to describe scenes from the article that remain most vivid in their mind. Then, in a discussion, challenge students to identify and analyze literary elements in the article that make these scenes memorable for them. They might consider irony, foreshadowing, suspense, symbolism, diction, connotations, imagery, and figurative language.

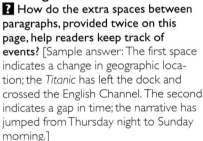
There was little fuss and fanfare at her sailing; her sister ship, the *Olympic*—slightly smaller than the *Titanic*—had been in service for some months and to her had gone the thunder of the cheers.

But the *Titanic* needed no whistling steamers or shouting crowds to call attention to her superlative qualities. Her bulk dwarfed the ships near her as longshoremen singled up her mooring lines and cast off the turns of heavy rope from the dock bollards.[2] She was not only the largest ship afloat, but was believed to be the safest. Carlisle, her builder, had given her double bottoms and had divided her hull into sixteen watertight compartments, which made her, men thought, unsinkable. She had been built to be and had been described as a gigantic lifeboat. Her designers' dreams of a triple-screw[3] giant, a luxurious, floating hotel, which could speed to New York at twenty-three knots, had been carefully translated from blueprints and mold loft lines at the Belfast yards into a living reality.

The *Titanic*'s sailing from Southampton, though quiet, was not wholly uneventful. As the liner moved slowly toward the end of her dock that April day, the surge of her passing sucked away from the quay[4] the steamer *New York*, moored just to seaward of the *Titanic*'s berth. There were sharp cracks as the manila mooring lines of the *New York* parted under the strain. The frayed ropes writhed and whistled through the air and snapped down among the waving crowd on the pier; the *New York* swung toward the *Titanic*'s bow, was checked and dragged back to the dock barely in time to avert a collision. Seamen muttered, thought it an ominous start.

Past Spithead and the Isle of Wight the *Titanic* steamed. She called at Cherbourg at dusk and then laid her course for Queenstown. At 1:30 P.M. on Thursday, April 11, she stood out of Queenstown harbor, screaming gulls soaring in

2. **bollards** (bäl′ərdz): strong posts on a pier or wharf for holding a ship's mooring ropes.
3. **triple-screw:** three-propellered.
4. **quay** (kē): dock.

her wake, with 2,201 persons—men, women, and children—aboard.

Occupying the Empire bedrooms and Georgian suites of the first-class accommodations were many well-known men and women— Colonel John Jacob Astor and his young bride; Major Archibald Butt, military aide to President Taft, and his friend Frank D. Millet, the painter; John B. Thayer, vice president of the Pennsylvania Railroad, and Charles M. Hays, president of the Grand Trunk Railway of Canada; W. T. Stead, the English journalist; Jacques Futrelle, French novelist; H. B. Harris, theatrical manager, and Mrs. Harris; Mr. and Mrs. Isidor Straus; and J. Bruce Ismay, chairman and managing director of the White Star Line.

Down in the plain wooden cabins of the steerage class were 706 immigrants to the land of promise, and trimly stowed in the great holds was a cargo valued at $420,000: oak beams, sponges, wine, calabashes,[5] and an odd miscellany of the common and the rare.

The *Titanic* took her departure on Fastnet Light[6] and, heading into the night, laid her course for New York. She was due at quarantine[7] the following Wednesday morning.

Sunday dawned fair and clear. The *Titanic* steamed smoothly toward the west, faint streamers of brownish smoke trailing from her funnels. The purser held services in the saloon in the morning; on the steerage deck aft[8] the immigrants were playing games and a Scotsman was puffing "The Campbells Are Coming" on his bagpipes in the midst of the uproar.

5. **calabashes** (kal′ə·bash′əz): large smoking pipes made from the necks of gourds.
6. **Fastnet Light:** lighthouse at the southwestern tip of Ireland. After the Fastnet Light, there is only open sea until the coast of North America.
7. **quarantine** (kwôr′ən·tēn): place where a ship is held in port after arrival to determine that its passengers and cargo are free of communicable diseases. *Quarantine* can also be used for the length of time a ship is held.
8. **aft:** in the rear of a ship.

WORDS TO OWN

superlative (sə·pur′lə·tiv) *adj.:* supreme; better than all others.

Message from the *Caronia*, warning of icebergs and tracts of floating ice.

Second Operator Harold Bride.

At 9:00 A.M. a message from the steamer *Caronia* sputtered into the wireless shack:

Captain, *Titanic*—Westbound steamers report bergs growlers and field ice 42 degrees N. from 49 degrees to 51 degrees W. 12th April.

Compliments—Barr.

It was cold in the afternoon; the sun was brilliant, but the *Titanic,* her screws turning over at seventy-five revolutions per minute, was approaching the Banks.[9]

In the Marconi cabin[10] Second Operator Harold Bride, earphones clamped on his head, was figuring accounts; he did not stop to answer when he heard *MWL*, Continental Morse for the nearby Leyland liner, *Californian,* calling the *Titanic*. The *Californian* had some message about three icebergs; he didn't bother then to take it down. About 1:42 P.M. the rasping spark of those days spoke again across the water. It was the *Baltic,* calling the *Titanic,* warning her of ice on the steamer track. Bride took the message down and sent it up to the

9. **Banks:** Grand Banks, shallow waters near the southeast coast of Newfoundland.
10. **Marconi cabin:** room where messages were received and sent by radio.

bridge.[11] The officer-of-the-deck glanced at it; sent it to the bearded master of the *Titanic,* Captain E. C. Smith, a veteran of the White Star service. It was lunchtime then; the captain, walking along the promenade deck, saw Mr. Ismay, stopped, and handed him the message without comment. Ismay read it, stuffed it in his pocket, told two ladies about the icebergs, and resumed his walk. Later, about 7:15 P.M., the captain requested the return of the message in order to post it in the chart room for the information of officers.

Dinner that night in the Jacobean dining room was gay. It was bitter on deck, but the night was calm and fine; the sky was moonless but studded with stars twinkling coldly in the clear air.

After dinner some of the second-class passengers gathered in the saloon, where the Reverend Mr. Carter conducted a "hymn singsong." It was almost ten o'clock and the stewards were waiting with biscuits and coffee as the group sang:

O, hear us when we cry to Thee
For those in peril on the sea.

On the bridge Second Officer Lightoller— short, stocky, efficient—was relieved at ten o'clock by First Officer Murdoch. Lightoller had talked with other officers about the proximity of ice; at least five wireless ice warnings had reached the ship; lookouts had been cautioned to be alert; captains and officers expected to reach the field at any time after 9:30 P.M. At twenty-two knots, its speed unslackened, the *Titanic* plowed on through the night.

Lightoller left the darkened bridge to his relief and turned in. Captain Smith went to his cabin. The steerage was long since quiet; in the first and second cabins lights were going out; voices were growing still; people were asleep. Murdoch paced back and forth on the bridge,

11. **bridge:** raised structure on a ship. The ship is controlled from the bridge.

R.M.S. TITANIC 393

E **Appreciating Language**
Combining Narration and Exposition
? Narrative techniques include the buildup of suspense. How does Baldwin build suspense in this paragraph? [Sample answer: He piles up instance upon instance in which iceberg warnings are ignored or treated lightly.]

F **Elements of Literature**
Irony
? How does the group's choice of song create dramatic irony? [Sample answer: The group members do not suspect that everyone there will soon be "in peril on the sea."]

G **Elements of Literature**
Irony
? How many causes for concern does Baldwin list in this paragraph? [four] What might one reasonably expect the captain and officers to do in response to these concerns? [Sample answer: alter course and/or reduce speed.] How is their actual response an example of situational irony? [Sample answer: They do the opposite of what one might expect, holding the course at full speed.]

H **English Language Learners**
Multiple Meanings
Tell students that *knot* can mean "nautical mile per hour," a measure of speed at sea. One knot is 1.15 statute miles per hour. Twenty-two knots is a little more than twenty-five miles per hour —far too fast to allow a forty-six-thousand-ton ship to stop or turn quickly.

Using Students' Strengths

Kinesthetic Learners
As students begin section III, explain that the water temperature at the site of the sinking of the *Titanic* was about 30°F. Use ice cubes and salt to reduce a partially filled container of water to 30°F. Then allow one or more volunteers to place their hands briefly in the container and to describe the initial shock of the water and the sensation of growing numbness. Follow up with a definition and discussion of hypothermia.

Interpersonal Learners
After students have read the article, ask them to imagine themselves overseeing the loading of the *Titanic's* lifeboats. Have students, in small groups, plan how they would get the job done efficiently and with a minimum of panic. Invite them to explain why the job was poorly done aboard the *Titanic* and to act out their versions of a properly executed lifeboat loading.

peering out over the dark water, glancing now and then at the compass in front of Quartermaster Hichens at the wheel.

In the crow's-nest, lookout Frederick Fleet and his partner, Leigh, gazed down at the water, still and unruffled in the dim, starlit darkness. Behind and below them the ship, a white shadow with here and there a last winking light; ahead of them a dark and silent and cold ocean.

Ⓐ There was a sudden clang. "Dong-dong. Dong-dong. Dong-dong. Dong!" The metal clapper of the great ship's bell struck out 11:30. Mindful of the warnings, Fleet strained his eyes, searching the darkness for the dreaded ice. But there were only the stars and the sea.

In the wireless room, where Phillips, first operator, had relieved Bride, the buzz of the *Californian*'s set again crackled into the earphones:

Californian: "Say, old man, we are stuck here, surrounded by ice."

Titanic: "Shut up, shut up; keep out. I am talking to Cape Race; you are jamming my signals."

Then, a few minutes later—about 11:40 . . .

Lookout Frederick Fleet.

First Operator Jack Phillips.

Ⓑ II

Ⓒ Out of the dark she came, a vast, dim, white, monstrous shape, directly in the *Titanic*'s path. For a moment Fleet doubted his eyes. But she was a deadly reality, this ghastly *thing*. Frantically, Fleet struck three bells—*something dead ahead*. He snatched the telephone and called the bridge:

"Iceberg! Right ahead!"

The first officer heard but did not stop to acknowledge the message.

Ⓓ "Hard-a-starboard!"

Hichens strained at the wheel; the bow swung slowly to port. The monster was almost upon them now.

Murdoch leaped to the engine-room telegraph. Bells clanged. Far below in the engine room those bells struck the first warning. Danger! The indicators on the dial faces swung round to "Stop!" Then "Full speed astern!" Frantically the engineers turned great valve wheels; answered the bridge bells . . .

Ⓔ There was a slight shock, a brief scraping, a small list to port. Shell ice—slabs and chunks of it—fell on the foredeck. Slowly the *Titanic* stopped.

Captain Smith hurried out of his cabin.

"What has the ship struck?"

Murdoch answered, "An iceberg, sir. I hard-a-starboarded and reversed the engines, and I was

394 THE NONFICTION COLLECTIONS

Getting Students Involved

Cooperative Learning

Living Pictures. After students have read the article, put them in small groups to create tableaus of the *Titanic* disaster. One student in each group will introduce the scene and will then tap each person in the tableau, one by one, allowing the character to come to life and share his or her experiences with the class.

• Have groups brainstorm to choose scenes and to plan their tableaus.

• Tell each group to choose one member who will serve as director/introducer. The others will play characters.

• If two students want to play the same character, have one student play the character's "public self" while a second student stands behind him or her and presents the character's personal thoughts.

• Encourage students to consult the article for specifics and insights into characters.

going to hard-a-port around it, but she was too close. I could not do any more. I have closed the watertight doors."

Fourth Officer Boxhall, other officers, the carpenter, came to the bridge. The captain sent Boxhall and the carpenter below to <u>ascertain</u> the damage.

A few lights switched on in the first and second cabins; sleepy passengers peered through porthole glass; some casually asked the stewards:

"Why have we stopped?"

"I don't know, sir, but I don't suppose it is anything much."

In the smoking room a quorum[12] of gamblers and their prey were still sitting round a poker table; the usual crowd of kibitzers[13] looked on. They had felt the slight jar of the collision and had seen an eighty-foot ice mountain glide by the smoking-room windows, but the night was calm and clear, the *Titanic* was "unsinkable"; they hadn't bothered to go on deck.

But far below, in the warren of passages on the starboard side forward, in the forward holds and boiler rooms, men could see that the *Titanic*'s hurt was mortal. In No. 6 boiler room, where the red glow from the furnaces lighted up the naked, sweaty chests of coal-blackened firemen, water was pouring through a great gash about two feet above the floor plates. This was no slow leak; the ship was open to the sea; in ten minutes there were eight feet of water in No. 6. Long before then the stokers had raked the flaming fires out of the furnaces and had scrambled through the watertight doors in No. 5 or had climbed up the long steel ladders to safety. When Boxhall looked at the mailroom in No. 3 hold, twenty-four feet above the keel, the mailbags were already floating about in the slushing water. In No. 5 boiler room a stream of water spurted into an empty bunker. All six compartments forward of No. 4 were open to the sea; in ten seconds the iceberg's jagged claw had ripped a three-hundred-foot slash in the bottom of the great *Titanic*.

---

12. **quorum** (kwôr′əm): the number of people required for a particular activity—in this case, for a game.
13. **kibitzers** (kib′its·ərz): talkative onlookers who often give unwanted advice.

Reports came to the bridge; Ismay in dressing gown ran out on deck in the cold, still, starlit night, climbed up the bridge ladder.

"What has happened?"

Captain Smith: "We have struck ice."

"Do you think she is seriously damaged?"

Captain Smith: "I'm afraid she is."

Ismay went below and passed Chief Engineer William Bell, fresh from an inspection of the damaged compartments. Bell <u>corroborated</u> the captain's statement; hurried back down the glistening steel ladders to his duty. Man after man followed him—Thomas Andrews, one of the ship's designers, Archie Frost, the builder's chief engineer, and his twenty assistants—men who had no posts of duty in the engine room but whose traditions called them there.

On deck, in corridor and stateroom, life flowed again. Men, women, and children awoke and questioned; orders were given to uncover the lifeboats; water rose into the firemen's quarters; half-dressed stokers streamed up on deck. But the passengers—most of them—did not know that the *Titanic* was sinking. The shock of the collision had been so slight that some were not awakened by it; the *Titanic* was so huge that she must be unsinkable; the night was too calm, too beautiful, to think of death at sea.

Captain Smith half ran to the door of the radio shack. Bride, partly dressed, eyes dulled with sleep, was standing behind Phillips, waiting.

"Send the call for assistance."

The blue spark danced: "CQD—CQD—CQD—CQ——"[14]

Miles away Marconi men heard. Cape Race heard it, and the steamships *La Provence* and *Mt. Temple*.

---

14. **CQD**: call by radio operators, inviting others to communicate with them.

WORDS TO OWN

ascertain (as′ər tān′) v.: find out with certainty; determine.

corroborated (kə·räb′ə·rāt′id) v.: supported; upheld the truth of.

F **Critical Thinking**
Analyzing
? Crew members and passengers respond with complacency. What role do you think complacency has played so far in the disaster? [Possible responses: If the captain, officers, and radio operators hadn't been so complacent about iceberg warnings, the collision might not have happened; complacency led to carelessness, which caused the collision.]

G **Appreciating Language**
Combining Narration and Exposition
? With matter-of-fact exposition, Baldwin takes us step by step along the starboard side, describing the damage. With what powerful narrative technique does he end the paragraph? [Sample answer: He uses figurative language; he creates an implied metaphor comparing the iceberg to a monster whose "jagged claw" has slashed the ship.]

H **Elements of Literature**
Repetition
As references to the blue spark of the radio call recur, the spark will come to suggest something larger—hope for rescue. Suggest that students stay alert for references to the spark and notice how they relate to the probability of rescue.

I **Historical Connections**
The Radiotelegraph
Italian engineer Guglielmo Marconi (1874–1937) invented the radiotelegraph, or wireless telegraphy, in 1895; he won the 1909 Nobel Prize in physics for his work. The technology was still in its infancy in 1912.

Getting Students Involved

Round Robin

What If . . .? After students finish reading the article, put them into groups of five to seven each to complete this sentence about the *Titanic* disaster: "More lives could have been saved if _____." Give the groups five minutes to pass around a sheet of paper, with each student adding his or her own ideas. Direct students to consider each stage of the disaster in their responses.

Then, have groups share their responses with the class. Ask students to note the following:
• which ideas appear most frequently
• which ideas show the most insightful or creative thinking

Speculating

? Lifeboat drills were standard procedure; why do you suppose none were held on the *Titanic*? [Possible responses: Maybe no one thought they were needed, since the ship was supposed to be unsinkable; maybe they had been postponed amid the fanfare of the maiden voyage.]

B Reading Skills and Strategies

Using Text Organizers

? Here Baldwin shifts from past tense to present, heightening the feeling of immediacy. Time notations now open many paragraphs. How do these notations clarify the narrative for readers? [Sample answers: They show the order of events; they show how quickly or slowly things happpen.]

C Elements of Literature

Irony

? How is this true-life event an example of situational irony? [Possible responses: One would expect the radio operator to stay on duty all night; one would expect the *Californian*, the nearest ship, to be of most help.]

D Elements of Literature

Irony

? What ironic details do you find in these paragraphs? [Possible responses: The women who want to avoid a "boat ride on an ice-strewn sea" don't know that drowning in an ice-strewn sea is the alternative; the breakfast that the men mention is far from the reality of what will come; the band plays breezy ragtime as if at a party, not a disaster.]

E Elements of Literature

Mood

Baldwin reinforces mood with repeated references to the band and to the type of music it is playing.

The sea was surging into the *Titanic*'s hold. At 12:20 the water burst into the seamen's quarters through a collapsed fore-and-aft wooden bulkhead. Pumps strained in the engine rooms—men and machinery making a futile fight against the sea. Steadily the water rose.

A The boats were swung out—slowly, for the deckhands were late in reaching their stations; there had been no boat drill, and many of the crew did not know to what boats they were assigned. Orders were shouted; the safety valves had lifted, and steam was blowing off in a great rushing roar. In the chart house Fourth Officer Boxhall bent above a chart, working rapidly with pencil and dividers.

B 12:25 A.M. Boxhall's position is sent out to a fleet of vessels: "Come at once; we have struck a berg."

To the Cunarder *Carpathia* (Arthur Henry Rostron, Master, New York to Liverpool, fifty-eight miles away): "It's a CQD, old man. Position 41–46N.; 50–14 W."

The blue spark dancing: "Sinking; cannot hear for noise of steam."

12:30 A.M. The word is passed: "Women and children in the boats." Stewards finish waking their passengers below; life preservers are tied on; some men smile at the precaution. "The *Titanic* is unsinkable." The *Mt. Temple* starts for the *Titanic*; the *Carpathia*, with a double watch in her stokeholds, radios, "Coming hard." **C** The CQD changes the course of many ships—but not of one; the operator of the *Californian*, nearby, has just put down his earphones and turned in.

The CQD flashes over land and sea from Cape Race to New York; newspaper city rooms leap to life and presses whir.

On the *Titanic,* water creeps over the bulkhead between Nos. 5 and 6 firerooms. She is going down by the head; the engineers—fighting a losing battle—are forced back foot by foot by the rising water. Down the promenade deck, Happy Jock Hume, the bandsman, runs with his instrument.

12:45 A.M. Murdoch, in charge on the starboard side, eyes tragic, but calm and cool, orders boat No. 7 lowered. The women hang

---

back; they want no boat ride on an ice-strewn sea; the *Titanic* is unsinkable. The men encourage them, explain that this is just a precautionary measure: "We'll see you again at breakfast." There is little confusion; passengers stream **D** slowly to the boat deck. In the steerage the immigrants chatter excitedly.

A sudden sharp hiss—a streaked flare against the night; Boxhall sends a rocket toward the sky. It explodes, and a parachute of white stars lights up the icy sea. "God! Rockets!" The band plays ragtime.

No. 8 is lowered, and No. 5. Ismay, still in dressing gown, calls for women and children, handles lines, stumbles in the way of an officer, is told to "get the hell out of here." Third Officer Pitman takes charge of No. 5; as he swings into the boat, Murdoch grasps his hand. "Goodbye and good luck, old man."

No. 6 goes over the side. There are only twenty-eight people in a lifeboat with a capacity of sixty-five.

A light stabs from the bridge; Boxhall is calling in Morse flashes, again and again, to a strange ship stopped in the ice jam five to ten miles away. Another rocket drops its shower of sparks above the ice-strewn sea and the dying ship.

1:00 A.M. Slowly the water creeps higher; the fore ports of the *Titanic* are dipping into the sea. Rope squeaks through blocks; lifeboats **E** drop jerkily seaward. Through the shouting on the decks comes the sound of the band playing ragtime.

The "Millionaires' Special" leaves the ship—boat No. 1, with a capacity of forty people, carries only Sir Cosmo and Lady Duff Gordon and ten others. Aft, the frightened immigrants mill and jostle and rush for a boat. An officer's fist flies out; three shots are fired in the air, and the panic is <u>quelled</u>. . . . Four Chinese sneak unseen into a boat and hide in the bottom.

1:20 A.M. Water is coming into No. 4 boiler room. Stokers slice and shovel as water laps

---

WORDS TO OWN
quelled (kweld) *v.*: quieted; subdued.

Crossing the Curriculum

Science

Invite interested students to prepare and present oral reports about icebergs. Among the questions they might consider in relation to "R.M.S. Titanic" are the following:

* How do icebergs form?
* How far south might the *Titanic* have had to sail to avoid icebergs in mid-April?
* How do ships deal with the threat of icebergs today?

Mathematics

Have students use a map to trace the course of the *Titanic* from Southampton (England) to Cherbourg (France), to Queenstown (County Cork, Ireland), and across the north Atlantic toward the Grand Banks. Tell them to find 41°46' N, 50°14' W, where she sank. Then, have them use the map's scale to calculate how far she had come and how far she still had to go before reaching New York.

Molly Brown (nicknamed "unsinkable" by the Associated Press) helped row a lifeboat and nurse survivors.

Colonel John Jacob Astor, wealthy hotel owner, went down with the *Titanic*.

about their ankles—steam for the dynamos, steam for the dancing spark! As the water rises, great ash hoes rake the flaming coals from the furnaces. Safety valves pop; the stokers retreat aft, and the watertight doors clang shut behind them.

The rockets fling their splendor toward the stars. The boats are more heavily loaded now, for the passengers know the *Titanic* is sinking. Women cling and sob. The great screws aft are rising clear of the sea. Half-filled boats are ordered to come alongside the cargo ports and take on more passengers, but the ports are never opened—and the boats are never filled. Others pull for the steamer's light miles away but never reach it; the lights disappear; the unknown ship steams off.

The water rises and the band plays ragtime.

1:30 A.M. Lightoller is getting the port boats off; Murdoch, the starboard. As one boat is lowered into the sea, a boat officer fires his gun along the ship's side to stop a rush from the lower decks. A woman tries to take her Great Dane into a boat with her; she is refused and steps out of the boat to die with her dog. Millet's "little smile which played on his lips all through the voyage" plays no more; his lips are grim, but he waves goodbye and brings wraps for the women.

Benjamin Guggenheim, in evening clothes, smiles and says, "We've dressed up in our best and are prepared to go down like gentlemen."

1:40 A.M. Boat 14 is clear, and then 13, 16, 15, and C. The lights still shine, but the *Baltic* hears the blue spark say, "Engine room getting flooded."

The *Olympia* signals, "Am lighting up all possible boilers as fast as can."

Major Butt helps women into the last boats and waves goodbye to them. Mrs. Straus puts her foot on the gunwale of a lifeboat; then she draws back and goes to her husband: "We have been together many years; where you go, I will go." Colonel John Jacob Astor puts his young wife in a lifeboat, steps back, taps cigarette on fingernail: "Goodbye, dearie; I'll join you later."

1:45 A.M. The foredeck is under water; the fo'c'sle[15] head almost awash; the great stern is lifted high toward the bright stars; and still the band plays. Mr. and Mrs. Harris approach a lifeboat arm in arm.

Officer: "Ladies first, please."

Harris bows, smiles, steps back: "Of course, certainly; ladies first."

Boxhall fires the last rocket, then leaves in charge of boat No. 2.

2:00 A.M. She is dying now; her bow goes deeper, her stern higher. But there must be steam. Below in the stokeholds the sweaty firemen keep steam up for the flaring lights and the dancing spark. The glowing coals slide and tumble over the slanted grate bars; the sea pounds behind that yielding bulkhead. But the spark dances on.

15. **fo'c'sle** (fōk′s'l): forecastle, front upper deck of a ship.

F **Reading Skills and Strategies**
Drawing Conclusions
? What would happen to the ship's radiotelegraph if the steam boilers stopped functioning? [Sample answer: Apparently, the radio runs on electricity from steam-driven dynamos; if the boilers stopped producing steam, the radio wouldn't work, and calls for help couldn't be sent.]

G **Appreciating Language**
Combining Narration and Exposition
? What techniques does Baldwin use to bring characters to life for readers? [Possible responses: He describes their looks (Millet's smile and Guggenheim's formal attire); he describes their actions; he includes poignant personal details (the woman and her Great Dane); he includes dialogue.]

H **Critical Thinking**
Extending the Text
? From information in this paragraph and in those above it, what generalizations might you make about human nature? [Possible responses: People can be courageous and altruistic in the face of disaster—as Mrs. Straus and Col. Astor demonstrate; people can become brutal and devoid of compassion in the face of disaster, as shown by the use of force to prevent steerage passengers from reaching the lifeboats.]

I **Elements of Literature**
Mood
? Again Baldwin uses the powerful narrative technique of figurative language to "put readers there." What mood does this personification of the *Titanic* evoke? [Sample answers: sorrow; awe; horror.]

Crossing the Curriculum

Social Studies

To deepen students' understanding of the historical setting of the *Titanic* disaster, put students into small groups, and have each group research one area of interest for 1912. They might examine world events, national events, standards of living, technology, entertainment, literature and other arts, sports, fashion, medicine, and so on. After groups have finished their research, direct each group to share its discussion of its research with the class. Have each group choose a moderator who will introduce and conclude the discussion and who will be sure each group member contributes significant facts. Encourage listeners to ask questions. After all groups have finished, challenge the class to form generalizations about differences between living in 1912 and today.

398 THE NONFICTION COLLECTIONS

Taking a Second Look

Review: Analyzing Cause and Effect

Remind students that many events have multiple causes and create multiple effects. Causes may be longer-term or immediate. In a complex event, such as the *Titanic* disaster, an incident can set off a cause-and-effect chain: A cause leads to an effect, which in turn becomes the cause of a new effect. For example, the gash in the hull causes water to pour in; the water floods boiler rooms and causes the ship's steam system to malfunction; the malfunctioning system causes a deafening roar of escaping steam.

Activities

1. Have students reread pp. 391–394 and list two longer-term causes and two immediate causes of the collision.
2. Have students reread sections II and III and trace a cause-and-effect chain set in motion by any one incident.

The *Asian* hears Phillips try the new signal—SOS.

Boat No. 4 has left now; boat D leaves ten minutes later. Jacques Futrelle clasps his wife: "For God's sake, go! It's your last chance; go!" Madame Futrelle is half forced into the boat. It clears the side.

There are about 660 people in the boats and 1,500 still on the sinking *Titanic*.

On top of the officers' quarters, men work frantically to get the two collapsibles stowed there over the side. Water is over the forward part of A deck now; it surges up the companion-ways toward the boat deck. In the radio shack, Bride has slipped a coat and life jacket about Phillips as the first operator sits hunched over his key, sending—still sending—"41-46 N.; 50-14 W. CQD—CQD—SOS—SOS——" **A**

The captain's tired white face appears at the radio-room door. "Men, you have done your full duty. You can do no more. Now, it's every man for himself." The captain disappears—back to his sinking bridge, where Painter, his personal steward, stands quietly waiting for orders. The spark dances on. Bride turns his back and goes into the inner cabin. As he does so, a stoker, grimed with coal, mad with fear, steals into the shack and reaches for the life jacket on Phillips's back. Bride wheels about and brains him with a wrench. **B**

2:10 A.M. Below decks the steam is still holding, though the pressure is falling—rapidly. In the gymnasium on the boat deck, the athletic instructor watches quietly as two gentlemen ride the bicycles and another swings casually at the punching bag. Mail clerks stagger up the boat-deck stairways, dragging soaked mail sacks. The spark still dances. The band still plays—but not ragtime: **C**

Nearer my God to Thee.
Nearer to Thee . . . **D**

A Elements of Literature
Repetition
Notice that the repeated image of Phillips calling for help adds an element of suspense—as if, in the liner's last moments, some help still might appear.

B Appreciating Language
Levels of Language
❓ Why do you suppose Baldwin abandons formal English here and uses the slang term "brains him"? [Possible responses: It shows that people are operating on an almost instinctual level; it's jarring, like the jarring actions that Baldwin describes.]

C Critical Thinking
Interpreting
❓ Though passengers and crew members now realize the ship is sinking, which details in this paragraph show that at least some people still expect to be rescued? [Possible responses: Some people are exercising in the gym; the mail clerks are trying to save the mail.]

D Elements of Literature
Mood
❓ What mood is suggested by the change in the band's choice of music? [Possible responses: fear; pleading; a need for comfort.]

Skill Link

Reading: Denotation and Connotation
This activity will give students background for the Language Link activity on p. 408. Tell students that skilled writers of narrative use connotations—the emotions and associations that a word suggests—to make character descriptions and action sequences compelling.

Activity
Ask students to take turns reading aloud narrative paragraphs on p. 397, from the "1:30 A.M." paragraph through the "2:00 A.M." paragraph. As each paragraph is read, have listeners jot down the words whose emotional impact seems strongest to them. After the reading, have students share the words they have listed, discussing their connotations and their effects on the narrative.

A few men take up the refrain; others kneel on the slanting decks to pray. Many run and scramble aft, where hundreds are clinging above the silent screws on the great uptilted stern. The spark still dances and the lights still flare; the engineers are on the job. The hymn comes to its close. Bandmaster Hartley, Yorkshireman violinist, taps his bow against a bulkhead, calls for "Autumn" as the water curls about his feet, and the eight musicians brace themselves against the ship's slant. People are leaping from the decks into the nearby water—the icy water. A woman cries, "Oh, save me, save me!" A man answers, "Good lady, save yourself. Only God can save you now." The band plays "Autumn":

> God of Mercy and Compassion!
> Look with pity on my pain . . .

The water creeps over the bridge where the *Titanic*'s master stands; heavily he steps out to meet it.

2:17 A.M. "CQ——" The *Virginian* hears a ragged, blurred CQ, then an abrupt stop. The blue spark dances no more. The lights flicker out; the engineers have lost their battle.

2:18 A.M. Men run about blackened decks; leap into the night; are swept into the sea by the curling wave that licks up the *Titanic*'s length. Lightoller does not leave the ship; the ship leaves him; there are hundreds like him, but only a few who live to tell of it. The funnels still swim above the water, but the ship is climbing to the perpendicular; the bridge is under and most of the foremast; the great stern rises like a squat leviathan.[16] Men swim away from the sinking ship; others drop from the stern.

The band plays in the darkness, the water lapping upward:

> Hold me up in mighty waters,
> Keep my eyes on things above,
> Righteousness, divine atonement,
> Peace and everlas . . .

16. **leviathan** (lə·vī′ə·thən): Biblical sea monster, perhaps a whale.

The forward funnel snaps and crashes into the sea; its steel tons hammer out of existence swimmers struggling in the freezing water. Streams of sparks, of smoke and steam, burst from the after funnels. The ship upends to 50—to 60 degrees.

Down in the black abyss of the stokeholds, of the engine rooms, where the dynamos have whirred at long last to a stop, the stokers and the engineers are reeling against the hot metal, the rising water clutching at their knees. The boilers, the engine cylinders, rip from their bed plates; crash through bulkheads; rumble—steel against steel.

The *Titanic* stands on end, <u>poised</u> briefly for the plunge. Slowly she slides to her grave—slowly at first, and then more quickly—quickly—quickly.

2:20 A.M. The greatest ship in the world has sunk. From the calm, dark waters, where the floating lifeboats move, there goes up, in the white wake of her passing, "one long continuous moan."

III

The boats that the *Titanic* had launched pulled safely away from the slight suction of the sinking ship, pulled away from the screams that came from the lips of the freezing men and women in the water. The boats were poorly manned and badly equipped, and they had been unevenly loaded. Some carried so few seamen that women bent to the oars. Mrs. Astor tugged at an oar handle; the Countess of Rothes took a tiller. Shivering stokers in sweaty, coal-blackened singlets and light trousers steered in some boats; stewards in white coats rowed in others. Ismay was in the last boat that left the ship from the starboard side; with Mr. Carter of Philadelphia and two seamen he tugged at the oars. In one of the lifeboats an Italian with a bro-

---

WORDS TO OWN

poised (poizd) v. used as *adj.*: balanced; in position.

Getting Students Involved

ken wrist—disguised in a woman's shawl and hat—huddled on the floorboards, ashamed now that fear had left him. In another rode the only baggage saved from the *Titanic*—the carryall of Samuel L. Goldenberg, one of the rescued passengers.

There were only a few boats that were heavily loaded; most of those that were half empty made but <u>perfunctory</u> efforts to pick up the moaning swimmers, their officers and crew fearing they would endanger the living if they pulled back into the midst of the dying. Some boats beat off the freezing victims; fear-crazed men and women struck with oars at the heads of swimmers. One woman drove her fist into the face of a half-dead man as he tried feebly to climb over the gunwale. Two other women helped him in and staunched the flow of blood from the ring cuts on his face.

One of the collapsible boats, which had floated off the top of the officers' quarters when the *Titanic* sank, was an icy haven for thirty or forty men. The boat had capsized as the ship sank; men swam to it, clung to it, climbed upon its slippery bottom, stood knee-deep in water in the freezing air. Chunks of ice swirled about their legs; their soaked clothing clutched their bodies in icy folds. Colonel Archibald Gracie was cast up there, Gracie who had leaped from the stern as the *Titanic* sank; young Thayer who had seen his father die; Lightoller who had twice been sucked down with the ship and twice blown to the surface by a belch of air; Bride, the second operator, and Phillips, the first. There were many stokers, half naked; it was a shivering company. They stood there in the icy sea, under the far stars, and sang and prayed—the Lord's Prayer. After a while a lifeboat came and picked them off, but Phillips was dead then or died soon afterward in the boat.

Only a few of the boats had lights; only one—No. 2—had a light that was of any use to the *Carpathia*, twisting through the ice field to the rescue. Other ships were "coming hard" too; one, the *Californian,* was still dead to opportunity.

The blue sparks still danced, but not the *Ti-*

---

tanic's. *La Provence* to *Celtic:* "Nobody has heard the *Titanic* for about two hours."

It was 2:40 when the *Carpathia* first sighted the green light from No. 2 boat; it was 4:10 when she picked up the first boat and learned that the *Titanic* had foundered.[17] The last of the moaning cries had just died away then.

Captain Rostron took the survivors aboard, boatload by boatload. He was ready for them, but only a small minority of them required much medical attention. Bride's feet were twisted and frozen; others were suffering from exposure; one died, and seven were dead when taken from the boats, and were buried at sea.

It was then that the fleet of racing ships learned they were too late; the *Parisian* heard the weak signals of *MPA*, the *Carpathia*, report the death of the *Titanic*. It was then—or soon afterward, when her radio operator put on his earphones—that the *Californian,* the ship that had been within sight as the *Titanic* was sinking, first learned of the disaster.

And it was then, in all its white-green majesty, that the *Titanic*'s survivors saw the iceberg, tinted with the sunrise, floating idly, pack ice jammed about its base, other bergs heaving slowly nearby on the blue breast of the sea.

IV

 But it was not until later that the world knew, for wireless then was not what wireless is today, and <u>garbled</u> messages had nourished a hope that all of the *Titanic*'s company were safe. Not until Monday evening, when P.A.S. Franklin, vice president of the International Mercantile Marine Company, received relayed messages in New York that left little hope, did the full extent of

17. **foundered:** filled with water, so that it sank; generally, collapsed or failed.

- -

WORDS TO OWN
perfunctory (pər·fuŋk′tə·rē) *adj.:* not exerting much effort; unconcerned.
garbled *v.* used as *adj.:* confused; mixed up.

- -

R.M.S. TITANIC 401

Assessing Learning

the disaster begin to be known. Partial and garbled lists of the survivors; rumors of heroism and cowardice; stories spun out of newspaper imagination, based on a few bare facts and many false reports, misled the world, terrified and frightened it. It was not until Thursday night, when the *Carpathia* steamed into the North River, that the full truth was pieced together.

Flashlights flared on the black river when the *Carpathia* stood up to her dock. Tugs nosed about her, shunted her toward Pier 54. Thirty thousand people jammed the streets; ambulances and stretchers stood on the pier; coroners and physicians waited.

In midstream the Cunarder dropped over the *Titanic*'s lifeboats; then she headed toward the dock. Beneath the customs letters on the pier stood relatives of the 711 survivors, relatives of the missing—hoping against hope. The *Carpathia* cast her lines ashore; stevedores[18] looped them over bollards. The dense throngs stood quiet as the first survivor stepped down the gangway. The woman half staggered—led by customs guards—beneath her letter. A "low wailing" moan came from the crowd; fell, grew in volume, and dropped again.

Thus ended the maiden voyage of the *Titanic.* The lifeboats brought to New York by the *Carpathia,* a few deck chairs and gratings awash in the ice field off the Grand Bank eight hundred miles from shore, were all that was left of the world's greatest ship.

V

The aftermath of weeping and regret, of recriminations and investigations, dragged on for weeks. Charges and countercharges were hurled about; the White Star Line was bitterly criticized; Ismay was denounced on the floor of the Senate as a coward but was defended by those who had been with him on the sinking *Titanic* and by the Board of Trade investigation in England.

18. **stevedores** (stē′və·dôrz′): persons who load and unload ships.

It was not until weeks later, when the hastily convened Senate investigation in the United States and the Board of Trade report in England had been completed, that the whole story was told. The Senate investigating committee, under the chairmanship of Senator Smith, who was attacked in both the American and the British press as a "backwoods politician," brought out numerous pertinent facts, though its proceedings verged at times on the farcical.[19] Senator Smith was ridiculed for his lack of knowledge of the sea when he asked witnesses, "Of what is an iceberg composed?" and "Did any of the passengers take refuge in the watertight compartments?" The senator seemed particularly interested in the marital status of Fleet, the lookout, who was saved. Fleet, puzzled, growled aside, "Wot questions they're arskin' me!"

The report of Lord Mersey, wreck commissioner in the British Board of Trade's investigation, was tersely damning.

The *Titanic* had carried boats enough for 1,178 persons, only one third of her capacity. Her sixteen boats and four collapsibles had saved but 711 persons; 400 people had needlessly lost their lives. The boats had been but partly loaded; officers in charge of launching them had been afraid the falls[20] would break or the boats buckle under their rated loads; boat crews had been slow in reaching their stations; launching arrangements were confused because no boat drill had been held; passengers were loaded into the boats haphazardly because no boat assignments had been made.

But that was not all. Lord Mersey found that sufficient warnings of ice on the steamer track had reached the *Titanic,* that her speed of twenty-two knots was "excessive under the

19. **farcical** (fär′si·kəl): absurd; ridiculous; like a farce (an exaggerated comedy).
20. **falls:** chains used for hoisting.

WORDS TO OWN

recriminations (ri·krim′ə·nā′shənz) *n.*: accusations against an accuser; countercharges.
pertinent (pur′tə·nənt) *adj.*: having some connection with the subject.

Making the Connections

Connecting to the Theme: "Being There!"

The theme works on multiple levels in Baldwin's article. As a journalist writing after the fact, Baldwin had to "be there" through research, which included obtaining information from participants who literally had been there. He also had to write in a way that lets readers feel that they "are there." He accomplishes this by using the techniques of narrative: characterization, figurative language, sensory imagery, irony, and selective repetition to reinforce mood and build suspense. Beyond the inherent dramatic irony of reporting a disaster that is well known, Baldwin highlights situational ironies, such as passengers exercising in the gym as the ship sinks. As a technical note, point out to students that this is an article, not a research paper, so Baldwin does not footnote facts or quotations.

circumstances," that "in view of the high speed at which the vessel was running it is not considered that the lookout was sufficient," and that her master made "a very grievous mistake"— but should not be blamed for negligence. Captain Rostron of the *Carpathia* was highly praised. "He did the very best that could be done." The *Californian* was damned. The testimony of her master, officers, and crew showed that she was not, at the most, more than nineteen miles away from the sinking *Titanic* and probably no more than five to ten miles distant. She had seen the *Titanic*'s lights; she had seen the rockets; she had not received the CQD calls because her radio operator was asleep. She had

attempted to get in communication with the ship she had sighted by flashing a light, but vainly.

"The night was clear," reported Lord Mersey, "and the sea was smooth. When she first saw the rockets, the *Californian* could have pushed through the ice to the open water without any serious risk and so have come to the assistance of the *Titanic*. Had she done so she might have saved many if not all of the lives that were lost.

"She made no attempt."

WORDS TO OWN
vainly *adv.:* without success; fruitlessly.

MEET THE WRITER
Journalist and Seaman
Hanson Weightman Baldwin
(1903–1991) was one of America's great journalists. He graduated with an ensign's commission from the U.S. Naval Academy at Annapolis. After only three years of service aboard battleships, Baldwin resigned from the Navy and launched a career as a military correspondent and editor. His longest hitch was with *The New York Times*.

During World War II Baldwin covered battles in North Africa and the D-day invasion of Normandy. His series of articles on the war in the South Pacific won him a Pulitzer Prize in 1943. After the war, he reported on the second atomic bomb test at Bikini Island, on guided-missile and rocket-firing installations, and on the organization of U.S. military forces in the nuclear age.

Relatively early in his writing career (1934), Baldwin wrote an article for *Harper's* magazine about the sinking of the *Titanic*, which had occurred twenty-two years earlier. His research was thorough: He pieced together information from ship logs, from interviews with survivors, and from written reports detailing the ship's design and launching. The subject of the *Titanic* was by no means new for Baldwin's readers. The sinking of the "unsinkable" ship had been fictionalized, sensationalized, and sentimentalized many times before 1934. Nevertheless, Baldwin's article became a textbook example of excellent reporting. His fast-paced account, with its mixture of factual details and irony, makes the disaster and all the human foibles associated with it seem tragically real again.

R.M.S. TITANIC 403

F Critical Thinking
Evaluating
? Do you consider Lord Mersey's condemnation of the *Californian* objective (based on fact) or subjective (based on emotion)? [Possible responses: objective, because Mersey cites numerous facts; subjective, because the facts are mixed with speculation.]

BROWSING IN THE FILES
About the Author. With the 1938 publication of *Admiral Death*, in which Baldwin examined twelve dramatic maritime disasters, he heard from many readers. He later published a letter from Karl Baarslag, a radio operator and fellow student of the *Titanic*. Baarslag wrote: "Evans [of the *Californian*], in my opinion the world's most unfortunate radio operator in that he might have saved 2,200 lives had he stayed up fifteen minutes longer, had been up and continuously on duty from 7 a.m. until 11:20 p.m., long past the usual time for him to go off watch. His ship was stopped by ice for the night, the crew, except a few on watch, were turned in, and there was no reason for him to continue on any longer. Even a $20 a month radioman is entitled to some sleep."

Resources ——————

Selection Assessment
Formal Assessment
• Selection Test, p. 66
Test Generator (One-Stop Planner)
• CD-ROM

Assessing Learning

Standardized Test Preparation
For practice with standardized test format specific to this selection, see
• *Standardized Test Preparation,* pp. 48, 50

Connections

This feature provides two eyewitness accounts of the sinking, one by a fireman who jumped into the water and survived and the second by a woman in a lifeboat.

Ⓐ Struggling Readers

Using Context Clues

❓ From clues in this paragraph, and from your reading of "R.M.S. Titanic," what do you think *fireman* means in this context? [Sample answer: someone who works with the ship's engines or furnaces.]

Ⓑ Critical Thinking

Making Connections

❓ Senior's "first lifeboat" was probably boat No. 1, the "Millionaires' Special" (p. 396). Baldwin states that the boat carried only twelve people, not thirteen, and that Ismay left the *Titanic* later, in another lifeboat. How might you explain these discrepancies? [Possible responses: Maybe Senior miscounted in the confusion; maybe Senior was biased against Ismay and assumed he would be in the "Millionaires' Special."]

The lifeboats of the "unsinkable" Titanic carried fewer than one third of the approximately 2,200 people aboard. A U.S. Senate investigating committee in 1912 found that a total of 1,517 lives were lost—a high proportion of them poor passengers who were far below decks in steerage.

J. Bruce Ismay, director of the White Star Line.

A Fireman's Story

Harry Senior

I was in my bunk when I felt a bump. One man said, "Hello. She has been struck." I went on deck and saw a great pile of ice on the well deck before the forecastle, but we all thought the ship would last some time, and we went back to our bunks. Then one of the firemen came running down and yelled, "All muster for the lifeboats." I ran on deck, and the captain said, "All firemen keep down on the well deck. If a man comes up, I'll shoot him."

Then I saw the first lifeboat lowered. Thirteen people were on board, eleven men and two women. Three were millionaires, and one was Ismay [J. Bruce Ismay, managing director of the White Star Line; a survivor].

Then I ran up onto the hurricane deck and helped to throw one of the collapsible boats onto the lower deck. I saw an Italian woman holding two babies. I took one of them and made the woman jump overboard with the baby, while I did the same with the other. When I came to the surface, the baby in my arms was dead. I saw the woman strike out in good style, but a boiler burst on the *Titanic* and started a big wave. When the woman saw that wave, she gave up. Then, as the child was dead, I let it sink too.

I swam around for about half an hour, and was swimming on my back when the *Titanic* went down. I tried to get aboard a boat, but some chap hit me over the head with an oar. There were too many in her. I got around to the other side of the boat and climbed in.

Mrs. J. Bruce Ismay.

"The *Titanic* orphans"—Edmond (age 2) and Michel (age 3) Navratil.

Connecting Across Texts

Connecting with "R.M.S. Titanic"

Whereas every detail in Baldwin's report on the *Titanic* is thoroughly researched, these eyewitness accounts are more subjective: fuzzier about some facts, perhaps, but fascinating as illustrations of "being there" in the most literal sense. Baldwin crafts his article carefully, with attention to literary elements, such as characterization, suspense, mood, and irony; the eyewitness accounts are less artful but no less compelling. They are clear and rich in detail, invaluable "amateur snapshots" of a tragedy almost a century old.

From a Lifeboat

Mrs. D. H. Bishop

We did not begin to understand the situation till we were perhaps a mile or more away from the *Titanic*. Then we could see the rows of lights along the decks begin to slant gradually upward from the bow. Very slowly, the lines of light began to point downward at a greater and greater angle. The sinking was so slow that you could not perceive the lights of the deck changing their position. The slant seemed to be greater about every quarter of an hour. That was the only difference.

In a couple of hours, though, she began to go down more rapidly. Then the fearful sight began. The people in the ship were just beginning to realize how great their danger was. When the forward part of the ship dropped suddenly at a faster rate, so that the upward slope became marked, there was a sudden rush of passengers on all the decks toward the stern. It was like a wave. We could see the great black mass of people in the steerage sweeping to the rear part of the boat and breaking through into the upper decks. At the distance of about a mile, we could distinguish everything through the night, which was perfectly clear. We could make out the increasing excitement on board the boat as the people, rushing to and fro, caused the deck lights to disappear and reappear as they passed in front of them.

This panic went on, it seemed, for an hour. Then suddenly the ship seemed to shoot up out of the water and stand there perpendicularly. It seemed to us that it stood upright in the water for four full minutes.

Then it began to slide gently downward. Its speed increased as it went down headfirst, so that the stern shot down with a rush.

The lights continued to burn till it sank. We could see the people packed densely in the stern till it was gone. . . .

As the ship sank, we could hear the screaming a mile away. Gradually it became fainter and fainter and died away. Some of the lifeboats that had room for more might have gone to their rescue, but it would have meant that those who were in the water would have swarmed aboard and sunk them.

Ruth Becker and her brother Richard survived in separate lifeboats.

Marion Wright from Somerset, England, married her fiancé when she arrived in New York City.

R.M.S. TITANIC **405**

C Reading Skills and Strategies

Using Text Organizers

❓ To Mrs. Bishop, it seemed that she watched from a distance for "a couple of hours" before the *Titanic* sank. According to Baldwin, how much time actually went by between the launching of the first lifeboat and the sinking of the *Titanic*? Scan the time notations in section II to find out. [Sample answer: about an hour and a half.]

D Critical Thinking

Recognizing Bias

❓ How might this description of steerage passengers suggest bias? [Possible response: It echoes the cliche of "the great, unwashed masses"; it suggests that Mrs. Bishop considers steerage passengers beneath her and does not see them as individuals.]

E Critical Thinking

Making Connections

❓ How does information in this paragraph differ from information provided by Baldwin on p. 400? [Possible responses: Baldwin says that the *Titanic*'s lights went out several minutes before it sank; Mrs. Bishop says, "The lights continued to burn till it sank."]

Assessing Learning

Check Test: Short Answer

1. Why was the *Titanic* considered unsinkable? [Sample answer: It had a double bottom and sixteen watertight compartments with watertight doors.]

2. Was the appearance of ice a surprise to the *Titanic*'s captain and crew? [Sample answer: No; several nearby ships had radioed warnings of ice.]

3. How did ships in the area respond to the *Titanic*'s distress call? [Sample answer: Most immediately headed for the *Titanic*. However, the telegraph operator of the nearest ship, the *Californian,* had gone to bed, so the *Californian* did not hear or respond.]

4. Even after the *Titanic* collided with the iceberg, why were some passengers still unaware that the boat was sinking? [Sample answers: Many were asleep, and the shock of the collision was so slight that they were not awakened; the boat was so huge, its sinking was gradual.]

5. List two criticisms of the *Titanic* listed by the investigators in their report. [Sample answers (any two): excessive speed in dangerous waters; too few lookouts; too few lifeboats; no lifeboat drills; haphazard loading and manning of lifeboats.]

MAKING MEANINGS

First Thoughts

1. Possible responses: interested but somewhat removed from most of them; very sympathetic toward some; frustrated with some; admiring of some; scornful of some; curious.

Shaping Interpretations

2. Sample answer: (1) events leading to the collision; (2) collision and sinking; (3) immediate aftermath and rescue of the survivors; (4) world's learning of the disaster and survivors' arrival in New York; (5) investigations and results. The divisions are logical in that they follow chronological order and break down a complex event into simpler segments.

3. Possible responses: Ismay's pocketing the iceberg warnings; Phillips's telling the *Californian* to "shut up" when it warned of ice; the *Californian*'s operator removing his headphones only minutes before the *Titanic* radioed for help; the band playing ragtime; the lifeboats being launched half-empty. Answers will vary as to which example of irony seems most incredible. Ask students to explain their choice.

4. Sample answer: Baldwin's research demonstrates that his aim is to be factual, and the article is certainly full of facts. However, he presents the facts in a way that engages readers' feelings and perhaps suggests his own.

5. Sample answer: The ragtime suggests fun or lightheartedness; the hymns suggest somberness or desperation. Other examples of repetition: the blue spark, which suggests hope; the moaning sound, which suggests sorrow.

Connecting with the Text

6. Possible disasters might include hurricanes, earthquakes, floods, plane crashes, riots, or terrorist attacks. Students will find instances of heroism, as well as selfishness. Encourage students to consider longer-term causes (analogous to the complacent attitudes of people on board the *Titanic*), as well as immediate causes (analogous to the *Titanic*'s collision with the iceberg).

MAKING MEANINGS

First Thoughts

[connect]

1. The *Titanic* sank a long time ago, and most of its survivors have since died. How did you feel about all the people involved in the disaster?

Shaping Interpretations

[analyze]

2. Baldwin uses numbers as **headings** to organize his text. Briefly summarize what is covered in each numbered part. Why are these divisions logical?

[analyze]

3. Find as many examples of **irony**—both **dramatic** and **situational**—in the story of the *Titanic* as you can. Which instance of irony do you think is the most incredible?

[evaluate]

4. Baldwin spent hundreds of hours sifting through reports of the sinking, the records of other ships, eyewitness accounts (see *Connections* on pages 404–405), and court proceedings. How **objective** (strictly factual) or **subjective** (based on opinions, feelings, and biases) do you think his report is? Explain.

[analyze]

5. Baldwin returns many times to the music played by the ship's band. What **moods** are suggested by the music? What other examples of **repetition** can you find, and how do these repeated details affect your feelings?

Connecting with the Text

[connect]

6. What more recent events remind you of this old tragedy at sea? Did any survivors of those events behave heroically or selfishly? What were the causes of those disasters?

[connect]

7. After reading about the events on board ship, how do you think (or hope) you would have acted if you'd been a passenger? a crew member? Look back at your Quickwrite to see whether you've changed your mind about how you'd behave in a catastrophe.

Extending the Text

[synthesize]

8. What, if any, truths about human nature can you **infer** from this story and from the survivors' eyewitness accounts (see *Connections* on pages 404–405)?

Scene from the movie *Titanic* (1997), starring Leonardo DiCaprio and Kate Winslet.

406 THE NONFICTION COLLECTIONS

Reading Check

a. What caused the *Titanic* to sink?

b. Why didn't the closest ship rush to the rescue?

c. Why weren't the lifeboats full?

d. Cite two heroic acts and two cowardly acts that took place aboard the *Titanic*.

Reading Check

a. It hit an iceberg at full speed, gashing its hull massively and irreparably.

b. Its radio operator had gone to bed, leaving no one on duty, just before the *Titanic* began calling for help.

c. Passengers were at first unwilling to get in the lifeboats; officers in charge of loading the boats feared that full boats would break the lines by which they were to be lowered into the water; no lifeboat drills had been held, so loading was confused and haphazard.

d. Sample answers: Heroic acts—stokers and engineers staying at work as engine rooms filled with water; the band playing until the end; Mrs. Straus turning back to be with her husband; women in a lifeboat rescuing a swimmer. Cowardly acts—a stoker trying to steal Phillips's life jacket; some people in lifeboats beating away drowning swimmers; a man dressing as a woman to get into a lifeboat.

CHOICES: Building Your Portfolio

Writer's Notebook

1. Collecting Ideas for a Research Paper

Listing questions. The *Titanic* never seems to go out of the news. You might be interested enough in the disaster to do further research. Start by skimming back over Baldwin's article, which was written in 1934. Jot down all the questions you have about the disaster and about details in the report. For example, have there been any new findings on the sunken ship: Are any of Baldwin's details now dated? One writer's first question is cited on the notepad below. (Be sure to save your notes.)

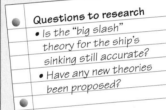

Questions to research
• Is the "big slash" theory for the ship's sinking still accurate?
• Have any new theories been proposed?

Writing a Summary

2. Just the Facts, Please

Write a one-page **summary** of "R.M.S. *Titanic*," including the most significant facts and Baldwin's most important conclusions. Before you write your summary, first **outline** the article, showing what Baldwin covers in each of the five numbered sections. (See page 334 for a model of an outline.) Include in your summary a **time line** showing the major events in the disaster.

Art

3. Disaster: An Artist's View

The illustration on pages 398–399 shows how one artist imagined the sinking *Titanic*. Create your own visual representation of the disaster (the impact of the iceberg, the ship's sinking, the unfilled lifeboats) in any medium you wish. If you prefer, illustrate a different disaster—the explosion of the *Challenger*, the San Francisco earthquake and fire, tornadoes—you choose.

Role-Play

4. A Senate Investigation

With a group, role-play an improvised sketch depicting a Senate hearing on the *Titanic* disaster. You'll need a table and chairs, several volunteers to play senators, including the chairperson, and witnesses. Senator Smith is a plum role. Other characters that you may want to include in your sketch are the crewman Fleet, the *Carpathia* captain Rostron, the radio operator Bride, and the shipping company chairman Ismay. Review the information about these characters in Baldwin's report. Then, use your imagination to further develop each role.

Comparing Responses to a Review

5. Why the Lineup?

Here's what one critic wrote about James Cameron's movie *Titanic* (1997):

> There's not a single superhero, alien, or bloodthirsty slasher in the three-hour tear-jerker. The story is crammed with ancient history, and everyone already knows that the ship sinks in the end.
> So, why are teens lining up for more?
>
> —Su Avasthi,
> *New York Post*

If you have seen the movie, compare your response to *Titanic* with the critic's. Then, try to explain the movie's enormous popularity. Be sure to cite details from the movie to support your responses.

7. Possible responses: fearfully, level-headedly, confusedly, dutifully, heroically.

Extending the Text

8. Possible responses: Human nature includes a tendency toward complacency that can prove disastrous; people have a great capacity for both cowardice and heroism; a crisis can cause people to behave in uncharacteristic ways.

Grading Timesaver

Rubrics for each Choices assignment appear on p. 138 in the *Portfolio Management System*.

CHOICES: Building Your Portfolio

1. **Writer's Notebook** Encourage students to brainstorm question lists with partners, aiming for a variety of *5W-How?* questions.
2. **Writing a Summary** Students can use either formal or informal outlines for their summaries.
3. **Art** Have each student prepare an information card about his or her representation.
4. **Role Play** Encourage students to consider how their character feels about participating.
5. **Comparing Responses to a Review** Remind students to state their responses clearly and to support them with reasons and specific details.

R.M.S. TITANIC **407**

Listening to Music

"Never an Absolution" by James Horner
The *Titanic* disaster continues to appeal to popular imagination, as the Oscar-winning 1997 film so clearly revealed. James Horner's music for the film also won an Oscar.

Activity
Play "Never an Absolution," and explain that it is the central instrumental theme of the film. Ask students, as they listen, to jot down words to describe the mood or feelings that the music evokes. Then, have them reread the nonfiction account to determine the author's mood or feelings.

LANGUAGE LINK

Students can use information from this mini-lesson as they plan and revise research papers for the Writer's Workshop on pp. 448–452.

Try It Out

1. Baldwin presents characters' looks, actions, and words without overtly evaluating them or editorializing about them.
2. Strong examples appear at the end of section I and throughout section II. Students may find that removing the dialogue deadens the article. Baldwin probably interviewed survivors and read primary source material, such as the Eyewitness Accounts included on pp. 404–405.
3. Baldwin uses detailed chronology and a loglike format, forcing readers to move slowly to the inevitable end of the narrative. He heightens suspense with selective repetition of words and images (the blue spark, the band music). He plays up the dramatic irony.

VOCABULARY

Synonyms and semantic features will vary widely. Encourage students to consult dictionary sample sentences and usage notes.

Possible synonyms:
superlative—outstanding; ascertain—determine; corroborated—supported; quelled—subdued; poised—ready; perfunctory—superficial; garbled—confused; recriminations—counter-charges; pertinent—relevant; vainly—unsuccessfully

Resources ———

Language
- *Grammar and Language Links* Worksheet, p. 45

Vocabulary
- *Words to Own* Worksheet, p. 24

LANGUAGE LINK   `MINI-LESSON`

Handbook
of
Literary
Terms
HELP

See Exposition and Narration.

Combining Narration and Exposition

In his long article about the *Titanic*, Baldwin combines a **chronological** account (a **narrative**, or story) with **factual** information (**exposition**). (On page 392 alone, see how many facts you can locate.) Facts enhance the narrative because they give information that allows us to feel like experts. The narrative techniques (**characterization,** use of **dialogue,** and **suspense**) make the article as compelling as a fast-paced adventure novel. In fact, Baldwin uses an old narrative device based on the ticking clock. A similar narrative device is used in the tense science fiction story "The Cold Equations" (page 9).

> ### Try It Out
>
> ➤Go back to the text as you look for these examples of Baldwin's narrative techniques.
>
> 1. Baldwin introduces us to some of the people involved in the disaster, and we learn more than their names. How does he "show, not tell," us about these **characters**?
>
> 2. Find places where Baldwin uses **dialogue** or **quotations.** Try reading those passages without the dialogue—what happens to the story? How do you suppose Baldwin discovered what these people said, or do you think he made up the dialogue?
>
> 3. Most readers know that the *Titanic* sank. What techniques does Baldwin use to create **suspense** in a story whose outcome is known?
>
> **A tip for writers:** Whenever you write an informative essay, look for places where you might use narrative devices (characterization, use of dialogue, and suspense) to make your information more interesting to your readers.

VOCABULARY   `HOW TO OWN A WORD`

WORD BANK

superlative
ascertain
corroborated
quelled
poised
perfunctory
garbled
recriminations
pertinent
vainly

Does It Apply? The Right Word

Would you use the word *superlative* to describe a person? How about *supreme*? When is a word appropriate, and when isn't it? The question isn't always easy to answer. Work with a partner or group to make **semantic features charts** like the one below. At the left, list one word in the Word Bank and a synonym. Along the top, list features (ideas, things, feelings, situations) to which the word might apply. Write a plus sign (+) if the word usually can be applied to that feature; write a minus sign (−) if it can't.

	Bomb	**Riot**	**Objections**	**Disturbance**
quell	−	+	+	+
subdue	−	+	−	+

408 THE NONFICTION COLLECTIONS

Language Link Quick Check

Use these questions to assess students' grasp of the literary genres of narration and exposition.

1. What is another term for a report of factual information? [exposition]

2. What is another term for a chronological account or story? [narration]

3. What are three narrative techniques that can enliven factual writing? [characterization, use of dialogue, and suspense]

Before You Read

NO NEWS FROM AUSCHWITZ

Make the Connection

Remembering History

In 1958, when A. M. Rosenthal was *The New York Times*'s correspondent in Warsaw, Poland, he visited the concentration camp at Auschwitz. About fourteen years had passed since the camps had been liberated, and virtually no mention of them had appeared in American newspapers for several years. There was "no news" to report from those sites, and Americans seemed all too willing to put the ugly memories behind them. Rosenthal's piece for *The Times* was a powerful reminder of the dangers that could befall people who forgot what had happened there.

Quickwrite

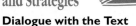

In a few sentences, write what you know about the Holocaust. (Perhaps you've read *The Diary of Anne Frank* or the speech from the Nuremberg trials on page 885. Save your notes.)

Reading Skills and Strategies

Dialogue with the Text

In your notebook, describe your feelings as you read this essay. Note the passages that you find most moving and your reactions to them.

 go.hrw.com
LE0 10-6

A. M. Rosenthal saw these photos of concentration camp prisoners when he visited the museum at Auschwitz in 1958.

Elements of Literature

Objective and Subjective Writing

At the moment, you are reading this book. That's a fact. You are somewhere. It is some hour of the day, some day of the week. All of these statements refer to **objective** facts, which means that they can be proved true.

You may also be interested or bored or worried about a test next period. These are **subjective,** or personal, feelings and judgments.

Two writers may start out with the same facts and yet report an event in vastly different ways. An encyclopedia article about the Holocaust, for example, that contains only facts and gives no clue to the writer's thoughts and feelings is **objective** writing. In revealing their own thoughts, judgments, feelings, and attitudes, writers are writing **subjectively**. As you read A. M. Rosenthal's report from Auschwitz, consider which type of writing—objective or subjective—is more important in his essay.

> **O**bjective writing reports only the facts; the writer is invisible. In **subjective** writing, the writer adds his or her opinions, judgments, or feelings.

NO NEWS FROM AUSCHWITZ **409**

OBJECTIVES

1. Read and interpret the essay
2. Identify objective and subjective writing and analyze an author's use of subjective writing
3. Monitor comprehension
4. Express understanding through writing, supporting an opinion, or visual arts/history

SKILLS

Literary
- Read and interpret the essay
- Identify objective and subjective writing and analyze an author's use of subjective writing

Reading
- Monitor comprehension through dialogue with the text

Writing
- List print and nonprint sources for a research paper
- Support an opinion about the objectivity or subjectivity of an essay

Visual Arts/History
- Create a visual memorial of a historic event

Viewing/Representing
- Analyze mood in art and literature (ATE)

Planning

- **Block Schedule**
  Block Scheduling Lesson Plans with Pacing Guide

- **Traditional Schedule**
  Lesson Plans Including Strategies for English-Language Learners

- **One-Stop Planner**
  CD-ROM with Test Generator

Resources: Print and Media

Reading
- *Graphic Organizers for Active Reading,* p. 25
- *Audio CD Library*
  Disc 12, Track 3

Elements of Literature
- *Literary Elements*
  Transparency 12
  Worksheet, p. 37

Writing and Language
- *Daily Oral Grammar*
  Transparency 25

Assessment
- *Formal Assessment,* p. 68
- *Portfolio Management System,* p. 140
- *Test Generator (One-Stop Planner CD-ROM)*

Internet
- go.hrw.com (keyword: LE0 10-6)

Summary ■ ■

Rosenthal reports on his visit to Auschwitz, now a "tourist center" at Brzezinka and Oświęcim, Poland. With the repeated, ironic observation that there is no longer news here to report, Rosenthal provides a look, both objective and subjective, at the partially restored camp (suffocation chambers and babies' shoes) and at visitors' reactions (reluctant steps, a "silent scream"). The understated, wrenching images achieve his purpose: to remember, for the sake of our own humanity and as a simple courtesy to those who died.

Resources

Listening
Audio CD Library
A recording of this essay is included in the *Audio CD Library:*
• Disc 12, Track 3

Elements of Literature
Objective and Subjective Writing
For additional instruction on objective and subjective writing, see *Literary Elements:*
• Transparency 12
• Worksheet, p. 37

No News from Auschwitz

A. M. Rosenthal

It all seemed frighteningly wrong . . . .

410 THE NONFICTION COLLECTIONS

Listening to Music

"Quartet for the End of Time" by Olivier
  Messiaen (1908–1992), performed by Tashi

The composer wrote this music while he was a prisoner in a concentration camp. The piece is scored for clarinet, violin, cello, and piano—instruments which were available to and played by some of the musically talented prisoners in the same camp.

Activity
After students have read the selection, have them listen to the music and describe their reactions to it. Some students may want to research information about artists who were imprisoned in concentration camps during World War II.

(Above) The abandoned Auschwitz II, or Birkenau, outside the town of Brzezinka, Poland, in February 1945. As the Soviet army advanced, Nazis moved prisoners to Dachau and other German concentration camps. (Left) Zdenka Gruenwald, age 15, who died in the Holocaust.

Brzezinka, Poland—The most terrible thing of all, somehow, was that at Brzezinka the sun was bright and warm, the rows of graceful poplars were lovely to look upon, and on the grass near the gates children played.

It all seemed frighteningly wrong, as in a nightmare, that at Brzezinka the sun should ever shine or that there should be light and greenness and the sound of young laughter. It would be fitting if at Brzezinka the sun never shone and the grass withered, because this is a place of unutterable terror.

And yet every day, from all over the world, people come to Brzezinka, quite possibly the most grisly tourist center on earth. They come for a variety of reasons—to see if it could really have been true, to remind themselves not to forget, to pay homage to the dead by the simple act of looking upon their place of suffering.

Brzezinka is a couple of miles from the better-known southern Polish town of Oświęcim.° Oświęcim has about 12,000 inhabitants, is situated about 171 miles from Warsaw, and lies in a damp, marshy area at the eastern end of the pass called the Moravian Gate. Brzezinka and Oświęcim together formed part of that minutely organized factory of torture and death that the Nazis called Konzentrationslager Auschwitz.

By now, fourteen years after the last batch of prisoners was herded naked into the gas chambers by dogs and guards, the story of Auschwitz has been told a great many times. Some of the inmates have written of those memories of which sane men cannot conceive. Rudolf Franz Ferdinand Hoess, the superintendent of the camp, before he was executed wrote his detailed memoirs of mass exterminations and the experiments on living bodies. Four million people died here, the Poles say.

°Oświęcim (ôsh·vyan′tsim): Polish name for Auschwitz.

No News from Auschwitz 411

Reaching All Students

A Reading Skills and Strategies

Dialogue with the Text

? What do you "hear" as you read this paragraph? What do you "see"? [Possible responses: hear—footsteps echoing in silence, a few low words from a guide; or see—empty rooms, wooden posts, a guide's impassive face, tourists' backs.]

B Elements of Literature

Objective and Subjective Writing

? What objective details do you find in these paragraphs? What subjectivity do you notice in the way they are presented? [Possible responses: Details: ruins of gas chambers and crematoria, daisies growing in rubble of gas chambers, displays of human hair and babies' shoes, suffocation cells; subjectivity: references to visitors' "horror," numbed stares, "shivering," a "silent scream," and the comment "Nothing more to see here."]

C Elements of Literature

Objective and Subjective Writing

? What might this subjective and very personal detail suggest about Rosenthal's purpose for writing? [Possible responses: Maybe one of his purposes is to come to terms with his feelings; maybe he's sharing this information in order to get readers to examine their own feelings about the Holocaust.]

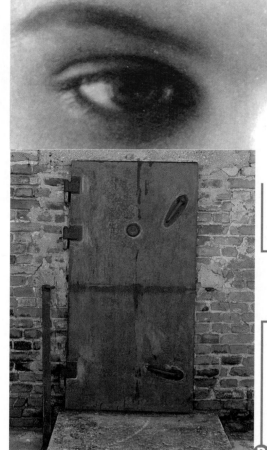

Entrance to one of the gas chambers at Auschwitz.

And so there is no news to report about Auschwitz. There is merely the compulsion to write something about it, a compulsion that grows out of a restless feeling that to have visited Auschwitz and then turned away without having said or written anything would somehow be a most grievous act of discourtesy to those who died here.

A Brzezinka and Oświęcim are very quiet places now; the screams can no longer be heard. The tourist walks silently, quickly at first to get it over with and then, as his mind peoples the barracks and the chambers and the dungeons and flogging posts, he walks draggingly. The guide does not say much either, because there is nothing much for him to say after he has pointed.

For every visitor there is one particular bit of horror that he knows he will never forget. For some it is seeing the rebuilt gas chamber at Oświęcim and being told that this is the "small one."

For others it is the fact that at Brzezinka, in the ruins of the gas chambers and the crematoria the Germans blew up when they retreated, there are daisies growing.

There are visitors who gaze blankly at the gas chambers and the furnaces because their minds simply cannot encompass them, but stand shivering before the great mounds of human hair behind the plate-glass window or the piles of **B** babies' shoes or the brick cells where men sentenced to death by suffocation were walled up.

One visitor opened his mouth in a silent scream simply at the sight of boxes—great stretches of three-tiered wooden boxes in the women's barracks. They were about six feet wide, about three feet high, and into them from five to ten prisoners were shoved for the night. The guide walks quickly through the barracks. Nothing more to see here.

A brick building where sterilization experiments were carried out on women prisoners. **C** The guide tries the door—it's locked. The visitor is grateful that he does not have to go in, and then flushes with shame.

Professional Notes

Cultural Diversity

Most of those whom Adolf Hitler sent to concentration camps were Jewish; more than six million Jews died at his direction. Other groups, however, also were imprisoned in the camps. These included Romanies (Gypsies), Polish and other Slavic people, criminals, political dissidents, homosexuals, conscientious objectors (such as Jehovah's Witnesses), the physically and mentally impaired, and prisoners not healthy enough to work.

Making the Connections

Connecting to the Theme: "Being There!"

Rosenthal maintains that this is not news journalism; yet his subtext is that—for such horror—his job as a reporter is indeed to share his personal experience of "being there." The essay is unabashedly subjective, though the device of describing "the visitor"—who very likely is the writer himself—adds some distance. The essay does the painful but necessary job of reawakening memories of Holocaust atrocities.

A long corridor where rows of faces stare from the walls. Thousands of pictures, the photographs of prisoners. They are all dead now, the men and women who stood before the cameras, and they all knew they were to die.

They all stare blank-faced, but one picture, in the middle of a row, seizes the eye and wrenches the mind. A girl, twenty-two years old, plumply pretty, blond. She is smiling gently, as at a sweet, treasured thought. What was the thought that passed through her young mind and is now her memorial on the wall of the dead at Auschwitz?

Into the suffocation dungeons the visitor is taken for a moment and feels himself strangling. Another visitor goes in, stumbles out, and crosses herself. There is no place to pray in Auschwitz.

The visitors look pleadingly at each other and say to the guide, "Enough."

There is nothing new to report about Auschwitz. It was a sunny day and the trees were green and at the gates the children played.

MEET THE WRITER

Journalist of Distinction

Abraham Michael Rosenthal (1922–   ) was born in Ontario, Canada, but moved with his family to New York City when he was four. For many years he served as the executive editor of *The New York Times*. When he "retired," he began to write a column for *The Times* called "On My Mind," in which he often takes a moral and ethical stand on events in the news.

In November 1959, after Rosenthal had written "No News from Auschwitz," the Polish government expelled him for his probing reporting. He won a Pulitzer Prize in May 1960 for the same reports. Rosenthal is also the author of *Thirty-Eight Witnesses* (1964), an account of a murder in a quiet New York City neighborhood. The title refers to the thirty-eight people who witnessed a young woman's murder but did nothing to help the victim.

When asked if he thought that reporters' opinions are slipping into news stories more often today than they did in the past, Rosenthal replied:

66 Yes, I do. But we don't try for objectivity, because there is no such thing as pristine objectivity. There is an approach to doing a fair job, . . . but if you start thinking the most important thing to do is present your opinion, by stealth or not, to change your readers' minds, then you can't do your job the same way. There are plenty of places in the paper to do that. . . .

The editorial writer gets paid to do it; if you don't like your job, become an editorial writer. Or stick around, be a reporter for thirty years, then become the executive editor, and then become a columnist. 99

D Reading Skills and Strategies

Dialogue with the Text

❓ What might the girl have been thinking about? [Possible responses: someone she loved; her home; a favorite piece of music or literature that she was mentally hearing; her religious faith.]

E Critical Thinking

Analyzing Purpose

❓ How does the sentence "There is nothing new to report about Auschwitz" help Rosenthal to achieve his purpose? [Possible responses: Its irony underscores the importance of the facts and feelings he has just shared; it suggests a commonly held view that Rosenthal hopes to change.]

Assessing Learning

Check Test: Short Answers

1. What seems "frighteningly wrong" about the scene in the opening paragraph? [Sample answer: that the sun shines, grass and trees grow, and children play at a former concentration camp.]
2. Why is Auschwitz "quite possibly the most grisly tourist center on earth"? [Sample answer: Four million people were killed there in horrible ways.]

3. In what country is Auschwitz located? [Poland]
4. What room at Auschwitz was locked when the visitor toured the site? [the room where the Nazis performed sterilization experiments]
5. Which image from Auschwitz does Rosenthal consider most wrenching and unforgettable? [Sample answer: a photograph of a girl who knows that she is to die and who is gently smiling.]

Standardized Test Preparation

For practice in proofreading and editing, see
• *Daily Oral Grammar,* Transparency 25

Summary

After seven weeks in a concentration camp, the young speaker recalls the bright yellow of the last butterfly he saw. He comforts himself with other images from nature and with the presence of "my people."

A **Reading Skills and Strategies**

Dialogue with the Text

? Which lines in the first stanzas strike you most strongly? What feelings or images do they create for you? [Possible responses: "… if the sun's tears would sing/against a white stone"— poignant blend of beauty and sorrow; "Such, such a yellow/Is carried lightly 'way up high"—a yellow butterfly against blue sky; a love and longing for freedom.]

B **Reading Skills and Strategies**

Making Inferences

? What time of year is implied by the references to dandelions and to the "white candle" blossoms of chestnut trees? [spring or summer] Would you normally expect to see many butterflies during that time of year? [yes]

Connections — A POEM

The Nazis used the Czech town of Terezín as a concentration camp between 1941 and 1945. From 1942 to 1944, a total of 15,000 children passed through the camp. Only about 100 of them survived. Pavel Friedmann, the writer of this poem, was one of the young people imprisoned in the camp. He died in Auschwitz in September 1944.

(Right) *Terezín Barracks* (detail) by Sonja Valdstein. (Below) *Flower and Butterfly* (detail) by Marika Friedman.

From *I never saw another butterfly* (Schocken Books, 1993). Courtesy U.S. Holocaust Memorial Museum, Washington, D.C.

The Butterfly
Pavel Friedmann

The last, the very last,
So richly, brightly, dazzlingly yellow.
    Perhaps if the sun's tears would sing
    against a white stone . . .

A
5 Such, such a yellow
Is carried lightly 'way up high.
It went away I'm sure because it wished to
    kiss the world goodbye.

For seven weeks I've lived in here,
10 Penned up inside this ghetto
But I have found my people here.
B The dandelions call to me
And the white chestnut candles in the court.
Only I never saw another butterfly.

15 That butterfly was the last one.
Butterflies don't live in here,
    in the ghetto.

Connecting Across Texts

Connecting with "No News from Auschwitz"

In both the poem and the essay, idyllic nature images contrast with the horrors of a concentration camp. Friedmann's poem describes a butterfly too fragile to stay in the harsh camp; readers may see an analogy to the young poet himself, who died in 1944 at Auschwitz.

Rosenthal describes sunny images from nature that he finds disquietingly inappropriate at the site of so many people's deaths. Yet he opens and closes his essay with these bright images, addressing an equally bright postwar world in danger of forgetting the Holocaust.

MAKING MEANINGS

First Thoughts

[connect]

1. If you had a chance to visit Auschwitz, would you go? Why or why not?

Shaping Interpretations

[explain]

2. Explain why the title of the essay is **ironic**. What "news" does Rosenthal want his readers to know?

[synthesize]

3. What **purpose,** or aim, do you think Rosenthal had in writing this essay?

Extending the Text

[analyze]

4. What relationship do you see between Rosenthal's essay and the poem "The Butterfly" (see **Connections** on page 414)?

Reading Check

Write a paragraph telling what this essay is about. Include the items below. Then, write a few sentences explaining what you learned about the Holocaust from the essay (refer to your Quickwrite notes).

Situation:_____

Setting: _____

What happens: _____

The writer's main idea:_____

_____

CHOICES: Building Your Portfolio

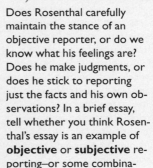

Writer's Notebook

1. Collecting Ideas for a Research Paper

Exploring sources.
For a topic you're considering researching, think about where you will find information. List and then explore some specific sources. Consider both **print sources** (books, magazines, encyclopedias) and **nonprint sources** (the Internet, on-line databases, TV documentaries, interviews). Before you finalize your topic, check to see if you can find enough information.

Visual Arts/History

2. Memorial

Maya Ying Lin was a 21-year-old architecture student when she submitted the winning design for the Vietnam Veterans Memorial in Washington, D.C.: two long black granite walls inscribed with the names of those who died in the war. With a partner, choose an important historic event that you want to portray. Then, create a poster, collage, exhibit, model, or drawing to memorialize the event. Display your work in a classroom mini-museum.

Supporting an Opinion

3. Objective? Subjective? Both?

Does Rosenthal carefully maintain the stance of an objective reporter, or do we know what his feelings are? Does he make judgments, or does he stick to reporting just the facts and his own observations? In a brief essay, tell whether you think Rosenthal's essay is an example of **objective** or **subjective** reporting—or some combination of both. Cite specific words, phrases, and sentences from the essay to support your view.

MAKING MEANINGS

First Thoughts

1. Possible responses: Yes, to learn and to pay respects; no, because it would be too disturbing.

Shaping Interpretations

2. The irony is that Rosenthal feels that there *is* important information at Auschwitz. Rosenthal wants readers to know what happened in the concentration camp and how visitors respond to what they see at the camp.

3. He hopes to dissuade people from pushing the ugly memories of Auschwitz (and of the Holocaust in general) out of their mind.

Extending the Text

4. Possible responses: Both contrast beautiful images with horrible ones; both offer wrenching reminders of the Holocaust.

Grading Timesaver

Rubrics for each Choices assignment appear on p. 140 in the *Portfolio Management System.*

CHOICES: Building Your Portfolio

1. Writer's Notebook Remind students to save their work for the Writer's Workshop on p. 448.

2. Visual Arts/History Have students form groups and brainstorm lists of events to commemorate.

3. Supporting an Opinion Give students self-adhesive notes to mark specific parts of the essay.

Reading Check

Sample paragraph:

Fourteen years after the liberation of Auschwitz, the infamous Nazi concentration camp, A.M. Rosenthal visits it as a tourist. His tour group sees the barracks, the crematoria, the displays of victims' pictures and belongings, and so on—and he sees that everyone in the group is troubled. His essay is, in part, a tribute to those who died; his main idea is that the Holocaust must not be forgotten.

Sample sentences:

Four million people died in just one concentration camp. People were walled in with bricks to die by suffocation. The retreating Germans blew up the gas chambers and crematoria as the war ended.

Resources

Elements of Literature
Essays and History
For additional instruction on essays and history, see *Literary Elements:*
• Transparency 11

Elements of Literature

This lesson contrasts essays and histories, defining both kinds of nonfiction and discussing their characteristics. It explores the roles of fact and opinion in each.

Mini-Lesson: Essays and History

You might use this mini-lesson to reinforce students' understanding of the material on pp. 416–417.

Have students summarize the differences between an essay and a history. [Sample answer: An essay may include facts, but it also presents and explores personal views, whereas a history focuses on presenting information, including research findings, clearly and accurately.]

Ask, "Given what you know about essays from reading about Montaigne, why would you call "No News from Auschwitz" an essay, but not "R.M.S. Titanic"? [Possible answer: "No News from Auschwitz" shares the author's thoughts and opinions about the topic, whereas "R.M.S. Titanic" is more matter-of-fact and objective.]

ESSAYS AND HISTORY: Thoughts and Reports

Though they dealt with real-life events, A. M. Rosenthal and Hanson W. Baldwin wrote two different kinds of nonfiction: "No News from Auschwitz" is an essay, and "R.M.S. *Titanic*" is a history.

Essays: Thinking on Paper

The personal **essay** is a younger genre (literary form) than history, biography, drama, or poetry. The personal essay was "born" in 1572, when a well-to-do Frenchman named Michel de Montaigne (män·tän′) retired from the practice of law, moved to his family's castle, and spent his time reading, thinking, writing, and enjoying himself. (Of course, a person who owns a family castle rarely has to worry about earning a living.)

Montaigne wrote short prose pieces on many different topics. He called them *essais* (French for "attempts" or "tries") because they were attempts to test his ideas and judgments on subjects that interested him.

Montaigne's essays were chatty, casual, and opinionated. They were also filled with digressions. The essays were written in the first person, but they weren't autobiographies because they weren't about Montaigne's life. They were about his thoughts—in fact, they *were* his thoughts.

Montaigne's success—and readers loved his three collections of *essais*—made the essay a popular form. In England, Francis Bacon took up the essayist's pen in 1597. Since then it's been used constantly.

Essays Today: From the Cosmos to Lost Socks

The subject matter of today's **personal** (or **informal**) **essays** is as wide as human experience—from the mysteries of the cosmos to the clothes dryer's habit of stealing and eating socks. The tone can range from somber, as in Rosenthal's essay on Auschwitz, to comic, as in essays by James Thurber, Dave Barry, and Erma Bombeck.

The Essayist's Art

Essayists take a particular subject—any subject—and examine it from different perspectives. It's like looking at an onion (or any other object) through a telescope, a microscope, and a kaleidoscope.

In "No News from Auschwitz" (page 410), for example, A. M. Rosenthal begins with what he sees at the gates: children playing, sun, grass, and trees. Then he moves deeper into Auschwitz and shows us the horrors visitors see and tells us how they feel. Though he doesn't state his insight directly, we know what he's telling us: We must not forget what happened there.

> "**E**very man has within himself the entire human condition."

Essays are thought journeys. "Every man has within himself the entire human condition," Montaigne once wrote. Essayists, writing about their own thoughts and feelings, touch us because they are writing about all of us.

History and Journalism: Reporting Information

Hanson W. Baldwin (page 390) isn't expressing his thoughts, his feelings, or his experiences. Baldwin is conveying information about events that he

Reaching All Students

English Language Learners

Point out that we still occasionally use the French meaning of *essay*. As a verb, it doesn't mean "to write an essay"; rather, it means "to try" or "to attempt," as in "We essayed to complete the project by Friday."

Advanced Learners

Share these quotations from the *Essais* of Michel de Montaigne. Invite students to explain each quotation and to consider how the quotations might apply to their own lives.

• "There are some defeats more triumphant than victories."
• "I speak truth, not so much as I would, but as much as I dare; and I dare a little the more, as I grow older."

• "There is no man so good who, were he to submit all his thoughts and actions to the laws, would not deserve hanging ten times in his life."
• "When I play with my cat, who knows whether I do not make her more sport than she makes me?"
• "Sits he on ever so high a throne, a man still sits on his bottom."

by Richard Cohen

hasn't experienced directly.

Part of the job of historians and reporters is to distinguish facts from opinions. A **fact** is something that can be proved true; an **opinion** is a belief that can't be proved. It is a fact that the *Titanic* struck an iceberg on the night of April 14, 1912; it is an opinion that the tragedy was avoidable.

Seeking "the Truth"

Writing **history** and **informative articles** is a formidable task. Suppose you're updating a U.S. history textbook, and your assignment is to write about the 1990s in ten pages. How would you choose which events to include? How would you know what to say about them? Where would you begin?

Before historians and reporters begin to write, they must seek "the truth" in a wilderness of facts and opinions. Generally there are too few facts or too many opinions. William Shakespeare, for example, left us the world's greatest poetry and drama, yet he provided amazingly few facts about his life.

The opposite problem—too many facts—can confuse the

researcher and make evaluation difficult. Who was to blame for the lives lost when the *Titanic* sank? Baldwin carefully provides us with facts so that we can answer this complex question for ourselves.

Luring the Reader

After spending countless hours in research—interviewing, reading, sorting, discarding, arranging, comparing, and summarizing—historians and reporters must evaluate and analyze the material they've collected. Is it true? Is it useful? How will it illuminate the story I'm telling?

Then they face the equally difficult job of selecting and presenting their material. More than two thousand people were on board the sinking *Titanic*. Baldwin had to decide which stories to tell, which details to include, and how to present them to give the reader a complete and realistic picture of the tragedy.

Nonfiction writers use all their skills, including storytelling techniques, to lure and hook readers who might otherwise be watching television, playing soccer, or talking on the telephone. The best

nonfiction writers make us eyewitnesses to events that really happened.

"Truth," the old saying goes, "is stranger than fiction." The writers in this collection present true stories that are just as exciting and entertaining as the world's best novels, short stories, and plays.

> *What Readers Demand: One Writer's Opinion*
>
> Those of us who are trying to write well about the world we live in, or to teach students to write well about the world they live in, are caught in a time warp, where literature by definition consists of forms that were certified as "literary" in the 19th century: novels and short stories and poems. But in fact these have become quite rarefied forms in American life. The great preponderance of what writers now write and sell, what book and magazine publishers publish, and what readers demand is nonfiction.
>
> —William Zinsser

Applying the Element
- As students read an excerpt from "Into Thin Air" (pp. 420–429) and "A Presentation of Whales" (pp. 434–442), tell them to decide whether each has more in common with an essay or with a history.
- Have students identify facts and opinions in each selection.
- You might then challenge students to decide which facts (and/or opinions) are crucial to the author's main idea.

Resources
Assessment
Formal Assessment
- Literary Elements Test, p. 74

Getting Students Involved

Cooperative Learning
Group Search and Share. To cultivate students' appreciation of the wide range of styles in nonfiction writing, have small groups of students prepare readings from essays. Groups may focus on a few writers, such as Barry Lopez or E. B. White, or they may focus on a theme. Tell them that each group will have around ten minutes to introduce and present its readings.

- Give groups three to four days to search for materials, make their selections, and practice their readings. After the group chooses an author or theme, each member should locate an essay and plan to read part or all of it.
- Afterward, have listeners discuss the role of facts and opinions, and of objectivity and subjectivity, in the essays they have heard.

OBJECTIVES

1. Read and interpret the report
2. Identify sensory imagery and analyze its use
3. Analyze text structure through cause and effect
4. Express understanding through writing, debate, research/ oral presentation, or creative writing/media
5. Use context to determine meanings of technical vocabulary
6. Understand and use new words
7. Read, understand, and complete verbal analogies

SKILLS

Literary
- Read and interpret the report
- Identify sensory imagery and analyze its use

Reading
- Analyze text structure through cause and effect

Writing
- Take notes for a research paper
- Write a descriptive essay
- Script a part of the selection as a movie scene

Speaking/Listening
- Debate an issue related to the selection
- Research a topic suggested by the selection and share findings in an oral presentation

Grammar/Language
- Use context to determine meanings of technical vocabulary

Vocabulary
- Read, understand, and complete verbal analogies

Before You Read

INTO THIN AIR

Make the Connection

Hot Story, Cold Mountain

You're standing on the 29,028-foot top of the world. The temperature is bone-numbing. Your oxygen is almost gone. The climb up Everest was grueling, and now you face the dangerous trek down. Can you imagine that experience? Jon Krakauer, the writer of this magazine article, lived through it.

Quickwrite

Why do you think some people are drawn to climb mountains? Would you like to? Briefly jot down why or why not.

Background

The Top of the World

The man who said he wanted to climb Mt. Everest "because it's there," George Leigh Mallory, disappeared in a mist near the summit in 1924. The first recorded conquest of the 29,028-foot peak was achieved by Edmund Hillary of New Zealand and Tenzing Norgay of Nepal in 1953. Since then more than 600 climbers have reached the summit, but 150 have lost their lives to the mountain.

The journalist who wrote this true story barely escaped with his. In 1996, *Outside* magazine financed Jon Krakauer as a client on an Everest expedition. The day he reached the summit, eight other climbers (including Krakauer's tour leader) died on the mountain. (This is the riskiest form of **participatory journalism,** in which a reporter actually takes part in the events.)

Since the May 1996 tragedy, more and more people have caught Everest fever, some paying $70,000 for a guided climb. Although many of these climbers are experts, some are inexperienced—a problem that creates grave dangers.

Making a Climb

Everest expeditions ascend the mountain in stages. From Base Camp at 17,600 feet, they make short trips up and down to acclimatize, or get used to higher elevations. This process may last several weeks before the final climb to the top, which is also done in stages. Krakauer's group made camp at 19,500 feet, 21,300 feet, 24,000 feet, and 26,000 feet. The area above 25,000 feet is known as the Death Zone. Here, the air is so poor in oxygen it's almost impossible to make rational decisions. Yet even at Base Camp, symptoms of altitude sickness can occur, including headaches, dizziness, and inability to eat or sleep. Note: No helicopter rescue has ever been made above 19,860 feet.

Elements of Literature

Imagery: What It Looks and Feels Like

Jon Krakauer takes us up Mt. Everest with him, shivering in icy winds, feeling numb fear in a blinding snow squall. It is **sensory images** that help us—safe in our chairs—feel that "we are there" in temperatures low enough to freeze flesh in minutes.

Reading Skills and Strategies

Understanding Cause and Effect

A **cause** is why something happens; an **effect** is the result of some event. A single effect may have several causes, and a single cause may lead to many effects. As you read, look for the causes that led to the disasters on Mt. Everest. Look for the effects of certain decisions made by the climbers. In fact, everything that happens in this tragic story is connected by a complex pattern of causes and effects. You might even draw a chart, linking causes and effects with arrows.

> **S**ensory details are specific images that appeal to our senses of sight, hearing, smell, taste, and touch. Sensory details are especially important in descriptive writing.

go.hrw.com
LEO 10-6

Preteaching Vocabulary

Words to Own

Tell students to read the definitions of the Words to Own at the bottom of the selection pages. Have students use the words to solve the following acrostics. The hidden words name two small items that play big roles in life-and-death struggles in the selection.

1. __ __ n __ __ __
2. __ u __ __ __ __
3. __ __ t __ __ __ __ __ __ __ t __
4. __ __ __ __ __ r __ __

5. __ __ __ u __ __ __ __
[Answers 1–5: benign, crucial, deteriorate, traverse, tenuous; hidden word: glove.]

6. __ o __ __ __ __ __ __ s
7. i __ __ __ __ __ __ __ __
8. __ __ __ c __ __ __ __ __
9. __ __ o __ __ d __ __ __ __
10. __ __ __ e __

[Answers 6–10: notorious, innocuous, speculate, jeopardize, apex; hidden words: ice ax.]

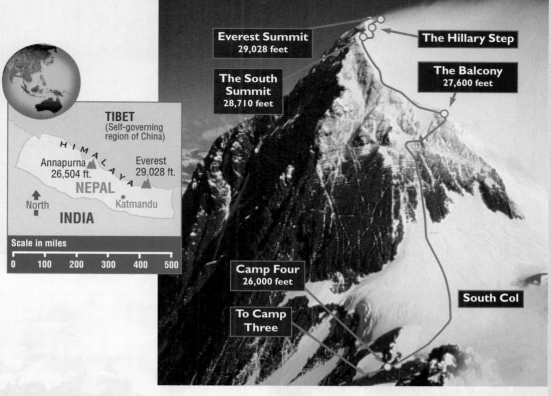

Everest Summit
29,028 feet

The Hillary Step

The South Summit
28,710 feet

The Balcony
27,600 feet

TIBET
(Self-governing region of China)

HIMALAYA

Annapurna
26,504 ft.

Everest
29,028 ft.

NEPAL

North

Katmandu

INDIA

Scale in miles

| 0 | 100 | 200 | 300 | 400 | 500 |

Camp Four
26,000 feet

South Col

To Camp Three

SOME OF THE CLIMBERS INVOLVED IN THE TRAGEDY

New Zealand-Based Team
① Rob Hall, *leader, head guide*
② Mike Groom, *guide*
③ Andy "Harold" Harris, *guide*
④ Doug Hansen, *client*
⑤ Jon Krakauer, *client, journalist*
⑥ Yasuko Namba, *client*
⑦ Beck Weathers, *client*
Lhakpa Chhiri Sherpa, *climbing Sherpa*

American-Based Team
Scott Fischer, *leader, head guide*
Anatoli Boukreev, *guide*

Taiwan Team
"Makalu" Gau Ming-Ho, *leader*

IMAX Film Crew
David Breashears, *leader, film director*
Ed Viesturs, *climber, film talent*

Members of Jon Krakauer's expedition team, led by Rob Hall. The numbers identify team members in the list of expedition members above.

 — *Resources: Print and Media* —

Reading
• *Graphic Organizers for Active Reading*, p. 26
• *Words to Own*, p. 25
• Audio CD Library
Disc 13, Track 2

Writing and Language
• *Daily Oral Grammar*
Transparency 26
• *Grammar and Language Links*
Worksheet, p. 47

• *Language Workshop CD-ROM*

Assessment
• *Formal Assessment*, p. 70
• *Portfolio Management System*, p. 141
• *Standardized Test Preparation*, p. 52
• *Test Generator (One-Stop Planner CD-ROM)*

Internet
• go.hrw.com (keyword: LE0 10-6)

Planning

• **Block Schedule**
Block Scheduling Lesson Plans with Pacing Guide
• **Traditional Schedule**
Lesson Plans Including Strategies for English-Language Learners
• **One-Stop Planner**
CD-ROM with Test Generator

Background

Since the 1953 triumph of Sir Edmund Hillary and Tenzing Norgay, many other people have climbed Mt. Everest—but never without a support team. Hillary and Norgay were part of a British team led by Lord John Hunt. Before Hillary and Norgay reached the summit, Hunt and two other team members had climbed to within four hundred feet of it and had then descended, leaving a cache of supplies that would later sustain Hillary and Norgay. After the successful climb, Hunt told a reporter that one cannot speak of "conquering" a mountain. "The relationship between a man and what he does on a mountain is one of humility," explained Hunt. ". . . [T]o feel that you've conquered them is a presumption."

Summary ▪ ▪

Krakauer's report covers seventy-two hours in May of 1996, when he was part of one of several pay-to-climb Everest expeditions that culminated in the mountain's worst tragedy to date. As his account opens, he stands at the summit, too ill and spent to savor the experience. He leaves in minutes. Dropping into an unexpected blizzard, he struggles to the base camp and survives; others, including several of his teammates, wait too long to descend —and die. Krakauer spikes his objective prose with gripping sensory images. His report implicitly calls into question the ethics of the burgeoning "ready-made adventure" industry.

Resources

Listening
Audio CD Library
A recording of this report is included in the *Audio CD Library:*
• Disc 13, Track 2

from

Into

Everest deals with trespassers harshly: The dead vanish beneath the snows, while the living struggle to explain what happened, and why. A survivor of the mountain's worst disaster examines the business of Mount Everest and the steep price of ambition.

420 THE NONFICTION COLLECTIONS

Reaching All Students

Struggling Readers
To help students follow the selection, pair them and instruct each pair to make a list of the people labeled in the photograph on p. 420. Explain that these people play significant roles in the selection. Tell students to stay alert, as they read, for references to each person and to add brief notes to their lists, tracking each person's experiences.

English Language Learners
You might discuss the idiom *into thin air.* Point out that it is usually used with the verb *to vanish* or *to disappear;* it means "completely and mysteriously." When students finish reading Krakauer's report, ask them to explain the double meaning of the title. For strategies for engaging English language learners with the literature, see
• *Lesson Plans Including Strategies for English-Language Learners*

Advanced Learners
Sir Edmund Hillary's *High in the Thin Cold Air* and Tenzing Norgay's *Tiger of the Snows* also report on climbing Everest. Invite students to compare one or both of these accounts with Krakauer's report. Encourage them to notice differences in tone and to consider how the differences relate to the authors' purposes.

Thin Air

Jon Krakauer

Straddling the top of the world, one foot in Tibet and the other in Nepal, I cleared the ice from my oxygen mask, hunched a shoulder against the wind, and stared absently at the vast sweep of earth below. I understood on some dim, detached level that it was a spectacular sight. I'd been fantasizing about this moment, and the release of emotion that would accompany it, for many months. But now that I was finally here, standing on the summit of Mount Everest, I just couldn't summon the energy to care.

It was the afternoon of May 10. I hadn't slept in 57 hours. The only food I'd been able to force down over the preceding three days was a bowl of Ramen soup and a handful of peanut M&M's. Weeks of violent coughing had left me with two separated ribs, making it excruciatingly painful to breathe. Twenty-nine thousand twenty-eight feet up in the troposphere, there was so little oxygen reaching my brain that my mental capacity was that of a slow child. Under the circumstances, I was incapable of feeling much of anything except cold and tired.

I'd arrived on the summit a few minutes after Anatoli Boukreev,[1] a Russian guide with an American expedition, and just ahead of Andy Harris, a guide with the New Zealand–based commercial team that I was a part of and someone with whom I'd grown to be friends during the last six weeks. I snapped four quick photos of Harris and Boukreev striking summit poses, and then turned and started down. My watch read 1:17 P.M. All told, I'd spent less than five minutes on the roof of the world.

After a few steps, I paused to take another photo, this one looking down the Southeast Ridge, the route we had ascended. Training my lens on a pair of climbers approaching the summit, I saw something that until that moment had escaped my attention. To the south, where the sky had been perfectly clear just an hour earlier, a blanket of clouds now hid Pumori, Ama Dablam, and the other lesser peaks surrounding Everest.

1. **Anatoli Boukreev:** Boukreev (pictured at left on Mt. Everest) was killed about a year and a half later, on December 26, 1997. He was trapped in an avalanche while climbing Annapurna, a mountain peak in the Himalayas.

INTO THIN AIR 421

Using Students' Strengths

Cause and Effect

❓ "Why" questions indicate that Krakauer not only will tell the story of the disastrous expedition but also will examine causes and effects of the disaster. On what causes does he focus here? [Sample answer: He wonders what caused guides to miss or ignore signs that a dangerous storm was approaching.]

B Elements of Literature

Sensory Imagery

❓ To which sense does Krakauer's description of the clouds appeal? [sight] Which words give you the clearest mental image of the clouds? [Sample responses: *wispy, gleaming, brilliant, puffs of condensation.*]

C Appreciating Language

Technical Vocabulary

❓ The terms *shank, corniced,* and *fin* have specialized meanings in mountaineering. Based on your reading of the paragraph, what do you think the three terms mean? [Sample answers: *shank*— segment of a ridge; *corniced*— with horizontal projections near the top; *fin*— a narrow vertical rock formation.]

D Reading Skills and Strategies

Making Inferences from Tone

❓ How does Krakauer seem to feel about the number of people climbing Everest? [Possible responses: annoyed, impatient, disapproving, nervous.] Why might he feel as he does? [Possible responses: They get in his way; they pose a safety risk; there are more people than the narrow route can accommodate.]

E Elements of Literature

Sensory Imagery

❓ What details help readers to share Krakauer's sensations when his oxygen valve is adjusted? [Possible responses: "My head cleared"; "Then, abruptly, I felt like I was suffocating"; "My vision dimmed and my head began to spin."]

Days later—after six bodies had been found, after a search for two others had been abandoned, after surgeons had amputated the gangrenous right hand of my teammate Beck Weathers—people would ask why, if the weather had begun to <u>deteriorate</u>, had climbers on the upper mountain not heeded the signs? Why did veteran Himalayan guides keep moving upward, leading a gaggle of amateurs, each of whom had paid as much as $65,000 to be ushered safely up Everest, into an apparent death trap?

Nobody can speak for the leaders of the two guided groups involved, for both men are now dead. But I can attest that nothing I saw early on the afternoon of May 10 suggested that a murderous storm was about to bear down on us. To my oxygen-depleted mind, the clouds drifting up the grand valley of ice known as the Western Cwm looked innocuous, wispy, insubstantial. Gleaming in the brilliant midday sun, they appeared no different from the harmless puffs of convection condensation that rose from the valley almost daily. As I began my descent, I was indeed anxious, but my concern had little to do with the weather. A check of the gauge on my oxygen tank had revealed that it was almost empty. I needed to get down, fast.

The uppermost shank of the Southeast Ridge is a slender, heavily corniced fin of rock and wind-scoured snow that snakes for a quarter-mile toward a secondary pinnacle known as the South Summit. Negotiating the serrated ridge presents few great technical hurdles, but the route is dreadfully exposed. After 15 minutes of cautious shuffling over a 7,000-foot abyss, I arrived at the notorious Hillary Step, a pronounced notch in the ridge named after Sir Edmund Hillary, the first Westerner to climb the mountain, and a spot that does require a fair amount of technical maneuvering. As I clipped into a fixed rope and prepared to rappel[2] over the lip, I was greeted by an alarming sight.

2. **rappel** (ra·pel′): descend a mountain by means of a double rope arranged around the climber's body so that he or she can control the slide downward.

Thirty feet below, some 20 people were queued up[3] at the base of the Step, and three climbers were hauling themselves up the rope that I was attempting to descend. I had no choice but to unclip from the line and step aside.

The traffic jam comprised climbers from three separate expeditions: the team I belonged to, a group of paying clients under the leadership of the celebrated New Zealand guide Rob Hall; another guided party headed by American Scott Fischer; and a nonguided team from Taiwan. Moving at the snail's pace that is the norm above 8,000 meters, the throng labored up the Hillary Step one by one, while I nervously bided my time.

Harris, who left the summit shortly after I did, soon pulled up behind me. Wanting to conserve whatever oxygen remained in my tank, I asked him to reach inside my backpack and turn off the valve on my regulator, which he did. For the next ten minutes I felt surprisingly good. My head cleared. I actually seemed less tired than with the gas turned on. Then, abruptly, I felt like I was suffocating. My vision dimmed and my head began to spin. I was on the brink of losing consciousness.

Instead of turning my oxygen off, Harris, in his hypoxically[4] impaired state, had mistakenly cranked the valve open to full flow, draining the tank. I'd just squandered the last of my gas going nowhere. There was another tank waiting for me at the South Summit, 250 feet below, but to get there I would have to descend the most exposed terrain on the entire route without benefit of supplemental oxygen.

But first I had to wait for the crowd to thin. I removed my now useless mask, planted my

3. **queued** (kyōōd) **up:** lined up.
4. **hypoxically:** characterized by hypoxia, a condition resulting from a decrease in the oxygen reaching body tissues. Hypoxia is a common condition at very high altitudes.

WORDS TO OWN

deteriorate (dē·tir′ē·ə·rāt) *v.:* worsen.
innocuous (in·näk′yōō·əs) *adj.:* harmless.
notorious (nō·tôr′ē·əs) *adj.:* famous, usually in an unfavorable sense.

Crossing the Curriculum

Science

Invite interested students to learn about climate patterns on Everest, about the types of rock that form the peak, and about the natural history of the region. They might share their findings with classmates by bringing in rock and plant samples or by creating illustrations, charts, cross sections, or dioramas.

Social Studies

Assign interested students to report on current political and social conditions in Tibet and Nepal. Challenge them to consider causes and effects in determining the role of Mt. Everest in the economic development of the region, and urge them to speculate about what the future holds for Mt. Everest.

ice ax into the mountain's frozen hide, and hunkered on the ridge crest. As I exchanged banal congratulations with the climbers filing past, inwardly I was frantic: "Hurry it up, hurry it up!" I silently pleaded. "While you guys are messing around here, I'm losing brain cells by the millions!"

Most of the passing crowd belonged to Fischer's group, but near the back of the parade two of my team-mates eventually appeared: Hall and Yasuko Namba. Girlish and reserved, the 47-year-old Namba was 40 minutes away from becoming the oldest woman to climb Everest and the second Japanese woman to reach the highest point on each continent, the so-called Seven Summits.

Later still, Doug Hansen—another member of our expedition, a postal worker from Seattle who had become my closest friend on the mountain—arrived atop the Step. "It's in the bag!" I yelled over the wind, trying to sound more upbeat than I felt. Plainly exhausted, Doug mumbled something from behind his oxygen mask that I didn't catch, shook my hand weakly, and continued plodding upward.

The last climber up the rope was Fischer, whom I knew casually from Seattle, where we both lived. His strength and drive were legendary—in 1994 he'd climbed Everest without using bottled oxygen—so I was surprised at how slowly he was moving and how hammered he looked when he pulled his mask aside to say hello. "Bruuuuuuce!" he wheezed with forced cheer, employing his trademark, fratboyish greeting. When I asked how he was doing, Fischer insisted he was feeling fine: "Just dragging a little today for some reason. No big deal." With the Hillary Step finally clear, I clipped into the strand of orange rope, swung quickly around Fischer as he slumped over his ice ax, and rappelled over the edge.

It was after 2:30 when I made it down to the South Summit. By now tendrils of mist were wrapping across the top of 27,890-foot Lhotse and lapping at Everest's summit pyramid. No longer did the weather look so <u>benign</u>. I

By the end of that long day, every minute would matter.

grabbed a fresh oxygen cylinder, jammed it onto my regulator, and hurried down into the gathering cloud.

Four hundred vertical feet above, where the summit was still washed in bright sunlight under an immaculate cobalt sky, my compadres were dallying, memorializing their arrival at the <u>apex</u> of the planet with photos and high-fives—and using up precious ticks of the clock. None of them imagined that a horrible ordeal was drawing nigh. None of them suspected that by the end of that long day, every minute would matter. . . .

At 3 P.M., within minutes of leaving the South Summit, I descended into clouds ahead of the others. Snow started to fall. In the flat, diminishing light, it became hard to tell where the mountain ended and where the sky began. It would have been very easy to blunder off the edge of the ridge and never be heard from again. The lower I went, the worse the weather became.

When I reached the Balcony again, about 4 P.M., I encountered Beck Weathers standing alone, shivering violently. Years earlier, Weathers had undergone radial keratotomy to correct his vision. A side effect, which he discovered on Everest and consequently hid from Hall, was that in the low barometric pressure at high altitude, his eyesight failed. Nearly blind when he'd left Camp Four in the middle of the night but hopeful that his vision would improve at daybreak, he stuck close to the person in front of him and kept climbing.

Upon reaching the Southeast Ridge shortly after sunrise, Weathers had confessed to Hall that he was having trouble seeing, at which point Hall declared, "Sorry, pal, you're going

---

WORDS TO OWN

benign (bi·nīn′) *adj.:* here, favorable or harmless.
apex (ā′peks′) *n.:* highest point; top.

F Elements of Literature

Sensory Imagery

❓ To which of your senses does this brief but vivid description appeal? [Sample answers: touch ("planted my ice ax," "the mountain's frozen hide"); sight ("hunkered on the ridge crest"); sound ("exchanged banal congratulations").]

G Elements of Literature

Sensory Imagery

❓ Krakauer is a master of concise character description. What sensory details in this description bring Doug Hansen's exhaustion home to you? [Possible answers: the mumble from behind his oxygen mask; the feel of his weak handshake; the sight of his plodding gait.]

H Elements of Literature

Sensory Imagery

❓ What sensory details "put you there" in the scene atop Everest? [Possible responses: visual images of the summit "washed in bright sunlight," of "an immaculate cobalt sky," and of climbers snapping photos and exchanging high-fives.]

I Elements of Literature

Suspense

❓ How does Krakauer build suspense in this part of the paragraph? [Possible responses: He uses the image of a ticking clock; he repeats the phrase "none of them"; he refers to ominous events to come.]

J Reading Skills and Strategies

Cause and Effect

❓ What do you suppose caused Weathers to keep climbing despite his near-blindness? [Possible responses: desire to reach the peak; poor judgment, caused by exhaustion and lack of oxygen; unwillingness to appear weaker than others who continued despite physical impairments (Krakauer's separated ribs, for example).]

Getting Students Involved

Cooperative Learning

Going Up! Put students in groups of four to report on other Everest expeditions. They might select expeditions by time period, by national affiliation, or by other characteristics (the first women to reach the summit, the oldest or youngest climber to reach the summit, and so on).

• Direct one group member to locate sources of information.

• Have the second member find relevant material in the sources and read it aloud to the third member, who will take notes.

• Tell groups to work together to formulate the notes into a report, to be dictated to the fourth member.

• Have each group member read a section of the report to the class.

down. I'll send one of the Sherpas[5] with you." Weathers countered that his vision was likely to improve as soon as the sun crept higher in the sky; Hall said he'd give Weathers 30 minutes to find out—after that, he'd have to wait there at 27,500 feet for Hall and the rest of the group to come back down. Hall didn't want Weathers descending alone. "I'm dead serious about this," Hall admonished his client. "Promise me that you'll sit right here until I return."

"I crossed my heart and hoped to die," Weathers recalls now, "and promised I wouldn't go anywhere." Shortly after noon, Hutchison, Taske, and Kasischke[6] passed by with their Sherpa escorts, but Weathers elected not to accompany them. "The weather was still good," he explains, "and I saw no reason to break my promise to Rob."

Ⓐ By the time I encountered Weathers, however, conditions were turning ugly. "Come down with me," I implored, "I'll get you down, no problem." He was nearly convinced, until I made the mistake of mentioning that Groom was on his way down, too. In a day of many mistakes, this would turn out to be a crucial one. "Thanks anyway," Weathers said. "I'll just wait for Mike. He's got a rope; he'll be able to

5. **Sherpas:** A Tibetan people living on the southern slopes of the Himalayas. As experienced mountain climbers, the Sherpas are hired by expeditions to haul loads and set up camps and ropes.
6. Stuart Hutchison, Dr. John Taske, and Lou Kasischke were three clients on Rob Hall's team.

short-rope[7] me." Secretly relieved, I hurried toward the South Col, 1,500 feet below.

These lower slopes proved to be the most difficult part of the descent. Six inches of powder snow blanketed outcroppings of loose shale. Climbing down them demanded unceasing concentration, an all but impossible feat in my current state. By 5:30, however, I was finally within 200 vertical feet of Camp Four, and only one obstacle stood between me and safety: a steep bulge of rock-hard ice that I'd have to descend without a rope. But the weather had deteriorated into a full-scale blizzard. Snow pellets born on 70-mph winds stung my face; any exposed skin was instantly frozen. The tents, no more than 200 horizontal yards away, were only intermittently visible through the whiteout. There was zero margin for error. Worried about making a critical blunder, I sat down to marshal my energy.

Ⓓ Suddenly, Harris[8] appeared out of the gloom and sat beside me. At this point there was no mistaking that he was in appalling shape. His cheeks were coated with an armor of frost, one

7. **short-rope:** assist a weak or injured climber by hauling him or her.
8. After writing this article, Krakauer discovered through conversations with Martin Adams (a client from Scott Fischer's team) that the person he thought was Harris was, in fact, Martin Adams.

WORDS TO OWN

crucial (krōō′shəl) *adj.:* extremely important; decisive.

Doug Hansen approaching the summit.

424 THE NONFICTION COLLECTIONS

eye was frozen shut, and his speech was slurred. He was frantic to reach the tents. After briefly discussing the best way to negotiate the ice, Harris started scooting down on his butt, facing forward. "Andy," I yelled after him, "it's crazy to try it like that!" He yelled something back, but the words were carried off by the screaming wind. A second later he lost his purchase[9] and was rocketing down on his back.

Two hundred feet below, I could make out Harris's motionless form. I was sure he'd broken at least a leg, maybe his neck. But then he stood up, waved that he was OK, and started stumbling toward camp, which was for the moment in plain sight, 150 yards beyond.

I could see three or four people shining lights outside the tents. I watched Harris walk across the flats to the edge of camp, a distance he covered in less than ten minutes. When the clouds closed in a moment later, cutting off my view, he was within 30 yards of the tents. I didn't see him again after that, but I was certain that he'd reached the security of camp, where Sherpas would be waiting with hot tea. Sitting out in the storm, with the ice bulge still standing between me and the tents, I felt a pang of envy. I was angry that my guide hadn't waited for me.

Twenty minutes later I was in camp. I fell into my tent with my crampons still on, zipped the door tight, and sprawled across the frost-covered floor. I was drained, more exhausted than I'd ever been in my life. But I was safe. Andy was safe. The others would be coming into camp soon. We'd done it. We'd climbed Mount Everest.

It would be many hours before I learned that everyone had in fact not made it back to camp—that one teammate was already dead and that 23 other men and women were caught in a desperate struggle for their lives. . . .

Meanwhile, Hall and Hansen were still on the frightfully exposed summit ridge, engaged in a grim struggle of their own. The 46-year-old Hansen, whom Hall had turned back just below this spot exactly a year ago, had been determined to bag the summit this time around.

9. **purchase:** firm hold.

"I want to get this thing done and out of my life," he'd told me a couple of days earlier. "I don't want to have to come back here."

Indeed Hansen had reached the top this time, though not until after 3 P.M., well after Hall's predetermined turnaround time. Given Hall's conservative, systematic nature, many people wonder why he didn't turn Hansen around when it became obvious that he was running late. It's not far-fetched to <u>speculate</u> that because Hall had talked Hansen into coming back to Everest this year, it would have been especially hard for him to deny Hansen the summit a second time—especially when all of Fischer's clients were still marching blithely toward the top.

"It's very difficult to turn someone around high on the mountain," cautions Guy Cotter, a New Zealand guide who summited Everest with Hall in 1992 and was guiding the peak for him in 1995 when Hansen made his first attempt. "If a client sees that the summit is close and they're dead set on getting there, they're going to laugh in your face and keep going up."

In any case, for whatever reason, Hall did not turn Hansen around. Instead, after reaching the summit at 2:10 P.M., Hall waited for more than an hour for Hansen to arrive and then headed down with him. Soon after they began their descent, just below the top, Hansen apparently ran out of oxygen and collapsed. "Pretty much the same thing happened to Doug in '95," says Ed Viesturs, an American who guided the peak for Hall that year. "He was fine during the ascent, but as soon as he started down he lost it mentally and physically. He turned into a real zombie, like he'd used everything up."

At 4:31 P.M., Hall radioed Base Camp to say that he and Hansen were above the Hillary Step and urgently needed oxygen. Two full bottles were waiting for them at the South Summit; if Hall had known this he could have retrieved the gas fairly quickly and then climbed back up to give Hansen a fresh tank. But Harris, in the throes of his

----

WORDS TO OWN

speculate (spek′yoo·lāt′) v.: think; guess.

D Elements of Literature

Sensory Imagery

? What sensory images reinforce Krakauer's statement that "Harris" (Adams) was in "appalling" condition? [Sample answers: sight of "an armor of frost" on his cheeks, one eye "frozen shut," his frantic movements ("scooting down on his butt") to reach the tents; "slurred" sound of his speech.]

E Critical Thinking

Challenging the Text

? Do you share Krakauer's certainty that Harris makes it to safety? Why or why not? [Possible responses: Yes, because Harris is only thirty yards from the tents and walking quickly, and people who can help him are visible; or no, because Krakauer last sees him thirty yards from the tents—a sudden whiteout still could disorient "Harris" and send him off into the storm.]

F Reading Skills and Strategies

Cause and Effect

? Hall and Hansen leave the summit late and are in danger from the rising storm. What does Krakauer suggest as possible causes of their predicament? [Sample answers: Hall may have felt obligated to get Hansen to the peak and descend with him; Hansen, though weakened and slow, may have refused to turn back; Hall may have decided to extend his deadline for returning when he saw members of another group still ascending.]

Taking a Second Look

Review: Distinguishing Between Fact and Opinion

Remind students that facts are verifiable; they can be proved true by using the five senses or by consulting reference sources. Opinions represent personal feelings and judgments. They can be supported, but they cannot be proved. "The expedition was a tragedy" is an opinion; "twelve people died" is a fact.

Activities

1. Direct students to reread p. 423 and to locate facts as well as opinions in Krakauer's descriptions of Namba and Hansen.
2. Have students reread p. 429 and decide which statements in Krakauer's final two paragraphs are facts and which are opinions.

A ⓐ Elements of Literature

Sensory Imagery

❓ Here Krakauer, quoting from a later interview, provides a gripping "sound track" of the disaster as it unfolds. What do the details of the accidental radio transmission convey to you? [Possible responses: the ferocity of the wind, so loud in the background that it distorted a voice near the microphone; the desperation of Hansen's and Hall's situation, conveyed by Hall's urgent shouts to "Keep moving!"]

B ⓑ Elements of Literature

Sensory Imagery

❓ What details of sound "put readers there" to receive the bleak news that Doug Hansen has died? [Sample answers: the flatness of Hall's statement that "Doug is gone"; the grim reference to ensuing silence about Hansen.]

C ⓒ Reading Skills and Strategies

Cause and Effect

❓ What might be causing Hall's uncontrollable shaking and loss of motor skills? [Possible responses: hypothermia; shock; exhaustion.] How do you think his condition might affect his chances for survival? [Possible responses: If he can't walk, his chances of making it to safety are minimal; if he can't use his legs, he can't move around to keep warm and is in danger of freezing to death.]

oxygen-starved dementia,[10] overheard the 4:31 radio call while descending the Southeast Ridge and broke in to tell Hall that all the bottles at the South Summit were empty. So Hall stayed with Hansen and tried to bring the helpless client down without oxygen, but could get him no farther than the top of the Hillary Step.

Cotter, a very close friend of both Hall and Harris, happened to be a few miles from Everest Base Camp at the time, guiding an expedition on Pumori. Overhearing the radio conversations between Hall and Base Camp, he called Hall at 5:36 and again at 5:57, urging his mate to leave Hansen and come down alone. . . . Hall, however, wouldn't consider going down without Hansen.

There was no further word from Hall until the middle of the night. At 2:46 A.M. on May 11, Cotter woke up to hear a long, broken transmission, probably unintended: Hall was wearing a remote microphone clipped to the shoulder strap of his backpack, which was occasionally keyed on by mistake. In this instance, says Cotter, "I suspect Rob didn't even know he was transmitting. I could hear someone yelling—it might have been Rob, but I couldn't be sure because the wind was so loud in the background. He was saying something like 'Keep moving! Keep going!' presumably to Doug, urging him on."

If that was indeed the case, it meant that in the wee hours of the morning Hall and Hansen were still struggling from the Hillary Step toward the South Summit, taking more than 12 hours to <u>traverse</u> a stretch of ridge typically covered by descending climbers in half an hour.

Hall's next call to Base Camp was at 4:43 A.M. He'd finally reached the South Summit but was unable to descend farther, and in a series of transmissions over the next two hours he sounded confused and irrational. "Harold[11] was with me last night," Hall insisted, when in fact Harris had reached the South Col at sunset. "But he doesn't seem to be with me now. He was very weak."

10. **dementia** (di·men′shə): mental impairment; madness.
11. **Harold:** Andy Harris's nickname.

Mackenzie[12] asked him how Hansen was doing. "Doug," Hall replied, "is gone." That was all he said, and it was the last mention he ever made of Hansen.

On May 23, when Breashears and Viesturs, of the IMAX team,[13] reached the summit, they found no sign of Hansen's body but they did find an ice ax planted about 50 feet below the Hillary Step, along a highly exposed section of ridge where the fixed ropes came to an end. It is quite possible that Hall managed to get Hansen down the ropes to this point, only to have him lose his footing and fall 7,000 feet down the sheer Southwest Face, leaving his ice ax jammed into the ridge crest where he slipped.

During the radio calls to Base Camp early on May 11, Hall revealed that something was wrong with his legs, that he was no longer able to walk and was shaking uncontrollably. This was very disturbing news to the people down below, but it was amazing that Hall was even alive after spending a night without shelter or oxygen at 28,700 feet in hurricane-force wind and minus-100-degree windchill.

At 5 A.M., Base Camp patched through a call on the satellite telephone to Jan Arnold, Hall's wife, seven months pregnant with their first child in Christchurch, New Zealand. Arnold, a respected physician, had summited Everest with Hall in 1993 and entertained no illusions about the gravity of her husband's predicament. "My heart really sank when I heard his voice," she recalls. "He was slurring his words markedly. He sounded like Major Tom[14] or something, like he was just floating away. I'd been up there; I knew what it could be like in bad weather. Rob and I had talked about the

12. **Mackenzie:** Dr. Caroline Mackenzie was Base Camp doctor for Rob Hall's team.
13. **IMAX team:** Another team of climbers, who were shooting a $5.5 million giant-screen movie about Mt. Everest. The movie was released in 1998.
14. **Major Tom:** refers to the song "Space Oddity" by David Bowie about an astronaut, Major Tom, who is lost and floating in space.

WORDS TO OWN
traverse (trə·vʉrs′) v.: cross.

Using Students' Strengths

Musical/Auditory Learners

Invite students to choose musical selections that relate to "Into Thin Air." Ask them to work in groups to present live readings of the report, accompanied by the music they have chosen. (They may present their own performances or play their selections on audiotape.) Direct them to create brief prologues explaining to listeners why they chose the music and providing background on it.

Interpersonal Learners

Some students may want to compose letters to Jon Krakauer, sharing their responses to his report, asking questions, and so on. If appropriate, show them (or have a librarian explain) how to find the address of Krakauer's publicist and how to mail or e-mail their letters.

impossibility of being rescued from the summit ridge. As he himself had put it, 'You might as well be on the moon.' "

By that time, Hall had located two full oxygen bottles, and after struggling for four hours trying to de-ice his mask, around 8:30 A.M. he finally started breathing the life-sustaining gas. Several times he announced that he was preparing to descend, only to change his mind and remain at the South Summit. The day had started out sunny and clear, but the wind remained fierce, and by late morning the upper mountain was wrapped with thick clouds. Climbers at Camp Two reported that the wind over the summit sounded like a squadron of 747s, even from 8,000 feet below. . . .

Throughout that day, Hall's friends begged him to make an effort to descend from the South Summit under his own power. At 3:20 P.M., after one such transmission from Cotter, Hall began to sound annoyed. "Look," he said, "if I thought I could manage the knots on the fixed ropes with me frostbitten hands, I would have gone down six hours ago, pal. Just send a couple of the boys up with a big thermos of something hot—then I'll be fine."

At 6:20 P.M., Hall was patched through a second time to Arnold in Christchurch. "Hi, my sweetheart," he said in a slow, painfully distorted voice. "I hope you're tucked up in a nice warm bed. How are you doing?"

"I can't tell you how much I'm thinking about you!" Arnold replied. "You sound so much better than I expected. . . . Are you warm, my darling?"

"In the context of the altitude, the setting, I'm reasonably comfortable," Hall answered, doing his best not to alarm her.

"How are your feet?"

"I haven't taken me boots off to check, but I think I may have a bit of frostbite."

Guide Rob Hall.

"I'm looking forward to making you completely better when you come home," said Arnold. "I just know you're going to be rescued. Don't feel that you're alone. I'm sending all my positive energy your way!" Before signing off, Hall told his wife, "I love you. Sleep well, my sweetheart. Please don't worry too much."

These would be the last words anyone would hear him utter. Attempts to make radio contact with Hall later that night and the next day went unanswered. Twelve days later, when Breashears and Viesturs climbed over the South Summit on their way to the top, they found Hall lying on his right side in a shallow ice-hollow, his upper body buried beneath a drift of snow.

Early on the morning of May 11, when I returned to Camp Four, Hutchison, standing in for Groom, who was unconscious in his tent, organized a team of four Sherpas to locate the bodies of our teammates Weathers and Namba. The Sherpa search party, headed by Lhakpa Chhiri, departed ahead of Hutchison, who was so exhausted and befuddled that he forgot to put his boots on and left camp in his light, smooth-soled liners. Only when Lhakpa Chhiri pointed out the blunder did Hutchison return for his boots. Following Boukreev's directions, the Sherpas had no trouble locating the two bodies at the edge of the Kangshung Face.

The first body turned out to be Namba, but Hutchison couldn't tell who it was until he knelt in the howling wind and chipped a three-inch-thick carapace of ice from her face. To his shock, he discovered that she was still breathing. Both her gloves were gone, and her bare hands appeared to be frozen solid. Her eyes were dilated. The skin on her face was the color of porcelain. "It was terrible," Hutchison recalls. "I was overwhelmed. She was very near death. I didn't know what to do."

INTO THIN AIR **427**

D Reading Skills and Strategies
Cause and Effect
❓ When Krakauer is at the summit, he de-ices his oxygen mask in less than five minutes. What could have caused the same task to take Hall four hours? [Sample answers: The blizzard must have caused a steep drop in temperature; Hall's fingers may be numb with cold or clumsy from exhaustion.]

E Elements of Literature
Suspense
❓ How does Krakauer let readers share the suspense and anxiety that those at Camp 4 felt about Hall? [Sample answer: Krakauer raises readers' hopes with details about the oxygen and about Hall's preparations to descend, then lowers hopes with details about Hall's wavering and about the storm.]

F Reading Skills and Strategies
Cause and Effect
❓ How does frostbite affect Hall's chances of survival? [Sample answer: With frostbitten hands, he can't use the ropes that are the only means of descent.]

G Elements of Literature
Sensory Imagery
❓ How do details of sound add to the poignancy of this segment? [Possible answers: Hall's conversation with his wife shows his tenderness; his "slow, painfully distorted voice" shows that he is suffering; silence—loss of radio contact—marks his death.]

H Elements of Literature
Sensory Imagery
❓ How do sensory details let readers share Hutchison's shock? [Sample answer: The clinical, precise visual images are shockingly vivid.]

Skill Link

Using Context Clues
(The following exercise will prepare students for the Language Link activity on p. T432.) Tell students that context clues may include mini-definitions, synonyms, antonyms, appositives, or general commentary. Have them use context clues to define the following underlined terms:

1. Digging through the <u>detritus</u> on the ridge, the climber found an underlying layer of firm rock. [accumulated debris]

2. The peak, in its thick <u>carapace</u> of ice, gleamed white in the sun. [shell]
3. She used <u>carabiners</u>—metal clips—to attach the rope to her climbing harness. [metal clips]
4. Was he still <u>on belay,</u> or had he already unfastened the fixed rope bearing his weight? [suspended from a fixed rope]
5. The trek leader <u>admonished</u> everyone about the danger of wasting oxygen. [warned]

He turned his attention to Weathers, who lay 20 feet away. His face was also caked with a thick armor of frost. Balls of ice the size of grapes were matted to his hair and eyelids. After cleaning the frozen detritus from his face, Hutchison discovered that he, too, was still alive: "Beck was mumbling something, I think, but I couldn't tell what he was trying to say. His right glove was missing and he had terrible frostbite. He was as close to death as a person can be and still be breathing."

Badly shaken, Hutchison went over to the Sherpas and asked Lhakpa Chhiri's advice. Lhakpa Chhiri, an Everest veteran respected by Sherpas and sahibs[15] alike for his mountain savvy, urged Hutchison to leave Weathers and Namba where they lay. Even if they survived long enough to be dragged back to Camp Four, they would certainly die before they could be carried down to Base Camp, and attempting a rescue would needlessly jeopardize the lives of the other climbers on the Col, most of whom were going to have enough trouble getting themselves down safely.

Hutchison decided that Chhiri was right. There was only one choice, however difficult: Let nature take its inevitable course with Weathers and Namba, and save the group's resources for those who could actually be helped. It was a classic act of triage.[16] When Hutchison returned to camp at 8:30 A.M. and told the rest of us of his decision, nobody doubted that it was the correct thing to do.

Later that day a rescue team headed by two of Everest's most experienced guides, Pete Athans and Todd Burleson, who were on the mountain with their own clients, arrived at Camp Four. Burleson was standing outside the tents about 4:30 P.M. when he noticed someone lurching slowly toward camp. The person's bare right hand, naked to the wind and horribly frostbitten, was outstretched in a weird, frozen salute. Whoever it was reminded Athans of a mummy in a low-budget horror film. The mummy turned out to be none other than Beck Weathers, somehow risen from the dead.

A couple of hours earlier, a light must have gone on in the reptilian core of Weathers' comatose brain, and he regained consciousness. "Initially I thought I was in a dream," he recalls. "Then I saw how badly frozen my right hand was, and that helped bring me around to reality. Finally I woke up enough to recognize that the cavalry wasn't coming so I better do something about it myself."

He was as close to death as a person can be and still be breathing.

Although Weathers was blind in his right eye and able to focus his left eye within a radius of only three or four feet, he started walking into the teeth of the wind, deducing correctly that camp lay in that direction. If he'd been wrong he would have stumbled immediately down the Kangshung Face, the edge of which was a few yards in the opposite direction. Ninety minutes later he encountered "some unnaturally smooth, bluish-looking rocks," which turned out to be the tents of Camp Four.

The next morning, May 12, Athans, Burleson, and climbers from the IMAX team short-roped Weathers down to Camp Two. On the morning of May 13, in a hazardous helicopter rescue, Weathers and Gau[17] were evacuated from the top of the icefall by Lieutenant Colonel Madan Khatri Chhetri of the Nepalese army. A month later, a team of Dallas surgeons would amputate Weather's dead right hand just below the wrist and use skin grafts to reconstruct his left hand.

After helping to load Weathers and Gau into the rescue chopper, I sat in the snow for a long while, staring at my boots, trying to get some

17. **Gau:** "Makalu" Gau Ming-Ho, leader of the Taiwanese National Expedition, another team climbing on Everest.

WORDS TO OWN

jeopardize (jep′ər·dīz′) *v.:* endanger.

15. **sahibs** (sä′ibz′): term used by Sherpas to refer to the paying members of the expeditions.
16. **triage** (trē·äzh′): assigning of priorities of medical care based on chances for survival.

Making the Connections

Connecting to the Theme: "Being There!"

"Into Thin Air" reveals a negative side of the thirst to "be there": In a quest for a peak experience, undertaken at the literal peak of the world, climbers fall victim to a chance storm and to their own imprudence. Krakauer's account of this contemporary disaster is a historian's treasure, a blend of thorough research and first-person reporting. Krakauer "puts readers there" as he and others struggle for their lives.

grip, however <u>tenuous</u>, on what had happened over the preceding 72 hours. Then, nervous as a cat, I headed down into the icefall for one last trip through the maze of decaying seracs.[18]

I'd always known, in the abstract, that climbing mountains was a dangerous pursuit. But until I climbed in the Himalayas this spring, I'd never actually seen death at close range. And there was so much of it: Including three members of an Indo-Tibetan team who died on the north side just below the summit in the same May 10 storm and an Austrian killed some days later, 11 men and women lost their lives on Everest in May 1996, a tie with 1982 for the worst single-season death toll in the peak's history. . . .[19]

18. **seracs:** pointed masses of ice.
19. It actually was the worst death toll on record. After Krakauer wrote this article, a twelfth death was discovered.

Climbing mountains will never be a safe, predictable, rule-bound enterprise. It is an activity that idealizes risk-taking; its most celebrated figures have always been those who stuck their necks out the farthest and managed to get away with it. Climbers, as a species, are simply not distinguished by an excess of common sense. And that holds especially true for Everest climbers: When presented with a chance to reach the planet's highest summit, people are surprisingly quick to abandon prudence altogether. "Eventually," warns Tom Hornbein, 33 years after his ascent of the West Ridge, "what happened on Everest this season is certain to happen again."

E

WORDS TO OWN

tenuous (ten′yo͞o·əs) *adj.:* weak, slight.

E **Critical Thinking**
Evaluating the Text
❓ Explain whether or not you think that there is a lesson to be found in Krakauer's experiences. [Possible responses: No—accidents happen and people make mistakes, and that's not news; yes—guides should not be allowed to take poorly qualified climbers up Everest.]

BROWSING IN THE FILES

About the Writer. In 1996, when Krakauer joined the Everest trek, he had already won critical and public acclaim for his *Into the Wild* (1995), an insightful report on an idealistic young loner whose dream of living deep in the Alaskan wilderness cost him his life.

A Critic's Comment. Reviewing *Into Thin Air* for *Time* magazine, John Skow observes: "[Krakauer's] fascinating and troubling account of the climb is no chronicle of triumph. . . . Krakauer, a thoughtful man and a fine writer . . . says the ratio of misery to pleasure on Everest was greater than on any other mountain he has climbed. He draws no ringing conclusions from the disaster. . . ."

MEET THE WRITER

Jon Krakauer (1954–) had mountain climbers as boyhood heroes instead of baseball players or movie stars. He made his first climb when he was only eight and after college became a "climbing bum." During the 1980s, he began writing articles on outdoor subjects.

In 1996, when *Outside* magazine asked Krakauer to write about Everest, he was an experienced climber but had never been above 17,200 feet. He later said,

❝If you don't understand Everest and appreciate its mystique, you're never going to understand this tragedy and why it's quite likely to be repeated. **❞**

After the disaster, Krakauer conducted dozens of interviews with other survivors. His article, completed five weeks after his return from Nepal, was published in September 1996. Krakauer still felt such a need to get the experience off his chest that he soon expanded the article into a book, *Into Thin Air*, which was an immediate bestseller. Despite that success, Krakauer has suffered grief and guilt over the disaster on Mt. Everest, and has said,

❝I'm never climbing it again, never. . . . I wish I hadn't gone this time. **❞**

INTO THIN AIR **429**

Assessing Learning

Check Test: Short Answers
[Sample answers are provided.]
1. How does Krakauer feel at the summit of Mt. Everest? [ill, tired, and dull]
2. Why don't those on the summit descend when the storm gathers? [The storm gathers below the summit; they are beneath blue sky, and their judgment is impaired by lack of oxygen.]
3. How strong are the winds of the blizzard? [seventy miles per hour]

4. What happens to Beck Weathers in the blizzard? [He loses his way, is later found by a search party, and is left for dead. He struggles to camp, one hand so badly frozen that it later must be amputated.]
5. How do the other climbers find out what is happening to Hall and Hansen? [Hall communicates via a small two-way radio.]

Standardized Test Preparation
For practice with standardized test format specific to this selection, see
• *Standardized Test Preparation*, p. 52
For practice in proofreading and editing, see
• *Daily Oral Grammar*, Transparency 26

MAKING MEANINGS

First Thoughts

1. Possible responses: Weathers, whose friends left him for dead; Jan Arnold, who was able to talk to her husband but not to save him; Namba, who seemed isolated and died alone; Hansen, who paid a horrible price for pushing himself too hard; Hall, who tried to help others but found that no one could help him.

Shaping Interpretations

2. Possible responses: sight of Namba's face after the ice was chipped off, because it was painful and graphic; suffocating feeling when Krakauer's oxygen gave out, because it was sudden and intense; sound of storm wind "like a squadron of 747s," because it was alarming; sight of Weathers lurching toward the tents, because it was wonderful and horrifying at the same time.

3. Sample answer: effect— death of Rob Hall; causes— unwillingness to turn Hansen back, waiting at the summit, wrong information from Harris about oxygen, surprise storm, refusal to abandon Hansen, hypoxia, frostbitten hands, exposure.

4. Possible responses: Hall is a hero because he gave his life to help Hansen; Weathers is a hero because he managed to save himself after everyone abandoned him; there are no heroes—they all took foolish risks and failed each other.

5. He concludes that mountain climbing will always be risky; that the higher the summit, the more readily some people "abandon prudence altogether" in an attempt to reach it. Some other risk-takers—deep sea explorers, race car drivers, and so on—seem equally imprudent.

Connecting with the Text

6. Possible passages: Krakauer's feelings at the summit; Hall's flat statement of Hansen's death; the decision to leave Namba and Weathers; the phone conversations between Hall and his wife. Students' opinions will vary.

Extending the Text

7. Possible responses: They should be barred because they endanger others as well as themselves; if they know the risks and still want to try, they should be allowed to, because everyone has a right to the pursuit of happiness.

T430

MAKING MEANINGS

First Thoughts

[connect]

1. Which person in this true story did you sympathize with most? Why?

Shaping Interpretations

[synthesize]

2. Which **sensory details** in Krakauer's descriptions have remained most vivid in your memory after reading the article? Why?

[analyze]

3. Choose one tragedy that happened on the mountain—for example, the death of Rob Hall or Doug Hansen or the loss of Beck Weathers's right hand. Draw a **cause-and-effect diagram** similar to the one below to show the complex causes that led to the tragedy.

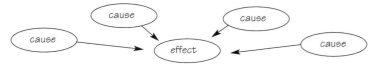

[respond]

4. Are there any real-life heroes in this story? If so, who are they, and why do you think they are heroes?

[analyze]

5. What conclusions does Krakauer draw at the end of this article? Do you think these conclusions can apply to other "risk takers" as well? Explain.

Connecting with the Text

[evaluate]

6. What passages in this narrative impressed you, puzzled you, shocked you, or caused other strong reactions? Read those passages aloud in a group. Discuss how the events described affected your previous opinion of mountain climbing. (Check your Quickwrite notes.)

Extending the Text

[evaluate]

7. Should inexperienced climbers be allowed to pay large sums of money to climb Mt. Everest, or should they be barred? Explain your opinion.

Challenging the Text

[evaluate]

8. Krakauer begins his article at the point when he reaches the top of Everest; then he reveals the nature of the tragedy that occurred. Does this beginning in the middle of the story spoil the element of surprise or **suspense**? Why or why not?

[evaluate]

9. This selection is filled with technical mountaineering details as well as specifics about time, place, and elevation. Did the difficulty of these details outweigh their usefulness for you, or did they enhance the piece? Explain.

Writer's Workshop

MAIN OBJECTIVE
Write a research paper

PROCESS OBJECTIVES

1. Use appropriate prewriting techniques to identify and develop a topic
2. Create a first draft
3. Use Evaluation Criteria as a basis for determining revision strategies
4. Revise the first draft, incorporating suggestions generated by self- or peer evaluation
5. Proofread and correct errors
6. Create a final draft
7. Choose an appropriate method of publication
8. Reflect on progress as a writer

Planning

- **Block Schedule**
  Block Scheduling Lesson Plans with Pacing Guide.

- **One-Stop Planner**
  CD-ROM with Test Generator

Introducing the Writer's Workshop

To help students identify possible topics for research, you may wish to bring a variety of newspapers and magazines to class. Have students leaf through these sources quickly, jotting down the titles of the publications and articles that attracted their attention. Discuss their reactions to various magazines and articles, asking students to generalize about what topics or features attracted their attention:

- Which magazines or newspaper did you want to pick up first? Why?
- Did you pay special attention to any articles? Why?
- Were there magazines or topics you skipped right over? Why?
- Did the same type of article in different magazines catch your interest? If so, what was the topic?

Technology HELP

See Writer's Workshop 2 CD-ROM. *Assignment: Informative Report.*

ASSIGNMENT

Write a research paper, using information gathered from several sources.

AIM

To inform.

AUDIENCE

Your teacher and classmates.

Broad topic: whales

↓

Narrower topic: dangers to whales

↓

Still narrower topic: recent theories about whale strandings

 go.hrw.com
LEO Research Paper

EXPOSITORY WRITING

RESEARCH PAPER

You'll be asked to write **research papers** throughout your school years—and possibly beyond. Researching is a two-part job. First you search for the most accurate, reliable information available, just as a scientist does. Then, like a reporter, you assemble those facts into an informative, accurate, and well-documented report.

Prewriting

1. Explore Topic Ideas

WORK IN PROGRESS

Review the entries in your Writer's Notebook to find a topic that interests you and that you think will interest your readers. If you can't find one there, try skimming magazines and newspapers or browsing the Internet. Cross out any topics on your list that seem too broad (the history of mountain climbing), too complex (how an ocean liner is built), or too hard to find information about. Keep in mind that you'll need to consult several sources.

2. Track Down Reliable Sources

As you gather information, you'll probably use both **secondary sources** (such as magazine and encyclopedia articles, textbooks, biographies, history books, and book reviews) and **primary sources** (such as interviews, journals, speeches, and literary works). Here's where to look:

- **Check out the library.** You'll find a variety of **print** and **non-print sources**—as well as librarians who can help you.

- **Log on.** Explore the Internet using one of the many available **search engines.** Each search engine works differently and gives varied results. Learn to use the search engines on your computer. (For more help with online searches, see Using the Internet in the Communications Handbook.) Through the Internet you can access databases, government documents, periodicals, professional Web sites, scholarly projects, and newsgroups. You can also **e-mail** experts and organizations to ask questions or request information.

 Resources: Print and Media

Writing and Language
- *Portfolio Management System*
  - Prewriting, p. 144
  - Peer Editing, p. 145
  - Assessment Rubric, p. 146

- *Workshop Resources*
  - Revision Strategy Teaching Notes, p. 27
  - Revision Strategy Transparencies 14, 15
- *Writer's Workshop 2 CD-ROM*
  - Informative Report

CHOICES: Building Your Portfolio

Writer's Notebook

1. Collecting Ideas for a Research Paper

Taking notes. In the midst of his ordeal while he was fighting to save his life, Krakauer continued to take notes in his spiral notebooks. (It was too cold for a tape recorder.) As you collect information on the topic you've chosen for your research paper (for the Writer's Workshop on page 448), take notes in a notebook or on cards. Be sure to record direct quotations exactly and to cite the sources of all facts, statistics, quotes, and paraphrases.

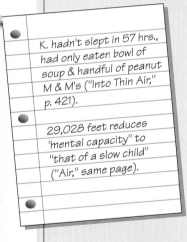

K. hadn't slept in 57 hrs., had only eaten bowl of soup & handful of peanut M & M's ("Into Thin Air," p. 421).

29,028 feet reduces "mental capacity" to "that of a slow child" ("Air," same page).

Debate

2. To Climb or Not?

With a small group of classmates, debate one of these questions: (a) *Is mountain climbing a foolhardy risk of life and limb, or a worthwhile adventure?* (b) *Should people pursuing dangerous sports or hobbies have to pass a test or be licensed?* Base your views on evidence as well as on personal feelings. If you focus on mountain climbing, you might want to read more of the book *Into Thin Air*.

Research/ Oral Presentation

3. Inquiring Minds

Had you ever heard of the Seven Summits before? or hypoxia? What do you know about Nepal and Tibet? What gear do you need to go mountain climbing? These are only a few of the many topics suggested by Krakauer's article that curious minds might want to investigate. Pick a topic that interests you and one or two partners. Draw up a list of research questions, and begin your investigation. Check the library, the Internet and databases, and experts, if you can. Report your findings to the class in an **oral presentation** using visuals or props or even demonstrations.

Descriptive Essay

4. What "Pulls" You?

About his decision to climb Everest, Krakauer said, "I'd had this secret desire to climb Everest that never left me from the time I was nine." Do you have something that "pulls" you, that you are passionate about? Maybe it's a sport, or music, or a hobby. In a brief essay, describe your "passion" in a way that communicates your love for your topic. Elaborate with specific **sensory details** that paint a clear "you are there" picture for readers.

Creative Writing/Media

5. Camera! Action!

Krakauer's story would make a good movie and, indeed, a film of his book was made for television. Pick a section from this selection, and work with a small group to write a movie script for the scene. Pick up dialogue that's there. You might even add some dialogue (be sure it sounds realistic) if you feel the scene needs expansion. Include camera and stage directions and notes about the setting (visual and sound effects) and characters (including costumes). Note: You'll find an example of a movie script on page 683.

Challenging the Text

8. Possible responses: It doesn't spoil the suspense because he doesn't specify who died or how, so readers are eager to find out; it spoils the suspense because it lets readers know from the beginning how the expedition will end.
9. Possible responses: The details help to make it real; the details interfere with the flow; the details slow a first reading but become useful when one rereads.

CHOICES: Building Your Portfolio

1. **Writer's Notebook** Encourage students to use abbreviations and other techniques to streamline their notetaking, as shown on p. 431.
2. **Debate** Remind students to prepare their cases carefully, providing facts and statistics to back up their reasons.
3. **Research/Oral Presentation** Invite students to involve listeners in their presentations. They might bring in cords and teach classmates to tie climbers' knots; challenge classmates to match photos with facts about the Seven Summits; or present details about Nepal and Tibet, then test classmates' recall in a game of Himalaya Jeopardy.
4. **Descriptive Essay** A sensory detail catalogue is one device for opening a descriptive essay. Without stating the topic, the writer describes sights, sounds, scents, tastes, and/or tactile impressions associated with it, piquing readers' interest. The writer then reveals the topic in the body of the essay.
5. **Creative Writing/Media** After students have chosen their scenes, suggest that they take roles and act out improvised versions. This will give them an idea of what stage directions are needed and what dialogue will sound realistic.

Assessing Learning

Self-Evaluation

Give students a scale of 1 (never) to 5 (always) to rate their use of reading skills and strategies with "Into Thin Air."

1. I made predictions and checked them.
2. I traced cause-and-effect text structures.
3. I constructed mental images based on sensory details in the text.
4. I asked questions about content.
5. I used context clues.

Try It Out
Possible Answers

1. *troposphere* (p. 421)— upper atmosphere; *gangrenous* (p. 422)— infected and decaying; *cwm* (p. 422)— mountain valley; *radial keratotomy* (p. 423)— vision surgery; *col* (p. 424)— gap in a mountain ridge
2. Sailing terms: *leeward, windward, tack, come about, jibe, capsize, boom, stays, sheets, heel.*
   Sentence: We accidentally jibed, and the awkward turn brought the wind gusting from behind to play havoc with the sail.

VOCABULARY

(See p. T1019 for a more in-depth treatment of analogies.)

Answers

1. apex
2. innocuous
3. jeopardize
4. crucial
5. speculate
6. benign
7. notorious
8. deteriorate
9. traverse
10. tenuous

Resources

Language
- *Grammar and Language Links* Worksheet, p. 47

Vocabulary
- *Words to Own*, Worksheet, p. 25

LANGUAGE LINK   MINI-LESSON

Technical Vocabulary—Widgets, Whatsits, Thingamajigs

If you are a football fan, you know the meaning of *touchdown*, *off-tackle*, and *scrimmage*. Before reading "Into Thin Air," did you know the meaning of *rappel* and *short-rope*?

> "As I clipped into a fixed rope and prepared to rappel over the lip, . . ." (page 422)

> "He's got a rope; he'll be able to short-rope me." (page 424)

Almost every kind of work or play has its own special **technical vocabulary**, or **jargon**. When writers cover a technical subject for a general audience, they must use technical terms in a way that readers will understand. Usually that means including **context clues** that will help the reader guess the meaning. Writers may also provide footnotes. (In fact, check the context clues and footnotes for *rappel* and *short-rope*. Could you explain the words to a friend?)

Try It Out

1. Find at least three technical terms in "Into Thin Air" that are not defined in footnotes. (They may be mountain climbing, scientific, or medical terms.) With a partner, use context clues to guess the meaning of each term. Check your guesses in a dictionary.

2. Write a list of technical terms for any field that you know well. Choose the most obscure term, and write a sentence using context clues that would enable a reader to understand the term.

➤ As you write your research paper (page 448), make sure that you include context clues for any technical terms you use.

VOCABULARY   HOW TO OWN A WORD

WORD BANK

deteriorate
innocuous
notorious
benign
apex
crucial
speculate
traverse
jeopardize
tenuous

Analogies

In an **analogy** the words in one pair relate to each other in the same way as the words in a second pair. Fill in each blank below with the word from the Word Bank that best completes the analogy. (Two words on the list are synonyms; they may be used interchangeably.) Analogies are sometimes written like this: *base: bottom:: _____ : top*

1. *Base* is to *bottom* as _____ is to *top*.
2. *Safe* is to *dangerous* as _____ is to *harmful*.
3. *Mislead* is to *deceive* as _____ is to *endanger*.
4. *Trivial* is to *minor* as _____ is to *important*.
5. *Try* is to *attempt* as _____ is to *guess*.
6. *Minor* is to *major* as _____ is to *malignant*.
7. *Famous* is to *star* as _____ is to *criminal*.
8. *Weaken* is to *strengthen* as _____ is to *improve*.
9. *Climb* is to *stairs* as _____ is to *bridge*.
10. *Strong* is to *powerful* as _____ is to *weak*.

432 THE NONFICTION COLLECTIONS

Language Link Quick Check

Use context clues to guess the meaning of the underlined word in each sentence.

1. <u>Crampons</u> attached to Krakauer's boots gave him traction on the ice. [cleats]
2. The climber secured his rope to a <u>piton</u> he had hammered into the rock. [a metal peg]
3. When people are caught in a blizzard, <u>hypothermia</u> can send them drifting into a deadly sleep. [dangerously low body temperature]
4. Crumbling plates of <u>shale</u> form some of the most treacherous rock areas on Everest. [a flat, brittle kind of rock]
5. In the <u>whiteout</u> caused by the blizzard, Krakauer could see only a few inches ahead. [loss of visibility due to blowing snow]

Before You Read

A PRESENTATION OF WHALES

Make the Connection

To the Rescue!

Suppose you are walking on a beach on a gray, windy day. You climb over a rocky ledge, and suddenly you are part of the scene in the photo below. How would you react?

Some people rise to such an occasion; some shrink from it; some just keep shooting video-tape. Being on the scene of a disaster can bring out unex-pected qualities in people. This report about rescuing whales is a sad story without a clear or simple moral. What would you have done if you'd been there?

Reading Skills and Strategies

Dialogue with the Text

Use a **KWL chart** to organize information about this report. KWL means "what I *know*, what I *want to know*, what I've *learned*." In the K (for *know*) column, write what you know about whales, especially beached whales. In the W column, write a few things you'd like to learn about whales. You'll fill in the L column after you read the report.

K	W	L

Elements of Literature

Ordering Information

You don't usually skip through a text. You start at the beginning and (unless you jump ahead—risking the loss of important in-formation) follow the sequence in which the writer has chosen to present information. In this report, Barry Lopez uses the fa-miliar order of narrative writing: **chronological order,** the se-quence in which events occur. "A Presentation of Whales" starts on a Saturday and ends the following Wednesday. See if you can find places where Lopez interrupts the chronological order, and try to figure out why he does so.

Chronological order is the order in which events occur in time.

Why did they come ashore?

(HRW) go.hrw.com
LEO 10-6

OBJECTIVES

1. Read and interpret the report
2. Identify chronological order and analyze its use
3. Use a KWL chart to organize information about a text
4. Express understanding through writing or speaking/listening
5. Identify topic sentences and use them in writing
6. Understand and use new words
7. Identify and use synonyms and antonyms

SKILLS

Literary
• Read and interpret the report
• Identify chronological order and analyze its use

Reading
• Use a KWL chart to organize information about a text

Writing
• Outline information for a research paper
• Write an extended analogy to explain a field, idea, or activity

Speaking/Listening
• Hold a panel discussion

Grammar/Language
• Identify topic sentences and use them in writing paragraphs

Vocabulary
• Identify and use synonyms and antonyms

Planning

• **Traditional Schedule**
  Lesson Plans Including Strategies for English-Language Learners

• **One-Stop Planner**
  CD-ROM with Test Generator

Preteaching Vocabulary

Words to Own

Have students, in pairs, read the definitions of the Words to Own at the bottom of the selection pages. To ensure familiarity with the words, have students explain their answers to the following:

1. How might a <u>callous</u> judge handle a <u>belliger-ent</u> criminal?
2. When in America's history has <u>elitism</u> <u>pre-cluded</u> justice?
3. How might Darth Vader treat a <u>numinous</u> being that appeared <u>precipitately</u>?
4. How might a chef's <u>ineptitude</u> lead to the creation of an <u>acrid</u>-tasting dessert?
5. What consequences would you expect if a <u>precipitous</u> rise in temperature <u>exacerbated</u> a drought?

Summary ▪▪

Lopez reports on—and invites readers to meditate on—the 1979 stranding of forty-one sperm whales on an Oregon beach. He proceeds chronologically through their slow death to the burning of their carcasses, breaking into the narrative once with facts and mysteries about sperm whales. The beach scene becomes a confused morality play, with police, press, environmentalists, scientists, veterinarians, and a huge crowd of onlookers all in conflict over the event's character: spiritual, tragic, scientifically momentous, or entertaining. Lopez expresses frustration at the circus, empathy for the concerned but inept experts, and awe for the whales.

Ⓐ Elements of Literature

Ordering Information

❷ What data does Lopez include to signal at the outset that his report will follow chronological order? [Sample answer: the date, June 16, 1979, and the fact that it is evening.]

A Presentation of Whales

Barry Lopez

A On that section of the central Oregon coast on the evening of June 16, 1979, gentle winds were blowing onshore from the southwest. It was fifty-eight degrees. Under partly cloudy skies the sea was running with four-foot swells at eight-second intervals. Moderately rough. State police cadets Jim Clark and Steve Bennett stood at the precipitous edge of a foredune a few miles south of the town of Florence, peering skeptically into the dimness over a flat, gently sloping beach. Near the water's edge they could make out a line of dark shapes, and what they had taken for a practical joke, the

WORDS TO OWN
precipitous (prē·sip′ə·təs) *adj.*: steep.

Resources: Print and Media

Reading
- *Graphic Organizers for Active Reading*, p. 27
- *Words to Own*, p. 26
- *Audio CD Library*
  Disc 14, Track 2

Elements of Literature
- *Literary Elements*
  Transparency 11
  Worksheet, p. 34

Writing and Language
- *Daily Oral Grammar*
  Transparency 27
- *Grammar and Language Links*
  Worksheet, p. 49
- *Language Workshop CD-ROM*

Viewing and Representing
- *Viewing and Representing*
  Fine Art Transparency 9
  Fine Art Worksheet, p. 36

Assessment
- *Formal Assessment*, p. 72
- *Portfolio Management System*, p. 143
- *Standardized Test Preparation*, p. 54
- *Test Generator (One-Stop Planner CD-ROM)*

Internet
- go.hrw.com (keyword: LE0 10-6)

Near the water's edge they could make out a line of dark shapes . . .

A PRESENTATION OF WHALES 435

Background

Before writing this essay, originally published in *Harper's* magazine, Barry Lopez not only witnessed the event but also did extensive research on "cetacean behavior, sperm whale physiology, and the history of such strandings." He waited months for scientists' studies of the whales to be completed so that he could include their results in his article.

Resources

Viewing and Representing
Fine Art Transparencies
You might use Adam Willaerts's *Sperm Whale Stranded on the North Sea Coast* as a discussion starter after reading. See the *Viewing and Representing Transparencies and Worksheets:*
- Transparency 9
- Worksheet, p. 36

Listening
Audio CD Library
A recording of this article is included in the *Audio CD Library:*
- Disc 14, Track 2

Elements of Literature
Essays and History
For additional instruction on essays and history, see *Literary Elements:*
- Transparency 11
- Worksheet, p. 34

Reaching All Students

Struggling Readers
As students work through the selection, have them note in their journals anything that creates a strong mental image or otherwise moves them. After they finish the selection, invite volunteers to read their notes aloud (or to have a partner read them aloud). Do not analyze the material shared; the purpose is to gather images that provide an overall impression of the selection.

English Language Learners
Show illustrations so that students can identify and compare sizes of killer whales (which they may have seen in films or at marine parks), gray whales, sperm whales, and giant squid. Ask students to share what they know about these marine creatures. For other strategies for engaging English language learners with the literature, see
- *Lesson Plans Including Strategies for English-Language Learners*

Advanced Learners
Have students approach the selection from a historical perspective, doing a little outside research if necessary. Encourage them to explore what has been learned about whales since 1979 and how rescue efforts today might differ. Challenge them to consider whether today's onlookers might behave differently from the onlookers Lopez describes.

exaggeration a few moments before of a man and a woman in a brown Dodge van with a broken headlight, now sank in for the truth.

Clark made a hasty, inaccurate count and plunged with Bennett down the back of the dune to their four-wheel-drive. Minutes before, they had heard the voice of Corporal Terry Crawford over the radio; they knew he was patrolling in Florence. Rather than call him, they drove the six miles into town and parked across the street from where he was issuing a citation to someone for excessive noise. When Crawford had finished, Clark went over and told him what they had seen. Crawford drove straight to the Florence State Police office and phoned his superiors in Newport, forty-eight miles up the coast. At that point the news went out over police radios: thirty-six large whales, stranded and apparently still alive, were on the beach a mile south of the mouth of the Siuslaw River.

There were, in fact, forty-one whales—twenty-eight females and thirteen males, at least one of them dying or already dead. There had never been a stranding quite like it. It was first assumed that they were gray whales, common along the coast, but they were sperm whales: *Physeter catodon.* Deep-ocean dwellers. They ranged in age from ten to fifty-six and in length from thirty to thirty-eight feet. They were apparently headed north when they beached around 7:30 P.M. on an ebbing high tide.

The information shot inland by phone, crossing the Coast Range to radio and television stations in the more populous interior of Oregon, in a highly charged form: giant whales stranded on a public beach accessible by paved road on a Saturday night, still alive. Radio announcers urged listeners to head for the coast to "save the whales." In Eugene and Portland, Greenpeace volunteers, already alerted by the police, were busy throwing sheets and blankets into their cars. They would soak them in the ocean, to cool the whales.

The news moved as quickly through private homes and taverns on the central Oregon coast, passed by people monitoring the police bands. In addition to phoning Greenpeace—an international organization with a special interest in protecting marine mammals—the police contacted the Oregon State University Marine Science Center in South Beach near Newport, and the Oregon Institute of Marine Biology in Charleston, fifty-eight miles south of Florence. Bruce Mate, a marine mammalogist at the OSU Center, phoned members of the Northwest Regional [Stranding] Alert Network and people in Washington, D.C.

By midnight, the curious and the awed were crowded on the beach, cutting the night with flashlights. Drunks, ignoring the whales' sudden thrashing, were trying to walk up and down on their backs. A collie barked incessantly; flash cubes burst at the huge, dark forms. Two men inquired about reserving some of the teeth, for scrimshaw.[1] A federal agent asked police to move people back, and the first mention of disease was in the air. Scientists arrived with specimen bags and rubber gloves and fishing knives. Greenpeace members, one dressed in a bright orange flight suit, came with a large banner. A man burdened with a television camera labored over the foredune after them. They wished to tie a rope to one whale's flukes,[2] to drag it back into the ocean. The police began to congregate with the scientists, looking for a rationale to control the incident.

In the intensifying confusion, as troopers motioned onlookers back (to "restrain the common herd of unqualified mankind," wrote one man later in an angry letter-to-the-editor), the thinking was that, somehow, the whales might be saved. Neal Langbehn, a federal protection officer with the National Marine Fisheries Service, denied permission to one scientist to begin removing teeth and taking blood samples. In his report later he would write: "It was my feeling that the whales should be given their best chance to survive."

This hope was soon deemed futile, as it had appeared to most of the scientists from the beginning—the animals were hemorrhaging[3] under the crushing weight of their own flesh

---

1. **scrimshaw:** intricate decoration and carving, usually done on whales' teeth and bones.
2. **flukes:** lobes of a whale's tail.
3. **hemorrhaging** (hem′ər·ij·iŋ′): bleeding heavily.

Using Students' Strengths

Logical/Mathematical Learners

Many of the points that Lopez makes could be classified under the heading of "What Went Wrong?" Invite students to keep a list of these failings by authorities, by scientists, and by the public. Then, in follow-up discussion, ask students to sum up what went wrong and what could have been done differently.

Intrapersonal Learners

After students finish reading, invite them to respond to the great unanswered question in the selection: Why did the whales come ashore? Writing as one of the beached whales, or as one of the sperm whales offshore, students should attempt an answer in prose or poetry.

and were beginning to suffer irreversible damage from heat exhaustion. The scientific task became one of securing as much data as possible.

As dawn bloomed along the eastern sky, people who had driven recreational vehicles illegally over the dunes and onto the beach were issued citations and turned back. Troopers continued to warn people over bullhorns to please stand away from the whales. The Oregon Parks Department, whose responsibility the beach was, wanted no part of the growing confusion. The U.S. Forest Service, with jurisdiction over land in the Oregon Dunes National Recreation Area down to the foredune, was willing to help, but among all the agencies there was concern over limited budgets; there were questions, gently essayed,[4] about the conflict of state and federal enforcement powers over the body parts of an endangered species. A <u>belligerent</u> few in the crowd shouted objections as the first syringes appeared, and yelled to scientists to produce permits that allowed them to interfere in the death of an endangered species.

Amid this chaos, the whales, sealed in their slick black neoprene[5] skins, mewed and clicked. They slammed glistening flukes on the beach, jarring the muscles of human thighs like Jell-O at a distance of a hundred yards. They rolled their dark, purple-brown eyes at the scene and blinked.

They lay on the western shore of North America like forty-one derailed boxcars at dawn on a Sunday morning, and in the days that followed, the worst and the best of human behavior were shown among them.

The sperm whale, for many, is the most awesome creature of the open seas. Imagine a forty-five-year-old male fifty feet long, a slim, shiny black animal with a white jaw and marbled belly cutting the surface of green ocean water at twenty knots. Its flat forehead protects a sealed chamber of exceedingly fine oil; sunlight sparkles in rivulets running off folds in its corrugated back. At fifty tons it is the largest carni-

4. **essayed** (e·sād′): tried out.
5. **neoprene** (nē′ō·prēn′): rubberlike. *Neoprene* is generally used to mean "a kind of synthetic rubber."

vore on earth. Its massive head, a third of its body length, is scarred with the beak, sucker, and claw marks of giant squid, snatched out of subterranean canyons a mile below, in a region without light, and brought writhing to the surface. Imagine a four-hundred-pound heart the size of a chest of drawers driving five gallons of blood at a stroke through its aorta: a meal of forty salmon moving slowly down twelve hundred feet of intestine; the blinding, <u>acrid</u> fragrance of a two-hundred-pound wad of gray ambergris[6] lodged somewhere along the way; producing sounds more shrill than we can hear—like children shouting on a distant playground—and able to sort a cacophony of noise: electric crackling of shrimp, groaning of undersea quakes, roar of upwellings, whining of porpoise, hum of oceanic cables. With skin as sensitive as the inside of your wrist.

What makes them awesome is not so much these things, which are discoverable, but the mysteries that shroud them. They live at a remarkable distance from us and we have no *Pioneer II* to penetrate their world. Virtually all we know of sperm whales we have learned on the slaughter decks of oceangoing whalers and on the ways at shore stations. We do not even know how many there are; in December 1978, the Scientific Committee of the International Whaling Commission said it could not set a quota for a worldwide sperm whale kill—so little was known that any number written down would be ridiculous.[7]

6. **ambergris** (am′bər·grēs′): substance from the intestines of sperm whales, used in some perfumes to make the scent last.
7. A quota of 5,000 was nevertheless set. In June 1979, within days of the Florence stranding but apparently unrelated to it, the IWC dropped the 1980 world sperm whale quota to 2,203 and set aside the Indian Ocean as a sanctuary. (By 1987 the quota was 0, though special exemptions permit some 200 sperm whales per year still to be taken worldwide.)—Author's note.

WORDS TO OWN

belligerent (bə·lij′ər·ənt) *adj.:* quarrelsome; ready to fight.

acrid (ak′rid) *adj.:* sharp or bitter smelling. *Acrid* is also used to describe tastes.

A PRESENTATION OF WHALES **437**

E Reading Skills and Strategies
Dialogue with the Text
? Lopez's prose brings readers in close enough to see, hear, and feel the whales. Which details surprise you? How do you feel toward the whales as you read this paragraph? [Possible responses: Surprises: They blink; their eyes are purple-brown; these huge creatures mew; they don't lie limp but move and communicate. Feelings: empathy; protectiveness; awe; a sense of relatedness.]

F Elements of Literature
Analogy
? Here Lopez extends what might have begun as a simile (the whales were as big as boxcars) to create an analogy. What might this analogy suggest about the whales? [Possible responses: that they carry something valuable; that they were on a journey but met with an accident; that their stranding is as traumatic as a train crash.]

G Elements of Literature
Ordering Information
? Lopez interrupts his chronological narrative to insert background information about sperm whales. What reasons might he have for placing it here, rather than at the beginning of the article? [Possible responses: Readers may find it more significant now that they've "met" the whales; action at the beginning of an essay is more of an audience grabber than background information is.]

Taking a Second Look

Chronological Order

Remind students that chronological order is the order in which events unfold in time. Writers can show chronological order by using tense shifts or by using transitional words and phrases, such as *first, next, in the beginning,* and *later.* Sometimes context shows chronological order; the things that happen fall into the same sequence that they would in real life.

Activities

1. Have students reread the second-to-last paragraph on p. 436 and decide if it is chronological. [yes]
2. Ask students to explain how the first paragraph on p. 437 demonstrates chronological order. [It begins with sunrise and moves forward in time; the phrases *as dawn bloomed* and *as the first syringes appeared* show the order of events.]

T437

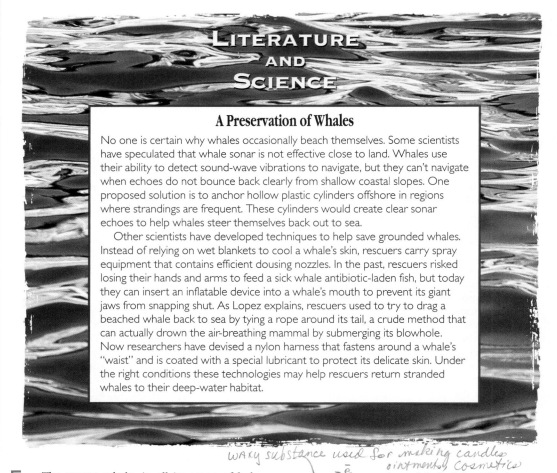

A Preservation of Whales

No one is certain why whales occasionally beach themselves. Some scientists have speculated that whale sonar is not effective close to land. Whales use their ability to detect sound-wave vibrations to navigate, but they can't navigate when echoes do not bounce back clearly from shallow coastal slopes. One proposed solution is to anchor hollow plastic cylinders offshore in regions where strandings are frequent. These cylinders would create clear sonar echoes to help whales steer themselves back out to sea.

Other scientists have developed techniques to help save grounded whales. Instead of relying on wet blankets to cool a whale's skin, rescuers carry spray equipment that contains efficient dousing nozzles. In the past, rescuers risked losing their hands and arms to feed a sick whale antibiotic-laden fish, but today they can insert an inflatable device into a whale's mouth to prevent its giant jaws from snapping shut. As Lopez explains, rescuers used to try to drag a beached whale back to sea by tying a rope around its tail, a crude method that can actually drown the air-breathing mammal by submerging its blowhole. Now researchers have devised a nylon harness that fastens around a whale's "waist" and is coated with a special lubricant to protect its delicate skin. Under the right conditions these technologies may help rescuers return stranded whales to their deep-water habitat.

waxy substance used for making candles ointments, cosmetics

Ⓐ The sperm whale, in all its range of behaviors—from the enraged white bull called Mocha Dick that stove[8] whaling ships off the coast of Peru in 1810, to a nameless female giving birth to a fourteen-foot, one-ton calf in equatorial waters in the Pacific—remains distant. The general mystery is enhanced by specific mysteries: The sperm whale's brain is larger than the brain of any other creature that ever lived. Beyond the storage of incomprehensible amounts of information, we do not know what purpose such size serves. And we do not know what to make of its most distinctive anatomical feature, the spermaceti organ. An article in *Scientific American,* published several months before the stranding, suggests that the whale can control the density of its spermaceti oil, thereby altering its specific gravity[9] to assist it in diving. It is argued also that the huge organ, located in the head, serves as a means of generating and focusing sound, but there is not yet any agreement on these speculations.

Of the many sperm whale strandings in recorded history, only three have been larger than the one in Oregon. The most recent was of

8. **stove:** punctured or smashed; broke up.

9. **specific gravity:** ratio of the weight of one object (in this case, a whale) to the weight of something else that takes up the same amount of space (in this case, water).

Crossing the Curriculum

Science

Invite teams of students to present oral reports about sperm whales. Among the questions they might consider are the following:
- Where can sperm whales be found?
- Do they migrate?
- Are sperm whales endangered?
- What might cause sperm whales to beach themselves?

Art

Photographs and paintings (including murals) of whales are very popular. Encourage students to find out who some of the artists in this field are and why those artists have devoted themselves to this special subject. Alternatively, have interested students plan and create a mural of whales. If possible, arrange to display the mural where other classes can enjoy it.

Social Studies

The only reason put forth for the stranding is that the whales "'were tired of running' from commercial whalers." Have interested students bring this legal aspect of the subject up to date by finding out how the International Whaling Commission operates today—how it sets limits, enforces its laws, and punishes illegal hunting. Students might design a poster to illustrate their findings.

fifty-six on the eastern Baja coast near Playa San Rafael on January 6, 1979. But the Florence stranding is perhaps the most remarkable. Trained scientists arrived almost immediately; the site was easily accessible, with even an airstrip close by. It was within an hour's drive of two major West Coast marine-science centers. And the stranding seemed to be of a whole social unit. That the animals were still alive meant live blood specimens could be taken. And by an uncanny coincidence, a convention of the American Society of Mammalogists was scheduled to convene June 18 at Oregon State University in Corvallis, less than a two-hour drive away. Marine experts from all over the country would be there. (As it turned out, some of them would not bother to come over; others would secure access to the beach only to take photographs; still others would show up in sports clothes—all they had—and plunge into the gore that by the afternoon of June 18 littered the beach.)

The state police calls to Greenpeace on the night of June 16 were attempts to reach informed people to direct a rescue. Michael Piper of Greenpeace, in Eugene, was the first to arrive with a small group at about 1:30 A.M., just after a low tide at 12:59 A.M.

"I ran right out of my shoes," Piper says. The thought that they would still be alive—clicking and murmuring, their eyes tracking human movement, lifting their flukes, whooshing warm air from their blowholes—had not penetrated. But as he ran into the surf to fill a bucket to splash water over their heads, the proportions of the stranding and the impending tragedy overwhelmed him.

"I knew, almost from the beginning, that we were not going to get them out of there, and that even if we did, their chances of survival were a million to one," Piper said.

Just before dawn, a second contingent of Greenpeace volunteers arrived from Portland. A Canadian, Michael Bailey, took charge and announced there was a chance with the incoming tide that one of the smaller animals could be floated off the beach and towed to sea (weights ranged from an estimated three and a half to

twenty-five tons). Bruce Mate, who would become both scientific and press coordinator on the beach (the latter to his regret), phoned the Port of Coos Bay to see if an oceangoing tug or fishing vessel would be available to anchor offshore and help—Bailey's crew would ferry lines through the surf with a Zodiac boat. No one in Coos Bay was interested. A commercial helicopter service with a Skycrane capable of lifting nine tons also begged off. A call to the Coast Guard produced a helicopter, but people there pronounced any attempt to sky-tow a whale too dangerous.

The refusal of help combined with the apparent futility of the effort precipitated a genuinely compassionate gesture: Bailey strode resolutely into the freezing water and, with twenty-five or thirty others, amid flailing flukes, got a rope around the tail of an animal that weighed perhaps three or four tons. The waves knocked them down and the whale yanked them over, but they came up sputtering, to pull again. With the buoyancy provided by the incoming tide they moved the animal about thirty feet. The effort was heroic and ludicrous. As the rope began to cut into the whale's flesh, as television cameramen and press photographers crowded in, Michael Piper gave up his place on the rope in frustration and waded ashore. Later he would remark that, for some, the whale was only the means to a political end—a dramatization of the plight of whales as a species. The distinction between the suffering individual, its internal organs hemorrhaging, its flukes sliced by the rope, and the larger issue, to save the species, confounded Piper.

A photograph of the Greenpeace volunteers pulling the whale showed up nationally in newspapers the next day. A week later, a marine mammalogist wondered if any more damaging picture could have been circulated. It would convince people something could have been done, when in fact, he said, the whales were doomed as soon as they came ashore.

For many, transfixed on the beach by their own helplessness, the value of the gesture transcended the fact.

By midmorning Piper was so disturbed, so

A PRESENTATION OF WHALES 439

B Elements of Literature
Ordering Information
❓ Lopez shifts smoothly from exposition back to his chronological narrative. What words help to signal the shift? [Sample answers: "But the Florence stranding . . ." "almost immediately."]

C Reading Skills and Strategies
Dialogue with the Text
❓ Have any of your questions about whales been answered so far? What might a reader learn about sperm whales from information in this segment? [Possible responses: They are unlikely to survive stranding; they can weigh from three and a half to twenty-five tons.]

D Reading Skills and Strategies
Making Inferences
❓ How would you describe Lopez's attitudes toward those who try to help and those who refuse to help? Which words suggest his attitudes? [Sample answer: Lopez admires those who try to help, calling them "genuinely compassionate." He finds those who refuse to help to be shallow or callous, as revealed in the lines "No one in Coos Bay was interested" and "A commercial helicopter . . . also begged off."]

Getting Students Involved

Cooperative Learning
Whale Gazette. Challenge the class to create a newspaper based on "A Presentation of Whales." Assign the following tasks and group sizes:
- lead story—three or four students
- features (interviews, background information, and so on)—two students each
- editorial—two or three students
- advertisements (related to the selection)—two students each

- art/design/layout—four or five students
Encourage students to supplement the information in the selection with research about whales and with their own thoughts and feelings about the stranding. If you have access to desktop publishing software, let students design the newspaper electronically and then print it.

A Critical Thinking

Challenging the Text

? Do you agree that it would have been better simply to keep the whales company than to try to tow them back to sea? Explain. [Possible responses: Yes, because the futile pulling just hurt and upset them; no, because there was a slight chance that they would recover in deeper water; no, they should have been left completely alone, in peace, in the company of each other.]

B Elements of Literature

Ordering Information

? Here Lopez jumps briefly forward in time, then briefly backward. How does he keep readers oriented about the order of events? [Sample answer: He uses the phrase "a week later" to signal the jump forward and "from the beginning" to signal the jump backward.]

C Elements of Literature

Analogy

? What feelings does Michael Gannon's analogy of a funeral suggest to you? [Possible responses: sorrow; frustration; confusion; numbness; the sense of something gone inexplicably awry.]

D Critical Thinking

Extending the Text

? Do you consider it an act of kindness to kill a suffering animal? Explain. [Possible responses: Yes, if the animal is definitely dying and if euthanasia will prevent prolonged fear and pain; no, because no one can predict with certainty that an animal will die, and no one really knows whether an animal being euthanized feels fear or pain.]

---

embarrassed by the drunks and by people wrangling to get up on the whales or in front of photographers, that he left. As he drove off through the crowds (arriving now by the hundreds, many in campers and motor homes), gray whales were seen offshore, with several circling sperm whales. "The best thing we could have done," Piper said, alluding to this, "was offer our presence, to be with them while they were alive, to show some compassion."

Irritated by a callous (to him) press that seemed to have only one question—Why did they come ashore?—Piper had blurted out that the whales might have come ashore "because they were tired of running" from commercial whalers. Scientists scoffed at the remark, but Piper, recalling it a week later, would not take it back. He said it was as logical as any other explanation offered in those first few hours.

Uneasy philosophical disagreement divided people on the beach from the beginning. Those for whom the stranding was a numinous event were estranged by the clowning of those who regarded it as principally entertainment. A few scientists irritated everyone with their preemptive, self-important air. When they put chain saws to the lower jaws of dead sperm whales lying only a few feet from whales not yet dead, there were angry shouts of condemnation. When townspeople kept at bay—"This is history, dammit," one man screamed at a state trooper, "and I want my kids to see it!"—saw twenty reporters, each claiming an affiliation with the same weekly newspaper, gain the closeness to the whales denied them, there were shouts of cynical derision.

"The effect of all this," said Michael Gannon, director of a national group called Oregonians Cooperating to Protect Whales, of the undercurrent of elitism and outrage, "was that it interfered with the spiritual and emotional ability of people to deal with the phenomenon. It was like being at a funeral where you are not allowed to mourn."

The least understood and perhaps most disruptive incident on the beach on that first day was the attempt of veterinarians to kill the whales, first by injecting M-99, a morphine-based drug, then by ramming pipes into their pleural cavities[10] to collapse their lungs, and finally by severing major arteries and letting them bleed to death. The techniques were crude, but no one knew enough sperm whale anatomy or physiology to make a clean job of it, and no one wanted to try some of the alternatives—from curare[11] to dynamite—that would have made the job quicker. The ineptitude of the veterinarians caused them a private embarrassment to which they gave little public expression. Their frustration at their own inability to do anything to "help" the whales was exacerbated by non-scientists demanding from the sidelines that the animals be "put out of their misery." (The reasons for attempting euthanasia[12] were poorly understood, philosophically and medically, and the issue nagged people long after the beach bore not a trace of the incident itself.)

As events unfolded on the beach, the first whale died shortly after the stranding, the last almost thirty-six hours later; suffocation and overheating were the primary causes. By waiting as long as they did to try to kill some of the animals and by allowing others to die in their own time, pathologists, toxicologists, parasitologists, geneticists,[13] and others got tissues of

---

10. **pleural** (ploor′əl) **cavities:** spaces that contain the lungs.
11. **curare** (kyōō·rä′rē): poison that causes paralysis.
12. **euthanasia** (yōō′thə·nā′zhə): deliberately causing death in order to bring an end to suffering.
13. **Pathologists** study the nature of disease. **Toxicologists** study poisons and their effects. **Parasitologists** study diseases caused by parasites. **Geneticists** study heredity.

WORDS TO OWN

callous (kal′əs) *adj.:* hardened; unfeeling; pitiless.
numinous (nōō′mə·nəs) *adj.:* deeply spiritual or mystical.
elitism (ā·lēt′iz′əm) *n.:* belief that one belongs to a group that is better than others.
ineptitude (in·ep′tə·tōōd′) *n.:* clumsiness; inefficiency.
exacerbated (eg·zas′ər·bāt′id) *v.:* increased; aggravated.

Assessing Learning

Self-Assessment

After students finish reading "A Presentation of Whales," ask them to give careful thought to completing the following sentences to evaluate their reading skills.

1. The reading strategy that helped me the most in understanding this selection was . . . .
2. The aspect of reading that I most needed to improve in my work with this selection was . . . .

poor quality to work with. The disappointment was all the deeper because never had so many scientists been in a position to gather so much information. (Even with this loss and an initial lack of suitable equipment—chemicals to preserve tissues, blood-analysis kits, bone saws, flensing knives[14]—the small core of twenty or so scientists "increased human knowledge about sperm whales several hundred percent," according to Mate.)

The fact that almost anything learned was likely to be valuable was meager consolation to scientists hurt by charges that they were cold and brutal people, irreverently jerking fetuses from the dead. Among these scientists were people who sat alone in silence, who departed in anger, and who broke down and cried.

"It was like being at a funeral where you are not allowed to mourn."

Beginning Sunday morning, scientists had their first chance to draw blood from live, unwounded sperm whales (they used comparatively tiny one-and-a-half-inch, 18-gauge hypodermic needles stuck in vessels near the surface of the skin on the flukes). With the help of a blue organic tracer, they estimated blood volume at five hundred gallons. In subsequent stages, blubber, eyes, teeth, testicles, ovaries, stomach contents, and specific tissues were removed—the teeth for aging, the eyes for corneal cells to discover genetic relationships within the group. Post-mortems[15] were performed on ten females; three near-term fetuses were removed. An attempt was made to photograph the animals systematically.

The atmosphere on the beach shifted perceptibly over the next six days. On Sunday, a cool, cloudy day during which it rained, as many as three thousand people may have been on the beach. Police finally closed the access road to the area to discourage more from coming. Attempts to euthanize the animals continued, the jaws of the dead were being sawed off, and in the words of one observer, "there was a televi-

14. **flensing knives:** knives designed to cut blubber and skin from a dead whale or seal.
15. **post-mortems** (pōst′môr′təmz): autopsies; detailed examinations of dead bodies to determine the causes of death.

sion crew with a backdrop of stranded whales every twenty feet on the foredune."

By Monday the crowds were larger, but, in the estimation of a Forest Service employee, "of a higher quality. The type of people who show up at an automobile accident were gone; these were people who really wanted to see the whales. It was a four-and-a-half-mile walk in from the highway, and I talked with a woman who was seven months pregnant who made it and a man in a business suit and dress shoes who drove all the way down from Seattle."

Monday afternoon the crowds thinned. The beach had become a scene of post-mortem gore sufficient to turn most people away. The outgoing tide had carried off gallons of blood and offal, drawing spiny dogfish sharks and smoothhound sharks into the breakers. As the animals died, scientists cut into them to relieve gaseous pressure—the resultant explosions could be heard half a mile away. A forty-pound chunk of liver whizzed by someone's back-turned shoulders; sixty feet of pearly-gray intestine unfurled with a snap against the sky. By evening the

E Reading Skills and Strategies
Dialogue with the Text
? How do these passages add to your store of knowledge about sperm whales? [Possible responses: They make it clear how little was known about them in 1979; they give data about skin thickness, blood volume, and ways to gauge age and familial relationships.]

F Elements of Literature
Ordering Information
? How do the opening words of paragraphs on this page and on the next show chronological order? [Sample answer: Lopez begins many of these paragraphs by naming a day of the week.]

G Appreciating Language
Topic Sentences
? In this paragraph, the second sentence serves as the topic sentence. How does this sentence alert readers about what to expect in the paragraph? [Possible responses: It refers to "gore," and the rest of the paragraph is certainly gory; it mentions that the scene would "turn most people away," warning readers that the paragraph will be graphic.]

Making the Connections

Connecting to the Theme: "Being There!"

This magazine article opens so objectively that the narrator may at first seem not to "be there" at all. As the article goes on, however, readers become aware of the narrator's watchful intelligence and realize that he is very much "there." As a reporter, he never puts himself in the action but uses sharp descriptive writing and striking quotations to bring the sad, gory scene to life for readers. One of Lopez's purposes in this article is to show the human species interacting with another species. He probes *who* should be there (the public, the press, scientists, novelists, artists, clergy, philosophers) and *how* to be there (what to do). Ultimately, in the whales' unfathomable dying, "being there"—a simple, compassionate presence—emerges as a primary value.

Writers on Writing. Barry Lopez comments: "The essays I write are most often based on a combination of personal experience in the field, background reading, and library research. In the case of 'A Presentation of Whales,' however, I had no time to prepare. As soon as I learned of the stranding I drove out to the Oregon coast—about one hundred miles from my home—and began asking questions. I familiarized myself with what had happened through a series of interviews, during which I also learned what the stranding meant to various people. As I pursued these interviews, I began to see the structure of the essay—it would be based on what the witnesses saw and imagined. I would write as a reporter, with my own feelings coming into the essay at the very end. And that's how the piece developed in the typewriter."

Ⓐ Reading Skills and Strategies
Connecting with the Text

❓ The whales in the pits are already dead. Why, then, does the image of their burning seem so horrible? [Possible responses: The images of sea creatures on fire is very strange; it sounds as if the whales are being tortured when Lopez describes them as boiling in their own oil.]

---

beach was covered with more than a hundred tons of intestines. Having to open the abdominal cavities so <u>precipitately</u> <u>precluded</u>, to the scientists' dismay, any chance of an uncontaminated examination.

By Tuesday the beach was closed to the public. The whale carcasses were being prepared for burning and burial, a task that would take four days, and reporters had given up asking why the stranding had happened, to comment on the stench.

Ⓐ On Wednesday afternoon the whales were ignited in pits at the foot of the foredune. As they burned they were rendered,[16] and when their oil caught fire they began to boil in it. The seething roar was muffled by a steady onshore breeze; the oily black smoke drifted southeast over the dunes, over English beach grass and pearly everlasting, sand verbena, and the purple flowers of beach pea, green leaves of sweet clover, and the bright yellow blooms of the monkey flower. It thinned until it disappeared against a weak-blue sky.

While fire cracked the blubber of one-eyed, jawless carcasses, a bulldozer the size of a two-car garage grunted in a trench being dug to the north for the last of them. These were still

16. **rendered:** melted down, releasing oil or fat.

---

sprawled at the water's edge. Up close, the black, blistered skin, bearing scars of knives and gouging fingernails, looked like the shriveled surface of a pond evaporated beneath a summer sun. Their gray-blue innards lay about on the sand like bags of discarded laundry. Their purple tongues were wedged in retreat in their throats. Spermaceti oil dripped from holes in their heads, solidifying in the wind to stand in translucent stalagmites twenty inches high. Around them were tidal pools opaque with coagulated blood and, beyond, a pink surf.

As far as I know, no novelist, no historian, no moral philosopher, no scholar of Melville, no rabbi, no painter, no theologian had been on the beach. No one had thought to call them or to fly them in. At the end they would not have been allowed past the barricades.

The whales made a sound, someone had said, like the sound a big fir makes breaking off the stump just as the saw is pulled away. A thin screech.

WORDS TO OWN
precipitately (prē·sip′ə·tit·lē) *adv.:* hurriedly; unexpectedly.
precluded (prē·klōōd′id) *v.:* prevented; made impossible.

MEET THE WRITER
Nature Is His Subject

Barry Lopez (1945–   ) is a writer who can't wait to get up in the morning. That is how another "nature writer," Edward Hoagland, described the author of *Arctic Dreams* (1986), a book that celebrates the northern landscape and the people and animals who live there. Lopez always combines observations of nature with insights into human life.

In a recent interview, Lopez identified two issues that matter most to him and the kind of writing he likes to do best:

❝ A writer has a certain handful of questions. Mine seem to be the issues of tolerance and dignity. You can't sit down and write directly about those things, but if they are on your mind and if you're a writer, they're going to come out in one form or another. The form I feel most comfortable with, where I do a lot of reading and aimless thinking, is natural history. ❞

Lopez also retold the Native American myths about the great trickster Coyote in a book subtitled *Coyote Builds North America* (1977). Lopez and his family live close to nature, beside the McKenzie River in western Oregon.

Assessing Learning

Check Test: Short Answers
1. Why is it unusual for sperm whales to beach themselves? [They are deep-sea dwellers, not common along the coast.]
2. How do environmentalists initially respond? [They keep the whales wet and try to drag one whale back to sea.]
3. Why do scientists arrive so quickly? [A convention of mammal specialists is meeting nearby, and there are two large marine research centers in the area.]

4. What other groups of people are at the site? [police, veterinarians, concerned members of the public, press, Forest Service, and entertainment-seeking onlookers]
5. What happens to the whales at the end? [They die, and their carcasses are burned and buried.]

Standardized Test Preparation
For practice with standardized test format specific to this section, see
• *Standardized Test Preparation*, p. 54
For practice in proofreading and editing, see
• *Daily Oral Grammar,* Transparency 27

MAKING MEANINGS

First Thoughts

[connect]

1. What details in "A Presentation of Whales" were disturbing to you? Are you glad or sorry that you read it? Why?

Shaping Interpretations

[synthesize]

2. What does Lopez think about the tragic events he describes? Does he state his **opinions** directly, or does he suggest them? Find passages that reveal his views on the whales and on the people at the beach.

[evaluate]

3. Has Lopez written this report so that the story has heroes and villains? Support your answer with specific details from the text.

[infer]

4. Reread Lopez's next to last paragraph. Why do you think he wrote it?

[apply]

5. Take out the **KWL** chart you began before you read this report. What can you now add to the L column? Skim the report again to be sure you have enough information to complete the column.

> ### Reading Check
> Make a **time line** showing the main events in this report in **chronological order**.

CHOICES: Building Your Portfolio

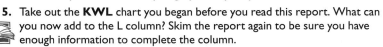

Writer's Notebook

1. Collecting Ideas for a Research Paper

Organizing information.

To write this report, Barry Lopez had to transform his notes into a coherent form. You'll face the same task in the Writer's Workshop on page 448. Find some notes you've made for a research paper, perhaps from another Writer's Notebook assignment in this collection. Try organizing your facts and details in **outline** form. (If you need help with outlining, see page 334).

Writing an Analogy

2. Science Is Like Art?

Go back to the text and find at least three passages in which Lopez uses **analogies,** or comparisons, to help us understand something about the whales. Scientist Polly Matzinger also uses analogies to explain something complex in this interview excerpt:

> **Q.** I'm told you dislike the way science and technology have become hyphenated terms—why?
> **A.** Because they are very different. Science is more like art and true scientists are more like artists. . . . Technology is about

vaccines and plastics and drugs and things that work in the world. Science is about describing nature, and so is art: We are painting nature.
Q. Do you think the scientific world is too solemn?
A. Oh, no. Not true science. It's art. Actually, it's a sandbox and scientists get to play all our lives.

Write your own analogy to explain some field or topic or activity that interests you—a sport, music, reading, cooking, running, etc. Elaborate on your analogy as Matzinger does.

Reading Check	Sample Time Line		
Saturday June 16	Whales beach themselves	Monday June 18	Mammalogists' convention opens at Corvallis Last whales die Crowds peak Post-mortems in progress
Sunday June 17	Greenpeace people try to tow whale back to sea Many whales die Veterinarians try to euthanize whales Scientists begin taking specimens	Tuesday June 19	Beach closed to public Carcasses prepared for disposal
		Wednesday June 20	Carcasses burned and buried

MAKING MEANINGS

First Thoughts

1. Disturbing details: refusals to help; brutal attempts at euthanasia; people walking on whales; scientists taking samples from living whales; exploding carcasses; dead whales burning. Possible responses: glad, because the report increases awareness of environmental issues; sorry, because the whales' death is sad and gruesome.

Shaping Interpretations

2. Sample answer: He suggests some opinions and states others. On the whales: "What makes them awesome is . . . the mysteries that shroud them." On the people: ". . . the worst and the best of human behavior were shown among them."

3. Sample answer: Lopez makes it clear that the real "villain" is the whales' desperate situation, coupled with people's lack of knowledge. He lauds environmental activists ("the effort was heroic"). He does condemn callous gawkers, pushy news crews, and a few scientists "with their preemptive, self-important air."

4. Possible responses: he believes that the event raises moral issues that should be dealt with; he believes that experts in the humanities, religion, and the arts could have offered insights that scientists could not.

5. Possible facts: A sperm whale's heart weighs four hundred pounds; its skin is as sensitive as the inside of our wrists; no one knows what the spermaceti organ does.

Grading Timesaver

Rubrics for each Choices assignment appear on p. 143 in the *Portfolio Management System*.

CHOICES: Building Your Portfolio

1. **Writer's Notebook** Remind students to save their work for the Writer's Workshop on p. 448.

2. **Writing an Analogy** Lopez's final paragraph is an analogy. More analogies appear in the third-to-last paragraph on p. 442.

Students can use information from this activity as they compose and revise paragraphs for research papers in the Writer's Workshop beginning on p. 448.

Try It Out
Possible Answer

Topic sentence—to be placed at the beginning of the paragraph: Problem-solving skills have become an important part of the curriculum in many schools today.

VOCABULARY

Answers

1. acrid
2. precluded
3. elitism
4. exacerbated
5. belligerent
6. precipitous
7. callous
8. precipitately
9. ineptitude
10. numinous

Resources

Language
- *Grammar and Language Links* Worksheet, p. 49

Vocabulary
- *Words to Own*, Worksheet, p. 26

LANGUAGE LINK [MINI-LESSON]

Topic Sentences

A **topic sentence,** which states the **main idea** of a paragraph, helps keep both writers and readers on track. A topic sentence helps the writer organize the paragraph, keeping out any unrelated, stray ideas. For the reader a topic sentence works as a signal, announcing the paragraph's main idea.

Not every kind of writing has topic sentences, but informative writing often does. Here are some examples from the beginning of "A Presentation of Whales." Look at the rest of the paragraph in which each appears to see how the topic sentence actually controls what is presented in the paragraph.

1. "The sperm whale, for many, is the most awesome creature of the open seas." (page 437)

2. "By Monday the crowds were larger, but, in the estimation of a Forest Service employee, 'of a higher quality.' " (page 441)

With a partner, find three more topic sentences in Lopez's article. They're usually at the beginning of a paragraph but sometimes appear at the end (to sum up the main idea) or in the middle.

Try It Out

Write a **topic sentence** for the following paragraph, and state where you'd insert it. Be sure to compare your sentences in class.

As part of their classes, kindergarten children are learning conflict resolution skills. In junior and senior high schools, peer mediators are being trained to help settle students' disputes without teachers or administrators. Mediators, who remain neutral in a dispute, help students focus on the problem and listen to one another respectfully.

➤ Select an essay or report from your writing portfolio, and check it for topic sentences. Did you use them? Are they effective? Do all the sentences in the paragraph stick to the main idea? If you haven't used topic sentences, try inserting some for clarity.

VOCABULARY [HOW TO OWN A WORD]

WORD BANK	Synonyms and Antonyms
precipitous	A **synonym** means the same (more or less) as another word. An **antonym** means the opposite.

WORD BANK
precipitous
belligerent
acrid
callous
numinous
elitism
ineptitude
exacerbated
precipitately
precluded

Synonyms and Antonyms

A **synonym** means the same (more or less) as another word. An **antonym** means the opposite.

1. What word means the opposite of *sweet-smelling*?
2. What word means the same as *prevented*?
3. What word refers to a belief that's the opposite of *equality*?
4. What word means the same as *worsened*?
5. What word means the opposite of *peace-loving*?
6. What word means the same as *steep*?
7. What word means the opposite of *sensitive*?
8. What word means the same as *hastily*?
9. What word means the opposite of *competence*?
10. What word means the same as *mystical* or *spiritual*?

Language Link Quick Check

Of the following four sentences, which is the best topic sentence, and why?

1. Rescuers of the past risked losing their arms when they tried to feed beached whales.
2. Scientists have recently found ways to help save whales that strand themselves.
3. Inflatable devices now safely keep whales' massive jaws from snapping shut.
4. Rescuers no longer use ropes to drag whales back to the ocean; they fasten canvas slings around the whales' midsections.

[Sentence 2 is the best, because it states a general idea, not specific details.]

EXTENDING *the theme*

A PROSE POEM

Celestial Combat by Nikolai Roerich (1874–1947).

Russian State Museum, St. Petersburg.

A Storm in the Mountains

Aleksandr Solzhenitsyn   *translated by Michael Glenny*

It caught us one pitch-black night at the foot of the pass. We crawled out of our tents and ran for shelter as it came towards us over the ridge.

Everything was black—no peaks, no valleys, no horizon to be seen, only the searing flashes of lightning separating darkness from light, and the gigantic peaks of Belaya-Kaya and Djuguturlyuchat[1] looming up out of the night. The huge black pine trees around us seemed as high as the mountains themselves. For a split second we felt ourselves on terra firma;[2] then once more everything would be plunged into darkness and chaos.

The lightning moved on, brilliant light alternating with pitch blackness, flashing white, then pink, then violet, the mountains and pines always springing back in the same place, their hugeness

1. **Belaya-Kaya** (bye·lī´ə kī´ə) **and Djuguturlyuchat** (djōō·gōō·tōōr·lyōō´chət): two mountains in Russia.
2. **terra firma** (ter´ə fûr´mə): Latin expression meaning "solid ground."

A STORM IN THE MOUNTAINS 445

WRITERS ON WRITING

In his 1970 Nobel Prize acceptance speech, Solzhenitsyn says: "Literature transmits condensed and irrefutable human experience. . . . It thus becomes the living memory of a nation. What has faded into history it thus keeps warm and preserves in a form that defies distortion and falsehood."

FINDING COMMON GROUND

1. If students need a starting point, suggest that they notice which words or images from the poem linger in their mind. Tell them to reread those parts, examining Solzhenitsyn's use of sensory details, rhythmic cadences, figurative language, and other elements.

2. Even after reading the definition of a prose poem, some students may not agree that "A Storm in the Mountains" can be classified as a poem. Urge them to support their opinions with reasons and specific details.

3. If students struggle with the last question, point out that the speaker in the poem ends by feeling "grateful" to be "part of this world." Have students consider why this feeling might be a gift and what responsibilities might accompany the gift.

---

filling us with awe; yet when they disappeared we could not believe that they had ever existed.

The voice of the thunder filled the gorge, drowning the ceaseless roar of the rivers. Like the arrows of Sabaoth,[3] the lightning flashes rained down on the peaks, then split up into serpentine streams as though bursting into

3. **Sabaoth** (sab´ā·äth´): biblical term meaning "armies."

spray against the rock face, or striking and then shattering like a living thing.

As for us, we forgot to be afraid of the lightning, the thunder, and the downpour, just as a droplet in the ocean has no fear of a hurricane. Insignificant yet grateful, we became part of this world—a primal world in creation before our eyes.

MEET THE WRITER
Russia's Nobel Laureate

Aleksandr Solzhenitsyn (sōl´zhə·nēt´sin) (1918–   ) spent many years in Soviet prisons. Solzhenitsyn catapulted to fame with the publication of his first novel, *One Day in the Life of Ivan Denisovich* (1962), which details the daily life of a political prisoner. Solzhenitsyn wrote from firsthand knowledge, for in 1945 he was arrested for criticizing Soviet leader Joseph Stalin and sentenced to eight years in prison and labor camps, plus three years in exile.

After his release, he taught mathematics and physics and continued writing. After the publication of *The Gulag Archipelago* (1974), he was exiled from Russia. In 1976 Solzhenitsyn and

his wife settled quietly in Vermont, where he continued to write and publish novels about Soviet life under the Communist regime.

In his acceptance speech for the 1970 Nobel Prize for Literature, Solzhenitsyn commented on the relationship between life and literature:

❝The sole substitute for an experience which we have not ourselves lived through is art and literature.❞

In 1994, with the Cold War over, and Russia's Communist regime out of power, Solzhenitsyn and his wife returned at last to their homeland.

FINDING COMMON GROUND

Get together with several classmates to share your Quickwrite notes. If you've lived in the same place for a long time, you may have written about the same event your classmates recalled. Discuss how your experiences are alike and different.

Then, **compare and contrast** your own experiences with Solzhenitsyn's. Let your group decide what you'd like to discuss, but if you need some help in setting your agenda, consider the following questions:

1. How does Solzhenitsyn manage to make his experience seem real, as if you are standing at his side?

2. What makes this description a **prose poem** (see page 605) rather than a news report—or some other kind of writing?

3. What does Solzhenitsyn conclude from his experience? If everyone shared this thought, how might people behave differently?

After your group finishes discussing Solzhenitsyn's prose poem, turn back to your Quickwrite notes. Write about your experience of "being there" in any form you choose: a journal entry, an eyewitness report, a poem or prose poem, or a letter. Try, as Solzhenitsyn does, to find a lesson or meaning in your experience.

Making the Connections

Connecting to the Theme: "Being There!"

Solzhenitsyn shares an instance of "being there" that is both literal and metaphoric. He "puts readers there" with him in a violent thunderstorm where he is camped, exposed and vulnerable, high in the mountains. At the same time, he brings readers into his vision of the storm as a primal union between earth and sky. In this vision, the world is in an ongoing state of creation, and humankind's great privilege is "being there"—witnessing and taking part.

READ ON

Nuclear Fallout

Hiroshima by John Hersey (Vintage) tells what happened on August 6, 1945, when the United States dropped the first atomic bomb on Hiroshima, Japan. Hersey's detailed, compelling narrative focuses on two women and four men, five Japanese and one German, who survived that day.

Witnessing the Civil Rights Movement

Eyes on the Prize by Juan Williams (Viking Penguin) documents eleven years (1954–1965) of the civil rights movement with text, photos, and oral histories that make you an eyewitness to the Montgomery bus boycott, the marches and freedom rides, and landmark desegregation cases.

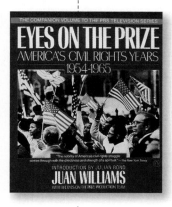

What Happened in Salem

Arthur Miller's great play *The Crucible* (Viking Penguin) puts a historical event onstage. The play takes place in Salem, Massachusetts, in 1692, when anyone could "cry witch" against a neighbor and twenty people were executed as witches. The McCarthy hearings (1952–1954), investigating suspected Communists in the United States, have been compared to these hysterical witch hunts in old Salem. Daniel Day-Lewis and Winona Ryder starred in the 1996 movie version, whose screenplay was written by Arthur Miller.

How They Lived

Alvin M. Josephy's lavishly illustrated *500 Nations: An Illustrated History of North American Indians* (Knopf) begins with origin stories, Mexican empires, and the way of life of the Indian nations before Columbus arrived. The text, photographs, and interviews with contemporary American Indians show the clashes with European settlers and the destruction of the old way of life.

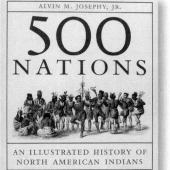

READ ON 447

BUILDING YOUR PORTFOLIO
Writer's Workshop

Technology HELP

See Writer's Workshop 2 CD-ROM. *Assignment: Informative Report.*

ASSIGNMENT

Write a research paper, using information gathered from several sources.

AIM

To inform.

AUDIENCE

Your teacher and classmates.

Broad topic: whales

↓

Narrower topic: dangers to whales

↓

Still narrower topic: recent theories about whale strandings

 go.hrw.com
LE0 Research Paper

448 THE NONFICTION COLLECTIONS

EXPOSITORY WRITING
RESEARCH PAPER

You'll be asked to write **research papers** throughout your school years—and possibly beyond. Researching is a two-part job. First you search for the most accurate, reliable information available, just as a scientist does. Then, like a reporter, you assemble those facts into an informative, accurate, and well-documented report.

Prewriting

1. Explore Topic Ideas

WORK IN PROGRESS

Review the entries in your Writer's Notebook to find a topic that interests you and that you think will interest your readers. If you can't find one there, try skimming magazines and newspapers or browsing the Internet. Cross out any topics on your list that seem too broad (the history of mountain climbing), too complex (how an ocean liner is built), or too hard to find information about. Keep in mind that you'll need to consult several sources.

2. Track Down Reliable Sources

As you gather information, you'll probably use both **secondary sources** (such as magazine and encyclopedia articles, textbooks, biographies, history books, and book reviews) and **primary sources** (such as interviews, journals, speeches, and literary works). Here's where to look:

- **Check out the library.** You'll find a variety of **print** and **non-print sources**—as well as librarians who can help you.

- **Log on.** Explore the Internet using one of the many available **search engines.** Each search engine works differently and gives varied results. Learn to use the search engines on your computer. (For more help with online searches, see Using the Internet in the Communications Handbook.) Through the Internet you can access databases, government documents, periodicals, professional Web sites, scholarly projects, and newsgroups. You can also **e-mail** experts and organizations to ask questions or request information.

The history
of the written
word is rich and
Once upon a time

- **Explore your community.** Visit a museum, contact a private organization or government agency, interview an expert, or conduct your own opinion poll or survey.

Before you use a source, be sure to **evaluate** its reliability; some sources are biased, inaccurate, outdated, or just plain silly. Be particularly careful with sources on the Internet, where anyone can post anything. Web sites with addresses ending in *gov* (government source) are the most reliable. (See pages 454 and 758 and the Communications Handbook for more on evaluating sources.)

3. Take Notes

As you research, take notes on any information you think you may want to use in your paper. Make a **source card** for each work, assigning it a number and recording the publication data; use a separate **note card** or page in a computer document for every fact or idea you record from that source. Avoid **plagiarism** (copying someone else's words or ideas without giving credit to the source) by putting information in your own words, enclosing quoted material in quotation marks, and giving credit to writers when you mention their ideas.

4. Document Your Sources

In your notes, be sure to record the source of every piece of information so that you can **document** it. The style set by the Modern Language Association (MLA), the style preferred by most English teachers, requires two types of documentation. You'll need both **parenthetical citations** (names of authors and page numbers enclosed in parentheses) within the paper and a **works**

PEANUTS reprinted by permission of United Features Syndicate, Inc.

Communications Handbook H E L P

See Research Strategies (Using a Media Center or Library, Using the Internet, Evaluating the Credibility of Web Sources).

Research Tip

To focus a Web search, familiarize yourself with each search engine's options for entering **key words** and **exact phrases.** They vary.

Try It Out

Choose a brief passage from one of the selections in this collection. Prepare three note cards:
1. Summarize the **main idea** of the passage, using your own words.
2. Paraphrase the entire passage (restate every sentence in your own words).
3. Directly quote the most important idea in the passage. Be sure to enclose the quoted words in quotation marks.

Prewriting

- Review the Prewriting steps outlined on pp. 448–450, and establish clearly your own standards for student performance. For example, many teachers specify the required length of the research paper or the number and types of research sources that must be cited.
- Be certain students see the cross-reference on p. 450 to the Communications Handbook. In this section of the textbook, students will find additional information on taking notes and on documenting sources. For up-to-date information on changes in the MLA or APA styles of documentation, be sure to check the HRW Internet site (keyword: research paper).

Reaching All Students

English Language Learners

The idea of doing research and documenting sources—along with the pressure to be interesting as well as accurate—may frustrate students learning English. For these students, it might be helpful to offer a cooperative writing option. Students in such a group should choose a topic that interests them all; then, they can divide the tasks as they research and write.

Before they begin, meet with students to help them establish realistic expectations for themselves. These goals should address both product and process. For example, a student could establish the product goal of generating a certain number of words and the process goal of using a certain number of primary and secondary sources. It may also be helpful to establish interim goals and schedules to help students keep on track.

Prewriting (continued)
Students should be made aware that the standards for citing and documenting sources vary over time. Establish what style is acceptable for this assignment, and caution students not to refer to other documentation guides, particularly older sources they may have at home.

Language/Grammar Link
H E L P

Combining Narration and Exposition: page 408. Technical Vocabulary: page 432. Topic Sentences: page 444.

Communications Handbook
H E L P

See Taking Notes and Documenting Sources.

Thesis statement: Scientists have learned a lot about whales, but they still don't know why whales become stranded.

I. Recent theories
  A. Sickness or injury
    1. Natural causes
      a. Ear infections
      b. Parasites
    2. Human causes
      a. Injuries resulting from swallowing plastic
      b. Injuries caused by fishing gear
      c. Injuries caused by boats
      d. Sickness caused by exposure to toxins
  B. Damage to echolocation (whale's sonar navigation)
    1. etc.

---

cited list (an alphabetical list of your sources with publication information) at the end. The box below shows some sample entries from a works cited list. (See the Communications Handbook for detailed guidelines and more examples of citations in the MLA style.)

> - **Book with two authors:**
>   Mallory, Kenneth, and Andrea Conley. <u>Rescue of the Stranded Whales</u>. New York: Simon and Schuster, 1989.
> - **Magazine article:**
>   Frantzis, A. "Does Acoustic Testing Strand Whales?" <u>Nature</u> 5 Mar. 1998: 29.
> - **On-line professional site:**
>   <u>National Aquarium, Marine Animal Rescue Program</u>. Baltimore. 23 Oct. 1999. <http://www.aqua.org/animals/environments/rescue.html>.
> - **E-mail:**
>   Morin, David (staff scientist, Cetacean Research Unit, Gloucester, Massachusetts). "Whale Strandings." E-mail to Pamela Ozaroff. 31 Oct. 1999.

5. Write a Thesis Statement

Before you start writing, draft a **thesis statement** that presents your paper's **main idea.** You may need to write several drafts before you come up with one that works.

EXAMPLE   Scientists still know very little about why whales become stranded, or beached.

6. Organize Your Information

The advantage of taking notes on separate index cards or computer pages is that you can sort them into piles, discarding any that seem weak or irrelevant. Arrange your note cards into "topic piles," and rearrange them as necessary until you find the topics and organization that make the most sense for your paper.

    When you have a basic structure in place, **outline** the body of your paper. Begin with your thesis statement; then, list every main idea and its supporting details. (Outlining will help you organize your thoughts as well as your information.) You can make either a **topic outline,** like the one at the left, with words and phrases as headings, or a **sentence outline,** with complete sentences as headings. If you put subheadings under a heading, you'll need at least two.

Reaching All Students

Struggling Writers

Making an outline is a critical step for students who have difficulty with extended writing assignments. Put students having difficulty in pairs, and give each pair 10 to 20 strips of paper. Have each student write one key idea for his or her paper on each strip. Then, have the pairs experiment with organizing the strips in the best order.

When the pairs have agreed to an organization, have them present the paper to you. If necessary, work with each person to reorganize his or her paper, paying particular attention to the subordination of ideas. If ideas are missing, add strips as needed. Have the writer tape the strips of paper together so that he or she has a starting draft for an outline.

Drafting

1. Elaborate on Your Thesis

Many writers draft the body of a paper first, leaving the introduction for later. Start by turning your notes into complete sentences; then, link the sentences to form paragraphs, with **topic sentences** based on your outline headings. Elaborate on each topic sentence with relevant **facts, descriptions, comparisons, quotations,** and other **supporting details.** Don't be afraid to depart from your outline or to drop information that no longer seems useful.

2. Begin and End

Begin your **introduction** by drawing your readers into your topic with an intriguing quotation, question, statistic, or description of the issue. Then, provide any necessary **background information,** and present your **thesis statement.**

In your **conclusion,** sum up by restating your thesis and perhaps adding a final comment on the topic. At the end of your paper, include your works cited list, giving complete publication information for every source referred to in your paper.

■ *Evaluation Criteria*

A good research report

1. *begins with a strong opener and a thesis statement*
2. *is organized logically*
3. *is based on a variety of reliable sources*
4. *elaborates on its main ideas with facts, quotations, examples, and other evidence*
5. *identifies quoted material and doesn't plagiarize*
6. *documents its sources in MLA or another approved style*
7. *ends with a restatement of the thesis statement*

Drafting

- Before students begin to write their drafts, have them read the Model provided on pp. 451–452. Review the on-page annotations with students, and continue the discussion, using the questions provided below.
- Remind students that today's writer is also a page designer. As students write, they should be alert to the potential of graphics to supplement or even replace complex text. Are there places in their paper where the use of a graph would make statistical information easier to read and understand? Is there a photograph that could add visual support to their thesis?
- Remind students to use only every other line when they write their drafts. They should also leave extra space in the right margin. These blank spaces will be used for comments and editing marks.

Model

FROM WHALE STRANDINGS: CURRENT THEORIES

[Introduction]

Nearly two decades have passed since the mass stranding of sperm whales that Barry Lopez describes in his essay "A Presentation of Whales." Since that 1979 incident, we have made much progress in our ability to rescue and rehabilitate stranded whales and other marine mammals. They are no longer simply left to die, with scientists and anguished observers "transfixed on the beach by their own helplessness" (439). Yet we still know very little about why these complex animals become stranded in the first place.

Opening paragraph refers to specific essay.

Essay already cited; only page number is needed. Thesis statement.

[From the body]

Scientists have proposed several theories to explain these mass strandings. Some involve human factors; others do not. One theory is that a sick or injured animal in a pod, or herd, becomes disoriented and heads toward shore. The rest of the pod follows (Morin), possibly in response to distress calls (Fulton). Whales become sick or injured for various reasons, some of which are related to human activity. Stranded animals have occasionally been found to have ear infections or parasites (Charles). Others

Topic sentence. Categorizes theories.

Cites electronic sources with no page numbers.

(continued on next page)

Reaching All Students

Struggling Writers

Go through the outlines prepared by struggling writers and suggest which points should be supported by in-text citations. You may also want to suggest places in the manuscript where quotations from sources would be particularly appropriate.

The *Writer's Workshop 2 CD-ROM* includes an electronic bibliography maker that will be helpful to students who find constructing a works-cited page especially difficult.

Evaluating and Revising

- Before students review their writing, have them read and analyze the Revision Model and Peer Comments on this page.
- Remind students to use the Evaluation Criteria provided on p. 451 as a guide to determining needed revisions.
- As students read and evaluate their writing, remind them to look for instances where information would be more comprehensible if presented in a graphic format.

Proofreading

Have students proofread their own paper first and then exchange it with another student. For this assignment, remind proofreaders to verify the format of source citations.

Publishing

Many Web sites are devoted to topical issues. If students have located Web sites related to their topics while completing this assignment, they may wish to submit their final draft to the site. *Students should have their parents' or guardians' permission before submitting any material for publication.*

If the content of their papers is appropriate, students may also wish to submit their research papers to a teacher in a related discipline for extra credit.

Reflecting

Organization is key to completing a research paper successfully. Have students answer the following questions and attach the responses to their papers before filing them in their portfolios:

1. Did I keep track of all my research sources? How could I have improved on my technique?
2. When writing from my notes, could I always tell what information was a direct quote and what had been paraphrased? How could I have improved my process?
3. How did I handle my time? Was I doing the bulk of the work in the last few days? How could I have improved my process?

Resources ———

Peer Editing Forms and Rubrics
- *Portfolio Management System,* p. 145

Revision Transparencies
- *Workshop Resources,* p. 27

Model (continued)

have swallowed plastic debris (National Aquarium), become entangled in fishing gear, or been struck by boats (National Marine Fisheries Service 10). Almost all stranded animals are contaminated by toxins (Geraci).

Cites examples of human-related injury.

[Conclusion]
The ancient Romans believed that stranded whales were being punished by the sea god Neptune. Today scientists have proposed many theories to explain whale strandings, but they are still simply "educated guesses" (Mallory and Conley 10). We have learned so much in the last twenty years about how to rescue and release stranded whales. Now we must learn how to prevent at least some of these tragedies from occurring in the first place.

Restates thesis.

Quotes phrase.

Ends with challenge for the future.

Proofreading Tip

Make sure that a source is given for every quotation and reference to another writer's ideas. Then, make sure that the works cited list is complete and correctly punctuated.

Sentence Workshop
H E L P

Correcting run-on sentences: page 453.

Communications Handbook
H E L P

See Proofreaders' Marks.

Evaluating and Revising

Ask a partner for suggestions for improving your report, using the evaluation criteria on page 451. Think about your partner's comments, and use this feedback to decide what changes to make. Don't be afraid to cut sentences or paragraphs, add new material, or rearrange ideas.

Revision Model

	Peer Comments
~~Scientists have proposed~~ There actually are several theories	*Use a stronger verb.*
to explain these mass strandings. ~~about this.~~ Some theories involve	*Explain "this." Be more specific.*
One theory is that human factors; others do not. A	*Is this one of the theories? Clarify.*
, or herd, sick or injured animal in a pod be-	*Define "pod"?*
disoriented and heads toward shore. comes ~~confused, the rest of the pod~~	*Fix run-on.*
(Morin), follows ~~the sick or injured whale,~~	*Repetitious.*
response to distress calls (Fulton). possibly ~~in order to help.~~	*Cite your source or sources.*

Grading Timesaver

Rubrics for this Writer's Workshop assignment appear on p. 146 of the *Portfolio Management System.*

BUILDING YOUR PORTFOLIO
Sentence Workshop

OBJECTIVES
1. Identify run-on sentences
2. Revise run-on sentences by using a variety of techniques

CORRECTING RUN-ON SENTENCES

Like a car running a red light or stop sign, a **run-on sentence** (like this one) doesn't stop when it's supposed to, it just keeps on going. A run-on sentence is made up of two or more sentences separated by a comma (like the preceding sentence) or with no punctuation. Here are three strategies you can use to correct run-on sentences:

1. Separate the run-on sentence into two sentences.

   RUN-ON   Forty-one whales were stranded on the beach all of them died.

   CORRECT   Forty-one whales were stranded on the beach. **A**ll of them died.

2. Change the run-on sentence to a compound sentence. You can use either a comma and a coordinating conjunction (such as *and, but, or,* or *so*) or a semicolon.

   RUN-ON   Volunteers tried to help, they failed.

   CORRECT   Volunteers tried to help**, but** they failed.

   CORRECT   Volunteers tried to help**;** they failed.

3. Make one of the sentences a subordinate clause.

   RUN-ON   Scientists arrived on the scene they could not save the whales.

   CORRECT   Scientists **who arrived on the scene** could not save the whales.

Notice that each of these run-on sentences could have been corrected in other ways:

   EXAMPLE   Volunteers **who tried to help** failed.

Writer's Workshop Follow-up: Proofreading

Reread the research paper that you wrote for the Writer's Workshop (page 448). As you read, focus on sentence structure. Do you see any run-on sentences? If so, correct them. Be sure to think carefully about which strategy you want to use to correct your run-ons.

Language Handbook
HELP

See Run-on Sentences, *page 1042.*

Technology
HELP

See Language Workshop CD-ROM. *Key word entry: run-on sentences.*

Try It Out

Act as an editor, and correct each run-on sentence two ways. Then, check the page cited to see how the professional writer wrote it.

1. A collie barked incessantly flash cubes burst at the huge, dark forms. (page 436)

2. I began my descent, I was indeed anxious, my concern had little to do with the weather. (page 422)

3. A woman tries to take her Great Dane into a boat with her she is refused and steps out of the boat to die with her dog. (page 397)

4. It was a sunny day the trees were green, at the gates the children played. (page 413)

5. They all stare blank-faced, one picture, in the middle of a row, seizes the eye and wrenches the mind. (page 413)

SENTENCE WORKSHOP **453**

Resources

Workshop Resources
• Worksheet, p. 65

Language Workshop CD-ROM
• Run-on Sentences

Try It Out
Possible Answers
1. A collie barked incessantly as the flash cubes burst at the huge, dark forms. (p. 436: "A collie barked incessantly; flash cubes burst at the huge, dark forms.")
2. Beginning my descent, I was indeed anxious, but my concern had little to do with the weather. (p. 422: "As I began my descent, I was indeed anxious, but my concern had little to do with the weather.")
3. A woman tries to take her Great Dane into a boat with her, but she is refused and steps out of the boat to die with her dog. (p. 397: "A woman tries to take her Great Dane into a boat with her; she is refused and steps out of the boat to die with her dog.")
4. It was a sunny day. The trees were green at the gates where the children played. (p. 413: "It was a sunny day and the trees were green and at the gates the children played.")
5. They all stare blank-faced, and yet one picture, in the middle of a row, seizes the eye and wrenches the mind. (p. 413: "They all stare blank-faced, but one picture, in the middle of a row, seizes the eye and wrenches the mind.")

Assessing Learning

Quick Check:
Correcting Run-on Sentences
Identify each sentence as *correct* or *run-on;* then, correct the errors. [Possible answers are shown in brackets.]

1. Investigative reporters work hard and often risk their lives. [correct]
2. One day they may be sitting behind a desk the next day they may be hiking through a steaming jungle. [Run-on: One day they may be sitting behind a desk; the next day they may be hiking through a steaming jungle.]

3. "Official" channels fail, these men and women often become undercover journalists. [Run-on: When "official" channels fail, these men and women often become undercover journalists.]
4. Some people think investigative reporters are just looking for publicity. [correct]
5. I disagree, they perform a valuable public service. [Run-on: I disagree. They perform a valuable public service.]

Reading for Life

Evaluating the Credibility of Sources: Print and Nonprint

Teaching the Lesson

Explain that evaluating the credibility of sources helps students obtain accurate, reliable information which they can then use in their writing and speaking. To help students understand the difference between kinds of sources, ask which of the following would be the most reliable source of information about whales:

a. remarks by visitors to an aquarium
b. an encyclopedia article on whales written by a marine biologist
c. a fiction book for children about a talking whale

Using the Strategies

Possible Answers

1. Videorecording of *Titanic;* Dave's *Titanic* Home Page; both are unreliable.
2. "Descent to the *Titanic*" in *il Petersen's Photographic Magazine;* "How We Found *Titanic*" and "Epilogue for the *Titanic*" in *National Geographic*
3. Photographs from the photographic magazine; video and pictures may be available on the NASA Web site.
4. With the exceptions of Dave's Home Page and the movie *Titanic,* the sources listed here would all be helpful to verify some facts. All of these sources, however, are more focused on finding and recovering objects from the *Titanic* than on giving a historical record of its sinking.

Situation

You and a friend have just seen the movie *Titanic,* and you disagree about the accuracy of the movie. To settle the argument, you decide to find out more about efforts to salvage artifacts from the R.M.S. *Titanic.* You've identified several sources (in the box at the right), but you want to focus only on those that will be the most accurate and reliable.

Strategies

Evaluate the source's credentials.
- If a writer is cited in the source, check to see if he or she is qualified to speak on the subject. For example, does the writer have an advanced degree in the field? Has the writer written other books or articles on this topic?
- Does the writer or producer have any biases toward the topic that you can detect, or any vested interest in a particular viewpoint?
- Is the writer or producer associated with a recognized institution?

Evaluate the medium.
- If the source is in a print medium, is it from a reputable publisher rather than a special interest group?

> ### List of Possible Sources of Information
> - *Titanic* (videorecording) starring Leonardo DiCaprio and Kate Winslet; directed by James Cameron. Paramount/20th Century Fox, 1997
> - "Descent to the *Titanic*" by P. Skinner. *il Petersen's Photographic Magazine,* Mar. 1989
> - "How We Found *Titanic*" by Dr. Robert D. Ballard (Woods Hole Oceanographic Institution). *National Geographic,* Dec. 1985
> - "Epilogue for the *Titanic*" by R. D. Ballard. *National Geographic,* Oct. 1987
> - Dave's *Titanic* Home Page (Web site)
> - Ocean Planet: How Deep Can They Go? RMS *Titanic's* Final Resting Place. http://seawifs.gsfc.nasa.gov/titanic.html (Web site)

- If the source is a videotape, is it a documentary?
- If the source is electronic, does the name of the Web site sound serious? Look for the abbreviations *.edu* (for educational) or *.gov* (for government) in the Internet address. Government sources and pages posted by a university are usually reliable. Someone's home page is not reliable.

Evaluate the source's timeliness.
- Check publication dates. Recent information may be more useful and accurate, but older information may provide important historical details.

Using the Strategies

1. For a formal research report, which sources cited in the box above would you definitely *not* use? Why?
2. For an article for a general interest magazine, which sources would you want to examine?
3. For a multimedia presentation, which sources might provide good visuals?
4. Of all the sources, which would be most reliable for checking your facts?

Extending the Strategies

Do research in a library or on the Internet to investigate sources available on another topic featured in this collection, such as the Holocaust or Mt. Everest expeditions.

454 THE NONFICTION COLLECTIONS

Reaching All Students

Struggling Readers
Provide specific examples of credentials (for example Ph.D.), organizations (for example, the Museum of Natural History or the University of Texas), publisher (for example, Holt Rinehart and Winston), and a film documentary (for example, a National Geographic Explorer film).

Advanced Students
Suggest that students report on sources quoted by a documentary film or nonfiction book about a topic that interests them. Point out that sources for film documentaries are usually cited at the end of the film and sources for nonfiction books appear at the beginning or end of the book on an acknowledgments page or in a preface.

Collection 7

Making a Point

Theme

Saying It! *To convince their readers and listeners, persuasive writers and speakers use both logical and emotional appeals. In this collection, Mark Twain uses satire and exaggeration to support his view of human nature. Roger Rosenblatt, Stephen King, and Pico Iyer use different strategies to persuade us of their views on the nature of heroism and the controversial content of TV shows.*

Reading the Anthology

Reaching Struggling Readers

The *Reading Skills and Strategies: Reaching Struggling Readers* binder provides materials coordinated with the Pupil's Edition (see the Collection Planner, p. T454B) to help students who have difficulty reading and comprehending text, or students who are reluctant readers. The binder for tenth grade is organized around sixteen individual skill areas and offers the following options:

- **MiniRead** MiniReads are short, easy texts that give students a chance to practice a particular skill and strategy before reading selections in the Pupil's Edition. Each MiniRead Skill Lesson can be taught independently or used in conjunction with a Selection Skill Lesson.

- **Selection Skill Lessons** Selection Skill Lessons allow students to apply skills introduced in the MiniReads. Each Selection Skill Lesson provides reading instruction and practice specific to a particular piece of literature in the Pupil's Edition.

Reading Beyond the Anthology

Read On

Collection 7 includes an annotated bibliography of books suitable for extended reading. The suggested books are related to works in this collection by theme, by author, or by subject. To preview the Read On for Collection 7, please turn to p. T491.

HRW Library

The *HRW Library* offers novels, plays, works of nonfiction, and short-story collections for extended reading. Each book in the Library includes one or more major works and thematically related Connections. Each book in the *HRW Library* is also accompanied by a Study Guide that provides teaching suggestions and worksheets. For Collection 7, the following titles are recommended.

THE FIRE NEXT TIME
James Baldwin
This ground-breaking essay by one of America's great writers helped millions of Americans to think differently about race.

ANIMAL FARM
George Orwell
Orwell satirizes totalitarian governments in this modern fable. An English farm is taken over by a group of animals who set up a socialist government. Everyone is equal— for a time.

Resources for this Collection

Note: All resources for this collection are available for preview on the *One-Stop Planner CD-ROM 1 with Test Generator.* All worksheets and blackline masters may be printed from the CD-ROM.

Internet Resources
go.hrw.com LE0 10-7

Selection or Feature	Reading and Literary Skills	Vocabulary, Language, and Grammar
The Lowest Animal (p. 456) Mark Twain **Connections: Gracious Goodness** (p. 464) Marge Piercy	• *Graphic Organizers for Active Reading,* Worksheet p. 28 • *Literary Elements:* Transparency 13 Worksheet p. 40	• *Words to Own,* Worksheet p. 27 • *Grammar and Language Links:* Using Commas, Worksheet p. 51 • *Language Workshop CD-ROM,* Punctuation • *Daily Oral Grammar,* Transparency 28
Elements of Literature: Persuasion (p. 468)	• *Literary Elements,* Transparency 13	
The Man in the Water (p. 470) Roger Rosenblatt	• *Reading Skills and Strategies: Reaching Struggling Readers* • MiniRead Skill Lesson, p. 158 • Selection Skill Lesson, p. 165 • *Graphic Organizers for Active Reading,* Worksheet p. 29	• *Words to Own,* Worksheet p. 28 • *Grammar and Language Links:* Wordiness, Worksheet p. 53 • *Language Workshop CD-ROM,* Wordiness • *Daily Oral Grammar,* Transparency 29
Now You Take "Bambi" or "Snow White"—That's Scary! (p. 479) Stephen King	• *Reading Skills and Strategies: Reaching Struggling Readers* • MiniRead Skill Lesson, p. 169 • Selection Skill Lesson, p. 176 • *Graphic Organizers for Active Reading,* Worksheet p. 30	• *Words to Own,* Worksheet p. 29 • *Grammar and Language Links:* Parentheticals, Worksheet p. 55 • *Language Workshop CD-ROM,* Parenthetical Expressions • *Daily Oral Grammar,* Transparency 30
Extending the Theme: The Unknown Rebel (p. 489) Pico Iyer	The Extending the Theme feature provides students with an unstructured opportunity to practice reading strategies using a selection that extends the theme of the collection.	
Writer's Workshop: Persuasive Essay (p. 492)		
Sentence Workshop: Varying Sentence Structure and Length (p. 497)		• *Workshop Resources,* p. 67 • *Language Workshop CD-ROM,* Sentence Structure
Learning for Life: Using Ads to Make Your Point (p. 499)		

Other Resources for this Collection

- *Cross-Curricular Activities,* p. 7
- *Portfolio Management System,* Introduction to Portfolio Assessment, p. 1
- *Formal Assessment,* Genre Test, p. 84
- *Test Generator,* Collection Test

Writing	Listening and Speaking Viewing and Representing	Assessment
• *Portfolio Management System,* Rubrics for Choices, p. 147	• *Visual Connections:* Videocassette A, Segment 7	• *Formal Assessment,* Selection Test, p. 76
	• *Audio CD Library,* Disc 15, Track 2	• *Test Generator (One-Stop Planner CD-ROM)*
	• *Portfolio Management System,* Rubrics for Choices, p. 147	
		• *Formal Assessment,* Literary Elements Test, p. 82
• *Portfolio Management System,* Rubrics for Choices, p. 148	• *Audio CD Library,* Disc 15, Track 3	• *Formal Assessment,* Selection Test, p. 78
	• *Portfolio Management System,* Rubrics for Choices, p. 148	• *Standardized Test Preparation,* p. 56
		• *Test Generator (One-Stop Planner CD-ROM)*
• *Portfolio Management System,* Rubrics for Choices, p. 149	• *Audio CD Library,* Disc 15, Track 4	• *Formal Assessment,* Selection Test, p. 80
	• *Viewing and Representing:* Fine Art Transparency 10 Worksheet p. 40	• *Standardized Test Preparation,* p. 58
	• *Portfolio Management System,* Rubrics for Choices, p. 149	• *Test Generator (One-Stop Planner CD-ROM)*
	• *Audio CD Library,* Disc 15, Track 5	
	• *Viewing and Representing:* Fine Art Transparency 11 Worksheet p. 44	
• *Workshop Resources,* p. 31	• *Viewing and Representing,* HRW Multimedia Presentation Maker	• *Portfolio Management System*
• *Writer's Workshop 2 CD-ROM,* Controversial Issue		• Prewriting, p. 150
• *Standardized Test Preparation:* Worksheet pp. 124, 132 Transparencies 1–12		• Peer Editing, p. 151
		• Assessment Rubric, p. 152
		• *Standardized Test Preparation:* Worksheet pp. 124, 132 Transparencies 1–12
		• *Portfolio Management System,* Rubrics, p. 153

 Transparency   CD-ROM   Video   Audio CD

Collection Planner

Collection 7 Making a Point
Skills Focus

Selection or Feature	Reading Skills and Strategies	Elements of Literature	Vocabulary/Language/ Grammar	Writing	Listening/ Speaking	Viewing/ Representing
The Lowest Animal (p. 456) Mark Twain	Identify the Writer's Purpose, pp. 456, 465 Identify the Writer's Point of View or Perspective, pp. 456, 465 Identify Generalizations, p. 465 Compare and Contrast, p. 465	Exaggeration, p. 456 Satire, pp. 456, 465 Irony, pp. 456, 465 Tall Tale, p. 466	Loaded Words, p. 467 Connotation and Denotation, p. 467 Suffixes, p. 467 Roots, p. 467 Noun-forming Suffixes, p. 467	Identify Topics for a Persuasive Essay, p. 466 Write a Rebuttal, p. 466 Write a Tall Tale, p. 466		Draw a Satiric Cartoon, p. 466
Elements of Literature: Persuasion (p. 468)		Persuasion, p. 468 Logical Argument, p. 468 Opinion, p. 468 Evidence, p. 468 Fallacies, p. 468 Emotional Appeals, p. 468				
The Man in the Water (p. 470) Roger Rosenblatt	Identify Supporting Details, p. 470 Summarize the Main Idea, pp. 470, 476	Main Idea, p. 470	Conciseness, p. 478 Synonyms and Connotations, p. 478	Write a Biographical Sketch, p. 477	Script and Present a Performance, p. 477	Make a Cluster Diagram, p. 477 Create a Gallery of Heroes, p. 477
Now You Take "Bambi" or "Snow White"— That's Scary! (p. 479) Stephen King	Make Generalizations, p. 486 Evaluate Motivation and Credibility, pp. 479, 486	Fact vs. Opinion, pp. 479, 486–487 Persuade, p. 486 Logical and Emotional Appeals, pp. 486–487 Compare and Contrast, p. 486	Parenthetical Expressions, p. 488 Synonyms, p. 488	Write a Parody, p. 487 Write a Persuasive Letter, p. 487 Write an Evaluative Essay, p. 487	Evaluate the Media, p. 487	Make a Pro-and-Con Chart, p. 487 Use a Venn Diagram, p. 488
Extending the Theme: The Unknown Rebel (p. 489) Pico Iyer	The Extending the Theme feature provides students with an unstructured opportunity to practice reading skills using a selection that extends the theme of the collection.					
Writer's Workshop: Persuasive Essay (p. 492)				Write a Persuasive Essay, pp. 492–496		
Sentence Workshop: Varying Sentence Structure and Length (p. 497)			Sentences, p. 497 • Simple • Compound • Compound-Complex	Revise Sentences to Vary Structure and Length, p. 497		
Reading for Life: Reading to Take Action (p. 498)	Strategies for Evaluating Persuasion, p. 498					
Learning for Life: Using Ads to Make Your Point (p. 499)				Write a Script, p. 499	Create a TV or Radio Spot, p. 499	Plan a Persuasive Ad Campaign, p. 499

MAKING A POINT

WRITING FOCUS: Persuasive Essay

In many ways writing is the act of saying I,

of imposing oneself upon other people, of saying

listen to me, see it my way, change your mind.
—Joan Didion

"I'M RIGHT." "YOU'RE WRONG." "NO, I'M RIGHT!" "NO, YOU'RE WRONG!"

Insisting on your view doesn't get you anywhere (unless, of course, you're a parent dealing with a small child or a supervisor overruling a worker). You're more likely to influence others if you use the strategies of persuasion. Persuasion relies on logic or emotion or both; it can be used fairly with skill, or it can be abused. As a citizen and a consumer exposed to persuasive writing and speaking, you must be able to think critically about persuasion, to distinguish between what's fair and reasonable and what's manipulative.

Responding to the Quotation

Didion's comment applies to fiction, poetry, and drama, as well as to nonfiction such as the persuasive essays that students will encounter in this collection. You might ask students if they feel that fiction, poetry, or drama can change readers' thinking as effectively as persuasive nonfiction can. Elicit a range of opinions, and encourage students to support their views. During the discussion, point out to students that they are using strategies of persuasion.

Writer's Notebook

Direct students to choose a specific commercial or speech, examining its persuasive strategies and the way the strategies affect students' thinking. Students might begin their entries with the "mind record" technique, transcribing their moment-to-moment thoughts and mental images while watching the commercial or speech.

Writer's Notebook

When you're watching a commercial or a political speech, notice what techniques are used to convince you that the product is worth buying or that the candidate is worth voting for. Write a brief reflection on the kinds of persuasive language you see on TV or in magazines and how you respond to them. Save your notes.

455

Writing Focus: Persuasive Essay

The following **Work in Progress** assignments build to a culminating **Writer's Workshop** at the end of the collection.

- The Lowest Animal   Brainstorming a topic (p. 466)
- The Man in the Water   Exploring the media for topics (p. 477)
- . . . That's Scary!   Listing pros and cons (p. 487)

Writer's Workshop: Persuasive Writing / Persuasive Essay (p. 492)

OBJECTIVES

1. Read and interpret the essay
2. Analyze satire
3. Determine writer's purpose and point of view
4. Express understanding through creative writing or drawing
5. Identify connotations and denotations and use loaded language
6. Understand and use new words
7. Recognize noun-forming suffixes

SKILLS

Literary and Reading
• Analyze satire
• Determine writer's purpose and point of view

Writing
• Brainstorm topics
• Write a rebuttal
• Rewrite an anecdote as a tall tale

Grammar/Language
• Identify connotations and denotations and use loaded language

Vocabulary and Art
• Recognize noun-forming suffixes
• Draw a satirical cartoon

Viewing/Representing
• Recognize satire in caricature (ATE)
• Compare techniques in art and poetry (ATE)

Planning

• **Block Schedule**
Block Scheduling Lesson Plans with Pacing Guide

• **Traditional Schedule**
Lesson Plans Including Strategies for English-Language Learners

• **One-Stop Planner**
CD-ROM with Test Generator

Before You Read

THE LOWEST ANIMAL

Make the Connection

Speaking Out—What's Wrong?

A utopia is a perfect world that exists only in the imagination. Utopian writers paint a picture of the way they think things should be—an ideal world in which everyone is happy and all needs are satisfied.

So what's wrong with the real world as you see it? And what can you do to fix it? In the essay you're about to read, Mark Twain directs his comic, stinging barbs against some of the things he thinks are wrong.

Quickwrite

In your notebook, list some things in life that you think should be changed to make the world better. Freewrite for several minutes.

 go.hrw.com
LEO 10-7

456 THE NONFICTION COLLECTIONS

Elements of Literature

Satire: The Weapon of Laughter

Mark Twain wrote that we have only "one really effective weapon—laughter. Power, money, persuasion, supplication—these can lift a colossal humbug—push it a little—weaken it a little, century by century; but only laughter can blow it to rags and atoms at a blast."

Satire uses humor to criticize all human beings or a particular person or institution. One of the favorite techniques of the satirist is **exaggeration**—overstating something to make it look absurd or worse than it is. Another favorite technique is **irony**—stating the opposite of what's really meant. Like many great satires, this famous essay is clearly outrageous. Twain doesn't really mean much of what he says. But sometimes the most exaggerated and maddening pieces of writing force us to think critically. You may disagree with a lot of what Twain says, but see if he also helps sharpen some of your own opinions about the world and what is wrong—or right—with it.

> **S**atire is the use of language to ridicule human weaknesses, vices, or stupidity, with the hope of bringing about social reform.
>
> *For more on Satire, see the Handbook of Literary Terms.*

Reading Skills and Strategies

What's the Writer's Purpose? What's the Point of View?

You should ask yourself two important questions when you read nonfiction: What is the writer's purpose? What is the writer's point of view? A writer's **purpose** may be to entertain, to share an experience, to inform, or to persuade. The **point of view,** or **perspective,** is the writer's position, thoughts, or feelings on a particular subject. A writer's purpose and point of view may be expressed directly—"This is what I think about X, and you should think so too because . . ." But most writers are not so direct. To determine a writer's purpose and point of view, follow these steps:

• Decide why this particular subject is important to the writer.

• Decide what the writer wants you to think about the subject.

Preteaching Vocabulary

Words to Own

Have students, either in pairs or individually, read the definitions of the Words to Own listed at the bottom of the selection pages. Then ask students to explain their answers to the following questions.

1. What would the Better Business Bureau do to **avaricious** salespeople who have not **scrupled** to lie about the validity of their products?

2. How might one **appease** toddlers who have cranky **dispositions**?

3. Should TV show the **sordid** details of an **atrocious** crime?

4. How might a pitcher of high **caliber** feel during the **transition** from the Major Leagues to the minors? Would he be tempted to renounce his **allegiance** to the team?

5. You see someone **wantonly** destroying the soccer team's equipment. What would you do?

T456

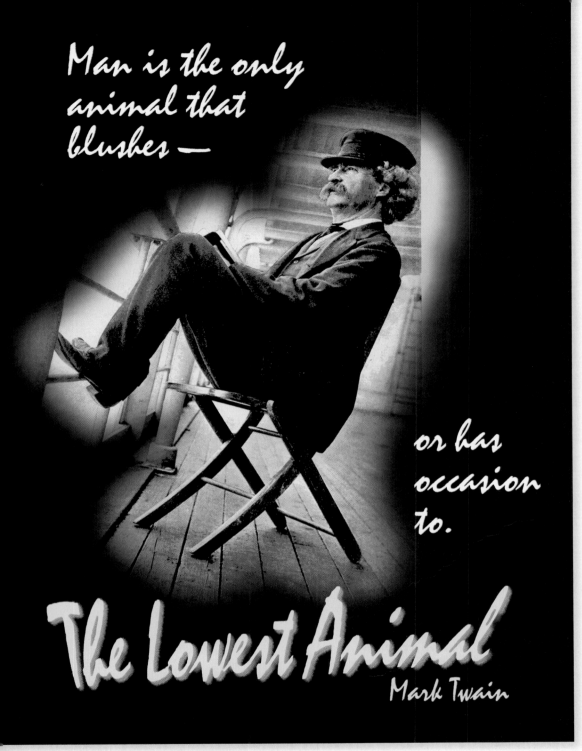

Man is the only animal that blushes —

or has occasion to.

The Lowest Animal
Mark Twain

Summary ■ ■ ■

Twain presents results of his "scientific method" that lead him to conclude that the ascent of humans from animals is really a descent. To show humans' incorrigible nature, he cites observations and examples from history and current events. He concludes that people—and only people—are cruel, avaricious, vengeful, vulgar, violent, irrational, and foolish. His clincher— which he claims to have proven by caging together people of dissimilar backgrounds—is that humans are incapable of learning to coexist.

Background

This essay, which Twain wrote around 1899, opens with a poke at Darwinism. Charles Darwin's *On the Origin of Species by Means of Natural Selection* had come out in 1859. This famous theory of biological evolution was one of the newer scientific ideas of the day.

Resources

Viewing and Representing
Videocassette A, Segment 7
This segment explores Twain's life and his role in American literature. For full lesson plans and worksheets, see *Visual Connections Teacher's Manual.*

Listening
Audio CD Library
An engaging recording of the essay is included in the *Audio CD Library:*
- Disc 15, Track 2

Resources: Print and Media

Reading
- *Graphic Organizers for Active Reading*, p. 28
- *Words to Own*, p. 27
- *Audio CD Library*
  Disc 15, Track 2

Elements of Literature
- *Literary Elements*
  Transparency 13
  Worksheet, p. 40

Writing and Language
- *Daily Oral Grammar*
  Transparency 28
- *Grammar and Language Links*
  Worksheet, p. 51
- *Language Workshop CD-ROM*

Viewing and Representing
- *Visual Connections*
  Videocassette A, Segment 7

Assessment
- *Formal Assessment*, p. 76
- *Portfolio Management System*, p. 147
- *Test Generator (One-Stop Planner CD-ROM)*

Internet
- go.hrw.com (keyword: LE0 10-7)

A Reading Skills and Strategies

Determining the Writer's Purpose/Point of View

❓ So far, does Twain's purpose seem to be to persuade or to entertain? **Explain.** [Sample answers: to persuade, since he directly states his new theory and seems to intend to prove it; to entertain, since his humorous tone suggests that he may not intend for his theory and proof to be taken seriously.]

B Elements of Literature

Satire

Twain's comically inflated diction is one early tip-off that the essay is satirical. Be sure students catch the exaggeration and irony in lines such as "I have not guessed or speculated or conjectured . . . ." and "These experiments . . . covered many months of painstaking and fatiguing work." Ask students to identify the target of Twain's satire in this paragraph. [Possible answers: scientists; the scientific method; scientific jargon.]

C Struggling Readers

Briticisms

Students may puzzle over the word *curious* used to describe experiments. Explain that in British (and earlier American) English, *curious* can mean "odd."

A I have been studying the traits and dispositions of the "lower animals" (so-called) and contrasting them with the traits and dispositions of man. I find the result humiliating to me. For it obliges me to renounce my allegiance to the Darwinian theory of the Ascent of Man from the Lower Animals, since it now seems plain to me that that theory ought to be vacated in favor of a new and truer one, this new and truer one to be named the *Descent of Man from the Higher Animals*.

B In proceeding toward this unpleasant conclusion, I have not guessed or speculated or conjectured, but have used what is commonly called the scientific method. That is to say, I have subjected every postulate[1] that presented itself to the crucial test of actual experiment and have adopted it or rejected it according to the result. Thus, I verified and established each step of my course in its turn before advancing to the next. These experiments were made in the London Zoological Gardens and covered many months of painstaking and fatiguing work.

Before particularizing any of the experiments, I wish to state one or two things which seem to more properly belong in this place than further along. This in the interest of clearness. The massed experiments established to my satisfaction certain generalizations, to wit:

1. That the human race is of one distinct species. It exhibits slight variations—in color, stature, mental caliber, and so on—due to climate, environment, and so forth; but it is a species by itself and not to be confounded with any other.

2. That the quadrupeds[2] are a distinct family, also. This family exhibits variations—in color, size, food preferences, and so on; but it is a family by itself.

3. That the other families—the birds, the fishes, the insects, the reptiles, etc.—are more or less distinct, also. They are in the procession. They are links in the chain which stretches down from the higher animals to man at the bottom.

C Some of my experiments were quite curious. In the course of my reading, I had come across a case where, many years ago, some hunters on our Great Plains organized a buffalo hunt for the entertainment of an English earl—that, and to provide some fresh meat for his larder.[3] They had charming sport. They killed seventy-two of those great animals and

---

1. **postulate** (päs′tyōō·lit): basic principle.
2. **quadrupeds** (kwä′drōō·pedz′): four-footed animals.
3. **larder**: supply of food or place where food supplies are kept.

WORDS TO OWN
dispositions (dis′pə·zish′ənz) *n.*: natures; temperaments.
allegiance (ə·lē′jəns) *n.*: loyalty or devotion.
caliber (kal′ə·bər) *n.*: quality or ability; worth.

Reaching All Students

Struggling Readers
Summarizing can help students recognize the author's purpose and point of view. It can also rescue students who are overwhelmed by Twain's style and diction. Have students jot down a one-line summary of each paragraph in the essay. Examples:
  1: Man is a lower animal.
  2: Conclusions come from experiments.
Students can refer to their summaries as they work on other activities for this selection.

English Language Learners
Students may need explanations of Twain's allusions to history: the slaughter of the buffalo, the Revolutionary War, the Spanish Inquisition, and so on. Have them form questions about what they don't understand and discuss answers with peer tutors. For strategies for engaging English language learners with the literature, see:
• *Lesson Plans Including Strategies for English-Language Learners*

Advanced Learners
Invite students to brainstorm a list of other forms of social satire that they have encountered. These might include cartoons, TV comedies, and satirical songs, films, and novels. Then, challenge students to identify techniques, beyond exaggeration and irony, that satirists use, such as loaded terms, understatement, non sequiturs, and stretched comparisons. Ask students to note Twain's use of these techniques.

ate part of one of them and left the seventy-one to rot. In order to determine the difference between an anaconda[4] and an earl—if any—I caused seven young calves to be turned into the anaconda's cage. The grateful reptile immediately crushed one of them and swallowed it, then lay back satisfied. It showed no further interest in the calves and no disposition to harm them. I tried this experiment with other anacondas, always with the same result. The fact stood proven that the difference between an earl and an anaconda is that the earl is cruel and the anaconda isn't; and that the earl wantonly destroys what he has no use for, but the anaconda doesn't. This seemed to suggest that the anaconda was not descended from the earl. It also seemed to suggest that the earl was descended from the anaconda, and had lost a good deal in the transition.

I was aware that many men who have accumulated more millions of money than they can ever use have shown a rabid hunger for more, and have not scrupled to cheat the ignorant and the helpless out of their poor servings in order to partially appease that appetite. I furnished a hundred different kinds of wild and tame animals the opportunity to accumulate vast stores of food, but none of them would do it. The squirrels and bees and certain birds made accumulations, but stopped when they had gathered a winter's supply and could not be persuaded to add to it either honestly or by chicane.[5] In order to bolster up a tottering reputation, the ant pretended to store up supplies, but I was not deceived. I know the ant. These experiments convinced me that there is this difference between man and the higher animals: He is avaricious and miserly, they are not.

In the course of my experiments, I convinced myself that among the animals man is the only one that harbors insults and injuries, broods over them, waits till a chance offers, then takes revenge. The passion of revenge is unknown to the higher animals.

Roosters keep harems, but it is by consent of their concubines;[6] therefore no wrong is done. Men keep harems, but it is by brute force, privileged by atrocious laws which the other sex was allowed no hand in making. In this matter man occupies a far lower place than the rooster.

---

4. **anaconda** (an′ə·kän′də): long, heavy snake that crushes its prey.
5. **chicane** (shi·kān′): clever deception; trickery. (*Chicanery* is the more common form.)
6. **concubines** (kän′kyo͞o·bīnz′): secondary wives.

- -

WORDS TO OWN

wantonly (wän′tən·lē) *adv.*: carelessly, often with deliberate malice.
transition (tran·zish′ən) *n.*: passing from one condition, form, or stage to another.
scrupled (skro͞o′pəld) *v.*: hesitated because of feelings of guilt.
appease (ə·pēz′) *v.*: satisfy; pacify.
avaricious (av′ə·rish′əs) *adj.*: greedy.
atrocious (ə·trō′shəs) *adj.*: evil; brutal; very bad.

- -

THE LOWEST ANIMAL **459**

D Critical Thinking
Analyzing
❓ Why, in your opinion, does Twain include the anecdote about the earl and the anacondas? [Possible responses: It supports Twain's theory that humans are lower or less humane than animals. The bizarre comparison creates humor.]

E Elements of Literature
Satire
❓ One technique of satire is exaggeration. What are some examples of exaggeration in this paragraph? [Possible responses: "a hundred different kinds of wild and tame animals"; "could not be persuaded to add to it either honestly or by chicane"; "to bolster up a tottering reputation, the ant pretended to store up supplies. . . ."]

F Advanced Learners
Argument
❓ How might you effectively counter the point that Twain makes in this paragraph? [Possible responses: No one knows whether or not hens "consent" to their living conditions. In some countries polygamy is a religious and cultural tradition supported by women as well as men.]

Skill Link

Using a Dictionary to Determine Meaning
Assign this activity before you teach the Language Link exercise on connotations and loaded language on p. 467. It will help you assess students' understanding of denotation vs. connotation.

From a dictionary, copy each word's first definition. Then write *positive* or *negative* to describe emotions that the word connotes.

1. slimy	6. honor
2. noble	7. bigot
3. tyranny	8. selfish
4. respectful	9. diligent
5. perseverance	10. coward

A ## Reading Skills and Strategies

Determining the Writer's Purpose/Point of View

❓ Twain states his point of view clearly here. How would you paraphrase it? [Possible responses: Humans do not reason. Their history shows that they don't. The proof lies in the fact that they see themselves as the top animal, when they are really the bottom one, according to their own ideas.]

B ## Elements of Literature

Satire

With the class, reread and discuss the information about *satire* on p. 456. Then ask students to compile a checklist of elements of satire in these two paragraphs. [Sample response:

√ persuasiveness √ humor
√ exaggeration   √ irony
√ ridicule   √ hope of reform]

Resources

Selection Assessment
Formal Assessment
• Selection Test, p. 76
Test Generator (One-Stop Planner)
• CD-ROM

A that whatever he is, he is *not* a reasoning animal. His record is the fantastic record of a maniac. I consider that the strongest count against his intelligence is the fact that with that record back of him, he blandly sets himself up as the head animal of the lot; whereas by his own standards, he is the bottom one.

In truth, man is incurably foolish. Simple things which the other animals easily learn he is incapable of learning. Among my experiments was this. In an hour I taught a cat and a dog to be friends. I put them in a cage. In another hour I taught them to be friends with a rabbit. In the course of two days I was able to add a fox, a goose, a squirrel, and some doves. Finally a monkey. They lived together in peace, even affectionately.

B Next, in another cage I confined an Irish Catholic from Tipperary, and as soon as he seemed tame I added a Scottish Presbyterian from Aberdeen. Next a Turk from Constantinople, a Greek Christian from Crete, an Armenian, a Methodist from the wilds of Arkansas, a Buddhist from China, a Brahman from Benares. Finally, a Salvation Army colonel from Wapping. Then I stayed away two whole days. When I came back to note results, the cage of Higher Animals was all right, but in the other there was but a chaos of gory odds and ends of turbans and fezzes and plaids and bones and flesh—not a specimen left alive. These Reasoning Animals had disagreed on a theological detail and carried the matter to a higher court.

MEET THE WRITER

The Voice of America

One of the many legends about **Mark Twain** (1835–1910) is that he was born on the day that Halley's comet appeared and died on the day of its return, seventy-five years later. Twain (who said that both he and the comet were "two unaccountable frauds") shifted from job to job when he was young, making and squandering fortunes. He was a great humorist who had a prickly disposition, a natural actor who lived a series of poses and disguises and believed in all of them—believed, along with his Connecticut Yankee, Hank Morgan, that "you can't throw too much style into a miracle."

Mark Twain was born Samuel Clemens in Florida, Missouri. He moved with his family to Hannibal, on the banks of the Mississippi, when he was four years old. (He later began to sign newspaper reports with the boatman's call "Mark Twain," which means "mark two fathoms [12 feet]," a safe depth for boats.) Twain seemed to have inherited the wit and vivacity of his beautiful mother and the extravagant temperament of his father. When the boy was eleven, his father died, almost bankrupt. Three of Twain's six brothers and sisters died in infancy, and a fourth, Henry, was killed in a steamboat accident at the age of twenty.

After his father's death, Twain left school to become a printer's apprentice, the first of a dozen jobs that failed to satisfy him during the next fifteen years. He tried soldiering, newspaper reporting, piloting a steamboat, prospecting, lecturing, and publishing. Through his various professions and lifestyles, however, two began to emerge as constants: that of a writer and that of a family man.

In 1869, Twain bought an interest in a Buffalo newspaper, believing that journalism

Taking a Second Look

Review: Evaluating Credibility of Sources

Remind students that their own common sense, experiences, and observations are among their best tools for evaluating credibility. Other tools include reference works, consultations with experts, and personal polls or surveys. For example, a history book could confirm the credibility of Twain's reference to atrocities committed by Richard I.

Activities

1. Have students recall what they know of the animals in the "experiment" in paragraph 2 on p. 462. Then, ask if Twain's results seem likely. Have students support their evaluations with their own observations.

2. Direct students to choose one other incident mentioned in the essay. Ask how they might confirm or refute the accuracy of the incident.

Listening to Music

Portrait for Orchestra ("Mark Twain") by Jerome Kern, performed by the Boston Pops

Activity

Have students listen to Kern's musical portrait of Mark Twain in conjunction with reading the "Meet the Author" feature. Then, have students work in pairs to create their own musical portrait of Twain or another author whose work appears in their text.

Mark Twain by "Spy," the pseudonym of English caricaturist Sir Leslie Ward (1851–1922). This illustration first appeared in *Vanity Fair* magazine.

would be his career. Then, almost immediately his fictionalized account of his European adventures, *Innocents Abroad,* was published and became a best-seller.

In 1870, he married the elegant and delicate Olivia Langdon of Elmira, New York, who would eventually inherit a quarter of a million dollars from her father. Twain sold his interest in the newspaper (at a loss) and moved to Hartford, Connecticut, where his first daughter, Susy, was born. The publication of *Roughing It* confirmed Twain's success as a writer, and he and his beloved "Livy"

built a house that was a monument to domesticity. (This elaborate three-storied turreted mansion is still a Hartford landmark.) Two more daughters, Clara and Jean, were born. The Clemenses lived in an atmosphere of intense familiarity, scarcely leaving one another's company except when Twain had to go on whirlwind lecture tours to pay for the cost of his extravagant establishment. The girls were educated at home. When Susy left home to attend college at Bryn Mawr, she was so homesick that she withdrew in the first year. When Clara went to Europe to study music, the whole family followed and set up housekeeping near her.

In the meantime, Twain wrote *The Adventures of Tom Sawyer* (1876) and *Adventures of Huckleberry Finn* (1884). *Huckleberry Finn* is generally considered a masterpiece of American fiction, yet in his own lifetime, Twain was thought of as a mere humorist and popular writer, seldom taken seriously by critics.

In an echo of his father's extravagance, Twain invested and lost more than $200,000 in an impractical typesetting machine. He was saved from bankruptcy by a Standard Oil executive, whom he insisted on paying back mainly with money earned from lecture tours that strained his health and robbed him of time to write.

Twain's last years were marked by a series of embittering misfortunes. Between 1902 and 1909, his wife and two of his treasured daughters died: Susy died of spinal meningitis, and Jean died during an epileptic seizure. Twain himself developed heart disease, and his energy declined as he struggled to complete novels and stories. There is no way he could have realized that within half a century he would stand as a literary giant, the one writer above all others who captured the American voice—vernacular, exuberant, ironic, and strong.

THE LOWEST ANIMAL 463

Assessing Learning

Grading Timesaver

Rubrics for each Choices assignment appear on p. 147 in the *Portfolio Management System*.

CHOICES:
Building Your Portfolio

1. **Writer's Notebook** With each selection, a Writer's Notebook activity appears as the first option in the Choices section. These brief, work-in-progress assignments build toward the writing assignment presented in the Writer's Workshop at the end of the collection. If students save their work for their Writer's Notebook activities as they move through the collection, they should be able to use some of them as starting points for the Workshop.

2. **Writing a Rebuttal** Students might use Twain's ploy of inventing imaginary experiments. If students have trouble beginning, write this starter sentence on the chalkboard: "Mr. Twain, I was so interested in your experiments with animals and humans that I decided to conduct a few experiments of my own."

3. **Creative Writing** Before students start, you might read aloud Twain's "The Celebrated Jumping Frog of Calaveras County" to show the blend of outrageous details and poker-face tone that characterizes tall tales.

4. **Drawing** Students may use computer animation software to create their cartoons.

CHOICES: Building Your Portfolio

Writer's Notebook
1. Collecting Ideas for a Persuasive Essay

Brainstorming a topic.
A topic for a persuasive essay, such as the one you'll write for the Writer's Workshop on page 492, should be

- debatable (Reasonable people have different opinions about it.)
- important (You should feel that it matters.)
- current (You should be able to gather information easily.)

For now jot down as many issues as you can think of. (Your Quickwrite list may give you ideas.) Then phrase your issues as questions. The issues can be local, national, or global. Maybe Twain's

—Rob Noyes, from *Voices of Youth*

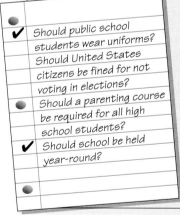

✔ Should public school students wear uniforms?
Should United States citizens be fined for not voting in elections?
Should a parenting course be required for all high school students?
✔ Should school be held year-round?

essay made you so angry that you'll find your topic there. Check the two issues you'd most like to write about.

Writing a Rebuttal
2. Dear Mr. Twain

Write a rebuttal of Twain's essay. Your rebuttal may be in any form you like: a letter to Mark Twain, a parody of Twain's essay, a serious essay, a dramatic sketch, a poem, an anecdote, a TV or newspaper editorial, or something else. Try to elaborate with specific examples, just as Twain does.

Creative Writing
3. That's a Tall Tale!

Twain, America's most celebrated humorist, was known for writing tall tales such as "The Celebrated Jumping Frog of Calaveras County." A **tall tale** is an exaggerated, far-fetched story that is obviously untrue but is told as though it should be believed. Stories

about Paul Bunyan and Pecos Bill are popular American tall tales.

Parts of this essay read almost like a tall tale—for example, Twain's "anecdote" about leaving several people alone in a cage and the mayhem that results. Obviously, this didn't really happen. Take a section of this essay, such as the one just mentioned, and rewrite it as a tall tale. Remember, your story must be exaggerated and untrue, but tell it with "a straight face."

Drawing
4. A Cartoon Satire

Draw a cartoon that satirizes an event or a situation that you think needs fixing. Rob Noyes, a high school student in Amherst, Massachusetts, won third place for the cartoon at the top of this page in a contest sponsored by a literary magazine. The cartoon probably would have delighted Mark Twain.

Mark Twain by "Spy," the pseudonym of English caricaturist Sir Leslie Ward (1851–1922). This illustration first appeared in *Vanity Fair* magazine.

would be his career. Then, almost immediately his fictionalized account of his European adventures, *Innocents Abroad,* was published and became a best-seller.

In 1870, he married the elegant and delicate Olivia Langdon of Elmira, New York, who would eventually inherit a quarter of a million dollars from her father. Twain sold his interest in the newspaper (at a loss) and moved to Hartford, Connecticut, where his first daughter, Susy, was born. The publication of *Roughing It* confirmed Twain's success as a writer, and he and his beloved "Livy"

built a house that was a monument to domesticity. (This elaborate three-storied turreted mansion is still a Hartford landmark.) Two more daughters, Clara and Jean, were born. The Clemenses lived in an atmosphere of intense familiarity, scarcely leaving one another's company except when Twain had to go on whirlwind lecture tours to pay for the cost of his extravagant establishment. The girls were educated at home. When Susy left home to attend college at Bryn Mawr, she was so homesick that she withdrew in the first year. When Clara went to Europe to study music, the whole family followed and set up housekeeping near her.

In the meantime, Twain wrote *The Adventures of Tom Sawyer* (1876) and *Adventures of Huckleberry Finn* (1884). *Huckleberry Finn* is generally considered a masterpiece of American fiction, yet in his own lifetime, Twain was thought of as a mere humorist and popular writer, seldom taken seriously by critics.

In an echo of his father's extravagance, Twain invested and lost more than $200,000 in an impractical typesetting machine. He was saved from bankruptcy by a Standard Oil executive, whom he insisted on paying back mainly with money earned from lecture tours that strained his health and robbed him of time to write.

Twain's last years were marked by a series of embittering misfortunes. Between 1902 and 1909, his wife and two of his treasured daughters died: Susy died of spinal meningitis, and Jean died during an epileptic seizure. Twain himself developed heart disease, and his energy declined as he struggled to complete novels and stories. There is no way he could have realized that within half a century he would stand as a literary giant, the one writer above all others who captured the American voice—vernacular, exuberant, ironic, and strong.

Assessing Learning

Check Test: Short Answer
"The Lowest Animal"
Answers may vary slightly.

1. What is Twain's central argument? [Man is the most savage form of animal life.]
2. Why is describing the earl's hunt as "charming sport" ironic? [It's not charming or sport to leave 71 slaughtered buffalo to rot.]
3. Which animal deals in war? [humankind]
4. What does Twain's experiment show that humans can't learn? [how to get along]

"Gracious Goodness"
5. Why does the royal tern "fall to the sand"? [It is impaled by a fishhook.]

Standardized Test Preparation
For practice in proofreading and editing, see
• *Daily Oral Grammar* Transparency 28

Connections

The speaker in this poem finds an injured royal tern while walking on the beach. She admires the bird as she and a friend remove the fishhook that has hurt it. As she watches the bird take flight, the speaker believes that her actions seem more "obviously right" than anything else she has ever done.

Ⓐ Appreciating Language

Connotations

? What adjectives connote power and majesty, despite the tern's perilous condition? [*muscular; glossy; strong*]

Ⓑ Elements of Literature

Metaphor

? How is virtue "a sunrise in the belly"? [Possible responses: It makes you feel warm inside; it creates hope and beauty.]

Ⓒ Critical Thinking

Extending the Text

? How would you answer this question? [Possible responses: because it healed an injury caused by other humans; because it was an act of pure compassion.]

Background

American poet, novelist, and social activist **Marge Piercy** (1936—   ) lives on Cape Cod, Massachusetts, near the ocean.

Royal Tern (1832) by John J. Audubon. Watercolor and graphite.

© Collection of the New-York Historical Society

Gracious Goodness

Marge Piercy

On the beach where we had been idly
telling the shell coins
cat's paw, crossbarred Venus, china cockle,
we both saw at once
5   the sea bird fall to the sand
and flap grotesquely.
He had taken a great barbed hook
out through the cheek and fixed
in the big wing.
10   He was pinned to himself to die,
a royal tern with a black crest blown back
as if he flew in his own private wind.
Ⓐ He felt good in my hands, not fragile
but muscular and glossy and strong,
15   the beak that could have split my hand
opening only to cry
as we yanked on the barbs.
We borrowed a clippers, cut and drew
out the hook.
Then the royal tern took off, wavering,
20   lurched twice,
then acrobat returned to his element,
dipped,
zoomed, and sailed out to dive for a fish.
Ⓑ Virtue: what a sunrise in the belly.
Why is there nothing
25   **Ⓒ** I have ever done with anybody
that seems to me so obviously right?

Connecting Across Texts

Connecting with "The Lowest Animal"

In a discussion, guide students in contrasting the episode of human conduct that Piercy narrates and the episodes that Twain narrates. Then ask them to contrast the overall impressions of humankind that they receive from Twain's essay and from Piercy's poem. [Possible responses: Piercy highlights an act of human virtue, while Twain recounts acts of human vice; Piercy shows humans acting superior—in a helpful way—to another animal, while Twain shows humans acting inferior to other animals. The main impression from Piercy's poem is guardedly positive (no other things the speaker has ever done have felt unquestionably right), whereas the main impression from Twain's essay is overwhelmingly negative.]

MAKING MEANINGS

First Thoughts

[respond]

1. What is your first response to Twain's essay?

Shaping Interpretations

[infer]

2. What is Twain's **purpose** in this essay? What is his **point of view**, or perspective—that is, what does he want you to think about humanity?

[comprehend]

3. What are the targets of Twain's **satire**, and where does he use **exaggeration** and **irony** to hit his targets? Does his satire work, or does he overdo it?

Extending the Text

[connect]

4. If Twain were alive today, what people, events, and institutions do you think he would satirize? How do Twain's targets compare with your Quickwrite list?

Challenging the Text

[evaluate]

5. Explain why you think "The Lowest Animal" is or isn't (a) convincing and (b) funny.

[synthesize]

6. A **generalization** is a statement that is meant to apply to every individual in a class. A valid generalization is true. (These examples are valid generalizations: Pigs have curly tails. All insects have six legs. These are *not* valid: Pigs are stupid. Insects carry disease.) Twain uses many often very funny generalizations. If you were debating with Twain, how would you attack his arguments?

[evaluate]

7. What aspects of humanity does Twain leave out? How is Piercy's poem (see *Connections* on page 464) an answer of sorts to Twain's arguments?

[contrast]

8. **Contrast** Twain's view of humanity with the view expressed by Roger Rosenblatt in his essay "The Man in the Water" (see page 471). Whose view comes closer to your own? Explain.

©The New Yorker Collection 1988
Bernard Schoenbaum from cartoonbank.com.
All Rights Reserved.

THE LOWEST ANIMAL 465

Reading Check

a. What three **generalizations** does Twain make as a result of his experiments at the London Zoo?

b. What animals does Twain compare to human beings?

c. Why does he think that each animal is superior to humans?

d. Twain repeats the following phrase several times: "Man is the only animal that . . ." List as many of these assertions as you can find.

Reading Check

a. Humans are all one distinct species; quadrupeds are a distinct family; other animal families are also distinct, and all form a hierarchy, with humans at the bottom.

b. anacondas, squirrels, bees, birds, ants, roosters, cats, dogs, rabbits, foxes, geese, squirrels, doves, and monkeys

c. Anacondas aren't cruel or destructive; squirrels, bees, birds, and ants aren't greedy; roosters and cats aren't immoral or sadistic;

the other animals can learn to get along with one another.

d. Man alone "harbors insults and injuries, broods over them, waits till a chance offers, then takes revenge," "laughs," "blushes," "is cruel," "inflicts pain for the pleasure of doing it," "deals in that atrocity of atrocities, war," "robs his helpless fellow of his country," "enslaves," shows patriotic or religious bigotry, is "unreasoning."

MAKING MEANINGS

First Thoughts

1. Possible responses:
   • It is funny, profound, bitter.
   • It isn't accurate.
   • Its reasoning is skewed.

Shaping Interpretations

2. Sample answers: *Purpose*—to persuade; to entertain and persuade. *Point of view*—that humans are more savage than animals.

3. Sample answers: *Targets*—human failings such as greed, cruelty, bigotry. *Exaggeration*—tirades against patriotism and religion; the anecdote of the caged people. *Irony*—"[I] have used . . . the scientific method," "They had charming sport," "He is alone in that distinction." Possible responses: The satire works because, as we laugh at Twain's exaggeration, we see the truth of his main point. The satire doesn't work because Twain is too extreme, damaging his credibility.

Extending the Text

4. Twain might satirize targets in politics, religion, education, science, environmental movements, the arts, or the media. Students' lists may include some of Twain's targets.

Challenging the Text

5. Possible responses: It is convincing because of the many accurate examples, and it's funny because the examples are so outrageous. It's not convincing because Twain ignores positive aspects of human nature, and it's too inaccurate and bitter to be funny.

6. Students might list incidents showing human honor, kindness, wisdom, or altruism.

7. Sample answer: Twain leaves out compassion, generosity, and love. Piercy's poem shows an act of compassion, countering Twain's generalization.

8. Possible response: Twain sees humans as purely cruel and self-serving; Rosenblatt's man in the water seems purely altruistic. Students' views will vary.

T465

Rubrics for each Choices assignment appear on p. 147 in the *Portfolio Management System*.

CHOICES:
Building Your Portfolio

1. **Writer's Notebook** With each selection, a Writer's Notebook activity appears as the first option in the Choices section. These brief, work-in-progress assignments build toward the writing assignment presented in the Writer's Workshop at the end of the collection. If students save their work for their Writer's Notebook activities as they move through the collection, they should be able to use some of them as starting points for the Workshop.

2. **Writing a Rebuttal** Students might use Twain's ploy of inventing imaginary experiments. If students have trouble beginning, write this starter sentence on the chalkboard: "Mr. Twain, I was so interested in your experiments with animals and humans that I decided to conduct a few experiments of my own."

3. **Creative Writing** Before students start, you might read aloud Twain's "The Celebrated Jumping Frog of Calaveras County" to show the blend of outrageous details and poker-face tone that characterizes tall tales.

4. **Drawing** Students may use computer animation software to create their cartoons.

CHOICES: Building Your Portfolio

Writer's Notebook
1. Collecting Ideas for a Persuasive Essay

Brainstorming a topic. A topic for a persuasive essay, such as the one you'll write for the Writer's Workshop on page 492, should be

- debatable (Reasonable people have different opinions about it.)
- important (You should feel that it matters.)
- current (You should be able to gather information easily.)

For now jot down as many issues as you can think of. (Your Quickwrite list may give you ideas.) Then phrase your issues as questions. The issues can be local, national, or global. Maybe Twain's

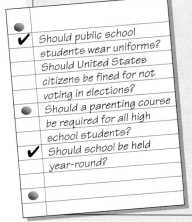

✔ Should public school students wear uniforms?
Should United States citizens be fined for not voting in elections?
Should a parenting course be required for all high school students?
✔ Should school be held year-round?

LOOK, FENTON... A NEW, PRISTINE, SAFE PLANET! THIS IS PERFECT... A NEW REPLACEMENT FOR OUR OWN DEPLETED, POLLUTED PLANET. MOUNTAINS... CLEAN AIR AND WATER... BLUE SKIES... JUST THINK, FENTON, A PLACE FOR THE HUMAN RACE TO START OVER AGAIN AND THIS TIME, DO IT RIGHT!

OK... THE COLONY AND RESORT GOES IN THAT SECTOR, WE'LL RAZE THAT FOREST TO PUT IN THE INDUSTRIAL PARK... THE MINI-MALL AND CASINO WILL GO WHERE THAT SWAMP GOES... HEY! WHERE DOES THE NUCLEAR PLANT GO?!

—Rob Noyes, from *Voices of Youth*

essay made you so angry that you'll find your topic there. Check the two issues you'd most like to write about.

Writing a Rebuttal
2. Dear Mr. Twain

Write a rebuttal of Twain's essay. Your rebuttal may be in any form you like: a letter to Mark Twain, a parody of Twain's essay, a serious essay, a dramatic sketch, a poem, an anecdote, a TV or newspaper editorial, or something else. Try to elaborate with specific examples, just as Twain does.

Creative Writing
3. That's a Tall Tale!

Twain, America's most celebrated humorist, was known for writing tall tales such as "The Celebrated Jumping Frog of Calaveras County." A **tall tale** is an exaggerated, far-fetched story that is obviously untrue but is told as though it should be believed. Stories about Paul Bunyan and Pecos Bill are popular American tall tales.

Parts of this essay read almost like a tall tale—for example, Twain's "anecdote" about leaving several people alone in a cage and the mayhem that results. Obviously, this didn't really happen. Take a section of this essay, such as the one just mentioned, and rewrite it as a tall tale. Remember, your story must be exaggerated and untrue, but tell it with "a straight face."

Drawing
4. A Cartoon Satire

Draw a cartoon that satirizes an event or a situation that you think needs fixing. Rob Noyes, a high school student in Amherst, Massachusetts, won third place for the cartoon at the top of this page in a contest sponsored by a literary magazine. The cartoon probably would have delighted Mark Twain.

466 THE NONFICTION COLLECTIONS

Connotations Give Loaded Words Their Punch

Handbook of Literary Terms
H E L P

See Connotations.

What do *patriotism, honesty,* and *truth* have in common with *terrorism, lazy, sneaky,* and *lies*? They're all **loaded words**, heavy with emotional associations, or **connotations**. The connotations of a word carry meaning beyond the word's literal meaning, or **denotation**. The first group above have positive connotations that make us feel good; the second group arouse negative feelings.

Skillful persuaders use loaded words to influence our feelings. "The lowest animal," for example, is a negatively loaded term. If Twain had called humans "a species that exhibits many contradictions," he would have been using neutral, unemotional terms. However, Twain wasn't interested in being unemotional; he was presenting a view he deeply believed in.

It's important to know when loaded words are being used to persuade you, often to get your vote or your money. Although loaded words are not necessarily bad, they're no substitute for reason and evidence. They are, however, very effective in arousing feelings.

Try It Out

➤ With a partner, reread a portion of Twain's essay, listing every loaded word or phrase you find. Substitute a neutral (unloaded) word for each loaded term. Which is more persuasive?

➤ Images can be loaded, too. Advertisers know that athletes, babies, young animals, and gardens have positive connotations. Find and share examples of positive and negative images in ads.

➤ If you've started to work on a persuasive essay, pull out your notes now and circle any loaded words you find. Do you see other places where you could use loaded words effectively?

VOCABULARY [HOW TO OWN A WORD]

WORD BANK

dispositions
allegiance
caliber
wantonly
transition
scrupled
appease
avaricious
atrocious
sordid

What's in a Noun? Suffixes That Form Nouns

A **suffix** is a word part added to the end of a word or to a **root** to create a new word. Certain suffixes change words into nouns—for example, *sordid* + *-ness* = *sordidness*. Study the following noun-forming suffixes and their meanings.

–ition	*meaning:*	action, result, state
–ance	*meaning:*	act, condition, quality
–ment	*meaning:*	means, result, action
–ness	*meaning:*	quality, state

Now, write down the words in the Word Bank, and indicate whether each is a noun. If it is a noun and it contains one of the noun-forming suffixes listed above, circle the suffix. If the word is *not* a noun, turn it into a noun by adding one of the suffixes above. (Note: For one of the words, you will have to remove a suffix before you add the noun-forming suffix. For another word, you need only remove its suffix to form a noun.) Finally, look up the meanings of the new words in a dictionary.

THE LOWEST ANIMAL 467

Students can use skills from this Language Link exercise when revising their persuasive essays for the Writer's Workshop at the end of the collection. Be sure students know that the use of loaded words is an appeal to readers' emotions and that appeals to emotion can augment sound reasoning but cannot replace it.

Try It Out
Possible Answers

1.

loaded words	neutral terms
lower animals	nonhuman animals
humiliating	informative
allegiance to	acceptance of
Ascent of Man	evolution of humans
truer	more accurate
Higher Animals	other animals

2. Some examples where students might find these images are in ads for snack foods, personal grooming products, cars, credit cards, or medicines.

VOCABULARY
Possible Answers

1. dispos<u>ition</u>s n.
2. alle<u>giance</u> n.
3. caliber n.
4. wantonly—wanton<u>ness</u>
5. trans<u>ition</u> n.
6. scrupled—scruple
7. appease—appease<u>ment</u>
8. avaricious—avarice
9. atrocious—atrocious<u>ness</u> (atrocity)
10. sordid—sordid<u>ness</u>

Resources

Language
• *Grammar and Language Links* Worksheet, p. 51

Vocabulary
• *Words to Own* Worksheet, p. 27

Language Link Quick Check

The words that follow appear in "The Lowest Animal." Indicate whether the connotation of each word is neutral, positive, or negative. Then suggest two words with similar meanings that have different connotations.

1. painstaking
2. accumulate
3. miserly
4. broods
5. slaughter
6. dispute
7. patriot
8. intelligence
9. confined
10. chaos

[Sample answers:
1. positive; careful, nitpicking
2. neutral; reap, hoard
3. negative; economical, thrifty
4. negative; thinks, meditates
5. negative; kill, terminate
6. neutral; debate, squabble
7. positive; citizen, isolationist
8. neutral; ingenuity, slyness
9. neutral; sheltered, caged
10. negative; disorder, complexity]

Resources

Elements of Literature
Persuasion
For additional instruction on persuasion, see *Literary Elements:*
• Transparency 13

Assessment
Formal Assessment
• Literary Elements Test, p. 82
Test Generator (One-Stop Planner)
• CD-ROM

Elements of Literature

This lesson discusses the persuasive aim in writing. It includes definitions and examples of logical appeals, logical fallacies, and emotional appeals, and explains positive and negative uses of emotional appeals.

PERSUASION: See It My Way

BIG BROTHER (*trying to persuade* LITTLE BROTHER *to stop using the TV screen for a video game so that he can watch a football game on TV):* If we watch the game together, you'll learn how to improve your game. I'll even give you some of the tips Coach Jackson taught us. If my team wins, I'll play "Demon Warrior" with you for an hour right after the game's over, and I'll wash the dishes for you tonight when it's really your turn.

If you were Little Brother, would you be persuaded?

Writers who have a **persuasive aim** are trying to lead you to think or act in a certain way—to agree with their opinions, buy their products, vote for their candidates, support their causes. In "The Lowest Animal," Mark Twain is trying to persuade you *not* to behave in certain ways—all the ways he ridicules.

Skillful persuaders have a whole trunkful of no-holds-barred techniques—just short of twisting your arm—designed to get you to see things their way. Learning these techniques will make your writing and speaking more forceful and convincing. It will also make you aware of the ways in which others try to persuade you.

Aim for the Brain: Logical Appeals

Logic is the science of correct reasoning that's been slowly built into your brain by your experiences in the world. It deals with things like "If this is true, then that must be true" and "This must be true because . . ." and "Yes, that makes sense to me." A logical **persuasive argument,** such as the one you'll present for the Writer's Workshop on page 492, is built on an **opinion** supported by reasons and evidence.

• **Reasons** tell *why* everyone should accept an opinion as **valid** (true).

Suppose you are in favor of all public school students' wearing uniforms. Two reasons to support your opinion might be that uniforms eliminate expensive competition over clothes and lessen classroom distractions.

Reasons can't stand alone; they need to be backed up by sufficient **evidence.**

• **Facts and statistics (number facts)** give strong support to your reasons because nobody can argue with them. A fact is, by definition, true (see page 479).

A recent survey shows that 61% of all students in this school and 86% of all their parents and guardians favor uniforms.

• **Expert testimony.** Statements made by an expert in the field are always convincing.

"Since we adopted uniforms two years ago," said Kate Applegate, Shaw's principal for the past twenty years, "school morale has definitely improved."

Beware of Faulty Reasoning: Fallacies

Some statements sound logical and factual, but they're not. Whenever someone tries to persuade you, ask yourself, "*How* is this person trying to convince me?" Be alert to these common kinds of faulty reasoning, or **logical fallacies,** and watch for them in your own writing and speaking.

• **Hasty generalization**—coming to a conclusion on the basis of insufficient evidence

All my friends prefer uniforms;

Reaching All Students

Struggling Readers
Before students begin reading, provide a three-part framework like the one in the next column. Direct them to fill it in as they read. When all students have finished reading the lesson, discuss, compare, and correct their frameworks.

• A logical persuasive argument is supported by _____ and _____ .
  Two types of evidence are _____ and _____ .
• An error in reasoning is called a _____ .
  Examples: _____, _____, _____, and _____ .
• An emotional appeal targets readers' _____ .
  Examples: _____, _____, and _____ .

by Richard Cohen

most tenth-graders would rather wear uniforms than faddish clothing.

- **Name calling**—attacking the person who holds the view rather than the view itself

Loren has been campaigning for school uniforms, but everyone knows what bad judgment he's shown in the past.

- **Either/or**—describing a situation as if there were only two choices when in fact there may be several

Either the school board requires that students wear uniforms, or we face increased disruptions in the classrooms and in the halls.

- **False cause and effect**—asserting that because Event B followed Event A, A caused B

Since he began to wear a uniform, Jed's been getting better grades on English tests.

Zeroing In on Feelings: Emotional Appeals

In the persuasive writing that you do for school, you'll be expected to rely mainly on logical appeals. But a little feeling never hurts. Think of emotional appeals as an extra nudge that moves the audience in your direction. The key point is that emotional appeals should reinforce logical arguments, not replace them.

- **Loaded words.** You've studied the power of loaded words on page 467. How many can you spot in this statement?

Neat, attractive school uniforms promote feelings of mutual respect and equality among students, who are judged by how they act rather than by the cost of their designer running shoes.

- **Glittering generalities.** A type of loaded words, they are so strongly positive that they "glitter" and make you feel good. Slogans are often glittering generalities.

School uniforms—they're all–American.

- **Bandwagon appeal.** This is the "Don't miss out" or "Don't be the last person to have one" appeal often used by advertisers.

In this district, all but two schools have voted to require uniforms for students.

- **Testimonials.** When a basketball star endorses a candidate for the Senate or a brand of cereal, he's making an emotional appeal to fans. Famous people who endorse products unrelated to their field of expertise are persuading by means of their talent, glamour, and fame.

Leila Lovelace, glamorous movie star, and Tyrone Washington, MVP quarterback, agree that they owe their success in life to wearing school uniforms as teenagers.

Check It Out

So there you have it. Effective persuasion is always built on logical appeals and sometimes on emotional appeals. It avoids all fallacies. Look for these characteristics of good persuasion in

- a commercial
- an editorial, a column, or a letter to the editor
- a political or campaign speech
- a persuasive argument made by a friend
- a persuasive argument you make

1. Read and interpret the essay
2. Identify the main idea
3. Summarize the main idea and supporting details
4. Express understanding through writing/drawing, or speaking/performing
5. Identify concise prose and streamline one's own writing
6. Understand and use new words
7. Recognize connotations

SKILLS
Literary
- Identify the main idea

Reading
- Summarize the main idea and supporting details

Writing
- Cluster ideas for a persuasive essay
- Write a biographical sketch

Speaking/Listening
- Prepare and present a theme-related performance

Grammar/Language
- Use concise prose

Vocabulary
- Recognize connotations

Art
- Create a poster or portrait

Viewing/Representing
- Discuss how a photograph relates to an essay (ATE)

Planning

- **Block Schedule**
  Block Scheduling Lesson Plans with Pacing Guide
- **Traditional Schedule**
  Lesson Plans Including Strategies for English-Language Learners
- **One-Stop Planner**
  CD-ROM with Test Generator

Before You Read

THE MAN IN THE WATER

Make the Connection

Who's a Hero?

Have you ever seen a real-life hero? We see so many inflated heroes in movies and on TV that the real thing is sometimes hard to recognize.

This essay is about a person who was unmistakably a hero, an ordinary man who didn't ask for the opportunity to display his courage. The disaster described in the essay occurred on the Potomac River, near Washington National Airport in Washington, D.C., in the winter of 1982.

Quickwrite

In your notebook, define *hero* and *heroism* in a sentence or two. Then list some people, past or present, famous or ordinary, whom you regard as heroes. Briefly tell why you think each person is a hero. Save your notes.

Elements of Literature

The Main Idea

When Rosenblatt sat down to write his feature article about the man in the water, he probably had his **main idea** in mind—some insight or message he wished to communicate about the tragedy. He was not writing a news article in which he'd have to report the facts of the event. That article had already been written. Rosenblatt wanted to do something else. He wanted to talk about something important that he saw in the incident. He had an idea to share.

> **A main idea** is an opinion, a message, an insight, or a lesson that is the focus of a piece of writing. Some essayists directly state their main idea. Others let us infer the idea for ourselves.

Reading Skills and Strategies

Summarizing the Main Idea

When you **summarize** an essay such as Rosenblatt's, you state its most important idea in your own words. You should also cite some of the essay's key **supporting details**. To find the **main idea** of Rosenblatt's—or any—essay, look for key statements that express the writer's opinion. You might want to organize your thoughts by filling out a chart like this:

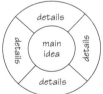

go.hrw.com
LEO 10-7

Preteaching Vocabulary

Words to Own

On the chalkboard, draw a shamrock graphic such as the one below.

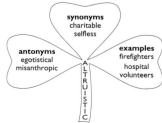

synonyms
charitable
selfless

antonyms
egotistical
misanthropic

examples
firefighters
hospital
volunteers

ALTRUISTIC

meaning: concerned for others' well-being

Have the class suggest more words to add to each of the three "leaves." Then tell pairs of students to read the definitions of the Words to Own listed at the bottom of the selection pages. [*flailing, abiding, pitted,* and *implacable*]. Direct the student partners to create and fill in a shamrock graphic for each Word to Own.

Like every other person on that flight, he was desperate to live.

The Man in the Water

Roger Rosenblatt

THE MAN IN THE WATER 471

Summary ▪ ▪

Reflecting on the crash of a plane into a Washington, D.C., bridge in the winter of 1982, Rosenblatt calls the disaster "two forms of nature in collision: the elements and human character." He examines the heroism of two helicopter rescuers who risked their lives to throw a lifeline to the five survivors in the icy Potomac; of a bystander who jumped in to drag a woman to shore; and of one crash victim who kept passing the lifeline to others—and then drowned. In the actions of this anonymous "man in the water," Rosenblatt sees the best of Everyman, the triumph of humanity and altruism over the impersonal and indifferent forces of nature.

Resources

Listening
Audio CD Library
A recording of this article is included in the *Audio CD Library:*
• Disc 15, Track 3

  Resources: Print and Media

Reading
• *Reading Skills and Strategies*
    MiniRead Skill Lesson, p. 158
    Selection Skill Lesson, p. 165
• *Graphic Organizers for Active Reading*, p. 29
• *Words to Own*, p. 28
• *Audio CD Library*
    Disc 15, Track 3

Writing and Language
• *Daily Oral Grammar*
    Transparency 29
• *Grammar and Language Links*
    Worksheet, p. 53
• *Language Workshop CD-ROM*

Assessment
• *Formal Assessment*, p. 78
• *Portfolio Management System*, p. 148
• *Standardized Test Preparation*, p. 56
• *Test Generator (One-Stop Planner CD-ROM)*

Internet
• go.hrw.com (keyword: LE0 10-7)

T471

A Reading Skills and Strategies

Summarizing the Main Idea

? This rhetorical question signals that Rosenblatt is about to contradict his first paragraph. How would you summarize the main point of the first paragraph? [Possible responses: There was nothing unique about the crash. The crash was terrible but not unusual in any way.]

B Appreciating Language

Style

Point out to students that Rosenblatt breaks his pattern of elegantly structured sentences at the end of the first paragraph and the beginning of the second by using three sentence fragments in a row. Explain that he has shifted from a "writing mode" to a "speaking mode," and ask students how this shift affects the reader. [Possible answers: It's as if the author were suddenly looking straight at the reader and talking one-on-one. Rosenblatt seems to be taking the reader into his confidence, creating a feeling of intimacy and intensity.]

C Elements of Literature

Main Idea

? This is the first of several places in which Rosenblatt states the main idea of his essay. What benefit might there be to stating it directly, here at the beginning, rather than waiting until the end or leaving it for readers to infer? [Sample answers: It gives readers a focus. It makes readers want to read more to find out exactly what he means.]

As disasters go, this one was terrible but not unique, certainly not among the worst on the roster of U.S. air crashes. There was the unusual element of the bridge, of course, and the fact that the plane clipped it at a moment of high traffic, one routine thus intersecting another and disrupting both. Then, too, there was the location of the event. Washington, the city of form and regulations, turned chaotic, deregulated, by a blast of real winter and a single slap of metal on metal. The jets from Washington National Airport that normally swoop around the presidential monuments like famished gulls were, for the moment, emblemized[1] by the one that fell; so there was that detail. And there was the aesthetic clash[2] as well—blue-and-green Air Florida, the name a flying garden, sunk down among gray chunks in a black river. All that was worth noticing, to be sure. Still, there was nothing very special in any of it, except death, which, while always special, does not necessarily bring millions to tears or to attention. Why, then, the shock here?

Perhaps because the nation saw in this disaster something more than a mechanical failure. Perhaps because people saw in it no failure at all, but rather something successful about their makeup. Here, after all, were two forms of nature in collision: the elements and human character. Last Wednesday, the elements, indifferent as ever, brought down Flight 90. And on that same afternoon, human nature—groping and flailing in mysteries of its own—rose to the occasion.

Of the four acknowledged heroes of the event, three are able to account for their behavior. Donald Usher and Eugene Windsor, a park-police helicopter team, risked their lives every time they dipped the skids[3] into the water to pick up survivors. On television, side by side in

1. **emblemized** (em′bləm·īzd′): represented; symbolized.
2. **aesthetic** (es·thet′ik) **clash:** unpleasant visual contrast.
3. **skids:** long, narrow pieces used in place of wheels for aircraft landing gear.

WORDS TO OWN
flailing (flāl′iŋ) v.: waving wildly.

---

472 THE NONFICTION COLLECTIONS

LITERATURE AND THE NEWS

The Last Conversation: A Database

Roger Rosenblatt's essay focuses on one aspect of a news event. Here are other facts:

Date: Wednesday, January 20, 1982; late afternoon.
Weather: Wet snow flurries.
Location: Plane hit 14th Street Bridge, crushing five cars and one truck, crashed into Potomac River, Washington, D.C.
Death toll: seventy-eight, including four motorists. Of the seventy-nine people aboard the plane, only five survived (four passengers, one flight attendant).
Probable cause of crash: ice on wings.

[Black box retrieved from wreckage of Air Florida Flight 90.]

COPILOT: It's been a while since we've been de-iced.
PILOT: Think I'll go home and . . .
COPILOT: Boy . . . this is a losing battle here on trying to de-ice those things . . . a false sense of security, that's all that does.
PILOT: That, ah, satisfies the Feds. Right there is where the icing truck, they oughta have two . . .
COPILOT: Yeah, and you taxi through kinda like a carwash or something.
PILOT: Hit that thing with about eight billion gallons of glycol . . .
COPILOT: Slushy runway. Do you want me to do anything special for this or just go for it?

Reaching All Students

Struggling Readers

Identifying the Main Idea was introduced on p. 470. For a lesson directly tied to this selection that teaches students to summarize the main idea with a strategy called Most Important Word, see the *Reading Skills and Strategies* binder:
• MiniRead Skill Lesson, p. 158
• Selection Skill Lesson, p. 165

English Language Learners

Rosenblatt calls the heroic passenger "the man in the water," "our man," and "man in nature," transforming the individual into an archetype. Be sure students understand that *man* can also mean "humankind." You might ask them to explain how this usage could cause confusion. For strategies for engaging English language learners with the literature, see
• *Lesson Plans Including Strategies for English-Language Learners*

Advanced Learners

The man in the water altruistically gives his life for others. In a discussion, challenge students to determine differences between heroic altruism and unhealthy self-sacrifice. Then have students brainstorm one list of literary characters who show heroic altruism and another list of characters who show unhealthy self-sacrifice. Explore disagreements and overlaps.

T472

PILOT: Unless you got anything special you'd like to do.

COPILOT: . . . just take off the hose wheel early like a soft-field takeoff . . . I'll pull it [the throttle] back to about one point five . . . supposed to be about one six depending on how scared we are . . . [Laughter]

[The plane is cleared for takeoff at 3:59 P.M., 45 minutes after its last de-icing.]

COPILOT: God, look at that thing.
COPILOT: That don't seem right, does it?
COPILOT: Ah, that's not right.
PILOT: Yes, it is, there's eighty.
COPILOT: Naw, I don't think that's right.
COPILOT: Ah, maybe it is.
PILOT: Hundred and twenty.
COPILOT: I don't know. . . .
PILOT: Come on, forward. . . .
PILOT: Just barely climb.
SPEAKER UNDETERMINED: Stalling, we're [falling].
COPILOT: Larry, we're going down, Larry.
PILOT: I know it. [Sound of impact]

bright blue jumpsuits, they described their courage as all in the line of duty. Lenny Skutnik, a 28-year-old employee of the Congressional Budget Office, said: "It's something I never thought I would do"—referring to his jumping into the water to drag an injured woman to shore. Skutnik added that "somebody had to go in the water," delivering every hero's line that is no less admirable for its repetitions. In fact, nobody had to go into the water. That somebody actually did so is part of the reason this particular tragedy sticks in the mind.

But the person most responsible for the emotional impact of the disaster is the one known at first simply as "the man in the water." (Balding, probably in his 50s, an extravagant moustache.) He was seen clinging with five other survivors to the tail section of the airplane. This man was described by Usher and Windsor as appearing alert and in control. Every time they lowered a lifeline and flotation ring to him, he passed it on to another of the passengers. "In a mass casualty, you'll find people like him," said Windsor. "But I've never seen one with that commitment." When the helicopter came back for him, the man had gone under. His selflessness was one reason the story held national attention; his anonymity another. The fact that he went unidentified invested him with a universal character. For a while he was Everyman, and thus proof (as if one needed it) that no man is ordinary.

Still, he could never have imagined such a capacity in himself. Only minutes before his character was tested, he was sitting in the ordinary plane among the ordinary passengers, dutifully listening to the stewardess telling him to fasten his seat belt and saying something about the "No Smoking" sign. So our man relaxed with the others, some of whom would owe their lives to him. Perhaps he started to read, or to doze, or to regret some harsh remark made in the office that morning. Then suddenly he knew that the trip would not be ordinary. Like every other person on that flight, he was desperate to live, which makes his final act so stunning.

For at some moment in the water he must have realized that he would not live if he contin-

THE MAN IN THE WATER **473**

LITERATURE AND THE NEWS
Point out that the black box transcript has no main idea. Ask students why. [It is raw data; it has not been composed by an author.] Remind students that data has no inherent main idea until an author shapes it. An author could use the transcript, the statistics, or both to express many ideas about the crash. Ask students what main ideas they might choose to organize the data into a poem. [Possible responses: Loss of life is tragic; nature is harsh; disaster can strike suddenly.]

D **Appreciating Language**
Streamlining
❓ With few words, Rosenblatt creates a striking image of the man in the water. What if Rosenblatt had been wordier? For the eight words in parentheses, try substituting these: *With a head of thinning hair that was becoming a bit sparse; essentially middle-aged, that is to say perhaps somewhere between the ages of 49 and 60; with a fairly unusual-looking mustache on his upper lip.* How might the impact of the paragraph change? [Possible responses: The extra words are distracting; the wordy version seems less focused.]

E **Literary Connections**
Everyman was originally an allegorical character in *The Summoning of Everyman,* an English morality play of the 1400s. Today, "Everyman" refers to any ordinary person who symbolizes the whole human race.

Using Students' Strengths

Auditory/Musical Learners
Play an audio or video recording of a professional broadcaster reading a news essay. Point out that the speaker stresses words, uses pauses, and makes dynamic vocal changes not just for emphasis but to achieve the controlled, rolling rhythm that marks broadcast journalism. Model a reading of the first paragraph of "The Man in the Water." Then have student volunteers read subsequent paragraphs aloud using a "broadcast voice."

Interpersonal Learners
TV stations often use emotional appeals in "teasers" for their newscasts: "Scientists share shocking news about a common food additive. Could it be dangerous? Find out at eleven." After students have read the essay, have partners create teasers for a news story about the man in the water. Remind them to appeal to viewers' emotions. [Sample answer: "Up next. The amazing story of one man's courage. Don't miss it."]

A park-police helicopter team airlifts one of the five survivors of Air Florida Flight 90 from the Potomac River's icy waters on January 20, 1982.

A Critical Thinking
Analyzing

After students have read the selection, point out that this haunting sentence marks a turning point in the essay. Ask students to speculate why.

[Possible response: Up to this point, Rosenblatt has narrated the events of the crash and rescue and has described the people involved. From this point on, he focuses more on his own reflections and insights.]

B Reading Skills and Strategies

Summarizing the Main Idea

? What two forces is Rosenblatt contrasting in this paragraph?

[humanity and nature]

RESPONDING TO THE ART

Activity. What elements in the photograph suggest the danger of the situation? [Possible responses: helicopter dangerously low; rescuer dangling from craft; survivor limp; lifeline thin; debris and ice in water.]
What is the effect of cropping the photo to show only a small part of the helicopter? [Possible responses: It puts our focus on the people, just as the essay does. It emphasizes that the rescuers' resources are limited, compared to the vastness of the icy water.]

ued to hand over the rope and ring to others. He *had* to know it, no matter how gradual the effect of the cold. In his judgment he had no choice. When the helicopter took off with what was to be the last survivor, he watched everything in the world move away from him, and he deliberately let it happen.

Yet there was something else about our man that kept our thoughts on him, and which keeps our thoughts on him still. He was *there,* in the essential, classic circumstance. Man in nature. The man in the water. For its part, nature cared nothing about the five passengers. Our man, on the other hand, cared totally. So the timeless battle commenced in the Potomac. For as long as that man could last, they went at each other, nature and man; the one making no distinctions of good and evil, acting on no principles, offering no lifelines; the other acting wholly on distinctions, principles, and, one supposes, on faith.

Since it was he who lost the fight, we ought to come again to the conclusion that people are powerless in the world. In reality, we believe the reverse, and it takes the act of the man in the water to remind us of our true feelings in

474 THE NONFICTION COLLECTIONS

Taking a Second Look

Review: Drawing Conclusions

Remind students that a conclusion is one kind of inference and that drawing a conclusion involves combining text information with prior knowledge. For example, after reading experts' warnings about ice on plane wings and recalling that ice forms within an hour when the air temperature is below freezing, a reader might conclude that hourly de-icing in winter can help to prevent plane crashes.

Activities

1. Have students reread paragraph 3 of the essay and then draw conclusions about the motivations behind heroic actions. Tell them to base their conclusions on the statements of Windsor, Usher, and Skutnik and on other heroic actions they have read about or witnessed.

2. After students finish the essay, have them reread paragraphs 4–7. Ask, "From these paragraphs, and from what you know of human nature, what conclusions might you draw about the motivations of the man in the water?" [Possible responses: He cared more for others than for himself. He believed he could save the others.]

this matter. It is not to say that everyone would have acted as he did, or as Usher, Windsor, and Skutnik. Yet whatever moved these men to challenge death on behalf of their fellows is not peculiar to them. Everyone feels the possibility in himself. That is the abiding wonder of the story. That is why we would not let go of it. If the man in the water gave a lifeline to the people gasping for survival, he was likewise giving a lifeline to those who observed him.

The odd thing is that we do not even really believe that the man in the water lost his fight. "Everything in Nature contains all the powers of Nature," said Emerson. Exactly. So the man in

the water had his own natural powers. He could not make ice storms, or freeze the water until it froze the blood. But he could hand life over to a stranger, and that is a power of nature too. The man in the water <u>pitted</u> himself against an <u>implacable</u>, impersonal enemy; he fought it with charity; and he held it to a standoff. He was the best we can do.

WORDS TO OWN

abiding *adj.:* continuing; lasting.
pitted *v.:* placed in competition.
implacable (im·plā′kə·bəl) *adj.:* relentless; not affected by attempts at change.

MEET THE WRITER

Searching for the Good

Roger Rosenblatt (1940–   ) has had a career's worth of practice in writing short opinion essays, first as the author of a weekly column for *The New Republic*, then as an editorial writer and columnist for *The Washington Post*, then as a commentator on Public Television's *MacNeil/Lehrer Newshour*.

After receiving a bachelor's degree from New York University and master's and doctoral degrees from Harvard, Rosenblatt taught literature for several years before turning to journalism. His 1983 book, *Children of War*, covers his journey through five war-torn countries—Ireland, Israel, Lebanon, Cambodia, and Vietnam. In each he interviewed children who had experienced war as a way of life.

Two years later, he followed that publication with *Witness: The World Since Hiroshima*. Both books, like "The Man in the Water," show Rosenblatt's search for the redeeming aspects of human existence.

Rosenblatt says that an expression of mystery characterizes his best essays and stories.

66 Often I will wait to write till the last possible minute before deadline, hoping not to solve a particular mystery, but to feel it more deeply. 'The Man in the Water' . . . was written in forty-five minutes, but I brooded about it for many days.

. . . Three full days that air crash led the evening news. I came to believe that the man in the water was the reason, yet no one had said so because he had done something people could not understand.

In too many ways the piece shows that it was written in forty-five minutes, but it resonated with readers at the time because it dwelt on the mystery of an act that people did not understand, or want to understand. Certain stories people do not want to understand. The mystery makes them feel closer to one another than would any solution. 99

❓ Here, Rosenblatt summarizes the main idea that the man's actions suggest to him. Why, in Rosenblatt's view, were people so riveted by the disaster? [Possible responses: Because the man's actions affirm something wonderful in human nature; because people need to see the good in humanity as much as the crash survivors needed a lifeline.]

⒟ Reading Skills and Strategies
Challenging the Text

❓ Do you agree that the man in the water won his fight? [Possible responses: No, because nature defeated him when he died. Yes, because he beat nature by saving others.]

⒠ Literary Connections

Ralph Waldo Emerson (1803–1882), American author and philosopher, saw human potential as infinite and nature as a source of transcendent insights.

Resources

Selection Assessment
Formal Assessment
• Selection Test, p. 78
Test Generator (One-Stop Planner)
• CD-ROM

BROWSING IN THE FILES

About the Author. Rosenblatt has written that Americans' sense of irony is vanishing: "Everyone is taken at his or her word. Not that people have to mean what they say; they merely have to sound that way. Thus in politics and other demonstrations of public life we are often confronted with the delightful combination of solemnity and insincerity. (The use of *delightful* here is ironic, by the way.) Why does the disappearance of irony matter? Because when people lose their sense of irony, they forfeit their ability to be teased out of adamancy; thus they also lose the chance to change their minds."

Assessing Learning

Check Test: Short Answer
Answers may vary slightly.
1. What heroic thing did the man in the water do? [He saved strangers' lives at the expense of his own.]
2. Which two qualities of the man made him fascinating, in Rosenblatt's opinion? [selflessness and anonymity]
3. What two forces are contrasted in the essay? [humanity and nature]

4. What is the victory of the man in the water? [His altruism is a victory over the indifference of nature.]

Standardized Test Preparation
For practice with standardized test format specific to this selection, see
• *Standardized Test Preparation*, p. 56

For practice in proofreading and editing, see
• *Daily Oral Grammar* Transparency 29

MAKING MEANINGS

First Thoughts

1. Possible responses: Sorrow at his unfair death—he helped everyone else and then died alone; the paradox of his story—he is ordinary and yet heroic.

Shaping Interpretations

2. Sample answer: Nature is harsh and indifferent, whereas the man in the water is compassionate and principled.

3. *Summary:* The man in the water, sacrificing his life to save strangers in a plane crash, shows human potential. Everyone has a capacity for caring that defies the indifference of nature. *Main idea:* Altruism is a powerful part of human nature (summarized in paragraph 8). *Support:* paragraphs 2, 7, 8, and 9.

4. Sample answer: Even ordinary people can have extraordinary qualities. Examples: friends/family members meeting challenges; community service workers; Sojourner Truth; Ishi; the unknown rebel (pp. 489–490); César Chavez; Anne Frank.

5. Possible responses: Agree—the man in the water shows the best in human nature; disagree—the fact that his gesture is seen as unusual suggests that we still have a long way to go.

Connecting with the Text

6. Possible responses: I would help but wouldn't risk my life, even for someone I loved; I might risk my life, as Usher, Windsor, and Skutnik did, but wouldn't purposely give my life—and I'm not certain that the man in the water purposely gave his.

Extending the Text

7. Sample answers: He counters Twain with an example of human altruism; he maintains that everyone has the capacity for heroic selflessness.

Challenging the Text

8. Possible responses: The details are few but show all we need to know; details of the man's thoughts and feelings are obviously made up, but effective. Sample questions: Is it ethical to make up certain details? Did you ever learn more about the man?

T476

MAKING MEANINGS

First Thoughts

[respond] **1.** As you read the essay, what did you think or feel about the man in the water? First, describe each response in a phrase; then elaborate.

Shaping Interpretations

[analyze] **2.** According to Rosenblatt, the man in the water symbolizes an "essential, classic circumstance": the conflict between human beings and nature. How does Rosenblatt characterize nature? How does nature differ from the man in the water?

[summarize] **3.** **Summarize** Rosenblatt's most important points, and state his **main idea**. Which passages support this idea most effectively? Does Rosenblatt ever state the idea directly? (Be sure to check the chart you made while reading.)

[interpret] **4.** Rosenblatt says that the man in the water is proof that "no man is ordinary." What do you think he means by this? What other people have proved that we are "not ordinary"?

[respond] **5.** The final two paragraphs of the essay make specific points about human nature. Tell how you feel about the opinions Rosenblatt expresses there.

Connecting with the Text

[connect] **6.** How would you react in a situation in which you might save a stranger's life but risk losing your own life? Would your behavior change if the person in danger was someone you loved? Talk about your responses to what the four heroes did.

Extending the Text

[analyze] **7.** Twain satirizes the bad in human nature (see page 457), and Rosenblatt praises the good. In what specific ways does Rosenblatt provide answers to Twain?

Challenging the Text

[evaluate] **8.** What do you think of the details the writer tells you—and doesn't tell you—about the man in the water? (What questions would you like to ask Rosenblatt?)

476 THE NONFICTION COLLECTIONS

Reading Check

a. Briefly describe the disaster.

b. What does Rosenblatt think the nation saw in this disaster?

c. Besides the man in the water, Rosenblatt mentions three other heroes. Who are they, and what did they do?

d. Describe what the man in the water looked like and what he did.

e. What ultimately happened to him?

Reading Check

a. An Air Florida jet crashed into the icy Potomac River after hitting the 14th Street Bridge in Washington, D.C., on January 20, 1982.

b. He believes the nation saw human nature rising to the occasion.

c. Donald Usher and Eugene Windsor, of the park police, used their helicopter to lift people to safety. Lenny Skutnik, of the Congressional Budget Office, jumped into the water to rescue an injured woman.

d. The man was balding, in his fifties, and had a mustache. He passed the lifeline to others rather than use it himself.

e. He drowned.

CHOICES: Building Your Portfolio

Writer's Notebook

1. Collecting Ideas for a Persuasive Essay

Looking in the news.
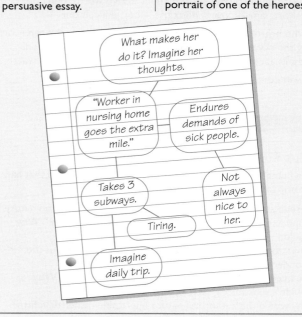
Did Rosenblatt's essay give you any ideas about where you might find topics for a persuasive essay of your own? (See the Writer's Workshop assignment on page 492.) Look through the papers (or watch TV) and find some news or sports stories that could contain some revelation about life. Make a cluster diagram for each news story to see if you can find enough material for a persuasive essay.

What makes her do it? Imagine her thoughts.

"Worker in nursing home goes the extra mile."

Endures demands of sick people.

Takes 3 subways.

Not always nice to her.

Tiring.

Imagine daily trip.

Creative Writing

2. A Biography of the Man in the Water

Give the man in the water a life. Imagine who he was, where he came from, where he was going, what his work and family were like. Then imagine his thoughts and feelings during and after the crash. Write an imaginary **biographical sketch** that elaborates on all these details. Read it aloud if you wish.

Writing/Drawing

3. A Gallery of Heroes

Create a poster or portrait of one of the heroes you listed in your Quickwrite notes. Show your hero in his or her surroundings. In a caption, tell a little about the person's life and why he or she is a hero. You might include quotations by and about your hero. You can work with other classmates to create a gallery of heroes for young readers or a bulletin-board display for your classroom. Remember that your hero can be ordinary. (He or she can be an "unsung" hero—someone anonymous, unlike the heroes made famous in poetry, songs, and books.)

Speaking/Performance

4. Life Is with People

With a group, prepare materials for a **performance** that presents your ideas on what people are capable of. You might organize your performance around human traits like courage, generosity, and kindness. You will have to decide what materials to present: Will you limit your performance to **readings** from poems, stories, and nonfiction pieces in this book? Will you include pieces from outside sources, like newspapers or even student publications? Will you include **music, art,** and photography? What title will you use? Who will your audience be?

Rubrics for each Choices assignment appear on p. 148 in the *Portfolio Management System*.

CHOICES: Building Your Portfolio

1. **Writer's Notebook** Remind students to save their work. They may use it as prewriting for the Writer's Workshop on p. 492.
2. **Creative Writing** You might suggest that students use a cluster diagram, shown below the first activity, as a way to organize details about the man before they begin to write.
3. **Writing/Drawing** Students might create borders for their portraits, including objects, dates, and people important in the life of the hero.
4. **Speaking/Performance** If student groups videotape their performances, they can compile a video anthology exploring what it means to be human.

Making the Connections

Connecting to the Theme: "Making a Point"

Ask students to discuss the collection theme after they have read the essay. You might point out that the essay is as much reflective as persuasive. Rosenblatt is both deciphering the point of an event and persuading readers to accept his point. He develops his idea by describing the man in the water and by imagining the man's thoughts before and after the crash (a purely emotional appeal). He also uses a logical appeal in an extended metaphor that compares human life to a battle with an indifferent enemy: nature. Readers' evaluations of Rosenblatt's extended metaphor may vary. Still, his empathic reflections make a case for his point—that concern for others is a redeeming and pervasive aspect of human nature. Invite students to name other moments of drama, in fiction or real life, in which people's acts of selflessness demonstrate Rosenblatt's point.

Introduce streamlining as part of editing. Streamlining during the earlier stages of the writing process may be counterproductive. Point out that streamlining involves both cutting and rewording. You might demonstrate how these two steps can lead to leaner prose:

1. Cut intensifiers (*really, quite, extremely, very,* and so on). Example: The plane's wings were <u>really quite</u> ice-coated. The plane's wings were ice-coated.
2. Replace vague verbs (forms of *to be, to make, to do*). Example: The plane's wings <u>were</u> ice-coated. Ice coated the plane's wings. Encourage students to use these steps in streamlining their prose.

Try It Out
Sample Inflated Passage
On television, as observed by the many home viewers who were watching, the two were shown together, appearing side by side in their working attire, which was jumpsuits of an extremely intense azure color, and they made a very modest description of their courage as all in the line of duty, as the saying goes.

Rosenblatt's original: "On television, side by side in bright blue jumpsuits, they described their courage as all in the line of duty."

VOCABULARY
Possible Answers
1. *Flailing* indicates struggle and desperation, whereas *waving* can be casual or playful.
2. *Abiding* adds the idea of permanence.
3. *Pitted* suggests deep determination and a fight to the finish; *set* is a more neutral term.
4. Unlike *firm, implacable* includes the idea that pleas are useless.

Resources

Language
• *Grammar and Language Links* Worksheet, p. 53

Vocabulary
• *Words to Own* Worksheet, p. 28

LANGUAGE LINK · MINI-LESSON

Technology HELP

See Language Workshop CD-ROM. *Key word entry: wordiness.*

Streamlining Your Prose

Compare these two sentences:

1. Every time, hoping to rescue him, they lowered a lifeline and flotation ring to him and hoped he would allow himself to be rescued out of the water, but he conveyed the rescue device to yet another one of the passengers who were in the plane with him, waiting in the water to be rescued after the crash.

2. *Rosenblatt:* "Every time they lowered a lifeline and flotation ring to him, he passed it on to another of the passengers."

Roger Rosenblatt's sentence is not only much better than the first sentence; it's also harder to write. That's because it's easier to be wordy than to write concisely. Rosenblatt states everything simply and in few words. When you are writing an informative essay, be concise. Avoid repetition. If you can say something in two words, don't use ten. If you can use a short, familiar word, don't use a long, difficult one.

WORDY — Those who heard about the airline disaster from reading the paper or watching the news expressed a desire to be enlightened with additional details about the life and identity of the passenger in the water.

IMPROVED — People wanted to know more about the man in the water.

Try It Out
Pick another short passage from "The Man in the Water" and inflate it, as shown in the first example. (By rewriting good, spare prose, you'll appreciate what makes it good.) Then ask a partner to pare your inflated passage to its essentials. Compare the "edited" version with Rosenblatt's. Did your partner come close to finding the original amid the wordiness?
► If you're like most writers, you probably could improve any page of prose you've written by cutting some words. Take a piece of prose you're working on or a piece from your writer's portfolio. See if you can do some pruning.

VOCABULARY · HOW TO OWN A WORD

WORD BANK
flailing
abiding
pitted
implacable

In Other Words: Synonyms and Connotations
From a number of **synonyms**, Rosenblatt chose the word that had the **connotations** he wanted. Examine his word choices.

1. Rosenblatt says that in the aftermath of the crash, human nature found itself "groping and <u>flailing</u> in mysteries of its own." Why wouldn't *waving* have the same effect as *flailing*?
2. What does <u>abiding</u> add to the author's conclusion about the "wonder of the story" that *lingering* wouldn't convey?
3. The man in the water "<u>pitted</u>" himself against nature. Why wouldn't substituting *set* for *pitted* work as well?
4. Why would the author call nature <u>implacable</u> rather than firm?

478 THE NONFICTION COLLECTIONS

Language Link Quick Check

Explain why each of the following sentences is true or false.

1. It is harder to write concise prose than wordy prose. [True; conciseness results from careful revision, requiring time, thought, and attention to word choice.]

2. Long, complicated words strengthen an informative essay. [False; simple, precise words increase clarity.]

3. Repetition usually helps to streamline informative prose. [False; unnecessary repetition can inflate prose.]

4. The following sentence needs streamlining: *He conveyed the rescue device to yet another one of the travelers who had occupied the aircraft.* [True. Possible revision: He passed the lifeline to another passenger.]

Before You Read

. . .That's Scary!

Make the Connection

Too Horrible for Kids

Horror and violence on television—do they harm kids? How to regulate what children watch on TV is an issue that concerns many parents, including Stephen King, who has become rich and famous by writing horror novels that have been turned into movies. Can you guess his position on the controversial issue of censoring scary TV shows?

Quickwrite

What do you remember about watching—or not being allowed to watch—scary movies and TV shows when you were little? In your notebook, write an anecdote or example.

Elements of Literature

Fact vs. Opinion

In this 1981 essay, King writes, "Three of my books have been made into films, and at this writing, two of them have been shown on TV." These are facts. A **fact** can be verified by consulting a reliable source or by personal observation.

About films of violent fairy tales, King writes, "All these films would certainly get G ratings if they were produced today." That's an **opinion** —a belief or conclusion that can't be proved. Although King may be confident that the films would get G ratings, there's no way to verify that conclusion.

 A **fact** is a statement that can be proved. An **opinion** is a statement of belief that can't be proved. It can only be supported.

For more on Facts and Opinions, see pages 468–469.

Reading Skills and Strategies

Evaluating Motivation and Credibility

King wants to persuade you to accept his opinion, so he uses facts, examples, and arguments to support that opinion. As a critical reader, you need to weigh his **motivation**—why is this issue especially important to him? You also need to evaluate the **credibility** of his information. Are his arguments convincing? Can they be substantiated or proved? Read carefully.

Planning

• **Block Schedule**
  Block Scheduling Lesson Plans with Pacing Guide

• **Traditional Schedule**
  Lesson Plans Including Strategies for English-Language Learners

• **One-Stop Planner**
  CD-ROM with Test Generator

Preteaching Vocabulary

Words to Own

Have students read the definitions of the Words to Own at the bottom of the selection pages. Then use the following activity to reinforce understanding of the words.

• Model using the dictionary to research the etymology of a word. Choose a word from Latin, such as *monster* (from *monere*, "to warn") or *serrated* (from *serra*, "saw blade").
• Direct students, either individually or in pairs, to look up the Latin derivations of the four Words to Own. [Dictionaries vary, but students' findings should approximate these: **specter**—from *spectare*, "to look at"; **appalled**—from *ad-*, "toward" + *pallere*, "to grow pale"; **arbitrarily**—from *arbiter*, "a judge"; **inherent**—from *in-* "inside" + *haerere*, "to stick."]
• Have students discuss their findings and speculate about the train of reasoning and associations leading from the ancient Latin definitions to the modern English ones.

Summary ▪▪

In this 1981 essay about children and television censorship, King maintains that violent and frightening programs should not be banned but should be broadcast in "later evening hours." He argues that 1) scariness is a variable, personal reaction, so censorship can't eliminate all potentially scary programs; 2) children have a right to and a need for the "catharsis" of scary programs; 3) parents should limit their children's "intake" of such fare.

Resources

Listening
Audio CD Library
A recording of this essay is included in the *Audio CD Library:*
• Disc 15, Track 4

Viewing and Representing
Fine Art Transparency
A transparency of Ben Verkaaik's *Children's Fantasy* can be used as a discussion starter after students read King's essay. See *The Viewing and Representing Transparencies and Worksheets:*
• Transparency 10
• Worksheet, p. 40

Ⓐ Reading Skills and Strategies
Evaluating Motivation and Credibility
King sets an informal tone by using the contraction *you'd* and the slang term *kids*. As they read further, ask students how the informality affects their impressions of King's credibility. [Possible responses: It makes King seem unpretentious and therefore trustworthy; it makes him seem unprofessional and therefore less trustworthy.]

NOW YOU TAKE "BAMBI" OR "SNOW WHITE"— THAT'S SCARY!
Stephen King

Ⓐ **R**ead the story synopsis below and ask yourself if it would make the sort of film you'd want your kids watching on the Friday- or Saturday-night movie:

A good but rather weak man discovers that, because of inflation, recession, and his second wife's fondness for overusing his credit cards, the family is tottering on the brink of financial ruin. In fact, they can expect to see the repossession men coming for the car, the almost

480 THE NONFICTION COLLECTIONS

 Resources: Print and Media

Reading
• *Reading Skills and Strategies*
  MiniRead Skill Lesson, p. 169
  Selection Skill Lesson, p. 176
• *Graphic Organizers for Active Reading,* p. 30
• *Words to Own,* p. 29
• *Audio CD Library*
  Disc 15, Track 4

Writing and Language
• *Daily Oral Grammar*
  Transparency 30
• *Grammar and Language Links*
  Worksheet, p. 55
• *Language Workshop CD-ROM*

Viewing and Representing
• *Viewing and Representing*
  Fine Art Transparency 10
  Fine Art Worksheet, p. 40
Assessment
• *Formal Assessment,* p. 80
• *Standardized Test Preparation,* p. 58
• *Portfolio Management System,* p. 149
• *Test Generator (One-Stop Planner CD-ROM)*

This essay originally appeared in *TV Guide* in June 1981 and includes references to two of Stephen King's early horror novels. In *Salem's Lot* (1975), a vampire spreads terror in a small Maine town. In *Carrie* (1974), a girl who is shunned and humiliated by schoolmates develops telekinetic powers and uses them to destroy her tormentors. Both novels are set in the present.

RESPONDING TO THE ART

You might discuss this illustration as an example of comic-book art. The lines are dark and heavy, and each shape is firmly outlined. Shadows are represented by groupings of parallel or crisscrossed lines called *hatching*. Though comic-book art is often taken less seriously than other mainstream art, the information it reveals is direct, the emotions intense.

Activity. Ask, "Which elements of the illustration suggest horror?" [wide-open eyes, fixed gaze, open mouth, beads of sweat, creased forehead, profusion of lines flying off at acute angles, darkness on right side of drawing]

Reaching All Students

Struggling Readers
Evaluating Motivation and Credibility was introduced on p. 479. For a lesson directly tied to this selection that teaches students to evaluate motivation and credibility with a strategy called Say Something, see the *Reading Skills and Strategies* binder:
- MiniRead Skill Lesson, p. 169
- Selection Skill Lesson, p. 176

English Language Learners
These students may need explanations of the fairy tales and children's literature to which King alludes. Ask volunteers to describe briefly *Bambi,* "Snow White," "Hansel and Gretel," "Bluebeard," "Little Red Riding Hood," and *The 500 Hats of Bartholomew Cubbins.* For strategies for engaging English language learners with the literature, see
- *Lesson Plans Including Strategies for English-Language Learners*

Advanced Learners
Challenge students to identify King's main points, then to support or counter each point with their own reasoning and observations. Students might stage a point/counterpoint panel discussion, with some presenting King's stance and others refuting it.

eight, and Owen, then three, did watch. Neither of them seemed to have any problems, either while watching it or in the middle of the night—when those problems most likely turn up.

I also have a tape of *Carrie,* a theatrical film first shown on TV about two and a half years ago. I elected to keep this one on what my kids call "the high shelf" (where I put the tapes that are forbidden to them), because I felt that its depiction of children turning against other children, the lead character's horrifying embarrassment at a school dance, and her later act of homicide would upset them. *Lot,* on the contrary, is a story that the children accepted as a fairy tale in modern dress.

Other tapes on my "high shelf" include *Night of the Living Dead* (cannibalism), *The Brood* (David Cronenberg's film of intergenerational breakdown and homicidal "children of rage" who are set free to murder and rampage), and *The Exorcist.* They are all up there for the same reason: They contain elements that I think might freak the kids out.

Not that it's possible to keep kids away from everything on TV (or in the movies, for that matter) that will freak them out; the movies that terrorized my own nights most thoroughly as a kid were not those through which Frankenstein's monster or the Wolfman lurched and growled, but the Disney cartoons. I watched Bambi's mother shot and Bambi running frantically to escape being burned up in a forest fire. I watched, appalled, dismayed, and sweaty with fear, as Snow White bit into the poisoned apple while the old crone giggled in evil ecstasy. I was similarly terrified by the walking brooms in *Fantasia* and the big, bad wolf who chased the fleeing pigs from house to house with such grim and homicidal intensity. More recently, Owen, who just turned four, crawled into bed with my wife and me. "Cruella DeVille is in my room," he said. Cruella DeVille is, of course, the villainess of *101 Dalmatians,* and I suppose Owen had decided that a woman who would want to turn puppies into dogskin coats might also be interested in little boys. All these films would certainly get G ratings if they were produced today,

and frightening excerpts of them have been shown on TV during "the children's hour."

Do I believe that all violent or horrifying programming should be banned from network TV? No, I do not. Do I believe it should be telecast only in the later evening hours, TV's version of the "high shelf"? Yes, I do. Do I believe that children should be forbidden all violent or horrifying programs? No, I do not. Like their elders, children have a right to experience the entire spectrum of drama, from such warm and mostly unthreatening programs as *Little House on the Prairie* and *The Waltons* to scarier fare. It's been suggested again and again that such entertainment offers us a catharsis[4]—a chance to enter for a little while a scary and yet controllable world, where we can express our fears, aggressions, and possibly even hostilities. Surely no one would suggest that children do not have their own fears and hostilities to face and overcome; those dark feelings are the basis of many of the fairy tales children love best.

Do I think a child's intake of violent or horrifying programs should be limited? Yes, I do, and that's why I have a high shelf. But the pressure groups who want to see all horror (and anything smacking of sex, for that matter) arbitrarily removed from television make me both uneasy and angry. The element of Big Brotherism[5] inherent in such an idea causes the unease; the idea of a bunch of people I don't even know presuming to dictate what is best for my children causes the anger. I feel that deciding such things myself is my right—and my responsibility.

---

4. **catharsis** (kə·thär′sis): release of emotional tension, often by some form of art.
5. **Big Brotherism:** invasion of people's privacy by the government, as in George Orwell's novel *1984.* This novel refers to the government as "Big Brother."

WORDS TO OWN
appalled (ə·pôld′) *v.* used as *adj.:* horrified.
arbitrarily (är′bə·trer′ə·lē) *adv.:* on the basis of whim or personal preference rather than reason.
inherent (in·hir′ənt) *adj.:* existing as a basic, essential part of something.

484 THE NONFICTION COLLECTIONS

Making the Connections

Connecting to the Theme:
"Making a Point"
As you discuss the theme with students, focus on the techniques King uses to make his point. His essay demonstrates the persuasive power of concrete examples (and the advantage of personal ones—they can't be easily disproved). His examples include a hypothetical, terrifying, modern-day "Hansel and Gretel"; his own children's reactions and his actions as a parent; and vivid descriptions of Disney films that "terrified"

him as a child. He crystallizes his opinions with a mixture of logic and emotion. This is not an argument backed by data and clarified by definition; its premise is developed through reason, experience, and charged language. Additional teaching points include King's failure to define the nature of the risk to children, his making a straw opponent of generalized "pressure groups," and his use of scare tactics in allusions to Big Brother.

MEET THE WRITER

Mr. Scary

Stephen King (1947–   ) is by far the best-known contemporary writer of horror fiction. His novels have sold more than a hundred million copies. Five of them have been on *The New York Times* best-seller list at the same time, and his name has remained on the list for more than ten years.

Born in Portland, Maine, King grew up in relative poverty after his father, a merchant sailor, deserted the family when King was two. King recalls that in his childhood he was subject to "very ordinary fears," such as fear of the dark. His love of horror movies and radio shows, he admits, contributed to scaring him. "I had friends and all that," King recalls, "but I often felt unhappy and different, estranged from other kids my age."

King is no longer estranged from the world: He is extraordinarily popular and has a happy family life in Bangor, Maine. In fact, people meeting him for the first time are often disappointed to find that he's so normal.

King sticks to a rigid writing schedule. After a brisk morning walk, he writes six pages every day ("and that's like engraved in stone," he says), revising in the afternoon. One odd aspect of his writing process is that he does his research *after* he writes his first draft, almost as if he's gathering facts to support a position he's already expressed.

WRITERS ON WRITING

Stephen King's sense of irony is apparent in his explanation of why he writes: "Writing is necessary for my sanity. As a writer, I can externalize my fears and insecurities and night terrors on paper, which is what people pay shrinks a small fortune to do. In my case, they pay me for psychoanalyzing myself in print."

Assessing Learning

Check Test: Short Answer

Answers may vary slightly.
1. What is King's main point in this essay? [Violent or horrifying programs should not be banned from TV.]
2. What kind of movies frightened King most when he was a child? [Disney cartoons]

3. What is "the high shelf"? [the shelf on which King keeps videos that he doesn't allow his children to watch]
4. In King's opinion, who should regulate children's TV viewing? [their parents]

Standardized Test Preparation

For practice with standardized test format specific to this selection, see
• *Standardized Test Preparation*, p. 58
For practice in proofreading and editing, see
• *Daily Oral Grammar* Transparency 30

MAKING MEANINGS

First Thoughts

1. Possible responses: He failed because his motives seem questionable; he succeeded because of his point that fear is subjective; I already opposed censorship for adults but am still not sure about it for children.

Shaping Interpretations

2. Sample answers: *Premise*—that TV programming should not be censored for violence or horror; *support*—he includes some facts, but also presents his own opinions as reasons; credibility of evidence is diminished by its personal and subjective nature.

3. Possible responses: logical appeals, because he argues from facts and valid opinions about children's literature, children's fears, and parents' responsibilities; emotional appeals, because he uses loaded language and implies negative things about his opponents.

4. Possible generalization: Television violence encourages asocial behavior in children. The studies weaken King's position that "children have a right to experience" violent, frightening programs.

Connecting with the Text

5. Some students, like King, may have been upset by fare usually considered tame: cartoons, clown shows, sitcoms, nature programs, or children's tales. Others may list predictably scary fare: ghost and horror tales, science fiction, crime shows, or the news.

Extending the Text

6. Possible responses: playful robots, heroic kitchen appliances, dinosaurs made soft and cuddly.

Challenging the Text

7. Possible responses: As a concerned parent and an intelligent, literate person, King is credible, regardless of his economic stake; King's economic stake skews his arguments.

8. Sample answers: Parents might agree with King if they like horror films, or disagree if they want their children protected; children might disagree, wanting to choose for themselves; writers and directors might agree because they want their work shown; broadcasters might agree because regulating the media threatens freedom of the press; psychologists might disagree because they know that children are impressionable.

MAKING MEANINGS

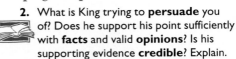

[connect]

First Thoughts

1. How convincing did you find King's essay? Did he fail to change your mind, or were you already on his side? Talk about some of your reactions.

Shaping Interpretations

[evaluate]

2. What is King trying to **persuade** you of? Does he support his point sufficiently with **facts** and valid **opinions**? Is his supporting evidence **credible**? Explain.

[identify]

3. Does King rely more on **logical** or **emotional appeals** to make his point? Support your view with evidence from the text.

[generalize]

4. Many people are concerned about the effects of television violence on viewers. Read "Children and TV Violence" on page 483, and see what **generalizations,** if any, you can make from the data given. Do the studies and surveys support or contradict King? Explain.

Connecting with the Text

[compare and contrast]

5. In your Quickwrite notes, you wrote about scary movies and TV programs you watched as a child. **Compare and contrast** your experiences with King's descriptions of his own and his children's experiences.

Extending the Text

[speculate]

6. Imagine that twenty years from now social pressures result in entertainment that contains no horror, violence, or sex. What might that entertainment contain? Brainstorm inventive possibilities.

Challenging the Text

[respond]

7. Respond to this comment: "Stephen King cannot possibly be objective on the issue of horror and violence. He is **motivated** by the fact that he makes money from his violent movies."

[evaluate]

8. How would you respond to this essay if you were a parent? a child? a writer? a broadcaster? a movie director? a psychologist?

Reading Check

a. What point does King make in his retelling of "Hansel and Gretel" and his summary of other fairy tales?

b. What does King put on his "high shelf"?

c. Name some movies that frightened King when he was a child.

d. What is King's position on banning all horror material from TV?

Robot on a Swing (1993) by Nam June Paik.

Courtesy Carl Solway Gallery, Cincinnati, Ohio.

Reading Check

a. Violence and horror are pervasive in traditional children's literature.

b. videotapes of *Carrie, Night of the Living Dead, The Brood,* and *The Exorcist*

c. *Bambi, Snow White, Fantasia,* "The Three Little Pigs"

d. He would not ban it but would have it shown only during late evening hours.

CHOICES: Building Your Portfolio

Writer's Notebook

1. Collecting Ideas for a Persuasive Essay

Pros and cons. King weighs the pros and cons of violence on TV. Choose a specific solution to some issue that you're interested in, and make a Pro and Con chart. At the top, write the proposed solution, stated in the form of a question. Under it, list the Pros (reasons to support that proposal) in one column and the Cons (reasons to oppose that proposal) in a second column. When you write your persuasive essay for the Writer's Workshop on page 492, listing pros and cons may help you support your position and anticipate opposing arguments.

Creative Writing

2. Updating a Fairy Tale

To make a point, King updates the old fairy tale about Hansel and Gretel. Bring to class one of the stories from *The Stinky Cheese Man and Other Fairly Stupid Tales* by Jon Scieszka (Viking) or a fable from *Fables for Our Time* by James Thurber (Harper). Using one of those **parodies** as a model, write an updated version of a fairy tale or fable. Focus on the **plot, characters, setting, resolution,** and **moral.**

Issue: Should horror movies be banned from TV?	
Pro [Yes, they should.]	**Con** [No, they shouldn't.]
1. They overexcite young children.	1. They're exciting.
2. They're not harmless—lead to nightmares and violence.	2. They're a safe way to express fears and aggression.
3. Very young children think they're real.	3. Everyone knows they're not real.
4. People should be protected from bad influences.	4. Censorship is wrong.

Persuasive Letter

3. What's Your Opinion?

Write a response to Stephen King's essay, stating your views on the subject of whether children should be allowed to watch horror movies and if so, how much and which ones. Put your response in the form of a letter to Stephen King or a letter to the editor of your local newspaper.

Critical Thinking and Listening

4. Evaluating the Media

Read, watch, or listen to one example of each of the following kinds of communication:

- newspaper editorial
- letter to the editor
- radio or television commercial
- magazine advertisement

What does each one try to **persuade** you to believe or do? Make some notes on **facts** and **opinions** (or their absence) and how they're used. Does each communication appeal to your **reason** or to your **emotions**? Does it contain **logical fallacies**? Write a brief essay evaluating all the communications. (You might want to review pages 468–469 for help.)

NOW YOU TAKE "BAMBI" OR "SNOW WHITE"—THAT'S SCARY! **487**

RESPONDING TO THE ART

Korean-born **Nam June Paik** (1932–   ) often includes working televisions in his art. His *Robot on a Swing* (p. 486) is a video sculpture; on the TV in the robot's "stomach," bright, abstract images move to music and voices. **Activity.** Students might discuss whether young children would find the sculpture entertaining or eerie.

Grading Timesaver

Rubrics for each Choices assignment appear on p. 149 in the *Portfolio Management System.*

CHOICES: Building Your Portfolio

1. **Writer's Notebook** Remind students to save their work. They may use it as prewriting for the Writer's Workshop on p. 492.
2. **Creative Writing** If students know only cartoon versions of fairy tales, share such classics from the brothers Grimm as "The Frog King," "Rapunzel," or "Sweetheart Roland."
3. **Persuasive Letter** If students' letters are effective, you might encourage them to send the letters to the author via his publisher or to the local newspaper.
4. **Critical Thinking and Listening** Students might use a chart like the one below to record and compare their data.

Media Type	Persuasion	Fact/ Opinion	Reason/ Emotion
Editorial			
Letter to Ed.			
Commercial			
Magazine Ad			

Skill Link

Researching Word Origins

Remind students that word origins can provide insights into meanings. Tell students that a dictionary may list word origins either at the beginning or at the end of an entry. If the information includes abbreviations, students can refer to the abbreviation key at the front of the dictionary. Urge students to explore cross-references. For example, an entry for *ghastly* may read, "from ME *gastli,* from *gasten,* to terrify. See also AGHAST." The key will show that *ME* means "Middle English." The entry for *aghast* will add that *gasten* comes from an Old English word meaning "ghost."

Activities

1. Have students research and record the origins of these words from King's essay: *catharsis, crone, homicide, horror.*
2. Ask students to explain how their knowledge of each word's origin might help them remember its meaning or understand its connotations.

GRAMMAR LINK

Students can use skills from this Grammar Link exercise when editing their persuasive essays for the Writer's Workshop at the end of the collection.

Try It Out
Possible Answers
1. Examples (p. 484):
   "—when those problems most likely turn up."
   "(where I put the tapes that are forbidden to them)"
   "(or in the movies, for that matter)"
   "—and my responsibility."
   Commas wouldn't do because dashes and parentheses indicate longer pauses.
2. **a.** No, because dashes and parentheses create greater pauses, and greater pauses would just make that aside sound awkward; **b.** Yes, parentheses would make the aside clearer than the confusing string of commas.

VOCABULARY

Possible content for Venn diagrams:
specter • any object of fear or dread; *synonym:* **ghost** • visible soul of a dead person (*overlap:* frightening thing to see)
arbitrary • based on whim, not reason; *synonym:* **tyrannical** • dictatorial, unjust (*overlap:* not governed by principle)
inherent • existing as a necessary part of something; *synonym:* **intrinsic** • part of the original makeup of something (*overlap:* basic)

Resources

Language
• *Grammar and Language Links* Worksheet, p. 55

Vocabulary
• *Words to Own* Worksheet, p. 29

GRAMMAR LINK   MINI-LESSON

Setting Off Parenthetical Information

Language Handbook HELP

See Commas, page 1052; Dashes, page 1057; Parentheses, page 1058.

Technology HELP

See Language Workshop CD-ROM. Key word entry: parenthetical expressions.

Parenthetical expressions are asides, remarks that are made almost as afterthoughts to a sentence. When you come to a parenthetical expression as you are reading aloud, you pause to set it off from the rest of the sentence.

1. ". . . even if you have already recognized the origin of this bloody little tale (and if you didn't, ask your kids: they probably will) as 'Hansel and Gretel' . . ." [parenthetical aside set off with parentheses]

2. "I have no wish to question any responsible parent's judgment—all parents raise their children in different ways—but it did strike me as passingly odd that a three-year-old should have been allowed to stay up that late to get scared." [parenthetical aside set off with dashes]

3. "*Lot,* on the contrary, is a story that the children accepted as a fairy tale in modern dress." [parenthetical expression set off with commas]

Try It Out

1. In King's essay, look for more sentences that contain parentheses and dashes. Check to see where each parenthetical remark begins and ends. Why wouldn't commas do in each situation?

2. Sometimes the use of punctuation is a judgment call. Could you use dashes or parentheses to set off the underscored words below?

   a. "Even on a weekend, and even for the oldest, an eleven o'clock bedtime is just not negotiable."

   b. "My two sons, Joe, eight, and Owen, then three, did watch."

VOCABULARY   HOW TO OWN A WORD

WORD BANK
specter
appalled
arbitrarily
inherent

Overlapping Synonyms: Venn Diagrams

Using a dictionary or the definitions provided in the text, find a **synonym** for each word in the Word Bank. You can explore the similarities and differences between the two synonyms by making a Venn diagram like the one below for the word *appalled*. In the overlapping area, write the meanings that apply to both words.

Appalled
• stunned
• suggests disgust and dismay at situation

shocked

Horrified
• filled with intense fear or loathing or terror

Grammar Link Quick Check

Set off the parenthetical information in each of the following statements.

1. Fairytales perhaps because they're so scary have remained popular for hundreds of years. [Fairytales, perhaps because they're so scary, have remained popular for hundreds of years.]

2. King makes a valid point though some might not agree about parental screening. [King makes a valid point—though some might not agree about parental screening.]

3. Some say that horror fiction causes violence although presumably there are multiple causes for violent behavior. [Some say that horror fiction causes violence (although presumably there are multiple causes for violent behavior).]

4. King's novels are blockbuster bestsellers though some critics despise them. [King's novels are blockbuster bestsellers—though some critics despise them.]

Quickwrite

What is the most courageous thing you have done? Write a brief account of your action, explaining what you did and why, if it was difficult, and how you felt during and after the experience. Was anything accomplished by your action?

EXTENDING *the theme*

A FEATURE ARTICLE

The Unknown Rebel

Pico Iyer

Almost nobody knew his name. Nobody outside his immediate neighborhood had read his words or heard him speak. Nobody knows what happened to him even one hour after his moment in the world's living rooms. But the man who stood before a column of tanks near Tiananmen Square—June 5, 1989—may have impressed his image on the global memory more vividly, more intimately than even Sun Yat-sen[1] did. Almost certainly he was seen in his moment of self-transcendence by more people than ever laid eyes on Winston Churchill, Albert Einstein, and James Joyce combined.

The meaning of his moment—it was no more than that—was instantly decipherable in any tongue, to any age: even the billions who cannot read and those who have never heard of Mao Tse-tung[2] could follow what the "tank man" did. A small, unexceptional figure in slacks and white shirt, carrying what looks to be his shopping, posts himself before an approaching tank, with a line of seventeen more tanks behind it. The tank swerves right; he, to block it, moves left. The tank swerves left; he

moves right. Then this anonymous bystander clambers up onto the vehicle of war and says something to its driver, which comes down to us as: "Why are you here? My city is in chaos because of you." One lone Everyman standing up to machinery, to force, to all the massed weight of the People's Republic—the largest nation

MOMENT OF TRUTH: THE LONE MAN IN 1989.

1. **Sun Yat-sen** (soon′ yät′sen′): leader of the revolution (1911–1912) that established a Chinese republic.
2. **Mao Tse-tung** (mou′ dzu′dŏŏn′): chairman of China's Communist Party from 1949 to 1976.

go.hrw.com
LEO 10-7

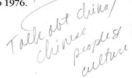

489

OBJECTIVES
1. Find thematic connections across genres
2. Generate relevant and interesting questions for discussion
3. Recognize distinctive and shared characteristics of culture through reading and discussion

Extending the Theme

Iyer reflects on the anonymous man who stood up to a column of tanks when the People's Republic of China cracked down on human-rights demonstrators in June 1989. Iyer describes the allegorical setting (the Avenue of Eternal Peace in the historic heart of China) and presents the man's actions as "self-transcendence"—as he resisted dehumanized force and injustice, he became all of humanity.

Reading Skills and Strategies
Analyzing Persuasion

In the second paragraph, the author uses facts and emotional appeals to recall the modern history of oppression in the People's Republic. Ask students to identify the loaded words that create powerful emotional images. [Examples: "One lone Everyman standing up to . . . force, to all the massed weight . . ."; "all-powerful leaders"; ". . . hiding somewhere within the bowels of the Great Hall of the People."] Then, have students identify facts that illuminate the extent of the oppression. ["the largest nation in the world"; "more than 1 billion people"]

Resources

Viewing and Representing
The Problem We All Live With by Norman Rockwell accompanies "The Unknown Rebel" by Pico Iyer.
• Fine Art Transparency 11
• Fine Art Worksheet, p. 44

Making the Connections

Connecting to the Theme:
"Making a Point"

With his controlled, even tone and his insights into Chinese history and culture, Iyer may seem to be exploring the significance of an event, rather than trying to drive home any particular point. His wealth of facts—names of people and places, significant dates, statistics—may at first appear purely informative. Yet they present logical appeals, just as Iyer's concise but powerful diction presents emotional appeals. You

might point out to students that they can gauge the persuasive power of the article by paying attention to their feelings after reading it. Invite students to share their responses. [Students may say they were touched by the heroism of the unknown rebel; angry at the entrenched and disinterested leaders who claimed ignorance of his fate; or even motivated to take their own stands, large or small, for human rights.]

Literary Connections

An **allegory** is a story in which characters, settings, and events stand for other people or for abstract ideas or qualities. Iyer examines both the positive and the negative aspects of human nature: The unknown rebel represents the positive; the forces he defies represent the negative. Ask students to identify the place names in the first paragraph on this page that lend an allegorical quality to these events. [Examples: Avenue of Eternal Peace; Gate of Heavenly Peace; Forbidden City.]

FINDING COMMON GROUND

As its name suggests, this feature requires students, through lively discussion, to discover areas of agreement about something related to the theme or about controversial issues in the literature.

1. Suggest that students use underlining to mark the parts of their Quickwrites that they consider most significant. Remind students that they need share only what they feel comfortable with.
2. After the group discussions, meet as a class and ask groups to summarize the points they touched on. Then ask students how they imagine Twain, Rosenblatt, King, and Iyer each might respond to the ideas that have been raised.

---

in the world, comprising more than 1 billion people—while its all-powerful leaders remain, as ever, in hiding somewhere within the bowels of the Great Hall of the People.

Occasionally, unexpectedly, history consents to disguise itself as allegory, and China, which traffics in grand impersonals, has often led the world in mass-producing symbols in block capitals. The man who defied the tank was standing, as it happens, on the Avenue of Eternal Peace, just a minute away from the Gate of Heavenly Peace, which leads into the Forbidden City. Nearby Tiananmen Square—the very heart of the Middle Kingdom, where students had demonstrated in 1919; where Mao had proclaimed a "People's Republic" in 1949 on behalf of the Chinese people who had "stood up"; and where leaders customarily inspect their People's Liberation Army troops—is a virtual monument to People Power in the abstract. Its western edge is taken up by the Great Hall of the People. Its eastern side is dominated by the Museum of Chinese Revolution. The Mao Tse-tung mausoleum swallows up its southern face.

For seven weeks, though, in the late spring of 1989—the modern year of revolutions—the Chinese people took back the square, first a few workers and students and teachers and soldiers, then more and more, until more than 1 million had assembled there. They set up, in the heart of the ancient nation, their own world within the world, complete with a daily newspaper, a broadcasting tent, even a 30-ft. plaster-covered statue they called the "Goddess of Democracy." Their "conference hall" was a Kentucky Fried Chicken parlor on the southwest corner of the square, and their spokesmen were 3,000 hunger strikers who spilled all over the central Monument to the People's Heroes. The unofficials even took over, and reversed, the formal symbolism of the government's ritual pageantry: when Mikhail Gorbachev[3] came to the Great Hall of the People for a grand state banquet during the demonstrations—the first visit by a

---

3. **Mikhail Gorbachev** (gôr′bə·chôf′): leader of the Soviet Union's Communist Party from 1985 to 1991.

490 THE NONFICTION COLLECTIONS

Soviet leader in 30 years—he had to steal in by the back door.

Then, in the dark early hours of June 4, the government struck back, sending tanks from all directions toward Tiananmen Square and killing hundreds of workers and students and doctors and children, many later found shot in the back. In the unnatural quiet after the massacre, with the six-lane streets eerily empty and a burned-out bus along the road, it fell to the tank man to serve as the last great defender of the peace, an Unknown Soldier in the struggle for human rights.

As soon as the man had descended from the tank, anxious onlookers pulled him to safety, and the waters of anonymity closed around him once more. Some people said he was called Wang Weilin, was 19 years old and a student; others said not even that much could be confirmed. Some said he was a factory worker's son, others that he looked like a provincial just arrived in the capital by train. When American newsmen asked Chinese leader Jiang Zemin a year later what had happened to the symbol of Chinese freedom—caught by foreign cameramen and broadcast around the world—he replied, not very ringingly, "I think never killed."

—from *Time*, April 13, 1998

FINDING COMMON GROUND

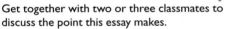

Get together with two or three classmates to discuss the point this essay makes.

1. Summarize your Quickwrite notes, and listen to your classmates' summaries of their experiences. Compare the circumstances surrounding the courageous acts and the results of the actions.
2. Use your experiences as a basis for understanding the unknown rebel's action near Tiananmen Square. You might discuss these questions:
   - Why do you think he risked his life?
   - What point did his action make to the watching world?
   - When is a grand gesture like this worth risking a life—or do you think it never is?

Using Students' Strengths

Visual Learners

Invite students to create a triptych, or three-panel artwork. One panel should reflect the image of humankind in Twain's "The Lowest Animal"; another, the image in Rosenblatt's "The Man in the Water"; and finally, the image in Iyer's "The Unknown Rebel." Direct students to devise a title for the triptych and to write annotations explaining likenesses and differences in the three panels.

Intrapersonal Learners

Have students write poems or song lyrics reflecting their insights from "The Unknown Rebel" and from other essays in this collection. Encourage volunteers to share their work or to post it on a classroom bulletin board.

Kinesthetic Learners

Tell students to bring in items related to the essays in this collection. For example, the Chinese character for "peace," a white shirt, or a Kentucky Fried Chicken box might recall images from "The Unknown Rebel"; a plastic buffalo or snake (Twain's anaconda) might suggest "The Lowest Animal." Have other students guess the significance of the items. In a class discussion, explore the ideas the objects stand for.

T490

READ ON

Beware of Pigs Who Act Like People

Mr. Jones is such a cruel farmer that the animals at Manor Farm revolt, renaming their farm Animal Farm. Things are cool for a while, as the animals run the farm themselves, but then a group of sly pigs proclaim, "Some animals are more equal than others." George Orwell's *Animal Farm* is a short, easy-to-read classic—a fable and a satire on totalitarian governments. (This title is available in the HRW library.)

Why No Songbirds Sing

Why are the birds dying, and what's happened to the butterflies? In 1962, Rachel Carson's award-winning *Silent Spring* (Fawcett) exposed the horrors of the pesticide DDT, which was in widespread use then, and set off the environmental movement.

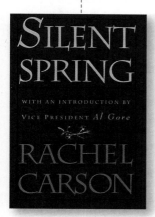

Our Country's Future

The Fire Next Time by James Baldwin (Dell) contains two essays—a letter to Baldwin's fourteen-year-old nephew James and an essay about Baldwin's experiences as an African American growing up in New York's Harlem. Baldwin, one of the first to proclaim that "black is beautiful," calls for an end to America's "racial nightmare." Written in 1963, the book remains a searing statement by one of America's finest novelists and essayists. (It is available in the HRW library.)

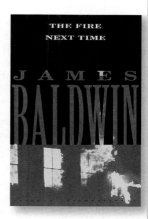

Remember Kindergarten?

So what did *you* learn there? Robert Fulghum claims *All I Really Need to Know I Learned in Kindergarten* (Ballantine). In his best-selling collection of short essays, Fulghum discovers wisdom and humor in everyday events and people.

READ ON
These Read On selections have been chosen for their appropriateness to the collection theme "Making a Point."

Portfolio Assessment Options
The following projects can help you evaluate and assess your students' reading accomplishments outside class. The projects themselves, or videotapes or photographs of the projects, can be included in students' portfolios.

- **Analyze the Theme** Have students write an essay in which they do the following:
  1. State what they think is the book's main theme.
  2. Support their statement with evidence from the book.
  3. State their agreement or disagreement with the book's theme.
  4. Support their opinion with evidence from their own experience and knowledge.
- **Write a Persuasive Essay** Suggest that students write an essay addressing the central issue raised by the book. In their essay, students should develop a thesis statement with supporting arguments, including examples and quotes from the book and from other sources. Encourage students to send their essays to the local school newspaper or to a community newspaper for publication. Students may also read their essays to the class.
- **Write a News Story** Direct students to write a front-page news story about an important incident from the book. Students should use the standard 5-W's and How as well as pyramid structure (important information first, followed by less important details) to write the news article.
- **Design a T-shirt** Students may design a T-shirt that reflects a theme or issue from their book. Encourage students to create thought-provoking designs and mottoes to convey a "message." Ask students to describe their project in writing, explaining their choices of design and text.

Writer's Workshop

MAIN OBJECTIVE
Write a persuasive essay

PROCESS OBJECTIVES

1. Use appropriate prewriting techniques to identify and develop a topic
2. Create a first draft
3. Use Evaluation Criteria as a basis for determining revision strategies
4. Revise the first draft, incorporating suggestions generated by self- or peer evaluation
5. Proofread and correct errors
6. Create a final draft
7. Choose an appropriate method of publication
8. Reflect on progress as a writer

Planning

- **Block Schedule**
  Block Scheduling Lesson Plans with Pacing Guide
- **One-Stop Planner**
  CD-ROM with Test Generator

Introducing the Writer's Workshop

Have students consider the selections in this collection. Why are these selections considered persuasive? Where might they have been published originally?

Technology HELP

See Writer's Workshop 2 CD-ROM. *Assignment: Controversial Issue.*

ASSIGNMENT

Write a persuasive essay on an issue that is important to you.

AIM

To persuade.

AUDIENCE

Your teacher, classmates, readers of a newspaper, a group or organization concerned about your topic. (You choose.)

PERSUASIVE WRITING

PERSUASIVE ESSAY

Whenever you try to persuade, you appeal to your readers or listeners to open their minds to the validity of your opinions and ideas. At the same time, you need to keep your own mind open so you can understand, anticipate, and refute the arguments of those who disagree with you. You use persuasion when you write a letter to a newspaper editor or review a book or a movie. You'll need to understand the techniques of persuasion to evaluate advertising claims and political speeches.

When you write persuasively, your goal is to express yourself convincingly so that readers understand the topic and your position. To do this, you provide reasons and support for your position.

Prewriting

1. Choose a Topic

In your Writer's Notebook, you've already jotted down ideas for a persuasive essay. If you haven't yet decided on a topic, check current news stories for topic ideas, such as the one in the model below. Reviewing the selections in this collection might also suggest a topic idea.

Professional Model

Appearances Are Destructive

As public schools reopen for the new year, strategies to curb school violence will once again be hotly debated. Installing metal detectors and hiring security guards will help, but the experience of my two sisters makes a compelling case for greater use of dress codes as a way to protect students and promote learning.

Introduction.

Opinion statement.

Shortly after my sisters arrived here from South Africa, I enrolled them at the local public school. I had great expectations for their educational experience. Compared with black schools under apartheid, American schools are Shangri-Las, with modern textbooks, school buses, computers, libraries, lunch programs, and dedicated teachers.

Despite these benefits, which students in many parts of the world

Reason 1 is a personal anecdote.

---

492 **THE NONFICTION COLLECTIONS**

— *Resources: Print and Media* —

Writing and Language
- *Portfolio Management System*
  Prewriting, p. 150
  Peer Editing, p. 151
  Assessment Rubric, p. 152
- *Workshop Resources*
  Evaluating and Revising Transparency, p. 31
  Revision Strategy Transparencies 16, 17

- *Writer's Workshop 2 CD-ROM*
  Controversial Issue

Assessment
- *Standardized Test Preparation*, pp. 124, 132;
  Transparencies 1-12

The history of the written word is rich and ... Once upon a time

Professional Model (continued)

only dream about, my sisters' efforts at learning were almost derailed. They were constantly taunted for their homely outfits. A couple of times they came home in tears. In South Africa students were required to wear uniforms, so my sisters had never been preoccupied with clothes and jewelry.

Loaded words: taunted, homely.

They became so distraught that they insisted on transferring to different schools, despite my reassurances that there was nothing wrong with them because of what they wore. . . .

Teachers shared their frustrations with me at being unable to teach those students willing to learn because classes are frequently disrupted by other students ogling themselves in mirrors, painting their fingernails, combing their hair, shining their gigantic shoes, or comparing designer labels on jackets, caps, and jewelry. . . .

Reason 2 deals with teachers' complaints. This is a generalization. How many teachers?

The argument by civil libertarians that dress codes infringe on freedom of expression is misleading. We observe dress codes in nearly every aspect of our lives without any diminution of our freedoms—as demonstrated by flight attendants, bus drivers, postal employees, high school bands, military personnel, sports teams, Girl and Boy Scouts, and employees of fast-food chains, restaurants, and hotels.

Here he deals with counterarguments — infringing on freedom.

In many countries where students outperform their American counterparts academically, school dress codes are observed as part of creating the proper learning environment. Their students tend to be neater, less disruptive in class, and more disciplined, mainly because their minds are focused more on learning and less on materialism.

Reason 3 is based on other countries' experiences with uniforms and learning.

It's time Americans realized that the benefits of safe and effective schools far outweigh any perceived curtailment of freedom of expression brought on by dress codes.

Conclusion sums up: pros outweigh cons.

—Mark Mathabane

2. Take a Stand: Formulate a Position

What is your initial reaction to your topic? Consider all sides of the issue, including the **pros** and **cons** (the arguments for and against). Then, write a clear one-sentence **opinion statement** expressing your position. Use this statement to focus

Communications Handbook HELP

See Using the Internet.

Teaching the Writer's Workshop

Prewriting

- Have students work in groups of three to think of possible topics: global, national, local, and school. Remind students that these topics should be issues of concern to them. Have students share their ideas for topics so that everyone has a rich assortment from which to choose.
- Have students read the five points for Prewriting, pp. 492–494, and then look closely at the Professional Model that begins on p. 492.

Using the Model

After reading the model aloud, discuss the side annotations with students. Then, focus discussion on the following:

? Can you identify the writer's topic? State it clearly.

? Does the writer take a stand? What is his position on the topic?

? What reasons and evidence does the writer give to support his position?

? Is the writer's argument well organized? Does he follow the outline model provided on p. 494?

? Does the writer's argument seem aimed at a particular audience? Who?

Using Students' Strengths

Visual Learners

Visual learners may need to imagine that their essay will be presented as the audio of a slide show. Tell them to sketch a "slide" for each of the following parts before writing the first draft: introduction, opinion statement, first reason, support for first reason (two slides), second reason, support for second reason (two slides), conclusion.

Evaluating and Revising

Have students use the Evaluation Criteria on p. 495 to review their drafts and determine needed revisions. In particular, encourage students to look carefully at word choices. Have they always chosen the most persuasive word or expression?

Proofreading

Have students proofread their own papers first and then exchange with another student. Encourage the proofreader to read the paper aloud while the writer listens. Does the reader know when to pause or stop? Can the reader rely on the writer's use of the conventions of punctuation to guide him or her?

Publishing

Encourage students to test the ideas from their persuasive essays on an audience.

- Have students rework their essays as letters to the editor, and send them to the editor of a school or local newspaper.
- Suggest students get together with classmates who've written about the same or a related issue and hold a panel discussion or debate.

Reflecting

If students decide to include this essay in their portfolios, they should date it and write a brief reflection on their experience. Which parts were easiest? hardest? What are the strongest parts of the essay? Who would be convinced by the argument presented? Which skills still need work?

Resources

Peer Editing Forms and Rubrics
- *Portfolio Management System,* p. 151.

Revision Transparencies
- *Workshop Resources,* p. 31.

Grading Timesaver

Rubrics for this Writer's Workshop assignment appear on p. 152 of the *Portfolio Management System.*

For some students, clothing is a form of expression. They express different tastes, ideas, and interests according to what they wear. My friend decorates all his T-shirts with designs and pictures. If the school board enforced a dress code, he would lose his right to express himself through his art. A dress code would inhibit students from expressing themselves, which is one of the most important parts of maturing.

Reason 3 uses details and opinions as support.

Although a dress code might eliminate some of the conditions that interfere with students' learning, it would cause more problems for them. Freedom of expression is what makes everyone unique, and taking it away strips students of their right to be individuals. Clearly, a dress code is not the best answer to school problems.

Conclusion anticipates a counterargument and refutes it with a strong restatement of the writer's opinion.

—Kimberly Phillips
Communications Arts High School
San Antonio, Texas

Language / Grammar Link
HELP

Loaded words: page 467. Streamlining prose: page 478. Parenthetical information: page 488.

Sentence Workshop
HELP

Varying sentences: page 497.

Communications Handbook
HELP

See Proofreaders' Marks.

Evaluating and Revising

Work with a partner, slowly reading each other's essays aloud. Ask your partner to point out confusing passages, wordiness, faulty reasoning (see pages 468–469), and lack of convincing support.

Revision Model

	Peer Comments
all over the country In many schools, students are	*Where are these schools?*
required to wear uniforms.	
As a plan to help They say that students learn	*Who is "they"?*
better, but uniforms fail to	
A dress code would be unfair and solve the problem. I think	*Use a stronger opinion statement.*
must not be forced upon students. uniforms are unfair.	

Assessing Learning

Standardized Test Preparation

For practice with standardized test prompts and formats, see
- *Standardized Test Preparation,* pp. 124, 132

Sentence Workshop

OBJECTIVES
1. Vary the length and structure of sentences
2. Recognize the structures of compound, complex, and compound-complex sentences

VARYING SENTENCE STRUCTURE AND LENGTH

Experienced writers use a variety of sentence structures and sentence lengths so that their paragraphs don't have the singsong sound of beginning readers' books.

1. A **simple sentence** has one independent clause and no subordinate clauses. Its subject or verb or both subject and verb may be compound.

   "Singhā, the lion, stands for courage and strength."
   —Pria Devi and Richard Kurin, *Aditi, the Living Arts of India*

2. A **compound sentence** has two or more independent clauses but no subordinate clause.

   "So we all went to bed, but none of us could get to sleep."
   —Anne Frank, *The Diary of a Young Girl*

3. A **complex sentence** has one independent clause and at least one subordinate clause. (Notice in the example below that the writer begins with the subordinate clause. In what other way could she have structured this sentence?)

   "Because it was the largest, most finely wrapped of all the boxes, she had noticed it for days."
   —Lorraine Hansberry, *To Be Young, Gifted and Black*

4. A **compound-complex** sentence has two or more independent clauses and at least one subordinate clause. (In what other ways could Dickens have begun the sentence below?)

   "The hours went on as he walked to and fro, and the clocks struck the numbers he would never hear again."
   —Charles Dickens, *A Tale of Two Cities*

Writer's Workshop Follow-up: Revising

Read your persuasive essay aloud, listening to the way the sentences flow together. If you find awkward, singsong passages, experiment with varying sentence structure and length.

Language Handbook HELP

See Classifying Sentences by Structure, pages 1040–1041.

Technology HELP

See Language Workshop CD-ROM. *Key word entry: sentence structure.*

Try It Out

Edit these choppy sentences by combining them into compound, complex, or compound-complex sentences. Check page 459 to see how Twain wrote them.

I caused seven young calves to be turned into the anaconda's cage. The grateful reptile immediately crushed one of them. It swallowed the calf. It then lay back satisfied. It showed no further interest in the calves. It showed no disposition to harm them. . . . The fact stood proven. The difference between an earl and an anaconda is that the earl is cruel. The anaconda isn't.

Resources ————

Workshop Resources
• Worksheet, p. 67

Language Workshop CD-ROM
• Sentence Structure

Try It Out
Possible Answer
I caused seven young calves to be turned into the anaconda's cage, and the grateful reptile immediately crushed and swallowed one of them. It then lay back satisfied, showed no further interest in the calves, and showed no disposition to harm them. The fact stood proven that the difference between an earl and an anaconda is that the earl is cruel and the anaconda isn't.

Assessing Learning

Quick Check: Varying Sentence Structure and Length

1. List three of the seven coordinating conjunctions that can join compound sentences.
   [Possible answers: *and, but, for, nor, or, so,* and *yet.*]

2. What punctuation is used between independent clauses in a compound sentence? Where does it go? [comma; before the coordinating conjunction]

3. When is a clause beginning with a subordinating conjunction set off by a comma?
   [when it comes before or in the middle of the independent clause]

4. What do you call a sentence with more than one independent clause and at least one subordinate clause? [compound-complex]

OBJECTIVES

1. Develop strategies for critical reading of persuasive text
2. Determine bias
3. Recognize logical fallacies
4. Identify emotional appeals
5. Evaluate the writer's objective
6. Use decision-making skills to determine a course of action

Reading for Life

Reading to Take Action

Teaching the Lesson

Discuss how some kinds of persuasive writing are intended to get the readers to take action—for example, to vote a certain way or to buy a product. Explain that being able to analyze and evaluate persuasive writing can help readers decide whether or not to take the recommended action.

Using the Strategies

Possible Answers

1. The editorial urges readers to take action to clean up San Jacinto Creek.
2. The logic in the editorial is the need to solve a problem. The logic is basically sound, with only one possible fallacy—a hasty generalization (unsupported by evidence) that "The city has done little to remedy the situation."
3. The writer appeals to the emotions by emphasizing readers' pride in the city. The sentence, "So, instead of being up the creek, let's take our creek back" uses the loaded phrase "up the creek" and has a kind of bandwagon appeal.
4. The proposed actions are reasonable and could lead to restoring the park.
5. Answers will vary. Most students would probably join the clean-up in order to enhance the community.

Situation

When you read or hear persuasive texts, such as editorials, political speeches, or petitions, you may feel moved to act on some issue. How do you decide whether or not to take action? The following strategies can help.

Strategies

Check the facts.
- Have the facts been reported accurately?
- Have important facts been omitted?
- Are reputable experts quoted? Are the experts unbiased?

Test the logic.
- Look for logical **fallacies** such as hasty generalizations, name-calling, either/or reasoning, and false cause and effect. (For more on these uses of persuasion, see pages 468–469.)

Be wary of emotional appeals.
- Notice loaded words, bandwagon appeals, and testimonials (see pages 468–469), and be aware of their effect on you.
- Remember that persuasive writing can touch your emotions, but it should also hold up under cooler, reasoned consideration.

(Clean) Up The Creek!

San Jacinto Creek has become a public disgrace in the past few years. It used to be a pleasant spot for family picnics. Now it's an eyesore—or worse, a potentially dangerous place, filled with litter, occupied by derelicts, and occasionally invaded by gangs. The city has done little to remedy the situation. So we are calling on our readers and other members of the San Jacinto community to take the following steps. First, sign the petition circulating around the city this week in support of a measure to clean up the creek and increase the police presence there. Second, appear at the next City Council meeting (7 P.M., Monday, September 14) to urge the Council to vote for this measure. Third, join the members of Up the Creek, a local organization formed to clean up the litter from San Jacinto Creek and patrol it, until the police are authorized by the city to do so.

Spending time at San Jacinto Creek used to be one of the greatest pleasures of living in this city. It could be again. So, instead of being up the creek, let's take our creek back.

Evaluate the objective.
- What are you being urged to do, and why?
- Who is urging the action?
- Does the objective seem well thought out, reasonable, and worthwhile?
- Is the objective personally meaningful to you?

Using the Strategies

1. What objective is urged in the editorial on this page?
2. Summarize the logic that runs through the editorial. Can you find any fallacies? Explain.

3. How has the writer appealed to your emotions?
4. Are the proposed actions likely to produce the desired result? Why or why not?
5. What, if any, actions would you take in response to the editorial, and why?

Extending the Strategies

Find an editorial in your local paper that urges some community action. With a group, examine the editorial using these strategies.

Using Students' Strengths

Visual Learners

Divide students into groups of three, and give each group a copy of the editorial and a set of highlighters in three colors. Have the small groups read the editorial together and determine whether each significant word is positive, negative, or neutral—from the writer's perspective. Students should highlight each word using the different colors and then make a list of the positive and negative words. Have students discuss the balance of positive and negative words. What impact does this have on the reader?

Alternatively, you may wish to do this by developing a list on the board as the class considers each word.

Learning for Life

Using Ads to Make Your Point

OBJECTIVES

1. Investigate advertising methods and messages
2. Plan an ad campaign to persuade a specific audience of an important message
3. Produce the ad campaign in the most effective advertising medium

Problem

Suppose you have an important message you want to get across to a group of your peers. How can you sell an idea, an action, or a cause to a group of teenagers?

Project

Work with a small group to produce an ad campaign designed to get a teenage audience to do something your group agrees is important.

Preparation

1. You'll want to investigate the kinds of appeals that speak to teenagers. Discuss in class any ads you think are particularly successful with teenage audiences. The ads can be from print media (newspapers or magazines), TV, radio, or billboards. Identify the images (pictures), words, music, story line, and **persuasive techniques** used in these ads. Summarize your findings.

2. Brainstorm to gather a list of **"messages"** or **issues** your classmates consider important (for example, fight racism; stay in school; don't drink). Join the creative team working on the issue or message that interests you most.

Procedure

1. With your group, brainstorm to find ideas about how to sell your message. What **facts** do you want to get across? What **advertising techniques** can you use?

2. Choose your **media**: print ads, radio spots, TV ads, billboards, or some combination of these. You might plan a walkathon or think of some unusual way to sell your message.

3. Plan your campaign, using some of the persuasive techniques you discovered in the ads you analyzed earlier.

4. Work with your creative team to produce a draft of your message or a detailed plan for your campaign. If you're using art, try out alternative layouts and create a storyboard like the ones ad agencies produce. (Your **storyboard** can be a large poster board with a series of rough sketches outlining the ad or video from beginning to end.)

5. Try out your draft with a focus group, a small sampling of your target audience. Ask members of the group what they like and dislike about the draft and what specific suggestions they have for improving it.

Presentation

Choose one of the following formats (or another your teacher approves):

1. Print Media

Create a series of newspaper or magazine ads, and tell where you'd place them to reach your audience. (If you have a school newspaper, that's one market for your campaign.) Think of other ways you might use print ads: on T-shirts? posters? billboards? flyers?

2. On the Air

Write a script or series of spot announcements for your school's radio or public address system. Get permission to broadcast your messages.

3. A Wider Audience

Contact local radio and TV stations to see what their requirements are for airing public-service messages. If you create a TV message, videotape it and submit it to the stations.

Processing

What did you learn about advertising techniques from doing this project? Do you think your attitudes and responses to advertisements have changed? If so, how?

Resources ——————

Viewing and Representing
HRW Multimedia Presentation Maker
Students may wish to use the *Multimedia Presentation Maker* to plan their ad campaigns.

Grading Timesaver

Rubrics for this Learning for Life project appear on p. 153 of the *Portfolio Management System.*

LEARNING FOR LIFE 499

Developing Workplace Competencies

Preparation	Procedure	Presentation
• Uses resources well • Works on teams • Acquires and evaluates data • Interprets information	• Communicates ideas and information • Reasons • Makes decisions • Monitors and corrects performance	• Communicates ideas and information • Thinks creatively • Demonstrates individual responsibility, self-esteem, and integrity

Responding to the Quotation

? American poet Robert Frost (1874–1963) won four Pulitzer Prizes and many other awards. Why might a poet find vagueness "tantalizing" rather than confusing or annoying? Remember that poetry addresses the world of feelings, sensations, and emotions—an ambiguous and abstract world. [Possible response: Vagueness would be tantalizing to a poet because it allows many possible interpretations and feelings. Perhaps it is the poet's task to put the tantalizing "vagueness" to use and to try to make some sense out of it.]

The Poetry Collections

A poem . . . begins as a lump in the throat, a sense of wrong, a homesickness, a lovesickness. It is never a thought to begin with. It is at its best when it is a tantalizing vagueness.

—**Robert Frost**

The Large Blue Horses (1911) by Franz Marc.

Collection Walker Art Center, Minneapolis.
Gift of the T. B. Walker Foundation, Gilbert M. Walker Fund, 1942.

Selection Readability

This Annotated Teacher's Edition provides a summary of each selection in the student book. Following each Summary heading, you will find one, two, or three small icons. These icons indicate, in an approximate sense, the reading level of the selection.

- ■ One icon indicates that the selection is easy.
- ■ ■ Two icons indicate that the selection is on an intermediate reading level.
- ■ ■ ■ Three icons indicate that the selection is challenging.

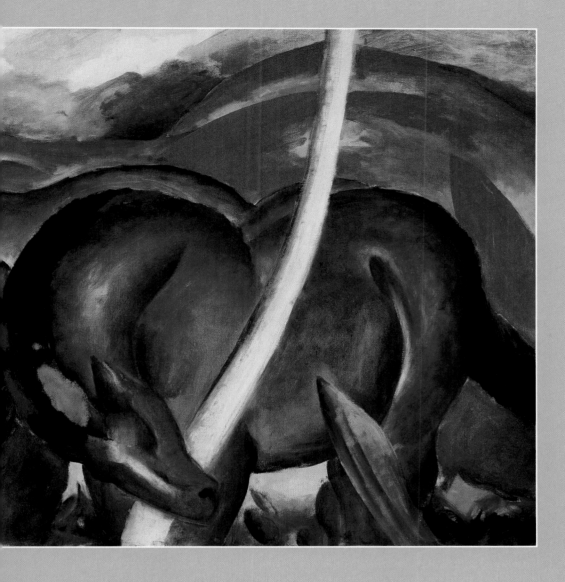

German expressionist **Franz Marc** (1880–1916) often used animals to symbolize feelings or states of being. In his later work, he favored intense colors and forms reduced to near-geometric simplicity. Marc died on a battlefield of World War I.

Activity. Ask students what the painting's glowing colors, blurred lines, and rounded forms suggest to them. Elicit various responses. [Possible answers: peace, strength, softness, joy, wistfulness, uncertainty, rhythm, movement.] Point out that the variety of their responses shows that more than one interpretation is possible. Discuss how the painting, like the best poems, demonstrates a "tantalizing vagueness."

You might also ask students to write a series of similes or metaphors describing what the painting makes them think of. They could start "The horses are like. . ." or "The painting reminds me of. . ."

501

Using Students' Strengths

Visual/Spatial Learners
Invite students to leaf through the text and find other fine art reproductions that might illustrate the quotation by Robert Frost on p. 500. Encourage students to show their choices to the class and to discuss their responses to the works they have chosen.

Naturalist Learners
Let students know that Franz Marc had a lifelong love for animals. He is said to have spent hours observing horses, deer, and other animals in the countryside. You might have students discuss how the horses in the illustration are, and are not, true to life. Explain that Marc saw animals as symbols of metaphysical purity, and invite students to explore the feelings for horses that the painting suggests.

Auditory Learners
Encourage students to choose or suggest music that could complement the painting and the quotation. If time permits, let students bring in tapes or CDs with the music they have chosen, play them for classmates, and discuss how the music relates to the art and the quotation.

A Conversation with Alice Walker. According to her mother, Alice Walker (1944–) was "writing" with a twig before she could stand. In this interview, Walker compares the birth of a poem to waiting for "a bubble from the spring" to come up, staying with the bubble as it surfaces, and then trying to understand "what is happening down in the depths." She describes her occasional struggle between resisting and complying when a poem "announces itself."

Additionally, Alice Walker recalls: "From the time I was eight, I kept a notebook. I found it lately and I was surprised. They were horrible poems, but they were poems. There was even a preface thanking all the people who were forced to hear them—my mother, my teacher, my blind Uncle Frank."

Ⓐ Critical Thinking
Making Connections

❓ How would you compare this statement to the quotation by Robert Frost on p. 500? [Possible responses: Both poets mention the importance of feelings in poetry; both poets mention sensitivity to unclear or ambiguous feelings—Frost in his reference to a "tantalizing vagueness" and Walker in her reference to "the slightest little bubble from the spring."]

Ⓑ Elements of Literature
Anecdote

❓ What point does Walker illustrate with this anecdote? [Possible responses: The point that subtle feelings play a major part in writing poetry; the point that poems can "announce themselves" at any time, and a poet must be ready.]

A WRITER ON POETRY
A CONVERSATION WITH ALICE WALKER

Alice Walker writes poems as well as nonfiction and fiction. (Her short story "Everyday Use" begins on page 70.)

Q: How young were you when you began to write?

Alice Walker: My mother says that when I was crawling, she would look for me and I would have crawled to the back of the house, having snatched the Sears Roebuck catalog. I would quietly sit scribbling in the catalog with a twig. That either meant that I came into this lifetime already writing and thinking about things that I had written before I got here, or that in some ways I was a neglected child because my parents always had to work, so I had to make my own diversions. I think I must have gone about it in a very contained way, because I didn't want to be underfoot. My parents were sharecroppers. Our housing was very shabby and small, and there were ten in the family. We lived in awful little shacks that leaked, and we couldn't get them warm in winter or cool in summer. But my mother planted flowers all around. I couldn't move anywhere without my eye hitting flowers. . . .

Q: Are there certain situations in which your creative juices are most likely to flow?

Walker: I have learned that I can't force poems. But if I spend a long time in silence, which I really love, that's very good for my writing. The main thing is just to live intensely and to feel. If there's the slightest little bubble from the spring coming up, I try to go with the bubble until it gets to the top of the water and then try to be there for it so that I can begin to understand what is happening down in the depths.

I can recall one morning in which I wrote five poems. I had gone to New York from California and was living with a friend. She put me in her guest room, and the bed was very short and lumpy. It didn't have good covers, and I was cold so I couldn't sleep. The surface of my brain was really busy with what it meant for someone to invite you to her house and to put you in a cold room with insufficient covers. I was thinking about that, and then, at about five o'clock in the morning, poetry just announced itself. It more or less said, "Well, it's time to write, so why don't you just put on something warm and get up?" And I did.

Sometimes writing poems is like falling in love. If you haven't done it for a long time, you can barely remember how wonderful it was, and you think that it probably won't happen again. That's why you resist. But that morning I gave in and liked every one of the poems that I wrote.

Reaching All Students

Struggling Readers
Guide students in using context clues to identify the meaning of *diversions, contained,* and *insufficient.* As context, students should cite, ". . . my parents always had to work," "I didn't want to be underfoot," and "It didn't have good covers…." *Diversions* means entertainment or amusing activities; *contained* means quiet and without taking up much space; *insufficient* means not adequate or good.

English Language Learners
Explain that *sharecroppers* are farmers who do not own their own land. They raise crops on land owned by someone else and pay for the use of the land by turning over a percentage (often most) of the crop to the owner. Many sharecroppers must live in housing provided by the landowners; such housing is often substandard.

Reading Skills and Strategies

Booking space on the Net:

OBJECTIVES
1. Recognize ways of making meaning from a poem
2. Understand the use of words with multiple meanings in a poem

READING A POEM

In some ways, reading a poem is just like reading a story or nonfiction. You respond to it with your experiences and feelings; you make meanings from the text. Yet reading poetry is also very different from reading prose. It requires strategies all its own.

1. **Read on—until there's a punctuation mark.** A poem's line breaks indicate thought groupings, but don't *brake* at the end of each line.

2. **If you're baffled, find the subject and verb.** Sometimes, when passages are difficult to understand, you can clarify the meaning by finding the subject, verb, and complement of each sentence. (For help, see pages 1038–1040 of the Language Handbook.) Try to **paraphrase**—say in your own words—a complicated passage.

3. **Look for figures of speech—and think about them. Figurative language** is part of what makes poetry poetry.

4. **Listen to the sounds.** Always read a poem aloud to yourself. Poets choose evocative words for their sound as well as their meaning.

5. **One reading isn't enough.** Respond to a poem on first meeting it, and then talk about the poem with other readers before you read it carefully again. On your second reading, you'll notice new details and develop new insights; and when you read it for the third time, the poem will feel comfortably "yours."

6. **Perform the poem.** When you give a poem a dramatic reading for an audience, you can emphasize the mood and feelings the words and images evoke. Then the poem really comes alive.

HOW TO OWN A WORD

Multiple Meanings—Specific Meanings

When a word has **multiple meanings**—and many words do—you have to choose the **specific meaning** that fits the context.

Take *back*, for instance. In the poem on the next page, the speaker describes a Bible as having a "broken back." Do you know what that phrase means? According to one dictionary, the word *back* used as a noun has ten meanings. Can you think of five more meanings to add to this cluster? Which meaning applies to the poem?

Now think of what the poet might have wanted to suggest by describing the Bible as having a *broken* back. Does he just want to suggest that someone read the Bible a lot? Does the phrase suggest violence instead—was the back broken deliberately?

Part of the pleasure of poetry is its suggestiveness. The answer to why the Bible's back is broken is up to *you*.

Apply the strategy on the next page.

READING SKILLS AND STRATEGIES 503

Reading Skills and Strategies

This feature presents strategies for reading a poem: being aware of punctuation, finding subject and verb, interpreting figures of speech, listening to sounds, rereading. In the accompanying poem, students have the opportunity to practice the strategies immediately.

Mini-Lesson:

Reading a Poem

Have students form groups of four and have each group apply the first four strategies to "Abandoned Farmhouse" on p. 504. (For strategy 1, ask the group how many thoughts they find in the poem.) Afterward, ask members of each group to summarize what they learned about the poem by applying these strategies. Students should see from the discussion that the fifth strategy is necessary: one reading is not enough.

Mini-Lesson:

How to Own a Word

To help students understand the importance of multiple meanings, ask them to work on a cluster for the word *abandoned* (from the title of Ted Kooser's poem on p. 504). Have a volunteer create the cluster on the board as class members consult dictionaries and dictate definitions. Then, discuss what feelings the poet suggests by describing the farmhouse as abandoned.

Using Students' Strengths

Visual/Spatial Learners

Invite students to draw the layout of the farm and farmhouse, working from details given in the poem on p. 504. Interested students might also draw interiors of specific rooms, or specific scenes from the outside of the house or from the fields.

Kinesthetic Learners

Students might enjoy tapping or drumming out the poem's irregular rhythm. Encourage them to notice subtle patterns (they may be surprised) and to make their sounds louder or softer, corresponding to the feelings that the lines of the poem suggest to them.

Summary ■ ■

In this evocative poem, Kooser lets an abandoned farmstead describe the family that once inhabited it: lonely, poor, not suited for farming, they "left in a nervous haste." Readers can add their own associations to the descriptions of meager, weathered belongings and draw their own conclusions about the former inhabitants of the farmhouse.

BROWSING IN THE FILES

About the Author. Volumes of poetry by American-born Ted Kooser (1939–   ) include *The Blizzard Voices* and *One World at a Time.*

Ⓐ Reading Skills and Strategies
Responding to the Text
❓ How would you feel if you stood in this abandoned house and saw what the speaker in the poem describes? [Possible responses: lonely, curious, apprehensive, sad.]

Ⓑ Elements of Literature
Personification
❓ Why do you think the poet gives the fields, the wall, the sandbox, and other things in the poem the ability to talk? [Possible responses: It emphasizes the feeling of loneliness—there are no people left to speak; it's an indirect way for the poet to make his points—it creates a "tantalizing vagueness."]

Ⓒ Reading Skills and Strategies
Connecting with the Text
❓ Why do you suppose the family in the poem abandoned the farmhouse? [Possible responses: a death or illness; a crop failure; despair over not making a living.]

Dialogue with the Text

The following notes were made by a student reading "Abandoned Farmhouse" for the first time. Cover her notes with a piece of paper, and jot down your own responses and questions. When you finish your first reading, **compare your responses** with Paula's.

I like the way they use the size of the shoes to show he was a big man—neat reference.

Good detail—I like the way it forms a picture in my mind.

This part reminds me of my house because we have the same sort of sand-box, and money was a problem for our family. My mom canned tomato juice and made different types of jelly.

The gravel road gives a lonely, sad feeling to the poem, like you're out in the middle of nowhere with no neighbors for miles.

What happened? Why did they have to leave? What was the hurry?

If his dad wasn't a farmer, why did the child have a toy tractor and plow?

Paula Stoller
—Paula Stoller
Eureka High School, Eureka, Illinois

504 THE POETRY COLLECTIONS

Abandoned (1994) by Robert Klein. Oil on canvas.
Courtesy Robert Klein.

Abandoned Farmhouse

Ted Kooser

He was a big man, says the size of his shoes
on a pile of broken dishes by the house;
a tall man too, says the length of the bed
in an upstairs room; and a good, God-fearing man,
5   says the Bible with a broken back
on the floor below the window, dusty with sun;
but not a man for farming, say the fields
cluttered with boulders and the leaky barn.

A woman lived with him, says the bedroom wall
10 papered with lilacs and the kitchen shelves
covered with oilcloth, and they had a child
says the sandbox made from a tractor tire.
Money was scarce, say the jars of plum preserves
and canned tomatoes sealed in the cellar-hole,
and the winters cold, say the rags in the window
15   frames.
It was lonely here, says the narrow gravel road.

Something went wrong, says the empty house
in the weed-choked yard. Stones in the fields
say he was not a farmer; the still-sealed jars
20 in the cellar say she left in a nervous haste.
And the child? Its toys are strewn in the yard
like branches after a storm—a rubber cow,
a rusty tractor with a broken plow,
a doll in overalls. Something went wrong, they say.

Reaching All Students

Struggling Readers
Some students lack confidence in their reading ability because they cannot recall details they have just read. Ask students to read through the poem, trying to remember three details from it. Then, tell them to close their books and write "First Reading" at the top and "Second Reading" in the center of a piece of paper. Have them list their first reading details before they read the poem a second time. After students have listed details from a second reading, invite them to compare their lists. Discuss how this strategic reading process can help build good reading skills.

How to Live

Theme

Seeing the World Clearly *The speakers in this collection's poems offer insights about what's most important in life. In setting, the poems range from a silent rural snowfall and New England's walled fields to the random violence of a city street. These poems, like all great poetry, celebrate human endurance in the face of hardship and the beauty of our home, the earth itself.*

Reading the Anthology

Reaching Struggling Readers

The *Reading Skills and Strategies: Reaching Struggling Readers* binder includes a Reading Strategies Handbook that offers concrete suggestions for helping students who have difficulty reading and comprehending text, or students who are reluctant readers. When a specific strategy is most appropriate for a selection, a correlation to the Handbook is provided at the bottom of the teacher's page under the head **Struggling Readers**. This head may also be used to introduce additional ideas for helping students read challenging texts.

Reading Beyond the Anthology

Read On An annotated bibliography of books suitable for extended reading is provided at the end of the poetry collections. The suggested books are related to works in these collections by theme, by author, or by subject. To preview the Read On for the poetry collections, please turn to p. T617.

Collection 8 How to Live

Resources for this Collection

Note: All resources for this collection are available for preview on the *One-Stop Planner CD-ROM 2 with Test Generator.* All worksheets and blackline masters may be printed from the CD-ROM.

Collection Planner

Selection or Feature	Reading and Literary Skills	Vocabulary, Language, and Grammar
Elements of Literature: Figurative Language (p. 506)	• *Literary Elements,* Transparency 14 	
Mother to Son (p. 508) Langston Hughes **Connections: The Power of a Poem** (p. 510) Susan Sheehan	• *Graphic Organizers for Active Reading,* Worksheet p. 31 • *Literary Elements:* Transparency 14 Worksheet p. 43	• *Daily Oral Grammar,* Transparency 31
Courage (p. 512) Anne Sexton	• *Graphic Organizers for Active Reading,* Worksheet p. 32	• *Words to Own,* Worksheet p. 30
Elements of Literature: Symbols (p. 515)	• *Literary Elements,* Transparency 9	
Stopping by Woods on a Snowy Evening (p. 516) Robert Frost	• *Graphic Organizers for Active Reading,* Worksheet p. 33	• *Words to Own,* Worksheet p. 30
Loveliest of Trees (p. 520) A. E. Housman **George Gray** (p. 522) Edgar Lee Masters	• *Graphic Organizers for Active Reading,* Worksheets pp. 34, 35 • *Literary Elements:* Transparency 14 Worksheet p. 43	• *Words to Own,* Worksheet p. 30 • *Daily Oral Grammar,* Transparency 32
Mending Wall (p. 526) Robert Frost **Connections: Mending Test** (p. 528) Penelope Bryant Turk **Connections: To the Editor** (p. 528) Jeffrey Meyers	• *Graphic Organizers for Active Reading,* Worksheet p. 36 • *Literary Elements:* Transparency 15 Worksheet p. 46	• *Words to Own,* Worksheet p. 30
The Legend Garrett Hongo (p. 530) **Connections: What I wanted ...** Garrett Hongo (p. 532) **Miss Rosie** Lucille Clifton (p. 534)	• *Graphic Organizers for Active Reading,* Worksheets pp. 37, 38 • *Literary Elements:* Poetry Transparencies 1–5 Teaching Notes, p. 69	• *Words to Own,* Worksheet p. 30
Extending the Theme: Is There Really Such a Thing as Talent? Annie Dillard (p. 538)	The Extending the Theme feature provides students with an unstructured opportunity to practice reading strategies using a selection that extends the theme of the collection.	
Writer's Workshop: Poetry (p. 541)		

Other Resources for this Collection

- *Cross-Curricular Activities,* p. 8
- *Portfolio Management System,* Introduction to Portfolio Assessment, p. 1
- *Test Generator,* Collection Test

Writing	Listening and Speaking Viewing and Representing	Assessment
		• *Formal Assessment,* Literary Elements Test, p. 94
• *Portfolio Management System,* Rubrics for Choices, p. 154	• *Audio CD Library,* Disc 16, Track 3 • *Portfolio Management System,* Rubrics for Choices, p. 154	• *Formal Assessment,* Selection Test, p. 88 • *Test Generator (One-Stop Planner CD-ROM)*
• *Portfolio Management System,* Rubrics for Choices, p. 155	• *Audio CD Library,* Disc 16, Track 4 • *Portfolio Management System,* Rubrics for Choices, p. 155	• *Formal Assessment,* Selection Test, p. 88 • *Test Generator (One-Stop Planner CD-ROM)*
		• *Formal Assessment,* Literary Elements Test, p. 96
• *Portfolio Management System,* Rubrics for Choices, p. 156	• *Visual Connections:* Videocassette B, Segment 8 • *Audio CD Library,* Disc 16, Track 5 • *Portfolio Management System,* Rubrics for Choices, p. 156	• *Formal Assessment,* Selection Test, p. 88 • *Standardized Test Preparation,* p. 60 • *Test Generator (One-Stop Planner CD-ROM)*
• *Portfolio Management System,* Rubrics for Choices, p. 157	• *Audio CD Library,* Disc 16, Tracks 6, 7 • *Viewing and Representing:* Fine Art Transparency 12 Worksheet p. 48 • *Portfolio Management System,* Rubrics for Choices, p. 157	• *Formal Assessment,* Selection Test, p. 90 • *Test Generator (One-Stop Planner CD-ROM)*
• *Portfolio Management System,* Rubrics for Choices, p. 158	• *Audio CD Library,* Disc 16, Track 8 • *Portfolio Management System,* Rubrics for Choices, p. 158	• *Formal Assessment,* Selection Test, p. 92 • *Standardized Test Preparation,* pp. 62, 64 • *Test Generator (One-Stop Planner CD-ROM)*
• *Portfolio Management System,* Rubrics for Choices, p. 159	• *Audio CD Library,* Disc 16, Tracks 9, 10 • *Portfolio Management System,* Rubrics for Choices, p. 159	• *Formal Assessment,* Selection Test, p. 92 • *Test Generator (One-Stop Planner CD-ROM)*
	• *Audio CD Library,* Disc 16, Track 11	

	• *Viewing and Representing,*
	HRW Multimedia Presentation Maker
		• *Portfolio Management System*
		  • Prewriting, p. 161
		  • Peer Editing, p. 162
		  • Assessment Rubric, p. 163

Transparency   CD-ROM   Video   Audio CD

Collection Planner

T504C

Skills Focus

Skills Focus

Selection or Feature	Reading Skills and Strategies	Elements of Literature	Vocabulary/Language/ Grammar	Writing	Listening/ Speaking	Viewing/ Representing
Elements of Literature: Figurative Language (p. 506)		Rhythm, p. 506 Simile, p. 506 Metaphor, p. 507 • Direct • Implied • Extended Personification, p. 507				
Mother to Son (p. 508) Langston Hughes		Extended Metaphor, pp. 508, 511		Extend a Metaphor, p. 511 Write a Memo Supporting an Opinion, p. 511		
Courage (p. 512) Anne Sexton	Dialogue with the Text, p. 512	Figures of Speech, pp. 512, 514 • Similes • Metaphors Comparisons, p. 514 Personification, p. 514 Themes, p. 514 Characters, p. 514		Write a Description Using Sensory Details, p. 514 Compile a List of Similes, p. 514 Write a Dialogue Comparing and Contrasting Poems, p. 514		
Elements of Literature: Symbols (p. 515)		Symbols, p. 515 Figures of Speech, p. 515				
Stopping by Woods on a Snowy Evening (p. 516) Robert Frost	Monitor Your Reading, pp. 516, 519	Symbols, pp. 516, 519 Metaphor, p. 519 Conflict, p. 519		Take Notes on Impressions and Images, p. 519 Write a Character Sketch, p. 519	Prepare and Present an Oral Interpretation of a Poem, p. 519	
Loveliest of Trees (p. 520) A. E. Housman George Gray (p. 522) Edgar Lee Masters	Compare Poems, pp. 524, 525 Identify Main Ideas, p. 525	Connotations, pp. 520, 525 Speaker, p. 522 Denotation, p. 525		List Sensory Details, p. 525 Create Metaphors, p. 525 Write Bumper Stickers, p. 525		Use a Chart to Organize Information, pp. 524, 525
Mending Wall (p. 526) Robert Frost	Identify Details That Support an Interpretation, p. 529	Ambiguity, pp. 526, 529 Characters, p. 529 Simile, p. 529 Symbol, p. 529 Meter, p. 529 Rhythm, p. 529 Parody, p. 529		Write a Poem, p. 529 Write a Letter or Journal Entry, p. 529 Write a Parody of a Poem or Song Lyric, p. 529		
The Legend (p. 530) Garrett Hongo Miss Rosie (p. 534) Lucille Clifton	Make Inferences, p. 537 Draw Conclusions, p. 537	Tone, pp. 530, 536–537 Idioms, pp. 534, 536–537 Symbol, p. 536 Figure of Speech, pp. 536–537 Sensory Details, p. 537 Images, p. 537	Conduct a Research Survey on Idioms, p. 537	Write Figures of Speech, p. 537 Write Additional Lines for a Poem, p. 537 Write a Poem Based on a News Story, p. 537	Conduct Interviews for an Oral History, p. 537 Discuss Poems as Social History, p. 537	Create a Visual Image of a Neighborhood, p. 537
Extending the Theme: Is There Really Such a Thing as Talent? (p. 538) Annie Dillard	Make Comparisons, p. 540	The Extending the Theme feature provides students with an unstructured opportunity to practice reading skills using a selection that extends the theme of the collection.				
Writer's Workshop: Poetry (p. 541)		Free Verse, p. 543 Iamb, p. 543 Trochee, p. 544 Couplet, p. 544 Quatrain, p. 544	Connotation, p. 542	Write a Poem or a Group of Poems, pp. 541–545		
Reading for Life: Reading Memos and E-Mail (p. 546)	Memos and E-Mail, p. 546 • Function • Form • Specific Content					

Skills Focus

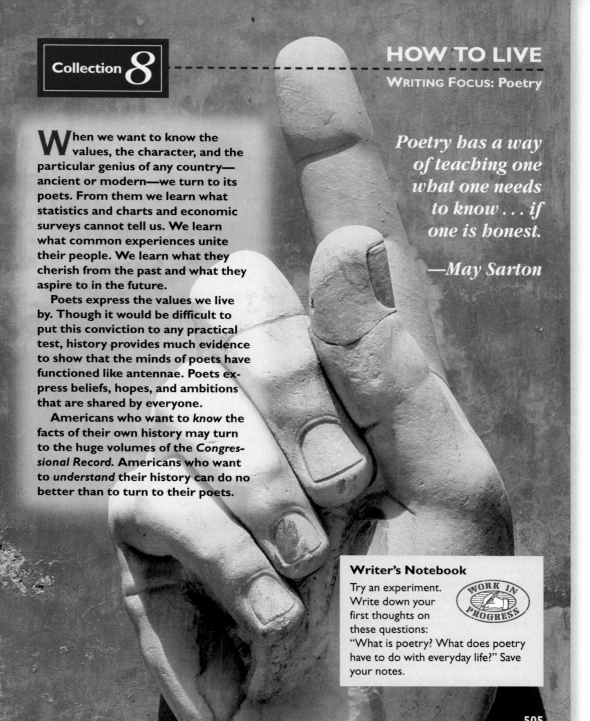

HOW TO LIVE

WRITING FOCUS: Poetry

When we want to know the values, the character, and the particular genius of any country—ancient or modern—we turn to its poets. From them we learn what statistics and charts and economic surveys cannot tell us. We learn what common experiences unite their people. We learn what they cherish from the past and what they aspire to in the future.

Poets express the values we live by. Though it would be difficult to put this conviction to any practical test, history provides much evidence to show that the minds of poets have functioned like antennae. Poets express beliefs, hopes, and ambitions that are shared by everyone.

Americans who want to *know* the facts of their own history may turn to the huge volumes of the *Congressional Record*. Americans who want to *understand* their history can do no better than to turn to their poets.

Poetry has a way of teaching one what one needs to know . . . if one is honest.

—May Sarton

Writer's Notebook

Try an experiment. Write down your first thoughts on these questions: "What is poetry? What does poetry have to do with everyday life?" Save your notes.

505

OBJECTIVES

1. Read poems focusing on the theme "How to Live"
2. Interpret literary elements in the poems, with special emphasis on figurative language and symbols
3. Apply a variety of reading strategies to the poems
4. Respond to the poems in a variety of modes
5. Learn and use new words
6. Plan, draft, revise, edit, proof, and publish a descriptive poem
7. Demonstrate the ability to read memos and e-mail

Responding to the Quotation

❓ **What might one most "need to know?"** [Possible responses: who you really are; how to be happy; the needs and wants of those you love; information about your immediate surroundings.] **Why does one need to be honest to know these things?** [Possible responses: To understand reality, you must honestly face issues and facts that seem negative as well as those that seem positive; if you're not honest with yourself about your feelings, you may lose the ability to recognize what's important.]

Writer's Notebook

Advise students to save their notes for possible use in the Writer's Workshop on p. 541. Allow volunteers to read their responses aloud.

Writing Focus: Poetry

The following **Work in Progress** assignments build to a culminating **Writer's Workshop** at the end of the collection.

• Mother to Son	Extending a metaphor (p. 511)
• Courage	Describing a person (p. 514)
• Stopping by Woods on a Snowy Evening	Describing a place (p. 519)
• Loveliest of Trees / George Gray	Using sensory details (p. 525)
• Mending Wall	Describing an experience (p. 529)
• The Legend / Miss Rosie	Using figures of speech (p. 537)

Writer's Workshop: Descriptive Writing / Poetry (p. 541)

OBJECTIVES

1. Recognize rhythm as a component of poetry
2. Appreciate the role of figurative language in poetry
3. Identify simile, metaphor, and personification

Resources

Elements of Literature
Figurative Language
For additional instruction on figurative language, see Literary Elements:
• Transparency 14

Assessment
Formal Assessment
• Literary Elements Test, p. 94

Elements of Literature

This essay defines and presents examples of similes, metaphors, and personification, discussing their function in poetry.

Mini-Lesson:
Figurative Language

You might use this lesson after students have read pp. 506–507, to ensure familiarity with the terms and concepts.

• Point out that some figurative language has been used so often that it has become stale.
• Offer examples of stale metaphors (he's a laugh a minute; she's a walking encyclopedia), similes (she can swim like a fish; the ground is as dry as a bone), and personification (the wind howled; the bills gobbled up his paychecks).
• Pair students, and have each pair create original metaphors, similes, and examples of personification to replace the stale examples.
• Invite volunteers to share their work with the class.

FIGURATIVE LANGUAGE: Language of the Imagination

Long before people began to communicate through writing, they uttered combinations of words having the sound of poetry. Yet after thousands of years, no one has produced a single definition of poetry that takes into account all the ways in which poetry makes itself heard. Though you can find enough definitions to fill a book, you won't be able to point to any one of them and say, "That's it!"

Recognizing Poetry When We Hear It

Yet we all know poetry when we hear it—whether it's a passage from the Bible, the chorus of a song, or some striking phrase overheard on a city street. Poetry is different from the plain prose we speak and from the flat language of the committee report we read. Poetry has a beat or a **rhythm**, a melody, and a texture. It's full of expressions that please us, surprise us, and make us laugh or cry. Our instincts alone tell us that when words are put together in a certain way, they are poetry. In the long run, our instinct for poetry may be more useful than a thousand definitions.

Speaking Figuratively

One of the elements that make poetry poetry is **figurative language**—language based on some sort of **comparison** that is not literally true. Such language is so natural to us that we use it every day. Let's say you read this in the newspaper:

The Budget Committee hammered at the Treasury secretary for three hours.

You don't ask in horror, "Will they be charged with murder?" You understand immediately from the context that the writer is speaking figuratively. A **figure of speech** is language shaped by the play of the imagination in which one thing (here, the continual questioning) is compared to something that seems to be entirely different (repeated blows with a hammer). A figure of speech is never literally true, but a good one always suggests a powerful truth to our imaginations.

Stated Likenesses: Similes

A **simile** is a figure of speech that uses the word *like, as, than,* or *resembles* to compare things that seem to have little or nothing in common. In a literal comparison, we might say,

"Remorse sits in my stomach like a piece of stale bread. How does that sound?"

Drawing by Booth: © 1991 The New Yorker Magazine, Inc.

"His face was as red as his father's." But when we use a simile, the comparison becomes more striking and imaginative: "His face was as red as a ripe tomato," or "His face was like a stoplight."

Similes are part of every poet's equipment. In a good simile, the comparison is unexpected but entirely reasonable. The nineteenth-century English poet William Wordsworth opened a poem with this now-famous simile:

I wandered lonely as a cloud

This simile helps us see at once that the wandering speaker has

Reaching All Students

Struggling Readers

The newspaper sports pages are rich in figurative language. Divide the class into mixed-ability groups of three students. Distribute sports pages, and have each group scan them for examples of metaphor, simile, and personification. Ask each group to list their findings and share their lists with the class.

English Language Learners

Be sure students know how to pronounce the tricky words *simile* and *metaphor*. Invite students to list figures of speech that they have noticed, puzzled over, or been amused by. (Some of these may be idioms, such as "nip it in the bud" or "in the wink of an eye.") Challenge students to classify them as similes, metaphors, or personification. Then, discuss the literal and figurative meanings of each figure of speech.

Advanced Learners

In a container, place folded slips of paper bearing the names of small, familiar objects: toothbrush, pencil, baseball, light bulb, orange, sock, and so on. Have each student take a slip and work independently to create a short poem about the object named. Direct students to include at least one metaphor, one simile, and one example of personification in each poem. Invite volunteers to share their work.

by John Malcolm Brinnin

no more sense of purpose or direction than a cloud driven by the wind. Wordsworth's simile was drawn from nature. Today a poet might make different connections, even ones taken from science or technology, as Marge Piercy does in describing city streets in a poem called "Some Collisions Bring Luck":

The streets shimmered
like laboratory beakers.

Making Identifications: Metaphors

A **metaphor** is another kind of comparison between unlike things in which some reasonable connection is instantly revealed. A metaphor is a more forceful version of a simile because the connective *like, as, resembles,* or *than* is not used. A **direct metaphor** says that something *is* something else: not "I wandered lonely as a cloud" but "I was a lonely cloud."

Metaphors, in fact, are basic to everyday conversation because they allow us to speak in a kind of imaginative shorthand. Suppose a man enters a diner and asks for two scrambled eggs on an English muffin.

The waiter might call to the kitchen "two wrecks on a raft!" The waiter is using an **implied metaphor**.

Many of the metaphors we use in conversation are implied: "the long arm of the law," "this neck of the woods," "the foot of the mountain." All these metaphors suggest comparisons between parts of the body and things quite different from the body.

Even single words can contain implied metaphors: "She *barked* her command" compares human speech to the sound a dog makes. Metaphors like these are now so familiar that we forget that once upon a time, they represented brand-new ways of seeing the world.

Metaphors in poetry can be startling. Here is how the American poet Robert Lowell uses metaphor to describe a construction site in Boston in a poem called "For the Union Dead":

. . . Behind their cage,
yellow dinosaur steamshovels
    were grunting
as they cropped up tons of
    mush and grass
to gouge their underworld
    garage.

Extending the Comparison

Metaphors are often **extended** over several lines of a poem and taken as far as they can logically go. Langston Hughes finds many points of comparison between a hard life and an old, torn-up stairway in the poem you'll read on page 508.

Humanizing the World: Personification

When we attribute human qualities to a nonhuman thing or to an abstract idea, we are using **personification**. We call computers "user-friendly," for example, or say that "misery loves company" or that "the future beckons." Personification is widely used by cartoonists, especially political cartoonists. You've probably seen justice personified as a blindfolded woman carrying scales and love personified as a chubby infant with a bow and arrow.

In poetry, figurative language is the most important means of imaginative expression. It is a tool that poets have used through the centuries to translate the experiences of their times into personal statements.

ELEMENTS OF LITERATURE: FIGURATIVE LANGUAGE 507

Crossing the Curriculum

Science

Challenge interested students to explain (or create their own) extended metaphors that shed light on scientific or physical processes. For example, students might explain why and how the heart can be compared to a pump or why a star can be called a nuclear furnace.

Social Studies

Define two specialized kinds of figurative language often found in social studies materials: *metonymy,* in which a word or phrase is substituted for another with which it is closely related (*the Kremlin* for *the Russian government*); and *synecdoche,* in which a part is used for the whole (*the man in the street* for *the general populace*). Have students skim social studies materials for examples and share their findings.

Applying the Element

As students read the poems in this collection, encourage them to note examples of simile, metaphor, and personification. Remind students to stay alert for implied metaphor. They might list their "finds" in a double-column reading journal, quoting the figurative language in one column and exploring its implications, and their responses, in the other.

OBJECTIVES

1. Read and interpret the poem
2. Interpret an extended metaphor
3. Express understanding through creative and persuasive writing

SKILLS

Literary
• Interpret an extended metaphor

Writing
• Extend a metaphor
• Support an opinion

Viewing/Representing
• Relate art to a poem (ATE)

Planning

• **Block Schedule**
  Block Scheduling Lesson Plans with Pacing Guide

• **Traditional Schedule**
  Lesson Plans Including Strategies for English-Language Learners

• **One-Stop Planner**
  CD-ROM with Test Generator

Before You Read

MOTHER TO SON

Make the Connection

Powerful Words

Sometimes words have the power to help a person through hard times. What effect do you think the words of the mother in this poem have on her son?

Quickwrite

If you were talking to a younger person about life and its struggles, what would you **compare** life to? Make a list of concrete "things" you might compare your life to. (*Keep your notes for use on page 511.*)

Elements of Literature

Extending the Metaphor

Starting in line 2 of this poem and continuing to the end, the mother makes many comparisons between her life and a particular kind of staircase. She is **extending** the **metaphor** stated in line 2 as far as she can logically take it.

> **A**n **extended metaphor** is a metaphor that develops its comparison over several lines of a poem or even throughout a whole poem.
>
> *For more on Metaphor, see pages 506–507 and the Handbook of Literary Terms.*

Mother to Son

Langston Hughes

Well, son, I'll tell you:
Life for me ain't been no crystal stair.
It's had tacks in it,
And splinters,
5   And boards torn up,
And places with no carpet on the floor—
Bare.
But all the time
I'se been a-climbin' on,
10 And reachin' landin's,
And turnin' corners,
And sometimes goin' in the dark
Where there ain't been no light.
So boy, don't you turn back.
15 Don't you set down on the steps
'Cause you finds it's kinder hard.
Don't you fall now—
For I'se still goin', honey,
I'se still climbin',
20 And life for me ain't been no crystal stair.

Proletarian (1934)
by Gordon Samstag.
Oil on canvas (48⁵⁄₁₆″ × 42″).

The Toledo Museum of Art,
Toledo, Ohio. Museum Purchase Fund. (1935.34)

go.hrw.com
LE0 10-8

 Resources: Print and Media

Reading
• *Graphic Organizers for Active Reading*, p. 31
• *Audio CD Library*, Disc 16, Track 3

Elements of Literature
• *Literary Elements*
    Transparency 14
    Worksheet, p. 43

Writing and Language
• *Daily Oral Grammar*
    Transparency 31

Assessment
• *Portfolio Management System*, p. 154
• *Test Generator (One-Stop Planner CD-ROM)*

Internet
• go.hrw.com (keyword: LE0 10-8)

Summary ▪ ▪

The speaker uses a stairway as an extended metaphor for her life. She says her life has been "no crystal stair," but one with "tacks" and "splinters," symbolizing hardships. Images of "reachin' landin's, /And turnin' corners" apply to the human struggle. Her message to her son is her example of perseverance.

Resources

Listening
Audio CD Library
For a recording of "Mother to Son," see the *Audio CD Library:*
• Disc 16, Track 3

Elements of Literature
Figurative Language
For additional instruction on metaphor, see *Literary Elements:*
• Transparency 14
• Worksheet, p. 43

Ⓐ Elements of Literature
Metaphor
❓ What connotations are suggested by the image of a crystal stairway? [Possible answers: a world of fairy tales; perfection; luxury; beauty.]

Ⓑ Appreciating Language
Dialect
❓ What does the use of dialect add to the poem? [Possible response: It creates a believable voice.]

Ⓒ Elements of Literature
Extended Metaphor
❓ In ll. 15–19, how does the speaker extend the metaphor of the staircase to encourage her son? [She tells him not to "set down on the steps" and not to "fall." She's "still climbin'."]

Reaching All Students

Struggling Readers
Have students work together in groups of three to respond to each of the poem's three parts: an account of hardships in the mother's life (ll. 1–7), her responses to hardship (ll. 8–13), her advice to her son (ll. 14–20). Suggest that each student prepare and read a section, and have the other two students listen and ask questions about it.

English Language Learners
Explain that a key feature of written dialect is the use of apostrophes to indicate missing letters: thus *climbin'* (l. 9) represents the word *climbing. I'se* stands for *I* and *has* or *I* and *is.* Note that in standard English *I'se* would be *I have* or *I am.* For other tips on dialect, see
• *Lesson Plans Including Strategies for English-Language Learners*

RESPONDING TO THE ART
Gordon Samstag (1906–1990), an American realist painter from New York, liked to paint people "at work."
Activity. Ask students to compare Hughes's mother to the woman in the painting. [Possible responses: They are both hard-working and dignified African American women.]

T509

Connections

Crystal, a tenth grader who is trying to finish high school while living in a group home, remembers Langston Hughes's poem from her classroom experience. She implies that she has faced problems and burdens similar to those described in Hughes's poem.

Ⓐ Reading Skills and Strategies
Making Inferences

❓ What does the writer imply about what Crystal might get out of school if she attended regularly? [Possible responses: She might discover other poems and ideas that are meaningful to her. Crystal might realize that many people face daily struggles.]

Ⓑ Reading Skills and Strategies
Connecting to the Text

At some time or another, everyone has read a poem, heard a song, or seen a movie and reacted as Crystal did to "Mother to Son." Ask students to explain why certain works have made them say "I understood that . . . ."

BROWSING IN THE FILES

A Critic's Comment. The biographer Donald C. Dickinson writes, "The basic ingredient of all [Hughes's] works is the essential honesty and optimism with which [he] viewed the world. The tragedies of black life are never denied, but the basic tragedy underlined in all his writing is the grievous condition of the poor and downtrodden everywhere."

MEET THE WRITER
In Harlem's Heart

Langston Hughes (1902–1967) was born in Joplin, Missouri, but is primarily identified with New York City's Harlem. A man of many talents, Hughes wrote plays, novels, screenplays, and prose sketches for newspapers. His work, he said, was an attempt to "explain and illuminate the Negro condition in America." Hughes made his most lasting contribution as a lyric poet, introducing to American poetry the rhythms of jazz and blues music and of black urban dialect.

Another poem by Hughes appears on page 376.

Connections — A BIOGRAPHICAL SKETCH

Crystal is a tenth-grader who has been in trouble with the law and is now living in a group home while trying to finish high school.

The Power of a Poem

Susan Sheehan

Crystal had continued to do poorly at Flushing High. She didn't do her homework, but once, when she was assigned by an English teacher to read a play of Shakespeare's ("That language was too much of a drag; there was too many complications," she says), she went to a movie theater to see *Macbeth* instead. "I remember witches, and a witch killed a man or a man killed a witch," she says. "It was OK, but it was corny. It was nothing like as good as *The Wizard of Oz.*" Crystal is unfamiliar with the names of most renowned poets—Keats, Emily Dickinson, and Countee Cullen, for example—but "one day at Flushing when I decided to play student out of the many days I cut," she was exposed to a Langston Hughes poem she admired and still half remembers: "Something about an old lady looking back and telling a little boy never to give up on hisself. She said something like, 'Life for me ain't been no crystal stairs; it had many boards torn up.' Because her life was not laid out on a red carpet, it made her want to do more, to get more better. It was saying to the boy even if he have to live in an apartment with no electricity, only candles, don't give up; you can always find something good at the end. I understood that poem."

—from "A Lost Childhood,"
The New Yorker

Connecting Across Texts

Connecting with "Mother to Son"
"The Power of a Poem." Crystal appears to need the advice that the mother in "Mother to Son" gives, so it is not surprising that she understands the poem and remembers it. Ask students to discuss some of the "tacks" and "splinters" Crystal might have experienced in her life. Then, have them take the voice of the mother in the poem and write a letter to Crystal offering her advice.

"Dark Symphony." This poem celebrates the work of Langston Hughes, especially "Mother to Son," and its significance in the lives of a young man and his mother. In the course of their daily routine, the young man and his mother allude to lines from Hughes's poem. Ask students why they think the mother recites "Life for me ain't been no crystal stair." [Possible answer: She identifies with the speaker and wants to pass on the encouraging message to her son.]

Getting Students Involved

Cooperative Learning
A Metaphorical Collage. Invite students to return to their lists of concrete "things" that represent their lives. Then, have groups of students create collages based on these metaphors. Students can divide tasks such as selecting metaphors that work, finding or creating illustrations, and designing the layout.

Dark Symphony

Reading Old Langston whose
Mulatto words stretched my mind to
   edge of knowing—
Good Langston made me proud to be
   the same color as black America's
Renaissance, brown as the dirt
   Momma plant those greens in.
Shoot, Europe has their Golden Age,
   we Black America got ours.

5

As I read of Simple° I quickly realize
I love his forgotten prose as much
   as his poetry.

Reciting Old Langston,
My mother yells with a burst of
   strength—
"Life for me ain't been no
   crystal stair,

10

You know who wrote that"
   with a sinful giggle she says
I say "yeah, Good Langston
   wrote that"
My mother then smiles
   and swallows me up in her love.
I'm older now, still reading.
   His stuff has set my mind free.

          —David Askia-Forbes
           Gonzaga College High School
           Washington, D.C.

6. Simple: the apparently simple but deeply
wise hero of a popular series of sketches that
Langston Hughes wrote in the 1940s.

MAKING MEANINGS
MOTHER TO SON

First Thoughts

[interpret] **1.** "Don't, don't," says the mother in
Hughes's poem. What is she really
telling her son to *do*?

Shaping Interpretations

[infer] **2.** What kinds of experiences do you
think the mother is talking about in
lines 3–7? What kinds of responses to
these experiences is she describing in
lines 8–13?

[hypothesize] **3.** What do you think might have
motivated this mother's "speech" to
her son?

CHOICES:
Building Your Portfolio

Writer's Notebook

1. Collecting Ideas for a Poem

Extending a metaphor. Look
back in your Quickwrite notes at
the list of things you compared life to. Try
extending one of these comparisons. Here,
for example, are three ways life is like a tennis match: We try to "win points," it's hard
work, it takes a lot of practice.

Supporting an Opinion

2. The Power of a Poem

Read the *Connections* on page 510 and
the student poem on this page. Then, think
about how Hughes's poem "Mother to
Son" could help young people who are having trouble. Write a **memo** to your principal telling why this poem should be displayed
on a school bulletin board.

The author of "Dark Symphony" reflects
on the poet Langston Hughes, writing
about Hughes's poetry, accomplishments, and contributions. Hughes's life
and work has had a great impact on the
student—giving rise to pride in himself
and opening his mind.

    When the author refers to "black
America's Renaissance" and to the
"Golden Age" of Black America, he is
speaking of the Harlem Renaissance—
the rich literary, artistic, and cultural
movement centered in Harlem during
the 1920s. Along with Jean Toomer,
Countee Cullen, and Zora Neale
Hurston, Langston Hughes was a
leading writer of this period.

MAKING MEANINGS
First Thoughts

1. She is telling him to keep striving, as
she has done.

Shaping Interpretations

2. In ll. 3–7 she may be alluding to
poverty, prejudice, illness, loss of
loved ones, or other setbacks. In ll.
8–13, she may be describing perse-
vering, making decisions, or having
faith in herself.

3. Her son may have experienced a
setback, expressed discouragement,
or failed at some task.

Grading Timesaver

Rubrics for each Choices assignment appear on p. 154 in the *Portfolio
Management System.*

CHOICES:
Building Your Portfolio

1. Writer's Notebook With each
selection, a Writer's Notebook
activity appears as the first option in
the Choices section. These brief
activities build toward the writing
assignment presented in the
Writer's Workshop on page 541.

2. Supporting an Opinion Have
students brainstorm a list of common problems that teenagers face.

Assessing Learning

Check Test: Short Answer

1. To what does the speaker compare her life?
[a stairway]

2. What is the speaker still doing? [climbing]

3. What kind of stairway is it? [rough: it has tacks
on it, splinters, torn boards, no carpet, bare,
dark]

4. What kind of stairway is the mother's life not
like? [It's not a crystal stair.]

5. What does the mother tell her son? [to keep
climbing, don't turn back, don't fall.]

Standardized Test Preparation

For practice in proofreading and editing, see

• *Daily Oral Grammar,* Transparency 31

Before You Read

COURAGE

Make the Connection

What It Takes

It takes courage to face life's difficulties, but not everyone views the same people or actions as courageous. In this poem, the speaker finds courage "in the small things." See if you agree.

Reading Skills and Strategies

Dialogue with the Text

List some examples from your own experience that illustrate your view of courage. As you read the poem, list the actions in each stanza that the speaker thinks are courageous. Do you agree that courage lies in acts like these? (*Keep your notes for use on page 514.*)

Elements of Literature

Figurative Language

Anne Sexton uses daring **figures of speech—similes** and **metaphors—** as "shock tactics" to grab our attention. Jot down responses to her unusual comparisons. If you're puzzled, see if the context helps you understand them.

> **F**igures of speech make unusual comparisons between two things that are basically unlike. Figures of speech are not meant to be taken literally.
>
> *For more on Figure of Speech, see pages 506–507 and the Handbook of Literary Terms.*

Courage
Anne Sexton

It is in the small things we see it.
The child's first step,
as awesome as an earthquake.
The first time you rode a bike,
5   wallowing up the sidewalk.
The first spanking when your heart
went on a journey all alone.
When they called you crybaby
or poor or fatty or crazy
10 Ⓐ and made you into an alien,
you drank their acid
and concealed it.

go.hrw.com
LEO 10-8

Later,
if you faced the death of bombs and bullets
15   you did not do it with a banner,
you did it with only a hat to   **B**
cover your heart.
You did not fondle the weakness inside you
though it was there.
20   Your courage was a small coal
that you kept swallowing.
If your buddy saved you
and died himself in so doing,
then his courage was not courage,
25   it was love; love as simple as shaving soap.

Later,
if you have endured a great despair,
then you did it alone,
getting a transfusion from the fire,
30   picking the scabs off your heart,
then wringing it out like a sock.
Next, my kinsman, you powdered your sorrow,
you gave it a back rub
and then you covered it with a blanket
35   and after it had slept a while
it woke to the wings of the roses
and was transformed.

Later,
when you face old age and its natural conclusion
40   your courage will still be shown in the little ways,
each spring will be a sword you'll sharpen,
those you love will live in a fever of love,   **C**
and you'll bargain with the calendar
and at the last moment
45   when death opens the back door
you'll put on your carpet slippers
and stride out.

MEET THE WRITER
Poet of Pain

Anne Sexton (1928–1974) was twenty-eight years old and a suburban homemaker in Newton, Massachusetts, when she began to study poetry. She made up for her late start with a stream of poems that were received enthusiastically both by general readers and by her fellow poets. In 1966, she won the Pulitzer Prize for poetry. Sexton was associated with a group of poets called "confessional" because they wrote openly about intimate and often painful details of their lives. Sexton believed that poetry should be a "shock to the senses," that "it should almost hurt."

66 . . . everyone said, 'You can't write this way. It's too personal; it's confessional; you can't write this, Anne,' and everyone was discouraging me. 99

Although much of Sexton's work is intensely personal, she also wrote about wider social issues, especially about the problems of women. One critic described her poetry as turning "wounds to words," and another said that it "delights even as it disturbs."

COURAGE 513

Summary ■ ■ ■

The speaker finds courage in the "small things" that people do and endure. Through unusual figures of speech, the ordinary trials of life are turned into extraordinary moments. The poem honors the courageous acts of people—from the first pain of child-hood through the anguish of war and the sorrows of adult life to the losses and fears of old age.

Resources

Listening
Audio CD Library
For a sensitive reading of the poem, see the *Audio CD Library*:
• Disc 16, Track 4

B **Reading Skills and Strategies**
Dialogue with the Text

❓ If you are confused about what a line means, ask yourself specific questions. For example, to explore what the poem is saying about courage, you might first ask: What does *banner* generally mean? [*Banner* means "a flag, a headline, a sign that's big and bold."] Then you might ask: So what might it mean to face death not "with a banner" but with "only a hat to cover your heart"? [It might mean that you faced death simply and modestly rather than with a flamboyant show of courage.]

C **Elements of Literature**
Figures of Speech
❓ Why would an old person's loved ones live in "a fever of love"? [Sample response: Fever can mean "a condition of heightened activity or excitement." Knowing that time is short, an aging person may devote extra attention to loved ones, and they may experience heightened feelings of love.]

Reaching All Students

Struggling Readers
These students may have difficulty understanding the figures of speech. For each figure of speech, have students list the two things being compared and then think of similarities between them. For example, in the first simile in the poem, the poet compares a child's first step to an earthquake. Both events are ones that cause major changes in people's lives, though on different scales. Have students analyze the poem's other comparisons in order to clarify them.

MAKING MEANINGS

First Thoughts

1. Possible responses: Yes, since small difficulties are more frequent and less predictable, they require more courage; or, no, big difficulties, by their nature, need stronger and more courageous reactions.

Shaping Interpretations

2. Acts include a child's first step, first bike ride, first spanking, and first cruel teasing by peers. They are "small" acts because they are commonplace. Examples of courage from students' reading notes will vary.

3. Similes and metaphors include: "as awesome as an earthquake"; "wallowing up the sidewalk"; "heart/went on a journey all alone"; "made you into an alien";"drank their acid/and concealed it." Students may cite the first, third, and fifth examples as heroic because the comparisons are exaggerated.

4. Line 20 compares courage to a coal that is eaten. Line 30 implies that the heart is a healing wound that is picked open again, and l. 31 compares the heart to a wet sock that needs wringing out. Students may say that the comparisons "work" because they create images of courage and pain or that the images are too far-fetched and jolting.

5. Each stanza describes a different stage of life. The first of the last three stanzas lauds bravery in battle; the second praises enduring suffering; and the last praises the courage to accept old age and death.

6. Lines 32–37 personify sorrow as a baby. Sorrow is transformed by care and the passage of time. Students may feel that sorrow should be accepted and be put to rest, and it will eventually be transformed, or that indulging in sorrow makes recovery more difficult.

Extending the Text

7. Possible answer: In both, people face death with dignity and composure after a life of courage and meaning.

Grading Timesaver

Rubrics for each Choices assignment appear on p. 155 in the *Portfolio Management System.*

MAKING MEANINGS
COURAGE

First Thoughts

[respond]

1. Do you agree that it's in small things that people show the most courage? Why?

Shaping Interpretations

[connect]

2. In what acts does the speaker see courage in childhood? How are these acts "small"? Compare the speaker's examples of courage with those you listed from your own experience in the notes you made while reading.

[identify]

3. List the **figures of speech** (**similes** and **implied metaphors**) in the first stanza. Which comparisons make these small acts seem large and heroic?

[evaluate]

4. What other unusual **comparisons** can you find in lines 20, 30, and 31? Do you think they all "work"? Why or why not?

[interpret]

5. The last three stanzas begin with the word *later.* What progression does each stanza represent? What acts of courage does the speaker praise in each?

[synthesize]

6. How does the speaker **personify** sorrow in lines 32–37? What seems to transform sorrow in the poem? Do you think this is true to life?

Extending the Text

[compare]

7. Can you see any connections between this poem and the story "With All Flags Flying," which begins on page 309? Talk over your responses.

CHOICES: Building Your Portfolio

Writer's Notebook

1. Collecting Ideas for a Poem

Finding a feeling. Poetry starts with feelings. Sexton's poem may have reminded you of a person you know who has shown courage—someone whose actions, large or small, touched your feelings. Try to **describe** the person with **sensory details**, especially ones that might "shock the senses."

Creative Writing
2. What Is Love?

Sexton's poem says: Love is "as simple as shaving soap." Create a list of **similes** about love: Love is as complicated as ____. Love is as sweet as ____. Love is as simple as ____.

Then, with a partner or group, list some "small things" that show love. Arrange your examples and similes into a poem about love that begins: "It is in the small things we see it."

Comparing and Contrasting Poems
3. A Conversation

Imagine that Langston Hughes and Anne Sexton met to talk about "Mother to Son" (page 508) and "Courage" (page 512). What similarities would they find in these two poems? what differences? Write a dialogue that Hughes and Sexton might have in which they discuss the poems' **themes**, **characters**, and **figurative language**.

CHOICES: Building Your Portfolio

1. Students should save their work for the Writer's Workshop.
2. Encourage students to be creative.
3. Students should support their dialogues with details from the poems.

Elements of Literature

OBJECTIVES
1. Define symbol and recognize the use of symbols in literature
2. Identify public symbols

SYMBOLS *by* John Malcolm Brinnin

What Symbols Stand For

A **symbol** is often an ordinary object, event, person, or animal to which we have attached extraordinary meaning and significance. We use a rectangle of dyed cloth to symbolize a country. We use a skull and crossbones to stand for poison or danger. We send red roses as a symbol of love.

Where Do Symbols Come From?

Symbols can be inherited or invented. The most familiar symbols have been inherited—that is, they have been handed down over time. For example, no one knows exactly who first thought of using the lion to symbolize power, courage, and domination. But once these qualities were associated with the animal, images of lions appeared on flags, banners, coats of arms, and castle walls, and the lion became a **public symbol** that shows up in art and literature even today.

People throughout history have endowed simple objects with meanings far beyond their simple functions: A crown symbolizes royalty, a dove symbolizes peace, a bull and bear symbolize the stock market, five linked rings symbolize the Olympics.

Symbols can also be invented. You probably have a symbol for your school. Writers often take a new object, character, or event and make it the embodiment of some human concern. Some invented symbols in literature have become so widely known that they have gained the status of public symbols. Peter Pan as the symbol of eternal childhood is an example.

Why Create Symbols?

You may ask why poets don't just come right out and say what they mean. Symbols, like all **figures of speech**, allow the poet to suggest layers and layers of meanings—possibilities that a simple, literal statement could never convey. A symbol is like a pebble cast into a pond: It sends off ever-widening ripples of meaning.

Some symbols are so rich in meanings that their significance has never been fully understood. Herman Melville's great white whale called Moby-Dick, for example, has traditionally been interpreted as a symbol of the mystery of evil. Yet for

> A symbol is like a pebble cast into a pond: It sends off ever-widening ripples of meaning.

more than a hundred years, this whale has provided research topics for students and scholars who still find new ways to look at Melville's famous monster.

Here is a very, very small poem that makes a big point about life by using two symbols from nature: dust and a rainbow. What do you think they stand for?

> Oh, God of dust and rainbows, help us see
> That without dust the rainbow would not be.
>
> —Langston Hughes

Resources

Elements of Literature
Symbol
For additional instruction on symbol, see *Literary Elements:*
• Transparency 9
Assessment
Formal Assessment
• Literary Elements Test, p. 96

Elements of Literature

Mini-Lesson: Symbols

Point out that symbols are found not just in literature but in many other aspects of life. Films, for example, often make good use of symbols to help extend the appeal of their stories. Discuss the following symbolic interpretation of the classic film *The Wizard of Oz:* a little girl stands for innocence, a lion represents bravery, a tin man stands for compassion, a scarecrow symbolizes intelligence, and a yellow brick road is a road to wisdom. Ask students how this symbolic interpretation of *The Wizard of Oz* affects our view of the movie. [Sample Response: It adds a universal layer of meaning to the story. This interpretation suggests that the story might be understood as a quest for happiness and completeness.]

Applying the Element

Challenge students to provide a symbolic reading of one of their favorite movies. [Possible response: Students might choose one of the *Star Wars* movies, in which the characters Obi-Wan Kenobi and Yoda symbolize wisdom, Darth Vader symbolizes evil, and Luke Skywalker symbolizes the quest for self-knowledge.]

Crossing the Curriculum

Social Studies/History

Students might enjoy researching pictographs, a form of symbol writing used by ancient civilizations throughout the world. Encourage students to find some examples of pictographs (such as those discovered in Texas or in southern France) or of hieroglyphs, a more sophisticated form of symbol writing. Students can display the examples and explain their meanings to the class.

Mathematics

To help students form a more concrete idea of the purpose of symbols, have them brainstorm a list of mathematical symbols. Ask students to discuss the meanings of the symbols and the value of using such symbols. [Universal mathematical symbols are part of a common language enabling mathematicians to communicate ideas with each other regardless of a mathematician's native language.] Students may design a poster that explains the meanings of some of these mathematical symbols.

OBJECTIVES

1. Read and interpret the poem
2. Interpret symbolic meaning
3. Monitor comprehension: Rereading
4. Express understanding through writing and speaking

SKILLS

Literary
- Interpret symbolic meaning

Reading
- Monitor comprehension: Rereading

Writing
- Collect ideas for a poem
- Write a character sketch

Speaking/Listening
- Interpret a poem orally

Viewing/Representing
- Relate art to a poem (ATE)

Planning

- **Block Schedule**
  Block Scheduling Lesson Plans with Pacing Guide
- **Traditional Schedule**
  Lesson Plans Including Strategies for English-Language Learners
- **One-Stop Planner**
  CD-ROM with Test Generator

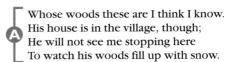

Before You Read

STOPPING BY WOODS ON A SNOWY EVENING

Make the Connection

More Than a Winter's Ride

This famous poem seems at first to be a simple account of a man who stops briefly to watch snow falling in the woods at night. Yet there's much more to this poem than a literal journey.

Reading Skills and Strategies

Monitoring Your Reading: Rereading

Read the poem several times. On your second reading, jot down what you *see* in the poem. On your third reading, jot down all the things you think are going through the *traveler's* mind as he gazes at the woods. *(Keep your notes for use on page 519.)*

Elements of Literature

Symbolic Meaning

Literally, snow is snow, a horse is a horse, and woods are woods. In the hands of a poet, however, ordinary things can become **symbols,** suggesting deep layers of meaning. As you read this poem, you must make those unspoken connections that only the imagination can make.

> **S**ymbolic meaning is the deeper layer of meaning suggested by a work's literal, or surface, meaning.
>
> *For more on Symbol, see pages 306–307 and 515 and the Handbook of Literary Terms.*

Stopping by Woods on a Snowy Evening

Robert Frost

> **A**
> Whose woods these are I think I know.
> His house is in the village, though;
> He will not see me stopping here
> To watch his woods fill up with snow.

> 5   My little horse must think it queer
> To stop without a farmhouse near
> Between the woods and frozen lake
> **B**   The darkest evening of the year.

> He gives his harness bells a shake
> 10   To ask if there is some mistake.
> The only other sound's the sweep
> Of easy wind and downy flake.

> **C**
> The woods are lovely, dark, and deep,
> But I have promises to keep,
> 15   And miles to go before I sleep,
> And miles to go before I sleep.

go.hrw.com
LE0 10-8

 — — *Resources: Print and Media* — 🗔 —

Reading
- *Graphic Organizers for Active Reading,* p. 33
- *Audio CD Library*
  Disc 16, Track 5

Viewing and Representing
- *Visual Connections*
  Videocassette B, Segment 8

Assessment
- *Portfolio Management System,* p. 156
- *Standardized Test Preparation,* p. 60
- *Test Generator (One-Stop Planner CD-ROM)*

Internet
- go.hrw.com (keyword: LE0 10-8)

Brooding Silence (detail) by John Fabian Carlson.
National Museum of American Art, Smithsonian Institution, Washington, D.C.

STOPPING BY WOODS ON A SNOWY EVENING 517

Summary ■

In this poem the speaker stops his horse near an isolated wood. In a literal interpretation, he is tempted to stay because the woods are "lovely, dark, and deep," but he reminds himself of his "promises" and the miles still before him. Symbolically, however, the "sleep" the speaker mentions may refer to the peace found in death or an escape from his life's duties. The speaker's "promises" may symbolize the responsibilities that keep him linked to his life.

Resources

Listening
Audio CD Library
For a dramatic reading of this poem, see the *Audio CD Library:*
• Disc 16, Track 5

Ⓐ Struggling Readers
Identifying Pronoun Antecedents
❓ In ll. 2–4, to whom do the pronouns "his" and "he" refer? [the owner of the woods]

Ⓑ Elements of Literature
Symbolic Meaning
❓ What might the "darkest evening of the year" symbolize? [It might literally be December 21, when night is longest. Symbolically, it could be a spiritual low point.]

Ⓒ Reading Skills and Strategies
Monitor Comprehension: Rereading
❓ Sometimes you can reread a poem in order to move to another level of interpretation—from the literal to the symbolic, for instance. Reread the last stanza. What might "miles to go" symbolize? [the years before the speaker will die]

Reaching All Students

English Language Learners
Students may need help understanding the first line of the poem, which is in inverted form. Help them to clarify the meaning of the first stanza by locating the subject *I* and restating the line as "I think I know whose woods these are." For additional strategies to supplement instruction for these students, see
• *Lesson Plans Including Strategies for English-Language Learners*

Advanced Learners
Tell students that Robert Frost always insisted that he did not repeat the last lines of "Stopping by Woods on a Snowy Evening" to invoke death. Instead, he claimed the repetition was supposed to suggest the speaker's dreamlike state. Ask students whether they believe Frost's statement or whether they think he intended those lines to symbolize the journey toward death.

RESPONDING TO THE ART
American artist **John Fabian Carlson** (1875–1945) depicts serene woods and creates a feeling of actually standing somewhere deep in the middle of the trees. **Activity.** Have students imagine that they are standing in the woods created by Carlson and ask them how they would feel.

T517

MEET THE WRITER
Only Seemingly Simple

Robert Frost (1874–1963), whom
most Americans consider the voice of
rural New England, was actually born in
San Francisco and lived as a child in the
industrial city of Lawrence, Massachusetts. He attended Dartmouth College
for a few months but left to write poetry
and work in a cotton mill. Years later,
after he had become a husband and
father, Frost returned to college but
left after two years, again to write
seriously.

In 1912, Frost moved his young family to England. During
the three years he spent there, he wrote and published two
books of poems—*A Boy's Will* (1913) and *North of Boston*
(1914)—that were immediate successes on both sides of
the Atlantic.

Frost went home to New England in 1915, finally able to
make his living as a poet. During his long career, he won
four Pulitzer Prizes and often gave public readings and lectures. One of his last public appearances was at the 1961
inauguration of President John F. Kennedy, where he recited
his poem "The Gift Outright."

Like the independent New England farmers he
frequently wrote about, Frost went his own way. He
refused to join his contemporaries in their experimental search for new poetic forms, finding all the freedom
he needed within the bounds of traditional verse.
Despite their apparently homespun subjects and traditional form, Frost's poems are only seemingly simple.
Beneath their surface is a complex and often dark
view of human life and personality. Frost said:

Robert Frost at President
John F. Kennedy's inauguration.

66 Like a piece of ice on a hot stove, the poem
must ride on its own melting. . . . Read it a hundred
times; it will forever keep its freshness as a metal
keeps its fragrance. It can never lose its sense of
a meaning that once unfolded by surprise as
it went. 99

You'll find another poem by Frost
on page 526.

Listening to Music

"Stopping by Woods on a Snowy Evening"
from *Frostiana* by Randall Thompson, performed by the New York Choral Society and
Manhattan Chamber Orchestra

Randall Thompson (1899–1984) was a celebrated music educator who taught at the
University of Virginia and wrote the well-known
basic music textbook *College Music*. As a composer, he is best known for his choral music,
though he has also written operas. He collaborated directly with Robert Frost in working on
Frostiana, and it was the poet himself who chose
the poems that Thompson set to music.

Activity
After students read "Stopping by Woods on a
Snowy Evening," have them listen to and comment on Thompson's musical version. Then, have
students work in small groups to discuss how
other poems in Collection 8—"Mother to Son"
(p. 508), for example, or "Loveliest of Trees"
(p. 520)—could be turned into choral pieces.

MAKING MEANINGS
STOPPING BY WOODS ON A SNOWY EVENING

First Thoughts

[respond]

1. What did you see happening in the poem? Check your rereading notes.

Shaping Interpretations

[hypothesize]

2. On the literal level, the speaker decides to keep going because he has promises to keep. What do you suppose his promises are?

[synthesize]

3. When the speaker first says he has miles to go before he can sleep, what is he probably thinking of? What other **metaphorical** sleep might he be referring to when he repeats the line?

[analyze]

4. The big question set up by the poem is what those lovely, dark, and deep woods **symbolize** to the traveler. What do you think? What has the speaker said no to in passing them by?

[infer]

5. Whatever the woods stand for, what has the speaker said yes to in deciding to go on? In other words, how has he resolved his **conflict**?

Connecting with the Text

[connect]

6. Do you think this poem is about a feeling that we all might have at one time or another in our lives? Explain.

CHOICES: Building Your Portfolio

Writer's Notebook

WORK IN PROGRESS

1. Collecting Ideas for a Poem

Finding a topic. Maybe the sight of the deep, dark woods on a winter night gave Frost the idea for this poem. Suppose you are passing a beautiful spot, a place you know well. You stop, stare, and start to think. What are you looking at? What time is it? Where are you heading? What are you thinking? Take notes describing your impressions and images. Your poem might open with Frost's line: "Whose _____ these are [this is] I think I know." (You may want to use these notes for the Writer's Workshop assignment on page 541.)

Describing a Character

2. Imagining the Speaker

Who is this traveler? Try to elaborate. Is it a man or a woman? Do you think the speaker is married or single? old or young? Is the speaker happy? sad? Write a brief **character sketch** of Frost's traveler.

Speaking

3. A Performance

Prepare to perform an **oral interpretation** of Frost's poem. You'll have to make these decisions: Will you use a single voice or several? Will you use a chorus? When will you slow down? speed up? pause for effect? You might even set the poem to music. Decide on your audience—for example, classmates, adults, or young children. What style of music would suit them best—ballad? hymn? rock? rap?

STOPPING BY WOODS ON A SNOWY EVENING 519

MAKING MEANINGS
First Thoughts

1. Responses may include the very literal (a person stops at the edge of a forest to watch the snow) or the symbolic (a person contemplates the peace of death and finds reasons to continue the journey through life).

Shaping Interpretations

2. Possible responses: The speaker's promises might include supporting and loving his family, helping his friends or community, or completing his work.

3. At first the traveler may be thinking of the distance he must go before sleeping that night. When he repeats the line, he might be referring to the metaphorical sleep of death.

4. Possible responses: The speaker may have said no to lingering, to his desire to rest, to abandoning life's struggles, or to giving up to death itself.

5. The traveler has decided to return to the duties and demands of life. He wants to fulfill the "promises" he has made.

Connecting with the Text

6. Most students will agree that the poem is about a universal feeling—the clash between fulfilling obligations and succumbing to personal desires.

Grading Timesaver

Rubrics for each Choices assignment appear on p. 156 in the *Portfolio Management System*.

CHOICES: Building Your Portfolio

1 and 2. Remind students to give specific details in their descriptions.

3. Imagining the speaker's appearance and personality will help students in their performance.

Assessing Learning

Check Test: True-False

1. The speaker does not know whose woods he is in. [False]
2. The horse is nervous or restless. [True]
3. The wind is loud in the woods. [False]
4. The speaker is frightened by the silence of the woods. [False]
5. The speaker leaves the woods regretfully. [True]

Standardized Test Preparation

For practice with standardized test format specific to this selection, see:
- *Standardized Test Preparation,* p. 60

**Loveliest of Trees /
George Gray**
1. Read and interpret the poems
2. Interpret connotations
3. Analyze speaker
4. Express understanding through critical and creative writing

SKILLS

Literary
• Interpret connotations
• Analyze speaker

Writing
• List sensory details describing a place
• Create metaphors
• Write bumper-sticker slogans
• Compare and contrast two poems

Viewing/Representing
• Discuss why art is appropriate to a poem (ATE)

Planning

• **Block Schedule**
  Block Scheduling Lesson Plans with Pacing Guide
• **Traditional Schedule**
  Lesson Plans Including Strategies for English-Language Learners
• **One-Stop Planner**
  CD-ROM with Test Generator

Before You Read

LOVELIEST OF TREES

Make the Connection

Capturing Time

A poem, like a snapshot, can capture a moment in words. What you might remember best about this poem is the image of the cherry tree. But look closely at those blossoms.

Quickwrite

Shut your eyes for a minute and think of your favorite place. It could be a place in nature, a city, or someplace indoors. Write down all that you see, smell, taste, feel, and hear. *(Keep your notes for use on page 525.)*

Elements of Literature

Connotations

If it weren't for **connotations** (associations and emotions that become attached to a word), poets would be out of business. Why, for example, do you think Housman uses the word *snow* in his last line?

> **C**onnotations are all the associations and emotions attached to a word.
>
> *For more on Connotations, see the Handbook of Literary Terms.*

Loveliest of Trees

A. E. Housman

Loveliest of trees, the cherry now
Is hung with bloom along the bough,
And stands about the woodland ride°
A Wearing white for Eastertide.

3. ride: path for horseback riding.

5 ⎡ Now, of my threescore years and ten,
  Twenty will not come again,
B And take from seventy springs a score,
  ⎣ It only leaves me fifty more.

And since to look at things in bloom
10 Fifty springs are little room,
About the woodlands I will go
To see the cherry hung with snow.

go.hrw.com
LE0 10-8

— *Resources: Print and Media* —

Reading
• *Graphic Organizers for Active Reading*, pp. 34, 35
• *Audio CD Library*, Disc 16, Tracks 6, 7

Elements of Literature
• *Literary Elements*
  Transparency 14
  Worksheet, p. 43

Writing and Language
• *Daily Oral Grammar*
  Transparency 32

Viewing and Representing
• *Viewing and Representing*
  Fine Art Transparency 12
  Fine Art Worksheet, p. 48

Assessment
• *Formal Assessment*, p. 90
• *Portfolio Management System*, p. 157
• *Test Generator (One-Stop Planner CD-ROM)*

Internet
• go.hrw.com (keyword: LE0 10-8)

Spring—Fruit Trees in Blossom (1873) by Claude Monet (1840–1926). Oil on canvas (24½″ × 39⅝″).

The Metropolitan Museum of Art, New York. Bequest of Mary Livingston Willard, 1926. (26.186.1) Photograph © 1984 The Metropolitan Museum of Art.

MEET THE WRITER

Poems as Clear as Water

A. E. Housman (1859–1936) spent the early years of his life near a part of western England called Shropshire. He wrote about its people, towns, and countryside in poems as clear as water from a brook. Housman is one of those rare poets whose whole career is associated with one book. In his case, that book is called *A Shropshire Lad.* Housman's themes are universal: the sad beauty of nature as it reminds us of our mortality, the brevity of youth, and regret for what has passed.

"Poetry is not the thing said but a way of saying it," Housman once said.

66 Experience has taught me, when I am shaving of a morning, to keep watch over my thoughts, because if a line of poetry strays into my memory, my skin bristles so that the razor ceases to act. This particular symptom is accompanied by a shiver down the spine; there is another which consists in a constriction of the throat and a precipitation of water to the eyes. . . . 99

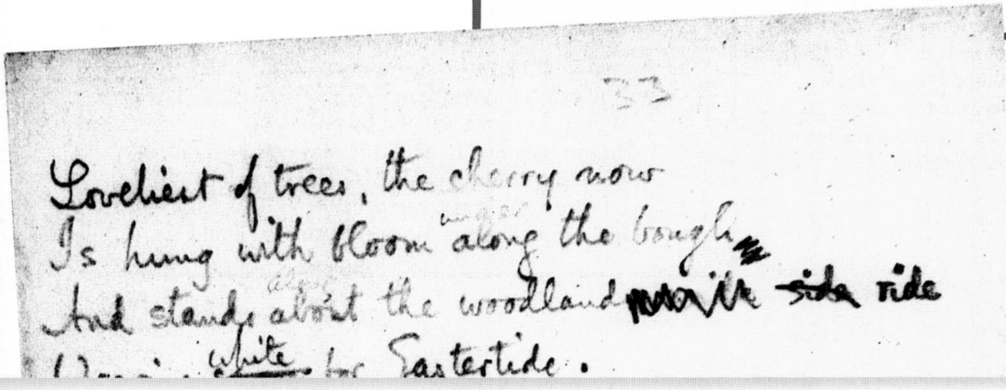

[handwritten manuscript:]

Loveliest of trees, the cherry now
Is hung with bloom along the bough,
And stands about the woodland side ride
. . . white for Eastertide.

521

Summary ■ ■

In this simple lyric poem, the young speaker says that the "loveliest of trees" is the cherry blooming in the spring. He then laments the fact that twenty years of his life have passed and he has only fifty more in which to enjoy the springtime. Conscious of his mortality and the rapid passage of time, he goes out to view the cherry trees with urgency. The final image reminds us again of death—the speaker sees the white blossoms as snow.

Resource 🎧

Listening

For a recording of this poem, see the *Audio CD Library:*
• Disc 16, Track 6

Ⓐ Elements of Literature

Connotations

❓ Explain to students that Eastertide is the period following Easter. At this time of year, Christians celebrate the rising of Jesus of Nazareth from the dead. How do the connotations of the Eastertide holiday fit the poem? [Since Easter celebrates a rebirth, it complements the image of cherry trees blooming again (rebirth) after winter (death).]

Ⓑ Struggling Readers

Making Inferences

Explain to students that *score* in l. 5 and l. 7 means "twenty." Ask them to figure out how old "threescore years and ten" is (three times twenty plus ten). [seventy years old] Explain that in l. 6, the speaker is saying he is twenty years old. Then, ask students how many years are left if you take a score from seventy. [fifty years]

> **RESPONDING TO THE ART**
> **Claude Monet** (1840–1926) is one of the foremost French Impressionists. This landscape captures the beauty of fruit trees in blossom. Note how the heavy, old branches are propped up.
> **Activity.** Discuss with students why the blooming cherry might be an appropriate symbol for fleeting time. [The blooms come and go quickly.]

Reaching All Students

English Language Learners
For strategies for these students, see
• *Lesson Plans Including Strategies for English-Language Learners*

Advanced Learners
Tell students that Housman was influenced by the simple folk ballads he heard when he was growing up: his lines are short, his words easy, his rhyme regular. Have students find examples in the poem of Housman's "keeping it simple."

Making the Connections

Cultural Connections
The people of Japan and the United States share the cultural tradition of appreciating cherry blossoms in spring. The Japanese enjoy daylong excursions to city parks and to the countryside to view the blooming cherry trees, a traditional symbol of prosperity. During the Cherry Blossom Festival in late March, Americans flock to Washington, D.C., to see the flowering Yoshino cherries around the Tidal Basin in Potomac Park.

Summary ▪▪

This short dramatic monologue, written in free verse, explores the speaker's regret at what he now sees as a life without meaning. Gazing at the symbol chiseled on his tombstone—"A boat with a furled sail at rest in a harbor"—the spirit of the deceased George Gray says the symbol represents his whole life. Because he refused to take chances—to risk the threat of failure—he did not experience deep suffering, but neither did he experience deep joy and excitement. He now sees that because he avoided risks, his life lacked meaning.

Resources ———

Listening
Audio CD Library
For a recording of this dramatic poem, see the *Audio CD Library:*
• Disc 16, Track 7

Viewing and Representing
Fine Art Transparency
The Fine Art transparency *Shelf with Two Candles* by Frank Wright can be used to relate the Frost and Masters poems to the theme "How to Live." (See p. T525 for more details.) See the *Viewing and Representing Transparencies and Worksheets:*
• Transparency 12
• Worksheet p. 48

FROM THE EDITOR'S DESK
We paired these two poems because both recommend that life be faced head-on and experienced. The differences between the two poems—in terms of language and messages—are also, of course, important and interesting.

Ⓐ Vocabulary Note
Using Context Clues
If students do not know the meaning of the word *furled* ("rolled up tightly"), have them compare the description of the sailboat in l. 3 with the contrasting description in ll. 10–12. Lead them to understand that the boat in l. 3 is at rest because its sail is rolled up tightly, while the boat in ll. 10–12 can "catch the winds of destiny" because its sail is unfurled, or unrolled.

Before You Read

GEORGE GRAY

Make the Connection
Looking Back at Life
Spoon River Anthology, from which this poem is taken, is one of the most famous books in American literature. Each poem in *Spoon River Anthology* is spoken by someone who once lived in Spoon River, Illinois. Each speaker now "sleeps" on the hill of Spoon River Cemetery. Here, George Gray comes forward to comment on the symbol chiseled on his tombstone. Read the poem aloud to hear the speaker's tone of voice.

Quickwrite
Someone asks you for advice: "What are the most important things in life?" Quickwrite your answer. (*Keep your notes for use on page 525.*)

Elements of Literature
The Poem's Speaker
All poems have speakers, and it's a mistake to think the writer and speaker are always the same. The **speaker** of a poem may be a fictional character, as George Gray is, or even an animal or object. Masters uses a whole graveyard full of people as the speakers of the poems in *Spoon River Anthology.*

The **speaker** is the voice that talks directly to us in a poem; the speaker is not always the poet.

For more on Speaker, see the Handbook of Literary Terms.

Background
What has made *Spoon River Anthology* so appealing to millions of readers is its combination of down-to-earth realism and poetic imagination. The realism comes from Edgar Lee Masters' close observation of life in a small Illinois town. The poetic imagination comes from the lawyer-poet's grasp of psychology. These gifts enable Masters to reveal the deeper and darker meanings of what, on the surface, looks like ordinary lives being lived by ordinary people. Underneath are lives full of drama and secret desires.

 go.hrw.com
LEO 10-8

George Gray Edgar Lee Masters

I have studied many times
The marble which was chiseled for me—
Ⓐ A boat with a furled sail at rest in a harbor.
Ⓑ In truth it pictures not my destination
5   But my life.
For love was offered me and I shrank from its disillusionment;
Sorrow knocked at my door, but I was afraid;
Ambition called to me, but I dreaded the chances.
Yet all the while I hungered for meaning in my life.
10   And now I know that we must lift the sail
Ⓒ And catch the winds of destiny
Wherever they drive the boat.
To put meaning in one's life may end in madness,
But life without meaning is the torture
15   Of restlessness and vague desire—
It is a boat longing for the sea and yet afraid.

522 THE POETRY COLLECTIONS

Reaching All Students

Struggling Readers
If students can't distinguish the poet from the speaker, point out the clue in the title. When a poem's title is a person's name, that person is often the speaker, especially if the poem is in the first person.

English Language Learners
For strategies for these students, see
• *Lesson Plans Including Strategies for English-Language Learners.*

Using Students' Strengths

Kinesthetic Learners
Ask students to think of a symbol for their lives. Tell them to think of objects or animals that connect on more than one level with their self-images. For instance, a person who selects a lightning bolt as a symbol should be able to make two or three comparisons between himself or herself and lightning. Next, encourage students to make models of their symbols and explain why they chose them.

Chelsea Wharf: Gray and Silver (c. 1875) by James A. McNeill Whistler (1834–1903). Oil on canvas (24¼" × 18⅛").

National Gallery of Art, Washington, D.C. Widener Collection/Courtesy Superstock.

Skill Link

Evaluating Performance Techniques

Using a somber tone of voice and weary gestures, model an effective dramatic reading of the first five lines of the poem. Then ask a volunteer to finish the job by performing the complete poem. Encourage the volunteer to incorporate gestures, body language, facial expressions, and perhaps even a simple prop such as a cane into the performance. Suggest that the student review the poem, especially ll. 6–10, to find actions to pantomime. After the performance, ask the class to assess the verbal and nonverbal techniques used in the performance in light of their own interpretations of the poem. Ask questions such as the following:

• How consistent and appropriate were the tone of voice, body language, and facial expressions?

• What phrases, words, or connotations of words in a given line supported the performer's interpretation?

• In what other ways might the same lines have been read?

• How well did the performer capture the personality of the speaker?

• How moved were you by the performance?

1. Read and interpret the poem
2. Analyze ambiguity
3. Express understanding through creative writing and music

SKILLS

Literary
• Analyze ambiguity

Writing
• Collect ideas for a poem
• Write a letter or journal entry
• Write a parody

Music
• Create a song lyric

Planning

• **Block Schedule**
  Block Scheduling Lesson Plans with Pacing Guide

• **Traditional Schedule**
  Lesson Plans Including Strategies for English-Language Learners

• **One-Stop Planner**
  CD-ROM with Test Generator

A **Reading Skills and Strategies**
Making Inferences

? What do these lines suggest about nature's response to a wall? [Possible answer: Nature operates without concern for human constructions such as walls, and as a result, does damage to them. Walls are unnatural barriers.]

Before You Read

MENDING WALL

Make the Connection

Frost vs. Walls

People who live in cold climates know that water freezing in the soil can dislocate stone walls, crack sidewalks, and push underground boulders onto the landscape. Frost's wall is made of boulders that are balanced one on another. Although low, this wall can effectively keep the neighbors at a distance.

Quickwrite

List all the different kinds of walls and boundaries you can think of. What's good about boundaries—and what's bad about them? (*Keep your notes for use on page 529.*)

Elements of Literature

A Matter of Interpretation

This is one of Frost's most controversial poems. The poem is **ambiguous**—that is, it allows for opposing interpretations. There are two mind-sets presented in the poem. The question is, which mind-set does the poet seem to favor: the neighbor's view that walls are good, or the speaker's view that walls should be torn down? There are other ambiguities: If the speaker dislikes walls, why does he initiate the wall mending each spring?

> **W**hen a work of literature allows for opposing interpretations, it is called **ambiguous**.

Mending Wall
Robert Frost

A

Something there is that doesn't love a wall,
That sends the frozen-ground-swell under it
And spills the upper boulders in the sun,
And makes gaps even two can pass abreast.
5   The work of hunters is another thing:
I have come after them and made repair
Where they have left not one stone on a stone,
But they would have the rabbit out of hiding,
To please the yelping dogs. The gaps I mean,
10 No one has seen them made or heard them made,
But at spring mending-time we find them there.
I let my neighbor know beyond the hill;
And on a day we meet to walk the line
And set the wall between us once again.
15 We keep the wall between us as we go.
To each the boulders that have fallen to each.
And some are loaves and some so nearly balls
We have to use a spell to make them balance:
"Stay where you are until our backs are turned!"
20 We wear our fingers rough with handling them.
Oh, just another kind of outdoor game,
One on a side. It comes to little more:
There where it is we do not need the wall:

go.hrw.com
LEO 10-8

Resources: Print and Media

Reading
• *Graphic Organizers for Active Reading*, p. 36
• *Audio CD Library*, Disc 16, Track 8

Elements of Literature
• *Literary Elements*
    Transparency 15
    Worksheet, p. 46

Assessment
• *Portfolio Management System*, p. 158
• *Standardized Test Preparation*, pp. 62, 64
• *Test Generator (One-Stop Planner CD-ROM)*

Internet
• go.hrw.com (keyword: LE0 10-8)

He is all pine and I am apple orchard.
25   My apple trees will never get across
And eat the cones under his pines, I tell him.
He only says, "Good fences make good neighbors." **B**
Spring is the mischief in me, and I wonder
If I could put a notion in his head:
30   "*Why* do they make good neighbors? Isn't it
Where there are cows? But here there are no cows.
Before I built a wall I'd ask to know
What I was walling in or walling out,
And to whom I was like to give offense. **C**
35   Something there is that doesn't love a wall,
That wants it down." I could say "Elves" to him,
But it's not elves exactly, and I'd rather
He said it for himself. I see him there,
Bringing a stone grasped firmly by the top
40   In each hand, like an old-stone savage armed. **D**
He moves in darkness as it seems to me,
Not of woods only and the shade of trees.
He will not go behind his father's saying,
And he likes having thought of it so well
45   He says again, "Good fences make good neighbors." **E**

MENDING WALL   527

Reaching All Students

Struggling Readers
To use the Read Rate Reread strategy with struggling readers, see p. 59 of the *Reading Strategies Handbook* in the *Reading Skills and Strategies* binder.

English Language Learners
Help students understand the idioms *walling in* ("enclosing") and *walling out* ("keeping out"). For additional strategies, see
• *Lesson Plans Including Strategies for English-Language Learners*

Advanced Learners
Share this quotation from Frost: "Poetry provides the one permissible way of saying one thing and meaning another. People say, 'Why don't you say what you mean?' We never do that, do we, being all of us too much poets." Discuss how this comment relates to the ambiguity of "Mending Wall." [It implies that the poem's ambiguity is deliberate, the result of Frost's poetic intent to say "one thing" and mean "another."]

Summary ■ ■

In spring the speaker and a neighbor meet to mend a stone wall between their properties. Their opposing views of the wall are expressed in the poem's opening and closing lines. The speaker states "Something there is that doesn't love a wall," and the neighbor replies "Good fences make good neighbors." The poem's ambiguity lies in the question of which viewpoint the poet supports.

Resources ———

Listening
Audio CD Library
For a strong reading of "Mending Wall," see the *Audio CD Library*:
• Disc 16, Track 8

Elements of Literature
Tone
For additional instruction in tone, see *Literary Elements*:
• Transparency 15
• Worksheet, p. 46

B Critical Thinking
Interpreting
? What does this expression mean? [To remain on friendly terms, neighbors should separate their properties clearly so they won't encroach on each other's territory.] How does the title relate to this expression? [Possible responses: Working together to repair a wall can improve ties between neighbors; mending a wall can mend a relationship.]

C Elements of Literature
Ambiguity
? How do the speaker's doubts about the wall contradict his behavior? [Possible answers: He helps mend the wall even though he doesn't think the wall is necessary; he enjoys mending the wall as a way to keep in touch with his neighbor, but he doubts that the wall makes good neighbors.]

D Elements of Literature
Simile
? Why does the speaker compare his neighbor to "an old-stone savage"? [He might be comparing him to the ignorance and suspicion associated with "savage" cavemen.]

E Elements of Literature
Ambiguity
? How does the repeated final line affect the meaning? [The neighbor has the last word, leaving us to wonder if the poet agrees with the speaker.]

T527

The poem "Mending Test" is a parody of Frost's poem "Mending Wall." A teacher implies that tests can serve the same function as walls: Tests can separate students from learning in the same way walls can divide people from one another.

The letter to *The New York Times* from Jeffrey Meyers continues the debate over the ambiguity of Frost's poem. Did Frost really believe that "Good fences make good neighbors" or was he simply being satirical?

Ⓐ Reading Skills and Strategies
Making Inferences
❓ What are the "gaps students often fall between"? [Sample response: When educators focus on test results, students who understand the curriculum but don't test well may fail and become lost academically.]

Ⓑ Reading Skills and Strategies
Making Connections
❓ What is the darkness to which the speaker refers? Is it different from the darkness in "Mending Wall"? [Sample responses: It is the darkness of power and single mindedness. The unwillingness of the district's high inquisitor to see a new point of view is similar to that of the neighbor in "Mending Wall."]

Ⓒ Appreciate Language
Puns
❓ If the "something" that doesn't love a wall is winter frost, what does the pun imply about the poet's opinion of walls? [It implies that he doesn't like them.]

Ⓓ Historical Connections
Berlin Wall
Remind students that the Berlin Wall was erected to keep East Germans from escaping to non-Communist West Germany. The Berlin Wall was torn down in 1989.

Connections

A PARODY

This poem was written by a teacher in Lakeside, California.

Mending Test
(Apologies to Robert Frost)
Penelope Bryant Turk

Ⓐ Something there is that doesn't love a test,
That sends the frozen mind-set under it
And spills the grade objectives in the room,
And makes gaps students often fall between.
5   No one has seen them made or heard them made
But at spring testing time we find them here.
I let my classes know within my room
And on a day we meet to take the test
And set the norms between us once again.
10   We wear our minds quite rough with handling them.
Oh, just another kind of indoor game,
One on a side. It comes to little more.
There where it is, we do not need the test.
The teachers can assess their goals, I tell him,
15   The district's high inquisitor, once more.
He only says, "Good tests will make good students."
Spring is the mischief in me, and I wonder
If I could put a notion in his head.
"Why do they make good students?" I inquire.
20   "Before I gave a test, I'd ask to know
What I was testing in or testing out.
And to whom I was like to do some good.
Something there is that doesn't love a test,
That wants it done." I could say this to him
25   But it's not politic, and then I'd rather
He said it for himself. I see him there
Bringing a test grasped firmly in each hand,
With pencils like an old-time pedant° armed.
Ⓑ He moves in darkness as it seems to me,
30   Not of woods only and the shade of trees.
He will not go behind the state's command,
And he likes having thought of it so well,
He says again, "Good tests will make good students."

28. pedant (ped′ 'nt): fussy, narrow-minded teacher.

A LETTER

In a 1995 opinion written for the Supreme Court, Justice Antonin Scalia justified a "high wall" separating the levels of government by quoting the neighbor in Frost's poem. The New York Times published an editorial reminding Justice Scalia that Frost did not think good fences made good neighbors. Here is one letter about the controversy.

To the Editor:

Robert Frost's "Mending Wall" has been subjected to many conflicting interpretations, but your April 22 editorial gives the correct one. The "pro-wall" speaker was Frost's French Canadian neighbor, Napoleon Guay. In the opening lines,

Something there is that doesn't love a wall,
That sends the frozen-ground-swell under it

Ⓒ the "something," a natural force that breaks down the wall and indicates the poet's point of view, is frost. Frost liked to pun on his name, calling his satire "frostbite."

Ⓓ When this poem was translated into Russian and printed in the newspapers for Frost's official visit to the Soviet Union in 1962, many writers and intellectuals saw a negative reference to the Berlin Wall put up by East Germany in 1961. So the Soviet translators jump-started the poem with line two.

—Jeffrey Meyers
Kensington, California
April 22, 1995

Connecting Across Texts

Connecting with "Mending Wall"
The parody "Mending Test" implies that tests, like walls, can separate people from what is really important. In "Mending Wall" the separation is between people; in "Mending Test" it is between students and knowledge. Discuss with students whether there are times when walls (and tests) are necessary and useful. Then, encourage them to talk about instances when it is better to break down walls and to use other methods of assessing knowledge.

Justice Scalia's opinion refers to his belief that "a high wall" should separate the levels of government. Ask students whether they believe that these walls are necessary—and what could happen if those walls were brought down. [Students might refer to the Constitution, which advocates a system of checks and balances among the branches of government to prevent conflicts of interest and overlapping jurisdictions.]

MAKING MEANINGS

MENDING WALL

First Thoughts

[respond]

1. Do you agree or disagree that "good fences make good neighbors"? Why?

Shaping Interpretations

[interpret]

2. Frost creates two **characters** in this poem, and we come to know them by what they say and do and think. How would you describe each character?

[synthesize]

3. What do you think the word *darkness* means in line 41? What could the **simile** in line 40 have to do with the darkness?

[infer]

4. What might the wall in the poem **symbolize**?

[interpret]

5. The poem is **ambiguous** and presents opposing views about the wall. Do you think Frost favors the view of the speaker or the neighbor? Which details lead you to this interpretation? Check the *Connections* on page 528.

Extending the Text

[generalize]

6. What other famous walls or boundaries have separated neighbors? (Be sure to check your Quickwrite notes.) Which speaker (maybe both?) would think these walls serve or served a useful purpose? What do you think?

CHOICES: Building Your Portfolio

Writer's Notebook

1. Collecting Ideas for a Poem

A poem about a poem. If you have feelings about walls and boundaries, **describe** an experience you've had with them. Frost writes his poem as a little story—a series of connected events that lead to a discovery. Think of a story to tell about your experience. Elaborate with descriptive details that might make the story more interesting. Also, notice how Frost's poem sounds like an informal conversation but is actually written in strict **meter**. (For more on meter, see pages 543–544 and 558–559.) You might start with Frost's first line and try to imitate his **rhythm**. Save your notes for the Writer's Workshop on page 541.

Creative Writing

2. Let's Hear It from the Neighbor

Using the **first-person point of view** (with "I" as the neighbor), write a letter or journal entry. Tell what you think about your neighbor (the speaker in "Mending Wall"), of the need to mend walls each spring, and of the way you've been portrayed in this poem. Make up details about your life.

Creative Writing/Music

3. Parody, Anyone?

A **parody** is a work that makes fun of another work by imitating some aspect of the writer's style. Penelope Bryant Turk's parody (see *Connections* on page 528), meaning no disrespect to Frost, offers her apologies at the outset. Work with a partner or group to parody the **style** or **format** of a poem or a song lyric.

MAKING MEANINGS

First Thoughts

1. Possible responses: Yes, they allow privacy and help define boundaries; no, they encourage separateness, isolation, and suspicion.

Shaping Interpretations

2. Possible answers: The speaker is open, hard-working, thoughtful, ironic. His neighbor is hard-working, traditional, closed-minded, unwilling to change.

3. Possible responses: It may mean the darkness of ignorance. By comparing his neighbor to a prehistoric thinker, Frost indicates that the man is unenlightened or closed-minded.

4. Students may cite such barriers to human communication as a class system or self-imposed obstacles, like snobbery, that separate people.

5. Possible responses: The poet Frost, like the frost in the earth, finds the wall unnatural, as does the speaker; or, the poet favors the neighbor's view, as shown by the speaker's ambiguity (he implies that he wants the wall down, but he rebuilds it) and by the neighbor's having the last say: "Good fences make good neighbors."

Extending the Text

6. Possible responses: The Berlin Wall, the Great Wall of China, and the Mason-Dixon line are examples of boundaries that have separated cultures, neighbors, and even families. The neighbor in the poem might have favored these boundaries; the speaker would probably be against them.

CHOICES: Building Your Portfolio

1. Remind students to elaborate their experiences with descriptive details.

2 and 3. Have students reread "Mending Wall" before beginning any writing activities.

Assessing Learning

Check Test: Short Answer

1. What does the wall separate? [the speaker's property from his neighbor's]

2. What force of nature shifts the boulders? [frost]

3. Why doesn't the speaker tell his neighbor what he thinks? [He'd rather the neighbor come to the conclusion by himself.]

4. Where did the neighbor learn the saying, "Good fences make good neighbors"? [from his father]

Standardized Test Preparation

For practice with standardized test format specific to this selection, see:

• *Standardized Test Preparation,* pp. 62, 64

OBJECTIVES

The Legend/Miss Rosie

1. Read and interpret the poems
2. Analyze tone
3. Interpret idioms
4. Express understanding through creative writing, visual arts, oral history, critical thinking, speaking and listening, or research

SKILLS

Literary
- Analyze tone
- Interpret idioms

Writing
- Write figures of speech
- Change the tone of a poem
- Write a poem

Speaking and Listening
- Participate in a group discussion

Research
- Conduct a survey

Art
- Create images of a neighborhood

Viewing/Representing
- Compare portraits created by poets and painters (ATE)
- Imagine a portrait (ATE)

Planning

- **Block Schedule**
  Block Scheduling Lesson Plans with Pacing Guide
- **Traditional Schedule**
  Lesson Plans Including Strategies for English-Language Learners
- **One-Stop Planner**
  CD-ROM with Test Generator

Before You Read

THE LEGEND

Make the Connection

Imagination's Eye

One night, Garrett Hongo saw a TV news story about an Asian man killed in an act of street violence. Much later, Hongo claims, the poem "just appeared." Which details do you think Hongo imagined?

Quickwrite

Look up, and focus on a person or a scene that you can observe closely. Note what you *see* and what you *imagine*. (*Keep your notes for use on page 537.*)

See	Imagine

Elements of Literature

Tone: An Attitude

A poet's attitude, or **tone,** can be inferred from words and details in the text. Read "The Legend" more than once to get the speaker's tone.

> **T**one is the attitude of the writer or the speaker toward the subject of the poem or toward the audience.
>
> *For more on Tone, see the Handbook of Literary Terms.*

Portrait of an Old Man in Red (c. 1652–1654) by Rembrandt. Oil on canvas (108 cm × 86 cm).

The Hermitage Museum, Saint Petersburg, Russia. Courtesy Scala/Art Resource, NY.

The Legend

Garrett Hongo

In Chicago, it is snowing softly
and a man has just done his wash for the week.
He steps into the twilight of early evening,
carrying a wrinkled shopping bag
5 full of neatly folded clothes,
and, for a moment, enjoys
the feel of warm laundry and crinkled paper,
flannellike against his gloveless hands.
There's a Rembrandt° glow on his face,

9. Rembrandt: Dutch painter (1606–1669), famous for his dramatic use of color and of light and shadow.

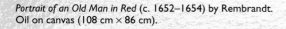

Resources: Print and Media

Reading
- *Graphic Organizers for Active Reading,* pp. 37, 38
- *Audio CD Library,* Disc 16, Tracks 9, 10

Elements of Literature
- *Literary Elements,* Poetry Transparencies 1-5; Teaching Notes, p. 69

Assessment
- *Portfolio Management System,* p. 159
- *Test Generator (One-Stop Planner CD-ROM)*

10 a triangle of orange in the hollow of his cheek
    as a last flash of sunset
    blazes the storefronts and lit windows of the street.

    He is Asian, Thai or Vietnamese,
    and very skinny, dressed as one of the poor
15 in rumpled suit pants and a plaid mackinaw,
    dingy and too large.
    He negotiates the slick of ice
    on the sidewalk by his car,
    opens the Fairlane's back door,
20 leans to place the laundry in,
    and turns, for an instant,
    toward the flurry of footsteps
    and cries of pedestrians
    as a boy—that's all he was—
25 backs from the corner package store
    shooting a pistol, firing it,
    once, at the dumbfounded man
    who falls forward,
    grabbing at his chest.

30 A few sounds escape from his mouth,
    a babbling no one understands
    as people surround him
    bewildered at his speech.
    The noises he makes are nothing to them.
35 The boy has gone, lost
    in the light array of foot traffic
    dappling the snow with fresh prints.
    Tonight, I read about Descartes' ⌐Ⓐ
    grand courage to doubt everything
40 except his own miraculous existence°
    and I feel so distinct
    from the wounded man lying on the concrete
    I am ashamed.

    Let the night sky cover him as he dies. ⌐
45 Let the weaver girl cross the bridge of heaven Ⓑ
    and take up his cold hands. ⌎

    IN MEMORY OF JAY KASHIWAMURA

    38–40. Descartes' . . . existence: René Descartes (1596–1650),
    French philosopher and mathematician, attempted to explain the
    universe by reason alone. In his search for truth, he discarded all
    traditional ideas and doubted everything. The one thing he could not
    doubt was the fact that he was doubting, which led him to conclude,
    "I think; therefore I am" (in Latin, *Cogito, ergo sum*).

    THE LEGEND 531

Summary ∎

This poem opens peacefully on a snowy street in Chicago, where a poor man of Asian descent is placing laundry in his car. Suddenly, he is shot by a boy who has just robbed a store. The speaker feels despair about the murder and shame at being "so distinct" from the victim. He ends his poem with a prayer for mercy (see Hongo's statement on pp. 532–533).

Resources 🎧

Listening
Audio CD Library
For a dramatic recording of "The Legend," see the *Audio CD Library:*
• Disc 16, Track 9

Ⓐ Critical Thinking
Interpreting
❓ How does the poem change, beginning at l. 38? [Lines 1–37 tell what the speaker sees. The rest of the poem describes what the speaker feels.]
What are the speaker's feelings about the events? [Possible responses: The speaker feels ashamed of putting reason, as represented by Descartes' beliefs, over feeling; the speaker feels compassion for the victim, as shown by his vision of the man's being cared for in the spiritual world.]

Ⓑ Elements of Literature
Tone
❓ How does the tone change in the poem's last three lines? What is the effect of this change? [Sample response: The tone becomes mystical, perhaps religious. The effect is one of benediction for the victim and closure to his tragic story.]

RESPONDING TO THE ART
Dutch painter **Rembrandt van Rijn** (1606–1669) is known for his use of shifting golden light to suggest emotional content.
Activity. Ask students to explain how the artist's use of light in the portrait relates to the poet's reference in l. 9. [Sample answer: The poet sees the Asian man as bathed in twilight but also glowing from an internal light, just as the old man in the painting is.]

Reaching All Students

English Language Learners
Explain the meanings of the following unfamiliar words: *mackinaw* in l. 15 denotes a plain, woolen jacket; and *Fairlane* in l. 19, a Ford automobile that was popular in the 1970s.
For additional strategies for English language learners, see
• *Lesson Plans Including Strategies for English-Language Learners*

Struggling Readers
Remind students that the poem is a response to a TV news story. Tell them to visualize the events in the poem as though they were being shown on TV news.

Advanced Learners
Invite these students to explore Descartes' beliefs. Ask them to contrast the intellectual ideas of Western tradition with the spiritual ideas of Asian legend, as suggested in the poem.

Connections

This reflection constitutes Garrett Hongo's answer when we questioned him about "The Legend." He goes on to relay a legend that he had heard during his childhood. It is an Asian creation story about a Weaver Maid and a Herd Boy whose sacrifice holds the universe together. The maid and the boy labor in distant parts of the universe, herding the star bands across the sky, without companionship or love. Yet for one night of the year, the universe, in its compassion, builds a footbridge of stars so that the two can spend one night together. The legend offers a promise that the universe is responsive to the human heart and that we will ultimately know the reason for our struggles and find a reward for them.

Ⓐ Reading Skills and Strategies
Drawing Conclusions

? Why do you think Hongo wants to believe that the universe is merciful? [Possible response: Without that belief, the events he has witnessed seem meaningless and unbearably cruel.]

Ⓑ Critical Thinking
Extending the Text

? Most people have felt the same need for mercy that Hongo feels. How do some of them meet their need? [Possible responses: They turn to a religion that allows for mercy; they turn to a philosophy that explains why things happen, giving their view of the universe some order and reason.]

Ⓒ Reading Skills and Strategies
Making Inferences

Invite students to explain how readers might infer that the culture in which the story of the Weaver Maid and the Herd Boy originated was rural as well as ancient. [Sample response: The image of the river of stars and the characters of the weaver and shepherd suggest a rural setting. The lack of technology in the story indicates an ancient era.]

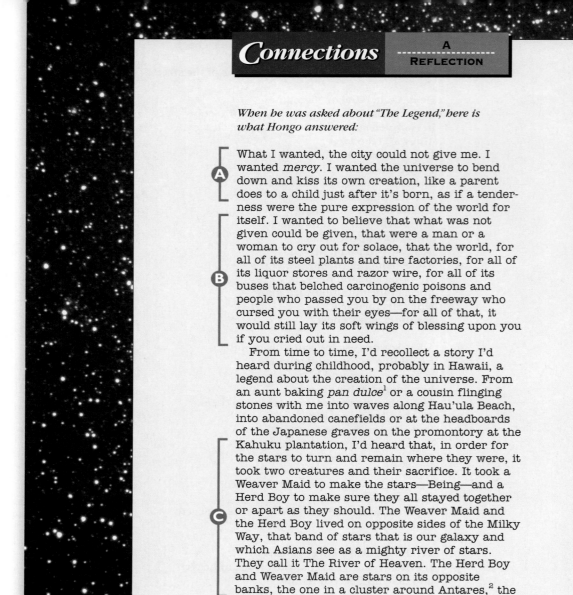

Connections

When he was asked about "The Legend," here is what Hongo answered:

Ⓐ What I wanted, the city could not give me. I wanted *mercy*. I wanted the universe to bend down and kiss its own creation, like a parent does to a child just after it's born, as if a tenderness were the pure expression of the world for itself.

Ⓑ I wanted to believe that what was not given could be given, that were a man or a woman to cry out for solace, that the world, for all of its steel plants and tire factories, for all of its liquor stores and razor wire, for all of its buses that belched carcinogenic poisons and people who passed you by on the freeway who cursed you with their eyes—for all of that, it would still lay its soft wings of blessing upon you if you cried out in need.

Ⓒ From time to time, I'd recollect a story I'd heard during childhood, probably in Hawaii, a legend about the creation of the universe. From an aunt baking *pan dulce*[1] or a cousin flinging stones with me into waves along Hau'ula Beach, into abandoned canefields or at the headboards of the Japanese graves on the promontory at the Kahuku plantation, I'd heard that, in order for the stars to turn and remain where they were, it took two creatures and their sacrifice. It took a Weaver Maid to make the stars—Being—and a Herd Boy to make sure they all stayed together or apart as they should. The Weaver Maid and the Herd Boy lived on opposite sides of the Milky Way, that band of stars that is our galaxy and which Asians see as a mighty river of stars. They call it The River of Heaven. The Herd Boy and Weaver Maid are stars on its opposite banks, the one in a cluster around Antares,[2] the

1. *pan dulce* (pän′ dool′sä): sweet bread.
2. **Antares** (an·ter′ēz′): brightest star in the constellation Scorpius; its name derives from the Greek for "rival of Ares" (Mars).

Getting Students Involved

Cooperative Learning
Since "The Legend" tells such a dramatic story, it lends itself well to a pantomime performance. Students can take the parts of the old man, the robber, and the bystanders. Other students might assume the task of finding music or sound effects to underscore the physical movements of the performers. One student might read the poem aloud as others act out the performance.

Researching Creation Legends
Students can work in small groups to research creation legends from other cultures. Members of each group can do research, provide visual aids, and orally present the legends and give relevant background information. Encourage students to discuss whether the legends promote the idea of a merciful—or at least a comprehensible—universe.

other far away and down along the flow, in a spot near Aldebaran.[3] They labor, dutifully fabricating the web and warp of Being, herding the star bands in an eternal solitude, celibate, without love or companionship. Yet, for one night of the year, on an evening when the star sky is said to be clearest, the universe is supposed to succumb to an overwhelming pity for the two lovers, living out lives in exile from each other, lives in deprivation of passion, without emotional compass or root in material certainties. In the form of a flock of compassionate starlings or swallows in the Japanese or Chinese versions, in the folded and gigantic wing of Crow in the Tlingit and Haida versions of the North Coast Pacific Indians, the universe, *one turning,* responds by making a footbridge across the River of Heaven out of its own interlocking bodies, out of its own need to create mercy and requital in a night of love for the effortful sacrifices of two of its children.

It is a vision of the afterlife, in a sense, a promise that the world will provide for us a reward and a reason for our struggles. It is a parable[4] about mercy and fulfillment, the response of the universe to needs of the human heart. The poem is the story of the Weaver Girl and the Herd Boy, told in inner-city, contemporary terms. It is about my own needs for mercy, for a fulfillment to a broad, urban, and contemporary story that baffled me.

3. **Aldebaran** (al·deb'ə·rən): brightest star in the constellation Taurus.
4. **parable** (par'ə·b'l): brief story that teaches a moral or religious lesson.

MEET THE WRITER

Looking for Mercy

Garrett Hongo (1951–   ) was born in Volcano, Hawaii, and grew up in Hawaii and Los Angeles. After graduating with honors from Pomona College, he toured Japan for a year and then returned to the United States to write and teach poetry. Hongo says he writes

66 for my father in a very personal way. He was a great example to me of a man who refused to hate or, being different himself, to be afraid of difference. . . . I want my poems to be equal to his heart. 99

D Vocabulary Note
Technical Words
Tell students that the terms *web* and *warp* are used in weaving. A web is a whole piece of cloth being woven on a loom. Warp is the name for the lengthwise threads in a woven fabric.

E Cultural Connections
? Why do you think Hongo mentions that this story exists in slightly different versions in these cultures? [Sample responses: Hongo wants readers to know that this story is powerful enough to have been transferred from one culture to another; he implies that the imagery of this story carries meaning for various cultures.]

F Struggling Readers
Summarizing
? Who are the two lovers in the legend? [the Weaver Maid and the Herd Boy] What does the universe do for these lovers one night a year? [It makes a footbridge across the River of Heaven so the lovers can be together.]

BROWSING IN THE FILES
About the Author. Garrett Hongo attended high school with Japanese, Caucasian, Chicano, and African-American students. He credits this early multicultural exposure with teaching him about the importance of cultural links.

Connecting Across Texts

Connecting with "The Legend"
At the end of this reflection, Hongo states that his poem "The Legend" is his rendition of the story of the Weaver Girl and Herd Boy. Invite students to explain how the story of the Asian man's murder relates to the story of the celestial lovers.

[Sample response: By mentioning the Weaver Girl at the end of the poem, Hongo hopes that in death the man might find the mercy he was not granted in life, just as the Weaver Girl and the Herd Boy are rewarded by a compassionate universe for their lives of sacrifice.]

Summary ■ ■

This poem's speaker uses strong figures of speech—"wrapped up like garbage" and "wet brown bag of a woman"—to depict the degradation of a once strong and beautiful woman. With the repeated idiom "I stand up," however, the speaker declares her respect for Miss Rosie.

Resources

Listening
Audio CD Library
For a heartfelt reading of "Miss Rosie," see the *Audio CD Library:*
• Disc 16, Track 10

RESPONDING TO THE ART

Catherine Howe (1959–   ), a figurative painter, is known for her powerful paintings of women. Howe uses bold expressionist brush strokes and often reflects colors from a background onto the bodies of her subjects.

Activity. Ask students to describe how the subject of *Mirage* resembles Miss Rosie both in her youth and in her present state. [Sample response: The subject of the painting is pretty and well-dressed and carries a hat that a young southern woman might wear, but her posture and facial expression make her seem isolated and possibly troubled.]

Make the Connection

Portrait of a Woman

No one can say that Clifton's portrait of Miss Rosie is very pretty. Yet beauty—and what can happen to it—is the subject of the poem. Notice how figures of speech help you see contrasting pictures, past and present, of Miss Rosie.

Quickwrite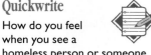

How do you feel when you see a homeless person or someone on the street asking for money? Write a few sentences in your notebook. (*Keep your notes for use on page 536.*)

Elements of Literature

Idioms: Not Literally True

An **idiom** is an expression that is peculiar to a certain language and that cannot be understood by a mere literal definition of its individual words. For example, the literal meaning of the expression "to fall in love" would be absurd. Like many idioms, this one implies a comparison. The experience of love can be so overwhelming that it feels like losing your footing or like falling into a trap, although not necessarily an unpleasant one.

One of the problems in translating a work from one language to another is the difficulty in translating the idioms.

If an idiom is unfamiliar to you—as the idiom "I stand up" in this poem may be—the context might help you understand it.

Mirage (1993) by Catherine Howe. Oil on canvas.
Collection Alan P. Power (Venice, California).

> **A**n **idiom** is an expression peculiar to a particular language. An idiom means something different from the literal meaning of each word.

Reaching All Students

Struggling Readers
Encourage students to go through the poem and chart the sensory details that Clifton uses to create her images. Suggest that students use a chart to organize words that appeal to the senses of sight, smell, and touch. Students can then use the chart to write brief descriptions of Miss Rosie as the speaker sees her.

English Language Learners
Students might not know the denotative and connotative meanings of the word *gal.* Explain that the word means "girl" and that it connotes a young woman who is lively and fun-loving. For additional strategies for engaging English language learners with the literature, see
• *Lesson Plans Including Strategies for English-Language Learners*

Miss Rosie

Lucille Clifton

When I watch you
wrapped up like garbage
sitting, surrounded by the smell
of too old potato peels
5   or
when I watch you
in your old man's shoes
with the little toe cut out
sitting, waiting for your mind  **A**
10 like next week's grocery
I say
when I watch you
you wet brown bag of a woman
who used to be the best looking gal in Georgia **B**
15 used to be called the Georgia Rose
I stand up
through your destruction **C**
I stand up

MEET THE WRITER

Celebrating Survival

Lucille Clifton (1936–) writes both fiction and poetry and has published many books for children. One of Clifton's best-known works is *Generations* (1976), a poetic memoir composed of portraits of five generations of her family. It begins with her great-great-grandmother, who was brought from Africa to New Orleans and sold into slavery. Like all of Clifton's work, *Generations* is honest but rarely bitter. As one critic observed, her purpose is perpetuation and celebration, not judgment.

Clifton says that family stories are part of the ingredients that make us who we are. She remembers hearing her own family's stories when she was growing up.

66 My father told those stories to me over and over. That made them seem important.

He told the stories to whoever was present, but I was the only person who listened. I think there is a matter of preserving the past for the future's sake. I think if we see our lives as an ongoing story, it's important to include all the ingredients of it and not have it in little compartments. I like to think of it as not just that was then, this is now, but that they all connect. For some reason, I've always been a person who found more interesting the stories between the stories. I've always wondered the hows and the whys to things. Why is this like this? What has gone into making us who we are? Is it good or not so good? What is destroying us? What will keep us warm? 99

MISS ROSIE **535**

Taking a Second Look

MAKING MEANINGS

First Thoughts

1. Sample responses: sadness, pity, and, perhaps, an initial feeling of revulsion toward Miss Rosie.

Shaping Interpretations

2. Possible responses: Such words as *snowing softly* and *glow* create a peaceful tone. Then the tone is harsher and hurried with such words as *slick*, *flurry*, and *cries*. At the end the tone is mystical, created by the phrase, "Let the night sky cover him" and the additional phrases *weaver girl* and *bridge of heaven*.

3. Possible responses: The tenderness of the weaver girl at the end of Hongo's poem supplies a vision of the mercy that he wants from the universe. Writing the poem seems to have satisfied Hongo's need to show mercy to a human victim, but some readers may continue to view the senseless murder as evidence of an uncaring universe.

4. Possible answers: "wrapped up like garbage," "waiting for your mind/like next week's grocery," "wet brown bag of a woman." Each figure creates a picture of sadness, wasted potential, or diminished capacity.

5. Possible responses: "Stand up" in the poem's context could mean "to protect, defend, salute." The image is of someone standing tall in the midst of disaster and refusing to be conquered. The speaker feels a link with Miss Rosie and remembers that she was once a beautiful and vital young woman. The speaker is standing up in spite of what happened to Miss Rosie.

6. Miss Rosie may symbolize all the people lost to poverty, homelessness, or hopelessness. She may symbolize the human capacity to endure and even triumph.

Extending the Text

7. Sample responses: The poems evoke the problems of poverty, despair, and urban violence. Many people can relate to the contrasting feelings the poets express: a desire to distance themselves from the problems and a desire to help individuals. Both poems call for mercy and seem to hope for some kind of redemption for the sufferers.

T536

MAKING MEANINGS

THE LEGEND
MISS ROSIE

First Thoughts

[respond]
1. In "The Legend" and "Miss Rosie," we meet two figures seen briefly on city streets. How do you feel about each of these people?

Shaping Interpretations

[interpret]
2. In "The Legend," an ordinary street scene is suddenly transformed by a tragic event. How would you describe the poem's **tone**? In other words, what is the poet's attitude toward the event he's made into a poem? List some of the words, phrases, and details that you think create the tone.

[evaluate]
3. Read Hongo's explanation of how he came to write "The Legend" (see ***Connections*** on page 532). Do you think the poem expresses what he wants it to? Talk about Hongo's comment about needing mercy.

[evaluate]
4. Which **figure of speech** in "Miss Rosie" do you think is most powerful? What picture of Miss Rosie does it create for you?

[infer]
5. The **idiom** "I stand up," used twice, gives the most important clue to how the writer wants us to feel about Miss Rosie. What does standing up in the face of Miss Rosie's destruction mean? (What does it make you *see*?) Why do you think the speaker is moved to "stand up" for Miss Rosie?

[infer]
6. In a way, Miss Rosie seems to represent something more than herself, something never named. What do you think she might **symbolize**?

Extending the Text

[connect]
7. What contemporary urban problems come alive in these poems by Hongo and Clifton? Do most people feel the way these poets felt about these problems? Talk about the ways in which people like Miss Rosie and events like the one in "The Legend" are regarded by society. (You may want to refer to your Quickwrite notes for "Miss Rosie.")

The Shoemaker (1945) by Jacob Lawrence.
Tempera on hardboard (30″ × 40″).

The Metropolitan Museum of Art, George A. Hearn Fund, 1946. (46.73.2) Courtesy of the artist and Francine Seders Gallery, Seattle, Washington. Photograph ©1985 The Metropolitan Museum of Art.

Assessing Learning

Check Test: Short Answer
"The Legend"

1. Just before he shoots the man, what has the boy been doing? [robbing a store]
2. What happens to the man and the boy? [The man dies, and the boy flees.]
3. Who understands the dying man's words? [no one]
4. What "legend" does the title refer to? [the legend of the Weaver Maid and the Herd Boy]

"Miss Rosie"

5. Whom is the speaker watching? [Miss Rosie]
6. What is Miss Rosie like now? [She seems to be a street person, homeless and emotionally ill.]
7. What was Miss Rosie once like? [She was the best looking gal in Georgia.]
8. What does the speaker vow to do through Miss Rosie's destruction? [stand up]

CHOICES: Building Your Portfolio

Writer's Notebook

1. Collecting Ideas for a Poem

Finding figures of speech.  Try to write figures of speech that tell what some person or scene reminds you of. Remember to think in **descriptive** images. Let your imagination free-associate; **comparisons** should come quickly to you. Write them all down, even those you might not totally understand. You might want to focus on the person or scene from your Quickwrite notes for "The Legend."

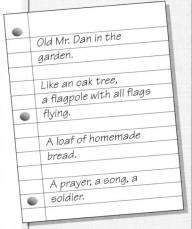

Old Mr. Dan in the garden.

Like an oak tree, a flagpole with all flags flying.

A loaf of homemade bread.

A prayer, a song, a soldier.

Creative Writing

2. Changing the Tone

Write at least three new lines to end "The Legend" and "Miss Rosie." Let your lines reveal a **tone**, or attitude toward the characters (the Asian man, Miss Rosie), that's different from the present tone of the poems. Use **figures of speech** and **sensory details** in your lines.

Visual Arts/Oral History

3. Portraits of a Neighborhood

In photographs, drawings, or paintings, show your neighborhood and the people who live there. **Interview** one person if you can, and add his or her words to your portrait. Try to elaborate with **images** that reveal the way you feel about this place.

Creative Writing

4. News Stories Are True Poems

"The true poem is the daily paper," wrote Walt Whitman in 1852. Write a poem that is based on a newspaper story or a television report. Follow Hongo's pattern in "The Legend": Begin with a close observation of the scene; focus on one or more unnamed characters; and then tell what happens, using present-tense verbs. End with a comment on your own feelings and thoughts about the event. Use your imagination to elaborate with **sensory details**.

Critical Thinking/Speaking and Listening

5. The Poems as Clues

Imagine that extraterrestrials visit America in the year 4000 and the only bits of writing they discover are these two poems. No other books or writings have survived. What might the newcomers **infer** about American life from these poems? Would their **conclusions** be valid? Discuss this scenario in a small group, and then report to the class.

Research/Survey

6. Idioms, Anyone?

With a small group, survey students in your school or your family or neighbors. Challenge them to think of as many idioms as they can, in English or in other languages. Read a few idioms to get them started—for example, "big shot," "go in one ear and out the other," and "He jumped out of his skin." Afterward, prepare a chart listing the idioms in one column, their literal meanings in the second column, and their real meanings in the third column. Do you have any favorites?

CHOICES: Building Your Portfolio

1. **Writer's Notebook** Remind students to save their work. They may use it as prewriting for the Writer's Workshop on p. 541.
2. **Creative Writing** Have students begin by identifying all the words and phrases that contribute to each poem's tone. They can then make more informed choices of words that will change the tone.
3. **Visual Arts/Oral History** Students might instead use a video camera and make a visual documentary. For every portrait, urge students to prepare questions before conducting their interviews.
4. **Creative Writing** Encourage students to choose a news story that inspires them to imagine sensory details. They can then convey their feelings about the event through these details.
5. **Critical Thinking/Speaking and Listening** Have students use a cluster diagram to organize the ideas about American life that they glean from each poem.
6. **Research/Survey** Encourage students to note which idioms are mentioned more than once. Is there any link among them? What could explain their popularity?

RESPONDING TO THE ART

New Jersey-born artist **Jacob Lawrence** (1917–   ) depicts African American life with intense colors and economical lines. (See pp. 346 and 377 for other Lawrence works).

Activity. Have students describe precisely what they see in this painting. Then, have them write a poem spoken by the man in the painting. The poem should fit into the theme "How to Live."

Making the Connections

Connecting to the Theme: "How to Live"

After students have read both poems, be sure to discuss the theme. In both poems, the speakers confront a moral and an ethical issue: how to respond to people in desperate circumstances or in great need. Encourage students to express and debate their views about whether everyone has a responsibility to help those who are in desperate trouble.

Grading Timesaver

Rubrics for each Choices assignment appear on p. 159 in the *Portfolio Management System.*

Extending the Theme

In her essay, Annie Dillard exhorts readers to face the "hard work" of making something of their lives. She admits to laziness herself and notes that we want to believe that achievers are both "natural wonders" and super-disciplined. Such a belief, she claims, makes us feel it is useless to expect much from ourselves. Using her experience, she counters that fallacy by noting that discipline comes from doing the task itself. Superhuman efforts are actually very human, done for love and respect of oneself, the world, and the task at hand.

Resources

Listening
Audio CD Library
For a recording of this essay, see the *Audio CD Library:*
• Disc 16, Track 11

Ⓐ Critical Thinking
Analyzing the Title
❓ After students have read the essay, point out that Dillard never uses the word *talent* in the body of the work. How does the essay answer the question posed in the title? [Sample response: It refutes the idea of talent by saying that it is love and dedication that allow people to do their work.]

Ⓑ Critical Thinking
Challenging the Text
❓ Is becoming a physicist or pitcher really "nothing but hard work"? Explain. [Sample answers: It is hard work to achieve these things, but there are rewards for the work—both personal and professional. These careers require special abilities as well as hard work.]

Ⓒ Reading Skills and Strategies
Drawing Conclusions
❓ What does Dillard mean by "it gets us off the hook"? [Believing that other people are extraordinary relieves us of the responsibility of trying hard to accomplish anything special—we can assume we lack the natural ability needed to do it.]

Quickwrite

Divide a page of your notebook into two columns. In one column, list all the jobs you think you'd like to have—if you could make a living doing them. In the other column, list (and don't be modest) your talents, the things you do well, and the things you really enjoy doing. Save your lists.

Is There Really Such a Thing as Talent?

Annie Dillard

> *The very thought of hard work makes me queasy.*

Ⓐ

Ⓑ It's hard work, doing something with your life. The very thought of hard work makes me queasy. I'd rather die in peace. Here we are, all equal and alike and none of us much to write home about—and some people choose to make themselves into physicists or thinkers or major-league pitchers, knowing perfectly well that it will be nothing but hard work. But I want to tell you that it's not as bad as it sounds. Doing something does not require discipline; it creates its own discipline—with a little help from caffeine.

People often ask me if I discipline myself to write, if I work a certain number of hours a day on a schedule. They ask this question with envy in their voices and awe on their faces and a sense of alienation all over them, as if they were addressing an armored tank or a talking giraffe or Niagara Falls. We want to believe that Ⓒ other people are natural wonders; it gets us off the hook.

Now, it happens that when I wrote my first book of prose, I worked an hour or two a day for a while, and then in the last two months, I got excited and worked very hard, for many hours a day. People can lift cars

Making the Connections

Connecting to the Theme: "How to Live"
About the theme "How to Live," Dillard herself says, "I would like to learn, or remember, how to live. . . . The weasel lives in necessity and we live in choice, hating necessity and dying at the last ignobly in its talons. I would like to live as I should. . . . And I suspect that for me the way is like the weasel's: open to time and death painlessly, noticing everything, remembering nothing, choosing the given with a fierce and pointed will." Discuss with students how Dillard's desire to live in necessity rather than in choice reflects the ideas she expresses in her essay. [In the essay she says that when we perform tasks out of necessity, that necessity can lead to love, which is an important part of the way she lives and essential to a successful life.]

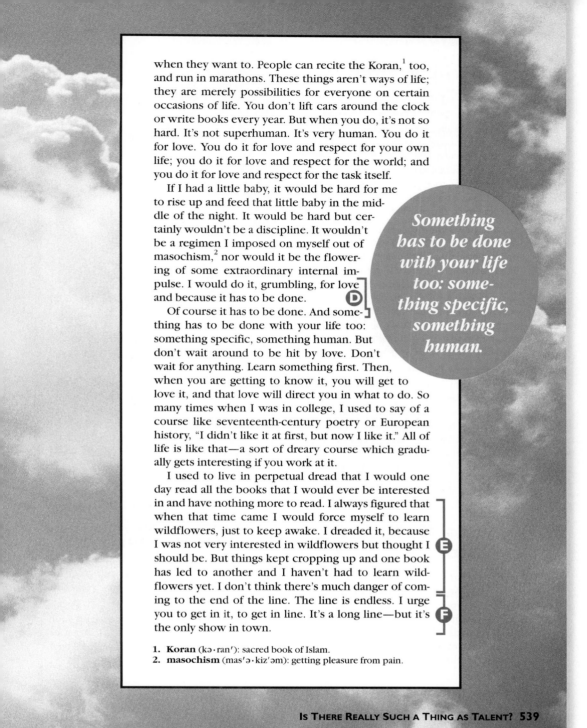

when they want to. People can recite the Koran,[1] too, and run in marathons. These things aren't ways of life; they are merely possibilities for everyone on certain occasions of life. You don't lift cars around the clock or write books every year. But when you do, it's not so hard. It's not superhuman. It's very human. You do it for love. You do it for love and respect for your own life; you do it for love and respect for the world; and you do it for love and respect for the task itself.

If I had a little baby, it would be hard for me to rise up and feed that little baby in the middle of the night. It would be hard but certainly wouldn't be a discipline. It wouldn't be a regimen I imposed on myself out of masochism,[2] nor would it be the flowering of some extraordinary internal impulse. I would do it, grumbling, for love and because it has to be done.

Of course it has to be done. And something has to be done with your life too: something specific, something human. But don't wait around to be hit by love. Don't wait for anything. Learn something first. Then, when you are getting to know it, you will get to love it, and that love will direct you in what to do. So many times when I was in college, I used to say of a course like seventeenth-century poetry or European history, "I didn't like it at first, but now I like it." All of life is like that—a sort of dreary course which gradually gets interesting if you work at it.

I used to live in perpetual dread that I would one day read all the books that I would ever be interested in and have nothing more to read. I always figured that when that time came I would force myself to learn wildflowers, just to keep awake. I dreaded it, because I was not very interested in wildflowers but thought I should be. But things kept cropping up and one book has led to another and I haven't had to learn wildflowers yet. I don't think there's much danger of coming to the end of the line. The line is endless. I urge you to get in it, to get in line. It's a long line—but it's the only show in town.

> *Something has to be done with your life too: something specific, something human.*

1. **Koran** (kə·ran′): sacred book of Islam.
2. **masochism** (mas′ə·kiz′əm): getting pleasure from pain.

D Reading Skills and Strategies
Comparing and Contrasting
? What is the difference between doing something "because it has to be done" and doing something "for love"? [Possible response: Doing something that has to be done is acting from a sense of obligation and duty. When love is added to the mix, the task gains meaning and importance.]

E Reading Skills and Strategies
Making Predictions
? What do you think would happen if the writer did force herself to learn wildflowers? What evidence supports your prediction? [Sample answer: With time and experience, she would probably grow to love the task. This can be inferred from her belief that while learning something, a person grows to love it.]

F English Language Learners
Idioms
Point out that Dillard uses the word *line* in two different idioms. Explain that by "the end of the line" she means the end of a series of interesting books. When she advises readers to "get in line," she is urging them to stay connected with life, learning, and work.

Taking a Second Look

Review: Recognize Author's Purpose
Remind students that authors have one or more purposes when they write. Often, the purpose is to inform, to persuade, or to entertain. Determining the author's purpose helps a reader evaluate, understand, and appreciate a text more fully.

1. Ask students to identify the intended audience for this piece of writing. Does it seem like an essay from a book? A talk presented to young people?

2. When students have decided what audience they think Dillard was writing for, ask them to determine her purpose in writing. Does she mean to inform, persuade, entertain, or does she have a combination of two or more purposes? Urge students to support their opinions with details from the essay. [Possible responses: Dillard's purpose is to persuade. She expresses her opinion about how to make something of one's life by engaging oneself in it—obviously she wants to inspire and persuade readers to be willing to carry out this idea in their own lives; or, Dillard has two purposes: to persuade and to inform—she gives factual examples from her own life as information, and she offers opinions about how to live and work.]

T539

FINDING COMMON GROUND

1. Possible questions for Dillard: "Do you believe there is no such thing as talent?" and "When did you first realize the importance of love?" Students might tell Dillard that they have received inspiration from her writing.

2. Have students who share common career goals work together to brainstorm ideas for how they can reach these goals. Possible areas to research include schools, vocational-training courses, and internships at companies or organizations where these positions are most available.

3. Some students may find inspiration in Dillard's assertion that there are many possibilities for success in life; others might feel intimidated by the idea that the strength to succeed and find meaning in life and work must come from within.

MEET THE WRITER

Rockhound, Naturalist, and Writer

When **Annie Dillard** (1945–   ) was twelve, her grandparents' paperboy handed her three shopping bags full of large rocks from an elderly neighbor. With the help of books, she identified each of the 340 rocks; she became a "rockhound," a rock collector. Later, looking out a car window at miles of dull gray rock, she realized:

66 But now I knew that even rock was interesting. . . . Even I could tap some shale just right, rain or shine, and open the rock to bones of fossil fish. There might be trilobites on the hilltops, star sapphires. . . . If even rock was interesting, if even this ugliness was worth whole shelves at the library, required sophisticated tools to study, and inspired grown men to crack mountains and saw crystals—then what wasn't? 99

Dillard's continuing interest in nature resulted in her Pulitzer Prize–winning first book, *Pilgrim at Tinker Creek* (1974). In it she chronicles a year's worth of observations of the beauties and terrors along a Virginia creek. Dillard's other works include an autobiography, *An American Childhood* (1987); essays on writing, *The Writing Life* (1989); and a novel,

The Living (1992).

To aspiring writers Dillard gives this advice:

66 You have enough experience by the time you're five years old. What you need is the library. What you have to learn is the best of what is being thought and said. If you had a choice between spending a summer in Nepal and spending a summer in the library, go to the library. 99

FINDING COMMON GROUND

Get together in small groups to discuss this essay. First, vote yes or no on the question in the title and explain your vote. Here is what you could focus on in your group discussions, though you can also set agendas of your own. Your purpose is to explore your responses to the text and **compare** them with the responses of other readers.

1. If Dillard visited your class, what questions would you ask? What would you tell her?

2. Share your Quickwrite notes about jobs you'd love to have. Is anyone else in your group interested in the same kinds of jobs? How could you get any of these jobs?

3. How did the essay make you feel about your future? What do you think of Dillard's advice about how to discover something you'll be happy doing?

540 THE POETRY COLLECTIONS

Assessing Learning

Check Test: True-False

1. According to the author, the act of doing something creates its own discipline. [True]
2. The author used a rigid schedule when she began to write her first book. [False]
3. The author once was afraid she would have nothing more to read. [True]
4. The author's main point is that we should study something until we begin to like it. [True]

Writer's Workshop

ASSIGNMENT

Write a poem or a group of poems that describe something or someone.

AIM

To express yourself; to create literature.

AUDIENCE

Your classmates, your family, or readers of a magazine of student writing. (You choose.)

I thought poetry was just something about dried roses and violets until I discovered that it could be about my shoestrings, about the neighborhood, about the sky, about my mother, about being a basketball player or a musician.

—Quincy Troupe

DESCRIPTIVE WRITING

POETRY

To write a poem is to give inner feelings outward expression. The process begins with finding the first word that will start the magic that translates what you feel into what you say.

In this workshop you will write a poem using **descriptive details**—sensory details that help the reader see, hear, smell, taste, even touch your subject.

Prewriting

1. Review Your Notebooks and Journals

When you are assigned to write a poem, your first reaction is likely to be, "What am I going to write about?" As you worked through the poems in this collection, you took notes on various subjects. You also experimented with **descriptive writing,** especially with figures of speech. Review your notes to find ideas for a poem.

2. Imagine You're a Camera

Here's a technique for finding a subject: Imagine that you've just been given a new camera and three rolls of film. You have nothing to do all day but wander wherever you'd like and snap anything you see. At first, you'll probably take shots of any object in range just because it's there. But as your supply of film gets lower and lower, you'll be more apt to snap things that have particular meaning for you. Make a list of subjects you might photograph.

- a corner of the schoolyard where you used to play in fourth grade
- your shoes
- the "For Sale" sign on your house
- your best friends
- a bird in flight
- your mom, the traffic officer
- rooftops silhouetted against the sky
- your dog, Gus, sleeping
- your father's chair
- your school cafeteria
- your favorite place

MAIN OBJECTIVE
Write a poem or a group of poems

PROCESS OBJECTIVES

1. Use appropriate prewriting techniques to identify and develop a topic
2. Create a first draft
3. Use Evaluation Criteria as a basis for determining revision strategies
4. Revise the first draft incorporating suggestions generated by self- or peer evaluation
5. Proofread and correct errors
6. Create a final draft
7. Choose an appropriate method of publication
8. Reflect on progress as a writer

Planning

- **Block Schedule**
  Block Scheduling Lesson Plans with Pacing Guide

- **One-Stop Planner**
  CD-ROM with Test Generator

Resources

Writing and Language
- *Portfolio Management System*
  Prewriting, p. 161
  Peer Editing, p. 162
  Assessment Rubric, p. 163

Introducing the Writer's Workshop

Have students go back through the poems they have studied and select one with which they feel a personal connection.

Ask students to consider what it is about the poem they have selected that speaks to them personally. List students' responses on the board, and then see if students can group their replies into two or three categories. Students' responses can probably be grouped in numerous ways, but the three categories below provide a convenient way to discuss poetry:

1. **Affective.** A response centered on feelings evoked by the poem: "This poem made me **feel** what it's like to _____."

2. **Cognitive.** A response centered on a thought or understanding prompted by the poem: "This poem helped me to **understand** or made me **think** about _____"

3. **Literary.** A response triggered by the form, structure, or use of language in the poem itself: "I just liked the way this poem **sounded**." "I thought comparing life to a crystal stair was interesting."

Discuss with students the ways in which poetry engages the reader. As students begin to write, they should be consciously considering the feeling, the message, and the poetic elements they will deal with in their poems.

Be sure to use the quotations from various poets that appear in the side margins of this workshop. The cartoon on p. 542 should amuse students who keep saying they have nothing to write about.

A Box of Descriptive Words

Can you add to the list?
Sight: radiant, flickering, lopsided, hazy, golden
Sound: roaring, raspy, tinkling, beeping, hissing
Smell: reeking, woodsy, fragrant, fresh-baked, rotting, flowery
Touch: icy, silken, yielding, prickly, gooey
Taste: spicy, buttery, salty, mouthwatering, tart, sweet

Handbook of Literary Terms
HELP

See Imagery, Description, Connotations, Figure of Speech.

Strategies for Elaboration

Team up with a partner to practice using your **descriptive skills.** Observe a place together. Without comparing impressions, jot down several details that appeal to your senses. Then, compare your perceptions. Did you and your partner notice the same things? Here are some settings you might observe:

- the school cafeteria
- an empty classroom
- a city street at 5:00 P.M.
- a back yard
- a storage room

Once you stop taking pictures of everything in sight, you'll begin to choose your subjects. Your choices are likely to be subjects that remind you of something else—an event, a person, a place—or that evoke a particular feeling you'd like to express.

3. Elaborating: Finding Descriptive Details

Once you've chosen your subject, the big question will be: "How can I make this thing and what I feel about it come alive for someone besides me?" The answer is _describe, describe, describe._ What you feel will be made apparent by the details you emphasize. So, as your next step, make another list.

a. Write down the details you want to emphasize.

b. Write down the colors, shapes, and textures of what you see.

c. Describe any sounds, tastes, smells, or movements you notice.

d. Be aware of the **connotations,** or suggestive powers, of the words and **figures of speech** you choose. Is that motorcycle leaning against the wall shining like a new toy, or does it look like a sinister war machine? Does the rain on that window look like tears or like a spray of diamonds? Does the wind in the trees sound like a moan or like a song? Try out some imaginative **comparisons** using the details you've listed.

At this point, jot down whatever comes into your mind. Later, you can select the descriptive details you will use. As you look over your list, you will also decide on your focus. Think of yourself again as a photographer: Will your picture be a wide-sweeping panorama, or will it be a tight close-up?

Drawing by Booth; © 1976 The New Yorker Magazine, Inc.

"Write about dogs."

Reaching All Students

Struggling Writers

If students are having difficulty thinking of experiences on which to base their poems, ask them to brainstorm with a partner or work with them individually to help them choose. Suggest that the students recall a memorable sports highlight video they have seen on television. Then, have students think of how their own lives could be made into a similar video. What events would they want to highlight? Why?

Using Students' Strengths

Visual/Kinesthetic Learners

Before attempting to write their poems, students may benefit from first composing a montage or collage. Students can gather visual images from their own personal photographs or from magazines and assemble them in a meaningful arrangement, perhaps on a piece of poster board. This activity will suggest words or phrases for the poem and may also serve as a visual accompaniment to the completed poem.

Drafting

1. Finding a Form

If you want to be informal or conversational about your chosen subject, write your poem in **free verse.** (See page 559.) If you want to be more structured, try using **meter** and **rhyme.** (See pages 558–559 and 588–589.)

2. Using Free Verse

a. If you choose free verse, be as economical as possible with words, phrases, and sentences. Don't "string out" what you mean in the casual language of a personal letter or the outpourings of school gossip. Pack your meaning into the smallest parcel that will contain it.

b. Free verse can be free-flowing and hypnotic, but it can also be as clipped and terse as something measured off with a ruler. In either case, free verse is free only to this extent: It allows natural **conversational rhythms** to do the work of meter, and it allows hard, precise images to carry the emotional weight of the poem. Find the proper images and your poem will almost write itself. Note the opening images in this poem describing a New England town.

> I must be mad, or very tired,
> When the curve of a blue bay beyond a railroad track
> Is shrill and sweet to me like the sudden springing of a tune,
> And the sight of a white church above thin trees in a city square
> Amazes my eyes as though it were the Parthenon.

> —Amy Lowell, from "Meeting-House Hill"

c. Try to open with a line that captures your reader's attention.

d. Pay special attention to where you end your lines. In writing free verse, poets may break a line to indicate a pause for breath or to show a natural break in thought.

e. Though free verse does not usually use end rhymes, it does often include **alliteration, onomatopoeia, internal rhyme,** and **approximate rhyme.**

3. Using Meter and Rhyme

a. If you are writing in a metric form, you will have to experiment until you find a pattern that suits your purpose. (You'll find the common meters under Meter in the Handbook of Literary Terms.) Try writing lines of three or four iambs. (An **iamb** is a pair of syllables made up of an unstressed syllable followed by a stressed syllable: daDAH daDAH daDAH daDAH.)

Poetry is a conversation with the world; poetry is a conversation with the words on the page in which you allow those words to speak back to you; and poetry is a conversation with yourself. Many times I meet students and see a little look of wariness in their faces—"I'm not sure I want to do this or I'm not sure I can do this"—I like to say, "Wait a minute. How nervous are you about the conversation you're going to have at lunch today with your friends?" And they say, "Oh, we're not nervous at all about that. We do that every day." Then I tell them they can come to feel the same way about writing. Writing doesn't have to be an exotic or stressful experience. You can just sit down with a piece of paper and begin talking and see what speaks back.

—Naomi Shihab Nye

**Handbook of
Literary Terms
H E L P**

*See Meter, Rhyme,
Couplet, Stanza.*

Teaching the Writer's Workshop

Prewriting

Review all the Prewriting suggestions on pp. 541–542, in particular, the strategies for elaboration (number 3 on p. 542). As students begin to select topics for their poems, remind them of the opening activity and ask them to jot down brief answers to the following:

- What do I want the reader to feel? Is there some emotion associated with the place or event I am describing?
- Do I have a message? Is there something I want to say that is important to me? Did I learn something important from the event or in the place I am describing?
- What type of sound structure and form will work best to convey the emotion and message I intend?

Drafting

- Before students begin to draft, read and discuss the Student Model provided on p. 544.
- As students draft their poems, encourage them to experiment with various forms before deciding which type of poetry they wish to write.
- Remind students to pause occasionally and read their poems aloud. Sound structure is an important element of poetry, and the best way to experience the sound structure of a poem is to hear it read aloud.

Read the model aloud with students. You may even wish to have students read the poem aloud together to ensure that they feel the rhythm and hear the sound structure. Follow the reading with a discussion focused on these questions:

? Do you think there is a specific feeling that this writer was trying to capture? [Possible responses: joy of childhood, love of the beach]

? Do you think the writer had any message for the reader? [Possible responses: No, she is just remembering her childhood. Yes, she is remembering how happy simple things made her as a child. I think she misses that and wants to feel that way again.]

? Did you notice any descriptive details? [Possible responses: little slab of gray porch; marigolds in black cauldrons; squawking gulls; warm, white sand; trim white boats, etc.]

Inside a Poem

*It doesn't always have to
    rhyme,
but there's the repeat of a
    beat, somewhere
an inner chime that makes
    you want to
tap your feet or swerve in
    a curve;
a lilt, a leap, a lightning-
    split:—
thunderstruck the
    consonants jut,
while the vowels open
    wide as waves in the
    noon-blue sea.*

*You hear with your heels,
    your eyes feel
what they never touched
    before:
fins on a bird, feathers on
    a deer;
taste all colors, inhale
memory and tomorrow
and always the tang is
    today.*

—Eve Merriam

b. For the most part, try to maintain your beat exactly, but allow for some variation so that your verse doesn't sound mechanical and forced. If you use a three-foot line, for example, you might occasionally vary the meter by beginning with a **trochee:** DAHda daDAH daDAH.

c. A simple form of rhyme is the **couplet**—two successive lines that rhyme. Another popular form of rhyme is the **quatrain**—four successive lines of verse that have a certain rhyme pattern.

4. Finding Your Own Style

A poem in meter and rhyme will amount to little unless you can overcome the mechanical sounds of the metrical form and let your own voice be heard. Think of meter and rhyme as a dress or suit hanging on a rack. Nobody can change its basic shape or cut; but anyone who tries it on will find a way to wear it that is just a little different from everyone else's way. That difference is called **style.**

Whether you write your poem in meter or in free verse (like the Student Model below), try out sounds and phrasings that sound like *you.* Read your poem aloud to yourself: Does it sound like your individual voice? Once you've found your voice, the resulting style will be all yours, and so will the poem.

OCEAN BEACH CHILDHOOD

I liked the little slab of gray porch
bordered by marigolds in black cauldrons.
I kicked the pebbles of the driveway
and over me squawked the gulls—
the same cry that woke me.
I sat on a rocky stool at the kitchen counter,
plum juice running down my chin,
spinning and spinning,
until the cool, dark rooms swirled, too.
Barefoot on the beach at sunset,
warm, white sand between my toes,
the ocean breeze flapped my clothing
and lurched trim white boats on the horizon
as it carried my laughter into the sky.

—Ann Marie Hoppel
Bishop George Ahr High School
Edison, New Jersey

*First appeared in Merlyn's Pen:
The National Magazines of Student
Writing*

Crossing the Curriculum

Technology
Have students type their poems for display, if possible. If they are using word processors, students may arrange and print their poems in significant shapes such as balloons, gift boxes, etc. Students may also wish to experiment with varied fonts and type sizes; however, caution students to use restraint and not use too many different fonts or type sizes.

Revising

See how many different words and lines E. E. Cummings tried out when he was revising "one wintry afternoon" (below). Tinker with words, phrases, images until you're satisfied that the poem says what you want it to say. Don't rush: The "right" word or image may take some time to appear—or it could pop into your brain immediately. Be sure to read the poem aloud as you revise it to hear its sound effects.

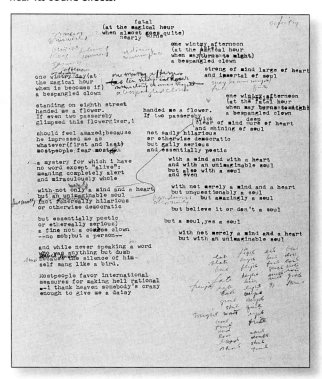

I wouldn't even know whether a poem was finished or not unless my ear told me.

—Paul Blackburn

Proofreading Tips

- Double-check your spelling.
- Read the poem aloud, checking to see that line breaks, punctuation, and indents indicate natural pauses or breaks in thought.

Communications Handbook HELP

See Proofreaders' Marks.

Publishing Tips

- Publish your favorite poem as a broadsheet (a poem published on a single page of good paper with an artistic design or illustration).
- Compile a classroom anthology, bulletin-board display, or audiotape of each student reading his or her favorite poem.
- Submit your poem to a magazine that publishes student writing.

Evaluating and Revising

Before they begin to revise, have students work in pairs and exchange poems. Each student should listen as his or her poem is read aloud. Is the intended mood obvious to the reader? Are there places where the reader loses the intended rhythm? Are there words or phrases that seem to grate on the ear? Do the line breaks support the intended meaning of the poem? Each writer should revise his or her poem based on this listening experience.

Be sure to examine the revised copy of E. E. Cummings's poem on this page. Notice the rhyming words he has listed at the right.

Proofreading

Have students proofread their own papers first. The personal nature of poetry allows more deviation from the traditional rules of mechanics, so it is important that the writer make the final judgments personally. Nevertheless, a peer reviewer should read the poem and mark misspellings or mechanical problems.

If time permits, the final copy should be put aside for at least a day before it is proofread for the final time by the author.

Publishing

If the class is creating an anthology, have them discuss methods of organization. How should poems be grouped and placed in relation to each other? Can thematic or topical links be useful for determining groupings? What are other alternatives to random placement?

Reflecting

Have students answer the following questions and attach their responses to their poems before filing them in their portfolios:

1. Did I select an appropriate event or place as the topic of my poem?
2. Did I select the right form of poetry to express my feelings?
3. What would I change if I had this assignment to do again?

Grading Timesaver

Rubrics for this Writer's Workshop assignment appear on p. 163 of the *Portfolio Management System.*

Resources

Peer Editing Forms and Rubrics
- *Portfolio Management System,* p. 162.

Teaching the Lesson

- Some students may be confused by the use of abbreviated names in e-mail addresses. Be certain students understand that people share these addresses the same way they share phone numbers. Also, most business people now put e-mail addresses on their business cards.

- You may need to clarify the different uses of memos and letters in the business world. Memos are informal correspondence and are generally restricted to use *within* a company. For communication with customers or clients, businesses use the letter form. If speed is essential, business letters may be faxed to the recipient with a hard copy sent by normal mail.

- E-mail is also an informal form of correspondence that is used primarily for intra-company communication. Once a friendly business relationship has been established, however, people with equivalent positions in different organizations may use e-mail for day-to-day business communication.

Using the Strategies

Possible Answers

1. The purpose of the memo is to have M. Gonzalez do preliminary research for a meeting. The memo also asks Gonzalez to attend the meeting.
2. M. Gonzalez is required to find information, including pictures, about the Weaver Maid and other similar figures in Japanese/Hawaiian folklore. The materials are to be delivered no later than Wednesday the 10th.
3. Gonzalez is also asked to attend a meeting on Thursday the 11th at 10.
4. KNAKA@aol.com

Situation

It's your first week at your dream job: helping to create film ideas for young adult audiences. You've just received an e-mail memo about an idea for a film. The following strategies will guide you in handling workplace memos and e-mail.

Strategies

Understand the function of memos and e-mail.

- A **memo** (short for "memorandum") is a type of print or electronic communication.

- In offices today, memos are increasingly sent in the form of **e-mail,** which arrives over an electronic computer network. E-mail can also be sent between people anywhere.

Be aware of the form of a memo.

- A memo begins with a heading that includes the date, the name of the person who wrote the memo, the person(s) to whom it is sent, and a brief description of the subject (look for the abbreviation *Re,* meaning "regarding"). The remainder of the memo deals with the subject.

- Learn to read an e-mail address, which includes some form of the person's name (or a chosen nickname) as

---

> **MEMORANDUM**
>
> **Date:** November 1, 1999
> **To:** Manuel Gonzalez, Research Associate, RightBrain, Inc.
> **From:** Cynthia Baddington, Director, RightBrain, Inc.
> **cc:** Michael Reilly, Art Director, RightBrain, Inc.
> Kay Nakagama
> **Subject:** "Weaver Maid"
>
> Kay Nakagama called this morning—she's been developing a treatment for a live-action film based on the Weaver Maid figure in Asian folklore. We'll meet with her next Thursday (the 11th) at 10 to discuss her ideas. (She'll try to get an outline to us Tuesday.) Please give me whatever relevant information, including visuals, you can find about the Weaver Maid. Actually, whatever you can find in the way of similar figures in Japanese/Hawaiian folklore would help. Could I have the material sometime on the day before our meeting? And please plan on coming to the meeting to take notes and to add anything relevant your research turns up.
>
> Thanks!

> **For e-mail**
>
> Date: 99-11-01 09:14:38 EST
> From: CYNBAD@rbi.com
> To: MGONZALEZ@rbi.com
> CC: MREILLY@rbi.com, KNAKA@aol.com
> Subj: "Weaver Maid"

---

well as the name of the e-mail server (the company providing the e-mail service).

Read the specific content.

- Note the date and subject. Timeliness is crucial.

- Does the memo require you to take any action?

- Notice who, besides you, was sent the memo. (The abbreviation "cc" stands for "courtesy copy," which is sent to someone only for information.)

- Is the memo important enough to be filed for reference?

Using the Strategies

1. What is the purpose of the memo above?

2. What is Manuel Gonzalez required to deliver to his supervisor, and by when?

3. What else is Gonzalez asked to do?

4. What is Kay Nakagama's e-mail address?

Extending the Strategies

Apart from the workplace, what other uses can you see for e-mail?

Can This Be Love?

Theme

When Poets Speak of Love *All poets, someone has said, write of our need for love and our struggle to defeat time. This collection presents poems from the ninth century to the twentieth, from Japan to England. Some poems are joyful: Love, Baca says, is like a warm coat; Cummings urges us to enjoy our beloved's kisses while we can. Some poems, like Dickinson's, are expressions of love's sorrows and disappointments. Can anything hurt like love?*

Reading the Anthology

Reaching Struggling Readers

The *Reading Skills and Strategies: Reaching Struggling Readers* binder includes a Reading Strategies Handbook that offers concrete suggestions for helping students who have difficulty reading and comprehending text, or students who are reluctant readers. When a specific strategy is most appropriate for a selection, a correlation to the Handbook is provided at the bottom of the teacher's page under the head Struggling Readers. This head may also be used to introduce additional ideas for helping students read challenging texts.

Reading Beyond the Anthology

Read On An annotated bibliography of books suitable for extended reading is provided at the end of the poetry collections. The suggested books are related to works in these collections by theme, by author, or by subject. To preview the Read On for the poetry collections, please turn to p. T617.

Collection 9 Can This Be Love?

Resources for this Collection

Note: All resources for this collection are available for preview on the *One-Stop Planner CD-ROM 2 with Test Generator.* All worksheets and blackline masters may be printed from the CD-ROM.

Selection or Feature	Reading and Literary Skills	Vocabulary, Language, and Grammar
Elements of Literature: Imagery (p. 548) • **Moons** (p. 549) John Haines • **The Moon was but a Chin of Gold** (p. 549) Emily Dickinson	• *Literary Elements,* Transparency 16	
I Am Offering This Poem (p. 550) Jimmy Santiago Baca **since feeling is first** (p. 552) E. E. Cummings	• *Graphic Organizers for Active Reading,* Worksheet pp. 39, 40 • *Literary Elements:* Transparency 16 Worksheet p. 49	• *Words to Own,* Worksheet p. 32 • *Daily Oral Grammar,* Transparency 33
Elements of Literature: The Sounds of Poetry (p. 558)	• *Literary Elements,* Transparency 17	
Shall I Compare Thee to a Summer's Day? (p. 560) William Shakespeare	• *Graphic Organizers for Active Reading,* Worksheet p. 41 • *Literary Elements:* Transparency 17 Worksheet p. 52	• *Words to Own,* Worksheet p. 32 • *Daily Oral Grammar,* Transparency 34
Bonny Barbara Allan (p. 564) Anonymous	• *Graphic Organizers for Active Reading,* Worksheet p. 42	• *Words to Own,* Worksheet p. 32
Heart! We will forget him! (p. 568) Emily Dickinson **Three Japanese Tankas** (p. 570) Ono Komachi *translated by* Jane Hirshfield *with* Mariko Aratani	• *Graphic Organizers for Active Reading,* Worksheet pp. 43, 44	• *Words to Own,* Worksheet p. 32
Hanging Fire (p. 574) Audre Lorde	• *Graphic Organizers for Active Reading,* Worksheet p. 45	• *Words to Own,* Worksheet p. 32
Extending the Theme: *from* **Don Quijote** (p. 577) Miguel de Cervantes *translated by* Burton Raffel	The Extending the Theme feature provides students with an unstructured opportunity to practice reading strategies using a selection that extends the theme of the collection.	
Writer's Workshop: Comparison-Contrast Essay (p. 580)		
Sentence Workshop: Varying Sentence Beginnings (p. 585)		• *Workshop Resources,* p. 69 • *Language Workshop CD-ROM,* Sentences

Other Resources for this Collection

- *Cross-Curricular Activities,* p. 9
- *Portfolio Management System,* Introduction to Portfolio Assessment, p. 1
- *Test Generator,* Collection Test 💿

Writing	Listening and Speaking Viewing and Representing	Assessment
		• *Formal Assessment,* Literary Elements Test, p. 103
• *Portfolio Management System,* Rubrics for Choices, p. 164	• *Audio CD Library,* Disc 17, Tracks 2, 3 🎧 • *Portfolio Management System,* Rubrics for Choices, p. 164	• *Formal Assessment,* Selection Test, p. 97 • *Standardized Test Preparation,* p. 66 • *Test Generator (One-Stop Planner CD-ROM)* 💿
		• *Formal Assessment,* Literary Elements Test, p. 105
• *Portfolio Management System,* Rubrics for Choices, p. 165	• *Audio CD Library,* Disc 17, Track 4 🎧 • *Portfolio Management System,* Rubrics for Choices, p. 165	• *Formal Assessment,* Selection Test, p. 99 • *Standardized Test Preparation,* p. 68 • *Test Generator (One-Stop Planner CD-ROM)* 💿
• *Portfolio Management System,* Rubrics for Choices, p. 166	• *Visual Connections:* Videocassette B, Segment 9 📼 • *Audio CD Library,* Disc 17, Tracks 5, 6 🎧 • *Portfolio Management System,* Rubrics for Choices, p. 166	• *Formal Assessment,* Selection Test, p. 99 • *Test Generator (One-Stop Planner CD-ROM)* 💿
• *Portfolio Management System,* Rubrics for Choices, p. 167	• *Audio CD Library,* Disc 17, Tracks 7, 8 🎧 • *Portfolio Management System,* Rubrics for Choices, p. 167	• *Formal Assessment,* Selection Test, p. 101 • *Standardized Test Preparation,* p. 70 • *Test Generator (One-Stop Planner CD-ROM)* 💿
• *Portfolio Management System,* Rubrics for Choices, p. 168	• *Audio CD Library,* Disc 17, Track 9 🎧 • *Portfolio Management System,* Rubrics for Choices, p. 168	• *Formal Assessment,* Selection Test, p. 101 • *Test Generator (One-Stop Planner CD-ROM)* 💿
	• *Audio CD Library,* Disc 17, Track 10 🎧 • *Viewing and Representing:* Fine Art Transparency 13 Worksheet p. 52	
• *Workshop Resources,* p. 35 • *Standardized Test Preparation:* Worksheet p. 148 Transparencies 19–24	• *Viewing and Representing,* HRW Multimedia Presentation Maker	• *Portfolio Management System* • Prewriting, p. 169 • Peer Editing, p. 170 • Assessment Rubric, p. 171 • *Standardized Test Preparation:* Worksheet p. 148 Transparencies 19–24

 Transparency   CD-ROM   Video   🎧 Audio CD

Collection 9 Can This Be Love?

Skills Focus

Selection or Feature	Reading Skills and Strategies	Elements of Literature	Vocabulary/Language/Grammar	Writing	Listening/Speaking	Viewing/Representing
Elements of Literature: Imagery (p. 548)	Compare Images, p. 548	Image, p. 548				
I Am Offering This Poem (p. 550) Jimmy Santiago Baca **since feeling is first** (p. 552) E. E. Cummings	Dialogue with the Text, p. 550 Double-Entry Journal, p. 550	Lyric Poetry, pp. 550, 556 Metaphor, pp. 552, 556 Comparison and Contrast, p. 556 Images, p. 556		Compare Poems, p. 557 Write a Response to a Poem, p. 557	Small Group Discussion, p. 557	Illustrate a Poem, p. 557
Elements of Literature: The Sounds of Poetry (p. 558)		Rhythm and Meter, p. 558 Stress, p. 558 Metrical Poetry, p. 558 Foot, p. 559 Free Verse, p. 559 Imagists, p. 559				
Shall I Compare Thee to a Summer's Day? (p. 560) William Shakespeare		Couplet, p. 560 Shakespearean Sonnet, pp. 560, 562 Image, p. 562 Rhythm, p. 562 Meter, p. 562 Tone, p. 563	Inverted Sentences, p. 563 Syntax, p. 563	Identify Comparable Subjects, p. 563 Write a Sonnet, p. 563	Present an Oral Response to a Poem, p. 563	
Bonny Barbara Allan (p. 564) Anonymous		Refrain, p. 564 Folk Ballad, p. 564 Ballad, pp. 564, 567 Meter, pp. 564, 567 Figurative Language, p. 567		Identify Points of Comparison, p. 567	Prepare and Present a Newscast Based on a Ballad, p. 567 Write a Melody for a Poem, p. 567	
Heart! We will forget him! (p. 568) Emily Dickinson **Three Japanese Tankas** (p. 570) Ono Komachi *translated by* Jane Hirshfield *with* Mariko Aratani		Personification, pp. 568, 573 Tanka Form, p. 570 Images, p. 573		Compare and Contrast Poems, p. 573 Write a Response to a Poem from a Character's Viewpoint, p. 573 Write a Tanka, p. 573		
Hanging Fire (p. 574) Audre Lorde		Speaker, pp. 574, 576 Title, p. 576 Refrain, p. 576		Identify Details to Compare or Contrast, p. 576	Present a Choral Reading of a Poem, p. 576 • Pitch • Tone • Expression	
Extending the Theme: *from* **Don Quijote** (p. 577) Miguel de Cervantes *translated by* Burton Raffel	Compare and Contrast, p. 579	The Extending the Theme feature provides students with an unstructured opportunity to practice reading skills using a selection that extends the theme of the collection.				
Writer's Workshop: Comparison-Contrast Essay (p. 580)			Words That Signal Comparison and Contrast, p. 583	Write an Essay Comparing and Contrasting Two Texts, pp. 580–584		
Sentence Workshop: Varying Sentence Beginnings (p. 585)			Modifier, p. 585 Prepositional Phrase, p. 585 Participial Phrase, p. 585 Subordinate Clause, p. 585	Revise Sentences for Variety, p. 585		
Reading for Life: Analyzing and Appreciating Art (p. 586)						Reading a Work of Art, p. 586 • Composition • Elements • Title

CAN THIS BE LOVE?
WRITING FOCUS: Comparison/Contrast Essay

Tête à tête am Wolkenkratzer 968 étage.
Color lithograph by Moriz Jung
(1885–1915). Postcard published by
Wiener Werkstätte, Vienna.

The Metropolitan Museum of Art, New York, Museum
Accession, 1943. (WW340) Photograph © 1981 The
Metropolitan Museum of Art.

W̲hat can you say about the joy
of love except that it's wonderful and about the pain of love except that it hurts? What can you say
that hasn't been said a million times
before? What's amazing is that
poets still manage to say anything
new about love at all. But they do,
as you'll see from the poems in this
collection. From tenth-century
Japan to the modern world, has love
stayed the same—or is love always
different?

All you need is love.
　　　　—The Beatles

What's love got to do with it?
　　　　—Tina Turner

Writer's Notebook

Think of two
popular songs
about love.
Are they alike
in feeling, or are they different?
Are their messages the same or
different? Are their styles the
same or different? Make some
notes and save them for the
Writer's Workshop (page 580).

Responding to the Quotations

Like love itself, the quotations are contradictory. The Beatles suggest that love is everything; Tina Turner implies that love is sometimes irrelevant. You might invite students to contrast the quotations and to explain whether their own views lean toward one or the other, or perhaps encompass both.

RESPONDING TO THE ART

The Wiener Werkstätte (Viennese Workshop) was a cooperative of artists that lasted from 1903 to 1932. These artists strove to restore to handicrafts and everyday items the aesthetics that mass production had stripped away. This decorative postcard is titled "Tête à Tête in the Skyscraper, 968th Floor." **Activity.** Ask students to describe the images and to interpret what the images convey about love. [new—power lines, high-rises, airplane; old—flowers, stars, two lovers, love causing people to do strange things]

Writing Focus: Comparison/Contrast Essay

The following **Work in Progress** assignments build to a culminating **Writer's Workshop** at the end of the collection.

OBJECTIVES
1. Recognize imagery
2. Relate imagery to feelings

Resources

Elements of Literature
Imagery
For additional instruction on imagery, see *Literary Elements*:
• Transparency 16

Assessment
Formal Assessment
• Literary Elements Test, p. 103
Test Generator (One-Stop Planner)
• CD-ROM

Elements of Literature

Imagery: Seeing with Our Minds
This lesson defines *image,* discusses links between imagery and feelings, and illustrates the use of imagery in poetry by comparing and contrasting images in two poems: "Moons" by John Haines and "The Moon was but a Chin of Gold" by Emily Dickinson.

Mini-Lesson: Imagery
You might use this Mini-Lesson after the main lesson, to guide students in exploring further how sensory imagery can evoke emotions. On the chalkboard, write the titles of the two poems. Encourage students to identify striking images from each poem and have a volunteer cluster the images around the appropriate poem titles. Then invite students to say what emotions each image evokes. Again, cluster their responses and encourage students to discuss them.

IMAGERY: Seeing with Our Minds

An **image** is a representation of anything we can see, hear, taste, touch, or smell. A realistic painter or sculptor can create an image of an apple so true to life that we'd like to eat it or feel its weight and roundness in our hands. A poet, using only words, can make us see and feel, taste and smell an apple by describing it as "rosy," "shiny," "heavy," "mushy," "sweet."

We can even distinguish poets on the basis of the imagery they use. Poets who live in the country, as Robert Frost did (pages 516 and 526), usually draw their images from nature. Poets who live in cities, as Langston Hughes did (page 508), usually draw their images from the sights, smells, and sounds of city life.

Calvin and Hobbes © 1989 Watterson. Reprinted with permission of Universal Press Syndicate. All rights reserved.

Two Poets, One Moon

To see how imagery works, look at two poems about the moon on the opposite page. The first poem, by John Haines, introduces many variations on the image of the moon. Can you find the image that tells us the poem was written sometime after 1969, when humans first disturbed the dust of the moon and left their debris on its surface? The second poem, by Emily Dickinson, was written more than a hundred years earlier than Haines's poem, long before the romantic "moon of the poet" had been soiled and scratched by scientific instruments. More important, Dickinson also wrote long before two terrible world wars changed the ways poets looked at the world.

Imagery and Feelings

These two moon poems show us something else that imagery

Images are not made just for the eye.

can do. The poets, through their evocative imagery, tell us how they *feel* about the moon. Haines's images of the "moon of the poet" are ironic and violent. As we see this moon in our minds, we share his sadness and even anger over the human capacity for destruction.

Dickinson, on the other hand, uses romantic images

RESPONDING TO THE ART

Activity. Ask students how the cartoon relates to Brinnin's statement that "images are not made just for the eye." [Sample responses: Images can appeal to all the senses, including touch. Some images hit readers at a more primal level—like a snowball in the face.]

Using Students' Strengths

Mathematical/Logical Learners
Have students poll classmates about the particular emotions that were evoked by the imagery in each of these two poems. Students might then create two pie charts (one for each poem) showing the results of their polls. Have students compare their charts and discuss the similarities and differences between them.

Visual Learners
Invite interested students to create two sketches—drawing one memorable image from each poem. Then, challenge students to analyze the lines and shapes in their sketches. Which poem's imagery generated sketches with more curving lines, more angles, thicker or thinner lines, symmetry or the lack of it, and so on? Invite students to share their work and to discuss the relationship between line and emotion.

by John Malcolm Brinnin

Moons

There are moons like continents,
diminishing to a white stone
softly smoking
in a fog-bound ocean.

5 Equinoctial° moons,
immense rainbarrels spilling
their yellow water.

Moons like eyes turned inward,
hard and bulging
10 on the blue cheek of eternity.

And moons half-broken,
eaten by eagle shadows . . .

But the moon of the poet
is soiled and scratched, its seas
15 are flowing with dust.

And other moons are rising,
swollen like boils—

in their bloodshot depths
the warfare of planets
20 silently drips and festers.

                —John Haines

5. equinoctial (ē′kwi·näk′shəl): of the spring and fall equinoxes, when day and night are of equal length.

The Moon was but a Chin of Gold

The Moon was but a Chin of Gold
A Night or two ago—
And now she turns Her perfect Face
Upon the World below—

5 Her Forehead is of Amplest Blonde—
Her Cheek—a Beryl° hewn—
Her Eye unto the Summer Dew
The likest I have known—

Her Lips of Amber never part—
10 But what must be the smile
Upon Her Friend she could confer
Were such Her Silver Will—

And what a privilege to be
But the remotest Star—
15 For Certainty She takes Her Way
Beside Your Palace Door—

Her Bonnet is the Firmament°—
The Universe—Her Shoe—
The Stars—the Trinkets at Her Belt—
20 Her Dimities°—of Blue—

                —Emily Dickinson

6. beryl: mineral that usually occurs in crystals of blue, green, pink, or yellow.
17. firmament: sky.
20. dimities: dresses made of dimity, a sheer, cool, cotton material.

that help us see another moon and share other feelings. Her moon is personified as a beautiful woman, even a queen, dressed in all the beauties of the night sky. Images of gold, beryl, dew, amber, silver, trinkets, and dimities help us share her feelings of wonder, admiration, and perhaps playfulness.

    Thus, images are not made just for the eye. When we read poetry, we must arrive at that point where we can say to the poet not only "I see the picture you are creating," but also "I see what you are feeling. I see what you mean."

ELEMENTS OF LITERATURE: IMAGERY 549

Applying the Element
As students read the poems in this collection, they can gain insight into imagery by filling in a Sensory Detail Chart for each poem. The charts will show how images target the senses and will provide fuel for a discussion of the way sensory images affect emotion. Below is a Sensory Detail Chart for the poem "Moons" that you might share with students as an example. Have students discuss how some images may target more than one sense.

	"Moons"
Sight	diminishing to a white stone yellow water eyes turned inward blue cheek moons half-broken eaten by eagle shadows bloodshot depths
Hearing	silently drips
Touch	hard and bulging scratched swollen like boils
Smell	softly smoking festers
Taste	—

Historical Connections
Manned Lunar Flights
The first manned craft to land on the moon, in 1969, was called *Eagle*. Its American astronauts not only scraped samples from the lunar surface, but also left debris including boots and backpacks. Subsequent expeditions took more samples and left more debris. These facts sharpen further Haines's images of "moons half-broken,/ eaten by eagle shadows" and "soiled and scratched."

Assessing Learning

Check Test: Short Answer

1. What are images? [Sample answer: representations of things we can see, hear, taste, touch, or smell.]

2. List any three images associated with the moon in Haines's poem. [Sample answer: white stone in an ocean, overflowing barrels of rain, bulging eyes.]

3. List any three images associated with the moon in Dickinson's poem. [Sample answer: a beautiful woman, amber lips, blue dresses.]

4. What two things should a reader look for in a poem's imagery? [Sample answer: the thing represented and the feelings.]

OBJECTIVES

I Am Offering This Poem / since feeling is first
1. Read and interpret the poems
2. Identify a lyric
3. Interpret metaphors
4. Monitor comprehension
5. Express understanding through writing, speaking/critical thinking, and visual arts

SKILLS

Literary
- Identify a lyric
- Interpret metaphors

Reading
- Monitor comprehension

Writing
- Compare and contrast themes
- Answer the speaker of a poem

Speaking/Critical Thinking
- Discuss themes

Art
- Illustrate a poem

Viewing/Representing
- Discuss how a work of art relates to a poem (ATE)
- Respond to a painting (ATE)

Planning

- **Block Schedule**
  Block Scheduling Lesson Plans with Pacing Guide
- **Traditional Schedule**
  Lesson Plans Including Strategies for English-Language Learners
- **One-Stop Planner**
  CD-ROM with Test Generator

Before You Read

I AM OFFERING THIS POEM

Make the Connection

The Gift of Love

Suppose someone said to you, "I have nothing to give you—except love." How would you feel? Think about whether love is a small gift or a great one.

Reading Skills and Strategies

Dialogue with the Text

Make a double-entry journal to track this poem's images and your responses to them. *(Keep your notes for use on pages 556–557.)*

Image	My Feeling/Response

Elements of Literature

Singing Your Feelings

Lyric poetry owes its name to the ancient Greeks, who used the word *lyrikos* to refer to brief poems they sang to the accompaniment of the lyre, a stringed instrument. Today most lyrics are still short and still musical. Lyrics use evocative words to suggest (rather than state directly) a single, strong emotion. Most of the poems in this collection are lyrics.

> **A lyric** is a short poem that expresses strong feelings. Unlike a narrative poem, a lyric does not tell a story.
>
> *For more about Lyric Poetry, see the Handbook of Literary Terms.*

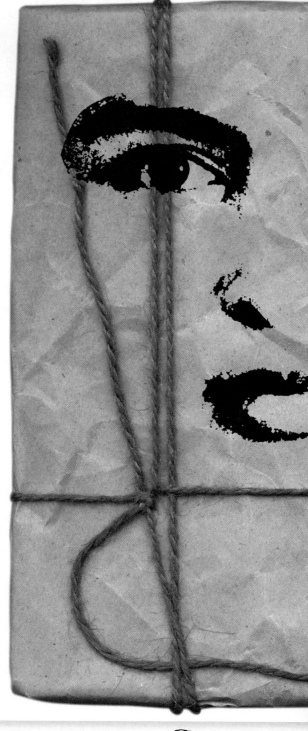

 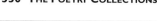 *Resources: Print and Media*

Reading
- *Graphic Organizers for Active Reading,* pp. 39, 40
- *Audio CD Library*
  Disc 17, Tracks 2, 3

Elements of Literature
- *Literary Elements*
  Transparency 16
  Worksheet, p. 49

Writing and Language
- *Daily Oral Grammar*
  Transparency 33

Assessment
- *Formal Assessment,* p. 97
- *Portfolio Management System,* p. 164
- *Standardized Test Preparation,* p. 66
- *Test Generator (One-Stop Planner CD-ROM)*

Internet
- go.hrw.com (keyword: LE0 10-9)

I Am Offering This Poem

Jimmy Santiago Baca

I am offering this poem to you,
since I have nothing else to give.
Keep it like a warm coat
when winter comes to cover you,
5 or like a pair of thick socks
the cold cannot bite through,

        I love you,

I have nothing else to give you,
so it is a pot full of yellow corn
10 to warm your belly in winter,
it is a scarf for your head, to wear
over your hair, to tie up around your face,

        I love you,

Keep it, treasure this as you would
15 if you were lost, needing direction,
in the wilderness life becomes when mature;
and in the corner of your drawer,
tucked away like a cabin or hogan
in dense trees, come knocking,
20 and I will answer, give you directions,
and let you warm yourself by this fire,
rest by this fire, and make you feel safe,

        I love you,

It's all I have to give,
25 and all anyone needs to live,
and to go on living inside,
when the world outside
no longer cares if you live or die;
remember,

30   I love you.

MEET THE WRITER
To Prove That He Exists

Jimmy Santiago Baca (1952–   ) says he began to write so the world would know he existed. Born in New Mexico of Mexican American and Apache ancestry, he was abandoned by his parents when he was two. His grandmother took care of him until he was sent to an orphanage at five. At eleven, he ran away, living on the streets until he landed in prison at eighteen for possessing drugs. In prison, he felt sure he was going to die:

    " And I had to tell somebody that I was here. . . . It's unthinkable to come to a universe, to live as a human being, and then to die and not have anyone ever know you were there. **"**

Baca taught himself to read and write in prison. He also began to keep a journal and eventually attended a poetry workshop. Then he "took a wild chance." He sent some poems to a magazine, and the magazine published them. Five books of poetry followed, along with essays, a screenplay, and a novel. Today Baca, his wife, and sons live in an old adobe house south of Albuquerque.

Summary ■

In this straightforward lyric, the speaker offers and expresses his love through a poem. The speaker's love is protective, comforting, and nurturing. It is described (among other homey figures of speech) as a warm coat, a pot of corn, and a cabin in thick woods. The speaker's final message is that love is "all anyone needs" to protect one's inner life from an indifferent world.

Resources ———

Elements of Literature
Imagery: Seeing with Our Minds
For additional instruction on imagery in this poem, see *Literary Elements:*
- Transparency 16
- Worksheet, p. 49

A Elements of Literature
Lyric
? Lyric poetry is a form for expressing strong feelings. What two strong feelings does this stanza suggest? [Possible answers: love; generosity.]

B Struggling Readers
Questioning
Explain that a *hogan* is a traditional Navajo log home, hexagonal in shape, with a roof of packed earth and a doorway facing east. Ask students to devise—and then to answer— a question exploring what the word *hogan* adds to the poem. [Possible response: How would the stanza be different if the word *home* were used instead of *hogan*? *Hogan* gives a more precise visual image and extends the ethnic context.]

WRITERS ON WRITING

In his book of reflections, *Working in the Dark,* Baca discusses the power of poetry: "I have seen poetry work its magic, reducing racists and bigots to impotent rage, impelling poor women and men to weep with joy because someone has touched their hearts and expressed a little of their lives. Poetry sits in God's chair when God is absent."

Reaching All Students

English Language Learners
Help students recognize the elliptical language in l. 16 and supply missing words in order to clarify the meaning: "in the wilderness [that] life becomes when [it is] mature. . . ."

Advanced Learners
In stanza 1, point out the exact rhyme (you/through) and in stanza 2, the slant internal rhyme (corn/warm). Challenge students to find other examples: [wear/hair, give/live, inside/outside; corner/drawer, cabin/hogan]

Making the Connections

Cultural Connections
Signs of Home. Some images in "I Am Offering This Poem" reflect the Native American and Mexican American cultures of New Mexico, where Baca was raised. Encourage students to identify these images (a pot of corn, a hogan). Invite students to write poems of their own, using images that reflect their home areas and cultures.

Summary ■■■

This lyric pits emotion against intellect, using grammar as a main metaphor. The speaker is trying to persuade his lover to join him in championing feeling over syntax (system), kisses over wisdom, a flutter of eyelids over an idea or thought, and life over a paragraph. The often quoted final line, "And death i think is no parenthesis," affirms love's power: Even death cannot interrupt love.

Resources ———

Listening
Audio CD Library
For a recording of this poem, see the *Audio CD Library*:
• Disc 17, Track 3

Ⓐ Reading Skills and Strategies
Paraphrasing
❓ How would you express ll. 1–4 in your own words? [Sample responses: In love, follow your heart, not your head; don't try to make love orderly or predictable, because then you can't love fully; don't overanalyze love.]

Ⓑ Reading Skills and Strategies
Dialogue with the Text
Invite students to write in their journals brief descriptions of the image(s) they find in each stanza of the poem. Encourage them to explore their responses to the images. Their entries can become source material for activities on pp. 556–557.

SINCE FEELING IS FIRST

Make the Connection
Feeling Your Way
At first sight, this poem looks difficult. Its lines break at unusual places, there's little capitalization, the punctuation isn't standard, and words are used in odd ways. But if you read the poem silently a couple of times and then read it aloud, you'll quickly "own" it—you'll be able to say "I see what you mean!"

Quickwrite
This poet is sending a message to all of us. After you've read the poem twice, write what you think that message is. To get the message, you have to know English grammar. *(Keep your notes for use on pages 556–557.)*

Elements of Literature

Metaphors: Grammar and Love
Lovers cannot bear to think of their love ending or of death separating them. Here, the poet sings of love and puts down death in two metaphors that only a writer would think of.

> **A** **metaphor** is a surprising comparison between two dissimilar things.
>
> *For more on Metaphor, see page 507 and the Handbook of Literary Terms.*

552 THE POETRY COLLECTIONS

---

since feeling is first

E. E. Cummings

Ⓐ since feeling is first
who pays any attention
to the syntax° of things
will never wholly kiss you;

5 Ⓑ wholly to be a fool
while Spring is in the world

Ⓒ my blood approves,
and kisses are a better fate
than wisdom
10 lady i swear by all flowers.   Don't cry
—the best gesture of my brain is less than
your eyelids' flutter which says

we are for each other:then
laugh,leaning back in my arms
15 Ⓓ for life's not a paragraph

Ⓔ And death i think is no parenthesis

---

3. syntax (sin'taks'): the arrangement of words, phrases, and clauses in sentences; here, a systematic, orderly arrangement.

The Lovers (1954–1955) by Marc Chagall (1887–1985). Watercolor, gouache, and ink on paper.
Collection Israel Museum, Jerusalem.
©1999 Artists Rights Society (ARS), New York/ADAGP, Paris.

 go.hrw.com
LEO 10-9

Reaching All Students

Struggling Readers
Explain that the poem contrasts order and feelings. Have students create a graphic organizer, a chart that displays the two aspects of the poem. Under the heading "Order," students should list aspects such as *syntax, wisdom, brain, paragraph,* and *parenthesis.* Invite students to add aspects related to feelings under "Emotion." [Possible responses: *kiss, fool, kisses, flowers, cry, eyelids' flutter, laugh, death.*]

Advanced Readers
E. E. Cummings is famous for not following the rules of punctuation, capitalization, and other mechanics. Have students find examples in this poem of the poet's purposeful, playful disregard of conventional syntax and mechanics, including run-together words, missing capitals, and ambiguous constructions. Invite students to consider and explain how these stylistic devices reflect and reinforce the poem's message.

Connecting with the Text

? Do you think that people in general agree that "kisses are a better fate/ than wisdom"? Explain. [Sample responses: Yes, when it comes to falling in love, many people let emotion take over; no, many people follow the voice of reason when building relationships.]

D Elements of Literature
Metaphor

? How is life not like a paragraph? Encourage students to explore this metaphor by pinpointing aspects of life that differ from those of a paragraph. [Possible responses: Life is more than an orderly, logical sequence—it is chaotic, joyous, unpredictable.]

E Vocabulary Note
Multiple Meanings

Let students know that *parenthesis* can have three distinct meanings: (1) a punctuation mark; one of a set of parentheses; (2) a grammatical structure, a word, phrase, or clause that interrupts a sentence; or (3) a literal interruption, a break in a state of affairs or in an activity or event. Ask students to decide which meaning of *parenthesis* best fits the context of the poem, and why. [Sample answer: a literal interruption, because the speaker is saying that death can't stop love.]

RESPONDING TO THE ART

Marc Chagall (1887–1985) was born in Vitebsk, Russia, and later lived in France. *The Lovers* shows huge, glowing lovers and flowers, floating above the outline of a town, suggesting that Chagall, like Cummings, values spontaneity over "syntax" and love above all. (For other Chagall art, see pp. 900–901.)

Activity. Ask students to decide what Chagall's painting and Cummings's poem have in common. [Both are unusual in form; both have lovers and flowers.]

Getting Students Involved

Creating Grammar Metaphors

In "since feeling is first," Cummings uses aspects of grammar as a metaphor for order, which contrasts with the spontaneity of love. Students might enjoy coming up with their own metaphors that compare aspects of grammar, language, or writing with something else. Offer these examples: A puppy is an action verb; boredom is a run-on sentence. Then invite students to write their own metaphors and share them with the class.

Browsing in the Files

About the Author. The following story about Cummings is from *The Little, Brown Book of Anecdotes:* "Departing with Marion, his wife, from a fashionable New Year's Eve party, Cummings realized that he did not have enough money for the subway fare. They stepped into the elevator, which was already occupied by a portly gentleman. 'Excuse me,' said Cummings politely, placing his hat with a flourish at the man's feet, 'would you care to step on my hat?' The man, somewhat taken aback but nevertheless impressed by Cummings's aristocratic demeanor, nodded assent. 'I'm afraid it will cost you five dollars,' added Cummings. The portly fellow stepped on the hat and paid his fee, enabling Cummings and his wife to travel home by taxi."

A Critic's Comment. Poet Horace Gregory points out that Cummings did not merely disregard conventional rules of mechanics. Rather, he devised new rules, "inflexible as laws in playing tennis, brilliantly stressed and pointed . . . orderly distortions and punctuations." Have students look again at "since feeling is first" and try to state one of Cummings's "rules." [Sample responses: Use capitals and periods for emphasis only; don't end with a period if you want your reader to go on thinking about what you've written; run words together when you want to speed up the tempo of the poem.]

Meet the Writer

"Nobody Else Can Be Alive for You"

E. E. (Edward Estlin) **Cummings** (1894–1962) was born in Cambridge, Massachusetts. This son of a Unitarian minister grew up "only a butterfly's glide" from Harvard and "attended four Cambridge schools: the first, private—where everybody was extraordinarily kind; and where (in addition to learning nothing) I burst into tears and nosebleeds—the other three, public; where I flourished like the wicked and learned what the wicked learn, and where almost nobody cared about somebody else."

After graduating from Harvard, Cummings joined a volunteer American ambulance corps in France. (The United States had not yet entered World War I.) A French censor decided that one of Cummings's odd-looking letters home was suspicious. So Cummings was arrested as a spy and held for three months in a prison camp, an experience he wrote about in a novel he called *The Enormous Room* (1922).

In his poetry, Cummings liked to use lowercase letters, space his words oddly across the page, and punctuate in his own style, although those oddities are only typographical. His themes are familiar: the joy, wonder, and mystery of life and the miracle of individual identity. He once advised young poets to be themselves:

> " . . . remember one thing only: that it's you—nobody else—who determines your destiny and decides your fate. Nobody else can be alive for you; nor can you be alive for anybody else. "

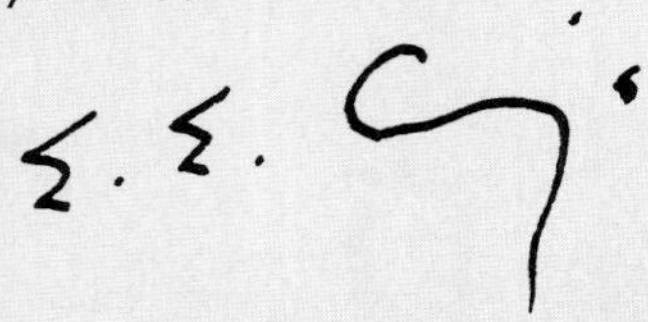

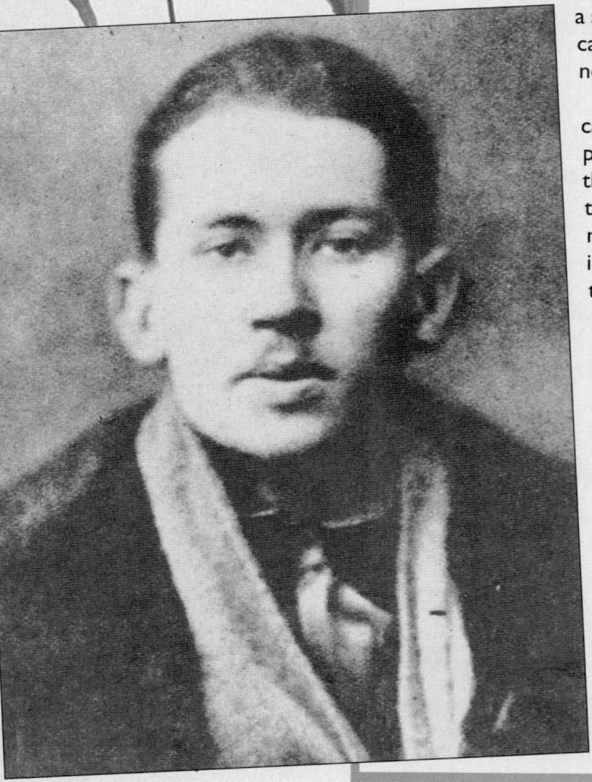

E. E. Cummings in 1933. "Since feeling is first" was published in 1926 in his fourth book of poems, which he titled *is 5*.

Using Students' Strengths

Auditory/Musical Learners
Ask students to choose music to complement Baca's and Cummings's poems. Their selections might include ragtime to complement Cummings's poem because ragtime uses unconventional rhythms and harmonies (as Cummings uses unconventional mechanics and syntax); acoustic folk music to complement Baca's poem because both are low-tech and reflect specific areas and cultures. Have students read the poems, accompanied by music.

Visual Learners
To help students organize information about the concept of love presented in each poem, ask them to work in pairs to create a cluster diagram for the word *love*. Have the pairs review the poems for images pertaining to love and add them to the diagram. Students might use different colors for each poem's images.

Just Another Love Poem

Maybe that's why I need you.
You, and
standing in the middle
of a
5   dark, raging thunderstorm
(the power making me tremble),
Riding in a
fast, sleek convertible
(30 over the limit),
10   Absorbing the
sensation of the
largest roller coaster
(seat belt discarded)
and
15   a 180-foot parachute free fall
all
somehow
give me the
unexplainable
20   thrill
of delighting in
something so
terribly,
wonderfully,
25   out of control.

—Erika Banick
    Warren Township High School
    Gurnee, Illinois

SINCE FEELING IS FIRST 555

Student to Student

Ⓐ Reading Skills and Strategies
Making Predictions

❓ What expectations about the speaker does the title set up? [Sample responses: Maybe the speaker thinks the poem is nothing special; maybe the speaker is being ironic and really plans to surprise readers with an unusual poem.] **Make predictions about what the speaker might say in the poem.** [Sample responses: The speaker might say it's hard to find an original way to express the power of love; the speaker might say she's tired of love poems or of love.]

Ⓑ Critical Thinking
Making Connections

❓ How do these images compare to the images in other love poems or songs that you know? [Possible responses: Most of Banick's images suggest powerful energy sources and technology, whereas Baca's images in his love poem are low-tech and homey; Banick describes a thunderstorm, and many other love poems and songs include nature images; Banick's images, like Baca's and Cummings's, reflect pleasure.]

Skill Link

Comparing and Contrasting Figurative Language

"Just Another Love Poem," "I Am Offering This Poem," and "since feeling is first" all include metaphors or similes, either direct or implied. To guide students in recognizing and analyzing these examples of figurative language, invite students to form small groups and to create charts such as the one shown. Each group's chart should show how the poems describe the feelings of love and the effects of love on a person.

I Am Offering This Poem	since feeling is first	Just Another Love Poem
Warm, like a coat or socks	Kisses are a better fate than wisdom	Powerful, like a thunderstorm

Encourage students to include as many examples as possible. Then ask each group to synthesize information from its chart into a general statement, comparing and contrasting figurative language in the three poems. [Sample answer: Figurative language in all three poems shows the power of love. In Baca's poem it's a calm power, in Cummings's it's spontaneous, and in Banick's it's wild.]

T555

MAKING MEANINGS

First Thoughts

1. Possible responses: Cummings's poem because it is unusual and playful, a little like a puzzle; Baca's poem because it is warm and nurturing, clear and powerful.

Shaping Interpretations

2. He uses images of a warm coat, a pair of thick socks, a pot full of yellow corn, and a scarf in winter's cold to show that his love provides warmth and comfort. Some students may like his use of everyday speech; others may appreciate the depth in phrases such as "the wilderness life becomes when mature."

3. Any person could be the recipient of the nurturing love that the speaker describes.

4. Possible response: The speaker addresses a lover, stressing feelings over thought. Possible message: One ought to enjoy life and love, not dull them by imposing order on them.

5. Metaphors include "death i think is no parenthesis," "kisses are a better fate than wisdom," and "life's not a paragraph." Some students may find these metaphors fresh and apt; others may find them abstract or obscure.

6. He contrasts wisdom with kisses; a gesture of the brain with the eyelids' flutter; life with a paragraph. He chooses kisses, fluttering eyelids, and life.

7. Possible response: Banick compares her love to dangerous thrills, such as standing in a thunderstorm, speeding in a convertible, riding a roller coaster with no seatbelt, and parachuting.

Extending the Texts

8. Possible responses: Cummings—joy as an exclamation point, relationship as more than an essay; Baca—mittens for warmth, a guiding lantern; Banick—the thrill of whitewater rafting or bungee jumping.

RESPONDING TO THE ART

Activity. Ask students to contrast this painting of two lovers with Chagall's on p. 553.

T556

MAKING MEANINGS
I AM OFFERING THIS POEM
SINCE FEELING IS FIRST

First Thoughts

[connect]

1. Which of these love poems (Baca's poem or Cummings's) would you like to receive? Which one do you wish you had written? Try to find reasons for your choices.

Shaping Interpretations

[respond]

2. What images does Baca use to suggest what his love will do for the person he's addressing? How do you feel about the way he's written this **lyric poem**? (Look back at your double-entry journal from page 550.)

[infer]

3. When we say "love poems," people often think of romantic love. Could Baca's poem be addressed to a child? a good friend? a parent? anyone else?

[interpret]

4. Describe the situation in Cummings's poem. Whom is the speaker addressing, and what is he saying? What message did you take away from eavesdropping on this conversation? (Look back at your Quickwrite notes for page 552.)

[evaluate]

5. What **metaphors** does Cummings use to express his feelings about love and even its power over death? How do you like his metaphors?

[contrast]

6. Notice the opposites Cummings uses in "since feeling is first." A person who pays attention "to the syntax of things" (lines 2–3) is **contrasted** with someone who is "wholly . . . a fool" (line 5). What opposites does he pose to wisdom (line 9), the brain (line 11), and life (line 15)? In each case, which of the opposites does the speaker choose?

[identify]

7. It's not easy to be original in a love poem—so many have been written over the ages. What exaggerated **comparisons** does Erika Banick use to express the wonder of love in her poem on page 555?

Extending the Texts

[synthesize]

8. For any one of these poems, think of more **images** or **comparisons** that the poet could have used if he or she had wanted to write another ten lines or so about love.

Portrait of a Man and Woman at a Casement by Fra Filippo Lippi (c. 1406–1469). Tempera on wood (25¼" × 16½").

The Metropolitan Museum of Art, New York. Gift of Henry G. Marquand, 1889. Marquand Collection. (89.15.19) Photograph © 1992 The Metropolitan Museum of Art.

556 THE POETRY COLLECTIONS

Assessing Learning

Check Test: True-False

"I Am Offering This Poem"

1. The poem's speaker is wealthy. [False]
2. The speaker believes that love is all a person needs to survive. [True]

"since feeling is first"

3. The poem's speaker values the heart over the mind. [True]
4. The speaker says that life is like a paragraph. [False]
5. The speaker reassures his love. [True]

Standardized Test Preparation

For practice with standardized test format specific to this selection, see
• *Standardized Test Preparation*, p. 66

For practice in proofreading and editing, see
• *Daily Oral Grammar*, Transparency 33

CHOICES: Building Your Portfolio

Writer's Notebook

1. Collecting Ideas for a Comparison/Contrast Essay

Noting similarities. When poems are grouped under a theme, you should be able to find some points of comparison or contrast between them. Look again at the poems by Baca and Cummings. Take notes on what each poet is saying about love. Try to put their messages in your own words. Then, take notes on this question: Are the poets' feelings the same in any way? (Be sure to check your double-entry journal and your Quickwrite.) Save your notes for the Writer's Workshop on page 580. The notebook below shows notes on two stories in the collection "Hearts That Love."

Creative Writing

2. What Do You Say?

"I Am Offering This Poem" and "since feeling is first" were both written by men. But could the **speakers** also be women? Suppose you were the person being addressed in Baca's or Cummings's poem. Write your answer to the speaker in a prose paragraph or in verse. Do you like what the speaker says to you or about you, or are your feelings something else? Who *is* the speaker, in your imagination? What **title** will you give your answer?

Speaking/Critical Thinking

3. What Love Is

Imagine that a poetry-loving scientist sends Baca's and Cummings's poems in an interstellar probe to deep space. Eventually, they are found and translated by aliens in a world without the concept of love. On the basis of these two poems alone, what might the aliens conclude about the nature of human love? Get together with a small group to discuss this question. Point to specific passages that you think would especially interest the curious aliens.

Visual Arts

4. Imagining Images

Suppose that you have been commissioned to illustrate either "I Am Offering This Poem" or "since feeling is first." Using whatever medium you prefer—pencil, paint, or collage—present the images suggested by the poem. Give your images a title, perhaps a line from the poem. Try to use colors that will capture the tone and the mood of the poem.

> "Distillation" (page 133): about a father's love and a child's memories.
>
> "Life Is Sweet at Kumansenu" (page 147): about a mother's love; ability to endure loss and pain.
>
> Both about great love of parent for child; both about the parent's pain.

Rubrics for each Choices assignment appear on p. 164 in the *Portfolio Management System*.

CHOICES: Building Your Portfolio

1. **Writer's Notebook** With each selection, a Writer's Notebook activity appears as the first option in the Choices section. These brief, work-in-progress assignments build toward the writing assignment presented in the Writer's Workshop at the end of the collection. If students save their work for their Writer's Notebook activities as they move through the collection, they should be able to use some of them as starting points for the Workshop.
2. **Creative Writing** Some students may find it helpful to work on this assignment in pairs. If they prefer, allow students to draft their responses in dialogue. Invite willing pairs to share their responses.
3. **Speaking/Critical Thinking** After discussion, students might enjoy creating a skit and taking on the roles of the aliens to present their conclusions to the class.
4. **Visual Arts** If students' artwork becomes too unwieldy for storage, have them take a photograph or make a slide transparency of the work for their portfolios.

Making the Connections

Connecting to the Theme: "Can This Be Love?"

Among your resources is the Fine Art Transparency *Wedding Above the Village* by Dr. T. F. Chen (see *Audiovisual Resources*, p. 282). It superimposes tender, happy images of a wedding, from Marc Chagall's *The Song of Songs,* onto the sky over the uneasily sleeping village of Vincent Van Gogh's *Starry Night.*

Use the transparency and the accompanying worksheet to liken the emotional appeal of visual images to the evocative power of verbal imagery in "I Am Offering This Poem" and "since feeling is first." Then ask students what message about life or love they can draw from the images in the art and the poems.

Assessing Learning

Self-Assessment

Ask students to use a chart like the following to evaluate their own appreciation and understanding of poetry.

1=yes   2=somewhat   3=not sure   4=no

1. My understanding of a poem improves with rereadings.	
2. I learn when I examine figurative language.	
3. I understand a poem better if I visualize the imagery.	

OBJECTIVES

1. Recognize rhythm
2. Distinguish between meter and free verse
3. Use scanning to understand stressed and unstressed syllables in metrical poetry
4. Recognize types of feet: iamb, trochee, anapest, dactyl, and spondee

Resources

Elements of Literature
The Sounds of Poetry: Rhythm and Meter

For additional instruction on rhythm and meter, see *Literary Elements:*
- Transparency 17

Assessment
Formal Assessment
- Literary Elements Test, p. 105

Test Generator (One-Stop Planner)
- CD-ROM

Elements of Literature

This lesson discusses characteristics of meter in structured poetry and rhythm in free verse. It guides students in scanning for iambic, trochaic, anapestic, dactylic, and spondaic feet.

Mini-Lesson: Rhythm and Meter

Before students begin the main lesson, you might use this Mini-Lesson to give them experience in recognizing the rhythms of language. First, lead students in reciting a familiar advertising jingle or nursery rhyme (such as "Twinkle, Twinkle, Little Star"), clapping on each stressed syllable. Then, divide the class into small groups and challenge each group to identify and to clap on the stressed syllables in the limerick on p. 558—including the unconventional last line. Have each group present and explain its analysis.

THE SOUNDS OF POETRY: Rhythm and Meter

Rhythm: Music in Speech

Poetry is a musical kind of speech. Like music, poetry is based on **rhythm**—that is, on the alternation of stressed and unstressed sounds that makes the voice rise and fall. Here's a little prayer that many children memorize and say at bedtime. Say it out loud, and you'll feel the regular rise and fall of its rhythm:

Now I lay me down to sleep.
I pray the Lord my soul to keep.
If I should die before I wake,
I pray the Lord my soul to take.

If you listen closely, you'll hear exactly four stressed syllables repeated in each line. This repetition of stressed syllables balanced by unstressed syllables creates the rhythm in the poem.

Poets have a choice in the kind of rhythm they can use. They can use **meter**—a strict rhythmic pattern of stressed and unstressed syllables in each line (as in "Now I lay me down to sleep"), or they can write in **free verse**—a loose kind of rhythm in which the sounds of long phrases are balanced against the sounds of short phrases. A poem written in free verse sounds more like natural speech than like formal poetry.

Meter: Patterns of Sounds

The emphasis given to a word or a syllable is called a **stress** or an accent. In **metrical poetry** (poetry that has a meter), stressed and unstressed syllables are arranged in a regular pattern.

Here's a famous stanza from a long poem called *The Rime of the Ancient Mariner* by Samuel Taylor Coleridge. Years ago schoolchildren could recite this poem from memory. The meter helped:

He prayeth best, who loveth best
All things both great and small;
For the dear God who loveth us,
He made and loveth all.

The mark ´ indicates a stressed syllable. The mark ˘ indicates an unstressed syllable. Indicating the stresses this way is called **scanning** the poem.

Welcome Variations

You'll notice how these four lines sound alike and are about the same length. Coleridge sets up his pattern in the first two lines and then sticks to it with only one variation. Read aloud the third line and hear how the first three syllables break the pattern.

In metrical poetry, variation is important. Without any variation at all, meter becomes mechanical and monotonous, like the steady ticktock ticktock of a clock or like a verse on a birthday card. An occasional change in rhythm, as in the third line of the stanza from *The Rime of the Ancient Mariner,* also allows the poet

There was a young man from Japan
Whose verses never would scan.
    When they said this was so,
    He said, "Yes, I know,
But I always try to get as many words in the last line
    as I possibly can."

Reaching All Students

Struggling Readers

Students who are sounding out words phonetically may find scanning extra challenging. You might guide them by presenting metrical poems on audiotape. If possible, provide at least one poem in iambic meter and others in anapestic or dactylic meter. On the first playing, direct students to listen for content. On subsequent playings, have students tap out the meters as they listen.

English Language Learners

Because songs feature exaggerated stresses, you might have students scan one or more simple songs. They can then move on to poems. Point out that recognizing meter can help them correctly pronounce new vocabulary words in metrical poems.

Advanced Learners

Provide complete copies of *The Rime of the Ancient Mariner* or another long metrical poem. Have students work in small groups to scan the poem in sections. Then, invite each group to prepare and present a dramatic reading of its section, reflecting the verses' metrical patterns and variations.

by John Malcolm Brinnin

to draw attention to key words in the poem.

Five Kinds of Feet

A line of metrical poetry is made up of metrical units called feet. A **foot** is a unit consisting of at least one stressed syllable and usually one or more unstressed syllables. There are five common types of feet used by poets writing in English, and their names come from Greek. Here are their names, with an example of a single word that matches the pattern of stressed and unstressed syllables in each foot:

iamb (insist)

trochee (double)

anapest (understand)

dactyl (excellent)

spondee (football).

(For more about these feet, see Meter in the Handbook of Literary Terms.)

Free Verse: Freedom from Rules

Early in this century, some American and English poets decided that they would rid poetry of its prettiness, senti-

From *The Beast in Me and Other Animals*. Copyright © 1948 James Thurber. Copyright © renewed 1976 Helen Thurber and Rosemary A. Thurber. Reprinted by arrangement with Rosemary A. Thurber and the Barbara Hogenson Agency.

A Trochee (left) encountering a Spondee.

mentality, and artificiality by concentrating on a new kind of poetry. Calling themselves **Imagists,** they declared that imagery alone—without any elaborate metrics or stanza patterns—could carry the full emotional message of a poem. They called their poetry **free verse** because it is free from the old metric rules.

Robert Frost, who disliked free verse, said that writing without the metric rules was "like playing tennis with the net down." What he meant was that the net on the tennis court is like meter in poetry— the essential part of the game that players must both respect and overcome. But in the twentieth century, more and more poets have accepted free verse as a challenge. Instead of conforming to meter, they write in cadences that follow "curves of thought" or "shapes

of speech." They trust their own sense of balance and measure to lead to poems as well composed as any written in meter.

Addressed to the Ear

As in ancient days, when poetry was not written down but only spoken or sung, poetry today is still addressed to the ear. You can't really say that you "know" a poem until you've heard it read aloud. Poets at work are not likely to be silent; they test what they're writing by reading it aloud to *hear* what it sounds like.

When you've heard the voices of many poets, chances are you'll have a favorite. And you'll probably find that you've chosen your favorite poet not only for what his or her poems *say* but also for the way they *sound.*

ELEMENTS OF LITERATURE: THE SOUNDS OF POETRY **559**

OBJECTIVES

1. Read and interpret the poem
2. Analyze the sonnet form
3. Express understanding through writing and speaking/listening
4. Identify and use inverted sentence structure

SKILLS

Literary
- Analyze the sonnet form

Writing
- Explore topics for comparison and contrast
- Write a sonnet

Speaking/Listening
- Prepare and present an oral response

Grammar/Language
- Use inverted sentence structure

Viewing/Representing
- Compare a portrait with a poem (ATE)

Planning

- **Block Schedule**
  Block Scheduling Lesson Plans with Pacing Guide
- **Traditional Schedule**
  Lesson Plans Including Strategies for English-Language Learners
- **One-Stop Planner**
  CD-ROM with Test Generator

Before You Read

SHALL I COMPARE THEE . . .

Make the Connection

Love in Fourteen Lines

In Shakespeare's day, every gentleman was expected to write sonnets in praise of his loved one. Writing a sonnet was a challenge, a kind of game. The speaker of this sonnet expresses passionate feelings within very strict rules—not an easy task.

Quickwrite

Before you read this poem, write your response to this question: Why would someone want to compare the person he loves to a summer's day? *(Keep your notes for use on pages 562–563.)*

Elements of Literature

The Sonnet: Strict Structure

The sonnet form favored (but not invented) by Shakespeare is the **Shakespearean**, or **English**, **sonnet**. Its fourteen lines are divided into three quatrains (rhyming groups of four lines) and a concluding **couplet** (pair of rhyming lines). Each quatrain makes a point or gives an example. The couplet sums it all up.

> **A sonnet** is a fourteen-line lyric poem written within very strict rules.
>
> *For more on the Sonnet, see the Handbook of Literary Terms.*

Alice Hilliard (end of the 16th century) by Nicholas Hilliard (1547–1619). Body color on vellum.

Victoria and Albert Museum, London/Art Resource, NY.

go.hrw.com
LE0 10-9

 Resources: Print and Media

Reading
- *Graphic Organizers for Active Reading,* p. 41
- *Audio CD Library*
  Disc 17, Track 4

Elements of Literature
- *Literary Elements*
  Transparency 17
  Worksheet, p. 52

Writing and Language
- *Daily Oral Grammar*
  Transparency 34

Assessment
- *Portfolio Management System,* p. 165
- *Standardized Test Preparation,* p. 68
- *Test Generator (One-Stop Planner CD-ROM)*

Internet
- go.hrw.com (keyword: LE0 10-9)

Shall I Compare Thee to a Summer's Day?

William Shakespeare

Shall I compare thee to a summer's day?
Thou art more lovely and more temperate.
Rough winds do shake the darling buds of May,
And summer's lease hath all too short a date.
5 Sometime too hot the eye of heaven shines,
And often is his gold complexion dimmed;
And every fair from fair sometime declines,
By chance, or nature's changing course, untrimmed;°
But thy eternal summer shall not fade,
10 Nor lose possession of that fair thou ow'st,°
Nor shall Death brag thou wand'rest in his shade,
When in eternal lines to time thou grow'st:
   So long as men can breathe or eyes can see,
   So long lives this, and this gives life to thee.

8. **untrimmed:** without trimmings (decorations).
10. **thou ow'st:** you own.

561

Summary ■ ■ ■

In this Shakespearean sonnet, the speaker proclaims his beloved "more lovely and more temperate" than a summer day. The first two quatrains argue that summer is fickle and fleeting. In the third quatrain and the final couplet, the beloved's qualities are presented as an "eternal summer," even defying death through the poem's "eternal lines." While clearly a tribute to a human lover, the poem also celebrates the immortalizing power of art, a characteristic Renaissance conceit.

Resources ─────

Elements of Literature
The Sounds of Poetry: Rhythm and Meter
For additional instruction on the sounds of poetry, see *Literary Elements*:
• Transparency 17
• Worksheet, p. 52

Ⓐ Appreciating Language
Word Choice
Help students understand that *temperate* means both "mild" and "constant" and that England's summer may be neither.

Ⓑ Elements of Literature
Sonnet
❓ How does this quatrain differ from the first two quatrains? [Sample answer: In the first two quatrains the speaker asks and answers a question focusing on summer's failings; here, he turns his attention to his beloved's eternal qualities.]

RESPONDING TO THE ART
The English artist **Nicholas Hilliard** (1547–1619) was a master of miniature portraiture. This portrait's border reads in Latin: "Alice Brandon, first wife of Nicholas Hilliard, painted by him; in the year of Our Lord 1578, aged 22."
Activity. Have students compare the effectiveness of the portrait and the poem in immortalizing their subjects. [Possible response: The portrait preserves the person's name and looks, while the poem preserves the speaker's feelings about the person.]

Reaching All Students

Struggling Readers
Guide students in paraphrasing ll. 3–4. (Example: "Stormy winds shake flower buds in May, and summer is too short.") Then have students work in small groups to paraphrase the rest of the sonnet, two lines at a time, as an aid to comprehension. To help students understand ll. 7–8, tell them that *fair* (l. 7) is a noun meaning "beauty."

English Language Learners
Point out examples of archaic language in the sonnet. Suggest that students create a two-column chart in which they list archaic words and their contemporary counterparts (thee/you; thou/you; do shake/shake; hath/has; thy/your; ow'st/own; wand'rest/wander; grow'st/grow). For other strategies for engaging English language learners, see
• *Lesson Plans Including Strategies for English-Language Learners*

Planning

RESPONDING TO THE ART

Activity. After students have read "Bonny Barbara Allan," they might enjoy creating a ballad based on the scene in *A Hunting Party*.

Before You Read

BONNY BARBARA ALLAN

Make the Connection

Love and Death

As you read this ballad, think about whether this love story is timely or out of date. Could it happen today?

Quickwrite

Write down the titles of some love songs popular today. Then take notes on these questions: Are the songs happy or tragic? Are any about betrayal? What are their refrains? *(Keep your notes for use on page 567.)*

Elements of Literature

The Ballad

"Bonny Barbara Allan" is a **ballad,** a story-poem meant to be sung. Most ballads use simple language and two of the oldest elements of poetry: a strong **meter** and a **refrain** (whole lines or stanzas repeated at regular intervals). **Folk ballads** such as this one, which have been passed down orally from generation to generation, often tell tales of love or violence. Folk ballads often use certain formulas—phrases such as "white as milk," "red, red lips," "red-roan steed," and "true, true love." The images of plants that grow on lovers' graves also are formulas. All of these formulas are part of the ballad singer's repertoire; whenever the singer needed to describe a woman's skin, for example, a formula was available.

564 THE POETRY COLLECTIONS

A Hunting Party (14th century), School of Paris. Ivory.

Victoria and Albert Museum, London/Art Resource, NY.

> **A** **ballad** is a song or songlike poem that tells a story.
>
> *For more about the Ballad, see the Handbook of Literary Terms.*

Resources: Print and Media

Bonny Barbara Allan

Anonymous

Oh, in the merry month of May,
When all things were a-blooming,
Sweet William came from the Western states
And courted Barbara Allan.

5　But he took sick, and very sick
And he sent for Barbara Allan,
And all she said when she got there,
"Young man, you are a-dying."

"Oh yes, I'm sick, and I'm very sick,
10　And I think that death's upon me;
But one sweet kiss from Barbara's lips
Will save me from my dying."

"But don't you remember the other day
You were down in town a-drinking?
15　You drank your health to the ladies all around,
And slighted Barbara Allan."

Summary ■ ■

In this folk ballad of unrequited and tragic love, William, a young man who has courted Barbara Allan, becomes ill and requests a curing kiss from her. Barbara Allan sees William but refuses to kiss him, claiming that he has slighted her, to which he responds, "Hardhearted Barbara Allan," and soon dies. Haunted by his final words, a refrain she seems to hear everywhere, she too succumbs to sudden death and is buried next to him. In an unexpected turn of events, "a red, red rose" grows from William's grave and entwines itself around a briar growing from Barbara Allan's grave in what becomes a "truelove knot," suggesting the redemptive power of love.

Resources ──

Viewing and Representing
Videocassette B, Segment 9
Available in Spanish and English. This segment explores the ballad as a poetic form. For full lesson plans, see *Visual Connections: Videocassette Program Teacher's Manual.*

Listening
Audio CD Library
For a vivid recording of "Bonny Barbara Allan," see the *Audio CD Library:*
• Disc 17, Track 5

Ⓐ Elements of Literature
Ballad
Point out "the merry month of May" as an example of a formulaic phrase found in many folk ballads.

Ⓑ Struggling Readers
Changing Your Reading Strategy
Read aloud the ballad's first few stanzas so that students can hear the meter. Then, ask them to "listen" in their minds for the meter as they read the rest of the poem silently. Suggest that when they lose track of the meter, they reread and try various stress patterns on the lines in question.

Ⓒ Reading Skills and Strategies
Responding to the Text
? What do you think of Barbara's response? [Possible responses: She seems petty and self-centered; or, she must feel deeply hurt.]

Reaching All Students

English Language Learners
Explain that the *a-* in the following words, "a-blooming," "a-dying," "a-drinking," "a-ringing," "a-singing," and "a-coming," is there for the sake of meter. Also, help students distinguish possessives ("Barbara's lips") from contractions ("death's upon me"; "don't"; "hadn't"; "I'll"). For additional strategies for engaging English language learners with the literature, see
• *Lesson Plans Including Strategies for English-Language Learners*

Advanced Learners
Suggest that students compare and contrast this melancholy ballad with Percy Montross's tragicomic "Clementine." Encourage students to scan both ("Clementine" is in iambic octameter) and to draw conclusions about the effects of metric patterns on mood and tone.

BROWSING IN THE FILES

A Critic's Comment. Editor Albert Friedman on English folk ballads: "Dialogue . . . bulks large in ballads, and it is the kind of dialogue that furthers action, not the kind that is introduced to develop the characters of the participants. For . . . ballads show no interest in the subtleties of character or in psychological motive-mongering." You might ask students to find a part of "Bonny Barbara Allan" that supports or refutes Friedman's point.

Ⓐ Elements of Literature
Ballad
❓ The repeated *ahh* sounds in the refrain "Hardhearted Barbara Allan" create the effect of groans or sighs. How do these sounds affect the ballad's mood? [They help to create a melancholy mood.]

Ⓑ Critical Thinking
Interpreting
❓ What might the rose and the briar symbolize? [Traditionally a red rose symbolizes love; here it might symbolize William's loving heart. Green often stands for jealousy, and Barbara seems upset by William's attention to other women; the thorny green briar could symbolize her jealous heart.]

Ⓒ Reading Skills and Strategies
Drawing Conclusions
❓ What message about love is suggested by this ballad's closing image? [Possible responses: Love is stronger than death; true love can conquer even a hard heart.]

"Oh yes, I remember the other day
I was down in town a-drinking;
I drank my health to the ladies all 'round,
20   But my love to Barbara Allan."

He turned his face to the wall;
She turned her back upon him;
The very last word she heard him say,
"Hardhearted Barbara Allan."

25 As she passed on through London Town,
She heard some bells a-ringing,
And every bell, it seemed to say,
"Hardhearted Barbara Allan."

She then passed on to the country road,
30 And heard some birds a-singing;
And every bird it seemed to say,
Ⓐ   "Hardhearted Barbara Allan."

She hadn't got more than a mile from town
When she saw his corpse a-coming;
35 "O bring him here, and ease him down,
And let me look upon him.

"Oh, take him away! Oh, take him away!
For I am sick and dying!
His death-cold features say to me,
40   'Hardhearted Barbara Allan.'

"O Father, O Father, go dig my grave,
And dig it long and narrow;
Sweet William died for me today;
I'll die for him tomorrow."

45 They buried them both in the old graveyard,
All side and side each other.
Ⓑ A red, red rose grew out of his grave,
And a green briar out of hers.

They grew and grew so very high
50 Ⓒ That they could grow no higher;
They lapped, they tied in a truelove knot—
The rose ran 'round the briar.

566 THE POETRY COLLECTIONS

🎵 **A Choral Reading: The Balladeers**

As far as we know, ballads were sung by individuals. Even so, here are some ideas for a choral reading of a ballad—no instruments required!

- First, examine the ballad: How many people are speaking? Which lines could be recited by a chorus? (Refrains are often a good choice for several speakers.)

- Next, think of how the speakers are feeling. (Usually in a ballad, feelings run pretty strong.) How can you express those feelings, using volume, pitch, and tone of voice? Where do feelings change?

- Will you use gestures? props? How will you dress?

- Finally, mark up a copy of your choral reading to use as a script. Watch the punctuation, and let it guide you in deciding where to pause and when to speed up. Indicate words to emphasize.

- Practice. Evaluate and adjust your performance before you present it to an audience. Have you and your fellow balladeers caught the texture of this sad story of love and betrayal?

Assessing Learning

Check Test: Short Answer
1. Why does William send for Barbara Allan? [He is dying and hopes her kiss will revive him.]
2. Why does she refuse his request? [She feels that he has slighted her.]
3. What words haunt Barbara Allan? ["Hard-hearted Barbara Allan"]
4. What grows above the lovers' graves? [a red rose and a green briar]

MAKING MEANINGS
BONNY BARBARA ALLAN

First Thoughts

[connect]

1. How did you feel about Barbara Allan and William as you began to read this poem? Did your feelings change by the end?

Shaping Interpretations

[analyze]

2. **Ballads** never tell the whole story. What details are left out of this one?

[interpret]

3. What evidence shows that Barbara Allan is indeed "hardhearted"? Does anything indicate that she is *not* hardhearted? Explain.

[interpret]

4. We'd expect the aggressive vines of a briar to grow around any nearby plant. Which plant entwines the other in this story? Which character and which emotion have triumphed?

[apply]

5. Read the ballad aloud. Then write it out on a separate piece of paper and **scan** it. Where does the singer vary the strict **meter** of the song?

Extending the Text

[analyze]

6. Are popular songs today at all like this old ballad? Check your Quickwrite notes.

CHOICES: Building Your Portfolio

Writer's Notebook

1. Collecting Ideas for a Comparison/Contrast Essay

Finding points of comparison. So you've chosen two works to compare. How do you begin? A good start is to list all the elements usually found in that type of writing. If you're comparing poems, you might start with **figurative language**. In your notebook, list all the other elements of poetry you can think of. Save your notes for the Writer's Workshop on page 580.

Speaking/Listening

2. Deaths Raise Doubts

Ballads often took their subjects from stories of domestic tragedy that would today be featured on the evening news. Prepare your own interpretation of the ballad as if it's tomorrow's **news story**. Remember that a good reporter answers *Who? What? When? Where? Why? How?* You might want to record your newscast presentation on videotape or audiotape.

Music

3. Love Set to Music

With a partner (or alone, if you prefer), try writing a melody for one poem you've read so far. Before you start, study your poem's **tone,** or mood. What type of music will best suit it? Folk? Rock? Country western? Rap?

Crossing the Curriculum

Social Studies

Encourage students to learn what a medieval English balladeer's life was like. Students might visit museums, interview experts, or consult reference works or the Internet to learn how balladeers dressed, where and for whom they performed, what training they had, what instruments they played, how and where they traveled and lodged, and so on. Students might present their findings in oral, written, or multimedia format.

Music

Invite students to gather and present recordings of ballads from a variety of eras and cultures. Libraries (as well as personal collections) might contain interesting examples of sung or spoken ballads such as "Hang Down Your Head, Tom Dooley" and "John Henry."

MAKING MEANINGS

First Thoughts

1. Some students may say that they liked William and disliked Barbara at the beginning of the poem, though later they forgave her. Others may at first think William is unfaithful, but later have doubts.

Shaping Interpretations

2. Possible responses: The ballad doesn't explain why Barbara is hardhearted; it also omits details about Barbara's and William's relationship before his illness. For instance, did she return his interest?

3. Possible response: Barbara's refusal of William's dying wish suggests that she is hardhearted. However, she does go to see him when he asks her to, and she suffers remorse.

4. The rose twines around the briar. William and love have triumphed.

5. Sample scanned stanza:
"As she passed on through London Town,
She heard some bells a-ringing
And every bell, it seemed to say,
"Hardhearted Barbara Allan."
Stanzas 4, 5, 6, 12 deviate from the regular iambic tetrameter and trimeter.

Extending the Text

6. Possible responses: Yes, many songs today deal with unrequited love; no, today's songs are more realistic.

CHOICES: Building Your Portfolio

1. **Writer's Notebook** Remind students to save their work for the Writer's Workshop on p. 580.
2. **Speaking/Listening** Give students tabloid stories as models.
3. **Music** If students don't know musical notation, have them tape their work.

Planning

- **Block Schedule**
  Block Scheduling Lesson Plans with Pacing Guide
- **Traditional Schedule**
  Lesson Plans Including Strategies for English-Language Learners
- **One-Stop Planner**
  CD-ROM with Test Generator

Before You Read

HEART! WE WILL FORGET HIM!

Make the Connection

Trying to Forget

In this poem, Emily Dickinson tells the old, sad story of unrequited love—of love that is not returned. The poem is about conflict: between will and emotion, between the thinking mind and the feeling heart.

Quickwrite

Which do you think is more powerful—the mind or the heart? Does one control the other, or are they completely independent systems? Think about your own experiences, and freewrite your response. *(Keep your notes for use on page 573.)*

Elements of Literature

Personification

In this poem the speaker addresses her heart as if it were a person who could listen, act, and feel. She's using **personification**, giving human qualities to something nonhuman.

> **P**ersonification is a kind of metaphor in which a nonhuman thing or quality is talked about as if it were human.
>
> *For more on Personification, see page 507 and the Handbook of Literary Terms.*

 go.hrw.com
LEO 10-9

568 THE POETRY COLLECTIONS

 Resources: Print and Media

Reading
- *Graphic Organizers for Active Reading,* pp. 43, 44
- *Audio CD Library*
  Disc 17, Tracks 7, 8

Assessment
- *Portfolio Management System,* p. 167
- *Standardized Test Preparation,* p. 70
- *Test Generator (One-Stop Planner CD-ROM)*

Internet
- go.hrw.com (keyword: LEO 10-9)

Heart! We will forget him!

Emily Dickinson

Heart! We will forget him!
You and I— tonight!
You may forget the warmth he gave—
I will forget the light!

When you have done, pray tell me
That I may straight begin!
Haste! lest while you're lagging
I remember him!

**Emily Dickinson (1848).
Oil over a photograph.**

The Granger Collection, New York.

MEET THE WRITER

Shy Woman in White

Emily Dickinson (1830–1886) rarely left Amherst, Massachusetts, her birthplace. There she lived unknown as a poet except to her family and a few friends, and there she produced almost eighteen hundred exquisite short poems that are now regarded as one of the great expressions of American genius.

She was the bright daughter of a well-to-do religious family; her father was a lawyer. As a girl at boarding school, she seemed high-spirited and happy. But something happened when she was a young woman (a love that was not, could not be requited, biographers speculate), and at thirty-one, she simply withdrew from the world. She dressed all in white, refused to leave her home or meet strangers, and devoted her life to her family—and to writing poetry. Of her own poetry, she wrote, "This is my letter to the World / That never wrote to Me. . . ."

She wrote her poems on little pieces of paper, tied them in neat packets, and occasionally gave them to relatives as valentine or birthday greetings or attached them to gifts of cookies or pies. In 1862, she sent four poems to the editor of *Atlantic Monthly*. Only seven of her poems were published (anonymously) during her lifetime. When she died at fifty-six, she had no notion that one day she would be honored as one of America's greatest poets.

Summary ▪ ▪

In this lyric about the pain of a love that has ended, the poet personifies her heart and instructs it to forget "the warmth he gave" while she forgets "the light." By separating the heart from the speaker, or emotion from reason, Dickinson implies that love cannot be easily tempered by rationality.

Resources

Listening
Audio CD Library
For a reading of this poem, see the *Audio CD Library:*
• Disc 17, Track 7

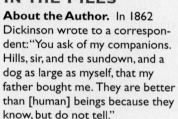

BROWSING IN THE FILES

About the Author. In 1862 Dickinson wrote to a correspondent: "You ask of my companions. Hills, sir, and the sundown, and a dog as large as myself, that my father bought me. They are better than [human] beings because they know, but do not tell."

Ⓐ Elements of Literature
Personification
❓ Why do you think the speaker treats her heart as a being separate from herself? [Possible responses: She may feel that she's not strong enough to forget on her own and needs an ally; she may feel that her emotions function separately from her mind.]

Ⓑ Struggling Readers
Paraphrasing
Tell students that *have done* means "have finished"; *pray* means "please"; and *straight* means "immediately." Ask them to paraphrase ll. 5–6 in modern English. [Sample answer: When you finish, please tell me, so I can start right in.]

Professional Notes

A Critic's Comment
Editor Howard E. Hugo notes one result of Dickinson's anonymity: "She could confide her poems to paper as if to a diary or journal, and therefore express and explore feelings too appalling to make public." Do you think that the feelings in this poem are in any way appalling? Why or why not? [Possible response: Most students will say the feelings are private but not appalling.]

Making the Connections

Connecting to the Theme
Have students recall Baca's, Cummings's, and Shakespeare's poems, and "Bonny Barbara Allan." Which speaker or character might best understand the feelings about love expressed in Dickinson's poem? Why? [Sample answers: The speaker in Baca's poem, since he knows life can be wintry without love; the speaker in Cummings's, since he respects the power of emotion; or Barbara Allan and William, who die for love.]

Summary ■ ■

Each of these Japanese tankas is prefaced with a one-line context and is built on a single image. The first poem might be paraphrased, "Should we pass by the opportunity to light up each other's life through love?" Its image is the night sky, which can be flooded with light when the clouds suddenly part for the moon. The second poem evokes the image of a "drifting ship" with the speaker aboard. Every day since falling in love, she's been drenched in painful, cold water. The third poem was sent attached to a rice stalk with empty husks that are likened to the speaker's life. This life has "emptied itself," presumably after the loss of a lover. In these poems love is a wistful, often disappointed longing.

Resources

Listening
Audio CD Library
For a reading of these classic tankas, see the *Audio CD Library:*
• Disc 17, Track 8

Ⓐ Elements of Literature

Poetic Form
❓ A tanka's five lines usually focus on a single image. As you read this tanka, what image emerges in your mind? [Possible responses: a cloudy night sky with the moon breaking through; a man and woman looking at the night sky together.]

Ⓑ Critical Thinking

Interpreting
❓ In this tanka, what might the "drifting ship" refer to? [Possible responses: The lover's indecisiveness or indifference; the speaker's insecurities.]

Ⓒ Reading Skills and Strategies

Connecting with the Text
❓ It was traditional to attach a tanka to a spray of flowers or colorful autumn leaves. How would you feel if someone sent you an empty grain stalk instead of a bouquet? [Possible responses: puzzled; upset; insulted.]

Make the Connection

Love's Obstacles

A loves B more than B loves A; B used to love A but feared rejection and has decided to snub A. If you think you hear a lot of that kind of gossip in your cafeteria, take a look at love in Japan more than a thousand years ago.

Quickwrite

In your notebook, finish these sentence starters with images or figures of speech:

Love is . . . Life is . . .
(Keep your notes for use on page 573.)

Elements of Literature

Tanka Structure

Japanese tankas, which date to the seventh century, are written within the strictest rules. Tankas have five unrhymed lines and a total of thirty-one syllables. Lines 1 and 3 have five syllables each. Lines 2, 4, and 5 have seven each. (The English translations don't always follow this strict syllable count.)

> Tanka poems, a Japanese **poetic form,** have five unrhymed lines and a total of thirty-one syllables. A tanka evokes a strong feeling with a single image.

Three Japanese Tankas

Ono Komachi

translated by Jane Hirshfield
with Mariko Aratani

1

Sent anonymously to a man who had passed in front of the screens of my room

Ⓐ Should the world of love
end in darkness,
without our glimpsing
that cloud-gap
where the moon's light fills the sky?

2

Sent to a man who seemed to have changed his mind

Ⓑ Since my heart placed me
on board your drifting ship,
not one day has passed
that I haven't been drenched
in cold waves.

3

Sent in a letter attached to a rice stalk with an empty seed husk

Ⓒ How sad that I hope
to see you even now,
after my life has emptied itself
like this stalk of grain
into the autumn wind.

go.hrw.com
LE0 10-9

Reaching All Students

Struggling Readers

Suggest that students isolate these tankas' images—darkness, cold waves, an empty seed husk—and ask themselves, "How is living without love like this image?" Have students answer in their own words from their experiences or from their reading. Such reflection may provide enough context for students to identify with Komachi's speakers.

English Language Learners

Help these students break down the compound construction *cloud-gap* in the first tanka into two separate words. Explain that the hyphen connects the meanings of these two words to create a single image. For more strategies for engaging English language learners with the literature, see
• *Lesson Plans Including Strategies for English-Language Learners*

五老峯年頼

The Poetess Ono
Komachi (c. 1820)
by Hokkei.
Surimono print
(20 cm × 17 cm).
Spencer Museum of
Art/University of Kansas.
The William Bridges
Thayer Memorial.

MEET THE WRITER

A Leading Lady and Poet

Ono Komachi (834–?) may have been the daughter of a ninth-century Japanese lord and may have served at the imperial court. Though little is known about her life, she is believed to have had at least one child and one grandchild. She was supposed to have been one of the most beautiful women of her time but is said to have died in poverty—aged and forgotten but still writing poetry.

Whatever the facts of her life, it is indisputable that Komachi was one of the great figures in an age when women dominated Japanese society and literature. In her hundred or so short poems that survive, she illuminated the subject of love through her understanding of Buddhist ideas about the fleeting nature of existence.

THREE JAPANESE TANKAS 571

Getting Students Involved

Cooperative Learning

The Whys and Hows. Have partners choose one tanka, and discuss these questions:
- Why does the speaker love the person to whom she writes?
- How does this person treat her?
- How might this person respond to her tanka?

Tell students to agree on a one-sentence answer to each question and to note how the tanka supports the answer. One partner can record, and the other can report to the class.

Using Students' Strengths

Visual Learners

Illustrated Tanka Gallery. Invite interested students to illustrate the tankas. Students might sketch, paint, or create collages based on the poems. Instruct them to provide a caption for each illustration, explaining how it reflects the imagery of the tanka. Then hold a gallery opening to celebrate and comment on the student artwork and its relationship to the various tankas.

LITERATURE AND HISTORY

The Heian era was not the only era in Japanese history to value poetry. Today, traditional poetry is experiencing new heights of popularity in Japan. Poetry is presented on television and radio programs, in magazines and newspapers, and in thousands of books. Japan's imperial poetry contest enjoys an audience equal to that of the Super Bowl in the United States. Clearly the Japanese have a passion for writing—and reading—poetry.

RESPONDING TO THE ART

In Japanese culture, the visual presentation of a poem is as important as the poem itself. The calligraphy here is a poem that reads: "One whom I met / Until yesterday / Is gone today, / Swept away / Like mountain clouds."

Activity. Ask students to write a tanka and then present it in an ornamental style.

LITERATURE AND HISTORY

Poetry in the Golden Age of Japan

In the imperial court of Heian-era Japan (794–1185), poetry had both private and public functions. In private, poetry was the accepted language of love. A gentleman showed his interest in a lady of the court by sending her an admiring five-line poem (a tanka). If the poem she wrote in reply was encouraging, he paid her a visit. Their exchange of poems continued throughout their relationship, and each new message had to be original and intriguing. Lovers also valued skillful calligraphy, exquisite paper, and a tasteful presentation. To match the mood of their poems, they covered tinted bamboo paper with scattered designs and tiny flecks of gold and silver foil. The final creation, carefully sealed with a twig or spray of flowers, was often lovely enough to decorate a folding screen.

Public poetry could be as romantic and beautiful as private poems, but it was presented and evaluated very differently. At popular poetry contests (*uta-awase*), competitors grouped themselves into two teams, Right and Left. A judge gave the teams a topic, such as "spring" or "names of things," and awarded a point to the side that created and recited the more pleasing composition. The team that had the most points after several rounds won. The government Office of Poetry preserved exceptional spoken poems in written anthologies.

Page from *Ishiyama-gire: Poems of Ki no Tsurayuki* (872?–c. 946). Calligraphy on ornamented paper.

Courtesy of the Freer Gallery of Art/Smithsonian Institution, Washington, D.C. (69.4)

Using Students' Strengths

Kinesthetic Learners

Pair students and invite them to play the Japanese tanka-writing game, *Karuta.* They might begin by viewing photographs or art for inspiration. Then invite them to collaborate on tankas. One partner should write the first three lines on a note card, and the other should write the last two lines on a different note card. Remind students to be sure to follow the tanka form. Review these points: The tanka focuses on one image, evokes a strong emotion, and has a strict format of five unrhymed lines and a total of thirty-one syllables. Tell partners to identify their own tanka by putting the same number on the backs of both cards. Then spread all the note cards from all the partners (tanka side up) on a table, and have students challenge each other to match the cards correctly.

Professional Notes

A Critic's Comment

Share this quotation about the Heian era from Jerrold M. Packard: "[In] that long-ago Japan, beauty was measured in extraordinarily precise degrees of social refinement, in subtle nuances of life that was lived, at its height, in . . . observed niceties." Ask where in the tankas students find attention to "subtle nuances" and social etiquette. [The prose introduction to each tanka reflects the etiquette for writing and "presenting" poetry.]

MAKING MEANINGS

HEART! WE WILL FORGET HIM!/THREE JAPANESE TANKAS

[connect]
First Thoughts

1. Do the three tankas leave you with the same feeling you get from Emily Dickinson's poem, or do they make you feel something different? Explain.

[interpret]
Shaping Interpretations

2. Dickinson **personifies** her heart by telling it to do things that only a person can do. What does she tell Heart? How would you paraphrase what she means by "warmth" and "light" (lines 3–4)?

[evaluate]
3. Refer to the Quickwrite on page 568. Which do you think is more powerful: the mind or the heart? How does Dickinson feel?

[synthesize]
4. Look back at the **images** in the tankas. What feelings do they suggest?

[connect]
Extending the Text

5. These poems were written many years ago—the tankas are centuries old. Are they dated? Could they still apply to people's feelings and experiences today?

CHOICES: Building Your Portfolio

Writer's Notebook

1. Collecting Ideas for a Comparison/Contrast Essay

Finding details.
Work out a chart like the following, in which you compare and contrast one of the tankas and Dickinson's poem according to the various elements of poetry you've looked at in these collections. Keep your notes for possible use in the Writer's

Elements	Dickinson	Tanka
Subject		
Mood/Feeling		
Images		
Figures of Speech		
Message		

Workshop on page 580.

Creative Writing

2. The Hidden Characters

These four poems contain hidden, unidentified characters—the men in Komachi's poems and the lost love in Dickinson's poem. Write a letter or journal entry in the voice of one of these hidden characters, responding to the way the poet/speaker has written about you and about your love.

Creative Writing

3. Try a Tanka

Review the information about Japanese poetry on page 572 and the **tanka form** on page 570. Then, in tanka style, write a series of poems that trace a relationship. Try to use the images or figures of speech that you created for the Quickwrite on page 570. Describe a symbolic object you might send with the tanka.

Assessing Learning

Check Test: True-False
Heart! We will forget him!

1. The speaker hates her heart. [False]
2. The speaker boasts that she can easily forget a lost love. [False]

Three Japanese Tankas

3. One tanka focuses on an image of cherry blossoms in moonlight. [False]
4. The speaker's heart, in one tanka, places her on a drifting ship. [True]
5. In these tankas love is disappointing. [True]

Standardized Test Preparation
For practice with standardized test format specific to this selection, see
- *Standardized Test Preparation,* p. 70

MAKING MEANINGS
First Thoughts

1. Possible responses: All the poems evoke a sense of disappointment in love; "Heart ..." evokes torment and determination, while the tankas evoke sad resignation; "Heart ..." evokes desperation, while the tankas seem more philosophical.

Shaping Interpretations

2. She tells Heart to help her get over a lost lover: Heart is to forget the lover's warmth and to let her know as soon as that's done. Possible paraphrases: *warmth*—love, kindness; *light*—carefreeness.
3. Possible responses: the mind, because it can see beyond emotions; the heart, because emotions affect us in spite of reason. Dickinson feels the heart is stronger, since it must do its work first; or, she feels the mind is stronger, since it is the "I" giving the orders.
4. Possible responses: Night clouds—gloom with a slim chance of joy; the wave-washed, drifting ship—loss and hopelessness; the empty husk—hollowness.

Extending the Texts

5. Possible responses: The poems still touch basic emotions that transcend time; Dickinson's language and the tankas' customs are too outdated for modern readers.

Grading Timesaver

Rubrics for each Choices assignment appear on p. 167 in the *Portfolio Management System.*

CHOICES: Building Your Portfolio

1. Remind students to compare as well as contrast the poems.
2. Pairs of students can brainstorm ideas.
3. Students should use the tankas on p. 570 as models.

Planning

- **Block Schedule**
  Block Scheduling Lesson Plans with Pacing Guide

- **Traditional Schedule**
  Lesson Plans Including Strategies for English-Language Learners

- **One-Stop Planner**
  CD-ROM with Test Generator

Before You Read

HANGING FIRE

Make the Connection

What the Title Tells

The expression *to hang fire* refers to shooting a gun. It means "to delay firing or to fail to fire." *Hang fire* has a general meaning too: "to be delayed."

Quickwrite

You're about to meet a speaker who has a lot of questions and worries. Right after you read the poem, jot down your impressions of the speaker. What does she seem to be waiting for? What's being delayed in her life? *(Keep your notes for use on page 576.)*

Elements of Literature

The Speaker

Every poem in this collection except "Bonny Barbara Allan" has a speaker who speaks as "I." When you come across poems like these, which speak in the first person, be sure you can identify the voice. Speakers are sometimes, but not always, the poet. In Langston Hughes's "Mother to Son" (page 508), the speaker is a woman addressing a young son. (The poet, of course, is a man.) In "George Gray" (page 522), the speaker is someone buried in Spoon River Cemetery, not the poet.

> The **speaker** in a poem is the voice talking to us. A speaker can be the poet, but he or she (or it) can also be almost anyone (or anything) else—even something nonhuman that can't speak at all.

Hanging Fire

Audre Lorde

I am fourteen
and my skin has betrayed me
the boy I cannot live without
still sucks his thumb
5   in secret
how come my knees are
always so ashy
what if I die
before morning
10   and momma's in the bedroom
with the door closed.

I have to learn how to dance
in time for the next party
my room is too small for me
15   suppose I die before graduation
A   they will sing sad melodies
but finally
tell the truth about me
There is nothing I want to do
20 **B**   and too much
that has to be done
and momma's in the bedroom
with the door closed.

Nobody even stops to think
25   about my side of it
I should have been on Math Team
my marks were better than his
why do I have to be
the one
30   wearing braces
I have nothing to wear tomorrow
will I live long enough
to grow up
and momma's in the bedroom
35   with the door closed.

Resources: Print and Media

Reading
- *Graphic Organizers for Active Reading*, p. 45
- *Audio CD Library*
  Disc 17, Track 9

Assessment
- *Portfolio Management System*, p. 168
- *Test Generator (One-Stop Planner CD-ROM)*

MEET THE WRITER

"I Am Black, Woman, and Poet"

Audre Lorde's (1934–1992) first published poem was rejected by her high school literary magazine as "much too romantic." Undaunted, she sent it to *Seventeen* magazine, which published it. She remembers how she started to write poems:

66 I used to speak in poetry. I would read poems, and I would memorize them. People would say, well, what do you think, Audre? What happened to you yesterday? And I would recite a poem, and somewhere in that poem would be a line or a feeling I would be sharing. In other words, I literally communicated through poetry. And when I couldn't find the poems to express the things I was feeling, that's what started me writing poetry, and that was when I was twelve or thirteen. 99

Lorde worked as a librarian and a teacher while her poetry began to accumulate honors and awards. Her poems deal with racial and feminist issues, love relationships (there is a recurring image of a mother who withholds her love, as in "Hanging Fire"), urban and nature images. Her language is unadorned, sometimes laced with fury.

"I am Black, Woman, and Poet," she once told an interviewer.

HANGING FIRE 575

Summary ▪

The speaker of this poem is a fourteen-year-old girl whose voice blends petulant self-absorption and sobering references to death. The speaker's focus veers wildly, but each stanza of musings is punctuated with a *what-if-I-die?* scenario and capped with the haunting refrain, "and momma's in the bedroom/with the door closed." The title sets up the idea of suspension—of waiting for adulthood or for life to begin, but also an unsettling premonition of early death.

Resources ———

Listening
Audio CD Library
For a recording of "Hanging Fire," see the *Audio CD Library:*
• Disc 17, Track 9

A Elements of Literature
Speaker
❓ What areas of her life is this speaker concerned about? [Sample answer: her appearance, boyfriend, death, mother, social life, future, and school work.]

B Critical Thinking
Interpreting
❓ How does this statement reflect the poem's title? [Possible responses: It suggests that the speaker is "hanging fire" when it comes to maturity; it suggests that she is "hanging fire" because she is overwhelmed.]

Reaching All Students

Struggling Readers
The fragmented nature of "Hanging Fire" makes the poem ideal for Popcorn Reading: a volunteer reads aloud several lines and then says "Popcorn!" and the name of another student who will begin to read from that point. Encourage the group to read through the poem several times. You might tape the reading for playback and discussion.

English Language Learners
With students, generate a list of idioms analogous to "hanging fire": "up in the air," "on ice," "on the back burner," "in limbo," "put off," and "in the wings." Discuss each idiom's connotations. Make sure students see the ominous overtones of *hanging fire*. For more strategies for engaging English language learners with the literature, see
• *Lesson Plans Including Strategies for English-Language Learners*

MAKING MEANINGS

First Thoughts

1. Possible responses:
Q. Why is the mother's door always closed? A. Perhaps she has her own problems. Q. Why does the speaker keep thinking about dying? A. She seems to be afraid she may never grow up.

Shaping Interpretations

2. "I" is a fourteen-year-old girl. Possible words: *insecure, honest, complaining, worried, resentful, sensitive, scared*.

3. Possible responses: She's waiting to grow up; she's waiting for her mother to care about her. The title's connotations are apt because the tensions in the speaker's life seem potentially destructive; or, another title, such as "Waiting," would be clearer.

4. Sample answer: The refrain suggests feelings of isolation and abandonment. This flat, repeated statement helps to create the poem's plaintive mood.

Connecting with the Text

5. Some students may point out that the poem deals with love between parent and child, as well as between two young people. Others may feel that the love indicated in the poem is uncertain. The speaker seems to ask "Can *this* be love?" in a painful, ironic way.

Grading Timesaver

Rubrics for each Choices assignment appear on p. 168 in the *Portfolio Management System*.

CHOICES:
Building Your Portfolio

1. Students should be specific with their details.
2. Photocopy the poem and make notes about pitch, pacing, etc.

MAKING MEANINGS
HANGING FIRE

[connect]
First Thoughts

1. What questions would you like to ask about this poem? How would you answer your own questions?

Shaping Interpretations

[analyze]
2. Who is the "I" in this poem? What are some words you'd use to describe this **speaker**?

[evaluate]
3. In what ways is this speaker "hanging fire"—waiting for things to happen? What do you think of this as the poem's **title**? (Review your Quickwrite notes.)

[synthesize]
4. What meanings and feelings does the poem's **refrain** suggest to you? How does this refrain help create the poem's mood?

Connecting with the Text

[synthesize]
5. What does this poem have to do with love? Could the question posed in the collection title be a question this speaker would ask? Talk over the poem's connection to love.

CHOICES: Building Your Portfolio

Writer's Notebook

1. Collecting Ideas for a Comparison/Contrast Essay

Finding details.
Here's another chance to find details in two poems that will help you compare and contrast them. Fill in this chart with details from "I Am Offering This Poem" by Jimmy Santiago Baca (page 551) and "Hanging Fire" by Audre Lorde (page 574). Keep your notes for possible use in the Writer's Workshop on page 580.

Elements	Baca	Lorde
Topic/Subject		
Message		
Feeling		
Refrain		
Images		
Figures of Speech		
Speaker		

Speaking/Listening

2. Choral Interpretation

In a group of four students, present a choral reading of "Hanging Fire." To prepare, read the poem carefully several times, and consider the speaker's **tone**, or **mood**. Think about the **structure of the poem**: Few lines have end punctuation, so where will you pause in your reading? Decide which lines will be read by each speaker. Experiment with **pitch**, **tone of voice**, and **facial expressions**. You may want the entire group to read the refrain. Present your choral interpretation to the class, and ask for their responses.

Assessing Learning

Check Test: Short Answer

1. How old is the speaker? [fourteen]
2. What does the speaker want to do before the next party? [learn to dance]
3. Where is the speaker's mother? [in the bedroom with the door closed]
4. List three of the speaker's complaints. [Possible responses: skin problems, ashy knees, small room, braces, "nothing to wear," not on math team, boyfriend sucks thumb, mother inaccessible.]

Background

One of the world's most famous books is a satiric Spanish novel about the power of love and idealism. Titled *The History of That Ingenious Gentleman Don Quijote de la Mancha*,[1] it is popularly known simply as *Don Quijote* (dän´kē·hōt′ē). Its hero is a faded old gentleman living in a backward village in the province of La Mancha, Spain, during the early 1600s. The old man has read so many **romances** (popular books about knights and their heroic deeds) that he has lost touch with reality. He now imagines himself a knight about to set off in quest of adventures, ready to rescue beautiful damsels and right the world's wrongs.

One day he goes into action: He takes his great-grandfather's suit of rusty armor out of a closet, attaches a cardboard visor to an old headpiece, and hits the road. He calls himself Don Quijote and names his skinny old horse Rocinante (rō·sē·nän′tā), roughly "worn-out old horse."

1. The English spelling is *Don Quixote*; in Spanish, the title is *El ingenioso hidalgo Don Quijote de la Mancha*.

go.hrw.com
LEO 10-9

EXTENDING *the theme*

A NOVEL EXCERPT

from Don Quijote

Miguel de Cervantes
translated by Burton Raffel

"A knight errant without love entanglements would be like a tree without leaves or fruit."

Well, with his armor scrubbed clean, and his helmet ready, and then his horse christened and himself confirmed, he realized that all he needed and had to hunt for was a lady to be in love with, since a knight errant without love entanglements would be like a tree without leaves or fruit, or a body without a soul. So he said to himself:

"Now, if for my sins, or by good fortune, I happen to find a giant right here in this neighborhood, which after all is something that usually happens to knights errant, and we have a go at it and I overthrow him, or maybe split him right down the middle, or, however it happens, conquer and utterly defeat him, wouldn't it be a good idea to have someone to whom I could send him, so he could go and kneel down in front of my sweet lady and say, his voice humble and submissive, 'I, my lady, am the giant Caraculiambro, lord of the island of Malindrania, defeated in man-to-man combat by that knight who can never be too much praised, Don Quijote de la Mancha, who has sent me here to offer myself at your pleasure, to be dealt with however your Grace may happen to think best'?"

Oh, how our good knight relished the delivery of this speech, especially once he'd decided who was going to be his lady love! It turns out, according to some people, that not too far from where he lived there was a very pretty peasant girl, with whom he was supposed, once upon a time, to have been in love,

DON QUIJOTE **577**

A Elements of Literature

Character

❓ What do you realize about Don Quijote from this description? [He has created his entire identity in his imagination.]

B Elements of Literature

Satire

❓ What key element of satire do you find in this phrase? What are some examples? [exaggeration—"endless wrongs," "endless injustices," "endless errors," "endless abuses," and "endless sins"]

RESPONDING TO THE ART

Pablo Picasso (1881–1973) is considered one of the greatest artists of the 20th century. He was unquestionably the most prolific, having created more than 20,000 works in various mediums in his lifetime.

Activity. The figure on the donkey at the left is Sancho Panza, a peasant who serves as Don Quijote's squire. This sketch shows Don Quijote just before his famous joust with the windmills (he thinks they are giants). Ask students to analyze the tone of the drawing (satiric) and compare it to the image of Don Quijote portrayed in the selection. Note the bony knight contrasted with the rotund peasant squire. Note also the elements in the sketch that give it a childlike quality.

Musée d'Art et d'Histoire, St. Denis, France.

Don Quixote (1955) by Pablo Picasso.

although (as the story goes) she never knew it nor did he ever say a word to her. Her name was Aldonza Lorenzo, and he thought it a fine idea to bestow on her the title of Mistress of his Thoughts. Hunting for a name as good as the one he'd given himself, a name that would be appropriate for that princess and noble lady, he decided to call her *Dulcinea del Toboso*, since Toboso was where she came from. To him it seemed a singularly musical name, rare, full of meaning, like all the others he'd assigned to himself and everything that belonged to him.

Having taken care of these arrangements, he had no desire to postpone his plan for even a moment longer, propelled by the thought of how badly the world might suffer if he delayed, for he intended to undo endless wrongs, set right endless injustices, correct endless errors, fix endless abuses, and atone for endless sins. One morning before dawn, on a steaming July day, without telling anyone what he was up to or being seen by a single soul, he put on all his armor, climbed onto Rocinante, settled his flimsy helmet into place, grasped his shield, picked up his spear and, riding through the back gate, set out for the open fields, wonderfully well content at how easily his noble desire had been set in motion.

Crossing the Curriculum

Art

Don Quijote has been the subject of paintings and drawings by artists other than Picasso. Have students research copies of paintings of the subject by Honoré Daumier and Gustave Doré and compare their interpretations of the famous knight to the drawing by Picasso.

Music

Don Quijote was the subject of a Broadway musical, *Man of LaMancha,* in 1965, and he is also the subject of a famous tone poem by Richard Strauss (*Don Quixote,* 1897). Invite interested students to obtain a recording of either the musical or the tone poem and describe their reactions. Encourage students to make comparisons with the excerpt from the novel.

Social Studies/History

Cervantes served in the Battle of Lepanto between Spain and Turkey in 1571. He later held a job furnishing supplies to the Spanish Armada in the late 1580s. Students might research either of these subjects and prepare a report for the class.

MEET THE WRITER

"Like a Madman Lived"

Miguel de Cervantes (1547–1616) wrote a best-selling novel—the first European novel, critics say—but he never received royalties. The publisher of *Don Quijote* (1605) and pirated editions pocketed all the profits from Cervantes' long, leisurely, episodic novel.

Cervantes' life was a tale of poverty, woe, and imprisonment. A poor young man from a town near Madrid, Spain, he enlisted in the army and was so gravely wounded in a famous naval battle that he lost permanent use of his left hand. Next, pirates captured him and held him as a slave in Algiers for years. Ransomed by his family, Cervantes worked as a playwright and tax collector before being thrown into debtors' prison. There he probably conceived the idea for *Don Quijote*, a **parody** (humorous imitation) of the wildly popular romances about knightly adventures.

In the preface to his great work, Cervantes wrote:

66 So what could my sterile, half-educated wit give birth to except the history of a whimper-ing child, withered, whining, its head stuffed with all kinds of thoughts no one else would even think of, like a man bred in a jail cell, where everything grates on your nerves and every new sound makes you still sadder. 99

Cervantes, who died within days of William Shakespeare, wrote his own epitaph:

66 For if he like a madman lived,
At least he like a wise one died. 99

FINDING COMMON GROUND

Get together in groups of three or four to talk about the *Don Quijote* excerpt.

1. You might start by reading aloud your Quickwrite notes. Then **compare and contrast** Don Quijote's quest for love with everyone's quest for someone to love and dedicate themselves to. How do people today seek and find love?

2. Does the prospect of love—having it, finding as well as searching for it—make us better people? Explain your response.

3. Don Quijote was inspired by the popular **romances** he read, stories like the heroic King Arthur tales (see pages 950–971),

in which every morning brought a new chance for glory for the knights of the Round Table. What elements of Don Quijote's story here are parodies of the old romances?

4. What stories do we read today? Do they inspire us to heroic deeds, to make the world a better place—or do they have different effects?

Share your group's conclusions in a whole-class discussion. Does everyone agree, or are there strongly different opinions? See if you can reach a consensus on some points.

FINDING COMMON GROUND

As its name suggests, this feature requires students to discover areas of agreement about elements of the selection from *Don Quijote*. Below are some possible responses to the questions.

1. People today seek love in various ways—by dedicating themselves to specific causes; by becoming involved with someone special; by taking care of a pet.

2. Most students will probably agree that searching for and finding love enhances a person's character and well-being—provided the search does not become desperate and obsessive.

3. Students may cite fighting for the love of a woman, slaying a giant (or dragon), protecting the kingdom from enemies, or assisting the weak and downtrodden.

4. Students may cite a variety of kinds of stories, including realistic fiction as well as science fiction and fantasy. Another genre that has become popular is the confessional biography or autobiography. In general, works of fiction and nonfiction can inspire heroism when the characters themselves display this quality.

Resources ———

Listening
Audio CD Library
A recording of this selection is available in the *Audio CD Library*:
• Disc 17, Track 10

Assessing Learning

Check Test: True-False

1. Don Quijote thinks his quest is incomplete without a lady to fight for. [True]
2. The knight's horse is named Rocinante. [True]
3. Don Quijote imagines that he will do battle with another knight like himself. [False]
4. He decides to call his lady Dulcinea. [True]
5. Don Quijote has impossible goals. [True]

Self-Reflection

Have students use their notes to complete the following statements.

1. I see similarities between the character of Don Quijote and _____ .
2. Compared to today's heroes, Don Quijote is _____.

To do a random evaluation, invite each student to submit one anonymous response to you; then, share several with the class.

Writer's Workshop

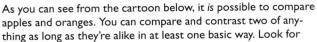

MAIN OBJECTIVE
Write a comparison/contrast essay

PROCESS OBJECTIVES

1. Use appropriate prewriting techniques to identify and develop a topic
2. Create a first draft
3. Use Evaluation Criteria as a basis for determining revision strategies
4. Revise the first draft incorporating suggestions generated by self- or peer evaluation
5. Proofread and correct errors
6. Create a final draft
7. Choose an appropriate method of publication
8. Reflect on progress as a writer

Planning

- **Block Schedule**
  Block Scheduling Lesson Plans with Pacing Guide
- **One-Stop Planner**
  CD-ROM with Test Generator

ASSIGNMENT

Write an essay comparing and contrasting two texts. The texts can be poems, stories, or essays or a combination of those forms.

AIM

To inform.

AUDIENCE

Your teacher, classmates, other English classes, readers of a magazine of student writing. (You choose.)

Relevant Features
Stories: subject, theme, plot, conflict, characters, point of view, setting, tone, style
Essays: subject, main idea or theme, purpose, subjective/objective details, tone, diction
Poems: subject, theme, imagery, figures of speech, speaker, tone, rhyme, rhythm and meter, other sound effects

580 THE POETRY COLLECTIONS

EXPOSITORY WRITING
COMPARISON/CONTRAST ESSAY

You use the skills of **comparing** (finding similarities) and **contrasting** (finding differences) all the time—to see how your sneakers are different from your friend's, to decide which TV show to watch next, to see how the war in Vietnam was different from World War II. These thinking skills—comparing and contrasting—are especially useful in talking and writing about literature. In this workshop, you'll write a **comparison/contrast essay,** which is one kind of **expository writing**—writing that explains or gives information.

Prewriting
1. Refer to Your Writer's Notebook

As you can see from the cartoon below, it *is* possible to compare apples and oranges. You can compare and contrast two of anything as long as they're alike in at least one basic way. Look for two works that are alike enough to give you something interesting to say about them. If you're not happy with the subjects you've been working on in your Writer's Notebook, choose two new ones now.

2. Find Relevant Features to Focus On

If you were judging a photography contest, the **features** you'd use to compare the photos might be lighting, color, composition, subject matter, and emotional effects. When you write about literature, finding the features is easy. You'll recognize them as the **elements of literature** you've been studying.

Resources: Print and Media

Writing and Language
- *Portfolio Management System*
  Prewriting, p. 169
  Peer Editing, p. 170
  Assessment Rubric, p. 171

- *Workshop Resources*
  Revision Strategy Teaching Notes, p. 35
  Revision Strategy Transparency 18

Assessment
  Standardized Test Preparation, p. 148

The history of the written word is rich and

3. Gather Information

Using a chart, take notes about how your works are alike and different, element by element. (The chart below shows the beginning of a comparison of two stories from the short-story collections in this book.)

Element	The Cold Equations (page 9)	The Pedestrian (page 173)
Subject	Power of technology to control our lives	Same
Message/Theme	Technology allows no room for human emotions.	Technology can limit our freedoms.
Tone	Sad, tragic	Bitter, satirical

4. Plan the Essay

You have two choices for organizing your information, and either one is fine. (See the chart on the right.)

- **Block Method**
  With this organization, you discuss the *works,* one at a time. First, you write about the elements of one work; then, you discuss the same elements in the same order for the second work.

- **Point-by-Point Method**
  With this method, you discuss the *elements,* one at a time. You might discuss the theme in work 1 and then the theme in work 2. In the next paragraph, you might talk about conflict in work 1 and then conflict in work 2. The Student Model on pages 582–583 uses the point-by-point method.

Drafting

1. Three Basic Parts

Like most essays, comparison/contrast essays have three parts:

- The **introduction**, usually a single paragraph, provides meat-and-potatoes information: titles and authors and necessary background. It also includes your **thesis statement**, in which you say briefly how the works are alike and different.

Block Method
Work 1: **"The Cold Equations"** Element 1: its subject Element 2: its theme Element 3: its tone
Work 2: **"The Pedestrian"** Element 1: its subject Element 2: its theme Element 3: its tone
Point-by-Point Method
Element 1: subject in "The Cold Equations" in "The Pedestrian"
Element 2: theme in "The Cold Equations" in "The Pedestrian"
Element 3: tone in "The Cold Equations" in "The Pedestrian"

Introducing the Writer's Workshop

- Ask students to list selections they have read that they feel are truly memorable. Next to each, write what they believe is the topic or theme. Are there two selections that share the same topic or theme? How are the two selections different?
- This activity will help to focus students on selections they may use for this assignment.

Teaching the Writer's Workshop

Read and discuss the information on Prewriting and Drafting (pp. 580–582).

Prewriting

- To help students plan, review the elements of literature that are commonly used to discuss literary works. Refer students to the boxed material on p. 581.
- Remind students to think about the audience they want to address. They also need to be sure that they define unfamiliar terms and give sufficient background information about the pieces of literature they are discussing.

Reaching All Students

Struggling Writers

Adapt the curriculum to allow students to participate actively while challenging them to meet individual goals. For example, students who have difficulty reading might bring favorite magazines to class to compare and contrast. Have them look at features such as contents, intended audience, use of color, etc. How are the magazines alike and different?

OBJECTIVES
1. Analyze and appreciate art
2. Describe the visual and emotional content of a work of art
3. Understand the composition of a painting
4. Identify the main elements of a painting: color, line, shape, and texture

Teaching the Lesson

If possible, bring art posters or books to class so that students can practice looking critically at various styles and types of art. In particular, students may be interested in seeing additional works by Renoir or by other Impressionist artists. If art books are not available, you may wish to select certain works of fine art in this text. See the Index of Art in the back of this book.

Using the Strategies

Students' responses to the painting will vary. A sample response is provided. **Content:** The painting shows a man and a woman dancing together. The position of the man's face and the expression on both his face and the woman's suggest that the man and woman are in love. Perhaps they are newlyweds. **How does the painting make me feel?** The painting makes me feel joy. **Composition:** The focus is on the couple, but particularly on the woman and her beautiful dress, which seems to form a triangle pointing to her face. The oval shape of the man's hat is complemented by the oval formed by his shoulders and her left arm. **The main elements of the painting:** The white color of the woman's dress predominates. It is highly contrasted against the dark blue of the man's suit. The man's dark beard and the woman's dark hair and red scarf are also contrasted against the woman's fair skin color. **The title:** The title is descriptive—the couple are dancing.

Reading for Life

Analyzing and Appreciating Art

Situation

You've probably noticed the fine art used in this book. Here are strategies you can use to learn more about how "to read" works of art.

Strategies

Describe the content.
- Describe *everything* you see in the painting.
- Tell what you think is happening. Do you see a "story" in the painting?

Try to pinpoint how the painting makes you feel.
- Art conveys emotions. What mood does the painting create?

Notice the composition of the painting.
- Artists take great care to draw viewers' eyes to the most important parts of the painting. This is composition: the arrangement of lines, shapes, and color.
- What do you first see in the painting—what is its *focus*? (Is it a face, a piece of light, a shape?)

Describe the main elements of the painting: colors, lines, shapes, and textures.
- **Color** helps create meaning by suggesting moods and associations. What color or colors dominate? Are certain colors repeated? What mood does the color create for you?
- What **lines** and **shapes** dominate the painting or catch your eye? Do you see curves, circles, angles? Do you see soft edges or hard edges? What **textures** do you see? What mood do these elements create?

Check the title.
- Titles of works of art are often merely descriptive (Picasso's *Three Musicians,* for example), but at times titles, such as Salvador Dali's *The Persistence of Memory,* might be revealing.

Dance at Bougival (1883) by Pierre Auguste Renoir. Oil on canvas (71⅝″ × 38⅝″).

Picture Fund, Courtesy, Museum of Fine Arts, Boston.

Using the Strategies

Apply each strategy to the Renoir painting above.

Extending the Strategies

Use these strategies to analyze another piece of fine art in this book. Be sure to discuss your "reading" of the art with other viewers.

Professional Note

About the Artist

This painting, *Le Bal à Bougival (Dance at Bougival)* by the French painter Pierre Auguste Renoir, was painted in 1883 and now hangs in the Museum of Fine Arts in Boston. Renoir is often thought of as an Impressionist painter, but this particular work comes from a time in his career when he was moving away from pure Impressionism. In this painting, Renoir uses black as a color, a technique that true Impressionists avoided. The painting showcases Renoir's ability to present women as almost floral beings whose skin tones echo the velvet texture of blossoms.

Collection 10

Dreams—Lost and Found

Theme

We Can't Live Without Them In some sense, literature is a record of humanity's dreams. The poems in this collection focus on dreams and their conflict with reality. With hard work and luck, some people manage to achieve their dreams. Others cling to their dreams and color their realities with hope; still others, looking back at their lives, long for past happiness.

Reading the Anthology

Reaching Struggling Readers

The *Reading Skills and Strategies: Reaching Struggling Readers* binder includes a Reading Strategies Handbook that offers concrete suggestions for helping students who have difficulty reading and comprehending text, or students who are reluctant readers. When a specific strategy is most appropriate for a selection, a correlation to the Handbook is provided at the bottom of the teacher's page under the head Struggling Readers. This head may also be used to introduce additional ideas for helping students read challenging texts.

Reading Beyond the Anthology

Read On An annotated bibliography of books suitable for extended reading is provided at the end of the poetry collections. The suggested books are related to works in these collections by theme, by author, or by subject. To preview the Read On for the poetry collections, please turn to p. T617.

Resources for this Collection

Note: All resources for this collection are available for preview on the *One-Stop Planner CD-ROM* 2 with *Test Generator.* All worksheets and blackline masters may be printed from the CD-ROM.

Internet Resources
go.hrw.com LE0 10-10

Selection or Feature	Reading and Literary Skills	Vocabulary, Language, and Grammar
Elements of Literature: Sound Effects (p. 588) **This is the land the Sunset washes** (p. 588) Emily Dickinson	• *Literary Elements,* Transparency 18	
Sea Fever (p. 590) John Masefield **Ex-Basketball Player** (p. 592) John Updike	• *Graphic Organizers for Active Reading,* Worksheets pp. 46, 47 • *Literary Elements:* Transparency 18 Worksheet p. 55	• *Words to Own,* Worksheet p. 34 • *Daily Oral Grammar,* Transparency 35
• **The Bean Eaters** (p. 598) • **We Real Cool** (p. 599) Gwendolyn Brooks	• *Graphic Organizers for Active Reading,* Worksheet p. 48	• *Words to Own,* Worksheet p. 34 • *Daily Oral Grammar,* Transparency 36
A Voice (p. 603) Pat Mora **Aunt Fannie Fixes Bison Bourguignon** (p. 605) Diane Glancy **Tony Went to the Bodega but He Didn't Buy Anything** (p. 607) Martín Espada **Connections: The Streets of the Barrio** (p. 610) Luis Rodriguez	• *Graphic Organizers for Active Reading,* Worksheets pp. 49, 50, 51	• *Words to Own,* Worksheet p. 34
Extending the Theme: The Ghost Dance at Wounded Knee (p. 612) *told by* Dick Fool Bull *recorded by* Richard Erdoes	The Extending the Theme feature provides students with an unstructured opportunity to practice reading strategies using a selection that extends the theme of the collection.	
Writer's Workshop: Supporting an Interpretation (p. 618)		
Sentence Workshop: Streamlining Wordy Sentences (p. 623)		• *Workshop Resources,* p. 71
Learning for Life: Presenting an Arts Festival (p. 625)		

Other Resources for this Collection

- *Cross-Curricular Activities,* p. 10
- *Portfolio Management System,* Introduction to Portfolio Assessment, p. 1
- *Formal Assessment,* Genre Test, p. 113
- *Test Generator,* Collection Test

Writing	Listening and Speaking / Viewing and Representing	Assessment
		• *Formal Assessment,* Literary Elements Test, p. 111
• *Portfolio Management System,* Rubrics for Choices, p. 172	• *Audio CD Library,* Disc 18, Tracks 2, 3 • *Portfolio Management System,* Rubrics for Choices, p. 172	• *Formal Assessment,* Selection Test, p. 107 • *Standardized Test Preparation,* p. 72 • *Test Generator (One-Stop Planner CD-ROM)*
• *Portfolio Management System,* Rubrics for Choices, p. 173	• *Audio CD Library,* Disc 18, Tracks 4, 5 • *Portfolio Management System,* Rubrics for Choices, p. 173	• *Formal Assessment,* Selection Test, p. 108 • *Test Generator (One-Stop Planner CD-ROM)*
• *Portfolio Management System,* Rubrics for Choices, p. 174	• *Visual Connections:* Videocassette B, Segment 10 • *Audio CD Library,* Disc 18, Tracks 6, 7, 8 • *Viewing and Representing:* Fine Art Transparency 14 Worksheet p. 56 • *Portfolio Management System,* Rubrics for Choices, p. 174	• *Formal Assessment,* Selection Test, p. 109 • *Test Generator (One-Stop Planner CD-ROM)*
	• *Audio CD Library,* Disc 18, Track 9	

• *Workshop Resources,* p. 39
• *Writer's Workshop 2 CD-ROM,* Interpretation
	• *Viewing and Representing,* HRW Multimedia Presentation Maker	• *Portfolio Management System*
		  • Prewriting, p. 176
		  • Peer Editing, p. 177
		  • Assessment Rubric, p. 178

		• *Portfolio Management System,* Rubrics, p. 179

 Transparency   CD-ROM   Video Audio CD

Collection Planner

Collection 10 Dreams—Lost and Found

Skills Focus

Selection or Feature	Reading Skills and Strategies	Elements of Literature	Vocabulary/Language/Grammar	Writing	Listening/Speaking	Viewing/Representing
Elements of Literature: Sound Effects (p. 588) **This is the land the Sunset washes** (p. 588) Emily Dickinson		Rhyme, p. 588 • End • Internal • Exact • Approximate Alliteration, p. 589 Onomatopoeia, p. 589				
Sea Fever (p. 590) John Masefield **Ex-Basketball Player** (p. 592) John Updike	Identify Comparisons, p. 596 Make an Inference, p. 597 Use Context Clues, p. 597	Rhythm, p. 590 Meter, p. 590 Structure, p. 592 Iambic Pentameter, p. 592 Internal Rhyme, p. 592 Alliteration, p. 592 Speaker, p. 596 Metaphor, p. 596 Personification, p. 596	Jargon/Technical Vocabulary, p. 597	Write an Essay, p. 597 Write a Poem from the Point of View of a Character, p. 597		
• **The Bean Eaters** (p. 598) • **We Real Cool** (p. 599) Gwendolyn Brooks	Identify the Speaker's Message, p. 601	Rhyme, pp. 598, 601 Irony, p. 601		Write a Poem Imitating a Model, p. 601	Prepare and Present a Reading of Two Poems, p. 601	
A Voice (p. 603) Pat Mora **Aunt Fannie Fixes Bison Bourguignon** (p. 605) Diane Glancy **Tony Went to the Bodega but He Didn't Buy Anything** (p. 607) Martín Espada		Tone, pp. 603, 610 Prose Poem, pp. 605, 610 Free Verse, pp. 607, 610 Speaker, p. 610		Interpret the Significance of a Title, p. 611 Write a Poem That Expresses a Dream, p. 611 Write About a Person, p. 611 Write a Poem About a Culture, p. 611	Engage in a Round-Table Discussion, p. 611	Draw a Story Map, p. 611
Extending the Theme: The Ghost Dance at Wounded Knee (p. 612) *told by* Dick Fool Bull *recorded by* Richard Erdoes	Dialogue with the Text, pp. 612, 616 KWL Chart, p. 612	The Extending the Theme feature provides students with an unstructured opportunity to practice reading skills using a selection that extends the theme of the collection.				
Writer's Workshop: Supporting an Interpretation (p. 618)	Paraphrase, p. 619			Write an Essay Supporting an Interpretation, pp. 618–622		
Sentence Workshop: Streamlining Wordy Sentences (p. 623)				Revising Wordy Sentences, p. 623		
Reading for Life: Interpreting Graphs (p. 624)	Types of Graphs, p. 624 Strategies, p. 624					
Learning for Life: Presenting an Arts Festival (p. 625)					Plan and Present a Poetry Reading, p. 625	Create a Documentary, p. 625

DREAMS—LOST AND FOUND

WRITING FOCUS: Supporting an Interpretation

Dreams are necessary to life.

—*Anaïs Nin*

Dreams *can* come true, but sometimes reality falls short of the dream. A family might dream of operating a farm and might work as hard as they can, but the realities of soil and weather might force them to find a new dream. Even successful dreams rarely turn out to be exactly as we imagined them. You may dream of becoming a movie star and make your dream come true—but you may also find that the life of a celebrity brings problems. The poems in this collection are about the imperfect fit between dream and reality—and the need to keep dreaming despite the imperfections.

Writer's Notebook

A dream sought by every generation in the United States is called the American Dream. What does this phrase mean to you? Jot down *your* interpretation of the phrase "American Dream." (You will have to use this kind of interpretive skill for the Writer's Workshop assignment on page 618.)

OBJECTIVES

1. Read poems on the theme "Dreams—Lost and Found"
2. Interpret literary elements used in the poems, with special emphasis on rhyme, alliteration, and onomatopoeia
3. Apply a variety of reading strategies
4. Respond to the poems in a variety of modes
5. Learn and use new words
6. Plan, draft, revise, proof, and publish an interpretive essay
7. Develop skills in streamlining wordy sentences
8. Put information into graphic form
9. Celebrate the imagination by holding a festival of the arts

Responding to the Quotation

? Do you agree that dreams are necessary to life? Why or why not?
[Possible responses: Some students may feel that dreams give a person purpose and make it easier to get through the day; they also provide an important outlet for human imagination. Other students may feel that dreams are unnecessary because they often lead to bitter disappointments and create frustrations.]

Writer's Notebook

Students may find it helpful to use a cluster diagram like the following one as a framework for their interpretations.

American Dream

Writing Focus: Supporting an Interpretation

The following **Work in Progress** assignments build to a culminating **Writer's Workshop** at the end of the collection.

- Sea Fever / Ex-Basketball Player
- The Bean Eaters / We Real Cool
- A Voice / Aunt Fannie Fixes Bison Bourguignon / Tony Went to the Bodega but He Didn't Buy Anything

Using details (p. 597)

Interpreting messages (p. 601)

Interpreting titles (p. 611)

Writer's Workshop: Expository Writing / Supporting an Interpretation (p. 618)

OBJECTIVES

Sea Fever / Ex-Basketball Player

1. Read and interpret the poems
2. Identify meter
3. Identify iambic pentameter
4. Express understanding through critical or creative writing
5. Understand and use work-related technical vocabulary, or jargon

SKILLS

Literary
- Identify meter
- Identify iambic pentameter

Writing
- Make inferences about a character from details in a poem
- Analyze sound effects in a poem
- Write a poem based on a model

Viewing/Representing
- Write a note from the viewpoint of the character in the Hopper painting (ATE)

Planning

- **Block Schedule**
  Block Scheduling Lesson Plans with Pacing Guide

- **Traditional Schedule**
  Lesson Plans Including Strategies for English-Language Learners

- **One-Stop Planner**
  CD-ROM with Test Generator

Before You Read

SEA FEVER

Make the Connection

A Sea Dream

Although supertankers and cruise ships are much taller than any sailing ship, the term *tall ship* still denotes a sailing vessel with high masts.

For millions of landlubbers, the image of a tall ship triggers dreams of romance, freedom, and adventure, just as it did for Masefield.

"The wheel's kick" in line 3 is a reference to what can happen when a sudden shift in the wind or the tide causes a ship's steering wheel to "kick over"—to spin out of control until the helmsman can grab it and put the ship back on course. "Trick" (line 12) is a sailing term for a round-trip voyage. Years ago, a "long trick" might have involved a voyage from England to China and back, a trip that could last for more than a year.

Quickwrite

Write down your initial interpretation of this poem's title. Does the title remind you of any other uses of the word *fever*? *(Keep your notes for use on pages 596–597.)*

Elements of Literature

Rhythms of the Sea

Read this famous poem aloud to hear how the poet's use of meter suggests the motion of a ship on the high seas. Where do you hear and feel the rolling rhythm of the sea swells? Where do you hear and feel the slap of waves against the ship?

> **M**eter is a pattern of stressed and unstressed syllables in poetry.
>
> *For more on Meter, see pages 558–559 and the Handbook of Literary Terms.*

 go.hrw.com
LEO 10-10

590 THE POETRY COLLECTIONS

Resources: Print and Media

Reading
- *Graphic Organizers for Active Reading,* pp. 46, 47
- *Audio CD Library* Disc 18, Tracks 2, 3

Elements of Literature
- *Literary Elements* Transparency 18 Worksheet, p. 55

Writing and Language
- *Daily Oral Grammar* Transparency 35

Assessment
- *Formal Assessment,* p. 107
- *Portfolio Management System,* p. 172
- *Standardized Test Preparation,* p. 72
- *Test Generator (One-Stop Planner CD-ROM)*

Internet
- go.hrw.com (keyword: LE0 10-10)

Sea Fever

John Masefield

I must go down to the seas again, to the lonely sea and the sky,
And all I ask is a tall ship and a star to steer her by;
And the wheel's kick and the wind's song and the white sail's shaking,
And a gray mist on the sea's face and a gray dawn breaking.

5   I must go down to the seas again, for the call of the running tide
Is a wild call and a clear call that may not be denied;
And all I ask is a windy day with the white clouds flying,
And the flung spray and the blown spume, and the sea gulls crying.

I must go down to the seas again, to the vagrant gypsy life,
To the gull's way and the whale's way where the wind's like a whetted
10   knife;
And all I ask is a merry yarn from a laughing fellow-rover.
And quiet sleep and a sweet dream when the long trick's over.

(A)

(B)
(C)

MEET THE WRITER

Sailor-Poet

John Masefield (1878–1967), born in England, was orphaned by the time he was thirteen years old. At once, as boys could do in those days, he joined the merchant navy and shipped around the world for several years. On a trip to New York, he jumped ship and lived for a time in the city as what we'd call today a homeless person. He began to write poetry after coming across a collection of Chaucer's *Canterbury Tales* in a New York bookstore.

Masefield is best remembered today for poems inspired by the years he spent as a sea-man, first on windjammers in the last days of the sailing ships and then on tramp steamers and ocean liners. No one has better evoked for the landlubber the sense of freedom and adventure, the taste of salt and spray associated with sailing "before the mast," or the pride that marked the crews of even the rustiest and dingiest of freighters.

For more than thirty years, Masefield served as Britain's poet laureate. Of his passion for sailing ships, the poet said:

66 They were the only youth I had, and the only beauty I knew in my youth, and now that I am old, not many greater beauties seem to be in the world. 99

SEA FEVER **591**

Reaching All Students

Struggling Readers
Some words in this poem might puzzle today's readers. Explain that *spume* means "foam" or "froth" and refers to the foam of the waves. *Whetted* means "sharpened as if on an old-fashioned whetstone." Ask students how the wind could be sharp. [A cold wind cuts through you like a knife.] Finally, make sure students realize that *yarn* in the context of l. 11 means "exaggerated story or tall tale."

English Language Learners
Students who are unfamiliar with the sea would benefit from hearing an audiotape of sea sounds before reading the poem. Students who have emigrated from islands or coastal nations may have memories of the sea to share. Ask them to explain the concept of sailing (navigating) by the stars or the term *running tide* (tide that carries one quickly out to sea).

Summary ■

In this hypnotic poem, the speaker hears "the call of the running tide" luring him back to the sea. Through vivid imagery —from gray mist to blown spume to crying gulls—Masefield conveys the speaker's feverish longing for the adventurous life he left behind.

Resources ————

Listening
Audio CD Library
The meter of this poem is so mesmerizing it can stay with you for a lifetime. To hear its rhythms, play the track in the *Audio CD Library:*
• Disc 18, Track 2

(A) Elements of Literature
Meter
Read the first line of the poem aloud, and then scan it on the chalkboard so students can hear and then see the pattern of stressed and unstressed syllables.
[I must go down to the seas again, to the lonely sea and the sky,]
Then ask students to select a line from the entire poem whose meter best captures the feel of the ocean's billowing swells. [Answers will vary, although many students will probably choose l. 1, 3, or 8.]

(B) Struggling Readers
Using Context Clues
Ask students to figure out the meaning of *vagrant,* using context, such as the nearby word *gypsy* and on l. 11 *fellow-rover.* [Both a rover and a gypsy are roamers or wanderers. *Vagrant* means "wandering."] Ask why this word is important to the poem's meaning. [Possible response: The speaker dreams of recapturing the carefree, adventurous life he once led.]

(C) Elements of Literature
Alliteration
❓ What aspect of life at sea is suggested by the repeated *w* and *wh* sounds? [the sound of the wind]

Summary ■

This lyric poem depicts the drab life of a former high school basketball star. Stuck in a dead-end job as a gas station attendant, Flick Webb lives in the past, with only the memories of his "glory days" to sustain him. The speaker senses an air of regret around Webb, who now clowns with an inner tube or loiters in a luncheonette.

FROM THE EDITOR'S DESK

The theme of this poem may strike a nerve with students who dream of an athletic career after high school. Be sensitive to students' aspirations while pointing out that many high school athletes do not achieve stardom.

Resources

Listening
Audio CD Library
For a recording of this poem, see the *Audio CD Library:*
• Disc 18, Track 3

Ⓐ Elements of Literature
Iambic Pentameter
Help students scan the third line and identify the five iambs.
[Before it has a chance to go two blocks]
Then ask the class to identify the lines in the first stanza that deviate from the meter. [ll. 1, 2, and 4]

Ⓑ Historical Connections
Students may be unfamiliar with the rounded, "bubble-head style" of gas pumps. To help them understand the metaphor comparing the pumps to high school basketball and football players, refer them to the artwork on p. 593. Also point out that the letters *E-S-S-O* spell Esso, the former name of the Exxon gasoline company.

Before You Read

Ex-Basketball Player

Make the Connection

Stuck in a Past Dream

Sometimes people get stuck in dreams of their past. They keep looking backward instead of forward. Every school has a sports hero, someone who is a "natural" at the game. But like the glittering stars whose brilliance fades overnight, some of these bright heroes seem to dim after graduation. Do you recognize Flick Webb in this poem?

Quickwrite

How important are school athletics to you? Do you think they prepare young people for life? Why? Jot down a brief response. *(Keep your notes for use on pages 596–597.)*

Elements of Literature

Sound Effects

Even though Updike's poem sounds free and conversational, it's really written within a tight **structure.** The basic beat is **iambic pentameter**—five iambs (˘ ´) to a line. This meter is closest to the rhythm of everyday English speech, and its use gives the poem an informal, conversational sound. You'll find the same meter providing the beat in a poem written centuries before Updike's—

Shakespeare's sonnet on page 561. Updike uses other sound devices: **Internal rhymes** and **alliteration** lend his unrhymed poem verbal music. Read it aloud.

> **I**ambic pentameter is a line of poetry made up of five iambs. An **iamb** contains one unstressed syllable followed by a stressed syllable.
>
> *For more on Meter, see pages 558–559 and the Handbook of Literary Terms.*

Ex-Basketball Player

John Updike

Pearl Avenue runs past the high-school lot,
Bends with the trolley tracks, and stops, cut off
Ⓐ Before it has a chance to go two blocks,
   At Colonel McComsky Plaza. Berth's Garage
5 Is on the corner facing west, and there,
   Most days, you'll find Flick Webb, who helps Berth out.

   Flick stands tall among the idiot pumps—
   Five on a side, the old bubble-head style,
   Their rubber elbows hanging loose and low.
10 Ⓑ One's nostrils are two S's, and his eyes
   An E and O. And one is squat, without
   A head at all—more of a football type.

   Once Flick played for the high-school team, the Wizards.
   He was good: in fact, the best. In '46

Reaching All Students

English Language Learners

For students unfamiliar with the game of basketball, play a videotape of a recent high school, college, or professional game. Have students who are familiar with the rules explain the scoring system of baskets, free throws, and three pointers and demonstrate moves such as dribbling and dunking. To put Flick's achievements in perspective, explain that the best professionals in the NBA average only 34 points a game. In addition, be sure that students know

that tires had inner tubes until fairly recently and that the brand names referred to in the last lines are types of candy.

Advanced Students

Have students compare the treatment of the theme of fading youthful glory in two of the following: the documentary film *Hoop Dreams,* the Bruce Springsteen song "Glory Days," the A. E. Housman poem "To an Athlete Dying Young." Allow students to suggest other possibilities.

Gas (1940) by Edward Hopper.
Oil on canvas (26¼″ × 40¼″).

The Museum of Modern Art, New York.
Mrs. Simon Guggenheim Fund. Photograph ©2000
The Museum of Modern Art, New York.

15   He bucketed three hundred ninety points,
    A county record still. The ball loved Flick.
    I saw him rack up thirty-eight or forty
    In one home game. His hands were like wild birds. **C**

    He never learned a trade, he just sells gas,
20   Checks oil, and changes flats. Once in a while,
    As a gag, he dribbles an inner tube,
    But most of us remember anyway.
    His hands are fine and nervous on the lug wrench.
    It makes no difference to the lug wrench, though.

25   Off work, he hangs around Mae's luncheonette.
    Grease-gray and kind of coiled, he plays pinball, **D**
    Smokes thin cigars, and nurses lemon phosphates.
    Flick seldom says a word to Mae, just nods
    Beyond her face toward bright applauding tiers **E**
30   Of Necco Wafers, Nibs, and Juju Beads.

EX-BASKETBALL PLAYER   593

C Appreciating Language

Technical Language

Have students speculate about the meanings of the terms *bucketed* and *rack up*. Then ask them to read the third stanza and see if these meanings make sense in the context of the poem. [*Bucketed* means "scored baskets"; *rack up* means "gain" or "collect."]

D Reading Skills and Strategies

Making Inferences

? What does the phrase "Grease-gray and kind of coiled" suggest about Flick's personality? [Possible response: His work has changed his appearance, but he seems constantly ready for action, or tensed. Gray suggests dullness.]

E Elements of Literature

Irony

? What is ironic about the poem's last three lines? [Possible response: Since he no longer has a real audience, Flick imagines that the rows of candy are applauding him.]

RESPONDING TO THE ART

American artist **Edward Hopper** (1882–1967) is one of the great realist painters of the twentieth century. The figures that inhabit his paintings convey a strong sense of alienation, isolation, and loneliness.

Activity. Ask students to imagine they're the man in *Gas,* and have them write a note responding to Updike's poem.

Skill Link

Adjusting Reading Strategies

Tell students that they can benefit from reading a poem several times, adjusting their reading strategy each time according to their purpose. Model this skill with "Ex-Basketball Player" as follows:

1. Read the poem aloud at a normal conversational rate, and have students give their initial responses to Updike's description of Flick Webb.
2. Now read the poem aloud slowly, with an emphasis on its meter. Tell students that this type of second reading is a good way to recognize and analyze a poem's rhyme and meter.
3. Point out that a careful silent reading is often necessary to interpret a poem's meaning. As students reread the poem silently, encourage them to stop, reread, and start again in order to obtain as much meaning as possible.
4. Finally, invite students to read the poem aloud again for their own enjoyment.

Using Students' Strengths

Kinesthetic Learners

Pairs of students may enjoy role-playing a scene between Flick Webb and a former teammate who has pulled into the service station for gas. Students can improvise or prepare a dialogue and use gestures, body language, tone of voice, and facial expressions to show each character's personality and behavior.

Selection Assessment
Formal Assessment
• Selection Test, p. 107
Test Generator (One-Stop Planner)
• CD-ROM

BROWSING IN THE FILES

About the Author. One of America's great contemporary writers, John Updike has written nearly fifty books since his volume of poems *The Carpentered Hen* appeared in 1958. Both "Ex-Basketball Player" and "Ace in the Hole"—a short story collected in *The Same Door* in 1959—can be seen as early sketches of Harry "Rabbit" Angstrom, Updike's most famous former high school athlete. About his subjects Updike writes, "The idea of a hero is aristocratic. Now either nobody is a hero or everyone is. I vote for everyone. My subject is the American Protestant small town middle class."

A Critic's Comment. The critic Richard Rupp found the following strengths in Updike's early work: "One reason for Updike's success rests on his celebrated style, a restless, exhaustive exploration of minute physical detail. . . ." Invite students to evaluate this comment in light of "Ex-Basketball Player."

MEET THE WRITER

Observer of American Life

John Updike (1932–   ) was born in the small town of Shillington, Pennsylvania. A year after he graduated from Harvard University, he got a job on the staff of *The New Yorker* magazine, which has published much of his writing ever since.

Though he has won fame for his novels and short stories, Updike is also a poet of great wit and craft. He is particularly drawn to occasional poetry—pieces inspired by odd or funny incidents reported in the newspapers or observed in the American suburban landscape of housing developments, service stations, and supermarkets. Despite his humorous approach, Updike is a sharp social observer and a serious moralist.

Among the most successful of Updike's novels are the Rabbit tales (the last two won Pulitzer Prizes): *Rabbit, Run* (1960), *Rabbit Redux* (1971), *Rabbit Is Rich* (1981), and *Rabbit at Rest* (1991). These novels chronicle the life of Harry "Rabbit" Angstrom, an ex-basketball player. Rabbit lives an outwardly conventional life in a small Pennsylvania town, but his hidden yearnings and disappointing relationships reveal the uncertainties of contemporary American life.

In accepting the American Book Award in 1982, Updike spoke to young writers:

66 Have faith. May you surround yourselves with parents, editors, mates, and children as supportive as mine have been. But the essential support and encouragement of course comes from within, arising out of the mad notion that your society needs to know what only you can tell it. 99

Assessing Learning

Standardized Test Preparation
For practice with standardized test format specific to this selection, see
• *Standardized Test Preparation,* p. 72
For practice in proofreading and editing, see
• *Daily Oral Grammar,* Transparency 35

Check Test: Questions and Answers
"Sea Fever"
1. Where does the speaker wish he could be? [at sea, on a sailing ship]
2. What appeals to him most about a seafaring life? [the sense of adventure, being free to roam, being close to nature]

"Ex-Basketball Player"
3. What is Flick Webb's claim to fame? [He was an outstanding high school basketball player.]
4. Where does Flick work? [at a gas station]
5. What does he think of while he works? [his past feats on the basketball court]

I Want to Be Somebody

Let me take you back to when I was just
  a child
with big wants and dreams,
but no one to encourage me on how   30
  to reach them.

5 I wanted to be a doctor
I wanted to be a teacher
I wanted to be the president
I wanted to be noticed
I wanted to be noticed

"You little Black child,
10 You ain't neva gonna be nobody.
You have big dreams.
Do you hear what I'm saying?
You ain't gonna be nobody."

I wanted to be a doctor
15 I wanted to be a teacher
I wanted to be the president
I wanted to be noticed
I wanted to be noticed

"You think you something!
20 You ain't no betta than nobody else.
You think you too good to get your hands
  dirty?
Black child, all you doing is dreamin'.
You ain't gonna be nobody."

I wanted to be the president
25 I wanted to be a millionaire
I wanted to be famous
I wanted to be noticed

"Yeah, I knew her when she was just a
  little sweet thang.
I knew she was gonna be somebody.
30 I even remember tellin' her
she was gonna be somebody."

I'm 4th in the nation
I'm 2nd in the nation as a forward
I'm 1st in the West Coast
35 I'm Angel Bagley #44
the best female basketball player in the
  West

I wanted to be the president
I wanted to be a millionaire
I wanted to be famous
40 I wanted to be noticed

All I wanted was to be somebody
I wanted to be somebody
I wanna be somebody
I'm somebody
45 I'm somebody

—Angel Bagley
Thomas Jefferson High School
Portland, Oregon

Student to Student

Angel Bagley's poem tells of her desire and determination to become somebody and to be noticed. She possesses a strong drive to succeed, even though she receives no encouragement. Her persistence helps her to realize her dream and, in the end, allows her to say "I'm somebody."

Ⓐ Critical Thinking
Expressing an Opinion
❓ Should adults encourage young people to pursue their dreams? Why or why not? [Sample responses: Yes, because encouragement from an older person is inspiring; no, because the strength to accomplish dreams comes from inside.]

Ⓑ Elements of Literature
Refrain
❓ What does the repetition of the lines "I wanted to be . . ." show about the speaker? [Possible response: The repetition shows the speaker's determination.]

Ⓒ Reading Skills and Strategies
Making Inferences
❓ Why has the tone of the poem's other voice suddenly changed in ll. 28–31? [Possible response: Now that the speaker is famous, everyone wants to take credit for encouraging her.]

Ⓓ Appreciating Language
Verb Tenses
❓ How do the changes in tense in the last five lines show a progression from dreams to reality? [*Wanted* shows a past desire; *wanna* shows a present desire; and the verb a*m (I'm)* shows that the speaker has arrived at her goal.]

Connecting Across Texts

Connecting with "Ex-Basketball Player"
Invite students to discuss how this student work connects with Updike's poem. How does the poet's dream in "I Want to Be Somebody" compare and contrast with Flick's dream in "Ex-Basketball Player"? [Possible responses: Angel is a highly ranked player at the time the poem is written, so she has fulfilled her dream of being noticed; Flick's days of being noticed on the basketball court are in the past. Some students may believe that Angel's success, like Flick's, may not last unless she is lucky or plans her future carefully. Others may argue that Angel seems more determined than Flick, so she may escape his fate.]

Making the Connections

Connecting to the Theme:
"Dreams—Lost and Found"
Have students review the poems and describe the ways in which all three poems connect with the theme. [Possible responses: The speaker of "Sea Fever" dreams of returning to a way of life at sea that he has lost. In "Ex-Basketball Player," Flick has lost his youthful stardom and now is reduced to dreaming about those past glories. In contrast, the speaker of "I Want to Be Somebody" is in the process of realizing her dream.]

MAKING MEANINGS

First Thoughts

1. When reading "Sea Fever," students might visualize a clear and windy day along a rocky seacoast. They might also visualize the tall masts of a sailing ship that is slapping through the waves. When reading "Ex-Basketball Player," students might see a younger Flick playing in a game; an old gas station; or a luncheonette with a pinball machine.

Shaping Interpretations

2. Possible response: The speaker in Masefield's poem is consumed by a fever to escape his daily routine. Other "fevers" students could mention include "gold-rush fever" and "Saturday night fever," as well as love and homesickness.

3. The speaker longs so badly to get to sea that many readers might suppose he leads a life full of drudgery.

4. The speaker compares life to a lengthy round-trip ocean voyage. The speaker wishes for an afterlife that resembles a quiet, refreshing slumber full of sweet dreams.

5. The street is cut off by a plaza, just as Flick's stardom was cut off after high school; the street doesn't go very far, just as Flick's basketball career never went very far.

6. The pumps are "Five on a side," like basketball players; they hold their "elbows hanging loose and low," again like basketball players. The word "idiot" modifies "pumps," which may be an unkind comment on Flick and other athletes. Flick "stands tall" among them, however, suggesting he had the ability to accomplish more than he did.

7. Flick sees the candy as a crowd at a basketball game. The personification suggests that Flick still fantasizes about being a star. He still is clinging to his old dreams, although they are not likely to come true at this point.

Connecting with the Text

8. Students may say they would try to get Flick interested in doing something else in the field of sports, such as coaching a basketball team or scouting; others may say they would try to convince Flick to transfer the energy he uses in remembering into planning for the future.

MAKING MEANINGS

SEA FEVER
EX-BASKETBALL PLAYER

First Thoughts

[respond]

1. What picture did you *see* as you read each poem?

Shaping Interpretations

[infer]

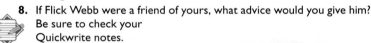

2. In what ways is the **speaker** of Masefield's poem in the grip of a "fever"? (Check your Quickwrite interpretation of the title.) Can you think of other "fevers"—like mountain fever or spring fever?

[infer/speculate]

3. Given the intensity of his feelings, what do you think the life of the speaker of "Sea Fever" is like?

[analyze]

4. In the final line of "Sea Fever," what **metaphor** describes life in terms of a sea voyage? What sort of afterlife does this speaker dream of?

[synthesize]

5. In "Ex-Basketball Player," look back at the opening description of Pearl Avenue. How can this street be seen as a **metaphor** for Flick's life?

[compare]

6. In stanza 2 of Updike's poem, find words that **personify** the gas pumps. Do you think Flick is similar to the pumps—why or why not?

[interpret]

7. In the last stanza of "Ex-Basketball Player," what is the candy **compared** to, and who sees it that way? What do you think this suggests about Flick's fantasies—or dreams?

Connecting with the Text

[connect]

8. If Flick Webb were a friend of yours, what advice would you give him? Be sure to check your Quickwrite notes.

Extending the Text

[compare]

9. How does Flick **compare** with the speaker in "I Want to Be Somebody" (page 595)?

596 THE POETRY COLLECTIONS

Extending the Text

9. While Flick seems passive, almost fatalistic, about his future, the speaker in "I Want to Be Somebody" works hard for her success and demonstrates pride in her accomplishments. Students may speculate that even if her basketball glory fades, Angel will have the determination to find and follow another dream.

CHOICES: Building Your Portfolio

Writer's Notebook

1. Collecting Ideas for an Interpretation

Using details. Make an **inference**, or informed guess, about why Flick lives the way he does. Jot down details from the poem that give clues to Flick's character and motives, and then list the inferences you can draw from these details. Save your notes.

Critical Thinking

2. What Makes It Tick?

Write a brief essay in which you discuss the **sound effects** of one of these poems—"Sea Fever" or "Ex-Basketball Player." First, on a separate piece of paper, type the poem you are examining (be sure to leave extra space between the lines). Then, scan the poem to see if you can determine its **meter.** (Reading aloud will help.) Next, circle all the **rhymes** and examples of **alliteration.** Is there a **refrain**? In your essay, describe how the poem's sound effects "work" and what they contribute to the poem as a whole.

Creative Writing

3. Flick's Poem

Imitate the structure of the student poem on page 595, and let Flick speak. You could keep the title "I Want to Be Somebody" and the first line if you think they work.

VOCABULARY   HOW TO OWN A WORD

Context Clues

When you come across unfamiliar **technical words,** look for **clues** in the words' **context** that will help you make an educated guess about meaning. For example, suppose you know nothing about basketball. What clues in Updike's poem would help you figure out what his basketball jargon means?

Remember: Always check your guesses in a dictionary. Sometimes context delivers no clues at all.

Jargon: Technical Vocabulary on the Job

Jargon is the specialized words, or **technical vocabulary,** used by people in particular jobs or groups. Doctors have jargon, as do athletes, actors, computer users, and sailors. Jargon often uses language in playful, imaginative ways—for example, "dunking" a basketball (as you might a doughnut) or, better yet, "slam-dunking" it.

Look at the sample chart below for the word *dunk*. Set up a chart similar to the one for *dunk* to study each of the basketball terms Updike uses in his poem. If you're hooked on sports jargon, do the same for other sports terms.

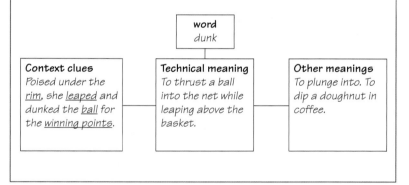

Rubrics for each Choices assignment appear on p. 172 in the *Portfolio Management System.*

CHOICES: Building Your Portfolio

1. **Writer's Notebook**   Remind students to save their work. It can be used as prewriting for the Writer's Workshop on p. 618.
2. **Critical Thinking**   If you have not already done so, demonstrate the process of scanning a poem by writing two lines of one of these poems on the chalkboard, reading them aloud, and marking the stressed and unstressed syllables.
3. **Creative Writing**   To help students get started, suggest that they imagine Flick revealing his feelings to a best friend, girlfriend, or former coach. What would he want that person to know about who he really is and how he really feels? What kind of help might he ask that person for?

VOCABULARY
Possible Answers

Word—*bucketed;* Context clues—*Three hundred ninety points;* Technical meaning—*Scored or threw into the basket;* Other meanings—*Carried.*
Word—*rack up;* Context clues—*Thirty-eight or forty;* Technical meaning—*To collect, achieve, or gain;* Other meanings—*To beat decisively.*
Word—*dribbles;* Context clues—*An inner tube, as a gag;* Technical meaning—*Bounces a ball or other object;* Other meanings—*Trickles.*

OBJECTIVES

The Bean Eaters / We Real Cool

1. Read and interpret the poems
2. Analyze rhyme
3. Express understanding through writing or speaking/listening

SKILLS

Literary
- Analyze rhyme

Reading
- Monitor comprehension

Writing
- Interpret the poems' messages
- Write a poem modeled on "We Real Cool"

Speaking/Listening
- Present a group reading

Viewing/Representing
- Speculate about characters in a painting (ATE)

Planning

- **Block Schedule**
  Block Scheduling Lesson Plans with Pacing Guide

- **Traditional Schedule**
  Lesson Plans Including Strategies for English-Language Learners

- **One-Stop Planner**
  CD-ROM with Test Generator

Resources

Listening
Audio CD Library
For a reading of "The Bean Eaters" and "We Real Cool," respectively, see the *Audio CD Library:*
- Disc 18, Track 4
- Disc 18, Track 5

THE BEAN EATERS
WE REAL COOL

Make the Connection

Slices of Life

Old people eating beans off chipped plates; young people playing pool. The old people spend their time remembering; the pool players spend their time acting cool. What happened to their dreams?

Quickwrite

Read the poems aloud several times, and imagine how the old couple and the young people look, dress, and move. Jot down what you visualize. *(Keep your notes for use on page 601.)*

Elements of Literature

Rhyme

Read both poems aloud to hear Brooks's use of **rhyme**. Is there a regular pattern of rhymes in each poem?

> **R**hyme is the repetition of accented vowel sounds and all sounds following them in words that are close together in a poem.
>
> *For more on Rhyme, see pages 588–589 and the Handbook of Literary Terms.*

go.hrw.com
LE0 10-10

Waiting Room (1984) by Phoebe Beasley. Collage (36″ × 36″).

Courtesy Mr. and Mrs. Samuel Casey, Chicago.

The Bean Eaters

Gwendolyn Brooks

They eat beans mostly, this old yellow pair.
Dinner is a casual affair.
A Plain chipware on a plain and creaking wood,
Tin flatware.

5   Two who are Mostly Good.
Two who have lived their day,
But keep on putting on their clothes
And putting things away.

And remembering . . .
10 **B** Remembering, with twinklings and twinges,
As they lean over the beans in their rented back room that
     is full of beads and receipts and dolls and cloths, tobacco
     crumbs, vases and fringes.

Resources: Print and Media

Reading
- *Graphic Organizers for Active Reading,* p. 48
- *Audio CD Library*
  Disc 18, Tracks 4, 5

Writing and Language
- *Daily Oral Grammar*
  Transparency 36

Assessment
- *Formal Assessment,* p. 108
- *Portfolio Management System,* p. 173
- *Test Generator (One-Stop Planner CD-ROM)*

Internet
- go.hrw.com (keyword: LE0 10-10)

We Real Cool

**The Pool Players.
Seven at The Golden Shovel.**

We real cool. We
Left school. We

Lurk late. We
Strike straight. We

Sing sin. We
Thin gin. We

Jazz June. We
Die soon.

—Gwendolyn Brooks

Summary ■ ■

The subjects of "The Bean Eaters" are a poor elderly couple whose dreams are behind them. The speaker evokes a bittersweet mood by describing their simple daily routines. They get dressed, eat beans off chipped plates, tidy up, and live through their memories.

A Appreciating Language
Invented Words

❓ What image of the couple's dining does the invented word *chipware* suggest? [It suggests that the couple have used their everyday plates for so long the plates are chipped; the image suggests habit, age, and poverty.]

B Critical Thinking
Interpreting

❓ How does the phrase "with twinklings and twinges" and the list of objects in ll. 12–13 affect the mood of the poem? [Possible responses: They brighten the mood by suggesting that the couple had had good times amidst the difficulties; or they make the old couple's pleasures and pains seem more pathetic.]

Summary ■ ■

The speakers of "We Real Cool" are young pool players. Although these young people boast about dropping out of school and doing "cool" things, such as staying out late and drinking, they know they are going to die soon.

C Elements of Literature
Rhyme

Brooks writes free verse "dotting a little rhyme here and there...." Ask students to find the internal rhyme in this stanza. [*late, straight*]

D Critical Thinking
Recognizing Author's Motivation

❓ What message is Brooks sending to young people in this poem? [Sample answers: She is suggesting that a "cool" lifestyle can end in early death; she hopes to convince other "pool players" to change their ways.]

Reaching All Students

English Language Learners
Although the "old yellow pair" in "The Bean Eaters" is an African American couple, be sure students understand the poem could be about any elderly couple living on a limited income. Point out that the expression "strike straight" in "We Real Cool" refers to striking the pool ball with a cue, although the phrase has other threatening connotations.

Advanced Learners
Remind students that each word in "The Bean Eaters" is carefully chosen. Have them analyze how line lengths and the more regular meter of stanza 2 and the piled-up words in stanza 3 mirror the content of each stanza.
[Possible responses: The regular rhyme and rhythm in stanza 2 reflect the couple's orderly daily routine; the long, loose lines in stanza 3 reflect the piles of mementos they have accumulated over the years.]

About the Author. In 1950, Gwendolyn Brooks became the first African American writer to win a Pulitzer Prize. Her poetry focuses on ordinary people in ordinary lives. As Brooks points out, however, she discovered early in life that "what was common could also be a flower." The idea that something common can be beautiful is essential to what Brooks calls her "G.B. voice." That voice has reached readers, young and old, for almost fifty years.

A Critic's Comment. According to the editors of *African American Writers,* "The Bean Eaters" treats a familiar theme in Brooks's poetry: ". . . the notion of the tiny, cramped physical and emotional space of the poor, which can be redeemed by the power of memory or the imagination to provide 'a streak or two streaks of sun. . . .'"

MAKING MEANINGS

First Thoughts

1. Possible responses: The characters in each poem seem sad, empty, and lonely; each poem conveys respect for the people described. (Students' responses usually change after a second reading.)

Shaping Interpretations

2. Possible response: The most important word in "The Bean Eaters" might be "remembering." The most important phrase in "We Real Cool" might be "die soon."

3. The bean eaters are old, quiet, "Mostly Good" people who do not have much money and live in memories of the past. The pool players are loud, self destructive, possibly dangerous young adults who live for the moment. Neither group has dreams for the future.

MEET THE WRITER
Chicago's Voice

Gwendolyn Brooks (1917–   ) was born in Topeka, Kansas, but for most of her life, she has been associated with Chicago, especially with its large African American population. Skilled in many different kinds of poetry, Brooks writes with both formal elegance and an ear for the natural speech rhythms of the people of Chicago's South Side. In an interview, Brooks answered questions about her work:

Q. Why do you write poetry?

A. I like the concentration, the crush; I like working with language, as others like working with paints and clay or notes.

Q. Has much of your poetry a racial element?

A. Yes. It is organic, not imposed. It is my privilege to state "Negroes" not as curios but as people.

Q. What is your poet's premise (basic principle)?

A. "Vivify the contemporary fact," said Whitman. I like to vivify the *universal* fact, when it occurs to me. But the universal wears contemporary clothing very well.

Book by Brooks
Brooks's novel *Maud Martha* (1953) is made up of a series of episodes that follow a young black girl as she grows up and finds her dream.

600

Assessing Learning

Check Test: True-False
"The Bean-Eaters"
1. The couple dine formally. [False]
2. This couple's accomplishments are behind them. [True]
3. Remembering is both pleasurable and painful for the pair. [True]

"We Real Cool"
4. The speaker is a high school student. [False]
5. The pool players have a dim future. [True]

Standardized Test Preparation
For practice in proofreading and editing, see
• *Daily Oral Grammar,* Transparency 36

MAKING MEANINGS

THE BEAN EATERS
WE REAL COOL

First Thoughts

[respond]

1. What were the first things you thought about after reading each poem? Try reading each poem a second time. Do your thoughts change?

Shaping Interpretations

[evaluate]

2. What do you think is the most important word or phrase in each poem?

[compare]

3. Are the bean eaters and the pool players alike at all? Explain. (Refer to your Quickwrite notes.)

[infer]

4. **Irony** is a discrepancy between expectations and reality. Do you think the poet believes the pool players are really "cool"? Why?

[interpret]

5. Were you surprised at the last thing the pool players say? Why do you think they believe they'll "die soon"?

[analyze]

6. How does Brooks use **rhyme** in each poem?

Extending the Text

[connect]

7. Are people like the bean eaters and the pool players found in our world today? Explain your response.

CHOICES: Building Your Portfolio

Writer's Notebook

1. Collecting Ideas for an Interpretation

Interpreting messages. What messages or social commentary do you find in these two poems? Take notes on the messages you find in each poem and on how they connect with life today. Save your notes for possible use in the workshop on page 618.

Creative Writing

2. Strike It Up in Spondees

"We Real Cool" may be the only poem in English written entirely in **spondees**. A spondee is two strongly accented syllables. Read the poem aloud. Are there any unaccented syllables? Try to write your own poem in imitation of "We Real Cool." You could open with Brooks's title. Who will your speakers be?

Speaking and Listening

3. A Reading

With a group, prepare and present these two poems in class. You'll have to decide if you'll use a single voice or several voices or even a chorus. You'll also have to decide if you'll use music as background. Be sure to prepare scripts indicating where your speakers will pause and how they'll vary their volume. Ask the audience to evaluate the class performances.

THE BEAN EATERS / WE REAL COOL 601

Shaping Interpretations (continued)

4. The poet suggests a tragic awareness of the pool players' live-fast, die-young attitude. She uses the word "cool" ironically.

5. The last line is a shock because the rhythm and rhymes make the poem seem lighthearted. The poem ends suddenly, with a sense of horror. The young people are living too hard and fast to last long; or they don't believe they have a future.

6. In "The Bean Eaters," Brooks uses end rhyme at least once in each stanza and links the first two stanzas with an exact rhyme (*wood/good*). In "We Real Cool," she uses internal rhyme in each stanza. (For a review of rhyme, see p. 588.)

Extending the Text

7. People who are old and have limited incomes, like the bean eaters, can be found today in many places. Sadly, young people without a sense of direction, like the pool players, exist in cities and towns all over the country.

Grading Timesaver

Rubrics for each Choices assignment appear on p. 173 in the *Portfolio Management System*.

CHOICES: Building Your Portfolio

1. Writer's Notebook Remind students to save their work for use in the Writer's Workshop on p. 618.

2. Creative Writing Encourage students to write about a group that arouses in them the same feelings Brooks has for the pool players.

3. Speaking and Listening Have students write directions for their reading performance on copies of the poem.

Making the Connections

Connecting to the Theme: "Dreams—Lost and Found"

The bean eaters' dreams are over. Perhaps they never found what they once dreamed of, but the past is rich with meaning and emotion for them. The subjects of "We Real Cool" have no dreams. They haven't lived long enough to have the kinds of memories that the bean eaters share, and it appears unlikely that they will live that long. Without dreams, these youths are doomed.

Getting Students Involved

Performing a Dialogue

The Way They Were. Ask partners to imagine that some memento, such as a receipt or a piece of cloth, sparks the bean eaters' memories of the past. Have the pair improvise a dialogue of the couple reliving their memories. Groups of three students could improvise a conversation between the couple and one of the young pool players.

**A Voice / Aunt Fannie Fixes . . . /
Tony Went to the Bodega . . .**

1. Read and interpret the poems
2. Identify tone
3. Analyze a prose poem
4. Identify free verse
5. Express understanding through writing, speaking and listening, or visuals

SKILLS

Literary
- Identify tone
- Analyze a prose poem
- Identify free verse

Writing
- Interpret a poem's title
- Write about a dream in a free-verse poem or a prose poem
- Write about a courageous person
- Write a poem about community

Speaking/Listening
- Role-play a round-table discussion

Visual Literacy/Mapping
- Map a character's life journey

Viewing/Representing
- Compare characters in a painting with those in a poem (ATE)

Planning

- **Block Schedule**
  Block Scheduling Lesson Plans with Pacing Guide
- **Traditional Schedule**
  Lesson Plans Including Strategies for English-Language Learners
- **One-Stop Planner**
  CD-ROM with Test Generator

The Spanish Family (1943) by Alice Neel. Oil on canvas (34″ × 28″).

© The Estate of Alice Neel. Courtesy Robert Miller Gallery, New York.

602 THE POETRY COLLECTIONS

 — Resources: Print and Media —

Reading
- *Graphic Organizers for Active Reading,* pp. 49, 50, 51
- *Audio CD Library*
  Disc 18, Tracks 6, 7, 8

Viewing and Representing
- *Viewing and Representing*
  Fine Art Transparency 14
  Fine Art Worksheet, p. 56

- *Visual Connections*
  Videocassette B, Segment 10

Assessment
- *Formal Assessment,* p. 109
- *Portfolio Management System,* p. 174
- *Test Generator (One-Stop Planner CD-ROM)*

Internet
- go.hrw.com (keyword: LE0 10-10)

A VOICE

Make the Connection

"This Is America, Mom"

Dreams take work. Sometimes that work requires courage. Perhaps it's the courage to move to a new country. Perhaps it's the courage to learn a new language. Pat Mora sees courage in something her mother did as a child. (Mora's mother grew up in El Paso, Texas. At home, the family spoke Spanish.)

Quickwrite

Write the name of someone who has fulfilled a dream. State what you admire about this person. *(Keep your notes for use on page 611.)*

Elements of Literature

Tone: What's the Attitude?

People reveal attitudes in the **tones** of their voices. They may sound humorous or sarcastic, cheerful or angry, sharp or sweet, bitter or sad. Read "A Voice" aloud. Do you hear more than one tone?

Tone is the attitude a writer takes toward the reader, a subject, or a character. In writing, tone is revealed by word choice.

For more on Tone, see the Handbook of Literary Terms.

---

go.hrw.com
LEO 10-10

A Voice

Pat Mora

Even the lights on the stage unrelenting
as the desert sun couldn't hide the other
students, their eyes also unrelenting,
students who spoke English every night

5   as they ate their meat, potatoes, gravy.
Not you. In your house that smelled like
rose powder, you spoke Spanish formal
as your father, the judge without a courtroom

in the country he floated to in the dark
10   on a flatbed truck. He walked slow
as a hot river down the narrow hall
of your house. You never dared to race past him

to say, "Please move," in the language
you learned effortlessly, as you learned to run,
15   the language forbidden at home, though your mother
said you learned it to fight with the neighbors.

You liked winning with words. You liked
writing speeches about patriotism and democracy.
You liked all the faces looking at you, all those eyes.
20   "How did I do it?" you ask me now. "How did I do it

when my parents didn't understand?"
The family story says your voice is the voice
of an aunt in Mexico, spunky as a peacock.
Family stories sing of what lives in the blood.

A VOICE 603

Summary ▪ ▪

In this poem, the speaker describes the only Mexican American girl in a large auditorium full of English-speaking students. At home, the girl's family speaks only formal Spanish; yet she learns to speak English well enough to compete in English speech contests. The speaker voices her admiration for this girl (now the speaker's mother), who has taught her children to speak up for themselves.

Resources

Viewing and Representing
Videocassette B, Segment 10
This segment on Mora talking about language is available in Spanish and English. Use it as a lesson preview. See also the *Visual Connections Teacher's Manual.*

Viewing and Representing
Fine Art Transparency
Use this cover art from the book *Like Water for Chocolate* to compare the speaker's mother and the woman making tortillas. See *Viewing and Representing*:
• Transparency 14
• Worksheet, p. 56

A Elements of Literature
Tone
❓ What is the poet's attitude toward the person she calls "you" in the poem?
[Possible response: She is proud of this person for learning English, even though her father forbade it at home.]

RESPONDING TO THE ART

American artist **Alice Neel** (1900–1984) once called herself "a collector of souls." She is best known for her expressive portrayals of the human condition found in modern American urban society. **Activity.** Ask students to note the tone of the colors in the painting (dark) and then to compare this family with the people in the poem. [Possible response: The family in the painting seems more somber.]

Reaching All Students

Struggling Readers
Some students may be confused by the fact that each stanza does not end with a complete thought. Model for them how to continue reading from the last line of one stanza to the first lines of the next.

English Language Learners
For strategies for engaging English language learners with the literature, see
• *Lesson Plans Including Strategies for English-Language Learners*

Making the Connections

Cultural Connections
As of 1996, nearly 10 percent of the population of the United States was born outside its borders. Of these 24.6 million immigrants, more than 6 million were born in Mexico. Like the speaker's mother, these immigrants faced the challenge of learning new customs and a new language and often had to combat ignorance or prejudice about their native traditions. Ask groups of students who have recently immigrated to discuss their experiences.

A Elements of Literature
   Tone
❓ What is the tone in the seventh stanza, and how does it change in the eighth? [Possible responses: The proud tone of the seventh stanza becomes fearful in the eighth; the respectful, admiring tone becomes anxious and despairing.]

B Critical Thinking
   Drawing Conclusions
❓ What is it that the girl can't do? [She can't speak up; she can't make herself known to all the strangers in the auditorium.]

C Appreciating Language
   Figurative Language
❓ What is the meaning of this figure of speech? [Possible responses: The mother's voice—the "breath" that pushes out words—has strongly influenced her children; in the same way that wind ripples the trees, the mother's interest in words has affected her daughter.]

BROWSING IN THE FILES

About the Author. Pat Mora refers to herself as a "Texican," because her Mexican and Texan heritage are blended so thoroughly. As a "Texican" writer, she considers herself "one of the many voices and not *the* voice, for we know the grand variety in our community, and we want others to recognize this human wealth."

---

25 You told me only once about the time you went
    to the state capitol, your family proud as if
    you'd been named governor. But when you looked
    around, the only Mexican in the auditorium,

    you wanted to hide from those strange faces.
30 Their eyes were pinpricks, and you faked
    hoarseness. You, who are never at a loss
    for words, felt your breath stick in your throat

    like an ice cube. "I can't," you whispered.
    "I can't." Yet you did. Not that day but years later.
35 You taught the four of us to speak up.
    This is America, Mom. The undoable is done

    in the next generation. Your breath moves
    through the family like the wind
    moves through the trees.

MEET THE WRITER
A Force of Words

Pat Mora (1942–   ) was born in El Paso, Texas, and received a master's degree from the University of Texas in El Paso. She has taught in public schools and college while writing a body of poetry that has been collected in several volumes, including *Chants* (1985) and *Borders* (1993). (You can find another one of her poems on page 65.) Mora offers these thoughts on "A Voice":

❝ This poem brings together two different experiences: hearing a story from my mother and hearing the sound of wind in the trees, the sound of an invisible force. My maternal grandparents came to El Paso, Texas, from Mexico. They did not speak English. My mother, though, knew English and Spanish when she started school. She was an excellent student and always liked participating in speech contests. One aspect of the poem is about her breath, her force, in our family. ❞

Using Students' Strengths

Verbal Learners
Like the young girl in this poem, some students may have found themselves overcome by stage fright. Have verbal learners make a list of symptoms of stage fright and suggestions for handling those symptoms. Ask verbal learners to tailor their tips to students with different learning styles or to those afraid of speaking up.

Auditory/Musical Learners
Ask students to read "A Voice" aloud and to try to convey with their voices the tone they detect in the poem's word choices and phrasing. Have students make a list of the characteristics of voice they use to read this poem (for example, proud, fearful, determined). Describing the voice in which they read should help students appreciate and understand the voice in the poem.

Before You Read

AUNT FANNIE FIXES BISON BOURGUIGNON

Make the Connection

Mixing Cultures

Bison, or buffalo, once roamed the American plains, supplying American Indians with food and the raw materials for clothing and shelter. Beef bourguignon (boor'gēn·yōn') is a French stew made of beef cooked in red wine. Why has the poet put bison in this French stew?

Quickwrite

How important to you is your specific ethnicity, religion, or culture? Rate its importance on a scale of 1 to 5, with 1 meaning "not important" and 5 meaning "very important." Freewrite for a few minutes, explaining your response. *(Keep your notes for use on page 611.)*

Elements of Literature

A Prose Poem

Although this little piece is written in ordinary paragraph form, it uses the elements of poetry—especially very powerful **images** that make the speaker's world easy to see and feel. Also, like most poetry, its message is elusive—its point is never directly stated. Like other poems, this **prose poem** by Diane Glancy allows us to enter the speaker's world and make

Granddaughter, I Am Teaching You (1993) by Joanna Osburn-Bigfeather (Western Band Cherokee). Clay with raku glaze (24″ × 17″).

Photograph by Neil McGreevy. Courtesy Joanna Osburn-Bigfeather.

our own meaning of it. After you've read Glancy's work once, read it aloud. Does it *sound* like a poem to you?

> **A** prose poem is a short piece that is written in the form of prose but uses the elements of poetry.

Summary ▪ ▪

In this prose poem with the odd title, a speaker describes the two worlds that framed her childhood: the white world of her mother and the Cherokee world of her father. Using images evoking moments of fracture and separation, she explains that she always carried a "sense of puzzlement & loss" as she moved among her white peers. She felt as if part of her heritage were just out of reach.

Background

Tell students that Diane Glancy, the author of this prose poem, is part Cherokee. At one time the Cherokee were the dominant Native American group in the southeastern United States. In 1827 they established the Cherokee Nation, modeled on the U.S. government, and boasted a constitution written in their own language. However, gold was discovered on Cherokee land, and in 1838 the U.S. government forced the nation to move to Oklahoma on an agonizing journey now called the Trail of Tears. Of the approximately 50,000 Cherokee alive today, most live on reservations in Oklahoma and North Carolina.

Resources

Listening
Audio CD Library
For a recording of this prose poem, see the *Audio CD Library:*
• Disc 18, Track 7

Reaching All Students

English Language Learners

Have students work in pairs to read the prose poem "Aunt Fannie Fixes Bison Bourguignon." Students can read the poem aloud, discuss their reactions, and explore connections to their own experiences as students living in two different cultures. For additional strategies for engaging English language learners with the literature, see
• *Lesson Plans Including Strategies for English-Language Learners*

Getting Students Involved

Cooperative Learning

A New Recipe. Have students work in groups of three or four. (If possible, group students of varying cultural backgrounds together.) Invite students to think of titles similar to Diane Glancy's that reflect their own cultural heritage. For example, a student whose background is Japanese and American could title a poem "Aunt Sachiko Fixes Pot Roast Teriyaki." Another whose background is Mexican and Italian could title a poem "Aunt Theresa Fixes Jalapeño Lasagna." Encourage groups to make their titles as varied, strange, or funny as they can. When groups are finished, they can share their titles with the class.

Aunt Fannie Fixes Bison Bourguignon

Diane Glancy

My father was Cherokee. My mother English & German. My father decided he would live in this world and migrated north to the stockyards in Kansas City. My mother also came north, from a small farm in Kansas. They married, struggled through the Depression, and bought a small house by the time I was born. I was integrated into my mother's white family. I went to a white grade school. In the winter our faces lined the window. Once my tongue stuck to the frost on the glass. I was just a little darker than the others, a little quieter. I walked home over the field, breaking thin plates of ice like locust wings. There was always a sense of puzzlement & loss. Something undefined wasn't there. The smell of old campfires? The green corn dance? I had the feeling I was always at the window, my tongue forever on the cold glass.

MEET THE WRITER

Reinventing Ceremony

Diane Glancy (1941–   ) was born in Kansas City, Missouri, graduated from the University of Missouri, and earned a master's degree in creative writing from the University of Iowa. She has explored her American Indian heritage in poetry and prose, including a series of reflections called *Claiming Breath*, which won the first North American Indian Prose Award in 1990. Presently Glancy is teaching writing and Native American literature at Macalester College in St. Paul, Minnesota. In her dedication to *Iron Woman* (1990), a book of poems, Glancy writes:

❝ I keep thinking why bother with my Native American heritage. What does it matter? Let it go. How does it relate to my life in this 'world that is' anyway? But I pass the Noguchi sculpture on my way to class at Macalester and I see 'Iron Woman.' I hear old footsteps of the ancestors in the leaves in autumn. In winter I feel a sense of loss that blows in the cold wind between the buildings. So I dedicate this book to the 'visage,' if that's the right word, the 'remains' of a heritage I feel every day. ❞

Making the Connections

Cultural Connections

The Green Corn Dance. For the Cherokee people, the growth and harvest of green corn is an important part of the cycle of seasons. The Green Corn celebration has two parts. In the New Green Corn Feast, a messenger collects one perfect ear of new corn from each of the seven Cherokee clans. Then hunters begin a six-day hunt while clan leaders start a six-day fast. On the seventh day, a festival begins, with prayers and offerings followed by a feast. Forty to fifty days later (when the corn is ripe), the Ripe Green Corn Feast takes place. Group members bring food offerings, and the men perform the Green Corn Dance—a series of seven dances in which the dancers imitate fields of green corn. The festival continues for four days and ends with a great feast.

ABINADER
GROCERY #6
COLD SANDWICHES · TROPICAL PRODUCTS

Summary ■

In this poem, Tony, whose father has left the family, goes to work at a neighborhood bodega in Long Island City. He works hard, gets a scholarship to law school, and moves to Boston. Feeling out of place, he walks to the city projects and a nearby bodega, where he can see familiar sights and feel comfortable. In time, Tony moves to an apartment above the Boston bodega.

FROM THE EDITOR'S DESK

We felt that this poem fit well with "Aunt Fannie Fixes Bison Bourguignon" and "A Voice" because all three poems explore the same dilemma: how to live in one world while retaining the customs of another.

Resources

Listening
Audio CD Library
For a recording of this upbeat free verse poem, see the *Audio CD Library*:
• Disc 18, Track 8

Before You Read

TONY WENT TO THE BODEGA BUT HE DIDN'T BUY ANYTHING

Make the Connection

A Rice and Beans Story

The course of a successful life is not always a straight line from where we are to where we want to be. Sometimes we move in unexpected directions, as Tony does in this "rice and beans success story."

Quickwrite

When you're an adult, how do you think you'll decide if you've succeeded or not? Write your thoughts on this question.

Elements of Literature

Free Verse

Like many contemporary poets, Martín Espada writes in **free verse**, using no regular meter or rhyme scheme. But the poem has a distinct rhythm, created by the use of long and short sentences and by the use of many run-on lines, lines that do not end with any mark of punctuation. To get their sense, you have to keep on reading, without pausing, to the next line. Read the poem aloud and listen to the rhythms. How would you

describe what you hear? Does the sound remind you of any particular type of music?

> **F**ree verse is poetry that has no regular meter or rhyme scheme. Free verse often creates its rhythm by alternating long and short sentences and by using run-on lines.
>
> *For more on Free Verse, see page 559 and the Handbook of Literary Terms.*

TONY WENT TO THE BODEGA BUT HE DIDN'T BUY ANYTHING **607**

Taking a Second Look

Review: Comparing and Contrasting Characters

Remind students that when they *compare* characters, they look for traits the characters share. When they *contrast* characters, they note differences. For example, one trait shared by the mother in "A Voice" and Tony in "Tony Went to the Bodega. . ." is the courage to learn a new language. One difference between the speaker in "Aunt Fannie Fixes Bison Bourguignon" and

Tony is a can-do attitude. The speaker feels frozen between two worlds; Tony is in motion.

Activity

Have students work in groups of three or four to brainstorm lists of character traits displayed by the mother in "A Voice," the speaker in "Aunt Fannie Fixes Bison Bourguignon," and Tony. Ask groups to create a chart like the one to the right to show similarities and differences.

	Mother	Speaker	Tony
Shared Traits			
Individual Traits			

The Drama Collection

A scene from Thornton Wilder's *Our Town,* as produced at the Long Wharf Theater, New Haven, Connecticut, December 1987.

Selection Readability

This Annotated Teacher's Edition provides a summary of each selection in the student book. Following each Summary heading, you will find one, two, or three small icons. These icons indicate, in an approximate sense, the reading level of the selection.

- ■ One icon indicates that the selection is easy.
- ■ ■ Two icons indicate that the selection is on an intermediate reading level.
- ■ ■ ■ Three icons indicate that the selection is challenging.